CORPORATE FINANCE

ASPEN SELECT SERIES

CORPORATE FINANCE

Second Edition

STEPHEN J. LUBBEN
Harvey Washington Wiley Chair in Corporate Governance & Business Ethics
Seton Hall University School of Law

To contact Customer Service, e-mail customer.service@wolterskluwer.com, call 1-800-234-1660, fax 1-800-901-9075, or mail correspondence to:

Wolters Kluwer
Attn: Order Department
PO Box 990
Frederick, MD 21705

Printed in the United States of America.

1 2 3 4 5 6 7 8 9 0

ISBN 978-1-4548-9195-6

About Wolters Kluwer Legal & Regulatory U.S.

Wolters Kluwer Legal & Regulatory U.S. delivers expert content and solutions in the areas of law, corporate compliance, health compliance, reimbursement, and legal education. Its practical solutions help customers successfully navigate the demands of a changing environment to drive their daily activities, enhance decision quality and inspire confident outcomes.

Serving customers worldwide, its legal and regulatory portfolio includes products under the Aspen Publishers, CCH Incorporated, Kluwer Law International, ftwilliam.com and MediRegs names. They are regarded as exceptional and trusted resources for general legal and practice-specific knowledge, compliance and risk management, dynamic workflow solutions, and expert commentary.

For J. and V.

SUMMARY OF CONTENTS

CONTENTS

14

BOND INDENTURES   219

15

BONDS AFTER THE INDENTURE   245

18

DERIVITIVES   381

19

ASSET SECURITIZATION   415

20

HEDGE FUNDS AND PRIVATE EQUITY FUNDS   461

30

CHAPTER 11 PLANS   831

PREFACE TO THE SECOND EDITION

Since the first edition was published, a lot has happened in both the corporate finance and law school worlds. This second edition reflects those changes. And following Benjamin Franklin's lead, this edition is also about "asking the advantages authors have in a second edition to correct some faults of the first."

The book is up to date as of March 2017. Obviously the political situation in Washington is somewhat fluid—to put it mildly—and regulatory changes might be coming that could effect this material. Or maybe not. Those will have to wait for the Third Edition.

As with everything I do, this edition benefited from the support of my spouse, Jennifer Hoyden. I value and appreciate every day with her.

My Seton Hall assistant, Silvia Cardoso, found the typos I could no longer see. The second edition is better than the first largely because of her attention to the fine details.

Thank you also to the users of the first edition—including both the faculty and the students—who pointed out its strengths and flaws. The second edition reflects the time you took to talk to me about the first.

New York, New York
Tuesday, March 28, 2017

ACKNOWLEDGMENTS

The author is grateful to the following authors, journals, and periodicals that granted permission to excerpt their work:

John D. Ayer et. al., *Welcome to the Jungle*, Am. Bankr. Inst. J., July/August 2003, at 24.

Robert P. Bartlett, III, *Venture Capital, Agency Costs, and the False Dichotomy of the Corporation*, 54 UCLA L. Rev. 37 (2006).

Stephanie Ben-Ishai & Stephen J. Lubben, "Involuntary Creditors and Corporate Bankruptcy" (2012) 45:2 UBC L Rev 253.

William W. Bratton, *The New Dividend Puzzle*, 93 Geo. L.J. 845 (2005).

Brian R. Cheffins & John Armour, *The Past, Present, and Future of Shareholder Activism by Hedge Funds*, 37 J. Corp. L. 51 (2011).

Lawrence A. Cunningham, *From Random Walks to Chaotic Crashes: The Linear Genealogy of the Efficient Capital Market Hypothesis*, 62 Geo. Wash. L. Rev. 546 (1994).

Ronald J. Gilson, *Engineering a Venture Capital Market: Lessons from the American Experience*, 55 Stan. L. Rev. 1067 (2003). Reproduced with permission of Stanford School of Law, Stanford University in the format republish in a book via Copyright Clearance Center.

Zohar Goshen, *Shareholder Dividend Options*, 104 Yale L.J. 881 (1995). Reproduced under license from The Yale Law Journal Company, Inc.

Michelle M. Harner, *The Search for an Unbiased Fiduciary in Corporate Reorganizations*, 86 Notre Dame L. Rev. 469 (2011).

Michelle M. Harner, *Trends in Distressed Debt Investing: An Empirical Study of Investors' Objectives*, 16 Am. Bankr. Inst. L. Rev. 69 (2008).

Espen Gaarder Haug & Nassim Nicholas Taleb, *Option Traders Use (Very) Sophisticated Heuristics, Never the Black–Scholes–Merton Formula*, J. Economic Behavior & Organization, Volume 77, Issue 2, February 2011, Pages 97-106. Reproduced with permission of Elsevier BV in the format reuse in a book/textbook via Copyright Clearance Center.

Claire A. Hill, *Securitization: A Low-Cost Sweetener for Lemons*, 74 Wash. U. L.Q. 1061 (1996).

Marcel Kahan, *Rethinking Corporate Bonds: The Trade–Off Between Individual and Collective Rights*, 77 NYU L. Rev. 1040 (2002).

Kenneth C. Kettering, *Securitization and Its Discontents: The Dynamics of Financial Product Development*, 29 Cardozo L. Rev. 1553 (2008).

Stephen J. Lubben & Rajesh P. Narayanan, *CDS and the Resolution of Financial Distress*, 24 J. Applied Corp. Fin. 129 (2012). © 2012 Morgan Stanley.

Daniel J. Morrissey, *Another Look at the Law of Dividends*, 54 U. Kan. L. Rev. 449 (2006).

Katherine Pratt, *The Debt-Equity Distinction in a Second-Best World*, 53 Vand. L. Rev. 1055 (2000).

Nicholas P. Saggese, et al., *A Practitioner's Guide to Exchange Offers and Consent Solicitations*, 24 Loy. L.A. L. Rev. 527 (1991).

Elizabeth Warren, *A Theory of Absolute Priority*, 1991 Ann. Surv. Am. L. 9, 37-38 (1992).

Arthur E. Wilmarth, Jr., *The Transformation of the U.S. Financial Services Industry*, 1975-2000: Competition, Consolidation, and Increased Risks, 2002 U. Ill. L. Rev. 215 (2002).

Harry Wilson, *Budget 2012: Perpetual bonds issue examined*, The Telegraph, 21 Mar. 2012. © Telegraph Media Group Limited 2012, used under license.

Sarah Pei Woo, *Regulatory Bankruptcy: How Bank Regulation Causes Fire Sales*, 99 Geo. L.J. 1615 (2011), used with the permission of Kenneth Wee.

Finally, while in practice I took a year off from the firm to earn an LL.M at Harvard. While there, I took Corporate Finance with Reinier Kraakman, and I would be remiss if I did not acknowledge the undoubted influence that course, as taught by him, had on my approach to this subject. Indeed, in my early years in academia, our two courses were virtually identical. Many thanks are due.

INTRODUCTION: WHY CORPORATE FINANCE?

In many ways, the Corporate Finance class can be seen as a collection of bits that were left out of other courses. The Trust Indenture Act of 1939 (Chapter 14) falls by the wayside for want of time in Securities Regulation. The more sophisticated corporate reorganization techniques (Chapters 27 & 29) tend to similarly get little treatment in the general Bankruptcy class that often barely has time to introduce chapter 11.

Now you might think that there is a reason why these things get dropped from other courses: maybe they're not so important?[1]

But I have repeatedly started my first class by explaining that Corporate Finance teaches topics that I wished I had learned before I became a first-year associate in New York. I learned these topics on the job, but this course gives you a chance to learn them in advance, so you can "hit the ground running." Given the current job market, that can't be a bad thing.

In short, this is a very functional course that teaches a collection of advanced skills that are useful for corporate lawyers of both the transactional and litigation variety. It also provides some useful skills for noncorporate lawyers, too, as I explain below.

This book is organized around four basic units: valuation (Chapters 1–11), finance (Chapters 12–21), mergers and acquisitions (Chapters 22–25), and financial distress (Chapters 26–30).

Valuation is the math-heavy part of the course, but it also introduces some finance theory. Understanding both the basics of the math and theory as taught in MBA programs will help you interact with bankers and accountants in practice.

Understanding the math is also helpful in several noncorporate contexts as well. For example, you need to understand how to value a business if you are going to practice family law. Families, you see, often own businesses. The same goes for any sort of estate planning or tax practice.

The goal is to help you understand the math, not necessarily to help you set up shop as an investment banker. Rather, when you find yourself negotiating a deal

---

1. *Cf.* 1 William Blackstone, *Commentaries on the Laws of England* 6 (1765).

in the future, some intuitive understanding of how the other side's banker got to a particular figure will help you do your job as a lawyer.

The second unit turns to specific financial instruments. Some, like common shares, are apt to be familiar; others—like swaps and CDOs—probably less so. But a working knowledge of the instruments covered in this section is vital to anyone who intends to practice with a big law firm anywhere in the world. Many of you might not practice on Wall Street, but your clients will inevitably have many, many interactions with Wall Street.

The third unit covers mergers and acquisitions, or M&A.

You might have covered the case law regarding mergers in your Business Associations class, but the aim of these chapters is to focus on the negotiation of the actual contracts involved in deals. You might have already studied *Revlon* and *Unocal*, but did you cover covenants, reps, and warranties? How about the choice between a merger and a sale of all of the company's assets?

The final unit covers financial distress, and examines the ways in which a corporation can work out of financial difficulties. This could mean bankruptcy, and several chapters examine chapter 11 as used by very large corporations like American Airlines and General Motors, but it might involve some sort of out-of-court workout, too. Chapter 26 in particular covers nonbankruptcy exchange offers, which involves the exchange of existing debt for new securities in an attempt to avoid bankruptcy. Chapter 27 examines prepackaged bankruptcy cases, which involves an attempt to use the Bankruptcy Code's power while only interacting with the bankruptcy process to a very minimal extent.

This material reflects the area where your author practiced, and thus is of special interest. But it should be of interest to any corporate lawyer, especially those who expect to have a transactional practice. By and large, corporate transactions are driven by either taxes or bankruptcy. Lawyers aim to structure the deal to avoid both.

A NOTE ON EDITING

While I like to provide a bit more of a case than many authors, entire sections have been chopped. Many citations have been removed to increase readability, and footnotes have often been removed. When retained, footnotes have been renumbered to conform to the chapter's numbering scheme.

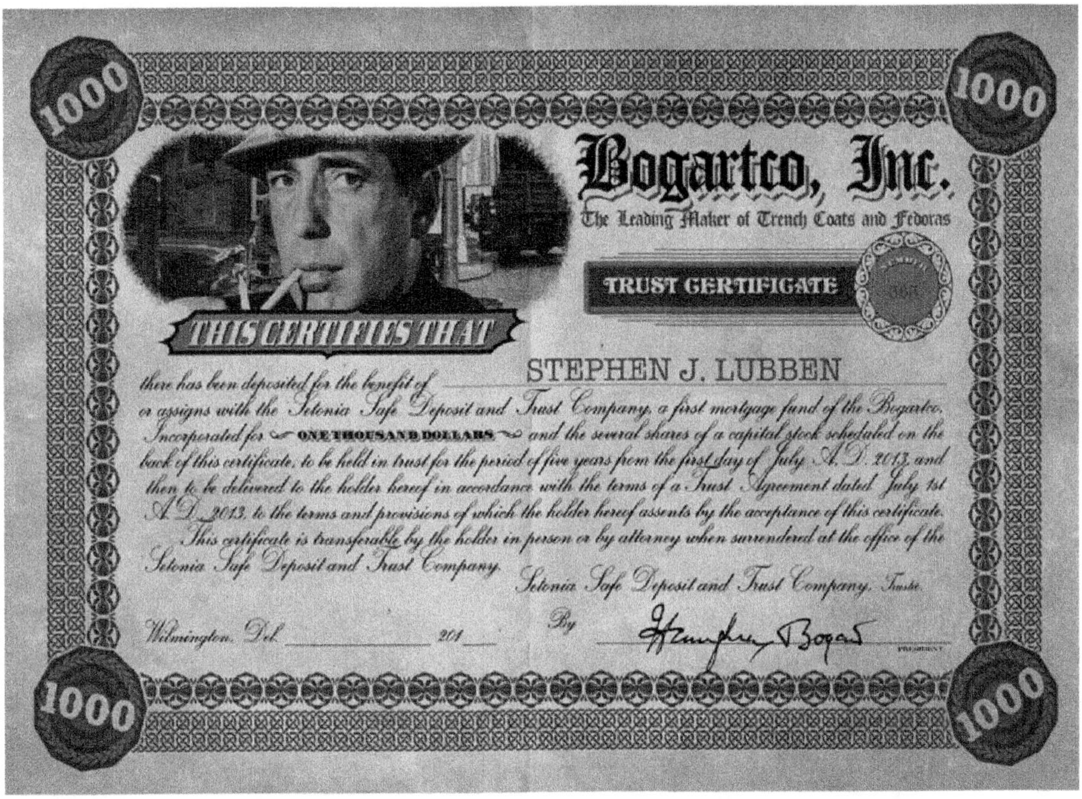

Graphic Artist: T.J. Bocchino

I

VALUATION

1

CORPORATE FINANCE, ACCOUNTING, AND CASH FLOWS

Corporate Finance texts, and finance articles, spend much time discussing "firms." For a law student, a firm is the source of a job, hopefully. But for purposes of this text and this class, firm means something more than law firm.

In finance a firm is any of the entities you studied in your Business Associations or Corporations class: sole proprietorships, partnerships, limited liability companies, and corporations. The firm is a way of organizing business and economic activity. The specific nature of each type of firm is a function of the law that created it.

There are many different types of businesses and each has its own unique set of transactions, but the fundamentals of all firms are basically the same. First, all firms have assets and liabilities. Assets are the things the firm *owns*, and liabilities are the things the firm *owes*. A factory is an asset—no matter how old and decrepit it might be—and a bank loan, a tort judgment against the firm, or a promise to pay employees is a liability.

But notice that for the bank, the loan to the firm is an asset. The bank has received a contract that will generate periodic interest payments, along with the return of the principal amount the bank lent. Many liabilities have this property: a liability for one firm is an asset to another.

Also notice that the only assets and liabilities that are shown on the balance sheet are those that can be reduced to dollar figures. The firm's good reputation might be thought of as an asset, but you won't find it on the balance sheet.

Next, all firms—at least all the firms covered in this class—have owners.[1] The owners' interest in the firm is called *equity*. It has nothing to do with justice. Equity can take the form of shares (in corporations), membership interests (LLCs), or any other ownership claim.

---

1. Not-for-profit firms have no owners, but do have beneficiaries.

With that background, you are ready to learn some basic accounting. Accounting is important, because much of corporate finance is based on an understanding of the firm's financial situation. The way to get that understanding is through the accounting statements.[2]

1. BALANCE SHEETS

A balance sheet is a picture of a firm's assets, liabilities, and equity at a point in time. As such, the balance sheet is often out of date one minute after it is prepared. The static nature of balance sheets can also be abused, as noted in the following excerpt from the Lehman Brothers examiner's report. An examiner is a neutral party appointed by a bankruptcy court to investigate some aspect of a company that has ended up in chapter 11.[3] In this case, the examiner was appointed to investigate the collapse of Lehman during the financial crisis of 2008.

IN RE LEHMAN BROTHERS HOLDINGS, INC.
(BANKR. S.D.N.Y. 2010)

Report of Anton R. Valukas, Examiner, pages 732–735

Lehman employed off-balance sheet devices, known within Lehman as "Repo 105" and "Repo 108" transactions, to temporarily remove securities inventory from its balance sheet, usually for a period of seven to ten days, and to create a materially misleading picture of the firm's financial condition in late 2007 and 2008.[4] Repo 105 transactions were nearly identical to standard repurchase and resale ("repo") transactions that Lehman (and other investment banks) used to secure short-term financing, with a critical difference: Lehman accounted for Repo 105 transactions as "sales" as opposed to financing transactions based upon the overcollateralization or higher than normal haircut in a Repo 105 transaction.[5] By recharacterizing the Repo 105 transaction as a "sale," Lehman removed the inventory from its balance sheet.

---

2. If offered at your school, a full accounting for lawyers class can be invaluable.

3. 11 U.S.C. §1104(c).

4. Unless otherwise noted, the Report uses the term "Repo 105" to refer to both Repo 105 and Repo 108 transactions. Lehman treated the two transactions identically under the same internal accounting policy and both transactions shared the same anatomy. They differed only in that Repo 105 transactions utilized fixed income securities and required a minimum five percent overcollateralization amount (i.e., a minimum of $105 worth of securities in exchange for $100 cash borrowed), while Repo 108 transactions utilized equities securities and required a minimum eight percent overcollateralization amount (i.e., a minimum of $108 worth of securities in exchange for $100 cash borrowed).

5. Sale and repurchase agreements ("repos") are agreements where one party transfers an asset or security to another party as collateral for a short-term borrowing of cash, while simultaneously agreeing to repay the cash and take back the collateral at a specific point in time. When the repo

Lehman regularly increased its use of Repo 105 transactions in the days prior to reporting periods to reduce its publicly reported net leverage and balance sheet. Lehman's periodic reports did not disclose the cash borrowing from the Repo 105 transaction—i.e., although Lehman had in effect borrowed tens of billions of dollars in these transactions, Lehman did not disclose the known obligation to repay the debt. Lehman used the cash from the Repo 105 transaction to pay down other liabilities, thereby reducing both the total liabilities and the total assets reported on its balance sheet and lowering its leverage ratios. Thus, Lehman's Repo 105 practice consisted of a two-step process: (1) undertaking Repo 105 transactions followed by (2) the use of Repo 105 cash borrowings to pay down liabilities, thereby reducing leverage. A few days after the new quarter began, Lehman would borrow the necessary funds to repay the cash borrowing plus interest, repurchase the securities, and restore the assets to its balance sheet.

Lehman never publicly disclosed its use of Repo 105 transactions, its accounting treatment for these transactions, the considerable escalation of its total Repo 105 usage in late 2007 and into 2008, or the material impact these transactions had on the firm's publicly reported net leverage ratio. According to former Global Financial Controller Martin Kelly, a careful review of Lehman's Forms 10-K and 10-Q [annual and quarterly reports filed with the SEC] would not reveal Lehman's use of Repo 105 transactions. Lehman failed to disclose its Repo 105 practice even though Kelly believed "that the only purpose or motive for the transactions was reduction in balance sheet"; felt that "there was no substance to the transactions"; and expressed concerns with Lehman's Repo 105 program to two consecutive Lehman Chief Financial Officers—Erin Callan and Ian Lowitt—advising them that the lack of economic substance to Repo 105 transactions meant "reputational risk" to Lehman if the firm's use of the transactions became known to the public. In addition to its material omissions, Lehman affirmatively misrepresented in its financial statements that the firm treated all repo transactions as financing transactions—i.e., not sales—for financial reporting purposes.

Starting in mid-2007, Lehman faced a crisis: market observers began demanding that investment banks reduce their leverage. The inability to reduce leverage could lead to a ratings downgrade, which would have had an immediate, tangible monetary impact on Lehman.

Despite the potential for abuse, the balance sheet provides useful information about the company. From a lender's perspective, the balance sheet provides some insight into the firm's ability to repay. From a supplier's perspective, the balance

---

transaction matures, the borrower repays the funds plus an agreed upon interest rate and takes back its collateral. . . . Overcollateralization amounts, or haircuts, in Repo 105 transactions were higher than the typical haircut applied to ordinary repos using similar securities.

sheet's discussion of liabilities reveals the degree to which other creditors have claims against the same firm, and the accounts payable line, over time, might offer the first sign of liquidity problems at the firm. When firms approach bankruptcy they often begin to "stretch the trade," which involves paying bills more slowly than in the past.

The balance sheet is said to comprise two sides: the left-hand side (assets) and the right-hand side (liabilities and equity). Visually you can think of an old-fashioned ledger that looks something like Table 1-1, even if modern balance sheets are rarely presented in this manner.

TABLE 1-1
Basic Balance Sheet

Assets	Liabilities
	Equity

The right side of the balance sheet is where most of the finance that is the subject of this class happens. But the asset side of the balance sheet can influence the financing choices that are made on the right side.

Table 1-2 puts some numbers on the balance sheet to make it a bit more realistic. Here is something you should notice right off the bat:

$$\text{Assets} = \text{Liabilities} + \text{Equity, and}$$
$$\text{Assets} - \text{Liabilities} = \text{Equity}$$

That is, the right side of the balance sheet balances with the left; hence the name.

The "equity" part of the balance sheet is the part that makes it balance, and reflects the owners' interest in the firm. Individuals, including individuals operating as "sole proprietorships," do not have equity, but their "net worth" is similar, at least from accounting perspective. Net worth represents the difference between an individual's assets and her liabilities.

TABLE 1-2
Bogartco, Inc. Balance Sheet

Bogartco, Inc., A Leading Maker of Trench Coats and Fedoras
(In millions)

	Year Ended December 31,	
	2012	2011
Assets		
Current assets:		
Cash and cash equivalents	**$8,161**	$5,505
Short-term investments (including securities loaned of $683 and $62)	**36,012**	31,283
Total cash, cash equivalents, and short-term investments	**44,173**	36,788
Accounts receivable, net of allowance for doubtful accounts of $312 and $375	**9,646**	13,014
Inventories	**1,242**	740
Deferred income taxes	**2,344**	2,184
Other	**2,176**	2,950
Total current assets	**59,581**	55,676
Property and equipment, net of accumulated depreciation of $8,942 and $8,629	**7,771**	7,630
Equity and other investments	**9,211**	7,754
Goodwill	**12,471**	12,394
Intangible assets, net	**1,077**	1,158
Other long-term assets	**1,429**	1,501
Total assets	**$91,540**	$86,113

	Year Ended December 31,	
	2012	2011
Liabilities and stockholders' equity		
Current liabilities:		
Accounts payable	**$3,654**	$4,025
Short-term debt	**1,000**	1,000
Accrued compensation	**2,252**	3,283
Income taxes	**2,136**	1,074
Short-term unearned revenue	**12,767**	13,652
Securities lending payable	**909**	182
Other	**3,139**	2,931
Total current liabilities	**25,857**	26,147
Long-term debt	**9,665**	4,939
Long-term unearned revenue	**1,152**	1,178
Deferred income taxes	**540**	229
Other long-term liabilities	**7,384**	7,445
Total liabilities	**44,598**	39,938
Commitments and contingencies		
Stockholders' equity:		
Common stock and paid-in capital—shares authorized 24,000; outstanding 8,562 and 8,668	**61,935**	62,856
Retained deficit, including accumulated other comprehensive income of $1,519 and $1,055	**(14,993)**	(16,681)
Total stockholders' equity	**46,942**	46,175
Total liabilities and stockholders' equity	**$91,540**	$86,113

Notice that some categories are now subdivided. Current assets are cash and things that can be turned into cash relatively quickly. Cash here means not only currency, but also bank account balances and other relatively riskless things like U.S. Treasury obligations.

Fixed or long-term assets are things than can only be turned into cash with some effort: Real estate is a classic example. Other less obvious examples include intellectual property, like trademarks. In normal times, these assets will not be turned into cash. Likewise, liabilities have been similarly subdivided among current liabilities (those due within a year) and long-term liabilities.

Total equity is equal to paid-in capital, the original price paid for stock at issuance, plus retained earnings. Paid-in capital is often further subdivided between stated capital or par value, a concept that you probably remember used to have some legal meaning, and additional paid-in capital. Retained earnings is money the company has earned, but not paid out as dividends to shareholders. When a company loses money in a year, retained earnings is the first item to absorb the loss.

Equity on the balance sheet has no direct relationship with the current market value of the firm's shares. A sustained period of negative earnings can make the book value of equity negative, even if the firm's shares are trading with a positive value in the markets.

Every entry on the right side of the balance sheet must have a corresponding entry on the left to maintain the basic equality or balance we already discussed. This is what is often referred to as *double-entry bookkeeping.* If the company adds more money to the retained earnings line, what entry would it make on the left side of the balance sheet?

Because firms only prepare balance sheets periodically—maybe once per quarter—transactions occurring in between the balance sheets are recorded in a journal. Each account on the balance sheet – essentially, each line item on the balance sheet – will have a ledger. Journal entries are periodically posted to the appropriate ledgers, which are then used to update the balance sheet. Every entry in the journal and the ledger will appear in two places, again reflecting the double entry approach to recordkeeping. For example, if HB, the owner of Bogartco, contributes $100,000 to the business, that money will increase the "Cash and cash equivalents" ledger and the ledger associated with "Total stockholders' equity."

PROBLEM SET 1.1

1. If assets minus liabilities equals equity, as noted earlier, how would you interpret negative equity?
2. Under generally accepted accounting practices (GAAP) in the United States, balance sheets like the one seen in Table 1-2 value assets at cost. What risks arise from such a valuation of Bogartco's plant (included in "property and equipment")? In particular, what is the likely difference between the value on the balance sheet and market value?
3. Bacall Tin Whistles, Inc. has current assets of $5.7 million, fixed assets of $4.3 million, current liabilities of $3.9 million, and long-term debt of $1.1 million. Construct a simple balance sheet. What is the shareholder equity?

2. INCOME STATEMENTS

Income or net income refers to the total revenue that a firm takes in, less the cost of generating that revenue. That is

$$\text{Revenues} - \text{Expenses} = \text{Net Income}$$

Income statements partially make up for the weaknesses of a static balance sheet. In particular, an income statement shows the flow of money into and out of a firm during a particular year. These flows will have an effect on the overall balance sheet, with positive income items increasing the equity and negative income items decreasing it, but the income statement, a sample of which is shown in Table 1-3, shows how the balance sheet came to be.

TABLE 1-3
Simple Income Statement

Spade & Marlowe Corporation For the Year Ending December 31, 1937	
Revenues	$100
Less Expenses	24
Net Income	$76

The accuracy of the foregoing statement is tempered by the GAAP notion that revenues should be matched with their corresponding expenses. This is known as *accrual accounting*, as contrasted with *cash accounting*, which is the kind of accounting your bank uses for your checking account (cash in, cash out). All of the firms studied in this course will use accrual accounting.[6]

Thus, under accrual accounting, income is reported when a sale is made—even if the sale is on credit and the firm receives no actual cash until some point in the future. A firm could have lots of income and still be unable to pay its electricity bill. The utility company likes cash.

Likewise, under accrual accounting a firm would realize the cost of manufacturing a trench coat it sold in the same period as the sale. In the accrual accounting system, both revenue and expenses may be *accrued* or *deferred* relative to when money actually changes hands in the real world.

The most important concept related to this principle is *depreciation.* When an asset is depreciated, the cost of the asset is incurred over the life of the asset. This represents an attempt to match the cost with the revenue resulting from the asset. But depreciation is merely an estimate of how much a thing is used up, and a variety of tax policies might permit deviations for this norm.

---

6. Some law firms, especially smaller ones, still use cash accounting. Cash accounting has the advantage of being much more intuitive.

Depreciation affects the income statement by spreading out expenses over time. These expenses will reduce net income over a series of years, rather than all falling in a single year. Depreciation also gradually reduces the value of the depreciated asset on the balance sheet and the size of the equity line on the balance sheet, given the relationship between depreciation and net income. Note the consistency here with double-entry bookkeeping: as the book value of the asset declines with the application of depreciation, the net income (and thus equity) line also faces a corresponding reduction.

Thus, Bogartco might purchase a new fedora-creasing machine for $100,000. It expects the machine to last for ten years, after which it will have no value at all. Casually we might think that Bogartco will incur a cost of $100,000 in year one and revenues but no cost in the nine years thereafter. [7] But such straightforward thinking would put legions of attorneys and accountants out of work.

Instead, under GAAP, Bogartco will incur part of the $100,000 over each of the next ten years. If Bogartco uses "straight line" depreciation, it will incur a $10,000 cost each year. From a cash flow perspective, it has spent $100,000 in year one. From an accounting perspective, it has spent $10,000.

Amortization is the same idea applied to nontangible assets—in particular, goodwill.[8] *Depletion* is the same concept applied to natural resources like coal or timber.

Because accounting and "real" cash flows are often out of sync, a similar issue develops with regard to taxes. Namely, the amount of tax actually owed in a particular year might not match with the amount of tax that would seem to be due based on the accounting income. This is because actual income might be more or less than accounting income.

To adjust for this, income statements (see Table 1-4) typically report taxes as the sum of the "current" taxes, which represents the actual paid amount, and deferred taxes, which represents taxes that would be due based on the accounting income reported. In theory, the deferred and current taxes will balance out over the long term.[9]

---

7. If Bogartco were to do this, it would be engaging in "cash" accounting.

8. *Goodwill* is a kind of accounting catchall that covers the "intangibles" of a business. For example, if a company buys another company for $100 over book value, that extra $100 will appear as "goodwill" on the acquiring company's balance sheet.

9. *Cf.* John Maynard Keynes, *A Tract on Monetary Reform* 80 (1923) ("[T]his *long run* is a misleading guide to current affairs. *In the long run* we are all dead. Economists set themselves too easy, too useless a task if in tempestuous seasons they can only tell us that when the storm is long past the ocean will be flat again.").

TABLE 1-4
Bogartco, Inc. Income Statement

Bogartco, Inc., *A Leading Maker of Trench Coats and Fedoras*
Income Statement
(In millions, except per share amounts)

	Year Ended December 31,
	2012
Revenue	**$16,195**
Operating expenses:	
Cost of revenue	3,139
Research and development	2,196
Sales and marketing	2,806
General and administrative	938
Total operating expenses	9,079
Operating income	7,116
Other income	114
Income before income taxes	7,230
Provision for income taxes	1,820
Net income	$5,410
Earnings per share:	
Basic	$0.63
Diluted	$0.62
Weighted average shares outstanding:	
Basic	8,614
Diluted	8,695
Cash dividends declared per common share	$0.16

Net income is often expressed per share of stock outstanding—that is, as earnings per share. This allows for easy comparison of companies in similar industries. This is calculated as

$$EPS = Net\ Income \div Shares\ Outstanding$$

As discussed later, EBITDA is an even more useful measure of the firm's cash flow.

3. CASH FLOW STATEMENTS

The income statement shows how the firm made or lost money over a specific period—typically, a quarter or a year. The balance sheet shows the firm's overall financial condition at the end of that same period.

A cash flow statement, shown in Table 1-5 on the next page, then reconciles the firm's opening and closing cash balance for the same period. The focus here is specifically on cash, rather than income. The use of cash is detailed, then that use is compared to the prior cash balance to then calculate the final, end-of-period cash balance.

In the case of cash flows from operations, the cash flow statement starts with net income and then adjusts for noncash changes in net income that come from depreciation and amortization. Likewise, the cash flow statement will reflect changes in the type of assets and liabilities the firm shows on its balance sheet—for example, a reduction in accounts receivable is typically reflected in an increase in cash, assuming the reduction is a result of getting paid. An increase in inventory will likely reflect a corresponding decrease in cash, as the cash is used to pay for the inventory.

For nonoperating activities, the process works similarly. If the company pays off debt, it uses cash. If it issues new debt, the proceeds become new cash on the balance sheet. An increase in plant, property, and equipment is a use of cash, and new equity issuance is a source of cash.

4. CONSOLIDATED REPORTS

In casual conversation, it is common to speak of a firm, when legally we really mean a group of firms. For example, normal people (i.e., nonlawyers) often speak of "Bank of America." But in fact, the thing known as Bank of America is comprised of more than 2,000 separate legal entities, grouped under a single Delaware holding company based in North Carolina.

Although corporate law might treat Bank of America as thousands of entities, as a matter of securities and tax law it is treated as a single legal entity, and Bank of America will prepare a single set of consolidated financial statements under the accounting rules. Essentially a new, hypothetical entity is created as a matter of accounting, and it is this entity that files Securities and Exchange Commission (SEC) reports and pays taxes.

TABLE 1-5
Bogartco, Inc. Cash Flow Statement

Bogartco, Inc., A Leading Maker of Trench Coats and Fedoras
Cash Flow Statement
(In millions)

	Year Ended December 31,
	2012
Operations	
Net income	**$5,410**
Adjustments to reconcile net income to net cash from operations:	
Depreciation, amortization, and other noncash items	694
Stock-based compensation	528
Net recognized losses (gains) on investments and derivatives	(29)
Excess tax benefits from stock-based compensation	(5)
Deferred income taxes	(148)
Deferral of unearned revenue	5,881
Recognition of unearned revenue	(6,862)
Changes in operating assets and liabilities:	
Accounts receivable	3,674
Inventories	(468)
Other current assets	208
Other long-term assets	62
Accounts payable	(400)
Other current liabilities	(911)
Other long-term liabilities	560
Net cash from operations	8,194
Financing	
Short-term borrowings, maturities of 90 days or less, net	814
Proceeds from issuance of debt, maturities longer than 90 days	4,721
Repayments of debt, maturities longer than 90 days	(814)
Common stock issued	177
Common stock repurchased	(4,399)
Common stock cash dividends paid	(1,118)
Excess tax benefits from stock-based compensation	5
Other	(25)
Net cash used in financing	(639)

Investing

Additions to property and equipment	(564)
Acquisition of companies, net of cash acquired	0
Purchases of investments	(7,417)
Maturities of investments	870
Sales of investments	1,427
Securities lending payable	727
Net cash used in investing	(4,957)
Effect of exchange rates on cash and cash equivalents	58
Net change in cash and cash equivalents	2,656
Cash and cash equivalents, beginning of period	5,505
Cash and cash equivalents, end of period	$8,161

Every subsidiary that the parent company owns more than a 50 percent interest in will be consolidated within the consolidated entity. As a result, the parent company must eliminate transactions between the parent and its subsidiaries for accounts receivable and accounts payable to avoid counting revenue twice and giving the impression that the consolidated entity has more profits or owes more money than it actually does.

If the parent company owns all of the equity interests of its subsidiaries, the consolidated revenues will be equal to the aggregate revenues of the group, less intercompany sales, and net income should equal the aggregate net income of the group, less the effect of intercompany transactions. It is slightly more complicated if the subsidiary is majority owned, but not wholly owned. Then an adjustment must be made to account for the cash flows that belong to the minority shareholders.

If a parent company owns between 20 percent and 50 percent of another company, a proportional share of the subsidiary's net income will appear in the net income of the parent company. This proportional treatment is called the equity method of accounting.

5.   LIQUIDITY, CASH FLOW, AND MEASURES OF FIRM HEALTH

The following press release from 2002 relates to Dynegy, an energy company that is used as an example throughout the textbook. Apparently Dynegy was concerned that stock analysts, who typically work for brokerage houses and make recommendations to clients about whether a particular stock should be bought or sold, were penalizing the company for the gap between reported net income and actual operating cash flow. Dynegy set out to close the gap with a corporate finance transaction that had no real economic substance.

SEC PRESS RELEASE
DYNEGY SETTLES SECURITIES FRAUD CHARGES INVOLVING SPES, ROUND-TRIP ENERGY TRADES
FOR IMMEDIATE RELEASE
2002–140
COMPANY WILL PAY $3 MILLION CIVIL PENALTY, CEASE AND DESIST FROM
VIOLATING ANTI-FRAUD PROVISIONS OF FEDERAL SECURITIES LAWS

Washington, D.C., September 24, 2002—The Securities and Exchange Commission filed a settled enforcement action today against Dynegy Inc., in connection with accounting improprieties and misleading statements by the Houston-based energy production, distribution and trading company. The Commission's case arises from (i) Dynegy's improper accounting for and misleading disclosures relating to a $300 million financing transaction, known as Project Alpha, involving special-purpose entities (SPEs), and (ii) Dynegy's overstatement of its energy-trading activity resulting from "round-trip" or "wash" trades—simultaneous, pre-arranged buy-sell trades of energy with the same counter-party, at the same price and volume, and over the same term, resulting in neither profit nor loss to either transacting party.

The Commission found that Dynegy engaged in securities fraud in connection with its disclosures and accounting for Project Alpha, and negligently included materially misleading information about the round-trip energy trades in two press releases it issued in early 2002. In settlement of the Commission's enforcement action, Dynegy, without admitting or denying the Commission's findings, has agreed to the entry of the cease-and-desist order and to pay a $3 million penalty in a related civil suit filed in U.S. district court in Houston. The Commission's investigation is continuing as to others.

More specifically, the Commission's Order finds as follows.

PROJECT ALPHA

By 2000, some energy analysts following Dynegy had noticed a widening gap between Dynegy's net income and operating cash flow. The gap resulted from Dynegy's recognition of net income in the form of unrealized gains from net forward positions,[10] and the fact that the net forward positions generate no current cash flow. This treatment of unrealized gains as net income was required under "mark-to-market" accounting principles. In April of 2001, Dynegy closed on Project Alpha, a complex web of transactions involving SPEs, to boost its 2001 operating cash flow by $300 million, or 37%, and thereby reduce the gap between its net income and operating cash flow, as well as to achieve a $79 million tax benefit.

---

10. A forward is a contract for purchase or sale of an item at some point in the future. *See* Chapter 17. —AUTHOR

Dynegy defrauded the investing public by failing to disclose in its 2001 Form 10-K the true financing, as opposed to operating, nature of the $300 million. In reality, the $300 million was a loan masquerading as operating cash flow on Dynegy's 2001 Statement of Cash Flows. This is particularly significant for two reasons: first, analysts view operating cash flow as a key indicator of the financial health of energy trading firms such as Dynegy; and second, historically, the Statement of Cash Flows has been considered immune from cosmetic tampering.

In addition, Dynegy's accounting in its financial statements for the $300 million failed to conform to GAAP in at least two respects. Under Financial Accounting Standard 95, Dynegy should have accounted for the Alpha-related cash flow as financing, rather than operating, cash flow. Moreover, Dynegy failed to comply with the 3% at-risk requirement for SPEs. Consequently, Dynegy overstated net income in 2001 by 12%—the amount of the purported $79 million Alpha-linked tax benefit.

ROUND-TRIP ENERGY TRADES

Dynegy issued materially misleading information to the investing public about the amount of trading on its electronic trading platform, Dynegydirect. On November 15, 2001, Dynegy entered into two massive "round-trip" electricity transactions. In a January 2002 press release, Dynegy included the notional trading value (multiple of volume, price and term) from one of these trades in a discussion of an increase in trading traffic on Dynegydirect. In an April 2002 press release, Dynegy included the results of these trades in its reported energy trading volume and in its first quarter 2002 revenues and cost of sales.

In both releases, Dynegy negligently failed to disclose that the resulting increases in energy trading volume, revenue and notional trading value were materially attributable to the round-trip trades. The contents of the press releases were also used in the offer and sale of securities. Because the round-trip trades lacked economic substance, Dynegy's statements were materially misleading to the investing public. This case is the first enforcement action resulting from an energy trading company's misleading disclosures regarding use of "round-trip" or "wash" trades.

DYNEGY'S CONDUCT AFTER CONTACT BY COMMISSION STAFF

Dynegy disclosed Alpha's impact on its financial performance in a Form 8-K that the company filed with the Commission on April 25, 2002, only after the Commission staff expressed to Dynegy concerns about Alpha. After those concerns were first raised, but before the filing of the Form 8-K, Dynegy's former Chief Financial Officer falsely stated to the public that Alpha's "primary purpose" was to secure a long-term natural gas supply, and Dynegy continued to assert that its obtaining a long-term gas supply was a principal purpose of Alpha. Dynegy officials did not, prior to Dynegy's filing of the Form 8-K, acknowledge that Alpha's principal purposes were, in fact, to minimize the gap between

Dynegy's reported net income and reported operating cash flow and to realize an associated tax benefit.

———————

As the foregoing indicates, net income is a widely reported measure that is often of limited practical value.[11]

EBITDA is a considerably more important measure than net income, and one that is often referenced in corporate finance transactions. EBITDA is pronounced exactly as it is spelled—E-BIT-DA. It stands for earnings before interest, taxes, depreciation, and amortization. The idea is to get a measure of the firm's cash flow that does not depend on accounting entries that often reflect noncash events. In the debt context in particular, documents will often demand a certain level of EBITDA, which gives the lender confidence that the debt will actually be paid. EBITDA is also often used as part of financial ratio—for example, EBITDA over total debt is a commonly used measure of the viability of a company. One of the most common methods to value businesses being acquired is by using multiples of EBITDA. Attorneys need to understand how these financial ratios work in conjunction with the contracts they are negotiating.

EBITDA can be overused and abused too. For example, taking out depreciation can lead one to forget that fedora creasing machines do not last forever. The cost of replacing worn out bits of the business will be incurred sometime, if the business is going to continue as a going concern. More generally, EBITDA must be compared to actual cash flow to insure that EBITDA corresponds to cash generation as expected. For example, if debt is rising, interest expense—which is also ignored in EBITDA—will be rising too. One can have rising EBITDA, but still go broke.

TABLE 1-6
Common Financial Ratios

Name	*Formula*
Earnings per share	Net earnings/# of shares
Debt ratio	Liabilities/Assets
Debt/equity ratio	Liabilities/Equity
Quick ratio	Current assets-(Inventory & Prepayments)/Current liabilities
Current ratio	Current assets/Current liabilities
Cash ratio	Cash/Current liabilities
Profit or operating margin	Net income/Sales
EBITDA margin	EBITDA/Sales
Return on equity (ROE)	Net income/Total equity

———————

11. The excerpt also introduces a series of SEC reports, which are discussed in the next section.

Myriad other ratios are used to measure a firm's health. Each ratio measures something slightly different, and which ratio is appropriate depends on the goal. Table 1-6 summarizes some of the most common financial ratios; think about their purpose as you read the table. One—EPS—you have already seen. Other ratios will be introduced later—like the price/earnings calculations we do in Chapter 12.

When using financial ratios always keep in mind that the ratios reflect accounting principles. For example, a ratio that uses "assets" is typically using book value, which will be quite different from "real" value.

6. SEC REPORTS

If a firm's shares are traded on a regulated stock exchange—like the New York Stock Exchange—the firm must file a series of reports with the SEC. These forms include the following:

Form 10-K—Annual report, must be filed by companies that have registered securities under Section 12 of the 1934 Act.

Form 10-Q—Quarterly report required for each of the first three quarters of the fiscal year.

Form 8-K—Current report required to be filed when certain key events occur.

Basically the 10-K and 10-Qs are routine forms, and the 8-K is used to report something exciting. The 10-K and 10-Q forms contain much of the accounting information discussed early in the chapter. The SEC's web page (*www.sec.gov*) allows you to search and find these forms for all publicly traded companies.

Typically, a company will file the 10-K sometime around March of the following year. For example, the Dynegy 2010 10-K, discussed in the next section, was filed in March 2011.

7. DYNEGY's 2010 FORM 10-K

Corporate documents from Dynegy are used throughout this text to illustrate many of the transactions. On its web page, Dynegy explains itself as follows:

Dynegy provides wholesale power, capacity and ancillary services to utilities, cooperatives, municipalities and other energy companies in six states in our key U.S. regions of the Midwest, the Northeast and the West Coast. The company's power generation portfolio consists of approximately 11,600 megawatts of baseload, intermediate and peaking power plants fueled by a mix of coal, fuel oil and natural gas. Our geographic, dispatch and fuel diversity contribute to a portfolio that is well-positioned to capitalize on regional differences in power prices and weather-driven demand.[12]

Or as the company states more concisely on another part of the web page:

We are a power generation company producing approximately 11,800 megawatts of electricity in 6 states.

For a junior associate tasked with reading the company's 10-K, terms like "baseload, intermediate and peaking" are apt to be quite foreign. That will be the case whenever you begin to learn about a new client, in a new industry. But hopefully the foregoing gives you at least some sense that Dynegy is an energy company that operates pretty much across the country, with the exception of the South.[13]

A common assignment for newly minted attorneys is to write a memo summarizing a new client's business, or for the associate to "get smart" on the client's business.

The easiest way to do this is to get your hands on a copy of the company's most recent 10-K. Maybe you will also pull a copy of the most recent 10-Q, especially if your assignment comes several months after March, and some recent 8-Ks, too.

Please read the Dynegy 2010 10-K, which is available on the course web page. When reading the 10-K, focus especially on the following sections that are apt to be of importance to lawyers:

- Item 1: Business
- Item 1A: Risk Factors
- Item 3: Legal Proceedings
- Item 7: Management's Discussion and Analysis of Financial Condition and Results of Operations
- Item 8: Financial Statements and Supplementary Data
- Notes to Consolidated Financial Statements

The Notes are especially important for lawyers. All of the nuances—the stuff of lawyers—will appear there.

For those of you who are disinclined to read a very long document this early in the class, keep in mind that we will return to Dynegy throughout the course. The better you understand the business now, the easier it will be to understand the company's bond indenture or merger agreement in the future. And how would your client—and your supervising partner—take it if you showed up to the meeting unprepared?

---

12. http://www.dynegy.com/about_dynegy/about_dynegy.asp.
13. Somewhat ironically, since the company has its headquarters in Texas.

2

THE TIME VALUE OF MONEY

Intuitively you probably understand that getting $100 today is different from getting $100 one year from today. For one, you might worry that you will not actually receive the money one year from now. We will ignore the issue of risk for now, but it certainly plays an important role in all corporate finance and will be the subject or subtext of many future chapters.

What other differences are there between $100 today and the same in one year? Having taken the risk of nonpayment off the table, you might be somewhat stumped. After all, $100 is $100, right?

Well, no. If you get $100 today, you can put it in the bank and earn a little interest on it over the next year. That lost interest—which you can think of as the value of getting to use the $100 for a year; in this case you are letting the bank use it and they are paying you—is the heart of the difference between the two payments of $100.

This chapter looks at various ways of accounting for the time value of money. It recognizes that $100 today is not the same as $100 in the future. This chapter is also the first of a few chapters that involve some math. The point is not to review your high school math course, or to make you into a math whiz. Rather, having at least a basic understanding of the math behind valuation techniques will aid you in future interactions with accountants and investment bankers. For example, how can you possibly cross-examine investment bankers if your eyes glaze over when they present their valuation of a company?

Take a deep breath, and if it is of any comfort, know that your author was a history major in college.

1.   ONE PERIOD PRESENT AND FUTURE VALUES

Suppose you take the $100 today and put it in the bank. How much will you have in a year if the interest rate is 5 percent? Intuitively you probably understand that you will have \$5 in interest,[1] and \$100, representing the return of your principal.

Mathematically this can be expressed as:

$$C_1 = C_0 \times (1 + r)$$

where r is the interest rate and C_0 represents the principal amount in question. C_1 is the total value one period in the future—one year in this case.

This is known as a future value calculation. Such formal math probably seems overdone in this case, but understanding this basic form now will make it easier to understand some of the topics addressed in the next section. The future value formula also helps us understand present value calculations. To figure out how much the \$100 you get in one year is worth today, we use the following formula:

$$C_0 = C_1 \div (1 + r)$$

Note that this is just an algebraic transformation of the future value formula, achieved by dividing each side of the first equation by $(1 + r)$. In short, the current or present value (C_0) is equal to the future payment (C_1) divided by the interest rate (r) added to the full principal (here represented by 1, which means 100 percent).

Because r is used to reduce the value of the sum to today's value, it is often referred to as the *discount rate*.[2] The process of calculating the reduced present value of a future payment is known as *discounting*.

Using the numbers from before, imagine you will get \$100 in one year, and if you had the money today you could earn 5 percent on it from the bank. How much is that future payment worth today?

$$C_0 = C_1 \div (1 + r)$$
$$PV = \$100 \div (1.05) = \$95.24$$

Whereas \$100 today is worth \$100, \$100 in one year is worth just over \$95. Which would you rather have?

Note also that the utility of this comparison is highly dependent on the interest rate. If 5 percent is not a useful or relevant interest rate, the result (\$95.24) is largely meaningless. For example, if banks are really paying 2 percent on savings accounts

$$C_0 = C_1 \div (1 + r)$$
$$PV = \$100 \div (1.02) = \$98.04$$

This is a much smaller difference, although if the sum in question is \$100 million, rather than just \$100, the different between \$95 million and \$98 million

---

1. \$100 × 0.05 = \$5. Remember that .05 represents 5 percent in decimal form.

2. In the financial press you will often hear mention of the discount rate, but in that context it refers to the rate at which the local Federal Reserve Bank will lend to commercial banks.

can hardly be ignored. Nonetheless, you have just learned one important lesson: when interest rates are low, the difference between getting money today or getting it in the future is small.

The goal here is to translate all future cash flows into "today dollars." Only by making this adjustment can you directly compare the amounts. But the translation has to be done correctly.

When we introduce risk into the calculation in subsequent chapters, picking the appropriate discount rate becomes even more challenging.

PROBLEM SET 2.1

1.   The preferred stock of Bogartco offers an 8.5 percent rate of return. The stock is currently priced at $200 per share. What is the amount of the annual dividend?

2.   Suppose your client P sues D for breach of contract. D agrees to settle the suit for a payment of $1,000 in one year, which D asserts has a value of $943. What would you want to know?

3.   Given a 10 percent interest rate, why should an investor be indifferent between $100 today and $110 in one year?

4.   What happens to a future value when you decrease r? A present value?

5.   One year ago, you invested $3,000. Today it is worth $3,142.50. What rate of interest did you earn?

6.   You list your apartment for sale and receive two offers. The first offer is for $189,000 in cash. The second offer is for $100,000 today and an additional $100,000 a year from today. If the applicable discount rate is 8.75 percent, which offer should you accept and why?

2.   MULTIPLE PERIOD PRESENT AND FUTURE VALUES

What if you are offered your choice of $100 today or $1,000 in five years? Which is the better choice?

First, start with the question of how much $100 might be worth five years from now, if the bank pays 5 percent. Your first answer might be $125. That is, $5 times five years, plus the original $100.

That calculation is known as *simple interest*. Almost no real world transaction uses simple interest.[3] Instead interest is usually *compounded*—that is, interest is earned on interest. Interest earned in year one is added to principal and then all subsequent years' interest is based on that larger principal amount. For example,

---

3. Gotham Partners, L.P. v. Hallwood Realty Partners, L.P., 817 A.2d 160, 173 (Del. 2002) (quoting the chancery court, explaining that "in Delaware, 'no rule of simple interest exists in the General Corporation Law' and '[t]he rule or practice of awarding simple interest, in this day and age, has nothing to commend it—except that it has always been done that way in the past.'").

in year two you would earn 5 percent interest on $105 in your account, assuming annual compounding.

The formula to calculate compound interest should look very familiar:

$$C_t = C_0 \times (1+r)^t$$

Other than that pesky little t, this is just the future value formula you saw earlier. Indeed, the exponent added to the $1 + r$ was there in section 1, but we could safely ignore it because it was equal to 1.[4] The t is just the number of time periods involved in the calculation.

So if $100 is worth $125 in five years with simple interest, how much is it worth with annual compounding?

$$C_t = C_0 \times (1+r)^t$$
$$C_5 = \$100 \times (1.05)^5 = \$127.63$$

In short, annual compounding would result in an extra return of $2.63.

An important thing to note and understand right at the beginning is this: The formulas in this chapter all involve a payment one period in the future. That is, in the foregoing problem we assumed that the first interest payment would be made one year hence. If there is an interest payment made today, and then every year for five years going forward, you have to add the first interest payment into the first cash flow:

$$C_5 = \$105 \times (1.05)^5 = \$134.01$$

Notice that having that extra $5 in there at the start results in an extra $1.38 at the end.[5]

What if compounding happened more frequently, say monthly? Here you have to remember that t can represent any time period—but you have to be consistent and only compare like time periods to like time periods, both in terms of t and r. In particular, 5 percent is an annual interest rate, but if we are going to use a monthly time period, we need to adjust the rate accordingly. Thus, we get something that looks like this:

$$C_{60} = \$100 \times (1.0042)^{60} = \$128.59$$

where 0.0042 is equal to .05 divided by 12, and 60 is equal to 12 times 5. We get about 70 cents more with monthly compounding than with annual compounding.

Once you understand how to calculate future values with compound interest, you are ready to calculate present values of payments that will be made several periods into the future. Notice the intentional use of "periods," instead of "years." Any time period will work here, too, you just need to remember to keep your periods and rates in the same units.

---

4. Recall that $x^1 = x$.

5. ($134.01 - $105) - ($127.63 - $100) = $1.38.

The present value formula, and the calculation of the present value of $100 received in five years then is:

$$C_0 = C_t \div (1 + r)^t$$
$$PV = \$100 \div (1.05)^5 = \$78.35$$

$100 in five years is worth just over $78 today.

PROBLEM SET 2.2

1. If you want to put some money in the bank today so that you will have $10,000 in ten years, and the bank will pay you 4 percent on a ten-year certificate of deposit (CD), how much should you deposit?
2. What is the difference between $100 in a five-year CD that pays 2 percent and the same CD that pays 2.5 percent, assuming monthly compounding?
3. You are comparing two investments that cost the same. Both will provide you with $30,000 of income. Investment 1 pays five annual payments starting with $10,000 the first year followed by four annual payments of $5,000 each. Investment 2 pays five annual payments of $6,000 each. Which is better?
4. If you have a choice to earn simple interest on $100,000 for three years at 10 percent or annually compounded interest at 9.5 percent for three years, which one will pay more and by how much?
5. You are considering a side job that will pay you $5,000 next year, $7,000 the following year, and $6,000 the third year. What is the present value of these cash flows, given a 7 percent discount rate?

3. PERPETUITIES

BUDGET 2012: PERPETUAL BONDS ISSUE EXAMINED

Harry Wilson, *The Telegraph*, 21 March 2012

The [UK] Treasury is consulting with investors on issuing gilts [government bonds] with maturities of more than 50 years and potentially looking at selling the first perpetual government bond—which pays a coupon but has no redemption date—in more than 60 years.

UK government perpetual bonds are extremely rare and are the oldest gilts still in issue. One bond dates back as far as 1853, though just £900,000 of this issue remains outstanding. In total eight perpetual bonds, worth a combined £2.7bn, remain out of a total gilt stock of £1 trillion.

Anthony Peters, a strategist at SwissInvest, said he thought there would be strong investor demand for a new perpetual gilt if it offered a coupon of 4.5pc, but that below this level the bond would not be attractive. Mr Osborne's [the

Chancellor of the Exchequer] decision to look again at issuing perpetual debt is likely to have come after demand from pension funds for longer-dated bonds and comes as UK interest rates are at a historic low.

"I think the Treasury has probably had a lot of enquiries from investors," said one banker.

As you will learn in subsequent chapters, a bond is simply a debt contract. The borrower agrees to pay back the principal borrowed at some point in the future, and agrees to pay interest on the amount borrowed during the life of the loan.

But note that the article mentions £900,000 of British government debt outstanding from 1853—the year the Crimean War started. When precisely is the bond due? Never.

The British Consols are the most famous real world example of a perpetuity; some were issued in the mid-1700s, but those from the nineteenth century are the oldest currently outstanding.[6] The British government can pay off the debt at its option. Otherwise, the debt remains outstanding and the holder receives periodic interest payments. Obviously no individual buyer from 1853 is still holding the debt, but holders who bought from an original holder or who inherited the bonds are holding the debt and receiving the payments.

How much should you expect to pay to buy an 1853 Consol today? Under the Consol, Her Majesty's Government promises to repay the principal—we will assume £1,000—at some indefinite point in the future.

If we assume the interest rate on the debt is 3 percent, and interest is paid annually, you could do a present value calculation. To keep the math somewhat manageable, we will start with 100 years as our duration.

$$C_0 = C_t \div (1 + r)^t$$
$$PV = £1,000 \div (1.03)^{100} = £52.03$$

What if we had wanted to be a bit more precise, and use 1,000 years in our calculation? Given the size of the exponent, it will be easier to do this calculation with Excel, if you know how to use it.[7]

$$C_0 = C_t \div (1 + r)^t$$
$$PV = £1,000 \div (1.03)^{1000} = £0$$

What happened? Remember that this calculation measures the value of getting our £1,000 principal back at some point (t) in the future. If you go out long enough, the value of getting your money back begins to approach zero. For

----

6. Mentions of Consols can be found in *David Copperfield, Howards End,* and other classic British works.

7. If not, don't worry, it will be covered in a later chapter.

example, using these numbers at 350 years out, the Consol is worth about 3 pence.

This makes some sense. If you were an investor in 1853, would you have ever given the British government £1,000 for 350 years—with instructions to repay your great-great ... grandchildren with interest in 2203? Given all the important historical events that have already happened since 1853—two World Wars, and the collapse of the British Empire, among other things—can you really know if the British government will be in a position to repay at a date that is still some 190 years in the future? It makes some sense that you might have been willing to pay 3 pence, and not much more, for the chance your distant relations would realize £1,000.

Does that mean a perpetuity is worthless? No. At least not if the perpetuity pays the interest during its life, rather than holding it until some unknown maturity at the end.

For a perpetuity that pays periodic interest and then returns principal at the end, the proper way to value the perpetuity is actually to do a series of present value calculations that separate out the interest payments from the principal; for example, 1,000 present value calculations to find the value of the interest payment (£30) over the next ten centuries, then another calculation to value the return of the principal. And then add the whole lot together. Needless to say, this would be quite cumbersome.

The calculations we originally did provide an important insight: namely, most of the value of a perpetuity resides in the early years, and the return of principal is of little import if it is far enough out. For example, we already discovered that at 100 years the principal is worth £52.03. At 50 years it would be worth £228.11, so you can see how quickly the value drops after even the 50th year.

Thus we can value the perpetuity based on the early interest payments alone and ignore the return of principal at the end. Moreover, only the interest payments in the near term really matter, because anything beyond 50 years or so is of increasingly lesser importance. The formula looks like this:

$$PV = \frac{C}{r}$$

Here C is the periodic interest payment, and r is the periodic discount rate.[8] One way to think about this that makes it tangible is to consider that you are one person in a long chain of people who have bought a specific Consol since 1853. Each of you holds it for about 50 years or so, and then sells it to a new young person who continues the cycle. It goes on like that forever, or at least until the British government decides to redeem the debt just prior to joining the United Federation of Planets.

---

8. For those of you who must know where this formula comes from, it is derived from the annuity formula we are about to cover. Basically, insert ∞ for t, and simplify to get the perpetuity formula.

The calculation for our 1853 Consol looks like this:

$$PV = \frac{C}{r} = \frac{£30}{0.03} = £1,000$$

The £30 is just the principal amount multiplied by 3 percent. So today you should expect to pay about £1,000 for your right to take your turn with the 1853 Consol.

There are few examples of perpetual debt in the United States, but it is often found abroad. European banks often issue perpetual debt, for example.[9] But an important and broader insight from this exercise is that if something pays a steady cash flow for enough years—approximately 50 or more—we can treat it as if it were a perpetuity, because the back end does not really affect the math all that much. So, for example, if you win a lottery that promises to pay you $1,000 per year for life, we can treat it as if it were a perpetuity, assuming you are less than 50 years old.[10] If we use a 3 percent discount rate again, your payment stream is worth just over $33,000.

What if your lottery winnings include an adjustment to account for expected increases in the cost of living? For example, what if payout starts at $1,000 and increases by 2 percent each year? This is known as a growing perpetuity, for obvious reasons, and the formula you can use to value it is as follows:

$$PV = \frac{C}{r - g}$$

One qualification: The growth rate must be less than the initial discount rate. If the growth rate equals r, you will end up with zero on the bottom. You also cannot get sensible results if you have a negative number on the bottom. Finally, remember that this assumes a constant rate of growth.

Plugging in the numbers in the example, we get

$$PV = \frac{C}{r - g} = \frac{\$1,000}{0.01} = \$100,000$$

In short, your lottery winnings are worth a lot more with the inflation adjustment built into the payment.

PROBLEM SET 2.3

1. A friend who owns a perpetuity that promises to pay $10,000 at the end of each year, forever, comes to you and offers to sell you all of the

---

9. https://goo.gl/ffV0DW.

10. Even better if you are less than 30, but textbook authors who have just turned 45 are sensitive to this sort of thing.

payments to be received after the 25th year for a price of $10,000. At an interest rate of 10 percent, should you pay the $10,000 today to receive payments numbered 26 and onward? What does this suggest to you about the value of perpetual payments?

2. Your grandmother establishes a trust in your name and deposits $1 million in it. The trust pays a guaranteed 3 percent rate of return. How much will you receive each year if the trust is required to pay you all of the interest earnings on an annual basis?

3. You are to receive $20,000 per year indefinitely. The market rate of interest for these types of payments is 6 percent. What is the value of your payment stream?

4. Following an unfortunate incident involving your laptop, the manufacturer promises to pay you $25,000 a year for life. You further negotiate to have the payment increased by 3 percent per year, which represents the average inflation rate over the past decade. If you want to sell this payment stream to get some immediate cash, how should you price it? You estimate that an appropriate discount rate would be 5 percent.

5. If the relevant interest rate is 5 percent, and a perpetuity pays $100 per year, what is the difference between a 3 percent and 4 percent growth rate?

6. Is a perpetual bond comparable to a fixed amount of currency that pays interest?

4. ANNUITIES

You might have some vague notion that an annuity has something to do with insurance. Insurance companies do offer contracts called annuities, but these are just one example of the larger group of cash flows that can be considered annuities.[11]

Essentially an *annuity* is any regular, periodic payment that does not constitute a perpetuity. For example, suppose you want to borrow money to buy a house. You are considering a 15-year or a 30-year loan. From the lender's perspective, the payments you make on these loans can be seen as 15- or 30-year annuities. Likewise, if you buy a Treasury bond from the U.S. Government, you will receive a series of interest payments and then the return of your principal at the end. As you will see later, this can be valued as an annuity (interest payments) plus the present value of the return of the principal.

In all cases these are perpetuities with the end years cut off. If you understand an annuity in this way, the following equation for the present value of an annuity will be a bit less intimidating:

---

11. *See* http://www.sec.gov/answers/annuity.htm.

$$PV = \frac{C}{r} \times \left[1 - \frac{1}{(1+r)^t}\right]$$

The first term is the present value of a perpetuity. Hopefully you already know all about that. If not, get some coffee and read the prior section again.

The second term, which is always less than one, tells you how much less the annuity is worth because it doesn't continue forever—because you don't get the payments from year n + 1 to infinity. For example, if the second term is equal to 0.40, you know that the annuity is worth 60 percent less than a perpetuity with the same basic terms.[12] In short, the present value of an annuity is the value of the perpetuity less the part you do not receive, because the annuity does not go on forever.

For example, suppose you decide to lease a car for five years, at $400 per month, at a time when annual interest rates are 4 percent. What is the cost of the lease?

$$PV = \frac{C}{r} \times \left[1 - \frac{1}{(1+r)^t}\right] = \frac{\$400}{0.0033} \times \left[1 - \frac{1}{(1.0033)^{60}}\right]$$

Solving the equation, we get a total cost of $21,719.63. Notice that the 4 percent interest rate has been converted into a monthly interest rate, to correspond with the monthly payments reflected in the exponent (t).

We should also consider the future value of an annuity. For example, what if you put $20,000 into a bank account at the end of every year, and the bank pays you 8 percent. What is the value at the end of year five?

Notice this is a different question from that in section 2, where we considered a lump sum placed in a bank account at the beginning of our time period. Here there are a series of sums that go into the account over time. The formula for the future value of an annuity is as follows:

$$FV = C \times \left[\frac{(1+r)^t - 1}{r}\right]$$

Plugging in the numbers from the hypothetical, we get

$$FV = \$20,000 \times \left[\frac{(1.08)^5 - 1}{0.08}\right] = \$117,332$$

You will have saved just over $117,000 by the end of the fifth year, about $17,000 more than the principal you have put into the account.

---

12. 60 percent less, because you are multiplying the perpetuity value by .4, which means you are "keeping" 40 percent of the total value.

If you are beginning to think all this valuation stuff is entirely too hypothetical, we interrupt the chapter to present a case. This involves annuities of the insurance company variety, and the question of how to properly value them for estate tax purposes.

ESTATE OF JOHN A. HANCE, PERCY L. HANCE, EXECUTOR, PETITIONER, v. COMMISSIONER OF INTERNAL REVENUE, RESPONDENT

18 T.C. 499
Tax Court of the United States
June 11, 1952

OPPER, Judge:

Respondent determined a deficiency in estate tax of $125,580.69, based on a number of adjustments of which only one now remains in controversy. An overpayment of $14,791.55 is claimed. The single issue relates to the valuation of seven survivorship annuities taken out by decedent during his life. All of the facts have been stipulated and are hereby so found. The estate tax return was filed with the collector for the third district of New York.

The factual background and the question presented are well summarized in petitioner's brief from which we quote verbatim (pp. 2–3):

*** Decedent John A. Hance died February 22, 1947, survived by his widow. The estate tax return was duly filed and the executor elected to have the gross estate valued as of the optional date in accordance with Section 811 (j) of the Internal Revenue Code. Among the assets reported in the return were seven single premium annuity contracts issued by five life insurance companies. Each of these contracts provided for the payment of a specified annuity to decedent during his lifetime and thereafter to his widow for her life. The widow died May 15, 1947, at the age of 83 years and 9 months. In the estate tax return these contracts were valued at an aggregate amount of $44,632.92. This valuation was arrived at by discounting at the rate of 4% the total payments which would have been received by the widow on the basis of her life expectancy at the time of decedent's death, without regard for the fact that she died on May 15, 1947. For present purposes it is conceded that this method of valuation was incorrect.

The Commissioner has determined that these contracts should be valued on the basis of the cost of similar policies issued on the date of decedent's death to a female applicant of the same age as the surviving widow. It has been stipulated that the total cost of such policies would be $121,905.27. This increase in the valuation of the annuities, coupled with several minor changes not in issue, results in the assessed deficiency of $125,580.69.

Petitioner concedes that the Commissioner has correctly valued the annuity policies as of the date of decedent's death but contends that, because of the election to have the estate valued as of the date one year after death, the

Commissioner erred in failing to allow an adjustment for the difference in value as of the later date not due to mere lapse of time.

The point where the parties are really at odds is the correct interpretations of section 811(j), Internal Revenue Code, [which allows the estate to make] "adjustment for any difference in its value as of [one year after death] not due to mere lapse of time."

The error of respondent's position may be described as his insistence that the widow's actual intervening death did not affect the value of the annuities on the optional date because the possibility of her death within that period was one of the factors taken into account in appraising the property as of the date of decedent's death.

But possibility is all that an actuarial computation can deal with. Actuality is an opposite concept. If we were confined to an appraisal of the facts as they existed at decedent's death, the possibility would be the limit of our concern...

The present situation was, however, envisioned, and we think correctly dealt with, in the *Welliver* case, where we said, referring to the actual intervening death of an annuitant: "*** by such event the interest or estate would not be affected merely by the lapse of time and express provision is made for adjustment on the later date because of a contingency other than the lapse of time."

Respondent in fact expressly a disavows any contention "that death is an event due to mere lapse of time." But it was precisely the widow's death which made the annuities totally worthless by the time the optional date arrived. The statute requires "adjustment for (such) difference in its value as of the later date ***," and there is of course nothing in respondent's regulations to the contrary.

Petitioner proposes to make the requisite adjustment by comparing the cost of annuities of the character involved on the date of decedent's death and of that of the widow. The difference, slightly over $5,000, which is in effect the value of the payments during the interval, is treated as the amount due to mere lapse of time. This appears reasonable considering that an annuitant situated as was decedent's widow would collect the differential by merely remaining alive.

The ultimate effect of this process is to include in the estate the figure representing in substance the payments actually received by the widow, notwithstanding that as of the optional date the annuities were entirely worthless. It is a reasonable result, since that is what turned out to be the dimensions of the property which decedent actually left, and it neither excludes the entire amount nor includes all of an item which by the optional date had ceased to exist. That is exactly what Congress said and we see no reason why they should not also have meant it.

———————————

The court ultimately rejects both parties' valuation of the annuities. What value does it use? Why was the IRS's valuation of the annuities rejected? What is the relationship between the IRS's proffered valuation and those just discussed in this text?

Just as with perpetuities, annuities can have growth features built into the periodic payments. As before, to calculate the present value of a growing annuity, we need to introduce the growth rate (g) at various points in the formula

$$PV = \frac{C}{r-g} \times \left[1 - \left(\frac{1+g}{1+r}\right)^t\right]$$

Be careful to note that sometimes you need to subtract g, but sometimes you are adding g.

For example, a pension might pay $40,000 per year for 30 years with a 5 percent cost of living increase each year. If current interest rates are 8 percent, then

$$PV = \frac{\$40,000}{.08 - .05} \times \left[1 - \left(\frac{1+.05}{1+.08}\right)^{30}\right]$$

$$PV = 1.33m \times 0.5705$$
$$PV = \$760,666.67$$

The recipient owns a stream of cash flows that is currently worth just over $760,000. In this example more of the steps are shown to highlight the fact that a growing perpetuity under these terms would be worth $1.33 million, whereas the 30-year annuity is worth about 60 percent as much.

PROBLEM SET 2.4

1. What is the present value of a four-year annuity of $100 per year that makes its first payment two years from today if the discount rate is 4 percent?
2. A settlement gave an accident victim four payments of $50,000 to be paid at the end of each of the next four years. Using a discount rate of 2 percent, what is the value of the settlement? What if the discount rate were 3 percent?
3. Goldman Sachs currently has notes outstanding that pay 5.95 percent interest on the $1,000 face amount of each note. Interest is paid every six months, and the notes mature January 16, 2027. What is the present value of the interest payments from January 15, 2013 until maturity?
4. There are three factors that affect the future value of an annuity. How will an increase in each affect the future value of the annuity?
5. You represent Nick in a divorce. He is married to Charles, who is retired and has a pension that entitles him to a monthly benefit of $1,200 on the date of separation. Charles has a life expectancy of 30 years. The pension company is well established, and you believe a reasonable rate of return

would be 3.0 percent above 20-year Treasury bonds—or 6 percent compounded monthly. If the entire pension was earned during marriage, what is its current value as a marital asset?

6. An investment that costs $800,000 will pay you $170,000 a year for ten years. Investments with similar risk pay 14 percent interest. What is the value of the investment? What can you conclude by comparing the value of the investment to its cost?

3

DISCOUNT RATES

To this point we have used a discount rate that was stated in the problem, or assumed that the cash flows at hand could be discounted using a low-risk or risk-free interest rate, like the government bond rate or a bank account rate. But the real world rarely works that way, so now that we have the basics of valuation under our belts, we need to examine the factors that go into a proper discount rate.

You can think of interest as the rent that a debtor has to pay a creditor for use of the creditor's money. If the creditor can get 5 percent by lending its money to the federal government, then you will have to pay something more than 5 percent to get the creditor to lend the money to you instead. Likewise, if you want to borrow money for five years, and the creditor can lend the money for two years and get 3 percent, you will likely have to pay something more than 3 percent to borrow for five years.

Imbedded in these and other questions are important issues of risk, capital structure, and inflation. But first we talk about two foundation issues: the concepts of expected return and opportunity cost of capital.

1. EXPECTED RETURN

Suppose you loan your friend $1,000 for a year, and she promises to pay you back with 5 percent interest. In friendly terms, you might say that you expect to get $1,050 from this transaction.

But is that really right? You might not think about it, but there is probably some chance, however slight, that your friend won't pay you back. It might be for "bad" reasons, like she decides she would rather use the money for a new boogie board. Or she might not pay for a "good" reason, like she ended up in the hospital after an "incident" while boogie boarding in Santa Monica (piers are hard).

In any event, there is some chance you will not get paid. Let's say that chance is 5 percent—in other words, your friend pays you back 95 percent of the time. Then the possible outcomes for this transaction are:

Paid back	$1,050
Not paid back	$0

Putting the outcomes together with the probability that each will happen, you could calculate a weighted average of the outcomes:

$$ER= (.05)\$0 + (.95)\$1,050$$
$$ER=\$997.50$$

This is an expected return calculation as used in economics and finance. Your real expected return at the outset of this transaction is about $52 less than you thought it was.

Notice also that the expected return is not necessarily a return that will actually happen—instead, it's an average. In the current example the possible outcomes are rather binary—all or nothing—and there is no way to actually achieve a return of $997.

But as we discuss later in this chapter, the expected return might influence your decision about whether 5 percent is the right interest rate to charge on this loan. Notice that you are "buying" an investment for $1,000 that has an expected return of less than $1,000. That should give you pause.

And then there is the time value of money. You are paying $1,000 for an expected return of $997 in one year. As we saw in the prior chapter, it is very unlikely that $997 in one year is worth $1,000 today.

PROBLEM SET 3.1

1. Joe is considering an investment in London Calling, Inc. He expects that if the economy does poorly the investment will lose about 10 percent, but if the economy is booming it will make 10 percent. He thinks there is about an equal chance of either outcome. On the other hand, if the economy stays about as it is, which he thinks has a 50 percent chance of happening, his investment will return 4 percent. What is the expected return?

2. It is reported that in the early 1800s the Prince of Wales was short of cash and thus offered, on his ascension to the throne, to give £10,000 and a lordship in Ireland to anyone who would give him £5,000 right away.[1] Assume you are a wealthy investor in 1800. How would you evaluate this   "investment?"

---

1. See the second volume of J.F. Molloy, *Court Life Below Stairs* (rev ed. 1885).

2.   OPPORTUNITY COST OF CAPITAL

As has been suggested before, one sensible way of evaluating investments is to consider the alternatives. If you can put your $1,000 in the bank for a year and earn 5 percent, there probably is no reason to lend the money to your friend at the same rate, unless you are a very good friend indeed. After all, the FDIC insures bank accounts in the United States for up to $250,000, so the probability of the bad outcome from that investment is 0 percent.[2]

That tells you that your loan should carry an interest rate of more than 5 percent, but it does not tell you what interest rate you should charge. For example, what if the proper comparison is the Standard & Poor's (S&P) 500, an index of the return of the 500 largest U.S. company stocks?[3]

For the past three years that index returned an average of 8.52 percent per year.[4] Of course, over the past ten years the index returned only 4.67 percent per year, reflecting the inclusion of the period around the Lehman Brothers bankruptcy in September 2008. If the loan carries similar risks as stocks of large corporations, the S&P 500 reflects an appropriate return for the loan.

In short, making the loan to your friend has a positive cost. If you have $1,000 available, you could invest it in a variety of projects, only one of which is the loan to your friend. Assuming your funds are finite—which they are for most everyone besides the Federal Reserve—choosing one project precludes another.

This is the concept of opportunity cost of capital. The corresponding rule is that the "opportunity cost of capital" is always the right rate at which to discount cash flows. Why?

If the bank pays 5 percent on one-year deposits, and your friend will also pay 5 percent, but with a chance of default, 5 percent is the minimum applicable discount rate because that is what you are giving up by making the loan. And the real cost or value of the loan is what your friend would pay if she obtained the loan in the market, in an arm's-length transaction. If you want to give your friend a break, that's fine. But the value of the loan is still measured by the opportunity cost of giving it.

PROBLEM SET 3.2

1.   Ziggy has a chance to invest in his friend David's new startup company, Sound & Vision, Ltd. David has promised Ziggy that if he makes a $100,000 investment, Sound & Vision will begin paying a 10 percent return in five years. David expects this return to continue at that level for decades to come. Ziggy currently earns 5 percent on his account at Aladdin Bank, 6 percent on his investment in Scary Monsters Industries,

---

2. If you've been burying gold in your backyard because of your fears of the size of the federal government's debts, feel free to replace 0 percent with "really, really small."

3. http://us.spindices.com/indices/equity/sp-500.

4. In all cases, measured from the end of April 2016.

a large NYSE traded company, and 7 percent on his investment in Major Tom Bakeries, a company started by another friend. Should Ziggy make the investment in David's new company?

ATLANTIC RICHFIELD COMPANY v. FARM CREDIT BANK OF WICHITA

226 F.3d 1138

United States Court of Appeals, Tenth Circuit.
Sept. 13, 2000.

BRISCOE, Circuit Judge.

This complex litigation involves several oil and gas leases. The lessee, plaintiff Atlantic Richfield Company ("ARCO"), filed a claim for declaratory relief. The defendant lessors [are] the Farm Credit Bank of Wichita ("FCB"), . . . and members of the Garcia family ("the Garcias").

I. BACKGROUND

In the 1970s, ARCO discovered that carbon dioxide ("CO_2") can be used to increase recovery from certain types of oil reservoirs. This process is commonly referred to as "tertiary recovery" or "enhanced oil recovery" ("EOR"). In 1975, ARCO acquired oil and gas leases for lands in Huerfano County, Colorado with the potential for CO_2 production. FCB ... and the Garcias own royalty interests in these leases, which were [consolidated] into a "Sheep Mountain Unit" ("SMU") for the exploration, development, and production of CO_2. Because the nearest market is approximately 400 miles away, ARCO constructed a pipeline (the "Pipeline") to transport the CO_2 from the SMU to the Permian Basin in West Texas.

As intended, CO_2 from the SMU is sold, used in kind, or exchanged to increase oil production in West Texas. To determine the "wellhead" value of the CO_2 and the lessors' royalties, ARCO uses a "work back" or "net back" method. ARCO calculates the wellhead value of the CO_2 by subtracting transportation and conditioning costs from the value of the CO_2 in the West Texas market. The costs deducted by ARCO fall into three categories: (1) operations and maintenance costs; (2) depreciation costs, which include interest during construction ("IDC"); and (3) cost of capital ("COC"). ARCO defines IDC as the cost of money used to build a facility, or the "[i]nterest charged on the investments made prior to commencement of operations." ARCO defines COC as the "opportunity cost" of capital, including the cost of building a facility through debt or equity financing. In other words, COC is "the rate of return that is required to induce investors to purchase the securities of a firm. This rate of return is the same as an investor's opportunity cost of capital, which is the rate of return that an investor can earn on an investment of similar risk."

ARCO initiated this litigation by filing suit against FCB . . . and other parties in July 1995. Among other things, the company requested a judicial declaration that "it has been and continues to be proper for ARCO to deduct the allocated share of all costs associated with transporting the CO^2 Gas from the point of production at the Sheep Mountain Unit to the West Texas market from royalty payments."

. . .

C. THE COMPONENTS OF THE TRANSPORTATION DEDUCTION

1. IDC and COC

Whether IDC and COC are deductible transportation expenses depends in part on the language of the parties' lease contracts. We begin with the Garcias' lease contract, which permits "reasonable" deductions for the "cost of transporting" CO^2 from the SMU to the point of use. Accordingly, our first task is to determine whether the phrase "cost of transporting" in the Garcias' lease unambiguously includes or excludes IDC and COC. If we conclude that the phrase is indeed unambiguous and that it includes IDC and COC, our next task is to determine whether the reasonableness of ARCO's deductions is a disputed issue of material fact.

We need not complete the second task, because the phrase "cost of transporting" is decidedly ambiguous. The phrase does not expressly include IDC and COC. Nor does it expressly exclude IDC and COC. Moreover, several permutations of the word "cost" have been deemed ambiguous by Colorado courts. For example, in *Tripp v. Cotter Corp.*, 701 P.2d 124 (Colo.Ct.App.1985), a Colorado court of appeals concluded that the phrase "cost of milling" was ambiguous:

> [T]he mining contract at issue here does not expressly describe the components to be included in calculating the costs of milling. There is nothing in the contract which defined the phrase "cost of ... milling," nor were there any provisions which described what the phrase encompassed in terms of those costs. The phrase in question is therefore ambiguous, and testimony offered for the purpose of explaining and interpreting it should not have been excluded.

Id. at 126. Other Colorado cases reach similar results.

Generic dictionary definitions also provide little assistance in resolving this ambiguity. The leading definition of "cost" is "the amount or equivalent paid or given or charged or engaged to be paid or given for anything bought or taken in barter or for service rendered." *Webster's Third New Int'l Dictionary* 515 (unabridged ed.1993); *see also Black's Law Dictionary* 345 (6th ed.1990) (defining "cost" as "expense," "price," and "[t]he sum or equivalent expended, paid or charged for something"). "Transport" is normally defined as "to transfer or convey from one person or place to another," and "transportation" is commonly thought to mean "an act, process, or instance of transporting or being transported." *Webster's Third New Int'l Dictionary* 2430 (unabridged ed.1993); *see also Black's Law Dictionary* 1499 (6th ed.1990) (defining "transport" as "[t]o carry or convey from one place to another," and "transportation" as "[t]he movement of goods or persons from one place to another, by a carrier"). It is not obvious whether IDC and COC—i.e., the returns that might have been achieved through alternative investments—constitute "amounts paid or given or charged" to "transfer or convey" something from one place to another. Given the uncertain meaning of the Garcias' lease, we reverse the district court's grant of summary judgment and remand this issue for additional proceedings.

Next we address FCB's lease contract, which does not contain the phrase "cost of transporting." Because FCB's lease does not address the deductibility of transportation expenses, our review of the contract is governed by *Garman.* *Garman* and its progeny establish that lessees may deduct reasonable "transportation costs," absent a lease provision to the contrary. *See Rogers,* 986 P.2d at 971, 975. Hence, under the *Garman-Rogers* rubric ARCO's IDC and COC are deductible if they (1) qualify as transportation costs, and (2) are reasonable. The definition of "transportation costs" is a question of law, while the reasonableness of any given transportation expense is a question of fact. *Cf. Garman,* 886 P.2d at 661 n. 28 (remarking that the deductibility of certain post-production marketing costs is "a question of fact to be decided based on competent evidence in the record"); *Rogers,* 986 P.2d at 972 (echoing that "whether any specific post-production cost" is incurred to make a product marketable or to enhance its value is "to be determined by the fact-finder in each case").

We conclude that IDC and COC are, in fact, deductible unless the parties provide otherwise in the lease contract. No Colorado case directly addresses this issue. Nonetheless, at least two other sources of authority suggest that IDC and COC fall within the definition of "transportation costs" for purposes of royalty deductions. First, as the Colorado Supreme Court intimated in *Garman,* federal regulations governing deductions for post-production expenses are "instructive." 886 P.2d at 661 n. 28. These regulations permit a "transportation allowance" based on the "reasonable actual costs" incurred by certain lessees. 30 C.F.R. § 206.157(b) (1998). As implemented by the Minerals Management Service (a bureau of the United States Department of the Interior), federal regulations allow ARCO to deduct IDC and COC when calculating royalties on government leases. Second, Colorado tax regulations enacted in 1996 allow "return on investment" and "return of investment" deductions for transportation equipment. These regulations likewise suggest that IDC and COC constitute deductible expenses ... We REVERSE the district court's ruling that the phrase "cost of transporting" in the Garcias' lease unambiguously excludes IDC and COC, and REMAND this issue for additional proceedings. On remand the district court should again determine what extrinsic evidence, if any, is relevant and admissible for the purpose of clarifying the meaning of the phrase "cost of transporting" as it appears in the Garcias' contract.

As regards FCB's lease which was silent as to transportation costs, we REVERSE the district court's ruling that IDC and COC do not constitute "transportation costs" under *Garman* and its progeny. Unless the parties intended something to the contrary in their contracts, IDC and COC are "transportation costs" under *Garman* and its progeny. If the district court or a jury determines on remand that FCB's lease permits ARCO to deduct transportation expenses, then IDC and COC should be included in the calculation.

––––––––––––––

What role does "cost of capital" play in this case? Do you find the court's distinction between the two leases persuasive? Before taking this class, would you have considered IDC and COC as part of the cost of producing a product? Should they be part of the cost?

3. RISK

Up until now, we have largely skirted around the question of risk by either stipulating that the risk-free rate applied or by stating the amount of risk involved in a particular project. Not so anymore.

Risk is one of the biggest drivers of corporate finance transactions, but it is also an extremely broad concept. Take the prior problem, where Ziggy:

- Gives Sound & Vision $100,000 with no fixed promise of repayment.
- Waits five years to begin receiving returns.
- Receives a fixed return once the return begins.

Each of these elements presents risk. For example, the first bullet point highlights the liquidity risk associated with this investment. We are not told if the investment takes the form of a loan or equity (shares), but in any event there is no obvious way for Ziggy to get his money out if he needs it. The second bullet point reminds us that Ziggy turns over his money to Sound & Vision and then has to trust that the company will honor its end of the bargain. In your first year of law school you took an entire class about people breaching their contracts— investment contracts are no different. And the final bullet point reminds us that Ziggy is locking in a return that looks good today, but might look very bad in the future.

In general, risk in finance relates to future changes that will cause a particular deal to become more expensive or otherwise less attractive. These changes will alter the return of the project.

The other thing to understand about risk and corporate finance is that risk comes with a price. The United States currently borrows money for five years at less than 2 percent interest—in May 2016 it was about 1.25 percent. The highest rated corporations currently borrow for the same term at about 1.4 percent.[5] That is, although these highly regarded corporations are considered essentially risk free—they have the same credit ratings as Norway and Switzerland—the market perceives there is slightly more risk lending to a corporation rather than the U.S. government. Perhaps this reflects the ability of the U.S. government to raise taxes, or even "print" money, to satisfy its obligations. Whatever the reason, the corporation pays more to borrow money.

As you will see throughout this book, risk and return are closely related. In May 2016 another five-year debt obligation was paying a return of just under 4.5 percent. Why so much more? The debt was issued by Puerto Rico, or more precisely the Puerto Rico Electric Power Authority. As you may know, the Commonwealth is presently facing serious debt problems, and has recently defaulted on some of its debt. In short, there is doubt about Puerto Rico's ability to repay.

A lesson to learn now is that if five-year U.S. government debt is paying 1.25 percent, the only way to earn more than that is to take on more risk.[6] You might lend the money for a longer time period, or you might lend it to a riskier borrower. But you will take on more risk. Anybody who tells you otherwise is lying.

4.   CAPITAL STRUCTURE AND THE ABSOLUTE PRIORITY RULE

One key element of risk in corporate finance involves the investor's standing on default. For example, imagine a simple company that defaults on its debts with a balance sheet as follows:

Assets	*Liabilities & Equity*
$100	$100 unsecured loan
	100 shares of common stock

Who gets what? The short answer is that the creditors—who gave the loan—take the assets and the shareholders get nothing. In bankruptcy this ordering of claimants is known as the absolute priority rule.[7]

---

5. This specifically refers to the yield on a Johnson & Johnson note as of May 2016.

6. The assumption here is that we are dealing with efficient or liquid markets—like the market for U.S. government debt. In some less efficient markets it might be possible to find mispriced assets, but the price will still be higher than the corresponding U.S. government interest rate.

7. Case v. Los Angeles Lumber Products Co., 308 U.S. 106, 117, 60 S. Ct. 1, 8, 84 L. Ed. 110 (1939).

ELIZABETH WARREN, *A THEORY OF ABSOLUTE PRIORITY*

1991 Ann. Surv. Am. L. 9, 37–38 (1992)

The legal rule of absolute priority had its genesis in the long-standing common law maxim that creditors would be paid ahead of equity. This rule assured those who did business with the corporation that if the business were dissolved the creditors would be paid before the insiders would recover their investments. In the case of collapse, the creditors could count on payment in full before equity collected anything from the business assets.

The provision is a form of creditor protection, one of many that attempt to restrict the ability of corporate owners and insiders from depleting a failing business for their own benefit, leaving the creditors with only the empty shell of a business. In part, the rule is designed to offset some of the consequences of superior information and control necessarily available to equity owners when they manage the business or exercise close supervision over the nominal managers. The rules of absolute priority satisfy concerns similar to those of state law rules of dividend distribution, for example, which require that the corporation only distribute stock dividends from earned surplus rather than from general assets of the business. As any good law-and-economics devotee could point out, creditors could have insisted on such provisions in advance, but the law provides an off-the-rack ordering among the parties that is nearest to what the parties would likely have negotiated for themselves, requiring that the owners/insiders restrict their abilities to take assets from the business to the injury of the creditors.

The basic idea is that secured creditors (creditors with liens or mortgages) get paid before unsecured creditors who get paid before shareholders.

Each of these financial instruments is examined in greater detail in subsequent chapters, but the goal now is to understand how the rule affects the cost of financing. Return to the simple example of the $100 asset firm at the start of this section—once you understand the absolute priority rule you can understand why the company will have to pay a greater return to its shareholders than it pays to unsecured creditors. Unless the firm can dupe its investors. But that is a trick that typically only works once; thereafter, investors get wise.

It is a simple matter of risk, opportunity costs, and expected return: The shareholders face a higher risk of losing their investment, so they will demand a higher return on their investment. Otherwise they might as well put their money in the bank. Or U.S government debt.

As a result of the absolute priority rule, investors higher in the capital structure face lower risks and get correspondingly lower returns. Of course, this does not mean that there is no risk—if there are no assets to liquidate, the pain will quickly move up the capital structure.

Imagine, for example, the investors in a manual typewriter manufacturer. How much will the machinery in the factory sell for? The secured creditors might be first in line to receive nothing.

PROBLEM SET 3.3

1. Siouxsie & Banshees, Inc. has 100 shareholders, each holding one share, and the following creditors: a $10 million secured bank loan, $400,000 owed to various trade creditors, $500,000 owed to unsecured bondholders, and $300,000 owed on a tort judgment. If its assets equal $11 million, who gets what on liquidation? Would you expect the bank loan or the unsecured bonds to have the higher interest rate? What about the trade creditors and the tort judgment?

5.   THE ROLE OF INFLATION

If you took a history class in college you probably associate inflation with Germany of the 1920s, when people had to bring wheelbarrows full of bills to the store just to buy a lamb chop. [8] Strictly speaking, that is an example of hyperinflation: The money lost so much value that German Marks were sold in London's East End as decorative paper to line kitchen shelves. The notes were sold by weight.

Inflation is the rate at which prices are rising and purchasing power is falling. For example, if inflation is 3 percent, a bottle of soda that costs $1 now will cost $1.03 in a year.[9] Conversely, for every dollar in wages you can buy increasingly less soda each year (which is probably for the best, anyway).

One of the most common measures of inflation is the Consumer Price Index (CPI), which measures the average change over time of prices paid by urban consumers for a basket of several hundred consumer goods and services. There are actually several versions of the CPI. One of the most common, shown in Figure 3-1, is called the All Items Consumer Price Index for All Urban Consumers (CPI-U) for the U.S. City Average. Another commonly used measure, which is also shown on the chart, is the same measure less food and energy costs. This is often referred to as "core" inflation, as the items that are removed tend to be more volatile than inflation generally.

As shown, the United States briefly experienced deflation in the immediate aftermath of the recent financial crisis. Typically, central banks—like the U.S. Federal Reserve—try to manage inflation to keep it from getting too high, while also avoiding deflation, which can have serious economic consequences. An

---

8. http://en.wikipedia.org/wiki/German_reichsmark.

9. For those of you wondering about the realism of this example, we can concede that the manufacturer likely will absorb the price increase for a year or two and then raise the price to some nice round number, say $1.25.

inflation rate of 2 to 3 percent is often said to be ideal. As you can see, the core rate of inflation only recently returned to those levels.

In finance, inflation (or deflation) is a key risk factor, especially in transactions that involve a fixed rate of return. Inflation is a risk here because the investor does not know what its *real rate of return* will be. For example, if you loan your friend $1,000 at 5 percent for a year, and inflation rate is currently 3 percent per year, then the real return on your loan would be 2 percent at year's end. And if the Federal Reserve stumbles a bit, and inflation goes to 5 percent, you have received no real return whatsoever—you've essentially treaded water.

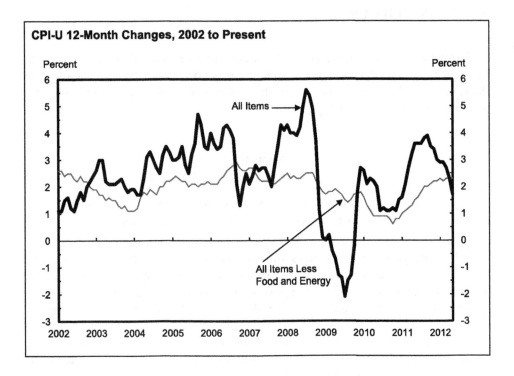

FIGURE 3-1
CPI-U 12-Month Changes, 2002 to 2012.
Source: **U.S. Bureau of Labor Statistics.**

Thus when we speak of inflation as a risk, we are referring to the uncertainty over the future real value of an investment. The risk increases the longer the term of the investment, simply because if there is some uncertainty about inflation next year, there is even more uncertainty regarding the level of inflation in years thereafter.

PROBLEM SET 3.4

1. Bauhaus Bank is considering making a ten-year loan to Peter. Peter would like a fixed-rate loan. The bank wants to make a floating-rate loan, whereby Peter would pay interest equal to the U.S. government bond rate plus a spread. What risks do Peter and Bank face with either approach?
2. Explain how inflation and deflation affect the interests of debtors and creditors.

6.   THE YIELD CURVE

The *term structure of interest rates*, also known as the *yield curve*, refers to the typical pattern of interest rates where rates get progressively higher the longer the term of the lending. Table 3-1 illustrates this with U.S government bond rates at the beginning of May 2016.[10]

TABLE 3-1
U.S. Government Bond Rates

	1 Mo	3 Mo	6 Mo	1 Yr	2 Yr	3 Yr	5 Yr	7 Yr	10 Yr	20 Yr	30 Yr
05/02/16	0.11	0.22	0.41	0.55	0.80	0.96	1.32	1.64	1.88	2.31	2.71

When the yield curve displays this pattern it is said to be *upward sloping*, because if you graphed the rates the result would be an upward sloping curve. The longer the money is lent to the government, the greater the return.

This is a normal situation because short-term debts generally hold less risk than long-term debts; the further into the future a debt's maturity, the more time and, therefore, uncertainty the creditor faces before being paid back its principal. There is risk of nonpayment and risk of unforeseen inflation. To invest in one instrument for a longer period of time, an investor needs to be compensated for undertaking the additional risk.

Other situations can arise. For example, sometimes the yield curve will "flatten." In these situations, long-term interest rates are very close to short-term interest rates. This often indicates periods of market uncertainty. For example, the U.S. government bond rates shown in Table 3-2 were quoted at the beginning of 2008. Notice how close the three-month and five-year rates are.

---

10. For the current rates, see http://goo.gl/BLjf1.

TABLE 3-2
U.S. Government Bond Rates, 2008

	1 Mo	3 Mo	6 Mo	1 Yr	2 Yr	3 Yr	5 Yr	7 Yr	10 Yr	20 Yr	30 Yr
1/2/08	3.09	3.26	3.32	3.17	2.88	2.89	3.28	3.54	3.91	4.39	4.35

In especially rare situations, the yield curve can invert. One reason why this might happen could be a rush of investors locking in long-term rates, because they expect rates to decline as the economy is entering recession (or worse). Table 3-2 shows some evidence of inversion—compare the one-, three-, and six-month rates with the two- and three-year rates. Recall that Lehman Brothers filed its bankruptcy petition in September of that year. If you had correctly interpreted the yield curve in January, you might have made a lot of money (or at least avoided some losses).

The key lesson here is that interest rates—and thus discount rates—vary a good deal based on their term. Thus, when discounting, it is vital to use an interest rate that reflects the term of the project you are discounting. For example, it would make no sense to discount the one-year loan to your friend using the five-year government bond rate.[11] Inasmuch as the term structure of rates reflects the risks involved in lending over various periods, you can think of this rule as a subset of the larger rule that you should always discount at the opportunity cost of capital.

PROBLEM SET 3.5

1. Andrew wants to borrow some money from Floodland Bank so he can buy a drum machine for his new gothic rock band. As it happens, Andrew is so very wealthy that the bank considers the loan nearly risk free, and they will charge Andrew the government bond rate plus 0.05 percent. If the loan is made in May 2016, how much interest would Andrew pay if he borrowed $5,000 for three, five, or seven years? What is the present value of these loans? Be ready to discuss the implications of these calculations.

7. DISCOUNTING WITH RISK

As we have seen in this chapter, calculating present or future values in a meaningful way requires the use of an appropriate discount rate. We have shown "appropriate" to mean a discount or interest rate that takes into account the risk

---

11. That actually involves two errors, as we have discussed: the term is wrong, and lending to your friend entails greater default risk than lending to the U.S. government.

of nonpayment (the default risk), the inflation risk, and the duration risk. As part of duration, you might also consider liquidity risk: how easy will be it for one party to sell their position if they need quick cash?

Considering the expected return of a particular project will lead you to understand the actual return for a project, assuming that you correctly weight each of the possible outcomes. In the real world, assigning probabilities to outcomes is much less precise than it is in a law school classroom.

That expected return should then be expressed in present value terms by discounting using the opportunity cost of capital, which will encapsulate all the risks discussed in this chapter. Note also how the decisions made in the expected value calculation—for example, what is the probability of nonpayment?—will tend to influence the choices made with regard to the appropriate opportunity cost of capital.

For example, remember that we decided at the beginning of the chapter that the $1,000 loan to your friend had a 5 percent chance of default, resulting in an expected return of $997 on your $1,000 investment. You would then look around for a comparable investment: a one-year investment, with similar risk of nonperformance. But the latter exercise presupposes that we correctly estimated your friend's likelihood of default: if the probability the friend will not repay is instead 8 percent, we need to consider a different opportunity cost of capital.

PROBLEM SET 3.6

1. Review pages 95 to 96 of the 2010 Dynegy 10-K (regarding the pension obligations) and be prepared to discuss.

4

THE NET PRESENT VALUE RULE AND SOME COMPETITORS

Given an investment opportunity, a firm needs to decide whether undertaking the investment will generate net economic profits or losses for the company. To do this, the firm estimates the future cash flows of the project and discounts them using a discount rate that represents the project's opportunity cost of capital. Subtracting this number from the initial cash outlay required for the investment provides the net present value of the investment.

In short, return minus cost gives you the value of the investment. If the value is positive, it's a good investment. If the value is negative, you are losing money on the deal. That's the essence of the net present value (NPV) rule.

For example, remember your loan to a friend. The net present value of that loan is the difference between the present value of its benefits (e.g., the interest the friend will pay you) and the present value of its costs (e.g., the loss of use of the money for a year, or the risk of nonpayment).

$$NPV = PV\,(Benefits) - PV\,(Costs)$$

But traditionally we actually write the formula this way:

$$NPV = PV\,(Costs) + PV\,(Benefits)$$
$$or$$
$$NPV = C_0 + C_1 \ldots + C_t$$

The reason is that this puts the cash flows in time order: The costs typically come before the benefits. The trick is to remember that costs are a *negative* cash flow, as you are paying money out.

If the NPV of a prospective project is positive, it should be accepted. However, if the NPV is negative, the project should be rejected because cash flows will also be negative. This is the *NPV rule*.

So you loan your friend $1,000 for a year, and she promises to pay you back with 5 percent interest. You now know about expected return, and the opportunity cost of capital, so after thinking about it for a while you decide that an appropriate discount rate is 7 percent for this investment.

Now right off the bat you should intuitively see the problem: When the discount rate is higher than the return on the project, the project can never have a positive NPV. But it is very important not to solve this problem by fooling yourself and rationalizing your way into a discount rate that is below 5 percent.

This is also why understanding the role of the discount rate is vital. When you find yourself cross-examining a witness who is explaining why the defendant bank manager's loan to his friend was perfectly proper based on an NPV calculation, that witness is never going to say "and I used a 4 percent discount rate because that's the only way I could get the numbers to 'work.'" You must be able to show the judge or jury that the witness manipulated the NPV formula to achieve a desired result.

Just to confirm that you understand this, let's prove what we already intuitively know. Here is the NPV calculation for the loan to your friend:

$$NPV = C_0 + C_1$$

$$NPV = -1{,}000 + \frac{997}{1.07} = -68.22$$

Notice that we used the expected cash flow here, not the "best case" cash flow. If your discount rate already accounts for the risk of default, you could argue that this overpenalizes your friend for the risk of nonpayment. If you are comfortable with your discount rate assumptions, you might use $1,000 instead of $997 for the final cash flow.

In either case, the project has a negative NPV and thus should be rejected under the "NPV rule." Of course, this is your friend, and maybe the amorphous benefits of helping your friend make up the difference.

But in most business transactions, conducted at arm's length, the lender has no desire to subsidize the other side of the deal. And that makes sense: Why should the shareholders of JP Morgan Chase subsidize the shareholders of some other big corporation that borrows from the bank? Indeed, if you see one firm making a negative NPV investment in another firm, you should immediately question why this is happening. Maybe there is a common controlling shareholder? Or maybe the officers of one of the corporations are breaching their duty of loyalty?

PROBLEM SET 4.1

1. In exchange for $500 today, you will receive $550 in one year with certainty. If the risk-free rate is 3 percent, what is the NPV of this investment? What if the risk-free rate were 8 percent?

2. A company can spend $28,000 today for a machine that it expects will help the company make $12,500 next year and $19,500 the following year, but only $3,000 in the third year, as the machine begins to break down and needs to be replaced. If the company's discount rate is 12 percent, should the company buy the machine?

1. COMPARING COMPETING PROJECTS: MORE ON THE NPV RULE

For the most part, clients do not typically sit around with infinite piles of money, considering possible investments. Instead, a decision to invest in one project necessarily precludes another project.

How does the NPV rule work here? It works quite well, thanks for asking. This is also a good place to introduce Excel, the big green X on your computer that you've probably only opened by mistake and then quickly closed. Open it up now and follow along, because it is important to get over your fears about the program. After all, many of your clients will use it, and they are not apt to be too impressed if you will not even open a spreadsheet they send you.

Imagine that you have created a small business while in law school that delivers coffee, tea, and other caffeinated products to students throughout the law school based on orders placed via Snapchat or Twitter, or whatever it is the youngsters are using these days. Business is booming, and you think you could sell the operation to the dean or a 1L for $300,000.

It costs you about $20,000 per year to run the business, which generates $70,000 a year in net income, and you could still sell the business for $300,000 in two years when you graduate. If you did not have to study so much, you think the business could generate more income—maybe $100,000. You could hire an employee to run the business for you, but that would increase costs up to $50,000. So you will only net $50,000. The advantage of this approach is that you suspect you could keep the business operating for at least a decade with very little day-to-day involvement. You figure the business at that point would have a remaining value of maybe $100,000.

In the background is your belief that you could receive a 5 percent return, with similar risk, if you invested your money elsewhere. How do you compare your various options?

First, we will make some simplifying assumptions: All costs are incurred now, but net income from the "own" or "operate" options is received only at the end of this year (which we will further assume is twelve months from now), and every year thereafter. This results in the cash flows shown in the table below. Note that because the "operate" and "own" options involve net cash flows going forward, you need to be careful not to include costs twice.

Consider three options that appear in the problem:

- Sell the business now and use the $300,000 to pay off some of your student loans.
- Continue to operate the business and sell it at the end of the year you graduate.
- Continue to own the business, but not operate it personally, for 10 years, at which point it will have a smaller residual value.

Each option can then be valued and considered with the NPV rule. The cash flows look like this:

	Today	End 2L	End 3L
Sell	$300,000	$0	$0
Operate	−$20,000	$70,000	$370,000
Own	−$50,000	$50,000	$50,000...

Notice that if you retain ownership of the business, but delegate operations to an employee, you simply hold an annuity that generates $100,000 per year, but to keep it going you have to incur $50,000 of cost for the next several years, so you net $50,000.[1] And the basic question is whether $300,000 in hand is worth more than $370,000 next year or the annuity. In evaluating the annuity option, we also have to remember the ability to sell the business in the future.

If you open the spreadsheet for this chapter, available on the course webpage, in the tab labeled "NPV hypo" you will see something that looks like this:

	Today	End 2L	End 3L	NPV	Excel Formula
Sell	$300,000	$0	$0	300,000.00	
Operate	($20,000)	$70,000	$370,000	382,267.57	=B3+NPV(5%, C3:D3)
Own	($50,000)	$50,000	$50,000...	394,554.68	=B4+PV(5%, 10, -C4) +(100000/(1.05^11))

The left side looks just like this table, but on the right we have added two new columns. The first, helpfully entitled "NPV," provides the answers to this problem. More on that in a moment.

First, note the column on the far right. This shows the formula that you can also see if you click on the answer in the NPV column. That is, $382,267.57 is the answer provided by the formula =B3+NPV(5%, C3:D3). What does this mean in English?

Excel's NPV formula is essentially not an NPV formula, but rather a present value formula, as it leaves out the "net" bit. It assumes that the first cash flow starts in one time period in the future. That means to actually do an NPV calculation you have to manually enter the first payment, which is typically a negative. That explains the "B3+" part of the formula, as that tells Excel to add the contents of box (or cell) B3—column B, row 3—to the results of the NPV formula.

The Excel NPV formula itself generates the present value of a range of numbers—here the numbers in cells C3 through D3—at a specified interest rate, which in this problem is given as 5 percent.

As you might expect given the perplexing nature of the NPV formula, the PV formula is also not quite a present value formula. It is a present value of an

---

1. There is an unrealistic assumption about inflation here—do you see it?

annuity formula. Thus, "PV(5%, 10, -C4)" provides the present value of an annuity at a 5 percent discount rate, with ten periods (starting one period from today), paying the negative of the amount shown in cell C4.

The formula is set up for outbound cash flows—that is, there is an implied negative in the formula—so if you omit the negative sign shown above, your result will be negative and you will get the wrong answer once you do the addition to reach the NPV. If you are using the formula to find the present value of a loan—or any other transaction with periodic inbound cash payments—the formula works "as is" and does not require the negative sign.

Despite these quirks, using Excel is obviously much easier than using the manual formulas discussed in Chapter 2. Of course, only by looking at the formulas can you understand the intuitions involved, which is likely to be of greater use in your future career. That, in short, is why the mean old author is only introducing Excel now.

Returning to the hypothetical, you can see that owning the business, and running it with an employee, is the best option, with an NPV that is more than $12,000 greater than the next best option. This is the result of the residual value we have assigned to the business after the end of the annuity. This is represented in the Excel formula by the "+(100000/(1.05^11)" which is tagged onto the end of our annuity formula.

We have assumed that you do not receive both the payout from the business and the value of selling the business in year ten. That is, the formula as shown assumes you earn your net payout from the business in year ten and then sell it the next year. If it were possible to both obtain the full cash flow from the business and sell it in the same year, we would change our exponent to 10, in which case the NPV of this option would increase by about $3,000. You can see this by changing the exponent in the spreadsheet yourself.

But if you were to delete the entire part of the formula that relates to the residual value, you would see that operating the business for two more years and then selling it is the highest value option, worth almost $50,000 more than the next best option. That cautions us that one easy way to slip up in these calculations would be to overestimate the residual value. In a real transaction—where the numbers are typically not given from "on high" (as your author likes to refer to himself) —you would want to look at the residual value quite carefully.

PROBLEM SET 4.2

1. How would the hypothetical above change if the discount rate were 19 percent? Or 1 percent?
2. Bogartco is considering expanding from its traditional trench coats and fedoras into a new product line. It can fund up to $400,000 in new projects, and its cost of capital is 8 percent. Bogartco will liquidate whatever project it chooses at year four. Which of the following should it choose?

	Initial Cost	Year 1 Cash Flow	Year 2 Cash Flow	Year 3 Cash Flow	Value at end of Year 4
Lead falcon statues	$100,000	$50,000	$50,000	$50,000	$60,000
Piano covers	$200,000	$20,000	$20,000	$20,000	$100,000
High Sierra brand tonic water	$300,000		$50,000	$50,000	$250,000
Badges	$400,000	$10,000	$10,000	$10,000	$100,000

2.   COMPARING COMPETING PROJECTS: INTERNAL RATE OF RETURN

As the last problem of the foregoing problem set shows, NPV can help you choose among competing projects. But the results are often somewhat less than intuitive. For example, how would you explain in plain English your decision to pick a certain project over another in the prior problem?

The internal rate of return (IRR) rule provides more intuitive results, but it would not be easy to use it for Problem 2, for reasons that will soon become clear. First, we need to understand IRR.

IRR is defined as the interest rate that will set a particular NPV calculation to zero. Finding the IRR of a particular project thus involves solving the NPV equation for r. You could probably do the math for a simple, two-cash-flow NPV equation. But with multiple cash flows, the math becomes cumbersome.

Business school textbooks typically describe three ways to find an IRR without higher math. Only one of these is likely to be of relevance to you.

First, you can graph an NPV profile—basically just the graph of the NPV values (on the y axis) that result from a range of discount rates (on the x axis). The point at which the graph crosses zero is your IRR. Better find that graph paper you have left over from junior high school! The other method involves trial and error. In short, start plugging in possible discount rates, narrowing down the range until you get an NPV close to zero.

Both of these methods are useful if you find yourself transported back to the 1940s (and forget to take your laptop). But since at least the waning days of the Carter administration, the only likely way that you would calculate an IRR is with a spreadsheet, which today probably means Excel, unless you're an anti-Microsoft fanatic.

Take the example of Bogartco's badge manufacturing business from Problem Set 4.2. The cash flows looked like this:

Today	Year 1	Year 2	Year 3	Year 4
($400,000)	$10,000	$10,000	$10,000	$100,000

To calculate the IRR, you simply put these numbers into a spreadsheet and use the IRR formula in reference to them. For example, in a new spreadsheet your formula would look like this:

$$= IRR(A1:E1)$$

That returns a result of -27 percent. Negative 27 percent sounds bad. Much more intuitive than the negative dollars you obtained in the NPV calculation.

Beyond its intuitive appeal, the IRR also provides a good check on how sensitive a particular NPV calculation is to the assumed discount rate. Namely, because IRR is the point at which NPV crosses over to a negative number, we can subtract the assumed cost of capital from the IRR to find the margin of error in our estimate.

So if we have a particular project with an IRR of 37 percent, and we subtract our discount rate of 8 percent from that, we know that even if our discount rate is seriously in error, the project will still have a positive NPV. On the other hand, if you calculate that the IRR is very close to the discount rate, you know that a small change in the discount rate could tip the project from one you should accept to one you should reject. For example, if a project has an IRR of 5 percent and our cost of capital is 4.5 percent, just a 1 percent mistake in our cost of capital (or discount rate) will entirely change the NPV analysis.

This also leads us to a clear statement of the *IRR rule*: Take any project where the IRR exceeds the cost of capital, and reject any project where the IRR is less than the cost of capital.

The IRR rule is predicated on a traditional pattern of cash flows, where cash is paid out at the beginning and returned at various periods thereafter. If you reverse the pattern—say you receive $1,000 today, but pay out $100 over the next five years—what you are really examining is a loan. In that case, the rule must be flipped: Only accept the project if the IRR is *less than* the cost of capital.

Indeed, the IRR method really only works with the prototypical example of cash paid out at T_0 and cash paid back over several periods. For example, if cash is paid into the project at several points—after the project has begun to return cash—there will be several possible IRRs, as the plot of NPV values crosses zero every time the project's cash flows change their sign.

There can also be instances where there is no IRR for a particular project—imagine a project with NPV values that are uniformly positive or uniformly negative. The plot never crosses the x-axis in either case.

Most important, you cannot directly compare IRRs when projects differ in their scale (different amounts of money are involved), their timing (cash flows come at different times), or their riskiness. To examine this, let's return to your law school business from the beginning of the chapter. Recall that you had the following opportunities:

- Sell the business now and use the $300,000 to pay off student loans.
- Continue to operate the business and sell it at the end of the year you graduate.

- Continue to own the business, but not operate it personally, for ten years (with cash flows commencing twelve months from today), and then realize the residual value.

These resulted in the following cash flows:

	Today	End 2L	End 3L	NPV
Sell	$300,000	$0	$0	$300,000.00
Operate	($20,000)	$70,000	$370,000	$382,267.57
Own	($50,000)	$50,000	$50,000…	$394,554.68

Under the NPV rule, and using a 5 percent discount rate, we decided you would be best off operating the business for a decade and then selling it. How would this analysis look under IRR?

Let's focus our analysis on the decision between "operate" and "sell," because once you pick between those, you can then decide if the return from the better project beats what you could do with $300,000 (the "sell" option) over the same time period.

You might be tempted to do something like this, especially if you have not been reading very closely:

	Today	End 2L	End 3L	IRR
Operate	($20,000)	$70,000	$370,000	539%
Own	($50,000)	$50,000	$50,000…	100%

Then you say *voilà!* Only a moron would turn down 539 percent! Especially when compared to 100 percent, which you are quite sure is less than 539 percent.

But wait a second, didn't the NPV rule tell us to take the "own" project? What is going on? This is an example of the "conflicting signals" problem that can occur when you try to compare unequal projects using IRR: note that the *own* project is of much longer duration than the *operate* project.

To see an even plainer example where using IRR would lead to the completely wrong result, look at the following table, which involves comparison of projects with a 5 percent discount rate:

	Today	Year One	Year Two	Year Three	IRR	NPV
Monty's Project	(750,000.00)	310,000.00	430,000.00	330,000.00	19.83%	220,327.18
Pat's Project	(2,100,000.00)	1,200,000.00	760,000.00	850,000.00	17.36%	466,461.51

If you are an IRR fanatic, you would take Monty's project, which has the higher rate of return. But what about Pat's project, with the higher NPV? The problem is that Monty's project offers a higher rate of return on a smaller amount of money.

Is it really better to get 19.8 percent on an investment of $750,000, or should you take 17.36 percent on an investment of much more money?

To answer this question, you need to calculate an *incremental IRR* and compare that to the relevant cost of capital (sometimes also referred to as a "hurdle rate"—5 percent in this case).

This involves creating a hypothetical project where you give up the seemingly higher returning project but smaller project by subtracting it from the larger, but seemingly lower returning project. You then calculate the IRR for that new project.

	Today	*Year One*	*Year Two*	*Year Three*	*IRR*	*NPV*
Monty's Project	(750,000.00)	310,000.00	430,000.00	330,000.00	19.83%	220,327.18
Pat's Project	(2,100,000.00)	1,200,000.00	760,000.00	850,000.00	17.36%	466,461.51
P-M	(1,350,000.00)	890,000.00	330,000.00	520,000.00	15.78%	

The result—15 percent—is well above our 5 percent hurdle rate, so we should take Pat's project and reject Monty's. Notice that the incremental IRR calculation accounts for the fact that we are unable to undertake both projects: picking Pat's project requires us to lose out on Monty's, but even under that condition the return on Pat's project is higher than our opportunity cost of capital.

The Monty-Pat conundrum is an example of projects of *unequal scale*. The same basic rule applies for projects of *unequal duration*. IRR assumes that you can always reinvest your funds at the same IRR, which is often not actually true. Relying on IRR alone overemphasizes the short term. Which project would you rather invest in?

- Franklin's project lasts for one year and offers a 100 percent IRR. Your money doubles.
- Winston's project lasts for five years and offers a lower IRR of 58 percent, but a higher NPV.

Franklin's project would indeed be better, if you could reinvest the proceeds for four more years at a 100 percent annual rate of return. If you can only reinvest at a lower market rate, say 10 percent, Winston's project is better. Only by calculating an incremental IRR, where you consider if Winston's project is still attractive even after giving up the gains of Franklin's project, can you really understand which project is the better investment.

PROBLEM SET 4.3

1. Calculate the incremental IRR for the "own" versus "operate" decision discussed earlier:

	Today	End 2L	End 3L	IRR
Operate	($20,000)	$70,000	$370,000	539%
Own	($50,000)	$50,000	$50,000...	100%

2. Compare the IRR for two projects. In Project 1 you invest $100 and receive $150 back in year. In Project 2, you invest $100 and receive $750.38 back in five years. If the cost of capital is 10 percent, which project do you choose? What is the IRR and NPV for each project?

3. Assume we have the following two projects, with the following payouts:

	Project A	Project B
2012	−$100,000	−$100,000
2013	+$50,000	0
2014	+$50,000	0
2015	+$50,000	+$152,087.50

The cost of capital for both projects is 10 percent. Find the NPV and IRR for each. Which project should you choose?

3.   PAYBACK AND HURDLE RATES

Payback rules and hurdle rates are largely tangential to understanding finance from a legal perspective. Because your client might mention them, though, it helps to know what they are. After all, blank stares don't inspire confidence.

Hurdle rates were mentioned in passing before, but warrant a fuller discussion. Virtually all businesses have some sort of hurdle rate, even if it is implicit, but the easiest way to understand this idea is to look at financial institutions. If a bank has to pay 5 percent to its depositors, then the "hurdle rate" for its projects (i.e., loans) must be at least 5 percent. That is, unless it wants to experience insolvency, it has to take in more than it pays out.

That's the basic ideal with a hurdle rate: The firm sets some bar over which all projects must pass.[2] At the very least this hurdle rate should be the opportunity cost of capital—for the reasons we discussed in prior chapters. As we will discuss in Chapter 11, many firms use a hurdle rate above their actual cost of capital.

Payback rules are similar rules of thumb that companies use when evaluating projects. The idea is that all projects must "pay back" their initial investment within a specified period of time. This does tend to reject long-term projects, but

2. In the hedge fund context, it has the related meaning of the minimum return that the fund must earn before the manager starts to collect management fees. *See* Chapter 20.

it also preserves liquidity for the firm, because the firm's cash must come back within the specified period.

To calculate the payback period for a particular project, simply add up the number of cash flows needed to return the nominal amount of cash originally invested in the project. For example, if a project involves a $50,000 investment and returns $10,000 per year, the payback period is five years.

Rarely will the calculation be this tidy, and thus calculation of a payback period often involves prorating the final payment over the final year. If we again take the $50,000 investment, but posit $12,000 per year cash flows, the calculation becomes

$$PP = 4 + \left[\frac{50,000 - 48,000}{12,000} \right]$$
$$PP = 4 + 0.167$$
$$PP = 4.167$$

where PP is the payback period, which we find is 4.167 years.

Neither of these rules is a substitute for the NPV or IRR analysis described earlier, but rather you will tend to see them used in conjunction with other tools for evaluating projects.

PROBLEM SET 4.4

1.   Consider the projects outlined in Problem 3 of Problem Set 4.3. What is the payback period for each? If Bogartco uses a two-year payback rule, which project will it pick?
2.   If Bogartco has an internal hurdle rate of 10 percent and finds that a particular new project has an IRR of 12 percent, should it necessarily go forward with the project?

5

VALUING BONDS

A *bond* is a security sold by a government or corporation. In essence, it is a contract whereby an investor (the creditor) gives the government or corporation (the debtor) some money and the borrower promises to repay that money at some point in the future.

The bond markets are massive in the United States, representing almost $35 trillion of investments—about three and a half times the size of the better known stock market. The largest single borrower in that market is the U.S. government. As of this writing, there was approximately $19 trillion of U.S. Treasury debt outstanding.[1]

Bonds will be the subject of several classes in this course, but for now we consider bonds from a valuation perspective.[2] Of course, to value bonds you first have to understand them, so we begin with a basic primer of bond types and how they "work."

1. TYPES OF BONDS

In North America, corporate bonds typically come in $1,000 increments and pay interest semiannually.[3] Thus, if you hold a single "Goldman Sachs Group 5.95% Note due 01/15/27," the company owes you $1,000 in 2027 and will pay you 2.975 percent interest on $1,000 every six months.[4] The 5.95 percent in the bond's title is simply the semiannual interest rate multiplied by two, as by convention bonds quote annual interest rates.

---

1. http://www.treasurydirect.gov/NP/debt/current.

2. *See also* Chapters 14 and 15.

3. In other jurisdictions, you might find that bonds pay interest quarterly or annually.

4. These bonds—or notes—were issued in November 2006. The issuer is the parent holding company of the bank with the same name.

PRELIMINARY REOFFERING CIRCULAR DATED JULY 15, 2013

Existing Issues Reoffered

On the date of original issuance of the Bonds, Sidley Austin LLP, Bond Counsel, delivered its opinion that interest on the Bonds would be exempt from personal income taxes imposed by the State of New York or any political subdivision thereof, including the City, and assuming continuing compliance with the provisions of the Internal Revenue Code of 1986, as amended (the "Code"), interest on the Bonds is not includable in the gross income of the owners thereof for federal income tax purposes. In connection with the reoffering, Fulbright & Jaworski LLP, Bond Counsel to the City for Tax Matters, will deliver its opinion (i) with respect to any of the Bonds that are not treated as reissued under the Code, that the conversion to a fixed rate to maturity of the interest rate will not in and of itself adversely affect the exclusion of interest on such Bonds from gross income for purposes of federal income taxation and (ii) with respect to any of the Bonds that are treated as reissued under the Code, that interest on such Bonds will be exempt from personal income taxes imposed by the State of New York or any political subdivision thereof, including the City, and assuming compliance with the provisions of the Code, interest on such Bonds is not includable in the gross income of the owners thereof for federal income tax purposes. See "SECTION III: MISCELLANEOUS —Tax Matters" herein for further information.

$135,000,000*
The City of New York
Tax-Exempt General Obligation Bonds
Fiscal 2014 Subseries 1

Conversion Date: August 15, 2013*   Due: As shown on the inside cover page

The outstanding bonds of (i) Fiscal 1994 Series A, Subseries A-8, A-9 and A-10 that are scheduled to mature in the years 2016 through 2018, inclusive, (ii) Fiscal 1994 Series B, Subseries B-3 that are scheduled to mature in the years 2017 and 2018, (iii) Fiscal 1994 Series H, Subseries H-3 that are scheduled to mature in 2014 and (iv) Fiscal 2006 Series E, Subseries E-2, E-3 and E-4 that would have been mandatorily redeemed in the years 2017 through 2021, inclusive, will be converted to the Fixed Rate Mode. To the extent such conversions constitute a reissuance under the Code, the related Bonds will be redesignated Fiscal 2014, Subseries 1 and, to the extent such conversions do not constitute a reissuance under the Code, the related Bonds will retain their original designation.

The Bonds are registered in the nominee name of The Depository Trust Company, New York, New York, which acts as securities depository for the Bonds.

Interest on the Bonds will be payable on each February 1 and August 1, commencing February 1, 2014. The Bonds can be purchased in principal amounts of $5,000 or any integral multiple thereof. Other terms of the Bonds are described herein. *A detailed schedule of the Bonds is set forth on the inside cover page.*

Effective upon the conversion of the Bonds to the Fixed Rate Mode, the Bonds will not be subject to tender for purchase and the former liquidity and letter of credit providers, as applicable, will have no liability with respect to the Bonds. The Bonds are subject to redemption as set forth herein.

In connection with the change in the method of determining the interest rates and other modifications of the Bonds, certain legal matters will be passed upon by Sidley Austin LLP, New York, New York, Bond Counsel to the City. Certain legal matters will be passed upon for the City by Fulbright & Jaworski LLP, a member of Norton Rose Fulbright, New York, New York, Bond Counsel to the City for Tax Matters. Certain legal matters in connection with the preparation of this Reoffering Circular will be passed upon for the City by Orrick, Herrington & Sutcliffe LLP, New York, New York, Special Disclosure Counsel to the City. Certain legal matters will be passed upon for the Underwriters by Squire Sanders (US) LLP, New York, New York, and D. Seaton and Associates, New York, New York, Co-Counsel to the Underwriters. It is expected that the Bonds will be available for delivery in New York, New York, on their date of conversion which is expected to be on or about August 15, 2013.

	J.P. Morgan	
BofA Merrill Lynch		**Citigroup**
Jefferies	**Morgan Stanley**	**Siebert Brandford Shank & Co., L.L.C.**
Barclays Capital	**M.R. Beal & Company**	**Fidelity Capital Markets**
Goldman, Sachs & Co.	**Janney Montgomery Scott LLC**	**Lebenthal & Co., LLC**
Loop Capital Markets LLC	**PNC Capital Markets LLC**	**Ramirez & Co., Inc.**
Raymond James	**RBC Capital Markets**	**Rice Financial Products Company**
Roosevelt & Cross Incorporated	**Southwest Securities, Inc.**	**Wells Fargo Securities**
Blaylock Robert Van, LLC	**Cabrera Capital Markets, LLC**	**Drexel Hamilton LLC**
	TD Securities (USA) LLC	

July   , 2013

_____
*   Subject to change.

Each interest payment is referred to as a *coupon*. In the old days—and still today with respect to some European bonds—bonds were bearer instruments. Whoever had physical possession of the bond was the owner. To get an interest payment, the holder had to cut off a coupon attached to the bond and send it in to the issuer or the issuer's agent (often a bank).

The $1,000 value of the bond is the principal lent to the issuer. It is also referred to as the bond's par or face value. *Zero coupon bonds* are bonds that make no periodic interest payments during their life. Instead, they are issued at a discount to par. In municipal finance these are often called *capital appreciation bonds*.

For example, a company might sell a one-year zero coupon bond to an investor for $960. The investor gets $1,000 in 12 months. The difference between the face value of the bond and the purchase price is effectively interest, and the IRS will treat it as such for tax purposes. U.S. government Treasury Bills— which have a maturity of less than one year—and U.S. Savings Bonds are common examples of zero coupon bonds.

Bonds that are issued at less than par are said to have "original issue discount" (OID). All zero coupon bonds have OID by definition—but interest-paying bonds may also be issued with OID. Can you describe what the effect is of combining OID and a stated interest rate?

As noted before, bonds can be issued by corporations or governments, and the issuing entity could be either foreign or domestic. For example, you might have heard that Greece recently engaged in a restructuring of its debt—bonds that it had issued to borrow money for various governmental purposes.

Bonds are also issued by cities, counties, and states within the United States. Under U.S. tax law, interest paid on this state and municipal debt is not subject to federal tax, and interest paid by the investor's "home state" is typically exempt from state and local tax, too. This gives these *municipal bonds* a special advantage in the marketplace.[5]

For example, assume a corporate bond has a yield of 8 percent, and a municipal bond has a yield of 6 percent. If your tax rate is 40 percent, which would you prefer?

It should also be noted that cities and counties can file for bankruptcy under chapter 9 of the Bankruptcy Code–Detroit being a recent example, whereas states are not presently eligible to file (and some argue could never be for constitutional reasons).[6] How would this affect the value of a California bond as compared with a bond issued by the City of Los Angeles?

---

5. Municipal bonds are often issued in increments of $5,000, unlike corporate bonds.

6. Melissa B. Jacoby, *Federalism Form and Function in the Detroit Bankruptcy*, 33 Yale J. on Reg. 55 (2016).

Final Term Sheet
USD 3,000,000,000 4.75% Global Notes due May 15, 2012

Terms:

Issuer:	KfW
Guarantor:	Federal Republic of Germany
Aggregate Principal Amount:	USD 3,000,000,000
Denomination:	USD 1,000
Maturity:	May 15, 2012
Redemption Amount:	100%
Interest Rate:	4.75% per annum, payable semiannually in arrears
Date of Pricing:	April 24, 2007
Closing Date:	April 30, 2007
Interest Payment Dates:	May 15 and November 15 in each year
First Interest Payment Date:	November 15, 2007
Interest Payable on First Payment Date:	USD 77,187,500
Currency of Payments:	USD
Price to Public/Issue Price:	99.665%
Underwriting Commissions:	0.10%
Proceeds to Issuer:	99.565%
Format:	SEC-registered global notes
Listing:	Luxembourg Stock Exchange (regulated market)
Business Day:	New York
Business Day Convention:	Following, unadjusted
Day Count Fraction:	30/360
Governing Law/Jurisdiction:	German Law; District Court Frankfurt am Main

FIGURE 5-1
KfW Bond Sheet

2.   BOND PRICING AND THE PRICE/YIELD RELATIONSHIP

As noted previously, corporate bonds are typically issued in $1,000 increments. Nonetheless, bond prices are quoted in the market in terms of 100. You can either think of this as a percentage, or the price without one of the trailing zeros. Thus, a bond priced at 100 is trading at par value—its original $1,000 issued price. But bonds don't necessarily trade at par. Instead, bonds can trade at a premium or a discount to par, and movements away from par are particularly common with long-term debt instruments. For example, the Goldman Sachs notes discussed earlier were issued in late 2006 at par, but in July 2012 were priced at 103.93800, meaning you could sell the note for more than the face value the holder will receive when the note matures in 2027. [7] Why might that be?

Remember back in Chapter 3, when we talked about interest rates? There we noted that ten-year U.S. government bonds were paying 1.88 percent interest and 20-year government bonds were paying 2.31 percent. The Goldman Sachs bonds—which are due in 15 years—have a 5.95 percent coupon.

Although Goldman Sachs plainly presents more risk than the U.S. government—the financial crisis made that clear—in a low interest rate environment the 5.95 percent coupon is so desirable that investors are willing to pay more than par to buy the bonds.

What is the effect of paying more than par? In short, it reduces the return or yield the bondholder receives. Rather than receiving 5.95 percent, as a par buyer would, a Goldman Sachs noteholder who buys at 103.93800 will receive a lower yield—closer to 5.5 percent.

When a bond's interest rate is higher than prevailing rates, the bond's price will go up—beyond par value. When a bond's interest rate is lower than prevailing rates, the bond price will go down. In short, this is the fundamental law of bond prices: Prices and yields move in opposite directions. If market interest rates go up, prices will go down, and vice versa.

---

[7] In February 2017, these instruments were trading at 113.5973.

PROBLEM SET 5.1

1. Review and explain the following table, which shows actual bond quotes as of July 2012:

	Coupon	Maturity	Qty.	Price	Min	Max	Accrued Interest	Estimated Total Cost
Johnson & Johnson Notes	6.95	9/1/29	25	150.541	1	372	$661.22	$38,296.47
Wal-Mart Notes	5.875	4/5/27	25	132.29302	2	50	$420.23	$33,493.49
Gen Elec Cap Cp Med Trm Nt	5.1	2/15/19	6	111.66667	6	6	$130.05	$6,830.05
Ge Captal Bonds	5.55	5/4/20	25	116.459	1	104	$285.21	$29,399.96
Gen Elec Cap Cp Med Trm	3.5	4/15/22	25	102.8	1	541	$221.18	$25,921.18
Ralston Purina Debenture	8.625	2/15/22	5	144.772	1	5	$183.28	$7,421.88
Merck & Co Inc Deb	6.4	3/1/28	25	138.72202	10	44	$608.89	$35,289.39
Genl Elec Cap Cp	6.75	4/15/18	12	118.49	1	12	$209.25	$14,428.05

3.   VALUING A BOND AS AN ANNUITY

The value of a bond is the sum of the present values of all coupon payments plus the present value of the returned par value at maturity of the bond. In short, you need to value (1) a stream of cash flows (semiannual interest payments), and (2) the return of $1,000 at some point in the future, and then add the two together.

Valuing a stream of cash flows we already know how to do—that's an annuity. And you know how to value the return of a lump sum at some point in the future. Putting it together, the formula for valuing a bond is then

$$\text{PV of bond} = \frac{I}{r}\left[1 - \frac{1}{(1+r)^t}\right] + \frac{\$1,000}{(1+r)^t}$$

where I is equal to the periodic interest payment. Remember that you will typically have to divide the stated interest rate by two and multiply that by $1,000 to calculate I. Also remember that the entire formula here will have to be based on a t of some number of six-month periods. For example, if you are valuing a ten-year bond, t will equal 20, and your discount rate (r) will have to be a six-month interest rate as well.

This assumes that you find yourself valuing a bond one day after an interest payment. Quite often, that will not be the case. Instead, some amount of interest will have accrued and the valuation will need to take that into account.

You saw an example of this in Problem Set 5.1. The price with the extra accrued interest is referred to as the "dirty" price for the bond, and you see that price listed in the column on the far right.

Figuring out how much interest is accrued but unpaid since the last interest payment is somewhat trickier than it might appear at first blush. The problem arises because you need to know how many days are in a year—as calculated under the terms of the bond in question. That is, although we all know that most years have 365 days, unless it's a leap year with 366, any sort of corporate finance document is free to adopt a different day count convention.

U.S. government debt uses the actual days of the year to calculate interest payments, but most corporate bonds do not. The actual day count convention might appear easier—it's certainly more intuitive—but remember that for any fraction of a year you have to account for months with 30 days, others have 31 days, and then there is the oddness that is February. Because of this, most bonds instead provide that all months are deemed to have 30 days, and all years are deemed to have 360 days. Then, a bond sold between semiannual interest payments accrues interest at the rate of 1/180th of the six-month interest payment per day.

Look at the KfW term sheet on page 64. What was the day count convention used there?

Next, recall the Goldman Sachs Group 5.95 percent notes. The semiannual interest is calculated as 0.0595 divided by two, or 0.02975, times $1,000. That results in a semiannual interest payment of $29.75. If we are now two months past the last interest payment, we know that $9.917 of interest has accrued. Do you see why?

PROBLEM SET 5.2

For all problems in this set, assume the market rate of interest is 6 percent per year.

1. Value the Goldman Sachs notes described in the prior section as of January 1, 2013, assuming that there is no accrued interest. Then assume that two months of interest have accrued (see above). What is the total value of the bond? What price would you expect to pay for the bond?
2. Value a ten-year zero coupon bond. What price would you expect it to sell for today? Would a zero coupon bond ever trade at a premium?

4. YIELD TO MATURITY

Yield to maturity (YTM) is a useful concept for comparing various bonds of different durations and prices in the market. YTM calculates the yield for a particular bond, given its current market price, if held to maturity. In other words, what *r* will give you a value for the bond that is equal to its current price? This should sound very familiar.

YTM is essentially an application of internal rate of return (IRR) to bonds. By finding the *r* that sets the bond's present value equal to its price, we are also finding the *r* that gives us a zero NPV if we were evaluating a project comprised of investing in the bond.

As with IRR, calculating YTM by hand would be quite burdensome, and after about 1980 only a math fanatic would do such a thing. Instead, use the "Yield" function in Excel.

For example, to calculate the YTM for the Goldman Sachs Group 5.95 percent notes discussed earlier (which mature on January 15, 2027), and using July 13, 2012 as "today," when the notes were trading at just over 105, you would enter the following into Excel:

=YIELD (Start, Maturity, Rate, Price, Redemption, Frequency)

=YIELD ("7/13/2012", "1/15/2027", 0.0595, 105.139, 100, 2)

which gives you a YTM of 5.4 percent. Note that the interest rate is put in at its annual rate, and then the "2" toward the end of the formula tells Excel to use semiannual payments. The number corresponds to the number of annual payments—for example, 12 would indicate monthly payments.

While we're at it, you should also know about another useful formula, the "Price" function in Excel. This allows you to calculate the price or value of a bond, given certain pieces of information. Wouldn't that have been helpful in the prior section?

Again, consider the Goldman Sachs notes:

=PRICE (Settlement, Maturity, Rate, Yield, Redemption, Frequency)

=PRICE ("7/13/2012", "1/15/2027", 0.0595, 0.0543, 100, 2)

As you can see, this function works much like the yield function, but here we are solving for price given the *required* yield (i.e., market yield) or a YTM. The formula above refers to the YTM we previously calculated, and we see that the result is the same as the actual market price used in the yield calculation earlier.

PROBLEM SET 5.3

1. Schnoodleman Ltd. issued a 30-year bond on March 15, 2003, with a 5 percent coupon. The bond currently trades at 120. What is the bond's YTM? What is the YTM if the bond currently trades at 85?
2. B. B. Worth, Inc. issued some bonds that have 20 years to go until maturity. The bonds have a 4 percent coupon, but similar companies are issuing new 20-year debt with 5 percent coupons. What is the current price of the bonds?

3. Hugo & Monkey Newspapers, Inc. just issued 30-year bonds, with a 3.5 percent coupon. Find the price for these bonds at years 3, 5, 10, 20, 25, and 29 if similar bonds yield 4.5 percent throughout. What if similar bonds instead yield 3 percent?

5. BOND RATINGS

Bond ratings are an assessment of an issuer's ability to repay its debt, based on its history of borrowing, repayment, and other factors. Currently three companies dominate the ratings business: Fitch, Moody's, and Standard & Poor's. S&P uses letters ranging from AAA—the highest rated companies, like Microsoft—to D, which means the company is in default. The corresponding Moody's ratings are Aaa and C.

Ratings reflect an assessment of an issuer's creditworthiness, and thus lower ratings should correspond with higher yields. Bonds in the lower range, but not in default, are referred to as "junk" or high-yield bonds.[8]

This, of course, assumes that the rating agencies are doing a good job. During the financial crisis, it came out that an employee of a leading ratings agency had said that "We rate every deal. It could be structured by cows and we would rate it."

ABU DHABI COMMERCIAL BANK v. MORGAN STANLEY & CO., ET AL.

651 F.Supp.2d 155

United States District Court, S.D. New York

Sept. 2, 2009

SHIRA A. SCHEINDLIN, District Judge.

I. INTRODUCTION

Two institutional investors, King County, Washington ("King County") and Abu Dhabi Commercial Bank ("ADCB" and, together with King County, "plaintiffs"), bring this class action to recover losses stemming from the liquidation of notes issued by a structured investment vehicle ("SIV") between October 2004 and October 2007. Plaintiffs have sued eight defendants . . . [including] Moody's Investors Service, Inc. and its affiliates, including wholly-owned and controlled subsidiary Moody's Investors Service Ltd. (collectively, "Moody's"); The McGraw–Hill Companies, Inc. and its affiliates, including its wholly-owned and controlled business division Standard & Poor's Rating Services (collectively, "S & P," and, together with Moody's, the "Rating Agencies") (collectively, "defendants"). Plaintiffs bring thirty-two claims of common law fraud, negligent misrepresentation, negligence, breach of fiduciary

---

8. From BB (S&P) or Bb (Moody's), to C or Ca.

duty, breach of contract and related contract claims, unjust enrichment, and aiding and abetting against defendants. Defendants now move to dismiss the First Amended Complaint . . .

II. BACKGROUND

A. FACTS

1. Credit Ratings and the Cheyne SIV

Beginning in approximately 2004, investors, including plaintiffs, began purchasing interests issued by non-party Cheyne Finance PLC (now known as SIV Portfolio PLC) ("Cheyne PLC"), which is now in receivership as a bankrupt entity, and its wholly-owned subsidiaries Cheyne Finance LLC and Cheyne Capital Notes LLC (collectively, "Cheyne LLC," and together with Cheyne PLC, the "Cheyne SIV"). The Cheyne SIV, as is typical of SIVs, issued three categories of notes, Commercial Paper, Medium-Term Notes (together with Commercial Paper, "Senior Notes"), and Mezzanine Capital Notes ("Capital Notes" and, together with the Senior Notes, "Rated Notes"), each of which was rated by the Rating Agencies.

The notes that SIV investors purchase typically receive ratings from rating agencies as a condition precedent to purchase. Rating agencies, like Moody's and S & P, evaluate a debt offering based on public, and sometimes nonpublic, information regarding the assets of an issuer and assign the debt offering a rating to convey information to a potential creditor/investor about the creditworthiness of the issuer's debt.

Historically, however, this was not always a rating agency's role. Prior to 1975, rating agencies provided unsolicited ratings on the creditworthiness of corporations, which were derived from publicly available information about the corporation, such as Securities and Exchange Commission ("SEC") filings, and charged a fee to the investor to view the rating. Over time, the market came to trust rating agencies for their integrity and unbiased approach to evaluating issuers and their debt offerings. Then, in 1975, the SEC created a special status to distinguish the most credible and reliable rating agencies, identifying them as "nationally recognized statistical rating organizations" or "NRSROs" to help ensure the integrity of the ratings process. According to the SEC, the "single most important criterion" to granting NRSRO status is that "the rating organization is recognized in the United States as an issuer of credible and reliable ratings by the predominant users of securities ratings" and that part of awarding the NRSRO label to the company hinges on "the rating organization's independence from the companies it rates."

A credit rating is important to both issuers and investors. The Second Circuit has recognized that:

> [Issuers] have their securities rated for two reasons. First, once the security or debt has received a favorable rating, that rating makes it easier to sell the security to investors,

who rely upon [the rating agency's] analysis and evaluation. The second reason is that a favorable rating carries with it a regulatory benefit as well. Fitch, along with its direct competitors Amici Moody's Investors Service, Inc. ("Moody's") and Standard & Poor's ("S & P"), has been designated by the Securities and Exchange Commission ("SEC") as a "nationally recognized statistical rating organization" ("NRSRO") whose endorsement of a given security has regulatory significance, as many regulated institutional investors are limited in what types of securities they may invest based on the securities' NRSRO rating.

A credit rating also provides important information to potential investors in an SIV because an SIV's success depends on the credit quality of the assets acquired by the SIV. If stable instruments comprise the SIV, then SIV investors are much less likely to suffer a loss. These stable instruments are typically assigned high ratings of "top rated" or "investment grade" and are commonly understood in the marketplace to be stable, secure, and safe. Accordingly, arrangers of the investments—Morgan Stanley in this case—are able to pay investors relatively low interest rates.

An SIV's assets typically include some combination of "investment grade" rated asset-backed securities ("ABS"), residential mortgage backed securities ("RMBS"), and collateralized debt obligations ("CDOs"). The Cheyne SIV and its Rated Notes were invested, in part, in RMBS securities. Accordingly, the Cheyne SIV's Senior Notes were "top rated" notes, meaning that they received the highest possible credit ratings from the Rating Agencies. Moody's rated the Senior Notes "Prime–1" and "AAA," and S & P rated the Senior Notes "A–1+" and "AAA." These ratings are the same as those usually assigned by the Rating Agencies to bonds backed by the full faith and credit of the United States Government, such as Treasury Bills. The Cheyne SIV's Capital Notes received similarly high ratings of "investment grade" and "A3/A" by Moody's and S & P, respectively. These were the highest credit ratings ever given to capital notes in any SIV. These ratings were then included in the Cheyne SIV's Information Memoranda and other Selling Documents that Morgan Stanley distributed to potential investors for the purpose of issuing up to twenty billion dollars in "top rated" Senior Notes and three billion dollars in "investment grade" Capital Notes. The Selling Documents were distributed with the knowledge and approval of the Rating Agencies and BoNY.

2. Defendants' Roles in the Cheyne SIV

Although a rating agency's role as an unbiased reporter of information typically requires the rating agency to remain independent of the issuers for which it rates notes, the Rating Agencies played a more integral role in the structuring and issuing of the Cheyne SIV's Rated Notes. Here, the Rating Agencies worked directly with Morgan Stanley to structure the Rated Notes in such a way that they could qualify for the Rating Agencies' highest ratings. For example, the Rating Agencies helped to determine how much equity was required at each level of the SIV in order to support the Senior Notes' "top ratings" and the Capital Notes' "investment grade" ratings. This determination was made, with the Rating Agencies' instruction, at the inception of the Cheyne SIV and on an ongoing basis throughout the alleged Class Period. Based on assistance from the Rating Agencies, on an asset-by-asset basis, the Cheyne SIV would set aside a predetermined amount of capital for the protection of the Rated Notes in order to preserve their respective ratings. The Rating Agencies also monitored the Cheyne SIV's portfolio and provided instructions on which types of assets the Cheyne SIV could acquire.

In exchange for the services the Rating Agencies provided, including issuing "top ratings" for the Cheyne SIV's Rated Notes, the Rating Agencies received fees in the range of ten or more basis points at the "launch" of the SIV approximately six million dollars. In addition, the Rating Agencies were paid ongoing fees following the launch. They shared annual remuneration with several other parties of a flat fee of approximately $1,200,000 plus 0.055 percent of the market value of the collateral assets. As a result, the Rating Agencies each received fees in excess of three times their normal fees for rating the Cheyne SIV and fees that increased in tandem with the Cheyne SIV's growth. The Rating Agencies' large fees were drawn from the proceeds of the Rated Notes' issuance and income owed to Rated Notes investors. Unbeknownst to investors at the time, the Rating Agencies' compensation was contingent upon the receipt of desired ratings for the Cheyne SIV's Rated Notes, and only in the event that the transaction closed with those ratings. . . .

4. The Collapse of the Cheyne SIV

The Cheyne SIV collapsed amid the credit crisis and the increasing awareness of the actual quality and value of the subprime mortgages that secured the Rated Notes in the summer of 2007. Because of the low quality of its assets, the Cheyne SIV was unable to repay its senior debt as it came due. In August 2007, the Cheyne SIV declared bankruptcy. Cheyne PLC was then restructured, and an auction process was instituted. As a result of the liquidation of the Rated Notes at severe discounts, holders of the Senior Notes have recovered only a "fraction of their investment," and the Capital Notes "are now worthless." Plaintiffs now bring this action to recover their losses. . . .

The Rating Agencies argue that plaintiffs have not pled an actionable misrepresentation because (1) the Rating Agencies are entitled to immunity under the First Amendment, and (2) even if the Rating Agencies could be held liable, their ratings are nonactionable opinions.

It is well-established that under typical circumstances, the First Amendment protects rating agencies, subject to an "actual malice" exception, from liability arising out of their issuance of ratings and reports because their ratings are considered matters of public concern. However, where a rating agency has disseminated their ratings to a select group of investors rather than to the public at large, the rating agency is not afforded the same protection. Here, plaintiffs have plainly alleged that the Cheyne SIV's ratings were never widely disseminated, but were provided instead in connection with a private placement to a select group of investors. Thus, the Rating Agencies' First Amendment argument is rejected.

I also reject the argument that the Rating Agencies' ratings in this case are nonactionable opinions. "[A]n opinion may still be actionable if the speaker does not genuinely and reasonably believe it or if it is without basis in fact." For the reasons discussed below, plaintiffs have sufficiently pled that the Rating Agencies did not genuinely or reasonably believe that the ratings they assigned to the Rated Notes were accurate and had a basis in fact. As a result, the Rating Agencies' ratings were not mere opinions but rather actionable misrepresentations.

For the same reasons, the disclaimers in the Information Memoranda that "[a] credit rating represents a Rating Agency's opinion regarding credit quality and is not a guarantee of performance or a recommendation to buy, sell or hold any securities," are unavailing and insufficient to protect the Rating Agencies from liability for promulgating misleading ratings. I conclude that plaintiffs have sufficiently alleged that the ratings issued by the Rating Agencies on the Rated Notes are actionable misstatements.

6

RISK AND RETURN

This chapter begins the transition from some basic, building block segments on valuation to the final chapters in the valuation unit, which put these building blocks together to provide a more sophisticated discussion of valuation. To complete that transition, you need to understand five more concepts that will undergird the coming chapters.

We begin first with *diversification*, a concept that you might have some intuitive understanding of, but that we need to solidify before moving on to portfolio theory, the Modigliani-Miller theorems, and the Capital Asset Pricing Model (CAPM) in coming chapters. Closely related to diversification are the ideas of separating risk into systematic and firm-specific risk, and then measuring a firm's relationship to systematic or market risk with beta (β). Integral to this entire analysis is some understanding of the law of one price—the idea that an asset should have but one price, no matter how many forms or locations it might be sold in—and the limits to this theoretical law that exist in reality.

1. DIVERSIFICATION

At its most basic level, the idea behind diversification is that spreading out investments across several projects will reduce risk, and might even increase return.[1] For example, if there are ten large, high-quality companies you might invest in, each of which looks equally good now, but only one of which will do really well over the next few years, putting all of your money in a single company constitutes a high-risk, potentially high-return strategy. If you correctly guess the high-performing company, you win. But you have a 90 percent chance of selecting a disappointment.

---

1. *See* Kelli A. Alces, *Legal Diversification*, 113 Colum. L. Rev. 1977, 1985-86 (2013).

IN RE JP MORGAN CHASE BANK

27 Misc. 3d 1205(A), 910 N.Y.S.2d 405
Unreported Disposition
Surrogate's Court, Westchester County, New York
March 31, 2010

ANTHONY A. SCARPINO, JR., J.

This is a contested proceeding to judicially settle the final accounting of JP Morgan Chase Bank, N.A. (formerly Lincoln First Bank of Rochester [the Bank]), as co-trustee of a trust created under the will of Blanche D. Hunter (decedent) for the benefit of Pamela Townley Creighton (Pamela), decedent's granddaughter, for the periods March 27, 1973 through August 13, 1996 (the intermediate account) and August 14, 1996 through January 17, 2003.

From June 22, 2009 through July 1, 2009, the court conducted a trial on the amended verified objections to the accounting which were filed and/or adopted by Margaret Hunter (Pamela's mother) and Pomona College, as testamentary appointees under Pamela's will, and the Office of the New York State Attorney General (the AG), on behalf of the charitable beneficiaries (collectively, objectants).

BACKGROUND

[Under her will the decedent created two trusts for the benefit of her granddaughters Alice and Pamela. The decedent passed away in 1972, and the two trusts were funded with large blocks of Kodak stock—in Pamela's case, she received more than 13,000 shares of Kodak.]

In March 1980, Alice died . . . [and] the Bank . . . transferred all of [her trust's] assets, including 12,981 Kodak shares with a value, as of that date, of $598,424.10 ($46.10 per share), to [Pamela's] Trust, bringing the total number of Kodak shares in [Pamela's] Trust to 26,016 with a value of $1,560,498.13

In May 2002, Pamela filed objections to the [Bank's request for approval of its fees], claiming, that the Bank had acted improperly, as co-executor and as co-trustee of the [two trusts]. She alleged that the Bank should not have retained such a high concentration of Kodak shares in the estate and the trusts from 1973 through the early 1980's, when there was a precipitous decrease in the value of those shares. Pamela sought a surcharge against the Bank for breaching multiple fiduciary duties . . .

By decision and order dated December 31, 2002 (December 2002 order), this court dismissed certain of Pamela's objections which sought to surcharge the Bank for improprieties as co-executor of decedent's estate and/or as co-trustee of the Trust. However, the court did not dismiss those of Pamela's objections which sought to surcharge the Bank for its failure, as co-trustee of [Pamela's] Trust, to object to any of its actions as co-executor of the estate and as co-trustee of the Trust.

. . . T]he primary issue at trial was the Bank's liability for the alleged retention of a concentration of common stock in Eastman Kodak Company (Kodak shares) in the trust. At the trial, objectants and the AG called James Lieb, the Bank's administrative officer for [Pamela's] Trust from 1993 through mid-1997 (Lieb), and John Teegardin, the Bank's investment officer for [Pamela's] Trust from 1977 to 1997 (Teegardin) as adverse witnesses; Loren Ross, as their liability expert (Ross), and Frank Torchio, as their damages expert. The Bank called two witnesses: William J. Wilkie, the Chief Fiduciary Officer for Banker's Trust Company, as its liability expert (Wilkie) and William Schwert, as its damages expert . . .

DIVERSIFICATION/RETENTION OF KODAK SHARES

Objectants contend that, as a result of the Bank's imprudence, they have sustained compensatory damages in a sum not less than $9 million as of January 17, 2003, plus prejudgment statutory interest, compounded annually.

[The court then reviews the testimony, concluding with] Ross's opinion, under the circumstances here where the Bank had already held onto a concentration of Kodak shares for more than 10 years, a prudent fiduciary would have sold 95% of Kodak stock in the summer of 1987. The court accepts and credits Ross's testimony.

The foregoing proof demonstrates that at no time during the administration of the trust did the Bank formulate any investment plan, let alone establish a plan to diversify its concentration of Kodak. The Bank acted contrary to its internal policies to restrict its holding of any one stock to certain circumstances, none of which were presented here. Following the enactment of the Prudent Investor Act, on January 1, 1995, the Bank continued to hold a concentration of Kodak shares in violation of the statutory requirement to "diversify assets unless the trustee reasonably determines that it is in the interests of the beneficiaries not to diversify, taking into account the purposes and terms and provisions of the governing instrument" (EPTL 11–2.3[b][3][C]). The record is clear that, after January 1, 1995, the Bank continued to hold a concentration of Kodak shares in the trust. The Bank failed to rebut such proof and establish that it took steps to determine whether it was in the interests of the beneficiaries not to diversify in relation to the purposes and terms of the trust and under the provisions of the governing instrument.

In addition, the Bank failed to consider the best interests of the persons interested in the trust. The proof establishes that the Bank paid limited attention to the needs of the income beneficiary and virtually no attention to the remainder interests.

Teegardin makes reference to the income beneficiary, the family's purported desire to hold onto the stock, and in one letter, noted the existence of potential tax consequences. The record is devoid of any proof that the Bank was proactive by assessing the volatility resulting from the concentration of Kodak and the benefit to selling and diversifying the portfolio, obtaining Pamela's written consent to retaining Kodak stock, ascertaining the tax consequences, if any, to

Pamela and determining whether the concentration jeopardized the remainder interest.

As in *Janes* [a NY Court of Appeals case on diversification], notably absent here is any proof that the Bank considered the increased risk to the trust portfolio by its continued concentration of one security in the portfolio. Also consistent with *Janes*, the record here establishes that the Bank: 1) failed to undertake a formal analysis of the trust by creating an investment plan; and 2) failed to conduct more than a superficial review of its holding of Kodak shares and consider alternative investments.

Introduced into evidence is a graph upon which the market price for Kodak stock during the period 1960 through August 2008 is shown on one side together with the dates when the trust was funded with the stock and the dates when the Bank sold its Kodak shares. The graph provides a useful depiction of the volatility of Kodak stock.

Between the initial funding of the trust in 1977, and the distribution from [Alice's trust] in 1980, the value of Kodak shares fell. Thereafter, the stock experienced an increase in its value in the early 1980s followed by another decrease in value in the mid-1980s and then began a steady climb to a peak in July, 1987. Teegardin acknowledged that in mid 1987, the Bank was aware that the price of Kodak was on the rise and testified that in July and August, 1987, the stock was "fairly valued." Yet, Teegardin made a deliberate decision in the summer of 1987 not to sell the Kodak shares.

Kodak suffered significant losses in value when the market turned in October, 1987. Not until August 17, 1989, did the Bank next sell stock, 5,000 shares and then on November 20, 1991, the Bank sold 6,100 shares. Thereafter, the Bank sold shares of Kodak during most of the years from 1989 through October 25, 2000, during which period there were gains and some losses.

Contrary to the Bank's assertions, the proof demonstrates that it considered the price of Kodak stock to be the determinative factor on whether to sell. Essentially, the Bank asks the court to consider the net gain to find that there is no liability. While the Bank repeatedly characterizes objectants' arguments as hindsight, it is the Bank that has engaged in hindsight by suggesting that an overall gain in the trust corpus protects it from surcharge . . .

Under the circumstances here, an experienced, careful investor should have seen that in the early summer of 1987, the market for the sale of Kodak shares had improved to the point that it was prudent to sell at least 95% of the Kodak shares, in order to eliminate the concentration in the portfolio and recoup the unrealized loss in the trust . . . Giving the Bank a reasonable period to implement the sale of Kodak, the court finds that the Bank should have sold 95% of the Kodak shares on July 30, 1987.

The record here demonstrates a pattern of neglect which rises to a breach of fiduciary duty by the Bank for over a 20 year period. Based upon such facts the court awards statutory interest [9%], compounded annually . . .

Accordingly, the proper measure of damages for "lost capital" shall be calculated by: (1) determining the gross value of 95% of the Kodak shares remaining in the B Trust on July 31, 1987, measured by the average of the high and low value of the stock on that day, (2) less any capital gains tax which would have been incurred upon the sale of such shares to obtain the net value of those shares on that date (the rolling balance). (On July 31, 1987, the trust held 22,686 Kodak shares, of which 95% equaled 21,552 shares.).

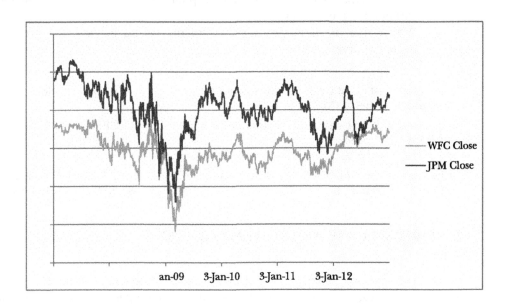

FIGURE 6-1
Share Prices of JP Morgan Chase and Wells Fargo.

Eastman Kodak Company filed for chapter 11 bankruptcy in January 2012, a victim of the growth of digital cameras and smartphones. Unfortunately, Pamela had also passed away by the time of the court's opinion, and thus her heirs were the primary beneficiaries of the court's decision.

The basic idea behind diversification is one you already know: "Don't put all your eggs in one basket." There is also an additional idea imbedded in diversification that turns on the concept of *correlation*. Correlation is a concept that you might have encountered if you took a college statistics class—if the values of two variables line up on a plot, they are correlated.

Investments can also be correlated: For example, you might expect that the share prices of similarly sized companies in the same industry will be highly correlated. For example, Figure 6-1 shows the share prices of JP Morgan Chase and Wells Fargo over the five years from the start of 2007 to the end of 2012. Until 2012—when Chase was the subject of some specific concerns, regarding its "London Whale" trade—the two shares were quite correlated.

If an investor assembles a portfolio that spreads investments across various, uncorrelated investments, then they are said to be well diversified.

PROBLEM SET 6.1

1. On July 31, 1987, Kodak shares closed at $93.87. On March 31, 2010, when the court's decision was issued, the shares closed at $5.79. On July 16, 2012, when this chapter was written, the shares closed at $0.28. How much damages were Pamela's heirs entitled to? What amounts should be offset against that figure (beyond capital gains taxes, as noted in the earlier excerpted opinion)?
2. Which five of the following investments would achieve the greatest degree of diversification?

East Coast Railroad	East Coast Coal Mining Co.	Midwestern Utility Co.	FedEx	Nestle SA
West Coast Railroad	West Coast Coal Mining Co.	California Tech. Co.	UPS	Pfizer, Inc.
Chevron Corp.	Wal-Mart Stores, Inc.	British Petroleum	Royal Dutch Shell PLC	France Telecom SA

2.   FIRM-SPECIFIC AND SYSTEMATIC RISK

Postwar finance theory (sometimes called "modern" finance) slices investments across several dimensions, two of which are particularly relevant for lawyers to understand. First, investments can be either "risk-free" or risky. Although an utterly risk-free investment is more of an academic invention, typically the debt of stable countries that borrow in their own currency are treated as risk free for these purposes. This includes not only the United States, but countries such as Canada, Japan, Norway, Switzerland, Australia, and the like. Germany and the Netherlands, even though they do not borrow in their own currency, undoubtedly belong in this group, too.

Risky assets are everything else, be it Belgian debt, gold bars, or shares in ExxonMobil or Pets.com.[2] To varying degrees, each of these investments could return less than the investor originally paid. Hence, they are risky investments.

Of course, as we noted in the prior chapter, there are degrees of risk. Shares in Exxon are clearly less risky than Pets.com shares (20/20 hindsight being what it is).

The risks faced by risky assets are then divided into two forms: systematic risk and firm-specific risk. *Systematic risk* is the risk that the value of an investment will go up or down as "the market" goes up or down. Inflation, war, and general economic conditions are all examples of systematic risk. In short, it is the risk that all investments face. To some degree, the definition of systematic

---

2. http://en.wikipedia.org/wiki/Pets.com.

risk depends on your frame of reference. For example, are the relevant economic conditions global or simply relevant to the U.S. economy?

To use a U.S. example, consider that Goldman Sachs' shares were down during the 2008 financial crisis by about 60 percent. During that time the entire S&P 500 went down about 13 percent. You might consider 13 percent to be a reflection of systematic risk, and the additional decline in Goldman's share price might be attributed to firm-specific risk.

As this implies, *firm-specific risks* are those that are unique to a particular firm or investment. These risks include the risk that Exxon will spill oil and incur cleanup costs, that Pets.com will try to gain market share by offering free shipping on heavy boxes of dog food, or that a new gold vein will be discovered in the rocks under Central Park, driving down the price of gold worldwide. Each of these affects the specific investment in question, lowering its value, but the money Pets.com loses offering free shipping has little effect on the price of gold, and vice versa.

This conception of risk leads to a couple of important insights. First, by diversifying, an investor can reduce his or her exposure to firm-specific risk. But diversification will not resolve systematic risk. Specifically, by splitting your money between Chase and Wells Fargo, you hedge against the chance that one of them will fail, but you don't avoid a general decline in U.S. financial institutions. In short, you have not done a very good job at diversification.

Spreading your money between Chase and the Union Pacific Corporation takes care of the risk specifically associated with financial institutions, but it still leaves you exposed to general declines in the U.S. economy. Buying Chase and Nestle takes care of the concentrated exposure to the domestic economy—although both firms have some large degree of exposure to the U.S. economic climate—but you are still exposed to global economic slowdowns, and the United States is the largest single economy.

The other insight comes from considering assets or investments as risk-free or risky. Namely, the price that risk-free assets pay investors must operate as a kind of floor to what risky assets will pay. Or, stated another way, if investors are even somewhat rational, they will demand that risky assets pay the risk-free rate of return plus some premium.

Otherwise the expected return of the risky asset will be lower than the expected return of the risk-free asset, and who would take a lower expected return?

3.   MEASURING SENSITIVITY TO SYSTEMATIC RISK—BETA

Once we realize that systematic risk—at least if measured broadly—is largely unavoidable, it becomes important to understand how a particular investment reacts to such risk. For example, when the world economy slows, if one investment will decline by 5 percent and another by 10 percent, an investor would like to know that before investing. Indeed, the sensitivity to systematic risk must be accounted for when valuing the investment.

The most common way to measure this sensitivity is through something called beta (β)—because using a Greek letter makes the concept more approachable.

Beta is a ratio. As such, it measures a particular investment relative to something else. As a matter of theory, the appropriate comparison is the "market." Measuring the performance of all investments worldwide is quite difficult—think not only stocks and bonds, but also commodities broadly defined and any other available investment—and thus more often investments are compared to their relevant submarket.

For equity investments in large U.S. companies, the point of comparison is the Standard & Poor's 500 Index. For bonds, the Lehman Aggregate Bond Index, which tracks U.S. Treasury securities, U.S. government agency bonds, mortgage-backed bonds, corporate bonds, and foreign bonds traded in the United States, has been used for a long time. (But, for obvious reasons, the index is now called the Bloomberg Barclays US Aggregate Bond Index.)

Beta is typically calculated historically, comparing the investment's volatility relative to the index over the past three or five years. Mathematically, beta is calculated as the ratio of the covariance of the stock with the market (or index being used as a proxy for the market) to the variance of the market:

$$\beta_i = \frac{Cov\ (Investment,\ Market)}{Var\ (Market)}$$

Variance and covariance are statistical terms that you probably forgot from your college statistics course. Variance is squared standard deviation. I'm sure that was helpful.

Perhaps more helpful is to remember that variance is the average of all squared deviations from the mean (average). To calculate the variance, take each difference, square it, and then average the result. So if a particular investment returns, on average, $5, but one year it returns $10, another year it returns $0, and another year it returns $5, you calculate variance as

$$(10 - 5)^2 + (0 - 5)^2 + (5 - 5)^2 = \$^2 50,$$
then divide by 3, to get $\$^2 16.67$.

That is, the variance is 16.67 squared dollars, whatever that means.

You are probably now remembering why standard deviation is useful—you take the square root of 16.67 squared dollars and then say, "This investment has a standard deviation of $4.08."

If you remember some rules from your college stats—and make the grand assumption that the investment's returns are "normally" distributed[3]—you can make some bold pronouncements like, "95 percent of the time this investment

---

3. That is, the historical returns fall into a bell-shaped curve.

will return $5 ± $8. You could earn up to $13."[4] Hopefully your audience won't notice that standard deviations work in both directions, and that the returns might not be normally distributed, and you are ready to sell mortgage-backed securities.[5]

Covariance, the top part of the beta calculation, is the sum of the investment's deviation from the mean multiplied by the market's deviation from the mean, for each year, divided by the number of years less one. That's a bit much, but the basic idea is that this measures the degree to which two items move in tandem.[6]

A positive covariance means that asset returns move together. A negative covariance means returns move inversely; in short, the ratio of the degree to which the investment moves with the market over the overall market movement. By definition, the beta of the S&P 500 is 1.0—after all, it is used as the proxy for the "market" and x over x always equals one.

An investment with a beta of 1.10 tends to perform 10 percent better than the market in up markets and 10 percent worse in down markets. Often high betas are deemed riskier investments, although a low beta might only indicate that the investment's volatility relative to the market is low, not that the investment has low risk.

You could calculate beta with Excel,[7] but more often you would probably look it up on a commercial service like Bloomberg, because the calculation requires three to five years of relevant market data. For casual use, Yahoo! Finance, MSN Money, and Google Finance all report stock beta values, too.[8]

PROBLEM SET 6.2

1. How would you interpret a beta of 1, 2, 3? How about −1, −2, −3?
2. Compare Coca-Cola's beta to that for Dow Chemical (DOW).[9] What can you conclude?
3. What are the limitations of beta when calculated on historical data?

---

4. For those of you who don't remember, the shorthand, rule of thumb is that if you have a bell-shaped curve, 95 percent of the data will be within two standard deviations of the mean (average).

5. Don't worry; this will make more sense once you have covered asset securitization in Chapter 19.

6. For those of you interested in the math, let's use the numbers from above, and assume a market return of $2, $3, and $5 for each of the three years. That gives us an average market return of $3.33. For year one you have (10 − 5), the investment calculation, multiplied by (2 − 3.33), the market calculation. You add that to the same calculations for years two and three, and divide by two (three years minus one). Or you use the "COVAR" function in Excel. That would look like this:

= COVAR ({refer to range of market numbers}, {refer to range of investment numbers})

7. = COVAR({refer to range of market numbers}, {refer to range of investment numbers})/VARP ({refer to range of market numbers}).

8. For example, go to https://www.google.com/finance?client=ob&q=NYSE:KO to see the report for The Coca-Cola Company (or just Google "NYSE:KO," and click over to Google Finance). What is its beta? How would you interpret that?

9. Google "NYSE:DOW."

4.   What would you expect to find if you examined the relationship between price and beta?

4.   THE LAW OF ONE PRICE (AND A BIT ON SHORT SELLING)

The law of one price is an implicit assumption in much of the finance theory we are about to encounter, so it bears making it explicit and exploring its limitations. The law of one price holds that in an efficient market[10] all oranges of equal quality must have equal prices.

We have already assumed something like this was at work. Think back to the last chapter on bond valuation—remember how we equated the value of a bond with its price? The reason for doing that is an assumption—the law of one price—that large deviations between price and value will not be long tolerated in liquid markets.

Of course, the rule applies to things other than oranges. For example, imagine a company (Bogartco Ltd.) that owns half of another company (High Sierra, Inc.) and has no other assets. And let's further assume that High Sierra's only asset is a bank account with a $100,000 balance. If both companies' shares are traded on the stock exchange, and Bogartco gets no special benefits from owning a large block of High Sierra shares, what should we expect regarding the value of these two companies?

Bogartco should be worth exactly half of High Sierra, or $50,000. What if instead Bogartco was trading at a price that implied it was worth $60,000? Smart investors should sell Bogartco shares and buy High Sierra shares, because they amount to the same thing. In short, the equivalent assets will have the same price before long.

What if we only had High Sierra, Inc., without Bogartco, and the price of High Sierra implied its value was $110,000? That is, the price implied a value $10,000 higher than reality. If you already own the High Sierra shares, now is a good time to sell. But what if the High Sierra shareholders are all blockheads, who can't see what is readily apparent to everyone else? Does the law of one price get suspended? (Maybe we call it the Blockhead Exception?)

Not really, because at least according to the theory, arbitrage will come into play. *Arbitrage* refers to an opportunity to make money with little or no risk. Typically it involves the selling of overpriced assets or the buying of underpriced assets, with the effect that prices and value come together.

For example, if oranges are selling in Los Angeles for $10 a bag, but in New York City for $20 a bag, there is a potential arbitrage opportunity. Namely, so long as I can transport oranges to New York for less than $10 per bag, I can sell

---

10. This is a concept that itself will be explored in coming chapters. In short, this means a market where buyers do not face any hindrances in examining goods and comparing prices; that is, information is freely available and costs of moving among sellers are low.

LA oranges in New York City. Eventually the price in New York should approach the LA price plus the cost of transport.

In the case of High Sierra, the arbitrage would take the form of short sales. Namely, an investor borrows High Sierra shares and then sells them, promising to return the borrowed shares at some point in the future. The expectation, of course, is that the share price will go down and the investor will be able to buy them back on the cheap. The investor then makes money on the difference between the sale proceeds and the cost of buying the replacement shares.

Arbitrage is an important element in the law of one price. As we consider finance theory going forward, we must be mindful of instances where arbitrage is not possible. For example, if you believe that your neighbor is overvaluing the shares of the local dry cleaners they own, there is not much you can do about it. Nobody is going to lend you dry cleaners shares to short. More often the limits to arbitrage are less obvious, and thus require deeper consideration of the issue.

For example, the noted economist John Maynard Keynes is reported to have said "[m]arkets can remain irrational a lot longer than you and I can remain solvent." The next case examines the truth of that pronouncement.

ZLOTNICK, ALBERT M. v. TIE COMMUNICATIONS & L.W. KIFER

836 F.2d 818
United States Court of Appeals, Third Circuit
Jan. 6, 1988

JAMES HUNTER, III, Circuit Judge:
Appellant Albert Zlotnick filed this class action against Appellees TIE Communications, Inc. ("TIE") and L.W. Kifer, alleging violations of §§9 and 10(b) of the Securities Exchange Act of 1934 and of the RICO Act. Zlotnick claims that appellees' misrepresentations artificially inflated the price of a stock which he had sold short, causing him to lose money when he made the purchase necessary to cover the short sale. The District Court dismissed for failure to state a claim, 665 F.Supp. 397. Zlotnick now seeks a reversal and the reinstatement of his complaint.

I.   BACKGROUND

A.   THE ALLEGATIONS

In reviewing a dismissal under Fed.R.Civ.P. 12(b)(6), the court must accept as true both the factual allegations contained in the complaint and all the reasonable inferences that can be drawn from those allegations. We therefore accept the facts as presented in Zlotnick's allegations.

In 1981, appellees TIE and Kifer formed Technicom International, Inc. ("Technicom"), a manufacturer of systems to monitor and control the moisture level of communication cables. At all relevant times in this case, TIE was the parent of Technicom and owned a majority of its stock, and Kifer was the

Chairman and CEO of Technicom and held a significant equity interest in the company. In March, 1982, TIE and Technicom entered into a "distribution agreement" whereby each would distribute the products of the other. Shortly thereafter, Technicom made a public offering of its common stock, selling approximately 625,000 shares at a price of $9.75 per share. The price of Technicom stock rose steadily throughout 1982, selling at six times its offering price by the end of the year.

On January 6, 1983, Zlotnick sold short 1,000 shares of Technicom at $16.875 per share. Five days later he sold short another 1,000 shares at an average price of $19.30. Zlotnick sold the stock short because he concluded that the stock was overvalued. He based this conclusion in part on his analysis of the company's earnings and prospects, finding that the stock was then selling at a ratio of approximately 50 times current annualized earnings. Zlotnick also based his conclusion on his belief that Technicom faced increasing competition that would diminish its profit margins and depress future earnings. At the time of his short sale Zlotnick was unaware of any wrongdoing or misrepresentations by appellees; and he did not base his decision to sell short on a belief that appellees were deceiving investors.

In early 1983, subsequent to Zlotnick's short sales, appellees undertook to inflate artificially the price of Technicom stock. Specifically, TIE and Kifer caused Technicom to issue several press releases which misrepresented the company's sales agreements and earnings prospects. They also caused Technicom to engage in illusory sales to TIE. Both misrepresentations falsely inflated the company's reported sales and earnings for the fourth quarter and entire fiscal year of 1982 to record levels. By March 14, 1983, the price of Technicom stock had risen to approximately $33.00 per share. Zlotnick, unaware of any deceptive practices by appellees, decided to cut his losses by making the purchases necessary to cover his short position; ultimately, he realized a loss of about $35,000.

The price of Technicom stock did not begin to fall until the summer of 1983. Thereafter, due in part to more realistic statements by Technicom, the value of the stock dropped sharply. On June 30, 1984, the stock was trading at $4.12 per share. Following further reported losses, Technicom merged with its parent TIE via a transaction in which Technicom stockholders received .29 shares of TIE stock for every share of Technicom; the value to shareholders of this transaction was approximately $2.50 per share of Technicom. This represented a drop in value of approximately 90% from the high of the previous year.

Zlotnick instituted this action on March 13, 1985 by filing a complaint on behalf of himself and all similarly situated investors. The complaint was amended on June 6, 1985. Appellees moved for dismissal on September 16, 1985 . . . [and the District Court] held that Zlotnick had not sufficiently alleged reliance on appellees' deception, and therefore had not stated a claim upon which relief could be granted. Zlotnick filed a notice of appeal on June 26, 1987.

B.   SHORT SELLING

Because this case turns to some extent on the nature of short selling as an investment strategy, we set out here our understanding of that process. Where the traditional investor seeks to profit by trading a stock the value of which he expects to rise, the short seller seeks to profit by trading stocks which he expects to decline in value. A typical short seller expects decline because, based on his view of the underlying strengths and weaknesses of a business, he concludes that the market overvalues the business' stock. As demonstrated by the allegations, these underlying facts can concern the present—such as the fact that a stock trades at fifty times its earnings—or they can concern the future—such as the fact that a business will face increased competition.

Short selling is accomplished by selling stock which the investor does not yet own; normally this is done by borrowing shares from a broker at an agreed upon fee or rate of interest. At this point the investor's commitment to the buyer of the stock is complete; the buyer has his shares and the short seller his purchase price. The short seller is obligated, however, to buy an equivalent number of shares in order to return the borrowed shares. In theory, the short seller makes this covering purchase using the funds he received from selling the borrowed stock. Herein lies the short seller's potential for profit: if the price of the stock declines after the short sale, he does not need all the funds to make his covering purchase; the short seller then pockets the difference. On the other hand, there is no limit to the short seller's potential loss: if the price of the stock rises, so too does the short seller's loss, and since there is no cap to a stock's price, there is no limitation on the short seller's risk. There is no time limit on this obligation to cover.

"Selling short," therefore, actually involves two separate transactions: the short sale itself and the subsequent covering purchase. We reject appellees' suggestion that the two components of selling short be considered one transaction. When the short seller transfers borrowed stock to a buyer, its obligations to that buyer are ended.

His only obligation is an open-ended one to the person who loaned him the stock. A short seller's default on this obligation will not affect the prior transfer. Also, the short seller exercises real discretion in choosing when to purchase shares, and this latter transaction actually determines his profit or loss. Thus, this investment, like most investments, involves two transactions: a purchase and a sale. That the sale occurs "before" the purchase does not affect our consideration of each separate transaction for the possible effects of fraud.

II.   STANDING

Appellees challenge Zlotnick's standing to bring suit under the securities laws. They claim that since Zlotnick, in effect, sold his stock before he purchased it, he never owned any Technicom stock. Therefore, they argue, he has no standing under the Supreme Court's ruling in *Blue Chip Stamps v. Manor Drug Stores*, 421 U.S. 723, 95 S. Ct. 1917, 44 L.Ed.2d 539 (1975). Appellees also seek to distinguish the short seller from the traditional investor, arguing that while the traditional investor hopes to profit from the company's good fortune, the short seller gains his profit from the company's decline. In effect, the short seller "bets against" the company, and so should not be treated as an investor in it. Appellees also analogize the short seller to the options trader, whom several courts have found unprotected by the anti-fraud provisions of the securities acts.

Appellees' standing arguments are without merit . . .

B.   THE INTEGRITY OF THE MARKET

Zlotnick argues that, as a short seller, he relied upon the integrity of the market. Though he believed the price of the stock overvalued at the time of the short sale, he relied on the market's ability, given accurate information, to correct its valuation of the stock and set a better price. By falsely inflating the price of the stock, defendants interfered with the market's ability to correct itself. Once he had sold short, Zlotnick was unable to protect himself from this fraud. Therefore, he argues, requiring him to prove individual reliance on defendant's misrepresentations "'imposes an unreasonable and irrelevant evidentiary burden.'" *Peil*, 806 F.2d at 1160 (quoting *Blackie v. Barrack*, 524 F.2d 891, 907 (9th Cir. 1975), *cert. denied*, 429 U.S. 816, 97 S. Ct. 57, 50 L.Ed.2d 75 (1976)).

Reliance on the integrity of the *market* in a stock differs from reliance on the integrity of the market *price* in that stock. An investor relying on the integrity of a market price in fact relies on other investors to interpret the relevant data and arrive at a price which, at the time of the transaction, reflects the true worth of the company. By contrast, an investor relying on the integrity of the market relies on the continuing ability of investors to interpret data subsequent to the transaction; he relies on future conditions. In the context of a short sale, the difference between these two types of reliance is more pronounced. The traditional purchaser depends on the "market" to determine a present value for the stock that allows the purchaser an adequate return on his investment. On the other hand, the short seller depends for a return on his investment on the "market" realizing that the value of the stock at the time of the short sale does not allow for an adequate return on the investment. This realization is what drives the price of the stock down and allows the short seller his profit.

More important, reliance on the integrity of the market price is actual, if indirect, reliance. The short seller is not injured because he knew of or depended on the misrepresentation; he is injured because others investing in the stock so relied. The fraud of which Zlotnick complains was truly perpetrated "on the market," and not, even indirectly, on Zlotnick as an investor in the market. We are mindful that reliance is not an abstract requirement in the securities laws: plaintiff must prove reliance in order to prove that the misrepresentation caused actual injury. "Reliance is therefore one aspect of the ubiquitous requirement that losses be causally related to the defendant's wrongful acts." *Sharp v. Coopers & Lybrand*, 649 F.2d 175, 186 (3d Cir. 1981), *cert. denied*, 455 U.S. 938, 102 S. Ct. 1427, 71 L.Ed.2d 648 (1982). Zlotnick may, as discussed above, be able to prove his own actual, indirect reliance upon the market price. However, to the extent

Zlotnick argues he is entitled to recover for the reliance of third parties, we reject his claim.

Zlotnick alleges that defendants misrepresented the truth, and that such misrepresentations caused the price of the stock to rise at the time he sold short. He concludes that since the fraudulently-induced rise in the stock caused him to lose money, he is entitled to recover. Under Zlotnick's theory, he would be allowed to recover even if he purchased after deciding, based solely on accurate information, that the stock was not overvalued and his short sale was ill-conceived. Yet, in such a case, Zlotnick is no different from the traditional purchaser who buys at a fraudulently-inflated price but actually relies solely on accurate information in purchasing: both have made bad valuations of the stock, but those valuations were independent of any alleged fraud. Zlotnick cannot recover his loss on his covering purchase unless he shows that his decision to cover was somehow connected with the fraud.

C.   INDIRECT RELIANCE

That Zlotnick states his claim in terms of reliance on the market's integrity does not preclude the conclusion that a fraudulent market price was a material factor in his decision to cover. Zlotnick might have changed his investment strategy and actually relied on the "integrity" of the inflated market price. The rise in price itself may have changed his opinion of the stock's value. The rise may also have increased his risk of loss beyond acceptable levels, causing him to purchase. It may have led him to conclude that the stock would take so long to decline in value that the cost of maintaining his short position would exceed his potential gain. In *Peil*, this court accepted that a market price which reflects a defendant's misrepresentation may pass that misrepresentation on to potential purchasers. It is only logical to hold that the same price which may communicate a misrepresentation to the traditional investor may also communicate a misrepresentation to the short seller.

Zlotnick is entitled to have this court consider as true both his allegations and all reasonable inferences from those allegations. *Wisniewski, supra.* We find Zlotnick's amended complaint sufficient to support a reasonable inference of actual, if indirect, reliance.[11] Defendants, on the other hand, have not made sufficient proof of either the reason for Zlotnick's decision to cover or the materiality of the price in these circumstances to entitle them to dismissal. We will therefore vacate the District Court's order dismissing the complaint and remand for further proceedings. However, unlike the plaintiff in *Peil*, Zlotnick is not entitled to a presumption at trial that the market price did actually pass defendants' misrepresentations on to him, or that he did actually rely on the

---

11. Zlotnick does not allege facts sufficient to establish fraud in his initial decision to sell short. He does not allege misrepresentation of the underlying strength of the business that induced his short sale: false inflation of the company's earnings would discourage his short sale by reducing the price/earnings ratio. Also, false inflation of the market price prior to his short sale would act to increase his potential profit.

inflated market price in making his decision to cover. We hold no more than that Zlotnick is entitled to a chance to prove such actual reliance to a finder of fact.

CONCLUSION

For the reasons stated above, this court will vacate the order of the District Court dismissing the complaint, and remand for further proceedings consistent with this opinion.

———————

What other ways might the law of one price break down?

7

THE CAPITAL ASSET PRICING MODEL

You now have a basic understanding of the time value of money, valuation, and the ideas that go into consideration of investments.[1]

This chapter begins to put together the lessons of prior chapters to explain the key elements of "modern" (post–World War II) finance theory. This chapter explains portfolio theory, the efficient capital markets hypothesis, and then the capital asset pricing model (CAPM), which is a common method for finding the "r" used in many valuation calculations, especially when we are valuing equity (common stock). The final section of this chapter notes some of the alternatives to CAPM, which you will see has some flaws. Namely, CAPM gives but a very rough estimate of the return of any specific investment. Unfortunately, so do most of the alternatives.

Nonetheless, CAPM combined with the weighted average cost of capital (WACC, covered in Chapter 11) are some of the valuation methods you are most apt to encounter in practice, probably because most corporate lawyers and judges understand them.

1. PORTFOLIO THEORY

According to lore, before Harry Markowitz came along in the 1950s, investors looked at individual stocks and considered a specific company's risk and return in isolation before investing. If this resulted in a portfolio of all railroads, so be it. If you find it hard to believe that investors before World War II were quite this dopey, join the club. As one profile of Professor Markowitz notes, "[i]nvestors already had been spreading their risks ever since the first bull market on Wall Street in 1792."[2]

---

1. Assuming, of course, you've done the reading and attended class.
2. http://goo.gl/SVAvC.

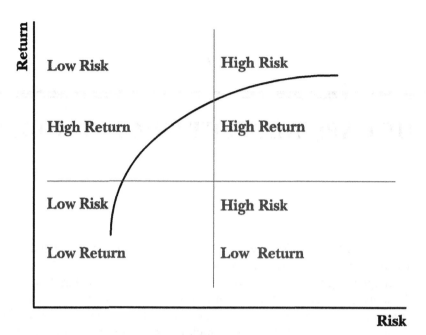

FIGURE 7-1
The Efficient Frontier

The real insight that Markowitz provided was that investors would be better served by looking at the correlation of their entire portfolio, moving away from the risk and return of individual investments.[3] He explained that all the possible investment portfolios could be graphed with their expected return plotted against standard deviation or variance, which Markowitz proposed as a measure of risk. Essentially, volatility and expected return stand in for the basic concepts of risk and return.

Out of the entire universe of possible portfolios, certain portfolios will best balance risk and reward. These comprise what Markowitz called an efficient frontier of portfolios—the portfolios that lay along the upper left-hand edge of the graph of all portfolios (see Figure 7-1). According to Markowitz, a rational investor should pick a portfolio that lies on the efficient frontier.

Although the tendency is to think of this in terms of stock market investments, the following excerpt makes clear that Professor Markowitz's insights work with regard to most any sort of investment.

---

3. His book is available online at http://goo.gl/FxGHz.

SARAH PEI WOO, *REGULATORY BANKRUPTCY: HOW BANK REGULATION CAUSES FIRE SALES*

99 GEO. L.J. 1615, 1631-1632 (2011)

Every bank maintains a portfolio of loans and assets whose value and risk profile is not simply the sum of its parts. The assessment of the risk of a loan within a portfolio is different from an assessment of that same loan in isolation, due to portfolio composition effects such as diversification of risk.[4]

Of particular interest to regulators is whether a bank's portfolio composition will cause, over the short or long term, uncompensated losses that will threaten the bank and require outside intervention to protect depositors or the economy. [There are] complex interlinkages among capital adequacy, portfolio composition, and the debtor-creditor relationship.

———

Another professor—James Tobin—came along next and extended Markowitz's work to develop the Capital Market Line (CML). Basically, Tobin asked "What if we consider that investors can invest in a risk-free asset, and they can borrow money to invest, too?"

You can think of the "risk-free asset" as a Treasury Bill to make it more tangible. And borrowing to invest has existed for a long time: Stockbrokers allow customers to borrow on "margin" so that they can buy many more shares than they might be able to with their cash on hand. Brokers, of course, get paid interest for offering this service.

Tobin then showed that investors should want to invest in some combination of one portfolio (M) on the efficient frontier and the risk-free asset, because of higher returns for a given level of risk everywhere except at the tangential point. You can see this in Figure 7-2.

By mixing in the risk-free asset, investors can move along the CML, which provides higher expected returns with equal or lower risk. The tangential point reflects investing 100 percent of your money in the portfolio. Anywhere to the left of that point reflects a lower percentage of the portfolio, with the balance made up of the risk-free asset. When you hit the axis, you have reached 100 percent risk-free asset.

Moving to the right of the tangential point, you are investing in more than 100 percent of the Markowitz portfolio. How is that possible? You borrow money and use it to buy more of the portfolio.

———

4. The concept of "Markowitz diversification" is used in this Article, being commonly used in portfolio risk management in the United States by banks and regulators. A "key contribution of Markowitz diversification is the formulation of an asset's risk in terms of a portfolio," rather than in isolation. *See* Frank J. Fabozzi, Harry M. Markowitz & Francis Gupta, *Portfolio Selection*, in The Theory and Practice of Investment Management 15, 29 (Frank J. Fabozzi & Harry M. Markowitz eds., 2002).

Note a couple of unrealistic points here: First, the CML assumes you are borrowing at the same rate as you are lending. That is, the only reason the line is straight is that it assumes you can borrow from your stockbroker to move to the right of the tangential point at the same interest rate (r_f) that you lend money to the government at. Most people can't borrow from their stockbroker at the same rate as the U.S. Treasury—for the simple reason that your stockbroker has figured out that you're not as good of a credit risk.

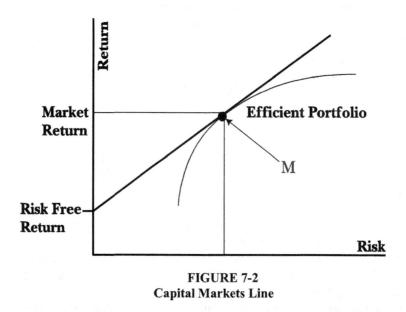

FIGURE 7-2
Capital Markets Line

Similarly, although the graph implies that you can go off to the right side into infinity, since the 1929 stock market crash, when lots of investors got in trouble buying stocks on margin, the Federal Reserve has limited margin lending.[5] The initial margin requirement represents the minimum amount of funds that investors must put up to purchase stocks on credit. The current rate, set in 1974, is 50 percent, which means that an investor can only borrow up to half the value of a share from the broker.[6]

And also note the oddity of using variance or standard deviation as a measure of risk. Under this approach, both downside and upside movements count as risk.[7] Are most investors all that concerned with unexpected upside movements? Oh darn, my investment went up more than I expected it to!

---

5. Timothy A. Canova, *Financial Market Failure as a Crisis in the Rule of Law: From Market Fundamentalism to a New Keynesian Regulatory Model*, 3 Harv. L. & Pol'y Rev. 369, 374 (2009).

6. Federal Reserve Regulations T and U. The Fed only sets the initial margin. After purchase, the minimum margin required as a result of price fluctuations, typically 25 percent, is set by stock exchange rules. Brokers, of course, can set higher limits as part of their normal risk management.

7. Michael C. Macchiarola, *Beware of Risk Everywhere: An Important Lesson from the Current Credit Crisis*, 5 Hastings Bus. L.J. 267, 277 (2009).

This is part of a larger problem of assuming that risk and return are symmetric and could equally go in either direction. It bakes in the idea that investors can never beat the market, a concept that in turn becomes the foundation of the efficient capital markets hypothesis we discuss later. Moreover, symmetric returns are simply not true for most mainstream investments.[8] As you learned in your Business Associations class, corporate shareholders benefit from limited liability. Thus, share prices can never go below zero, meaning that returns on the left side of the distribution are artificially truncated.

Nonetheless, from the combination of Markowitz and Tobin we can get the *one-fund theorem*, which says that the investors will trade only in the risk-free asset and one portfolio (consisting of only risky assets). All possible combined portfolios lie on the CML, and all are efficient portfolios. And this work provides the foundation for CAPM. But first, we must pick up one other theory.

Think about something before we move on, though: What is the relationship between portfolio theory and the separation of risk into systematic and nonsystematic risk, discussed in the prior chapter?

2. THE EFFICIENT CAPITAL MARKETS HYPOTHESIS

Recall both in the prior chapter and the first part of this chapter that passing mention was made to "efficient" or well-functioning capital markets and "rational" investors. Now is the time to formalize these ideas.

French mathematician Louis Bachelier performed the first notable analysis of stock market returns in his 1900 dissertation. He documented the statistical independence of stock returns—meaning that today's return signals nothing about the direction or magnitude of tomorrow's return—and this led him to model stock returns as a "random walk."

This view was not prevalent, however. Instead, most prewar investors probably agreed with John Maynard Keynes's beauty contest analogy, in which each analyst recommends not the stock he thinks best, but rather the stock he thinks most other analysts think is best. In Keynes's view, stock prices are based more on speculation, and analysts' fears about being wrong, than on economic fundamentals.[9]

In the 25 years following the war, financial theory began to return to Bachelier's approach, which fit nicely with other developments in the field. By 1978, well-known economist Michael Jensen would famously say that "there is no other proposition in economics which has more solid empirical evidence supporting it than the Efficient Market Hypothesis."

---

8. But remember, this only applies to mainstream investments like stocks and bonds. As you will see in Chapter 18, derivatives can be quite different.

9. http://goo.gl/xj0fFg.

LAWRENCE A. CUNNINGHAM, *FROM RANDOM WALKS TO CHAOTIC CRASHES: THE LINEAR GENEALOGY OF THE EFFICIENT CAPITAL MARKET HYPOTHESIS*

62 GEO. WASH. L. REV. 546, 559-563 (1994)

The perfect market is a heuristic invented by stipulating the following assumptions concerning a market: there are a large number of participants such that the actions of any individual participant cannot materially affect the market; participants are fully informed, have equal access to the market, and act rationally; the commodity is homogeneous; and there are no transaction costs. Under these assumptions, the perfect market model would predict precisely what the random walk model was implying: that prices of goods (securities) in the public capital markets should adjust instantaneously and accurately to new information concerning them. That prediction was embodied in the ECMH as first propounded: in its broadest terms, the ECMH held that the prices of securities traded in public capital markets fully reflect all information concerning those securities.

1.   THREE FORMS OF EFFICIENCY

Under this broad statement, the ECMH explains more than the random walk model required: the random walk model holds simply that successive price changes are independent or uncorrelated, whereas the ECMH explains that holding by saying that public security prices fully reflect all information—not just price histories—about a security. As a result, virtually since the emergence of the ECMH as an explanation of the random walk model, the ECMH has been divided into three forms, defined in terms of specified categories of information. The three forms were first proposed to classify empirical tests of price behavior given specified kinds of information. The weak form tested the random walk model itself, using autocorrelation tests and run analysis to investigate whether past prices indicate anything about future prices. Semi-strong form testing investigated whether publicly available information other than prices was reflected in prevailing prices, and strong-form testing investigated whether private information was reflected in prevailing prices.

As the wealth of tests and discussion proceeded in the 1970s, the three forms of the ECMH came to be used to refer to the conclusions those tests suggested. Thus, the forms of the ECMH are now specified as follows: the weak form holds that current security prices fully reflect all information consisting of past security prices; the semi-strong form holds that current security prices fully reflect all information that is currently publicly available; and the strong form holds that current security prices fully reflect all currently existing information, whether publicly available or not. Finally, each of these three forms may be respecified in terms of their implications: a market is efficient with respect to an information set (defined, for example, as price histories, publicly available information, or private information) when it is not possible to generate above-normal returns by trading on the basis of that information set.

There is thus a direct and logical link between the random walk model and weak-form efficiency and a more attenuated and contingent link between the random walk model and stronger forms of the ECMH. Recall that the random walk model held that price changes are independent of or uncorrelated with prior price changes. That means that technical analysis of past price changes—sometimes called chartist analysis—cannot aid prediction of future price changes in any systematic way. Weak-form efficiency explains this independence and its implications for prediction by hypothesizing that the current price impounds all information contained in prior prices. Thus, any price change can only be the result of new information, the production of which is itself assumed to be random. This process of information absorption continues and thus explains the absence of substantial linear dependence in successive price changes discovered in the autocorrelation and run tests described above. It also leads to the stronger forms of the hypothesis.

The semi-strong form of the ECMH posits not only that current security prices reflect all information consisting of prior security prices but also that they reflect all publicly available information about the security in question. Testing this more ambitious claim requires a focus not on correlation analysis of price changes but on the relative swiftness with which prices change given new information. Despite this different testing methodology, semi-strong efficiency depends on the validity of the random walk model, which depends in turn on empirical conclusions concerning the absence of statistical dependence in security price data. In other words, if future price changes are dependent on prior price changes, then any price change the semi-strong form tests cannot be attributable solely to new information the test is evaluating. Thus, weak-form and semi-strong-form efficiency each depend on the proof provided by linear testing models.

The strong form of the ECMH extends much further than the random walk model suggested. Indeed, the strong form is a theological proposition, holding that public capital markets are infinitely wise: even non-public information is reflected in public security prices. Numerous studies have investigated whether persons possessing non-public information could, by using that information as a basis for trading decisions, achieve abnormal market returns. The theory is that, if market prices reflect less than all information, then those with the excess (private) information should be able to outperform the rest of the market. The insider trading scandals of the 1980s are among the many proofs that the strong form of the ECMH is invalid.

Because the strong form of the ECMH is widely discredited, debate concerning the ECMH centers on the semi-strong and weak forms. Debate over the weak form generally is defined by analysis of the random walk model itself, usually in terms of linear empirical models used to test the relationship between successive price changes, although more recent attention is being paid to nonlinear testing and nonlinear models. Debate over the semi-strong form traditionally has been defined in terms of anomaly studies—empirical models demonstrating that above-normal returns can be achieved by using specified information sets that are publicly available.

Although the theory applies to all types of investment assets, most of the testing has been done on common stocks. After all, stocks have the most liquid and transparent trading markets, so if the theory applies anywhere, it should apply to stocks.

As noted in the excerpt, most of the battle about the utility of ECMH has taken place at the point of semistrong efficiency. This version of the doctrine holds that it is (generally) impossible to make money from publicly available information. And if any small deviations in price do exist, sophisticated traders will quickly remove them via arbitrage.

Noted economist Joseph Stiglitz has observed that this is kind of impossible. Namely, if it really were impossible to beat the markets with public information, why would sophisticated investors spend any time trying to find mispricings? Indeed, there would not be any need for market analysts at all if the markets are highly efficient.

There is also little discussion of the reality of investing: namely, most people do not invest directly into the stock market. Instead, they invest through agents like pension fund managers, mutual fund managers, hedge fund managers, or stockbrokers. Even a big investor like a bank invests through its agents—the bank employees. These agents have their own incentives—namely, getting paid—that could sometimes conflict with the interests and rationality of the investor.

Perhaps most puzzling, in the early 1990s Eugene Fama, often credited as the father of ECMH, and Kenneth French published a large empirical survey of stock market returns since 1940 and found several ways in which returns were not random.[10] Small company stocks returned more than they "should," and value investing, which involves buying stocks that appear "cheap" relative to asset value, could get an investor "excessive" returns for long periods of time. Sometimes an investor could make money simply by buying a stock whose share price had recently been on the upswing.

There are other assumptions built in here, too, that we will look at again in connection with CAPM, which is codependent on ECMH. For example, there is an assumption that returns are normally distributed—that is, they fall out in a bell-shaped curve pattern. And remember that all of this is tested with historical data—but how much of the historical data should you use? Market data in the United States goes back to the 1890s, although the number of stocks traded back then was small (mostly railroads). Should the models be tested using all that data,

---

10. Other assumptions are built into the model, too, but we will save the rest for our discussion of CAPM, which is codependent on ECMH.

or just the data after 1945? After all, is data from 1904 really comparable to data from today?

Despite this ongoing debate, there was and is some faith that markets function efficiently most of the time, aggregating vast amounts of disparate information into a single number—the price—on the basis of which millions of decisions are made.

But the 2008 financial crisis called into question how often "most of the time" might be. In late 2011, a survey of sophisticated investors by RBC Capital Markets and the *Economist* Intelligence Unit found that

> More than half (56%) now have doubts about such tenets of modern finance as efficient markets hypothesis, the capital asset pricing model and portfolio theory; only one in four (27%) accept these concepts unquestioningly. More than half of fund managers (53%) question the value of diversification in mitigating portfolio risk. While the basic theory seems sound, there is uncertainty about how to apply it as assets become more closely correlated.

PROBLEM SET 7.1

1. On May 13, 2009, your author was quoted as a corporate bankruptcy expert in the *Wall Street Journal*, where I said that General Motors' share price of about $1.50 per share "might be about $1.45 a share too much."[11] On June 1, 2009, GM filed its chapter 11 petition, and soon thereafter it filed a reorganization plan that provided for no recovery by shareholders. Its share price was about 75 cents the Friday before the bankruptcy petition. What does this tell us about the ECMH? Does it matter that GM was part of the Dow Jones Industrial Index, an index of the largest U.S. companies, until June 8?

2. A study by the London Business School found that, since 1900, buying British stocks with the best performance the prior year would have turned £1 into £1.95 million (before costs and tax) by the end of 2008; the same sum invested in the worst performers would have grown to just £31. Is this consistent with the ECMH?

3. Bernard Madoff promised his investors returns that beat the S&P 500 with less volatility. Indeed, he provided such returns (no negative returns for months!) for many years. Even if you are an ECMH skeptic, explain why investors might have been suspicious sooner.

4. The following question was asked by the Buttonwood columnist for *The Economist* in March 2009:

> If regulators thought markets were too efficient to interfere with, how come they allowed banks to get involved in an activity which, after bonuses, was a game they collectively could not win?

---

11. http://goo.gl/fE9WQ.

Do you have an answer? (No, "I have not taken Banking Regulation/Financial Institutions" does not count.)[12]

5. One of the implications of portfolio theory and the ECMH is that most investors would be better off buying an index fund, thus buying "the market," rather than attempting to pick specific stocks that will provide extra return. But portfolio theory also describes the benefits of diversification, and at present, almost 20 percent of the S&P 500 index is made up of ten really big companies.[13] An investor who buys the index invests more in Apple alone than in the smallest 100 companies in the index. Can these ideas be reconciled?

3.   THE CAPITAL ASSETS PRICING MODEL

CAPM is a model for determining what the expected return (r) should be on any given security. As such, it puts together many of the concepts we have covered both in this chapter and prior chapters. As you will see in subsequent chapters, CAPM is often used along with the WACC method to value a company.

CAPM is the result of work done in the early 1960s by William F. Sharpe, which builds on the work of Markowitz, Tobin, and others, including an early version of the ECMH, which Fama wrote about later.

CAPM states that the risk of an asset and its expected return are a function of beta, which you will recall is a measure of an asset's variance in relation to the market's variance.

The model begins with some strong assumptions, which we will come back to at the end. First, it assumes that all investors are mean-variance investors. That means that all investors simply slide along Tobin's line, deciding how much variance (risk) they are willing to tolerate.

That is, mean-variance analysis assumes that all investors have the same beliefs about the market and the relationship among different assets. And as we discussed before, mean-variance analysis assumes all investors can borrow at the risk-free rate, without transaction costs. For example, your stockbroker does not charge you anything to buy or sell. Finally, all assets you might want to buy are liquid under this analysis—if you want to buy or sell, there is never a problem finding somebody who will take the other side of the trade.

Once we make these heady assumptions, then it becomes easy to say that all investors will thus own only mixtures of the portfolio at the intersection point of the Tobin line and the risk-free asset. We call that intersection portfolio M for convenience (see Figure 7-2).

---

12. http://www.economist.com/node/13240822/print.

13. As of mid-2016: ExxonMobil, Apple, Microsoft, Facebook, Johnson & Johnson, General Electric, JP Morgan Chase, Amazon, AT&T, and Berkshire Hathaway.

Notice then that if a security is traded, it has to be one of the securities that makes up M, because this is the only portfolio the investors will even consider. Stated another way, all securities must be in M, because otherwise they would not even be looked at by investors and wouldn't really count as securities.

That means that the sum of all traded securities is M, and M is therefore "the market." Thus, according to CAPM, all investors should hold the market portfolio, complemented with greater or lesser positions in the risk-free asset, as Tobin described. Under Sharpe's CAPM analysis, not only does the market portfolio (M) sit on the efficient frontier, but it *is* Tobin's efficient portfolio.

CAPM thus relates the return that an individual security must provide to the entire market, as Professor Sharpe concluded that most of an investment's risk comes from its sensitivity to the market. After all, remember that Markowitz had already shown that firm-specific risks could be diversified away. An investor with low risk tolerance will have most of her money in the risk-free security, whereas a person with high risk tolerance will borrow to finance the purchase of extra investments in the market portfolio.

Thus, the value of any asset is a function of the return on the risk-free asset plus a return that is tied to how that asset responds to movements in the overall market. You already know how to measure the relationship between an asset's return and the market return, that's beta. CAPM is thus written as

$$r = r_f + \beta \, (r_m - \{r_f\})$$

where r_f is the risk-free rate, and the term $(r_m - r_f)$ is often referred to as the spread, as it reflects the return on the market portfolio (r_m) beyond the risk-free rate.

Now the CAPM formula might seem very mysterious and "mathy," but I'm sure that somewhere deep in the recesses of your brain, you can remember some school teacher incanting

$$y = ax + b$$

Move the b to the other side and compare that formula with CAPM:

$$y = b + ax$$

$$r = r_f + \beta(r_m - r_f)$$

CAPM is just the formula for a line, often referred to as the Security Market Line (which you should not confuse with the CML). The risk-free rate of return is the intercept, and beta acts as the slope of the line. That is, it assumes that there is a linear relationship between risk (measured by variance) and return for all investments.

In prior chapters we talked about how investors need to be compensated for the time value of money. To paraphrase the old cartoon, a hamburger today is worth more than a hamburger tomorrow. If I'm going to let you use my money, so that I can't buy a hamburger today, I want something in return.

But investors also need to be compensated for risk, otherwise the expected return on lending out or investing the money is not the same as just keeping it or putting it in a government-insured bank account, where I hopefully make enough to at least keep pace with inflation.

Let's consider a simple example, to make all this more concrete. Assume that one-year U.S. Treasury debt is paying 1 percent, and the S&P 500 has returned an average of 3 percent over the past few years. Bogartco's stock has a beta of 2.3. What rate should we use to discount an investment in Bogartco? This involves plugging in the numbers to the CAPM formula, and because we have been given all the relevant data, we can find the expected return for Bogartco:

$$r = r_f + \beta(r_m - r_f)$$

$$r = 0.01 + 2.3(0.03 - 0.01)$$

$$r = 0.056 \text{ or } 5.6\%$$

A risk-free investment returns 1 percent, the market returns 3 percent, and Bogartco should return 5.6 percent, which makes sense given the beta of 2.3.

Now is a good time to go back and think about the assumptions built into CAPM, and its foundations. We noted the key ones at the outset, but here is a fuller list of the assumptions behind CAPM:

- There are many investors. They behave competitively (that is, they are all price takers).
- All investors are looking ahead over the same (one period) planning horizon.
- *All* investors have equal access to *all* securities.
- There are no taxes.
- There are no brokerage commissions or other trading costs.
- Each investor cares only about expected return and standard deviation.
- *All* investors have the exact same (or "homogeneous") beliefs about
  - o   the investment opportunities, and
  - o   all correlations for the universe of risky assets.
- Investors can borrow and lend at a single risk free rate.
- Investors can short *any* asset, and hold any fraction of an asset.

You might also consider how CAPM applies beyond the S&P 500. That is, do the assumptions hold when applied to stocks traded not in New York or London, but also Lagos?[14] How about real estate located in Nevada or Florida or Damascus? Or the markets in frozen concentrated orange juice[15] or in autographed Don Ameche photographs?[16]

---

14. *See* Erb, Harvey and Viskanta, *Expected Returns and Volatility in 135 Countries*, J. Portfolio Management, Spring 1996 at 46. The authors find that CAPM has some problems when applied to nondeveloped markets.

15. http://goo.gl/KP5iAJ.

16. http://en.wikipedia.org/wiki/Don_Ameche.

PROBLEM SET 7.2

1. Which of the following investments are correctly priced if the risk-free rate of return is 1.5 percent and the market rate of return is 3.5 percent?

Investment	Beta	Expected Return
A	0.85	3.5%
B	1.08	4.1%
C	1.69	5.1%
D	0.71	2.9%
E	1.45	4.4%

2. Sam Spade is considering buying some shares in Bogartco, which trades on the market for $50 per share. He concludes that the expected rate of return on this investment is 10 percent per year. If the risk-free rate is 3 percent, the market return is 7 percent, and the stock's beta is 1.5, is this a good buy or not? What if the risk-free rate changes to 5 percent? What are the limitations of this analysis?

4. ALTERNATIVES TO CAPM

In financial academia, CAPM lives on primarily in old articles, and most researchers have moved on to newer asset pricing models. But in law, CAPM still plays an important role, in part because of its (relative) simplicity.

The fact that betas are scaled around one provides for a simple intuitive understanding: An investment with a beta of 1.2 is a bit more risky than the average investment in the market. Even math-phobic lawyers can understand that.

Because of all the simplifying assumptions built into the CAPM model, however, it provides but a rough estimate of a proper expected return or discount rate. As we have seen earlier, even small changes in discount rates can sometimes result in big differences in valuation.

And the CAPM model becomes even wobblier the further we get away from its core competence: namely, the valuation of very large company shares traded on well-developed stock exchanges. CAPM is also somewhat dependent on the ECMH, which itself is the subject of some skepticism.[17]

---

17. Claire A. Hill, *Why Financial Appearances Might Matter: An Explanation for "Dirty Pooling" and Some Other Types of Financial Cosmetics*, 22 Del. J. Corp. L. 141, 149 & n.22 (1997).

One commonly seen alternative is the Arbitrage Pricing Model, also called arbitrage pricing theory. It was developed by Steven Ross, a professor at MIT.[18] His basic idea was that several factors can affect return, and betas should be estimated for each of these factors.

If you took statistics in college, you will recognize that this moves from a univariate model, with CAPM, to a multivariate model. But it's still a linear model. And the hard part is specifically what factors should be included in the model. For example, the share price of the Union Pacific Railroad is probably very sensitive to diesel fuel prices, but the share price of JP Morgan Chase, not so much.

Some newer versions of this, which tend to be called multifactor models, use historical data to develop relevant factors for future stock prices. Well-known examples include three- and five-factor models proposed by Eugene F. Fama and Kenneth R. French.[19] Fama and French started with the observation that two classes of stocks have tended to do better than the market as a whole: small caps and stocks with a high book-value-to-price ratio (often called "value" stocks; their opposites are called "growth" stocks). They then added two factors to CAPM to reflect a portfolio's exposure to these two classes, and thus the three-factor model was born. The Fama-French five-factor model added two more factors – profitability and investment.

Your statistics professor—if you had one—would have called it data mining, and frowned on it.[20]

In essence, the APM is simply an invitation to construct your own model. Not surprisingly, even sophisticated courts and corporate lawyers have tended to decline.

Many additional models have been developed, but none have been shown to be without faults. That, in addition to its simplicity, might be the ultimate reason why CAPM continues to prevail in legal circles.

---

18. Edward S. Adams & David E. Runkle, *Solving a Profound Flaw in Fraud-on-the-Market Theory: Utilizing a Derivative of Arbitrage Pricing Theory to Measure Rule 10b-5 Damages*, 145 U. Pa. L. Rev. 1097, 1129 (1997).

19. Eugene F. Fama & Kenneth R. French, *A Five-Factor Asset Pricing Model*, 116 J. Fin. Econ. 1 (2015).

20. Your statistics professor probably did not have any money on the line either.

8

CAPITAL STRUCTURE AS ECONOMIC DREAM

Companies have two basic choices when deciding on a financial structure: debt or equity. More realistically, the company (or its managers) needs to decide what portion of debt should be used to finance the firm—equity being something of the default choice.

As a theoretical matter, the optimal capital structure is easily explained. Namely, an optimal capital structure is one that minimizes the costs to the firm while maximizing the firm's ability to take on any project with a positive NPV that it desires.[1]

When the firm is first incorporated, its capital structure is made up of only equity. If it needs more funds—either to provide liquidity for daily operations or to purchase more assets—it then faces the choice. It could sell more shares. Doing so will reduce the ownership stake of existing shareholders, unless they are willing to buy the new shares. Or the company can borrow money. This could either take the form of a loan from a bank or the sale of bonds. In either case, the firm has contractually promised to repay the money with interest at some point in the future. That means that the company has committed to a fixed obligation, whereas shareholders have no contractual entitlement to dividends. If the company is uncertain about its ability to repay, this tips the balance in favor of issuing more shares.

Many investors look for "strong" balance sheets, which is typically taken to mean limited debt. On the other hand, using debt instead of equity to pursue profitable investments means that upside gains are shared with a smaller group of shareholders. Debt holders only get a fixed return; shareholders take the rest. This, of course, assumes that the firm makes more on its projects than it pays on its debts.

---

1. George S. Geis, *The Space Between Markets and Hierarchies*, 95 Va. L. Rev. 99, 114 (2009).

1.   THE MODIGLIANI AND MILLER CAPITAL STRUCTURE IRRELEVANCE THEOREM (PART I)

Given the practical concerns just outlined, you might be surprised to learn that Professors Modigliani and Miller promoted a widely discussed theory that all of this is a waste of time.[2] And one of them got a Nobel Prize for it.

M&M Proposition I, the first part of their capital structure irrelevance theorem, states that the value of a firm does *not* depend on its capital structure.[3] As explained by Professor Modigliani himself in 1990:

> With well-functioning markets (and neutral taxes) and rational investors, who can "undo" the corporate financial structure by holding positive or negative amounts of debt, the market value of the firm—debt plus equity—depends *only* on the income stream generated by its assets. It follows, in particular, that the value of the firm should not be affected by the share of debt in its financial structure or by what will be done with the returns—paid out as dividends or reinvested (profitably).[4]

There is a lot here. Here is how one lawyer unpacks the capital structure irrelevance theorem.

CLAIRE A. HILL, *SECURITIZATION: A LOW-COST SWEETENER FOR LEMONS*

74 Wash. U. L.Q. 1061, 1084-1085 (1996)

Modigliani and Miller's famous irrelevance theorem holds that capital structure does not affect firm value: a firm cannot increase its value by having one capital structure rather than another. But clearly, firms spend enormous time, energy and expense choosing among, and sometimes developing, different capital structures. This behavior can be seen as rational only in a world where the theorem's underlying assumptions are violated, and the theorem therefore does not hold.

The Modigliani and Miller assumptions can be stated as follows:

(1) Financing decisions are independent of investment decisions, broadly construed: a firm's capital structure decision will not affect its future receipts and expenditures (cash flows). Agency, regulatory, and other costs affect a firm's future cash flows; financing decision independence

---

2. Robert P. Bartlett III, *Taking Finance Seriously: How Debt Financing Distorts Bidding Outcomes in Corporate Takeovers*, 76 Fordham L. Rev. 1975, 1981 (2008).

3. D. Bruce Johnsen, *The Quasi-Rent Structure of Corporate Enterprise: A Transaction Cost Theory*, 44 Emory L.J. 1277, 1278 (1995).

4. *Quoted in* Anne P. Villamil, *The Modigliani-Miller Theorem*, in The New Palgrave Dictionary of Economics.

means that there are no such costs which a firm's capital structure can affect.

(2) Financial markets are perfect. . . . This also means that there are no transaction costs to issue, buy, or sell.

(3) Financial markets are complete. For my purposes, this means principally that perfect substitutes for everything are available.

(4) Financial markets do not discriminate between those seeking financing and those providing financing: each has the same opportunities available to them on the same terms.

The first assumption, coupled with the traditional finance principle that a firm's value is the net present value of its expected future cash flows, implies that there is only one correct value for a firm, regardless of its capital structure. The remainder of the assumptions imply that a price difference between two equally valuable firms (or cash flow streams) should not persist as it would be arbitraged away. And it is not only differences between equally valuable firms or cash flow streams that will be arbitraged away. Each firm (and cash flow stream) has a correct price; if perfect arbitrage is possible, it also will assure that the relationship between the price of any two firms or cash flow streams is correct.

The world of Modigliani and Miller's theorem is, of course, not our world. In our world, there are many costs, including information costs, agency costs, regulatory costs, and transaction costs. And there are benefits which particular capital structures can provide.

In short, in a *very* stylized world, it does not matter what mix of equity and debt a firm uses, the value of the firm will be the same. Under these special conditions, firm value is like a pie (or a pizza, if you prefer): It does not matter how you slice it, the overall size of the pie stays the same. That is, there is no benefit to the firm of separating cash flows into different types of claims on the firm as that just concerns distribution, not overall value.

If debt could increase the value of the corporation, investors would create "homemade" debt, and would rather purchase a less expensive comparable company with money borrowed from their broker.

Nobody, probably not even the authors of the theory, thought that M&M Proposition I described reality. But by understanding M&M's theory, we can better understand kinds of market imperfections we need to look for and pay attention to.[5] As we'll see in coming chapters, the issues that are most likely to make a difference are taxes, the costs of insolvency or bankruptcy, and the costs of writing and enforcing complicated investment contracts.

---

5. Peter H. Huang & Michael S. Knoll, *Corporate Finance, Corporate Law and Finance Theory*, 74 S. Cal. L. Rev. 175, 179 (2000).

PROBLEM SET 8.1

1. Bogartco, a leading manufacturer of trenchcoats and fedoras, as you know, has a capital structure of 1,000 common shares. The firm earns $1,000 per year in profits. Then HB, the chief executive, decides Bogartco should issue $10,000 of debt to fund a new project. Bogartco will pay 10 percent interest per year on this debt. If we are in an "M&M world," what is the value of the firm before and after the debt is issued? Why? (Hint: Start by considering what the share price should be, with and without debt.)

2. Problem 1 gives us a chance to talk about another aspect of Modigliani and Miller: their "dividend irrelevance" proposition. The idea is that what a firm pays in dividends is irrelevant and that stockholders are indifferent about receiving dividends, given the same assumptions as we have thus far made regarding capital structure. Why might this be?

2.   THE MODIGLIANI AND MILLER CAPITAL STRUCTURE IRRELEVANCE THEOREM (PART II)

The second part of the capital structure irrelevance theorem is called M&M Proposition II. It holds that the greater the percentage of debt in the capital structure, the greater the rate of return required by equity holders.[6] This is the natural corollary of the first M&M proposition: If firm value stays the same after the addition of a senior claim on the firm, something must have happened elsewhere in the capital structure.

M&M Proposition II essentially views firm capital structure as a zero-sum game, where additions of senior claims will result in lower claimants demanding greater returns to compensate for greater risks to their returns.

That is, the expected return on equity of the firm is positive and a function of the debt-to-equity ratio. The increase in expected equity return reflects increased risk. The increase in debt increases the degree of variation in cash flows available to shareholders, as the debt holders have first claim on the cash flows.[7]

Assume Bogartco has a discount rate (and thus required return) of 12.5 percent and 100 shares outstanding. It earns $250 per year. Bogartco decides that it wants to try to increase value by issuing $1,000 of debt and using the proceeds to repurchase shares. Bogartco can issue debt at a risk-free rate of 10 percent. With the $1,000, Bogartco is able to purchase 50 shares, so there are 50 shares

---

6. Herwig J. Schlunk, *The Zen of Corporate Capital Structure Neutrality*, 99 Mich. L. Rev. 410, 436 (2000).

7. Note that the risk to shareholders here is not the risk of default, as M&M Proposition II is based on the idea that small amounts of debt are virtually risk free, and thus they treated the debt in their model as risk free. Of course, in reality even a company with an AAA credit rating pays slightly more for its debt than the U.S. government (which we treat as risk free, despite the reality of some political risk).

outstanding. What is the required rate of return on its shares, assuming the M&M assumptions are in place?

M&M Proposition I tells us that the firm value will not change, despite Bogartco's best efforts. That is, the overall return on this firm will remain 12.5 percent. But M&M Proposition II tells us that to achieve this result, the return to equity will have to go up. That is, although the average return of the firm remains 12.5 percent, the return to shareholders has to increase because their expected return decreases as some of the firm's cash flows are now promised elsewhere.

In numbers, we can find this required return by using the formula that M&M provided. Remember that they said that return to equity increases in a linear fashion as the proportion of debt in the firm increases. Taking what we already know from CAPM, we can say that the return on equity in this firm would then look like this:

$$r_e = r_f + \frac{Debt}{Equity}(r_f - r_d)$$

Note that r_f represents the firm rate of return without debt (and not the risk-free rate, as it did in CAPM). Like CAPM, the equation is for a line, with the basic rate of return for the firm, plus a spread that increases as the amount of debt increases in the firm, giving the return on equity. Using the numbers, we get

$$r_e = 12.5\% + \frac{1,000}{1,000}(12.5\% - 10\%)$$
$$r_e = 15\%$$

We can check our result in this case quite easily, as debt and equity are balanced. Thus, the average of the two returns should equal the firm rate of return, 12.5 percent.

PROBLEM SET 8.2

1. Describe the range of outcomes for shareholder's returns in (a) an all-equity-financed firm, and (b) a firm with 50 percent debt and 50 percent equity.
2. If in the preceding hypothetical, Bogartco instead had $1,500 of debt or $500 of debt, how would this change the results?
3. A company is currently an all-equity firm that pays no taxes. The market value of the firm's equity is $3 million. The return on this company's shares is 15 percent per year. The company plans to issue $600,000 in debt and use the proceeds to repurchase stock. The cost of debt is 4 percent annually. After the repurchase, what will the cost of equity be? Explain.

9

SOME REAL-WORLD CONSIDERATIONS
(PART 1)

In this chapter and the next, we examine the reasons why the M&M propositions do not hold in the real world. If you understand these considerations, you can often discover the motives for many of the financial instruments and transactions we cover in subsequent chapters.

In this chapter we look at not only M&M Propositions I and II, but also their claim that a firm's dividend policy does not matter. Recall that this was related to their larger points that capital structure is irrelevant. If capital structure is irrelevant, it also makes sense that details about the securities that make up the capital structure also do not matter. In particular, M&M argued that shareholders could create their own "dividends" by selling some shares if they need cash—and that managers should simply focus on increasing the value of the firm.

Of course, in the real world managers do spend a good bit of time thinking about dividends. And historically the taxation of dividends meant that there was some difference between selling shares and paying dividends.[1]

Moreover, much of the M&M propositions were based on perfectly functioning financial markets. Later, we examine how more realistic assumptions in this regard make the financing and cash retention decisions of actual corporations more understandable. In the final section we look at the creation of corporate conglomerates and the spinoff of parts of corporations. Both should not matter in the idealized world of M&M, but reality is somewhat different.

1. DIVIDEND POLICY

Once the firm has decided on a mix of debt and equity, it also faces the question of whether it should pay dividends to shareholders.[2] Some firms have

---

1. And such a situation might return with changes to the tax code.

paid dividends since time immemorial, and if they stop paying dividends, it becomes big news. General Motors is an obvious example. Other firms pay dividends reluctantly, if at all. Apple, Inc. is a good example here. It only recently started to pay dividends, despite a growing amount of cash on its balance sheet.

Some investors favor dividend-paying stocks, which are seen as safer investments. The thinking is that even in a down market, these stocks provide income, if not share appreciation. Moreover, dividend-paying companies are often seen as "stable" firms.

Of course, AIG was considered just such a firm in 2007. And during the 2008 financial crisis, many such stable firms—like Bank of America, General Motors, Pfizer, and GE—either suspended or cut their dividends.

From the company's perspective, returning money to shareholders only makes sense if there is not a better use for the funds. Nonetheless, many managers feel pressure to return cash to shareholders, particularly if, as in Apple's case, there is no immediate need for the funds that managers can point to.

DANIEL J. MORRISSEY, *ANOTHER LOOK AT THE LAW OF DIVIDENDS*

54 U. Kan. L. Rev. 449, 453, 461-468 (2006)

A.   THE CURRENT LAW OF DIVIDENDS

Dividends are the conventional vehicle by which corporations distribute their profits to shareholders. Those equity stakeholders, however, have no direct control over the firms in which they invest. Corporations exist as separate legal entities run by their directors. Among other powers vested in those managers is the authority to declare and set the amount of dividend payments. . .

IV.   THE HISTORY OF DIVIDEND POLICY

A.   THE EARLY DAYS OF LIBERAL DIVIDENDS

The corporation developed in nineteenth-century America as the premier form of business organization that could gather capital from numerous and widespread investors. Through the early part of the twentieth century, those entities retained little of their earnings, and paid out almost all of them regularly as dividends. There were two principal reasons for that early practice.

First, corporations in the nineteenth century typically made few financial disclosures to their public shareholders. Dividends were thus the only real way a firm would keep its shareholders' faith and provide them income from its operations. Second, such payments were the only viable means for shareholders

---

2. A dividend payment is a payout of portion of a company's profits or retained earnings to stockholders.

to make a return on their investments because trading markets for those instruments were either nonexistent or in their infancy.

C. THE MOVE TO MORE CONSERVATIVE DIVIDEND POLICIES

[L]egal reluctance to second-guess management coincided with the increasing separation of ownership from corporate control that occurred in the early decades of the twentieth century. As Berle and Means famously found, by the 1930s equity investment in most large corporations had become so widely dispersed that hardly any shareholders had effective power in their enterprises. Governance of public firms had been ceded to a managerial class.

As business boomed after World War I, industrial leaders used the earnings of their firms to expand their operations. . .

In those times, shareholders also began to favor a steady pattern of regular, if reduced, dividends over the boom-or-bust payouts of the nineteenth century.

D. THE ERA OF THE DIVIDEND PUZZLE

[D]uring the past seventy-five years, dividends have easily accounted for more than half of the long-term returns on the stocks of large, publicly held companies.

Through the 1960s, '70s, and '80s, companies listed in the Standard and Poors 500 (S&P 500) annually paid dividends in the range of three to five percent of their stocks' prices. The approach peaked in 1980 when more than ninety percent of firms listed in the S&P 500 paid dividends in that range.

Influential financial experts found this inclination to declare dividends puzzling, and they argued that dividend payment was really irrelevant. Not only were there substantial disincentives in the tax code to pay dividends, but shareholders of publicly traded companies really did not need them. Instead, those shareholders could get a cash equivalent whenever they wanted by selling some of their shares or borrowing against them.

Shareholders, said these economists, really should be "indifferent" to a firm's dividend policy. From a wealth-generating perspective, it should not matter whether a firm pays out its income directly to shareholders or redeploys it in a way that will grow the business and thus build up the price of its shares. So long as the firm's expected rate of return is greater than its opportunity costs, such an investment will be productive. And because a trading market exists, any shareholders who believe they can put those funds to better use can access that gain by selling their shares.

Even more incongruous, according to those theorists, was the practice of many firms to pay dividends while at the same time going to the public market to finance new ventures. Such companies could easily and cheaply fund their projects with internally generated cash instead of bearing all the transaction costs of those offerings.

Various explanations were put forward to justify the seemingly illogical approach of those firms. Shareholders were said to value cash received in hand by way of dividends more highly than the mere "paper" appreciation of their shares. Others theorized that dividends sent favorable signals to skeptical shareholders that their firms were prospering. Studies seemed to bear out this second theory. Management distributed dividends out of sensitivity to a perceived shareholder preference for steady payments. According to conventional wisdom, it was better to follow such a systematic, if conservative, pattern than to vary dividends with fluctuations in earnings. Many believed firms should not even raise dividends in good times for fear that they might anger shareholders by cutting them back when conditions reversed. A fortiori, corporate officials were reluctant to lower them in hard times for fear of adverse publicity and would even seek alternate funding to keep paying them when profits fell off.

Another justification for the payment of dividends was the so-called "clientele" theory. It postulated that different groups of investors would gravitate toward firms that met their particular needs. For instance, tax-exempt institutions or conservative investors who preferred steady payments would place their funds with companies that paid ample dividends. Others, more concerned about long-term growth and tax deferral, would opt for firms that offered little or no such yields.

Given such diverse corporate practices and shareholder expectations, Professor Victor Brudney wrote an influential article in 1980 arguing that federal law ought to compel publicly traded firms to make meaningful disclosures about how they planned to use their income streams. Dividend decisions would thus be open to public scrutiny. Not only would such transparency, he said, give investors a better idea of what to expect in the deployment of corporate earnings, but it also would provide a check on the inherent tendency of management to make suboptimal use of a firm's earnings in ways that advanced their own interests to the detriment of their shareholders.

Several years later Professor (now Judge) Frank Easterbrook continued that theme in a scholarly piece that offered two justifications for the puzzling tendency of shareholders to favor dividends over the reinvestment of corporate earnings. First, corporate officials are agents of shareholders and thus at all times should act to further their interests. But because opportunities often arise that can lead management to favor themselves at the expense of their shareholders, vigilance is needed to restrain corporate officials from such behavior. A commitment to regular dividends, Easterbrook argues, disciplines management by forcing it to go to the public market to finance new projects. This process monitors management activity in a way that no individual shareholder has sufficient incentive to do. Second, the payment of dividends helps overcome management's natural inclination to risk-adverse behavior and forces it to adhere to its profit-maximizing mission. Taking funds out of the firm's net worth account increases the level of debt over equity. Such higher leveraging benefits shareholders because debt holders are owed only their interest fixed by contract. Any gain over and above those payments goes to the shareholders. Shareholders thus make more with the same amount of their money at risk.

E. THE DISAPPEARING DIVIDEND AND THE ALTERNATIVE OF SHARE REPURCHASES

In the booming market of the 1990s, dividend payments tailed off substantially. As one observer put it, "[d]uring the last decade, dividends were scarcely a market focal point. Investors sought growth, and companies plowed profits back into their businesses to achieve it, especially in the heady days of the late 1990s." By 2000, the average dividend yield of stocks in the S&P 500 was down to 1.1%.

As of mid 2016, the S&P 500 dividend yield was 2.14 percent. The foregoing article primarily discusses dividends from the investor perspective, which of course influences the behavior of firms to the extent they cater to investor wants and desires. The basic point is that firms *do* spend time worrying about dividends despite finance theory.

Finance theory itself was slow to develop any theory of dividends. Arthur Stone Dewing (a big name in finance from about 1900 to the 1950s and the author of a leading corporate finance text)[3] had done some descriptive papers on dividends, but there was not really any theory. The one exception was John Lintner, who interviewed a sample of corporate managers in the mid-1950s. From those interviews he came up with some basic facts about dividend policy, and they are generally a good description of real-world practice even today.

One of the primary findings of the interviews was that a high portion of managers wanted—above all else—to maintain a stable, regular dividend. As Professor Lintner put it, managers demonstrate "a reluctance (common to all companies) to reduce regular rates once established and a consequent conservatism in raising regular rates."

But companies that lock themselves into fixed dividends are in effect turning their equity into bonds and taking away the primary benefit of using equity, namely the flexibility that comes from not having a fixed payment obligation.

As noted in the preceding excerpt, there are some defenders of this approach. The drawbacks include dividend payments that are lower than they could be and the potential that some firms might get locked into unsustainable dividends and end up in much worse trouble.

PROBLEM SET 9.1

1. In some countries, firms pay a percentage of their net income as dividends each year. Is there an advantage to this approach? If so, why might it be that large U.S. companies have been slow to adopt it?

---

3. https://goo.gl/V7mgmu.

2. Can you think of other, objective measures that a company might use to
    commit to return cash to shareholders, without locking itself into an
    unsustainable dividend policy?

2.   DIVIDENDS AND THE ROLE OF SHARE BUYBACKS

For many years, the big American automakers would maintain a low regular
dividend, but declare "special" dividends whenever they had extra cash. But the
U.S. Tax Code changed to provide that capital gains would be taxed at a lower
rate than income and dividends, which were treated as regular income. This
provided a justification for companies to buy back their own shares instead of
paying extra dividends, although one that came late to the game—the tax
difference long predated the move to buybacks.[4] Then the law changed yet again.

WILLIAM W. BRATTON, *THE NEW DIVIDEND PUZZLE*

93 Geo. L.J. 845 (2005)

The Jobs and Growth Tax Relief Reconciliation Act of 2003 (the "JGTRRA")
aligns tax rates on shareholder capital gains and dividend income at a maximum
fifteen percent, departing from the classical rate preference for capital gains and
ameliorating the tax system's longstanding bias against dividends. According to
the JGTRRA's proponents, this adjustment will help jumpstart a staggering
economy, jolt stock prices upward, and release a cascade of corporate cash into
the pockets of upscale consumers. Several high profile dividend increases since
the JGTRRA's enactment and an increase in the overall amount paid out create
an appearance of immediate success. Cooler heads point out that these increases
fail to impress when viewed in historical context. This Article joins the cooler
heads to predict that no fundamental shift in payout practice should be expected
in the wake of the JGTRRA. But it simultaneously enters a governance objection:
Corporate boards should take the occasion of the JGTRRA to reconsider
prevailing assumptions about payouts, in particular the relative advantages of
dividends and stock repurchases.

During the two decades preceding the JGTRRA, corporate boards steadily
moved away from the dividend—the traditional vehicle for distributing profits to
shareholders—diverting about half of the cash they distribute to shareholders to
open-market repurchases of their firms' own common stock ("OMRs"). The shift
seemed desirable for four reasons. First, OMRs offered the lower capital gains
rate to the selling shareholders, along with a tax deferral and the same lower rate
for nonselling shareholders. Second, OMRs increased earnings per share by
reducing the number of shares outstanding. Third, OMRs signaled good news

---

4. Steven A. Bank, *Is Double Taxation a Scapegoat for Declining Dividends? Evidence from
History*, 56 Tax L. Rev. 463, 464 (2003).

and supported the firm's stock price in the market. Fourth, because OMRs suited management's preferences, they facilitated payout and reduced the risk of suboptimal earnings retention. Old-fashioned dividends, in contrast, carried a tax disadvantage for most shareholders, did nothing for earnings per share, did less than OMRs to support the stock price, and overly constrained cash flow management. Rate parity under the JGTRRA substantially removes the first of the four justifications, inviting reconsideration of the emphasis accorded the second, third, and fourth.

This Article moots the proposition that, given tax-rate parity under the JGTRRA, dividends could rise to relative superiority over repurchases for shareholders of many firms. Prior to rate parity, straightforward reasoning supported a preference for repurchases over dividends. Rate parity brings the relative advantages of dividends and OMRs into much closer balance, turning the choice into a puzzle. In addition to tax-rate parity, four factors favor dividends. First, dividends are transparent, but OMRs can fly under the radar of the disclosure system. Second, dividends treat all shareholders equally, but OMRs can divide shareholders into groups of winners and losers. Third, dividends discipline managers, but OMRs augment management discretion respecting the marginal dollar's payout. Fourth, repurchases help managers line their own pockets by supporting the value of their stock options even as they obscure the options' cost.

Corporate boards should confront the puzzle, reviewing payout policy de novo and actively monitoring it on an ongoing basis. Unfortunately, in the corporate governance system's present posture, boards are unlikely to confront the puzzle, much less to attempt to solve it from the shareholder's point of view. Managers retain a bias in favor of OMRs, stemming in part from their interest in their own stock option compensation and from their dislike of the disciplinary effect of dividends. Corporate and securities law inadvertently support this bias.

———————

As this excerpt notes, the most obvious reason for favoring buybacks disappeared once the taxation of dividends was equalized with that for capital gains.

There might be other reasons to favor buybacks. For example, because capital gains are taxed only when shares are sold, a taxable investor generally has incentives to minimize her personal tax liability by deferring the realization of capital gains. In other words, an investor derives value from the tax-timing option embedded in her shares. That value is better served by a buyback, in which shareholder participation is optional, as compared with a dividend.

On the other hand, many shareholders are exempt from U.S. taxes—pensions, foreign investors, and individuals holding assets in tax-deferred retirement accounts, among the most obvious examples. They should be largely indifferent as between dividends and buybacks.

PROBLEM SET 9.2

1. Based on your knowledge of corporate law, which do you think the author is alluding to at the end of the excerpt? *Cf.* Robert J. Rhee, *Intrafirm Monitoring of Executive Compensation*, 69 Vand. L. Rev. 695, 705 (2016).
2. Subject to the comments above, would a shareholder really be indifferent as between a dividend or a share buyback?

3.   CORPORATE CASH RETENTION

One of the key assumptions of the M&M theories is that the financial markets work perfectly. Thus, if a firm has a good project, it does not matter if it pays out its cash as a dividend or uses it to fund the project, because in the first case the firm can always borrow the needed funding from the markets. Likewise, the flexibility embedded in the use of equity in place of debt is unneeded, because the financial markets stand ready to provide for the firm's liquidity needs.

Managers often object that some amount of cash must be retained within a firm to provide for a potential rainy day. In recent decades, scholars have been skeptical.

ZOHAR GOSHEN, *SHAREHOLDER DIVIDEND OPTIONS*

104 Yale L.J. 881, 8820883 (1995)

A firm's dividend policy reflects management's decision as to what portion of accumulated earnings will be distributed to shareholders and what portion will be retained for reinvestment.[5] A firm's retained earnings represent the amount of financing that the firm can utilize without having to compete against other firms in the capital markets. Because dividend policy wholly determines the amount of earnings that a firm retains, dividend policy also determines the extent to which a firm can escape the scrutiny of participants in the capital markets.

Retained earnings are the greatest source of capital for firms. The typical U.S. industrial corporation finances almost seventy-five percent of its capital expenditures from retained earnings, whereas new equity issues provide a negligible fraction of corporate funding.[6] Scholars have long recognized firms'

---

5. The result of this decision is referred to as the firm's dividend payout ratio: the ratio between earnings distributed as dividends and total earnings (dividends/total earnings = payout ratio).

6. From 1981 to 1991, U.S. corporations financed 74.7% of their new investments from internally generated cash flow. The figure of 74.7% represents net income plus depreciation minus dividends. Between 1981 and 1991, average new equity financing was about −11%, as firms repurchased more shares than they issued. *See* Stephen A. Ross et al., *Corporate Finance* 406 tbl. 14.1 (3d ed. 1993). Moreover, on average, publicly traded firms issue "seasoned" equity— additional equity issued by a firm whose shares are already traded in public markets—only once

significant dependence on retained earnings and negligible dependence on equity financing.[7] This phenomenon led Professor Baumol to the inescapable conclusion that a substantial proportion of firms "manage to avoid the *direct* disciplining influences of the securities market, or at least to evade the type of discipline which can be imposed by the provision of funds to inefficient firms only on extremely unfavorable terms."[8] Unfortunately for the sake of allocative efficiency, in recent years, most firms have also managed to avoid even the *indirect* disciplining influences of the market for corporate control.[9]

Inefficient managers might try to escape a market inspection of their performance by adopting a low-payout dividend policy and avoiding the competitive external market for financing.[10]

But perhaps this skeptical view might change in light of recent events.

---

every 18.5 years. *See* Lynn A. Stout, *The Unimportance of Being Efficient: An Economic Analysis of Stock Market Pricing and Securities Regulation*, 87 Mich. L. Rev. 613, 647 n.186 (1988). The portion of corporate funding that does not come from either retained earnings or equity is raised through debt financing. *See id.* at 648.

7. *See, e.g.*, William J. Baumol, *The Stock Market and Economic Efficiency* 69 (1965); Gordon Donaldson, *Corporate Debt Capacity* 56 (1961). The proclivity of U.S. firms to finance their capital expenditures from internally generated cash flows is almost without parallel in the world of international corporate finance. Compared to U.S. corporations, firms in other countries finance much less of their capital expenditures from internal cash flow and much more of their capital expenditures from new equity issues. Germany is the only major industrial country whose firms generate as much financing internally as do U.S. firms.

8. Baumol, *supra*, at 70. For this reason, Baumol noted that "[o]ne might almost venture to conclude ... that the market in fact does not allocate much of the economy's capital." *Id.* at 79. Market pricing of new stock issues directly influences the allocative efficiency of the economy by determining firms' cost of capital. The fact that the market allocates so little capital, however, has provided grounds for doubting the importance of capital markets efficiency. *See* Stout, *supra* note 2, at 617-618.

9. *See* Stout, *supra*, at 691 (contending that managerial defensive tactics and state antitakeover legislation have raised costs of hostile takeover significantly above that which would be incurred in free market for corporate control).

10. The risk of managerial abuse of discretion is known as agency cost. *See* Michael C. Jensen & William H. Meckling, *Theory of the Firm: Managerial Behavior, Agency Costs and Ownership Structure*, 3 J. Fin. Econ. 305, 310-311 (1976). Indeed, as some of the literature on takeovers suggests, many managers do abuse their discretion and retain excessive earnings. *See, e.g.*, Michael C. Jensen, *Agency Costs of Free Cash Flow, Corporate Finance, and Takeovers*, 76 Am. Econ. Rev. 323 (1986).

IN RE LEHMAN BROTHERS HOLDINGS, INC., ET AL., DEBTORS.

416 B.R. 392
United States Bankruptcy Court, S.D. New York
Sept. 25, 2009

JAMES M. PECK, Bankruptcy Judge.

INTRODUCTION

This dispute involves one of the loans held by State Street Bank and Trust Company ("State Street") that is part of a pool of commercial loans transferred pursuant to the terms of a master repurchase agreement (the "MRA").[11] Under the MRA, State Street paid approximately $1 billion to purchase this portfolio of financial assets from Lehman Commercial Paper, Inc. ("LCPI"). The transaction evidenced by the MRA contemplated that LCPI would repurchase these assets and repay State Street in accordance with the agreement, but LCPI filed for relief under chapter 11 and has defaulted under the MRA. The result is that State Street now owns these assets, including the loan in question made to LH 1440 LLC ("LH 1440") as borrower.

Plaintiff LH 1440 complains that the transfer of this loan to State Street adversely impacted its rights under other contemporaneous loan documentation. In substance, LH 1440 contends that it entered into three integrated loans that were intended to function as a unified financing package for the acquisition and improvement of certain commercial real estate. It claims that its expectations have been frustrated due to the sale of only one of these loans to State Street under the terms of the MRA. The splitting up of the financing and the selection of one loan for inclusion in the pool of loans sold to State Street allegedly has exposed Plaintiff to the risk of a mortgage foreclosure action at a time when it is unable to obtain advances needed to support the project under the remaining loans still held by LCPI. Plaintiff argues that State Street, as purchaser of this pool of assets, should be placed in the shoes of the original lender and be required to advance funds to LH 1440 even though financing documents for these other loans were not included within the pool of assets acquired by State Street. . . .

On June 8, 2007, LH 1440, as borrower, and LBHI, as lender, entered into real estate financing arrangements documented by means of two separate loan agreements, the Acquisition and Project Loan Agreement and the Building Loan Agreement. In addition, the parties executed a Consolidated, Amended and Restated Acquisition Loan Mortgage and Security Agreement, and an Option Agreement referencing three loans: 1) the Acquisition Loan of $15,649,568.31; 2) the Project Loan of $6,232,323.69; and 3) the Building Loan of $4,875,819.00. The loans were secured by three separate promissory notes. A single

---

11. Recall the discussion of "repo" agreements in Chapter 1 with regard to Lehman's "Repo 105" transactions.—AUTHOR

Participation Fee of 28.5% and a single Interest Rate Cap of $26,757,711.00 applied to the loans.

The Acquisition Loan was used to acquire certain real property located at 1440 Story Avenue in the Bronx, New York. The Project and Building Loans have been used to maintain and improve the acquired property and to fund interest payments on the Acquisition Loan. The Acquisition Loan is fully funded, and the Project and Building Loans have future funding obligations. Thus, the holder of the Acquisition Loan is under no direct obligation to advance funds to LH 1440. At some point, LCPI acquired the above referenced loans from LBHI.

On May 1, 2007, State Street entered into the MRA with LCPI, and as evidenced by a July 2007 confirmation letter, purchased a pool of commercial loans for $1 billion. Pursuant to the MRA, LCPI was entitled to substitute loans, as long as the value of those assets, in the aggregate, exceeded $1 billion. On September 17, 2008, State Street gave LCPI a notice of default under the MRA. When LCPI failed to repurchase the loans, State Street took possession of the mortgages and promissory notes for those assets. At that time, the promissory note for the Acquisition Loan was one of thirty-six commercial loans within the pool of assets held by State Street, but the promissory notes for the Project Loan and the Building Loan were not included among those assets.

On March 31, 2009, LH 1440 filed this adversary proceeding to obtain a declaratory judgment that the loan agreements together constitute an integrated loan to LH 1440 and that State Street necessarily acquired the Acquisition Loan, Project Loan, and Building Loan when it exercised its rights as counterparty under the MRA and took possession of the commercial loans described in the MRA. Thereafter, on May 1, 2009, State Street filed the Motion based on the failure to state a claim upon which relief may be granted. LBHI and LCPI have joined in the Motion. Following oral argument, the Court reserved judgment....

The Court concludes that it would be inconsistent with customary market practices to expect the counterparty in a repo transaction to conduct a time consuming investigation regarding the assets that are included in the transaction. This is particularly true in consideration of the fact that other assets often can be substituted, and the focus of the transaction is on the aggregate value of the assets, rather than the specific assets within the pool. LH 1440 has not alleged that State Street as repo counterparty had any reason to know about or a duty to discover the alleged connection between the Acquisition Loan Note and other instruments executed by LH 1440 and LBHI. The complaint as to State Street seeks a remedy from a party that owes no duty to LH 1440 and fails to state a claim that rises above the speculative level. For that reason, the Motion is granted as to State Street, but LH 1440 shall be granted the opportunity to reformulate its allegations in an amended complaint.

The Motion is denied as to LBHI and LCPI. While the transfer provisions and the splitting clause establish that the loans were separately transferable, the underlying documents indicate that the transaction appears to have been intended to function as an interrelated loan. The loans were to be used in tandem; the Acquisition Loan, now fully funded, provided funds to purchase the property, while the Project and Building Loans, with ongoing funding obligations, would allow the borrower to maintain and improve the acquired property. The single Participation Fee and the single Interest Rate Cap Agreement also may be indicative of a single loan transaction. . . .

Even in late 2012, long after Lehman's bankruptcy filing in 2008, the company continued to hold more than $3 billion in loans it had made to other corporations.

PROBLEM SET 9.3

1. The text suggests that the recent failures of financial institutions might change attitudes toward companies that finance expansion with retained earnings. How so?
2. Why would a shareholder object to a corporation that kept a large cash balance in its bank account (or money market fund)?
3. In 1968 the Pennsylvania Railroad and the New York Central Railroad merged to form the PennCentral Railroad. Two years later, PennCentral unexpectedly filed what was then the largest corporate bankruptcy case in American history. PennCentral had financed its operations with more than $70 million in money market paper, and the default had the effect of dislocating the money markets in the United States for several weeks. Investors lost confidence in other corporate issuers and stopped refinancing maturing commercial paper. Within three weeks of PennCentral's bankruptcy, the amount of corporate commercial paper outstanding had dropped almost 10 percent. As a result, most large corporations began to keep lines of credit with large banks as a "backup" in case such an event happened again. Does the case above suggest the limitations to that strategy?

4.   CONGLOMERATES

The diversified corporation or conglomerate, was the way big business was done until the 1980s. There were several reasons for this:

The diversified corporation became the dominant form of industrial firm in the United States over the course of the twentieth century. During the 1920s, DuPont and General Motors pioneered the use of the multi-divisional form (or M-form) to produce and market a number of related products through separate divisions, and this organizational structure subsequently spread (Chandler 1962). The M-form also allowed easy integration of acquired businesses, which enabled firms to grow through acquisition. Following the enactment of the Celler-Kefauver Act in 1950, horizontal and vertical acquisitions (buying competitors, buyers, or suppliers) fell out of regulatory favor, and firms seeking to grow through acquisition were forced to diversify into other industries. This fueled the conglomerate mergers of the late 1960s and 1970s (Fligstein 1991). The strategy of growth through acquiring firms in unrelated lines of business and structuring them as a collection of separate business units reflected an under-lying model of appropriate corporate practice—the "firm-as-portfolio" model. By 1980, the triumph of the firm-as-portfolio model seemed complete, as growth through diversification was perhaps the most widely used corporate strategy among large firms (Porter 1987), and fewer than 25 percent of the *Fortune* 500 largest industrial corporations made all their sales within a single broadly-defined (2-digit SIC) industry.[12]

In short, antitrust law discouraged buying firms within a related industry, so managers began buying unrelated firms. The prototypical example was ITT, which began life as International Telephone & Telegraph in 1920, but ended up owning the Sheraton Hotel chain, the ITT Technical Institute of afternoon TV fame, a major insurance company, the maker of Wonder Bread, and the Avis rental car company. All while becoming heavily involved in South American politics along with the CIA.[13]

The key justification for this hodge-podge of companies was diversification.[14] When one part of the firm was in the dumps, another would be doing well and overall the arrangement would provide for slow and steady corporate profits.

Today it seems incredible that managers would be allowed to assemble what amounts to a mutual fund, when they were typically paid based on the size of the company they managed. But it is important to remember that in the 1960s and early 1970s mutual funds were expensive, and brokerage fees were high. That is, it was not cheap or easy to assemble a diversified portfolio, despite what finance theory at the time suggested.

By the 1980s neither of these two factors were at play, as brokerage fees had become deregulated, and mutual funds were going mainstream. In short, the notion that investors needed managers to achieve diversification—which conflicted with much of modern finance theory, and represented a rather extreme attempt to finance projects "internally"—largely came to an end.

The key exception is in the financial industry, where even after the recent financial crisis conglomerates control increasingly large parts of finance.[15] Widely admired companies like General Electric and United Technologies Corporation, and international firms like Unilever and Siemens, also suggest that the conglomerate is not completely gone.

---

12. Gerald F. Davis, et al., *The Decline and Fall of the Conglomerate Firm in the 1980s: The Deinstitutionalization of an Organizational Form*, 59 American Sociological Rev. 547 (1994).

13. http://foia.state.gov/reports/churchreport.asp.

14. Richard A. Booth, *Five Decades of Corporation Law: From Conglomeration to Equity Compensation*, 53 Vill. L. Rev. 459, 464 (2008).

15. Arthur E. Wilmarth, Jr., *The Dark Side of Universal Banking: Financial Conglomerates and the Origins of the Subprime Financial Crisis*, 41 Conn. L. Rev. 963 (2009).

But were the conglomerates justified by their times? Even that is a bit unclear. For example, one author found

> [N]o evidence that diversified firms are valued more than single segment firms in the 1960s and early 1970s; on the contrary, for several years diversified firms sell at a substantial discount when compared to single segment firms. This discount is large and significant over the 1961-1970 period, but it becomes small and insignificant in 1973-1976. These results hold after controlling for industry effects and for differences between diversified and undiversified firms in profitability, leverage, and investment policy. The largest increase in diversification takes place over the 1970-1976 period when the penalty imposed by capital markets is small. Thus, the firms that diversified at that time did not impose a cost on their shareholders.[16]

In short, originally the conglomerates did seem to impose a cost on shareholders—the parts were worth more than the whole—but eventually the harm seems to have gone away. Why is unclear.

PROBLEM SET 9.4

1. During the 1960s it was thought that conglomerates added value, by providing shareholders with a diversified return that reduced overall risk. More recently, it has been suggested that "spinoffs," which involve the separation of large corporations into smaller, more coherent parts, might create real value for shareholders. Is either view consistent with the M&M propositions?

2. In a 2014 article in *The Economist*, it was observed that:

   > AN INVESTOR who bought one Berkshire Hathaway share at just over $11 when Warren Buffett took control of the firm 50 years ago, and kept it, would have seen its value hit an all-time peak above $190,000 in recent days, an annual return of 21%. . .
   >
   > Berkshire is into all manner of business, from insurance to ice-cream parlours. Normally, such diverse groups suffer a "conglomerate discount"; but Berkshire's shares trade at a 40% premium to the book value of its holdings. Mr Buffett's proven formula has been to seek solid firms with good defences against competitors, leave their managers to run them as before, and hang on to them for the long term. His success over the past half-century makes him living disproof of the "efficient-markets hypothesis," which argues that even the shrewdest investor cannot, over the long term, buck the collective wisdom of the market and consistently outperform it.[17]

   Does the example of Berkshire Hathaway undermine the argument against conglomerates, or is it the "exception that proves the rule"?

---

16. Henri Servaes, *The Value of Diversification During the Conglomerate Merger Wave*, 51 J. Fin. 1201, 1203 (1996).

17. http://goo.gl/Q1inAu.

10

SOME REAL-WORLD CONSIDERATIONS (PART 2)

In Chapter 9 we examined some of the reasons why the M&M propositions, and some other related elements of finance theory, do not hold in the real world. For example, if a company favors "internal" financing instead of paying dividends and financing in the market, this violates M&M dividend irrelevance. But it could also be seen as a violation of the ECMH, to the extent the firm makes this choice because it believes that the market will not appreciate the value of its new project.

Our focus in Chapter 9 was largely on issues affecting the firm's equity. Now we turn to debt and the issues that influence the firm's use of debt despite the M&M propositions.

1. DEBT AND TAXES

Although the choice between debt and equity does not matter in the M&M world, in a world with a tax code, the choice matters very much.

KATHERINE PRATT, *THE DEBT-EQUITY DISTINCTION IN A SECOND-BEST WORLD*

53 Vand. L. Rev. 1055, 1059-1065 (2000)

Our federal income tax system treats corporations as taxpaying entities.[1] Each year, a corporation must pay tax on its income for the year. The tax is on

---

[1]. I.R.C. §11 imposes tax on "C" corporations. *See* I.R.C. §11 (1994). For purposes of this Article, assume that the corporation is a "C" corporation, which is any corporation that has not elected to be treated as an "S" corporation. C corporations and S corporations are named for the subchapters of the Code that apply to those types of corporations. A corporation can be an S corporation only if it has 75 or fewer shareholders, no foreign or entity shareholders, and only one class of stock. *See id.* §1361(b)(1) (1994) (amended 1998). S Corporations are not taxpaying entities; instead S Corporation income and other tax items pass through to the shareholders and

net income, not gross income, so corporations can deduct the costs of earning their income.

Corporations finance their operations by raising debt and equity capital. A corporation, acting as a borrower, can issue debt (e.g., bonds) to debtholders, the creditors, in exchange for cash or other property. The corporation can also issue stock to shareholders in exchange for cash or other property.[2] As compensation for the use of the debtholders' money, the corporation pays the debtholders interest.[3] As compensation for the use of the shareholders' money, the corporation pays the shareholders distributions in the form of dividends.

Although, for reasons discussed later, the Internal Revenue Code (the "Code") should treat debt and equity similarly for tax purposes, the Code has always distinguished between debt and equity. There are numerous tax differences between debt and equity. Some of these differences relate to the tax consequences to the corporate issuer of the debt or equity.[4] Some relate to the tax consequences to the holder of the debt or equity.[5]

---

each shareholder reports her allocable share of those items on her individual tax return. *See id.*§1366 (1994) (amended 1996).

2. The stock proceeds the corporate issuer receives from the shareholder are not included in the corporation's income. *See* I.R.C. §1032(a) (1994).

3. The corporate borrower also eventually returns to the bondholders the amount they loaned the corporation. Interest paid on the bond includes a pure time value of money element (with an inflation component) and compensation for the risk that the issuer will default.

4. For example, the tax consequences of a corporation retiring its stock or debt differ. A corporation does not have income when it receives cash or other property in exchange for its stock. *See* I.R.C. §1032(a) (1994). If the corporation later repurchases the stock for an amount of cash less than the amount for which the stock was issued, the corporation recognizes no income. See I.R.C. §311(a) (1994). Section 1032(a), which insulates the corporate issuer from gain on the issuance of stock in exchange from property, does not technically apply to the issuer's repurchase of the stock. *See id.*§1032(a) (1994). Treasury Regulations provide that §1032 does not apply to a corporation's acquisition of its own shares unless the corporation acquires the shares in exchange for its own stock (although the regulation cross references the §311 regulations). *See* Treas. Reg. §1.1032-1(b). Section 311(a) provides that a corporation does not recognize gain on the distribution of property with respect to its stock. *See* I.R.C §311(a) (1994). Property includes cash under I.R.C. §317(a). *See id.*§317 (a) (1994); *see also* Bittker & Eustice, *supra*, at 4-71 (6th ed. 1998) ("Upon redeeming or repurchasing its own stock, a corporation recognizes no gain, even if the amount paid is less than the stock's par or stated value or the amount received when it was issued; any corporate level gain on the transaction is instead treated as a tax-free capital contribution under I.R.C. §118(a), as a distribution covered by I.R.C. §311(a)(2), or simply as a nontaxable capital adjustment.") (footnote omitted).

A corporation does not have to include proceeds from the issuance of debt in income. If a corporation retires debt for less than the amount owed on the debt, however, the corporation must generally include in income the difference between the amount owed on the debt and the amount paid to discharge the debt. *See* I.R.C. §61(a)(12) (1994); United States v. Kirby Lumber Co., 284 U.S. 1, 3 (1931). If the debt discharge occurs in a bankruptcy proceeding, I.R.C. §108(a)(1)(A) permits the corporation to exclude the debt discharge income completely. *See* I.R.C. §108(a)(1)(A) (1994). If the debt discharge does not occur in a bankruptcy proceeding, I.R.C. §108(a)(1)(B) and (3), and (d)(3) permit the corporation to exclude the debt discharge income to the extent of the corporation's insolvency (the corporation's liabilities less assets) prior to the discharge. *See id.*

This Article will focus on the most important difference between debt and equity at the level of the corporate issuer: a corporation can deduct interest paid or accrued on the debt it issues but cannot deduct the dividends it pays on the shares it issues.[6] It will also consider investor level character and timing differences between debt and equity because these differences affect the amount of debt and equity in corporate capital structures.

First consider the character differences. Debtholders pay tax at ordinary income tax rates on interest paid or accrued on the corporate debt they own.... If a corporation retains earnings, instead of distributing them as dividends, the value of the assets of the corporation will increase, which will in turn increase the value of the stock of the corporation held by its shareholders. If a shareholder sells stock that has appreciated, the shareholder will realize gain equal to the amount for which the stock was sold less the amount the shareholder paid for the stock. (The gain from the sale of the stock [and now dividends are] usually taxed at preferential capital gains rates.) In summary, shareholders typically pay tax on undistributed corporate earnings when they sell their stock.

Second, consider the timing differences between the investor level tax consequences of stock and debt. Shareholders typically include dividends when they receive the dividends and include gain from the sale of stock when they sell the stock. In other words, corporate earnings are not typically taxed at the shareholder level until the corporation pays a dividend or the shareholder sells appreciated stock. Stock is therefore taxed using what is sometimes called a "wait-and-see" method.

Debtholders include (and the issuer deducts) interest as it is paid or as it accrues. Interest on corporate debt may be stated interest or unstated interest. If all of the interest is stated, the debtholders include the interest and the issuer deducts the interest as it is paid. If the debt instrument bears unstated interest,

---

§§108(a)(1)(B), (a)(3), (d)(3) (1994). Section 108(a) often just defers the tax on debt discharge income because debt discharge income excluded under I.R.C. §108(a) reduces the corporation's net operating losses. *See id.* §108(b)(2)(A) (1994). A net operating loss for one tax year can be used to reduce the corporate taxpayer's tax liability for other profitable years. Net operating losses can be carried back two years and forward 20 years. *See id.* §172(b) (1994). If the corporation that has excluded debt discharge income later begins earning income again, the §108(b) reduction in its net operating losses will increase its tax liability because the net operating losses would otherwise have reduced the corporation's income.

5. Stock and debt instruments are generally "capital assets," so that gain from the sale of such securities qualifies for preferential capital gain rates and loss from the sale of such securities is subject to special loss limitation rules. *See* I.R.C. §§1(h) (amended 1997), 1201(amended 1997), 1211, 1221, 1222 (1994); Van Suetendael v. Commissioner, 13 T.C.M. 1071, 1075-76 (T.C. 1944), aff'd, 152 F.2d 654 (2d Cir. 1945) (holding that sale by an individual who traded securities generated capital gain, not ordinary income).

Special rules may apply, however, that distinguish between stock and debt instruments in certain circumstances. For example, I.R.C. §306, which recharacterizes all or a part of the capital gain from the sale of preferred stock as ordinary income, does not apply to debt instruments. *See* I.R.C. §306(a)(1) (1994).

6. *See* I.R.C. §163(a) (1994) (amended 1998).

which the Code refers to as original issue discount ("OID"), the debtholder includes the OID and the issuer deducts the OID as it accrues. In other words, the bondholder's interest inclusion and corporate issuer's interest deduction may precede the payment of that interest. . .

To summarize, the corporate earnings distributed or allocable to the debtholders as interest are taxed once at the debtholder level because the corporate issuer deducts the interest on its tax return and the bondholder includes the interest as income on her tax return. On the other hand, corporate earnings distributed to shareholders as dividends are taxed twice, first at the corporate level (since the corporation cannot deduct the dividends paid to shareholders) and second at the shareholder level when the dividends are paid. The corporate earnings that are not distributed are also taxed twice, first at the corporate level, and second at the shareholder level when the shareholder sells the stock, which has appreciated to reflect the earnings retained by the corporation.

From the firm's perspective, the deductibility of interest payments makes debt more attractive than equity. The value of the extra benefit of debt is equal to the corporation's tax rate multiplied by the amount of interest it pays in any year. For example, if Bogartco pays $1,000 per year in interest on its debt, and has a tax rate of 30 percent, the benefit of using debt would be $300 per year. Over a period of several years, we can assume the value of the tax deduction is either a perpetuity or an annuity and value accordingly.

This extra value to debt that results from corporate tax law is referred to as the "tax shield." In the preceding example, Bogartco can "protect" up to $1,000 of corporate income from taxation because of the deductibility of its interest payments.

M&M recognized the effect of taxes and revised their propositions to take taxes into account. First, recall the original M&M Proposition I provided that firm value does not change with changes in the capital structure ($V_L = V_U$). In the revised M&M world with taxes, Proposition I now holds that firm value increases with leverage (i.e., the use of debt). Mathematically, we would write this new Proposition I as

$$V_L = V_U + T_C B$$

The initial terms are the old Proposition I, but now the value of the "leveraged" firm is the value of the unleveraged firm plus the value of the tax shield.

Similarly, M&M modified their Proposition II to account for taxes. Remember that originally this proposition had described efforts to "slice up" the capital structure as a zero-sum game: Increased use of debt simply resulted in higher costs of equity. But when we add in taxes, the new Proposition II instead holds that some of the increase in equity risk and return is offset by the interest tax shield.

PROBLEM SET 10.1

1. What might be the policy justification for allowing corporations to deduct interest payments but not dividend payments?

2. You own all the equity in a company. The company has no debt. The company's annual cash flow is $1,000, before interest and taxes. The corporate tax rate is 40 percent. You have the option to exchange half of your equity position for $1,000 in 10 percent debt. Should you do this and why?

In addition to the traditional favoritism toward debt shown by the Tax Code, the Code also distorts financial decisions made by corporate groups that operate across borders. In particular, as of mid-2016, large American corporate groups held more than $1 trillion in cash on their balance sheets. This money was earned by foreign subsidiaries, but American companies resist returning the cash to the United States because doing so will subject the funds to taxation.

Unlike most other countries, the U.S. taxes corporations on earnings generated anywhere in the world. American companies owe taxes at the full corporate tax rate of 35 percent on profits they earn around the world. They then get credits for tax payments to foreign governments, but most foreign jurisdictions tax at a rate lower than 35 percent. The American companies do not pay the residual U.S. tax until they bring the money home.

This also provides an incentive to "move" income abroad. For example, technology and pharmaceutical companies whose profits stem from intellectual property often place those property rights in a subsidiary incorporated in a low tax jurisdiction, like Ireland.

One of the most notable companies in this situation is Apple, which reports $216 billion in cash on its balance sheet, 93 percent of which is held abroad. Apple has gone so far as to issue debt, which of course is tax deductible, to pay share dividends, even while it holds billions in cash through foreign subsidiaries.

In a further irony, most of the cash held by foreign subsidiaries of American companies is actually parked in bank accounts in New York or invested in U.S. government securities.[7] In short, it is not really "abroad," but rather trapped in the corporate structure.

***

As this edition of the book was going to press, a new president was sworn in, and it was not the person many had expected. In addition, for the first time since 2008, both houses of Congress and the White House are under the control of a single political party. As a result, significant changes to the Tax Code are under discussion; in particular, changes to the current corporate tax regime.

---

7. http://goo.gl/NYOhSr.

Among other things, proposals under consideration would end the deductibility of interest payments in connection with lowering the corporate tax rate from the current 35% to 20%, while imposing a border adjustment (taxing imports at the full rate and exempting exports). The new tax would apply to all domestic sales while exempting foreign ones, making the corporate tax regime more like a sales tax (or value-added tax) than an income tax. These changes would clearly effect the foregoing discussion. Whether any will actually be enacted will have to await the third edition.

2.   THE EFFECTS OF LEVERAGE

Online,[8] you can find a chart that compares the return of two exchange traded funds (ETFs).[9] One (SPY)[10] tracks the S&P 500 index and the other (UPRO)[11] aims to provide three times the return of the index. How could the second fund do that?

If your answer is "by buying three times as many stocks" take a moment and think about that. If the S&P 500 returns 10 percent, do I get a three times greater return by investing $300 instead of $100? Nope. I still get a 10 percent return, it's just on a bigger amount now.

The ProShares UltraPro S&P 500 Fund's (UPRO) disclosures give us some indication of how it achieves its returns:

> The fund invests in equity securities and derivatives that [the fund manager] believes, in combination, should have similar daily return characteristics as three times (3x) the daily return of the index.

Derivatives, which we cover in a later chapter, are one way of achieving leverage. But the more traditional way of achieving leverage is by using debt. A home mortgage loan is a common example of the use of leverage. If you have $100,000 to spend on a house, without leverage that is the maximum value of the house you can buy. But if a bank will lend you 80 percent of the purchase price of a house, you can buy a $500,000 house. That means you have five times as much exposure to the local real estate market.

In good times, the use of the loan benefits you tremendously. For example, if home prices double you would now have a $100,000 gain if you had bought your

---

8. http://goo.gl/PKE0G.

9. An ETF is a mutual fund that trades throughout the day like a stock. A mutual fund is a fund that investors buy to get exposure to a portfolio of securities. For example, if you have $1,000 to invest, it would be hard to obtain a diversified portfolio by buying individual stocks. But if you bought shares in a mutual fund that itself owned a diversified portfolio, you get the benefits of diversification. Of course, it is costlier to buy shares through a mutual fund (the manager gets paid) than to buy them directly.

10. http://goo.gl/ScL33.

11. http://goo.gl/WCHIz.

house with cash ($100,000 × 2). But with the loan, you have a $500,000 gain—your house is worth $1 million, less the $400,000 you owe to the bank and your $100,000 investment. With the same initial investment, you have obtained a 500 percent return as opposed to a 100 percent return if you used only cash.

But leverage also works the other way around as well. If home prices decline, cutting values in half, your cash-purchased home is worth $50,000, and you have a $50,000 loss. But your finer home, purchased with the help of the bank, is now worth $250,000. Your initial investment is gone and you owe the bank $150,000 beyond the value of the home. In the vernacular, you are "underwater" by $150,000. The lesson is that leverage magnifies returns–*in both directions*.

It works with corporations, too. And given the tax benefits already described, it provides a strong temptation for managers to use at least some leverage to amplify their returns. After all, shareholders are diversified (or they should be) and limited liability means that at most shareholders will lose their investment (unlike the mortgage example, involving an individual borrower).

On the eve of the financial crisis, Merrill Lynch led all financial institutions with a leverage ratio of 40 to 1. That is, the right-hand side of Merrill's balance sheet was comprised of 2.5% equity (1 divided by 40), and the remainder debt.

PROBLEM SET 10.2

1. Consider the following table. If it had been around, how much would the ProShares UltraPro S&P 500 fund (UPRO) have returned in the two best and worst years for the index?

History	2006	2007	2008	2009	2010	2011	2012	2013	2014	2015
SPX	13.62	3.53	-38.49	23.45	12.78	0.00	13.41	29.60	11.39	-0.73

2. Why might managers decline to use as much leverage as shareholders might like? Alternatively, recall the Bratton article in Chapter 9 and the discussion of manager compensation. Why might managers decide to use lots of leverage?
3. What are the systematic risks that might occur for the use of high levels of leverage?

3.   THE COSTS OF DEBT

Recall that one of the M&M assumptions was that debt was essentially risk free. In the real world, of course, corporate debt is not risk free. American Airlines (and every other major U.S. airline), Lehman Brothers, Kodak, Blockbuster Video, Border's Books, and the Los Angeles Dodgers all remind us that sometimes corporations do not pay their debts.

STEPHEN J. LUBBEN, *WHAT WE "KNOW" ABOUT CHAPTER 11 COST IS WRONG*

17 FORDHAM J. CORP. & FIN. L. 141, 147-167 (2012)

The costs of corporate reorganization are compelling in any recession, and particularly so in a financial crisis, such as the one we are currently experiencing. To the casual reader of the *Wall Street Journal* who still thinks of bankruptcy as the equivalent to corporate death, the millions of dollars paid by "bankrupt" or "insolvent" firms like Lehman Brothers, or Enron before it, often seems quite extreme.

A similar phenomenon can be seen in academic literature, dating back to Modigliani and Miller in 1958, and the notion that a firm's capital structure amounts to little more than slices in a pie. In this world, debtor-firms are typically discussed relative to a backdrop of complete contracts and zero transaction costs. Accordingly, firms that encounter financial distress—that is, having liquid assets insufficient to meet current fixed claims—simply renegotiate their obligations and proceed accordingly. Slight deviations from the background assumptions can be assumed and then addressed by neatly automated contractual responses. That Kmart, a large discount store chain, would pay more than $134 million to professionals to do so is inconsistent with this idealized understanding of the world, and thus each dollar spent is evidence of inefficiency.

Of course, both views of "bankruptcy" are based on basic misunderstanding or oversimplification. Both assume that financial distress is costless, whereas even liquidation does not happen by itself. Indeed, only abandonment of a distressed firm might be costless—if we limit our conception of cost to actual "out of pocket" expenditures by the debtor-firm. More broadly, understanding the cost of a corporate reorganization system is important because debtor-firms face the reality of a world with incomplete contracts, incomplete information, uncertain asset values, and complex capital structures that highlight the many ways in which assumptions about capital structure irrelevance or managerial rationality, or both, fail. Given these truths, and the added reality of asset market disruptions, it is generally thought that reorganization structures are important tools to avoid excessive and economically disruptive liquidation of assets. If given a choice of possible approaches to reorganization, the cost of any particular system, weighed against its benefits, provides an obvious metric for evaluation. . . .

[My] dataset is non-random, comprising all 2004 bankruptcy cases listed in the "Major Bankruptcies" database on www.bankruptcydata.com (published by New Generation Research, Inc.) except for cases initially filed under chapter 7 and not converted to chapter 11 and cases filed under former section 304 of the Bankruptcy Code.[12]

. . . In a chapter 11 case, all professionals that are to be paid with estate funds are required to have their retention approved at the start of the case.[13] And the bulk of those professionals are also required to have their fees and expenses approved by the bankruptcy court before being paid from the estate.[14] In short, there is both *ex ante* and *ex post* oversight of most professionals by the bankruptcy court.

The debtor's bankruptcy estate is responsible for paying for all professionals it retained in the case. In addition, the estate is responsible for paying the expenses of any professionals retained by official—that is, court appointed—committees in the case.[15] Finally, the estate is also responsible for paying any court appointed "neutrals," and their professionals, including trustees and examiners. All of these expenses count as costs of administration of the estate, and are thus entitled to priority payment.[16] . . .

Throughout the literature, it has become common to report fees as a percentage of debtor size. The advantage of such a measure is obvious—namely it provides an easy "rule of thumb" for considering whether a particular case is above or below the average cost. But as Professor LoPucki has noted, the relationship between debtor size and cost is highly sensitive to the size of the cases under study, meaning that use of such "rules of thumb" will often result in substantial errors.

This same effect is evident in the present study, where the average cost of the smallest quartile of cases is 10% of size,[17] while in the largest cases cost is 2% of size. Based on the ratios of cost to size shown on Table 7B, it appears that there are substantial economies of scale to chapter 11 cases. . . . The relationship between size and standardized cost demonstrates a strong downward trend, further suggesting that there may be significant fixed costs to chapter 11, and thus a declining cost for the largest of debtors.

---

12. Section 304 was repealed in 2005 as part of the enactment of new chapter 15. Both section 304 and new chapter 15 deal with the recognition of foreign bankruptcy proceedings in the United States. *See* Jay Lawrence Westbrook *Chapter 15 at Last*, 79 Am. Bankr. L. J. 713 (2005).

13. 11 U.S.C. §327(a).

14. *See* 11 U.S.C. §§327, 330, 331.

15. 11 U.S.C. §§1103; 330.

16. 11 U.S.C. §§507(a)(2); 503(b)(2).

17. Defined as the average of assets and debts.

TABLE 7B
Standardized Chapter 11 Cost by Size Quartiles (Big Case Dataset)

	Mean	Std. Err.	[95% Conf.	Interval]
Total cost over size				
1 (smallest)	0.101	0.017	0.067	0.135
2	0.089	0.015	0.059	0.119
3	0.042	0.006	0.029	0.055
4	0.021	0.006	0.010	0.033
Mean debtor size (USD)				
1	7,080,907.00	981,618.40	5,131,608.00	9,030,207.00
2	44,700,000.00	4,120,754.00	36,500,000.00	52,900,000.00
3	242,000,000.00	21,800,000.00	198,000,000.00	285,000,000.00
4	2,410,000,000.00	609,000,000.00	1,200,000,000.00	3,620,000,000.00
n = 94				

———————

The costs of corporate bankruptcy or reorganization are often considered to encompass two concepts. First, there are the direct costs, made up chiefly of the professional fees associated with reorganization, but also including other lesser costs like court filing fees and, in the United States, quarterly fees due to the U.S. Trustee's office.[18] The excerpt examines these costs.

In addition, there are also indirect costs of a firm's bankruptcy, which are more abstract but include things like lost revenues, lost opportunities, and lost goodwill. Some of these costs might be of concern to the firm's stakeholders, but not to policymakers if, for example, financial distress simply results in the shifting of sales from the distressed firm to a competitor firm—unless the competitor is abroad.

Although there have been some efforts to study indirect costs empirically, and one recent study suggests that the total expected cost of financial distress might be as high as 4.5 percent of the firm's predistress assets,[19] more often efforts to examine these costs have been theoretical, particularly in the legal literature.[20] In addition, studies of indirect costs have been limited to publicly held companies,

---

18. The U.S. Trustee Program is a component of the Department of Justice that monitors bankruptcy cases for fraud and the like. It is distinct from the bankruptcy trustee appointed in all chapter 7 and some chapter 11 cases.

19. Heitor Almeida & Tomas Philippon, *The Risk-Adjusted Cost of Financial Distress*, 62 J. Fin. 2557 (2007).

20. Barry E. Adler, *Bankruptcy and Risk Allocation*, 77 Cornell L. Rev. 439 (1992); James J. White, *Harvey's Silence*, 69 Am. Bankr. L.J. 467 (1995).

and it is unknown if the results found in that context will translate to privately held firms, which make up the vast majority of debtors.

In addition, there might be "agency costs" associated with the use of debt. For example, managers and shareholders might collude to take extra risks, knowing that limited liability will protect them from the downside, while all the upside will result in extra return for them. Creditors suffer when this happens, and in Chapters 14 and 15 of this text we will talk about how creditors protect themselves against these costs.

The more debt a firm has, the greater the probability that they will encounter financial distress, and thus the greater the probability that the firm will incur the direct and indirect costs associated with financial distress. Whereas taxes suggest a firm should use as much debt as its managers and shareholders can stand, the risk of bankruptcy pushes in the other direction, particularly if creditors are able to pass on the projected costs of bankruptcy to the borrower in the form of higher interest rates.

PROBLEM SET 10.3

1. How might you integrate taxes and financial distress costs into an overall theory of firm value?
2. How could it be that chapter 11 is efficient if it costs millions of dollars to complete a case?
3. If the taxation of debt and equity were equalized, how might bankruptcy costs affect the use of debt?

11

VALUING A FIRM

CONSOLIDATED ROCK PRODUCTS CO. v. DU BOIS

312 U.S. 510
Supreme Court of the United States
March 3, 1941

Mr. Justice Douglas delivered the opinion of the Court.

This case involves questions as to the fairness under §77B of the Bankruptcy Act [a predecessor to today's chapter 11], of a plan of reorganization for a parent corporation (Consolidated Rock Products Co.) and its two wholly owned subsidiaries—Union Rock Co. and Consumers Rock and Gravel Co., Inc. The District Court confirmed the plan; the Circuit Court of Appeals reversed. We granted the petitions for certiorari because of the importance in the administration of the reorganization provisions of the Act of certain principles enunciated by the Circuit Court of Appeals.

The stock of Union and Consumers is held by Consolidated. Union has outstanding in the hands of the public $1,877,000 of 6% bonds secured by an indenture on its property, with accrued and unpaid interest thereon of $403,555— a total mortgage indebtedness of $2,280,555. Consumers has outstanding in the hands of the public $1,137,000 of 6% bonds secured by an indenture on its property, with accrued and unpaid interest thereon of $221,715—a total mortgage indebtedness of $1,358,715. Consolidated has outstanding 285,947 shares of no par value preferred stock and 397,455 shares of no par common stock.

The plan of reorganization calls for the formation of a new corporation to which will be transferred all of the assets of Consolidated, Union, and Consumers free of all claims.[1] The securities of the new corporation are to be distributed as follows:

Union and Consumers bonds held by the public will be exchanged for income bonds and preferred stock of the new company. For 50 per cent of the principal amounts of their claims, those bondholders will receive income bonds secured by a mortgage on all of the property of the new company; for the balance they will receive an equal amount of par value preferred stock. Their claims to accrued

---

1. The claims of general creditors will be paid in full or assumed by the new company.

interest are to be extinguished, no new securities being issued therefor. Thus Union bondholders for their claims of $2,280,555 will receive income bonds and preferred stock in the face amount of $1,877,000; Consumers bondholders for their claims of $1,358,715 will receive income bonds and preferred stock in the face amount of $1,137,000. Each share of new preferred stock will have a warrant for the purchase of two shares of new $2 par value common stock at prices ranging from $2 per share within six months of issuance, to $6 per share during the fifth year after issuance.

Preferred stockholders of Consolidated will receive one share of new common stock ($2 par value) for each share of old preferred or an aggregate of 285,947 shares of new common.

A warrant to purchase one share of new common for $1 within three months of issuance will be given to the common stockholders of Consolidated for each five shares of old common.

The bonds of Union and Consumers held by Consolidated, the stock of those companies held by Consolidated, and the intercompany claims (discussed hereafter) will be cancelled.

In 1929 when Consolidated acquired control of these various properties, they were appraised in excess of $16,000,000 and it was estimated that their annual net earnings would be $500,000. In 1931 they were appraised by officers at about $4,400,000, "exclusive of going concern, good will and current assets." The District Court did not find specific values for the separate properties of Consolidated, Union, or Consumers, or for the properties of the enterprise as a unit. The average of the valuations (apparently based on physical factors) given by three witnesses at the hearing before the master were $2,202,733 for Union as against a mortgage indebtedness of $2,280,555; $1,151,033 for Consumers as against a mortgage indebtedness of $1,358,715. Relying on similar testimony, Consolidated argues that the value of its property, to be contributed to the new company, is over $1,359,000, or exclusive of an alleged good will of $500,000, $859,784. These estimated values somewhat conflict with the consolidated balance sheet (as at June 30, 1938) which shows assets of $3,723,738.15 and liabilities (exclusive of capital and surplus) of $4,253,224.41. More important, the earnings record of the enterprise casts grave doubts on the soundness of the estimated values. No dividends were ever paid on Consolidated's common stock; and except for five quarterly dividends in 1929 and 1931, none on its preferred stock. For the eight and a half years from April 1, 1929, to September 30, 1937, Consolidated had a loss of about $1,200,000 before bond interest but after depreciation and depletion. And except for the year 1929, Consolidated had no net operating profit, after bond interest and amortization, depreciation and depletion, in any year down to September 30, 1937. Yet on this record the District Court found that the present fair value of all the assets of the several companies, exclusive of good will and going concern value, was in excess of the total bonded indebtedness, plus accrued and unpaid interest. And it also found that such value, including good will and going concern value, was insufficient to pay the bonded indebtedness plus accrued and unpaid interest and the liquidation preferences and accrued dividends on Consolidated preferred stock. It further found that the present fair value of the assets admittedly subject to the trust indentures of Union and Consumers was insufficient to pay the face amount, plus accrued and unpaid interest of the respective bond issues. In spite of that finding, the District Court also found that "it would be physically impossible to determine and segregate with any degree of accuracy or fairness properties which originally belonged to the companies separately"; that as a result of unified operation properties of every character "have been commingled and are now in the main held by Consolidated without any way of ascertaining what part, if any thereof, belongs to each or any of the companies separately"; and that, as a consequence, an appraisal "would be of such an indefinite and unsatisfactory nature as to produce further confusion."

We agree with the Circuit Court of Appeals that it was error to confirm this plan of reorganization.

On this record no determination of the fairness of any plan of reorganization could be made. Absent the requisite valuation data, the court was in no position to exercise the "informed, independent judgment" (National Surety Co. v. Coriell, 289 U.S. 426, 436, 53 S.Ct. 678, 681, 682, 77 L.Ed. 1300, 88 A.L.R. 1231) which appraisal of the fairness of a plan of reorganization entails. Case v. Los Angeles Lumber Products Co., 308 U.S. 106, 60 S.Ct. 1, 84 L.Ed. 110. And see First National Bank v. Flershem, 290 U.S. 504, 525, 54 S.Ct. 298, 306, 78 L.Ed. 465, 90 A.L.R. 391. There are two aspects of that valuation problem.

In the first place, there must be a determination of what assets are subject to the payment of the respective claims. This obvious requirement was not met....

In the second place, there is the question of the method of valuation. From this record it is apparent that little, if any, effort was made to value the whole enterprise by a capitalization of prospective earnings. The necessity for such an inquiry is emphasized by the poor earnings record of this enterprise in the past. Findings as to the earning capacity of an enterprise are essential to a determination of the feasibility as well as the fairness of a plan of reorganization. Whether or not the earnings may reasonably be expected to meet the interest and dividend requirements of the new securities is a sine qua non to a determination of the integrity and practicability of the new capital structure. It is also essential for satisfaction of the absolute priority rule of Case v. Los Angeles Lumber Products Co., supra. Unless meticulous regard for earning capacity be had, indefensible participation of junior securities in plans of reorganization may result.

As Mr. Justice Holmes said in Galveston, Harrisburg & San Antonio Ry. Co. v. Texas, 210 U.S. 217, 226, 28 S.Ct. 638, 639, 52 L.Ed. 1031, "the commercial value of property consists in the expectation of income from it." Such criterion is the appropriate one here, since we are dealing with the issue of solvency arising in connection with reorganization plans involving productive properties. It is plain that valuations for other purposes are not relevant to or helpful in a determination of that issue, except as they may indirectly bear on earning capacity. The criterion of earning capacity is the essential one if the enterprise is to be freed from the heavy hand of past errors, miscalculations or disaster, and if the allocation of securities among the various claimants is to be fair and equitable. Since its application requires a prediction as to what will occur in the future, an estimate, as distinguished from mathematical certitude, is all that can be made. But that estimate must be based on an informed judgment which embraces all facts relevant to future earning capacity and hence to present worth, including, of course, the nature and condition of the properties, the past earnings record, and all circumstances which indicate whether or not that record is a reliable criterion of future performance. A sum of values based on physical factors and assigned to separate units of the property without regard to the earning capacity of the whole enterprise is plainly inadequate. But hardly more than that was done here.

The case should dispel any notion that the concepts of valuation that we have discussed in prior chapters are a new invention. In this chapter we apply these concepts to value an entire company, as the Supreme Court did in the *Consolidated Rock* case.

1.   WACC

In prior classes we have noted that the proper discount rate to use when valuing any project is the opportunity cost. As Justice Douglas notes, a firm can be valued as a project, too. Here the opportunity cost is the firm's own cost of capital. That is, how much return does it have to promise investors to get them to invest?

For an all equity firm, at least one that is publicly traded, you already know how to do this. The capital assets pricing model (CAPM) provides the expected return on shares in such a firm.

But what if the firm has some debt? CAPM still provides the return for the equity, but M&M have already shown us, the cost of equity is influenced by amount of debt outstanding. What we really need to find is the firm's cost of capital, which is the blended rate of its entire capital structure, taking into account both debt and equity.

The conventional technique for obtaining this weighted average is known as the weighted average cost of capital (WACC). The method relies on M&M principles and makes use of CAPM to find the cost of equity, which is then weighted along with the cost of debt. In short

$$WACC = \left[\frac{Equity}{Equity + Debt} \times R_E \right] + \left[\frac{Debt}{Equity + Debt} \times R_D \times (1 - T) \right]$$

The first term in each bracket represents the proportion of the overall capital structure that is equity or debt, respectively. These terms weight the returns paid on equity (R_E) and debt (R_D) by the proportion of each in the capital structure.

The second bracket also includes the term $(1-T)$, which is just one minus the corporation's tax rate. This accounts for the tax-privileged status of debt—namely, the firm does not ultimately pay for the entire cost of debt. For example, if the tax rate is 25 percent, then the firm only pays 75 percent of the cost of its debt, as the remainder offsets taxes that would otherwise be due.

We have already noted that CAPM can be used to find the firm's cost of equity (R_E). What about the cost of debt? Yield to maturity (YTM) of the firm's outstanding debt can provide an estimate of how much it would cost the firm to issue debt today.

The result of this calculation is the rate that should be used to discount any project where one believes that the project's risk is equal to the risk of the firm as a whole (and the project has the same leverage as the firm as a whole), or to value the firm, as described in the next section.

But first, we need some practice on WACC. The problems that follow are best done in a spreadsheet (remember, for example, the Yield function in Excel if you need to find YTM).

PROBLEM SET 11.1

1. Bogartco has 80,000 bonds outstanding. Bonds with similar characteristics are yielding 10.5 percent. The company also has 10 million shares of common stock outstanding. The stock has a beta of 1.1 and sells for $40 a share. The U.S. Treasury bill is yielding 4 percent and the market risk premium is 8 percent. Bogartco's tax rate is 35 percent. What is Bogartco's weighted average cost of capital?

2. Merciful Release, Inc. is considering financing a new band called Doktor Avalanche. Merciful expects to spend about $72 million up front promoting the band and estimates the band will return $13.5 million a year for five years. Merciful has a debt/equity ratio of one. The firm's cost of equity is 13 percent, the cost of debt is 9 percent, and the tax rate is 34 percent. What is the appropriate discount rate? What assumptions about Doktor Avalanche does your calculation entail? Should Merciful undertake the investment in Doktor Avalanche?

2.   DCF

Discounted cash flow (DCF) valuation is essentially the valuation referred to by Justice Douglas in the *Consolidated Rock* case. It is the most common valuation method used in many legal settings.[2]

The basic idea is to find the present value of the company's projected earnings. Earnings are projected over a number of years—often five or ten—and then the value of the firm at the end of this income stream is added onto the equation. Typically for this final or terminal value the firm will be valued as a perpetuity, or, more precisely, a growing perpetuity, based on projected earnings at that final time period and some projected growth rate.

In short, DCF valuation involves an annuity (the projected cash flows for five years) plus a perpetuity, which reflects the "terminal value" of the company. The WACC provides the appropriate discount rate for these present value calculations. In practice, you will often see DCF combined with some other valuation model.

CEDE & CO. v. JRC ACQUISITION CORP.

29 Del. J. Corp. L. 887
Court of Chancery of Delaware
Feb. 10, 2004

CHANDLER, J.

This action, brought under 8 *Del. C.* §262, seeks an appraisal of 652,400 shares of 800-JR Cigar, Inc. ("Respondent," "JR Cigar" or the "Company") held of record by Cede & Co. ("Petitioner" or "Cede") for the benefit of various investment funds. This Opinion determines the fair value of those shares, together with an appropriate rate of interest. For the reasons set forth in greater detail below, I conclude that the fair value of JR Cigar stock as of the merger date is $13.58 per share. The Company must pay Petitioner $8,859,592. In addition, I award Petitioner 4.73% interest on the principal, compounded monthly, from October 4, 2000 to the date of payment.

I.   BACKGROUND

A.   THE STIPULATED FACTS

On August 29, 2000, pursuant to a merger agreement dated the day before, the Rothman family commenced an offer to purchase all shares of common stock of JR Cigar that they did not already own. The Rothmans, before the offer, owned 78% of the outstanding common shares of JR Cigar. After the offer closed on September 26, 2000, the Rothmans, through an acquisition corporation owned by

---

2. *E.g.*, Bernard Trujillo, *Patterns in a Complex System: An Empirical Study of Valuation in Business Bankruptcy Cases*, 53 UCLA L. Rev. 357, 384 (2005).

them, beneficially owned over 90% of the outstanding shares of JR Cigar. Because the Rothmans owned more than 90% of the outstanding shares following the offer, the merger was accomplished pursuant to 8 *Del. C.*§253. The merger became effective on October 4, 2000.

Under the merger agreement, each share of common stock outstanding immediately before the merger was converted into the right to receive $13.00 per share in cash.

The only issue in this case is the fair value of Petitioner's shares, together with the appropriate rate of interest.

B.   THE EXPERTS

Cede's expert, Charles DeVinney, has his MBA in Finance, is Vice President of Curtis Financial Group, Inc., an Accredited Senior Appraiser, and a Chartered Financial Analyst. DeVinney is in the business of appraising companies. He used two methods to value JR Cigar. First, he looked at transactions comparable to the acquisition of JR Cigar. Based on these purportedly comparable transactions, DeVinney found that JR Cigar was worth $16.80 per share as of October 4, 2000, the date the merger became effective. Second, DeVinney performed a discounted cash flow ("DCF") analysis. His DCF analysis resulted in an estimated fair value of $19.80 per share. Placing equal weight on the two valuation methods, DeVinney opined that JR Cigar was worth between $16.80 and $19.80 per share.

JR Cigar's expert, Dr. Gregg Jarrell, is a Professor of Economics and Finance at the University of Rochester's William E. Simon Graduate School of Business. Jarrell holds a Ph.D. in Business Economics and was formerly the Chief Economist for the SEC. He teaches graduate courses in finance, is well-published, and has served as an expert witness in several valuation cases. In rendering his opinion, Jarrell relied principally on a DCF analysis, but he also conducted two market-based analyses to verify his DCF analysis. First, he performed what he referred to as a "market check," which consisted of a determination of whether other reasonably *bona fide* offers were made for JR Cigar. Second, Jarrell conducted an analysis of the control premium in this case as compared to control premiums obtained in over 2,000 other deals during a five-year period. He concluded that the fair value of JR Cigar was $12.67 per share.

[B]oth experts testified at trial. Additionally, both experts prepared a report shortly before trial summarizing their valuation work. Those reports, along with numerous other documents, were introduced as exhibits at trial.

II.   LEGAL FRAMEWORK

Under 8 *Del. C.*§262, dissenting stockholders are entitled to their *pro rata* share of the "fair value" of the corporation in which they held stock before the merger. "Accordingly, the Court of Chancery's task in an appraisal proceeding is to value what has been taken from the shareholder, *i.e.*, the proportionate interest in the going concern."[3] "The application of a discount to a shareholder is contrary to the requirement that the company be viewed as a 'going concern.'" But the valuation is "exclusive of any element of value arising from the accomplishment or expectation of the merger," although it may "encompass known elements of value" not the product of speculation.[4]

The corporation may be valued "by any techniques or methods which are generally considered acceptable in the financial community and otherwise admissible in court."[5] In recent years, the DCF valuation methodology has featured prominently in this Court because it "is the approach that merits the greatest confidence" within the financial community. In appropriate cases, this Court has relied exclusively on DCF models. Regardless of the methodology, however, this Court prefers valuations based on management projections available as of the date of the merger and holds a healthy skepticism for post-merger adjustments to management projections or the creation of new projections entirely. Expert valuations that disregard contemporaneous management projections are sometimes completely discounted.

In this proceeding, "both sides have the burden of proving their respective valuation positions by a preponderance of the evidence." If neither party satisfies its burden, however, the Court must use its own independent judgment to determine fair value. The Court can reject the views of both experts.

III.   ANALYSIS

In this section, I evaluate the respective valuations of the parties' experts. I begin with DeVinney's comparable transactions analysis, turn to the dueling DCF models, assess Jarrell's "market checks," and then reach the Court's determination as to the fair value of JR Cigar as of October 4, 2000.

A.   DEVINNEY'S COMPARABLE TRANSACTIONS ANALYSIS

DeVinney used the comparable transactions found in Merrill Lynch's "Presentation to the Special Committee of the Board of Directors of Leaf."[6] A special committee of JR Cigar's Board of Directors retained Merrill Lynch to advise them in connection with the then-proposed merger, and it rendered a fairness opinion dated August 28, 2000. "Merrill Lynch noted that nearly all of the Comparable Transactions represent the acquisition of control of the target company which may not be directly comparable to the acquisition of a minority stake of a target company, as in the Offer and the Merger." Nonetheless, "Merrill Lynch determined a reference multiple range LTM [latest twelve months] EBITDA [earnings before interest, taxes, depreciation, and amortization] for the Company of 6.0x to 7.5x, resulting in a reference range for an implied value per

---

3. *Cede & Co. v. Technicolor, Inc.*, 684 A.2d 289, 298 (Del.1996) (citing *Cavalier Oil Corp. v. Harnett*, 564 A.2d 1137, 1145 (Del.1989)).

4. *Cede & Co.*, 684 A.2d at 299 (citing *Weinberger v. UOP*, 457 A.2d 701, 713 (Del.1983)).

5. *Weinberger*, 457 A.2d at 713.

6. Leaf was the codename for JR Cigar.

Share of $12.00 to $15.50." Merrill Lynch found that "the most comparable transaction," one involving Swisher International, "represents 6.2x LTM EBITDA or $12.00 per share." The Swisher International transaction was the most comparable because, like the JR Cigar deal, it did not involve a change of control. But even that transaction, as well as all the other "comparable" transactions, involved companies that manufacture cigars and related products. JR Cigar is not a manufacturer; it only sells cigars, cigarettes, and related products.

DeVinney looked at the same set of transactions as Merrill Lynch, but altered their calculations in one significant respect. One of the transactions reviewed by Merrill Lynch was Swedish Match's acquisition of General Cigar. Merrill Lynch calculated the LTM EBITDA multiple in that transaction at 10.4x. DeVinney calculated the multiple at 12.8x because he included EBITDA of General Cigar for a 13-week period ending after the transaction was announced. During this period, General Cigar's EBITDA declined, which has the effect of inflating the transaction multiple. I cannot discern any principled basis for this alteration of General Cigar's EBITDA. As DeVinney admitted on cross-examination, Swedish Match did not use the post-transaction EBITDA data in arriving at its offer price. Moreover, Merrill Lynch did not use the post-transaction EBITDA data, even though it advised Swedish Match on the transaction and had "expertise in evaluating similar transactions."

Moreover, contrary to DeVinney's expert report, the Swedish Match transaction is not comparable to the transaction in this case. Swedish Match's acquisition of General Cigar was, unlike the going private merger here, a strategic acquisition. The synergistic nature of the deal accounts for some of the premium, which DeVinney conceded on cross-examination. Additionally, Swedish Match was acquiring 64% of the equity of General Cigar. Again, DeVinney testified on cross-examination that this "may explain some of the premium." Merrill Lynch, also Swedish Match's advisor, determined that the transaction in that case was not the most comparable to the JR Cigar merger. Merrill Lynch's opinion was that the Swisher International transaction was the most comparable. The Swisher transaction multiple was 6.2x, less than half of the "adjusted" multiple DeVinney derived for the Swedish Match transaction.

The problems identified above render DeVinney's comparable transactions analysis unreliable. Most of these errors were exposed on cross-examination, as he was unable to fully defend his methodology. Witnessing DeVinney's testimony first-hand convinces me once again that "no substitute has ever been found for cross-examination as a means of ... reducing exaggerated statements to their true dimensions."[7]

B. DISCOUNTED CASH FLOW ANALYSIS OF DEVINNEY AND JARRELL

The DCF method estimates the value of a business such as JR Cigar based on projected future free cash flows that are discounted to present value. Based on a

---

7. Francis L. Wellman, *The Art of Cross-Examination* 7 (4th rev. ed. 1948).

DCF analysis, DeVinney concluded that the fair value of JR Cigar was $19.80 per share. Jarrell, using the same basic DCF methodology, concluded that the range of fair value of JR Cigar was from $11.76 to $13.58 per share. By way of comparison, Merrill Lynch performed a DCF analysis in connection with its fairness opinion that produced a reference range for an implied value per share of $9.49 to $12.63.

The parties agree that most of the difference between the experts' DCF calculations is the result of four variables: (1) JR Cigar's estimated growth rate in perpetuity; (2) the Company's debt-to-equity ratio; (3) the *Ibbotson* equity size premium applied in the capital asset pricing model (CAPM); and (4) JR Cigar's tax rate. The latter three factors collectively contribute to JR Cigar's weighted average cost of capital (WACC), which is used to discount future cash flows. I will discuss each variable in turn.

1.   *Growth Rate in Perpetuity*

In a DCF valuation, the cash flow is projected for each year into the future for a period of years, typically five. After that point, one uses a single value representing all subsequent cash flows to calculate a company's terminal value. The terminal value may be determined by using multiples from comparable transactions, referred to as an exit multiple, or may be ascertained by assuming a constant growth rate after the initial five year forecast period, *i.e.*, the growth rate in perpetuity. The terminal value calculation is critical here because it represents well over half of JR Cigar's total estimated present value.

Jarrell used the perpetuity growth approach and computed a range of values based on growth rates of 2.5% to 3.5%, rates equal to or exceeding the long-term rate of inflation. DeVinney used both the comparable transactions approach and the perpetuity growth approach to calculate JR Cigar's terminal value. DeVinney used the multiple of 8.5x (ascertained in his comparable transaction analysis) and applied that multiple to JR Cigar's estimated 2004 EBITDA. DeVinney also used a perpetuity growth rate of 5%. DeVinney opined that each method of calculating terminal value is equally appropriate and averaged the two indications of value.

Regardless of whether ascertaining a company's terminal value by applying a transaction multiple is appropriate as a matter of finance theory, I have already determined that the 8.5x multiple derived by DeVinney is unreliable and should not be used in any DCF analysis. As such, in determining the terminal value of JR Cigar, the analysis is necessarily limited to the appropriate perpetual growth rate. DeVinney on cross-examination agreed that this was the appropriate route if the Court concluded that his comparable transaction analysis was not valid.

Although DeVinney's report is silent as to the rationale for using a 5% growth rate into perpetuity, at trial he indicated reliance on a document prepared by Fleet Bank, N.A.[8] DeVinney testified on direct examination that "it appears that there were management projections provided to Fleet that utilized a five percent growth rate through 2009." The document at issue does in fact show 5% growth

---

8. Fleet provided part of a $55 million loan to finance the merger.

from 2000 through 2009 and includes small type in the lower left that reads "Management Case." Jarrell testified, however, that upon conversation with JR Cigar's CFO Michael Colleton, he understood that JR Cigar had not prepared projections beyond five years. Moreover, he testified that it appeared from the face of the document that Fleet merely extrapolated upon management's five-year projections. This conclusion is sustainable given that only five-year projections are shown in another portion of the document that discusses the "Management Case."

Petitioner is anxious to have the Fleet document characterized as a "management projection" because of the Court's preference for such projections. After reviewing the document and after considering the testimony of both experts, however, I cannot conclude with confidence that the projections in the Fleet document for the years 2004 to 2009 are actually "management projections." Petitioner attempts to create the inference that the later year projections were management's with several novel arguments that, to be candid, are mostly sophistry. The bottom line is that nothing in the document states affirmatively that JR Cigar provided Fleet with ten-year projections *and* Colleton stated that this was because JR Cigar did not give Fleet such projections.

Because I cannot safely conclude that management projected growth of 5% after 2004 does not mean that calculating JR Cigar's terminal value based on such a growth rate is inaccurate. Nor does it mean, presumptively, that Jarrell's lower perpetual growth rate of 2.5% to 3.5% is accurate. The lack of definite, long-term management projections simply means that the experts, and ultimately this Court, must ascertain some independently justifiable growth rate with which to calculate JR Cigar's terminal value.

In Jarrell's opinion, JR Cigar's likely growth rate in the long-term was only at or slightly above the rate of inflation. Jarrell based this opinion initially on the fact that the management forecasted growth rate of 5% for 2000 to 2004 was modest and that it is "quite common and normal in discounted cash flow analysis to observe a higher growth rate in the forecast period than in the perpetuity period." Jarrell buttressed this opinion with empirical and contemporaneous evidence that sales of JR Cigar's two main products, cigars and cigarettes, were on the decline. Merrill Lynch's presentation to JR Cigar shows that sales of premium cigars were on the decline. Rothman testified in his deposition that sales of premium cigars were on the decline. And since the early 1980s, there has been a "steep and steady" decline in the domestic consumption of cigarettes. Based on the foregoing, Jarrell testified that it was "conservative on behalf of the petitioners, to assume that over the long haul after 2004 that this company's sales, dollar sales, will keep up with the inflation rate."

In support of using a 5% perpetual growth rate, Petitioner turns back to the Fleet document. In that document, prepared as part of a credit offering, Fleet notes JR Cigar's impressive pre-2000 results and that "the U.S. cigar market [was] expected to grow by 2.0% to 5.0% in the medium to long term." Additionally, in his deposition, Rothman noted that, although cigar prices were declining, JR Cigar's revenues grew by 10.6% in 1999 and that the Company increased its market share. Perhaps realizing that JR Cigar's performance before 2000 was no indication of growth beyond the year 2004, especially given the declining state of the domestic market, Petitioner offered a couple of other rationales for a 5% perpetual growth rate. First, DeVinney testified that JR Cigar could eliminate competitors in a declining market due to its advantageous distribution systems. Second, Petitioner hypothesized that JR Cigar could have seized upon international sales, sales over the internet, and sales in non-tobacco related products to grow at 5% in perpetuity in spite of a declining domestic market.

As to international expansion, there is simply no record support for this theory. It is the product of speculation. As to the sale of non-tobacco related products, again, there is no record support that JR Cigar had any plans to enhance revenue in this fashion. In fact, JR Cigar's already minimal sales of fragrances and other merchandise declined in 2000 from the previous year.

The most compelling rationale offered by Petitioner for JR Cigar's ability to maintain growth at 5% is through the elimination of competitors. This rationale has some historical support. Rothman testified that JR Cigar increased revenues and market share in the late 1990s even though the tobacco market was beginning to contract. Notwithstanding Rothman's testimony, there is no persuasive evidence that JR Cigar's ability to sustain growth in the face of an initial market decline would have translated into long-term growth prospects. Increased market share could explain the 5% growth forecasted by management in years 2000 to 2004, but it does not follow that JR Cigar would grow by 5% per year into perpetuity. Additionally, increasing market share when the market is declining overall is not a recipe for growth: half of two is one, but all of one is still one.

The problem with ascertaining a growth rate in perpetuity is that it is an inherently speculative enterprise, Jarrell, under questioning by the Court, was refreshingly candid when he stated: "Who knows what the growth rate in perpetuity is going to be. It's a judgment call." The experts, and ultimately the Court, are asked to surmise what rate a company will grow at five years into the future. This is hardly an exact science. In this type of circumstance it is difficult (if not impossible) for litigants to "prov[e] their respective valuation positions by a preponderance of the evidence." Nevertheless, the Court must assess whether one expert's judgment is more defensible than the other. And, on this record, it appears that Jarrell's judgment that JR Cigar's growth rate in perpetuity is at or slightly above the rate of inflation is more credible. Jarrell used a range of 2.5% (roughly equal to the long-term rate of inflation in 2000) to 3.5% in his DCF analysis. In my opinion, the upper end of that range is appropriate and fair. Using a rate of 3.5% accounts for the possibility, however marginal, that JR Cigar may be able to expand in an otherwise declining domestic market for cigars and cigarettes.

2. *Debt-to-Equity Ratio*

Under a DCF analysis, JR Cigar's future cash flows must be discounted to present value. DeVinney and Jarrell based their discount rates on the weighted average cost of capital ("WACC") methodology. DeVinney explained WACC quite concisely at trial: "It's the cost of equity times the percentage of equity in the capital structure plus the cost of debt times that percentage of debt." The parties dispute the "percentage of debt" part of this equation, primarily because the more weight one gives to debt, the lower the discount rate and the higher the valuation. Petitioner argues that the appropriate percentage of debt to ascribe to JR Cigar is 25%. Respondent urges a debt percentage of 10% or less.

Respondent's position that 10% debt is appropriate is based on three factors. First, before the merger, JR Cigar had no debt. Second, Jarrell testified that at the time of the transaction JR Cigar did not anticipate any large capital expenditures and that management believed that the Company optimally was run with minimal debt. Third, Jarrell noted that the only other publicly-traded retail cigar company operated with no debt.

Petitioner's support for 25% debt-allocation is based on four factors. First, Petitioner points to JR Cigar's pre-IPO capital structure, which was approximately 17% debt. Second, DeVinney opined that 25% debt was similar to that of comparable companies. Third, Petitioner argues that JR Cigar had expansion opportunities that would require additional capital. And, fourth, Petitioner notes that JR Cigar borrowed $55 million for the merger.

Reviewing the record and submissions by the parties, I am convinced that the appropriate percentage of debt for the WACC calculation is 10%. The pre-IPO structure is not indicative of JR Cigar's going-forward capital structure precisely because it was "pre-IPO." The IPO was in 1997, three years before the valuation date, and the IPO was used to reduce JR Cigar's debt. Moreover, the comparable companies relied upon by Petitioner are not comparable. The companies used as reference points by DeVinney are manufacturing companies, not retailers. DeVinney conceded on cross-examination that the capital structure of those companies "would be different most likely." As noted above, the only other publicly-traded retail cigar company had no debt. Finally, although I agree that JR Cigar may have pursued expansion opportunities, no evidence exists to suggest that those opportunities would have required such debt as to justify a 25% capital allocation, especially since management did not plan on incurring significant debt and since the Company already had over $13 million in cash and equivalents as of June 30, 2000.

Petitioner's final justification for a 25% debt allocation is that JR Cigar incurred $55 million of debt to finance the merger. Petitioner's argument is that "[t]he merger did not enhance JR Cigar's ability to borrow; therefore valuing it based on its optimal capital structure instead of its actual capital structure does not contravene, but instead comports with, 8 *Del C.* 262(h)."

[T]he fact that the merger did not enhance JR Cigar's ability to borrow does not condone ignoring its actual capital structure in favor of some "optimal capital structure." In *In re Radiology Assocs., Inc.*, the petitioner argued that the respondent's debt to equity ratio should mimic the overall industry's debt-to-equity ratio because it was more efficacious than the respondent's actual debt-to-equity ratio. The Court dismissed this effort because an appraisal proceeding does "not attempt [...] to determine the potential maximum value of the company." I must value JR Cigar, "not some theoretical company."

JR Cigar had no debt before the merger. Petitioner has introduced no evidence of non-speculative plans to incur significant debt that is not due to the accomplishment of the merger. Therefore, a capital structure of 25% debt is not appropriate. A debt ratio of 10% is, however, reasonable and accounts for the probability that JR Cigar may seek to incur limited debt to pursue expansion opportunities.

3.   Ibbotson *Equity Size Premium*

The parties also disagree about another component of the WACC formula—the cost of equity. A standard method of ascertaining the cost of equity is CAPM. CAPM is based on the premise that the expected return of a security equals the rate on a risk-free security plus a risk premium. Under CAPM the cost of equity is equal to the risk-free rate (the yield on 20 year Treasury bonds) plus a large company equity risk premium multiplied by the specific company adjusted beta for JR Cigar. Added to this figure is an equity size premium. An equity size premium is added because smaller companies have higher returns on average than larger ones,[9] *i.e.*, small companies have a higher cost of equity. The equity size premium for all sized companies is published by Ibbotson Associates.

Both experts used CAPM to derive JR Cigar's cost of equity, but applied different equity size premiums. Both used a chart published in *Ibbotson* to find the premium. The *Ibbotson* chart indicates that the size premium for companies with capitalization between $192 and $840 million is 1.1%, the "low-cap" category. The premium is 2.6% for companies with capitalization below $192 million, the "micro-cap" category. DeVinney added an equity size premium of 1.1%, while Jarrell added 2.6%. Jarrell placed JR Cigar in the micro-cap category because its market capitalization, based on the traded price of the stock before the announcement of the merger (or based on the merger price), was well below $192 million. On the other hand, DeVinney placed JR Cigar in the low-cap category because he "determined that the value, the market capitalization, should be more at the fair value implied market capitalization." DeVinney made this determination because the stock price was, in his opinion, depressed.

Respondent argues that basing the equity size premium on JR Cigar's implied fair value contravenes finance theory. When asked on cross-examination if the *Ibbotson* text suggested that his methodology was sound, DeVinney answered in the negative. Jarrell testified that implying the fair value, rather than using a market measurement, is somewhat circular because the whole purpose of the

---

9. Ibbotson Associates, *Ibbotson, Stocks, Bonds, Bills and Inflation: Valuation Edition 2001 Yearbook* 107 (2001) ("Ibbotson").

DCF analysis is to ascertain JR Cigar's fair value. Additionally, Jarrell testified that the *Ibbotson* data already incorporates illiquidity and depressed values since it is derived exclusively from traded stock prices. Although one valuation textbook suggests that simply estimating the market value of the equity is appropriate for some WACC calculations, it does not state whether it is appropriate to imply a fair value to determine the equity size premium, a number derived from actual market prices.

Regardless of whether or not adjusting the equity size premium based on implied fair value is appropriate in some circumstances, I ultimately determine that the record in this case does not support DeVinney's methodology. According to Petitioner, JR Cigar's stock was depressed because Rothman held an abnormally large majority position and because the minority portion of the stock was very illiquid. In order for Petitioner's argument to stand, JR Cigar's stock would have needed to be depressed by over five dollars per share-over half its value. Petitioner cites to two First Union presentations as support for this position. These documents reveal that First Union believed JR Cigar's shares were discounted in the public markets because of Respondent's "[s]mall public float," i.e., the number of shares available for trading, "[s]ignificant inside ownership," and "[l]ack of research coverage." But the same documents indicate that the stock was also depressed because of JR Cigar's small market capitalization and "[n]egative public, legal and governmental sentiment toward tobacco." These documents offer mixed support for the position that JR Cigar's stock was significantly depressed because they do not quantify the extent to which the stock was depressed by illiquidity as opposed to generalized industry factors. The sour state of the tobacco market would undoubtedly depress JR Cigar's stock price, but would also depress JR Cigar's fair value.

The failure to isolate the specific impact of JR Cigar's illiquidity on its stock price undermines Petitioner's analysis. The illiquidity of a particular security is usually measured by the size of the bid/ask spread. In general, the lower the liquidity, the higher the bid/ask spread. And when the spread is higher, the "discount" to a firm's fundamental value increases. Petitioner introduced no evidence regarding JR Cigar's bid/ask spread. The only evidence introduced related to JR Cigar's trading volume. That evidence shows that 7.9 million shares of JR Cigar were traded during the 12 months preceding the announcement of the merger—more than double the number of shares not controlled by Rothman. During this period, JR Cigar's stock price never rose above $12.75 per share— well within the *Ibbotson* micro-cap category.

Even assuming that JR Cigar's stock price was depressed because of its illiquidity, Petitioner cannot justify categorizing JR Cigar as a low-cap, rather than micro-cap, company (for the purposes of CAPM) based on this fact. CAPM identifies the expected return on a particular security, an expected return that is inputted into the WACC and used to discount JR Cigar's future cash flows to present value. The *Ibbotson* size premium number reflects the empirical evidence that smaller firms have higher returns than larger firms. Petitioner's position that JR Cigar is a low-cap company (rather than a micro-cap company) decreases the expected rate of return on JR Cigar's stock by lowering the "size premium" applied. The problem with using liquidity as a basis for justifying a lower expected return, however, is that low liquidity is associated with higher expected returns. Investors seek compensation for the high transaction costs of illiquid securities, *e.g.*, the bid/ask spread. In other words, even if JR Cigar had a higher market capitalization than the market price of its stock suggested *because of its illiquidity*, investors would still expect higher returns *because of its illiquidity*.

Petitioner also seeks to justify the categorization of JR Cigar as a low-cap company based on its beta. A company's beta is the measure of its volatility in relation to the overall market, in this case the S & P 500. Petitioner's argument is that JR Cigar's adjusted beta, calculated by DeVinney at .62, is much lower than the betas of the other companies in its *Ibbotson* micro-cap group.[10] This argument is unavailing for several reasons. First, there is no evidence that DeVinney categorized JR Cigar as a low-cap company based on its low beta. DeVinney only testified that he thought that JR Cigar's stock was "depressed." Second, Petitioner did not introduce evidence that JR Cigar's beta is outside the ranges of betas for the micro-cap category. Lastly, the size premium is not dependent on the beta of the firm. In fact, it is because the beta does not capture all the systemic risk that a size premium is included. "[E]ven after adjusting for the systematic (beta) risk of small stocks, they outperform large stocks."

4.   *Tax Rate*

Petitioner argues that JR Cigar's tax rate is 36%. DeVinney arrived at this figure after reviewing JR Cigar's income statement contained in Merrill Lynch's August 28, 2000 presentation to the JR Cigar Board. The income statement does not actually list JR Cigar's tax rate, but the rate used by Merrill Lynch can be deduced by calculating the difference between the yearly EBIT and net income figures over the historical and forecast period. Merrill Lynch's figures imply a tax rate near the 36% rate used by DeVinney. The August 28, 2000 presentation, as well as other documents, indicate that Merrill Lynch's income statement was based on management forecasts and estimates. It is unclear from the face of these documents, however, what exactly JR Cigar management provided to Merrill Lynch. Merrill Lynch's due diligence request list does not show that Merrill Lynch ever asked for JR Cigar's effective tax rate. No evidence indicates that Merrill Lynch ever received such information.

Even if management did provide Merrill Lynch with information regarding its effective tax rate, the presentation upon which Petitioner relies does not imply

---

10. DeVinney calculated a beta of .62 based on a period beginning six months after JR Cigar's IPO. Tr. at 84–85. Jarrell calculated a beta of .67 based on a period beginning a week after the IPO. *Id.* Neither period is presumptively valid. A longer period of time, such as the period used by Jarrell, is generally preferred. A five-year period, longer than the period used by either expert, is the most common. Shannon P. Pratt, *Cost of Capital: Estimations and Applications* 82 (2d ed. 2002). Petitioner's argument that the stock should be given time to "season" after an IPO is understandable, but I am unsure why this takes six months.

that management gave Merrill Lynch the 36% figure that DeVinney used for his calculations. A colloquy between DeVinney and Respondent's counsel on cross-examination demonstrated that the Merrill Lynch presentation may have included other items in JR Cigar's net income, resulting in an implied tax rate lower than the actual tax rate. DeVinney could have made some inquiry, but did not speak to anybody at Merrill Lynch or JR Cigar to identify the actual effective tax rate.

Fortunately, the Court does not need to engage in guesswork to determine JR Cigar's tax rate. Note 6 to JR Cigar's financial statements in its 1999 Annual Report explicitly states that the tax rate was 40.9% in 1997, 40.1% in 1998, and 40.2% in 1999. This information came from management. Nothing indicates that management understood that the 40% tax rate would decline. JR Cigar's CFO indicated that the tax rate was 40% and, generally, 40% is a common tax rate to use. At the end, JR Cigar's historical tax rate published in its annual report is more reliable than speculation regarding Merrill Lynch's analysis.

5.   *Reconciling the Differences in the DCF Analyses*

The parties anticipated that the validity of the DCF calculations would hinge on the four differing assumptions examined above. Respondent introduced a demonstrative exhibit at trial that purported to recast DeVinney's DCF analysis by integrating Jarrell's assumptions. Respondent, for example, introduced a demonstrative exhibit that showed the impact that changing the tax rate had on DeVinney's DCF calculations. According to Respondent, changing the four variables discussed at length in this section has the effect of reducing DeVinney's imputed fair value by $9.95 per share. In its opening brief, Petitioner took issue with these calculations and stated that the composite effect of the four variables is to decrease DeVinney's DCF value per share by $8.03. In other words, the parties put Jarrell's assumptions into DeVinney's model and came up with *two different values.* [11]

Failing to adhere to elementary principles and to "show your work," the Court was unable to ascertain the nature of the $1.92 (the difference between $9.95 and $8.03) discrepancy. Nonetheless curious as to why the DCF estimates were off by almost two dollars per share, I sought the parties input on this issue. The parties' responses were less than satisfactory as they largely regurgitated exhibits already submitted at trial. Although Respondent was able to ascertain some of the discrepancy, it was ultimately unable to reconcile $0.69 per share difference. Despite having the benefit of Respondent's submission, Petitioner was unable to explain the reason for *any* of the discrepancy.[12] As such, insufficient evidence has been presented to enable the Court to integrate Jarrell's assumptions (those

---

11. This discrepancy is in addition to the fact that Jarrell's model generates a fair value per share that is different from using his assumptions in DeVinney's model.

12. Petitioner's submission was a day late and (almost literally) a dollar short. Letter from Mondros to Chandler, C. of 1/13/04. Importantly, Petitioner did not deny that DeVinney made calculation errors.

largely accepted by the Court) into DeVinney's DCF model.[13] Consequently, the Court must rely on Jarrell's DCF model exclusively.

C.   JARRELL'S MARKET-BASED ANALYSIS

1.   *Measurement of Control Premiums*

Jarrell, in addition to his DCF analysis, looked at how the premium paid in the JR Cigar merger compared with control premiums paid in 2,077 deals between January 1995 and August 2000. For that sample, the median one-day control premium was 25% and the mean one-day control premium was 30.4%. Isolating the 31 mergers out of 2,077 where the buyer already owned 75% or more of the stock (as is the case here), Jarrell found that the median one-day control premium for those 31 transactions was 17%, as compared with the 21% premium paid by the Rothmans. Petitioner argues, among other things, that this analysis "violate[s] any concept of comparability, including the 'law of one price.'" I agree.

The only thing that the transactions in Jarrell's sample have in common are that they are all transactions. The data is not segmented by industry or date. The one-day premiums vary considerable; the standard deviation is 32%. Additionally, it is not clear that any analysis of premiums over all transactions has any bearing on "fair value" in an appraisal action, even if it may bear on how efficiencies arising from a merger could equitably be apportioned between the buyer and the sellers.

2.   *"Market Check"*

Jarrell considered the fact that First Union was unable to find any interested potential acquirers and that none emerged once the deal was publicly announced at $13 per share. He testified that "in my judgment, the evidence clearly indicated that there were no such offers and that there were no such folks out there willing to pay that, because if there were, they would have shown up."

Although Jarrell's testimony has a certain intuitive appeal, there is insufficient record support from which a reliable conclusion can be drawn about this "market check." First Union, JR Cigar's financial advisor at the time, was only authorized to conduct a "limited market check." As such, First Union only contacted two possible buyers. Little can be drawn from the fact that these two buyers declined to make an offer. Additionally, simply because no rival bidders appeared after the announcement of the going private proposal does not help the Court ascertain the fair value of JR Cigar.

---

13. This problem was compounded by Petitioner's decision to not comply with my request to "provide the Court with electronic versions (Microsoft Excel compatible) of the DCF worksheets," *e.g.*, "Exhibit 4 of Prof. Jarrell's report." Letter from Chandler, C. to Counsel of 1/2/04, at 2. Only Respondent complied with this request.

D. THE COURT'S DETERMINATION

The comparable transactions looked at by DeVinney are not reliable indicators of the fair value of JR Cigar. The only transaction worth noting is the Swisher International transaction that was, in the opinion of Merrill Lynch, the most comparable to the JR Cigar transaction. That transaction implies a fair value of $12.00 per share. Jarrell's market based analysis, the measurement of control premiums and his "market check," are not reliable indicators of JR Cigar's fair value. In my opinion, the more "reliable" indicator of JR Cigar's fair value is a DCF analysis.

The four key DCF variables identified by the parties are JR Cigar's growth rate in perpetuity, its debt to equity ratio, the equity size premium, and JR Cigar's tax rate. As discussed earlier in the Court's analysis, the appropriate growth rate in perpetuity is 3.5%, the WACC calculation should reflect a 10% debt ratio, the equity size premium included in the CAPM calculation should be 2.6, and JR Cigar's effective tax rate is 40%. Jarrell's DCF calculations include an equity size premium of 2.6 and a tax rate of 40%. Jarrell uses a range of growth rates (2.5% to 3.5%) and a range of discount rates (13% to 15%). The range of discount rates reflect a debt weighting of 0% to 10% (13% discount rate reflecting 10% debt). Looking at the upper end of Jarrell's ranges, *i.e.*, 10% debt and 3.5% growth, his DCF model produces a value of $13.58 per share....

The last matter for consideration is the form of interest. "The compounding interval should ... reflect the interval available to the petitioners had they the use of their funds as well as, if possible, the interval actually received by the corporation." Petitioner requests that interest be compounded daily. Although I have commented that daily compounding may be appropriate in some cases, Petitioner has not introduced evidence that daily compounding is appropriate in this case. In fact, DeVinney compounded interest annually in his report. JR Cigar's post-trial brief is silent regarding the compound interval, as is Jarrell's report. Jarrell does, however, compound the prime rate on a monthly basis in order to determine JR Cigar's annual borrowing costs. Ultimately, given that neither side has provided evidence as to the appropriate interval, "I find that the dual purposes of compensation and restitution may only be served by a compounding interval at least as frequent as one month."

PROBLEM SET 11.2

1. What was the net gain to the petitioners by bringing this action?
2. How hard would it have been for the petitioner to introduce evidence of an alternative investment that paid daily compound interest? Could the court have taken judicial notice of such an investment? Should it have done so?
3. As we discuss in the next chapter, Cede & Co. was acting as an agent for the true shareholders in this case. Those shareholders were a group of well-known small cap mutual funds.

3.   A QUICK NOTE ON DISCOUNT RATES

As you have just seen, courts typically use WACC to find a firm's discount rate or cost of capital. But many studies in the financial literature have found that firms often use an even higher discount rate when evaluating projects internally. For example, while WACC might suggest Bogartco has a WACC of 8 percent, its managers might use 12 percent when deciding whether or not to invest in a new line of trench coats. Why might that be?

One recent article argues that "firms expecting plentiful investment opportunities, binding operational constraints, and high idiosyncratic risk increase their discount rate the most."[14] The authors further summarize their findings as follows:

> We find that, although most firms use WACC as a basis for their discount rates, they almost always augment it before using it to evaluate projects. The firms adding the biggest premiums are exposed to high levels of idiosyncratic risk and maintain large cash holdings. Because these firms are not financially constrained based on either survey or accounting measures, we conclude that they anticipate valuable investment opportunities to arise in the future and hoard cash to position themselves to exploit those opportunities as soon as they emerge.
>
> But even when firms are not financially constrained, operational issues can prevent them from taking all profitable opportunities. For example, it takes time to expand a workforce, particularly one reliant on firm-specific human capital. Limited managerial bandwidth can also force firms to forgo profitable projects. We find that firms in such circumstances inflate their discount rates above their cost of financial capital to account for such constraints.

What implications, if any, does this have in a legal setting?

---

14. R. Jagannathan et al., *Why Do Firms Use High Discount Rates?*, 116 J. Fin. Econ. 445, 459 (2016).

II

FINANCE

12

COMMON SHARES

By the time you get to this chapter, it is likely that you have either already taken or are well into a Corporations or Business Associations class. Thus you already know lots about corporations, and a fair amount about the rights of their common shareholders. If a corporation contains nothing else in its capital structure, it has common shares.

BCE INC. AND BELL CANADA v. 1976 DEBENTUREHOLDERS

2008 SCC 69, [2008] 3 SCR 560
Supreme Court of Canada.
Reasons delivered: December 19, 2008.

The following is the judgment delivered by

THE COURT —

V. ANALYSIS

A. OVERVIEW OF RIGHTS, OBLIGATIONS AND REMEDIES UNDER THE CBCA

[34] An essential component of a corporation is its capital stock, which is divided into fractional parts, the shares: *Bradbury v. English Sewing Cotton Co.*, [1923] A.C. 744 (H.L.), at p. 767; *Zwicker v. Stanbury*, [1953] 2 S.C.R. 438. While the corporation is ongoing, shares confer no right to its underlying assets.

[35] A share "is not an isolated piece of property . . . [but] a 'bundle' of interrelated rights and liabilities": *Sparling v. Quebec (Caisse de dépôt et placement du Québec)*, [1988] 2 S.C.R. 1015, at p. 1025, *per* La Forest J. These rights include the right to a proportionate part of the assets of the corporation upon winding-up and the right to oversee the management of the corporation by its board of directors by way of votes at shareholder meetings.

[36] The directors are responsible for the governance of the corporation. In the performance of this role, the directors are subject to two duties: a fiduciary duty to the corporation under s. 122(1)(*a*) (the fiduciary duty); and a duty to exercise

the care, diligence and skill of a reasonably prudent person in comparable circumstances under s. 122(1)(*b*) (the duty of care).

———————

Shares measure the investor's stake in the corporation. That stake often, but not always, entitles the shareholder to vote and receive dividends.[1] As the Canadian Supreme Court explains, it also entitles the shareholder to receive a proportionate distribution upon dissolution of the corporation, subject to the absolute priority rule and firm not being insolvent.

1.   THE STOCK MARKET AND IPOS

To the extent you encountered common shares before law school, it was probably in connection with the trading of shares in the *secondary market*, as opposed to the *primary market*, which involves the initial sale of shares by a firm to the public.

When a firm enters the primary market, it typically does so by way of an *initial public offering* (IPO). When companies that already have publicly traded shares sell more shares into the market, it is termed a *secondary offering*.

In the first case, this involves compliance with the "33 Act," the Securities Act of 1933. Issuers must register their securities by filing the registration statement with the Securities and Exchange Commission before selling or advertising the securities in ways that implicate interstate commerce. This is covered in more detail in the Securities Regulation course.

Once the securities are sold to the public, the firm becomes subject to the "34 Act," the Securities Exchange Act of 1934. This requires ongoing disclosure—an example of which you saw in Chapter 1 when we reviewed the Dynegy 10-K.

Trading in the secondary market typically does not implicate the issuing firm. For example, if you want to buy shares of Apple, you would place a trade with a broker, who in turn would send the order to a stock exchange for execution. The stock exchange would match your order with a willing seller of Apple shares.

In the case of Apple, this exchange would be NASDAQ, the second largest stock exchange in the world, and home to many California-based tech firms. NASDAQ is a computerized exchange, in which multiple market makers post bids on a computer system indicating the prices at which they are willing to buy and sell Apple and other NASDAQ listed shares. When an order is submitted, the system automatically matches the order with the best offer. Apple would have no involvement in the transaction.

Shares in Apple, the world's biggest and most heavily traded company, turn over more than $3 billion each day. But that is dwarfed by the biggest exchange

———————

1. *See* Del. Code Ann. tit. 8, §211(b). *See also* Cal. Corp. Code § 700.

traded fund (ETF), State Street's SPDR S&P 500, which tracks the index.[2] That fund trades more than $14 billion each day. Five of the world's seven most heavily traded equity securities are ETFs.

The largest stock exchange in the world is the New York Stock Exchange (NYSE), which operates more traditionally and is where many traditional companies list their shares (*e.g.*, Exxon, General Electric, and Wells Fargo).[3] The NYSE is a physical place in lower Manhattan where orders from buyers and sellers are routed to dedicated market makers in a particular stock. Unlike NASDAQ, the NYSE only has one market maker per listed company. But trading on the NYSE is increasingly done through computers, just like NASDAQ.[4]

Both of the exchanges have various requirements for listing shares. Oscala's Roast Beef & Smoothie Palace, Inc. is not going to be traded on the "Big Board," as the NYSE is sometimes called, or NASDAQ anytime soon. Moreover, companies on the decline could be involuntarily delisted from an exchange. Shares that are not listed on a market, or those that have become delisted, trade "over the counter" or OTC. Many companies are traded OTC in the United States because their primary listing is on a foreign exchange. Food products giant Nestle is a good example: It is a Swiss company, traded on the exchange in Zurich and OTC in the United States.

There are two electronic quotation services on the OTC market: the OTC Bulletin Board (OTCBB) and the Pink Sheets. Pink sheet stocks got their name because their quotes actually were printed on pink paper, and OTC stocks were referred to as such because trades happened with no physical stock exchange or meeting place for the deal—just a guy with a desk and a telephone selling shares from an office in lower Manhattan.

Market makers provide two price quotes for each share—a *bid price* (the price at which they are willing to buy) and the *ask price* (the price at which they are willing to sell). Ask prices are always higher than bid prices, resulting in the bid-ask spread. This is how market makers earn a profit. The size of the bid-ask spread also provides some information on market efficiency, as lower spreads indicate more liquid, efficient markets.

From an investor's perspective, the bid-ask spread is a transaction cost in addition to any brokerage fees associated with the trade.

---

2. Both traditional mutual funds and ETFs are collections of securities packaged into a fund. Investors buy a share in the fund. Almost all ETFs track an index, as do some index-tracking mutual funds. The difference is that mutual funds are "open-ended"—investors can buy directly into the fund or withdraw from it. This is done once a day, at prices set at the close of business. With an ETF, investors buy and sell shares without directly adding to or taking away from the fund itself. Instead, the shares trade on an exchange and market makers buy, sell, and create new shares to ensure they move in line with the value of the fund.

3. The next largest stock exchanges are London and Tokyo, respectively. Together these four exchanges account for about 75 percent of the total stock trade volume worldwide.

4. *See* Onnig H. Dombalagian, *Exchanges, Listless?: The Disintermediation of the Listing Function*, 50 Wake Forest L. Rev. 579, 591 (2015).

Buying long is the traditional way to buy common stock. When you hear your grandmother talk about the AT&T shares she bought 50 years ago, she's talking about buying long. The Facebook stock you bought last year was also bought long. This is in contrast with selling short, which we looked at back in Chapter 6.

PROBLEM SET 12.1

1. Why is the bid-ask spread a transaction cost?
2. Toyota's common shares are available to trade as an ADR, a foreign stock (also known as an "ordinary") in the U.S. OTC market, and as a foreign ordinary on the Tokyo Stock Exchange in Japan, where the company is actually listed. American Depositary Receipts (ADRs) are certificates that trade in the United States, issued by a U.S. bank, representing foreign shares held by the bank, usually by a branch or correspondent in the country of issue.[5] One ADR may represent a portion of a foreign share, one share, or a bundle of shares of a foreign corporation.[6] In the case of Toyota, the ADR trades on the NYSE under the symbol TM and represents two of the Japanese shares. What is the purpose of Toyota offering its shares in so many places?

2.   LEGAL ASPECTS OF SHARE OWNERSHIP

Consider the story of SJL, as we'll call him, to protect him from shame. He's a young associate, the first week on the job in the mid-1990s. A partner asks him to pull a client's shareholder list in anticipation of a possible restructuring. He does so, and finds three entries on the list. "It seems that Cede & Co. owns almost 95 percent," he reports to the partner.

You'll understand the humor at the end of this section.

Shares are commonly held in one of two ways. First, a shareholder might have possession of a physical certificate. That's increasingly rare, but it does sometimes happen. For example, if you want to give your spouse 1,000 shares of Hermes[7] (he really likes their purses), presenting the certificate is much nicer than a brokerage statement.[8]

But most shareholders, whether individuals or institutions, like mutual funds, hold shares through their brokerage account. This is more convenient if the

---

5. ADRs have custody fees that are levied on a regular basis, such as annually or quarterly.

6. For example, one ADR for Anheuser-Busch InBev represents one share in the company, but one ADR for Diageo represents four ordinary shares in the company, to take a boozy example.

7. More formally, Hermes International SCA: http://goo.gl/GxsDW.

8. Assuming you can get a certificate. Companies are increasingly providing shares in "book entry" form only, which means the shares exist only as a computer file somewhere. Even if you can get a certificate, there typically will be an extra charge associated with preparing it.

investor intends to trade the securities, and it avoids the problem of losing or damaging a physical certificate.

In this case, the shares are typically held in "street name," that is, all shares in a particular company are kept in the name of the broker. The broker then internally allocates the shares to individual customers. For a large brokerage, some of those individual customers might be smaller brokerage firms that use the big brokerage to execute trades. In these instances, street name registration of the shares obscures multiple layers of claims on the shares.

The true, ultimate owner of a share is called the *beneficial owner*. To further confuse the issue, even the big brokerage firm that is the top-level street name holder probably does not hold the shares in its own name. Rather, to facilitate easy transfers of shares among brokerage firms, most register their shares with the Depository Trust Company (DTC).[9] The actual holder of these shares is Cede & Co., a DTC subsidiary, or "nominee" in brokerage speak.[10]

Thus, when Brokerage A's clients sell Apple shares and Brokerage B's clients buy, the actual exchange of ownership will take place on the books of DTC, rather than on the shareholder list of the company, which, by the way, is also provided by DTC.

The list DTC provides, and which SJL obtained in the story above, is a list of registered owners. Registered owners correspond with beneficial owners only to the limited degree that shareholders hold in their own name—which is largely comprised of those few shareholders who hold physical certificates. In most cases Cede & Co. will instead be the record holder, but obviously not the beneficial holder.

Thus, to get in touch with the actual "owners" of the securities, you have to drill through many layers: DTC/Cede—Big Broker—Small Broker—Customer. And note that there is ambiguity here, in that Big Broker might be holding for a customer or it might be holding for its own trading purposes.

To address the distinction between record and beneficial ownership, the SEC has created rules to allow firms to communicate with beneficial owners through broker or other intermediaries.[11] The rules allow brokers to disclose to a company the identity of those beneficial owners who do not object to such disclosure. Those who object are known as "objecting beneficial owners" (OBOs) under the SEC's rules. The company cannot contact OBOs directly.

The company may, however, have direct contact with shareowners who have designated themselves "non-objecting beneficial owners" (NOBOs), owners who do not object to having their identity known to the issuing company.

---

9. DTC's parent company is DTCC, Depository Trust & Clearing Corporation.

10 NOMINEE, Black's Law Dictionary (10th ed. 2014): 1. Someone who is proposed for an office, membership, award, or like title or status. • An individual seeking nomination, election, or appointment is a candidate. A candidate for election becomes a nominee after being formally nominated. See candidate. 2. A person designated to act in place of another, usu. in a very limited way. 3. A party who holds bare legal title for the benefit of others or who receives and distributes funds for the benefit of others.

11. *See* Rules 14b-1 and 14b-2 under the 34 Act.

To get a list of NOBOs, you might think you would have to go to each and every broker. Most brokers, but not all, delegate this responsibility to an agent, in almost all cases Broadridge Financial Solutions, Inc.[12] Broadridge provides a single list of all NOBOs. The NOBO list includes the name, address, and securities position for each NOBO. Because Broadridge does not disclose the identity of a NOBO's broker or bank intermediary, brokers like this approach because it prevents outsiders from figuring out who their customers are.

The NOBO list from Broadridge provides some insight into the beneficial owners, but remember not all brokers participate. You (or, more likely, the client issuer) would have to get lists from those brokerages individually. However, while companies may communicate directly with NOBOs, SEC rules require that proxies and proxy materials nonetheless be forwarded by broker and bank intermediaries, not by companies. So you still have to work through the brokerage firms to actually effectuate most transactions.

And let's not forget the OBOs. All indications are that the bulk of brokerage customers are OBOs, so they will remain behind the veil of a brokerage name— so even if you see the name of a big brokerage house on a list from Broadridge, you still do not know if that broker holds for itself, for one customer, or for a million customers.

Working with a firm that specializes in these matters, you can pass information to the shareholders through the brokerages. But you will still never know if the broker's 100 customers all hold roughly equal amounts of shares or if one customer holds the vast bulk of the client's shares.

To make matters more confusing, state corporate law provides for voting by the record holder. As a result, the company cannot send a proxy card and proxy materials directly to each beneficial owner, but must provide the proxy card to the record holder. To delegate voting authority under state law to the beneficial owner, first, as the record holder of shares held in street name, DTC executes an "omnibus" proxy in favor of all brokers and banks who hold the company's shares through DTC's facilities.

In turn, after being vested with voting authority by DTC, the broker requests voting instructions from the beneficial owner. Typically, Broadridge sends the requests for voting instructions on behalf of the broker, and beneficial owners return instructions as to how the proxies should be voted to Broadridge, which then tabulates the voting instructions received and fills out a proxy for each intermediary broker for which it acts as agent, aggregating the voting instructions received from all beneficial owners from a particular broker.

The issuing company pays brokers and Broadridge for the services they provide under this system at levels fixed by the NYSE. The following case looks at this complex system in a real world context, with real world consequences, as noted at the end.

---

12. Before 2007, Broadridge was a subsidiary of a company called ADP, so many older attorneys will still refer to it as "getting the NOBO list from ADP."

IN RE: APPRAISAL OF DELL INC.

2016 WL 3030909; 2016 BL 149950
Court of Chancery of Delaware.
May 11, 2016

LASTER, Vice Chancellor.

Respondent Dell Inc. completed a merger (the "Merger") that gave rise to appraisal rights. A stockholder only can pursue an appraisal if the stockholder "neither voted in favor of the merger . . . nor consented thereto in writing." 8 *Del. C.* § 262(a) (the "Dissenter Requirement"). The appraisal statute defines the term "stockholder" as "a holder of record of stock in a corporation." *Id.* (the "Record Holder Requirement").

Fourteen of the appraisal petitioners are mutual funds sponsored by T. Rowe Price & Associates, Inc. ("T. Rowe") or institutions that relied on T. Rowe to direct the voting of their shares (collectively, the "T. Rowe Petitioners"). The T. Rowe Petitioners were not holders of record. They held their shares through a custodial bank, State Street Bank & Trust Company ("State Street"). For purposes of Delaware law, State Street was not a holder of record either. It was a participant member of the Depository Trust Company ("DTC").

DTC held the T. Rowe Petitioners' shares in the name of its nominee, Cede & Co. For purposes of Delaware law, Cede was the holder of record. As such, Cede had the legal right under Delaware law to vote the shares and demand appraisal.

But Delaware law formed only part of a Byzantine and path-dependent system by which stockholders voted on the Merger. Federal law, the Uniform Commercial Code, stock exchange listing standards, and private contracts combined to create an overarching superstructure of requirements and practices. The resultant legal web constrained Cede to vote the T. Rowe Petitioners' shares as T. Rowe directed.

I. FACTUAL BACKGROUND

Dell originally moved for entry of summary judgment against the T. Rowe Petitioners because of their failure to satisfy the Dissenter Requirement. The parties agreed to defer briefing until after trial, and the materials that they deemed relevant were introduced into the trial record. The factual findings in this decision are drawn from the trial record.

A. THE MERGER

On February 5, 2013, Dell's board of directors (the "Board") approved an agreement and plan of merger (the "Merger Agreement") between Dell and three counterparties: Denali Holding Inc., Denali Intermediate Inc., and Denali Acquiror Inc. Dell's counterparties under the Merger Agreement were affiliates of Dell's eponymous founder, Michael Dell, and Silver Lake Management LLC (the "Buyout Group"). The Merger Agreement contemplated that each share of common stock of Dell not held by a member of the Buyout Group would be converted into the right to receive $13.75 in cash. The Merger therefore gave rise to appraisal rights. *See* 8 *Del. C.* § 262(b).

Under Section 251(c) of the Delaware General Corporation Law (the "DGCL"), a merger agreement "shall be submitted to the stockholders of each constituent corporation at an annual or special meeting for the purpose of acting on the agreement." *Id.* § 251(c). The Board scheduled a meeting of stockholders for July 18, 2013 (the "July Meeting"). The Board set a record date of June 3 for the meeting.

On May 31, 2013, Dell filed its definitive proxy statement for the July Meeting (including amendments, the "Proxy Statement"). The Proxy Statement announced the meeting date and the record date, solicited proxies from Dell's stockholders, and asked them to vote "FOR" the Merger.

B.   THE T. ROWE PETITIONERS' SHARES

The T. Rowe Petitioners had invested in Dell common stock. They did not, however, hold legal title to any shares. They were beneficial owners who held through State Street.

State Street did not hold legal title either. Legal title rested with Cede, the nominee of DTC. DTC's role in the ownership structure of publicly traded domestic corporations stems from the federal policy of share immobilization, adopted in response to a paperwork crisis on Wall Street during the late 1960s and early 1970s. To achieve share immobilization, the Securities and Exchange Commission placed a new entity—the depository institution—at the bottom of the ownership chain. DTC emerged as the only domestic depository. Today, over 800 custodial banks and brokers are participating members of DTC and maintain accounts with that institution.

DTC primarily holds shares on behalf of its participants in fungible bulk, meaning that all of the shares are issued in the name of Cede "without any subdivision into separate accounts of the custodian's customers." Marcel Kahan & Edward Rock, *The Hanging Chads of Corporate Voting,* 96 Geo. L.J. 1227, 1239 (2008). Through a Fast Automated Securities Transfer account (the "FAST Account"), DTC tracks the number of shares that each participant holds using an electronic book entry system.

When the Board approved the Merger, the shares of Dell common stock that State Street held at DTC on behalf of the T. Rowe Petitioners were part of the FAST Account. Beginning on July 12, 2013, however, T. Rowe caused Cede to send letters demanding appraisal on behalf of the T. Rowe Petitioners. Cede sent a separate demand letter for each T. Rowe Petitioner, and each demand letter made clear that Cede was seeking appraisal on behalf of a specified block of shares owned by a client of one of its participants. In standardized language, each demand stated that Cede was the record holder of shares of Dell common stock and was "informed by its Participant" that a specified number of shares was "beneficially owned by" an identified beneficial owner, characterized as a "customer of Participant." Each demand concluded, "[i]n accordance with instructions received from Participant on behalf of its customer, we hereby assert appraisal rights with respect to the Shares."

[W]hen the T. Rowe Petitioners caused Cede to demand appraisal, DTC removed the shares covered by the demand from the FAST Account and requested paper certificates from Dell's transfer agent. From that point on, the shares that State Street held as custodian were maintained in certificated form in DTC's vault.

The following illustration depicts the manner in which the T. Rowe Petitioners held their shares and the multiple levels of ownership involved. The figure identifying Cede's ownership encompasses both shares held in fungible bulk and shares that are certificated in Cede's name.

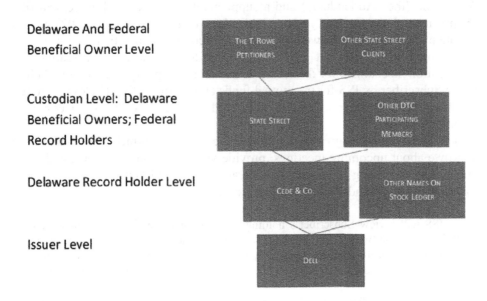

C. T. ROWE'S RELATIONSHIP WITH ISS

As one of the largest institutional investors in the United States, T. Rowe is called upon to submit voting instructions at a large number of stockholder meetings. To facilitate the submission of voting instructions, T. Rowe has adopted a set of default voting policies. T. Rowe also has entered into an agreement with [Institutional Shareholder Services Inc. ("ISS")] under which ISS provides a range of voting-related services (the "ISS Master Agreement").

As defined in an attachment to the ISS Master Agreement, the services provided by ISS included an "administrative portion" that encompasses "vote execution" and "record keeping and reporting services."

Under vote execution, ISS tracks User/Subscriber's holdings by account to ensure votes are recorded on time and casts votes based on User/Subscriber's guidelines.

For record keeping and reporting, ISS records the meeting name, CUSIP, meeting date, shares voted, proxy proposals, management recommendation, and vote cast. ISS also provides standard reports for each company voted, all votes for a single account, and other specialized reports.

Under the heading *"PERFORMANCE STANDARDS,"* the attachment stated: "Subscriber/User requires that at least ninety-nine (99%) of all meetings be voted and voted as instructed."

For the period beginning January 1, 2013, T. Rowe and ISS clarified their contractual relationship by entering into an addendum to the ISS Master Agreement (the "Addendum") and a supplemental service level agreement (the "Supplemental Agreement"). The Addendum elaborated on how ISS would maintain and provide T. Rowe with access to records documenting how its shares were voted. It stated that ISS would provide "[a] web-based search and presentation mechanism for disclosure of any archived proxy votes cast on behalf of the Subscriber by ISS for the mutual funds and accounts listed below. Through a link on the Subscriber's web site, users will be able to seamlessly access vote records."

The Supplemental Agreement specified the manner in which ISS would notify T. Rowe about upcoming meetings, provide voting recommendations, and carry out T. Rowe's voting instructions. A paragraph entitled "Delivery of Research, Recommendations and Voting Services" stated:

> ISS will review Subscriber's holdings file and/or the ballots received for the Subscriber and match the holdings and/or the ballots against the upcoming shareholders meeting list maintained by ISS. In the event of a match, an entry will be created on the electronic web-based delivery platform regarding the meeting.

For each match for Subscriber's common equity holdings, ISS will prepare a research report and make a vote recommendation with respect to each item to be voted on the shareholders meeting. The research report and vote recommendations will be prepared in accordance with Subscriber's custom voting policy as provided by Subscriber to ISS.... Research and recommendations will be presented via ISS' electronic web-based delivery system.

The "web-based delivery platform" was part of a computerized voting system maintained by ISS called Proxy Exchange (the "ISS Voting System").

The Supplemental Agreement elaborated on ISS's obligation to implement T. Rowe's voting instructions accurately. A provision titled "Voting Services" stated:

> ISS must accurately vote [REDACTED] of Subscriber's ballots. If ISS fails to meet this target due to an ISS error (including voting ballots contrary to

Subscribers [sic] instructions received in good order), then ISS shall provide the Subscriber with a service credit of [REDACTED] of ballot fees.

Under these agreements, when ISS learned that an issuer had scheduled a meeting of stockholders, the ISS Voting System would notify T. Rowe by generating a communication called a meeting record. T. Rowe personnel would view the meeting record through T. Rowe's Proxy Recommendation System (the "T. Rowe Voting System"). The T. Rowe Voting System would pre-populate the meeting record with voting instructions that matched T. Rowe's standard voting policies. When T. Rowe received a meeting record, the T. Rowe Voting System would send an email automatically to the portfolio managers of the T. Rowe funds who were invested in that issuer so that they could review the meeting record and determine whether to depart from T. Rowe's standard voting policies. To vote, a T. Rowe portfolio manager could either leave the pre-populated voting instructions in place or submit different instructions. Once finalized, the voting instructions would be sent to ISS.

D. T. Rowe Provides Voting Instructions for the July Meeting

For the July Meeting, the ISS Voting System generated a meeting record on July 9, 2013 (the "July Meeting Record"). It identified three agenda items. Item 1 was the approval of the Merger Agreement. Item 2 was an advisory vote on golden parachute compensation payable in connection with the Merger. Item 3 was a proposal giving Dell authority to adjourn the July Meeting. For a transaction that is supported by management, the T. Rowe default voting position was to vote "FOR" the transaction and "FOR" the authority to adjourn. The default voting position was to vote "AGAINST" an advisory vote on golden parachute compensation.

The T. Rowe Voting System pre-populated the July Meeting Record with T. Rowe's default voting positions and sent an email to all of the T. Rowe portfolio managers who held Dell stock in actively managed accounts. Six of the portfolio managers decided to vote against the Merger. They communicated their determinations to a T. Rowe Vice President and Corporate Governance Specialist.

On July 16, 2013, the Corporate Governance Specialist logged into the T. Rowe Voting System and changed the voting instructions for the first and third items in the July Meeting Record to "AGAINST." As a result, the July Meeting Record contemplated T. Rowe voting against all three items. The T. Rowe Voting System sent the specialist an email confirming those instructions.

That same day, relying on the voting instructions entered into the July Meeting Record by the Corporate Governance Specialist, a T. Rowe Business Analyst entered the "AGAINST" instructions into the ISS Voting System. The analyst clicked "submit" on the web-based portal, transmitting those voting instructions to ISS.

Also that same day, a T. Rowe Price Assistant Vice President and Senior Manager emailed ISS to confirm that ISS had received the instructions to vote "AGAINST" all three proposals. ISS confirmed receipt of the instructions.

E. DELL PUSHES OFF THE JULY MEETING THREE TIMES

On July 18, 2013, Dell convened the July Meeting for the sole purpose of adjourning it until July 24. ISS updated the date of the meeting, but did not send out a new meeting record for the adjourned meeting. The T. Rowe Corporate Governance Specialist nevertheless confirmed that T. Rowe's instructions to vote "AGAINST" remained operative in both the T. Rowe Voting System and the ISS Voting System.

On July 23, 2013, the Buyout Group delivered a revised proposal that increased the merger consideration to $13.75. Dell rejected the proposal, but adjourned the stockholder meeting until August 2. ISS updated the date of the meeting, but did not send out a new meeting record for the adjourned meeting. The T. Rowe Corporate Governance Specialist reconfirmed that T. Rowe's instructions to vote "AGAINST" remained operative in both the T. Rowe Voting System and the ISS Voting System.

On July 31, 2013, the Buyout Group proposed a one-time special cash dividend that effectively increased the merger consideration to the final figure of $13.88 per share. On August 2, Dell accepted the revised proposal. Also on August 2, Dell convened the adjourned meeting for the sole purpose of adjourning it again until September 12 (the "September Meeting"). Dell set a new record date of August 13 for the September Meeting.

On August 12, 2013, ISS updated the date of the meeting to September 12, but the ISS Voting System did not generate a new meeting record. The T. Rowe Corporate Governance Specialist confirmed for a third time that T. Rowe's instructions to vote "AGAINST" all three proposals remained operative in both the T. Rowe Voting System and the ISS Voting System.

F. THE VOTING MIX–UP FOR THE SEPTEMBER MEETING

On September 4, 2013, the ISS Voting System generated a new meeting record for the re-scheduled meeting (the "September Meeting Record"). The T. Rowe Voting System showed both the July Meeting Record and the September Meeting Record. In the ISS Voting System, however, the September Meeting Record replaced the July Meeting Record. This had the effect of deleting the voting instructions that had been entered in the ISS Voting System.

The T. Rowe Voting System automatically pre-populated the September Meeting Record with the default voting instructions called for by T. Rowe's voting policies. As a result, the T. Rowe Voting System populated the September Meeting Record with instructions to vote "FOR" the Merger, "AGAINST" the advisory resolution on golden parachutes, and "FOR" authority to adjourn the meeting.

No one from T. Rowe's proxy team logged into the ISS Proxy System to check the status of T. Rowe's voting instructions. As part of the routine operation of the two systems, the default instructions in the September Meeting Record were conveyed automatically to ISS.

G. BROADRIDGE VOTES THE SHARES

Simply by providing instructions to ISS, the T. Rowe Petitioners had not yet voted their shares. Getting to the actual voting required three more steps: the transfer of the voting instructions from ISS to Broadridge [Financial Solutions, Inc.], the transfer of voting authority from Cede to Broadridge, and the execution and delivery by Broadridge of a client proxy that voted the shares over which it had received voting authority in accordance with the voting instructions it had received.

1. The Sources of Broadridge's Authority

Under Delaware law, the legal authority to vote at a meeting of stockholders rests with the stockholders of record at the time of the meeting, and for that purpose, the stock ledger constitutes "the only evidence as to who are the stockholders entitled . . . to vote in person or by proxy at any meeting of stockholders." 8 *Del. C.* § 219(c). The stock ledger "is a compilation of the transfers by and to each individual stockholder, with each transaction separately posted to separately maintained stockholder accounts."

Because shares are freely alienable by default, the identity of a corporation's stockholder base is typically in flux—and for a public corporation constantly so. It is therefore necessary to define a specific population of stockholders who are entitled to receive notice of a meeting of stockholders and vote at the meeting. The DGCL addresses this need by empowering a board of directors to set either a single record date for both purposes, or to pick two separate record dates, one for notice and another for voting. Based on the record date that will control the exercise of voting rights, the DGCL contemplates that "[t]he officer who has charge of the stock ledger of a corporation shall prepare and make . . . a complete list of the stockholders entitled to vote at the meeting." § 219(a). The resulting list identifies the stockholders of record on the selected date, "arranged in alphabetical order, and showing the address of each stockholder and the number of shares registered in the name of each stockholder." *Id.* It thus converts the transactions on the stock ledger into a list of owners with legal authority to exercise voting rights at the meeting.

Dell outsourced the obligation to maintain its stock ledger and generate a stock list to its transfer agent, American Stock Transfer & Trust Company, LLC ("American"). Using the record date of August 13, 2013, American generated a list of stockholders showing Dell's holders of record under state law for purposes of the September Meeting. The stock list identified Cede as the holder of record for 1,535,558,891 shares, with 240,996,342 shares certificated in its own name and 1,294,562,549 in the FAST Account. Within the 240,996,342 shares held in Cede's own name were the T. Rowe Petitioners' shares, which had been certificated when the T. Rowe Petitioners caused Cede to demand appraisal.

Under the federal regime that created the depository system, DTC is not a record holder and cannot simply vote the shares held in Cede's name. The record holders for purposes of federal law are the DTC participants. *See* 17 C.F.R. § 240.14c–1(i). In this case, State Street was the DTC participant and record holder for purposes of federal law. To transfer its state-law voting rights to the federal-law record holders, DTC executed an omnibus proxy in favor of its participants.

The voting rights handoff did not stop there. When a DTC participant holds shares as a fiduciary for its clients, as State Street did, then the participant is obligated to provide its clients with proxy cards or voting instruction forms and carry out any instructions it receives. That task is an administrative headache, and many participants have outsourced it.

State Street is one of the custodians that has outsourced a variety of voting-related functions to Broadridge. In this case, a services agreement between State Street and Broadridge provided that "Broadridge shall fulfill all annual meeting, proxy voting (contested and uncontested) and consent gathering communications requested by a corporate or other issuer (a 'Registrant') on behalf of [State Street]." They agreed that "Broadridge does not transmit signed proxies to beneficial shareholders or member organizations but uses a standard voting instruction form (a 'Voting Information Instruction Form') in lieu thereof."

As part of the contractual arrangement, Broadridge committed to provide State Street with the following recordkeeping services:

> (1) In connection with each meeting of a Registrants [sic] with respect to which Broadridge provides Services, Broadridge keeps and maintains for a period of seven (7) years from the date of such meeting, or such longer period as shall be reasonably requested in writing by [State Street]:
> (a) Voting Instruction Forms that are returned with the beneficial shareholders' voting instructions;
> (b) a record of all voting instructions received from beneficial shareholders verbally or electronically;
> (c) copies of all multiple client proxies sent to Registrants; and
> (d) copies of [State Street] voting confirmations which inform [State Street] of all the voting results for each proxy job processed by Broadridge on behalf of [State Street].
> (2) Broadridge shall, during reasonable business hours, make available to [State Street] the above records during such periods.

State Street granted Broadridge a power of attorney that gave Broadridge the authority to perform the contracted-for services. The power of attorney in effect for purposes of the September Meeting appointed three Broadridge representatives individually, with full power of substitution, the undersigned's true and lawful attorney in the undersigned's name, place and stead for the sole purpose of executing proxies issued by any and all corporate or other issuers with respect to any and all of the securities of any such corporate or other issuer registered in the name of the undersigned or its nominee and owned by the undersigned, or registered in the name of the undersigned or its nominee and beneficially owned by clients of the undersigned. . . .

The power of attorney limited this broad grant of authority to executing proxies "only in accordance with the voting instructions of the undersigned or the beneficial owners of any such securities indicated on the returned proxies or voting instruction forms," unless stock exchange rules or SEC rules allowed Broadridge to vote without instructions from the beneficial owners.

Through these contractual arrangements, Broadridge ended up with the legal authority to vote the shares held of record by Cede on behalf of the T. Rowe Petitioners for which State Street was custodian. The omnibus proxy transferred to State Street the authority that the DGCL imbued in DTC, and State Street had a standing arrangement transferring the right to exercise that authority to Broadridge under the power of attorney.

In this case, the T. Rowe Petitioners had demanded appraisal, which caused DTC to certificate their shares. State Street therefore had to take the additional step of manually entering the T. Rowe Petitioners' ownership positions into Broadridge's system. When this occurred, Broadridge's computer system generated an internal control number for each position. State Street provided the control numbers for twelve of the T. Rowe Petitioners to ISS so that ISS could submit voting instructions for those positions to Broadridge.

2. Broadridge Receives Instructions and Votes the Shares

On September 9, 2013, ISS transmitted to Broadridge the voting instructions for the T. Rowe Petitioners' positions as they appeared in the ISS Voting System. Those voting instructions were found in the September Meeting Record, matched T. Rowe's default voting policies, and called for voting "FOR" the Merger, "AGAINST" the advisory vote on golden parachute compensation, and "FOR" authority to adjourn the meeting.

In the next step in the voting process, Broadridge delivered a series of "Broadridge Client Proxies" to Dell's proxy solicitor. The first proxy was dated September 10, 2013, and revoked all prior proxies. Broadridge delivered supplemental client proxies as it received additional voting instructions from its broker and custodian clients. Each client proxy was issued "pursuant to powers of attorney executed by each listed brokerage firm or nominee which are in full force and effect as of the date hereof" and "on file with the offices of Broadridge." JX 694 at 3. Through its client proxy cards, Broadridge voted each of the positions held by the T. Rowe Petitioners "FNF," meaning "FOR" the Merger, "AGAINST" the advisory resolution on golden parachute compensation, and "FOR" authority to adjourn the meeting. Each Broadridge Client Proxy disclosed aggregate votes by client. None of the Broadridge Client Proxies broke out the shares by accounts or beneficial owners.

The following illustration depicts the flow of voting power and instructions.

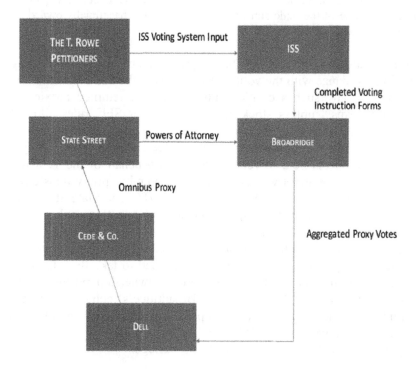

In this case, the record establishes how Cede voted the T. Rowe Petitioners' shares because the Broadridge internal control numbers serve as a unique identifier for each position held by a Broadridge client. Although Broadridge does not provide its control numbers to the issuer or the public, it does make them available upon request to its clients, such as State Street. The following table identifies the T. Rowe Petitioner, its unique Broadridge control number, its corresponding identification on the verified list of appraisal petitioners, and the number of shares voted in favor of the Merger.

T. Rowe Petitioner	Control No.	Verified List No.	Shares
T. Rowe Price Equity Income Fund, Inc.	902401246009	1	16,500,000
T. Rowe Price Science and Technology Fund	902401256207	2	7,045,780
John Hancock Variable Insurance Trust—Equity Income Trust	902401251707	5	1,271,400
John Hancock Funds II—Equity Income Fund	902401258409	7	1,010,600
T. Rowe Price Equity Income Trust, a sub-trust of T. Rowe Price Institutional Common Trust Fund	902401240403	9	965,100
T. Rowe Price Institutional Equity Funds, Inc., on behalf of T. Rowe Price Institutional Large Cap Value Fund	902401257303	10	954,800
John Hancock Funds II—Science & Technology Fund	344965119305	13 & 39	1,090,800
T. Rowe Price Equity Series, Inc., on behalf of T. Rowe Price Equity Income Series, Inc.	902401249307	15	685,800
John Hancock Variable Insurance Trust Science & Technology Fund	902401254005	18	458,900
T. Rowe Price U.S. Equities Trust	902401262001	23 & 24	552,100

T. Rowe Petitioner	Control No.	Verified List No.	Shares
Prudential Retirement Insurance & Annuity Co., on behalf of Separate Account SA-5T2	902401281301	26	256,500
John Hancock Funds II—Spectrum Income Fund	902401261905	42	93,900
Tyco International Retirement Savings & Investment Plan Master Trust	902401276603	43	86,450
The Bureau of National Affairs, Inc.	344996356596	45	80,000

H. THE RESULTS OF THE SEPTEMBER MEETING

Each Broadridge Client Proxy appointed two Dell representatives to vote the shares represented by the proxy at the September Meeting in accordance with the instructions on the proxy. Dell's proxy solicitor aggregated all of the proxies, and the two Dell representatives voted them. IVS Associates, Inc., the inspector of the election, counted the votes. IVS reported that stockholders present at the meeting had approved the Merger, stating:

> At the close of business on August 13, 2013, the record date for determination of stockholders entitled to vote at the Meeting, there were issued and outstanding 1,758,001,669 shares of the Company's common stock, each share being entitled to one vote at the Meeting and representing all of the outstanding voting securities of the Company. . . .
> At the Meeting, the holders of 1,452,545,285 shares of the Company's common stock were represented in person or by proxy, constituting a quorum. . . .

At the Meeting, the vote on a proposal to adopt the Agreement and Plan of Merger, dated as of February 5, 2013, as amended on August 2, 2013, by and among Denali Holding Inc., Denali Intermediate Inc., Denali Acquiror Inc. and the Company, as it may be further amended from time to time ("Proposal 1"), was as follows:

For	Against	Abstain
1,013,326,409	399,608,525	39,610,350

Excluding the shares to be voted by the Affiliated Stockholders from the total shares voted FOR above, the vote on Proposal 1 was at least as follows:

For	Against
733,998,074	399,608,525

The report that IVS prepared certified that Cede had voted as follows:

For	Against	Abstain
803,734,618	397,961,172	39,574,205

The votes recorded on Cede's behalf included the shares voted pursuant to the Broadridge Client Proxies, which implemented the instructions that T. Rowe provided to ISS and ISS conveyed to Broadridge.

I. ADDITIONAL EVIDENCE OF HOW THE T. ROWE PETITIONERS VOTED

Eight of the T. Rowe Petitioners are mutual funds. Federal law requires that they file a Form N–PX disclosing how they voted their securities during the most recent twelve-month period ended June 30.

In August 2014, the eight T. Rowe Petitioners filed their forms. ISS generated the forms using data pulled from the ISS Voting System. T. Rowe personnel checked the forms for accuracy and filed them. The forms stated that the eight T. Rowe Petitioners had voted "FOR" the Merger.

Because T. Rowe had opposed the Merger publicly, the disclosure that eight of the T. Rowe Petitioners had voted "FOR" the Merger generated inquiries. T. Rowe began to investigate what happened. On October 28, 2014, an ISS representative explained to T. Rowe personnel by email that it had provided Broadridge with instructions to vote the T. Rowe Petitioners' shares in favor of the Merger. The email stated:

[T]he Dell Inc. meeting situation was very fluid during the July–Sept 2013 period and delayed several times. Ultimately, the proxy contest (and applicable ballots) was canceled and a special meeting was held for shareholders to vote on the proposed merger. New ballots were issued for the Special meeting which were voted in-line with the [T. Rowe] Policy Recommendations; the majority of the ballots being voted 4–6 days prior to the meeting.

Given this factual record, Dell has proven by a preponderance of the evidence that the T. Rowe Petitioners shares were voted "FOR" the Merger. Broadridge voted those shares in favor of the Merger through the Broadridge client proxies, which exercised the voting authority that Broadridge received from State Street through a power of attorney, and which State Street had received from Cede through the DTC omnibus proxy.

II. LEGAL ANALYSIS

Delaware cases uniformly place the burden of proof on the petitioner to demonstrate compliance with the requirements of the appraisal statute. The Dissenter Requirement is one of those requirements. It therefore might seem intuitive that to satisfy the Dissenter Requirement, a petitioner would bear the burden of proving that Cede, as record holder, had not voted the shares for which appraisal was sought in favor of the merger giving rise to appraisal rights.

Two Delaware Supreme Court cases support that conclusion. *See Olivetti Underwood Corp. v. Jacques Coe & Co. (Olivetti II),* 217 A.2d 683 (Del.1966); *Reynolds Metals Co. v. Colonial Realty Corp. (Reynolds II*), 190 A.2d 752 (Del.1963). In three more recent cases, however, this court declined to require a petitioner to make this showing, which the decisions helpfully labeled a "share-tracing requirement." All three cases involved situations where investors purchased shares in the open market after the record date for a merger for the purpose of pursuing appraisal. This practice is known colloquially as "appraisal arbitrage," so it is convenient to call them the "Appraisal Arbitrage Decisions."

Although the Delaware Supreme Court has not yet spoken on this issue, I believe that each of the Appraisal Arbitrage Decisions was decided correctly in light of the arguments that the parties advanced and the record they presented to the court. In none of the three cases was there evidence showing how the record holder voted the shares for which appraisal was sought. To the contrary, in each case, the parties agreed that it was impossible for either side—the investors or the corporation—to show how Cede voted particular shares. Imposing a share-tracing requirement therefore implied that no stockholder who held through Cede could seek appraisal. Investors who bought after the record date would not be able to trace their shares to a prior beneficial owner with the legal authority to direct how the shares were voted. More broadly, investors who held on the record date would not be able to prove how Cede voted the shares for which appraisal was sought. As the parties presented it, a share-tracing requirement would foreclose street-name holders from seeking appraisal.

Not surprisingly, the Appraisal Arbitrage Decisions rejected a share-tracing requirement. They did so by stressing that the Record Holder Requirement called for considering only Cede's actions. But the decisions then took the additional step of seemingly equating the analysis of Cede's voting behavior with an exclusive focus on the aggregate voting totals provided at the meeting. In a case where everyone agreed that no one could show anything more, stopping there made sense. Before this case, the Delaware courts had never confronted a situation in which the evidence showed that Cede in fact voted the shares for which appraisal was sought in favor of the merger giving rise to appraisal rights.

The existence of evidence showing how Cede voted the T. Rowe Petitioners' shares warrants distinguishing the Appraisal Arbitrage Decisions as addressing situations in which there was an evidentiary vacuum. That scenario necessarily prevails at the pleading stage, and it may persist after discovery, as it did in those cases. The holdings of the Appraisal Arbitrage Decisions mean that a petitioner can establish a *prima facie* case that the Dissenter Requirement was met by showing that Cede held a sufficient number of shares that were not voted in favor of a merger to cover the appraisal class. At that point, the burden shifts to the respondent corporation to adduce evidence showing how Cede actually voted the shares for which appraisal was sought. If the corporation can rebut the petitioner's *prima facie* case and demonstrate that Cede actually voted the particular shares in favor of the merger, then the appraisal petitioner cannot satisfy the Dissenter Requirement for those shares.

In my view, distinguishing the Appraisal Arbitrage Decisions on this ground is necessary to avoid an absurd result. If a court cannot examine evidence regarding how Cede actually voted, then the combination of that evidentiary limitation and the Record Holder Requirement will permit an appraisal petitioner who holds in street name to give instructions to vote its shares in favor of a merger, have those instructions carried out by the record holder, and then nevertheless seek an appraisal for the very same shares, as long as there were sufficient shares that Cede had not voted in favor of the merger to cover the appraisal class. Under that scenario, a non-dissenter can pursue dissenters' rights. It seems absurd to interpret one statutory provision (the Record Holder Requirement) so broadly that investors can act directly contrary to a second statutory provision (the Dissenter Requirement).

In this case, Dell proved that Cede (through Broadridge) voted the shares for which the T. Rowe Petitioners now seek appraisal in favor of the Merger. The Dissenter Requirement was not met for these shares, so no one can seek appraisal for them . . .

For present purposes, the "realities of modern stock practices" encompass a first-level transfer of voting authority from Cede to the DTC participants through the omnibus proxy, a second-level transfer of voting authority from the DTC participants to Broadridge through powers of attorney, and a third-level role for Broadridge in collecting voting instructions *and carrying them out* by voting Cede's shares through the Broadridge Client Proxies. By using Broadridge's internal control numbers and other voting authentication materials, it is possible to determine how Cede voted particular blocks of shares.

In my view, the fact that Cede outsourced these parts of the voting process does not mean an iron curtain has descended to isolate the resulting evidence from the legal system. It simply means that the litigants must obtain the information from Broadridge, and they readily can.

The evidence showing how Cede voted particular blocks of shares provides a basis for distinguishing the Appraisal Arbitrage Decisions. Under those opinions, an appraisal petitioner that held in street name can establish a *prima facie* case that the Dissenter Requirement was met by showing that there were sufficient shares at Cede that were not voted in favor of the merger to cover the appraisal class. This showing satisfies the petitioner's initial burden and enables the case to proceed. If there is no other evidence, then as in the Appraisal Arbitrage Decisions, the *prima facie* showing is dispositive.

The analysis, however, need not stop there. Once the appraisal petitioner has made out a *prima facie* case, the burden shifts to the corporation to show that Cede actually voted the shares for which the petitioner seeks appraisal in favor of the merger. The corporation can do this by pointing to documents that are publicly available, such as a Form N–PX. Or the corporation can introduce evidence from Broadridge, ISS, and other providers of voting services, such as internal control numbers and voting authentication records. If the evidence that the corporation adduces is not sufficient to demonstrate that Cede actually voted the shares for which the petitioner seeks appraisal in favor of the merger, then the petitioner can continue to maintain an appraisal action. But if the corporation demonstrates that Cede actually voted the shares for which the petitioner seeks appraisal in favor of the merger, then the Dissenter Requirement is no longer met, and the petitioner cannot obtain seek appraisal for those shares. . . .

F. THE T. ROWE PETITIONERS' OTHER ARGUMENTS

To avoid the implications of the Dissenter Requirement, the T. Rowe Petitioners seek to shift the focus elsewhere, away from the voting instructions that the T. Rowe Voting System submitted to ISS, which ISS provided to Broadridge, and which Broadridge carried out. First, the T. Rowe Petitioners argue that they submitted the voting instructions mistakenly, which they did, and that they should not lose their appraisal rights because of an inadvertent error. Second, they point to language in the Proxy Statement which they interpret as saying that earlier votes would remain effective, and they argue that Dell should be estopped from treating Broadridge's later votes in favor of the Merger as Cede's actual votes. Third, they argue that because of the ruling that this court reached in the *Dell Ownership* decision, the voting instructions that they provided should not matter. None of these arguments carries the day. . . .

When an investor elects to use intermediaries, the investor assumes the risk that the intermediaries will err or otherwise fail to act in accordance with the investor's wishes. That general rule applies to the appraisal statute. Ironically, by making this argument, the T. Rowe Petitioners are effectively contending that Broadridge acted without actual authority (albeit with apparent authority) because of the mistaken conveyance of voting instructions by ISS. . . .

By choosing to rely on ISS to transmit its voting instructions, T. Rowe accepted the risk that ISS might transmit voting instructions inconsistent with T. Rowe's true intentions.

Nor would the mistake disappear if the court treated State Street as the record holder. Through the power of attorney in its services agreement with Broadridge,

State Street granted Broadridge authority to vote its shares in accordance with instructions received from the beneficial holders. In this case, the T. Rowe Voting System communicated instructions to ISS, which communicated them to Broadridge, which carried them out. For purposes of this case, the outcome remains the same if the analysis were to focus on State Street rather than on Cede.

. . . The T. Rowe Petitioners creatively propose to amend their petitions to substitute Cede as the petitioner. That would not matter. Cede cannot obtain appraisal of shares it voted in favor of the Merger. No one can seek appraisal for those shares.

In an opinion published a few days later, Vice Chancellor Laster found that Dell shares were worth about $17.62 at the time of the 2013 leveraged buyout, rather than the $13.75 that Mr. Dell and Silver Lake paid. There was "widespread and compelling evidence of a valuation gap" between the market's perception of Dell's performance and the company's "operative reality," Laster ruled. But in the opinion you just read, the Vice Chancellor had disqualified about 29 million of the 34 million shares that had sought appraisal in connection with the merger.

PROBLEM SET 12.2

1. What is the consequence of the foregoing system for the issuing firm? For those who would like to mount a takeover of the firm? What justification might there be for the existing system? Note that in most other countries, issuing firms can and do communicate directly with their investors. *See* Del. Gen. Corp. Law §113.
2. Take another look at the *JRC Acquisition Corp* in Chapter 11. Does the opening paragraph make more sense now?
3. How much did the shareholders of the T. Rowe Price Equity Income Fund lose out on as a result of the *Dell* decision? Who should bear that loss?

3.   VALUING SHARES

As we have learned in prior chapters, the value of an asset is the expected cash flows it will generate—including any cash flows generated by sale of the asset. For a common share, you might think it easiest to simply value the shares based on the earnings of the company, with earnings being a kind of proxy for cash flows.

But we have already discussed how some investors might have prior claims on the cash flows, claims that are fixed and thus not subject to the board's discretion.

Additionally, the firm might decide to provide cash flows (i.e., dividends) to shareholders even in the absence of earnings. We have already discussed why that might be, too.

The dividends thing might give you an idea: What about valuing the shares like an annuity? After all, this is essentially what we did when we valued companies using the DCF method. In particular, if a company pays dividends, you could value the company as a string of dividends followed by the money you receive upon sale of the shares.

That works, but what will you receive when you sell the share? That is, how to value the terminal value? Well, if you were buying the shares, you might value it based on the future dividends you will receive. That is, if you value the shares as an annuity, you might end up valuing it as a series of dividend payments you will receive, and then the value of a series of dividend payments the next owner will receive.

This is beginning to look less like an annuity and more like a perpetuity. And if you want to get fancy, you might consider valuing the shares as a growing perpetuity to account for the trend of future dividend payments.

This is the essence of the *dividend discount model* (DDM) or Gordon growth model, as it is also called. Dividend-paying shares are valued as a growing perpetuity:

$$P_t = D_t \times (1 + g) / (r - g)$$

While the Gordon growth model or the DDM is a simple approach to valuing equity, its use is limited to firms that are growing at a stable rate.

You should have two questions immediately: How do I estimate the r and the g? The r used in this formula is often calculated as the shares' dividend yield. Dividend yield is a simple ratio of the annual dividend payment over the current share price. It is also widely reported, if you are fully "mathed out" at this point in the class. Alternatively, you might find r using CAPM.

Then how do we find g, which figures so importantly in our growing perpetuity formula? That's a bit more complex, and even small changes in the assumed g can have big effects on the estimated share price under the DDM. As the growth rate approaches the cost of equity, the value per share approaches infinity. If the growth rate exceeds the cost of equity, the value per share becomes negative, which is more than a bit confusing.

In short, g is frequently estimated as the firm's retention ratio[13] multiplied by the firm's return on retained earnings; that is, how much the firm keeps (the retention ratio) and what it earns on what it keeps (the return on retained earnings).

_____

13. The ratio of retained earnings to total earnings.

Because return on retained earnings is very difficult for an outside observer to project, most often it will be replaced with the historical return on equity (ROE), which is widely reported and easily calculated. This, of course, assumes that today's managers will do just as good of a job as past managers.

$$g = ROE \times RR$$

with *RR* being the retention ratio.

ROE is calculated as net income over shareholder equity. You can find net income on the income statement. Shareholder equity, meanwhile, is located on the balance sheet, in both cases as we saw in Chapter 1.

PROBLEM SET 12.3

1. Calculate the value of a common stock using the DDM (Gordon growth model):

Risk-free rate	**3%**
Equity risk premium	6%
Beta	1.2
Current dividend	$2
Dividend growth rate	5%
Current stock price	$24

2. Given your understanding of balance sheets, what problems might you foresee with ROE and its use in the DDM?
3. What other limitations might there be to DDM beyond those discussed in the text?

4.   A NOTE ON THE P/E RATIO AND OTHER "MULTIPLES"

In Chapter 1 we introduced a variety of ratios that are derived from a firm's balance sheet and other financial statements. ROE is one example we have seen in this chapter.

Another share valuation ratio that is tied to the financial statements is the *price/earnings (P/E) ratio*. This ratio is calculated as the current share price over the earnings per share, or alternatively, total market value over net income.

The PE ratio is a simple measure that reports the cost of the firm's shares in relation to its earnings. Thus, if Exxon's shares are trading at $87.90 and its EPS is 9.23, it has a P/E ratio of 9.52. That is, its current share price is 9.52 times its current EPS.

Whether that means the share price is low or high depends on your point of reference. Most important, particular industries tend to have particular P/E ratios.

Thus, if you compared Exxon to Google—which as of August 2012 had a P/E ratio of 20.4—you might think that Exxon is massively underpriced. But then note that Apple has a ratio of 15.83, Hermes is at 39.57, and Chevron has a ratio of 9.23.

P/E is an example of a multiple. Financial advisors and investment bankers use multiples all the time—in comparable company analysis, comparable transaction analysis, in LBO valuation, in fairness opinions of all sorts—so it is helpful for lawyers to understand what they are talking about. It is also important to understand the problems with overreliance on multiples.

A multiple can be used to compare firms of different sizes. For example, Exxon is extremely large, but when valuing a smaller oil company we might consider what share price would be implied by using a similar 9.52 P/E ratio.

Of course, none of this takes into account firm-specific differences. For example, British Petroleum (at the same point in 2012) traded at a multiple of 7.8. Before assuming it is cheap relative to Exxon and Chevron, one might want to consider the effects of a certain oil spill in 2010.[14] Similarly, if two firms have different accounting policies, comparing multiples might lead to misleading results, especially for those multiples (like P/E ratio) that do not take into account capital structure.[15] Firms, even in the same industry, can have drastically different expected growth rates, returns on invested capital, and capital structures.

Another common form of *relative valuation*—which is a general term for valuation by comparing multiples instead of *absolute, or intrinsic valuation,* which involves discounting cash flows—is EV/EBITDA, which stands for enterprise value over EBITDA. This is known as the *EBITDA multiple* or *enterprise multiple.*

To calculate EV, you start with a company's market value (the number of shares times the market price). You then add the amount of debt the firm has outstanding, both short-term and long-term, at current market value. Then you subtract the amount of cash the firm has. The last part essentially means that EV is market value of equity plus *net debt,* which is debt less available cash.

To take one more example, distressed debt investors often talk about *creation multiples.* We talk more about distressed debt investing in Chapter 15, but in short, it involves investing in companies that are experiencing *financial distress,* which is a fancy way of saying they are on the ropes.

A creation multiple typically refers to the number of years of EBITDA required to cover the cost of the investment. For example, if an investor buys a debt that is second in the capital structure, after a bank loan, the creation multiple would take into account not only the cost the investor paid, but also the face

---

14. http://en.wikipedia.org/wiki/Deepwater_Horizon_oil_spill.

15. EBITDA-based multiples are popular because they are less affected by these issues, as they measure firm cash flows before depreciation and amortization, which underlie many differences among firms.

value of the senior loan that must be paid off first. This is the absolute priority rule from Chapter 3 in action.

To take a simple example, imagine a firm with $100 million a year of EBITDA, $500 million of senior bank loans, and $500 million of bond debt. The investor buys all the junior bond debt. If everything is trading at par, the creation multiple for the junior debt investor would be 10x. But because we are talking about distressed investing, the real creation multiple will be lower than that, because the junior debt is apt to trade below par.

So to make the example more realistic, let's assume the bank loan is currently priced at 60 and the bonds are priced at 40. The junior creditors still have to pay off the senior creditors before they can get paid, so the creation multiple here would be 7x. That is comprised of 5x to pay off the senior creditors and 2x to cover the cost of the junior debt ($500 million in face value, but $200 million in actual cost). On the other hand, an investor who bought the bank loan would have a creation multiple of just 3x. That is, the company only needs to operate for three years for the investor to recoup its cost, while the junior investor needs seven years of cash flow to break even.

PROBLEM SET 12.4

1. In a recent press report, it was observed that by "borrowing up to 3.5 times the combined forecast [EBITDA] for 2016, the enlarged Bayer could take on just over $30 billion of new debt." What does this mean? What are the limitations of this analysis?
2. The EIBTDA multiple requires use of debt market values. If those are not available, it is common to use book values instead. How does that change the analysis?
3. Review the following paragraph, taken from the 2016 proxy statement issued in connection with the proposed merger of Huntington Bancshares and FirstMerit, two regional banking groups:

> *Illustrative Discounted Dividend Analyses for FirstMerit on a Stand-Alone Basis*
>
> Using the Forecasts, Goldman Sachs performed illustrative discounted dividend analyses, as of December 31, 2015, on FirstMerit, on a stand-alone basis, to derive a range of illustrative present values per share of FirstMerit common stock on a stand-alone basis.
>
> Using discount rates ranging from 10.2% to 11.2% reflecting estimates of the cost of equity for FirstMerit on a stand-alone basis, Goldman Sachs discounted to present value as of December 31, 2015 (a) the forecasted dividends to FirstMerit common shareholders on a stand-alone basis for the years 2016 to 2021, using a target tangible common equity to tangible assets ratio, or "TCE/TA," of 8.0% as instructed by

Huntington management,[16] and (b) a range of illustrative terminal values for FirstMerit on a stand-alone basis, as of December 31, 2021, calculated by applying price/tangible book value multiples ranging from 1.5x to 1.9x, to an estimate of the post-dividend tangible book value of FirstMerit on a stand-alone basis as of December 31, 2021, as reflected in the Forecasts. Then, by adding the ranges of present values it derived as described above and dividing these values by the total number of fully diluted shares of FirstMerit common stock outstanding as of December 31, 2015, as provided by FirstMerit management, Goldman Sachs derived illustrative present values per share of FirstMerit common stock on a stand-alone basis ranging from $18.32 to $22.29.

How would you explain this in "plain English"? As of January 2016, Goldman also estimated that FirstMerit shareholders would receive total consideration per share of $20.74 under the proposed merger.

---

16. Author's note: The following quote from an American Banker web post might help you understand this ratio:

> . . . though, many in the investment community are saying that the tangible-common-equity-to-total-assets ratio is actually the truest measure of a bank's health because—and this is them talking—it shows just how strong a bank's first line of defense is, without any muddling from such intangibles as goodwill, servicing rights and deferred tax assets. The higher the TCE/TA ratio, the less the banks would have to dig into regulatory capital to cover defaults.
>
> Investors and analysts started paying closer attention to this ratio around the time the Treasury Department began investing in banks, and now much of the industry is obsessed with it. Banks that never before mentioned it in the capital ratio section of earnings announcements are doing so prominently. And the Treasury is floating a proposal to convert government-held preferred shares into common equity, in large part to boost TCE ratios.
>
> Since common equity provides a cushion against credit losses, investors obviously want the TCE ratio to be as high as possible, and they start to get uncomfortable when it falls below 5 percent of assets.
>
> But it's worth noting that several of the nation's largest and, by regulatory capital measures, healthiest banking companies, including Wells Fargo & Co. and PNC Financial Services Group, have ratios of less than 5 percent. And, as an industry expert recently pointed out, Washington Mutual Inc. had a very high TCE ratio on the September day it failed.

Alan Kline, *Past the Point of Debate on TCE Ratio*, http://www.americanbanker.com/magazine /119_6/-380004-1.html.

13

PREFERRED SHARES

It is often noted that preferred shares are a hybrid between debt and equity. A less polite observer might note that a preferred shareholder is either a shareholder without voting power or a deeply subordinated debtholder.[1]

Financial institutions are some of the biggest issuers of preferred shares in the United States, as preferred shares' equity status provides regulatory benefits under the applicable capital requirements. Before the 2008 financial crisis, financial institutions experimented with a wide variety of instruments that appeared to be equity for regulatory purposes, while acting as debt for tax purposes. Although these instruments had lots of clever names, in the financial industry it was widely thought that these instruments were more often sold rather than bought. Large, staid businesses historically also issued a good bit of preferred stock, often to meet the putative demand from retirees seeking steady income.[2]

Other specialized uses of preferred stock include the U.S. Treasury's bailout of financial institutions in late 2008—its investment in AIG, for example, came in the form of convertible preferred shares—and venture capitalists, who often invest in companies by way of convertible preferred shares.[3] Convertible shares, which allow the holder to transform their investment into some number of common shares, are covered in the subsequent chapter on options and convertible instruments. Venture capital investments are also the subject of a separate chapter.

The term *preferred* means that a firm must pay the dividends due on its preferred shares before it pays any common stock dividends. Also, in theory, if a company goes bankrupt, preferred holders have priority over common stock shareholders. In many cases, the liquidation preference might entitle the preferred shareholders to be first in line to receive nothing. The absolute priority still applies, and thus means creditors first.

---

1. *See* Ben Walther, *The Peril and Promise of Preferred Stock*, 39 Del. J. Corp. L. 161, 167-68 (2014).

2. Whether this demand was actually the result of investors' demands or the result of marketing efforts by the banks that underwrote the preferred shares remains uncertain.

3. *See* Chapter 21.

1.   STRUCTURAL ISSUES (THE TERMS OF THE DEAL)

As a matter of general corporate law, simply calling a particular class of "preferred" shares does nothing.[4] The shares remain common shares, entitled to all the normal rights of shareholders that are the subject of your basic Business Associations class.[5]

Any special rights, therefore, must be specified by some other document.[6] Typically this other document is either the firm's certificate of incorporation itself, or a document known as a certificate of designation.

CERTIFICATE OF DESIGNATION OF TERMS OF 6.75% NON-CUMULATIVE PREFERRED STOCK, SERIES Q

CUSIP Number: 313586778

1.   DESIGNATION, PAR VALUE AND NUMBER OF SHARES.

The designation of the series of preferred stock of the Federal National Mortgage Association ("Fannie Mae") created by this resolution shall be "6.75% Non-Cumulative Preferred Stock, Series Q" (the "Series Q Preferred Stock"), and the number of shares initially constituting the Series Q Preferred Stock is 15,000,000. Shares of Series Q Preferred Stock will have no par value and a stated value of $25 per share. Shares of Series Q Preferred Stock will have no stated maturity date, and, subject to Section 3 below, will be perpetual. The Board of Directors of Fannie Mae, or a duly authorized committee thereof, in its sole discretion, may reduce the number of shares of Series Q Preferred Stock, provided such reduction is not below the number of shares of Series Q Preferred Stock then outstanding.

2.   DIVIDENDS.

(a) Holders of record of Series Q Preferred Stock (each individually a "Holder," or collectively the "Holders") will be entitled to receive, when, as and if declared by the Board of Directors of Fannie Mae, or a duly authorized committee thereof, in its sole discretion out of funds legally available therefor, non-cumulative quarterly dividends. . . .

(b) No dividend (other than dividends or distributions paid in shares of, or options, warrants or rights to subscribe for or purchase shares of, the common stock of Fannie Mae or any other stock of Fannie Mae ranking, as to the payment of dividends and the distribution of assets upon dissolution, liquidation or winding up of Fannie Mae, junior to the Series Q Preferred Stock) may be declared or paid or set apart for payment on Fannie Mae's common stock (or on

---

4. *Shanghai Power Co. v. Del. Trust Co.,* 316 A.2d 589, 593 (Del. Ch. 1974).

5. Del. Gen. Corp. Law §212(a).

6. Richard M. Buxbaum, *Preferred Stock and Draftsmanship*, 42 Cal. L. Rev. 243, 303 (1954).

any other stock of Fannie Mae ranking, as to the payment of dividends, junior to the Series Q Preferred Stock) unless dividends have been declared and paid or set apart (or ordered to be set apart) on the Series Q Preferred Stock for the then-current quarterly Dividend Period; provided, however, that the foregoing dividend preference shall not be cumulative and shall not in any way create any claim or right in favor of the Holders of Series Q Preferred Stock in the event that dividends have not been declared or paid or set apart. . . .

(c) The Board of Directors of Fannie Mae, or a duly authorized committee thereof, may, in its discretion, choose to pay dividends on the Series Q Preferred Stock without the payment of any dividends on Fannie Mae's common stock (or any other stock of Fannie Mae ranking, as to the payment of dividends, junior to the Series Q Preferred Stock).

(d) No full dividends shall be declared or paid or set apart for payment on any stock of Fannie Mae ranking, as to the payment of dividends, on a parity with the Series Q Preferred Stock for any period unless full dividends have been declared and paid or set apart for payment on the Series Q Preferred Stock for the then-current quarterly Dividend Period. When dividends are not paid in full upon the Series Q Preferred Stock and all other classes or series of stock of Fannie Mae, if any, ranking, as to the payment of dividends, on a parity with the Series Q Preferred Stock, all dividends declared upon shares of Series Q Preferred Stock and all such other stock of Fannie Mae will be declared pro rata so that the amount of dividends declared per share of Series Q Preferred Stock and all such other stock will in all cases bear to each other the same ratio that accrued dividends per share of Series Q Preferred Stock (but without, in the case of any noncumulative preferred stock, accumulation of unpaid dividends for prior Dividend Periods) and such other stock bear to each other.

(e) No dividends may be declared or paid or set apart for payment on any shares of Series Q Preferred Stock if at the same time any arrears exist or default exists in the payment of dividends on any outstanding class or series of stock of Fannie Mae ranking, as to the payment of dividends, prior to the Series Q Preferred Stock.

(f) Holders of Series Q Preferred Stock will not be entitled to any dividends, whether payable in cash or property, other than as herein provided and will not be entitled to interest, or any sum in lieu of interest, in respect of any dividend payment.

3. OPTIONAL REDEMPTION.

(a) The Series Q Preferred Stock shall not be redeemable prior to September 30, 2010. On and after that date, subject to (x) the notice provisions set forth in Section 3(b) below, (y) the receipt of any required regulatory approvals and (z) any further limitations which may be imposed by law, Fannie Mae may redeem the Series Q Preferred Stock, in whole or in part, at any time or from time to time, out of funds legally available therefor, at the redemption price of $25 per share plus an amount equal to the amount of the dividend (whether or not declared) for the then-current quarterly Dividend Period accrued to but excluding the date of such redemption, but without accumulation of unpaid dividends on the Series Q Preferred Stock for prior Dividend Periods.

(d) The Series Q Preferred Stock will not be subject to any mandatory redemption, sinking fund or other similar provisions. In addition, Holders of Series Q Preferred Stock will have no right to require redemption of any shares of Series Q Preferred Stock.

4.   LIQUIDATION RIGHTS.

(a) Upon any voluntary or involuntary dissolution, liquidation or winding up of Fannie Mae, after payment or provision for the liabilities of Fannie Mae and the expenses of such dissolution, liquidation or winding up, the Holders of outstanding shares of the Series Q Preferred Stock will be entitled to receive out of the assets of Fannie Mae or proceeds thereof available for distribution to stockholders, before any payment or distribution of assets is made to holders of Fannie Mae's common stock (or any other stock of Fannie Mae ranking, as to the distribution of assets upon dissolution, liquidation or winding up of Fannie Mae, junior to the Series Q Preferred Stock), the amount of $25 per share plus an amount, determined in accordance with Section 2 above, equal to the dividend (whether or not declared) for the then-current quarterly Dividend Period accrued to but excluding the date of such liquidation payment, but without accumulation of unpaid dividends on the Series Q Preferred Stock for prior Dividend Periods.

(b) If the assets of Fannie Mae available for distribution in such event are insufficient to pay in full the aggregate amount payable to Holders of Series Q Preferred Stock and holders of all other classes or series of stock of Fannie Mae, if any, ranking, as to the distribution of assets upon dissolution, liquidation or winding up of Fannie Mae, on a parity with the Series Q Preferred Stock, the assets will be distributed to the Holders of Series Q Preferred Stock and holders of all such other stock pro rata, based on the full respective preferential amounts to which they are entitled (but without, in the case of any noncumulative preferred stock, accumulation of unpaid dividends for prior Dividend Periods).

(c) Notwithstanding the foregoing, Holders of Series Q Preferred Stock will not be entitled to be paid any amount in respect of a dissolution, liquidation or winding up of Fannie Mae until holders of any classes or series of stock of Fannie Mae ranking, as to the distribution of assets upon dissolution, liquidation or winding up of Fannie Mae, prior to the Series Q Preferred Stock have been paid all amounts to which such classes or series are entitled.

(d) Neither the sale, lease or exchange (for cash, shares of stock, securities or other consideration) of all or substantially all of the property and assets of Fannie Mae, nor the merger, consolidation or combination of Fannie Mae into or with any other entity or the merger, consolidation or combination of any other entity into or with Fannie Mae, shall be deemed to be a dissolution, liquidation or winding up, voluntary or involuntary, for the purposes of this Section 4.

(e) After payment of the full amount of the distribution of assets upon dissolution, liquidation or winding up of Fannie Mae to which they are entitled pursuant to paragraphs (a), (b) and (c) of this Section 4, the Holders of Series Q

Preferred Stock will not be entitled to any further participation in any distribution of assets by Fannie Mae. . . .

7. VOTING RIGHTS; AMENDMENTS.

(a) Except as provided below, the Holders of Series Q Preferred Stock will not be entitled to any voting rights, either general or special. . . .

(c) Except as set forth in paragraph (b) of this Section 7, the terms of this Certificate or the Series Q Preferred Stock may be amended, altered, supplemented, or repealed only with the consent of the Holders of at least two-thirds of the shares of Series Q Preferred Stock then outstanding, given in person or by proxy, either in writing or at a meeting of stockholders at which the Holders of Series Q Preferred Stock shall vote separately as a class. On matters requiring their consent, Holders of Series Q Preferred Stock will be entitled to one vote per share.

8. ADDITIONAL CLASSES OR SERIES OF STOCK.

The Board of Directors of Fannie Mae, or a duly authorized committee thereof, shall have the right at any time in the future to authorize, create and issue, by resolution or resolutions, one or more additional classes or series of stock of Fannie Mae, and to determine and fix the distinguishing characteristics and the relative rights, preferences, privileges and other terms of the shares thereof. Any such class or series of stock may rank prior to, on a parity with or junior to the Series Q Preferred Stock as to the payment of dividends or the distribution of assets upon dissolution, liquidation or winding up of Fannie Mae, or otherwise.

PROBLEM SET 13.1

1. What are the dividend, voting, and preference rights of a holder of the Series Q Preferred Stock? What risks does the holder face based on the terms presented?
2. Contrast the dividends in the foregoing shares to those provided by the following provision:

> The holders of shares of the outstanding Preferred Stock shall be entitled, when, as and if declared by the Board of Directors out of funds of the Corporation legally available therefor, to receive cumulative cash dividends at the rate per annum of 4.50% per share on the Liquidation Preference (equivalent to $2.25 per annum per share), payable quarterly in arrears (the "Dividend Rate") . . . Such dividends shall be cumulative . . . (whether or not in any dividend period or periods the Board of Directors shall have declared such dividends or there shall be funds of the Corporation legally available for the payment of such dividends) and shall accumulate on a day-to-day basis, whether or not earned or declared, from and after the Issue Date. Dividends payable for any partial dividend

period shall be computed on the basis of days elapsed over a 360-day year consisting of twelve 30-day months. Accumulated unpaid dividends accrue and cumulate dividends at the annual rate of 4.50% and are payable in the manner provided in this Section 3.

3. Unlike common shares, preferred shares typically remain close to their initial issue price, and rarely go over their initial issue price. Why?

2.   INTERPRETING THE TERMS

ELLIOTT ASSOCIATES, L.P., v. AVATEX CORPORATION

715 A.2d 843
Supreme Court of Delaware.
Aug. 28, 1998.

VEASEY, Chief Justice:

In this case of first impression, we hold that certain preferred stockholders have the right to a class vote in a merger where: (1) the certificate of incorporation expressly provides such a right in the event of any "amendment, alteration or repeal, whether by merger, consolidation or otherwise" of any of the provisions of the certificate of incorporation; (2) the certificate of incorporation that provides protections for the preferred stock is nullified and thereby repealed by the merger; and (3) the result of the transaction would materially and adversely affect the rights, preferences, privileges or voting power of those preferred stockholders. In so holding, we distinguish prior Delaware precedent narrowly because of the inclusion by the drafters of the phrase, "whether by merger, consolidation or otherwise."

FACTS

Defendant Avatex Corporation ("Avatex") is a Delaware corporation that has outstanding both common and preferred stock. The latter includes two distinct series of outstanding preferred stock: "First Series Preferred" and "Series A Preferred." Plaintiffs in these consolidated cases are all preferred stockholders of defendant Avatex. The individual defendants are all members of the Avatex board of directors.

Avatex created and incorporated Xetava Corporation ("Xetava") as its wholly-owned subsidiary on April 13, 1998, and the following day announced its intention to merge with and into Xetava. Under the terms of the proposed merger, Xetava is to be the surviving corporation. Once the transaction is consummated, Xetava will immediately change its name to Avatex Corporation. The proposed merger would cause a conversion of the preferred stock of Avatex into common stock of Xetava. The merger will effectively eliminate Avatex' certificate of incorporation, which includes the certificate of designations creating the Avatex preferred stock and setting forth its rights and preferences.[7] The terms of the merger do not call for a class vote of these preferred stockholders. Herein lies the heart of the legal issue presented in this case.

Plaintiffs filed suit in the Court of Chancery to enjoin the proposed merger, arguing, among other things, that the transaction required the consent of two-thirds of the holders of the First Series Preferred stock. Defendants responded with a motion for judgment on the pleadings, which the Court of Chancery granted, finding that the provisions governing the rights of the First Series Preferred stockholders do not require such consent.

The plaintiffs allege that, because of Avatex' anemic financial state, "all the value of Avatex is [currently] in the preferred stock." By forcing the conversion of the preferred shares into common stock of the surviving corporation, however, the merger would place current preferred stockholders of Avatex on an even footing with its common stockholders. In fact, the Avatex preferred stockholders will receive in exchange for their preferred stock approximately 73% of Xetava common stock, and the common stockholders of Avatex will receive approximately 27% of the common stock of Xetava.

Under the terms of the Avatex certificate of incorporation, First Series stockholders have no right to vote except on:

(a) any "amendment, alteration or repeal" of the certificate of incorporation "whether by merger, consolidation or otherwise," that

(b) "materially and adversely" affects the rights of the First Series stockholders.

The text of the terms governing the voting rights of the First Series Preferred Stock is set forth in the certificate of designations as follows:

> Except as expressly provided hereinafter in this Section (6) or as otherwise . . . required by law, the First Series Preferred Stock shall have no voting rights. . . .
>
> So long as any shares of First Series Preferred Stock remain outstanding, the *consent* of the holders of at least two-thirds of the shares of the *First Series Preferred Stock* outstanding at the time (voting separately as a class . . .) . . . *shall be necessary to permit, effect or validate* any one or more of the following:
>
> . . .
>
> (b) *The amendment, alteration or repeal, whether by merger, consolidation or otherwise, of any of the provisions of the* Restated *Certificate* of Incorporation or of [the certificate of designations] which would *materially and adversely affect any right, preference, privilege or voting power of the First Series Preferred Stock or of the holders thereof.* . . .

These are the operative terms of Section 6 of the certificate of designations (with emphasis supplied) setting forth the rights and preferences of the First

---

7. When certificates of designations become effective, they constitute amendments to the certificate of incorporation so that the rights of preferred stockholders become part of the certificate of incorporation. Accordingly, we will use the term "certificate" to refer to the certificate of designations as integrated into the certificate of incorporation. See Kaiser Aluminum Corp. v. Matheson, Del.Supr., 681 A.2d 392, 394 n. 3 (1996) (citing 8 Del. C. §§102(a)(4), 151(g)).

Series Preferred stock that became effective March 18, 1983. On September 14, 1983 a new certificate of designations became effective with respect to the Second Series Preferred stock. There is, however, no Second Series Preferred stock outstanding. Unlike the First Series certificate, Section 6 of the Second Series certificate expressly provides the Second Series Preferred stock with a right to vote on any consolidation or merger (with certain exceptions not relevant here) to which Avatex is a party:

> So long as any shares of the Second Series Preferred Stock remain outstanding, the consent of the holders of at least a majority of the shares of the Second Series Preferred Stock outstanding at the time...shall be necessary to permit or approve any of the following:
>
>   . . .
>
> (b) The consolidation or merger of the Corporation with or into any other corporation unless. . . .

We discuss this provision further in our analysis of the legal issue involved.

ANALYSIS

Delaware law permits corporations to create and issue stock that carries no voting power. Professor Buxbaum, in his seminal article on preferred stock nearly 45 years ago, noted, among many other cogent observations, that: (a) statutes often permit alteration of preferred stock rights and preferences by merger; (b) the merger may be with a "paper subsidiary created for that purpose with no independent business validity"; (c) "corporate articles [often] require consent of two-thirds (or a majority) of the preferred shareholders as a class for the consummation of any merger . . . "; and (d) courts have struggled with "controls in the name . . . of 'fairness' and generally abandoned them [, which] is as it should be [since the] issue is one of corporate power."

The Avatex certificate of incorporation provides that Avatex preferred shares have no right to vote except on matters set forth therein or required by law. This denial of the right to vote is subject to an exception carved out for any "amendment, alteration or repeal" of the certificate "whether by merger, consolidation or otherwise" that "materially and adversely" affects the rights of the preferred stockholders. Such an event requires the consent of two-thirds of the First Series Preferred stockholders voting as a class.

This appeal, then, reduces to a narrow legal question: whether the "amendment, alteration or repeal" of the certificate of incorporation is caused "by merger, consolidation or otherwise" thereby requiring a two-thirds class vote of the First Series Preferred stockholders, it being assumed for purposes of this appeal that their rights would be "materially and adversely" affected. The Court of Chancery answered this question in the negative. Although we respect that Court's craftsmanlike analysis, we are constrained to disagree with its conclusion.

Relying primarily on *Warner Communications Inc. v. Chris-Craft Industries Inc.*, the Court of Chancery held that it was only the *conversion* of the stock as a result of the merger, and not the *amendment, alteration or repeal* of the certificate, that would adversely affect the preferred stockholders. It is important to keep in mind, however, that the terms of the preferred stock in *Warner* were significantly different from those present here, because in *Warner* the phrase "whether by merger, consolidation or otherwise" was not included. The issue here, therefore, is whether the presence of this additional phrase in the Avatex certificate is an outcome-determinative distinction from *Warner*.

In *Warner*, the question was whether the Series B preferred stock of Warner Communications, Inc. had the right to a class vote on a proposed merger of Warner with Time, Inc. (renamed Time Warner Inc.) and TW Sub, its wholly-owned subsidiary. As the first step in a two-step transaction, Time had acquired approximately 50% of Warner's common stock in a tender offer. The second step was the "back-end" merger in which TW Sub was merged into Warner, which survived as a wholly-owned subsidiary of Time. The Warner common stock not held by Time was converted into cash, securities and other property. In the merger, the Warner Series B preferred would be converted into Time Series BB preferred stock. The parties stipulated that the Warner Series B stockholders would thereby be adversely affected.

The Chancellor held that the drafters of the Warner Series B certificate of designations did not intend for two-thirds of the Series B stockholders to have a veto over every merger in which their interest would be adversely affected because the right to vote was conferred expressly (as it must under Delaware law), and "only in narrowly defined circumstances . . . not present here."

Here the First Series Preferred stock of Avatex is converted to common stock of the surviving corporation, Xetava, a newly formed corporation admittedly a wholly owned subsidiary of Avatex created for the sole purpose of effecting this merger and eliminating the rights of the Avatex First Series Preferred. In *Warner*, the Warner, Series B Preferred also received a new security—Time Series BB Preferred—a senior security issued by the surviving corporation, Time (renamed Time Warner). This was accomplished by using TW Sub, Time's wholly-owned subsidiary, as the merger partner of Warner. Since we do not reach the question of the economic quality of the transaction, it makes no difference for purposes of this analysis (as plaintiffs argue) that in *Warner* there were two distinct acts that operated independently—that the substitution of charters was between Warner and TW Sub and the exchange of shares was between Warner and Time. The operative events here are that the proposed downstream merger of Avatex into Xetava results in the conversion of Avatex stock to Xetava stock and the elimination "by merger" of the certificate protections granted to the Avatex First Series Preferred. Thus, it is *both* the stock conversion *and* the repeal of the Avatex certificate that causes the adverse effect to the First Series Preferred. In *Warner*, it was only the stock conversion that caused the adverse effect because the phrase, "whether by merger, consolidation or otherwise" was not present.

The relevant statutory provisions are found in Sections 251(b) and 251(e) of the Delaware General Corporation Law ("DGCL") . . .

Avatex argued below, and the Court of Chancery appears to have agreed, that *only* a Section 251(b)(3) Amendment to the surviving corporation's charter amounts to an "amendment, alteration or repeal" within the meaning of the provisions defining the voting rights of the preferred stockholders. Accordingly, the argument runs, these provisions would apply *only* in the circumstance (not present here) where Avatex survives the merger and its certificate is amended thereby. Since the proposed merger with Xetava does not contemplate any such amendments to the disappearing Avatex certificate, the argument goes, the transaction can go forward without a First Series class vote.

The first question is: What will happen as a result of the merger to the "rights, preferences, privileges or voting power" of the Avatex First Series Preferred stock as set forth in the existing Avatex certificate? They disappear when the preferred stockholders of Avatex become common stockholders of Xetava under its certificate that does not contain those protections. We assume, as did the trial court, that their elimination would affect the First Series Preferred stockholders adversely.

The second question is: What act or event will cause this adverse effect if the merger is consummated? The trial court held that, "[a]s in *Warner*," the adverse effect on the plaintiffs "will not flow from any 'amendment, alteration or repeal' of the First Series Certificate (however accomplished) but from the conversion into common stock of the First Series Preferred in the Proposed Merger." The Court so held notwithstanding that it had noted the distinguishing language of the certificate here—not present in *Warner*—" whether by merger, consolidation or otherwise." But the Court dismissed this distinction by concluding that this "language only modifies the phrase 'amendment, alteration and repeal' and does not independently create a right to a class vote in the case of *every merger*. "But that is not the issue here where there is no contention that the First Series Preferred have a right to a class vote on *every merger*.

In our view, the merger does cause the adverse effect because the merger is the corporate act that renders the Avatex certificate that protects the preferred stockholders a "legal nullity," in defendants' words. That elimination certainly fits within the ambit of one or more of the three terms in the certificate: *amendment* or *alteration* or *repeal*. The word *repeal* is especially fitting in this context because it contemplates a nullification, which is what defendants concede happens to the Avatex certificate.

Articulation of the rights of preferred stockholders is fundamentally the function of corporate drafters. Construction of the terms of preferred stock is the function of courts. This Court's function is essentially one of contract interpretation against the background of Delaware precedent. These precedential parameters are simply stated: Any rights, preferences and limitations of preferred stock that distinguish that stock from common stock must be expressly and clearly stated, as provided by statute. Therefore, these rights, preferences and limitations will not be presumed or implied. The other doctrine states that when there is a hopeless ambiguity attributable to the corporate drafter that could mislead a reasonable investor such ambiguity must be construed in favor of the reasonable expectation of the investor and against the drafter. This latter doctrine is not applicable here because there is no ambiguity.

In our view, the rights of the First Series Preferred are expressly and clearly stated in the Avatex certificate. The drafters of this instrument could not reasonably have intended any consequence other than granting to the First Series Preferred stock the right to consent by a two-thirds class vote to any merger that would result in the elimination of the protections in the Avatex certificate if the rights of the holders of that stock would thereby be adversely affected. The First Series Preferred stock rights granted by the corporate drafters here are the functional equivalent of a provision that would expressly require such consent if a merger were to eliminate any provision of the Avatex certificate resulting in materially adverse consequences to the holders of that security.

The drafters were navigating around several alternatives. First, all parties agree that pure amendment protection available to the First Series Preferred stockholders as granted by Section 242(b)(2) of the DGCL and Section 4 of the certificate does not—absent the very phrase at issue here—apply to this merger. Although *Warner* was decided after the Avatex certificate of designations became effective, *Warner* clearly supports this view and it continues to be valid precedent for that proposition. Second, all parties agree that if Avatex would have been the survivor, and its certificate were amended in the merger as contemplated by 8 *Del.C.*§251(c)(3), the First Series Preferred would have the right to consent by two-thirds class vote. Third, all parties agree that the right to consent to *any* merger that was granted (subject to certain exceptions not relevant here) to the Second Series Preferred stock (of which none is outstanding) was not intended to be granted to the First Series holders whose rights are more narrowly circumscribed. In their case: (a) the merger must be the cause of an "amendment alteration or repeal" of the certificate (not all mergers do this); and (b) their rights must be adversely affected (which does not inevitably occur in a merger).

If Section 6 of the certificate does not guarantee a class vote to the First Series Preferred in this merger, what could it conceivably be interpreted to mean? Defendants argue that the certificate can be construed to apply *only* in the second instance noted above-namely, in the case where Avatex is the survivor and its certificate is amended, altered or repealed, as contemplated by Section 251(b)(3). But, as plaintiffs point out, this cannot be the *only* outcome the drafters intended because the certificate grants the First Series Preferred this protection in a consolidation where Section 251(b)(3) does not apply. Because the word *consolidation* is included, it cannot reasonably be argued that the protections of Section 6 of the certificate applicable to the First Series Preferred are confined to a Section 251(b)(3) amendment. Therefore, the term *consolidation* cannot be ignored or wished away as surplusage, as defendants argue. It is well established that a court interpreting any contractual provision, including preferred stock provisions, must give effect to all terms of the instrument, must read the instrument as a whole, and, if possible, reconcile all the provisions of the instrument.

POLING v. CAPLEASE, INC.

2016 WL 1749803
Court of Special Appeals of Maryland.
May 3, 2016.

NAZARIAN, J.

The challenge in this appeal lies more in framing the question than in reaching the answer. John Poling, a preferred stockholder of CapLease, Inc. ("CapLease" or the "Company"), sued individually and on behalf of a putative class of Series B and C preferred stockholders ("Preferred Stockholders"), alleging that the terms of the Company's 2013 merger (the "Merger") with American Realty Capital Properties, Inc. ("ARCP") breached the Preferred Stockholders' contractual rights. Mr. Poling's theory of the case begins with the Articles Supplementary as the analytical starting point, and contends that the absence of any provision specifically defining the Preferred Stockholders' rights in a transaction like this Merger precluded the Company from exchanging the preferred shares to ARCP for cash. We agree with the Circuit Court for Baltimore City, though, that Mr. Poling has the analysis inverted: the Corporations and Associations Article of the Maryland Code authorized the Company to enter and close the Merger, and nothing in the Articles otherwise limited it. We affirm the circuit court's decision to grant the Company's motion to dismiss with prejudice.

I. BACKGROUND

Before the Merger, CapLease was a Maryland corporation that owned and managed single-tenant commercial properties and operated as a real estate investment trust ("REIT") for federal income tax purposes. On April 8, 2012, CapLease filed the Series B Articles Supplementary with the Maryland State Department of Assessments and Taxation. The original Series B Articles authorized CapLease to issue 2,300,000 shares of Series B preferred stock; an amendment authorized an additional one million Series B shares. On January 18, 2013, CapLease filed the Articles Supplementary authorizing 850,000 shares of Series C preferred stock. Pursuant to Section 3 of the Articles, Series B and C holders were entitled to receive annual dividends of 8.375% and 7.25%, respectively, as approved by the board of directors and permitted by the Company. The Articles further provided that the preferred stock could not be redeemed prior to April 19, 2017 and January 25, 2018, respectively, after which the Company could redeem any or all preferred stock at its option. The Articles also contained certain protections for Preferred Stockholders. Among other things, Section 7 precluded the Company (or a successor) from issuing additional shares or materially altering the Preferred Stockholders' rights, preferences, privileges or voting power without a two-thirds vote of the existing Preferred Stockholders. And Section 9 allowed Preferred Stockholders to convert their shares into cash—$25.00 per share plus accumulated and unpaid dividends—in the event of a Change of Control, a defined term that encompassed transactions in which the acquiring entity was not publicly traded.

On May 28, 2013, CapLease and ARCP, a Maryland corporation that also operated as a REIT and invested in single-tenant commercial real estate properties, announced the Merger. As part of the consideration, ARCP agreed to pay $25.00 cash per share plus any accumulated and unpaid dividends for each outstanding share of preferred stock. The Merger closed on November 5, 2013, after which CapLease and its partner companies ceased to exist and its directors resigned from their positions. Because ARCP was and is publicly traded, the Merger did not qualify as a Change of Control that would allow Preferred Stockholders to convert shares pursuant to Section 9 (although, as it turns out, they received the same cash consideration in the Merger as they would have in a conversion).

On October 8, 2013, four months after the Merger was announced, Mr. Poling filed a complaint (the "Complaint"), on behalf of himself and a putative class including the Series B and C Preferred Stockholders, in which he alleged that the cash-out transaction violated the Preferred Stockholder's contractual rights, as defined in the Articles. . . .

The defendants—CapLease and its directors, ARCP, and various Merger-related subsidiaries—moved to dismiss the Complaint, and Mr. Poling opposed the motion. The circuit court held a hearing on May 15, 2015, and granted the motion to dismiss. . . . Mr. Poling filed a timely notice of appeal.

II. DISCUSSION

Mr. Poling's five appellate questions really boil down to two: did the circuit court err in granting CapLease's motion to dismiss, and in doing so with prejudice? He maintains that CapLease was not entitled to enter into a merger that cashed out the Preferred Stockholders' shares; that the terms of this Merger violated the Preferred Stockholders' rights as defined in the Articles. . . . CapLease responds that Maryland corporate law permitted the Company to merge with ARCP and to exchange the Preferred Stock for cash as part of the consideration for the Merger, unless the Articles provided otherwise, which, CapLease says, they didn't.

A. CAPLEASE HAD THE AUTHORITY TO EXCHANGE THE PREFERRED SHARES FOR CASH AS CONSIDERATION FOR THE MERGER.

Mr. Poling phrases the question here as "whether the *[Articles] permitted* [CapLease] to involuntarily defease the Preferred Stockholders by converting their Series B and C shares to cash to effectuate the merger." (Emphasis added.) He claims that CapLease breached the Preferred Stockholders' contract with the Company—the Articles—by exchanging the preferred stock for cash. Citing the Articles and the Prospectus, he contends that the preferred stockholders' shares cannot be defeased, as he puts it, except under the "five very limited circumstances" listed in the Articles. And since none of these five circumstances occurred in connection with this Merger, he argues that the preferred stockholders' interests in the preferred stock survived the Merger, and ARCP should have "assumed" the shares (along with the obligation to continue paying dividends).

His argument, though, proceeds from the analytically backward assumption that the Articles are the starting point for understanding the Company's rights and obligations vis-à-vis the Preferred Stockholders, and thus that the Company needs authority from the Articles in order to proceed with the Merger. We disagree. CapLease was a Maryland corporation governed by the Corporations and Associations Article of the Maryland Code ("CA"). And although preferred stock may have attributes of other instruments, such as a defined stream of dividends, at its core, it's still stock. . . . Corporations owning capital stock may merge with other corporations, CA § 3–102(a), and the Code allows merging corporations to exchange their stock, including preferred stock, or convert it into any consideration, including money, as part of such a transaction. CA § 3–103.

The difference between common stock and preferred stock lies in preferred stock's preferential rights, which are defined by contract (in this case the Articles) and can include a broad range of terms and conditions. *See* Scott v. B & O R.R. Co., 93 Md. 475, 497 (1901) (preferred stock "has about it no elements or rights other than those that are conferred upon it by the statute or contract to the authority of which it owes its existence"). "Any rights, preferences and limitations of preferred stock that distinguish that stock from common stock must be expressly and clearly stated, as provided by statute. Therefore, these rights, preferences and limitations will not be presumed or implied." Matulich v. Aegis Commc'ns Grp., Inc., 942 A.2d 596, 601 (Del.2008) (internal quotations and citations omitted).[8]

CapLease's preferred stock entitled its holders to prospects its common stockholders didn't have, most notably a specified stream of dividends and the opportunity to redeem the shares for cash. The Articles also specified the Preferred Stockholders' rights under certain circumstances, such as a corporate

---

8. Maryland courts "deem decisions of the Delaware Supreme Court and Court of Chancery to be highly persuasive. . . ." *Kramer v. Liberty Prop. Tr.,* 408 Md. 1, 24–25 (2009) (noting similarities in Maryland's and Delaware's business law statutes, as well as Delaware courts' reputation for their expertise in matters of corporate law).

liquidation or a Change in Control, a term defined in the Articles to encompass mergers where the acquirer is not publicly traded. That said, the Articles state, in Section 13, that "[t]he Series B Preferred Stock shall not have any preferences, conversion or other rights, voting powers, restrictions, limitations as to dividends or other distributions, qualifications or terms or conditions of redemption other than expressly set forth in the Charter and these Series B Terms." Thus, the Articles themselves recognize their limitations—they define the Preferred Stockholders' rights, but only those rights delineated in the Articles distinguish the preferred stock from the common.

In the Complaint, Mr. Poling classified the transaction as a redemption by the Company. At the motions hearing in the circuit court, he recharacterized the transaction as a conversion. But as those terms are defined in the Articles, it's neither. Whatever one calls it, we agree with the circuit court that nothing in the Articles forbade a cash-out merger and that CapLease had the authority to enter into and consummate this transaction.

Mr. Poling points primarily to Section 9 of the Articles, which allows Preferred Stockholders to convert their shares into cash if a carefully defined Change in Control[9] occurs:

> 9. *Conversion.* The shares of Series B Preferred Stock are not *convertible* into or exchangeable for any other property or securities of the Company, except as provided in Section 9.
>
> (a) Upon the occurrence of a Change of Control, *each holder of shares of Series B Preferred Stock shall have the right* . . . to convert some or all of the shares of Series B Preferred Stock held by such holder . . . into a number of Common Stock per share of Series B Preferred Stock to be converted. . . .
> * * *
> (e) *In order to exercise the Change of Control Conversion Right, a holder of shares of Series B Preferred Stock shall be required to* deliver . . . the certificates representing the shares. . . .

(Emphasis added.) According to Mr. Poling, this provision represents the *only* instance in which preferred stock can be cashed out. He argues that the conversion rights conferred in Section 9 apply to both stockholders and the Company, and so both the Preferred Stockholders and the Company have the same rights and limitations. And he insists that because both parties agree a

---

9. A Change of Control, as defined in the Articles, Section 6(a), occurs when (i) there is a merger and (ii) neither the Company (CapLease) nor the surviving entity (ARCP) have a class of common securities listed on the NYSE or NASDAQ. ARCP is a publicly traded company on the NYSE, and so the parties agree that the Merger was not a Change of Control.

Many of the provisions in the Articles are not triggered until there is a Change of Control. As CapLease explains, such provisions, including Section 9, serve to "ensur[e] that, as the result of a particular type of transaction, preferred stockholders are not left holding preferred stock in a privately held company with no opportunity either to exercise voting rights or liquidate their holdings."

Change of Control did not result from the Merger, neither he nor CapLease had any ability to convert the preferred shares into cash.

CapLease responds that Section 9 creates a conversion right only in the *holders* of preferred stock, and the plain language supports this reading. CapLease points as well to the definition of "convertible," which indicates "[a] security (usually a bond or preferred stock) that may be exchanged by the owner for another security." We agree with the circuit court that "[Section 9] establishes a limitation upon the right of Preferred Stockholders to convert their stock ...," and that this right, whatever its bounds, isn't triggered by this Merger.

Mr. Poling points as well to Sections 3, 4, 5, and 6 of the Articles, each of which, he claims, defines the limited circumstances under which Preferred Stockholders can be "defeased." We agree with the Company, though, that in defining the rights and obligations they define, none of these provisions limits CapLease from taking any other action authorized by Maryland corporate law. If anything, the Articles' careful delineation of the Preferred Stockholders' rights and CapLease's obligations bolsters our view that the Articles left CapLease free to close this Merger.

Section 3 establishes a preferential right to dividends: "Holders of Series B Preferred Stock shall be entitled to receive, when and as authorized by the Board of Directors and declared by the Company . . . cumulative preferential cash dividends at the rate of. . . ." Section 4 explains the stockholders' rights in the event of the Company's liquidation, dissolution or winding up (as Section 4 defines a liquidation, this Merger is not an event that triggers liquidation rights). Section 5 states that preferred stock may not be redeemed before a specified date unless necessary for the Company to maintain REIT status, and the stock is otherwise redeemable at the Company's option after the specified dates. The clause sets the redemption price at $25 per share plus accumulated and unpaid dividends. Section 6 provides CapLease with a "Special Option Redemption," under which CapLease may redeem some or all stock at the redemption price upon a Change of Control. Section 7 clarifies that preferred stockholders do "not have any voting rights, except as set forth" in that section. Nothing in these provisions supports Mr. Poling's views of the Company's rights vis-à-vis the Preferred Stockholders; the Articles themselves, read as a whole, reinforce the circuit court's decision and our agreement with it.

We agree with the circuit court as well that Rauch v. RCA Corp., 861 F.2d 29 (2d Cir.1988), is instructive. In that case, RCA merged with General Electric Company and converted preferred stock into the right to receive cash. The stockholder claimed the transaction was an illegal redemption, but the court found it to be a permissible conversion. As we have here, *Rauch* looked first to Delaware statutory corporate law, which authorized mergers and the conversion of shares to cash to effectuate a merger. *See* id. at 30 (noting that a conversion to cash was "legally distinct" from a redemption of shares by the corporation). The court then examined the Preferred Stockholders' contract with RCA and found nothing expressly prohibiting a cash-out merger: "Nothing in RCA's [contract] indicated that the holders of Preferred Stock could initiate a redemption, nor was there provision for any specified event, such as the [merger], to trigger a redemption." The circuit court here conducted its inquiry in the same manner as the *Rauch* court—statute first, then contract—and achieved the same result.

Rauch relied heavily on *Rothschild Int'l Corp. v. Liggett Grp.,* in which the Supreme Court of Delaware explained that "where a merger of corporations is permitted by law, a shareholder's preferential rights are subject to defeasance. Stockholders are charged with knowledge of this possibility at the time they acquire their shares." 474 A.2d 133, 136–37 (Del.1984). Just as the circuit court did here, *Rauch* held that "because the merger [ ] was permitted by law, [the company] legitimately chose to structure their transaction in the most effective way to achieve the desired corporate reorganization, and were subject only to a similar duty to deal fairly." Rauch, 861 F.2d at 32.

When analyzed against the correct legal backdrop, Mr. Poling's breach of contract claim could not survive CapLease's motion to dismiss. "[A] complaint alleging a breach of contract 'must of necessity allege with certainty and definiteness *facts* showing a contractual obligation owed by the defendant to the plaintiff and a breach of that obligation by defendant.' As we've explained, it doesn't matter that the Merger did not fit the criteria specified in the Articles for redemption or conversion, and he's wrong that the absence of these "defeasance" conditions means the Company lacked authority to exchange the preferred stock for cash as a condition of the Merger. The authority to merge on the agreed terms, including the exchange of preferred shares for cash, flowed to the Company from the Code, and nothing in the Articles limited it.

PROBLEM SET 13.2

1. The preferred shareholders won in the *Avatex* case, but should preferred shareholders generally look to the Delaware courts for protection?
2. Does DGCL §242(b) provide greater protection for preferred shareholders if the company instead proceeds by way of charter amendment? *See* Hartford Accident & Indemnity Co. v. W.S. Dickey Clay Mfg. Co., 24 A.2d 315 (Del. 1942). Would preferred shareholders be better off under California law? California Corporations Code §903.
3. Draft a term to provide Mr. Poling the protection he apparently wanted as a preferred shareholder of CapLease, Inc.

3.   APPRAISAL RIGHTS OF PREFERRED SHARES

IN RE APPRAISAL OF METROMEDIA INTERNATIONAL GROUP, INC.

971 A.2d 893
Court of Chancery of Delaware
April 16, 2009

CHANDLER, Chancellor.

In this consolidated appraisal proceeding, dissenting petitioners seek a judicial determination of the "fair value" of the 7.25% Cumulative Convertible Preferred Stock of respondent Metromedia International Group, Inc. ("MIG"). This litigation arises from the August 22, 2007 merger of CaucusCom Mergerco Corp. ("MergerSub"), a wholly-owned subsidiary of CaucusCom Ventures, L.P. ("CaucusCom"), with MIG, in which MIG was the surviving entity. The merger occurred after MergerSub had already acquired in a tender offer approximately 77% of MIG's outstanding common shares. After the tender offer, the merger agreement between MIG, CaucusCom, and MergerSub granted MergerSub the option (referred to as the "Top-Up Option"), which MergerSub exercised, to obtain additional common shares from MIG in order to raise MergerSub's ownership stake to 90%. The Top-Up Option was followed by a short-form merger under 8 *Del. C.*§253 in which the remaining common shares were cashed out, and which led to this appraisal proceeding.

MIG asserts that the highest value of the preferred shares is based on the preferred's being converted into common shares under the certificate of designation. According to MIG, the certificate of designation imposed limitations on the consideration that preferred holders would receive upon conversion, which tops out at $18.07 for each preferred share. In contrast, petitioners rely upon three different valuation approaches, which yield a range of values from $67.50 per share to $79.76 per share. They view their methodologies as vindicated by virtue of their "convergence" on the preferred stock's $79.76 redemption price under the certificate of designation, even though (as I determine) no redemption has ever occurred.

The case was tried before the Court on December 12, 15, 16, and 17, 2008. This is the Court's post-trial decision. After considering the record of over 220 exhibits, the testimony of one fact and three expert witnesses, and having weighed all of the evidence, I determine the fair value of MIG preferred shares on August 22, 2007 to be $38.92 for each share. I also award interest on this amount at the statutorily prescribed rate.

In September 1997, when MIG issued the preferred shares, MIG's total enterprise value was approximately $1 billion. MIG owned all or part of telecommunications businesses in fourteen countries throughout Eastern Europe, the republics of the former Soviet Union, and other emerging markets. . . . As of the time of the Merger, the accrued and unpaid dividends totaled $121,732,028, or $29.40 for each preferred share. . . . Salford Capital Partners Inc. ("Salford")] is a private equity investment management firm that specializes in the former Soviet Union and other Central and Eastern European countries. . . . Sun Capital Partners Ltd., a United Kingdom principal investment group ("Sun"), joined Salford as a partner in the discussions with MIG regarding a tender offer. . . . Salford and Sun agreed with MIG to include a back-end merger as part of the transaction

II. ANALYSIS

A preferred shareholder's rights are defined in either the corporation's certificate of incorporation or in the certificate of designation, which acts as an amendment to a certificate of incorporation. Thus, rights of preferred shareholders are contractual in nature and the "construction of preferred stock provisions are matters of contract interpretation for the courts."

This proposition of contract interpretation for preferred stock is interwoven with a stockholder's statutory right of appraisal. Generally, in an appraisal action, this Court has broad discretion and uses a "liberal approach" in considering "all relevant factors involving the value of a company," to independently determine the "fair price" of the stock. Narrowly interpreted "speculative elements of value," usually contemplated synergies or speculative *pro forma* projections, are eliminated from consideration. Moreover, this Court will consider "proof of value by any techniques or methods which are generally considered acceptable in the financial community and otherwise admissible in court." Methods approved by this Court in determining fair value include the discounted cash flow valuation methodology, the comparable transactions approach, and the comparable company analysis. Each approach is dependent on the reliability of its inputs and is limited by the similarities between the companies or transactions being compared.

The law of Delaware governing contracts is clear: a valid contract will be enforced unless the contract violates public policy or positive law, or unless a party's non-performance is excused. Given the contractual nature of preferred stock, a clear contractual provision that establishes the value of preferred stock in the event of a cash-out merger is not inconsistent with the language or the policy of §262. Thus, the most critical question in this action is whether the certificate of designation, which establishes the rights of MIG's preferred shares, contractually establishes the metric for valuing the preferred shares in the event of a merger. I conclude that it does, which effectively renders irrelevant many of the underlying disputes among the testifying experts over the competing valuation models.

Unlike common stock, the value of preferred stock is determined solely from the contract rights conferred upon it in the certificate of designation. The only reported post-*Weinberger* opinion involving an appraisal of preferred stock, *In re Appraisal of Ford Holdings, Inc. Preferred Stock*, demonstrates the primacy of contract as the measure of the preferred's value. There, former-Chancellor Allen analyzed the rights conferred upon preferred shareholders by the certificate of designation because, "[t]o the extent it possesses any special rights or powers and to the extent it is restricted or limited in any way, the relation between the holder of the preferred and the corporation is contractual." When determining the fair value of preferred stock, therefore, I must first look to the contract upon which the preferred stock's value is based. In other words, the valuation of preferred stock must be viewed through the defining lens of its certificate of designation, unless the certificate is ambiguous or conflicts with positive law. As former-Chancellor Allen recognized in *Ford Holdings*, statutory appraisal rights can be modified or relinquished by contract, but in the case of unclear or indirect drafting, this Court will not "cut stockholders off from a statutory right" to judicial appraisal of their preferred shares.

Turning to the facts of this case, I conclude that MIG's certificate of designation clearly and unambiguously delimits the value to which preferred stockholders are entitled in the event of a merger. The certificate fixes the precise value to be paid to the preferred holders upon a merger event. I begin with Section 8(a) of the certificate of designation, which provides:

> Each holder of Preferred Stock shall have the right, at its option, at any time and from time to time from the Issue Date to convert, *subject to the terms and provisions of this Section 8*, any or all of such holder's shares of Preferred Stock. In such a case, the shares of Preferred Stock shall be converted into such number of fully paid and nonassessable shares of Common Stock as is equal, *subject to Section 8(g)*, to the product of the number of shares of Preferred Stock being so converted multiplied by the quotient of (i) the Liquidation Preference plus any Accumulated Dividends and any Accrued Dividends to and including the date of conversion divided by (ii) the Conversion Price (as defined below) then in effect, except that with respect to any share which shall be called for redemption such right shall terminate at the close of business on the date of redemption of such share, unless the Company shall default in performance or payment due upon exchange or redemption thereof. The Conversion Price shall be $15.00, subject to adjustment as set forth in Section 8(c).

The rights granted to the preferred shares in Section 8(a), however, are "subject to" the provisions of Section 8(g). Turning to Section 8(g), it states in part:

> In case of any capital reorganization or reclassification or other change of outstanding shares of Common Stock (other than a change in par value . . .) or *in case of any consolidation or merger* of the Company with or into another Person . . . *each share of Preferred Stock then outstanding shall, without the consent of any holder of Preferred Stock, become convertible only into* the kind and amount of shares of stock or other securities (of the Company or another issuer) or *property or cash receivable upon such [merger] by a holder of the number of shares of Common Stock into which such share of Preferred Stock could have been converted immediately prior to such [merger]* after giving effect to any adjustment event. The provisions of this Section 8(g) and any equivalent thereof in any such certificate similarly shall apply to successive [mergers]. *The provisions of this Section 8(g) shall be the sole right of holders of Preferred Stock*

3. **Appraisal Rights of Preferred Shares**

in connection with any [merger] and such holders shall have no separate vote thereon.

Section 8(g) effectively determines the value to be paid to preferred holders upon certain events. It is triggered by a merger, and the preferred holders' shares, without their consent, are to be valued as if they had been converted immediately before the merger. Here, a short-form merger followed immediately after the tender offer closed. Thus, the "sole right" available to MIG's preferred holders under the certificate of designation was the non-consensual conversion procedure under Section 8(g).

Section 8(g) also defines the formula for determining the value of preferred shares upon a merger or like transaction:

> [E]ach share of Preferred Stock then outstanding *shall, without the consent of any holder of Preferred Stock, become convertible only into* the kind and amount of shares of stock or other securities . . . or property or *cash receivable upon such [merger] by a holder of the number of shares of Common Stock into which such share of Preferred Stock could have been converted* immediately prior to such [merger] after giving effect to any adjustment event.

This language defines the consideration to which preferred shares are entitled in a merger because it stipulates that the preferred "becomes convertible" into the cash received in the merger by the number of common shares into which the preferred holder "could have been converted" immediately before the merger. In this case, pursuant to Section 8(a), every preferred holder immediately before the merger could have converted each preferred share into 5.29 shares of common stock.

Importantly, Section 8(g) operates as a non-consensual conversion provision, treating the preferred on a merger event as though they have converted ("become convertible" and "which could have been converted"). It could not be more clear on this point: if there is a merger, the preferred holder must accept ("without consent") a conversion into common stock, calculated pursuant to the certificate's formula in Section 8(a).

Therefore, because the cash receivable upon the merger for each common share was $1.80, Section 8(a) sets the amount receivable after the merger for each preferred holder to $9.52 per share (1.80 × 5.29). Section 8(g), however, is not the only value-adding contractual provision triggered by the merger. Section 8(b) also mandates that:

> When shares of Preferred Stock are converted *pursuant to this Section 8, all Accumulated Dividends and all Accrued Dividends* (whether or not declared or currently payable) on the Preferred Stock so converted to (and not including) the date of conversion *shall be immediately due and payable*, at the Company's option, (i) in cash; (ii) in a number of fully paid and nonassessable shares of Common Stock equal to the quotient of (A) the amount of Accumulated Dividends and Accrued Dividends payable to the holders of Preferred Stock hereunder,

divided by (B) the Market Value for the period ending on the date of conversion; or (iii) a combination thereof.

Since 8(g) is triggered by the merger, mandating the conversion of each preferred share into 5.29 common shares, 8(b) is also triggered, mandating the payment of the $29.40 in accumulated and accrued dividends. This provision 8(b) is applicable to Section 8 in its entirety and is not subordinate to Section 8(g). Section 8(b) is incorporated into the calculation of value under 8(g) by the clear provision that Section 8(b) applies to *all* of Section 8.

Turning briefly to the gist of petitioners' arguments, they insist that there are alternative value-adding provisions in the certificate of designation (other than Sections 8(g) and 8(b)) that were triggered by the merger. Specifically, they point to: (1) Section 7, granting the preferred shares a liquidation preference amounting to $50.00 for each preferred share, and (2) Section 3, granting MIG the right to redeem each preferred share at $50.00. Petitioners essentially ask this Court to award an appraisal value based on "hypothetical" scenarios—what preferred holders would have been entitled to had their stock been redeemed or had there been a liquidation event. Their expert's valuation models turn on assumptions about what an economically rational MIG board "ought" to do in the future— whether redeem or liquidate—in order to meet notions of an efficient capital market. These views are based on a fundamental misconception of the contractual obligations imposed by the certificate, a few examples of which should illustrate the fallacy of petitioners' position.

I turn first to the fallacy that the merger constituted a redemption under Section 3 of the certificate of designation. Section 3 defines the redemption value of the preferred shares by setting the redemption price at $50.00 for each share. Section 3.1 grants MIG the option to redeem the preferred shares. Under the certificate of designation, redemption would also trigger payment of the $29.40 in accrued and unpaid dividends.

Petitioners argue that redemption of the preferred shares will occur because it is likely that Salford will seek a liquidity event for MIG in the next three to five years. Salford is a private equity investor. Robert Brokaw, petitioners' expert witness, testified that a redemption period of three to five years is industry standard for private equity investors and provides the best internal rates of return on investments. Brokaw also opined that in the event Salford exits its investment in MIG, it would make no sense to keep the preferred shares in perpetuity and not pay dividends because defaulted securities in the capital structure will impair Salford's ability to achieve the highest multiple in a sale. Thus, the theory goes, Salford will leave money on the table when it attempts to exit its investment in MIG unless it voluntarily redeems the preferred shares and becomes current on the accumulated and accrued dividends.

The problem with this argument is that petitioners assume that Salford's exit will result in a redemption. In so assuming, they fail to consider various exit strategies available to Salford that would not require redemption of the preferred shares. For example, a potential buyer could enter into a transaction similar to the transaction Salford and MIG effectuated in this case, such as a tender offer and the purchase of the common shares directly from Salford. Alternatively, MIG could conduct an IPO of MIG or sell its shares in Magticom. Brokaw's assumption is thus speculative in that it assumes the probability of a future event, that is not certain to occur, and that has not occurred as of the appraisal date. Salford has every incentive to avoid entering into a transaction that would cause redemption of the preferred shares. Moreover, the preferred holders are only entitled to the value provided for in the certificate of designation. The certificate does not contemplate the probability of future events, regardless of the industry standard or what would amount to Salford's optimal outcome. The probability that redemption will occur seems remote, is at least speculative, and is not supported by the certificate of designation. Thus, it is no basis on which I may determine "fair value" in this appraisal proceeding.

Petitioners further contend that the events of the merger constituted an effective redemption because the common shareholders received value ahead of the preferred holders in violation of the preferred's seniority in MIG's capital structure. As I stated above, the events of the merger complied with the provisions of the certificate of designation. The common shareholders did not receive any value that violated any expressly contemplated rights granted to the preferred under the certificate. If the parties had intended that a transaction, such as the merger, constituted an "effective redemption" of the preferred holders then they should have included language to that effect in the contract. The absence of such language in an otherwise clear and unambiguous contract leads me to the opposite conclusion—the events of the merger did not operate as an effective redemption of the preferred shares.

I turn finally, and briefly, to the liquidation value of the preferred shares under Section 7 of the certificate of designation. Section 7.1 provides:

> In the event of any liquidation, dissolution or winding-up of the Company, whether voluntary or involuntary, the holders of the shares of Preferred Stock shall be entitled to receive out of the assets of the Company available for distribution to stockholders up to the Liquidation Preference plus Accumulated Dividends and Accrued Dividends thereon in preference to the holders of, and before any distribution is made on, any Junior stock, including, without limitation, on any Common Stock.

Petitioners argue that the merger resulted in a liquidation of MIG entitling the preferred shares to the liquidation preference of $50.00 for each share plus the accumulated and accrued dividends. This argument is equally without merit. "The right to be paid the amount due in the event of a liquidation or a redemption arises only in the circumstances specified in the preferred stock terms." Section 7.2 of the certificate of designation specifically states that:

> Neither the sale, conveyance, exchange or transfer . . . of all or substantially all the property and assets of the Company nor the merger or consolidation of the Company into or with any other corporation . . . shall be deemed to be a

liquidation, dissolution or winding up, voluntary or involuntary, for the purposes of this Section 7.

Salford purchased the common shares of MIG pursuant to a tender offer, a Top-Up Option, and a §253 short-form merger. Under a plain reading of the certificate of designation, these events have not resulted in a "liquidation," "dissolution" or "winding-up" of MIG. To the contrary, MIG continues as a going concern. No event triggering the liquidation provision has occurred, and thus to base valuation decisions on assumptions that it did would be error.

None of the alternative value-adding sections of MIG's certificate of designation have been triggered and, thus, these untriggered contract rights offer no non-speculative value upon which this Court is entitled to rely in an appraisal proceeding. Accordingly, the "sole right" available to the preferred holders in the event of merger, as explicitly set forth in the certificate of designation, is the nonconsensual conversion right under Section 8(g), which also triggered payment of the accumulated and accrued dividends under Section 8(b). As described above, that right, the preferred holders "sole right" under the certificate, yields a value of $38.92 per share of preferred stock. Preferred holders who acquired their stock in 1997 for $50 may be disappointed that ten years later their stock was worth only 78% of its original issuance price, just as common stockholders who paid $12 in 1997 are no doubt disappointed to realize only 15% of their purchase price, but these consequences flow from the certificate and the market, not from the vagaries of financial methodologies applied in appraisal proceedings. Where the rights of preferred shareholders in the event of a merger are clearly stated in the certificate of designation, those shareholders cannot come to this Court seeking additional consideration in the merger through the appraisal process.

PROBLEM SET 13.3

1. The court interprets section 8(g)—"*each share of Preferred Stock then outstanding shall, without the consent of any holder of Preferred Stock, become convertible only into the kind and amount of shares of stock or other securities*"—as effectively requiring conversion of the shares. What is the effect of this interpretation, and what other interpretation might the preferred shareholders have argued for?

2. Why might the preferred shareholders wanted to have exited the firm after the merger? *Dalton v. Am. Inv. Co.,* 501 A.2d 1238 (Del. 1985).

3. The appraisal remedy is often thought to have its roots in the historic ability of shareholders to veto mergers—throughout most of the nineteenth century mergers required unanimous shareholder approval. Appraisal rights were given in exchange for loss of these strong voting rights. In this context, does it make sense to allow preferred shareholders to bring appraisal actions?

4. Note that appraisal rights can be modified or waived by the terms of the preferred shares. *Matter of Appraisal of Ford Holdings, Inc. Preferred Stock*, 698 A.2d 973 (Del. Ch. 1997).

4. FIDUCIARY DUTIES TO PREFERRED SHAREHOLDERS

As you no doubt remember from Business Associations, or earlier in this course, the primary protections for shareholders under state corporate law are voting rights and fiduciary duties. Because preferred shareholders often have given up their voting rights by contract, fiduciary duties remain their only possible means of protection if the terms of the contract come up short.

MARILYN JEDWAB v. MGM GRAND HOTELS, INC.

509 A.2d 584

Court of Chancery of Delaware, New Castle County.

April 11, 1986.

ALLEN, Chancellor.

MGM Grand Hotels, Inc., a Delaware corporation ("MGM Grand" or the "Company") that owns and operates resort hotels and gaming establishments in Las Vegas and Reno, Nevada, has entered into an agreement with Bally Manufacturing Corporation, also a Delaware corporation, ("Bally") contemplating a merger between a Bally subsidiary and the Company. On the effectuation of such merger, all classes of the Company's presently outstanding stock will be converted into the right to receive cash.

Defendant Kerkorian individually and through Tracinda Corporation, which he wholly owns, beneficially owns 69% of MGM Grand's issued and outstanding common stock and 74% of its only other class of stock, its Series A Redeemable Preferred Stock (the "preferred stock" or simply the "preferred"). Mr. Kerkorian took an active part in negotiating the proposed merger with Bally and agreed with Bally to vote his stock in favor of the merger. Since neither the merger agreement nor the Company's charter contains a provision conditioning such a transaction on receipt of approval by a greater than majority vote, Mr. Kerkorian's agreement to vote in favor of the merger assured its approval.

Neither Kerkorian nor any director or officer of MGM Grand is affiliated with Bally either as an owner of its stock, or as an officer or director. Nor, so far as the record discloses, has any such person had a business or social relationship with Bally or any director, officer or controlling person of Bally. Bally—at least prior to its obtaining an option on Kerkorian's shares as part of the negotiation of the agreement of merger—has owned no stock in MGM Grand.

Plaintiff is an owner of the Company's preferred stock. She brings this action as a class action on behalf of all owners of such stock other than Kerkorian and Tracinda and seeks to enjoin preliminarily and permanently the effectuation of the proposed merger. The gist of the theory urged as justifying the relief sought is that the effectuation of the proposed merger would constitute a breach of a duty to deal fairly with the preferred shareholders owed to such shareholders by Kerkorian, as a controlling shareholder of MGM Grand, and by the directors of the Company. The merger is said to constitute a wrong to the preferred shareholders principally in that it allegedly contemplates an unfair apportionment among the Company's shareholders of the total consideration to be paid by Bally upon effectuation of the merger. Pending is plaintiff's motion for a preliminary injunction.

II.

Plaintiff claims that the proposed merger constitutes a breach of a fiduciary duty owed by the directors of MGM Grand and its controlling shareholder to the preferred stockholders. As developed at oral argument, the central aspect of plaintiff's theory of liability involves a breach of the duty of loyalty, although plaintiff contends as well that the manner in which the merger was negotiated and approved constitutes a breach of a duty of care.

The main argument advanced by plaintiff is premised upon the assertion that the directors of a Delaware corporation have a duty in a merger transaction to negotiate and approve only a merger that apportions the merger consideration fairly among classes of the company's stock. To unfairly favor one class of stock over another is, on this view, a breach of the duty of loyalty that a director owes to the corporation and, by extension, that he owes equally to all of its shareholders. Asserting factually that under all the circumstances the two outstanding classes of MGM Grand's stock represent equivalent values, plaintiff contends that the proposed Bally merger which does not apportion the merger consideration equally breaches this duty.

Intertwined with this central contention, are a host of other liability theories, including arguments (1) that the board of MGM Grand violated its duty of care in negotiating and approving the merger (relying heavily in that connection on the recent holding of our Supreme Court in *Smith v. Van Gorkom*, Del.Supr., 488 A.2d 858 (1985)); (2) that in instigating the merger at this time and in arrogating to himself the power to negotiate the terms of the merger on behalf of the corporation, Kerkorian (without regard to the specific terms ultimately agreed upon) acted without legal authority and in breach of duties to the preferred; and (3) that the merger constitutes a manipulation of the corporate machinery of the Company in order to avoid paying the preferred a $20 redemption price.

IV.

Initially I address two preliminary although critical legal questions: first, whether, in these circumstances, defendants owe any fiduciary duties to the preferred at all and, second, what standard—entire fairness or business judgment—is appropriate to assess the probability of ultimate success.

A.

Issue on the merits of claims alleged is first joined on the fundamental question whether the directors of MGM Grand owe *any* duty to the holders of the preferred stock other than the duty to accord to such holders the rights, powers and preferences set out in the certificate designating and defining the legal rights of the preferred. As I understand plaintiff's principal theories of liability each is premised upon the existence of a supervening fiduciary duty recognized in equity that requires directors and controlling shareholders to treat shareholders fairly. *See, Weinberger v. UOP, Inc.*, Del.Supr., 457 A.2d 701 (1983); *Sterling v. Mayflower Hotel Corp.*, Del.Supr., 93 A.2d 107 (1952); *Guth v. Loft, Inc.*, Del.Supr., 5 A.2d 503 (1939). If there is no such duty insofar as preferred stockholders are concerned plaintiff's theories of liability would seem fatally flawed.

Defendants contend there is no broad duty of fidelity owed to preferred stock if that duty is understood to extend beyond the specific contractual terms defining the special rights, preferences or limitations of the preferred. In support of its position on this point defendants cite such cases as *Rothschild International Corp. v. Liggett Group, Inc.*, Del.Supr., 474 A.2d 133 (1984); *Wood v. Coastal States Gas Corp.*, Del.Supr., 401 A.2d 932 (1979) and *Dart v. Kohlberg, Kravis, Roberts & Co.*, Del.Ch., C.A. No. 7366, Hartnett, V.C. (May 6, 1985). Broadly speaking these cases apply the rule that "preferential rights are contractual in nature and therefore are governed by the express provisions of a company's certificate of incorporation" *Rothschild, supra*, 474 A.2d at 136. Defendants restate this accepted principle as meaning "all rights of preferred shareholders are contractual in nature." They then go on to argue (analogizing to the wholly contractual rights of bondholders—as to which no "fiduciary" duties extend) that the only duties directors have to preferred shareholders are those necessary to accord the preferred rights set out in their contract, i.e., the document designating the rights, preferences, etc., of their special stock.

The flaw in this argument lies in a failure to distinguish between "preferential" rights (and special limitations) on the one hand and rights associated with all stock on the other. At common law and in the absence of an agreement to the contrary all shares of stock are equal. *Shanghai Power Co. v. Delaware Trust Co.*, Del. Ch., 316 A.2d 589 (1974). Thus preferences and limitations associated with preferred stock exist only by virtue of an express provision (contractual in nature) creating such rights or limitations. But absent negotiated provision conferring rights on preference stock, it does not follow that no right exists. The point may be conclusively demonstrated by two examples. If a certificate designating rights, preferences, etc. of special stock contains *no* provision dealing with voting rights or *no* provision creating rights upon liquidation, it is not the fact that such stock has no voting rights or no rights upon liquidation. Rather, in such circumstances, the preferred stock has the same voting rights as common stock (8 *Del.C.*§212(a); *Rice & Hutchins, Inc. v. Triplex Shoe Co.*, Del.Ch., 147 A. 317 (1929) *aff'd.*, 152 A. 342 (1930)) or the same rights to participate in the liquidation of the corporation as has such stock (11 W. Fletcher Cyclopedia of the Law of Private Corporations §5303 (rev. perm. ed. 1971); *Continental Insurance Company v. Reading Company*, 259 U.S. 156, 42 S.Ct. 540, 66 L.Ed. 71, 871 (1922)).

Thus, with respect to matters relating to preferences or limitations that distinguish preferred stock from common, the duty of the corporation and its directors is essentially contractual and the scope of the duty is appropriately defined by reference to the specific words evidencing that contract; where however the right asserted is not to a preference as against the common stock but rather a right shared equally with the common, the existence of such right and the scope of the correlative duty may be measured by equitable as well as legal standards.

With this distinction in mind the Delaware cases which frequently analyze rights of and duties towards preferred stock in legal (i.e., contractual) terminology (*e.g., Wood v. Coastal States Gas Corp., supra; Judah v. Delaware Trust Company*, Del.Supr., 378 A.2d 624 (1977); *Rothschild International Corp. v. Liggett Group, Inc., supra*) may be made consistent with those cases that apply fiduciary standards to claims of preferred shareholders (*e.g., David J. Greene & Co. v. Schenley Industries, Inc.*, Del.Ch., 281 A.2d 30 (1971); *Lewis v. Great Western United Corporation*, Del.Ch., C.A. No. 5397, Brown, V.C. (September 15, 1977)).

Accordingly, without prejudging the validity of any of plaintiff's liability theories, I conclude that her claim (a) to a "fair" allocation of the proceeds of the merger; (b) to have the defendants exercise appropriate care in negotiating the proposed merger and (c) to be free of overreaching by Mr. Kerkorian (as to the timing of the merger for his benefit) fairly implicate fiduciary duties and ought not be evaluated wholly from the point of view of the contractual terms of the preferred stock designations.

B.

Assuming that plaintiff and the other preferred shareholders have a "right" recognized in equity to a fair apportionment of the merger consideration (and such a right to require directors to exercise appropriate care) it becomes material to know what legal standard is to be used to assess the probability that a violation of that right will ultimately be proven. Plaintiff asserts that the appropriate test is one of entire or intrinsic fairness. That test is the familiar one employed when fiduciaries elect to utilize their power over the corporation to effectuate a transaction in which they have an interest that diverges from that of the corporation or the minority shareholders. *See, Weinberger v. UOP, Inc., supra; Gottlieb v. Heyden Chemical Corp.*, Del.Supr., 91 A.2d 57 (1952).

Our Supreme Court has made it quite clear that the heightened judicial scrutiny called for by the test of intrinsic or entire fairness is not called forth simply by a demonstration that a controlling shareholder fixes the terms of a transaction and, by exercise of voting power or by domination of the board, compels its effectuation. (The apparent situation presented in this action.) It is in each instance essential to show as well that the fiduciary has an interest with respect to the transaction that conflicts with the interests of minority shareholders. *Aronson v. Lewis*, Del.Supr., 473 A.2d 805, 812 (1984). Speaking in the context of a parent dealing with a controlled but not wholly-owned subsidiary our Supreme Court has said:

> The basic situation for the application of the rule [requiring a fiduciary to assume the burden to show intrinsic fairness] is the one in which the parent has received a benefit to the exclusion and at the expense of the subsidiary.

A parent does indeed owe a fiduciary duty to its subsidiary when there are parent-subsidiary dealings. However, this alone will not evoke the intrinsic fairness standard. This standard will be applied only when the fiduciary duty is accompanied by self-dealing—the situation when a parent is on both sides of a transaction with its subsidiary. Self-dealing occurs when the parent, by virtue of its domination of the subsidiary, causes the subsidiary to act in such a way that the parent receives something from the subsidiary to the exclusion of, and detriment to, the minority stockholders of the subsidiary.

Sinclair Oil Corporation v. Levien, Del.Supr., 280 A.2d 717, 720 (1971).

As to what appears to be the material element of the negotiation of the Bally merger—the $440,000,000 cash price—Mr. Kerkorian had no conflicting interest of a kind that would support invocation of the intrinsic fairness test. With respect to total price, his interest was to extract the maximum available price. Moreover, as to the apportionment of the merger consideration between the two classes of the Company's stock, Mr. Kerkorian's interest again appears to create no significant bias on his part since his ownership of each class is not only great but substantially equal. Indeed, as indicated, Kerkorian's ownership of the preferred is proportionately somewhat greater.

Thus, had Kerkorian apportioned the merger consideration equally among members of each class of the Company's stockholders (as distinguished from equally between classes of stock on a per share basis), then the fact of his substantially equivalent ownership of each class of stock would have supported invocation of the legal test known as the business judgment rule. *Aronson v. Lewis*, Del.Supr., 473 A.2d 805 (1984). The fact that each class was treated differently would not itself require application of the intrinsic fairness test. *See, MacFarlane v. North American Cement Corp.*, Del.Ch., 157 A. 396 (1928); *Bodell v. General Gas & Electric Corp.*, Del.Supr., 140 A. 264 (1927).

But Kerkorian directed the apportionment of merger consideration in a way that treated himself differently from other holders of common stock. He accorded to himself less cash per common share ($12.24) but, in the License Agreement, arrogated to himself the right to use or designate the use of the MGM Grand name and, under the Price Adjustment Agreement, he is to assume certain obligations and acquire certain rights with respect to pending property insurance claims of the Company.

I conclude [. . .] that, in apportioning that element of consideration wholly to his own shares to the exclusion of others Kerkorian was exercising power of a kind and in circumstances justifying invocation of the heightened standard of judicial review.

V.

I also conclude that, as to the claim of the preferred to an equal or fair share of the merger proceeds, the defendants are likely to meet the burden thus imposed upon them. It follows that plaintiff has failed to demonstrate a reasonable probability of success on this issue.

First, it seems elementary that the preferred has no *legal* right to equivalent consideration in the merger. Neither the certificate of incorporation nor the certificate of designation of the preferred stock expressly creates such a right. Nor does it appear that such a right may be fairly implied from those documents when read in the light of the terms of the 1982 Exchange Offer. *Cf., Katz v. Oak Industries, Inc.*, Del.Ch., 508 A.2d 873 (1986). Nor do I perceive any basis to recognize an *equitable* right to mathematically equal consideration based upon the conduct of Kerkorian as a fiduciary. Some of what is said below supports this conclusion.

As to a right of the preferred to have the total consideration fairly (as distinguished from equally) apportioned, the current record provides no persuasive basis to conclude that the allocation contemplated by the Bally merger is unfair.

Plaintiff's claim of unfairness in an apportionment of $18 per share to the common stockholders and $14 a share to the preferred, in my opinion, involves a fundamental defect: it rests upon an invalid comparison. The pertinent comparison, if one is treating a right to fair apportionment among classes of stock, is between what those *classes* receive in the merger, on a per share basis, not between what the class of preferred receive per share and what the public holders of common stock are to receive . . . when the financial value of the appropriate comparison is developed (to the extent the current record permits the development and evaluation of that comparison) it does not appear very great and certainly does not at this stage appear unsustainable in light of the differences in the rights of common and preferred stockholders and the historical treatment of both classes of stock by the market.

The foregoing evaluation of the probabilities of ultimate success forecloses the necessity for an evaluation of plaintiff's claim of irreparable injury. However, in denying the pending motion, I am sensitive to the interests of the public common stockholder and of Bally to have the proposed merger effectuated without judicial interference. While the complaint in conclusory language alleges that Bally knowingly participated in a breach of fiduciary duty, no specific facts are alleged—nor so far as the present record discloses have facts been uncovered in discovery—that would support that conclusion. In these circumstances, Bally's contract rights—while not dispositive—present an additional circumstance supporting the denial of the pending motion.

PROBLEM SET 13.4

1. What precisely is Chancellor Allen's approach to the duties owed to preferred shareholders?
2. One noted corporate law scholar has argued that preferred shareholder's rights should start and end with the terms of the preferred shares. [10] Beyond its ease of application, what arguments for and against such an approach can you think of?

---

10. http://goo.gl/6sbhN.

14

BOND INDENTURES

Before Virginia's colonial economy was rooted in African slavery, it first experimented with labor provided by indentured servants. The term *indenture* here refers to the contract that bound the laborers to terms of otherwise unpaid service in exchange for their passage to the New World from England.[1]

In early English law, an indenture was often used for conditional contracts, the name apparently coming from the ability to split the agreement in two parts along a notch at the top, so that each party could retain a piece of the agreement. As explained by a legal historian, when parties agreed to a debt that was conditional on performance of a number of terms, a

> sophisticated method, which was very commonly employed in the case of bilateral agreements, was to set out the terms of the agreement in the form of covenants in an indenture under seal; both parties could then retain one part of the indenture which they had executed. They could then both execute bonds of even date with the indenture, binding themselves to pay a sum of money unless the covenants in the indenture were performed.[2]

Today these terms—indenture, covenant, and bond—are all still used with regard to corporate and sovereign debt, but the agreements have been collapsed to a single, if still formidable, writing.

---

1. *See generally* Edmund S. Morgan, *American Slavery American Freedom: The Ordeal of Colonial Virginia* (1975).

2. A.W. Brian Simpson, *A History of the Common Law of Contract* 91 (1975).

QUADRANT STRUCTURED PRODUCTS CO., LTD. v. VERTIN

23 N.Y.3d 549
Court of Appeals of New York.
June 10, 2014.

RIVERA, J.

I.

The Delaware litigation underlying the certified questions is a reminder of the continued effects of the 2008 financial crisis and the economic fallout associated with the utilization of complex financial instruments that mask investment risk levels—*see generally* Kristin N. Johnson, *Things Fall Apart: Regulating the Credit Default Swap Commons*, 82 U. Colo. L. Rev. 167 [2011]. . . .

Against this backdrop of high-stakes securities transactions and downward spiraling financial fortunes, the certified questions present for our consideration familiar efforts to prohibit individual lawsuits of securityholders, by the use of a contractual provision referred to as a "no-action" clause.

II.

Quadrant Structured Products Company, Ltd. (Quadrant) sued several defendants in the Delaware Court of Chancery for alleged wrongdoing related to notes purchased by Quadrant and issued by defendant Athilon Capital Corp. (Athilon), a business which plaintiff alleges is now insolvent. Defendant EBF & Associates, LP (EBF) acquired Athilon in 2010, installed and now controls its Board. Like Quadrant, EBF holds certain Athilon issued securities. Defendants moved to dismiss the suit as barred by a no-action clause contained in the indenture agreement governing Quadrant's notes. The notes and indenture were a necessary part of Athilon's financing scheme, which has its roots in Athilon's initial formation. Athilon was founded in 2004 with $100 million in equity and, along with its wholly owned subsidiary Athilon Asset Acceptance Corp., sold credit derivative products in the form of "credit default swaps" which afforded credit protection for large financial institutions. . . . These credit default swaps provided that Athilon would pay the purchaser in the case of a default on the debt that was the subject of the swap. As a risk containment measure, Athilon's operating guidelines mandated that it invest conservatively, and that when certain "suspension events" occurred, enter "runoff mode"—a period during which it could not issue new credit swaps and was required to pay off existing swaps as claims arose.

As part of its capital raising strategy, Athilon incurred debt through the issuance of a series of securities, as relevant here, consisting of $350 million in senior subordinated notes, $200 million in three series of subordinated notes and $50 million in junior notes. Athilon raised $600 million in capital through this debt structure. Debt subordination is common in commercial finance, and as the name of these different classes of notes implies, payment of senior subordinated notes takes priority over payment of junior notes. Quadrant owns certain classes of these subordinated notes, including senior subordinated notes, while EBF owns junior notes.

As part of this debt financing, Athilon entered agreements, referred to as trust indentures (indentures), with two separate Trustees, who serve as third-party administrators of the issuance of the securities.[3] An indenture is essentially a written agreement that bestows legal title of the securities in a single Trustee to protect the interests of individual investors who may be numerous or unknown to each other. As is typical of these agreements, the Athilon indentures set forth Athilon's obligations as the issuer of the securities, the securityholders' rights and remedies in the case of Athilon's default on the provisions of the indenture, and the duties and obligations of the Trustee.

By 2008, Athilon had undertaken $50 billion in nominal credit default risk, far exceeding its $700 million in capital reserves . . . [and] in the aftermath of the 2008 financial crisis, in early 2009, Athilon and its subsidiary sustained several suspension events and entered into runoff mode as per its operating guidelines.

In October 2011, Quadrant sued Athilon, Athilon's officers and directors, EBF, and EBF affiliate Athilon Structured Investment Advisors LLC (ASIA), asserting various counts directly and derivatively as a creditor of Athilon. . . .

Defendants moved to dismiss, asserting that Quadrant's claims were barred by a no-action clause (Athilon clause) contained in article 7, § 7.06 of the indenture governing the subordinated notes. The Athilon clause provides:

> *"Limitations on Suits by Securityholder.* No holder of any Security shall have any right by virtue or by availing of any provision of this Indenture to institute any action or proceeding at law or in equity or in bankruptcy or otherwise upon or under or with respect to this Indenture, or for the appointment of a trustee, receiver, liquidator, custodian or other similar official or for any other remedy hereunder, unless such holder previously shall have given to the Trustee written notice of default in respect of the series of Securities held by such Securityholder and of the continuance thereof, as hereinbefore provided, and unless also the holders of not less than 50% of the aggregate principal amount of the relevant series of Securities at the time Outstanding shall have made written request upon the Trustee to institute such action or proceedings in its own name as trustee hereunder and shall have offered to the Trustee such reasonable indemnity as it may require against the costs, expenses and liabilities to be incurred therein or thereby and the Trustee for 60 days after its receipt of such notice, request and offer of indemnity shall have failed to institute any such action or proceedings and no direction inconsistent with such written request shall have been given to the Trustee pursuant to Section 7.08 hereof within such 60 days."

Defendants argued that the clause permitted only Trustee-initiated suits upon request of a majority of securityholders, and prohibited individual securityholder actions. In support of this argument defendants relied on . . . Delaware Court of

---

3. Deutsche Bank Trust Company serves as Trustee under the indenture governing subordinated notes, and The Bank of New York serves as Trustee pursuant to the indenture governing senior subordinated notes.

Chancery cases applying New York law, wherein the court dismissed the respective plaintiffs' claims based on a no-action clause. The clauses at issue in those cases barred a securityholder's action "with respect to this Indenture *or the Securities* unless [specified conditions are met]"

[T]he Delaware Supreme Court certified the following question[] to us:

"(1) A trust indenture no-action clause expressly precludes a security holder[,] who fails to comply with that clause's preconditions, from initiating any action or proceeding upon or under or with respect to 'this Indenture,' but makes no reference to actions or proceedings pertaining to 'the Securities.'"

III.

A.

In response to the first question, for the reasons discussed in detail below, we conclude that a no-action clause which by its language applies to rights and remedies under the provisions of the indenture agreement, but makes no mention of individual suits on the securities, does not preclude enforcement of a securityholder's independent common-law or statutory rights. We reach this conclusion based on the legal standards applicable to indenture agreements, as well as the analyses of no-action clauses in [the previous Delaware Court of Chancery cases], and cases from New York.

A trust indenture is a contract, and under New York law "[i]nterpretation of indenture provisions is a matter of basic contract law" (Sharon Steel Corp. v. Chase Manhattan Bank, N.A., 691 F.2d 1039, 1049 [2d Cir.1982]; *see also* . . . Racepoint Partners, LLC v. JP Morgan Chase Bank, N.A., 14 N.Y.3d 419 [2010] [same].

In construing a contract we look to its language, for "a written agreement that is complete, clear and unambiguous on its face must be enforced according to the plain meaning of its terms.". . .

Applying these well-established principles of contract interpretation, and with the understanding that no-action clauses are to be construed strictly and thus read narrowly, we turn to the language of the no-action clause presented by the certified question. The no-action clause here states that no securityholder "shall have any right *by virtue or by availing of any provision of this Indenture* to institute any action or proceeding at law or in equity or in bankruptcy or otherwise *upon or under or with respect to this Indenture. . . .*" The clear and unambiguous text of this no-action clause, with its specific reference to the indenture, on its face limits the clause to the contract rights recognized by the indenture agreement itself. Further supporting this construction of the clause is the sole textual reference to securities, which is contained in the clause's provision for a Trustee-initiated suit for a continuing "default in respect of the series of Securities." This part of the no-action clause permits the trustee to sue in its name, after notice by a securityholder of a continuing default and upon approval of the suit by a majority of securityholders. Thus, the clear import of the no-action clause is to leave a securityholder free to pursue independent claims involving rights not arising from the indenture agreement . . .

Defendants' argument that interpreting the no-action clause to exclude certain claims would upset the contracting parties' expectations is unpersuasive. The indenture itself defines "indenture" and "securities" separately, recognizing them as distinct. Therefore, defendants' functional equivalency argument is merely another version of the argument we have already rejected on the law: that the parties intended other than what the words in the document mean. As our law makes clear, we rely on the unambiguous terms of the agreement when construing contract provisions like the indenture no-action clause. Quadrant's claims are based not on the indenture agreement—under which the Trustee administers the debt issuance by Athilon—but rather arise from Quadrant's status as a securityholder. The parties could not have expected otherwise, given the plain language of the clause. If the parties sought to prohibit these types of suits, they were free to include them within the Athilon no-action clause.

What is the distinction between the indenture and the securities issued under the indenture that the New York Court of Appeals is drawing in this case? Do you find it convincing? Why might you want a "no action" clause in an indenture? What are the risks of such a clause?

MARCEL KAHAN, *RETHINKING CORPORATE BONDS: THE TRADE–OFF BETWEEN INDIVIDUAL AND COLLECTIVE RIGHTS*

77 NYU L. Rev. 1040, 1044–1047 (2002)

I.   THE STRUCTURE OF BONDHOLDER RIGHTS

With few exceptions, the bond indenture must comply with the provisions in the Trust Indenture Act. The Trust Indenture Act requires that a trustee be appointed as representative of the bondholders and specifies certain ground rules relating to eligibility and disqualification of the trustee. Most aspects of bondholder rights, however—including the substantive content of bondholder rights and most provisions relating to the modification and enforcement of these rights—are not regulated by the Trust Indenture Act and are thus left open to contracting. Though this means that each bond indenture could contain widely varying provisions, many bond provisions are standardized and included in a virtually identical form in each indenture.

A.   AN OVERVIEW OF SUBSTANTIVE BONDHOLDER RIGHTS

The contractual rights of bondholders fall into three categories: financial terms, protective covenants, and miscellaneous provisions. Beyond their contractual rights, bondholders—as creditors and security holders—have rights that arise under statutory and common law.

The most important right of bondholders is the right to receive payments of interest at stated intervals and payment of principal when the bonds mature. In addition, corporate bonds often contain other financial terms, the most important of which are optional redemption rights, sinking funds, put rights, conversion rights, and subordination clauses. Optional redemption (or call) provisions grant the company a right to repay its bonds prior to their maturity. By contrast, sinking fund (or mandatory redemption) provisions obligate the company to repay a specified portion of a bond issue prior to the final maturity of all bonds in that issue. Put rights, in turn, obligate the company, in specified circumstances, to repay the bonds of those bondholders who have elected to exercise their rights. Conversion rights permit bondholders to exchange their bonds for other securities, usually common stock, of the issuing company. Subordination clauses contain an agreement by bondholders to subordinate their right to receive payments from the company to the rights of other specified creditors.

Protective covenants are a second important set of bondholder rights. Designed to protect the bondholders' entitlement to receive payments from the company, protective covenants are limitations on the company's conduct of its business. The most common types of protective covenants in publicly issued bonds are debt restrictions, dividend restrictions, asset sale restrictions, investment restrictions, restrictions on mergers, restrictions on liens and sale/leasebacks, and restrictions on transactions with affiliates.

Beyond financial terms and protective covenants, and beyond the provisions related to amendment and enforcement . . . , bond indentures provide for a host of other bondholder rights. These provisions relate to matters such as the right to receive a replacement bond certificate should one's certificate get lost or stolen; the right to receive notice of a special payment date for the payment of defaulted interest; the right to receive notice of a redemption of bonds or of the fact that a put right has become exercisable; the right to have the conversion price adjusted in certain events; or the right of holders of subordinated bonds to be subrogated to the rights of holders of senior debt once all senior debt is paid in full.

In addition to these contractual rights, bondholders have rights that result from their status as creditors and securityholders. These include rights under fraudulent conveyance law, under provisions of corporation law designed to protect creditors, under federal securities laws and state blue-sky laws, under federal bankruptcy law, and under the common law of fraud.

1.   THE TRUST INDENTURE ACT

Until the New Deal, the terms of a bond indenture were subject to the normal rules of contract, supplemented by whatever moral obligation was felt by the key parties—namely the issuer and its underwriter bank. Following the 1929 Crash, and the subsequent Depression, this began to change.

In particular, future Supreme Court justice William O. Douglas led a series of SEC hearings into the treatment of bondholders in "equity receiverships," the corporate bankruptcy proceedings of the times.[4] Ultimately these hearings led to the federalization of corporate bankruptcy, and the enactment of the Trust Indenture Act.[5]

IN THE MATTER OF J.P. MORGAN & CO.
INCORPORATED FILE NO. 25-1
SECURITIES AND EXCHANGE COMMISSION

1941 SEC LEXIS 1210; 10 S.E.C. 119
September 19, 1941

FINDINGS AND OPINION OF THE COMMISSION

The questions before us in this proceeding concern the eligibility, under the Trust Indenture Act of 1939, of J.P. Morgan & Co. Incorporated to serve as indenture trustee for securities which may be issued and sold in the future by an obligor or obligors, at present unknown, for which Morgan Stanley & Co. Incorporated is or may be an underwriter.

By Sections 305(b) and 307(c) of the Act it is provided that this Commission, in an appropriate proceeding, shall issue an order refusing to permit a registration statement or application for the qualification of an indenture to become effective if the Commission finds, among other things, that any person designated as trustee under the indenture has any "conflicting interest," as that term is defined in Section 310(b) of the Act. As will be more fully developed further on in this opinion, one of the primary objectives of the Act is to ensure that the holders of bonds, debentures, notes, and other debt securities (referred to as "indenture securities") issued subject to the Act shall have the services of an effective and independent trustee. Among the conflicting interests which the Congress deemed detrimental to that objective, and which the Act provides shall render a person ineligible to serve as trustee under an indenture, are those which exist if—"(3) such trustee directly or indirectly controls or is directly or indirectly controlled by or is under direct or indirect common control with an obligor upon the indenture securities *or an underwriter for such an obligor"*; or if—"(6) such trustee is the beneficial owner of . . . (A) 5 per centum or more of the voting securities, or 10 per centum or more of any other class of security, of an obligor upon the indenture securities . . . or (B) *10 per centum or more of any class of security of an underwriter for any such obligor; . . .*"

The partnership of J.P. Morgan & Co., formed in 1894 as successor to the partnership of Drexel, Morgan & Co., carried on a commercial banking and agency business until 1940 and, until 1934, also a securities underwriting

---

4. Stephen J. Lubben, *Railroad Receiverships and Modern Bankruptcy Theory*, 89 Cornell L. Rev. 1420 (2004). *See also* Report on the Study and Investigation of the Work, Activities, Personnel and Functions of Protective and Reorganization Committees (1936).

5. 15 U.S.C. §§77aaa-77bbbb.

business. These businesses were carried on in New York under the name of J.P. Morgan & Co., and in Philadelphia under the name of Drexel & Co.

The requirement of the Banking Act of 1933 [commonly known as the Glass-Steagall Act] that the business of underwriting securities be separated from the business of commercial banking became effective in June of 1934. The major part of the business of J.P. Morgan & Co. had always been in the commercial banking and agency fields, and in addition, the securities markets had then been dormant for some time. Thus, when faced with the necessity of electing between commercial banking and the underwriting business, the partnership elected to continue its commercial banking activities.

3.   OBJECTIVES OF THE TRUST INDENTURE ACT.

The facts bearing on the relationship between the trust company and underwriter here involved must be considered in the light of the purposes and history of the Trust Indenture Act, with particular reference to the objectives Congress had in mind when it defined the conflicts of interest disqualifying the indenture trustee.

Among the primary purposes of the Act was the purpose to "assure that the security holders [holders of bonds, notes, debentures, and similar securities] will have the services of a *disinterested indenture trustee*. . . .

With this end in view, it is obvious why an indenture trustee should not be permitted to have a community of interest with an obligor on the indenture securities: for the creditor interests represented by the trustee will clearly be adverse to the interests of the obligor and its stockholders in the event of a default, or in a period when default is near. Moreover, their interests will be adverse in many ways throughout the life of the indenture securities, in respect of such matters as substitution of collateral, compliance with negative pledge clauses, disclosure of financial condition, declaration and payment of dividends, wasting or diversion of assets, and other matters.

It is equally true that there is danger in a community of interest between the indenture trustee and an underwriter for the obligor. Significantly, the Act treats such relationships as a problem to be met and a practice to be eliminated on virtually the same basis as a community of interest between the trustee and the obligor itself. Section 302 declares that

"the national public interest and the interest of investors in notes, bonds, debentures . . . [etc.], which are offered to the public, are adversely affected—

"(1) when the obligor fails to provide a trustee to protect and enforce the rights and to represent the interests of such investors . . .

"(2) when the trustee does not have adequate rights and powers, or adequate duties and responsibilities, in connection with matters relating to the protection and enforcement of the rights of such investors . . .

"*(3) When the trustee . . . has any relationship to or connection with the obligor or any underwriter of any securities of the obligor, or holds, beneficially or otherwise, any interest in the obligor or any such underwriter, which relationship,*

connection, or interest involves a material conflict with the interests of such investors;
"(b) Practices of the character above enumerated have existed to such an extent that, unless regulated, the public offering of notes, bonds, debentures, evidences of indebtedness, and certificates of interest or participation therein, by the use of means and instruments of transportation and communication in interstate commerce and of the mails, is injurious to the capital markets, to investors, and to the general public; *and it is hereby declared to be the policy of this title, in accordance with which policy all the provisions of this title shall be interpreted, to meet the problems and eliminate the practices, enumerated in this section, connected with such public offerings.*" (Italics supplied.)

Under clauses (2) to (6), inclusive, of Section 310(b), which defines various situations in which the indenture trustee shall be deemed to have a conflicting interest, various relationships with the underwriter are treated in exactly the same manner as relationships with the obligor. Thus a trustee is disqualified: if the trustee or any of its directors or executive officers is an *obligor* on the indenture securities or an *underwriter* for such an obligor (310(b)(2)); if the trustee controls, or is controlled by, or is under common control with, such an *obligor* or an *underwriter* for such an obligor (310(b)(3)); if the trustee or any of its directors or executive officers is a director, officer, partner, employee, appointee, or representative of such an *obligor* or of an *underwriter* for such an obligor (with certain exceptions favoring limited representation of the trustee in the management of the obligor) (310(b)(4)); if specified percentages of the trustee's voting securities are beneficially owned by such an *obligor*, its directors, partners or executive officers, or by an *underwriter* for such an obligor or by its directors, partners or executive officers (the test being more stringent with respect to the underwriter) (310(b)(5)); and if the trustee beneficially owns 5% of the voting securities or 10% of any other class of security of such an *obligor*, or 10% of any class of security of an *underwriter* for such an obligor (310(b)(6)).

The reasons impelling Congress to treat relationships with an underwriter on the same basis as relationships with the obligor are declared in the legislative history of the Act. It was, of course, recognized that indenture trustees must be given not only the power but also the duty to take affirmative action promptly for the benefit of their beneficiaries, and "should be made to live up to the responsibility which nearly every purchaser assumes it has, and which it represents to the public as having undertaken, in a sense, by the very advertisement of the designation 'trustee.'" Yet conferring adequate powers and imposing necessary duties upon the trustee in the indenture was not considered enough for the purpose. "Few of the indentures examined contained any restrictions upon the possession or acquisition by the trustee of interests materially conflicting with those of the bondholders. Some of the indentures specifically permitted them. It is difficult in many cases quantitatively to estimate the effect of too close affiliations with the obligor *or with the underwriters* of its outstanding securities . . . *It is clear, however, that the existence of such relationships does have a tendency to dilute the loyalty of the indenture trustee.*"

As was said by Commissioner (now Mr. Justice) Douglas, testifying before a subcommittee of the Senate:

"A further danger lurks in affiliations which a corporate trustee may have with the underwriters of the bonds under its indenture . . .

"*Such affiliations of the trustee with the underwriter*, whose objectives in reorganizations are frequently incompatible with those of investors, *tend to submerge the interests of the security holders and to make them subordinate to the wishes, desires, and possible selfish interests of the underwriter. The trustee will be either unable or unwilling to look at the situation coldly and objectively with a single eye to the protection of his beneficiaries.*"

Situations in which the interests of the underwriter were found to be incompatible with those of the security holders represented by the indenture trustee included default situations, in which the underwriters found it to their interest to conceal defaults and delay action thereon by the trustee at least long enough to permit them to set the stage for reorganization and obtain control of reorganization committees:

"In the minds of bondholders, default itself creates distrust and suspicion of the houses which originated and sold the bonds. Not much is required to fan this feeling of growing distrust and suspicion into a blazing fire of resentment against the houses of issue which may result in adverse publicity, litigation, and damage to any future business. In every default situation, regardless of the guilt or innocence of the houses of issue, there is present the possibility that a committee not controlled by the houses may take aggressive action of this sort. On the other hand, control of the committee—whether exerted by placing members of the house of issue directly on the committee or by insuring the selection of men acceptable to the house of issue—means control over the version of the situation presented to the bondholders through committee circulars, advertisements and answers to inquiries. It also means that if a friendly and cooperative plan of reorganization were worked out, the true facts as to the value of the property and the relation of the houses of issue to it could be kept permanently in their possession and not brought to light. It also means that there will not be a thorough investigation of possible causes of action against the houses of issue nor will there be litigation by the committees against them.

"In this manner the houses of issue will minimize the risk of their own liability to bondholders. In this manner they will also 'save face.' Through their mouthpiece—the protective committee—they can minimize the seriousness of the situation. They can blame mortgagors, depressions, and business cycles. They can divert criticism to those causes. They can, perhaps completely prevent the searching light of publicity being cast on their own misdeeds. They can, perhaps, lull bondholders into some sense of security by virtue of the fact that they, the houses of issue, are working assiduously in the cause of the investor. In this manner they can perhaps avoid facing the clamor of bondholders. By this method of control the bondholders may not get scent of the facts surrounding the issuance and sale of the securities. In this way perhaps vast majorities of bondholders can be induced to deposit their securities with the house of issue. Once that is accomplished effective control over foreclosure and reorganization has been attained. Minorities are rendered quite impotent. They cannot marshal enough support to make up the percentage necessary under the trust indenture to demand foreclosure or other enforcement of the security underlying the bonds by the trustee. Likewise, the trust indenture may prohibit suit on their non-deposited bonds unless the trustee refuses to act after demand by holders of a specified percentage of bonds. Thus dissenting groups are slowed up and made ineffective, if not completely stilled and rendered impotent. . . .

"In such a manner do protective committees controlled or dominated by houses of issue stand in a peculiarly strategic position to protect the house of issue against its own misdeeds. In such a manner do deposit agreements serve as insulation for trustees (or their principals) against assertions of fraud, duress, and deception practiced on their beneficiaries."[6] . . .

"*To obtain such control over the reorganization the underwriter normally needs a friendly or complacent trustee—a trustee who will not sound a cry of warning to the security holders; a* trustee *who by inaction or by compliance with the wishes of the underwriter will take no steps contrary to the desires of the underwriter.* The underwriter had such a trustee in the real estate bond field. He will be likely to have such a trustee in any field if it is an affiliated interest. In such cases the interests of the underwriter and security holder frequently become antithetical. In the same manner the interests of the affiliated trustee become incompatible with those of its beneficiaries."

Under all the circumstances of this case, we are of the opinion that the persons in control of the two corporations have such a community of interest as to preclude a finding by us that the trust company is not "under direct or indirect common control" with the underwriter. The provisions and intent of Section 310(b)(3) of the Act are such that under existing circumstances, for the purposes of Sections 305(b) and 307(c), we are unable to conclude that the applicant trust company is eligible to act as indenture trustee in respect of securities of any obligor for which Morgan Stanley & Co. Incorporated is or may be an underwriter

---

The Trust Indenture Act of 1939 was amended in 1990 with the stated goal of recognizing changes in debt-financing techniques that had evolved in the more than 50 years since the TIA's original adoption.

Sections 310–318 of the Trust Indenture Act set forth indenture provisions that are mandatory, and they apply as a matter of federal law and those that

---

6. *Report on the Study and Investigation of the Work, Activities, Personnel and Functions of Protective and Reorganization Committees* (Government Printing Office, 1936), Part III, at 85–87, 90; quoted *id.*, Part VI, at 105–106. Such report was made by this Commission to Congress pursuant to Section 211 of the Securities Exchange Act of 1934. In the Trust Indenture Act, Section 302(a) entitled "Necessity for Regulation" begins with the recitation: "Upon the basis of facts disclosed by reports of the Securities and Exchange Commission made to Congress pursuant to Section 211 of the Securities Exchange Act of 1934 and otherwise disclosed and ascertained, it is hereby declared . . ." etc.

impose duties on any person are automatically deemed included in every qualified indenture whether or not actually set forth therein.

The most important mandatory provisions can be briefly summarized as follows:

- Section 310, the subject of the SEC opinion excerpted above, sets standards of eligibility for trustees and lists the conflicts of interest that will result in disqualification of trustees.
- Section 315(b) requires the trustee to notify holders of defaults of which the trustee is aware.
- Upon default, section 315(c) requires the trustee to exercise its rights and powers under the indenture according to a "prudent-person" standard.
- Section 316(b) states that the right of any bondholder to receive payment of principal and interest on his indenture securities, and to institute suit for enforcement of such payment, shall not be impaired without her consent. Notice that section 316(b) protects two discrete, albeit related rights: (i) "the right of any holder of any indenture security to receive payment of the principal of and interest on such indenture security"; and (ii) the right of such holder "to institute suit for the enforcement of any such payment."
- Section 317 authorizes the trustee, in case of a default in payment of principal or interest on the indenture securities, in its own name as trustee, to recover judgment against the obligor on the indenture securities and to file proofs of claim in any bankruptcy proceedings.
- Finally, section 318 provides that the mandatory provisions of the TIA will override any conflicting provision of the indenture.

The TIA also requires the "qualification" of most indentures before they can become effective. Since adoption of the 1990 amendments, the SEC no longer reviews indentures to determine their conformity with the TIA. The SEC's role is confined to determining that the debt securities being registered will be issued under an indenture and that the designated trustee is eligible to serve as such and not disqualified.

The SEC has no enforcement authority over the terms of the indenture once the registration statement becomes effective, but the TIA contains criminal liability for certain willful violations and misrepresentations and express civil liability for any omission or misstatement in the filing documents. Courts have also implied a federal private right of action against indenture trustees for violations of the TIA and the terms of indentures issues thereunder.[7]

One final note of relevance to future chapters: Section 304 of the TIA and section 1145 of the Bankruptcy Code[8] contain certain exemptions from the requirements of the TIA. For example, under section 1145(d) of the Bankruptcy

---

7. Zeffiro v. First Pennsylvania Banking & Trust Co., 623 F.2d 290, 298 (3d Cir. 1980).
8. 11 U.S.C. §1145.

Code, a note issued under a reorganization plan that matures no later than one year after the effective date of the plan is exempt from compliance with the TIA.

PROBLEM SET 14.1

1. What is the purpose of section 316(b)'s prohibition on changes to the indenture? Note that sovereign debt, which is not subject to the TIA, often contains a "collective action clause" that allows these terms to be changed by majority or supermajority vote. Before the Great Depression, corporate bonds and notes also contained such provisions.
2. Review the TIA in your statutory supplement and be prepared to discuss in class. Does the TIA still have a role to play decades after its enactment?

2. NEGOTIATING THE INDENTURE

CHESAPEAKE ENERGY CORP. v. BANK OF NEW YORK MELLON TRUST CO.

773 F.3d 110

United States Court of Appeals, Second Circuit.
Nov. 25, 2014.

LEVAL, Circuit Judge:

Defendant Bank of New York Mellon Trust Company, N.A. ("BNY Mellon") appeals from the judgment of the United States District Court for the Southern District of New York (Engelmayer, *J.*) declaring that the Notice of Special Early Redemption issued by plaintiff Chesapeake Energy Corporation ("Chesapeake") on March 15, 2013 was timely and effective to redeem certain senior notes (the "Notes") at the "Special Price" of 100% of the principal amount, plus interest accrued to the date of redemption. BNY Mellon brings this appeal in its capacity as indenture trustee for the benefit of the noteholders.

After an expedited bench trial, the district court adopted Chesapeake's argument, construing the Ninth Supplemental Indenture (the "Supplemental Indenture"), which governed the Notes, as unambiguously authorizing Chesapeake to redeem the Notes at the Special Price by giving notice of redemption during the Special Early Redemption Period—between November 15, 2012 and March 15, 2013—and redeeming the Notes 30 to 60 days thereafter. BNY Mellon contends that the Supplemental Indenture authorized Chesapeake to redeem the Notes at the Special Price only if the redemption would be accomplished within the Special Early Redemption Period, i.e., no later than March 15, 2013, with notice of 30 to 60 days given during the Special Early Redemption Period. We agree with BNY Mellon. Accordingly, we reverse the judgment and remand for consideration of Chesapeake's second claim for declaratory relief.

BACKGROUND

a.   FACTUAL BACKGROUND

In February 2012, Chesapeake issued $1.3 billion in senior notes due on March 15, 2019 bearing an interest rate of 6.775%. The Notes were issued under two indentures—a pre-existing Base Indenture, dated August 2, 2010, which applied to several series of notes, and the Supplemental Indenture, dated February 16, 2012, which specifically governed this series.

This dispute centers on the meaning of § 1.7 of the Supplemental Indenture, which governs Chesapeake's option to make a Special Early Redemption of the Notes. This section provides:

> (a) The Company [Chesapeake] shall have no obligation to redeem, purchase or repay the Notes pursuant to any mandatory redemption, sinking fund or analogous provisions or at the option of a Holder thereof.
> (b) At any time from and including November 15, 2012 to and including March 15, 2013 (the *"Special Early Redemption Period "*), the Company, at its option, *may redeem the Notes in whole or from time to time in part for a price equal to 100% of the principal amount of the Notes to be redeemed,* plus accrued and unpaid interest on the Notes to be redeemed to the date of redemption; provided, however, that, immediately following any redemption of the Notes in part (and not in whole) pursuant to this Section 1.7(b), at least $250 million aggregate principal amount of the Notes remains outstanding. The Company shall be permitted to exercise its option to redeem the Notes pursuant to this Section 1.7 *so long as it gives the notice of redemption pursuant to Section 3.04 of the Base Indenture during the Special Early Redemption Period.* Any redemption pursuant to this Section 1.7(b) shall be conducted, to the extent applicable, pursuant to the provisions of Sections 3.02 through 3.07 of the Base Indenture.
> (c) At any time after March 15, 2013 to the Maturity Date, the Company, at its option, may redeem the Notes in whole or from time to time in part for an amount equal to the Make–Whole Price plus accrued and unpaid interest to the date of redemption in accordance with the Form of Note.

Section 1.7(b) cross-references § 3.04 of the Base Indenture, which provides:

> (a) At least 30 days but not more than 60 days before a redemption date, [Chesapeake] shall mail a notice of redemption by first-class mail to each Holder of Securities to be redeemed at such Holder's registered address.

These provisions allowed Chesapeake two elective options for early redemption. Pursuant to § 1.7(b), Chesapeake could elect early redemption of Notes at the Special Price during the Special Early Redemption Period. Pursuant to § 1.7(c), Chesapeake could elect early redemption of Notes after the Special Early Redemption Period at a substantially higher "Make–Whole Price."

On February 20, 2013, twenty-three days prior to the end of the Special Early Redemption Period, Chesapeake announced that it planned to redeem the Notes at the Special Price pursuant to § 1.7(b). Later that day, however, a hedge fund, which had purchased a large amount of the Notes, protested that the time allowed for notice of redemption at the Special Price had expired because redemption at the Special Price was permitted solely within the Special Early Redemption Period and no less than 30 days following the giving of notice, which was no longer possible.

On February 22, 2013, BNY Mellon notified Chesapeake that it would not participate in the proposed redemption. On February 28, 2013, BNY Mellon told Chesapeake that if Chesapeake issued a notice of redemption, BNY Mellon might deem the notice as having triggered redemption at the Make–Whole Price pursuant to § 1.7(c). Chesapeake nonetheless issued a Notice of Special Early Redemption on March 15, 2013, calling for redemption at the Special Price on May 15, 2013.

b. THE TRIAL AND THE DISTRICT COURT'S DECISION

On March 8, 2013, Chesapeake filed this action against BNY Mellon seeking declaratory judgment that its Notice of Special Early Redemption at the Special Price would be timely and effective if mailed by March 15, 2013. In the event the court ruled that the notice was not timely to effectuate early redemption at the Special Price, the complaint also sought a declaratory ruling that the notice would not trigger redemption at the Make–Whole Price.

The court held an expedited bench trial on April 23–25, 2013 with closing arguments on April 30, 2013. On May 8, 2013, only eight days later, and with the date noticed for redemption only one week away, the court issued a detailed 92–page decision, and entered judgment thereon, ruling that § 1.7(b) of the Supplemental Indenture was unambiguous in setting March 15, 2013 as the deadline for notice of redemption at the Special Price, and in allowing actual redemption to occur 30 to 60 days thereafter. Chesapeake Energy Corp. v. Bank of N.Y. Mellon Trust Co., N.A., 957 F.Supp.2d 316, 339 – 40 (S.D.N.Y.2013). The court further ruled that, even if the indenture provisions were deemed ambiguous, "the extrinsic evidence convincingly establishes a meeting of the minds among the negotiating parties" that "these parties intended and agreed that March 15, 2013 would serve as the deadline for Chesapeake to give notice of redemption." Id. at 359.

BNY Mellon appeals, arguing that § 1.7(b) authorized redemption at the Special Price only if accomplished no later than March 15, 2013, with notice given 30 to 60 days before, also during the Special Early Redemption Period.

DISCUSSION

We conclude that the terms of § 1.7 unambiguously terminated Chesapeake's right to redeem the Notes at the Special Price on March 15, 2013. Notice of such redemption needed to be given no later than February 13, 2013; the notice given by Chesapeake on March 15, 2013 of redemption to occur on May 15, 2013 was, therefore, untimely.

When interpreting a contract, our "primary objective . . . is to give effect to the intent of the parties as revealed by the language of their agreement." "[T]he words and phrases [in a contract] should be given their plain meaning, and the contract should be construed so as to give full meaning and effect to all of its provisions."

Under New York law, a contract is ambiguous if its terms "could suggest more than one meaning when viewed objectively by a reasonably intelligent person who has examined the context of the entire integrated agreement and who is cognizant of the customs, practices, usages and terminology as generally understood in the particular trade or business."

The district court adopted Chesapeake's argument. It read § 1.7(b)'s Special Early Redemption Period as fixing the period during which Chesapeake could begin the redemption process by providing notice, and not requiring actual redemption within that period. Accordingly, it read the term "may redeem," in the first sentence of § 1.7(b) to mean "may commence the redemption process [by giving notice]." In the court's view, this interpretation was required in order to avoid what the court perceived to be an "irreconcilable conflict" in the indenture's terms.

Because the first sentence of § 1.7(b) provides that Chesapeake "may redeem" the Notes at the Special Price "[a]t any time from and including November 15, 2012 to and including March 15, 2013," the court interpreted that sentence as guaranteeing Chesapeake four full months in which it could effectuate the redemption. However, the second sentence of § 1.7(b) (incorporating by reference § 3.04 of the Base Indenture) required Chesapeake to give 30 to 60 days notice, which notice was required to be given during the same four-month period. The notice obligation provided by the second sentence thus prevented Chesapeake from redeeming during the first 30 days of the specified Special Early Redemption Period. The effect of the second sentence was, thus, to allow three months during which Chesapeake could effectuate the redemption. In the court's view this created an irreconcilable conflict. The court explained,

> Under BNY Mellon's reading of § 1.7(b), there is no four-month period for doing *anything,* including for giving notice or for a redemption. Rather, there is, implicitly, a three-month period for a notice of at-par redemption (November 15, 2012 through February 13, 2013) and a separate, implicit three-month period for redemption itself on such terms (December 15, 2012 through March 15, 2013).

While the court's observation (that Chesapeake did not have four months in which it could redeem) was correct, we respectfully disagree that this created an irreconcilable conflict. Chesapeake's interpretation is flawed in several respects.

The Supplemental Indenture does not purport to give Chesapeake four months in which to accomplish redemption at the Special Price, or four months in which to give notice of the redemption. Nor does the indenture purport to give Chesapeake the opportunity to redeem *at any time* between November 15, 2012 and March 15, 2013. The indenture was simply drafted using a "so long as" clause, in the nature of a proviso, which limited the scope of a prior provision.

It is true that the first sentence of § 1.7(b) of the Supplemental Indenture, if it were written in isolation, would give Chesapeake the right to redeem Notes at the Special Price "at any time from and including November 15, 2012 to and including March 15, 2013," defined as the "Special Early Redemption Period." But that first sentence does not appear in isolation. The immediately following sentence makes clear that Chesapeake's right of redemption set forth in the first sentence is subjected to a limiting qualification. The second sentence states, "[Chesapeake] shall be permitted to exercise its option to redeem the Notes pursuant to this Section 1.7 *so long as it gives the notice* of redemption pursuant to Section 3.04 of the Base Indenture *during the Special Early Redemption Period*." (emphasis added.)

Reading the first and second sentences together makes clear that Chesapeake may exercise this right of early redemption only during the Special Early Redemption Period and only after giving the required notice of 30 to 60 days *"during the Special Early Redemption Period."* (emphasis added.)

When a proposition is followed by a clause beginning with "so long as," the "so long as" clause typically serves as a proviso, introducing a condition that narrows the broader initial proposition. *See, e.g., Burrage v. United States,* 571 U.S. ——, 134 S.Ct. 881, 888, 187 L.Ed.2d 715 (2014) ("[I]f poison is administered to a man debilitated by multiple diseases, it is a but-for cause of his death even if those diseases played a part in his demise, so long as, without the incremental effect of the poison, he would have lived."); *The Chicago Manual of Style* § 4.3 (16th ed. 2010) ("Whenever a book or article, poem or lecture, database or drama comes into the world, it is automatically covered by copyright so long as it is 'fixed' in some 'tangible' form and embodies original expression."). Section 1.7(b)'s "so long as" clause is not in conflict with the first sentence; it is a proviso, which limits the scope of Chesapeake's right.

The use of such a proviso in a contract can indeed narrow the scope of a contract term, but it does so in a manner dictated by the contractual text. As employed in the Supplemental Indenture, this common linguistic device was used to set forth the different components of a set of rights and obligations in separate sentences. The contractual text required reading these different sentences in tandem. When read in tandem, these sentences communicated a clearly defined right, contingent on the performance of clearly specified obligations.

If instead of describing the Special Early Redemption process in two consecutive sentences, the indenture had stated in a single sentence, "At any time during the Special Early Redemption Period from November 15, 2012 to March 15, 2013, Chesapeake may redeem the Notes at the Special Price, so long as it gives notice pursuant to Section 3.04 of the Base Indenture during the Special Early Redemption Period," what Chesapeake calls an "irreconcilable conflict" would be equally present, and yet no one could fail to understand that both notice and redemption must occur during the Special Early Redemption Period. By spreading those provisions through two successive sentences, the indenture perhaps required more patience on the part of the reader, but it had the same unmistakable meaning. . . .

CONCLUSION

For the reasons stated above, we REVERSE the district court's judgment and REMAND for consideration of Chesapeake's second claim for declaratory judgment that the redemption notice given by Chesapeake on March 15, 2013 should not be deemed to have noticed redemption at the Make–Whole Price.

FAILLA, District Judge, dissenting:

Both the district court and the majority have it half-right: the majority is correct that Section 1.7(b) of the Supplemental Indenture cannot be read to unambiguously support Chesapeake's position, and the district court is correct that it cannot be read to unambiguously support BNY Mellon's position. The text is ambiguous, and the case should be remanded to the district court to reevaluate the extrinsic evidence with due regard for the principles of unmanifested subjective intent and course of performance . . .

How convincing do you find the majority's resort to the *Chicago Manual of Style* when interpreting a bond indenture? Could Chesapeake have given the required notice in advance of the "Special Early Redemption Period," thus providing it with the full four months? How could Chesapeake (or its attorneys) have better drafted the language in question to achieve their apparent goals?

In May 2016, the *Wall Street Journal* reported that Chesapeake "would swap 4.1% of its shares outstanding for debt, the latest move by the beleaguered energy company to ease its debt load as it struggles with low natural-gas prices." Does that suggest that the bondholders should have let Chesapeake redeem? What role did the indenture trustee play in the decision to object to the redemption?

RACEPOINT PARTNERS, LLC, ET AL. v. JP MORGAN CHASE BANK, N.A.

14 N.Y.3d 419
Court of Appeals of New York.
April 1, 2010.

PIGOTT, J.

On February 7, 2001, the energy company Enron executed an indenture agreement with Chase Manhattan Bank (Chase), naming Chase as the indenture trustee for the holders of certain Enron notes. The agreement contained, in section 4.02, a standard provision setting forth a covenant by Enron

> "[to] file with the Trustee [i.e., Chase], within 15 days after it files the same with the SEC [Securities and Exchange Commission], copies of its annual reports and of the information, documents and other reports . . . which the Company [i.e., Enron] is required to file with the SEC pursuant to Section 13 or 15(d) of the [Securities] Exchange Act. Delivery of such reports, information and documents to the Trustee is for informational purposes only and the Trustee's receipt of such shall not constitute constructive notice of any information contained therein or determinable from information contained therein, including the Issuer's compliance with any of its covenants hereunder (as to which the Trustee is entitled to rely exclusively on Officers' Certificates). The Issuer also shall comply with any other provisions of Trust Indenture Act Section 314(a)."

The agreement also set forth various circumstances or events that would constitute default by either party, including failure by Enron to comply with this provision, if not corrected within 60 days of notification by Chase.

In December 2001, in the wake of the major accounting fraud scandal with which it has become synonymous, Enron filed for bankruptcy. Thereafter, plaintiffs Racepoint Partners, LLC, and Willow Capital–II, L.L.C., bought approximately $1 billion of the notes from their holders. Plaintiffs, which, as secondary holders of the notes, are vested with the claims and demands of the sellers, then brought this common-law action against Chase alleging, among other things, breach of contract. Plaintiffs claim, first, that Enron defaulted under the indenture agreement and, second, that Chase had actual knowledge of this default and that its failure to notify Enron and the noteholders of the default constituted breach of the agreement. The issue in this appeal is the allegation of contractual default by Enron in filing reports that were false.

Plaintiffs point to the fact that Enron agreed in section 4.02 to file with Chase copies of all reports that it was "required to file with the SEC pursuant to Section 13 or 15(d) of the [Securities] Exchange Act." Section 13 of the Act requires publicly traded companies to keep records accurately reflecting their transactions and assets, and to file annual and quarterly reports with the Securities and Exchange Commission (*see* 15 USC §78m). Plaintiffs argue that because the financial reports filed by Enron with Chase were inaccurate and did not comply with federal securities law, they were not the reports Enron was "required to file with the SEC." Plaintiffs posit that, by filing these same fraudulent reports with Chase, Enron failed to satisfy its section 4.02 covenant, and thus defaulted.

Chase moved to dismiss the complaint under CPLR 3211. Supreme Court denied Chase's motion. The Appellate Division reversed, granting the motion (57 A.D.3d 378, 869 N.Y.S.2d 489 [2008]). We granted leave to appeal (12 N.Y.3d 706, 879 N.Y.S.2d 52, 906 N.E.2d 1086 [2009]), and now affirm.

Section 4.02 of the indenture agreement is a mandated provision based on the requirements of section 314(a)(1) of the Trust Indenture Act of 1939:

> "Each person who, as set forth in the registration statement or application, is or is to be an obligor upon the indenture securities covered thereby shall . . .
>
> "file with the indenture trustee copies of the annual reports and of the information, documents, and other reports (or copies of such portions of any of the foregoing as the [Securities and Exchange] Commission may by rules and regulations prescribe) which such obligor is required to file with the Commission pursuant to section 13 or section 15(d) of the Securities Exchange Act of 1934 [15 USC §78m or §78o(d)]; or, if the obligor is not required to file information, documents, or reports pursuant to either of such sections, then to file with the indenture trustee and the [Securities and Exchange] Commission, in accordance with rules and regulations prescribed by the Commission, such of the supplementary and periodic information, documents, and reports which may be required pursuant to section 13 of the Securities Exchange Act of 1934 [15 USC §78m], in respect of a security listed and registered on a national securities exchange as may be prescribed in such rules and regulations" (codified at 15 USC §77nnn [a][1]).

Plaintiffs concede that the parties' intent in section 4.02 may be equated with congressional intent with respect to section 314(a) of the Trust Indenture Act of 1939. In drafting the Trust Indenture Act, Congress intended simply to ensure that an indenture trustee was provided with up-to-date reports on a company's financial status, by requiring the company to send the trustee a copy of filed financial reports. In the 1930s, when section 314(a) was drafted, computer-based technologies, whereby copies of SEC reports can now be obtained, did not exist.

The legislative history of section 314(a) suggests that Congress intended to create a delivery requirement and no more. The 1939 House Report highlighted the legislators' concern that trustees and bondholders at the time did not receive periodic reports from companies issuing bonds.

"In a substantial portion of the indentures . . . the issuer was under no obligation to file an annual report with the indenture trustee. None of the indentures . . . required the transmission to the bondholders of periodic reports, such as stockholders customarily receive. None of them established machinery for the transmission of such reports. . . ." (HR Rep. 1016, 76th Cong., 1st Sess., at 35 [1939].)

It is apparent that section 314(a) was designed to mandate such a mechanism of delivery of reports to indenture trustees. The same House Report, observing that in many cases a company "will already be required to file periodic reports with the [Securities and Exchange] Commission under section 13 or section 15(d)," stated that the bill under consideration "merely requires that copies of such reports ... be filed with the indenture trustee" (HR Rep. 1016, 76th Cong., 1st Sess., at 35).

As federal courts have observed, when considering indenture agreement provisions very similar to the one at issue here,

> "the provision merely requires the company to transmit to the trustee copies of whatever reports it *actually* files with the SEC ...
>
> "[A]ny duty actually to file the reports is imposed 'pursuant to Section 13 or 15(d) of the Exchange Act' and *not* pursuant to the indenture itself. The provision does not incorporate the Exchange Act; it merely refers to it in order to establish which reports must be forwarded. ...
>
> "[It] impose[s] nothing more than the ministerial duty to forward copies of certain reports, identified by reference to the Exchange Act, within fifteen days of actually filing the reports with the SEC" (*UnitedHealth Group Inc. v. Wilmington Trust Co.*, 548 F.3d 1124, 1128–1130 [8th Cir.2008]; *see also e.g. Affiliated Computer Servs., Inc. v. Wilmington Trust Co.*, 565 F.3d 924, 930–931 [5th Cir.2009]; *American Stock Transfer & Trust Co. v. Par Pharm. Cos., Inc.*, 2009 WL 1754473, *4–5, 2009 U.S. Dist LEXIS 52602, *10–13 [SD N.Y.2009]).

It is clear therefore that indenture agreements containing the required delivery provisions pursuant to section 314(a) refer to the Securities Exchange Act only to identify the types of report that should be forwarded to indenture trustees. They do not create contractual duties on the part of the trustee to assure that the information contained in any report filed is true and accurate. That is simply not the mission or purpose of the trustee or the contract under which it undertakes its duties.

Of course, companies have a duty to file accurate reports with the SEC. That obligation, however, derives from the Securities Exchange Act, not from indenture agreements.

Our holding that section 4.02 of the indenture agreement simply embodies a delivery requirement, and does not imply a duty on the part of the trustee to assure the filing of accurate reports or risk default, is consistent with the limited, "ministerial" functions of indenture trustees (*AG Capital Funding Partners, L.P. v. State St. Bank & Trust Co.*, 11 N.Y.3d 146, 157, 866 N.Y.S.2d 578, 896 N.E.2d 61 [2008]), and with the plain language of section 4.02, which states that "[d]elivery of such reports, information and documents [filed with the SEC] to the Trustee is for informational purposes only." Plaintiffs' proposed interpretation, on the other hand, would require indenture trustees to review the substance of SEC filings, so as to reduce the risk of liability, greatly expanding indenture trustees' recognized administrative duties far beyond anything found in the contract.

Accordingly, the order of the Appellate Division should be affirmed, with costs.

Order affirmed, with costs.

This second case reaffirms the basic notion in corporate finance that if you want something, you had better negotiate for it in the contract. And it had better be expressly set forth in the contract. This point will be the subject of the next chapter.

Actually, the terms of the indenture are not so much negotiated; rather the parties negotiate the section of the offering memorandum entitled "Description of Notes" or "Bond" or whatever debt instrument is being issued.[9] That section will set forth, verbatim, the desired covenants of the indenture, with the remainder of the indenture consisting of so-called "boilerplate" that the junior associate cuts and pastes in from a prior deal.[10]

Often bonds or notes are first sold privately, under exemptions from the securities laws like Rule 144A, and later exchanged for public bonds in an "A/B" exchange offer registered with the SEC.[11] Sometimes bonds or notes are sold without registration rights, as "144A for life."

In all cases the investors are bargaining about the terms of a relationship that will last from 10 to 30 years, if not longer. The covenants in the indenture not only act directly, by prohibiting certain conduct, but also by triggering opportunities for renegotiation during the life of the agreement. The issuer-debtor would like to limit those events, to allow maximum flexibility when running its business. The investor-creditors worry that they will be abused by the debtor at a point when their leverage over the debtor might be quite minimal.[12]

Before 1980, there was a relatively standard set of traditional protective covenants that were included in most bond indentures. Since then the strength of covenants has ebbed and flowed with the bond markets. Before the 2008 financial crisis, some issuers were able to place "covenant light" debt, meaning debt that had few if any covenants. Following the crisis, there is some sense that covenants that had been forgotten are reappearing in indentures. But low interest rates and high demand for bond debt has also pushed in the other direction in recent years, and more stories about "Cov Light" appear in the financial press each day.

As a general rule, high-yield (junk) debt will contain more covenants than investment-grade debt.

---

9. This difference in terms relates to their duration—notes are issued for ten years or less.

10. *See* Stephen J. Choi and G. Mitu Gulati, *Innovation in Boilerplate Contracts: The Case of Sovereign Bonds*, 53 Emory L. J. 929 (2004).

11. Exchange offers are discussed later in the course.

12. Marcel Kahan, *The Qualified Case Against Mandatory Terms in Bonds*, 89 Nw. U. L. Rev. 565, 572 (1995).

3.   CALL PROVISIONS AND OTHER COVENANTS

Callable or redeemable bonds are bonds that can be redeemed or paid off by the issuer prior to the bonds' maturity date. When an issuer calls its bonds, it pays investors the call price, which may simply be the face value of the bonds, together with accrued interest to date. In many respects this is the corporate equivalent of refinancing your house (or your parents refinancing their house)—the old debt is paid off, often with the proceeds of a new loan.

Call provisions are often part of corporate and municipal bonds, but not bonds issued by the federal government. Even bonds with call provisions are typically not callable during the early years of the bond's term.

PROBLEM SET 14.2

1. A call option is an advantage for the issuer and a disadvantage to the investor. Why is this?
2. In what situations might the issuer want to exercise the call?
3. A make-whole call feature allows the issuer to call the security prior to the stated maturity date at the greater of par or par plus the "make whole premium." Here is the description of the clause from a Goldman Sachs offering memorandum:

> We will have the option to redeem the subordinated notes, in whole or in part, at our option at any time, at a redemption price equal to the greater of (1) 100% of the principal amount of the subordinated notes to be redeemed or (2) as determined by the quotation agent described below, the sum of the present values of the remaining scheduled payments of principal and interest on the subordinated notes to be redeemed, not including any portion of these payments of interest accrued as of the date on which the subordinated notes are to be redeemed, discounted to the date on which the subordinated notes are to be redeemed on a semi-annual basis assuming a 360-day year consisting of twelve 30-day months, at the adjusted U.S. treasury rate described below plus 20 basis points, plus, in each case, accrued interest on the subordinated notes to be redeemed to the date on which the subordinated notes are to be redeemed.

What is the purpose of this clause? What is the effect of the interest rate described in this text? How does this clause compare to a straight call provision?

A *change of control covenant* is designed to protect bondholders most directly from leveraged buyouts or other transactions where a change in ownership of the firm could impair the firm's creditworthiness. The covenant generally gives bondholders the opportunity to put their bonds back to the issuer before a change at 101 percent of the face amount. This commonly applies following a transaction that affects "all or substantially all," of the firm and, sometimes, its subsidiaries.[13]

The covenants often have an exception to their operation if the surviving corporation assumes the debt, and there is no immediate event of default. Other limitations of this covenant include uncertainty about when a sale of all or substantially all assets has occurred. This is especially true if the firm has engaged in a series of transactions.

A *negative pledge clause* is quite common and often quite useless. The basic idea is to prevent the issuer from granting liens on its assets. In short, the goal is to prevent the insertion of senior debt into the capital structure. But what is the remedy for breach of such a clause? Typically, there are exceptions for small liens and mortgages on real property.

PROBLEM SET 14.3

1. Bogartco, Inc. has a clause in its 20 Year Senior Unsecured Floating Rate Notes that prohibits the granting of "any lien, security interest, charge, mortgage, pledge or other encumbrance of any kind including any conditional sale or other title retention agreement, any lease in the nature thereof, and any agreement to give any security interest other than an agreement to secure indebtedness equally and ratably upon the incurrence of other secured indebtedness." What risks does this leave open? For example, would it prohibit Bogartco's plans to issue $200 million in new Senior Unsecured Floating Rate Notes?

2. Many negative pledge clauses contain exceptions for new borrowing under existing bank loans and borrowing at the subsidiary level. What risks do these exceptions present to the bondholder?

Limitations on debt are meant to restrict the total claims on a company. They solve some of the problems of negative pledge clauses. What the definition of "debt" is will make or break the utility of this kind of clause.

Typically, the clause allows for the incurrence of debt so long as a specified financial ratio is satisfied. Often this is a ratio of EBITDA to interest expense or debt to EBITDA. Once the ratio no longer meets the standard, new debt (however defined) is no longer permitted. You knew there was a reason to learn what EBITDA was.

A *subordination provision* is a contractual agreement by one group of bondholders to defer getting paid until another group of bondholders gets paid in full. Importantly, such a provision is enforceable under the Bankruptcy Code.[14]

Such a provision does not, however, guarantee that the senior bondholders will get paid in full. Why not? If a company has senior and subordinated debt, what would you assume about the coupons on the respective bonds?

---

13. *Cf.* DGCL §271.
14. 11 U.S.C. §510(a).

A *restricted payment covenant* typically restricts an issuer's ability to make distributions to shareholders or pay off subordinated debt. Such a covenant also constrains an issuer's ability to make "restricted investments." These are investments in "unrestricted subsidiaries"—that is, subsidiaries not subject to the indenture covenants—as well as other investments that are not "permitted investments," such as joint ventures with other companies.

Finally, consider who is borrowing the money under an indenture. Often an indenture will require guarantees by all key subsidiaries. These guarantees mean that the corporate group is liable for the debt, and not just the specific parent company corporate entity. Why include such a provision?

4.   THE DYNEGY BOND INDENTURE AND NOTE

Please read the sample bond indenture provided online, especially Articles II and III. Look for the clauses discussed earlier. Consider the definitional questions raised in the preceding discussion.

How much is being borrowed? What are the rights of the creditors? Who is obligated to repay the amounts borrowed and when? What remedies (beyond a suit for breach of contract) are contained in this indenture?

15

BONDS AFTER THE INDENTURE

Once the bond indenture is signed, it can be the beginning of what might be a long-term relationship between issuer and bondholder, and a very long-term relationship if you buy into the century-long debt once commonly issued by railroads and recently issued by companies like Disney to take advantage of low interest rates. Universities also issue a good deal of long-term debt. For example, in 2011 the University of Southern California issued debt that will mature in October 2111. It has a make-whole call provision, a coupon of 5.250%, and in early 2017 was trading at 115.833.

One should not be too literal about this. After all, bondholders always have the ability to sell their bonds if they no longer believe in their earlier investment. Of course, the new owner of the bond will at least partially base the price they are willing to pay on the terms of the indenture.

In all events, the primary avenue for subsequent change, or to resolve disagreements about the terms of the previously negotiated indenture, is through negotiation. Typically, these negotiations will happen between a group of large bondholders—that is, bondholders who hold many bonds, not linebacker bondholders—and the issuer.

These negotiations take place in the shadow of the existing case law regarding bond indentures. That is, the parties will argue about which prior case is more like the current situation, and beliefs regarding that case law will dictate who has power in the negotiations.

Thus, case law is important here even if most indentures will never result in litigation. Because most bonds sold in the United States have a New York choice of law clause—and bonds worldwide tend to have either a New York or English choice of law clause—cases from New York, including the federal courts therein, are especially important. Delaware sees a lot of these cases, too, although often it finds itself applying New York law.[1]

---

1. Bankruptcy courts in New York and Delaware, where most of the big chapter 11 cases are filed, also end up interpreting a lot of indentures after default.

1.   INTERPRETING THE INDENTURE

SHARON STEEL CORPORATION v. THE CHASE MANHATTAN BANK, N.A., AND MANUFACTURERS HANOVER TRUST COMPANY

691 F.2d 1039
United States Court of Appeals, Second Circuit.
Sept. 28, 1982.

Ralph K. WINTER, Circuit Judge

BACKGROUND

1.   THE INDENTURES

Between 1965 and 1977, UV issued debt instruments pursuant to five separate indentures, the salient terms of which we briefly summarize. In 1965, UV issued approximately $23 million of 53/8% subordinated debentures due in 1995, under an indenture naming The Chase Manhattan Bank, N.A. ("Chase") as the trustee ("First Chase Indenture"). The current principal amount of the debentures outstanding under that indenture is approximately $14 million.

In 1968, the City of Port Huron, Michigan, issued approximately $22 million in Industrial Development Revenue Bonds, bearing 6 1/4% interest and due in 1993, under an indenture also naming Chase as the trustee ("Second Chase Indenture"). These bonds were issued by Port Huron to raise funds for the construction of a facility to be leased by Mueller Brass Company, a UV subsidiary. The rent paid by Mueller Brass covers the principal and interest on the bonds. Moreover, UV executed an unconditional guaranty of these obligations of its subsidiary ("Chase Lease Guaranty"). The principal amount presently outstanding is approximately $16.5 million.

Similarly, in 1968, the County of Itawamba, Mississippi, issued approximately $13 million in Industrial Development Revenue Bonds due in 1993, under an indenture naming Union Planters National Bank of Memphis as the trustee ("Union Planters Indenture"). These bonds were also issued to fund construction of facilities to be leased by Mueller Brass, the rent payments being sufficient to satisfy the debt service on the bonds. Again, UV guaranteed Mueller Brass' lease obligations ("Union Planters Lease Guaranty"). Approximately $9.78 million principal amount of these Itawamba County bonds remains outstanding.

In 1977, UV issued $75 million of 8 7/8% debentures due in 1997 under an indenture naming Manufacturers Hanover Trust Company ("Manufacturers") as the trustee ("Manufacturers Indenture"). The principal amount of these debentures has been reduced to approximately $66.78 million. At the same time, UV issued $25 million of 9 1/4% senior subordinated notes due in 1987 pursuant to an indenture under which United States Trust Company of New York ("U.S.

Trust") is the trustee ("U.S. Trust Indenture"). Approximately $16 million principal amount of these notes remains outstanding.

The debentures, notes and guaranties are general obligations of UV. Each instrument contains clauses permitting redemption by UV prior to the maturity date, in exchange for payment of a fixed redemption price (which includes principal, accrued interest and a redemption premium) and clauses allowing acceleration as a non-exclusive remedy in case of a default. The First Chase Indenture,[2] the Port Huron Lease Guaranty, the Union Planters Lease Guaranty, the Manufacturers Indenture and the U.S. Trust Indenture each contains a "successor obligor" provision allowing UV to assign its debt to a corporate successor which purchases "all or substantially all" of UV's assets. If the debt is not assigned to such a purchaser, UV must pay off the debt. While the successor

---

2. Section 13.01 of the First Chase Indenture reads as follows:

> Nothing in this Indenture or any of the Debentures contained shall prevent any merger or consolidation of any other corporation or corporations into or with the Company, or any merger or consolidation of the Company (either singly or with one or more corporations), into or with any other corporation, or any sale, lease, transfer or other disposition of all or substantially all of its property to any corporation lawfully entitled to acquire the same or prevent successive similar consolidations, mergers, sales, leases, transfers or other dispositions to which the Company or its successors or assigns or any subsequent successors or assigns shall be a party; provided, however, and the Company convenants and agrees, that any such consolidation or merger of the Company or any such sale, lease, transfer or other disposition of all or substantially all of its property, shall be upon the condition that the due and punctual payment of the principal of, interest and premium, if any, on, all of the Debentures, according to their tenor, and the due and punctual performance and observance of all the terms, covenants and conditions of this Indenture to be kept or performed by the Company shall, by an indenture supplemental hereto, executed and delivered to the Trustee, be assumed by any corporation formed by or resulting from any such consolidation or merger, or to which all or substantially all of the property of the Company shall have been sold, leased, transferred or otherwise disposed of (such corporation being herein called the "successor corporation"), just as fully and effectively as if the successor corporation had been the original party of the first part hereto, and such supplemental indenture shall be construed as and shall constitute a novation thereby releasing the Company (unless its identity be merged into or consolidated with that of the successor corporation) from all liability upon, under or with respect to any of the covenants or agreements of this Indenture but not, however, from its liability upon the Debentures.
>
> After the execution and delivery of the supplemental indenture referred to in the preceding paragraph, any order, certificate, resolution or other instrument of the Board of Directors or officers of the Company may be made by the like board or officers of the successor corporation. The Trustee shall receive an Officers' Certificate that the foregoing conditions are complied with, and an Opinion of Counsel that any such indenture supplemental hereto complies with the foregoing conditions and provisions of this Section 13.01. Subject to the provisions of Section 10.01, such Officers' Certificate and Opinion shall be full warrant to the Trustee for any action taken in reliance thereon.

obligor clauses vary in language, the parties agree that the differences are not relevant to the outcome of this case.

2.   THE LIQUIDATION OF UV

During 1977 and 1978, UV operated three separate lines of business. One line, electrical equipment and components, was carried on by Federal Pacific Electric Company ("Federal"). In 1978, Federal generated 60% of UV's operating revenue and 81% of its operating profits. It constituted 44% of the book value of UV's assets and 53% of operating assets. UV also owned and operated oil and gas properties, producing 2% of its operating revenue and 6% of operating profits. These were 5% of book value assets and 6% of operating assets. UV also was involved in copper and brass fabrication, through Mueller Brass, and metals mining, which together produced 13% of profits, 38% of revenue and constituted 34% of book value assets and 41% of operating assets. In addition to these operating assets, UV had cash or other liquid assets amounting to 17% of book value assets.

On December 19, 1978, UV's Board of Directors announced a plan to sell Federal. On January 19, 1979, the UV Board announced its intention to liquidate UV, subject to shareholder approval. On February 20, 1979, UV distributed proxy materials, recommending approval of (i) the sale of Federal for $345,000,000 to a subsidiary of Reliance Electric Company and (ii) a Plan of Liquidation and Dissolution to sell the remaining assets of UV over a 12-month period. The proceeds of these sales and the liquid assets were to be distributed to shareholders.

On March 26, 1979, UV's shareholders approved the sale of Federal and the liquidation plan. The following day, UV filed its Statement of Intent to Dissolve with the Secretary of State of Maine, its state of incorporation. On March 29, the sale of Federal to the Reliance Electric subsidiary for $345 million in cash was consummated. On April 9, UV announced an $18 per share initial liquidating distribution to take place on Monday, April 30.

The Indenture Trustees were aware that UV contemplated making an $18 per share liquidating distribution since at least February 20, 1979 (the date the proxy materials were distributed). On April 26, representatives of Chase, Manufacturers and U.S. Trust met with UV officers and directors and collectively demanded that UV pay off all the debentures within 30 days or, alternatively, that UV establish a trust fund of $180 million to secure the debt. There was testimony that at least one of the Indenture Trustees threatened to sue to enjoin UV from paying the $18 liquidating distribution on the grounds that a liquidating distribution prior to payment of UV's debts would violate Maine law,[3] which provides, as to a liquidating corporation, that:

---

3. The Indenture Trustees apparently concede that as of the April 26 meeting none of the Indentures was in default and the forthcoming $18 distribution would not be a default under any of the indentures. Such an interpretation by the Trustees is evidenced by two letters written by

> *After* paying or adequately providing for the payment of all its obligations, the corporation shall distribute the remainder of its assets . . . among its shareholders . . .
> Me.Rev.Stat.Ann.Tit. 13-A, §1106(4) (1971) (emphasis added).

The outcome of this meeting was an "Agreement for Treatment of Certain Obligations of UV Industries, Inc.," dated April 27, 1979, between UV and the Indenture Trustees ("April Document"). Under the April Document, UV agreed, *inter alia*, to set aside a cash fund of $155 million to secure its public debt and to present a proposal for the satisfaction and discharge of that debt to the Indenture Trustees within 90 days. The Indenture Trustees agreed not to seek an injunction against the payment of the $18 per share liquidating distribution. The April Document provided that all obligations thereunder would terminate upon the payment of UV's public debt or upon UV's abandonment of the plan of liquidation.

On July 23, 1979, UV announced that it had entered into an agreement for the sale of most of its oil and gas properties to Tenneco Oil Company for $135 million cash. The deal was consummated as of October 2, 1979 and resulted in a net gain of $105 million to UV.

3. THE SALE TO SHARON STEEL

In November, 1979, Sharon proposed to buy UV's remaining assets. Another company, Reliance Group (unrelated to Reliance Electric), had made a similar offer. After a brief bidding contest, UV and Sharon entered into an "Agreement for Purchase of Assets" and an "Instrument of Assumption of Liabilities" on November 26, 1979. Under the purchase agreement, Sharon purchased all of the assets owned by UV on November 26 (*i.e.*, Mueller Brass, UV's mining properties and $322 million in cash or the equivalent) for $518 million ($411 million of Sharon subordinated debentures due in 2000—then valued at 86% or

---

Manufacturers and U. S. Trust, respectively, to debentureholders. The letter from Manufacturers to one of its debentureholders, dated June 22, 1979, states, in pertinent part:

> In our opinion and in the opinion of our counsel, neither the approval by stockholders [of UV] of the Plan of Liquidation and Dissolution, nor the initial liquidating dividend constitutes a default under the Indenture. Nor are we aware of any other act or omission on the part of UV which constitutes a default under the Indenture. Absent a default under the Indenture, neither the Trustee nor the Debentureholders can, in our opinion, require UV to call the Debentures or in any other way compel payment of the Debentures other than in accordance with the terms of the Debentures and of the Indenture.

A similar conclusion was expressed by U. S. Trust in a letter to a debentureholder dated June 13, 1979, which reads in part:

> We advise, as Trustee, less complete Liquidation and Dissolution, that nothing has come to our attention that caused us to believe that [UV] was not in compliance with any of the covenants or agreements of the governing Indenture.

$353,460,000—plus $107 million in cash). Under the assumption agreement, Sharon assumed all of UV's liabilities, including the public debt issued under the indentures. UV thereupon announced that it had no further obligations under the indentures or lease guaranties, based upon the successor obligor clauses.

On December 6, 1979, in an attempt to formalize its position as successor obligor, Sharon delivered to the Indenture Trustees supplemental indentures executed by UV and Sharon. The Indenture Trustees refused to sign. Similarly, Sharon delivered an assumption of the lease guaranties to both Chase and Union Planters but those Indenture Trustees also refused to sign.

4.   THE PROCEEDINGS IN THE DISTRICT COURT

By letters dated December 24, 1979, Chase, U.S. Trust and Manufacturers issued virtually identical notices of default as a result of UV's purported assignment of its obligations to Sharon. Each demanded that the default be cured within 90 days or that the debentures be redeemed. Chase and U.S. Trust brought separate actions in New York County Supreme Court against UV and Sharon for redemption of the debentures; Manufacturers subsequently initiated a similar lawsuit. On December 26, 1979, Sharon initiated this action against Chase, U.S. Trust and Manufacturers. The state court actions have been stayed pending disposition of this case.

Chase, U.S. Trust and Manufacturers sought specific performance of the redemption provisions by counterclaim.

[The district court largely ruled in favor of the indenture trustees.]

DISCUSSION

1.   THE SUCCESSOR OBLIGOR CLAUSES

Sharon Steel argues that Judge Werker erred in not submitting to the jury issues going to the meaning of the successor obligor clauses. We disagree. Successor obligor clauses are "boilerplate" or contractual provisions which are standard in a certain genre of contracts. Successor obligor clauses are thus found in virtually all indentures. Such boilerplate must be distinguished from contractual provisions which are peculiar to a particular indenture and must be given a consistent, uniform interpretation. As the American Bar Foundation *Commentaries on Indentures* (1971) ("*Commentaries*") state:

> Since there is seldom any difference in the intended meaning [boilerplate] provisions are susceptible of standardized expression. The use of standardized language can result in a better and quicker understanding of those provisions and a substantial saving of time not only for the draftsman but also for the parties and all others who must comply with or refer to the indenture, including governmental bodies whose approval or authorization of the issuance of the securities is required by law.

Id.

Boilerplate provisions are thus not the consequence of the relationship of particular borrowers and lenders and do not depend upon particularized intentions of the parties to an indenture. There are no adjudicative facts relating to the parties to the litigation for a jury to find and the meaning of boilerplate provisions is, therefore, a matter of law rather than fact.

Moreover, uniformity in interpretation is important to the efficiency of capital markets. . . .

We turn now to the meaning of the successor obligor clauses. Interpretation of indenture provisions is a matter of basic contract law. As the *Commentaries* at 2 state:

> The second fundamental characteristic of long term debt financing is that the rights of holders of the debt securities are largely a matter of contract. There is no governing body of statutory or common law that protects the holder of unsecured debt securities against harmful acts by the debtor except in the most extreme situations . . . [T]he debt securityholder can do nothing to protect himself against actions of the borrower which jeopardize its ability to pay the debt unless he . . . establishes his rights through contractual provisions set forth in the . . . indenture.

Contract language is thus the starting point in the search for meaning and Sharon argues strenuously that the language of the successor obligor clauses clearly permits its assumption of UV's public debt. Sharon's argument is a masterpiece of simplicity: on November 26, 1979, it bought everything UV owned; therefore, the transaction was a "sale" of "all" UV's "assets." In Sharon's view, the contention of the Indenture Trustees and Debenture holders that proceeds from earlier sales in a predetermined plan of piecemeal liquidation may not be counted in determining whether a later sale that involves "all assets" must be rejected because it imports a meaning not evident in the language.

Sharon's literalist approach simply proves too much. If proceeds from earlier piecemeal sales are "assets," then UV continued to own "all" its "assets" even after the Sharon transaction since the proceeds of that transaction, including the $107 million cash for cash "sale," went into the UV treasury. If the language is to be given the "literal" meaning attributed to it by Sharon, therefore, UV's "assets" were not "sold" on November 26 and the ensuing liquidation requires the redemption of the debentures by UV. Sharon's literal approach is thus self-defeating.

The words "all or substantially all" are used in a variety of statutory and contractual provisions relating to transfers of assets and have been given meaning in light of the particular context and evident purpose.

Sharon argues that such decisions are distinguishable because they serve the purpose of either shareholder protection or enforcement of the substance of the Internal Revenue Code. Even if such distinctions are valid, these cases nevertheless demonstrate that a literal reading of the words "all or substantially all" is not helpful apart from reference to the underlying purpose to be served. We turn, therefore, to that purpose.

Sharon argues that the sole purpose of successor obligor clauses is to leave the borrower free to merge, liquidate or to sell its assets in order to enter a wholly new business free of public debt and that they are not intended to offer any protection to lenders. On their face, however, they seem designed to protect lenders as well by assuring a degree of continuity of assets. Thus, a borrower which sells all its assets does not have an option to continue holding the debt. It must either assign the debt or pay it off. As the *Commentaries* state at 290:

> The decision to invest in the debt obligations of a corporation is based on the repayment potential of a business enterprise possessing specific financial characteristics. The ability of the enterprise to produce earnings often depends on particular assets which it owns. Obviously, if the enterprise is changed through consolidation with or merged into another corporation or through disposition of assets, the financial characteristics and repayment potential on which the lender relied may be altered adversely.

The single reported decision construing a successor obligor clause, *B. S. F. Company v. Philadelphia National Bank*, 42 Del.Ch. 106, 204 A.2d 746 (1964), clearly held that one purpose of the clause was to insure that the principal operating assets of a borrower are available for satisfaction of the debt.

Sharon seeks to rebut such inferences by arguing that a number of transactions which seriously dilute the assets of a company are perfectly permissible under such clauses. For example, UV might merge with, or sell its assets to, a company which has a miniscule equity base and is debt heavy. They argue from these examples that the successor obligor clause was not intended to protect borrowers from the kind of transaction in which UV and Sharon engaged.

We disagree. In fact, a substantial degree of protection against diluting transactions exists for the lender. Lenders can rely, for example, on the self-interest of equityholders for protection against mergers which result in a firm with a substantially greater danger of insolvency. So far as the sale of assets to such a firm is concerned, that can occur but substantial protection exists even there since the more debt heavy the purchaser, the less likely it is that the seller's equityholders would accept anything but cash for the assets. A sale to a truly crippled firm is thus unlikely given the self-interest of the equityholders. After a sale, moreover, the lenders would continue to have the protection of the original assets. In both mergers and sales, complete protection against an increase in the borrower's risk is not available in the absence of more specific restrictions, but the self-interest of equityholders imposes a real and substantial limit to that increase in risk. The failure of successor obligor clauses to provide even more protection hardly permits an inference that they are designed solely for the benefit of borrowers.

We hold, therefore, that protection for borrowers as well as for lenders may be fairly inferred from the nature of successor obligor clauses. The former are enabled to sell entire businesses and liquidate, to consolidate or merge with another corporation, or to liquidate their operating assets and enter a new field free of the public debt. Lenders, on the other hand, are assured a degree of continuity of assets. . . .

We hold, therefore, that boilerplate successor obligor clauses do not permit assignment of the public debt to another party in the course of a liquidation unless "all or substantially all" of the assets of the company at the time the plan of liquidation is determined upon are transferred to a single purchaser.

The application of this rule to the present case is not difficult. The plan of liquidation was approved by UV's shareholders on March 26, 1978. Since the Indenture Trustees make no claim as to an earlier time, *e.g.*, the date of the Board recommendation, we accept March 26 as the appropriate reference date. The question then is whether "all or substantially all" of the assets held by UV on that date were transferred to Sharon. That is easily answered. The assets owned by UV on March 26 and later transferred to Sharon were Mueller Brass, certain metals mining property, and substantial amounts of cash and other liquid assets. UV's Form 10-K and Sharon's Form S-7 state that Mueller Brass and the metals mining properties were responsible for only 38% of UV's 1978 operating revenues and 13% of its operating profits. They constitute 41% of the book value of UV's operating properties. When the cash and other liquid assets are added, the transaction still involved only 51% of the book value of UV's total assets.

Since we do not regard the question in this case as even close, we need not determine how the substantiality of corporate assets is to be measured, what percentage meets the "all or substantially all" test or what role a jury might play in determining those issues. Even when the liquid assets (other than proceeds from the sale of Federal and the oil and gas properties) are aggregated with the operating properties, the transfer to Sharon accounted for only 51% of the total book value of UV's assets. In no sense, therefore, are they "all or substantially all" of those assets. The successor obligor clauses are, therefore, not applicable. UV is thus in default on the indentures and the debentures are due and payable. For that reason, we need not reach the question whether the April Document was breached by UV.

3. THE REDEMPTION PREMIUM

Judge Werker held that the redemption premium under the indentures need not be paid by UV. His reasoning was essentially that UV defaulted under the indenture agreement and that the default provisions provide for acceleration rather than a redemption premium. We do not agree. The acceleration provisions of the indentures are explicitly permissive and not exclusive of other remedies. We see no bar, therefore, to the Indenture Trustees seeking specific performance of the redemption provisions where the debtor causes the debentures to become due and payable by its voluntary actions.

Sharon Steel has become the leading case on interpretation of bond indentures, and its discussion of how such indentures should be read in light of their "boilerplate" nature is quoted in many of the opinions in this chapter.

PROBLEM SET 15.1

1. What precisely is the protection provided by the successor clause in this case? Could UV/Sharon Steel have achieved their desired ends if UV had been less transparent about its plans to liquidate? *Bank of New York Mellon Trust Co. v. Liberty Media Corp.*, 29 A.3d 225, 243 (Del. 2011).

2. Can you reconcile Judge Winter's discussion of boilerplate with his subsequent interpretation of the clause? In particular, do you find it odd that he investigates the background and meaning of the clause rather than simply reading the "four corners" of the text? *See* Diane Lourdes Dick, *Confronting the Certainty Imperative in Corporate Finance Jurisprudence*, 2011 Utah L. Rev. 1461, 1476 (2011).

3. Why did Sharon and UV want to avoid paying off these bonds and notes?

IN RE DURA AUTOMOTIVE SYSTEMS, INC., ET AL., DEBTORS

379 B.R. 257
United States Bankruptcy Court, D. Delaware.
Dec. 7, 2007.

Kevin J. CAREY, Bankruptcy Judge.

On October 30, 2006 (the "Petition Date"), Dura Automotive Systems, Inc. and related entities (the "Debtors") filed voluntary petitions for relief under chapter 11 of title 11 of the United States Code in the United States Bankruptcy Court for the District of Delaware. The Debtors are operating their businesses and managing their properties as debtors-in-possession pursuant to Bankruptcy Code sections 1107(a) and 1108.

The Debtors filed a proposed plan of reorganization (as amended, the "Plan") and corresponding disclosure statement (as amended, the "Disclosure Statement") on August 22, 2007. Revised versions of the Plan and Disclosure Statement were filed on September 28, 2007 and October 4, 2007. The Disclosure Statement was approved by the Court on October 4, 2007. The deadline for filing objections to the Plan was November 5, 2007 and the deadline for creditors to vote whether to accept or reject the Plan was November 15, 2007. Hearing on confirmation of the Plan is now scheduled for December 11, 2007.

Thomas A. and Pattiann Kurak (the "Plaintiffs") assert that they are beneficial holders of $81.5 million of certain subordinated notes issued by Debtor Dura Operating Corp. ("Dura OpCo") pursuant to the Subordinated Note Indenture (described in more detail below), who argue that the Debtors' Plan improperly excludes them from all distributions and recovery. On September 19, 2007, the Plaintiffs filed this adversary proceeding against the Debtors, seeking a declaratory judgment that the Debtors' Plan violates applicable law by failing to provide for a distribution to Plaintiffs of New Common Stock (as defined below) and by failing to allow the Plaintiffs to participate in the Rights Offering (as defined below).

By order dated October 15, 2007, the Bank of New York Trust Company, N.A. ("BNY" or the "Senior Notes Trustee") was authorized to intervene as a defendant in this adversary proceeding.

UNDISPUTED FACTS

From the parties' respective submissions, I discern the following undisputed facts, upon which I rely in my analysis of the Motions.

A.   THE INDENTURES.

In April 1999, Series A and Series B of the 9% Notes, denominated $300 million (U.S.) and $100 million, respectively, were issued pursuant to two indentures, each dated as of April 22, 1999 (as amended or supplemented, the "April 1999 Indentures"), among Dura OpCo, as issuer, U.S. Bank Trust National Association ("US Bank"), as indenture trustee, and certain of the Defendants listed on the signature pages thereto as guarantors (the "Guarantors"). Subsequently, Dura OpCo issued an additional $158.5 million in 9% Notes, Series C and D, pursuant to that certain indenture, dated as of June 22, 2001 (as amended or supplemented, the "June 2001 Indenture" and, together with the April 1999 Indentures, the "Subordinated Note Indenture"), among Dura OpCo, as issuer, U.S. Bank, as indenture trustee, and the Guarantors, as guarantors. The holders of notes issued under the Subordinated Note Indenture are known herein as the "Subordinated Noteholders" or the "9% Noteholders."

In April of 2002, Dura OpCo issued the 8 5/8% Senior Notes (the "Senior Notes") in the aggregate principal amount of $400 million, pursuant to that certain indenture dated as of April 18, 2002 (as amended or supplemented, the "Senior Notes Indenture") among Dura OpCo, as issuer, BNY, as indenture trustee, and certain Defendants listed on the signature pages thereto as guarantors.

Article 10 of the Subordinated Note Indenture is entitled "Subordination" and contains the following provision:

Section 10.01 Agreement to Subordinate.

The Company agrees, and each Holder by accepting a Note agrees, that the Indebtedness evidenced by the Notes is subordinated in right of payment, to the extent and in the manner provided in this Article 10, to the prior payment in full of all Senior Debt of the Company, including Senior Debt incurred after the date of this Indenture, and that the subordination is for the benefit of the holders of Senior Debt.

The term "Company" is defined in the Subordinated Notes Indenture as "Dura Operating Corp., and any and all successors thereto." The Subordinated Note Indenture also provides a specific provision addressing the subordination in the event of a chapter 11:

> Section 10.02. Liquidation; Dissolution; Bankruptcy.
>
> Upon any distribution to creditors of the Company in a liquidation or dissolution of the Company, in a bankruptcy, reorganization, insolvency, receivership or similar proceeding relating to the Company or its property, in an assignment for the benefit of creditors or in any marshalling of the Company's assets and liabilities:
>
> (i) holders of Senior Debt shall be entitled to receive payment in full of all Obligations due in respect of such Senior Debt (including interest after the commencement of any such proceeding at the rate specified in the applicable Senior Debt) before Holders of the Notes shall be entitled to receive any payment with respect to the Notes (***except that Holders may receive (i) Permitted Junior Securities*** and (ii) payments and other distributions made from any defeasance trust created pursuant to Section 8.01 hereof); and
>
> (ii) until all Obligations with respect to Senior Debt (as provided in subsection (i) above) are paid in full, any distribution to which Holders would be entitled but for this Article 10 shall be made to the holders of Senior Debt (***except that Holders of Notes may receive (i) Permitted Junior Securities*** and (ii) payments and other distributions made from any defeasance trust created pursuant to Section 8.01 hereof), as their interests may appear.

See Subordinated Notes Indenture, §10.03 (adding emphasis to the language at issue, known as the "X–Clause"). The term "Permitted Junior Securities" is defined in Section 1.01 as follows and is reproduced here precisely as it appears in the Subordinated Notes Indenture:

> "*Permitted Junior Securities*" means:
> (1) Equity Interests in the Company, DASI or any Guarantor; or
> (2) debt securities that are subordinated to all Senior Debt and any debt securities issued in exchange for Senior Debt to substantially the same extent as, or to a greater extent than, the Notes and the Guaranties are subordinated to Senior Debt under this Indenture.

B.   THE PLAN.

The Debtors' prepetition non-current debt structure is approximately $1.3 billion and comprised of: (a) credit facilities secured by first and second liens providing for aggregate borrowings of $325 million; (b) the Senior Notes, in principal face amount of $400 million; (c) the Subordinated Notes, in principal face amount of approximately $536.6 million (using the exchange rate applicable on the Petition Date for those Subordinated Notes denominated in Euros), and (d) certain convertible subordinated debentures, in principal face amount of $55.2 million (the "Convertible Notes").

The Plan contemplates a rights offering ("Rights Offering") of between $140 million and $160 million in new cash investments in exchange for between 39.3% and 42.6% of the common stock of the reorganized company (the "New Common Stock"), with the balance of the New Common Stock being distributed to holders of the Senior Notes and certain large trade creditors. Based on the valuations set forth in the Disclosure Statement, the Plan provides for holders of Senior Notes and other unsecured claimants to receive substantially less than full recovery on their claims.

The Plan provides the following classification and treatment of the Debtors' unsecured notes:

Class 3—Senior Notes Claims. The Plan provides that claims in Class 3, the Senior Notes claims, will receive their pro rata share of New Common Stock (including the New Common Stock that would otherwise be distributable to the holders of the Subordinated Notes and the Convertible Notes but for the subordination provision) and be afforded the right to participate in the rights offering. (*See* Plan at III.B.3.) Even with the enforcement of the subordination provisions, it is estimated that holders of Senior Notes Claims will receive a recovery of only approximately 55% of the value of their claim. (*See* Disclosure Statement at xiii.)

Class 4—Subordinated Notes Claims. With respect to claims in Class 4, the 9% Subordinated Notes claims, the Plan provides that "Holders of Subordinated Notes Claims shall neither receive nor retain any property under the Plan, pursuant to the Subordinated Notes Indenture, which subordinate their right to payment to the right of holders of Senior Notes Claims to payment in full prior to any distribution being made to holders of 9% Subordinated Notes Claims." (*See* Plan at III.B.4.) The Plan further provides that holders of 9% Subordinated Notes claims are not entitled to vote, as they are "conclusively deemed to reject the Plan." (*Id.*)

Class 6—Convertible Notes Claims. Similarly, with respect to claims in Class 6, the Convertible Notes claims, the Plan provides that "Holders of Convertible Subordinated Debentures Claims shall neither receive nor retain any property under the Plan, pursuant to the Convertible Subordinated Indenture, which subordinates their right to payment to the right of holders of Senior Notes Claims to payment in full prior to any distribution being made to holders of Convertible Subordinated Debentures Claims." (*See* Plan at III.B.6.) The Plan further provides that holders of Convertible Notes claims are not entitled to vote, as they are "conclusively deemed to reject the Plan." (*Id.*)

The Subordinated Notes are not permitted to participate in the Rights Offering. Any New Common Stock otherwise distributable to the Subordinated Noteholders will instead be distributed to the 8 5/8% Noteholders.

DISCUSSION

B.   THE MOTIONS FOR SUMMARY JUDGMENT.

(2)   The "X-Clause."

All of the parties agree on the following principles:

1. The Subordinated Notes Indenture should be enforced in accordance with its terms;
2. The X-Clause is enforceable in bankruptcy, Bankruptcy Code §510(a);
3. The Court must look to state law—in this case the law of New York state—to interpret the Subordinated Notes Indenture and to determine the intent of the parties; and
4. The contract provisions at issue here are not ambiguous.

It is also not disputed that the purpose of subordination provisions in the Subordinated Notes Indenture is to assure payment in full of the Senior Notes before there is any recovery on the Subordinated Notes.

Plaintiffs' argument is straightforward: they are entitled to receive New Common Stock because, by operation of the unconditional and absolute obligation of the Debtors to repay the 9% Notes and Section 1129(b) of the Bankruptcy Code, the 9% Notes must receive the same distribution as any other general unsecured creditor of the Debtors, unless there is some basis for disparate treatment of the 9% Notes. The subordination provisions of the 9% Indenture provides this basis in most circumstances; however, Permitted Junior Securities are unambiguously excepted from the subordination provisions by the X-Clause, and therefore holders of the 9% Notes may receive such securities *even if the 8 5/8% Notes have not yet received payment in full.* Because New Common Stock and the Rights Offering clearly fall within the definition of Permitted Junior Securities, Plaintiffs and all other holders of the 9% Notes must share in the distribution of New Common Stock and be permitted to participate in the Rights Offering on a *pari passu* basis with holders of the 8 5/8% Notes. Otherwise, the Plan is in clear violation of section 1129(b) of the Bankruptcy Code [prohibiting unfair discrimination between classes of creditors of equal priority].

The key to this position rests upon the Plaintiffs' assertion that the Subordinated Notes Indenture's definition of "Permitted Junior Securities" sets forth phrases (1) and (2) as independent clauses. This interpretation rests on the use of a semi-colon and the word "or" at the end of phrase (1), a blank line, and the break which separates phrase (2). The consequence of this reading places "Equity Interests" within the definition without qualification, while "debt securities," the subject of phrase (2), are "Permitted Junior Securities" only if subordinated to the Senior Notes. Since the term "Equity Interests" would include, in this case, the distribution of New Common Stock and the right to participate in the Rights Offering, the Plaintiffs claim that the X-Clause exception to subordination applies, and the Subordinated Noteholders are entitled to retain their share of the Plan's distribution to general unsecured creditors.

The Defendants respond to this by pointing out that "every subordinated noteholder that has litigated this issue has made precisely the same argument . . ." and lost. *See* Reply Memorandum of BNY (docket no. 42) at p. 23. The Defendants cite to three reported decisions (and one unreported decision) in support of this view. All three reported decisions are by circuit courts of appeals.

Despite an invitation extended by this Court at oral argument, neither BNY nor the Debtor would acknowledge that the X-Clause at issue here was poorly drafted. However, like the X-clause in [the Seventh Circuit's opinion in *In re Envirodyne Industries, Inc.,* 29 F.3d 301 (7th Cir.1994) (Posner, J.)] the X-Clause here, while not legally ambiguous, lacks the utter clarity that BNY and the Debtor would now surely prefer.

But, like the *Envirodyne* courts, in interpreting the contract language before me, I will: *"read the contract as a whole* and consider all parts of the whole and not give undue force to certain words or phrases that would distort or confuse the primary and dominant purpose of the contract."

The X-Clause must be read in context. When read as a whole, the Subordinated Note Indenture clearly manifests the intent to assure payment in full of the Senior Notes before permitting payment (in whatever form) to the Subordinated Noteholders. The Plaintiffs argue, in counterpoint, that the purpose of an x-clause is to carve out certain distributions from the otherwise applicable subordination provisions. Therefore, the X-Clause should be read generously in favor of those who are its intended beneficiaries so as to give the fullest effect to this intention. This argument must fail because an x-clause, as a general proposition, creates only limited exceptions to the otherwise applicable subordination provisions and, therefore, must be read narrowly, and in harmony, with the entire contract. This principle applies equally to the X-Clause at issue here.

In an opinion authored by the late Chief Judge Becker, the Third Circuit Court of Appeals followed *Envirodyne. In re PWS Holding Corp.,* 228 F.3d 224 (3d Cir.2000).

In *PWS*, the debtor's plan provided no distribution to a subordinated noteholder. The subordinated noteholder argued that the x-clause created an affirmative obligation by the debtor to distribute securities, so long as the securities distributed to the subordinated noteholder were junior to those issued to senior debt. *Id.* at 244–245. The x-clause in *PWS* provided:

[u]ntil all Obligations with respect to Senior Indebtedness (as provided in Subsection above) are paid in full in cash or cash equivalent, any distribution to which holders would be entitled but for this article shall be made to holders of Senior Indebtedness (except that Holder may receive . . . securities that are subordinated to at least the same extent as the Securities to (a) Senior Indebtedness and (b) any securities issue [sic] in exchange for Senior Indebtedness), as their interests may appear.

The Court, citing the *Envirodyne* decision, explained that the purpose of the x-clause was to avoid the cumbersome procedure that would require junior creditors to pay over securities received pursuant to a plan of reorganization and then take the securities back once the senior creditors were paid in full.

The Plaintiffs contend that *PWS* is not dispositive of this dispute because *PWS* involved a dispute over whether the x-clause at issue there *required* the debtor, when making a distribution to senior debt that was not excluded by the x-clause from the subordination provisions, to make a separate and distinct subordinated distribution to the junior creditors of a different class of security.

Plaintiffs argue, correctly, that each x-clause is different and must be considered only in the specific context of the applicable contract. Considering the X–Clause before me, I conclude that it must not be considered based upon its grammatical structure alone, but also within the context of the entire agreement, which, here, is more reflective of the parties' intent: that except in very limited circumstances, no payment can be made to the Subordinated Noteholders until (1) the Senior Notes are paid in full, or (2) the Senior Noteholders consent. Neither circumstance is present here. I conclude that the language which follows the words "debt securities" in phrase (2) of the "Permitted Junior Securities" definition modifies both phrase (1) and phrase (2). To interpret the X-Clause to include the New Common Stock and the Rights Offering in the definition of "Permitted Junior Securities" would eviscerate the purpose of the subordination provisions in the Subordinated Notes Indenture and expand the limited carve out beyond its intended scope. As the bankruptcy court in *Envirodyne* said, the interpretation advanced by the Subordinated Noteholders "defies explanation and logic. A senior creditor simply would not agree to a subordination agreement in which its priority depended upon the form of consideration chosen by the debtor." *Envirodyne*, 161 B.R. at 448.10

PROBLEM SET 15.2

1. In the *Envirodyne* case, Judge Posner noted that the x-clause was poorly drafted. So did this court, even though the indenture in this case was drafted five years after the *Envirodyne* opinion. Are bond lawyers ignoring Circuit Court opinions?

2. Notice that the plaintiff bondholders in this case were not originally subordinated, but agreed to future subordination. Why might the issuer-debtor have sought to subordinate bondholders from inception?

3. Before the New Deal, it was common for corporate reorganizations to distribute new securities using "relative priority," rather than "absolute priority," as reflected in the "absolute priority rule" we discussed in Chapter 3. That is, securities were distributed to old investors in a way that maintained their relative rank within the capital structure, without following the rule that senior creditors must be paid in full before junior creditors can get anything. With this background, does the purpose of the x-clause become clearer? Does it still have a role to play?

2.   ENFORCING THE INDENTURE

HARRIS TRUST AND SAVINGS BANK v. E-II HOLDINGS, INCORPORATED

926 F.2d 636
United States Court of Appeals, Seventh Circuit.
Feb. 21, 1991.

Harrington WOOD, Jr., Circuit Judge.

Technically, they are high yield debt securities, but in common parlance we call them junk bonds. It is an unflattering and unwelcome appellation, due in no small part to the fact that oftentimes the securities are, quite literally, junk. *See* Kuhn, *Junk: The Weak and the Strong*, Fortune, Oct. 23, 1989, at 17. The appellants, trustees of high yield debt securities with a face value of $1.5 billion, are before this court in an attempt to assuage their fears that the worst has occurred. We cannot provide the reassurance they seek, however; we lack subject matter jurisdiction over most of the complaint and the remainder fails to state a claim.

The facts are straightforward and, for purposes of this decision, undisputed. In 1987, BCI Holdings Corp. ("BCI") engineered a $6.2 billion leveraged acquisition of Beatrice Companies, Inc ("Beatrice"). During the reshuffling that ensued, BCI created E-II Holdings, Inc. ("E-II"), and capitalized it with an initial portfolio of fifteen business concerns that were once part of Beatrice. Soon thereafter, E-II made a registered public offering of $1.5 billion in high yield debt securities: $750,000,000 of 12.85% senior subordinated notes and $750,000,000 of 13.05% subordinated debentures. The trustee under the note indenture was Harris Trust and Savings Bank ("Harris"). The trustee under the debenture indenture was LaSalle National Bank ("LaSalle") (collectively, the "Trustees").

E-II was not immune to the takeover mania that victimized the 1980s, and in December 1987 it launched a hostile takeover bid for American Brands, Inc. ("American Brands"). American Brands countered with a bid for E-II-the so-called "pac man" defense. And when the dust settled, it was American Brands, and not E-II, that prevailed.

Following its unsuccessful takeover attempt, E-II was involved in a number of business transactions that gave rise to uneasiness on the part of the Trustees. For example, on February 29, 1988, E-II became a wholly owned direct subsidiary of American Brands. On July 1, 1988, American Brands sold E-II to McGregor Acquisition Corp. ("McGregor"). And one day after that sale, McGregor made a "capital contribution" to E-II of all of the issued and outstanding stock of its subsidiary, Faberge, Inc. ("Faberge"), in exchange for 840 shares of E-II and a "dividend" of $925,000,000. In all, the Trustees have concerns about some fourteen different transactions (the parties refer to them as "Extraordinary Transactions") occurring between February and December of 1988.

The Trustees were not alone in their concern. A significant number, though not a majority, of investors filed notices of default with the Trustees during the summer and fall of 1988. These notices alleged that a default had occurred because the transaction involving Faberge was in violation of the Indentures.[4]

The Trustees sought to quell their own concerns, as well as those of the investors, by going directly to the source. In addition to the officers' certificates and opinions of counsel required under the Indentures, the Trustees demanded that E-II provide additional information about the Extraordinary Transactions. In particular, the Trustees asked E-II to disclose the factual information on which the certificates and opinions were based. E-II was not accommodating, however; it provided the certificates and opinions required under the Indentures but did not disclose the factual bases of those certificates and opinions. E-II refused to provide the additional information on the ground that the Indentures did not provide such a right.[5]

In the Trustees' view, E-II's failure to cooperate placed them in a quandary the likes of Scylla and Charybdis. If they acted immediately and declared E-II in default, then the declaration could trigger cross-default provisions in other loan agreements and thereby catapult E-II into involuntary bankruptcy. And if it was later discovered that the Trustees were wrong and that E-II had not been in default, then the disgruntled investors would likely sue the Trustees. On the other hand, the Trustees were also amenable to suit if they failed to act and the investors later discovered that, in fact, E-II's actions had breached the Indentures' covenants. Neither course of action seemed prudent in view of what the Trustees perceived as the insufficient nature of the information in their possession.

Paralyzed by indecision, the Trustees searched for someone to make their decision for them. On January 10, 1989, the Trustees filed a declaratory judgment action against E-II and asserted that the following issues were "matter[s] in dispute":

> a. Whether the acquisition of E-II by American Brands was in compliance with the terms of the Indentures and principles of applicable law and equity, including the implied covenants of good faith and fair dealing;

> b. Whether the post-acquisition Extraordinary Transactions…were in compliance with the terms of the Indentures and principles of applicable law and equity, including the implied covenants of good faith and fair dealing;

> c. Whether E-II has complied with the provisions of the [Trust Indenture Act ("Act"), 15 U.S.C. §§77aaa-bbbb,] including but not limited to Section 314, [id. §77nnn,] which requires evidence of compliance with indenture provisions;

---

4. Under section 6.01(3) of the Indentures, a "Default" occurs if E-II "fails to comply in any respect with any of its other agreements contained in the Securities or this Indenture." This "Default" does not become an "Event of Default" (allowing the Trustees to accelerate payment, etc.) until E-II (1) receives written notice from the Trustees or a majority of the investors and (2) fails to correct the Default within 30 days of receiving the notice. Indentures §6.01.

5. E-II apparently would have provided some of the information on a confidential basis, but the Trustees did not believe that their fiduciary duties would allow them to withhold information from the investors and they declined E-II's offer.

d. Whether an Event of Default has occurred on the Notes or the Debentures within the meaning of Section 315 of the [Act, 15 U.S.C. §77000];

e. What action the Trustees should take with respect to the Notices of Default . . . received . . . ;

f. Whether or not the assets remaining in E-II are sufficient to generate sufficient revenues to ensure payment of principal, interest, and sinking fund obligations of the Notes and Debentures;

g. Whether any future asset sales by E-II can be permitted and, if so, under what circumstances; and

h. To what information are the Trustees entitled in order to determine if unusual occurrences, such as the Extraordinary Transactions, violate the terms of the Indentures.

The Trustees closed their complaint with a request for a judicial declaration concerning each of these "matter[s] in dispute."

E-II, however, and subsequently the district court, were hard pressed to determine the Trustees' positions with respect to the alleged "matter[s] in dispute." And in fact, the Trustees had failed to take a position with respect to virtually every one of the issues for which they sought a judicial declaration. The Trustees did argue that they were entitled to more information than E-II was giving them (the eighth "matter in dispute"), but otherwise peppered their submissions with qualifiers—"may," "could," and other verbalisms that failed to indicate a stance.

On E-II's motion to dismiss under rules 12(b)(1) and 12(b)(6) of the Federal Rules of Civil Procedure, the district court held that it had no subject matter jurisdiction to decide those issues for which the Trustees failed to take a position. That failure, the district court concluded, precluded jurisdiction because it evidenced the lack of a case or controversy. As to the dispute over the Trustees' entitlement to additional information, the district court concluded that a case or controversy existed because the parties disputed the quantity and quality of disclosure required of E-II. The district court then found no legal basis to support the Trustees' claim that they were entitled to more information than E-II was willing to disclose. As such, it dismissed the request for information on the ground that it failed to state a cause of action. The district court also denied a subsequent motion by the Trustees to alter or amend the judgment.

On appeal, the Trustees continue to assert that it is neither necessary nor appropriate for them to commit to a position. Indeed, they assert that their request for "judicial guidance" and "judicial instruction" is the paradigm on which all declaratory judgment cases are built. And in so doing, they seal their fate: "Frequently, an issue of this sort will come before [this court] clad, so to speak, in sheep's clothing: the potential of the asserted principle to effect important change . . . is not immediately evident, and must be discerned by a careful and perceptive analysis. But this wolf comes as a wolf." [6]

As a predicate to relief, the Declaratory Judgment Act requires that the case be one of "actual controversy." 28 U.S.C. §2201(a). That predicate, which tracks the "cases" or "controversies" requirement of article III, saves the statute from unconstitutionally expanding the federal courts' jurisdiction. *See Aetna Life Ins. Co. v. Haworth*, 300 U.S. 227, 57 S.Ct. 461, 81 L.Ed. 617 (1937) (upholding Act); U.S. Const. art. III, §2.10 The often unspoken, but yet obvious, corollary of the "actual controversy" predicate is that the dispute must exist *between the parties to the declaratory judgment action.*

The only issue in the Trustees' complaint that does appear to present a case or controversy is the dispute over the quantity and quality of information that the Trustees are entitled to receive from E-II. This dispute fails to clear a different hurdle, however; the Trustees have not put forth a cognizable legal basis under which they might be entitled to the information that they seek. Of the three bases offered—express covenant, implied covenant, and the Act—not one can support the Trustees' demand for additional information.

The first potential basis for relief—the express language of the Indentures—is a latecomer to this litigation; the Trustees failed to raise this argument until they filed a motion to alter or amend the judgment.

Even if we were to reach the merits on this issue, we would feel compelled to agree with the district court. The argument that section 11.05 expressly requires E-II to provide the requested information is more wishful thinking than anything else. As the district court observed, section 11.05 is limited by its express terms to a "certificate" or "opinion." Nowhere does it require E-II to disclose the facts underlying these documents. Indeed, when more disclosure is necessary, the Indentures make express provisions for that disclosure. *See, e.g.*, Indentures §4.07 (if E-II knows of a "Default" or "Event of Default," "the certificate shall describe any such Default or Event of Default and its status"); *Id.*§5.01(5) (certificate shall contain a statement of compliance and have attached "arithmetic computations" demonstrating compliance with the Consolidated Interest Expense Ratio).

The second potential basis for relief—the implied covenant of good faith and fair dealing—presents a more difficult question. The parties agree that New York law applies and that every contract governed by New York law contains an implied covenant to perform the contract fairly and in good faith. The parties are in relatively sharp disagreement, however, as to what that implied covenant requires in this case.

Courts often use broad and unqualified language in describing the content of the implied covenant of good faith. *See, e.g., Metropolitan Life Ins. Co. v. RJR Nabisco, Inc.*, 716 F.Supp. 1504, 1516–18 (S.D.N.Y.1989). In contrast to their broad definitional language, however, their analyses indicate that the "party who

---

6. *Morrison v. Olson*, 487 U.S. 654, 699, 108 S.Ct. 2597, 2623, 101 L.Ed.2d 569 (1988) (Scalia, J., dissenting).

asserts the existence of an implied-in-fact covenant bears a heavy burden." And from these analyses, we discern that New York law appears to invoke the implied covenant of good faith and fair dealing only in those instances where one party has violated the spirit, although not the letter, of a contract. *See Metropolitan Life*, 716 F.Supp. at 1517 (implied covenant appropriate where, while the express terms of the contract "may not have been technically breached, one party has nonetheless effectively deprived the other of those express, explicitly bargained-for benefits.").

Here, as in *Metropolitan Life*, the relevant contracts do not support the interpretation that the Trustees now advocate. The Trustees allude to the "fruits" of the investors' bargain but fail to demonstrate, especially in light of the limited requirements of section 11.05, how a reasonable investor would be justified in assuming that E-II promised to disclose the factual bases underlying its certificates and opinions. Indeed, their language suggests, without basis, that E-II has a continuing duty to reassure the investors that they have made a good investment—the same type of argument rejected in *Metropolitan Life*. New York law does not, as the Trustees would have us believe, imply a covenant merely on the basis of strong societal concerns; the foundation of the implied covenant is the express covenant, and the Trustees' claim simply fails to provide that foundation.

True, the Indentures do not preclude the Trustees from obtaining the information they now seek, but that does not mean that we should imply such a right of access.

Implying the covenant requested by the Trustees would also be "troublesome" in view of the fact that the Indentures "could easily have been drafted to incorporate expressly the terms the [Trustees] now urge this court to imply." Section 603(f) of the Model Debenture Indenture Provisions even provides a basic model for such a provision:

> Except as otherwise provided in Section 601: . . .
> (f) the Trustee shall not be bound to make any investigation into the facts or matters stated in any resolution, certificate, statement, instrument, opinion, report, notice, request, direction, consent, order, bond, debenture, coupon or other paper or document but the Trustee, in its discretion, may make such further inquiry or investigation into such facts or matters as it may see fit, and, if the Trustee shall determine to make such further inquiry or investigation, it shall be entitled to examine the books, records and premises of the Company, personally or by agent or attorney. . . .

The third potential basis for relief—the Act—fares no better than its predecessors. Section 314(e) of the Act specifies the "evidence of compliance" (with a condition or covenant) that an issuer must furnish to an indenture trustee. 15 U.S.C. §77nnn(e). That section (like section 11.05 of the Indentures) requires certificates and opinions but does not require issuers to disclose the factual bases of certificates or opinions. Moreover, although section 314(a)(2) of the Act, 15 U.S.C. §77nnn(a)(2), allows the SEC to promulgate rules or regulations that could require E-II to provide additional "evidence of compliance," the SEC to date has failed to promulgate any such rule or regulation. *See* 17 C.F.R. §§260.0-1 to 260.14a-1. Last, section 314(f) dispositively states:

> Nothing in this section shall be construed either as requiring the inclusion in the indenture to be qualified of provisions that the obligor upon the indenture securities shall furnish to the indenture trustee any other evidence of compliance with the conditions and covenants provided for in the indenture than the evidence specified in this section, or as preventing the inclusion of such provisions in such indentures, if the parties so agree.

Id. §77nnn(f). This freedom-of-contract mentality leaves no room for the interpretation that the Trustees would thrust upon the Act.

The doors to the federal courthouse remain open to the Trustees as they remain open to all litigants: subject to such prerequisites as subject matter jurisdiction and stating a cognizable claim. Until the Trustees are willing and able to meet those prerequisites, however, we must turn them away.

PROBLEM SET 15.3

1. How could this problem have been avoided? Is it a problem?
2. What would you advise a trustee in a similar position in the future to do in these circumstances?

MARBLEGATE ASSET MANAGEMENT, LLC v. EDUCATION MANAGEMENT FINANCE CORP.

846 F.3d 1

United States Court of Appeals,
Second Circuit.
January 17, 2017

LOHIER, Circuit Judge:

Defendant–appellant Education Management Corporation ("EDMC") and its subsidiaries appeal from a judgment following a bench trial before the United States District Court for the Southern District of New York (Failla, J.). The District Court held that a series of transactions meant to restructure EDMC's debt over the objections of certain noteholders violated Section 316(b) of the Trust Indenture Act of 1939, 15 U.S.C. § 77ppp(b). The transactions at issue, the District Court determined, stripped the non-consenting noteholders, plaintiffs–appellees Marblegate Asset Management, LLC and Marblegate Special Opportunity Master Fund, L.P. (together, "Marblegate"), of their practical ability to collect payment on notes purchased from EDMC's subsidiaries. As a result, the District Court ordered EDMC to continue to guarantee Marblegate's notes and pay them in full.

On appeal, EDMC argues that it complied with Section 316(b) because the transactions did not formally amend the payment terms of the indenture that governed the notes. We agree with EDMC and conclude that Section 316(b) prohibits only non-consensual amendments to an indenture's core payment terms. We therefore VACATE the judgment and REMAND to the District Court for further proceedings consistent with this opinion.

BACKGROUND

1. FACTS

EDMC is a for-profit higher education company that relies heavily on federal funding through Title IV of the Higher Education Act of 1965, 20 U.S.C. §§ 1070–1099. EDMC is the parent company of defendants–appellants Education Management, LLC and Education Management Finance Corporation (together, the "EDM Issuer").

In 2014 EDMC found itself in severe financial distress. Its enterprise value had fallen well below its $1.5 billion in outstanding debt. But restructuring its debt by resorting to bankruptcy court was not a realistic option for EDMC, which, the parties agree, would lose its eligibility for Title IV funds if it filed for bankruptcy and discontinued as an ongoing concern. EDMC therefore had to cooperate with its creditors outside of the bankruptcy process if it hoped to restructure its debt and persist as a viable entity.

EDMC's outstanding debt consisted of both secured debt (roughly $1.3 billion) and unsecured debt ($217 million). The secured debt was governed by a 2010 credit agreement between the EDM Issuer and secured creditors (the "2010 Credit Agreement"). The 2010 Credit Agreement gave EDMC's secured creditors the right, upon default, to deal with the collateral securing the loans "fully and completely" as the "absolute owner" for "all purposes." The collateral securing the debt consisted of virtually all of EDMC's assets.

The unsecured debt, to which we will refer as the "Notes," was also issued by the EDM Issuer and governed by an indenture executed in March 2013 and qualified under the Trust Indenture Act of 1939 (the "Indenture"). The Notes were guaranteed by EDMC as the parent company of the EDM Issuer (we refer to this guarantee as the "Notes Parent Guarantee") and carried a high effective interest rate—nearly 20 percent per year—to compensate for the riskier nature of the unsecured debt. Both the Indenture and the offering circular relating to the Notes informed lenders who had purchased them (the "Noteholders") about their rights and obligations as junior, unsecured creditors. For example, the offering circular explained that the Notes Parent Guarantee was issued solely to satisfy EDMC's reporting obligations, that it could be released solely by operation of the release of any later guarantee EDMC issued to secured creditors, and that Noteholders should therefore not assign any value to the Notes Parent Guarantee. Marblegate holds Notes with a face value of $14 million but never held any secured debt.

As EDMC's financial position deteriorated, its debt burden became unsustainable. After negotiating with EDMC, a majority of secured creditors agreed in September 2014 to relieve the EDM Issuer of certain imminent payment obligations and covenants under the 2010 Credit Agreement. The resulting agreement was a new amended credit agreement entered in the fall of 2014 (the "2014 Credit Agreement"). As consideration for these changes, EDMC agreed to guarantee the secured loans (the "Secured Parent Guarantee").

Around the same time, a group of creditors formed an Ad Hoc Committee of Term Loan Lenders (the "Ad Hoc Committee") and established a Steering Committee, which is an intervenor–appellant in this appeal, to negotiate with EDMC.[7] The Steering Committee and EDMC eventually devised two potential avenues to relieve EDMC of its debt obligations.

The first option, which obtained only if creditors unanimously consented, was designed to result in (1) most of EDMC's outstanding secured debt being exchanged for $400 million in new secured term loans and new stock convertible into roughly 77 percent of EDMC's common stock, and (2) the Notes being exchanged for equity worth roughly 19 percent of EDMC's common stock. EDMC estimated that this first option would amount to roughly a 45 percent reduction in value for secured lenders and a 67 percent reduction in value for Noteholders.

The second option would arise only if one or more creditors refused to consent. Under that circumstance, a number of events would occur that together constituted the "Intercompany Sale." Secured creditors consenting to the Intercompany Sale would first exercise their preexisting rights under the 2014 Credit Agreement and Article 9 of the Uniform Commercial Code (UCC) to foreclose on EDMC's assets. In addition, the secured creditors would release EDMC from the Secured Parent Guarantee. That release in turn would effect a release of the Notes Parent Guarantee under the Indenture. With the consent of the secured creditors (but without needing the consent of the unsecured creditors), the collateral agent would then sell the foreclosed assets to a subsidiary of EDMC newly constituted for purposes of the Intercompany Sale. Finally, the new EDMC subsidiary would distribute debt and equity only to consenting creditors and continue the business.

The Intercompany Sale was structured to incentivize creditors to consent. While non-consenting secured creditors would still receive debt in the new EDMC subsidiary, that debt would be junior to the debt of consenting secured creditors. Non-consenting Noteholders would not receive anything from the new company: though not a single term of the Indenture was altered and Noteholders therefore retained a contractual right to collect payments due under the Notes, the foreclosure would transform the EDM Issuer into an empty shell. In offering to exchange the Notes for equity in the new EDMC subsidiary, therefore, EDMC

---

7. The Ad Hoc Committee held 80.6 percent of the secured debt and 80.7 percent of the Notes. Of that total, the Steering Committee of the Ad Hoc Committee held 35.8 percent of secured debt and 73.1 percent of the Notes.

and the Ad Hoc Committee explicitly warned Noteholders that they would not receive payment if they did not consent to the Intercompany Sale.

Except for Marblegate, all of EDMC's creditors (representing 98 percent of its debt) eventually consented to the Intercompany Sale.

2. PROCEDURAL HISTORY

Marblegate, the sole holdout, sued to enjoin the Intercompany Sale on the ground that it violated Section 316(b) of the Trust Indenture Act of 1939 (the "TIA"), 15 U.S.C. § 77ppp(b). Marblegate Asset Mgmt. v. Educ. Mgmt. Corp., 75 F. Supp. 3d 592 (S.D.N.Y. 2014) ("Marblegate I"). Section 316(b) of the TIA, entitled "Prohibition of impairment of holder's right to payment," provides as follows:

> Notwithstanding any other provision of the indenture to be qualified, the right of any holder of any indenture security to receive payment of the principal of and interest on such indenture security, on or after the respective due dates expressed in such indenture security, or to institute suit for the enforcement of any such payment on or after such respective dates, shall not be impaired or affected without the consent of such holder, except as to a postponement of an interest payment consented to as provided in paragraph (2) of subsection (a) of this section, and except that such indenture may contain provisions limiting or denying the right of any such holder to institute any such suit, if and to the extent that the institution or prosecution thereof or the entry of judgment therein would, under applicable law, result in the surrender, impairment, waiver, or loss of the lien of such indenture upon any property subject to such lien.

15 U.S.C. § 77ppp(b) (emphasis added) . . .

Since the bulk of the Intercompany Sale was already completed, the subsequent bench trial focused on whether the District Court should permanently enjoin release of the Notes Parent Guarantee and thereby force EDMC to continue its guaranteed payment on Marblegate's Notes. On that question, the District Court ultimately sided with Marblegate by reiterating that the release of the Notes Parent Guarantee would violate Section 316(b).

This appeal followed. At present, because EDMC was able to reduce its debt burden through the very transaction to which Marblegate objected, it currently has the assets to pay on Marblegate's Notes. Marblegate, as the owner of Notes that had been poised to receive only limited additional payments because of EDMC's pending insolvency, is now the only creditor receiving full payouts according to the original face value of its Notes.

DISCUSSION

EDMC appeals the judgment on the ground that the District Court misinterpreted Section 316(b) of the TIA. We review the District Court's conclusions of law de novo . . .

1. TEXT

The core disagreement in this case is whether the phrase "right . . . to receive payment" forecloses more than formal amendments to payment terms that eliminate the right to sue for payment. 15 U.S.C. § 77ppp(b). We agree with the District Court that the text of Section 316(b) is ambiguous insofar as it "lends itself to multiple interpretations" that arguably favor either side on that issue. Likewise, Marblegate conceded at oral argument that the interpretation it advances is not supported by reference to the plain text alone.

On the one hand, Congress's use of the term "right" to describe what it sought to protect from non-consensual amendment suggests a concern with the legally enforceable obligation to pay that is contained in the Indenture, not with a creditor's <u>practical</u> ability to collect on payments. On the other hand, adding that such a right cannot be "impaired or affected" arguably suggests that it cannot be diminished, relaxed, or "otherwise affect[ed] in an injurious manner."

To be sure, Marblegate's broad reading of the term "right" as including the practical ability to collect payment leads to both improbable results and interpretive problems. Among other things, interpreting "impaired or affected" to mean any <u>possible</u> effect would transform a single provision of the TIA into a broad prohibition on any conduct that could influence the value of a note or a bondholder's practical ability to collect payment. Furthermore, if the "right . . . to receive payment" means a bondholder's practical ability to collect payment, then protecting the "right ... to institute suit for the enforcement of any such payment" would be superfluous, because limiting the right to file a lawsuit for payment constitutes one of the most obvious impairments of the creditor's practical ability to collect payment. The "right . . . to receive payment" is not, in other words, so broad as to encompass the "right . . . to institute suit." If for no other reason than the "general rule" that different statutory phrases "can indicate that different meanings were intended," these two rights are best viewed as distinct from one another. The former right, it seems to us, prohibits non-consensual amendments of core payment terms (that is, the amount of principal and interest owed, and the date of maturity). It bars, for example, so-called "collective-action clauses"—indenture provisions that authorize a majority of bondholders to approve changes to payment terms and force those changes on all bondholders. The latter right (to sue) ensures that individual bondholders can freely sue to collect payments owed under the indenture. So construed, the right to sue clearly bars so-called "no-action clauses," which preclude individual bondholders from suing the issuer for breaches of the indenture, leaving the indenture trustee as the sole initiator of suit. An indenture that contains only a collective-action clause violates the "payment" right, not the "suit" right; an indenture that contains only a no-action clause violates the "suit" right, not the "payment" right.

Regardless, we agree with the District Court that the plain text of Section 316(b) is ultimately ambiguous and fails to resolve the principal question before us.

Nor does any party seriously contend that the structure of the TIA provides a clear answer to that question, as the dissenting opinion suggests. At best, we have observed that "[n]othing in Section 316(b), or the TIA in general, requires that bondholders be afforded 'absolute and unconditional' rights to payment."

2. LEGISLATIVE HISTORY

Because the text of Section 316(b) is ambiguous and the TIA's structure fails to remove the ambiguity, we turn to legislative history.

Marblegate argues that the history of Section 316(b) demonstrates Congress's broad intent to prohibit "an out–of–court debt restructuring that has the purpose and effect of eliminating <u>any</u> possibility of receiving payment under their notes." The District Court effectively adopted this view . . .

Based on our review of the legislative history of Section 316(b), we conclude that Congress did not intend the broad reading that Marblegate urges and the District Court embraced. Starting in 1936, the Securities and Exchange Commission (SEC) published a comprehensive eight-part report examining the role of protective committees in reorganizations. Part VI of that report, published in 1936 and entitled "Trustees Under Indentures" (the "1936 SEC Report"), led to enactment of the TIA. <u>See</u> 15 U.S.C. § 77bbb(a) (citing "reports of the [SEC]" as "the basis of facts" for promulgating the TIA). Subsequent congressional reports, testimony, and other contemporaneous statements by SEC officials relating to earlier bills also shaped the final legislation enacted in 1939.

Among other things, the drafters of the TIA appear to have been well aware of the range of possible forms of reorganization available to issuers, up to and including foreclosures like the one that occurred in this case but that the District Court concluded violated Section 316(b). Indeed, foreclosure-based reorganizations were widely used at the time the TIA was drafted. As we explain below, the history of the TIA, and of Section 316(b) in particular, shows that it does not prohibit foreclosures even when they affect a bondholder's ability to receive full payment. Rather, the relevant portions of the TIA's legislative history exclusively addressed <u>formal</u> amendments and indenture provisions like collective-action and no-action clauses.

A. The 1936 SEC Report

Two sections of the 1936 SEC Report are relevant to the competing interpretations of Section 316(b) offered by the parties on appeal. Neither section supports Marblegate's position that Section 316(b) meant to prohibit involuntary debt restructurings like foreclosures . . .

In 1938 then-SEC Chairman William O. Douglas, an expert in the field of corporate reorganizations, testified before Congress in support of the proposed Trust Indenture Act of 1938. Because Douglas had been the principal draftsman of the 1936 SEC Report and the "main proponent" of the legislation before Congress, the District Court appropriately paid significant attention to his testimony.

Like the 1936 SEC Report, Chairman Douglas's testimony narrowly addressed collective-action clauses and formal amendments to core payment terms. Quoting at length from the "Reorganization by contract" section of the 1936 SEC Report and responding to the "bogey" that the proposed legislation would require unanimous consent of bondholders to amend any indenture term, Douglas assured critics of the proposed legislation that "[t]here is absolutely nothing in the bill to prevent" amendment of the indenture by a majority, with one exception, which he described as follows:

> The effect of this exception is <u>merely to prohibit</u> <u>provisions</u> authorizing such a majority to force a non-assenting security holder to accept a reduction or postponement of his claim for principal, or a reduction of his claim for interest or a postponement thereof for more than 1 year. <u>In other words, this</u> <u>provision merely restricts the power of the majority</u> to change those particular phases of the contract.

Douglas thus explained that Section 7(m)(3) of the 1938 bill (which evolved into Section 316(b) of the TIA) meant "merely" to prohibit indenture "provisions" that would allow majorities to amend core payment terms . . .

Our review of the testimony and reports leading up to and immediately following the enactment of Section 316(b) convinces us, in sum, that Congress sought to prohibit formal modifications to indentures without the consent of all bondholders, but did not intend to go further by banning other well-known forms of reorganization like foreclosures . . .

F. Textual Changes

Marblegate separately points to the evolution of the text of Section 316(b) through its enactment in 1939 to argue that the final text substantively broadened the TIA's protections of the minority bondholder's right from "a mere right to sue into a more substantive right" to actually "receive payment of the principal and interest. We are not persuaded.

We find little if any textual support for the proposition that a new substantive right to receive payment was added to the final version of Section 316(b) . . .

3. WORKABILITY AND DISSENTING BONDHOLDER REMEDIES

Finally, we highlight an additional difficulty with Marblegate's interpretation of Section 316(b) and address a potential concern with our holding.

Marblegate's interpretation of Section 316(b) requires that courts determine in each case whether a challenged transaction constitutes an "out–of–court debt restructuring . . . designed to eliminate a non–consenting holder's ability to receive payment." The interpretation thus turns on the subjective intent of the issuer or majority bondholders, not the transactional techniques used. But we have expressed a particular distaste for interpreting boilerplate indenture provisions based on the "relationship of particular borrowers and lenders" or the "particularized intentions of the parties to an indenture," both of which undermine "uniformity in interpretation." *See* Sharon Steel Corp. v. Chase Manhattan Bank, N.A., 691 F.2d 1039, 1048 (2d Cir. 1982).[8]

Marblegate similarly argues that the right to receive payment is impaired "when the source of assets for that payment is deliberately placed beyond the reach of non–consenting noteholders." But this description could apply to <u>every</u> foreclosure in which the value of the collateral is insufficient to pay creditors in full. Marblegate and the District Court respond that Section 316(b) permits "genuinely adversarial" foreclosures but prohibits the type of foreclosure that occurred here. But neither the text nor the legislative history of Section 316(b) supports a distinction between adversarial and "friendly" foreclosures.[19] Nor do we agree with the District Court's description of the negotiations. To the contrary, our reading of the record convinces us that the negotiations were clearly adversarial before the parties agreed on a course to preserve the value of the assets. The negotiations leading to the creation and release of the Secured Parent Guarantee were, in our view, also adversarial.

Limiting Section 316(b) to formal indenture amendments to core payment rights will not leave dissenting bondholders at the mercy of bondholder majorities. Our holding leaves Marblegate with some recourse. By preserving the legal right to receive payment, we permit creditors to pursue available State and federal law remedies. (And of course, sophisticated creditors, like Marblegate, can insist on credit agreements that forbid transactions like the Intercompany Sale.) Having foregone the protection of bankruptcy in this case, the secured creditors and EDMC have also shed the protection of the Bankruptcy Code, including a discharge order. The foreclosure in this case therefore may be challenged by other creditors under State law. Moreover, where creditors foreclose on a debtor's collateral and sell the collateral to a new entity meant to carry on the business, the debtor's other creditors may be able to sue the new entity under State law theories of successor liability or fraudulent conveyance. We obviously take no view on the potential merit of any State law or federal law claims in the context of the Intercompany Sale at issue here.

CONCLUSION

To summarize, we hold that Section 316(b) of the TIA does not prohibit the Intercompany Sale in this case. The transaction did not amend any terms of the Indenture. Nor did it prevent any dissenting bondholders from initiating suit to collect payments due on the dates specified by the Indenture. Marblegate retains its legal right to obtain payment by suing the EDM Issuer, among others. Absent changes to the Indenture's core payment terms, however, Marblegate cannot

---

8. *Compare* Sharon Steel, 691 F.3d at 1048 ("Just such uncertainties would be created if interpretation of boilerplate provisions were submitted to juries sitting in every judicial district in the nation."), *with* BOKF, N.A. v. Caesars Entm't Corp., 144 F. Supp. 3d 459, 474–75 & n.86 (S.D.N.Y. 2015) (adopting Marblegate's interpretation of Section 316(b), but sending to the factfinder the question of whether the "overall effect" of the transactions at issue was "a debt restructuring or a series of routine corporate transactions").

invoke Section 316(b) to retain an "absolute and unconditional" right to payment of its notes.

STRAUB, Circuit Judge, dissenting:

The question before this Court is whether Section 316(b) of the Trust Indenture Act (the "TIA") prohibits Defendant–appellant Education Management Corporation ("EDMC") from engaging in an out-of-court restructuring that is collusively engineered to ensure that certain minority bondholders receive no payment on their notes, despite the fact that the terms of the indenture governing those notes remain unchanged. Because the plain text of the statute compels the conclusion that it does, I would answer that question in the affirmative and uphold the judgment of the District Court. I therefore respectfully dissent . . .

Had Congress intended merely to protect against modification of an indenture's payment terms, it could have so stated. Nothing in the language of Section 316(b), however, cabins the prohibition on impairing or affecting the "right . . . to receive payment" to mere *amendment* of the indenture. In fact, that Congress used the broad phrase "impaired or affected" implies that it did not intend Section 316(b) to be limited in its scope to mere amendments. Because we are compelled to give every term in a statute effect, our reading of the statute must account for rather than ignore this phraseology. Further, Section 316(b) is written in the passive voice; its prohibition is nowhere limited to actions taken by a noteholder majority. Despite Appellants' arguments to the contrary, nothing in the text of the statute requires the narrow reading that Section 316(b) merely prohibits modification of an indenture's core payment terms (amount and due date) by noteholder majority action without consent of the individual noteholder . . .

I am cognizant of the parade of horrors that Appellants predict will result from interpreting the TIA in the manner above. However, threatening dire commercial consequences from the refusal to read a statute in a manner inconsistent with its plain language is not a sufficient basis to override the correct interpretation of the law. We must not forget the long–standing imperative that *making* law is the job of the legislature and not of the courts . . . [9] The bond market has surely undergone significant alterations since the enactment of the TIA, including that the main players are now sophisticated corporate entities on both sides. But it is not for this Court to alter the TIA on its own accord, and "none of this establishes why the plaintiffs should be barred from vindicating their rights under the [TIA]" as it currently stands. "Our role is not to craft a resolution that will solve all the problems that might arise in hypothetical future litigation involving other bonds

---

9. Significantly, Congress recently abandoned two proposals to amend § 316(b), first through a 2015 highway bill rider and then through an omnibus appropriations legislation rider. The proposals would have narrowed the definitions of impairment of the right to payment and the right to institute suit for nonpayment. In response to the latter proposal, 18 law professors sent a letter to members of Congress urging them to reject the proposed amendment, which would have been undertaken without legislative hearings or public comment, because the amendment "could have broad negative unintended consequences in the securities market."

and other [parties]," but it is instead to interpret the TIA in as fastidious a manner as we are able. In so doing I would hold that Section 316(b) of the TIA bars the actions at issue in this case.

CONCLUSION

Because the Intercompany Sale as proposed under the Restructuring Support Agreement would have the effect of imposing on Marblegate a choice between a modification of their core payment terms or receiving no payment at all—thereby clearly impairing Marblegate's right to receive payment under the original terms of the indenture—I would hold that it violates the plain text of Section 316(b) of the Trust Indenture Act and affirm the judgment of the District Court. Our system of governance is organized such that Congress is tasked with writing the law and the federal courts are tasked with applying, not rewriting, it. If Congress and the parties affected by the TIA are unsatisfied with the law's consequences, it is for Congress rather than this Court to amend it. I therefore respectfully dissent.

PROBLEM SET 15.4

1. What role does the TIA play in this dispute?
2. What indenture amendments are permissible under the Second Circuit's approach?

3. IMPLIED RIGHTS OF BONDHOLDERS

METROPOLITAN LIFE INSURANCE COMPANY v. RJR NABISCO, INC.

716 F.Supp. 1504
United States District Court, S.D. New York.
June 1, 1989.

WALKER, District Judge:

I. INTRODUCTION

The corporate parties to this action are among the country's most sophisticated financial institutions, as familiar with the Wall Street investment community and the securities market as American consumers are with the Oreo cookies and Winston cigarettes made by defendant RJR Nabisco, Inc. (sometimes "the company" or "RJR Nabisco"). The present action traces its origins to October 20, 1988, when F. Ross Johnson, then the Chief Executive Officer of RJR Nabisco, proposed a $17 billion leveraged buy-out ("LBO") of the company's shareholders, at $75 per share.[10] Within a few days, a bidding war

---

10. A leveraged buy-out occurs when a group of investors, usually including members of a company's management team, buy the company under financial arrangements that include little

developed among the investment group led by Johnson and the investment firm of Kohlberg Kravis Roberts & Co. ("KKR"), and others. On December 1, 1988, a special committee of RJR Nabisco directors, established by the company specifically to consider the competing proposals, recommended that the company accept the KKR proposal, a $24 billion LBO that called for the purchase of the company's outstanding stock at roughly $109 per share.

The flurry of activity late last year that accompanied the bidding war for RJR Nabisco spawned at least eight lawsuits, filed before this Court, charging the company and its former CEO with a variety of securities and common law violations. The Court agreed to hear the present action—filed even before the company accepted the KKR proposal—on an expedited basis, with an eye toward March 1, 1989, when RJR Nabisco was expected to merge with the KKR holding entities created to facilitate the LBO. On that date, RJR Nabisco was also scheduled to assume roughly $19 billion of new debt. After a delay unrelated to the present action, the merger was ultimately completed during the week of April 24, 1989.

Plaintiffs now allege, in short, that RJR Nabisco's actions have drastically impaired the value of bonds previously issued to plaintiffs by, in effect, misappropriating the value of those bonds to help finance the LBO and to distribute an enormous windfall to the company's shareholders. As a result, plaintiffs argue, they have unfairly suffered a multimillion dollar loss in the value of their bonds.[11]

On February 16, 1989, this Court heard oral argument on plaintiffs' motions. At the hearing, the Court denied plaintiffs' request for a preliminary injunction, based on their insufficient showing of irreparable harm. An exchange between the Court and plaintiffs' counsel, like the submissions before it, convinced the Court that plaintiffs had failed to meet their heavy burden:

> THE COURT: How do you respond to [defendants'] statements on irreparable harm? What we're looking at now is whether or not there's a basis for a preliminary injunction and if there's no irreparable harm then we're in a damage action and that changes . . . the contours of the suit. . . . We're talking about the ability . . . of the company to satisfy any judgment.
>
> PLAINTIFFS: That's correct. And our point . . . is that if we receive a judgment at any time, six months from now, after a trial for example, that

---

equity and significant new debt. The necessary debt financing typically includes mortgages or high risk/high yield bonds, popularly known as "junk bonds." Additionally, a portion of this debt is generally secured by the company's assets. Some of the acquired company's assets are usually sold after the transaction is completed in order to reduce the debt incurred in the acquisition.

11. Agencies like Standard & Poor's and Moody's generally rate bonds in two broad categories: investment grade and speculative grade. Standard & Poor's rates investment grade bonds from "AAA" to "BBB." Moody's rates those bonds from "AAA" to "Baa3." Speculative grade bonds are rated either "BB" and lower, or "Ba1" and lower, by Standard & Poor's and Moody's, respectively. *See, e.g., Standard and Poor's Debt Rating Criteria* at 10–11. No one disputes that, subsequent to the announcement of the LBO, the RJR Nabisco bonds lost their "A" ratings.

judgment will almost inevitably be the basis for a judgment for everyone else. . . . But if we get a judgment, everyone else will get one as well. . . .

THE COURT: [Y]ou're . . . asking me . . . [to] infer a huge number of plaintiffs and a lot more damages than your clients could ever recover as being the basis for deciding the question of irreparable harm. And those [potential] actions aren't before me.

PLAINTIFFS: I think that's correct. . . .

Plaintiffs failed to respond convincingly to defendants' arguments that, although plaintiffs have invested roughly $350 million in RJR Nabisco, their potential damages nonetheless remain relatively small and that, upon completion of the merger, the company will retain an equity base of $5 billion. *See, e.g.*, Tr. at 32, 35; D. Opp. at 48, 49. Given plaintiffs' failure to show irreparable harm, the Court denied their request for injunctive relief. This initial ruling, however, left intact plaintiffs' underlying motions, which, together with defendants' cross-motions, now require attention.

Although the numbers involved in this case are large, and the financing necessary to complete the LBO unprecedented,[12] the legal principles nonetheless remain discrete and familiar. Yet while the instant motions thus primarily require the Court to evaluate and apply traditional rules of equity and contract interpretation, plaintiffs do raise issues of first impression in the context of an LBO. At the heart of the present motions lies plaintiffs' claim that RJR Nabisco violated a restrictive covenant—not an explicit covenant found within the four corners of the relevant bond indentures, but rather an *implied* covenant of good faith and fair dealing—not to incur the debt necessary to facilitate the LBO and thereby betray what plaintiffs claim was the fundamental basis of their bargain with the company. The company, plaintiffs assert, consistently reassured its bondholders that it had a "mandate" from its Board of Directors to maintain RJR Nabisco's preferred credit rating. Plaintiffs ask this Court first to imply a covenant of good faith and fair dealing that would prevent the recent transaction, then to hold that this covenant has been breached, and finally to require RJR Nabisco to redeem their bonds.

RJR Nabisco defends the LBO by pointing to express provisions in the bond indentures that, *inter alia*, permit mergers and the assumption of additional debt. These provisions, as well as others that could have been included but were not, were known to the market and to plaintiffs, sophisticated investors who freely bought the bonds and were equally free to sell them at any time. Any attempt by this Court to create contractual terms *post hoc*, defendants contend, not only finds no basis in the controlling law and undisputed facts of this case, but also would

---

12. On February 9, 1989, KKR completed its tender offer for roughly 74 percent of RJR Nabisco's common stock (of which approximately 97% of the outstanding shares were tendered) and all of its Series B Cumulative Preferred Stock (of which approximately 95% of the outstanding shares were tendered). Approximately $18 billion in cash was paid out to these stockholders. KKR acquired the remaining stock in the late April merger through the issuance of roughly $4.1 billion of pay-in-kind exchangeable preferred stock and roughly $1.8 billion in face amount of convertible debentures.

constitute an impermissible invasion into the free and open operation of the marketplace.

For the reasons set forth below, this Court agrees with defendants. There being no express covenant between the parties that would restrict the incurrence of new debt, and no perceived direction to that end from covenants that are express, this Court will not imply a covenant to prevent the recent LBO and thereby create an indenture term that, while bargained for in other contexts, was not bargained for here and was not even within the mutual contemplation of the parties.

II.   BACKGROUND

A.   THE PARTIES:

Metropolitan Life Insurance Co. ("MetLife"), incorporated in New York, is a life insurance company that provides pension benefits for 42 million individuals. According to its most recent annual report, MetLife's assets exceed $88 billion and its debt securities holdings exceed $49 billion. MetLife is a mutual company and therefore has no stockholders and is instead operated for the benefit of its policyholders. MetLife alleges that it owns $340,542,000 in principal amount of six separate RJR Nabisco debt issues, bonds allegedly purchased between July 1975 and July 1988. Some bonds become due as early as this year; others will not become due until 2017. The bonds bear interest rates of anywhere from 8 to 10.25 percent. MetLife also owned 186,000 shares of RJR Nabisco common stock at the time this suit was filed.

RJR Nabisco, a Delaware corporation, is a consumer products holding company that owns some of the country's best known product lines, including LifeSavers candy, Oreo cookies, and Winston cigarettes. The company was formed in 1985, when R.J. Reynolds Industries, Inc. ("R.J. Reynolds") merged with Nabisco Brands, Inc. ("Nabisco Brands"). In 1979, and thus before the R.J. Reynolds-Nabisco Brands merger, R.J. Reynolds acquired the Del Monte Corporation ("Del Monte"), which distributes canned fruits and vegetables. From January 1987 until February 1989, co-defendant Johnson served as the company's CEO. KKR, a private investment firm, organizes funds through which investors provide pools of equity to finance LBOs.

B.   THE INDENTURES:

The bonds implicated by this suit are governed by long, detailed indentures, which in turn are governed by New York contract law. No one disputes that the holders of public bond issues, like plaintiffs here, often enter the market after the indentures have been negotiated and memorialized. Thus, those indentures are often not the product of face-to-face negotiations between the ultimate holders and the issuing company. What remains equally true, however, is that underwriters ordinarily negotiate the terms of the indentures with the issuers. Since the underwriters must then sell or place the bonds, they necessarily negotiate in part with the interests of the buyers in mind. Moreover, these indentures were not secret agreements foisted upon unwitting participants in the bond market. No successive holder is required to accept or to continue to hold the bonds, governed by their accompanying indentures; indeed, plaintiffs readily admit that they could have sold their bonds right up until the announcement of the LBO. Instead, sophisticated investors like plaintiffs are well aware of the indenture terms and, presumably, review them carefully before lending hundreds of millions of dollars to any company.

Indeed, the prospectuses for the indentures contain a statement relevant to this action:

> The Indenture contains no restrictions on the creation of unsecured short-term debt by [RJR Nabisco] or its subsidiaries, no restriction on the creation of unsecured Funded Debt by [RJR Nabisco] or its subsidiaries which are not Restricted Subsidiaries, and no restriction on the payment of dividends by [RJR Nabisco].

Further, as plaintiffs themselves note, the contracts at issue "[do] not impose debt limits, since debt is assumed to be used for productive purposes."

2. *The elimination of restrictive covenants:*

In its Amended Complaint, MetLife lists the six debt issues on which it bases its claims. Indentures for two of those issues—the 10.25 percent Notes due in 1990, of which MetLife continues to hold $10 million, and the 8.9 percent Debentures due in 1996, of which MetLife continues to hold $50 million—once contained express covenants that, among other things, restricted the company's ability to incur precisely the sort of debt involved in the recent LBO. In order to eliminate those restrictions, the parties to this action renegotiated the terms of those indentures, first in 1983 and then again in 1985.

MetLife acquired $50 million principal amount of 10.25 percent Notes from Del Monte in July of 1975. To cover the $50 million, MetLife and Del Monte entered into a loan agreement. That agreement restricted Del Monte's ability, among other things, to incur the sort of indebtedness involved in the RJR Nabisco LBO. Reynolds—the corporate predecessor to RJR Nabisco—purchased Del Monte and assumed its indebtedness. Then, in December of 1983, R.J. Reynolds requested MetLife to agree to deletions of those restrictive covenants in exchange for various guarantees from R.J. Reynolds. A few months later, MetLife and R.J. Reynolds entered into a guarantee and amendment agreement reflecting those terms. Pursuant to that agreement, and in the words of Robert E. Chappell, Jr., MetLife's Executive Vice President, MetLife thus "gave up the restrictive covenants applicable to the Del Monte debt ... in return for [the parent company's] guarantee and public covenants."

MetLife acquired the 8.9 percent Debentures from R.J. Reynolds in October of 1976 in a private placement. A promissory note evidenced MetLife's $100 million loan. That note, like the Del Monte agreement, contained covenants that restricted R.J. Reynolds' ability to incur new debt. In June of 1985, R.J. Reynolds announced its plans to acquire Nabisco Brands in a $3.6 billion transaction that involved the incurrence of a significant amount of new debt. R.J. Reynolds requested MetLife to waive compliance with these restrictive covenants in light of the Nabisco acquisition.

In exchange for certain benefits, MetLife agreed to exchange its 8.9 percent debentures—which *did* contain explicit debt limitations—for debentures issued under a public indenture—which contain no explicit limits on new debt. An internal MetLife memorandum explained the parties' understanding:

> [MetLife's $100 million financing of the Nabisco Brands purchase] had its origins in discussions with RJR regarding potential covenant violations in the 8.90% Notes. More specifically, *in its acquisition of Nabisco Brands, RJR was slated to incur significant new long-term debt, which would have caused a violation in the funded indebtedness incurrence tests in the 8.90% Notes.* In the discussions regarding [MetLife's] willingness to consent to the additional indebtedness, *it was determined that a mutually beneficial approach to the problem* was to 1) agree on a new financing having a rate and a maturity desirable for [MetLife] and 2) modify the 8.90% Notes. The former was accomplished with agreement on the proposed financing, while the latter was accomplished by [MetLife] agreeing to substitute RJR's public indenture covenants for the covenants in the 8.90% Notes. In addition to the covenant substitution, RJR has agreed to "debenturize" the 8.90% Notes upon [MetLife's] request. This will permit [MetLife] to sell the 8.90% Notes to the public.

3.   *The recognition and effect of the LBO trend:*

Other internal MetLife documents help frame the background to this action, for they accurately describe the changing securities markets and the responses those changes engendered from sophisticated market participants....At least as early as 1982, MetLife recognized an LBO's effect on bond values.[13] In the spring of that year, MetLife participated in the financing of an LBO of a company called Reeves Brothers ("Reeves"). At the time of that LBO, MetLife also held bonds in that company. Subsequent to the LBO, as a MetLife memorandum explained, the "Debentures of Reeves were downgraded by Standard & Poor's from BBB to B and by Moody's from Baal to Ba3, thereby lowering the value of the Notes and Debentures held by [MetLife]."

MetLife further recognized its "inability to force any type of payout of the [Reeves'] Notes or the Debentures as a result of the buy-out [which] was somewhat disturbing at the time we considered a participation in the new financing. However," the memorandum continued,

---

13. MetLife itself began investing in LBOs as early as 1980. *See* MetLife Special Projects Memorandum, dated June 17, 1989, attached as Bradley Aff.Exh. V, at 1 ("[MetLife's] history of investing in leveraged buyout transactions dates back to 1980; and through 1984, [MetLife] reviewed a large number of LBO investment opportunities presented to us by various investment banking firms and LBO specialists. Over this five-year period, [MetLife] invested, on a direct basis, approximately $430 million to purchase debt and equity securities in 10 such transactions . . .").

our concern was tempered since, as a stockholder in [the holding company used to facilitate the transaction], we would benefit from the increased net income attributable to the continued presence of the low coupon indebtedness. The recent downgrading of the Reeves Debentures and the consequent "loss" in value has again raised questions regarding our ability to have forced a payout. *Questions have also been raised about our ability to force payouts in similar future situations, particularly when we would not be participating in the buy-out financing.*

Id. (emphasis added). In the memorandum, MetLife sought to answer those very "questions" about how it might force payouts in "similar future situations."

> *A method of closing this apparent "loophole," thereby forcing a payout of [MetLife's] holdings, would be through a covenant dealing with a change in ownership.* Such a covenant is fairly standard in financings with privately-held companies. . . . It provides the lender with an option to end a particular borrowing relationship via some type of special redemption. . . .

(Emphasis added.)

A more comprehensive memorandum, prepared in late 1985, evaluated and explained several aspects of the corporate world's increasing use of mergers, takeovers and other debt-financed transactions. That memorandum first reviewed the available protection for lenders such as MetLife:

> Covenants are incorporated into loan documents to ensure that after a lender makes a loan, the creditworthiness of the borrower and the lender's ability to reach the borrower's assets do not deteriorate substantially. *Restrictions on the incurrence of debt,* sale of assets, mergers, dividends, restricted payments and loans and advances to affiliates *are some of the traditional negative covenants that can help protect lenders in the event their obligors become involved in undesirable merger/takeover situations.*

MetLife Northeastern Office Memorandum, dated November 27, 1985 (emphasis added). The memorandum then surveyed market realities:

> Because almost any industrial company is apt to engineer a takeover or be taken over itself, *Business Week* says that investors are beginning to view debt securities of high grade industrial corporations as Wall Street's riskiest investments. In addition, *because public bondholders do not enjoy the protection of any restrictive covenants,* owners of high grade corporates face substantial losses from takeover situations, if not immediately, then when the bond market finally adjusts.... [T]here have been 10–15 merger/takeover/LBO situations where, *due to the lack of covenant protection, [MetLife] has had no choice but to remain a lender to a less creditworthy obligor.* . . . The fact that the quality of our investment portfolio is greater than the other large insurance companies . . . may indicate that we have negotiated better covenant protection than other institutions, thus generally being able to require prepayment when situations become too risky. . . . [However,] a problem exists. And *because the current merger craze is*

not likely to decelerate and because there exist vehicles to circumvent traditional covenants, the problem will probably continue. Therefore, *perhaps it is time to institute appropriate language designed to protect Metropolitan from the negative implications of mergers and takeovers.*

Id. at 2–4 (emphasis added).

Indeed, MetLife does not dispute that, as a member of a bondholders' association, it received and discussed a proposed model indenture, which included a "comprehensive covenant" entitled "Limitations on Shareholders' Payments." As becomes clear from reading the proposed-but never adopted- provision, it was "intend[ed] to provide protection against all of the types of situations in which shareholders profit at the expense of bondholders." *Id.* The provision dictated that the "[c]orporation will not, and will not permit any [s]ubsidiary to, directly or indirectly, make any [s]hareholder [p]ayment unless . . . (1) the aggregate amount of all [s]hareholder payments during the period [at issue] . . . shall not exceed [figure left blank]." The term "shareholder payments" is defined to include "restructuring distributions, stock repurchases, debt incurred or guaranteed to finance merger payments to shareholders, etc."

These documents must be read in conjunction with plaintiffs' Amended Complaint. That document asserts that the LBO "undermines the foundation of the investment grade debt market . . . ,"; that, although "the indentures do not purport to limit dividends or debt . . . [s]uch covenants were believed unnecessary with blue chip companies . . .,"; that "the transaction contradicts the premise of the investment grade market . . .,"; and, finally, that "[t]his buy-out was not contemplated at the time the debt was issued, contradicts the premise of the investment grade ratings that RJR Nabisco actively solicited and received, and is inconsistent with the understandings of the market . . . which [p]laintiffs relied upon."

Solely for the purposes of these motions, the Court accepts various factual assertions advanced by plaintiffs: first, that RJR Nabisco actively solicited "investment grade" ratings for its debt; second, that it relied on descriptions of its strong capital structure and earnings record which included prominent display of its ability to pay the interest obligations on its long-term debt several times over, and third, that the company made express or implied representations not contained in the relevant indentures concerning its future creditworthiness. In support of those allegations, plaintiffs have marshaled a number of speeches made by co-defendant Johnson and other executives of RJR Nabisco. In addition, plaintiffs rely on an affidavit sworn to by John Dowdle, the former Treasurer and then Senior Vice President of RJR Nabisco from 1970 until 1987. In his opinion, the LBO "clearly undermines the fundamental premise of the [c]ompany's bargain with the bondholders, and the commitment that I believe the [c]ompany made to the bondholders. . . . I firmly believe that the company made commitments . . . that require it to redeem [these bonds and notes] before paying out the value to the shareholders."

III.   DISCUSSION

At the outset, the Court notes that nothing in its evaluation is substantively altered by the speeches given or remarks made by RJR Nabisco executives, or the opinions of various individuals—what, for instance, former RJR Nabisco Treasurer Dowdle personally did or did not "firmly believe" the indentures meant. *See supra*, and *generally* Chappell, Dowdle and Howard Affidavits. The parol evidence rule bars plaintiffs from arguing that the speeches made by company executives prove defendants agreed or acquiesced to a term that does not appear in the indentures.

The indentures at issue clearly address the eventuality of a merger. They impose certain related restrictions not at issue in this suit, but no restriction that would prevent the recent RJR Nabisco merger transaction. The indentures also explicitly set forth provisions for the adoption of new covenants, if such a course is deemed appropriate. While it may be true that no explicit provision either permits or prohibits an LBO, such contractual silence itself cannot create ambiguity to avoid the dictates of the parole evidence rule, particularly where the indentures impose no debt limitations.

Under certain circumstances, however, courts will, as plaintiffs note, consider extrinsic evidence to evaluate the scope of an implied covenant of good faith. However, the Second Circuit has established a different rule for customary, or boilerplate, provisions of detailed indentures used and relied upon throughout the securities market, such as those at issue. Thus, in *Sharon Steel Corporation v. Chase Manhattan Bank, N.A.*, 691 F.2d 1039 (2d Cir.1982), Judge Winter concluded that

> [b]oilerplate provisions are . . . not the consequences of the relationship of particular borrowers and lenders and do not depend upon particularized intentions of the parties to an indenture. There are no adjudicative facts relating to the parties to the litigation for a jury to find and the meaning of boilerplate provisions is, therefore, a matter of law rather than fact. Moreover, uniformity in interpretation is important to the efficiency of capital markets. . . . Whereas participants in the capital market can adjust their affairs according to a uniform interpretation, whether it be correct or not as an initial proposition, the creation of enduring uncertainties as to the meaning of boilerplate provisions would decrease the value of all debenture issues and greatly impair the efficient working of capital markets. . . . Just such uncertainties would be created if interpretation of boilerplate provisions were submitted to juries sitting in every judicial district in the nation.

Id. at 1048. *See also Morgan Stanley & Co. v. Archer Daniels Midland Co.*, 570 F.Supp. 1529, 1535–36 (S.D.N.Y.1983) (Sand, J.) ("[Plaintiff concedes that the legality of [the transaction at issue] would depend on a factual inquiry... This case-by-case approach is problematic. . . . [Plaintiff's theory] appears keyed to the subjective expectations of the bondholders . . . and reads a subjective element into what presumably should be an objective determination based on the language appearing in the bond agreement."). Ignoring these principles, plaintiffs would have this Court vary what they themselves have admitted is "indenture boilerplate," of "standard" agreements, to comport with collateral representations and their subjective understandings.

A.   PLAINTIFFS' CASE AGAINST THE RJR NABISCO LBO:

1.   Count One: The implied covenant:

In their first count, plaintiffs assert that

> [d]efendant RJR Nabisco owes a continuing duty of good faith and fair dealing in connection with the contract [i.e., the indentures] through which it borrowed money from MetLife, Jefferson-Pilot and other holders of its debt, including a duty not to frustrate the purpose of the contracts to the debtholders or to deprive the debtholders of the intended object of the contracts-purchase of investment-grade securities.
>
> In the "buy-out," the [c]ompany breaches the duty [or implied covenant] of good faith and fair dealing by, *inter alia*, destroying the investment grade quality of the debt and transferring that value to the "buy-out" proponents and to the shareholders.

In effect, plaintiffs contend that express covenants were not necessary because an *implied* covenant would prevent what defendants have now done. A plaintiff always can allege a violation of an express covenant. If there has been such a violation, of course, the court need not reach the question of whether or not an *implied* covenant has been violated. That inquiry surfaces where, while the express terms may not have been technically breached, one party has nonetheless effectively deprived the other of those express, explicitly bargained-for benefits. In such a case, a court will read an implied covenant of good faith and fair dealing into a contract to ensure that neither party deprives the other of "the fruits of the agreement." Such a covenant is implied only where the implied term "is consistent with other mutually agreed upon terms in the contract." In other words, the implied covenant will only aid and further the explicit terms of the agreement and will never impose an obligation "'which would be inconsistent with other terms of the contractual relationship.'" Viewed another way, the implied covenant of good faith is breached only when one party seeks to prevent the contract's performance or to withhold its benefits. As a result, it thus ensures that parties to a contract perform the substantive, bargained-for terms of their agreement.

In contracts like bond indentures, "an implied covenant...derives its substance directly from the language of the Indenture, and 'cannot give the holders of Debentures any rights inconsistent with those set out in the Indenture.'*[Where] plaintiffs' contractual rights [have not been] violated, there can have been no breach of an implied covenant."*

The appropriate analysis, then, is first to examine the indentures to determine "the fruits of the agreement" between the parties, and then to decide whether those "fruits" have been spoiled—which is to say, whether plaintiffs' contractual rights have been violated by defendants.

A review of the parties' submissions and the indentures themselves satisfies the Court that the substantive "fruits" guaranteed by those contracts and relevant to the present motions include the periodic and regular payment of interest and the eventual repayment of principal. According to a typical indenture, a default shall occur if the company either (1) fails to pay principal when due; (2) fails to make a timely sinking fund payment; (3) fails to pay within 30 days of the due date thereof any interest on the date; or (4) fails duly to observe or perform any of the express covenants or agreements set forth in the agreement. Plaintiffs' Amended Complaint nowhere alleges that RJR Nabisco has breached these contractual obligations; interest payments continue and there is no reason to believe that the principal will not be paid when due.

It is not necessary to decide that indentures like those at issue could never support a finding of additional benefits, under different circumstances with different parties. Rather, for present purposes, it is sufficient to conclude what obligation is *not* covered, either explicitly or implicitly, by these contracts held by these plaintiffs. Accordingly, this Court holds that the "fruits" of these indentures do not include an implied restrictive covenant that would prevent the incurrence of new debt to facilitate the recent LBO. To hold otherwise would permit these plaintiffs to straightjacket the company in order to guarantee their investment. These plaintiffs do not invoke an implied covenant of good faith to protect a legitimate, mutually contemplated benefit of the indentures; rather, they seek to have this Court create an additional benefit for which they did not bargain.

Although the indentures generally permit mergers and the incurrence of new debt, there admittedly is not an explicit indenture provision to the contrary of what plaintiffs now claim the implied covenant requires. That absence, however, does *not* mean that the Court should imply into those very same indentures a covenant of good faith so broad that it imposes a new, substantive term of enormous scope. This is so particularly where, as here, that very term—a limitation on the incurrence of additional debt—has in other past contexts been expressly bargained for; particularly where the indentures grant the company broad discretion in the management of its affairs, as plaintiffs admit, particularly where the indentures explicitly set forth specific provisions for the adoption of new covenants and restrictions, and *especially* where there has been no breach of the parties' bargained-for contractual rights on which the implied covenant necessarily is based. While the Court stands ready to employ an implied covenant of good faith to ensure that such bargained-for rights are performed and upheld, it will not, however, permit an implied covenant to shoehorn into an indenture additional terms plaintiffs now wish had been included.

Plaintiffs argue in the most general terms that the fundamental basis of all these indentures was that an LBO along the lines of the recent RJR Nabisco transaction would never be undertaken, that indeed *no* action would be taken, intentionally or not, that would significantly deplete the company's assets.

Accepting plaintiffs' theory, their fundamental bargain with defendants dictated that nothing would be done to jeopardize the extremely high probability that the company would remain able to make interest payments and repay principal over the 20 to 30 year indenture term—and perhaps by logical extension even included the right to ask a court "to make sure that plaintiffs had made a good investment." *Gardner*, 589 F.Supp. at 674. But as Judge Knapp aptly concluded in *Gardner*, "Defendants . . . were under a duty to carry out the terms of the contract, but not to make sure that plaintiffs had made a good investment."

To respond to changed market forces, new indenture provisions can be negotiated, such as provisions that were in fact once included in the 8.9 percent and 10.25 percent debentures implicated by this action. New provisions could include special debt restrictions or change-of-control covenants. There is no guarantee, of course, that companies like RJR Nabisco would accept such new covenants; parties retain the freedom to enter into contracts as they choose. But presumably, multi-billion dollar investors like plaintiffs have some say in the terms of the investments they make and continue to hold. And, presumably, companies like RJR Nabisco need the infusions of capital such investors are capable of providing.

Whatever else may be true about this case, it certainly does not present an example of the classic sort of form contract or contract of adhesion often frowned upon by courts. In those cases, what motivates a court is the strikingly inequitable nature of the parties' respective bargaining positions. *See generally*, Rakoff, *Contracts of Adhesion: An Essay in Reconstruction*, 96 Harv.L.Rev. 1173 (1982). Plaintiffs here entered this "liquid trading market," with their eyes open and were free to leave at any time. Instead they remained there notwithstanding its well understood risks.

Ultimately, plaintiffs cannot escape the inherent illogic of their argument. On the one hand, it is undisputed that investors like plaintiffs recognized that companies like RJR Nabisco strenuously opposed additional restrictive covenants that might limit the incurrence of new debt or the company's ability to engage in a merger. Furthermore, plaintiffs argue that they had no choice other than to accept the indentures as written, without additional restrictive covenants, or to "abandon" the market.

Yet on the other hand, plaintiffs ask this Court to imply a covenant that would have just that restrictive effect because, they contend, it reflects precisely the fundamental assumption of the market and the fundamental basis of their bargain with defendants. If that truly were the case here, it is difficult to imagine why an insistence on that term would have forced the plaintiffs to abandon the market. The Second Circuit has offered a better explanation: "[a] promise by the defendant should be implied only if the court may rightfully assume that the parties would have included it in their written agreement had their attention been called to it. . . . *Any such assumption in this case would be completely unwarranted.*"

2.   Count Five: In Equity:

Count Five substantially restates and realleges the contract claims advanced in Count I.

In their papers, plaintiffs variously attempt to justify Count V as being based on unjust enrichment, frustration of purpose, an alleged breach of something approaching a fiduciary duty, or a general claim of unconscionability. Each claim fails.

[P]laintiffs advance a claim that remains based, their assertions to the contrary notwithstanding, on an alleged breach of a fiduciary duty. Defendants go to great lengths to prove that the law of Delaware, and not New York, governs this question. Defendants' attempt to rely on Delaware law is readily explained by even a cursory reading of *Simons v. Cogan*, 549 A.2d 300, 303 (Del.1988), the recent Delaware Supreme Court ruling which held, *inter alia*, that a corporate bond "represents a contractual entitlement to the repayment of a debt and does not represent an equitable interest in the issuing corporation necessary for the imposition of a trust relationship with concomitant fiduciary duties." Before such a fiduciary duty arises, "an existing property right or equitable interest supporting such a duty must exist." A bondholder, that court concluded, "acquires no equitable interest, and remains a creditor of the corporation whose interests are protected by the contractual terms of the indenture." Defendants argue that New York law is not to the contrary, but the single Supreme Court case they cite—a case decided over fifty years ago that was not squarely presented with the issue addressed by the *Simons* court—provides something less than dispositive support. For their part, plaintiffs more convincingly demonstrate that New York law applies than that New York law recognizes their claim.

Regardless, this Court finds *Simons* persuasive, and believes that a New York court would agree with that conclusion. In the venerable case of *Meinhard v. Salmon*, 249 N.Y. 458, 164 N.E. 545 (1928), then Chief Judge Cardozo explained the obligations imposed on a fiduciary, and why those obligations are so special and rare:

> Many forms of conduct permissible in a workaday world for those acting at arm's length, are forbidden to those bound by fiduciary ties. A trustee is held to something stricter than the morals of the market place. Not honesty alone, but the punctilio of an honor the most sensitive, is then the standard of behavior. As to this there has developed a tradition that is unbending and inveterate. Uncompromising rigidity has been the attitude of courts of equity when petitioned to undermine the rule of undivided loyalty. . . . Only thus has the level of conduct for fiduciaries been kept at a level higher than that trodden by the crowd.

Before a court recognizes the duty of a "punctilio of an honor the most sensitive," it must be certain that the complainant is entitled to more than the "morals of the market place," and the protections offered by actions based on fraud, state statutes or the panoply of available federal securities laws. This Court has concluded that the plaintiffs presently before it—sophisticated investors who are unsecured creditors—are not entitled to such additional protections.

PROBLEM SET 15.5

1. *MetLife* is often cited for the proposition that bondholders have no rights beyond the terms expressly set forth in the indenture. Do you agree with that interpretation of the case?
2. Would an individual bondholder have made a better plaintiff in this case?
3. From MetLife's perspective, how has it been harmed? After all, it obtained full payment on its bonds (as we now know that RJR did not enter bankruptcy).[14]

4.   FIGHTS WITHIN THE CAPITAL STRUCTURE

IN RE MPM SILICONES, LLC

531 B.R. 321
United States District Court, S.D. New York.
May 4, 2015.

BRICCETTI, District Judge.
This case involves related appeals from proceedings in the United States Bankruptcy Court for the Southern District of New York (Robert D. Drain, Judge), during which the Joint Chapter 11 Plan (the "Plan") of Reorganization for Momentive Performance Materials Inc. ("MPM") and its affiliated debtors (collectively with MPM, the "Debtors") was confirmed.

Appellant U.S. Bank National Association ("U.S. Bank") contends the Bankruptcy Court erred in confirming the Plan despite the Plan's failure to provide any distributions to holders of subordinated notes (the "Subordinated Notes") issued pursuant to an indenture agreement dated December 4, 2006 (the "2006 Indenture").

Appellants BOKF, N.A., and Wilmington Trust, National Association, contend the Bankruptcy Court . . . erred in confirming the Plan despite the Plan's failure to provide a "make-whole" payment to holders of senior lien notes issued pursuant to indentures dated May 25 and October 25, 2012 (the "2012 Indentures").

For the following reasons, the Bankruptcy Court's Orders are AFFIRMED.

BACKGROUND

MPM, together with its Debtor and non-Debtor subsidiaries (collectively, the "Company"), is one of the world's largest producers of silicones and silicone

---

14. http://www.businessweek.com/archives/1991/b322820.arc.htm.

derivatives, which are used in the manufacture of a myriad of industrial and household products. The Company began as the Advanced Materials business of General Electric Company ("GE"). In 2006, investment funds affiliated with Apollo Global Management, LLC (collectively, "Apollo"), acquired the Company from GE.

I. FACTS LEADING UP TO BANKRUPTCY

At the time Apollo acquired the Company, the Debtors issued substantial debt obligations, including the Subordinated Notes. The Subordinated Notes were issued pursuant to the 2006 Indenture, which describes the relative ranking of the Subordinated Notes in comparison with other debt obligations issued by the Debtors. The 2006 Indenture provides that the Subordinated Notes are "subordinated in right of payment ... to the prior payment in full of all existing and future Senior Indebtedness of the Company."

In 2010, the Debtors issued springing second lien notes (the "Second Lien Notes"). The Second Lien Notes were unsecured when issued, but would become secured if all second lien notes issued in 2009 were redeemed. When the Second Lien Notes were issued, the Debtors stated that "[p]rior to and following the Springing Lien Trigger Date, the [Second Lien] Notes ... will be senior indebtedness" and rank "senior in right of payment to ... the Company's existing subordinated notes." (Debtors' Subordinated Notes Ex. 3). In November 2012, the Second Lien Notes became secured by a junior lien—that is, the lien "sprung"—because all of the second lien notes issued in 2009 were redeemed.

In 2012, the Debtors issued two additional classes of senior secured notes—the 1.5 Lien Notes and the First Lien Notes (collectively, the "Senior Lien Notes"). The 1.5 Lien Notes were issued at an interest rate of 10% pursuant to an indenture dated May 25, 2012, and the First Lien Notes were issued at an interest rate of 8.875% pursuant to an indenture dated October 25, 2012. The Senior Lien Notes had a maturity date of October 15, 2020.

In addition, the Senior Lien Notes provide for the payment of a "make-whole" premium if the Senior Lien Notes are redeemed before October 15, 2015:

> [P]rior to October 15, 2015, the Issuer may redeem the [Senior Lien] Notes at its option, in whole at any time or in part from time to time ... at a redemption price equal to 100% of the principal amount of the [Senior Lien] Notes redeemed plus the Applicable Premium as of, and accrued and unpaid interest and Additional Interest, if any, to the applicable redemption date.

The Applicable Premium is the make-whole payment.

However, the 2012 Indentures, which govern the Senior Lien Notes, contain an acceleration provision. The acceleration provision is triggered upon an "Event of Default," which includes the voluntary commencement of a bankruptcy proceeding. If such an Event of Default is triggered, "the principal of, premium, if any, and interest on all the [Senior Lien] Notes shall ipso facto become and be immediately due and payable."

The Senior Lien Notes, along with certain other debt (collectively, the "Senior Secured Loans") are secured by the same collateral (the "Common Collateral") as the Second Lien Notes. An intercreditor agreement (the "Intercreditor Agreement") governs the relationship between the classes of notes. The Intercreditor Agreement provides that the Second Lien Notes are subordinated to the Senior Secured Loans with respect to their position in the Common Collateral. Moreover, the Intercreditor Agreement provides that it does not alter the Second Lien Noteholders' rights as unsecured creditors.

II. THE PLAN

The Plan provides no distributions to the holders of the Subordinated Notes.

The Plan also provides that if the holders of the Senior Lien Notes vote in favor of the plan, all outstanding principal and accrued interest on the Senior Lien Notes would be paid in cash to the Senior Lien Noteholders on the effective date of the Plan. However, no make-whole premium would be allowed. According to the Plan, if the holders of the Senior Lien Notes vote against the Plan, they would receive "Replacement ... Notes [the "Replacement Notes"] with a present value equal to the Allowed amount of such holder's Claim," which could—at the Bankruptcy Court's discretion—include a make-whole premium. The Senior Lien Noteholders voted against the Plan. The Bankruptcy Court then determined the Senior Lien Noteholders were not entitled to a make-whole premium.

DISCUSSION

II. SUBORDINATION DISPUTE

On behalf of the Subordinated Noteholders, U.S. Bank contends the Plan violates [the Bankruptcy Code] . . . by denying them any recovery while providing distributions to the Second Lien Noteholders. Whether the Second Lien Noteholders are entitled to recovery ahead of the Subordinated Noteholders turns on whether the Second Lien Notes are Senior Indebtedness under the 2006 Indenture (which governs the Subordinated Notes).

The 2006 Indenture provides that the Subordinated Notes are "subordinated in right of payment . . . to the prior payment in full of all existing and future Senior Indebtedness of the Company." Senior Indebtedness is defined as:

> all Indebtedness . . . unless the instrument creating or evidencing the same or pursuant to which the same is outstanding expressly provides that such obligations are subordinated in right of payment to any other Indebtedness of the Company[;] [the "Base Definition"] . . . *provided, however,* that Senior Indebtedness shall not include, as applicable
> 4) any Indebtedness or obligation of the Company or any Restricted Subsidiary that by its terms is subordinate or junior in any respect to any other Indebtedness or obligation of the Company . . . including any Pari Passu Indebtedness.

U.S. Bank argues that according to the plain language of the Indenture, Senior Indebtedness cannot include debt that is "subordinated in right of payment" (the "in right of payment" clause) or "subordinate or junior in any respect" to any other debt (the "in any respect" clause). Because the Second Lien Notes are secured by a junior lien, U.S. Bank argues they cannot be Senior Indebtedness under the "in any respect" clause. The Debtors argue, and the Bankruptcy Court held, that both clauses exclude payment subordination—rather than lien subordination—from the definition of Senior Indebtedness, and thus the Second Lien Notes are Senior Indebtedness.

The Court agrees with the Debtors and the Bankruptcy Court.

Before delving into the language of the 2006 Indenture, it is important to understand the difference between lien subordination and payment subordination. Under a lien subordination agreement, "the subordinating party agrees to demote the priority of its lien to that of another secured creditor, thereby delaying its recourse to the identified collateral until the other party's secured claim has been satisfied." Ryan E. Manns & Camisha L. Simmons, *Safeguarding Enforcement of Lien Subordination Agreements,* 32 Am. Bankr. Inst. J. 52, 52 (2013). In contrast, payment, or debt, subordination, "entitles the senior creditor to full satisfaction of its superior debt before the subordinated creditor receives payment on its debt."

An examination of the plain language of the definition of Senior Indebtedness reveals that only indebtedness subject to *payment* subordination, and not indebtedness subject to *lien* subordination, is excluded. The Base Definition of Senior Indebtedness excludes debt that is "subordinated in right of payment" to any other debt. The words "in right of payment" clearly refer only to payment subordination; thus, the Base Definition excludes only indebtedness subordinated by payment from the definition of Senior Indebtedness.

Six provisos follow the Base Definition. The fourth of those provisos—the "in any respect" clause—provides Senior Indebtedness cannot include debt that is "subordinate or junior in any respect" to other debt. U.S. Bank rests much of its argument on this clause, as upon first glance, it appears to be as broad as possible, thus encompassing *both* payment and lien subordination. However, closer consideration reveals this is not the case.

First, the six provisos appended to the Base Definition of Senior Indebtedness must be read in conjunction with the Base Definition. As described above, the Base Definition excludes debt subordinated by payment from the definition of Senior Indebtedness. The provisos can only clarify or augment the Base Definition; they are not a substitute for the Base Definition. Thus, when looking to determine the meaning of the "in any respect" clause, the Court is mindful of the words the drafters of the 2006 Indenture chose to use in the Base Definition.

With that in mind, the "in any respect" clause unambiguously clarifies the Base Definition by ensuring the exclusion of indebtedness that is subordinated by payment to other indebtedness "by its terms," even if the instrument creating the indebtedness does not expressly create that subordination. The "in right of payment" clause excludes indebtedness expressly subordinated in right of payment, while the "in any respect" clause excludes indebtedness subordinated in right of payment "by its terms."

Second, as the Bankruptcy Court correctly noted, if the "in any respect" clause is read—as U.S. Bank contends it must be—to encompass both payment and lien subordination, it would entirely subsume the exclusion of indebtedness "subordinated in right of payment" contained in the Base Definition. Such a construction violates bedrock principles of contract interpretation. The structure of the definition of Senior Indebtedness renders this interpretation even more implausible; only a tortured interpretation of a contract could read a proviso as entirely subsuming language contained in the Base Definition.

U.S. Bank faults this interpretation of the "in any respect" clause, arguing it fails to give meaning to the words "in any respect." U.S. Bank is wrong. The "in any respect" clause excludes from the definition of Senior Indebtedness "any Indebtedness or obligation of the Company ... that by its terms is subordinate or junior in any respect to any other Indebtedness." "In any respect," placed in context, makes clear that all types of payment subordination—no matter how that payment subordination is created—precludes an obligation from being Senior Indebtedness. It makes perfect sense that the drafters of the Indenture would have included the words "in any respect" when seeking to emphasize that all debt subordinated by right of payment through *any* non-explicit means is excluded from the definition of Senior Indebtedness.

U.S. Bank next argues this interpretation of Senior Indebtedness—just like the interpretation U.S. Bank proposes—also violates principles of contract construction by rendering the "in right of payment" clause superfluous. U.S. Bank contends debt subordinated in right of payment "by its terms" must include debt "expressly" subordinated in right of payment. However, this type of surplusage—if any exists—is far easier to swallow than that created by the interpretation U.S. Bank proposes. Reading the "in any respect" clause to apply to both lien and payment subordination substitutes the proviso entirely for the Base Definition. Reading the "in any respect" clause to add ways in which payment subordination can be expressed allows the proviso to augment the Base Definition.

Thus, the plain language of the definition of Senior Indebtedness unambiguously provides that Senior Indebtedness excludes *only* debt subordinated by payment, and not debt secured by a junior lien. The "in any respect" clause augments the Base Definition, clarifying that the instrument creating the debt does not have to render that debt explicitly subordinated by right of payment to other debt; the debt is still excluded from the definition of Senior Indebtedness if it is "by its terms . . . in any respect" subordinated by right of payment.

Moreover, U.S. Bank concedes that if the lien securing the Second Lien Notes had never sprung, those Notes would constitute Senior Indebtedness. In U.S. Bank's view, the Second Lien Notes were senior to the Subordinated Notes when they were unsecured, but became *pari passu* with the Subordinated Notes when the junior lien sprang. As the Bankruptcy Court correctly noted, this is an absurd result that should be avoided.

Thus, the 2006 Indenture provides that Senior Indebtedness unambiguously excludes only debt subordinated by payment; it does not exclude debt secured by a junior lien.

U.S. Bank also contends the Second Lien Notes are subordinated by payment to the Senior Secured Loans by the Intercreditor Agreement. The Court does not agree. The Intercreditor Agreement addresses only the relative priorities of the liens securing the Senior Secured Loans and the Second Lien Notes. Further, the Intercreditor Agreement provides that it does not alter the Second Lien Noteholders' rights as unsecured creditors.

Finally, U.S. Bank contends the "primary feature of the [Second Lien Noteholders'] subordination is the requirement that they must wait in line to have their *debt* paid as to a substantial portion of the Debtor's assets," that is, the Common Collateral. Thus, even in the provisions of the Intercreditor Agreement that U.S. Bank contends connote payment subordination, "[t]he focus still is on the collateral that was agreed to be secured by the liens." That describes lien—not payment—subordination.

Because the Second Lien Notes are Senior Indebtedness, the Plan—which provides no distributions to the holders of the Subordinated Notes—does not run afoul of [the Bankruptcy Code].

IV. THE MAKE–WHOLE DISPUTE

[BOKF, as Trustee for the First Lien Noteholders, and Wilmington Trust, as Trustee for the 1.5 Lien Noteholders (collectively, the "Senior Lien Appellants")] contend the Bankruptcy Court erred in failing to award them a "make-whole" premium. Whether the Senior Lien Appellants are owed a make-whole premium turns on language in both the 2012 Indentures and the Senior Lien Notes themselves. The Senior Lien Notes provide for the payment of a make-whole premium if the Senior Lien Notes are redeemed before October 15, 2015. However, the 2012 Indentures, which govern the Senior Lien Notes, contain an acceleration clause triggered by the voluntary commencement of a bankruptcy proceeding. The acceleration clause provides that in the event of a bankruptcy proceeding, "the principal of, premium, if any, and interest on all the [Senior Lien] Notes shall ipso facto become and be immediately due and payable."

The Senior Lien Appellants contend the Debtors' commencement of the Chapter 11 proceeding constituted a redemption of the Senior Lien Notes prior to October 15, 2015, such that the Senior Lien Noteholders are entitled to a make-whole payment. The Debtors contend that the acceleration provision was triggered when they filed for bankruptcy, negating the Senior Lien Appellants' right to a make-whole premium.

The Court agrees with the Debtors and the Bankruptcy Court that the Senior Lien Appellants are not entitled to a make-whole premium. As described above, the "[i]nterpretation of Indenture provisions is a matter of basic contract law."

The parties agree New York law governs the interpretation of the 2012 Indentures and the Senior Lien Notes.

Section 6.01(f) of the 2012 Indentures provides that the commencement of a Chapter 11 proceeding is an Event of Default. *See* 2012 Indentures § 6.01(f) ("An 'Event of Default' occurs if ... the Company or any Significant Subsidiary pursuant to or within the meaning of any Bankruptcy Law commences a voluntary case."). Further, a Section 601(f) Event of Default triggers the acceleration clause contained in Section 6.02 of the 2012 Indentures. That acceleration clause provides:

> If an Event of Default (other than an Event of Default specified in Section 601(f) . . .) occurs and is continuing, the Trustee or the Holders of at least 25% in principal amount of outstanding [Senior Lien] Notes, by notice to the Company may declare the principal of, premium, if any, and accrued but unpaid interest on all the [Senior Lien] Notes to be due and payable. . . . If an Event of Default specified in Section 6.01(f) . . . occurs, the principal of, premium, if any, and interest on all the [Senior Lien] Notes shall ipso facto become and be immediately due and payable without any declaration or other act on the part of the Trustee or any Holders. The Holders of a majority in principal amount of outstanding [Senior Lien] Notes by notice to the Trustee may rescind any such acceleration with respect to the Notes and its consequences.

Thus, acceleration can be invoked at the noteholders' option for non-bankruptcy events, but acceleration is mandatory in the case of the voluntary filing of a bankruptcy petition.

Having determined the filing of the bankruptcy case triggered an automatic acceleration of the Senior Lien debt, the Court must determine whether a make-whole payment is due to the Senior Lien Noteholders under such circumstances. Under New York law, "[g]enerally, a lender forfeits the right to a prepayment consideration by accelerating the balance of the loan. The rationale most commonly cited for this rule is that acceleration of the debt advances the maturity date of the loan, and any subsequent payment by definition cannot be a prepayment." However, courts recognize an exception to this rule "when a clear and unambiguous clause ... calls for payment of the prepayment premium."

Two separate clauses of the agreements potentially provide for a make-whole provision in the context of an acceleration of debt first, the acceleration clause, and second, the make-whole provision itself.

The acceleration clause does not clearly and unambiguously call for the payment of the make-whole premium in the event of an acceleration of debt. To the contrary, the acceleration clause provides the "premium, if any" shall become immediately payable upon the triggering of the acceleration clause. This language is not sufficient to create an unambiguous right to a make-whole payment. Courts allowing make-whole payments under these circumstances have largely required the contract to provide explicitly for a make-whole premium in the event of an acceleration of debt or a default.

Neither does the make-whole provision contained in paragraph 5 of the Senior Lien Notes clearly and unambiguously call for the payment of the make-whole premium upon acceleration of debt. The Senior Lien Appellants contend that, under the make-whole provision, regardless of whether the voluntary commencement of the bankruptcy case was an Event of Default triggering a mandatory acceleration of the debt, the early payment of the debt constituted a redemption prior to October 15, 2015.

However, under New York law, the payment of debt pursuant to an acceleration clause does not constitute an early redemption. Instead, the automatic acceleration of the debt under Section 6.02 of the 2012 Indentures "changed the date of maturity from some point in the future . . . to an earlier date based on the debtor's default under the contract." Thus, "[w]hen the event of default occurred and the debt accelerated, the new maturity date for the debt was [the date of the filing of the bankruptcy case]." Consequently, the repayment of the debt in connection with the bankruptcy proceeding is not a redemption because "'[p]repayment can only occur *prior* to the maturity date.'"

The Senior Lien Appellants contend such a result "makes no commercial sense, contrary to the tenet of New York contract law that courts should avoid interpretations that would be absurd, commercially unreasonable, or contrary to the reasonable expectations of the parties." However, this result is exactly what the Senior Lien Appellants bargained for under the 2012 Indentures.

PROBLEM SET 15.6

1. How does reading the "in any respect" clause to apply to both lien and payment subordination substitute the proviso entirely for the Base Definition, as the court suggests? Why did the intercreditor agreement not provide a basis for subordination?
2. Does this case suggest that bond indentures should not provide for automatic acceleration of the debt upon bankruptcy?
3. In late 2016, the U.S. Court of Appeals for the Third Circuit held that noteholders in Energy Future Holdings Corp. were entitled to payment of an optional redemption premium at the make-whole price because of the repayment of their notes in a bankruptcy proceeding. *In re Energy Future Holdings Corp.*, 842 F.3d 247 (3d Cir. 2016). In its ruling, the Third Circuit declined to follow the *Momentive* decision. Instead, the Third Circuit placed the onus on the issuer to make it clear in the indenture that an optional redemption provision was not applicable following acceleration. "[I]f [Energy Future] wanted its duty to pay the make-whole on optional redemption to terminate on acceleration of its debt, it needed to make clear" in the indenture that acceleration cuts off the optional redemption provision. Which is the better approach? How would you advise a client drafting a new bond indenture?

5.   DISTRESSED DEBT INVESTORS

Debt investing was once seen as the safe part of the investing market, reserved for retirees and life insurance companies. That, of course, changed with the growth of the junk bond market in the 1980s, and the intentional issuance of debt that offered high yield in exchange for high risk.

Recent years have also seen the growth of investors that intentionally target the debt of underperforming companies. Indeed, these sorts of investors are important clients of all the major law firms.[15]

MICHELLE M. HARNER, *TRENDS IN DISTRESSED DEBT INVESTING: AN EMPIRICAL STUDY OF INVESTORS' OBJECTIVES*

16 Am. Bankr. Inst. L. Rev. 69, 75-77 (2008)

A distressed debt investor is an entity that purchases the debt of a financially troubled company at a discount against the face value of the debt. The amount of the discount varies by situation, but can range from a low discount of 20% to a high discount of 60% or perhaps even 80%. The investor seeks to make a profit on its investment primarily by reselling the debt, through recoveries on the debt in the restructuring process or by converting the debt into an equity position in the reorganized debtor.

The practice of distressed debt investing is not new; however, the market for distressed debt has expanded significantly since its inception.[16] Trade vendors no longer are the only creditors that desire to liquidate their claims against a debtor quickly. Rather, traditional financial institutions and long-term institutional investors, such as banks and insurance companies, are now quick to sell troubled credits. Banks and other traditional lenders also are increasingly syndicating commercial loans at the outset. These practices make it easy for traditional

---

15. For an interview with one prominent distressed investor, see http://goo.gl/wPNMm.

16. For a discussion of the history of the distressed debt market, see Hilary Rosenberg, *The Vulture Investors* 16–19 (John Wiley & Sons, Inc., 2000) (detailing growth of "vultures" during 1980s, and how they had an increased role in "restructuring of corporate America . . ." and changed "dynamics of bankruptcy" so creditors have increased influence. By the late 1990s, the "vulture market had matured" so "new activist" players were raising money to invest in these "downtrodden companies . . ."). *See also* Jay Krasoff & John O'Neill, *The Role of Distressed Investing and Hedge Funds in Turnarounds and Buyouts and How This Affects Middle-Market Companies*, J. Private Equity, Spring 2006, at 17 (explaining how distressed debt investing has a long history, stretching as far back as moneychangers in Bible, and noting changes accompanying "credit-oriented hedge funds" becoming more "proactive in the distressed investing market and the accompanying restructuring process"). For a discussion of the growth in the market, see Heidi Moore, *Distressed Debt Fundraising Hits Record*, Fin. News (Online US), July 13, 2007. Ms. Moore's article states that "high leverage levels and sub-prime downgrades" created doubt with respect to credit markets, noting that distressed-debt firms raised more in the first six months of 2007 than at the end of 2006, and observing that some "firms are rushing to get part of the distressed-debt markets." *Id.*

lenders and investors to exit, and hedge funds, private equity firms and other nontraditional lenders to enter, troubled situations.

The presence of nontraditional lenders in troubled situations changes the dynamics of corporate restructurings, including corporate chapter 11 cases. As one commentator observed, most distressed debt investors are "far less image conscious—they do not have the white-shoe, gentlemanly workout orientation of commercial banks, previously the biggest creditors in bankruptcies." The concept of "relationship lending," where a bank would work with a troubled company to develop a mutually-agreeable restructuring plan to foster repeat business with the company, is now the rare exception rather than the rule. Most distressed debt investors are repeat players in the market, but not with respect to a particular company or management team.

The upshot for troubled companies is that they now face increasing demands and pressures from their debt holders. Even before the filing of a chapter 11 case, the company may lose control of its restructuring process to one or more distressed debt investors. Investors may obtain this type of leverage over a company through contractual covenants, promises of post-bankruptcy financing, statutory rights under Article 9 of the Uniform Commercial Code or chapter 11 of the Bankruptcy Code or some combination of the foregoing. The end result is a more creditor-controlled restructuring process.

At its simplest, distressed debt investing involves purchasing debt obligations trading at a distressed level—for example at 30 percent of par value—with the expectation that the true value is somewhat higher. In short, distressed debt traders are looking for investments where the debt obligations are fundamentally mispriced and will rebound in value.

This involves a variety of legal issues as these investors explore their legal rights under the debt instrument and how those rights might allow them to obtain value from the instrument, especially if the market price for the debt does not rebound or the debtor decides to restructure its debt obligations before such rebound.

While distressed debt investors on the whole are a closed-mouthed bunch, in a 2010 interview, one prominent distressed debt investor provided a short example of how this might work in practice:

[W]e became involved with Six Flags, a US amusement park company which had around USD1 billion of bank debt, USD400 million of senior bonds and USD800 million of subordinated debt. It had been financed at around ten times EBITDA, but the company could not refinance that debt and went into bankruptcy. We got control of the company through the process, mainly because we had bought the bank debt at around 60-65 cents on the dollar and the senior bonds at 40-50 cents. It was clear the bank debt would be paid off and the bonds would become the new equity—under US bankruptcy law, unless you are paid off at par, you get the equity in the company.

What is he referring to at the end of quote? What was the approximate return on this investment? What happened to the subordinated bondholders?

16

SYNDICATED LOAN AGREEMENTS

Corporations often borrow from banks, just like real people. Corporations' lending needs are quite a bit larger than yours or mine—even if you are quite wealthy (textbook authors are not).

Accordingly, specialized legal and financial structures have developed around large loans to corporations.[1] Moreover, a secondary market in these loans has developed, and a trade association, The Loan Syndications and Trading Association (LSTA), has established standardized documentation for loan trading and model credit agreement provisions to facilitate trading.[2]

Large corporate loans typically take one of two forms, which we take up in the first two sections of this chapter. We first consider syndicated loans, which is our primary focus in this chapter. Then we will consider loan "participations," which, as you will see, involve a much less active role for the investor.

Syndication means that the loan is made by a group of lenders. Thus, a $100 million loan to Bogartco might be made under a loan agreement whereby ten lenders agree to contribute $10 million to the whole. You can think of this as a kind of diversification strategy by the lending financial institutions.

A syndicated loan is typically structured and priced by a lead arranger, book runner, or agent, which can be one or more banks, which then sells portions of the credit (i.e., the loan) to other lenders or investor groups. After the loan is closed, the arranger often becomes the lead or administrative agent. In general terms, the role of a lead agent is to communicate with the borrower on a day-to-day basis and to perform the ministerial tasks associated with the loan for the benefit of the syndicate lenders.

The lenders often appoint a collateral agent, distinct from the lead agent, to serve as the secured party on their collective behalf. This includes serving as agent with respect to perfecting security interests in the borrower's assets.

---

1. Douglas G. Baird & Robert K. Rasmussen, *Antibankruptcy*, 119 Yale L.J. 648, 667 (2010).

2. Elisabeth de Fontenay, *Do the Securities Laws Matter? The Rise of the Leveraged Loan Market*, 39 J. Corp. L. 725 (2014); *see also* Stephen J. Lubben, *Credit Derivatives and the Future of Chapter 11*, 81 Am. Bankr. L.J. 405, 426 (2007).

In a syndication, each lender has a legal relationship with the borrower. Essentially a syndication is either a joint loan or an assignment of an interest in the loan, which means that the lead bank that may have organized the loan no longer has any performance obligation on the syndicated pieces of the loan.[3]

Each colender typically acquires a promissory note in the amount of such colender's share of the loan, made by the borrower payable to the order of such colender, as payee. However, the notes often provide that the payments made under the note be sent to the lead agent, who collects the payments and distributes to each colender its respective share of the funds.

1.   SYNDICATED LOANS

MORGAN STANLEY   BANK OF AMERICA
                                                     MERRILL LYNCH

April 10, 2011

Project Kansas Commitment Letter
Endo Pharmaceuticals Holdings Inc.
100 Endo Boulevard
Chadds Ford, Pennsylvania 19317
Ladies and Gentlemen:

You (the "Borrower") have advised Morgan Stanley Senior Funding, Inc. ("MSSF") and Merrill Lynch, Pierce, Fenner & Smith Incorporated ("MLPFS" and, collectively with MSSF, the "Lead Arrangers") and Bank of America, N.A. ("BANA" and, collectively with MSSF, the "Commitment Parties"; together with the Lead Arrangers, "we" or "us") that you intend to acquire the Target and consummate the other transactions described in the introductory paragraphs of the Summary of Terms and Conditions in respect of the Senior Secured Facilities attached as Exhibit A hereto (the "Senior Term Sheet" and, collectively with the Summary of Terms and Conditions in respect of the Bridge Facility attached as Exhibit B hereto (the "Bridge Term Sheet"), the "Term Sheet"). Capitalized terms used but not defined herein are used with the meanings assigned to them in the applicable Term Sheet.

In connection with the foregoing, you have requested that MSSF and MLPFS agree to (i) structure, arrange and syndicate a bridge loan facility to the Borrower in an aggregate principal amount of $700,000,000 (the "Bridge Facility"), (ii) arrange a senior secured term loan "A" facility in an aggregate principal amount of $1,500,000,000 (the "Term Loan A Facility"), (iii) arrange a senior

---

3. Loan syndications have been around for a while. *E.g.*, Coffin v. President, etc., of Grand Rapids Hydraulic Co., 18 N.Y.S. 782, 783 (Super. 1892) *aff'd*, 136 N.Y. 655, 32 N.E. 1076 (1893).

secured term loan "B" facility in an aggregate principal amount of $900,000,000 (the "Term Loan B Facility" and, together with the Term Loan A Facility, the "Term Loan Facilities") and (iv) arrange a multicurrency revolving credit facility in an initial aggregate principal amount of $500,000,000 (the "Revolving Credit Facility," and together with the Term Loan Facilities, the "Senior Secured Facilities" and, together with the Bridge Facility, the "Facilities" and each such facility individually, a "Facility"). You have also requested that (w) MSSF commit to provide fifty percent (50%) of each of the Facilities on the Closing Date (as hereinafter defined), (x) BANA commit to provide fifty percent (50%) of each of the Facilities on the Closing Date, (y) MSSF agree to serve as administrative agent for the Facilities (other than the Bridge Facility) and as syndication agent for the Bridge Facility and (z) BANA agree to serve as administrative agent for the Bridge Facility and syndication agent for the Facilities (other than the Bridge Facility).

The Lead Arrangers are pleased to advise you that they are willing to act as joint lead arrangers and joint bookrunners for the Facilities. Furthermore, in connection with the foregoing, (i) MSSF is pleased to advise you of its several (but not joint) commitment to provide 50% of the aggregate principal amount of the Senior Secured Facilities on the Closing Date, and, in the event that the Borrower does not issue the full amount of the Senior Notes or other Securities (as defined in the Fee Letter) at or prior to the time the Acquisition is consummated, 50% of the aggregate principal amount of the Bridge Facility on the Closing Date and (ii) BANA is pleased to advise you of its several (but not joint) commitment to provide 50% of the aggregate principal amount of the Senior Secured Facilities on the Closing Date, and, in the event that the Borrower does not issue the full amount of the Senior Notes or other Securities at or prior to the time the Acquisition is consummated, 50% of the aggregate principal amount of the Bridge Facility on the Closing Date, in each case upon the terms and subject to the conditions set forth in this commitment letter and in the Term Sheet (together with this commitment letter, the "Commitment Letter").

It is agreed that MSSF will act as the sole and exclusive administrative agent (the "Administrative Agent") for the Facilities (other than the Bridge Facility) and as sole and exclusive syndication agent for the Bridge Facility, that BANA will act as the sole and exclusive administrative agent for the Bridge Facility and as sole and exclusive syndication agent for the Facilities (other than the Bridge Facility) and that the Lead Arrangers will act as joint lead arrangers and joint bookrunners for the Facilities. It is agreed that MSSF will have "left placement" and MLPFS will have "right placement" on the top line in the Confidential Information Memorandum referred to below and in all other marketing materials or advertisements related to the Facilities (or, in the case of any such materials or advertisements solely in respect of the Bridge Facility, MLPFS will have "left placement" and MSSF will have "right placement" on the top line thereof). You agree that no other agents, co-agents, co-managers, bookrunners or arrangers will be appointed, no other titles will be awarded and no compensation (other than that expressly contemplated by the Term Sheet and the Fee Letters referred to below) will be paid in connection with the Facilities unless you and we shall so agree; provided that, in consultation with us, you may appoint prior to May 1, 2011, up to two additional joint bookrunners in respect of the Bridge Facility (the "Additional Bookrunners") so long as each such bookrunner assumes a commitment in respect of no less than 10% of the aggregate principal amount of the Bridge Facility pursuant to a joinder or amendment to this Commitment Letter in form and substance reasonably acceptable to you and us (subject to an aggregate maximum commitment of the Additional Bookrunners in respect of the Bridge Facility not to exceed 20% thereof) (and shall have agreed to become a Lender in the general syndication of the Revolving Credit Facility and the Term Loan A Facility in an aggregate amount as shall be mutually agreed between you and us), it being understood that the commitments of MSSF and BANA in respect of the Bridge Facility shall be ratably reduced by any commitments assumed by any Additional Bookrunner, and it is agreed that such Additional Bookrunners will be listed alphabetically on the second line in the Confidential Information Memorandum referred to below and in all other marketing materials or advertisements related to the Bridge Facility.

The Lead Arrangers intend to syndicate the Facilities (including, in our discretion, all or part of each Commitment Party's commitment hereunder) to a syndicate of financial institutions identified by the Lead Arrangers in consultation with you (together with MSSF and BANA, the "Lenders"); provided that notwithstanding the Lead Arrangers' right to syndicate the Facilities and receive commitments with respect thereto, other than with respect to the commitments allocated to, and assumed by, the Additional Bookrunners under the Bridge Facility as described in the preceding paragraph, (i) the Commitment Parties shall not be relieved, released or novated from their respective obligations hereunder (including their obligation to fund the Facilities on the Closing Date) in connection with any syndication, assignment or participation of the Facilities, including its commitments in respect thereof, until after the Closing Date has occurred, (ii) no assignment or novation shall become effective with respect to all or any portion of the Commitment Parties' commitments in respect of the Facilities until the initial funding of the Facilities, (iii) unless you otherwise agree in writing, the Commitment Parties shall retain exclusive control over all rights and obligations with respect to its commitments in respect of the Facilities, including all rights with respect to consents, modifications, supplements, waivers and amendments, until the Closing Date has occurred and (iv) your consent shall be required with respect to any assignment if, prior to the first anniversary of the Closing Date, the Commitment Parties and the Additional Bookrunners would hold, in the aggregate, less than a majority of the outstanding loans under the Bridge Facility. The Lead Arrangers intend to commence syndication efforts promptly upon the execution of this Commitment Letter, and until the earlier of (x) the date of completion of a Successful Syndication (as defined in the Fee Letter) and (y) the date that is 90 days after the Closing Date (such earlier date, the "Syndication Date"), you agree actively to assist, and to use your commercially reasonable efforts to cause the Target to actively assist, the Lead

Arrangers in completing the syndication. Such assistance shall include (a) your using commercially reasonable efforts to ensure that the syndication efforts benefit materially from your and, to the extent practical and appropriate, the Target's existing lending relationships, (b) direct contact between senior management and advisors of the Borrower (and using your commercially reasonable efforts to arrange for direct contact between senior management and advisors of the Target) and the proposed Lenders at times and locations mutually agreed upon, (c) the hosting, with the Lead Arrangers, of one or more meetings of prospective Lenders at times and locations mutually agreed upon and (d) as set forth below, assistance in the preparation of customary materials to be used in connection with the syndication (collectively with the Term Sheet, the "Information Materials"). The Borrower shall use commercially reasonably efforts to obtain, at its expense, corporate credit or family ratings of the Borrower after giving effect to the Transaction and monitored public ratings of the Senior Secured Facilities and the Senior Notes from each of Moody's Investor Service, Inc. and Standard and Poor's Rating Services, a division of The McGraw Hill Companies, Inc. for the Borrower, the Senior Secured Facilities and the Senior Notes no later than the Marketing Period Commencement Date (as defined in the Bridge Term Sheet). The Borrower shall participate actively in the process of securing such ratings, including, having senior management of the Borrower meet with such ratings agencies. The Borrower shall also cause senior management of the Borrower and other representatives to participate in any customary "roadshow" in connection with the placement of the Senior Notes during the Marketing Period (as defined in the Bridge Term Sheet). Notwithstanding anything to the contrary contained in the Commitment Letter or the Fee Letters but subject to the Syndication Period Condition (as defined below), none of the completion of the syndication of the Facilities, a Successful Syndication or the receipt of any ratings shall constitute a condition precedent to the availability of the Facilities on the Closing Date.

Unfunded loan commitments, whether syndications or participations, are often in the form of a revolving credit agreement—ominously termed the "revolver," in industry slang.[4] Revolving credit is like your credit card: The company can borrow, and pay, and borrow and pay against the same loan for the entire term of the agreement.

A term loan, on the other hand, is more like a bond. The loan is typically funded at the outset, and repayable on a set schedule. One key distinction from a bond, however, is that bank loans typically have floating interest rates, whereas bonds are most often fixed rate instruments. Thus, whereas bonds involve both credit risk and interest rate risk, investments in loans arguably involve only credit risk.

---

4. Another common unfunded loan interest relates to letters of credit.

In addition to the floating interest rate, most credit facilities charge a variety of fees. A commitment fee, or unused credit line fee, is the amount paid on the unused portion of the loan commitment. This is specified as a percentage of the undrawn amount, and is paid on a schedule similar to interest. Because banks are required by bank regulators to maintain capital against their commitments, these fees essentially pass the cost on to the potential borrowers.

If the loan is syndicated, the borrower often pays an additional annual fee to compensate the agent bank for its duties. Typically the borrower will also have to pay the agent bank's expenses in connection with the loan.

The borrower also often does its banking with the lead bank on the loan. This may provide the lender with an ability to seize the debtor's cash upon bankruptcy, and it provides the lead bank with another benefit from managing the loan.

Exhibit A
PROJECT KANSAS SENIOR SECURED FACILITIES
Summary of Terms and Conditions
April 10, 2011

Capitalized terms used but not defined in this Exhibit A shall have the meanings set forth in the Commitment Letter to which this Exhibit A is attached.

Endo Pharmaceuticals Holdings Inc. (the "Borrower") intends to acquire (the "Acquisition") a company previously identified to us and code-named "Kansas" (the "Target"), all as previously described to the Commitment Parties and the Lead Arrangers. In connection therewith: (a) the Borrower will enter into an Agreement and Plan of Merger (in form and substance reasonably acceptable to the Lead Arrangers and Commitment Parties) by and among the Borrower, the Target and NIKA Merger Sub, Inc. (together with all exhibits, schedules and disclosure letters thereto, the "Acquisition Agreement") pursuant to which a subsidiary of the Borrower will merge with and into the Target, with the Target surviving as a wholly-owned subsidiary of the Borrower and (b) the Borrower will obtain the Facilities described in the Commitment Letter.

The Lead Arrangers and the Commitment Parties acknowledge and agree that the Acquisition Agreement delivered to them on April 10, 2011 and identified to them as the "execution copy," together with all exhibits, schedules and disclosure letters thereto delivered to them at 1:50 a.m. (Eastern time) on April 11, 2011, is reasonably acceptable to each of them.

The Acquisition and other transactions described above are collectively referred to herein as the "Transaction".

Set forth below is a summary of the terms and conditions for the Senior Secured Facilities.

I. **Parties**

Borrower: Endo Pharmaceuticals Holdings Inc. (the "Borrower").

Guarantors: The Borrower's material direct and indirect domestic subsidiaries (as required by and consistent with the materiality standards set forth in the Existing Credit Agreement, the "Guarantors") shall unconditionally guaranty all of the Borrower's obligations under and in connection with the Senior Secured Facilities (as defined below) and certain interest rate swaps, currency or other hedging obligations and cash management obligations owing to any Lender or any affiliate thereof; provided that no "unrestricted subsidiary" or, consistent with the terms of the Existing Credit Agreement, any non-wholly owned domestic subsidiary that is a joint venture with an unaffiliated third party (each, a "JV Subsidiary") shall be required to act as a Guarantor.

Collateral: The obligations of the Borrower and the Guarantors shall be secured by a first priority perfected security interest (subject to exceptions permitted by the Credit Documentation) in and lien on the existing and future assets and property of the Borrower and each Guarantor consistent with and subject to the terms of the Existing Credit Agreement and the Security Agreement (as defined in the Existing Credit Agreement (as defined below)).

Joint Lead Arrangers and Joint Bookrunners: Morgan Stanley Senior Funding, Inc. ("MSSF") and Merrill Lynch, Pierce, Fenner & Smith Incorporated ("MLPFS" and collectively with MSSF in such capacity, the "Lead Arrangers").

Administrative Agent: MSSF (in such capacity, the "Administrative Agent").

Syndication Agent: Bank of America, N.A. ("BANA").

Lenders: A syndicate of banks, financial institutions and other entities, including MSSF and BANA, arranged by the Lead Arrangers in consultation with the Borrower (collectively, the "Lenders").

**II.   The Senior
Secured Facilities**

**A. Revolving
Credit Facility**

Type and Amount
of Facility:

Revolving credit facility (the "Revolving Credit Facility") in the U.S. Dollar equivalent amount of $500,000,000 (the loans thereunder, the "Revolving Credit Loans") which shall be made available by all of the Lenders in euro, Japanese Yen and such other foreign currencies as may be agreed to by the Administrative Agent and the Lenders (collectively with U.S. Dollars, the "Agreed Currencies").

Availability:

The Revolving Credit Facility shall be available on a revolving basis during the period commencing on the Closing Date and ending on the date that is the five-year anniversary of the Closing Date (the "Revolving Credit Termination Date"); provided that the Credit Documentation shall provide the right for individual Lenders to agree to extend the maturity of their commitments under the Revolving Credit Facility upon the request of the Borrower to all Lenders under the Revolving Credit Facility ratably and without the consent of any other Lender, subject to customary conditions precedent.

Letters of Credit:

A portion of the Revolving Credit Facility not in excess of the U.S. Dollar equivalent of $50,000,000 shall be available for the issuance of letters of credit (the "Letters of Credit") in Agreed Currencies by MSSF (in such capacity, the "Issuing Lender"). No Letter of Credit shall have an expiration date after the earlier of (a) one year after the date of issuance and (b) five business days prior to the Revolving Credit Termination Date, provided that any Letter of Credit with a one-year tenor may provide for the renewal thereof for additional one-year periods (which shall in no event extend beyond the date referred to in clause (b) above).

Drawings under any Letter of Credit shall be reimbursed by the Borrower (whether with its own funds or with the proceeds of Revolving Credit Loans) on the same business day. To the extent that the Borrower does not so reimburse the Issuing Lender, the Lenders under the Revolving Credit Facility shall be irrevocably and unconditionally obligated to reimburse the Issuing Lender on a pro rata basis.

Swing Line Loans:

A portion of the Revolving Credit Facility not in excess of $50,000,000 shall be available for swing line loans in U.S. Dollars (the "Swing Line Loans") from MSSF (in such capacity, the "Swing Line Lender") on same-day notice. Any such Swing Line Loans will reduce availability under the Revolving Credit Facility on a dollar-for-dollar basis. Each Lender under the Revolving Credit Facility shall acquire, under certain circumstances, an irrevocable and unconditional pro rata participation in each Swing Line Loan.

Maturity: The Revolving Credit Termination Date.

Purpose: The proceeds of the Revolving Credit Loans shall be used to finance the Acquisition, for general corporate purposes (including permitted acquisitions) of the Borrower and its subsidiaries and to refinance the (i) Credit Agreement, dated as of November 30, 2010, among the Borrower, certain lenders and JPMorgan Chase Bank, N.A., as administrative agent (the "Existing Credit Agreement"), (ii) Credit and Guaranty Agreement, dated as of July 20, 2006, among the Target, certain guarantors, certain lenders and CIT HEATHCARE LLC, as administrative agent (the "Existing Target Credit Agreement," as such agreement may be replaced on or prior to April 20, 2011 by an up to $250,000,000 senior secured revolving credit facility evidenced by a credit agreement in substantially the form presented to the Lead Arrangers on April 10, 2011, with such amendments, supplements or other modifications thereafter (whether in such credit agreement, pursuant to a separate agreement or otherwise) not materially adverse to the Lenders or the Borrower (it being understood that any increase in the aggregate commitments in excess of $250,000,000 thereunder shall be deemed to be materially adverse to the Lenders and the Borrower) (the "Proposed Target Credit Facility") so long as prior to or concurrently with the effectiveness of the Proposed Target Credit Facility (w) if there are any amounts then outstanding under the Existing Target Credit Agreement, the Borrower shall use its reasonable best efforts to obtain a customary payoff letter confirming that all indebtedness under the Existing Target Credit Agreement shall have been fully repaid (except to the extent being so repaid with the proceeds of the initial loans and to the extent outstanding letters of credit are continued under the Proposed Target Credit Facility), (x) all outstanding indebtedness and other obligations under the Existing Target Credit Agreement shall in fact have been paid in full, (y) all commitments under the Existing Target Credit Agreement shall have been terminated and cancelled and (z) all liens in connection therewith shall have been terminated and released, the "Target Credit Agreement"), (iii) 31/4% Convertible Senior Subordinated Notes Due 2036 (the "Target 2036 Notes") and (iv) 4.00% Convertible Senior Subordinated Notes Due 2041 (the "Target 2041 Notes," and together with the Target 2036 Notes, the "<u>Existing Target Notes</u>"); provided, that the aggregate principal amount of the loans under the Revolving Credit Facility on the Closing Date shall not exceed $250,000,000.

B. Term Loan Facilities

1. Term Loan A Facility

A term loan "A" facility (the "<u>Term Loan A Facility</u>") in the amount of $1,500,000,000 (the "<u>Term Loan A Commitment</u>" and the loans thereunder, the "<u>Term A Loans</u>"

Type and Amount of Facility:

The Term A Loans shall be made available in a single drawing on the Closing Date (as defined below).

Term Loan Availability:

The Term A Loans will amortize according to the following percentages for the following years, in each case with payments to be made on a quarterly basis:

Amortization:

Year 1:   3.75%
Year 2:   7.5%
Year 3:   10%
Year 4:   10%
Year 5:   15%

Maturity:

The Term A Loans will mature on the date that is five years after the Closing Date (the "<u>Term Loan A Maturity Date</u>"); provided that the Credit Documentation shall provide the right for individual Lenders to agree to extend the maturity date of the outstanding loans under the Term Loan A Facility upon the request of the Borrower to all Lenders under the Term Loan A Facility ratably and without the consent of any other Lender, subject to customary conditions precedent. The remaining aggregate principal amount of the Term A Loans will be repayable on the Term Loan A Maturity Date.

Purpose:

The proceeds of the Term A Loans shall be used to finance the Acquisition and to refinance loans under the Existing Credit Agreement and the Target Credit Agreement and the Existing Target Notes.

2. Term Loan B Facility

Type and Amount of Facility:

A term loan "B" facility (the "<u>Term Loan B Facility</u>"; and collectively with the Revolving Credit Facility, and the Term Loan A Facility, the "<u>Senior Secured Facilities</u>") in the amount of $900,000,000 (the "<u>Term Loan B Commitment</u>," and the loans thereunder, the "<u>Term B Loans</u>"; and collectively with the Term A Loans, the "Term Loans; and collectively with the Revolving Credit Loans, the "Loans").

Term Loan Availability:

The Term B Loans shall be made available in a single drawing on the Closing Date (as defined below).

Amortization:

The Term B Loans will amortize at 1% per year, in each case with payments to be made on a quarterly basis.

Maturity:

The Term B Loans will mature on the date that is seven years after the Closing Date (the "Term Loan B Maturity Date"); provided that the Credit Documentation shall provide the right for individual Lenders to agree to extend the maturity date of the outstanding loans under the Term Loan B Facility upon the request of the Borrower to all Lenders under the Term Loan B Facility ratably and without the consent of any other Lender, subject to customary conditions precedent. The remaining aggregate principal amount of the Term B Loans will be repayable on the Term Loan B Maturity Date.

Purpose:

The proceeds of the Term B Loans shall be used to finance the Acquisition (including the refinancing of loans under the Target Credit Agreement, the Existing Credit Agreement and the Existing Target Notes).

* * *

Voting:

Amendments and waivers with respect to the Credit Documentation shall require the approval of Lenders holding greater than 50% of the aggregate amount of the Term Loans, Revolving Credit Loans, participations in Letters of Credit and Swing Line Loans and unused commitments under the Revolving Credit Facility (with customary tranche voting to be agreed upon), except that (a) the consent of each Lender directly affected thereby shall be required with respect to (i) reductions in the amount or extensions of the scheduled date of amortization or final maturity of any Loan, (ii) reductions in the rate of interest or any fee or extensions of any due date thereof and (iii) increases in the amount or extensions of the expiry date of any Lender's commitment and (b) the consent of 100% of the Lenders shall be required with respect to (i) modifications to any of the voting percentages and (ii) releases of all or substantially all of the Guarantors or all or substantially all of the Collateral.

Assignments and Participations:

The Lenders shall be permitted to assign all or a portion of their Loans and commitments with the consent, not to be unreasonably withheld, of (a) the Borrower (provided that the Borrower shall be deemed to have consented to any such assignment unless it shall object thereto by written notice to the Administrative Agent within ten business days after having received notice thereof), unless (i) the assignee is a Lender, an affiliate of a Lender or an approved fund or (ii) an event of default has occurred and is continuing, (b) the Administrative Agent, unless a Term Loan is being assigned to a Lender, an affiliate of a Lender or an approved fund, and (c) the Issuing Lender, unless a Term Loan is being assigned to a Lender, an affiliate of a Lender or an approved fund. In the case of partial assignments (other than to another Lender, to an affiliate of a Lender or an approved fund), the minimum assignment amount shall be $5,000,000, in the case of a commitment under the Revolving Credit Facility, and $1,000,000, in the case of a Term Loan, unless otherwise agreed by the Borrower and the Administrative Agent.

Yield Protection:

The Credit Documentation shall contain customary provisions consistent with current market conditions (a) protecting the Lenders against increased costs or loss of yield resulting from changes in reserve, tax, capital adequacy and other requirements of law and from the imposition of or changes in withholding or other taxes and (b) indemnifying the Lenders for "breakage costs" incurred in connection with, among other things, any prepayment of a Eurocurrency Loan (as defined in Annex I) on a day other than the last day of an interest period with respect thereto.

Expenses and Indemnification:

The Borrower shall pay (a) all reasonable out-of-pocket expenses of the Administrative Agent and the Lead Arrangers and their affiliates associated with the syndication of the Senior Secured Facilities and the preparation, execution, delivery and administration of the Credit Documentation and any amendment or waiver with respect thereto (including the reasonable fees, disbursements and other charges of one primary counsel (with exceptions for conflicts of interest) and one local counsel in each relevant jurisdiction) and (b) all out-of-pocket expenses of the Administrative Agent and the Lenders (including the fees, disbursements and other charges of one primary counsel (with exceptions for conflicts of interest) and one local counsel in each relevant jurisdiction) in connection with the enforcement of the Credit Documentation, in each case on the same terms as set forth in the Existing Credit Agreement.

The Administrative Agent, the Lead Arrangers and the Lenders (and their affiliates and their respective officers, directors, employees, advisors and agents) will have no liability for, and will be indemnified and held harmless against, any loss, liability, cost or expense incurred in respect of the financing contemplated hereby or the use or the proposed use of proceeds thereof (except to the extent determined by a court by a final and non-appealable judgment to have resulted from the gross negligence or willful misconduct of the relevant indemnified party or any Related Indemnified Party of such indemnified party).

Defaulting
Lenders:
The Credit Documentation shall contain the Administrative Agent's customary provisions in respect of defaulting lenders.

Governing Law
and Forum:
State of New York.

PROBLEM SET 16.1

1. Diagram the loans set forth in the documents above. How much is being borrowed, and under what terms? Be prepared to discuss in class.
2. The loan features a "swing line" that allows the borrower to obtain funds on short notice. What are the costs and benefits of this feature to both borrower and its banks?
3. One distinction between a large corporate loan and a bond is the floating interest rate typically seen in a loan. Another distinction is that loan agreements are often secured, although there is no requirement that they be secured—and some highly rated borrowers do obtain unsecured syndicated loans. What are the trade-offs from the borrowing firm's perspective when deciding whether or not to obtain a secured loan, an unsecured loan, or issue bond debt?

2.   PARTICIPATIONS

In a loan participation, as contrasted with a syndication, the participant will have no direct relationship with the borrower. Instead, the buyer of a loan participation simply obtains an interest in a relationship that the lender has already established with the borrower—somewhat like a sublease.[5]

When buying a loan participation, the participant will typically not receive its own note and will have but limited rights to control the lending relationship.

PARTICIPATION AGREEMENT

This PARTICIPATION AGREEMENT (this "**Agreement**") is entered into as of _____, 20 _____ by and between _____, a [n] _____ ("**Lead Lender**") and _____, a _____ ("**Participant** ").

---

5. In re Okura & Co. (Am.), Inc., 249 B.R. 596, 604 (Bankr. S.D.N.Y. 2000).

A. Lead Lender has made or is making the loan (the "**Loan**") identified in the Summary of Terms (defined below) (1) to the borrower indicated in the Summary of Terms ("**Borrower**"), (2) in the principal amount indicated in the Summary of Terms and (3) secured by a mortgage, deed of trust or similar instrument ("**Mortgage**") on the project indicated in the Summary of Terms ("**Project**").

B. Lead Lender and Participant have agreed that Lead Lender shall sell and transfer, and Participant shall purchase and assume, an undivided participation interest in the Loan on the terms and conditions set forth herein.

IN CONSIDERATION of the agreements, provisions and covenants herein contained, the parties hereto agree as follows:

SECTION 4
LOAN ADMINISTRATION

4.1 <u>Loan Administration</u>. Subject to the provisions of <u>Section 4.2</u>, Participant hereby authorizes Lead Lender to: (a) negotiate, manage and administer the Loan, (b) give consents, approvals or waivers in connection with the Loan Documents, (c) amend the Loan Documents; (d) take or refrain from taking any action and make any determination provided for herein or in the Loan Documents, (e) retain the original Loan Documents, (f) collect all payments made under the Loan Documents, (g) require funding by the parties hereto (in their respective Percentages) of Protective Advances or other Costs (to the extent not paid by Borrower); (h) realize or manage and dispose of Collateral; and (i) exercise all other powers as are available to the holder of the Loan. Lead Lender shall administer the Loan in a manner consistent with the standard of care applied by Lead Lender in administering loans owned entirely for its own account.

4.2 <u>Major Decisions</u>. Notwithstanding <u>Section 4.1</u>, Lead Lender shall not take the following actions (each a "Major Decision") with respect to the Loan without the prior written consent of Participant (provided, however, Lead Lender shall be authorized to take any of the following actions without the consent of Participant if Participant has defaulted in funding an Advance and failed to cure such default within the period set forth in Section 2.4):

> (a) Release the Mortgage, in any material respect, or release any guaranty of the Loan, except in connection with the full repayment of the Loan or pursuant to the express terms of the Loan Documents;
> (b) Subordinate the Mortgage to other indebtedness;
> (c) Amend, modify or waive any provision of the Loan Documents so as to (a) reduce or forgive the amount of any interest or principal payable required under the Loan Documents; (b) change or modify the interest rate under the Loan Documents; (c) extend the maturity date of the Loan; (d) postpone or defer any date for payment of principal or interest under any Loan Document; or (e) increase

the principal amount of the Loan except for (x) Advances to be made after the date hereof pursuant to the Loan Documents, and (y) any Protective Advances; or

(d) Approve a sale of the Project by Borrower.

In no event shall the decision to assess or waive late charges or default interest be a Major Decision.

4.3 <u>Response to Requests</u>. Participant shall respond to a written request for approval or consent from Lead Lender within five (5) Business Days after such request. A failure to respond within such time period shall be deemed an approval or consent. If Lead Lender and Participant are unable to reach an agreement on any Major Decision within five (5) Business Days following the disapproval of the request, then Lead Lender shall have the option to exercise its rights under <u>Section 6.1</u>.

What are the risks the original lender faces in selling participations in an unfunded loan? What are its remedies?

3. DECISION MAKING

Loan agreements typically come with more covenants and disclosure obligations than bond debt. But if the lenders are to exercise these extra rights in a meaningful way, they need to provide for some internal governance structures to resolve disputes amongst lenders. A syndicated loan agreement is an agreement between the borrower and every bank in the credit line. As such, the syndicate banks may be less inclined to delegate to the lead or agent bank. But the borrower will want to make sure that the lead lender can make as many decisions as possible without having to go to all the other lenders for approval, which may prove time consuming and burdensome. Thus the agreement typically provides that the lead bank can make certain decisions, other decisions can be made only upon majority vote of the lenders, and other decisions require unanimous consent.

IN RE CHRYSLER LLC, ET AL., DEBTORS

405 B.R. 84
United States Bankruptcy Court, S.D. New York.
May 31, 2009.

Arthur J. GONZALEZ, Bankruptcy Judge.
Before the Court is a motion seeking authority to sell substantially all of the debtors' operating assets, free and clear of liens, claims, interests and encumbrances to a successful bidder and to authorize the assumption and assignment of certain executory contracts and unexpired leases in connection

with the sale, as well as certain other related relief. The sale transaction for which authorization is sought (the "Sale Transaction" or "Fiat Transaction") is similar to that presented in other cases in which exigent circumstances warrant an expeditious sale of assets prior to confirmation of a plan. The fact that the U.S. government is the primary source of funding does not alter the analysis under bankruptcy law.

The Debtors and their non-debtor direct and indirect subsidiaries (collectively, the "Chrysler Companies") comprise one of the largest manufacturers and distributors of automobiles and other vehicles, together with related parts and accessories. At the Petition Date,[6] Chrysler had 32 manufacturing and assembly facilities and 24 parts depots worldwide; and in addition, at the Petition Date, it had a network of 3,200 independent dealerships in the United States, with 72% of Chrysler sales occurring in the United States.

Chrysler's ultimate parent company is Chrysler Holding LLC ("Holding"). The owners of Holding are Cerberus Capital Management L.P. ("Cerberus") and Daimler AG ("Daimler"). As of the Petition Date, Cerberus or its affiliates held 80.1% of the membership interests in Holding, and Daimler or its affiliates held 19.9% of its membership interests.

Pursuant to an Amended and Restated First Lien Credit Agreement dated as of November 29, 2007 (the "First Lien Credit Agreement") a $10 billion term loan that matures on August 2, 2013 was made available to Chrysler. JP Morgan Chase Bank N.A. is the administrative agent (the "Administrative Agent") under the First Lien Credit Agreement. Chrysler's obligations under the First Lien Credit Agreement are secured by a security interest in and first lien on substantially all of Chrysler's assets. In addition, those obligations are guaranteed by certain other Debtors. The guarantees by these "other" Debtors are secured by a first priority lien on substantially all of such Debtors' respective assets. On the Petition Date, Chrysler owed the first-lien prepetition lenders (the "First–Lien Lenders") approximately $6.9 billion under that term loan.

In the fall of 2008, a global credit crisis affecting the liquidity markets impacted the availability of loans both to dealers and consumers, resulting in the erosion of consumer confidence and a sharp drop in vehicle sales. Chrysler was forced to use cash reserves to compensate for the reduction in cash flow and the resulting losses. The losses eliminated the gains that Chrysler had made early in its restructuring effort. Moreover, other OEM's were impacted, forcing them to confront their own liquidity issues.

As a result, in late 2008, Chrysler and other entities sought assistance from the government to obtain new financing to fund their operations to carry them through the liquidity crunch. In response, the TARP Financing was provided. Chrysler sought $7 billion and they were given $4 billion. Pursuant to the terms of the loan, Chrysler was required to submit a plan showing that it was able to achieve and sustain long-term viability, energy efficiency, rationalization of costs

---

6. The date the bankruptcy case was commenced; the date the bankruptcy petition was filed with the court. —AUTHOR

and competitiveness in the U.S. marketplace (the "Viability Plan"), which would indicate Chrysler's ability to repay the TARP Financing.

The Debtors used the $4 million TARP Loan to operate their business, including paying vendors and other ordinary course payables, and to fund their effort to pursue the Viability Plan. At the same time, Chrysler continued to pursue an alliance with Fiat; Chrysler considered Fiat to be a good prospect because it viewed Fiat's products and distribution network as complementary to those of Chrysler.

On January 16, 2009, Chrysler entered into a term sheet with Fiat for a strategic alliance (the "Fiat Alliance") pursuant to which Fiat would acquire 35% of the equity of Chrysler and would provide access to competitive fuel-efficient vehicle platforms, distribution capabilities in key growth markets and substantial cost-saving opportunities. The Fiat Alliance also would provide Chrysler with a distribution network outside of the North American region.

On May 19, 2009, the Indiana State Teachers Retirement Fund, Indiana State Police Pension Trust, and Indiana Major Moves Construction (the "Indiana Funds"), which oversee the investment of retirement assets for certain civil servants in the state of Indiana, filed an objection to the Sale Motion. The Indiana Funds hold approximately $42 million of the $6.9 billion in first priority secured claims, which represents less than 1% of the first-lien debt. In their objection, the Indiana Funds argue that pursuant to the Sale Motion, the First–Lien Lenders' collateral would be stripped and, in return, those lenders would be paid 29 cents on the dollar. The collateral would then be transferred to New Chrysler, where, according to the Indiana Funds, it would be worth significantly more than the money paid to the First-Lien Lenders. The Indiana Funds further argue that unsecured deficiency claims would not be paid while unsecured trade debt would be paid in full. In addition, the Indiana Funds contend that their senior claims will be impaired while the Governmental Entities, as junior lienholders and VEBA and the UAW, as unsecured creditors, will receive value . . .

The Indiana Funds are parties to the First Lien Credit Agreement as assignees to a portion of the debt. As previously noted, Chrysler's obligation to repay the loans under the First Lien Credit Agreement is secured by liens on most of its assets. Consequently, two additional documents are relevant: an Amended and Restated Collateral Trust Agreement, dated November 29, 2007 (as amended, the "CTA"), pursuant to which Wilmington Trust Company is the collateral trustee (the "Collateral Trustee"); and the Security Agreement, pursuant to which Chrysler grants a security interest in most of its assets, and the proceeds thereof, to the Collateral Trustee. *Security Agreement*, §2(a). Thus, while the liens are for the benefit of the lenders under the First Lien Credit Agreement, the liens themselves were granted to and are held by the Collateral Trustee. *See CTA* at p. 1.

Each lender under the First Lien Credit Agreement irrevocably designated the Administrative Agent to act as such lender's agent in exercising the powers delegated to the Administrative Agent and to be bound by its action. *First Lien Credit Agreement*, §§8.1, 8.4. The lenders, including the Indiana Funds, agreed to be bound by the Administrative Agents' action made at the request of lenders holding a majority of the indebtedness under the First Lien Credit Agreement (the "Required Lenders"). *Id.* at §1.1 & §8.4.

The commencement of the Debtors' bankruptcy cases was an event of default under the First Lien Credit Agreement, *Id.* at §7(e)(i)(A). The CTA defines the Administrative Agent as the "Controlling Party" as long as the first and second secured obligations have not been paid. *CTA*§1.1. Upon receipt of a "notice of event of default", the Collateral Trustee exercises the rights and remedies provided for in the CTA, and related security documents, "subject to the direction of the Controlling Party." *CTA*§2.1(a). A notice of event of default is deemed to be in effect whenever there is a bankruptcy filing. *CTA*§2.1(b). While such notice of an event of default is in effect, the Collateral Trustee has power to take any Collateral Enforcement Actions permitted under the security documents or any action it "deems necessary to protect or preserve the Collateral and to realize upon the Collateral", including selling all or any of the Collateral. CTA §§2.2. & 2.3. A Collateral Enforcement Action is defined, with respect to any secured party, as exercising, instituting or maintaining or participating "in any action or proceeding with respect to, any rights or remedies with respect to any Collateral, including . . . exercising any other right or remedy under the Uniform Commercial Code or any applicable jurisdiction or under any Bankruptcy Law or other applicable law." CTA §1.1.

Further, section 2.5(b) of the CTA provides that the Administrative Agent, as Controlling Party, has the right to direct, among other things, "the taking or the refraining from taking of any action authorized by this Collateral Trust Agreement or any Trust Security Document." Further, section 2.5(c) of the CTA provides, in relevant part:

> Whether or not any Insolvency Proceeding has been commenced by or against any of the [Chrysler parties to the CTA], no . . . [secured party] shall do any of the following without the consent of the Controlling Party; (i) take any Collateral Enforcement Action ... or (ii) object to, contest or take any other action that is reasonably likely to hinder (1) any Collateral Enforcement Action initiated by the Collateral Trustee, (2) any release of Collateral permitted under Section 6.12, whether or not done in consultation with or with notice to such Secured Party or (3) any decision by the Controlling Party to forbear or refrain from bringing or pursuing any such Collateral Enforcement Action or to effect any such release.

Thus, section 2.5, concerning the exercise of powers, gives the Collateral Trustee the exclusive right to pursue all of the lenders' rights and remedies concerning the Collateral and, further, gives the Administrative Agent, as Controlling Party, the exclusive authority to direct the Collateral Trustee's action concerning the Collateral.

In accordance with the direction of the Administrative Agent, the Collateral Trustee, who is the holder of the liens, has consented to the Fiat Transaction. The right to consent to the sale of the Debtors' assets that constitute Collateral is a Collateral Enforcement Action. It is an exercise of a right pursuant to Bankruptcy Law concerning the Collateral. *CTA*, §1.1. The Administrative Agent has received the concurrence of 92.5% of the outstanding principal amount of the loans under the First Lien Credit Agreement. Thus, the Administrative Agent has obtained the needed support of the Required Lenders. Consequently, pursuant to the CTA, the Administrative Agent properly directed the Collateral Trustee, who holds the liens, to consent to the section 363 sale of the Collateral. Moreover, the Administrative Agent acted as agent to the Indiana Funds and on their behalf. Thus, the Indiana Funds are bound by the Administrative Agent's action in that regard. *First Lien Credit Agreement*, §§8.1(a), 8.4. Therefore, the Administrative Agent's consent to the sale of the assets and its direction to the Collateral Trustee to consent, under section 363(f)(2) of the Bankruptcy Code, satisfies that section and allow for the purchased assets to be sold free and clear of the liens on the property held by the Collateral Trustee.

The Indiana Funds direct the Court's attention to section 9.1(a)(iii) of the First Lien Credit Agreement and argue that it requires the Administrative Agent to receive the consent of all Lenders before it can release collateral. The section referenced by the Indiana Funds, however, concerns waivers, amendments, supplements or modifications to the First Lien Credit Agreement and related documents. The transfer of the purchased assets to New Chrysler pursuant to section 363 of the Bankruptcy Code does not require any amendment, supplement or modification to the loan documents. *See In re GWLS Holdings, Inc.*, No. 08–12430, 2009 WL 453110, 2009 Bankr. LEXIS 378 (Bankr.D.Del. Feb. 23, 2009) (concluding that a provision concerning waivers, amendments, supplements or modifications after execution of certain related credit agreements did not override the provision concerning the right of the lenders' agent to credit bid). *See also Beal Sav. Bank v. Sommer*, 8 N.Y.3d 318 328–29, 834 N.Y.S.2d 44, 865 N.E.2d 1210 (2007) (concluding that provisions in a syndicate loan arrangement requiring unanimous consent by participating lenders in order to amend, modify or waive terms of related loan agreements did not preclude application of specific provisions which accomplished the parties' agreed-upon intent for collective action through an agent upon default by borrower). The purpose of section 9.1(a)(iii) of the First Lien Credit Agreement is to ensure that, unless there is unanimous consent by all lenders under the related loan agreements, the terms of those agreements cannot be altered in a manner that is inconsistent with the terms originally agreed to by the parties. *See id.* It does not concern collective action to enforce rights as authorized under the agreed-upon specific provisions of the parties' loan agreements.

Upon an Event of Default, the CTA expressly granted the Collateral Trustee the right to sell any or all of the Collateral. Thus, the loan documents authorized the Collateral Trustee to consent to the sale without the need to amend or modify the loan documents. Further, the Administrative Agent and Collateral Trustee are operating under their exclusive authority to take any Collateral Enforcement Action necessary to realize upon the Collateral. Moreover, it is not a "release" of collateral because the lien attaches to the proceeds of the sale, which remain as collateral to secure the loan made by the Lenders. Finally, even if the action were viewed as an amendment to the loan documents, the prohibition against releasing collateral without the consent of all lenders under section 9.1(iii) of the First Lien Credit Agreement, itself has an exception where the action is otherwise provided for in the loan documents. Here, the loan documents expressly provide for the Administrative Agent to direct the Collateral Trustee to take Enforcement Actions, including the sale of all or any of the Collateral.

The Court concludes that the purpose of the relevant provisions of the First Lien Credit Agreement, the CTA, and the Security Agreements is to have the Administrative Agent and Collateral Trustee act in the collective interest of the lenders. Restricting enforcement to a single agent to engage in unified action for the interests of a group of lenders, based upon a majority vote, avoids chaos and prevents a single lender from being preferred over others. Pursuant to the CTA, the Indiana Funds are bound by the Administrative Agent's direction to the Collateral Trustee to consent to the sale of its collateral free and clear of liens and other interests in exchange for the $2 billion cash payment.

Finally, with respect to the consenting First-Lien Lenders, the Indiana Funds question their independence in entering into the compromise to allow the sale of the assets free and clear of the lien. Inasmuch as certain of the individual-consenting lenders were recipients of government loans under the TARP program, the objecting lenders seek to portray the TARP-recipient lenders as being intimidated by the government. A compromise that is not based upon business considerations, including an assessment of litigation risks, would raise issues regarding the Administrative Agent's obligations, if any to the Indiana Funds, under the agreement. Clearly, that issue is not before this Court.

The Indiana Funds seem to be asking that, if the Court finds that they are bound under the governance provisions of the First Lien Credit Agreement, the Court should nullify the consent given because it was brought about by undue pressure by the U.S. government on the TARP-recipient lenders, who voted to give consent to the transaction before the Court.

In the first instance, it is not clear that this Court would even have jurisdiction over this inter-creditor dispute. However, the suggestion that the TARP-recipient lenders have been pressured to the point that they would breach their fiduciary duty and capitulate to the settlements presented is without any evidentiary support. It is mere speculation and without merit.

The Indiana Funds contracted away their right to act inconsistently with the determination of the Required Lenders. In that regard, if they did not want to waive such rights, they should not have invested in an investment with such restrictions. The fact that they do not like the outcome is not a basis to ignore the governance provisions of the relevant agreements.

The First-Lien Lenders had limited options: demand a liquidation of the collateral, negotiate with the only available source of funding, i.e., the Governmental Entities, or provide funding to sustain the Debtors on a stand-alone basis. The First-Lien Lenders, operating under their governance structure, decided to concentrate their efforts on negotiating with the only available source of funding, the Governmental Entities, and to accept their proposal.

Although loan syndication enables lenders to increase diversification and engage in transactions they might otherwise be inclined to reject, lenders within a syndicate group give up the ability to make decisions independently. In this context, disputes can arise regarding the role and authority of the group as contrasted with its individual members.

The New York Court of Appeals, in *Beal Savings Bank v. Sommer*, 8 N.Y.3d 318 (2007), found that one member of a lending group could not, in contravention of the syndicate's decision, take action against a guarantor of debt obligations following the default on that debt. As the court noted, "[h]ad the parties intended that an individual have a right to proceed independently, the Credit Agreement . . . should have expressly so provided." That is not quite the same thing as saying the contract clearly provides for majority rule, but the *Beal* case provides the foundation for decisions like the one you just read.

The governance issues at play in *Chrysler* were mild compared with those that might arise under some of the more complex loan structures. For example, in loan structures involving both senior lenders and subordinate lenders, the lender relationship may be arranged such that only senior lenders have the right to be involved in decision-making.

The most common structure—often referred to as an *A/B loan structure*—is for a first lien loan to be secured by all the available assets and a second lien loan relying on the same collateral pool, very much like a second mortgage on a home. In a typical transaction, a bank or other lender (or a lending group) takes a first lien on most of a borrower's assets. The debt is often guaranteed by affiliated companies or secured by their assets. Another lender (or another lending group), then extends credit to the same borrower, taking a second lien on the same assets upon which the first secured creditor has a lien.

Often the two pieces of the loan are referred to as the A and B *tranches*. *Tranche* is a French word that the syndicated loan market has borrowed from asset securitization, as we will see in an upcoming chapter. Essentially, *tranche* for these purposes means "layer" or "slice." Apparently, the word *slice* was seen as too pedestrian.

The A tranche is targeted at the commercial banks since generally they will hold only the revolver and the shortest term loan. The B tranche is targeted to other institutional investors, like mutual funds and hedge funds. It tends to be made up of bond-like structures with longer maturities—six or seven years is typical—and deferred amortizations.

Generally an *intercreditor agreement* will require the second lien holder to release its second lien on the collateral whenever the first lien holder has elected to release the first lien on such collateral under the terms of the first lien loan documents. In these cases, governance of the entire loan package is essentially under the control of the senior lenders. For example, the second lien or B interest typically must give up any right to call the loan, file a bankruptcy petition, or exercise any rights in a bankruptcy proceeding. These sorts of B loans are often referred to as "silent seconds."

In contrast to the A/B loan structure described above, a *unitranche facility* is structured as a single loan, secured by a single first lien in collateral, but with two tranches of debt — a "first out" tranche and a "last out" tranche. The first out tranche may contain a revolver plus a senior term loan.

As the names imply, the first out tranche of the facility has priority of payment over the last out tranche. But that priority comes solely by contract. Instead of separate notes and security agreements for two classes of debt with an intercreditor agreement harmonizing the two sets of documents, unitranche transactions are governed by a single document, typically called the Agreement Among Lenders (AAL). It is worth noting that the borrower typically is not a party to the AAL, and from the borrower's perspective a unitranche facility is essentially a single loan. However, it remains uncertain how courts will view the relationships among the various lenders and how potential disputes among those lenders will affect borrowers.

PROBLEM SET 16.2

1. Why might it make sense for syndicated loans to adopt majority rule for important changes? What are the risks?
2. In an A/B intercreditor agreement, it is common to provide that (a) the agent bank has control over routine matters, (b) the B lenders (the subordinated lenders) have control over all other decisions, (c) unless the collateral is appraised at a sufficient low level that the B lenders will either have to guarantee the A lender claims or allow the A lenders to take control. Does it surprise you that the B lenders have control even though they are subordinated?
3. Look back at the Endo Pharmaceuticals loan documents above. What kind of loan structure was used in that transaction?
4. Would the Indiana Pension Funds have had a better argument in *Chrysler* if their investment was made under the loan participation agreement set forth above?
5. The court notes that "the suggestion that the TARP-recipient lenders have been pressured to the point that they would breach their fiduciary duty and capitulate to the settlements presented is without any evidentiary support." There are some indications that there was some pressure applied to TARP recipients. For example, some regulators conducting the "stress tests" of a major financial institution allegedly suggested that the institution "would be crazy to vote against the Chrysler sale." Should that have influenced the court's decision?

4. DUTIES OF THE LEAD BANK

Given that many loan agreements delegate considerable powers to the lead or agent bank, other participants in the loan have to trust that the agent bank's incentives are properly aligned. Yet often these large financial institutions interact with the borrower on a variety of levels beyond the loan agreement.

UNICREDITO ITALIANO SPA v. JPMORGAN CHASE BANK

288 F.Supp.2d 485
United States District Court, S.D. New York.
Oct. 14, 2003.

SWAIN, District Judge.

This action concerns loans, made by Plaintiffs to or for the benefit of the Enron Corporation, that were administered by JP Morgan Chase Bank and Citibank. Plaintiffs contend that Defendants defrauded them in connection with the formation of certain syndicated credit facilities and payments under those facilities.

Defendants now move pursuant to Rules 12(b)(6) and 9(b) of the Federal Rules of Civil Procedure for an order dismissing the Second Amended Complaint. The Court has considered thoroughly all arguments and submissions in connection with the instant motions. For the following reasons, Defendants' motions are granted in part and denied in part.

BACKGROUND

The following factual recitation is drawn from the Second Amended Complaint (the "Complaint"), statements or documents incorporated in the Complaint by reference, public disclosure documents filed with the SEC, and/or documents that Plaintiffs either possessed or knew about and upon which they relied in bringing this action. All of Plaintiffs' allegations are taken as true for the purposes of this recitation.

Plaintiff UniCredito Italiano SpA ("UCI") is an Italian financial institution with headquarters in Milan, Italy. Plaintiff Bank Polska Kasa Opieki SA, also known as Bank Pekao SA ("Pekao") is a Polish financial institution with headquarters in Warsaw, Poland.

Defendant JP Morgan Chase & Co. ("JPMC & Co.") is a Delaware corporation with its principal place of business in New York. Its primary banking subsidiary is Defendant JP Morgan Chase Bank; its primary investment banking or securities subsidiary is Defendant J.P. Morgan Securities Inc. Defendant JP Morgan Chase Bank is a New York corporation, with its principal place of business in New York. Defendant J.P. Morgan Securities Inc. is a Delaware corporation with offices in New York.

Defendant Citigroup, Inc. ("Citigroup") is a Delaware corporation with its principal place of business in New York. Citigroup's primary banking subsidiary is Defendant Citibank, N.A. ("Citibank"); its primary investment banking or securities subsidiary is Defendant Salomon Smith Barney. Citibank is a national banking association with its principal place of business in New York. Defendant Salomon Smith Barney is a New York corporation with its principal place of business in New York.

[The Defendants were involved in a series of transactions designed to hide the true financial conditional of Enron.]

THE CREDIT FACILITIES

The bulk of Plaintiffs' damages claims in this action arise from losses sustained on investments in credit facilities for Enron for which the Defendant banks served as Administrative and/or Paying Agents or, in the case of JP Morgan Chase Bank with respect to a 2001 letter of credit facility, the Issuing Bank, and which were marketed by the Defendant securities subsidiaries.

Defendants JP Morgan Chase Bank (through its predecessor in interest, The Chase Manhattan Bank) and Citibank were the Co-Administrative Agents for three Enron credit facilities in which Plaintiffs participated: 1) a $1.25 billion medium-term credit facility entered into on May 18, 2000 (the "2000 Credit Facility"), 2) a $1.75 billion short-term facility entered into on May 14, 2001 (the "2001 Credit Facility"), and 3) a $500 million letter of credit facility entered into on May 14, 2001 (the "2001 L/C Facility) (collectively, the "Syndicated Facilities"). Citibank was also the Paying Agent for the 2000 and 2001 Credit Facilities, and The Chase Manhattan Bank was the Paying Agent and Issuing Bank for the 2001 L/C Facility.

The agreements establishing each of the Syndicated Facilities contained disclaimer, covenant, and acknowledgment provisions identical in all relevant respects to the following provisions of the 2000 Credit Facility:

Section 7.02 *Paying Agent's Reliance, Etc.*
[T]he Paying Agent shall not have, by reason of this Agreement or any other Loan Document a fiduciary relationship in respect of any Bank or the holder of any Note; and nothing in this Agreement or any other Loan Document, expressed or implied, is intended or shall be so construed as to impose upon the Paying Agent any obligations in respect of this Agreement or any other Loan Document except as expressly set forth herein. Without limitation of the generality of the foregoing, the Paying Agent ... (iii) makes no warranty or representation to any Bank for any statements, warranties or representations (whether written or oral) made in or in connection with any Loan Document or any other instrument or document furnished pursuant hereto or in connection herewith; (iv) shall not have any duty to ascertain or to inquire as to the performance or observance of any of the terms, covenants or conditions of any Loan Document or any other instrument or document furnished pursuant hereto or in connection herewith on the part of the Borrower or to inspect the property (including the books and records) of the Borrower;

Section 7.03 *Paying Agent and Its Affiliates*

With respect to its Commitment, the Advances made by it and the Note issued to it, each Bank which is also the Paying Agent shall have the same rights and powers under the Loan Documents as any other Bank and may exercise the same as though it were not the Paying Agent; the term "Bank" or "Banks" shall, unless otherwise expressly indicated, include any Bank serving as the Paying Agent in its individual capacity. Any Bank serving as the Paying Agent and its affiliates may accept deposits from, lend money to, act as trustee under indentures of, accept investment banking engagements from and generally engage in any kind of business with, the Borrower, any of the Subsidiaries and any Person who may do business with or own securities of the Borrower or any Subsidiary, all as if such Bank were not the Paying Agent and without any duty to account therefor to the Banks.

Section 7.04 *Bank Credit Decision*

Each Bank acknowledges that it has, independently and without reliance upon the Paying Agent or any other Bank and based on the financial statements referred to in Section 4.01(d) and such other documents and information as it has deemed appropriate, made its own credit analysis and decision to enter into this Agreement. Each Bank also acknowledges that it will, independently and without reliance upon the Paying Agent or any other Bank and based on such documents and information as it shall deem appropriate at the time, continue to make its own credit decisions in taking or not taking action under this Agreement and the other Loan Documents. The Paying Agent shall not have any duty or responsibility, either initially or on a continuing basis, to provide any Bank or the holder of any Note with any credit or other information with respect thereto, whether coming into its possession before the making of the Advances or at any time or times thereafter.

As noted above, JP Morgan Chase Bank was also designated as the "Issuing Bank" under the 2001 L/C Facility Agreement, which provided that the "Issuing Bank," in selling to the participating banks their pro rata share of the obligation under any letter of credit issued pursuant to the agreement, "represents and warrants to [the participating bank] that the Issuing Bank is the legal and beneficial owner of such interest being sold by it, free and clear of any liens, but makes no other representation or warranty. The Issuing Bank shall have no responsibility or liability to any other [participating bank] with respect to any [letter of credit obligation] or any such participation [.]" Section 7.03 of the 2001 L/C Facility Agreement provided that the Issuing Bank and its affiliates had the right to engage in transactions with Enron "with no duty to account therefor" to the participating banks, and section 7.04 contains the acknowledgment of participating banks that they had not relied on the Issuing Bank in making the decision to enter into the agreement and that they would make their continuing decisions as to whether or not to take action under the agreement or letters of credit issued under the agreement "independently and without reliance upon . . . the Issuing Bank[.]"

In each of the agreements for the Syndicated Facilities, Enron (which was referred to in the agreements as the "Borrower") entered into certain covenants concerning the participating banks' due diligence rights. These covenants were identical in all relevant respects to the covenants in the 2000 Credit Facility Agreement, the pertinent provisions of which follow:

> Section 5.01 *Affirmative Covenants.*
> (a) Reporting Requirements [the Borrower will furnish to each Bank:]
> (viii) such other information respecting the condition or operations, financial or otherwise, of the Borrower or any of its Subsidiaries as any Bank through the Paying Agent may from time to time reasonably request.
>
> . . .
>
> (f) *Visitation Rights* At any reasonable time and from time to time, after reasonable notice, [the Borrower will] permit the Paying Agent or any of the Banks or any agents or representatives thereof, to examine the records and books of account of, and visit the properties of, the Borrower and any of its Principal Subsidiaries, and to discuss the affairs, finances and accounts of the Borrower and any of its Principal Subsidiaries with any of their respective officers or directors.

Defendants Salomon Smith Barney and J.P. Morgan Securities (the "Securities Subsidiaries") were co-lead arrangers of the Syndicated Facilities. They distributed to participant banks offering memoranda and invitations to offer in connection with the Syndicated Facilities. Those documents contained and referred to publicly filed financial information about Enron. (*Id.*) The offering memoranda contained the following section entitled "Disclaimer":

> The information contained in this Information Memorandum has been supplied by or on behalf of Enron Corp. (the "Company"). Neither Salomon Smith Barney Inc. and Chase Securities Inc. (as "Co-Lead Arrangers") nor any of their affiliates has independently verified such information and the same is being provided by the Co-Lead Arrangers for informational purposes only. The Co-Lead Arrangers do not make any representation or warranty as to the accuracy or completeness of such information and does not [sic] assume any undertaking to supplement such information as further information becomes available or in light of changing circumstances. The Co-Lead Arrangers shall not have any liability for any representations or warranties (express or implied) contained in, or any omissions from, the Information Memorandum or any other written or oral communication transmitted to the recipient in the course of its evaluation of the proposed financing or otherwise.
>
> The information contained herein has been prepared to assist interested parties in making their own evaluation of the proposed financing for the Company and for no other purpose. The information does not purport to be all-inclusive or to contain all information that a prospective lender may desire. It is understood that each recipient of this Information Memorandum will perform its own independent investigation and analysis of the proposed financing and the creditworthiness of the Company, based on such information as it deems relevant and without reliance on Co-Lead Arrangers. The information contained herein is not a substitute for the recipient's independent investigation and analysis.
>
> Plaintiff UCI contributed $10,416,667.67 under the 2000 Credit Facility, $11,666,666.67 under the 2001 Credit Facility, and $3,333,333.33 under the 2001

L/C Facility. Plaintiff Pekao purchased a participating interest in the 2000 Credit Facility in the amount of $6.25 million.

THE OCTOBER 25, 2001 BORROWING REQUESTS

Under the credit agreements governing the 2000 and 2001 Credit Facilities, Enron had to satisfy certain conditions before it could receive loan funds, including compliance with all laws and the maintenance of a 65% debt-to-capitalization ratio. On October 25, 2001, Plaintiff UCI received borrowing demands at 11:48 a.m. and 12 noon, conveyed through Citibank, for immediate payment of its shares of the 2000 and 2001 Credit Facilities, and Plaintiff Pekao received a demand at 12 noon, conveyed through Citibank, to fund immediately its share of the 2000 Credit Facility.

At 2:45 p.m., the Managing Director of JP Morgan Chase Securities, Claire O'Connor, notified UCI that Enron would explain its need for cash to redeem its commercial paper at a conference call at 3:00 p.m. The Defendant banks helped manage Enron's commercial paper program, but O'Connor did not mention their role. O'Connor falsely stated that Enron was drawing down the funds to reestablish market confidence. At the 3:00 p.m. conference call, Enron's CFO explained that Enron needed the full amounts of the 2000 and 2001 Credit Facilities so that Enron could redeem its commercial paper. The Defendant banks participated in the conference call, but said nothing about Enron's defaults under the credit agreements, defaults of which they were aware.

At 4:06 p.m., UCI received a facsimile from Citibank conveying Enron's certification that its representations and warranties, including those in the credit agreements, continued to be correct, and that there was no default or event of default under the credit agreements. UCI and Pekao subsequently forwarded their respective contributions under the credit facilities to Citibank, to be conveyed to Enron.

Pursuant to section 6.01 of the credit agreements governing the 2000 and 2001 Credit Facilities, if a majority of the participating banks had determined that a default or event of default had occurred that relieved them of their obligations under the agreements, the banks could have instructed Citibank to declare the termination of each bank's obligation to make advances. Defendants knew that Enron's debt-to-capitalization ratio put it in breach of the credit agreements, and their concealment of that breach prevented Plaintiffs from exercising their rights under section 6.01.

The Defendant banks, who were also participants in the 2000 and 2001 Credit Facilities, contributed their shares of the October 25, 2001 funding. The credit facilities enabled the banks to reduce their aggregate exposure and take a "smaller hit" with respect to Enron.

On November 1, 2001, the Defendant banks announced that they were negotiating to extend $1 billion in secured loans to Enron. Citibank conditioned its participation in that secured loan on Enron's payment of an earlier $250 million unsecured Citibank loan.

UCI AND THE 2001 L/C FACILITY

After its October 25, 2001 payments, UCI sought from JP Morgan Chase Bank the identification of all letters of credit that had been issued under the 2001 L/C Facility and information as to the current status of those letters of credit. On November 26, 2001, JP Morgan Chase Bank identified eleven letters of credit that it said had been issued under the 2001 L/C Facility, two of which had expired. On Friday, November 30, 2001, UCI received a request to fund $1,050,000 under a letter of credit for Enron, and made the requested payment to JP Morgan Chase Bank.

Enron filed for bankruptcy protection on Sunday, December 2, 2001. On December 3, 2001, UCI received a different list from JP Morgan Chase of letters of credit purportedly issued under the 2001 L/C Facility. The second list included a $150 million letter of credit dated October 9, 2001 in favor of an entity called Mahonia. The Mahonia letter of credit was drawn down on December 11, 2001.

Under the agreement governing the 2001 L/C Facility, Enron's breach of its covenants, representations, and warranties would have permitted a majority of the participating banks in that facility to demand security from Enron, including requiring Enron to deposit an amount equal to the undrawn letter of credit amounts into a cash collateral account.

Defendant JP Morgan Chase Bank has continued to demand payments from UCI under the 2001 L/C Facility, including a demand in May 2002. Plaintiff has refused to make any further payments under the 2001 L/C Facility. On June 4, 2002, JP Morgan Chase Bank advised UCI and other participating banks that JP Morgan Chase Bank had erroneously applied letters of credit in an aggregate amount exceeding the maximum authorized under that facility. UCI was advised that it would be paid its proportionate share of such excess. To date, no such payment has been made.

UCI has made repeated requests of JP Morgan Chase Bank for information, to which UCI is entitled to as a participant in the 2001 L/C Facility and which JP Morgan Chase Bank has made available to other participating banks, about the letters of credit that have been issued under that Facility; those requests have been refused. JP Morgan Chase Bank has failed to allow UCI to have access to a repository or central file of documents relating to the 2001 L/C Facility, including documents that UCI has specifically requested.

JP Morgan Chase Bank has submitted and continues to submit bills for legal expenses to UCI that JP Morgan Chase Bank claims are subject to indemnification under the 2001 L/C Facility.

THE 2000 L/C FACILITY

In May 2000, the same month UCI approved its participation in the 2000 Credit Facility, it also, under a separate agreement with Enron, approved a $10 million letter of credit facility for Enron, which was increased to $30 million in August 2000 (the "2000 L/C Facility"). UCI would not have taken part in the 2000 L/C Facility had it not been for Defendants' participation in falsifying

Enron's financial statements, including its Form 10-K and 10-Q, specifically the disclosures concerning revenues, earning, liabilities, and debt. Defendants knew that UCI had established the 2000 L/C Facility, but they did not advise UCI of Enron's actual financial condition.

On August 31, 2000, at the direction of Enron, UCI issued a standby letter of credit in favor of CalPX Trading Services in the amount of $10 million. On December 12, 2000, that amount was increased to $25 million at the direction of Enron. The maturity date was extended several times at Enron's request, including by an agreement on October 24, 2001, to extend the maturity date to November 30, 2001. After the October extension, UCI and Enron began negotiations concerning Enron providing collateral for the letters of credit that UCI had issued. By the third week of November 2001, Enron had delivered to UCI a form of agreement under which Enron was to provide the collateral.

On or about November 26, 2001, UCI received a phone call from Claire O'Connor. O'Connor asked UCI if it would be interested in contributing its $25 million exposure on the 2000 L/C Facility to a new letter of credit facility for the benefit of Enron that JP Morgan Chase Bank was proposing to arrange. UCI declined to participate, and explained that it expected to enter an agreement under which it would receive cash collateral from Enron for its 2000 L/C Facility exposure.

UCI and Enron never executed the proposed agreement for collateral. On November 30, 2001, the letter of credit was drawn down in the full amount of $25 million.

CHOICE OF LAW

The credit agreements for the Syndicated Facilities provide that they are governed by New York law.

PLAINTIFFS' CAUSES OF ACTION

Plaintiffs UCI and Pekao assert common law claims against all Defendants for fraudulent concealment (Count I), fraudulent inducement (Count II), aiding and abetting fraud by Enron (Count III), negligent misrepresentation (Count IV), civil conspiracy (Count V), and unjust enrichment (Count VII). Plaintiffs assert a claim against JP Morgan Chase Bank and Citibank for breach of an implied duty of good faith in connection with the Syndicated Facilities (Count VI). Plaintiff UCI also seeks declaratory relief against Defendant JP Morgan Chase Bank with respect to the 2001 L/C Facility (Count VIII).

PLAINTIFFS' FRAUD AND NEGLIGENT MISREPRESENTATION CLAIMS

. . . Plaintiffs' fraud and misrepresentation claims must be dismissed because the contracts pursuant to which they made their Enron loan investments preclude them from establishing essential elements of those claims, namely, that the Defendant banks had a duty to disclose information regarding or gained from their business dealings with Enron, and that any reliance by Plaintiffs on misrepresentations by the Defendants was reasonable . . .

The operative documents also, on their face, preclude Plaintiffs from claiming that they relied reasonably on any alleged representations by the Defendants . . .

PLAINTIFFS' AIDING AND ABETTING FRAUD CLAIM

Plaintiffs have stated a claim for aiding and abetting fraud. Plaintiffs allege that Defendants knowingly participated in and helped structure the transactions . . . that enabled Enron to distort its public financial statements, specifically with respect to Enron's revenues and its ratio of balance sheet debt to balance sheet capital. Furthermore, Plaintiffs allege that Defendant's participation in those transactions contributed to Enron's collapse, and thus its inability to meet its obligations under the credit agreements. In addition, by identifying Enron's fraudulent statements, that is, the revenue and debt-to-equity figures in Enron's public financial statements, and specifying the way in which those figures misrepresented the reality of Enron's revenues and liabilities, Plaintiffs have plead Enron's fraud with sufficient particularity to satisfy the requirements of Rule 9(b) of the Federal Rules of Civil Procedure. Accordingly, Defendants' motions are denied to the extent they seek dismissal of Count III.

PLAINTIFFS' CLAIM FOR BREACH OF THE IMPLIED DUTY OF GOOD FAITH AND UCI'S CLAIM FOR DECLARATORY RELIEF

The express disclaimers in the credit agreements preclude Plaintiffs' claim for breach of the implied duty of good faith in those agreements to the extent that claim is premised on the allegedly fraudulent conduct addressed above. Plaintiffs allege that the failure of Defendant banks to disclose Enron's true financial condition in connection with the credit transactions prevented Plaintiffs from taking advantage of their various rights under the credit agreements. Although New York law implies a duty of good faith and fair dealing in every contract, "no obligation can be implied that would be inconsistent with other terms of the contractual relationship." Here, as explained above, the operative contracts specifically absolve the Defendant banks from any duty to disclose financial information regarding Enron and contain Plaintiffs' undertakings to rely on their own credit analyses in making the relevant decisions. Implication of a duty, notwithstanding these provisions, of the banks to make disclosures regarding Enron's financial conditions would clearly be inconsistent with the governing contracts . . .

PROBLEM SET 16.3

1. Is the opinion's treatment of the Defendant's as agents consistent with the agency law you learned in Business Associations?

2. Given the many hats worn by large financial institutions, why do buyers of loan interests and participations agree to exculpatory clauses like those seen in this case?

5.   DEFAULTING AND UNWANTED LENDERS

One consequence of the increasing trend toward sale of bits of corporate loans is that the borrower is less apt to know who its lender is, and could end up with a group of lenders that it finds it is unable to work with. This might be especially likely to occur as the debtor's credit quality changes over time—for example, the group of staid insurance companies and banks that once owned the loan might be replaced by a new group of distressed debt investors who have very different goals and interests.

Short of refinancing the loan, the borrower has limited recourse. One potentially relevant provision is known as the "yank-a-bank" clause. It typically provides something like this:

12.24 REPLACEMENT OF LENDERS

If any Lender requests compensation under **Section 3.3**, or if the Borrowers are required to pay any additional amount to any Lender or any Governmental Authority for the account of any Lender pursuant to **Section 3.1**, or if any Lender is a Defaulting Lender or under the circumstance set forth in the last paragraph of **Section 11.1** [refusal to consent to a loan amendment, that has been agreed to a majority of lenders], then the Borrowers may, at their sole expense and effort, upon notice to such Lender and the Agent, require such Lender to assign and delegate, without recourse (in accordance with and subject to the restrictions contained in, and consents required by, **Section 11.2**), all of its interests, rights and obligations under this Agreement and the related Loan Documents to an assignee that shall assume such obligations (which assignee may be another Lender, if a Lender accepts such assignment); provided that:

(a) the Borrower shall have paid to the Agent the processing fee specified in **Section 11.2(a)**;

(b) such Lender shall have received payment of an amount equal to the outstanding principal of its Loans (including the L/C Loans), accrued interest thereon, accrued fees and all other amounts payable to it hereunder and under the other Loan Documents (including any amounts under **Section 3.5**) from the assignee (to the extent of such outstanding principal and accrued interest and fees) or the Borrowers (in the case of all other amounts);

(c) in the case of any such assignment resulting from a claim for compensation under **Section 3.3** or payments required to be made pursuant to **Section 3.1**, such assignment will result in a reduction in such compensation or payments thereafter; and

(d)   such assignment does not conflict with Applicable Laws. A Lender shall not be required to make any such assignment or delegation if, prior thereto, as a result of a waiver by such Lender or otherwise, the circumstances entitling the Borrowers to require such assignment and delegation cease to apply.

This clause might also become relevant if a particular lender in the bank line fails to perform. Before 2008, the idea that a major financial institution would fail to fund a loan it had agreed to make was almost unthinkable. Then Lehman Brothers filed for bankruptcy, throwing into doubt financing for several major construction projects.

The issue of "defaulting lenders" also arises with regard to letters of credit outstanding on a bank loan. If and when a complying draw is made under the letter of credit (and the borrower does not reimburse the issuer), the issuing bank must turn to the other lenders to fund their part of these LCs.[7]

PROBLEM SET 16.4

1.   How useful would the yank-a-bank clause set forth previously have been during the financial crisis, if Chrysler had wanted to replace the Indiana pension funds as a lender in its loan agreement? How about a borrower that wanted to replace Lehman as lender in an outstanding but unfunded loan agreement?

2.   If an issuing bank sells participations in the credit risk to the other lenders, and those participations are in turn sold to other investors, what are the potential issues that might arise? In particular, what concerns should the issuing bank or the borrower have? Would the following sort of clause (taken from LSTA model documents) help? Would the lead lenders be eager to agree to such a clause?

> "Disqualified Institution" means, on any date, (a) any Person designated by the Borrower as a "Disqualified Institution" by written notice delivered to the Administrative Agent on or prior to the date hereof and (b) any other Person that is a Competitor of the Borrower or any of its Subsidiaries, which Person has been designated by the Borrower as a "Disqualified Institution" by written notice to [the Administrative Agent and the Lenders (including by posting such notice to the Platform) not less than [_] Business Day[s] prior to such date]; provided that "Disqualified Institutions" shall exclude any Person that the Borrower has designated as no longer being a "Disqualified Institution" by written notice delivered to the Administrative Agent from time to time.

7. R.J. Miles, et al., *Syndicated Lending Update: Defaulting Lender Issues*, 126 Banking L.J. 165 (2009).

6. TRADING PIECES OF LOANS

TAEL ONE PARTNERS LIMITED v.
MORGAN STANLEY & CO. INT'L PLC

United Kingdom Supreme Court
Hilary Term
[2015] UKSC 12
11 March 2015

LORD REED: (with whom LORD NEUBERGER, LORD KERR, LORD TOULSON and LORD HODGE agree)

1   This appeal raises a question of contractual interpretation. Its significance lies in the fact that the contractual condition in question forms part of the Loan Market Association standard terms and conditions for par trade transactions ("the LMA terms"), which are a recommended set of terms published by the LMA and commonly used in the secondary loan market. There is no dispute as to the relevant legal principles.

2   Loan agreements normally entitle the lender to charge interest on the principal sum. They may also entitle the lender to the payment of a further lump sum at the time when the principal is repaid. This is sometimes known as a payment premium. If the lender assigns his rights to an assignee for value, provision will normally be made as to whether the assignee should account to the assignor for any interest which may have accrued but be unpaid at the date of the assignment. If a payment premium is due on the repayment of the loan, a question may also arise as to whether the assignee should account to the assignor for any part of the premium which can be said to be attributable to the period prior to the assignment. That depends on the terms of the assignment.

3   In the present case, the appellant, Tael, was one of a number of lenders under a loan agreement. During the currency of the loan, it assigned its rights in respect of part of its lending (or, in the jargon, transferred part of its participation) to the respondent, Morgan Stanley, under a contract which incorporated the LMA terms. The loan was subsequently repaid, together with a payment premium. Tael claims that, under the terms of the transfer to Morgan Stanley, it is entitled to be paid the part of the payment premium which relates to the amount transferred, to the extent that (as Tael argues) it pertains to the period prior to the date of the transfer. Whether it is so entitled depends on the construction of the LMA terms.

THE FACTUAL BACKGROUND

4   In terms of a facility agreement concluded in 2009, Tael agreed to participate, together with a number of other lenders, in the advance of a US $100m syndicated loan to Finspace SA. The loan facility was for a period of 24 months. The facility agreement provided for payment of interest at the rate of 11.25% per annum, accruing daily but payable three monthly in arrears. It also provided for a payment premium, to be paid by the borrower at the same time as prepayment or repayment of the principal of the loan, which enhanced the rate of return to the lenders to a total of either 17% or 20% per annum, depending on the circumstances in which the loan was prepaid or repaid. Clause 24 of the facility agreement permitted a lender to transfer part or all of its participation in the loan facility.

5   In January 2010 Tael transferred US $11m, out of its total US $32m participation, to Morgan Stanley. The parties documented the transfer in a transfer certificate and a LMA trade confirmation which incorporated the LMA terms. The confirmation defined the trade date and the settlement date as being 14 January 2010.

6   A purchase price letter was also executed on 14 January 2010 by both parties. It provided that in accordance with the LMA terms the amount payable by Morgan Stanley was agreed to be as set out in the schedule. The schedule provided that the total purchase price due to Tael from Morgan Stanley was US $11m plus accrued interest for the period between 16 October 2009 and 14 January 2010 in an amount of US $309,375. The purchase was also conditional on Tael's lending US $11m to a third party. The purchase price letter did not provide for any further payment by Morgan Stanley, and in particular did not provide for any payment to be made in respect of the payment premium.

7   In March 2010 Morgan Stanley sold its participation in the facility agreement to Spinnaker Global Strategic Fund Limited.

8   On 16 December 2010 the borrower refinanced the loan under the facility agreement, prepaying it in full. In accordance with the facility agreement, the borrower paid the payment premium to all lenders as at that date. Those lenders included Tael, which was still a participant in the loan, and Spinnaker, but not Morgan Stanley.

9   Tael claims that Morgan Stanley is required by the LMA terms to pay it the payment premium in respect of Tael's US $11m participation in the facility agreement that was transferred to Morgan Stanley, so far as it had accrued as at 14 January 2010.

10   Those being the facts in summary, it is necessary next to examine the relevant contractual terms.

THE LMA TERMS

23   Condition 7.1 provides:
"The transaction shall be settled on the Settlement Date by the taking of all necessary action to complete the transaction. . . ."

24   Condition 7.3 provides:
"The action necessary to complete a transaction shall include the payment for the Purchased Assets on the Settlement Date . . ."

25   Condition 11 deals with interest and fees. Condition 11.1 provides:
"All interest and fees referred to in this Condition 11 which are expressed to accrue by reference to time elapsed are based on the rates contained in the Credit Agreement [ie the facility agreement]."

26   Conditions 11.2, 11.3, 11.5 and 11.6 deal with each of the four bases on which, in terms of the trade confirmation, the parties can agree that the transfer should be settled. In the present case, the agreed basis was "Paid on settlement date," which is addressed in condition 11.3. It will however be necessary to refer also to the other conditions in order to understand how condition 11.9 is intended to operate.

27   Condition 11.2 applies where the agreed basis is "Settled without accrued interest." It provides:
"(a) . . . if "Settled Without Accrued Interest" is specified in the Agreed Terms then, subject to paragraph (b) of Condition 7.2 *(Delayed Settlement)* if applicable, upon receipt by the Buyer of any interest or fees accrued up to but excluding the Settlement Date in respect of the Purchased Assets (other than (i) PIK Interest and (ii) the fees referred to in paragraph (b) of Condition 11.9 *(Allocation of interest and fees)* which are payable after the Trade Date), the Buyer shall promptly pay to the Seller an amount equal to the amount of such interest or fees.
(b)   If the Buyer pays any amount to the Seller in accordance with paragraph (a) above and . . . the Buyer does not receive all or part of such amount [from the borrower] . . . then the Seller shall promptly, after demand by the Buyer, repay to the Buyer the whole or a proportionate part of such payment."

PIK interest is defined as meaning "any interest, fees or other amounts . . . which are either: (a) automatically deferred or capitalised; or (b) deferred or capitalised at the option of any Obligor", and is dealt with separately in condition 11.11.

28   Where, as in this case, the parties have specified "Paid on Settlement Date" in their trade confirmation, condition 11.3 provides:
"(a) . . . the Buyer shall pay to the Seller on the Settlement Date an amount equal to the amount of any interest or fees accrued up to but excluding the Settlement Date in respect of the Purchased Assets (other than (i) PIK Interest and (ii) the fees referred to in paragraph (b) of Condition 11.9 *(Allocation of interest and fees)* which are payable after the Trade Date).
(b) . . . if, on or after the Settlement Date, any interest or fees accrued up to but excluding the Settlement Date in respect of the Purchased Assets are paid to the

Seller, the Seller shall promptly after receipt pay a corresponding amount to the Buyer.

(c) The Buyer shall have no right of recourse to the Seller in relation to any amounts paid to the Seller in accordance with paragraph (a) above including, without limitation, in circumstances where the Buyer does not receive all or part of any interest or fees on their due date . . ."

29   Condition 11.5 provides for the situation where the parties have specified "Discounted from next roll-over date" in the trade confirmation. It provides:

". . . any interest or fees accrued up to but excluding the Settlement Date in respect of the Purchased Assets (other than PIK Interest) but which are not payable until the next roll-over date applicable under the Credit Agreement shall be discounted from such roll-over date back to the Settlement Date at IBOR. . . ."

30   Condition 11.6 provides for the situation where the parties have specified "N/A" in the trade confirmation. It provides:

". . . subject to Condition 11.10 [*sic:* condition 11.11 is meant] *(PIK Interest),* the Buyer shall not be obliged to make any payment to the Seller in respect of accrued interest or accrued fees, either on the Settlement Date or on receipt of any such interest or fees."

31   Condition 11.9, headed "Allocation of interest and fees", provides:

"Unless these Conditions otherwise provide . . .

(a) any interest or fees (other than PIK Interest) which are payable under the Credit Agreement in respect of the Purchased Assets and which are expressed to accrue by reference to the lapse of time shall, to the extent they accrue in respect of the period before (and not including) the Settlement Date, be for the account of the Seller and, to the extent they accrue in respect of the period after (and including) the Settlement Date, be for the account of the Buyer; and

(b) all other fees shall, to the extent attributable to the Purchased Assets and payable after the Trade Date, be for the account of the Buyer."

THE PROCEEDINGS BELOW

32   Tael commenced proceedings against Morgan Stanley and applied for summary judgment. Morgan Stanley responded by also applying for summary judgment. Both applications came before Popplewell J, who granted Tael's application and dismissed Morgan Stanley's: [2012] EWHC 1858 (Comm); [2013] 1 CLC 879. He considered that the payment premium was similar to interest and performed an analogous function. The cost of the borrowing was more than the interest of 11.25% per annum, but only that amount required to be paid out of cash flow three monthly in arrears. The remainder of the cost of borrowing was deferred and became payable, in the form of the payment premium, whenever the loan was repaid to a particular lender or all the lenders. The payment premium was therefore part of the consideration for the loan, and was calculated by

reference to the period for which the borrower had the use of the money in just the same way as was the entitlement to "interest" described as such.

33   Since the payment premium was incapable of quantification on 14 January 2010, it could not be said to have "accrued up to" that date, and therefore did not fall within condition 11.3(a) of the LMA terms. That condition was concerned with something which had accrued at an identified point of time, namely the settlement date. It was to be distinguished from condition 11.9(a), which was concerned with interest and fees which might only accrue at a later date but which accrued "in respect of" an earlier period. The payment premium fell in his view within the scope of condition 11.9(a), as "fees . . . which are expressed to accrue by reference to the lapse of time." The portion of the payment premium which was attributable to the US $11m transferred to Morgan Stanley, and was in respect of the period prior to 14 January 2010, was therefore due by Morgan Stanley to Tael under condition 11.9(a), since fees falling within the scope of that condition "shall, to the extent they accrue in respect of the period before (and not including) the Settlement Date, be for the account of the Seller."

34   The judge reached that conclusion principally on the basis of an analysis of the language of the LMA terms. In his view, "accrual," in the sense in which the term (or its cognates) are employed in conditions 11.3(a) and 11.9(a), is concerned with the vesting of rights. A fee accrued, in his view, when there was a vested right to an ascertained or ascertainable sum. The fee could accrue notwithstanding that it was payable at a future date which was uncertain. It could not however accrue if the existence of the right to payment, or the amount payable, was contingent upon an uncertain future event. In response to the argument that, adopting that approach, the payment premium could not be said to "accrue by reference to the lapse of time," the judge stated that those words were

> ". . . apposite to describe a right to payment of a sum which is earned to some extent from day to day but at a rate which cannot be calculated until a future event which then vests the right to payment of a sum calculated by reference to that period of time."

The judge also observed that, if condition 11.9(a) was to add anything to condition 11.3(a), it must cover a wider range of fees and interest:

> "It must therefore envisage that something may *accrue by reference to the lapse of time* and accrue *in respect of* the period prior to the settlement date, but not have accrued *up to* the settlement date. The two conditions must be construed as using the word accrue in the same sense and giving the word its natural meaning of the vesting of rights. It follows that condition 11.9(a) must treat accrual *by reference to* the lapse of time as addressing the *nature of the right* which accrues, rather than its *time of vesting*." (Original emphasis.)

35   An appeal against that decision was allowed by the Court of Appeal: [2013] EWCA Civ 473; [2013] 1 CLC 879. Longmore LJ, with whose judgment Rimer and Tomlinson LJJ agreed, observed that the words "which are expressed to accrue by reference to the lapse of time", in

condition 11.9(a), echo the introductory condition 11.1, which provides that the interest and fees "which are expressed to accrue by reference to time elapsed" are based on the rates contained in the credit agreement (in this case, the facility agreement). Like the judge, Longmore LJ considered that the payment premium was an amount which was "expressed to accrue by reference to time elapsed," since it was an "additional amount ... which together with [other sums] equates to an internal rate of return equal to the Loan IRR calculated . . . from the date of disbursement up to the date of payment or prepayment."

36   Longmore LJ considered however that condition 11.9(a) did not confer any additional entitlement beyond what was said to be payable in condition 11.3(a): the words "expressed to accrue by reference to the lapse of time" were merely words of description designed to encompass the interest and fees that were payable by reference to those parts of condition 11 which imposed obligations. Condition 11.9(a) was headed "Allocation of interest and fees" and, in contrast to other conditions of the LMA terms, did not use the words "shall pay," "payment," "be payable" or "paid," but used the phrase "shall . . . be for the account of. . . ." That phrase was in his view apt to describe how sums already payable, by reason of obligations imposed by other conditions, should be dealt with in any accounting exercise undertaken by the parties.

37   In that connection, Longmore LJ observed that, if condition 11.9(a) were intended to confer an extra entitlement in respect of sums not accrued by the settlement date but only accruing thereafter (albeit accruing by reference to a period before the settlement date), the contract specified no mechanism for the implementation of such an entitlement. It so happened that, in the present case, Tael retained part of the loan it originally made, and therefore knew when the loan was repaid. If Tael had sold the whole of the loan, it would not have known when the loan was repaid. It would be necessary to imply into the sale and purchase agreement a term that the buyer would inform the seller when the loan was repaid; otherwise the seller would not know when he could make a claim for the payment premium. If, moreover, as in the present case, the buyer had disposed of the whole loan to another party (such as Spinnaker), one would have not only to imply a term into that sub-sale contract to the same effect but also a further term into the Tael/Morgan Stanley agreement that Morgan Stanley would enforce the implied term in their own sub-sale contract. It was, in his view, difficult to think that this series of implications could have been intended. This of itself militated against condition 11.9(a) constituting an entitlement to sums not accrued at the settlement date.

38   A further difficulty, in his view, was that the payment premium might not in fact be paid at the termination of the loan, for example because there was an earlier default or because the borrower had insufficient funds to pay when payment was due. On Tael's argument, the payment premium would be due and would to some extent have accrued in respect of the period

before the settlement date. It would then be "for the account of the Seller." If that phrase meant that the buyer must pay it when it fell due, the buyer would be accountable for (and would have to pay out) money he had never received. That consequence could be avoided only if there were some implication that the words "for the account of the Seller" extended only to sums if and when they were received by the Buyer. But it was more natural not to read the words of condition 11.9(a) as giving rise to any entitlement beyond that which was conferred by condition 11.3(a), rather than as giving rise to an entitlement which then had to be restricted by some implication.

39   Longmore LJ acknowledged that, on his reading of condition 11.9(a), it probably added little or nothing to the rights conferred on the seller by condition 11.3(a), but observed that that was not altogether surprising in a 20-page document of some complexity. In the light of the difficulties resulting from the alternative construction, he did not regard the argument from redundancy as particularly compelling.

DISCUSSION

40   Although the arguments presented in the appeal ranged somewhat more widely than the judgments of the courts below, the most important points remain those which were discussed in those judgments. I can therefore proceed directly to a discussion of those points.

41   The starting point is the words the parties have used in condition 11.9(a):

"any interest or fees (other than PIK interest) which are payable under the Credit Agreement in respect of the Purchased Assets and which are expressed to accrue by reference to the lapse of time shall, to the extent they accrue in respect of the period before (and not including) the Settlement Date, be for the account of the Seller and, to the extent they accrue in respect of the period after (and including) the Settlement Date, be for the account of the Buyer. . . ."

There is room for argument as to whether the payment premium would naturally be described, in the context of this agreement, as "interest or fees," or whether it might fall within the definition of PIK interest. What appears to me to be clear, however, is that it is not "expressed to accrue by reference to the lapse of time." It is true that a period of time enters into the calculation of the amount of the payment premium. Counsel for Tael argued that that was sufficient: "expressed to accrue by reference to the lapse of time" should, he submitted, be understood as meaning "calculated by reference to the lapse of time." But that is not what the condition says; and it is not the natural meaning of what it says.

42   The word "accrue" is generally used to describe the coming into being of a right or an obligation (as, for example, in *Aitken v South Hams District Council* [1995] 1 AC 262), so that the person in question then has an accrued right, or is subject to an accrued liability, as the case may be. That

is the meaning which accrual usually bears, in particular, in relation to interest and other payments. The amount to which there is an entitlement may not be payable until a future date, but an entitlement may nevertheless have accrued. For example, under section 2 of the Apportionment Act 1870, rents, annuities, dividends and other periodical payments may be considered as accruing from day to day, although they may be payable at longer intervals (*In re Howell* [1895] 1 QB 844); and a bequest of an "accruing dividend" carried the dividend for the period during which the death occurred, although the dividend was not declared until a later date (*In re Lysaght* [1898] 1 Ch 115). Situations can readily be envisaged in which interest or fees might accrue, in that sense, by reference to the lapse of time: indeed, interest invariably accrues by reference to the lapse of time, as do recurring fees such as commitment fees. This is not however such a situation. An entitlement to a payment premium under the facility agreement accrues on a defined event.

43   It can of course be said that the purpose of the payment premium is to reward the lender for the borrower's use of the money over a period of time. But that does not mean that the payment premium is "expressed to accrue by reference to the lapse of time." It is expressed as an amount equal to the difference between the total of several other amounts, on the one hand, and an amount equal to interest calculated at a given rate, on the other hand. So interest, and therefore time, enter into the calculation. That being so, there is a sense in which it might be said that part of the payment premium relates to the period before the settlement date. That does not however mean that the payment premium can be regarded, retrospectively, as having notionally accrued over that period. The method of calculation of the payment premium should not be confused with the accrual of the right to the premium.

44   That conclusion, derived from the text of condition 11.9(a), is reinforced by the commercial context, and in particular by the first of the considerations to which Longmore LJ referred (para 37 above). The LMA terms are intended for use in a market in which loans are traded. A loan may be traded many times, between many different parties, over a number of years. One would not readily infer that a contract for the sale of a loan in a market of that nature was intended to create continuing rights and obligations between the parties to that contract, in respect of payment, which might exist over a substantial period of time. In that regard, it is significant that the LMA terms do not make provision for any mechanism enabling the holder of the putative right to a payment premium, following the sale of his interest in the loan, to know when his right has vested, or in what amount. Unless he happened to have retained some participation in the loan in question, as in the present case, he would not normally know when he had become entitled to payment, or how much he was entitled to be paid. It would be more natural, in such circumstances, to expect the potential value

of the right to receive the payment premium to be reflected in the consideration for which the loan was transferred.

45   That conclusion is sufficient to dispose of the appeal. It leaves open, however, two related questions which may be of significance. First, does this construction of condition 11.9(a) render it redundant? In my view, it does not. As I shall explain, condition 11.9(a) can be seen to have a purpose if it is read together with the provision made as to the payment of interest and fees in conditions 11.2, 11.3, and 11.9(b). Secondly, does condition 11.9(a) provide a right to payment, additional to that conferred by the other provisions of condition 11? In my view, it does not.

46   It is necessary to note, in the first place, that fees falling within condition 11.9(b) are expressly excluded from the scope of conditions 11.2(a) and 11.3(a). Condition 11.9(b) is however dependent on condition 11.9(a): it applies to "all other fees" which are payable after the trade date: that is to say, the date when the contract for the transfer of the loan is concluded. "Other" fees are fees other than those falling within the scope of condition 11.9(a).

47   Condition 11.2(a) therefore requires the buyer to pay to the seller, promptly on receipt, any interest or fees accrued prior to the settlement date, other than (i) PIK interest and (ii) fees not falling within condition 11.9(a), which are payable after the date when the contract was concluded. Condition 11.3(a) requires the buyer to pay to the seller, on the settlement date, any interest or fees accrued prior to the settlement date, subject to the same exceptions. The result is that conditions 11.2(a) and 11.3(a) (and also condition 11.4) can only be applied together with conditions 11.9(a) and (b). The conditions have to be taken together in order to determine the amount or amounts to be paid in respect of interest and fees.

48   This can be illustrated by taking condition 11.9 as the starting point. It divides interest and fees between those which are for the account of the seller and those which are for the account of the buyer. In the former category are any interest and fees (other than PIK interest) which are expressed to accrue by reference to the lapse of time, to the extent that they accrue in respect of the period prior to the settlement date (condition 11.9(a)). Any such interest and fees which accrue in respect of the period on or after the settlement date, and all other fees which are payable after the trade date, are for the account of the buyer (conditions 11.9(a) and (b)). This must be intended to be an exhaustive allocation (other than in respect of PIK interest). Putting the matter broadly, the practical effect is that interest and recurring fees (other than PIK interest) which accrue prior to the settlement date are for the account of the seller, whereas if they accrue in a later period they are for the account of the buyer. All other fees payable after the trade date (other than PIK interest) are for the account of the buyer.

49   That allocation under condition 11.9 is reflected in the provisions as to payment. Where condition 11.2(a) applies, its practical effect is to require

the buyer to pay the seller, on receipt, an amount equal to any interest or fees accrued prior to the settlement date, other than PIK interest and non-recurring fees which are payable after the trade date. The practical effect of condition 11.3 is similar, except that the buyer pays the relevant amount on the settlement date and bears the risk that he may not receive that amount from the borrower. Condition 11.5 provides a variant on the same principle. Condition 11.6 applies where the parties have opted for no payments to be made by the buyer in respect of accrued interest or fees, and therefore has the practical effect of discharging the buyer from any liability which might otherwise have arisen.

50   Is it however possible for condition 11.9(a) to confer a right to payment of an amount to which there is no right to payment under conditions 11.2(a) or 11.3(a)? That question arises because of the difference in wording between "accrued up to . . . the Settlement Date" (the words used in conditions 11.2(a) and 11.3(a)), and "accrue in respect of the period before . . . the Settlement Date" (the words used in condition 11.9(a)). Notwithstanding that difference in wording, the language used elsewhere in condition 11.9 suggests that it is not intended to confer an additional right to payment. It allocates interest and fees (as the heading indicates) as being "for the account of" one party to the transaction or the other. Other conditions then impose an obligation to "pay" in accordance with that account (or, in the case of condition 11.6, make it clear that no such obligation is imposed). The absence from condition 11.9 of any provision for payment is therefore one indication that it is not intended to impose such an obligation. The absence of any provisions addressing the possibility of default by the borrower, such as one finds in conditions 11.2(b) and 11.3(c), is a further indication that it is not intended to confer a right to additional payment.

CONCLUSION

51   I would therefore uphold the decision of the Court of Appeal, although for somewhat different reasons, and dismiss the appeal.

The LMA is the European equivalent of the LSTA. What do you think may have motivated this litigation?

STONEHILL CAPITAL MANAGEMENT, LLC v. BANK OF THE WEST

28 N.Y.3d 439
Court of Appeals of New York.
Dec. 20, 2016.

RIVERA, J.

Plaintiffs Stonehill Capital Management LLC, Stonehill Institutional Partners, L.P. and Stonehill Master Fund Ltd (collectively Stonehill) are affiliated commercial entities that seek to enforce the auction sale of a syndicated loan against defendant Bank of the West (BOTW). BOTW concedes that it accepted Stonehill's bid and then refused to transfer the loan, but claims it had no legal obligation to do so because the parties never executed a written sales agreement and Stonehill failed to submit a timely cash deposit. However, these prerequisites are not conditions precedent to formation of the parties' contract and do not render their agreement unenforceable. Therefore, Stonehill has established its entitlement to summary judgment.

I.

BOTW, a lender of various non-performing mortgage loans, retained co-defendant Mission Capital Advisors, LLC (Mission) to manage a competitive online sealed-bid auction of several of these loans. As part of the bid process, in March 2012 Mission issued an Offering Memorandum (Memorandum), which announced its solicitation of indicative bids for the purchase of the loans, individually or in any combination, and invited non-contingent final offers. The auction portfolio included a syndicated loan—with an aggregate principal value of $8,787,141—known to the parties as the "Goett Loan." The Goett Loan is the underlying subject of the parties' dispute.

The Memorandum set forth information about the loan portfolio and the asset pools contained therein. In the description of the "Loan Sale Process," the Memorandum informed interested parties that:

> "[a]fter receipt of the indicative bids, Mission, in conjunction with the Seller, will select Final Bidders to complete final due diligence before submitting non-contingent offers on the Final Bid Date (the acceptance of which by Seller will require immediate execution of pre-negotiated Asset Sale Agreement(s) by Prospective Bidder accompanied by a 10% non-refundable wire funds deposit)."

The asset sale agreement would be made available for review to final bidders. The Memorandum also included the following disclaimer: "The seller reserves the right, at their sole and absolute discretion, to withdraw any or all of the assets from the loan sale, at any time. . . . Only those representations and warranties that are made by the seller to a prospective bidder in a definitive, executed loan sale agreement shall have any legal effect."

After Stonehill expressed an interest in the Goett Loan, Mission forwarded a proposed asset sale agreement, referred to as the "Loan Sale Agreement" (LSA). Two days later, on April 18, Stonehill submitted to Mission a $2,363,142 final bid on the Goett Loan. The same day, by separate correspondence, Stonehill informed Mission that the LSA was not the proper document to effectuate a syndicated loan transfer, and offered to "either make the minor modifications required to that document to account for the agent's approval process, etc, or use an LSTA syndicated loan document, whichever the seller prefers."

Mission notified Stonehill by telephone on April 20 that it had submitted the winning bid for the Goett Loan. On April 23, Stonehill sent Mission a modified redlined version of the proposed LSA, purportedly at Mission's request, containing what Stonehill considered to be the necessary technical changes that would enable the LSA to effectuate the sale and assignment of the Goett syndicated loan. Mission's representative replied that it was "a substantially larger markup than I was expecting to see. I can't actually say that our lawyer is going to use it." Then, on April 24, BOTW's counsel sent Mission an email stating that if the Goett Loan was a syndicated credit "the LSTA form agreement is actually pretty good," to which Mission's representative responded that he was "99.9% certain that [Stonehill] is right about this being a syndicated credit."

On Friday, April 27, Mission emailed Stonehill written confirmation that BOTW agreed to the Stonehill bid. The correspondence stated:

> "Subject to mutual execution of an acceptable [LSA], [BOTW] has agreed to the Stonehill [ ] bid of:
>
> Mixed Portfolio—$8,787,141 UPB
>
> Purchase Price—$2,363,142
>
> As discussed, counsel representing [BOTW] will be sending you an executable [LSA] by Tuesday, May 1st. An executed signature page and 10% non-refundable deposit is expected no later than 2:00 pm EDT on Wednesday, May 2nd."

The email also included wiring instructions for the deposit and closing.

That same day, BOTW's counsel sent Stonehill an email in which counsel explained that he was previously unaware that the Goett Loan was syndicated and that he "prefer[red] to use LSTA documentation for syndicated credits." He pushed for an early May closing on the loan transfer because "[m]ost trade agents won't approve trades at the end of the month" and said that he would send the trade agreements the following week.

On Friday, May 4, BOTW's counsel was still preparing the documents and initiated a series of email exchanges to move the deal ahead. Counsel first informed Stonehill that he was working on sending the documents by Monday and requested that, "in the meantime," Stonehill send him the term sheet from a previous trade specified by counsel. Stonehill wrote back that the requested term sheet was confidential but that Stonehill would provide an LSTA form reflecting the terms of the Goett Loan transaction, stressing, "we hope this arrangement will be acceptable to you and will enable us to move forward to close quickly." BOTW's counsel responded that he "assumed as much" and it was "fine to proceed as [Stonehill] indicated."

As promised, two days later Stonehill sent the LSTA form to BOTW's counsel with the terms for the loan transaction and related documents. In this same correspondence, Stonehill informed counsel that it was forwarding the Credit Agreement Transfer Forms to Wells Fargo, the Credit Agreement agent, and this was a necessary step to complete and record the transfer of the Goett Loan to Stonehill.

On May 8, Stonehill informed BOTW's counsel that Wells Fargo approved the Credit Transfer Forms. Under the credit agreement, Stonehill needed the promissory note endorsed in order to close on the Goett Loan, so Stonehill also sent counsel a standard allonge form for the promissory note on the Goett Loan issued to BOTW.

Around this time, BOTW learned that Stonehill was refinancing the Goett Loan. This would apparently increase the value of the loan, which led BOTW to consider its options with respect to the loan sale. An internal BOTW memorandum circulated on May 10 detailed both the refinancing and the auction sale to Stonehill. The memorandum explained that

> "there is a question as to the direction [BOTW] should take; sale or not to sale [sic], given that no formal written commitments are executed between [BOTW]/Mission Capital and Stonehill that would obligate [BOTW] to sale [sic] the Goett Note. Fact remains that [BOTW] acted in good faith and has verbally committed to the Goett Note sale to Stonehill."

It further stated that Stonehill had proceeded with various steps to finalize the refinancing and Stonehill funding was highly likely.

On May 14, Stonehill contacted BOTW's counsel for an update. Counsel, apparently surprised by Stonehill's inquiry, forwarded the email to Mission. Then on May 16, Mission informed Stonehill by telephone that BOTW would not proceed with the trade. Over a week later, on May 25, Mission forwarded to Stonehill a May 18 email from BOTW to Mission declaring that it would not sell to Stonehill:

> "[BOTW] will not proceed with this trade because it has no obligation to do so. There are no agreements (oral or written) between [BOTW] and Stonehill Capital. The Offering Memorandum specifically permits [BOTW] to withdraw any loan from the auction at any time. Specifically, it states 'The Seller reserve [s] the right, at their sole and absolute discretion, to withdraw any or all of the assets from the loan sale, at any time.' In addition, Mission Capital's bid response e-mail to Stonehill conditioned [BOTW's] response upon the execution of a definitive loan sale agreement."

As a consequence of the refinancing and the cancellation of the sale to Stonehill, on June 21 BOTW received $4,197,441 on the Goett Loan, an excess of approximately $1.8 million over Stonehill's bid.

Stonehill commenced the present action against BOTW and Mission, alleging breach of contract and breach of the implied covenant of good faith and fair dealing, and seeking indemnification. In its Amended Complaint, Stonehill added a cause of action for unjust enrichment and demanded $1.5 million in damages.

Supreme Court denied BOTW's motion to dismiss and cross motion for summary judgment, and granted Stonehill's motion for summary judgment on the breach of contract cause of action. Supreme Court held that because the purchase and sale agreement was pre-negotiated, BOTW's acceptance of Stonehill's bid created a binding contract. BOTW appealed and the Appellate Division reversed, granted BOTW's cross motion for summary judgment and dismissed the complaint as against BOTW, holding that Stonehill had failed to establish a valid acceptance

II.

A. SUMMARY JUDGMENT STANDARD

It is well established that "the proponent of a summary judgment motion must make a prima facie showing of entitlement to judgment as a matter of law, tendering sufficient evidence to demonstrate the absence of any material issues of fact". Once the movant makes the proper showing, "the burden shifts to the party opposing the motion for summary judgment to produce evidentiary proof in admissible form sufficient to establish the existence of material issues of fact which require a trial of the action".

B. BREACH OF CONTRACT CLAIM

To establish a prima facie breach of contract, Stonehill must show that BOTW breached a binding agreement between the parties, which damaged Stonehill. To form a binding contract there must be a "meeting of the minds", such that there is "a manifestation of mutual assent sufficiently definite to assure that the parties are truly in agreement with respect to all material terms".

Stonehill maintains that BOTW's acceptance of its bid constitutes a contract to sell the Goett Loan. In response, BOTW asserts it conditioned the sale on the parties' execution of a written agreement and Stonehill's submission of a 10% deposit, neither of which was satisfied prior to BOTW's withdrawal from the transaction. We conclude, based on the totality of the parties' actions and communications, that they agreed to an enforceable contract, with express material terms and post-formation requirements.

BOTW, through Mission as its auctioneer, solicited bids on a loan portfolio and its component parts. The Offering Memorandum stated that the bids were non-contingent final offers that, if accepted by the seller, required execution by the bidder of a pre-negotiated asset sale agreement and an accompanying 10%

deposit. The Memorandum additionally informed prospective bidders that the loans sold at auction were "subject only to those representations and warranties explicitly stated in the asset sale agreement," which was included with the Memorandum. Thus, the terms of the sale were pre-set.

In response, Stonehill submitted a bid and separately informed Mission that the LSA included with the Memorandum was inappropriate for the type of asset that was the subject of the auction, specifically a syndicated credit facility. Stonehill offered to make the necessary modifications or use LSTA documents instead. When BOTW accepted Stonehill's offer it confirmed the bid in a correspondence setting forth the sale price, the specific loan to be sold, the timing of the closing, and the manner of payment and wire transfer instructions—terms material to the agreement. BOTW in no way indicated that the LSTA form or any modifications were unacceptable. At no time during the period between when BOTW accepted Stonehill's bid and when it withdrew from the transaction, did BOTW communicate its objection to the LSTA form that Stonehill had sent to BOTW's counsel or indicate that the proposed modifications were "deal breakers." In fact, counsel emailed Stonehill that once he became aware that the asset was a syndicated loan, he too preferred to use the LSTA documentation.

In future correspondence counsel did not mention any problems with the LSTA form that Stonehill had sent, but instead requested documentation from Stonehill to move the transaction along towards a mid-May closing date. Specifically, in the Friday, May 4th email thread, BOTW's counsel said he was working on getting the documents to Stonehill the following Monday and requested a term sheet to further the process. After Stonehill responded that it could not return the specific term sheet requested because of confidentiality provisions, offering instead to send an LSTA form for the Goett Loan transaction, BOTW's counsel informed Stonehill that it could proceed as described.

The totality of the parties' conduct and the "objective manifestations" of their intent is evidenced by BOTW's inclusion of pre-negotiated auction terms in the Offering Memorandum, BOTW's acceptance of Stonehill's bid in correspondence that communicated the terms of the purchase and the date and instructions for the closing, the email exchanges between BOTW's counsel and Stonehill which indicated the sale was moving ahead and included references to documents necessary for closing the transaction, and BOTW's utter failure to identify or explain any objections to the LSTA form prior to the May 18th correspondence announcing its withdrawal from the sale. This established the parties' intent to enter a binding agreement in which BOTW would sell the Goett Loan to Stonehill at the accepted final price.

BOTW argues that an executed signed agreement and a 10% deposit were preconditions to the contract which were never fulfilled and so BOTW was not bound to sell the Goett Loan to Stonehill. It claims that, at best, the parties had an unenforceable agreement to agree. BOTW relies on the April 27th email to Stonehill, which provides that "subject to mutual execution of an acceptable Loan Sale Agreement, [BOTW] has agreed to the StoneHill . . . bid" and which also set a due date for the executed signature page and the 10% deposit. BOTW argues the "subject to" language made the sale contingent on satisfaction of these two unmet conditions. This argument is unsupported by the record.

Certainly, "when a party gives forthright, reasonable signals that it means to be bound only by a written agreement, courts should not frustrate that intent" (*R.G. Grp., Inc. v. Horn & Hardart Co.,* 751 F.2d 69, 75 [2d Cir1984][applying New York contract law]).

Such a forthright, reasonable signal is not obvious from the mere inclusion in an auction bid form of such formulaic language that the parties are "subject to" some future act or event. Less ambiguous and more certain language is necessary to remove any doubt of the parties' intent not to be bound absent a writing . . .

We disagree with BOTW that the "subject to" language in the April 27th email clearly expresses an intent not to be bound to the sale of the Goett Loan. This email stated that closure of the transaction required execution of a signed document and Stonehill's tender of the 10% deposit. That, however, is not the same as a clear expression that the parties were not bound to consummate the sale and that BOTW could withdraw at any time, for any reason. Nor did BOTW make known its desire for an unrestricted exit from the deal before accepting Stonehill's bid or anytime before it withdrew from the transaction.

This was never made explicit before the bid was accepted either. There is a difference between conditions precedent to performance and those prefatory to the formation of a binding agreement. In *IDT Corp. v. Tyco Group, S.A.R.L.* the Court explained the legal distinction:

> "A condition precedent is an act or event, other than a lapse of time, which unless the condition is excused, must occur before a duty to perform a promise in the agreement arises . . . Most conditions precedent describe acts or events which must occur before a party is obliged to perform a promise made pursuant to an existing contract, a situation to be distinguished conceptually from a condition precedent to the formation or existence of the contract itself."

Here, the signed writing and deposit were post-agreement requirements necessary for the consummation of the transfer, as established by the continued exchange of documents necessary to the asset transfer. To adopt BOTW's argument would mean that the auction was neither final nor binding—in direct contravention of the auction sale terms and the usual manner in which reserve auctions proceed.

Truman Capital Advisors LP v. Nationstar Mortg., LLC (2014 WL 4188090 [SDNY Aug 25, 2014], *aff'd* 599 F App'x 6 [2d Cir2015]), cited by BOTW, is distinguishable. In that breach of contract action, Truman bid on loans put up for auction by Nationstar. Nationstar reneged, relying on language in the auction terms that "No obligation to sell shall be binding on Seller unless and until a written contract of sale or loan sale agreement is signed and delivered by Seller". The court held that Nationstar's "right to reject the winning bid was implicitly reserved through the inclusion of the term requiring that Nationstar return a signed contract of sale or loan sale agreement in order for the transaction to be consummated". The Second Circuit affirmed, reiterating that the clause in the auction terms prevented Nationstar from being forced to sell even after Truman was determined to be the winning bidder.

By comparison, the Memorandum and the April 27th email are not affirmative declarations foreclosing a sale "unless and until a written contract . . . is signed and delivered." Instead, the language in these documents requires that the sale be completed upon the execution of a signed writing and the tender of the 10% deposit—post-agreement requirements the parties were obliged to perform pursuant to an existing agreement. The fact that the parties anticipate and identify future events necessary to close the sale is not the legal equivalent of an intent to delay formation of a binding contract absent the passage of those events.

Furthermore, there is no indication that these events were an actual obstacle to the sale. BOTW proffered no evidence to suggest that Stonehill refused to enter a signed agreement or to submit the deposit. Quite the opposite. Stonehill was responsive to all of BOTW's requests for documentation, expressed its eagerness to close the deal, took necessary steps to achieve that end (including securing approval of the Credit Agreement from Wells Fargo), and never implied its inability or unwillingness to turn over the deposit.

BOTW's withdrawal was not without consequences for Stonehill, which suffered losses totaling over $1.8 million, reflecting the difference between the refinanced Discounted Payoff proceeds on account of the loan received by BOTW ($4,197,441) and the accepted bid sale price ($2,363,142). In other words, BOTW's breach of contract resulted in Stonehill not being able to realize the increased valuation of the Goett Loan.

We conclude therefore that Stonehill met its prima facie burden on summary judgment by showing that BOTW accepted Stonehill's bid to purchase the Goett Loan and the parties entered a binding agreement to complete the sale, BOTW breached that agreement, and the breach caused Stonehill to suffer monetary damages.[4] Moreover, Stonehill asserted—and BOTW did not dispute—that Stonehill was ready, willing and able to close.

In response, BOTW failed to establish the existence of material issues of fact. . . . In addition to the acceptance, the correspondence, and the LSTA form exchange, the clear objective of both parties upon the acceptance of the offer was to sell the Goett Loan to Stonehill for the bid amount. While that objective remained unchanged for Stonehill, BOTW reconsidered the sale—not because of the failure to execute a written agreement or because Stonehill had not tendered the 10% deposit, but because BOTW concluded it would make more money by reneging on the sale. That choice was a breach of its agreement with Stonehill.

III.

Accordingly, the order of the Appellate Division, insofar as appealed from, should be reversed, with costs, and the judgment of Supreme Court in favor of the Stonehill plaintiffs on their breach of contract claim against BOTW reinstated.

If the parties are bound without signing an agreement, why bother to sign one?

7. THE DYNEGY LOAN AGREEMENT

Take a look at the materials regarding the 2007 Dynegy Credit Agreement that are available online. As you review it, the following points might help you structure your reading:

- Who are the lenders?
- What types of agents are there?
- Who are the borrowers?
- Is the loan secured or unsecured?
- What types of loans are being made?
- What interest rates and fees are associated with the loan?
- How much can the borrower(s) get under the loan, and when can they and when must they pay it back?
- What covenants have the borrower(s) agreed to? In particular, what financial covenants apply and what limitations on the borrower(s) apply?
- How can the borrower(s) default under the agreement? What are the implications of a default?

17

OPTIONS, WARRANTS, AND CONVERTIBLES

This chapter addresses three related instruments of long pedigree. If you encountered "rights of first refusal" in your 1L property class, you have already seen an option in action. Basically any contract that gives one party the choice to perform at some future date can be deemed an *option*.

As you will see, *warrants* and *convertible instruments* are simply options in other forms. For example, convertible instruments are often bonds or preferred stocks with options imbedded in their documentation.

1. OPTIONS

For the purchaser, an option represents the right, but not the obligation, to buy or sell the reference, or underlying, asset within a specified time period for a specified price, known as the strike price. The underlying asset could be almost anything: an individual security, a real asset, a market index, or a currency.

Options are divided into calls and puts. A *call* option gives the holder or buyer the right to buy the underlying asset, whereas a *put* option gives the holder the right to sell.

The option buyer is the party that has the "option"—the seller or writer of an option must perform if the holder exercises their option. That is, the choice is not bilateral in an option, because the seller always has to perform if requested.

At expiration, an option is either valuable or "out of the money." For example, a call option to buy shares of Bogartco at $5 per share is valuable only if Bogartco's shares are currently trading at more than $5 per share. And the ultimate value of the option depends on the degree to which the current price exceeds $5 per share, the call option's "strike price."

Note that the strike price or exercise price is distinct from any cost you incur to buy the option itself. The cost of the option is incurred up front, and sometimes periodically during the life of the option, and will always be incurred, whether the holder exercises the option or not.

If the share price is less than $5 per share, exercise of the option would be nonsensical, because the option holder could buy shares on the open market. Thus the option expires without being exercised, and the holder is out the cost of the option.

You can thus see that options, unlike many other securities we have discussed to date, are a zero sum game. Gain for the option holder in the given example is loss for the option writer. In theory, the losses to the option writer in a call option are unlimited—the greater the rise in Bogartco's share price, the bigger the losses. Even if Bogartco shares zoom up to $100,000,000,000,000 per share, the option writer is still obligated to sell for $5 per share.

Because of this exposure, option seller therefore typically uses a portion of the option buyer's premium payment to finance a hedge of its position under the options. We will talk about hedging in the next chapter, but the basic idea is that option seller or call writer will typically enter into another option transaction, with another party, that puts some of the risk on that third party. Because the option seller is typically a bank or broker-dealer, it pays a lower premium to enter into its hedge than the option buyer pays to it. Overall, option seller's profit is the amount of the premium paid by the option buyer, less the cost of any hedge of its position under the option that it may enter into.

Because of limited liability, the exposure is somewhat more limited for the writer of a put. Do you see why?

Most options used in financial transactions are so-called *American options*, a term that no longer has geographic significance, but instead refers to the holder's ability to exercise the option at any point up until expiration. This is in contrast with the so-called *European option*, which is only exercisable on the maturity date.

Thus, if your call option just described was a March 2016 Bogartco option, you could exercise it any time Bogartco's share price exceeded $5 per share before March 2016. More precisely, options typically expire on the Saturday following the third Friday of the expiration month. Practically, this means the option expires on the third Friday in March 2016 in our example, as brokerages are not typically open for business on Saturdays. If you want to exercise the option, you will have to pay the strike price by Friday.

Both put and call options can be either physically settled or cash settled. A physically settled call option buyer has the right to acquire shares from the seller at the strike price on the exercise date. A cash-settled call option buyer has the right to a payment from the option seller if on the exercise date the spot or settlement price of the agreed-upon underlying shares is greater than the strike price set. The amount of the payment is equal to the difference between the settlement price and the strike price multiplied by the number of shares specified in the trade. This calculation is repeated and aggregated for each different type of share if the option is on a basket of shares or index.

Figure 17-1 shows the options available from a major brokerage firm with respect to Coca-Cola (a real company, unlike Bogartco).

Coca Cola Company (KO)
Last Trade: 4:00:38PM ET

Last	Change	Bid	Ask	High	Low	Volume
37.40	+0.26	37.40	37.54	37.58	37.15	20,711,518

Calls						Strike	Puts					
Last	Change	Bid	Ask	Volume	OI		Last	Change	Bid	Ask	Volume	OI
KO 2/16/2013 (Expires: 166 days from today)												
5.15	+0.05	5.00	5.10	19	215	32.50	0.51	-0.03	0.48	0.50	7	784
4.15	0.00	3.90	4.05	0	135	33.75	0.66	-0.06	0.68	0.70	33	2,639
2.97	-0.08	2.95	3.05	2	235	35.00	0.94	-0.08	0.98	1.00	76	6,464
2.14	+0.21	2.11	2.14	1,226	607	36.25	1.43	+0.13	1.39	1.42	97	1,966
1.41	-0.05	1.40	1.43	60	1,913	37.50	2.05	+0.14	1.94	1.98	1	767
0.88	+0.06	0.86	0.89	575	2,023	38.75	2.64	+0.08	2.66	2.69	25	627
0.50	0.00	0.49	0.51	966	9,702	40.00	3.52	0.00	3.50	3.60	0	556
0.27	0.00	0.26	0.28	13	3,522	41.25	4.60	+0.70	4.50	4.60	40	311
KO 1/18/2014 (Expires: 502 days from today)												
5.80	+0.20	5.65	5.75	10	28,399	32.50	1.90	0.00	1.89	1.95	0	12,930
4.90	+0.15	4.80	4.90	42	3,518	33.75	2.20	0.00	2.32	2.37	0	28,958
4.10	+0.20	4.00	4.05	275	14,916	35.00	2.93	0.00	2.81	2.87	0	12,927
3.30	0.00	3.25	3.35	46	6,682	36.25	3.45	0.00	3.35	3.45	0	1,344
2.74	+0.09	2.64	2.70	101	5,500	37.50	4.00	-0.06	4.00	4.10	4	105,243
2.09	-0.05	2.09	2.15	50	3,090	38.75	4.60	0.00	4.75	4.85	0	2,125
1.68	+0.06	1.65	1.70	122	4,763	40.00	5.55	-0.15	5.55	5.65	7	934
1.25	-0.01	1.26	1.31	2	1,594	41.25	6.45	0.00	6.40	6.55	0	306

FIGURE 17-1
Coca-Cola Options

At the top right of Figure 17-1, you see the then current (September 2012) market price for the shares. Below that you see prices for calls (on the left) and puts (on the right). The strike prices for each are in the column in the center. OI stands for open interest, which indicates the number of contracts outstanding at a particular strike price. The shading indicates options that are "in the money."

The options are to buy or sell round lots of shares—100 shares—but are quoted at their per share price. Thus, the put option priced at $6.45 (bottom right) would actually cost $645 to buy. Because it gives you the right to sell shares currently worth $3,740 for $4,125, for an instant profit of $385, the high cost is perhaps understandable. After all, you have until January 2014 to make even more profit if KO prices were to decline.

PROBLEM SET 17.1

1. If you had bought the put option priced at $6.45 (bottom right) in September 2012, and in early May 2013 the KO share price was $42.24, where would you stand?
2. If in September 2012 you bought a January 2014 put with a strike price of $32.50, and also owned 100 shares of KO, what have you achieved?
3. If in September 2012 you own 100 KO shares and sell a January 2014 call with a $41.25 strike price, what will you have in January 2014 if the share price is (a) $40.00, (b) $42.00, or (c) $60.00?
4. Compare the following investments:
   A. Buy a $1,000 Bogartco bond and a call option on the company's shares with a strike price of $10 per share;
   B. Buy 100 shares of Bogartco and a put option with a strike price of $10 per share.

How are these similar?

2.   WARRANTS

In many respects a warrant is just like a call option. The distinction is that a warrant is issued by the firm whose stock is the underlying asset.

For example, Coca-Cola might sell warrants to buy its own shares. Exercise of a warrant thus increases the amount of outstanding shares, unless the company takes action to buy back a corresponding amount of its own shares on the open market.

Warrants tend to have longer maturity periods than exchange-traded options. They also tend to be issued in specialized situations. For example, in a bankruptcy case where it is unclear if the equity should receive any value, the reorganization plan might give warrants to the old shareholders, with a strike price that only puts them in the money if the company's post-bankruptcy share price exceeds some level that will result in full payment of creditors. We saw an example of this in the Supreme Court's *Consolidated Rock* opinion in Chapter 11.

PAUL R. LOHNES v. LEVEL 3 COMMUNICATIONS, INC.

272 F.3d 49
United States Court of Appeals, First Circuit.
Nov. 30, 2001.

SELYA, Circuit Judge.

The primary issue raised in this appeal is whether the terms "capital reorganization" and/or "reclassification of stock," as used in a stock warrant, encompass a stock split. Asserting the affirmative of this proposition, a warrantholder, plaintiff-appellant Paul R. Lohnes, claims that a stock split effectuated by defendant-appellee Level 3 Communications, Inc. (Level 3) triggered an antidilution provision in the warrant that automatically increased the number of shares of stock to which he was entitled. Level 3 resists this claim. The district court concluded that the language of the warrant could not reasonably be construed to encompass a stock split and, accordingly, granted Level 3's motion for summary judgment. We affirm.

I. BACKGROUND

Consistent with the conventional summary judgment praxis, our account of the relevant facts construes the record in the light most favorable to the nonmoving party (here, the appellant).

The appellant is both a trustee and a beneficiary of C.E.M. Realty Trust (the Trust). In February of 1998, the Trust leased 40,000 square feet of commercial space to XCOM Technologies, Inc. (XCOM). The details of the lease transaction need not concern us, save for the fact that, as part of the consideration, XCOM issued a stock warrant to the appellant. The parties negotiated the principal terms of the warrant—the number of shares, the exercise price, and the expiration date—and XCOM's lawyer then drafted the document. The warrant specified that its exercise would be governed by Massachusetts law. It empowered the holder to purchase, at his discretion but within a fixed period, 100,000 shares of XCOM common stock at $0.30 per share.

Unbeknownst to the appellant, XCOM's days as an independent entity were numbered. Shortly after the appellant executed the lease and accepted the warrant, Level 3 acquired XCOM in a stock-for-stock transaction and converted XCOM into a wholly-owned subsidiary. As part of this transaction, Level 3 agreed to assume XCOM's warrant obligations and satisfy them with shares of Level 3's common stock (using a designated share exchange formula). Following this paradigm, the appellant's unexercised warrant for XCOM shares was duly converted into a warrant to purchase 8,541 shares of Level 3's common stock. The appellant does not challenge this conversion (which took effect in April of 1998).

The next significant development occurred on July 14, 1998. On that date, Level 3's board of directors authorized a two-for-one stock split, to be effectuated in the form of a stock dividend granting common shareholders one new share of stock for each share held.[1]

The board set the record date as July 30, 1998. On July 20, Level 3 issued a press release announcing the stock split, but it did not provide the appellant with personalized notice.

The split occurred as scheduled. Adhering to generally accepted accounting practices, Level 3 adjusted its balance sheet to account for the split by increasing its common stock account in the amount of $1,000,000 and reducing paid-in-capital by a like amount. These accounting entries had no net effect on either the retained earnings or the net equity of the company.

Despite the sharp reduction in the share price that accompanied the stock split, the appellant paid no heed until approximately three months after the record date. When his belated inquiry revealed what had transpired, the appellant contacted Level 3 to confirm that the stock split had triggered a share adjustment provision, thus entitling him to 17,082 shares (twice the number of shares specified in the warrant). Level 3 demurred on the ground that the warrant did not provide for any share adjustment based upon the occurrence of a stock split effected as a stock dividend.

Dissatisfied by Level 3's response, the appellant exercised the warrant and received 8,541 shares of Level 3's common stock. He then sued Level 3 in a Massachusetts state court alleging breach of both the warrant and the implied duty of good faith and fair dealing. Citing diversity of citizenship and the existence of a controversy in the requisite amount, Level 3 removed the action to the federal district court. The parties then engaged in a protracted period of pretrial discovery.

Discovery closed on October 30, 2000. Thereafter, Level 3 moved for summary judgment. *See* Fed.R.Civ.P. 56.

In due course, the district court ruled that, as a matter of law, a stock split, effected as a stock dividend, did not constitute a "capital reorganization" as that term was used in the warrant and, accordingly, granted the motion for summary judgment.

---

1. A corporation effects a "stock split" by increasing the number of shares outstanding without changing the proportional ownership interests of each shareholder. Companies typically execute a stock split by issuing a "stock dividend" to current shareholders, i.e., "paid in stock expressed as a percentage of the number of shares already held by a shareholder." Black's Law Dict. 493 (7th ed.1999) (cross-referencing definition of "dividend"). Stock splits lower the price per share, thereby fostering increased marketability and wider distribution of shares.

Technically, not all stock dividends are stock splits, and the two may, in limited instances, receive different accounting treatment. In the instant matter, however, "stock split" and "stock dividend" are two sides of the same coin, and we use the terms interchangeably.

II.   METHODOLOGY OF REVIEW

We begin our analysis by outlining the legal framework that governs our review. Next, we apply well-worn principles of contract interpretation to resolve the appellant's contention that the terms "capital reorganization" and "reclassification of stock" encompass a stock split implemented as a stock dividend. In this endeavor, our principal task is to determine the ambiguity *vel non* of the disputed terms. Thus, we investigate whether either term is reasonably susceptible to the interpretation urged by the appellant. As part of this exercise, we consider (and reject) the appellant's belated attempt to introduce expert testimony bearing on this question. We conclude by addressing the appellant's claim that Level 3 breached the implied duty of good faith and fair dealing inherent in the warrant.

III.   THE CONTRACT INTERPRETATION CLAIMS

A stock warrant is an instrument that grants the warrantholder an option to purchase shares of stock at a fixed price. Against the backdrop of this well-established definition, we turn to the appellant's contract interpretation claims.

B.   PARSING THE WARRANT.

The warrant at issue here contained a two-paragraph antidilution provision which, upon the occurrence of certain described events, automatically adjusted the number of shares to which the warrantholder would be entitled upon exercise of the warrant. In all, share adjustments were engendered by five separate contingencies: capital reorganization, reclassification of common stock, merger, consolidation, and sale of all (or substantially all) the capital stock or assets. However, the warrant did not explicitly provide for an adjustment of shares in the event of a stock split. The appellant attempts to plug this lacuna by equating a stock split with a capital reorganization and/or a reclassification of stock. This argument brings the following paragraph of the antidilution provision into play:

> *Reorganizations and Reclassifications.* If there shall occur any capital reorganization or reclassification of the Common Stock, then, as part of any such reorganization or reclassification, lawful provision shall be made so that the Holder shall have the right thereafter to receive upon the exercise hereof the kind and amount of shares of stock or other securities or property which such Holder would have been entitled to receive if, immediately prior to any such reorganization or reclassification, such Holder had held the number of shares of Common Stock which were then purchasable upon the exercise of this Warrant.

Building upon the premise that either "capital reorganization" or "reclassification of stock" encompasses a stock split, the appellant concludes that Level 3's stock split activated the share adjustment mechanism set forth in the quoted paragraph.

As said, the appellant bears the burden of establishing the existence of a genuine issue of material fact. Given the circumstances of this case, the only way for him to succeed in this endeavor is by showing that one of the disputed terms ("capital reorganization" or "reclassification of stock") is shrouded in ambiguity, that is, that reasonable minds plausibly could reach opposite conclusions as to whether either term extended to stock splits. To appraise the success of the appellant's efforts, we ponder each term separately.

C.   CAPITAL REORGANIZATION.

Since the warrant does not elaborate upon the meaning of "capital reorganization," we turn to other sources. Massachusetts law offers no discernible guidance. . . .

Moving beyond the case law, the meaning of the term "capital reorganization" in common legal parlance seemingly belies the appellant's ambitious definition. The preeminent legal lexicon defines "reorganization," in pertinent part, as a "[g]eneral term describing corporate amalgamations or readjustments occurring, for example, when one corporation acquires another in a merger or acquisition, a single corporation divides into two or more entities, or a corporation makes a substantial change in its capital structure." *Black's Law Dict.* 1298 (6th ed.1990). The first two prongs of this definition are clearly inapposite here. That leaves only the question of whether a stock split entails a "substantial change in [a corporation's] capital structure." We think not.

First and foremost, the accounting mechanics that accompany a stock split are mere window dressing. To be sure, a stock split effected through the distribution of shares in the form of a stock dividend results in an increase in the common stock at par account and an offsetting decrease in additional paid-in capital, but this subtle set of entries has no effect on total shareholder equity or on any other substantive aspect of the balance sheet. Because a stock split does not entail a substantial change in a corporation's capital structure, the unelaborated term "capital reorganization" cannot plausibly include a stock split effected as a stock dividend.

D.   RECLASSIFICATION OF STOCK.

We turn next to the phrase "reclassification of stock." Two Massachusetts cases seem worthy of mention. In the first, a corporation took advantage of a new statute authorizing the issuance of preferred stock and amended its charter to divide its previously undifferentiated stock into common and preferred shares. *Page v. Whittenton Mfg. Co.*, 211 Mass. 424, 97 N.E. 1006, 1007–08 (1912). The Massachusetts Supreme Judicial Court approved the corporation's actions. It held that a corporation could classify stock into common and preferred shares (providing preferred shareholders with cumulative dividends and a liquidation preference) so long as that classification was effected through a charter amendment. *Id.* at 1007. Although *Page* uses the verb "classify," we view what transpired as a reclassification. *See* XIII *Oxford English Dict.* 339 (2d ed.1989) (defining "reclassify" as "[t]o classify again; to alter the classification of").

In *Boston Safe Deposit & Trust Co. v. State Tax Comm'n*, 340 Mass. 250, 163 N.E.2d 637 (Mass.1960), the court considered the tax implications of a reclassification of stock. The reclassification in question involved the partial substitution of redeemable, convertible, cumulative, nonvoting shares for nonredeemable, nonconvertible, noncumulative, voting shares. *Id.* at 642. The court held that the reclassification constituted a taxable event under Massachusetts law. *Id.* at 643.

Our reading of the Massachusetts cases leads us to conclude that the sine qua non of a reclassification of stock is the modification of existing shares into something fundamentally different. At the end of the day, the stockholders in *Page* held a different class of shares, while the stockholders in *Boston Safe* gained some privileges while losing the right to vote. Thus, *Page* and *Boston Safe*, respectively, illustrate two ways in which a security can be altered fundamentally: (a) by changing the class of stock, or (b) by modifying important rights or preferences linked to stock.

Stock splits effected as stock dividends do not entail any such fundamental alteration of the character of an existing security. For example, Level 3's stock split in no way altered its shareholders' proportionate ownership interests, varied the class of securities held, or revised any of the attributes associated with the stock. What is more, the stock split did not have a meaningful impact on either the corporation's balance sheet or capital structure. For those reasons, we perceive no principled basis on which to stretch the definition of "reclassification of stock" to encompass a stock split.

E. THE OVERALL PLAN OF REORGANIZATION.

The appellant also makes a conclusory claim that the July 1998 stock split was part and parcel of a comprehensive corporate reorganization (and, thus, animated the warrant's antidilution provision). He did very little to develop this claim below, and he has not remedied that shortfall on appeal. For that reason, we deem the claim abandoned.

In any event, the claim lacks merit. As best we can understand it, the appellant hypothesizes that the stock split was an offshoot of a corporate reorganization launched by Level 3 in 1997. In that year, Level 3 shifted direction away from construction and mining activities in order to pursue its interests in communications and business services. Between August 1997 and May 1998, the company dramatically modified its capital structure by splitting off its construction business and eliminating two series of stock. Although none of these transactions involved XCOM or otherwise impacted the appellant, he implies that the July 1998 stock split, effected to increase the marketability of the company's shares as a prelude to raising capital in the public markets, should be viewed as an essential component of the company's overall capital reorganization and stock reclassification, thereby triggering the warrant's antidilution provision.

We reject the appellant's intimation that the stock split is magically transformed into a capital reorganization or reclassification of stock based upon its inclusion in a long-term business plan that also contains a number of more complex financial maneuvers. Taken to its logical extreme, the appellant's argument invites us to deem *any* corporate activity engaged in by Level 3 while in the midst of reorganizing its capital structure as a capital reorganization and reclassification of stock. We are unable to perceive any principled basis on which we could accept this invitation.

G.   THE DENOUEMENT.

[T]he appellant plainly is fishing in an empty stream. We have found no legal usage of the terms "capital reorganization" or "reclassification of stock" that supports the proposition that a reasonable person plausibly could have believed that either term encompassed a stock split. This is made crystal clear when one contrasts the warrant received by the appellant with a warrant issued by XCOM approximately ten months earlier to a different party—a warrant that contained more than six full pages of antidilution protections (including explicitly-worded share adjustments for stock splits and stock dividends). Moreover, the appellant has failed to adduce any credible evidence that the parties here somehow intended to adopt such an unusually expansive interpretation of the terms "capital reorganization" and/or "reclassification of stock."

If more were needed—and we doubt that it is—the maxim *expressio unius est exclusio alterius* instructs that, "when parties list specific items in a document, any item not so listed is typically thought to be excluded." Here, the warrant's antidilution protection extended expressly to five designated contingencies: capital reorganizations, reclassification of the common stock, merger, consolidation, or sale of all (or substantially all) the capital stock or assets. Since nothing within the four corners of the warrant hints at additional contingencies, we apply this maxim and conclude that the parties intended stock splits to be excluded from the list of events capable of triggering the share adjustment machinery.

The appellant is left, then, with his reliance on the principle of *contra proferentum*—the hoary aphorism that ambiguities must be construed against the drafter of an instrument. This reliance is mislaid. In order to invoke this principle, the proponent first must demonstrate that there is an ambiguity. Here, the appellant has failed to show that the interpretation which he urges is, "under all the circumstances, a reasonable and practical one." *Id.* Accordingly, we have no occasion to apply the principle of *contra proferentum.*

IV.   THE IMPLIED COVENANT OF GOOD FAITH AND FAIR DEALING

Although the terms "capital reorganization" and "reclassification of stock," as they appear in the warrant, are inherently unambiguous and do not encompass stock splits, the appellant mounts one further attack. He posits that Level 3 had a legal obligation, under the implied contractual covenant of good faith and fair dealing, to provide him with personalized, advance warning of the stock split. The appellant further argues that Level 3 breached this obligation by failing to advise him specifically about the adverse impact that the stock split would have on the warrant if the appellant did not exercise it before the record date. This argument lacks force.

Under Massachusetts law, every contract includes an implied duty of good faith and fair dealing. *Anthony's Pier Four, Inc. v. HBC Assocs.*, 411 Mass. 451, 583 N.E.2d 806, 820 (1991). This implied covenant forbids a party from doing "anything which will have the effect of destroying or injuring the rights of the other party to receive the fruits of the contract."

The most prominent flaw in the appellant's attempt to wield this club is that he misperceives the fruits of the bargain that he struck. After all, a warrantholder does not become a shareholder unless and until he exercises his purchase option. Consequently, a warrantholder's right to insist that the corporation maintain the integrity of the shares described in the warrant, if it exists at all, must be found in the text of the warrant itself. Put another way, the fruits of the contract were limited to those enumerated in the warrant.

An examination of the warrant reveals quite clearly that Level 3 was not contractually bound to provide the appellant with individualized notice of the stock split. The warrant contained language stating that "[u]ntil the exercise of this Warrant, the Holder shall not have or exercise any rights by virtue hereof as a stockholder of the Company." This disclaimer hardly could have been written more plainly.

Furthermore, the warrant contained a notice provision which, by its terms, pertained to "notices, requests and other communications hereunder." Applying the settled definition of "hereunder," Level 3 was only obligated to provide notice for events contemplated in the warrant agreement. *See* VII *Oxford English Dict.* 165 (2d ed.1989) (defining "hereunder"). Because the warrant contained no provision that even arguably required Level 3 to furnish individualized notice of the stock split to the appellant, the failure to give such notice could not constitute a breach of the implied duty of good faith and fair dealing.[2]

V.   CONCLUSION

We need go no further. In light of the appellant's inability to show that a reasonable person plausibly could construe either "capital reorganization" or "reclassification of stock" to include stock splits, we conclude that these terms, as they appear in the warrant, were unambiguous and did not cover the contingency of a stock split effected as a stock dividend. It follows that the stock split in question here did not trip the warrant's antidilution provision. By like token, Level 3 did not breach the implied covenant of good faith and fair dealing by

---

2. We note in passing that Level 3's general press release announced the stock split ten days in advance of the record date and provided the appellant with constructive notice of the stock split. Thus, the appellant had ample opportunity to exercise the warrant and avoid the dilutive effects of which he now complains.

neglecting to give special notice beyond what the warrant itself required. The bottom line, then, is that the district court was correct in granting Level 3's motion for summary judgment.

PROBLEM SET 17.2

1. Should the Appellant's original attorney be worried by this decision?
2. The court suggests that the Appellant could have avoided his fate even given the shortcomings in the drafting of the warrant—how exactly?

3. OPTION PRICING

Option pricing is a highly developed area of corporate finance theory that might or might not have real-world applications. The most famous theory of option pricing comes from work done by Fischer Black and Myron Scholes in the early 1970s, and expanded by Robert C. Merton. The original Black-Scholes option pricing formula prices European put or call options on a stock that does not pay a dividend or make other distributions. The formula assumes the underlying stock price follows a geometric Brownian motion with constant volatility. Merton and Scholes received the 1997 Nobel Prize in Economics for their work, Professor Black being ineligible due to his earlier death.

The original formula looks like this:

$$C_0 = S \times N(d_1) - Ee^{-Rt} \times N(d_2)$$

where N(d) is a cumulative standard normal distribution function[3] and:

$$d_1 = \frac{\ln(S/E) + (R + \frac{\sigma^2}{2})t}{\sigma\sqrt{t}}$$

and:

$$d_2 = d_1 - \sigma\sqrt{t}$$

S is the current stock price, R is the risk-free interest rate, e is your friend the imaginary number, t is the time until maturity, and the big E is the exercise price of the option. The lowercase sigma—as in, Ὀδυσσεύς (Odysseus)—represents our old friend standard deviation, in this case of the underlying stock price. Think of that as a measure of the stock's volatility.

---

3. You can think of this as a probability calculation. It involves calculus, which, if you took it, you have likely forgotten. It involved things like calculating how many cows could fit into a two-dimensional pen.

Brownian motion refers to the observations that English botanist Robert Brown made in 1828. While looking at pollen, he noticed that very small particles of pollen in water exhibited an incessant, irregular motion. Albert Einstein explained why this happens in a 1905 paper.

Assuming your math skills are somewhat less than Einstein's, even if he did work without a calculator or Excel, we will not dwell on the math behind Black-Scholes in this class, but you should understand its intuitions.

Moreover, you should understand that although Black-Scholes is the best-known option pricing theory, it provides at best an estimate of what an option's price should be, subject to a significant margin of error. It's a bit like CAPM in that regard.

ARTHUR E. WILMARTH, JR., *THE TRANSFORMATION OF THE U.S. FINANCIAL SERVICES INDUSTRY, 1975-2000: COMPETITION, CONSOLIDATION, AND INCREASED RISKS*

2002 U. Ill. L. Rev. 215, 343-44

The Black-Scholes theory determines the value of a particular option based on five factors: exercise price, time to expiration, risk-free interest rate, current price of the underlying asset, and anticipated volatility in the underlying's price until expiration. Of these factors, anticipated volatility in the underlying's price cannot be derived from existing market data or established by agreement between the parties. Instead, volatility must be estimated based on historical data and predictions about future movements in the underlying's market price.

The Black-Scholes model simplifies the problem of estimating volatility by assuming that future market prices for the underlying will exhibit a "constant volatility" and will follow a pattern consistent with "a lognormal probability distribution." Unfortunately, both assumptions create the potential for serious error. The observed volatility of prices in financial markets is not constant and changes frequently in response to altered economic conditions. Moreover, actual price distributions for assets traded in financial markets typically exhibit "fat tails." The presence of "fat tails" means that higher percentages of actual prices fall within the extreme negative and positive ends of the pricing spectrum than would be predicted under the "normal" distribution assumed in the Black-Scholes model. Indeed, equity markets and other financial markets appear to operate with fatter tails on the left or extreme negative end of the pricing spectrum because "crashes occur more frequently than sudden sharp increases in stock prices."

In addition to the faulty assumptions regarding constant volatility and "normal" distribution of prices, the Black-Scholes option pricing theory depends on the following unrealistic assumptions regarding market conditions: (i) trading will occur continuously and instantaneously in the relevant derivatives market and in all related markets; (ii) arbitrageurs will quickly eliminate any discrepancies between the value of a derivative and the price of the underlying;

and (iii) transaction costs involved in such arbitrage will be negligible. [A]ll three of these assumed conditions often fail to describe actual market behavior, which includes liquidity crunches, financial constraints on arbitrage, and large transaction costs, especially during periods of market stress.

ESPEN GAARDER HAUG[4] & NASSIM NICHOLAS TALEB[5], *OPTION TRADERS USE (VERY) SOPHISTICATED HEURISTICS, NEVER THE BLACK–SCHOLES–MERTON FORMULA*

77 J. Economic Behavior & Organization 97 (February 2011)

Option traders call the formula they use the "Black–Scholes–Merton" formula without being aware that by some irony, of all the possible options formulas that have been produced in the past century, what is called the Black–Scholes–Merton "formula" (after [Black and Scholes, 1973] and [Merton, 1973]) is the one the furthest away from what they are using. In fact of the formulas written down in a long history it is the only formula that is fragile to jumps and tail events.

First, something seems to have been lost in translation: Black and Scholes (1973) and Merton (1973) actually never came up with a *new* option formula, but only a theoretical economic *argument* built on a new way of "deriving," rather re-deriving, an already existing—and well known formula. The argument, we will see, is extremely fragile to assumptions. The foundations of option hedging and pricing were already far more firmly laid down before them. The Black–Scholes–Merton argument, simply, is that an option can be hedged using a certain methodology called "dynamic hedging" and then turned into a risk-free instrument, as the portfolio would no longer be stochastic.[6] Indeed what Black, Scholes and Merton did was "marketing," finding a way to make a well-known formula palatable to the economics establishment of the time, little else, and in fact distorting its essence.

Such argument requires strange far-fetched assumptions: some liquidity at the level of transactions, knowledge of the probabilities of future events (in a neoclassical Arrow–Debreu style),[7] and, more critically, a certain mathematical structure that requires "thin-tails," or mild randomness, on which, [more] later. The entire argument is indeed, quite strange and rather inapplicable for someone clinically and observation-driven standing outside conventional neoclassical

---

4. Independent Option Trader, London, United Kingdom.

5. NYU Poly, 6 Metrotech Center, Brooklyn, USA.

6. Random and variable. —AUTHOR

7. Of all the misplaced assumptions of Black–Scholes that cause it to be a mere thought experiment, though an extremely elegant one, a flaw shared with modern portfolio theory, is the certain knowledge of future delivered variance for the random variable (or, equivalently, all the future probabilities). This is what makes it clash with practice—the rectification by the market fattening the tails is a negation of the Black–Scholes thought experiment.

economics. Simply, the dynamic hedging argument is dangerous in practice as it subjects you to blowups; it makes no sense unless you are concerned with neoclassical economic theory. The Black–Scholes–Merton argument and equation flow a top-down general equilibrium theory, built upon the assumptions of operators working *in full knowledge* of the probability distribution of future outcomes—in addition to a collection of assumptions that . . . are highly invalid mathematically, the main one being the ability to cut the risks using continuous trading which only works in the very narrowly special case of thin-tailed distributions (or, possibly, jumps of a well-known structure). But it is not just these flaws that make it inapplicable: option traders do not "buy theories," particularly speculative general equilibrium ones, which they find too risky for them and extremely lacking in standards of reliability. A normative theory is, simply, not good for decision-making under uncertainty (particularly if it is in chronic disagreement with empirical evidence). Operators may take decisions based on heuristics under the impression of using speculative theories, but avoid the fragility of theories in running their risks.

Yet professional traders, including, initially, the authors (and, alas, the Swedish Academy of Science) have operated under the illusion that it was the Black–Scholes–Merton "formula" they actually used—we were told so. This myth has been progressively reinforced in the literature and in business schools, as the original sources have been lost or frowned upon as "anecdotal" (Merton, 1992). [S]imple random jumps represent too large a share of the variability of returns to make the Black–Scholes–Merton argument scientifically acceptable— the Swedish Academy does not grant the Nobel in Medicine to works that are grounded in the assumption that men were mice. . . .

There are indeed two myths:

- That we had to wait for the Black–Scholes–Merton options formula to trade the product, price options, and manage option books. In fact the introduction of the Black, Scholes, and Merton argument increased our risks and set us back in risk management. More generally, it is a myth that traders rely on theories, even less a general equilibrium theory, to price options.
- That we "use" the Black–Scholes–Merton options "pricing formula." We simply don't. . . .

[T]here is evidence that while both the Chicago Board Options Exchange and the Black–Scholes–Merton formula came about in 1973, the model was "rarely used by traders" before the 1980s (O'Connell, 2001). When one of the authors (Taleb) became a pit trader in 1992, almost two decades after Black–Scholes– Merton, he was surprised to find that many traders still priced options heuristically . . . without recourse to any formula. . . .

We conclude with the following remark. Sadly, all the equations, from the first (Bachelier), to the last pre-Black–Scholes–Merton (Thorp) accommodate a [simpler model]. The notion of explicitly removing the expectation [of the distribution of future outcomes] from the forward was present in Keynes (1924) and later by Blau (1944)—and long a call short a put of the same strike equals a forward. These simple and effective arbitrage relationships appeared to be well known heuristics in 1904.

One could easily attribute the explosion in option volume to the computer age and the ease of processing transactions, added to the long stretch of peaceful economic growth and absence of hyperinflation. From the evidence (once one removes the propaganda), the development of scholastic finance appears to be an epiphenomenon rather than a cause of option trading. Once again, lecturing birds how to fly does not allow one to take subsequent credit.

This is why we call the equation Bachelier–Thorp. We have been using it all along and gave it the wrong name, after the wrong method and with attribution to the wrong persons. It does not mean that dynamic hedging is out of the question; it is just not a central part of the pricing paradigm. It led to the writing down of a certain stochastic process that may have its uses, some day, should markets "spiral towards dynamic completeness." But not in the present.

The second excerpt is a challenging article, but it is an important one to remember if you ever find yourself negotiating against somebody who purports to be using Black-Scholes or cross-examining a finance professor.

To understand the pricing of options we need to understand not only the factors that affect price in a Black-Scholes world, but also those factors that affect price in the real world. Most important, an option's price will be greatly affected by the selling broker's ability to hedge the option, which means that supply and demand for a particular option, and the broker's assessment of the risks of its hedging strategy, will be important, too.

Returning to the Black-Scholes world, the formula provides that the following issues affect option price in the following ways:

		Call	Put
1.	Asset price	+	−
2.	Exercise price	−	+
3.	Interest rate	+	−
4.	Volatility in the asset price	+	+
5.	Expiration date	+	+

That is, rising asset prices increase the value of the call, and decrease the value of a put. Hopefully that is self-evident.

The other factors might be less intuitive, but think about them and be prepared to discuss in class why it might be that volatility, for example, is good for both types of option holder.

SECURITIES AND EXCHANGE COMMISSION (S.E.C.)
IN THE MATTER OF DAVID J. LUBBEN, RESPONDENT

Administrative Proceeding File No. 3–13374
February 19, 2009
17 C.F.R.230; 240

Order Instituting Administrative Proceedings Pursuant to Rule 102(E) of the Commission's Rules of Practice, Making Findings, and Imposing Remedial Sanctions

I.

The Securities and Exchange Commission ("Commission") deems it appropriate and in the public interest that public administrative proceedings be, and hereby are, instituted against David J. Lubben ("Respondent" or "Lubben") pursuant to Rule 102(e)(3)(i) of the Commission's Rules of Practice.[8]

II.

In anticipation of the institution of these proceedings, Respondent has submitted an Offer of Settlement (the "Offer") which the Commission has determined to accept. Solely for the purpose of these proceedings and any other proceedings brought by or on behalf of the Commission, or to which the Commission is a party, and without admitting or denying the findings herein, except as to the Commission's jurisdiction over him and the subject matter of these proceedings, and the findings contained in Section III. 3. below, which are admitted, Respondent consents to the entry of this Order Instituting Administrative Proceedings Pursuant to Rule 102(e) of the Commission's Rules of Practice, Making Findings, and Imposing Remedial Sanctions ("Order"), as set forth below.

III.

On the basis of this Order and Respondent's Offer, the Commission finds that:

1. Lubben, age fifty-six (56), is and has been an attorney licensed to practice in the State of Minnesota. From 1996 until late 2006, he served as General Counsel to UnitedHealth Group Inc. ("UnitedHealth").
2. UnitedHealth is and was, at all relevant times, a Minnesota corporation with its principal place of business in Minnetonka, Minnesota.

---

8. Rule 102(e)(3)(i) provides, in relevant part, that:

The Commission, with due regard to the public interest and without preliminary hearing, may, by order,... suspend from appearing or practicing before it any attorney ... who has been by name: (A) permanently enjoined by any court of competent jurisdiction, by reason of his or her misconduct in an action brought by the Commission, from violating or aiding and abetting the violation of any provision of the Federal securities laws or of the rules and regulations thereunder.

UnitedHealth is a diversified health and well-being company offering a variety of insurance and other products and services to approximately 70 million individuals through six operating businesses. UnitedHealth's securities are registered with the Commission pursuant to Section 12(b) of the Securities Exchange Act of 1934 ("Exchange Act") and are listed on the New York Stock Exchange.

3. On January 23, 2009, a final judgment was entered against Respondent in the civil action entitled *Securities and Exchange Commission v. David J. Lubben*, 08-cv-6454, in the United States District Court for the District of Minnesota. The final judgment permanently enjoined Lubben from future violations of Section 17(a) of the Securities Act of 1933 ("Securities Act") and Sections 10(b), 13(b)(5), 14(a) and 16(a) of the Exchange Act and Rules 10b-5, 13b2-1, 14a-9 and 16a-3 thereunder, and from aiding and abetting violations of Sections 13(a), 13(b)(2)(A), 13(b)(2)(B) and 16(a) of the Exchange Act and Rules 12b-20, 13a-1, 13a-11, 13a-13 and 16a-3 thereunder. The final judgment also ordered that Lubben is liable for $1,403,310 in disgorgement, plus $347,211 in prejudgment interest, and a $575,000 civil money penalty.

4. The Commission's complaint alleged, among other things, that Lubben participated in a stock options backdating scheme at UnitedHealth, in which hindsight was used to pick advantageous grant dates for the Company's nonqualified stock options, which dates corresponded to dates of historically low annual or quarterly closing prices for UnitedHealth's common stock. The complaint further alleged that various individuals, including Lubben or others acting at his direction, created false or misleading Company records indicating that the grants had occurred on the earlier dates when the Company's stock price had been at a low. According to the complaint, because of the undisclosed backdating, for fiscal years 1996 through 2005, UnitedHealth filed with the Commission and disseminated to investors quarterly and annual reports, proxy statements and registration statements that Lubben knew, or was reckless in not knowing, contained or incorporated by reference materially false and misleading statements pertaining to the true grant dates of UnitedHealth options and materially false and misleading financial statements, which underreported compensation expenses. In addition, the complaint alleged that Lubben received and exercised backdated options on shares of UnitedHealth stock, and thus personally benefited from the backdating.

IV.

In view of the foregoing, the Commission deems it appropriate and in the public interest to impose the sanction agreed to in Respondent Lubben's Offer.

Accordingly, it is hereby ORDERED, effective immediately, that:

Lubben is suspended from appearing or practicing before the Commission as an attorney for three (3) years. Furthermore, before appearing and resuming practice before the Commission, Lubben must submit an affidavit to the Commission's Office of General Counsel truthfully stating, under penalty of perjury, that he has complied with the Order; that he is not the subject of any suspension or disbarment as an attorney by a court of the United States or of any state, territory, district, commonwealth, or possession; and that he has not been convicted of a felony or misdemeanor involving moral turpitude as set forth in Rule 102(e)(2) of the Commission's Rules of Practice.

By the Commission.
Elizabeth M. Murphy
Secretary

What was the point of the conduct alleged in paragraph 4?

4.   CONVERTIBLES

Convertible securities are stocks or bonds that have an option to convert built into them. Typically the securities are preferred shares or debt that have an option to convert into common shares.

The call option is exercised any time before the instrument either matures or is called. The holder exchanges the debt or preferred shares for common shares at an exchange rate that is set in the instrument.

Assume that Bogartco issues 1 million, 4.5 percent convertible preferred shares priced at $100 per share. The shareholders are entitled to a 4.5 percent dividend before the common shareholders get anything, and they also have priority in liquidation, just like any other preferred share. But if Bogartco's common shares rise, so that the option to purchase common shares by trading in the preferred share goes "into the money," then preferred shareholders have an additional way to earn returns on their investment. For example, if the conversion ratio set forth in the Bogartco preferred shares is five, any price above $20 per share for the common stocks makes the conversion feature valuable.[9]

As with other financial instruments we have seen, the precise terms of the deal can be quite important.

---

9. 100/5 =$20.

BANC OF AMERICA SECURITIES LLC
PROSPECTUS SUPPLEMENT TO PROSPECTUS DATED MAY 5, 2006

6,000,000 Shares of 7.25% Non-Cumulative Perpetual Convertible Preferred Stock, Series L

Bank of America Corporation is offering 6,000,000 shares of 7.25% Non-Cumulative Perpetual Convertible Preferred Stock, Series L, $0.01 par value, with a liquidation preference of $1,000 per share (the "Preferred Stock").

We will pay dividends on the Preferred Stock, when, as, and if declared by our board of directors or a duly authorized committee of our board, quarterly, in arrears, on January 30, April 30, July 30, and October 30 of each year, beginning on April 30, 2008. For each quarterly dividend period from the issue date of the Preferred Stock, we will pay declared dividends at a rate of 7.25% per annum. Dividends on the Preferred Stock will not be cumulative.

Each share of the Preferred Stock may be converted at any time, at the option of the holder, into 20 shares of our common stock, $0.01 par value (the "common stock") (which reflects an initial conversion price of $50.00 per share of common stock, which is approximately a 25% premium over the VWAP (as defined herein) of our common stock from 2:30 p.m. EST on January 23, 2008 to 4:00 p.m. on the pricing date for the offering), plus cash in lieu of fractional shares, subject to anti-dilution adjustments. The conversion rate will be adjusted as described herein upon the occurrence of certain other events.

The Preferred Stock is not redeemable by us at any time. On or after January 30, 2013, if the closing price of our common stock exceeds 130% of the then-applicable conversion price for 20 trading days during any period of 30 consecutive trading days, we may at our option cause some or all of the Preferred Stock to be automatically converted into common stock at the then prevailing conversion rate.

We have applied to list the Preferred Stock on the New York Stock Exchange under the symbol "BAC PrL." If approved for listing, we expect trading of the Preferred Stock to begin within 30 days after we issue the Preferred Stock.

***

"VWAP" per share of our common stock on any trading day means the per share volume-weighted average price as displayed under the heading "Bloomberg VWAP" on Bloomberg page "BAC UN equity AQR" (or its equivalent successor if such page is not available) in respect of the period from the open of trading on the relevant trading day until the close of trading on the relevant trading day (or if such volume-weighted average price is unavailable, the market price of one share of our common stock on such trading days determined, using a volume-weighted average method, by a nationally recognized investment banking firm (unaffiliated with us) retained for this purpose by us). For purposes of determining the conversion price, VWAP may refer to a partial trading day.

Google "nyse:bac" and calculate the current desirability of converting these shares. Based on what you find, how would you value the preferred shares? What is the effect of the bank's ability to convert the shares when they exceed 130 percent of the conversion price?[10]

The same basic idea holds for convertible debt, except that debt typically involves trading in increments of $1,000—or $5,000 in Europe—of debt in exchange for common shares.

Both instruments also operate under a kind of floor. That is, once the call option on the debt or preferred shares becomes sufficiently out of the money, you can treat the instrument as a straight bond or preferred stock, because the conversion feature likely will never be exercised.

WILLIAM F. LORENZ v. CSX CORPORATION et al.

1 F.3d 1406
United States Court of Appeals, Third Circuit.
Aug. 6, 1993.

COWEN, Circuit Judge.

Prior to December 13, 1977, the plaintiffs in these two related actions purchased convertible debentures issued by the defendant Baltimore and Ohio Railroad Company ("B & O"). At that time, 99.63% of the B & O's shares were owned by defendant Chesapeake and Ohio Railroad Company, which in turn was a wholly-owned subsidiary of Chessie Systems, Inc., the corporate predecessor to defendant CSX Corporation ("CSX"). The indenture trustee was defendant Chase Manhattan Bank. Plaintiffs allege that the defendants defrauded them from 1977 to 1986 by failing to disclose material information which would have enabled them to convert their debentures into B & O common stock and receive a lucrative dividend. Plaintiffs appeal the dismissal of their claims for breach of fiduciary duty, breach of the implied covenant of good faith and fair dealing, civil RICO, and violations of section 10(b) and Rule 10b-5 of the Securities Exchange Act of 1934 ("'34 Act"). We will affirm.

I.   FACTS AND PROCEDURAL HISTORY

The defendants have been involved in litigation against their debentureholders for the past fifteen years in a series of closely related actions. A detailed description of the facts and procedural history can be found in earlier district and circuit court opinions in the *Pittsburgh Terminal Corp./ Guttmann* litigation. *See, e.g., Pittsburgh Terminal Corp. v. Baltimore & Ohio R.R. Co.*, 509 F.Supp. 1002 (W.D.Pa.1981), *aff'd in part, rev'd in part*, 680 F.2d 933 (3d Cir.), *cert. denied*, 459 U.S. 1056, 103 S.Ct. 475, 74 L.Ed.2d 621 (1982); *Pittsburgh Terminal Corp.*

---

10. You can find the current trading price for the preferred shares by going to Nasdaq.com, and entering BAC.PRL in the search box.

v. Baltimore & Ohio R.R. Co., 824 F.2d 249 (3d Cir.1987) (*PTC IV*). We will recite only those facts which are relevant to these appeals.

The plaintiffs were holders of debentures in the B & O Railroad as of December 13, 1977. The debentures were convertible into B & O common stock at any time before maturing in the year 2010. To avoid Interstate Commerce Commission regulations hindering the development of non-rail assets owned by railroads, B & O devised a plan to segregate its rail and non-rail assets. Non-rail assets were transferred to a wholly owned subsidiary, Mid Allegheny Corporation ("MAC"), and MAC common stock was distributed as a dividend on a share-for-share basis to B & O shareholders. B & O sought to avoid the registration of its shares with the Securities and Exchange Commission ("SEC"), a time-consuming process which would have required appraisals of the transferred assets. Because B & O had few shareholders, the company thought that the SEC would issue a "no-action" letter excusing the registration of MAC stock. This plan would have been foiled if large numbers of B & O debentureholders exercised their conversion option in order to receive the MAC dividend.

To avoid this occurrence, B & O transferred its non-rail assets to MAC on December 13, 1977 and declared the dividend in MAC stock on the same date, without prior notice. As a result, the debentureholders could not convert their shares in time to receive the MAC dividend. Some of the debentureholders brought actions, later consolidated, under section 10(b) of the '34 Act against B & O, C & O, and Chessie Systems.[11] This suit is known as the *PTC/Guttmann* litigation. In 1978 and 1979, B & O and Chase Manhattan Bank entered into a series of letter agreements, whereby B & O agreed that if the *PTC/Guttmann* plaintiffs prevailed or obtained a settlement, debentureholders would be allowed to participate equally in that judgment or settlement regardless of whether they had converted their debentures.

The *PTC/Guttmann* plaintiffs moved for class certification. The district court denied the motion, at least in part because Chessie Systems' general counsel, Robert F. Hochwarth, filed an affidavit dated May 2, 1980 memorializing the earlier letter agreements with Chase Manhattan Bank. The affidavit, known as the "Hochwarth Stipulation," states that if plaintiffs prevail or a settlement is reached, "all holders of debentures as of December 13, 1977, whether or not they were subsequently converted, will be permitted to participate in the Court judgment or settlement on the same terms as the plaintiffs." App. at 279.

After a bench trial, the district court entered judgment in favor of the defendants. *Pittsburgh Terminal Corp.*, 509 F.Supp. at 1017–18. We reversed. A divided panel agreed only that the failure to provide the debentureholders with advance notice of the dividend violated Rule 10b-17 of the '34 Act. *Pittsburgh Terminal Corp. v. Baltimore & Ohio R.R. Co.*, 680 F.2d 933, 941–42 (3d Cir.) (*PTC II*), *cert. denied*, 459 U.S. 1056, 103 S.Ct. 475, 74 L.Ed.2d 621 (1982); *id.* at 945–46 (Garth, J., concurring in part and concurring in the judgment). We

---

11. Chessie Systems later merged into defendant CSX Corporation.

remanded to the district court to fashion an appropriate remedy. On May 8, 1984, the district court granted plaintiffs the opportunity to convert their debentures into shares and receive the MAC dividend plus dividend income accruing since December 13, 1977. *Pittsburgh Terminal Corp. v. Baltimore & Ohio R.R. Co.*, 586 F.Supp. 1297, 1304–05 (W.D.Pa.1984), *aff'd*, 760 F.2d 257 (3d Cir.), *cert. denied*, 474 U.S. 919, 106 S.Ct. 247, 88 L.Ed.2d 256 (1985). The district court, construing the Hochwarth Stipulation, described the scope of the remedy:

> The remedy ordered here is limited to those persons who owned the subject debentures at the time of the violation, December 13, 1977, and who still own those debentures. Those persons who owned debentures on December 13, 1977 and subsequently converted to B & O common stock may also elect to participate in this remedy, obtaining MAC and its dividends, offset by interest accruing on the debentures after December 13, 1977. . . . Those persons who owned B & O debentures on December 13, 1977 and subsequently sold their debentures are not within the scope of . . . this action. . . .

Id. at 1305. The defendants were ordered to give notice to the debentureholders of the district court's order. In December of 1986, after the denial of certiorari, defendants published notice of the remedy in the *New York Times* and *Wall Street Journal*. In a subsequent appeal, we held that under the terms of the Hochwarth Stipulation, the district court's remedy also included persons who held B & O debentures on December 13, 1977, converted them to B & O common stock, and subsequently sold the stock. *PTC IV*, 824 F.2d at 256.

The plaintiffs in the present actions are those persons who are outside the scope of the *PTC/Guttmann* remedy. They held debentures on December 13, 1977 but subsequently sold them without having ever converted them into stock. On July 25, 1986, plaintiff Ethel B. Savin filed her complaint in the United States District Court for the Southern District of New York on behalf of a class of similarly situated former B & O debentureholders. The case was transferred to the Western District of Pennsylvania because of the related litigation there. On April 23, 1987, the *Lorenz* plaintiffs filed their complaint in the United States District Court for the Western District of Pennsylvania on behalf of a class of similarly situated former B & O debentureholders. The complaint alleged . . . breach of fiduciary duty.

In July of 1987, the defendants moved to dismiss under Fed.R.Civ.P. 12(b)(6).

On November 3, 1992, the district court dismissed *Savin* for the reasons stated in its *Lorenz* opinion of August 18. Plaintiffs filed these appeals.

We accept all factual allegations in the complaints and all reasonable inferences to be drawn therefrom in the light most favorable to the plaintiffs. We may affirm only if it is certain that no relief could be granted under any set of facts which could be proven.

IV.   BREACH OF IMPLIED COVENANT OF GOOD FAITH AND FAIR DEALING CLAIMS
         AGAINST DEFENDANT CHASE MANHATTAN BANK

The district court dismissed plaintiffs' claims against the indenture trustee Chase Manhattan Bank for breach of the implied covenant of good faith and fair dealing, allegedly arising from the bank's failure to inform them of the MAC dividend, the letter agreements with B & O, and the *PTC/Guttmann* judgment. Because the indenture specifies that the liability of the trustee shall be determined under New York law, we will apply New York law.

The courts of New York consistently have held that the duties of an indenture trustee, unlike those of a typical trustee, are defined exclusively by the terms of the indenture. The sole exception to this rule is that the indenture trustee must avoid conflicts of interest with the debentureholders.

The plaintiffs specifically claim that Chase Manhattan Bank violated the implied covenant of good faith and fair dealing which, under New York law, is contained in every contract. The implied covenant prohibits either party from doing anything which would prevent the other party from receiving the fruits of the contract. The covenant, however, cannot be used to insert new terms that were not bargained for. A covenant is implied only when it is consistent with the express terms of the contract.

An indenture is, of course, a contract. Unless the indenture trustee has deprived the debentureholders of a right or benefit specifically provided to them in the indenture, there is no violation of the implied covenant of good faith and fair dealing. *cf. Metropolitan Life Ins. Co. v. RJR Nabisco, Inc.*, 716 F.Supp. 1504, 1517–22 (S.D.N.Y.1989) (no breach of implied covenant under New York law where corporation's incurrence of debt to fund leveraged buyout depleted the value of its debentures, as the indenture lacked any terms prohibiting the transaction). We therefore will consider whether the indenture in this case contains provisions which entitled the debentureholders to receive notice of the MAC dividend, the letter agreements with B & O, or any of the remedies in the *PTC/Guttmann* action.

The indenture contains no provisions which explicitly require the trustee to provide notice of any kind to the debentureholders. Plaintiffs cite two provisions which they claim implicitly require notice. First, the indenture states:

> The Indenture permits the amendment thereof and the modification or alteration, in any respect, of the rights and obligations of the Company and the rights of the holders of the Debentures ... at any time by the concurrent action of the Company and of the holders of 66 2/3% in principal amount of the Debentures then outstanding affected by such amendment, modification or alteration (including, in the case of a modification of the terms of conversion of this Debenture into common stock of the Company or of payment of the principal of, or the premium or interest on, this Debenture, the consent of the holder hereof), all as more fully provided in the Indenture.

Plaintiffs claim that the letter agreements between B & O and Chase Manhattan Bank altered their rights under the Indenture. Those agreements provided that the debentureholders would be allowed to participate equally in any judgment against B & O or any settlement regardless of whether they converted their debentures to common stock. Because the quoted language gives the debentureholders the right to vote regarding any change in their or the company's rights and obligations under the indenture, the plaintiffs argue that they were entitled to notice of the letter agreements.

Second, the indenture provides:

> At any meeting at which there shall be a quorum the holders of the Affected Debentures shall have the power by resolution adopted as hereinafter provided:
>
> (*a*) to authorize the Trustee to join with the Company in making any modification, alteration, repeal of or addition to any provision of this Indenture or of the Debentures, and any modification of or addition to the rights and obligations of the Company or the rights of the holders of the Debentures...under this Indenture or under the Debentures. . . .

The plaintiffs claim that the letter agreements between B & O and Chase Manhattan Bank were supplemental indentures which modified or added to their rights under the indenture. Because the debentureholders have the right to vote on whether to permit the indenture trustee and company to execute a supplemental indenture, the plaintiffs argue that they were entitled to notice.

Both provisions cited by plaintiffs provide debentureholders with the right to vote, and arguably therefore to receive notice, only if there is some modification of the debentureholders' rights or the company's obligations under the indenture. We agree with the district court that the letter agreements did not affect their rights under the indenture and cannot be characterized as supplemental indentures. The agreements pertained only to the scope of a possible remedy under the federal securities laws in the *PTC/Guttmann* litigation, in the event of a judgment against the defendant corporations or a settlement. The plaintiffs' contractual rights under the indenture itself, including rights regarding conversion of shares, were never modified.

It would have been advantageous for the plaintiffs to have been informed of the letter agreements and thus of potential violations of securities laws committed by B & O. They may have sued the defendant corporations years earlier. However, so long as an indenture trustee fulfills its obligations under the express terms of the indenture, it owes the debentureholders no additional, implicit duties or obligations, except to avoid conflicts of interest. There is no provision in the indenture which obligated the trustee Chase Manhattan Bank to inform the debentureholders that they possibly had rights against B & O and its parent companies under the federal securities laws. Because the bank did not deprive the plaintiff of any right under the indenture, the bank could not have breached the implied covenant of good faith and fair dealing.

In the present case . . . the indenture does not have any provision which required the bank to provide notice regarding B & O's alleged violations of securities laws and the resulting litigation. To infer such a requirement would, in effect, add a new term to the indenture, and the implied covenant can never be used for that purpose. The district court correctly dismissed the claims against Chase Manhattan Bank for breach of the implied covenant of good faith and fair dealing.

V.   BREACH OF FIDUCIARY DUTY CLAIMS AGAINST DEFENDANTS CSX AND C & O

Plaintiffs claim that defendants CSX and C & O, as controlling shareholders of B & O, breached a fiduciary duty to disclose material information. The district court concluded that the defendants owed no duties to the plaintiff debentureholders aside from those specified in the indenture. Finding no breach of the indenture, the district court dismissed the breach of fiduciary duty claims.

It is well-established that a corporation does not have a fiduciary relationship with its debt security holders, as with its shareholders. The relationship between a corporation and its debentureholders is contractual in nature. Just as an indenture trustee's duties are strictly defined by the indenture, a corporation is under no duty to act for the benefit of its debentureholders, or to refrain from action which dilutes their interest, except as provided in the indenture. *Parkinson v. West End St. Ry. Co.*, 173 Mass. 446, 448, 53 N.E. 891, 892 (1899) (Holmes, J.). Even if the debentures are convertible, the debentureholder is merely a creditor who is owed no fiduciary duty until conversion takes place.

As we stated in Part IV *supra* with respect to the indenture trustee's liability, the indenture contains no provisions which entitled the debentureholders to receive notice of the Hochwarth Stipulation, the letter agreements between B & O and Chase Manhattan Bank, or events in the *PTC/Guttmann* litigation. Plaintiffs have not identified, nor have we found, any additional provisions which impose upon B & O or its controlling shareholders a duty to disclose such information. The district court, therefore, correctly dismissed the breach of fiduciary duty claims.

PROBLEM SET 17.3

1. Compare the opinion above to an earlier opinion involving the same bonds:

Whatever may be the fiduciary duty of majority stockholders and corporate directors under Maryland law to general unsecured creditors, we are here dealing with securities having an equity option feature. Maryland follows the settled rule that a control stockholder owes a fiduciary obligation not to exercise that control to the disadvantage of minority equity participants. . . . Similarly, Maryland directors must act as fiduciaries to all equity participants. Although no Maryland case has been called to our attention presenting the precise issue of fiduciary obligations to holders of securities containing stock options, we would be very much surprised if Maryland or any other state would today hold that no such obligations were owed by an issuer of such securities and its directors.

Pittsburgh Terminal Corp. v. Baltimore & Ohio R. Co., 680 F.2d 933, 941 (3d Cir. 1982). Notably, only Judge Gibbons joined in this part of the opinion.

Which is the better rule?

The opinion excerpted above, rather than Judge Gibbons's, probably reflects the majority approach. *E.g.*, Pittelman v. Pearce, 6 Cal. App. 4th 1436, 1444, 8 Cal. Rptr. 2d 359, 364 (1992) (decided under California law, but holding that there was no difference with Delaware law).

2. Sophisticated investors often purchase convertible bonds as a convertible arbitrage strategy (simultaneous purchase of a company's convertible bond and shorting of the company's stock). How could that work?

3. Issuers of convertible notes or bonds that will be settled in shares must remember that they will need to maintain sufficient authorized and unissued shares under their certificate of incorporation to satisfy all conversions, especially when contemplating other equity issuances (including through compensation plans) that might use up those unissued shares.

4. Alternatively, for convertible notes that require or permit the issuer to settle all or a portion of their conversion obligations in cash, issuers must ensure that they have sufficient cash on hand, and the ability to use that cash, to satisfy their conversion obligations. Loan agreements and senior bond indentures often have restrictions on the ability of issuers to use cash to pay junior debt.

5. "DEATH SPIRAL" CONVERTIBLES

As the next case indicates, convertibles are not always the staid investments we have covered thus far.

LOG ON AMERICA, INC. v. PROMETHEAN ASSET MANAGEMENT L.L.C.

223 F.Supp.2d 435
United States District Court, S.D. New York.
Dec. 10, 2001

BERMAN, District Judge.

On or about August 18, 2000, Plaintiff Log On America, Inc. ("Plaintiff" or "LOA") filed this action against defendants Promethean Asset Management L.L.C. ("Promethean") and HFTP Investment L.L.C. ("HFTP" and, together with Promethean, the "Promethean Defendants"); Fisher Capital Ltd. ("Fisher"), Wingate Capital Ltd. ("Wingate") and Citadel Limited Partnership ("Citadel" and, together with Fisher and Wingate, the "Citadel Defendants"); and Marshall Capital Management, Inc. ("Marshall") (the Promethean Defendants, the Citadel

Defendants and Marshall are collectively, the "Defendants"), asserting claims under the Securities Exchange Act of 1934, as amended (the "1934 Act"), specifically Section 10(b), 15 U.S.C. §78j(b), Section 13(d), 15 U.S.C. §78m(d), and Section 16(b), 15 U.S.C. §78p(b); and claims for common law fraud, breach of contract, and breach of the covenants of good faith and fair dealing under New York law. Plaintiff seeks damages, injunctive relief, declaratory relief, rescission, disgorgement, and costs. Defendants now move to dismiss Plaintiff's claims pursuant to Rule 12(b)(6) of the Federal Rules of Civil Procedure ("Fed. R. Civ.P."). For the reasons stated below, Defendants' motion to dismiss is granted.

I.   BACKGROUND

Plaintiff is a Delaware corporation with its principal place of business in Providence, Rhode Island. Plaintiff provides telephone service, high-speed Internet access, and cable programming to homes and businesses throughout the Northeast of the United States.

Defendant HFTP is a limited liability company, organized and doing business in New York, engaged principally in the business of investments and financial services. Defendant Promethean, a New York company, is an affiliate of HFTP and also its investment advisor. Defendants Fisher and Wingate are limited partnerships organized under the laws of the Cayman Islands and have offices in Chicago, Illinois. Fisher and Wingate are venture capital lenders. Defendant Citadel, a limited partnership, is a registered broker-dealer and is the trading manager of both Fisher and Wingate. Defendant Marshall, an Illinois (venture capital) investor corporation doing business in New York, is a wholly-owned subsidiary of Credit Suisse Group and an affiliate of Credit Suisse First Boston Corporation.

On February 23, 2000, LOA entered into the following financial agreements with HFTP, Fisher, Wingate, and Marshall: (i) Securities Purchase Agreement (the "Agreement"); (ii) Registration Rights Agreement ("Registration Agreement"); and (iii) Certificate of Designations, Preferences and Rights of Series A Convertible Preferred Stock of Log On America, Inc. (the "Certificate of Designations") (collectively, the "Transaction Documents"). Under the Transaction Documents, HFTP, Fisher, Wingate, and Marshall (cumulatively) paid to LOA $15 million in exchange for: (i) 15,000 shares of LOA's Series A Convertible Preferred Stock ("Preferred Stock");[12] and (ii) 594,204 warrants (the "Warrants") for the purchase of LOA common shares ("Common Stock").

Plaintiff acknowledged that "its obligation to issue Conversion Shares upon conversion of the Preferred Shares...is...absolute and unconditional regardless of

---

12. Defendants were granted the right to convert their Preferred Stock into Common Stock at a fixed discount to market at the time of conversion. Plaintiff states that this type of Preferred Stock, which is based on a "floating" conversion ratio, is known as "floorless convertible," "toxic convertible," or "death spiral convertible." According to Plaintiff, the lower the market price of the common stock at the time of conversion, the greater the number of shares Defendants would receive upon conversion of Preferred Stock.

the dilutive effect that such issuance may have on the ownership interests of other stockholders of [LOA]." The Certificate of Designations contains a "conversion cap" (or "blocker") limiting the beneficial ownership by any holder of Preferred Stock and its affiliates to 4.99% of the total outstanding shares of Plaintiff's common stock.

The Agreement provided that Defendants were acquiring the Preferred Stock and Warrants "for investment only." It did not by its terms constrain Defendants to hold the securities for any minimum period of time...

Defendants were granted the right to sell short LOA Common Stock. However, they agreed not to sell short more than 594,204 shares of Common Stock for a certain period of time...

Pursuant to the Agreement, Plaintiff was required to file a Registration Statement covering resale of the common stock underlying the Preferred Stock and Warrants and to request the Securities and Exchange Commission ("SEC") to declare the Registration Statement effective "as soon as practicable, but in no event later than 180 days after [February 23, 2000]." Plaintiff filed a Registration Statement with the SEC on or about April 26, 2000 to register shares of Common Stock on behalf of the holders of Preferred Stock, but the Registration Statement was not declared effective before the 180 day period expired on August 21, 2000.

Plaintiff alleges in the instant Complaint that Defendants "wrongfully utilized 'floorless' convertible stocks ... to launch an unlawful scheme to 'short sell' Plaintiff's stock in sufficient volume to drive down its price knowing that they would be in a position to cover the short sales by converting their preferred stock at depressed market prices." Plaintiff maintains that Defendants violated the Federal Securities Laws and breached the terms of the Transaction Documents by artificially manipulating the market prices of LOA's common stock through massive and unlawful short sales while in possession of material non-public information concerning LOA's business."

Defendants state that "[t]he fundamental problem with Plaintiff's claims is that short selling was expressly contemplated and authorized under the Agreement" and that "what Plaintiff is really complaining of here is not fraud or breach of contract, but of having to live up to its obligations under the Agreement." "Indeed, Plaintiff admitted in its Registration Statement that the holders of Preferred Stock could engage in short sales as a legitimate hedging strategy."

1. MISREPRESENTATION

Plaintiff alleges that Defendants' conduct was "manipulative" and "fraudulent" because it was allegedly contrary to written representations that Defendants would not engage in short sales and that they would hold the Preferred Stock as a long-term investment. The Court finds that these misrepresentation claims as currently stated are inadequate.

To maintain a misrepresentation claim under Section 10(b) of the 1934 Act and Rule 10b–5, "a plaintiff must plead that in connection with the purchase or sale of securities, the defendant, acting with scienter, made a false representation or omitted to disclose material information and that the plaintiff's reliance on the defendant's action caused the plaintiff injury."

Short Sales

Section 4(*o*) of the Agreement explicitly authorizes Defendants to make short sales of up to 594,204 shares of Common Stock. **"[E]ach Buyer and its Affiliates are entitled to engage in transactions which constitute Short Sales to the extent that following such transaction the aggregate net short position of such Buyer and its Affiliates does not exceed ... the number of shares of Common Stock equal to the aggregate number of Warrant Shares which such Buyer and its Affiliates have the right to acquire upon exercise of the Warrants held by such Buyer and its Affiliates (without regard to limitations on exercises of the Warrants)."** (Emphasis added.) Plaintiff contends that this "'carve out,' upon which Defendants rely [for the right to sell short] never 'matured'" because "the Warrants were never 'in the money.'" Plaintiff cites no language in the Agreement in support of its position. "[The Agreement] says nothing about being in the money or out of the money."

The Court finds that the language in Section 4(*o*) is plain and unambiguous. It authorizes the very activity Plaintiff says is impermissible, namely short sales. Plaintiff's interpretation, as noted by Defendants, "would strain the contract language beyond its reasonable and ordinary meaning."

Investment Intent

The Agreement (itself) makes clear that while they were purchasing for investment, Defendants were not obligated to hold the Preferred Stock for any specified period of time. **"[B]y making the representations herein, such Buyer does not agree to hold any of the securities for any minimum or other specific term and reserves the right to dispose of the securities at any time in accordance with or pursuant to a registration statement or an exemption under the 1933 Act."** (Emphasis added.) It is difficult to ascertain the basis for a misrepresentation claim upon the instant conclusory pleadings as to investment intent.

2.   MARKET MANIPULATION

Preliminarily, the Court addresses Defendants' challenge to Plaintiff's "standing." Under Section 10(b) of the 1934 Act or Rule 10-b, a plaintiff must be a purchaser or seller of securities. *See Blue Chip Stamps*, 421 U.S. at 730–31, 95 S.Ct. 1917.18 In *Global Intellicom v. Thomson Kernaghan & Co.*, United States District Court Judge Denise J. Cote confronted a similar standing challenge and determined that the plaintiff (there) was neither a purchaser nor a seller: "[Plaintiff] has no standing to bring such a claim since it does not allege that it purchased or sold securities in connection with the alleged manipulation." *Global Intellicom*, 1999 WL 544708, at *9.

LOA does not here allege to have acted as a purchaser or seller with respect to the securities allegedly sold short by Defendants, apart from its view that the conversion feature of the Preferred Stock qualifies as a contract for the purchase or sale of a security. Neither *Pittsburgh Terminal* nor *FS Photo* stands for the proposition that the sale of a convertible security provides an issuer with standing to challenge the kinds of activity alleged here. *See Pittsburgh Terminal*, 680 F.2d at 938–40; *FS Photo*, 61 F.Supp.2d at 478.

C.   COMMON LAW FRAUD

To support a claim of fraud where, as here, a contract exists, a plaintiff must either: "(i) demonstrate a legal duty separate from the duty to perform under the contract; or (ii) demonstrate a fraudulent misrepresentation collateral or extraneous to the contract; or (iii) seek special damages that are caused by the misrepresentations and unrecoverable as contract damages."

Plaintiff's (fraud) claim meets none of these requirements. First, no (fiduciary) duty, according to the Agreement, existed between LOA and Defendants apart from the duty to perform pursuant to the Agreement as reflected in the pleadings. Second, each of the misrepresentations alleged in the Complaint is based upon the Securities Purchase Agreement. Plaintiff's conclusory assertion that "Defendants fail[ed] to disclose information concerning Defendants' true intent," without more, does not adequately specify the requisite fraudulent conduct. *See* Fed.R.Civ.P. 9(b).

D.   BREACH OF CONTRACT

LOA asserts that "Defendants are in material breach of the ['Investment Purpose' and 'Restriction on Short Sales'] provisions contained in the Securities Purchase Agreement." Defendants counter that: (i) Plaintiff has failed to allege breach; and (ii) Plaintiff has failed to allege its own performance.

To state a breach of contract claim under New York law, a complaint must allege "(1) the existence of an agreement, (2) adequate performance of the contract by the plaintiff, (3) breach of contract by the defendant, and (4) damages." For the reasons already discussed *supra*, the Court finds that Plaintiff has failed sufficiently to plead that Defendants' alleged conduct breached the provision(s) of the Agreement.

F.   DECLARATORY RELIEF AND RESCISSION

Plaintiff seeks declarations under both Section 29(b) of the 1934 Act, 15 U.S.C. §78cc(b), and the Declaratory Judgment Act, 28 U.S.C. §2201 that, because of Defendants' alleged fraudulent conduct, Plaintiff is relieved of its obligations and liabilities under the Transaction Documents. "By reason of the fraud, illegality and manipulative conduct . . . LOA is entitled to a declaration that ... it is relieved of its obligations and liabilities under the [Transaction Documents] and that the Defendants have no right to have their Convertible Preferred Stock exchanged for LOA common stock." Plaintiff also seeks rescission of the Securities Purchase Agreement "by reason of the fraud, illegality and manipulative conduct. . . ." Defendants assert that declaratory relief is unwarranted because the claims "are premised upon inadequate allegations of fraud, breach of contract and Sections 13(d) and 16(b) violations." Defendants also contend that the claim for rescission must be dismissed because Plaintiff has not alleged actionable (securities) fraud.

To establish a violation under Section 29(b) of the 1934 Act, a plaintiff must "show that (1) the contract involved a prohibited transaction, (2) he is in contractual privity with the defendant, and (3) he is in the class of persons the [1934] Act was designed to protect." The Court finds that Plaintiff has not adequately pled these requirements. Specifically, because the underlying claims have been dismissed, Plaintiff has not (sufficiently) alleged that the Agreement involved a "prohibited transaction."

IV.   CONCLUSION

For the foregoing reasons, Defendants' motion to dismiss is granted as to all claims without prejudice.

PROBLEM SET 17.4

1. How, precisely, do the short selling allegations connect with the "death spiral convertibles"?
2. Why did LOA enter into this agreement in the first instance?
3. Why do convertibles exist at all? How might convertible debt different from straight debt of comparable maturities? Would you pay more or less for the conversion feature? *See* William A. Klien, *The Convertible Bond: A Peculiar Package*, 123 U. Pa. L. Rev. 547, 555–561 (1975).

18

DERIVATIVES

Derivatives are considered inherently complex instruments, and the 2008 financial crisis did nothing to change that perception. But derivatives remain in widespread use, not only among financial institutions, but also by corporations. Indeed, virtually every corporation of any noteworthy size will have some derivatives on its balance sheet.[1] It is important to remember that, at heart, all derivatives are contracts. Try to keep that in mind if you begin to feel overwhelmed.

Although there is no universal definition of *derivative*, it can be broadly defined as an instrument that derives its value from some other asset or measure, like an index. That primary asset or reference point is referred to as the *underlying* or the *reference asset*. For example, the reference asset of an S&P 500 futures contract (described later) is the S&P 500 index.

You have already seen derivatives in Chapter 17, as options clearly meet the definition. Other types of derivatives, like forwards and futures, have been around for more than a century and were designed to allow farmers and merchants to hedge risk stemming from uncertainty and instability of future commodity prices. Exchanges were eventually established to provide a marketplace with standardized contract terms and open price discovery.

The exchanges also created clearinghouses that act as buyer for every contract seller and as seller to every contract buyer, thereby limiting *counterparty risk* for market participants. The clearinghouse essentially becomes a hub in the middle of all transactions.

The clearinghouse protects itself from the risk of nonperformance by requiring market participants to maintain deposits, called *margin*. Like a bank that requires a customer to maintain a savings account before obtaining a loan, margin accounts provide a source of recovery for the clearinghouse if a market participant defaults.

---

1. *See generally* Kimberly D. Krawiec, *Derivatives, Corporate Hedging, and Shareholder Wealth: Modigliani-Miller Forty Years Later*, 1998 U. Ill. L. Rev. 1039 (1998).

But margin is small relative to the size of the trades that market participants are allowed to undertake, which represents one key aspect of the leverage inherent in most derivative trades. We come back to this point in Section 4.

In the 1970s, exchanges such as the Chicago Mercantile Exchange, New York Mercantile Exchange, and Chicago Board of Trade expanded beyond their commodity-based instruments to trade derivative contracts based on financial markets, including futures and options on securities indexes and foreign currencies. S&P 500 futures started trading on the Chicago Mercantile Exchange in 1982 and soon their trading volume exceeded that of physical shares.

Advances in computer technology also facilitated rapid expansion of over-the-counter (OTC) derivative markets. OTC derivatives are negotiated between the parties, without an exchange as the intermediary. Unlike exchange-traded derivatives, OTC contracts are not guaranteed by a clearinghouse and involve potentially significant counterparty risk, an issue that came to the fore in the recent financial crisis. In addition, OTC instruments can be more complicated to liquidate, and might require approval from the counterparty in the event of a proposed sale or transfer (called a "novation" in the industry).

Historically OTC swap markets were opaque and transactions were dominated by banks and brokers, who were parties to most trades. But the recently enacted Dodd-Frank Act might change that. In particular, Dodd-Frank does the following:

- Requires as many OTC derivative products as possible to be centrally cleared and traded on exchanges or other trading facilities.
- Subjects OTC swap dealers and major OTC swap participants to registration with either the Commodity Futures Trading Commission (CFTC) or SEC.
- Imposes capital, margin and reporting requirements on OTC swap dealers and large OTC swap participants.
- Requires public reporting of transaction and pricing data on both cleared and uncleared swaps.

Generally, Dodd-Frank contemplates transforming the OTC market for swaps into a market that will bear a strong resemblance to the futures markets, including standardized terms and daily "mark to market" adjustment to cash margin balances.[2]

Following Dodd-Frank, regulation of the OTC derivatives market is divided between the CFTC and the SEC, with the CFTC having jurisdiction over "swaps," and the SEC having jurisdiction over "security-based swaps." A *swap* is defined to include most types of OTC derivatives, except "security-based swaps"

---

2. Stephen J. Lubben, *Failure of the Clearinghouse: Dodd-Frank's Fatal Flaw?*, 10 Va. L. & Bus. Rev. 127 (2015).

and certain other specified exceptions.[3] A *security-based swap* is defined as a swap that references a security index or a single security or loan.[4]

Although OTC contracts are theoretically customized, many are based on standardized agreements (e.g., the International Swaps and Derivatives Association, Inc. [ISDA] Master Agreement), with individual trade confirmations that provide the customized specifics to the agreement. The basic terms of most deals thus tend to be quite similar.

1. FORWARDS AND FUTURES

A *forward* is a contract that obligates each party to the contract to trade an underlying asset at a specified price at a specified date upcoming. In some respects, most of your first-year Contracts class was devoted to forwards— although I bet the professor never used that word. But a contract signed today to buy wheat or widgets in the future, at a price set today, is a forward.

For example, a foreign exchange (FX) forward involves the exchange of one currency for another, on a future date and at a forward price established today. The winners and losers in this deal will be determined by the actual market (or spot) exchange rate on the future date.

Forward contracts are traded OTC and therefore include exposure to counterparty credit risk. Even in the Dodd-Frank era, forwards are likely to remain customized products that are not cleared or exchange traded.

A *future*, which is a specialized kind of forward, is a standardized contract to purchase or sell an underlying asset in the future at a specified price and date. A futures contract is an agreement between two parties: a short position—the party who agrees to sell a commodity—and a long position—the party who agrees to buy a commodity.

Unlike forwards, futures are exchange-traded derivatives. That means that all trades go through a central clearinghouse, which stands in as the short party on one leg of the transaction, and the long party on the other leg of the transaction. If one party fails to perform, the clearinghouse's central position means the other party does not face any counterparty risk. As already noted, when you trade futures contracts you are required to post some margin to back up your performance on the contracts, which reduces the risk to the clearinghouse.

When you hear about trading in gold, rice, pork bellies, oranges, and so on, it is often in the futures market, where everyone trades the exact same contracts. Like a forward, a future involves agreeing to buy or sell something in the future at a price you are fixing today.

Forwards and futures may be either physically settled or cash settled, just as with options. In a physically settled forward or futures contract, the buyer of the contract receives physical delivery of the underlying commodity or shares on the

---

3. 7 U.S.C. §1a(47)(A).
4. 15 U.S.C. §78c(a)(68).

contract's settlement date. A cash-settled forward or futures contract is settled by the payment from one party to the other of a cash amount equal to the difference between the price specified in the contract and the actual price of the underlying commodity or shares on the contract's settlement date. If you understood expectation damages in your 1L contracts class, you already understand cash settlement.

That said, even physically settled futures contracts are often never actually physically settled. Rather, many physically settled futures contracts do not reach their settlement date, as they are traded throughout the life of the contract and the positions are then closed out just before delivery in what is known as an "offsetting" or "closing" sale. Forwards, as customized, OTC transactions are more apt to involve actual physical delivery of the "underlying."

To take an example, imagine an investor, call him HB, who thinks Bogartco shares are going to rise from their current price of $10. In what is referred to as the "opening purchase," HB enters into a three-month futures contract on Bogartco shares at $15 per share. HB in this instance is speculating that the value of the shares will rise in the next three months to more than $15.

If Bogartco's share price rises to $17 on the future's expiration date, HB will have made $2 per share. If his contract specifies physical delivery, he can take delivery of the shares and sell them for the gain. Alternatively, he could sell the futures contract in the market at the then-current market price in an offsetting or closing sale and realize the same gains. If the contract provided for cash settlement, he would receive $2 per share from his counterparty—the clearinghouse in most cases. The key difference is that under a cash settled contract there is no option to take and hold the shares, if HB so desired.

PROBLEM SET 18.1

1. What benefits are there to standardizing futures contracts?
2. A derivative can provide some information about broader sentiment, which might in turn influence trading in the underlying. Dow Jones Industrial Average futures contracts begin trading on the Chicago Board of Trade at 8:20 a.m. EST, and S&P 500 and Nasdaq 100 futures both open at 8:30 a.m. EST and trade on the Chicago Mercantile Exchange. In all cases this means the futures have been trading for at least an hour before the NYSE opens. If you have access to international markets, trading in S&P 500 futures begins in Tokyo the evening before the market opens in the United States.
3. There two basic uses for derivatives: hedging and speculating. A hedger faces some sort of exposure to the underlying asset. For example, a farmer might use futures to hedge against changes in the value of her crop, particularly to avoid the risk of large price drops. What type of future position would she take? Of course by doing so, she gives up some of the potential upside if prices rise. A speculator is somebody who is

betting on the price of the crop, without any exposure to the underlying. For example, people in $3,000 suits in Chicago and New York typically do not have large fields of growing crops, but they still might buy and sell futures tied to agricultural commodities. There is a vigorous policy debate about whether such traders (a) provide valuable liquidity to derivatives markets or (b) induce excess volatility in commodities markets, which effects food, fuel, and other consumer prices. *See* http://goo.gl/18KNp.

4. A contract for differences (CFD) is similar to a cash-settled futures contract. CFDs give the holder exposure to the change in price of an underlying financial asset without having legal ownership of the asset itself. The cash settlement represents the difference between the underlying price set at the outset of the contract and its market price on the date of the settlement of the contract. CFDs can be long or short. Unlike forwards and futures, CFDs are open-ended, with no fixed settlement date, and, unlike swaps, they can be closed out by the holder on demand.

2. SWAPS

STEPHEN J. LUBBEN, *CREDIT DERIVATIVES AND THE FUTURE OF CHAPTER 11*

81 Am. Bankr. L.J. 405, 408–417 (2007)

A. DERIVATIVES GENERALLY

Financial derivatives are contracts that derive their value from interest rates, the outcome of specific events, or the price of underlying assets such as debt or equities. These contracts have no value in seclusion, but rather derive their value from movements in the value of other more substantive matter. Options, futures, and forwards are all long-recognized types of derivatives.

The heart of the modern derivatives markets was born in the early 1980s with the advent of swap agreements.[5] A swap is a contract between two parties to exchange cash flows at specified intervals. Unlike securities or futures contracts, which are standardized for easy trading on national exchanges, swaps are party-specific bilateral contracts and are thus traded over the counter.

One of the most common swaps is an interest rate swap, where the parties (or "counterparties") agree to exchange a fixed rate cash flow for a floating rate cash flow. The amount of the cash flows is determined by reference to a hypothetical

---

5. *See* Bank One Corp. v. Comm'r, 120 T.C. 174, 186 (2003) ("The origin of the swaps market is generally traced to a currency swap negotiated between the World Bank and IBM in 1981. That transaction involved an exchange of payments in Swiss francs for payments in deutschmarks. The first interest rate swap was negotiated with the Student Loan Marketing Association in 1982.").

or "notional" amount of money that is never actually exchanged between the parties.

For example, assume two parties swap a fixed 4% payment for the three-month London Interbank Offered Rate (LIBOR)[6] plus 150 basis points,[7] based on a $100 million notional amount.[8] If LIBOR starts at 2.5% and rises to 5%, the cash flows on this swap look like this:

FIXED owes FLOATING $4 million
FLOATING owes FIXED $6.5 million
FLOATING pays FIXED $2.5 million [9]

By entering into this swap, the fixed rate payer has essentially replaced its interest rate risk with the credit risk of the floating rate payer, perhaps because it has a corresponding $100 million floating rate loan obligation. If the credit exposure issues appear acute, the risks of default are often balanced by posting collateral [i.e., margin], typically in the form of government securities. ISDA estimated that about $1.34 trillion of collateral was in use at the end of 2006.

B.   CREDIT DERIVATIVES

Credit derivatives are a class of privately negotiated contracts designed with the express purpose of transferring credit risk from one party to another. As with other derivatives, credit derivatives do not themselves involve a credit relationship, but rather look to the credit consequences of other financial instruments or conditions to find their value.

In June of 2001, the first time the trade group ISDA conducted surveys of credit derivatives, the outstanding notional amount of credit derivatives was just over $631 billion. By June 2005, only four years later, the notional amount of outstanding credit default swaps, the key credit derivative instrument, stood at more than $12 trillion—almost a twenty-fold increase. About forty percent of outstanding credit derivatives are held by national banks, whose holdings are equally split between buyer and seller positions. Emerging market credit

---

6. This is the rate of interest at which banks can borrow funds from other banks in the London interbank market. It is commonly used as a reference floating interest rate in swaps.

7. 0.01%= 1 basis point. Because swaps typically have net present values equal to zero at inception—that is, the swap is balanced and no payment is owing in either direction—the example implies a LIBOR rate of 2.5%. *See* Linda M. Beale, *Book-Tax Conformity and the Corporate Tax Shelter Debate: Assessing the Proposed Section 475 Mark-To-Market Safe Harbor*, 24 Va. Tax Rev. 301, 389–90 (2004).

8. For simplicity, I assume all payments are made annually, but actual practice varies by jurisdiction. In the United States fixed payments are often made semi-annually and floating payments are made quarterly. The numbers in the example also do not take into account date conventions. For example, in the United States many swaps trade under an actual/360 day count convention.

9. Conversely, if the LIBOR rate fell below 2.5%, so that the floating payment was less than 4% in total, FIXED would make payments to FLOATING equal to the difference in the two rates.

derivatives, the newest segment of the market, are expected to exceed \$650 billion by this year.

The speedy growth of the credit derivatives market can be seen as a further extension of a larger, ongoing trend toward disaggregation of financial obligations, albeit one that is just now approaching the level of development on the default side that has been seen in the interest rate swap markets for over a decade. While syndication of loans and securitization of receivables have long provided ways for the initial lender to reduce their exposure to the debtor, the subsequent investor still acquires something more than pure credit or default risk, while the initial lender necessarily incurs a corresponding reduction in its claim against the debtor. Credit derivatives, on the other hand, allow for the sale of the default risk of a loan separate from any other element of ownership. In addition, the growth of credit markets has allowed for "shorting" of bonds, something that was often impossible before-hand due to the limited liquidity of the corporate bond markets. Credit derivatives also allow investors an opportunity to invest in debt that trades in foreign markets without bearing currency risk.

As noted, the most important credit derivative instrument is the credit default swap, also known as a single-name credit default swap. This type of swap is a contract covering the risk that a specified debtor defaults. One party (the "protection seller") acquires the credit risk associated with a debt or class of debts in exchange for an annual fee from the counterparty (the "protection buyer"). The debtor on the referenced obligation is not a party to the swap, and in most cases is unaware of the transaction.

If the reference obligation goes into default, the protection buyer receives a payment meant to compensate it for its losses.[10] More specifically, the protection seller's payment obligation is triggered by the occurrence of a "credit event" with regard to a specified class of obligations incurred by the reference entity. Commonly used credit events include "bankruptcy,"[11] "failure to pay,"[12] and "restructuring."[13] Swaps written on sovereign or emerging markets debt add

---

10. Whether a credit event has occurred is sometimes subject to dispute, as when Argentina announced a debt exchange in 2001. *Eternity Global Master Fund Ltd.* v. *Morgan Guar. Trust Co.*, 375 F.3d 168 (2d Cir. 2004); *see also* Stephen J. Choi & G. Mitu Gulati, *Contract as Statute*, 104 Mich. L. Rev. 1129, 1142–44 (2006).

11. ISDA, 2003 ISDA Credit Derivatives Definitions §4.2.

12. *Id.*§4.5. "Failure to Pay" is defined, in part, as the failure of the reference entity to make "payments in an aggregate amount of not less than the Payment Requirement." "Payment Requirement" is a term that the parties can define, but otherwise defaults to obligations of at least \$1 million. *Id.*§4.8(d).

13. *Id.*§4.7. The restructuring must relate to debt in excess of the "Default Requirement," which is set at \$10 million unless the parties agree otherwise. *Id.*§4.8(a). The definition of restructuring is not uniform among jurisdictions; for example, in the North American corporate market the definition is usually modified—and thus referred to as "Modified Restructuring"—by electing additional limitations on the maturity and transferability of the debt that can be delivered under the swap. *Id.*§2.32; *see also* Frank Packer & Haibin Zhu, *Contractual Terms and CDS Pricing*, Bis Q. Rev. (Mar. 2005) available at http://www.bis.org/publ/qtrpdf/r_qt0503.htm.

provisions regarding repudiations or debt moratoriums.[14] In the North American and European corporate markets, these events typically must occur with respect to "borrowed money"—effectively any obligation owed to voluntary creditors of the reference entity or its subsidiaries, if the parent guaranteed the subsidiaries' obligations—in excess of the $1 million and $10 million limitations built into the definitions of failure to pay and restructuring, respectively.

[Sometimes] the swap will call for "physical settlement" upon the occurrence of a credit event, meaning that the buyer will deliver a defaulted bond to the seller in exchange for payment of the full face value of the bond. Unlike insurance, credit default swaps do not require proof of actual loss, so the buyer can purchase a bond post-default and deliver it to the seller.[15]

The types of obligations that can be delivered to settle the swap are typically set forth in the documentation, although market practice does tend to give the protection buyer a choice within a range of debt instruments. This gives rise to the so-called "cheapest to deliver" option in a triggered swap; namely, the ability of a buyer to maximize recovery under the swap by purchasing the least valuable debt instrument that will satisfy the contractual provisions of the swap. In the North American and European corporate markets, swaps regularly allow for the delivery of any bond or loan issued by the reference entity, provided that, among other things, the obligation is not subordinated, is not bearer paper, and does not mature more than thirty years from the settlement date.

In a credit default swap transaction, the protection buyer gives up the risk of default by the debtor and takes on the risk of concurrent default by both the protection seller and the underlying debtor. While the risk of mutual default is likely remote, especially given the strong credit quality of many swap dealers, it is not inconceivable that a major corporate default could cause one or two financial institutions severe financial distress. The protection seller takes on the default risk of the debtor, as if it had lent money to the debtor. For this reason, the seller is sometimes described as a "synthetic" lender, albeit a short-term lender, as the duration of swaps tends to extend for no more than a few years; whereas, a bond could last twenty or more years.[16]

---

14. ISDA, 2003 ISDA Credit Derivatives Definitions §4.6.

15. INSOL International, Credit Derivatives in Restructurings 12 (2006). This might occur if the buyer used the credit default swap to hedge an illiquid debt, such as a bank loan with transfer restrictions, or simply because the buyer was making a speculative bet on the reference debtor's credit worthiness. Cf. N.Y. Ins. Law §3401 (McKinney 2007) ("No contract or policy of insurance on property made or issued in this state, or made or issued upon any property in this state, shall be enforceable except for the benefit of some person having an insurable interest in the property insured. In this article, 'insurable interest' shall include any lawful and substantial economic interest in the safety or preservation of property from loss, destruction or pecuniary damage.").

16. According to one industry source, "the most liquid CDS is the five-year contract, followed by the three-year.... The fact that a physical asset does not need to be sourced means that it is generally easier to transact in large round sizes with CDS." Dominic O'Kane, et al., Lehman Brothers, The Lehman Brothers Guide to Exotic Credit Derivatives 6 (2003), available at http://investinginbonds.com/assets/files/LehmanExoticCredDerivs.pdf.

Because of General Motors' recent financial difficulties, pricing information for its credit default swaps has been readily available. Table 2 illustrates the information conveyed by this new market in a firm's credit prospects. Because prices for long-term coverage are lower than mid-term protection, the market apparently believes that General Motors faces the biggest challenges in the next three or four years, after which the risks apparently moderate. By early 2007, General Motors' prospects had substantially improved, at least in the market's eyes, and five-year CDS spreads had shrunk to just over 330 basis points.

TABLE 2
General Motors CDS Spreads

Spread Over Risk Free Rate; As of March 30, 2006

	1 Year	2 Year	3 Year	5 Year	7 Year	10 Year
Spread (in basis points)	967.24	1199.32	1145.15	1083.29	1040.54	1012.21

Source: www.markit.com.

Credit default swaps are used for speculation, hedging credit risk, and as building blocks in creating more complex financial products. For example, a credit default swap can be used to construct a synthetic asset securitization, where the risk of loss is transferred to the special purpose vehicle but all other aspects of ownership remain with the originator.

More recently, credit default swaps have moved from simple, single-name products to swaps that look to groups of reference entities. One product—known as an "nth to default" swap—protects the buyer against the nth default to occur among a group of debtors and then terminates. Similarly, swaps written on indexes give the protection buyer a hedge against a pool of representative debtors with similar credit profiles.

For example, the Dow Jones CDX IG portfolio consists of 125 North American investment grade bond issuers, each equally weighted in the index. Assume a swap written on this index with notional amount of $100 million. Upon a default of a single index element, the protection buyer would deliver bonds with a par value of $800,000 to the protection seller in exchange for a payment of $800,000 in cash.[17] The transaction continues until a predetermined "roll date," when the index is adjusted and reissued with a revised group of 125 issuers. Similar products exist for the foreign and high-yield markets.

The sudden growth of the credit derivative market has exposed several areas of structural underdevelopment, at least two of which are important for present purposes. First, even when it works as described, this market is rather opaque and is arguably not truly a "market" in the conventional sense.

Consisting entirely of privately negotiated bilateral contracts, one of the oft cited benefits of the market is the ability of lenders to hedge or diversify their credit exposure without incurring any relationship costs with respect to the

---

17. $800,000 = (1/125)($100 million).

borrower. Recently, however, it has become widely known that many credit default swaps were assigned to new protection buyers without the prior consent of the seller. Under the terms of the ISDA Master Agreement,[18] the prior written consent of the other party is required when its counterparty in a trade wishes to assign its position in a trade to a third party. However, this non-conforming practice has apparently been tolerated in the community. Thus, upon a chapter 11 filing, it may not be clear which creditors are protected from losses, even among the parties to swaps. ISDA has moved to address regulatory concerns regarding assignments, so the problem of unauthorized transfers should hopefully disappear from the market. The larger question of which creditors have bought or sold protection will loom large in chapter 11 cases in the future.

Second, the rapid growth of the credit derivatives market has recently led to supply and demand problems upon a default. After the recent chapter 11 filing of automotive parts manufacturer Delphi Automotive, $2 billion of bonds were said to be in circulation when it filed for bankruptcy. However, the notional amount of outstanding derivatives was more than $20 billion, which initially had the explicable, although still strange, effect of driving up the market prices of the bonds just as Delphi filed for chapter 11. ISDA has stepped in to mitigate this problem through a series of "protocols," which were successfully deployed in not only the Delphi case but also in connection with other recent chapter 11 cases. Essentially, these protocols use an auction mechanism to set a price for the debtor's bonds, and then use that price to allow settlement of index credit default swaps without need for actual delivery of bonds.[19] Removing index swaps from the mix reduces but does not eliminate the supply and demand effects on the bond markets.

---

18. Most of the derivatives in the global derivatives market are documented under ISDA documentation. The ISDA Master Agreement, the most current version of which is the 2002 ISDA Master Agreement, is a standard agreement, used in the industry, to provide a set of default terms for a series of derivative transactions between a set of counterparties. A "schedule" is attached to the Master Agreement to account for party-specific terms of the deal. The economic terms of individual derivative transactions are reflected in "confirmation" term sheets, which are deemed to be part of the single Master Agreement between the parties, somewhat like the schedules of equipment used in long-term equipment leases. Each confirmation will incorporate by reference a relevant set of ISDA definitions. In the credit derivatives context, this is typically the 2003 ISDA Credit Derivatives Definitions. Also commonly used are documents related to credit support, which are used when parties are of differing credit quality and provide for the lower credit quality party to provide collateral to reduce the credit risk associated with the transaction. *See generally* www.isda.org; *see also* Ursa Minor Ltd. v. Aon Fin. Prods., Inc., No. 00 Civ. 2474 (AGS), 2000 U.S. Dist. LEXIS 10166, at *6–8 (S.D.N.Y. July 21, 2000).

19. While traditionally these settlement procedures have been used only in conjunction with index products, the process was recently extended to single name swaps. See Press Release, Creditex and Markit Announce Results of Dura Credit Event Fixing for Defaulted Bonds (Nov. 28, 2006), available at http://www.creditex.com/press/dura.pdf. [The more recent practice is to cash settle CDS contracts.]

As noted in the excerpt, interest rate swaps often rely on LIBOR as the basis for the floating rate leg of the trade. LIBOR is also used as a base rate in other floating rate securities, such as syndicated bank loans and asset securitization.

LIBOR is an interest rate set in London among large banks. Every day a group of leading banks submits the interest rates at which they are willing to lend to other large financial institutions. They suggest rates in 10 currencies covering 15 different loan terms, ranging from overnight to 12 months.

The most important rate is the three-month dollar LIBOR. The rates submitted are what the banks estimate they would pay other banks to borrow dollars for three months if they borrowed money on the day the rate is being set. Then an average is calculated.

The problem is that during the 2008 financial crisis traders at several banks conspired to influence the final average rate that results by agreeing among themselves to submit rates that were either higher or lower than their actual estimates. Barclays traders reportedly first manipulated LIBOR a few years before the crisis so that their colleagues could make profits on derivatives pegged to the base rate.

During the crisis, large banks allegedly moved LIBOR in whatever direction would help the banks survive on any given day. For example, some banks manipulated LIBOR downward by telling LIBOR calculators that it could borrow money at relatively inexpensive rates to make the bank appear less risky. The result was that trillions of dollars of financial instruments were priced at the wrong rate or at least at a rate artificially created by bank insiders.

More than a half-dozen global banks have paid more than $10 billion to settle charges with regulators and law enforcement agencies that they conspired to rig LIBOR. Two former Rabobank traders were sentenced to prison in early 2016 in the first U.S. criminal trial arising from global investigations into the manipulation of LIBOR. The other person to be sentenced to date is a former UBS AG and Citigroup trader currently serving an 11-year sentence after being convicted in a London trial involving yen LIBOR manipulation.

The Second Circuit recently ruled that banks could face possible antitrust liability for their involvement in LIBOR manipulation.

* * *

In recent years, most CDS contracts, of all types, have moved to cash settlement. As with most derivatives, CDS contracts that are not centrally cleared involve counterparty risk.

In addition to counterparty risk, any swap transaction might involve *basis risk*. This risk arises from a disconnect between what the swap measures and the risk the swap buyer is trying to hedge. In some cases, that risk might be another swap, as we will see below.

AON FINANCIAL PRODUCTS, INC. v. SOCIÉTÉ GÉNÉRALE

476 F.3d 90
United States Court of Appeals, Second Circuit.
Feb. 5, 2007.

SACK, Circuit Judge:

On August 8, 2000, the plaintiffs, Aon Corp. and its subsidiary, Aon Financial Products, Inc. ("AFP", together "Aon"), brought suit in the United States District Court for the Southern District of New York seeking recovery in breach of contract against Société Générale ("SG") under a $10 million credit default swap agreement between them dated March 8, 1999 (the "Aon/SG CDS contract").

The Aon/SG CDS contract provides that if a "Credit Event" occurs before the defined "Termination Date" of the agreement and Aon notifies SG of that Credit Event, then SG must pay Aon $10 million. Aon contends that a Credit Event occurred when the Government Service Insurance System ("GSIS"), an agency of the Philippine Government, defaulted on a surety bond that GSIS had issued to cover investments in a project with respect to which Bear Stearns International Limited ("BSIL") later made a loan. BSIL, in an effort to protect itself against the risk of GSIS defaulting on the bond, entered into a Credit Default Swap Agreement with Aon (the "BSIL/Aon CDS contract"). In a separate suit, the district court determined that a Credit Event occurred under the BSIL/Aon CDS contract when GSIS defaulted on the surety bond.

BACKGROUND

This case arises out of one of a series of transactions related to the financing of a condominium complex in the Philippines. In 1999, BSIL agreed to loan Ecobel Land, Inc. ("Ecobel") $9.3 million to build the condominiums. Ecobel was obligated under this agreement to repay BSIL $10 million on March 7, 2000. As a condition precedent to that loan, BSIL required that Ecobel procure a surety bond from GSIS that guaranteed repayment of the full $10 million in the event that Ecobel defaulted on its loan. GSIS then purportedly transferred to BSIL as obligee a $10 million GSIS surety bond covering Ecobel's borrowings for the condominium project dated March 11, 1998, but apparently issued on February 5, 1999 (the "Surety Bond"), which listed Ecobel as principal and Philippine Veterans Bank as obligee. Section 9 of the statute establishing GSIS states that "the government of the Republic of the Philippines . . . guarantees the fulfillment of the obligations of [GSIS] when and as they shall become due."

In order to protect itself against the risk of GSIS defaulting on the Surety Bond, BSIL entered into the BSIL/Aon CDS contract on February 4, 1999. According to the agreement, Aon promised to pay BSIL $10 million upon the occurrence of a "Credit Event," which the contract defined as a "Failure to Pay," that is, "the failure by [GSIS] to make, when due, any payments under the

Obligations for whatever reason or cause."[20] The only "Obligation" referred to in the agreement was the Surety Bond. For this credit protection, BSIL paid Aon $425,000.

To reduce its own risk exposure, on February 9, 1999, Aon entered into a separate credit default swap agreement with SG. In it, SG promised to pay Aon $10 million upon the occurrence of a "Credit Event," defined as one of five occurrences: a "Failure to Pay," a "Sovereign Event," a "Cross Default," a "Repudiation," or a "Restructuring." But whereas the BSIL/Aon CDS contract defined "Reference Entity," whose obligations were the subject of the swap, as GSIS and any successors and assigns, the Aon/SG CDS contract defined "Reference Entity" as "Republic of Philippines and any successors." Similarly, while the "Reference Obligation," which was the subject of the BSIL/Aon CDS contract, was GSIS's $10 million Surety Bond, the "Reference Obligation" of the Aon/SG CDS contract was a $500 million Republic of Philippines treasury bond (US718286AE71, coupon rate 8.875%, maturing on April 15, 2008). For the credit protection under the Aon/SG CDS contract, Aon paid SG $328,000, nearly $100,000 less than the amount that BSIL had paid Aon for protection under the BSIL/Aon CDS contract.

About one year later, in March 2000, Ecobel defaulted on its BSIL loan. On March 9, 2000, Bankers Trustee Company, Ltd. ("Bankers"), to whom BSIL had assigned its rights under the various agreements relating to the loan, notified Aon that it had received a letter from GSIS stating that it did not intend to pay Bankers on the bond because it had not been appropriately authorized on GSIS's behalf. Aon responded the following day that it would not pay Bankers under the BSIL/Aon CDS contract because GSIS's statement that it intended to refuse to honor the Surety Bond did not constitute a "Credit Event" under the BSIL/Aon agreement. Aon then initiated a declaratory judgment action in the United States District Court for the Northern District of Illinois seeking clarification of its rights as against BSIL and SG under the various agreements.

Before the Illinois litigation was resolved, however, BSIL's assignees filed suit against Aon in the United States District Court for the Southern District of New York. The district court granted summary judgment in the action in favor of the assignees. The court concluded that the BSIL/Aon CDS contract specifically defined "Credit Event" as a failure *by GSIS,* the Reference Entity, to pay under the Surety Bond "'for whatever reason or cause,'" and that GSIS's default clearly satisfied that condition. The court noted that in the BSIL/Aon CDS contract, Aon

---

20. The document that defines "Credit Event," "Failure to Pay," and other relevant terms is known in the industry as the "confirmation." Parties to credit derivative swaps enter into a standard form "Master Agreement" created by the International Swaps and Derivatives Association, Inc. ("ISDA"), which governs the legal and credit relationship between the parties and other aspects of the agreement. Supplemental documents, such as confirmations, set forth economic terms and other transaction-specific modifications to the Master Agreement and other standard documents. The provisions of the BSIL/Aon CDS contract and the Aon/SG CDS contract that are at issue here are both contained in "confirmations," which incorporate materially similar versions of the ISDA Master Agreement.

had waived the defense of any illegality of the GSIS Surety Bond. The court concluded that Aon "bore the risk of non-payment by GSIS, for 'whatever reason or cause,' including a justifiable refusal to pay."

DISCUSSION

CDS agreements are . . . significantly different from insurance contracts. As *amicus* correctly points out, they "do not, and are not meant to, indemnify the buyer of protection against loss. Rather, CDS contracts allow parties to 'hedge' risk by buying and selling risks at different prices and with varying degrees of correlation." Br. of *amicus curiae* Int'l Swaps and Derivatives Ass'n, Inc. (ISDA), at 7 (footnote omitted). Aon bought from BSIL the risk of a "Credit Event" as defined by the BSIL/Aon CDS contract. With the Aon/SG CDS contract, Aon hedged the risk that it bought from BSIL by selling to SG the risk of a "Credit Event" as defined by the Aon/SG CDS contract. But the risk transferred *to* Aon and the risk transferred *by* it were not necessarily identical. The terms of each credit swap agreement independently define the risk being transferred.

To decide whether GSIS's failure to pay on the Surety Bond because GSIS took the position that it was not a legally binding obligation, an event that constituted a Credit Event as defined in the BSIL/Aon CDS contract, also constituted a "Credit Event" as defined in the Aon/SG CDS contract—the issue presently before us—we look first to the language of the contract. If it is unambiguous—which we think that it is—then "we are required to give effect to the contract as written."

The Aon/SG CDS contract defines "Credit Event" as, *inter alia,* a "Sovereign Event," which is

> a condition which is created by or results from any act or failure to act by the government of the Reference Entity or any agency or regulatory authority thereof, including the central bank of the Reference Entity, that has the effect ***97** of declaring a moratorium (whether de facto or de jure) on, or causing a failure to honour any obligation relating to, or cancelling or generally causing material changes to the terms and conditions of, any obligation issued by the government of the Reference Entity or the central bank of the Reference Entity.

The contract defines "Reference Entity" as "Republic of Philippines and any successors." Thus, for purposes of our analysis, after redacting inapplicable language, the Aon/SG CDS Contract provides that an event is a "Sovereign Event" if it is "a condition . . . created by or result[ing] from any act or failure to act by the government of [the Republic of Philippines and any Successors] or any agency or regulatory authority [thereof] . . . that has the effect of . . . causing a failure to honour any obligation relating to . . . any obligation issued by the government of [the Republic of Philippines]."

***

A literal reading of the Sovereign Event definition might suggest that the "act or failure to act" by the government of the Philippines that "had the effect of causing [the] failure [of GSIS] to honour" the Surety Bond was something other than the failure to pay on the Surety Bond itself. Hypothetically, for example, the "act" might have been the issuance of GSIS's letter to BSIL's assignees denying liability. Even if that were what Aon's complaint said, the argument would fail. The letter was, to be sure, an "act." But it did not *create* a separate "condition" which in turn *caused* the default on the Surety Bond.

Moreover, an "act or failure to act" in the context of a "Sovereign Event" seems to refer to such large-scale events as the restructuring of the Sovereign's— i.e., the government's—debt, taken in its capacity as a sovereign. The act of debt restructuring by a sovereign may well cause—indeed may be expected to cause—a general "condition" throughout the country (e.g., currency devaluation, restriction on exports of U.S. dollars, and the like) that in turn results in one or more defaults on one or more particular obligations against which an entity doing business with or within the country would want to protect itself. *Cf. Eternity Global,* 375 F.3d at 170 (addressing the operation of CDS contracts where "the government of the Republic of Argentina, in the grip of economic crisis, initiated a 'voluntary debt exchange'"). There was no such act or resulting condition here.

. . . And we can perceive of no basis for concluding that the district court's decision in *Ursa Minor* that there was a "Failure to Pay" Credit Event under the BSIL/Aon CDS contract implies that there was a "Sovereign Event" Credit Event under the Aon/SG CDS contract.

We therefore conclude that GSIS's default was not a "Sovereign Event" as that term is used in the Aon/SG CDS contract.

"Failure to Pay"

The district court considered only one of the five kinds of Credit Events referred to in the Aon/SG CDS contract—the Sovereign Event. Finding that there had been such a Credit Event under the terms of the Aon/SG CDS contract, the court declined to consider whether the events also constituted a "Failure to Pay," which is also one of the defined Credit Events under that agreement.

"Although we ordinarily will not review an issue the district court did not decide, whether we do so or not is a matter within our discretion." *Chertkova v. Connecticut General Life Ins. Co.,* 92 F.3d 81, 88 (2d Cir.1996) (citing *Singleton v. Wulff,* 428 U.S. 106, 120–21, 96 S.Ct. 2868, 49 L.Ed.2d 826 (1976)). We think this case an appropriate one for exercising that discretion. Apparently as a result of the district court's conclusion that a Sovereign Event had occurred, the parties devote little attention to the Failure to Pay issue in their briefs to us. But the parties amply presented arguments on that issue to the district court. In fact, there, the parties focused on the Failure to Pay language rather than the Sovereign Event provision upon which the district court eventually decided the motions. The interpretation of the unambiguous terms of a contract is, moreover, a matter of law that we may properly evaluate and decide ourselves.

As noted above, the Aon/SG CDS contract defines the "Reference Entity" as the "Republic of Philippines and any successors." Under the Aon/SG CDS contract, a *"Failure to Pay* means . . . the failure by the Reference Entity [*the Republic of Philippines* and any Successors] to make, when due, any payments equal to or exceeding the Payment Requirement (if any) under any Obligations." An "Obligation" under that agreement is: "With respect to the [Republic of Philippines], any obligation (whether present or future, contingent or otherwise, as principal or surety or otherwise) for the payment or repayment of money." The Reference Obligation is identified as:

Issuer/Borrower: Republic of Philippines

Maturity: April 15, 2008

Coupon. 8.8750%

Original Issue Amount: USD 500,000,000

The Payment Requirement is "USD 5,000,000 or its equivalent in any other currency at the time of the Credit Event."

Aon argues that GSIS itself qualifies as the "Reference Entity" of the Aon/SG CDS contract, that is, that "Republic of Philippines" includes GSIS. GSIS's default on the Surety Bond, therefore, is a "Failure to Pay" by the Reference Entity on an Obligation of the Reference Entity. Aon contends that because the ISDA Credit Derivatives Definitions, incorporated into the Aon/SG CDS contract, define "Sovereign" as "any state, political subdivision or government, or any agency, instrumentality, ministry, department or other authority (including, without limiting the foregoing, the central bank) thereof," the term "Republic of Philippines" must also include "any agency" of the state. We disagree.

It is clear from the face of the Aon/SG CDS contract that "Republic of Philippines" does not include GSIS or other government agencies like it. There is no language in the Reference Entity definition, or anywhere else in the agreement as we read it, suggesting that it does, or indicating that it incorporates the ISDA definition of "Sovereign." To incorporate that definition of "Sovereign" into the definition of "Reference Entity," we would expect the parties to use that word, "Sovereign," in the relevant portion of the contract. They did not. Rather, they use the words "Republic of Philippines." Where the contract uses the word "Sovereign," in the term "Sovereign Event," by contrast, the contract does clearly mean to incorporate the ISDA definition. "Sovereign Event" is the only term in the Aon/SG CDS contract that refers not only to the Reference Entity, but to "the Reference Entity or any agency or regulatory authority thereof, including the central bank of the Reference Entity."

If we were to credit Aon's argument as to the expansive meaning of "Republic of Philippines," it would follow that any CDS contract listing a sovereign nation as a Reference Entity will be incorporating the ISDA definition of "Sovereign" without using the term, or at least that the contract is ambiguous in that regard. We are given, and ourselves see, no reason to do so.

Instead, we look to Philippine law for guidance about the distinction between the Republic of the Philippines and its agencies and instrumentalities. . . . Before the district court, SG offered uncontested expert evidence that, under Philippine law, GSIS is considered a juridical entity distinct from the Republic. We conclude that, as a matter of Philippine law, GSIS is a separate juridical entity from the Republic of the Philippines. As such, GSIS is not the "Republic of Philippines"; its obligations are not the Republic of the Philippines' obligations; and a failure by GSIS to make a payment on its obligations is not equivalent to the failure of the Republic of the Philippines to make a payment on its obligations.

One might argue . . . although the plaintiffs do not, that the Republic's statutory guarantee of GSIS's debt was an Obligation of the Reference Entity, which the Republic failed to pay when the Surety Bond came due on March 7, 2000, and that this failure to pay was a Credit Event, triggering SG's payment obligations under the contract. This argument would also fail. To trigger SG's payment obligations, a Credit Event must occur before the Termination Date of the CDS agreement, March 31, 2000. But Aon did not send a Notice and Demand to the Government of the Republic of the Philippines until April 3, 2000, three days after the Termination Date of the Aon/SG CDS contract. And the Republic of the Philippines did not deny Aon's demand until April 14, 2000, two weeks after the Termination Date. Because the Republic's denial of liability did not occur before the Termination Date, it cannot constitute a Credit Event under the contract.

We therefore conclude that neither the default, which constituted a Failure to Pay under the BSIL/Aon CDS contract, nor the Republic's failure to honor its alleged statutory obligation, constituted a Failure to Pay under the Aon/SG CDS contract. For the same reasons, neither event constituted a "Repudiation." They similarly do not satisfy the other definitions of Credit Event enumerated in the Aon/SG CDS contract.

Credit Event Notice

Although not central to the result we reach, we note that the contract also provides that SG is obligated to pay Aon only after Aon serves SG with a "Credit Event Notice" and a demand for payment.

The district court concluded that Aon's March 22, 2000, letter constituted a Credit Event Notice. We disagree. The Aon/SG CDS contract defines "Credit Event Notice" as "an irrevocable notice (which may be oral, including by telephone) to the parties and the Calculation Agent that describes the occurrence of a Credit Event on or after the Effective Date and on or prior to the Scheduled Termination Date." In the March 22 letter, which does not use the term "Credit Event Notice," Aon informed SG that GSIS had declined to make payments on the Surety Bond and that BSIL had made a demand on Aon pursuant to the BSIL/Aon CDS agreement. The letter outlined Aon's position.

To be a "Credit Event Notice," the action taken must be "irrevocable." The March 22 letter was not irrevocable. Aon went to great lengths to explain in the letter the circumstances under which it would rescind its contention that SG "owed" Aon and would agree that no Credit Event had occurred under either CDS contract and that neither Aon nor SG was obligated to pay under them. This letter was not a Credit Event Notice and therefore could not have triggered SG's payment obligations under the contract.

CONCLUSION

As a matter of law and under the unambiguous language of the Aon/SG CDS contract, no Credit Event occurred thereunder and SG therefore did not breach that agreement by declining to pay Aon thereunder. We therefore reverse the judgment of the district court and enter judgment in favor of SG.

In addition to the two types of swaps described in the Lubben excerpt—interest rate and credit default swaps—currency swaps are another common type of swap, used by many businesses that operate internationally.

Like an FX forward, a *cross-currency swap* consists of the exchange of principal amounts (based on today's spot rate) and interest payments between counterparties. Unlike a forward, however, a cross-currency swap involves multiple exchanges of interest rather than a single exchange of interest at the end (as in an FX forward), as well as the exchange of principal at maturity. The final principal exchange reverses an initial principal exchange, which makes FX swaps unlike other swaps where the notional amount never changes hand. Thus, FX swaps can be viewed as FX collateralized borrowing and lending.

For example, consider a firm that receives USD interest and pays EUR interest under a currency swap. The front and back exchanges of principal amounts are based on the current spot rate, which means the profit or loss on the transaction (assuming no counterparty default) turns on the intermediate cash flows. The Euro cash flows are economically equivalent to issuing a Euro bond (as those are paid out by the firm); the USD cash flows are equivalent to investing in a USD bond, as they are received by the firm.

If the firm has engaged in USD borrowing, the swap converts the USD loan into a EUR loan. The firm pays interest on its loan in USD, but receives a corresponding payment under the swap that it can pass on to creditors.

If the swap is paired with a EUR investment, it converts the EUR asset into a USD asset. The asset throws off cash flows in EUR, which the firm then uses to pay its obligations under the swap, while the firm receives the USD cash flows from the swap.

Of course, these swaps can be used for currency speculation, too.

The examples given thus far have focused on "fixed for fixed" exchanges of currencies, known as a currency or cross-currency swap. A *cross-currency basis swap* is a contract with both legs of the swap linked to floating rates indices. For example, the three-month (3M) U.S. LIBOR for the U.S. leg of a trade versus 3M EURIBOR for the foreign leg of the trade.

A *basis swap* is an interest rate swap with two floating rate legs. In the United States, the prime rate has historically been about 300 basis points above the federal funds target rate and is used extensively as a reference for loans such as home equity loans, credit cards, and car and student loans. A prime/LIBOR basis swap is an exchange of (netted) cash flows where the prime leg is tied to the prime rate and the LIBOR leg is tied to a three-month LIBOR. Such a swap would be useful to a U.S. bank that funds itself in LIBOR-priced assets but makes loans that generate cash flows tied to the prime rate.

A cross-currency basis swap then combines a basis swap with a currency swap.

As with LIBOR, there have been allegations that the world's largest financial institutions conspired to manipulate the foreign exchange market as far back as 2003. The conspiracy allegedly affected dozens of pairs—the value of one currency versus another—including seven pairs with the highest market volume. The global investigation into whether the $5 trillion-a-day forex market was rigged has led to dozens of firings and prompted U.S. and U.K. authorities to impose more than $10 billion in fines on some of the world's largest banks. Some traders who were fired have maintained that they lost their jobs unfairly, saying they engaged in practices that were well understood by their superiors. Several have filed unfair dismissal claims with London employment tribunals.

3.   EQUITY DERIVATIVES

Options, which we covered in Chapter 17, are the most common equity derivatives because they directly grant the holder the right to buy or sell equity at a predetermined value. More complex equity derivatives include equity index swaps, equity swaps (such as total return swaps), and others.

Equity derivatives are typically divided between *"delta one" products* and products that have an optionlike payoff structure, which can accelerate in a nonlinear manner. Delta is the ratio of the change in the fair market value of a derivative to a small change in the fair market value of the number of shares of the equity security referenced by the derivative. The higher a derivative's delta, the better its fair market value tracks the fair market value of the underlying and the more economically equivalent it is to the underlying. "Delta one" refers to derivatives in which a change in the value of the underlying asset results in a change of the same, or nearly the same, proportion in the value of the derivative.[21] Some examples of delta one derivatives include equity swaps, forwards, futures, CFDs, and total return swaps. They all exhibit a linear relationship with the underlying.

In a basic *equity swap*, if the equity referenced in the trade confirmation has risen since the swap's execution or previous "measurement date," the "equity amount payer" pays to the "equity amount receiver" an amount equal to the value of that increase multiplied by the number of shares specified in the transaction confirmation. Conversely, if the value of underlying equity has declined, the "equity amount receiver" pays the "equity amount payer" an amount equal to the value of that decrease, again multiplied by the number of shares specified in the transaction confirmation.

The following excerpt briefly introduces *total return swaps*, one of the most common types of equity swaps.

STEPHEN J. LUBBEN, *THE BANKRUPTCY CODE WITHOUT SAFE HARBORS*

84 Am. Bankr. L.J. 123, 131–132 (2010)

[I]magine that Lehman Brothers has intermediated a total-return swap on a million shares of BOGARTCO stock where Party A receives and Lehman pays the BOGARTCO return. BOGARTCO shares are currently trading at $40. As the total return payer, Lehman makes payments to Party A equal to the cash flows (any dividend payments on the BOGARTCO stock) plus any appreciation on the reference asset (the BOGARTCO shares). The total return receiver pays a floating interest rate, generally one of the LIBOR rates plus some additional amount, termed a spread, and any depreciation on the reference asset. The total return payer (Lehman in the top transaction on Figure 2) realizes the same returns as if it had sold the reference asset short. Meanwhile, the total return receiver (Party A) realizes the same returns as if it owned the reference asset, and is said to be "long" in this transaction. But Party A never actually owns BOGARTCO shares in any legal sense.

Because it is obligated only to make a series of payments based on the return of BOGARTO, and is not purchasing the underlying shares from Lehman, Party A's investment in BOGARTCO is leveraged. For example, if Party A pays the 3-month LIBOR rate plus 100 basis points, it has effectively purchased stock and simultaneously financed the investment in the BOGARTCO shares by borrowing at the 3-month LIBOR rate plus 1%.

---

21. Somewhere in the recesses of your mind, you might recall that the Greek letter delta (Δ) is often used to symbolize change or the slope of a line. A slope of one would indicate a one-to-one relationship between x and y.

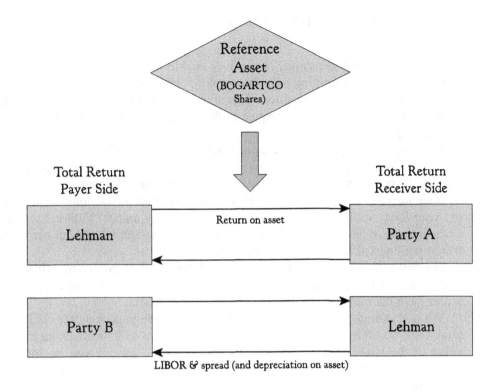

FIGURE 2
Total Return Swap Transaction

In the hypothetical, imagine that at the same time, Party B pays the return of BOGARTCO and Lehman receives the return of BOGARTCO for some period of time, during which Lehman pays Party B a floating interest rate payment, say LIBOR plus 50 basis points. Consequently, Lehman would earn 50 basis points, which is the difference in the spread between the two variable interest rate legs of these transactions.

Although the example described above involves a cash-settled total return swap, some total return swaps are physically settled. In a physically settled total return swap, the short party under the swap (the total return payer) provides shares to its counterparty, in place of the cash payments described in the excerpt.

In all cases, the total return receiver pays an initial amount to the total return payer at the inception of the transaction. This payment functions as a loan from the receiver to the payer, and is often used to fund the payer's purchase of hedging shares. The initial amount exchanged is therefore often equal to the purchase price of the underlying shares (or the swap's notional amount). This amount is repaid on the swap's expiration date.

4.   DERIVATIVES AND LEVERAGE

Unlike traditional securities, derivatives enable investors to purchase or sell exposure without committing cash in an amount equal to the economic exposure (the notional value) of the position. This should sound familiar, as it enables the same kind of magnification of exposure that we discussed with regard to debt-funded leverage.

For example, equity swaps and other equity derivatives are inherently leveraged. They allow an investor to obtain exposure to equity price movements without the cash outlay that would be required to purchase the shares.

Imagine you have $100 million. Don't linger on that bit too long. You could put your $100 million in the stock market, maybe buy an S&P 500 index fund. Then you would have $100 million of stock market exposure, and your net worth would rise and fall in lockstep with the market.

But what if you instead purchased S&P 500 futures contracts, which are traded on the Chicago Mercantile Exchange? These contracts run for a quarter of a year, with the first contract of any year expiring in March.

We will assume you're a positive sort, so you decide to go long the S&P 500. Each S&P 500 futures contract provides the equivalent to 250 times the current value of the index of exposure to the stock market. Thus, if you bought one contract when the index was at 1,000,[22] you would have gained $250,000 of exposure to the stock market. Because you are long, you will gain when the market goes up, and lose when the market goes down.

PROBLEM SET 18.2

1. How much exposure could you get to the stock market with your $100 million, if you purchase futures rather than actual securities? Remember that you will have to post margin in connection with the futures—assume that initially you post 5 percent and for this and the next problem, ignore any trading commissions you might pay.

2. What if you instead decided that you would like to obtain $100 million of exposure to the market and put the rest in a bank account. Assume that both your margin account and the bank account pay 4 percent per year. What would your cash flows look like if:

    a. On the following day, the S&P 500 Index Level increases by 100 (from 1,000 to 1,100).

    b. On the next day, the index level decreases by 200 (from 1,100 to 900).

    How would this compare to your cash flows if you had invested your $100 million directly into the index?

---

22. In reality, the index is currently (Feb. 2017) at 2,297.42. But we'll keep using 1,000 to make the math easier.

3. Return to the ProShares UltraPro S&P 500 (UPRO)[23] ETF from Chapter 10. Remember that it offered to provide investors with a return equal to three times the S&P 500, without using debt. How might that be? Look at its current holdings list.[24] Why so many total return swaps?[25] What is the drawback of having so many swaps that achieve the same ends?

5. ISDA AGREEMENTS, MARGIN, AND TERMINATION

Because OTC derivatives only provided the desired hedge or speculation if the other side performs, OTC derivatives entail counterparty risk.[26]

The Dodd-Frank Act attempts to solve that problem by making swaps more like futures, where a central clearinghouse stands ready to perform despite the failure of one party to the swap. That works, so long as the clearinghouse does not fail.

More generally, the parties to swaps and other derivatives have developed two additional methods to reduce counterparty risk. These involve the posting of margin and the ability of parties to terminate trades on the occurrence of certain events.

Margin refers to the amount of cash or other collateral[27] deposited by a derivatives purchaser or seller. For exchange-traded derivatives, the collateral will be held by the broker or clearinghouse. For OTC derivatives, the terms of the collateral requirements will be specified in the ISDA documents between the parties to the transaction. Before the financial crisis, these documents often put big brokers in charge of holding margin. After the failure of Lehman, there has been some move to post margin with third parties.

Margin is subdivided into *initial margin,* which is the amount of margin set aside when the position is opened, and *variation margin,* which reflects daily adjustments to the initial margin to reflect movements in the value of the contract. In addition, if the parties are of unequal credit quality, sometimes the lower quality party will have to post additional margin, which is called an "independent amount." Lehman Brothers, which had an investment grade credit rating until late 2008, held many hedge funds' independent amounts when it failed. Needless to say, there has been more skepticism about posting independent amounts in recent years.

It was the requirement to post margin that did in American International Group, Inc. ("AIG") during the financial crisis. AIG's London office had written many, many CDS contracts that referenced mortgage-backed securities (the

---

23. http://goo.gl/uXlIi.

24. http://goo.gl/iwuxg.

25. Note that the S&P 500 E-Mini is a futures contract with 50 times the value of the index (versus 250 times the value, as discussed previously).

26. Of course, so do most securities, but with derivatives the risk is distinct from the overall performance of the investment.

27. U.S. government debt is often used, too.

subject of the next chapter). AIG had a AAA credit rating, so it did not have to post much if any initial margin. But when these securities declined in value, and the probability increased that AIG would have to pay out on the CDS contracts, AIG had to post the variation margin. This obligation began to suck increasing amounts of cash out of the company.

In extreme cases, parties also have the right to terminate a derivative contract with a counterparty and replace it with a new one. The next case looks at these termination rights while also providing a nice overview of the ISDA documents used in most swap transactions and of the reality of the termination process.

LEHMAN BROTHERS INTERNATIONAL (EUROPE) (IN ADMINISTRATION), PLAINTIFF, v. AG FINANCIAL PRODUCTS, INC., DEFENDANT

Unreported Disposition
38 Misc.3d 1233(A)
Supreme Court, New York County, New York.
March 12, 2013.

Marcy S. FRIEDMAN, J.

This action arises out of a series of credit derivative transactions entered into between plaintiff Lehman Brothers International (Europe) (LBIE) and defendant AG Financial Products, Inc. (Assured Guaranty). Plaintiff alleges that defendant breached the contracts and the implied covenants of good faith and fair dealing by terminating nine transactions in December 2008 and 28 transactions in July 2009. Defendant moves, pursuant to CPLR 3211(a)(1) and (7), to dismiss the first and the third causes of action of the complaint, both for breach of the implied covenant.

FACTS

The facts, as alleged in the complaint, are undisputed unless otherwise stated. The parties, sophisticated commercial entities with the benefit of counsel, entered into 37 credit derivative transactions, each governed by three documents that form the contract for the transaction: a Master Agreement based on a 1992 template promulgated by the International Swaps and Derivatives Association; a negotiated Schedule to the Master Agreement; and a negotiated Confirmation for each transaction. The stated maturity date for each transaction is the maturity date of the underlying notes, referred to as the Reference Obligation.

As discussed below, the Master Agreement provides for termination of transactions upon "Event[s] of Default" which include bankruptcy, while the Confirmations for the transactions that were terminated in December 2008 enumerate "Additional Termination Events." The December 2008 terminations were based on the occurrence of an Additional Termination Event—namely, LBIE's failure to provide trustee reports for the underlying obligations. The July 2009 terminations were based on the occurrence of an Event of Default—namely, LBIE's entry into administration, the United Kingdom analogue of bankruptcy.

The contractual methodologies for calculating the payments due upon termination differ significantly for these different grounds for termination.

DISCUSSION

It is well settled that on a motion to dismiss addressed to the face of the pleading, "the pleading is to be afforded a liberal construction. . . ."

It is further settled that every contract contains an implied covenant of good faith and fair dealing. The implied covenant "embraces a pledge that neither party shall do anything which will have the effect of destroying or injuring the right of the other party to receive the fruits of the contract."

However, "the implied obligation is in aid and furtherance of other terms of the agreement of the parties. No obligation can be implied . . . which would be inconsistent with other terms of the contractual relationship.". . . As this Department explained in *Richbell Information Services, Inc. v. Jupiter Partners, L.P.* (309 A.D.2d 288, 302 [1st Dept 2003]), there is "tension between, on the one hand, the imposition of a good faith limitation on the exercise of a contract right and, on the other, the avoidance of using the implied covenant of good faith to create new duties that negate explicit rights under a contract." In the face of this tension, cases which uphold causes of action for breach of the implied covenant appear to fall into two main categories:

In the first, an implied covenant claim may be recognized where a contract provides for a party's exercise of discretion but does not expressly require that the discretion be exercised reasonably.

In the second, an implied covenant claim may be recognized where a party "exercise[s] a [contractual] right malevolently, for its own gain as part of a purposeful scheme to deprive plaintiffs of the benefits" of the contract. In support of the claim, a party may not merely assert that the opposing party should not be permitted to exercise an explicit contractual right or seek to "create new duties that negate specific rights under a contract" but, rather, must allege "bad faith targeted malevolence in the guise of business dealings." (*Richbell Info. Servs.*, 309 A.D.2d at 302 [denying motion to dismiss implied covenant claim where complaint alleged that defendant not only exercised contractual right to veto IPO that would have provided plaintiff with funds to repay note, but also entered into secret "bid rigging agreement" to orchestrate plaintiff's default on note, all for the purpose of enabling defendant to purchase plaintiff's stock at artificially low price]; *see also ABN AMRO Bank, N.V.*, 17 NY3d at 228–229 [denying motion to dismiss implied covenant claim by plaintiff-holders of financial guarantee insurance policies on structured finance products, based on allegation that defendants, by fraudulently transferring billions of dollars to subsidiary for no consideration, rendered defendant unable to meet its obligations under policies]. . . .

A negotiated contract provision cannot, however, be nullified by a conclusory allegation that a defendant acted "unfairly" or "contrived" to deprive the opposing party of the benefits of the contract. Nor, where a contract contains an express covenant governing a subject, will the courts imply a covenant with respect to the same subject. *Staffenberg v. Fairfield Pagma Assocs, L.P.*, 95 AD3d 873, 875 [2d Dept 2012] [on summary judgment motion, dismissing implied covenant claim where limited partnership agreement provided that client funds were to be invested with Madoff and "no other obligation to invest" could be implied under the agreement].)

DECEMBER 2008 TERMINATIONS

As noted above, the December 2008 terminations were based not on the Master Agreement but on the Confirmations which require that LBIE "obtain and provide [Assured Guaranty] with copies of all reports and other information relating to the Reference Obligation" that were required to be delivered to the holders of the Reference Obligation by any Reference Entity or its manager or servicer, or by a trustee. The Confirmations further provide that if LBIE fails to deliver the reports "promptly" or fails to cure within a 30–day period after written notice from Assured Guaranty, Assured Guaranty "may . . . declare an Additional Termination Event" and "designate an Early Termination Date" with respect to the subject transaction.

On November 13, 2008, Assured Guaranty sent LBIE nine "Notices of Failure to Deliver Reports," stating that LBIE had failed to provide Assured Guaranty with monthly trustee reports relating to the underlying Reference Obligations as required by Section 8(a)(ii) of the Confirmations. LBIE did not cure and, on December 23, 2008, Assured Guaranty sent Notices of Termination, designating December 24, 2008 as the Early Termination Date.

As the December 2008 terminations were based on an "Additional Termination Event," the Confirmations require LBIE to pay an Accrued Fixed Payment Amount. As pleaded in the complaint, and undisputed by defendant, the Accrued Fixed Payment Amount consists of the accrued and unpaid premiums that LBIE owed to Assured Guaranty as of the Early Termination Date. Upon the occurrence of an Additional Termination Event, "no amount (other than amounts due and not paid) is payable by either party in respect of the termination" of the transaction.[28] Both LBIE and Assured Guaranty refer to the Accrued Fixed Payment Amount as "walk-away money." On October 7, 2009, Assured Guaranty delivered a valuation statement, asserting that LBIE owed it an Accrued Fixed Payment Amount of $3,960,319.86.

LBIE argues that at the time of the terminations, the parties were engaged in settlement negotiations concerning possible novation of all 37 transactions, and that Assured Guaranty could have requested the reports from the negotiators or obtained them from other sources, including the trustee. LBIE acknowledges that Assured Guaranty had contractual authorization for the December 2008

---

28. The Accrued Fixed Payment Amount is defined as follows: "[A]s of any Early Termination Date, the accrued and unpaid Fixed Payments under the Transaction for the period from and including the [premium payment date] immediately preceding the Early Termination Date to but excluding the Early Termination Date, plus any Unpaid Amounts payable to [Assured Guaranty] and outstanding on the Early Termination Date."

terminations. However, LBIE contends that "act[s] consistent with a contract's express terms" do not bar a claim of breach of the implied covenant, and that the parties' "course of dealing" must be considered. Assured Guaranty, it claims, used the reports as a "pretext for termination" so that it could avail itself of the "more advantageous termination methodology" (the Accrued Fixed Payment Amount) available upon termination based on an Additional Termination Event.

Assured Guaranty contends that the implied covenant claim must be dismissed because it acted within its express contractual rights in terminating the transactions based on LBIE's failure to provide trustee reports. It further contends that in claiming a breach of the implied covenant, LBIE in effect invites the court to rewrite the parties' respective contractual rights and obligations by requiring Assured Guaranty to provide oral notice of LBIE's failure to deliver the reports in addition to the written notice provided for by the Confirmations, or to undertake an additional obligation to obtain the reports from other sources. Assured Guaranty argues that such obligations are inconsistent with the terms of the contract.

The court holds that LBIE fails to state a claim for breach of the implied covenant based on the December 2008 terminations. It is undisputed that Assured Guaranty's right to terminate the transactions based on LBIE's failure to provide trustee reports was a bargained-for provision of the contract, and that the transactions were terminated in compliance with that provision. LBIE's conclusory assertion that Assured Guaranty terminated the transactions pursuant to the provision in order to avail itself of a favorable payment methodology falls far short of alleging the kind of fraudulent or malevolent scheme to deprive LBIE of the benefits of the contract that would support an implied covenant claim. Moreover, to hold that Assured Guaranty was required to have requested the reports from the parties engaged in settlement negotiations or to have obtained the reports on its own would, as Assured Guaranty correctly argues, impose obligations upon it additional to those imposed by the Confirmations, and therefore inconsistent with its right under the Confirmations to terminate the transactions upon LBIE's failure to provide the reports.

JULY 2009 TERMINATIONS

The July 2009 terminations were based on the Early Termination provision of the Master Agreement which provides in pertinent part: "If at any time an Event of Default with respect to a party (the Defaulting Party') has occurred and is then continuing, the other party (the Non-defaulting Party') may, by not more than 20 days notice to the Defaulting Party specifying the relevant Event of Default, designate a day not earlier than the day such notice is effective as an Early Termination Date in respect of all outstanding Transactions." Under the Master Agreement, the bankruptcy of a party constitutes an Event of Default.

On September 15, 2008, LBIE entered into administration in the United Kingdom. On July 23, 2009, Assured Guaranty gave notice terminating the remaining 28 Transactions based on LBIE's entrance into bankruptcy administration, and designated July 23, 2009 as the Early Termination Date.

As the termination of these transactions was based on an Event of Default, the Master Agreement provides for the early termination payment to be "determined by the Non-defaulting Party." The Schedule in turn provides that in calculating the payment, the Non-defaulting Party must first use the "Market Quotation" payment measure and "Second [payment] Method."

The Market Quotation methodology requires the Non-defaulting Party to obtain quotations from leading dealers in the relevant market, known as "Reference Market-makers," to "step into the shoes" of the Defaulting Party for a replacement transaction. Under the Master Agreement, if three quotations cannot be obtained, "it will be deemed that the Market Quotation in respect of such Terminated Transaction or group of Terminated Transactions cannot be determined." The alternative Loss methodology may be used to calculate the early termination payment if "a Market Quotation cannot be determined or would not (in the reasonable belief of the party making the determination) produce a commercially reasonable result." Loss is defined as "an amount that party reasonably determines in good faith to be its total losses and costs (or gain, in which case expressed as a negative number) in connection with . . . [the] group of Terminated Transactions. . . ." The Loss methodology requires that a party "determine its Loss as of the relevant Early Termination Date, or, if that is not reasonably practicable, as of the earliest date thereafter as is reasonably practicable. A party may (but need not) determine its Loss by reference to quotations of relevant rates or prices from one or more leading dealers in the relevant markets."

According to plaintiff, Assured Guaranty represented that it could not obtain bids from at least three Reference Market-makers. Assured Guaranty therefore took the position that it could not use the Market Quotation method and instead applied the Loss method, determining that LBIE owed Assured Guaranty $24,799,972.85 for the July 2009 Terminations.

LBIE alleges that Assured Guaranty breached the implied covenant with respect to the July 2009 terminations by making the use of Market Quotation "impossible" in that it delayed its request for quotations "until well after the Early Termination Date," and then required the Reference Market-makers to agree to Assured Guaranty's onerous bidding procedures, including execution of a confidentiality agreement, thereby "effectively discouraging them from submitting bids." LBIE further contends that Assured Guaranty not only "bypass[ed]" the contractual requirement that the Market Quotation method be used, but also misapplied the Loss method. More particularly, LBIE claims that it is "accepted market practice to determine Loss by reference to the market price ... for replacing the terminated transactions," but that Assured Guaranty instead determined Loss by "calculating the purported present value of all payments that [Assured Guaranty] expected to receive from LBIE during the entire term of each Transaction and subtracting from it the sum of all payments [Assured Guaranty] purportedly determined that it would likely have to pay to LBIE during the term of each Transaction. . . ." Further, LBIE alleges that Assured Guaranty used its "own undisclosed internal assumptions and models about the shortfalls that would occur on the underlying securities" to determine the present value and "ignored the then-market consensus as to the likelihood of defaults."

In moving to dismiss the implied covenant claim based on the July 2009 terminations, Assured Guaranty contends that it is duplicative of the second cause of action for breach of contract. Assured Guaranty points to allegations in the breach of contract cause of action that Assured Guaranty "bypass[ed] Market Quotation" and "improperly calculate[d] Loss without reference to any market information and in a manner that was commercially unreasonable."

A cause of action for breach of the implied covenant will be dismissed as duplicative of a breach of contract cause of action where both claims arise from the same facts and seek identical damages. (*Amcan Holding, Inc. v. Canadian Imperial Bank of Commerce*, 70 AD3d 423, 426 [1st Dept 2010]; *see MBIA Ins. Corp. v. Merrill Lynch*, 81 AD3d 419, 419–420 [1st Dept 2011].)

Here, the allegations of the breach of contract and implied covenant causes of action overlap in significant respects. As discussed above, both allege that Assured Guaranty "bypassed" the contractually required Market Quotation and then applied the Loss methodology in an improper manner. The issue is therefore whether the implied covenant claim is maintainable based on the additional allegations, on which LBIE relies, that Assured Guaranty made the use of Market Quotation "impossible" by delaying its request for quotations and imposing unreasonable bidding procedures.

As to the allegation regarding delay, the Master Agreement contains a specific term requiring the party making the determination to request the Reference Market-makers to provide their quotations "to the extent reasonably practicable as of the same day and time . . . on or as soon as reasonably practicable after the relevant Early Termination Date," and further providing that "[t]he day and time on which those quotations are to be obtained will be selected in good faith." (Master Agreement, §14 "Market Quotation Definition.") The implied covenant cause of action, to the extent based on timing of the request for quotations, is thus duplicative of the contract cause of action.

As to the allegation regarding bidding, the Master Agreement imposes several requirements that the Market Quotation determination be made in good faith, including a requirement that the Replacement Transaction be "subject to such documentation as [the party making the calculation] and the Reference Market-maker may, in good faith, agree," and a requirement that the Reference Market-makers be selected "in good faith."

Significantly, the Master Agreement and other contract documents do not contain express directives as to the bidding procedures to be followed in obtaining the Market Quotations. Assured Guaranty has acknowledged that in making the determination of the Early Termination payment, it "had to act reasonably and in good faith subject to rights the contract specifically provided us." At this early juncture, however, the rights provided by the contract with respect to the bidding procedures are not settled.[29] The implied covenant claim, to the extent based on Assured Guaranty's conduct in the bidding process therefore cannot be said to be duplicative of the breach of contract cause of action. Moreover, LBIE's allegations regarding the bidding process, viewed in the light most favorable to LBIE, could rise to the level of deliberate conduct designed to deprive LBIE of the benefit of its bargain. Defendant's motion to dismiss will therefore be denied as to the implied covenant cause of action with respect to the July 2009 terminations.

It is accordingly hereby ORDERED that the motion of defendant AG Financial Products, Inc. to dismiss the first and third causes of action of the complaint is granted solely to the extent of dismissing the first cause of action.

There are presently two forms of the ISDA Master Agreement—often called either the "Master" or the "ISDA"—in use: the 1992 ISDA Master and the 2002 ISDA Master. Both are preprinted contracts designed for use with all types of OTC derivative transactions. A "Schedule" to the master agreement allows parties to modify and add provisions to the ISDA Master; the master agreement itself is not designed for anything other than signing. The terms of each individual transaction are then documented using a "confirmation." Section 1(c) of the master agreement, in both its 1992 and 2002 forms, provides that all the confirmations and the ISDA Master (including the Schedule) form a single agreement.

The entire contractual structure is supported by various ISDA published definitions, which are incorporated by reference into specific types of trades. For example, the 2014 ISDA Credit Derivatives Definitions apply to CDS trades made after February of that year. The 2011 ISDA Equity Derivatives Definitions apply to equity and total return swaps, while definitions published in 2006 apply to interest rate and currency swaps. Supplements and appendices have been published to many of these to further update them; for example, in 2016 the 49th supplement to the index and currency definitions changed some of the original definitions. All ISDA documents are available for sale on its web page, although in many cases at extremely high prices.

If you have taken Bankruptcy, you might wonder why LBIE's administration proceeding did not stop AG Financial from terminating these agreements. The answer is *not* that U.K. insolvency law is markedly different: Indeed, the result would be no different under U.S. bankruptcy law.

Under the Bankruptcy Code, clauses that allow parties to terminate a contract upon another party's bankruptcy or insolvency are unenforceable.[30] That is, that's the normal rule. Derivatives are subject to an alternative set of special rules.

---

29. Similarly, the Master Agreement does not set forth a detailed methodology for calculating Loss in the event a Market Quotation cannot be determined or would not produce a commercially reasonable result. (*See* Master Agreement, §14 "Loss" Definition.)

30. 11 U.S.C. §365(e).

STEPHEN J. LUBBEN, *THE BANKRUPTCY CODE WITHOUT SAFE HARBORS*

84 Am. Bankr. L.J. 123, 124–130 (2010)

A.   THE SAFE HARBORS

The safe harbor provisions of the Code developed incrementally, growing from narrowly targeted provisions that addressed specific concerns about the interaction of bankruptcy and certain financial products, to the wide-open provisions enacted in 2005. Following the 2005 amendments to the Code, it is hard to envision a derivative that is not subject to special treatment.[31]

The safe harbors cover a wide range of contracts that might be considered derivatives, including securities contracts,[32] commodities contracts,[33] forward contracts,[34] repurchase agreements,[35] and, most importantly, swap agreements.[36]

---

31. Michael Simkovic, *Secret Liens and the Financial Crisis of 2008*, 83 Am. Bankr. L.J. 253, 282 (2009).

32. The definition of "securities contract" in section 741(7) includes:

> a contract for the purchase, sale, or loan of a security, a certificate of deposit, a mortgage loan . . . or option on any of the foregoing, including an option to purchase or sell any such security, certificate of deposit, mortgage loan . . . including any repurchase or reverse repurchase transaction on any such security, certificate of deposit, mortgage loan. . . .

The definition of "securities contract" was amended in 2005 to conform to the definition in the Federal Deposit Insurance Act. The term "security" is itself defined in §101(49).

33. 11 U.S.C. §781(4). As explained in *Collier's*:

> The meaning of the term "commodity contract" differs depending upon the type of commodity broker at issue. A commodity contract with respect to a futures commission merchant is a contract for the purchase or sale of a commodity for future delivery on, or subject to the rules of, a contract market or board of trade. Such a contract is known in the commodities trade as a "commodity futures contract." A commodity contract with respect to a foreign futures commission merchant is a foreign future, and with respect to a leverage transaction merchant is a leverage transaction. A commodity contract with respect to a clearing organization is either a commodity futures contract that is cleared by such clearing organization or is a commodity option traded on, or subject to the rules of, a contract market or a board of trade that is cleared by such clearing organization. A commodity contract with respect to a commodity options dealer is a commodity option.

Collier on Bankruptcy ¶761.05 (footnotes omitted). Commodity is defined in §761(8) through cross-reference to the Commodity Exchange Act ("CEA"). CEA §1a(4) defines "commodity" to include agricultural products "and all other goods and articles, except onions as provided in section 13-1 of this title, and all services, rights, and interests in which contracts for future delivery are presently or in the future dealt in." The origins of the amusing "onion" exception are detailed in http://www.time.com/time/magazine/article/0,9171,891311,00.html. Several other parts of Code §761 also cross-reference the CEA. *See* Olympic Natural Gas, 294 F.3d 737, 740–41 (5th Cir. 2002) ("The term 'commodity contract' encompasses purchases and sales of commodities for future delivery on, or subject to the rules of, a contract market or board of trade.... In contrast, 'forward contracts' are 'contracts for the future purchase or sale of commodities that are not subject to the rules of a contract market or board of trade.'").

34. Forward contract is defined in §101(25), to include contracts (other than commodity contracts, see *supra* note 33) for the purchase, sale, or transfer of a commodity at least two days in

The latter has become a kind of "catch-all" definition that covers the whole of the derivatives market, present and future.

A protected contract, that is one that falls within one of the foregoing categories, is only protected if the holder is also a protected person, as defined in the Bankruptcy Code. Financial participants[37]—essentially very large financial institutions—are always protected. And with regard to each class of protected derivative contract this is also a more specific class of protected parties.[38]

In some cases these latter categories have some real meaning. For example, forward contracts are only subject to the safe harbors with regard to financial participants and "forward contract merchants." A forward contract merchant means either a Federal Reserve Bank or an entity "whose business consists in whole or in part of entering into forward contracts."[39] On the other hand, the current definitions of "repo participant"[40] and "swap participant"[41] are essentially vacuous, requiring nothing more than the person in question be party to a repo or swap with the debtor. In short, anyone with standing to invoke the safe harbors is apt to be a protected person with regard to these contracts.

The safe harbors provide non-bankrupt counterparties with the ability to exercise contractual rights allowing liquidation, termination or acceleration of derivative contracts upon bankruptcy,[42] the right to set off or net derivative

---

the future, and includes "a repurchase or reverse repurchase transaction . . . consignment, lease, swap, hedge transaction, deposit, loan, option, allocated transaction, unallocated transaction, or any other similar agreement."

35. 11 U.S.C. §101(47). A repurchase agreement or "repo," is essentially the sale of a financial instrument combined with a forward contract to repurchase the same. The initial "buyer" is compensated by the "seller" through a difference between the initial payment and the final payment. To qualify under the Code's definition, the repurchase obligation must occur within one year, but the definition expressly excludes a repurchase obligation under a participation in a commercial mortgage loan. Note, however, that these types of repos might constitute another type of protected contract, particularly a swap or securities contract. *See* In re Hamilton Taft & Co., 114 F.3d 991 (9th Cir. 1997).

36. 11 U.S.C. §101(53B). The definition includes not only obvious swaps, like CDS, interest rate swaps, and currency swaps, but also any instrument "of a type that has been, is presently, or in the future becomes, the subject of recurrent dealings in the swap markets" including "a forward, swap, future, option or spot transaction on one or more rates, currencies, commodities, equity securities, or other equity instruments, debt securities or other debt instruments, quantitative measures associated with an occurrence, extent of an occurrence, or contingency associated with a financial, commercial, or economic consequence, or economic or financial indices or measures of economic or financial risk or value." In short, every conceivable derivative contract.

37. 11 U.S.C. §101(22A) (defining "financial participant").

38. With regard to securities contracts with the debtor, the counterparty must be a "stockbroker," "financial institution," "financial participant" or "securities clearing agency."

39. 11 U.S.C. §101(26). *See also* In re Mirant Corp., 310 B.R. 548, 568 (Bankr. N.D. Tex. 2004).

40. 11 U.S.C. §101(46).

41. 11 U.S.C. §101(53C).

42. 11 U.S.C. §§555 (securities contracts), 556 (forward and commodities contracts), 559 (repurchase or "repo" agreements), 560 (swaps). The exceptions apply to a "contractual right," which includes rights provided for in a rule by various trade organizations or exchanges.

contracts free of the automatic stay,[43] and broad immunity from avoidance actions.[44] These protections also extend to derivative transactions nestled under a master agreement, even if the master agreement aggregates disparate types of derivative contracts.[45] Security agreements and other credit enhancements are also encompassed within the definitions of protected contracts, and thus subject to the safe harbors.[46]

Many authors, especially those that come from a restructuring background, have expressed some skepticism about the safe harbor provisions,[47] and it is worth noting that the new Orderly Liquidation Authority, Dodd-Frank's special bankruptcy system for financial institutions, provides for a 24-hour stay on any termination of a derivative contract.

---

43. 11 U.S.C. §§362(b)(6) (securities contracts, forwards and commodity contracts), 362(b)(7) (repos), 362(b)(17) (swaps). *See also* 11 U.S.C. §§362(o) (exercise of rights under the forgoing provisions not subject to any stays), 556 (forwards and commodity contracts protected parties' right to margin payments under those contracts shall not be stayed, avoided or limited), 560 (under a swap right to offset or net-out any termination values or payment amounts shall not be stayed, avoided or limited).

44. 11 U.S.C. §§546(e), (f), (g), (j), 548(d)(2)(B), (C), (D). The foregoing sections of section 546 prohibit the bringing of avoidance actions under sections 544, 545, 547, 548 (a)(1)(B), and 548 (b) of the Bankruptcy Code. The foregoing provisions of section 548 provide that a derivatives counterparty always takes for value, potentially complicating an attempt to recover a transfer as an actual fraudulent transfer. 11 U.S.C. §548(c).

This author is at a loss to explain how a derivative might be a statutory lien under section 545. These provisions do not seem to prohibit the lifting of the automatic stay to allow a creditor to bring an avoidance action under state or federal non-bankruptcy law, so long as the creditor did not bring such action on behalf of the estate. *Cf.* 11 U.S.C. §544(b)(1).

45. 11 U.S.C. §§362(b)(27) (allows setoffs and netting under master netting agreements) 561 (right to terminate, accelerate or liquidate, or to offset, or net termination values, payment amounts or other transfer obligations arising under or in connection with one or more securities contracts, commodity contracts, forward contracts, repurchase agreements, swap agreements or master netting agreements, shall not be stayed, avoided or limited by operation of the bankruptcy code or by order of a court or administrative agency). *See also* 11 U.S.C. §§101(38A) (definition of "master netting agreement"). The definitions of securities contracts, commodities, forward contracts, repurchase agreements, and swap agreements also include "a master agreement" that includes the defined contracts. Note the slight difference in terminology between "master agreement" and "master netting agreement."

46. *See, e.g.*, 11 U.S.C. §101(25)(E) (definition of "forward contract").

47. Frank Partnoy & David A. Skeel, Jr., *The Promise and Perils of Credit Derivatives*, 75 U. Cin. L. Rev. 1019, 1049 (2007) ("The first thing to note is that the standard explanation for the special treatment is not particularly compelling. It is far from clear that the exception reduces systemic risk; it may even increase this risk because it eliminates a possible curb on counter-parties' rush to close out their contracts in the event of a wave of failures.").

PROBLEM SET 18.3

1. The Lehman case above involved a "walkaway clause" that pays the nondefaulting party damages regardless of the underlying economic value of the swap. For example, Lehman might have been "in the money" on the swaps, but could have owed a payment to its counterparty nonetheless. Such clauses are not enforceable in bank receivership proceedings against the FDIC. Should they be enforceable in other contexts?

2. From the industry perspective, what benefits arise from the safe harboring of most swap agreements from the normal operation of the Bankruptcy Code? For example, how might the existence of the safe harbors influence the pricing of a swaps deal?

3. Based on what you know about contract law, what do you think of the provision in the ISDA master agreement that provides that all trades under a single master agreement constitute a single contract? Note that trades, and confirmations entered into in connection with those trades, might occur years, if not decades, after the master agreement was first signed.

19

ASSET SECURITIZATION

If you followed the 2008 financial crisis at all, you probably heard about asset securitization—the famed mortgage-backed securities (MBS) that were at the center of many discussions of the crisis are one form of asset securitization.

Even before the financial crisis, asset securitization (briefly) entered mainstream discourse when David Bowie[1] securitized his music royalties from albums made before 1990 in exchange for $55 million from the Prudential insurance company.[2] Bowie essentially gave up ten years of royalty payments in exchange for a (very) large check.[3]

1. MOTIVATIONS

Securitization is an awkwardly named substitute for secured lending. In a basic secured loan, the borrower-firm gives a bank a lien on an asset in exchange for cash. If the borrower fails to repay the loan, the bank can institute a foreclosure proceeding under state debtor-creditor law and take the asset. In the interim, there is some risk that the defaulting borrower will forestall this process by filing bankruptcy under the federal Bankruptcy Code. Bankruptcy, as discussed in later chapters, allows a firm to renegotiate its loans from a position of greater strength than it would enjoy under state law.

The possibility of a bankruptcy filing means that a secured lender cannot count on being able to quickly obtain the collateral upon default. In many cases it probably does not really want the collateral, but getting the collateral beats not

---

1. For those of you who are too young to know, David Bowie (1947–2016) was a musician of great importance to some textbook authors who were in their youth in the 1970s and 1980s.

2. http://en.wikipeedia.org/wiki/Bowie_Bonds.

3. Teresa N. Kerr, Comment, *Bowie Bonding in the Music Biz: Will Music Royalty Securitization Be the Key to the Gold for Music Industry Participants?*, 7 UCLA Ent. L. Rev. 367 (2000).

getting paid.[4] The delay associated with bankruptcy is thus a factor that should influence the lender's expected return calculation, and thus the interest rate the debtor pays the lender on the loan.

Securitization involves the isolation of the asset in a way that—in theory—allows the lender to price the loan solely on the value of the asset, free from any risk of bankruptcy.

To return to the case of David Bowie, he might have gotten a bank loan secured by his royalties. One risk the bank would have faced was the possibility that David might have filed a personal bankruptcy case and used the bankruptcy process to impose a new deal on the bank, perhaps paying off the loan over a longer term, while still retaining the rights to the royalties.

But when he securitized the royalties, they were moved into a separate legal entity, referred to as a Special Purpose Vehicle (SPV) or Entity (SPE), which did nothing but own the rights. The transfer would have been structured as a "true sale" that terminated David's rights in the royalties. A legal opinion would certify that some law firm really believes that this was actually a sale, and not simply a sham transaction (hence, the "true" sale).

The SPV paid David $55 million, and David gave the SPV the royalty rights. Where did the SPV get the $55 million? From Prudential. Why would Prudential give an SPV so much money? It's not because they're all Ziggy Stardust fanatics.

Prudential actually bought bonds issued by the SPV that promised to pay it a certain return, based on the expected payout that David Bowie's back catalog would generate over the course of ten years.[5]

And who was the "owner" of the SPV? That would be David Bowie. When the transaction was completed, and Prudential was all paid back, he could do what he wanted with the rights. But if Prudential had not been paid during the interim, as a creditor of the SPV they could have taken the rights.

And David's own bankruptcy case would have had no effect on the operation of the SPV. Just like your own bankruptcy case would have no effect on Apple or Exxon, even if you owned shares in those companies. More formally, one expert explains the process thusly.

KENNETH C. KETTERING, *SECURITIZATION AND ITS DISCONTENTS: THE DYNAMICS OF FINANCIAL PRODUCT DEVELOPMENT*

29 Cardozo L. Rev. 1553 (2008)

The main purpose of this paper is to consider the process of innovation in financial and commercial products. It takes as its point of departure one of the major financial innovations of recent decades, namely the financing technique variously known as "securitization" or "structured finance." These terms are not well defined, but they have acquired a certain cachet in the marketplace, and so

---

4. Ronald J. Mann, *Strategy and Force in the Liquidation of Secured Debt*, 96 Mich. L. Rev. 159 (1997).

5. http://ftalphaville.ft.com/2016/01/11/2149761/a-short-history-of-the-bowie-bond/.

are often applied very loosely to transactions that have almost nothing in common. As used in this paper, "securitization" refers to a transaction that, in the first place, involves the issuance to financiers of debt instruments that are backed by a designated pool of assets—typically rights to payment owned by the firm that effects the transaction (referred to herein as the "Originator"). That description, by itself, would encompass a simple loan to the Originator secured by the asset pool. The distinctive feature of securitization is that the transaction also is structured to isolate the asset pool from the Originator in such a way that, if the Originator later becomes subject to an insolvency proceeding, the proceeding will not interrupt the continued receipt by the financiers of the payments due to them, as and when due, through realization on the asset pool. If that goal is achieved, the credit risk to the financiers will depend solely on the assets in the pool, and so will be independent of the creditworthiness of the Originator. For brevity that goal sometimes may be referred to as "bankruptcy isolation" of the securitized assets.

The term "securitization" is thus a misnomer insofar as it suggests that the issuance of securities is the heart of the matter. The debt instruments issued to the financiers in a securitization transaction might be securities issued into the capital markets, but they need not be; they might just as well be loan obligations owed to a syndicate of banks, involving no securities at all. . . .

Securitization transactions, in the foregoing sense, were first employed in the late 1970s using asset pools comprised of mortgages. The first public transaction to securitize rights to payment other than mortgages (referred to as an "asset-backed" transaction, as opposed to a "mortgage-backed" transaction, in the somewhat illogical terminology conventional in the market) occurred in 1985. This infant was born under a lucky star, and from its birth it grew prodigiously: the volume of securities outstanding in securitization transactions at the end of 2006 aggregated $3.6 trillion. The growth of securitization indeed has been such as to move one scholar to predict the death of secured lending, as being hopelessly overshadowed by its more sophisticated relative.

This vast inverted pyramid of securitized debt is balanced uneasily on a pinpoint of legal doctrine: namely, that the structure employed for the purpose of isolating the pooled assets from the bankruptcy of the Originator will indeed achieve that purpose. From the beginning that doctrinal conclusion, or aspiration, was a shaky one. Even without detailed study the wobble is apparent from numerous outward signs. For example, in securitization transactions lawyers typically are asked to deliver opinions on the relevant points (or at least some of the relevant points) of bankruptcy doctrine. The opinion given is never a clean unqualified opinion that the structure works; rather, standard practice is to give a "reasoned" opinion, commonly dozens of pages long, which by its form and in its content signals substantial uncertainty about the result.

The dearth of case law is paralleled by the skimpiness of the academic literature casting a critical eye on the doctrinal foundations of the product. A vast amount has been written about securitization, understandably so because such transactions raise legal, tax, accounting, and other issues that are manifold, specialized, and arcane. But with few exceptions the literature is by and for practitioners, to assist in the doing of deals, and as such is naturally oriented toward cheerleading rather than skepticism.

I. The Prototypical Securitization, the Bankruptcy Tax, and Bankruptcy Policy

Structures for securitization transactions, or at least for transactions that are advertised as securitizations, are many and varied. This paper focuses on the structure that is commonly viewed as being prototypical, and that indeed is used as the exemplar in the major law school textbook dedicated to teaching securitization. The doctrinal discussion in this paper is at a sufficiently high level of generality to be applicable to other securitization structures. Some of the terminology associated with the prototypical securitization was introduced earlier in this paper, but it is well to describe the transaction here even at the cost of some repetition.

In its simplest form, the prototypical securitization begins with the firm that wishes to procure financing against assets that it owns, which are typically rights to payment owed to it. Because that firm ordinarily (though not necessarily) will have originated those rights to payment by lending money to or providing property or services to the obligors, it is convenient to refer to that firm as the "Originator." The Originator forms a wholly-owned subsidiary conventionally referred to as a "special purpose entity," or "SPE," because it is formed for the purpose of the transaction and its operations are limited to those required in connection with the transaction. This SPE is (in further industry argot) "bankruptcy remote," in that it is created subject to an array of constraints designed to eliminate, to the extent possible, the risk that the SPE might in the future become subject to a proceeding under the Bankruptcy Code, whether involuntarily, voluntarily, or through the SPE being substantively consolidated with its Originator in the event of the Originator's bankruptcy. Thus, involuntary bankruptcy is countered by provisions in the SPE's organic documents authorizing it to engage only in activities necessary to the securitization transaction and by obtaining waivers of the right to file an involuntary petition against the SPE from third parties who deal with the SPE. Voluntary bankruptcy is countered by provisions in the SPE's organic documents requiring a unanimous vote of the SPE's board of directors to authorize the filing of a voluntary bankruptcy petition and requiring one or more members of the SPE's board to be independent of the Originator. Substantive consolidation[6] with the Originator is countered by covenants requiring the Originator and SPE to avoid acting in ways that would permit the invocation of any of the usual grounds for substantive consolidation, i.e., the SPE is to comply with proper corporate formalities, its assets are not to be commingled with those of the Originator, and so on.

---

6. This is the bankruptcy counterpart of veil piercing, whereby a bankruptcy court can treat several related corporations as a single legal entity, pooling all assets and debts. —Author

After the SPE is formed, the Originator conveys the assets being securitized to the SPE. This conveyance, which is the key to the bankruptcy isolation that is sought for the securitized assets, is effected as a sale or a capital contribution. In the simplest structure, which might be referred to as "one tier," the securitization would then be completed by the SPE issuing debt instruments to financiers, secured by the securitized assets, and immediately passing the proceeds of the financing upstream to the Originator (by way of payment of the purchase price of the securitized assets or distribution on the SPE's equity, depending on how the conveyance of assets from the Originator to the SPE was effected). For accounting reasons, however, it is common to employ a slightly more elaborate structure referred to conventionally as "two tier." In the "two tier" structure, the SPE transfers the securitized assets to a second entity, typically a trust formed for the transaction ("SPE-2"), which issues the debt instruments to the financiers and passes the proceeds back to the SPE; the SPE is the residual beneficiary of SPE-2 and so is entitled to the residual value of the securitized assets after the financiers have been paid. In order to comply with the relevant accounting conventions the transfer of the assets from the SPE to SPE-2 need not be a sale for bankruptcy law purposes and it typically is not considered to be. Hence for purposes of bankruptcy analysis the "one tier" and "two tier" structures are practically identical, and for simplicity of exposition this paper will ignore SPE-2.

If the structure is respected, then the stream of payments to the financiers derived from collection of the securitized assets should not be affected by the subsequent bankruptcy of the Originator. Because the securitized assets are the property of the SPE, they will not be part of the Originator's bankruptcy estate. Moreover, the SPE should be practically immune from becoming the subject of a bankruptcy proceeding in its own right because of the bankruptcy remoteness conditions to which it is subject. The achievement of this "bankruptcy isolation" of the securitized assets is the purpose of the structure. The credit risk associated with the securitized debt issued to the financiers thus becomes independent of the creditworthiness of the Originator. The credit risk associated with the securitized debt is a function only of the amount and collectibility of the securitized assets and the amount of securitized debt issued against those assets.[7] The credit risk associated with the securitized debt when it is issued could be reduced as low as desired by providing a sufficiently high degree of overcollateralization.

---

7. That bankruptcy isolation of the securitized assets causes the credit risk of the securitized debt to be independent of the creditworthiness of the Originator is a good first approximation, but it is subject to qualifications. For example, the transfer of the securitized assets by the Originator to the SPE is typically subject to representations and warranties by the Originator about the identity and nature of those assets, breach of which would implicate the creditworthiness of the Originator. Likewise, the Originator commonly acts as the servicer of the securitized assets (i.e., it administers and collects them), and its creditworthiness would be implicated if it were to reject its duties as servicer in a bankruptcy proceeding, commingle collections of the securitized assets with other funds, or otherwise breach its duties as servicer. Steps can be taken to mitigate these risks, such as building into the financing structure a servicing fee sufficient to discourage the Originator from rejecting its servicing duties in bankruptcy and to permit ready engagement of a substitute servicer.

That result is very much in contrast to the result if the Originator were to effect the financing as a simple secured debt—that is, if the Originator simply borrowed directly from the financiers, securing its obligation by granting a security interest in the same assets. In that event the assets, still owned by the Originator, would be part of the Originator's bankruptcy estate in the event of the filing of a petition under the Bankruptcy Code by or against the Originator. The Bankruptcy Code then would impair substantially the financiers' power to enforce their security interest in those assets—or, to make the same point from the perspective of the Originator and its unsecured creditors, the Bankruptcy Code would preserve for the benefit of the bankruptcy estate certain rights in those assets notwithstanding the financiers' security interest. In the first place, the automatic stay would prevent the financiers from exercising remedies against those assets.[8] As a result of the automatic stay, a secured creditor in a reorganization case is typically compelled to wait a long time before realizing value on its secured claim. Although a secured creditor has the right to have the stay lifted if its interest is not adequately protected, adequate protection has not been construed to require the secured creditor to be paid interest by way of compensation for the delay in realization that the stay itself forces on the secured creditor. Other provisions of the Bankruptcy Code may entitle the secured creditor to postpetition interest to the extent he is overcollateralized, but a secured creditor who is undercollateralized, or who is not sufficiently overcollateralized to be entitled to postpetition interest for the duration of the bankruptcy proceeding, must suffer the delay in realization imposed by the stay without any compensation.

A second impairment imposed by the Bankruptcy Code on a financing structured as a secured loan to the Originator is that the bankruptcy estate would have the right to use the cash collections received on the collateral, so long as the secured creditor's interest is adequately protected. From the perspective of the debtor in possession, this is perhaps the most consequential of the rights it is granted by the Bankruptcy Code, for the bankruptcy estate typically is thirsty for cash and collections of such collateral can be used to slake that thirst, subject only to the constraint of providing the secured creditor adequate protection— which might be done by grant of a replacement lien on some illiquid substitute asset, or even by doing nothing at all, if there is a sufficient equity cushion in the collateral.

The Bankruptcy Code gives the bankruptcy estate numerous other rights in collateral that impair the nonbankruptcy rights of the secured creditor, but the two mentioned above are the most likely to be of importance to the bankruptcy estate in the case of assets of the type normally subjected to securitization. Borrowing from David Carlson, it is convenient to use the term "Bankruptcy Tax" to refer collectively to the rights that the Bankruptcy Code awards to the bankruptcy estate in collateral owned by the debtor that is subject to a security interest—or, if one prefers the view from the secured creditor's perspective, the

---

8. Bankruptcy Code §362(a).

collective set of impairments that the Bankruptcy Code imposes on the rights that the secured creditor has in the collateral under nonbankruptcy law. "Bankruptcy Tax" is useful both as a shorthand and as a metaphor that expresses an important truth: these impairments amount to a tax that the Bankruptcy Code levies on secured credit for the benefit of the bankruptcy estate as a whole. In a business bankruptcy, the main point of this Bankruptcy Tax is to improve the chances that a debtor that seeks to reorganize will be able to do so. The ultimate beneficiaries of the Bankruptcy Tax, therefore, are the unsecured creditors and other constituencies of the Originator that would benefit from a successful reorganization. Securitization thus can be viewed as a method of evading the Bankruptcy Tax.

The relief from the Bankruptcy Tax that securitization is designed to afford is securitization's reason for being. Because of this relief, securitized debt is rated by the credit rating agencies on the basis of the likelihood that the securitized assets will be sufficiently collectible to make the payments due under the securitized debt. The rating given to the securitized debt thus is independent of the credit rating of the Originator (that is, the rating that would be given to the Originator's ordinary unsecured debt). The securitized debt thus can achieve ratings much higher than the Originator's own credit rating. By contrast, simple secured debt issued by the Originator, even if so heavily overcollateralized that the secured creditor will eventually be paid in full, with interest, after a bankruptcy filing by the Originator, will not be rated much higher than the Originator's own credit rating. The reason is that a rating agency's rating of a debt instrument is predominantly a prediction of the likelihood that the debt will be paid in accordance with its terms. Ratings do give some weight to the amount of the recovery that the debtholder is likely to receive if the debt goes into default, but that weight is relatively modest. Payments on an Originator's secured debt will be interrupted by the Originator's bankruptcy filing, so no matter how well overcollateralized the debt may be, its rating will be based on the Originator's own rating, with only a modest bump upward, at best, to reflect the increased probability of an eventual good recovery on the secured debt as compared to unsecured debt. Neil Baron, the principal legal advisor to one of the two predominant rating agencies during the early days of securitization, stated the point as follows:

> A rating is a statement that payment will be made in accordance with the terms of an obligation. That means on time. A payment default on a triple-A rated bond is front page news. The fact that investors get paid fully at some later time makes page 11. Timeliness is an element rating agencies are obsessive about.

Substantially all of the benefits claimed for securitization are nothing more than consequences of the structure's purported avoidance of the Bankruptcy Tax, and the resulting willingness of the rating agencies to rate securitized debt on the assumption that payments thereon from collections of the securitized assets will not be interrupted by the bankruptcy of the Originator. The primary benefit claimed for securitization is that an Originator can use its securitizable assets to obtain financing at a substantially lower interest rate than the Originator would have to pay on non-securitized debt. That is simply the result of the fact that, because of the bankruptcy avoidance to which securitized debt is purportedly entitled, securitized debt will receive a better rating than would debt incurred directly by the Originator secured by the same assets, and so financiers are content with a lower yield on the former than they would require on the latter . . .

The proposition that securitization conflicts with bankruptcy policy argues itself, and so is much less interesting than attempts to deny it. Steven Schwarcz advanced a rebuttal that is worth quoting in full:

> [T]he argument that securitization . . . undermines bankruptcy policy is a chimera. The originator, after all, freely makes the choice of its financing transactions. Securitization has a lower cost precisely due to bankruptcy remoteness. If, therefore, the originator chooses securitization in order to benefit from that lower cost, it should not have the right to later complain. Moreover, the very availability of securitization as a financing option, by providing liquidity to otherwise viable originators unable to borrow, has been shown to facilitate the fundamental bankruptcy policy of debtor rehabilitation. This sets forth two arguments, which respectively implicate two long-running debates among scholars of bankruptcy and commercial law. Whatever the normative merits of these arguments, they are not consistent with the positive law of the Bankruptcy Code as it currently stands.

The final sentence of the quoted paragraph argues that avoidance of the Bankruptcy Tax provides liquidity for Originators who might be unable to borrow if their financiers had to suffer the Bankruptcy Tax (or, to make the point more generally, lower cost financing for all Originators who use the technique). That amounts to saying that the Bankruptcy Tax is bad policy—that debtors as a class, their unsecured creditors, and other affected constituencies are better off if debtors are allowed to do secured financing that is not subject to the Bankruptcy Tax (at least as to collateral of the type typically used to back securitizations). As a normative argument this is a special case of a more general decades-long academic debate as to the social utility of secured credit, played for lower stakes: the general debate considers the whole bundle of rights possessed by a secured creditor, while securitization involves only the relatively marginal increment of rights represented by the Bankruptcy Tax. The normative debate, though deeply interesting, is not to be confused with positive law. Congress has made its normative judgment on this point, and has ordained that secured creditors must bear the Bankruptcy Tax. A court adjudicating a challenge to a securitization transaction under the Bankruptcy Code as it currently stands is not at liberty to ignore that decision.

The other argument made by Schwarcz in the quoted paragraph is that an Originator who chooses to securitize, and thereby obtain the benefit of the lower-cost financing made available to it by the avoidance of the Bankruptcy Tax, should have no right after its bankruptcy to seek to impose the Bankruptcy Tax on the transaction. That amounts to saying that a debtor should have the power to enter into an enforceable prepetition waiver of the Bankruptcy Tax as to a secured financing (again, at least as to collateral of the type typically used to back securitizations), so long as the debtor receives consideration for the waiver. That argument implicates the long-running academic debate over "contract bankruptcy"—that is, the merits of replacing the current mandatory regime of bankruptcy rules with a regime that would allow each debtor to shape by contract in advance of its failure the rules that will apply to it following its failure. . . .

Here too, Professor Schwarcz substitutes argument from a highly unsettled normative debate for positive law. The prototypical securitization is a structural substitute for an explicit prepetition waiver by a debtor of the Bankruptcy Tax that would otherwise apply to its secured financing, made by the debtor at the outset of the financing. Under current law, such an explicit waiver would not be enforceable. . . .

To legal entrepreneurs seeking to avoid the Bankruptcy Tax on their secured financings, the pragmatic benefits of the securitization structure go beyond the obvious one of disguising the conflict with bankruptcy policy. It also shifts the burden of going forward in the event of the Originator's bankruptcy. In addition to its other defects, an express prepetition waiver of the Bankruptcy Tax given by the Originator to secured financiers would be of no avail to those financiers unless they place it before the bankruptcy judge and persuade him to enforce it. The securitization structure, by contrast, hums along without interruption after the Originator's bankruptcy. . . .

PROBLEM SET 19.1

1. What are the benefits to the debtor of financing its operations by asset securitization? Who pays the costs?
2. The excerpt notes that the theory behind the securitization is to allow creditors to continue to collect cash flows from the assets, and maintain control over the assets, even after the originator's bankruptcy. But if the assets are central to the debtor-originator's business, what might the more likely outcome be?
3. One of the perceived benefits of securitization involved its accounting treatment—perhaps another example of the tension between reality and finance theory? The fundamental benefit involved the ability to leave SPEs (or SPVs) "unconsolidated" so that they did not show up on the balance sheet of the company. Following the recent financial crisis, GAAP has been further revised to require consolidation in more instances. See FASB Statement No. 166, FASB Statement No. 167.

2. UNDERSTANDING THE STRUCTURES

As the next case shows, the structures of asset securitizations have become increasingly complex.

BNY CORPORATE TRUSTEE SERVICES LIMITED
v. NEUBERGER BERMAN EUROPE LTD
(ON BEHALF OF SEALINK FUNDING LTD)

United Kingdom Supreme Court
Easter Term
[2013] UKSC 28
9 May 2013

LORD WALKER (with whom Lord Mance, Lord Sumption and Lord Carnwath agree)

INTRODUCTION

1. Sections (1) and (2) of section 123 of the Insolvency Act 1986 ("the 1986 Act") provide as follows:

> "(1) A company is deemed unable to pay its debts—(a) [non-compliance with a statutory demand for a debt exceeding £750 presently due]
> (b) to (d) [unsatisfied execution on judgment debt in terms appropriate to England and Wales, Scotland and Northern Ireland respectively]
> (e) if it is proved to the satisfaction of the court that the company is unable to pay its debts as they fall due.
> (2) A company is also deemed unable to pay its debts if it is proved to the satisfaction of the court that the value of the company's assets is less than the amount of its liabilities, taking into account its contingent and prospective liabilities."

A company in the situation described in subsection (1)(e) is often said to be "cash-flow" insolvent. A company in the situation described in subsection (2) is often said to be "balance-sheet" insolvent, but that expression is not to be taken literally. It is a convenient shorthand expression, but a company's statutory balance sheet, properly prepared in accordance with the requirements of company law, may omit some contingent assets or some contingent liabilities. There is no statutory provision which links section 123(2) of the 1986 Act to the detailed provisions of the Companies Act 2006 as to the form and contents of a company's financial statements. This appeal is concerned with the construction and effect of section 123(1)(e) and (2) as incorporated into the documentation of an issue of loan notes.

2. The statutory provisions were incorporated, with some small modifications, into the conditions applicable to loan notes issued in the course of a securitisation transaction comprising a portfolio of non-conforming mortgage loans secured on residential property in the United Kingdom. The issuer is Eurosail-UK 2007-3BL plc ("Eurosail"), one of many similar single purpose entities ("SPEs") set up by the Lehman Brothers group (but off the balance sheet of any of that group's

companies) not long before its collapse. Eurosail is the principal respondent to this appeal, and it has a cross-appeal on a subsidiary issue. The other respondent appearing before this court, BNY Corporate Trustee Services Ltd ("the Trustee") is part of the BNY Mellon Group. It is the trustee for the holders ("Noteholders") of loan notes of various classes issued by Eurosail. It has adopted a neutral attitude in the proceedings (as explained in its written case), and has not appeared by counsel before this court. But it will, in the event that the appeal succeeds and the cross-appeal fails, have an important judgment to make as to material prejudice to the Noteholders' interests.

3. In 2007 Eurosail (described in the documentation as "the Issuer") acquired a portfolio of mortgage loans, secured on residential property in England and Scotland and denominated in sterling, to the principal amount of approximately £650m. Most of the mortgages were regarded as "non-conforming" in that they did not meet the lending requirements of building societies and banks. This purchase was funded by the issue on 16 July 2007 of loan notes in five principal classes (A, B, C, D and E) comprising 14 different subclasses, some denominated in sterling, some in US dollars and some in euros. In the designation of the classes "a" indicated that the loan was denominated in euros, "b" US dollars and "c" pounds sterling. The senior (class A) notes were divided into three sub-classes, denominated in one of the three currencies, designated and issued as follows:

> A1b US$200,000,000
> A1c £102,500,000
> A2a € 64,500,000
> A2b US$100,000,000
> A2c £ 63,000,000
> A3a €215,000,000
> A3c £ 64,500,000

The B, C, D and E Notes were issued in smaller amounts, with variations in currency but no subclasses having different priorities as between themselves. There were also some notes designated as ETc "revenue-backed" notes. The total sum raised was just under £660,000,000. After payment of costs and expenses of the issue the initial surplus of assets over prospective liabilities (if taken at face value) was quite small.

4. The provisions of section 123(1) and (2) of the 1986 Act are incorporated into an important provision in the conditions of issue of the Notes ("the Conditions"). Condition 9(a) (events of default) provides that the Trustee may on the occurrence of any of five specified events (an "Event of Default") serve on Eurosail a written notice (an "Enforcement Notice") declaring the Notes to be due and repayable. In some circumstances the Trustee is obliged to serve such a notice. In the absence

of an Event of Default the A1 Notes were repayable in 2027 at latest (in fact they have already been repaid, as have the revenue-backed notes). All the other Notes are repayable in 2045 at latest.

5. The Events of Default include (Condition 9(a)(iii)):

> "The Issuer, otherwise than for the purposes of such amalgamation or reconstruction as is referred to in sub-paragraph (iv) below, ceasing or, through or consequent upon an official action of the Board of Directors of the Issuer, threatens to cease to carry on business or a substantial part of its business or being unable to pay its debts as and when they fall due or, within the meaning of section 123(1) or (2) (as if the words 'it is proved to the satisfaction of the court' did not appear in section 123(2) of the Insolvency Act 1986 (as that section may be amended from time to time), being deemed unable to pay its debts..."

Under a proviso to Condition 9(a), an occurrence falling within sub-paragraph (iii) counts as an Event of Default only if the Trustee certifies to Eurosail that it is, in the Trustee's sole opinion, materially prejudicial to the interests of the Noteholders.

6. The service of an Enforcement Notice would have immediate and far-reaching consequences for all the Noteholders (other than the A1 and ETc Noteholders, whose Notes have already been fully redeemed). As described in more detail below, an Enforcement Notice shifts their rights from the regime prescribed in Condition 2(g) (priority of payments prior to enforcement) to the regime prescribed in Condition 2(h) (priority of payments post-enforcement). Under the latter regime Noteholders of Class A3 ("A3 Noteholders") rank pari passu with Noteholders of Class A2 ("A2 Noteholders") for repayment of principal. That is in contrast with the present regime, under which A2 and A3 Noteholders rank pari passu for interest payments (clause 2(g)(vi)) but A2 Noteholders have priority over A3 Noteholders in receiving repayments of principal out of funds representing principal sums received on the redemption of mortgages in the portfolio (those funds being included in the definition of "Actual Redemption Funds" in the preamble to the Conditions).

7. It is in these circumstances that the construction of section 123(2) of the 1986 Act, as incorporated into Condition 9(a)(iii), has assumed such importance. Eurosail, together with those of the A2 Noteholders who appeared below, succeeded before Sir Andrew Morritt C [2010] EWHC 2005 (Ch), [2011] 1 WLR 1200, and the Court of Appeal [2011] EWCA Civ 227, [2011] 1 WLR 2524. The Court of Appeal considered that section 123(2) should be interpreted broadly and in line with standards of commercial probity:

> "A balance has to be drawn between the right of an honest and prudent businessman, who is prepared to work hard, to continue to trade out of his difficulties if he can genuinely see a light at the end of the tunnel, and the

corresponding obligation to 'put up the shutters,' when, by continuing to trade, he would be doing so at the expense of his creditors and in disregard of those business considerations which a reasonable businessman is expected to observe."

(That is a quotation from paragraph 216 of the *Report of the Review Committee on Insolvency Law and Practice* (1982) (Cmnd 8558), better known as the Cork Report, reflecting the view of Professor Goode; this passage is quoted in para 54 of the judgment of Lord Neuberger MR in the Court of Appeal). The appellant A3 Noteholders say that this passage is not in point. They have argued for a much stricter construction. They have emphasised that a company's inability to pay its debts is no more than a precondition to the exercise of the court's jurisdiction, which is discretionary, to make a winding up order or an administration order. The precondition to be satisfied should be, they have argued, transparent and certain, leaving scope for the exercise of discretion on the hearing of the petition. There has also been argument as to whether the statutory text (as incorporated in an amended form, and also allowing for possible future legislative amendment) must bear the same meaning as it would in actual winding-up proceedings, or whether it can and should, as incorporated, take account of the commercial context of the Conditions.

8. Those, in outline summary, are the positions of the opposing parties on the appeal. The cross-appeal, which is relevant only if the appeal is successful, is concerned with the so-called Post-Enforcement Call Option ("PECO") which is a subsidiary (but technically important) part of the securitisation transaction.

9. Before going further into the complexities of the appeal I would comment that the image invoked by Professor Goode of an honest and prudent trader working hard to turn his business round relates, as was pointed out by Mr Moss QC for the appellants, to the law of insolvency as it applies to individuals. Even if translated into corporate terms, it has very little bearing on the situation in which Eurosail now finds itself. Its present financial position and future prospects are not matters for which Eurosail and its managers merit either praise or criticism, since those matters are almost entirely out of their control. They depend on three imponderables: first, (since the currency and interest-rate hedging arrangements with the Lehman Brothers group have failed, leaving Eurosail with a claim in its insolvency) the movements of the US dollar and the euro relative to the pound sterling; secondly, movements in LIBOR or equivalent interest rates on loans denominated in those three currencies; and thirdly, the performance of the United Kingdom economy in general, and the United Kingdom residential property market in particular, as influencing the performance of the mortgage portfolio.

THE TRANSACTION DOCUMENTS

10. The legal documents relating to the securitisation issue are, as Lord Neuberger MR put it, regrettably and forbiddingly voluminous. Apart from the Conditions themselves there was a formal trust deed made between the Trustee and Eurosail, a Liquidity Facility Agreement, currency swaps agreements, a Fixed/Floating Swap Agreement, a BBR Swap Agreement and other agreements relating to administrative matters (there is a full list of "transaction documents" in the definition of that expression in the preamble to the Conditions). Several expressions used in the Conditions involve a paperchase to other documents in order to find their definitions. Mr Moss [the barrister representing the Appellant] opened the documents very lightly, moving rapidly from Condition 9(a)(iii) to concentrate his submissions on the construction of section 123(1) and (2) of the 1986 Act. Mr Dicker QC (for Eurosail) went into the Conditions more fully to pave the way for his contextual arguments. Without pre-judging those arguments I think it is necessary, if only in order to appreciate the consequences of the opposing arguments, to have an outline understanding of how the SPE (which counsel concurred in describing as a "closed system" or "wrapper") operated before the collapse of Lehman Brothers, of how it operates now (after the collapse of Lehman Brothers but before any Enforcement Notice), and of how it would operate after the service of an Enforcement Notice.

11. Interest is payable on all unredeemed Notes quarterly in arrears, the first payment having been made on 13 September 2007. The annual rate of interest is linked to LIBOR or its dollar or euro equivalents, exceeding that rate by a margin which varies from 0.07% for A1b Notes to 4% for E Notes.

12. Mortgage interest received by Eurosail cascades down the metaphorical waterfall set out in the 24 sub-paragraphs of Condition 2(g). The first claims on the income stream are for remuneration, charges and expenses; then sums due to the Liquidity Facility Provider, and (sub-paragraph (v), but only until the collapse of Lehman Brothers) sums payable under or in connection with the Fixed/Floating Swap Agreement and the BBR Swap Agreement (but not any currency swaps). Payments to currency swaps counterparties were linked to interest payments to particular classes of Noteholders, so that payments to counterparties in respect of A Noteholders come into the provision for payment of interest to those Noteholders, which is made pari passu as between all the A sub-classes. The next priority was for payment-off of any A Principal Deficiency (another expression defined in the preamble), but in practice such a deficiency could arise only if all the junior classes of Notes had become valueless. Next in the waterfall come similar groups of provisions for payment of interest, sums due to the currency swaps

counterparties (and any B Principal Deficiency) in respect of B Notes and so on for all the other classes.

13. On 15 September 2008 Lehman Brothers Holdings Inc ("LBHI"), the guarantor of the swaps counterparty, Lehman Brothers Special Financing Ltd ("LBSF") filed for Chapter 11 bankruptcy, as did LBSF on 3 October 2008. The swaps were terminated on 13 November 2009. Eurosail has made a claim against LBHI's and LBSF's bankrupt estates for about $221,000,000. At the time of the hearings below, the claim had not been admitted and no distribution has been made in respect of it. During the last three years sterling has depreciated significantly against both the euro and the dollar, but the prevailing low level of interest rates has resulted in a surplus ("excess spread") of mortgage interest received by Eurosail, which has enabled it to continue to pay in full the interest on all the outstanding Notes of every class.

14. In the meantime, both before and after the collapse of Lehman Brothers, Eurosail received principal sums from time to time as principal secured by the mortgages was repaid, either by way of partial or total redemption by mortgagors, or by enforcement of the security against mortgagors who were in default. These sums have been and are at present applied under Condition 5(b)(i) as "Actual Redemption Funds," on each date for payment of interest, in repaying the principal of the Notes in the order of priority A1 (now fully repaid), A2, A3, B, and so on. There is a proviso to Condition 5(b) under which the order of priority may be altered. The first possible variation (proviso (A)) applies if all the A1 and A2 Notes have been redeemed and other (favourable) specified conditions are satisfied: the A3 to E1c Notes then rank pari passu. Conversely, under the other variation (proviso (B)), which applies if there is an A Principal Deficiency, priority is granted to the A Notes as a single class ranking pari passu.

15. Events of default are regulated by Condition 9. The events specified in Condition 9(a) are, apart from that already set out (para 5 above): default in payment for three business days of any principal or interest due on any of the Notes; breach by Eurosail of any of its obligations and failure to remedy the breach (if remediable) for 14 days after notice of the breach given by the Trustee; the making of an order or resolution for the winding up of Eurosail, otherwise than for an approved amalgamation or reconstruction; and the initiation of insolvency or administration proceedings, or the levying of execution (subject to various qualifications which it is unnecessary to set out in detail).

16. If the Event of Default is an event under Condition 9(a)(iii) or a breach of Eurosail's obligations, there is a further requirement that the Trustee shall have certified to Eurosail "that such event is, in its sole opinion, materially prejudicial to the interests of the Noteholders." For this purpose the Trustee may under the trust deed "have regard only to (i) the interests of the A Noteholders if, in the Trustee's sole opinion, there

is a conflict between the interests of the A Noteholders (or any Class thereof) and the interests of the B Noteholders, the C Noteholders, the D Noteholders and/or the E Noteholders." This provision does not indicate how the Trustee is to exercise its discretion in the event of a conflict (such as there now potentially is) between the interests of the A2 Noteholders and the A3 Noteholders. If there is an Event of Default (and, in the cases just mentioned, it is materially prejudicial) the Trustee may at its discretion serve an Enforcement Notice on Eurosail. Moreover it is obliged to do so if requested or directed (i) by holders of at least 25% of the outstanding "Most Senior Class of Notes" (defined as meaning the A Noteholders, rather than a subclass of them) or (ii) by an extraordinary resolution of the holders of that class. This court was not shown any evidence, and did not hear any submissions, as to whether either of those requirements would be likely to be satisfied in practice.

17. On service of the Enforcement Notice the Notes become immediately due and payable and the Noteholders' security becomes enforceable. Thereupon the order of priority shifts from that in Condition 2(g) to that in Condition 2(h). It is unnecessary to go through all the detail of Condition 2(h). The all-important change is that under Condition 2(h)(v) the available funds are applicable to pay "pari passu and pro rata (1) all amounts of interest and principal then due and payable on the A1c Notes, the A2c Notes and the A3c Notes and (2) [subject to provisions about currency swaps that have now lapsed] any interest and principal then due and payable on the A1b Notes, the A2a Notes, the A2b Notes and the A3a Notes, respectively." In practical terms, the A2 Notes would no longer have priority, in terms of principal, to the A3 Notes.

18. The opening words of condition 2(h) express the Trustee's obligation as being to make payments "to the extent of the funds available to [Eurosail] and from the proceeds of enforcement of the Security" (with exceptions that need not be detailed). The penultimate provision of Condition 2(h) provides: "The Noteholders have full recourse to [Eurosail] in respect of the payments prescribed above and accordingly are entitled to bring a claim under English law, subject to the Trust Deed, for the full amount of such payments in accordance with Condition 10 (Enforcement of Notes)." Mr Dicker did not challenge Mr Moss's submission that the opening words do not contradict the penultimate provision, and that seems to be correct. The opening words are directed to the Trustee's obligations, not to those of Eurosail.

19. Condition 5(j) contains the PECO (Post Enforcement Call Option) which is the subject of the cross-appeal. This option (which has been given effect to as a separate written agreement between the Trustee and a company named or referred to as OptionCo) is regarded in the industry as a means of achieving the effect of limited recourse without the adverse tax consequences that would then have followed from a simple express non-recourse provision. The operative part of Clause 5(j) is as follows:

"All of the Noteholders will, at the request of the holder of the Post Enforcement Call Option, sell all (but not some only) of their holdings of the Notes to the holder of the Post Enforcement Call Option, pursuant to the option granted to it by the Trustee (as agent for the Noteholders) to acquire all (but not some only) of the Notes (plus accrued interest thereon), for the consideration of one euro cent per Euro Note outstanding, one dollar cent per Dollar Note outstanding and one penny per Sterling Note outstanding (and for these purposes, each Global Note shall be one Note) in the event that the Security for the Notes is enforced, at any time after the date on which the Trustee determines that the proceeds of such enforcement are insufficient, after payment of all other claims ranking higher in priority to the Notes and pro rata payment of all claims ranking in equal priority to the Notes and after the application of any such proceeds to the Notes under the Deed of Charge, to pay any further principal and interest and any other amounts whatsoever due in respect of the Notes."

BANKRUPTCY REMOTENESS

20. "Bankruptcy remoteness" was the expression used by Standard & Poor's credit-rating agency, and generally in the industry, to describe one criterion for a SPE to obtain a satisfactory credit rating for its loan notes. This is not the place to consider either the reliability of the credit-rating agencies' judgments on Notes secured by sub-prime mortgages, or the influence that their judgments seem to have had in the market (caused, some have suggested, by the industry's general inability to comprehend the risks inherent in its own creations). But the notion of "bankruptcy remoteness," even if imperfectly understood, underlay many features of the Conditions and the arrangements of which they formed part.

21. In developing his contextual argument that this court should (if necessary) mould the meaning of section 123(1) and (2), as incorporated into Condition 9(a)(3) so as to take account of commercial realities, Mr Dicker [for the Respondents] drew particular attention to five features of the arrangements. They are set out and discussed in section B2 of Eurosail's case. Most of them have been mentioned already, at least in passing, but it may be helpful to bring them together in summary form. They are relevant not only (arguably) to the issue of construction but also (without room for argument) to determining the likely length of deferment of Eurosail's long-term liabilities under the Conditions, in the absence of an Event of Default which triggers an Enforcement Notice. These points are covered at some length in the witness statements of Mr Mark Filer, a director of Wilmington Trust SP Services (London) Ltd, Eurosail's corporate services provider.

22. The five salient features of the Conditions and the supporting documentation bearing on the likely deferment of Eurosail's obligations in respect of principal and interest are as follows:

(1) Condition 2(g) defines Eurosail's obligations for payment of interest on the Notes (after remuneration, charges and expenses) in terms of the Available Revenue Fund (see para 12 above). If that source is insufficient for payment of interest on any of the Junior Notes (that is, those which are not A Notes) the obligation is deferred (while accruing interest) under Condition 6(i) and (j), if necessary until the final redemption date in 2045.

(2) Temporary shortages of income can be provided for by the Liquidity Facility (reimbursements to which have a high order of priority under Condition 2(g)(iv)).

(3) As to principal, redemption of Notes (other than the redeemed A1 Notes and the revenue-backed Notes) is not due until 2045. Until then redemption is limited to the Actual Redemption Funds (as defined in the preamble) which are applied in the appropriate order of priority under Condition 5(b) (see para 14 above).

(4) Any loss of principal resulting from default on mortgages is termed a 'Principal Deficiency' and is recorded in the Principal Deficiency Ledger (the detailed provisions as to this are found not in the Conditions but in Clauses 8 and 9 of the Cash/Bond Administration Agreement). If there is surplus income from the mortgage payments, the 'excess spread' can be used to reduce or eliminate any Principal Deficiency on whatever is the highest-ranking class of Notes with a deficiency. Recoupment of a Principal Deficiency takes priority to the payment of interest on lower-ranking Notes (see para 12 above).

(5) Finally there is the PECO, which is intended to produce the same, or a similar result as an express limited-recourse provision (see paras 18 and 19 above).

    . . .

39. At first instance the Chancellor started with three propositions derived from the case law: that the assets to be valued are the present assets of the company; that "contingent and prospective liabilities" are not to be taken at their full face value; and that:

> "'Taking account of' must be recognised in the context of the overall question posed by the subsection, namely whether the company is to be deemed to be insolvent because the amount of its liabilities exceeds the value of its assets. This will involve consideration of the relevant facts of the case, including when the prospective liability falls due, whether it is payable in sterling or some other currency, what assets will be available to meet it and what if any provision is made for the allocation of losses in relation to those assets."

He then set out four reasons for concluding that the value of Eurosail's assets exceeded its liabilities, "having taken account of its contingent and prospective liabilities to such extent as appears to be necessary at this stage."

40. In the Court of Appeal Lord Neuberger MR did not disagree with anything in the Chancellor's judgment so far as it related to statutory

construction. He did however go further in his detailed discussion of section 123(2). He observed:

> "In practical terms, it would be rather extraordinary if section 123(2) was satisfied every time a company's liabilities exceeded the value of its assets. Many companies which are solvent and successful, and many companies early on in their lives, would be deemed unable to pay their debts if this was the meaning of section 123(2). Indeed, the issuer is a good example of this: its assets only just exceeded its liabilities when it was formed, and it was more than possible that, even if things went well, it would fall from time to time within the ambit of section 123(2) if the appellants are right as to the meaning of that provision."

41. Lord Neuberger MR developed this at paras 47 to 49 of his judgment:

> "47. More generally, I find it hard to discern any conceivable policy reason why a company should be at risk of being wound up simply because the aggregate value (however calculated) of its liabilities exceeds that of its assets. Many companies in that position are successful and creditworthy, and cannot in any way be characterised as 'unable to pay [their] debts.' Such a mechanistic, even artificial, reason for permitting a creditor to present a petition to wind up a company could, in my view, only be justified if the words of section 123(2) compelled that conclusion, and in my opinion they do not.
> 48. In my view, the purpose of section 123(2) has been accurately characterised by Professor Sir Roy Goode in *Principles of Corporate Insolvency Law*, 3rd ed (2005). Having referred to section 123(1)(e) as being the 'cash flow test' and to section 123(2) as being the 'balance sheet test,' he said this, at para 4–06: 'If the cash flow test were the only relevant test [for insolvency] then current and short-term creditors would in effect be paid at the expense of creditors to whom liabilities were incurred after the company had reached the point of no return because of an incurable deficiency in its assets.'
> 49. In my judgment, both the purpose and the applicable test of section 123(2) are accurately encapsulated in that brief passage."

42. Toulson LJ agreed with Lord Neuberger MR but expressed himself in a more guarded way. He agreed that Professor Sir Roy Goode had "rightly discerned the underlying policy" but added that Professor Goode's reference to a company having "reached the point of no return because of an incurable deficiency in its assets" illuminates the purpose of the subsection but does not purport to be a paraphrase of it. He continued:

> "Essentially, section 123(2) requires the court to make a judgment whether it has been established that, looking at the company's assets and making proper allowance for its prospective and contingent liabilities, it cannot reasonably be expected to be able to meet those liabilities. If so, it will be

deemed insolvent although it is currently able to pay its debts as they fall due. The more distant the liabilities, the harder this will be to establish."

I agree with what Toulson LJ said here, and with great respect to Lord Neuberger MR I consider that "the point of no return" should not pass into common usage as a paraphrase of the effect of section 123(2). But in the case of a company's liabilities that can as matters now stand be deferred for over 30 years, and where the company is (without any permanent increase in its borrowings) paying its debts as they fall due, the court should proceed with the greatest caution in deciding that the company is in a state of balance-sheet insolvency under section 123(2).

REASONING IN THE COURTS BELOW

43. Sir Andrew Morritt C, having set out some general propositions as to the effect of section 123 (1)(e) and (2), rejected the A3 Noteholders' submission that Eurosail was plainly insolvent for the purposes of section 123(2) as applied by Condition 9(a)(iii). He relied on four points, set out in paras 34 to 37 of his judgment. First, Eurosail's claims in the insolvencies of LBHI and LBSF, though not admitted, could not be ignored. The secondary market indicated that the claim was worth 35% to 37% of US$221m (that is, a value of the order of £60m). Second, a large part of the total deficiency that was claimed to exist was due to conversion into sterling at the prevailing spot rate of liabilities not due for payment until 2045. Third, the future liabilities were fully funded in the limited sense that deficiencies resulting from mortgage defaults reduced Eurosail's liability to the Noteholders through the operation of the Principal Deficiency Ledger. Fourth, the Chancellor was able to infer that a calculation of the then present values of assets and liabilities would not show a deficiency, since Eurosail was well able to pay its debts as they fell due, there was no deficiency on the Principal Deficiency Ledger, and projected redemptions of each class of A Notes were in advance of the maturity dates.

44. In the Court of Appeal counsel appearing for the A2 Noteholders did not feel able to give complete support to the Chancellor's second point, and Lord Neuberger MR accepted the submission of counsel for the appellants:

"As Mr Sheldon [then appearing for the A3 Noteholders] said, one has to value a future or contingent liability in a foreign currency at the present exchange rate. By definition, that is the present sterling market value of the liability."

I would also respectfully question the Chancellor's third point. The Chancellor had earlier in his judgment, at para 13, referred to clause 8 of the Cash/Bond Administration Agreement, which provides for the maintenance of Principal Deficiency Ledgers. That seems to be the basis of his point about liabilities being self-cancelling. But clause 8 seems to be concerned with no more than an accountancy exercise, not with a permanent extinction of liabilities. It operates to defer liabilities for principal until the final redemption date, if circumstances require, and provided that an Enforcement Notice is not given in the meantime. But Condition 2(h) provides for Eurosail to be liable on a full recourse basis post-enforcement, as already noted (para 18 above).

45. Lord Neuberger MR did not accept that a forecast deficiency based on then current exchange rates could be dismissed as entirely speculative. He started from Eurosail's audited accounts for the year ending 30 November 2009, which showed a net liability of £74.557m. He noted that this figure required two substantial amendments (one for the Lehman Brothers claim, and the other for the full recourse factor) "which, ironically and coincidentally, virtually cancel each other out." So his final discussion and conclusion starts with an assumed deficiency of the order of £75m.

46. Against that Lord Neuberger MR set three factors. The first was that a deficiency of £75m, with an aggregate principal sum of just over £420m outstanding on the mortgages, was less than 17% of the assets. Secondly, the deficit was largely based on the assumption that exchange rates would remain constant:

"Of course, they are as likely to move in an adverse direction as they are to move in a favourable direction, but the volatility of those rates tell against the appellants given that they have to establish that the issuer has reached the point of no return."

Thirdly, the court was looking a long way ahead:

"Not only do all the unredeemed notes have a final redemption date in 2045, but it appears from the evidence that the weighted average term of the remaining mortgages is in the region of 18 years, and the rate of early redemption has slowed significantly and is likely, according to expert assessment, to remain low for the time being."

47. Lord Neuberger MR accepted that there was a real possibility that, if no Enforcement Notice was served, events might turn out to the disadvantage of the A3 Noteholders:

"However, as mentioned, a future or contingent creditor of a company can very often show that he would be better off if the company were wound up rather than being permitted to carry on business. In a commercially sensible legal system that cannot of itself justify the creditor seeking to wind up the company."

Toulson and Wilson LJJ agreed with this reasoning. Toulson LJ emphasised the importance of the liabilities being distant in time (para 119, quoted in para 42 above). The appeal was therefore dismissed, as was the cross-appeal.

CONCLUSIONS

48. The crucial issue, to my mind, is how far the Court of Appeal's conclusion depended on the "point of no return" test. For reasons already mentioned, I consider that that is not the correct test, if and in so far as it goes beyond the need for a petitioner to satisfy the court, on the balance of probabilities, that a company has insufficient assets to be able to meet all its liabilities, including prospective and contingent liabilities. If it means no more than that, it is unhelpful, except as illuminating (as Toulson LJ put it) the purpose of section 123(2).

49. In my view the Court of Appeal would have reached the same conclusion without reference to any "point of no return" test; and I would myself reach the same conclusion. Eurosail's ability or inability to pay all its debts, present or future, may not be finally determined until much closer to 2045, that is more than 30 years from now. The complex documentation under which the loan notes were issued contains several mechanisms (identified in para 22(1) to (4) above, the PECO being disregarded for present purposes) for ensuring that liabilities in respect of principal are, if necessary, deferred until the final redemption date, unless the post-enforcement regime comes into operation. The movements of currencies and interest rates in the meantime, if not entirely speculative, are incapable of prediction with any confidence. The court cannot be satisfied that there will eventually be a deficiency.

50. I would therefore dismiss the appeal. I would also dismiss the cross-appeal, for the same reasons as were given by the Chancellor and the Court of Appeal. It is not necessary to consider Mr Dicker's arguments based on supposed inconsistencies and commercial realities....The loan notes documentation did indeed contain some provisions which are inconsistent with the post-enforcement regime being triggered by a temporary deficiency of assets. But the court might well have taken the view, on documents of such complexity, that the draftsman had simply failed to grasp all its many and various implications, and that it was not for the court to rewrite the documents for the parties.

LORD HOPE

51. I would dismiss the appeal for the reasons given by Lord Walker. I would also dismiss the cross-appeal, which concerns the effect of the

PECO on the application of section 123(2) of the 1986 Act as incorporated into Condition 9(a)(iii). The question which it raises no longer needs to be answered as the Noteholders' appeal on the question whether Eurosail ("the Issuer") was unable to pay its debts was not successful. But Sir Andrew Morritt C [2011] 1 WLR 122 gave his view on it in paras 39–44 of his judgment, and so too did Lord Neuberger MR in the Court of Appeal [2011] 1 WLR 2524 in paras 84–100. A PECO is widely used in securitisation transactions of the kind that was entered into in this case, and we have been told that the question is of some importance to the securitisation market more generally. So it is appropriate that we should give our reasons for agreeing with the Chancellor and the Court of Appeal that it has no effect on the way the liability of the Issuer to the Noteholders for the purposes of the default provision in Condition 9(a)(iii) is to be calculated.

52. The Trustee entered into a PECO Agreement on behalf of the Noteholders on 16 July 2007, which is the same date as that on which the Notes were issued. By Clause 3.1 it granted an option to a company called Eurosail Options Ltd (referred to in the Agreement as "OptionCo"):

> "to acquire all (but not some only) of the Notes (plus accrued interest thereon) in the event that the Security for the Notes is enforced and the Trustee, after the payment of the proceeds of such enforcement, determines that the proceeds of such enforcement are insufficient, after payment of all claims ranking in priority to or pari passu with the Notes pursuant to the Deed of Charge, to pay in full all principal and/or interest and any other amounts whatsoever due in respect of the Notes. The Trustee shall promptly after the Security is enforced and the proceeds of such enforcement are paid, make a determination of whether or not there is such an insufficiency. If the Trustee determines that there is such an insufficiency the Trustee shall forthwith give notice (the 'Insufficiency Notice') of such determination to OptionCo and the Issuer."

53. Clause 3.1 has to be read together with Condition 5(j) (see para 19, above), which provides that each Noteholder will, on the exercise of the option conferred on OptionCo, sell to the company the whole of his holding of notes for the nominal consideration for which the PECO provides. It also has to be read together with the Event of Default described in Condition 9(a)(iii): see para 5, above. Under that provision a default occurs, among other things, in the event of the Issuer:

> "being unable to pay its debts as and when they fall due or, within the meaning of section 123(1) or (2) (as if the words 'it is proved to the satisfaction of the court' did not appear in section 123(2)) of the Insolvency Act 1986 (as that section may be amended from time to time), being deemed unable to pay its debts."

54. The Prospectus at p 26 contains this explanation of the effect of these provisions, under the heading "Considerations related to the Instruments," for prospective purchasers:

"Although the Instruments will be full recourse obligations of the Issuer, upon enforcement of the security for the Instruments, the Trustee...will, in practice, have recourse only to the Loans and Collateral Security, and to any other assets of the Issuer then in existence as described in this document..."

55. The purpose of a PECO is to achieve bankruptcy remoteness for the issuer. Its aim is to prevent the issuer from being susceptible to insolvent winding up proceedings by ensuring so far as possible that, if its assets prove to be insufficient to meet its liabilities, a director of the issuer will not instigate bankruptcy proceedings in respect of it. Bankruptcy remoteness is one of the criteria used by the rating agencies which issuers of notes seek to satisfy so that their instruments will achieve the highest possible credit rating. That criterion is satisfied in other jurisdictions by provisions which limit the rights of noteholders against the issuer to the value of the issuer's assets. Until recent tax legislation altered the position, limited recourse provisions of that kind gave rise to UK stamp duty reserve tax at the rate of 1.5% of the amount subscribed for them. As the Chancellor explained in para 40, the PECO is designed to achieve the same result as limited recourse provisions, but without the adverse tax consequences.

56. The Issuer accepts that, as a matter of contract, the liabilities were unlimited in recourse. But it maintains that the commercial reality was that the liabilities alleged to be the debts that the issuer was unable to pay to the Noteholder were liabilities which it would never have to meet. In the event that the assets of the Issuer were exhausted, any claim that the Noteholder had against the Issuer would be assigned to the option holder. That, it is said, would bring an end to the claim. So it would be wrong to treat the Issuer as falling within section 123(2) as incorporated into Condition 9(a)(iii) on the ground that it was unable to pay its debts, as in practice it was never intended or expected that the liabilities would be paid except out of the underlying assets available to the Issuer.

57. The soundness of this approach depends however on whether, in law, the PECO affects the liability of the Issuer to the Noteholder. In answering this question it is important to appreciate that the question is not whether the Issuer should actually be wound up on the grounds described in section 123(2), but whether its financial position is such that it falls within that subsection for the purposes of the default provision in Condition 9(a)(iii). The answer to that question is to be found by examining the wording of the Condition in the context of the provisions of the transaction documents as a whole. Does the PECO in any way alter the conclusion that would otherwise be drawn that the

Issuer's assets were less than its liabilities and that it was unable to pay its debts?

58. The Chancellor based his judgment that it did not on the wording of section 123(2), as amended for the purposes of Condition 9(a)(iii). He held that if, in the application of that subsection the court concluded that the value of the company's assets was less than the amount of its liabilities, taking into account its contingent and prospective liabilities, the PECO had no effect on those liabilities at all: para 43. As he put it, the liabilities of the Issuer remain the same, whether or not there is a PECO or, if there is, whether or not the call option has been exercised. Unless and until the option holder releases the Issuer from all further liability, which it is under no obligation to do, the liability of the Issuer is unaffected.

59. Lord Neuberger reached the same conclusion, but for fuller reasons: see paras 92–97. He said that, reading the relevant provisions of the documents together, they established that the Issuer's liability to the Noteholders was to be treated as a liability of full recourse at least until the security was enforced and, arguably, until the option was exercised and the transfer to the option holder was completed. There was the statement in the Prospectus mentioned in para 54, above. It suggested a two-stage process, under which the Issuer's liability was treated initially as full recourse and liability would become limited recourse only on enforcement of the security. There was the closing part of clause 6.7 of the Deed of Charge which, having restricted the ability of the Trustee to enforce the Noteholders' rights on enforcement of the Security beyond the Issuer's assets, provided that this "shall not apply to and shall not limit the obligations of the Issuer to the [Noteholders] under the Instruments and this Deed." And there was the provision in Condition 2(h), which stated in terms that the Noteholders had full recourse to the Issuer in respect of payments due and that they were entitled to bring a claim under English law for the full amount of such payments.

60. Finally Lord Neuberger referred to the wording of Condition 9(a)(iii) itself. It was hard to see why any reference should be made in that Condition to section 123(2) if the Noteholders' rights against the Issuer were not to be treated as full recourse until the enforcement of the security. He also said that there was nothing commercially insensible in the conclusion that, for the purpose of Condition 9(a)(iii), the Noteholders' rights against the Issuer were treated as being of full recourse, notwithstanding the PECO: para 100.

61. The A3 Noteholders submit that the key operative provision is Clause 3.1 of the PECO itself. It makes it plain that it does not have the effect of limiting the liability of the Issuer in respect of the Notes to the value of the Issuer's assets. Its reference to there being an "insufficiency" of assets after enforcement to meet whatever is "due in respect of the Notes" is a clear indication that it contemplates that the

amount of the liabilities that the Notes have created must be capable of exceeding the value of the assets of the Issuer. Then there is the time at which the option is exercisable. It is not said to have any operative effect at all prior to enforcement of the security. So at all times prior to its exercise the Noteholders remain entitled to payment in accordance with the Conditions. And even when exercised all it does is provide a mechanism by which the right to be paid under the Notes is assigned to OptionCo.

62. As the Issuer relies on commercial reality rather than legal form, the legal effect of the documents is not really in dispute. The common intention of the parties is said by the Issuer to be quite different. Its argument is that, as inclusion of a PECO rather than a contractual limited recourse provision was done solely for tax reasons, it was not intended or understood to alter the commercial nature, effect and operation of the asset-backed securitisation. As a matter of contract the liabilities were unlimited in recourse. As a matter of commercial substance and in practice, they were the equivalent of a provision by which the rights of Noteholders were expressly limited. The Issuer's case is that its future obligations to pay principal under the Notes should be taken into account only to the extent that its assets were sufficient to pay for them. As Mr Dicker QC for the Issuer put it at the end of his argument, legal form should not triumph over commercial substance.

63. I do not think that it is possible to distinguish the intended commercial effect of these provisions from their legal effect in this way. The exercise that Condition 9(a)(iii) predicates is the quantification of the amount of the Issuers' assets and liabilities in order to determine whether there has been an Event of Default. The legal effect and the commercial effect of the PECO, on its true analysis, both point in the same direction. It has no effect, for the purpose of that quantification, on the amount of the Issuer's liabilities. To limit those liabilities as the Issuer contends would contradict the parties' clearly expressed commercial intention as found in the contractual documents. The fact that the economic result of the PECO may be the same as if the Noteholders' right of recourse had been limited to the Issuer's assets is beside the point. It can be expected to achieve bankruptcy remoteness as effectively. But it would not be in accordance with the true meaning of the documents to treat the two methods as if they had the same effect in law.

64. The ultimate aim in construing provisions of the kind that are in issue in this case, as it is when construing any contract, is to determine what the parties meant by the language that they have used. Commercial good sense has a role to play when the provisions are open to different interpretations. The court should adopt the more, rather than the less, commercial construction: *Rainy Sky SA v Kookmin Bank*[2011] UKSC 50, [2011] 1 WLR 2900. But, for the reasons given by the Chancellor

and Lord Neuberger MR, the meaning to be given to the language that the parties used in this case is not open to doubt. The suggestion that to give effect to that meaning is to surrender to legal form over commercial substance amounts, in effect, to an invitation to depart from the settled role of commercial good sense. Its role is to find out what the parties meant when they entered into the arrangement, not to replace it with something which is not to be found in the language of the documents at all.

Be ready to describe and discuss the rather intricate *Eurosail* transaction in class. Why might Lehman have wanted to enter into this transaction? What was the purpose of issuing so many layers of debt? What role did the swaps play?

Lord Hope's concurrence makes clear that this transaction is one where bankruptcy and tax issues intersect. Be sure you understand precisely how that is so.

3.   TRANCHE WARFARE

The title of this section might bring back high school or college memories of Wilfred Owen or Siegfried Sassoon, but you actually have already seen an example of this phenomenon in the *Eurosail* case. In short, we are talking about fights among the various tranches, which are apt to break out when there are not enough funds to go around. After the 2008 financial collapse, that happened with more frequency than ever before. The following case provides another, more extreme, example.

IN RE ZAIS INVESTMENT GRADE LIMITED VII

455 B.R. 839
United States Bankruptcy Court, D. New Jersey.
Aug. 26, 2011.

RAYMOND T. LYONS, Bankruptcy Judge.

INTRODUCTION

Hildene Capital Management and Hildene Opportunities Master Fund, LTD (collectively "Hildene" or "Movants"), noteholders in a junior tranche, move to dismiss this involuntary chapter 11 case filed by senior noteholders. Zais Group, LLC (the "Collateral Manager") and Babson Capital Management, a senior noteholder, join in the motion. Because the Debtor failed to contest the involuntary petition and the order for relief has been entered, Hildene may not challenge the involuntary petition. The Debtor has property in the United States and a place of business in the United States through a trustee and the Collateral

Manager; therefore, it is eligible to be a debtor under title 11, United States Code. The petitioning creditors have established a good faith basis for filing this involuntary petition in that they seek to maximize the value of the Debtor's assets by actively managing them freed of the strictures of the trust indenture. Motion denied.

FINDINGS OF FACT AND PROCEDURAL HISTORY

Zais Investment Grade Limited VII ("ZING VII" or the "Debtor") is a Cayman Islands corporation formed in 2005. Zais Group, LLC worked with an affiliate of Citigroup, Inc. to create this special purpose vehicle. It issued notes in the face amount of $365.5 million on the Irish Stock Exchange and used the proceeds to acquire securities. ZING VII then pledged those securities (Collateral Securities) as collateral for its obligations to the noteholders. The Bank of New York Mellon Trust Company, N.A. is Trustee under a trust indenture for the benefit of the noteholders. It holds ZING VII's assets in trust here in the United States. ZING VII also issued $40 million of so-called Income Notes that are not secured and are junior to all the secured notes. Under the indenture the Income Notes are treated as equity.

In Wall Street jargon ZING VII is a CDO Squared. "CDO" stands for collateralized debt obligation; i.e., ZING VII issued notes and pledged the securities as collateral. In addition, the Collateral Securities are made up primarily of CDO's issued by other entities—hence, CDO Squared. At the bottom of this pyramid of debt are, primarily, residential mortgages, but also commercial mortgages, corporate loans, auto loans, credit cards, student loans and others.

The noteholders are separated into classes (tranches) and are entitled to distributions from the trust in descending order of priority. The petitioning creditors hold Class A–1 notes, the first priority. Hildene holds Class A–2 notes—second in line. ZAIS Group, LLC is the Collateral Manager for ZING VII's securities. It was permitted to sell securities and replace those with other eligible securities. If all noteholders were satisfied in full, the Collateral Manager stood to share any excess proceeds with the Income Noteholders. There is a nominal shareholder of ZING VII but it has no right to any residual value realized through ZING VII's business. ZING VII has contracted away any right to benefit from its assets. Two individuals in the Cayman Islands serve as directors and maintain the corporate existence. ZING VII has no employees or officers and takes no role in the management of its assets. It merely exists.

An event of default under the indenture occurred on March 11, 2009. It was not a payment default but a covenant default. That triggered a provision in the indenture requiring the Trustee to hold the Collateral Securities intact. Therefore, the Trustee has merely been collecting payments under the securities it holds as collateral and distributing the money it collects. The Collateral Manager has not been managing the Collateral Securities but continues to monitor the assets. The senior noteholders accelerated their notes effective June 3, 2009. Following acceleration, all collections must be distributed to the Class A–1 noteholders until they are satisfied in full. Since default and acceleration the Trustee has collected and distributed significant amounts and reduced the principal balance on the Class A–1 notes.

The petitioning creditors, GRF Master Fund, L.P., Anchorage Illiquid Opportunities Master Offshore, L.P., Anchorage Capital Master Offshore, Ltd., and Anchorage Capital Group, L.L.C., are all funds managed by Anchorage Capital Group, L.L.C. ("Anchorage"). None of them was an original investor in ZING VII. They all acquired their notes after default, beginning in October 2009. Anchorage asserts that the collateral could yield a better return if it were managed, or liquidated in an orderly fashion, not just left to runoff by collection of the debt securities held in trust now. Anchorage attempted, without success, to convince ZING VII to rectify the passive holding of its assets. Under the trust indenture, the only way to achieve an orderly liquidation of the assets is to obtain the consent of 66.67% of all noteholders, which Anchorage deems highly unlikely, if not impossible. Secondly, Anchorage asserts that, even if managed well, the securities will never yield enough to satisfy the Class A–1 noteholders, so all other noteholders are out of the money.

An involuntary petition under chapter 11 of the Bankruptcy Code was filed on April 1, 2011 by the Anchorage entities; no other creditors joined the petition under section 303(c). No answer was filed, therefore, the court entered an order for relief by default on April 26, 2011. *See* 11 U.S.C. § 303(h). The Debtor filed schedules listing one small bank account with $500.00 in a Cayman Islands bank. The other assets are described as "Debt obligations held by the Indenture Trustee." The Trustee has submitted a declaration of an officer detailing the Collateral Securities it holds. Certificated securities are held in a vault in New York City. Un-certificated securities are registered with Depository Trust Company in New York City and Euroclear in Brussels. The Trustee also holds millions of dollars in cash in a bank account in the United States.

The petitioning creditors filed a plan of reorganization and disclosure statement. The plan was prepared prepetition and, according to Anchorage, garnered approval by 95% in amount of the Class A–1 noteholders before the case was filed. Hildene challenges the voting tabulation. The plan calls for all of the Collateral Securities to be transferred to Anchorage for management and orderly liquidation with the proceeds distributed to the Class A–1 noteholders.

Hildene, likewise, was not an original investor. It purchased junior notes after the involuntary petition was filed and on the eve of entry of the order for relief. Hildene's principal submitted a declaration that Hildene expects to realize a profit on its investment because it estimates the collections of the Collateral Securities will be more than the amount needed to satisfy the Class A–1 notes. In addition, Hildene holds junior positions in other CDO's, believes that CDO's should not be in bankruptcy, and that allowing ZING VII to be placed in involuntary bankruptcy sets a bad precedent for the CDO market. Hildene filed a motion to dismiss or abstain under sections 305 and 1112 of the Bankruptcy Code.

DISCUSSION

Movants argue that there are two threshold issues that warrant dismissal of this case: (1) ZING VII is not eligible to be a debtor under Section 109 of the Bankruptcy Code; or (2) the Anchorage entities are not qualified to be petitioning creditors.

ZING VII'S ELIGIBILITY TO BE A DEBTOR

Section 109(a) limits who may be a debtor under title 11 of the U.S.Code:

[O]nly a person that resides or has a domicile, a place of business, or property in the United States . . . may be a debtor under this title.

The burden of establishing eligibility is on the petitioners. *In re Global Ocean Carriers Limited,* 251 B.R. 31, 37 (Bankr.D.Del.2000). It is uncontroverted that ZING VII, a Cayman Islands corporation, does not reside in or have a domicile in the United States. The petition listed ZING VII's place of business in Red Bank, New Jersey, but that is the office of ZAIS Group, LLC, the Collateral Manager, a separate entity from ZING VII. Movants also contend that since ZING VII does not engage in business, it has no place of business. The business activities of collecting money from the Collateral Securities and distributing money to the noteholders are done by the Trustee, pursuant to a contract with ZING VII. To the extent the Collateral Securities were managed or are being managed, that is by the Collateral Manager, ZAIS Group LLP, under contract with ZING VII.

ZING VII can be characterized as a letterbox company. All that happens in the Cayman Islands are the necessities for maintaining registration. The important functions of investing, collecting, disbursing, recordkeeping and communicating with noteholders is primarily done in the U.S. The court finds that ZING VII does have a place of business in the United States for the purpose of section 109 through the Trustee and Collateral Manager.

Movants argues that ZING VII has no property in the United States. The schedules list one small bank account with $500.00 in a Cayman Islands bank. The other assets are described as "Debt obligations held by the Indenture Trustee." These securities are held in a vault in New York City or are registered in New York City and in Brussels. Millions of dollars in cash are in a bank account in the United States. These securities and cash, although pledged as collateral and held by the Trustee, are nominally the property of the Debtor and are located in the United States. In response to the motion to dismiss or abstain the Debtor has clarified its position that the assets held by the Trustee as collateral belong to the Debtor and are located in the United States. The Trustee, likewise, has filed a supplemental declaration disclaiming any beneficial interest in the cash or Collateral Securities.

ZING VII's Collateral Securities and cash are held or registered in the U.S. It is eligible to be a debtor under Section 109.

QUALIFICATION OF PETITIONING CREDITORS

Movants contend that the Anchorage Entities were not qualified to be petitioning creditors because their notes are non-recourse, they cannot be unsecured creditors. Section 303(b)(1) permits three or more entities holding claims aggregating at least $14,425 more than the value of any collateral securing such claims to file an involuntary petition. According to Movants, since the notes are non-recourse, the claims can never be more than the value of the collateral, i.e., the petitioning creditors are secured, but not unsecured creditors.

Only the alleged debtor may contest an involuntary petition, including challenging the qualifications of the petitioning creditors. 11 U.S.C. § 303(d); *In re QDN, LLC,* 363 Fed.Appx. 873, 875–6 (3d Cir.2010). Here, ZING VII failed to contest the petition and the order for relief was entered by default. Movants may not question the petitioning creditors' qualifications.

DISMISSAL

The court may dismiss a case for cause under Section 1112. Although not mentioned as one of the list of specific causes for dismissal, lack of good faith is recognized as grounds for dismissal. When a party files a motion to dismiss and places good faith "at issue" by presenting a *prima facie* case of bad faith in the filing, the non-moving party bears the burden of demonstrating good faith. Further, dismissal is appropriate when the petition lacks a "valid reorganizational purpose." *In re SGL Carbon Corp.,* 200 F.3d at 169 (holding that the filing of a chapter 11 merely to avoid the consequences of antitrust litigation while the company was otherwise financially stable did not meet the requirement of a "valid reorganizational purpose" and consequently the petition was not filed in good faith).

Initially, Movants invite the court to consider the eligibility of the debtor under section 109 and the qualification of the petitioners as indicia of bad faith. The court declines that invitation. As determined above, the debtor is eligible and the Movants may not challenge the qualifications of the petitioners. There is no reason to consider these factors as cause for dismissal.

Movants disparage the motives of the petitioning creditors alleging an attempt to gain an unfair advantage at the expense of other noteholders. However, if Anchorage is correct that under the best of circumstances no creditors beyond Class A–1 will ever receive a payment, no other noteholders are disadvantaged. Receiving zero under the plan is no worse than getting nothing from a runoff collection of the Collateral Securities. If the court were to find Anchorage's valuations incorrect, and that some other tranches are in the money, then Anchorage's plan cannot be confirmed. Furthermore, Anchorage's plan benefits all Class A–1 Noteholders, not just Anchorage. This case is distinguishable from *SGL Carbon* because the Debtor is in financial distress. An event of default under the indenture has occurred and is expected to persist. The Class A–1 notes have been accelerated and no junior classes will receive a distribution until the A1's have been paid.

Movants also contend that it is not a valid bankruptcy purpose to avoid the limitations on management of the Collateral Securities under the indenture. They point out that the petitioning creditors acquired their notes after default and acceleration when the requirement of the indenture that the Trustee hold the Collateral Securities intact had already become effective. Movants suggest that the sanctity of the contract should be upheld. However, sections 365(a) and 1123(b)(2) of the Bankruptcy Code specifically permit the rejection of an executory contract indicating that there are circumstances justifying overriding a burdensome contract. In addition, section 1123(b)(1) specifically provides that a plan may impair secured or unsecured claims or interests. Any knowledgeable attorney opining on the enforceability of a contract will disclaim the effects of bankruptcy law.

Lastly, Movants contend that the indenture is a subordination agreement that must be enforced under section 510(a) of the Bankruptcy Code. Although the indenture subordinates all tranches to the Class A–1 Notes, the Movants argue that the requirement to hold the Collateral Securities intact following default absent the consent of a supermajority of all noteholders is for their benefit and cannot be disregarded. One need only note that section 1129(b)(1) permits confirmation of a plan "notwithstanding section 510(a)." Movants cite *Ion Media Networks, Inc. v. Cyrus Select Opportunities Master Fund, Ltd. (In re Ion Media Networks, Inc.),* 419 B.R. 585 (Bankr.S.D.N.Y.2009) for the proposition that inter-creditor agreements barring certain bankruptcy actions will be enforced. Here, while the indenture prohibits the Trustee and junior noteholders from filing an involuntary petition against the debtor, Class A–1 noteholders are not mentioned in those provisions. To the contrary, the limitations expire one year and a day after senior noteholders have been paid in full, indicating that the non-petition clauses are for the benefit of senior noteholders, not a limitation on their rights to file a petition.

The arguments by the Movants do not constitute a *prima facie* case of bad faith, but even if they did, the court finds that the petitioning creditors have shown good faith in their desire to realize the greatest present value of the Collateral Securities for the benefit of the Class A–1 creditors without negatively impacting junior creditors who have no prospect of recovery under the status quo. It remains to be seen if the plan proponents can carry their burden of proof at confirmation.

CONCLUSION

The debtor is eligible to be in bankruptcy in the United States because it has a place of business and property here. The Movants may not challenge the involuntary petition and have not shown that it is the best interests of creditors and the debtor to abstain or dismiss the petition under section 305 of the Bankruptcy Code. The petitioning creditors have demonstrated a good faith basis for filing bankruptcy to maximize the value of the debtor's assets by actively managing them. While the court makes no finding regarding confirmation of the plan proposed by the petitioning creditors, the motion to dismiss or abstain is denied.

PROBLEM SET 19.2

1. Why bankruptcy in this case?
2. If ZING VII had timely contested the involuntary bankruptcy petition, would the outcome have changed? A Royal Bank of Scotland study of a small sampling of securitization transaction documents found pervasive use of non-petition clauses substantially similar to those in the ZING VII indenture.
3. Are ABS securities debt or equity? Does it matter? *See* IRS Notice 94-47, 1994-19 I.R.B. 9 (Apr. 18, 1994). Should the Trust Indenture Act apply to them? *Ret. Bd. of the Policemen's Annuity & Ben. Fund of the City of Chicago v. Bank of New York Mellon*, 775 F.3d 154, 163 (2d Cir. 2014) (deciding the TIA does not apply to one common ABS structure, but not addressing the issue more generally). *See also Blackrock Core Bond Portfolio v. U.S. Bank Nat'l Ass'n*, No. 14-CV-9401 (KBF), 2016 WL 796848, at *19 (S.D.N.Y. Feb. 26, 2016) (assuming TIA applies).
4. Securitization emerged as a means to generate new assets with (perceived) low credit risk but with higher yields. It did not turn out that way. Would it be accurate to say that was no party explicitly authorized, or if authorized, not satisfactorily incentivized (eg, through adequate fees), to conduct due diligence on securitizations deal-by-deal?

4. "SYNTHETIC" SECURITIZATION

BAYERISCHE LANDESBANK v. ALADDIN CAPITAL MANAGEMENT LLC

692 F.3d 42
United States Court of Appeals, Second Circuit.
Aug. 6, 2012.

RAKOFF, District Judge, sitting by designation.
In this case, we are called on to determine whether an investor in a special investment vehicle—a synthetic collateralized debt obligation ("CDO") that sold interests in a credit default swap—can bring an action against the manager of the investment portfolio for the loss of its investment where the investor was not a party to the contract that defined the manager's role and duties.

Plaintiffs–Appellants Bayerische Landesbank ("Bayerische") and Bayerische Landesbank New York Branch filed this action against Defendant–Appellee Aladdin Capital Management LLC ("Aladdin") for breach of contract and gross negligence based on Aladdin's alleged disregard of its obligation to manage the portfolio in favor of the investors. Aladdin's purportedly gross mis-management allegedly caused plaintiffs to lose their entire $60 million investment in the CDO. On January 31, 2011, plaintiff Bayerische Landesbank, New York Branch filed its original Complaint in the United States District Court for the Southern District of New York seeking to recover damages for the loss of its investment, and later filed an Amended Complaint joining its parent, Bayerische Landesbank, as co-plaintiff. Aladdin moved to dismiss the Amended Complaint, and, by Order dated July 8, 2011, the district court granted the motion. The district court held that, because of a provision of the contract limiting intended third-party beneficiaries to those "specifically provided herein," plaintiffs could not bring a third-party beneficiary breach of contract claim, and held also that plaintiffs could not "recast" their failed contract claim in tort. For the reasons described below, however, we conclude that plaintiffs have properly alleged both a breach of contract claim and a tort claim.

FACTUAL ALLEGATIONS

Plaintiff Bayerische Landesbank is a publically regulated bank incorporated in Germany with its principal place of business in Munich, Germany. Co-plaintiff Bayerische Landesbank, New York Branch is the New York branch of Bayerische Landesbank and is a federally chartered bank licensed by the United States Office of the Comptroller of the Currency. Defendant Aladdin is a Delaware limited liability company with its principal place of business in Stamford, Connecticut. Aladdin is a registered investment adviser under the Investment Advisers Act of 1940, and is a subsidiary of Aladdin Capital Holdings LLC ("ACH"), an investment bank.

In December 2006, plaintiffs invested $60 million in a collateralized debt obligation structured and marketed by defendant Aladdin and by non-parties Goldman Sachs & Co. and Goldman Sachs International (collectively, "Goldman Sachs"). A CDO is a financial instrument that sells interests (here in the form of "Notes") to investors and pays the investors based on the performance of the underlying asset held by the CDO. The CDO at issue in this case, called the Aladdin Synthetic CDO II ("Aladdin CDO") was a "synthetic" CDO, meaning that the asset it held for its investors was not a traditional asset like a stock or bond, but was instead a derivative instrument, *i.e.*, an instrument whose value was determined in reference to still other assets. The derivative instrument the Aladdin CDO held was a "credit default swap" entered into between the Aladdin CDO and Goldman Sachs Capital Markets, L.P. ("GSCM") based on the debt of approximately one hundred corporate entities and sovereign states that were referred to as the "Reference Entities" and comprised the "Reference Portfolio."

A credit default swap ("CDS") is a financial derivative that allows counterparties to buy and sell financial protection for the creditworthiness of specific corporations or sovereign entities, here the Reference Entities. A counterparty taking the position that the Reference Entities would *not* experience a "Credit Event"—such as bankruptcy, default, restructuring, or failure to pay a defined obligation—is said to be the "protection seller," similar to an insurance underwriter. A counterparty taking the position that the Reference Entities *would* experience a Credit Event is the "protection buyer," similar to an individual purchasing insurance. A credit default swap differs from traditional insurance in that the protection buyer need not actually own the underlying asset or security in order to purchase protection on it. More to the point, the protection seller is, in effect, taking a long position and betting that there will be no Credit Event, while the protection buyer is taking a short position and betting that there will be a Credit Event.

Here, Aladdin and Goldman Sachs created a shell entity, the "Issuer" of the Aladdin CDO, to serve as the protection seller, while GSCM served as the protection buyer. Thus, GSCM was to pay premiums to the Issuer in order to purchase protection against the occurrence of a Credit Event. The Issuer was also authorized to establish a separate "short" Reference Portfolio, which would reverse the counterparties' positions—*i.e.* the Issuer would be the protection buyer and GSCM would be the protection seller.

Since the Issuer was just a shell entity, Aladdin and Goldman Sachs, in order to fund the CDO and have money available to pay GSCM in the event of a Credit Event, marketed interests in the CDO to investors in the form of Notes. The Notes were formally issued by the Issuer, Aladdin Synthetic CDO II SPC, and the Co–Issuer, Aladdin Synthetic CDO II (Delaware) LLC, which are limited liability companies incorporated under the laws of the Cayman Islands and Delaware, respectively. Aladdin, as "Portfolio Manager," used the money received from investors who purchased the Notes to purchase interest-yielding securities that, together with the payment of premiums by GSCM, were intended to pay quarterly interest payments to Noteholders until the CDO matured in December 2013, when the principal would be returned to the Noteholders. The principal that investors paid to purchase the Notes was available to cover payments to GSCM as the protection buyer if there were a Credit Event.

The Issuer split the Notes into separate Series, each with different levels of risk and return. Each Series of Notes had a specific level of risk, or "subordination," that protected each Series of Notes against possible losses to the invested principal. For each Series issued, a separate "Indenture" spelled out the relationship between the Noteholders of that Series and the CDO. If a Reference Entity in the Reference Portfolio (*i.e.,* the securities underlying the CDS) suffered a Credit Event, GSCM would reduce the level of subordination for the affected Series by a certain percentage amount, depending on the weight of the relevant Reference Entity in the Reference Portfolio. The plaintiffs here purchased Notes in both Series B–1 and Series C–1. The level of subordination for plaintiffs' Series B–1 Notes was 5.15% and the level of subordination for the Series C–1 Notes was 4.65%.

The structure of the CDS entered into by the Issuer and GSCM allowed the Issuer to change the composition of the overall Reference Portfolio by trading Reference Entities into or out of the Reference Portfolio. This trading also affected the level of subordination. If the Issuer replaced a low-risk Reference

Entity (reflected by a smaller "spread" or insurance premium) with a higher-risk Reference Entity (reflected by a larger spread), that would increase the level of subordination for the Noteholders, and vice versa.

If the level of subordination for a Series went more than 1% below zero, the entire amount invested by the Noteholders in that Series would go to GSCM, and the Notes would become worthless and no longer deliver interest payments. Plaintiffs allege that the Series they invested in could sustain Credit Events with respect to approximately ten or eleven Reference Entities before their subordination levels fell to more than 1% below zero. Additionally, if Aladdin purchased protection for Reference Entities through the short portfolio, the Noteholders' subordination levels would be increased if those short Reference Entities experienced a Credit Event. Thus, the financial interests of GSCM and the Noteholders were adverse.

Since the Issuer was just a shell entity, the Noteholders needed someone to manage the Reference Portfolio, and, according to plaintiffs, protect the Noteholders by minimizing the occurrence of losses and avoiding Credit Events. Here, Goldman Sachs and Aladdin structured the CDO so that Aladdin would manage the CDO as an independent investment manager on behalf of the Noteholders.

Plaintiffs allege that they purchased their Notes in the Aladdin CDO after Aladdin and Goldman Sachs came to the offices of Bayerische's New York branch to present marketing materials regarding the then-proposed Aladdin CDO and to solicit plaintiffs' investment. In the marketing book defendant provided to plaintiffs, defendant Aladdin allegedly represented that its interests were aligned with the Noteholders' interests and that it would manage the Reference Portfolio in a conservative and defensive manner to avoid Credit Events and thus losses to Noteholders. Aladdin's formal responsibilities, however, were spelled out in the Portfolio Management Agreement ("PMA"), an agreement between Aladdin and the shell Issuer that was not signed by the Noteholders. Plaintiffs purchased $60 million of the total $100 million worth of Notes from Goldman Sachs, which underwrote the CDO (*i.e.,* Goldman used its own money to purchase the Notes from the Issuer before reselling those Notes to investors like plaintiffs).

Plaintiffs did not enter into any direct contract with Aladdin. Aladdin, as the Portfolio Manager, selected the initial approximately one-hundred Reference Entities that comprised the Reference Portfolio. Plaintiffs allege that, following the issuance of the Aladdin CDO on December 19, 2006, Aladdin managed the portfolio in a grossly negligent fashion, culminating in the Reference Entities sustaining 11 credit events just three years into the CDO's seven-year term, thereby causing plaintiffs' Notes to default. As a result, plaintiffs lost their entire $60 million principal investment and any future interest from the remaining four years of the CDO term. Plaintiffs allege that, had Aladdin simply left the initial Reference Portfolio in place, plaintiffs would not have suffered any losses whatsoever.

On the basis of the foregoing allegations, the Amended Complaint asserts two claims: (1) a claim in contract alleging that Aladdin breached its obligations under the PMA; and (2) a claim in tort alleging that Aladdin's conduct was grossly negligent, resulting in harm to the Noteholders. On May 23, 2011, Aladdin moved to dismiss the Amended Complaint for failure to state a claim, pursuant to Federal Rule of Civil Procedure 12(b)(6). On July 8, 2011, the district court held oral argument on defendant's motion to dismiss and dismissed the complaint from the bench.

DISCUSSION

Bayerische alleges that Aladdin breached its duty to manage the Reference Portfolio in the Noteholders' favor and failed to perform its obligations "using a degree of skill, care diligence and attention consistent with the practice and procedures followed by reasonable and prudent [portfolio managers]," in such a manner that its actions amounted to gross negligence and reckless disregard of its obligations. But, as already noted, Bayerische was not a party to the PMA, which sets forth Aladdin's duties as Portfolio Manager. Only the shell Issuer and Aladdin signed the PMA. Accordingly, Bayerische seeks to hold Aladdin liable through two avenues: (1) that Bayerische, as a Noteholder, was an intended third-party beneficiary of the PMA that can enforce the contract; or (2) that, in the alternative, the contract created a legal duty in tort that Aladdin owed to the Noteholders, and Bayerische can therefore sue for damages based on Aladdin's gross negligence. The district court rejected both theories of recovery; but we disagree.

(1) Breach of Contract: Third–Party Beneficiary. The PMA is governed by New York law. Under New York law, a third party may enforce a contract when "recognition of a right to performance in the beneficiary is appropriate to effectuate the intention of the parties and ... the circumstances indicate that the promisee intends to give the beneficiary the benefit of the promised performance."

Here, Aladdin argues that section 29 of the PMA expressly rules out any intent to benefit the Noteholders. Section 29 reads:

> *Beneficiaries*
>
> This Agreement is made solely for the benefit of the Issuers and the Portfolio Manager, their successors and assigns, and no other person shall have any right, benefit or interest under or because of this Agreement, *except as otherwise specifically provided herein.* The Swap Counterparty shall be an intended third party beneficiary of this Agreement.

(emphasis supplied.) Aladdin argues, and the district court found, that because section 29 expressly names GSCM, the Swap Counterparty, as an intended third-party beneficiary, but does not expressly name the Noteholders anywhere in the section, the Noteholders were not "otherwise specifically provided herein," and therefore the parties to the Agreement did not intend for the Noteholders to be third-party beneficiaries of the PMA. Bayerische argues that reading "otherwise specifically provided herein" as limited to the names expressly listed *within section 29,* reads the wording too narrowly and ignores the other provisions of the contract that, in Bayerische's view, show a specific intent by the shell Issuer and Aladdin to benefit the Noteholders.

On its face, we cannot conclude that section 29 precludes an intent by the parties to benefit the Noteholders. The "herein" in "except as otherwise specifically provided herein" is not defined. While it might be read to refer, as Aladdin argues, to only section 29, it could just as reasonably be read to refer, as Bayerische argues, to the PMA as a whole. Indeed, the latter interpretation seems more likely. The clause at issue comes at the end of a sentence that states "no other person shall have any right ... under ... this *Agreement,* except as otherwise specifically provided herein." (emphasis supplied.) The following sentence, which identifies the Swap Counterparty as "*an* intended third party beneficiary" (emphasis supplied) has no language of limitation and could reasonably be read as clarification that, whomever else might be a third-party beneficiary, the Swap Counterparty is for certain.

Accordingly, we must look beyond section 29 to the contract as a whole to determine whether "provided herein" should be read as limited to the Swap Counterparty or whether it can be fairly read to include the Noteholders like Bayerische. As it happens, other portions of the PMA evince an intent to benefit the Noteholders by defining Aladdin's obligations and delineating the scope of its liability to the Noteholders. For example, section 6 of the PMA states that "the Portfolio Manager shall use all reasonable efforts to ensure that [it takes no action that would] ... adversely affect the interests of the holders of the Notes in any material respect (other than as permitted under the Transaction Documents)." Even more tellingly, section 8 of the PMA, entitled "Benefit of this Agreement; Limit on Liability," states, in relevant part:

> The Portfolio Manager shall perform its obligations hereunder in accordance with the terms of this Agreement and the terms of the Transaction Documents applicable to it. The Portfolio Manager agrees that such obligations shall be enforceable at the insistence of each Issuer, the Trustee on behalf of the holders of the relevant Notes, or the requisite percentage of holders of the relevant Notes on behalf of themselves, as provided in the relevant Indenture.

Together, these sections plausibly demonstrate an intent to benefit the Noteholders.

Other sections of the contract further support this plausible interpretation. Section 11(c) of the PMA, for example, allows a majority of the Noteholders (or majority of the holders of each Series) to *remove* the Portfolio Manager for cause, where "cause" is defined, *inter alia,* as a "material breach" of the PMA. It would be odd to conclude that the parties intended to allow the Noteholders to remove Aladdin as Portfolio Manager for breaching its duties, but not allow them to sue Aladdin for damages resulting from that breach.

Drawing all inferences in favor of the plaintiff, a plausible reading of the parties' Agreement is that the PMA expressly requires the Portfolio Manager to perform various obligations—including managing the Reference Portfolio—on behalf of the Noteholders. The limitations on liability that discuss the Noteholders suggest that the parties intended that the Noteholders be able to sue Aladdin directly, albeit only for acts of gross negligence. Such a reading of the contract does not, as Aladdin argues, fail to give effect to the language of section 29, for section 29 would still prevent non-Noteholders from suing on the PMA. Moreover, given section 8's limitation on enforcement directly by the Noteholders to the "requisite percentage" in the Indenture, section 29 could plausibly be read as intended to exclude small Noteholders, or secondary market Noteholders, from suing Aladdin directly.

In short, it is more than plausible that the parties intended the PMA to inure to the benefit of the Noteholders. Otherwise, to read the ambiguous language of "specifically provided herein" as not encompassing these express obligations undertaken by Aladdin would leave these obligations enforceable only by the shell Issuer and the Swap Counterparty, GSCM, that, as the counterparty, had interests that were directly opposed to those of the Noteholders.

Thus, although section 29 is ambiguous, we need not look beyond the four corners of the contract as a whole to conclude that, drawing all inferences in Bayerische's favor, it is plausible that the parties intended the Noteholders to benefit from the PMA. Nonetheless, "where the contract language creates ambiguity, extrinsic evidence as to the parties' intent may properly be considered," and in the context of a motion to dismiss, "if a contract is ambiguous as applied to a particular set of facts, a court has insufficient data to dismiss a complaint for failure to state claim."

Here, the allegations set forth in the Amended Complaint regarding Bayerische's decision to invest in the CDO plausibly indicate that the parties intended the PMA to benefit the Noteholders such as Bayerische. The complaint alleges that Aladdin and Goldman Sachs came to Bayerische's office in New York to present marketing materials regarding the then-proposed Aladdin CDO and to solicit Bayerische's investment. In the marketing book, Aladdin represented that its interests were aligned with investors' interests in the CDO and that it would manage the Reference Portfolio in "a conservative and defensive manner" to avoid losses to the Noteholders, and gave some specifics as to the parameters it would use to manage the Portfolio conservatively. The Offering Circular that was included among the marketing materials specifically detailed how Aladdin could trade out Reference Entities, and explained that Aladdin and the CDO would use the PMA to define Aladdin's obligations. These allegations further support Bayerische's interpretation that Aladdin's obligations under the PMA were intended to protect the Noteholders.

We therefore conclude that the district court erred in dismissing Bayerische's contract claim.

(2) Duty of Care; Gross Negligence. We turn then to Bayerische's second, alternative, claim: that Aladdin breached a duty of care, in tort, to the Noteholders, by engaging in acts that amounted to gross negligence in its

management of the Reference Portfolio. Under New York law, a breach of contract will not give rise to a tort claim unless a legal duty independent of the contract itself has been violated. Such a "legal duty must spring from circumstances extraneous to, and not constituting elements of, the contract, although it may be connected with and dependent on the contract." Where an independent tort duty is present, a plaintiff may maintain both tort and contract claims arising out of the same allegedly wrongful conduct.

As discussed above, the Amended Complaint alleges, in effect, that Aladdin was aware that its work as Portfolio Manager would be relied on by Bayerische, a non-party to the contract. Before Bayerische invested in the CDO, Aladdin met with Bayerische at its offices in New York to explain the many ways that Aladdin, as Portfolio Manager, would competently and effectively protect Bayerische's interests as investors in the Aladdin CDO. Bayerische alleges that it relied on these representations, and the PMA, in protecting its interests. In such reliance, Bayerische committed to a $60 million investment, or 60% of the total value of the CDO. The Amended Complaint thus plausibly alleges facts evincing Aladdin's understanding that Noteholders would rely on Aladdin's care and competence in managing the Reference Portfolio.

Aladdin maintains, however, that Bayerische fails to satisfy the criteria set out by then-Chief Judge Cardozo in the seminal case of *Ultramares Corp. v. Touche,* 255 N.Y. 170, 174 N.E. 441. We are not persuaded. In *Ultramares,* the defendants were accountants who had prepared and certified a balance sheet for a rubber-importing business. *Id.* at 173, 174 N.E. 441. The rubber-importing business borrowed money to finance its purchases of rubber from the plaintiff, who requested a certified balance sheet before it would provide the loan. *Id.* at 175, 174 N.E. 441. After the rubber-importing business went bankrupt, the plaintiff sued the accountants for negligently certifying the balance sheet. *Id.* at 175–76, 174 N.E. 441. Chief Judge Cardozo concluded that the accountants could not be held to have a duty to anyone who relied on the rubber-importing company's balance sheet, as "the indeterminate class of persons who, presently or in the future, might deal with the [rubber-importing company] in reliance on the audit" did not have a relationship with the accountants that approached privity. *Id.* at 183, 174 N.E. 441. This was because "the service was primarily for the benefit of the [rubber] company, a convenient instrumentality for use in the development of the business, and only incidentally or collaterally for the use of those to whom [the company] might exhibit it." *Id.*

By contrast, Chief Judge Cardozo noted, in *Glanzer v. Shepard* (in which he had previously established a basis for finding a duty in tort to a third-party), "the service rendered by the defendant ... was primarily for the information of a third person, in effect, if not in name, a party to the contract, and only incidentally for that of the formal promisee." *Id.* (citing *Glanzer,* 233 N.Y. 236, 135 N.E. 275). Likewise, in this case there was allegedly no service being provided to the formal promisee (the Issuer), which was merely a shell entity. To the contrary, Aladdin is alleged to have been aware that its management of the Reference Portfolio would run specifically to the benefit of Bayerische, which Aladdin solicited to invest in the CDO. The "end and aim" of the PMA was to install Aladdin as the manager of the Reference Portfolio, on behalf of the Noteholders, and as relevant here, to Bayerische in particular.

We acknowledge that this is not quite as close as the relationship in *Glanzer*. Bayerische had already purchased the Notes, and was free to sell its Notes on the secondary market (subject to specific transfer restrictions), and the Offering Circular indicated that Goldman would make efforts to list the CDO on the Irish Stock Exchange, further increasing the liquidity of the Notes such that they could be resold to investors beyond those Aladdin specifically solicited, such as Bayerische. Even so, it is clear that Bayerische has properly alleged that (1) Aladdin was aware that the PMA had the particular purpose of installing Aladdin as the Portfolio Manager to manage the Reference Portfolio on behalf of the Noteholders; (2) Bayerische was known to Aladdin and relied on Aladdin to perform its obligations pursuant to the PMA; and (3) Aladdin's conduct in soliciting Bayerische's investment and its representation that it would manage the CDO in Bayerische's favor evinced an understanding by Aladdin that Bayerische would rely on its performance. Thus, Bayerische has properly alleged a relationship between Aladdin and the Noteholders sufficiently close that recognizing a duty running from Aladdin to Bayerische would not offend the limitations imposed by New York law on tort liability to non-privy third parties.

Finally, Aladdin argues that, even if such a relationship exists, the Noteholders have failed to allege facts that plausibly show Aladdin's conduct amounted to gross negligence. Again, we disagree.

Defendant's conduct in these regards may plausibly be said to have been an extreme departure from the standard of ordinary care, most obviously because there is no apparent reason why defendant would want to take this risk, especially since Bayerische alleges that the CDO was created with trading restrictions that were supposed to prevent defendant from adding Reference Entities to the Reference Portfolio with spreads of greater 500 basis points. Accepting below-market spreads with a below-market subordination adjustment appears to have allowed defendant to bypass the trading restrictions designed to protect Bayerische and keep the Reference Portfolio oriented on investment-grade Reference Entities.

Furthermore, accepting below-market spreads on risky Entities appears to have been contrary to how defendant explicitly represented it would manage the portfolio on behalf of the Noteholders. The stated objective of Aladdin's role as Portfolio Manager, according to the PMA, was to "minimize the occurrence" of any losses to the Noteholders. PMA § 2(i). Further, in the marketing presentation Goldman and Aladdin pitched to Bayerische in New York, Aladdin represented that, although its "typical trading [for the Portfolio] is defensive.... Aladdin can also take a view on a credit by taking out a tight spread name and replacing it with a wider name ... where Aladdin believes that the new credit is trading wider than is reflected by the fundamental credit risk. These trades will result in an increase in subordination." In effect, the representation was that where Aladdin believed the market spread for a given Entity was too high, it could substitute that Entity into the Reference Portfolio, thus increasing Bayerische's protection from default (by increasing subordination at the market spread), without a proportional increase in riskiness (given the difference between the market spread and what Aladdin thought the proper spread should be). But, according to Bayerische's allegations, here, Aladdin did the exact opposite. By substituting Reference Entities at a spread *below* the market spread, Aladdin increased what the market would have perceived as the riskiness of the Reference Portfolio without a proportional increase in protection to the Noteholders through subordination. Even if Aladdin had thought these Entities were not as risky as the market spread suggested, adding them to the Reference Portfolio did not give Bayerische any corresponding benefit through increased subordination. By adding these Entities to the Reference Portfolio at a below market spread, Aladdin in effect transferred the benefits of any bet on the market overpricing the riskiness of the Reference Entities from the Noteholders to GSCM, the Swap Counterparty.

The PMA outlines the specific trading procedures for swapping Reference Entities. First, Aladdin was to propose adding a new Reference Entity to the Portfolio. GSCM, the Swap Counterparty, would provide in good faith what it thought was the appropriate and commercially reasonable spread for the Reference Entity. Aladdin could either accept GSCM's spread or seek a market quotation spread from a neutral "Reference Dealer," which would be binding on Goldman. Once the trade was completed, GSCM would make the appropriate adjustments to the Noteholders' subordination levels that reflected the change in the riskiness of the Reference Portfolio, but Aladdin had the responsibility to challenge GSCM on behalf of Noteholders when GSCM acted improperly. Throughout this pricing and subordination adjustment procedure, it was Aladdin's role to protect the Noteholders' interests vis-à-vis their adverse counterparty, GSCM. Further, given that Bayerische alleges that the market based spreads were in fact *above* the 500 basis point trading restriction, it is reasonable to infer these were particularly risky trades in the context of the overall CDO that would demand some level of heightened scrutiny on the part of Aladdin.

Admittedly, Bayerische does not allege with particularity what the source of an objective market-based spread would be. Bayerische also does not allege whether Aladdin ever challenged GSCM's pricing on the Reference Entities, or made any efforts to confirm that the spreads were reasonably tied to the market spread through the Reference Dealer procedures outlined in the PMA. But this is not a claim for fraud, which pursuant to Federal Rule of Civil Procedure 9(b), would require Bayerische to plead with particularity. Fed.R.Civ.P. 9(b). Rather, gross negligence and breach of contract claims fall under Rule 8(a), and thus require only a "short and plain statement of the claim," so long as the facts alleged and any reasonable inferences that can be drawn in Bayerische's favor give rise to a plausible claim for relief. Fed.R.Civ.P. 8(a) . . . Here, the allegations do just that.

Bayerische alleges further facts that, when taken together with all reasonable inferences in Bayerische's favor, are sufficient to allege a claim for gross negligence, even if they might not be sufficient standing alone. Specifically, plaintiffs allege that Aladdin "tripled down" when adding Icelandic bank debt to the Reference Portfolio, *i.e.,* adding two more Icelandic bank Reference Entities to the existing Icelandic bank in the Reference Portfolio, which exposed the Noteholders to the entirety of the Icelandic bank industry at a time when there was an abundance of information regarding the deteriorating position of these banks and the risks associated with them. Bayerische alleges that this concentration in one small country and one specific industry was contrary to Aladdin's representation that it would maintain a diverse portfolio to avoid multiple credit events. When all three banks failed in October 2008, thus sustaining Credit Events, Bayerische alleges that the losses from these entities represented more than a quarter of Bayerische's loss of subordination that led to the loss of its entire investment.

Defendant argues that the express terms of the transaction documents did not prohibit such an industry or geographic concentration. But Bayerische alleges that no reasonable portfolio manager would triple down on such Entities when it was managing the portfolio to avoid Credit Events. Bayerische is not required to show a violation of the trading restrictions in order to plausibly allege that Aladdin acted recklessly in how it managed the portfolio.

Defendant also argues, relying on two decisions in litigation arising out of Bernard Madoff's Ponzi scheme, that Bayerische's failure to plead that defendant was aware of Bayerische's alleged "red flags" means the gross negligence claim must be dismissed. But the complaint in this case is subject to the requirements only of Fed.R.Civ.P. 8, not Rule 9 or the Private Securities Litigation Reform Act of 1995, 15 U.S.C. § 78u–4; and one can reasonably infer from the allegations that the concerns surrounding certain risky Reference Entities were publically-known, and that the sophisticated investment managers at Aladdin were aware of those concerns and invested in those Entities anyway, notwithstanding Aladdin's commitment to manage the Reference Portfolio so as to avoid Credit Events. We note that Bayerische alleges that had Aladdin simply left the original Reference Portfolio as it was, Bayerische would not have lost its investment.

Bayerische also alleges that Aladdin failed to manage the Portfolio in its favor because it failed to establish the short portfolio that could have been used to further increase Bayerische's subordination and protect it from losing its principal if a Credit Event occurred. By itself, this allegation does not suggest recklessness or intentional wrongdoing. There easily may have been a legitimate investment reason for not establishing the short portfolio (*e.g.,* reducing interest payments to Noteholders). Alternatively, it could have been merely an oversight that did not amount to gross negligence. But although this allegation is insufficient by itself, it can be aggregated with the other allegations described above. Taking the allegations as a whole and drawing all reasonable inferences in Bayerische's favor, we conclude that Bayerische has sufficiently alleged facts plausibly suggesting Aladdin abandoned its role to manage the Reference Portfolio in favor of the Noteholders.

After discovery, the facts that come to light may show a different story. But at this preliminary motion-to-dismiss stage, drawing all inferences in Bayerische's favor, Bayerische has plausibly alleged that Aladdin's gross negligence exposed Bayerische to greater risk that it would lose its entire investment than would have otherwise been the case.

PROBLEM SET 19.3

1. How could it be that a super senior tranche of a CDO that buys low-grade MBS earns the same credit rating as the governments of Switzerland or Norway?
2. The credit rating agencies note that until 2007, there had never been such a broad, steep decline in housing prices since the end of World War II. Why might that last qualification be important for utility of the improved models, discussed at the outset of this section?
3. Suppose you set up an SPV and put a CDS contract in it. The CDS "reference entity," instead of being an operating company, could be an existing CDO or MBS. If the SPV were to then sell debt securities to investors, what might this look like? Are there any special risks to be concerned about here?
4. What if you take a bunch of CDOs that you own and put them into an SPV. If the SPV were to then sell debt securities to investors, what might this look like? What if instead of owning the CDOs, you own CDS contracts that reference the CDOs? What if you kept repeating this process (putting CDS contracts in SPVs that reference CDOs that are made up of CDS contracts that reference CDOs . . .)?

5.   A NOTE ON COVERED BONDS

Covered bonds are bonds issued by banks and other financial institutions. They are quite common in Europe and might become more common in North America if investors decide that securitization is not worth the risk.

A covered bond is collateralized by a dedicated pool of mortgages, known as the cover pool. Unlike mortgages or other assets that are removed from the bank's balance sheet and moved into an SPV when securitized, the mortgages in the cover pool remain on the balance sheet, and the bank must hold capital against potential losses just like any other loan. Like securitization, the issuance of covered bonds converts illiquid assets into a funding source for the bank.

One of the key reasons why securitization became so popular in this country is because it enabled banks to remove loans from their balance sheets and to free up capital they would have had to hold on their balance sheet.[9] Investors might have liked securitized assets because they provided a low-cost way of gaining some exposure to the real estate market without getting broader exposure to all the risks associated with a bank. This was probably especially true in the period between 2001 and 2007, when interest rates on traditional debt were quite low.

By contrast, covered bonds do not offer investors any exposure to the residential mortgage market even though they are backed by residential mortgages. There is no exposure because the interest and principal payments are the bank's obligation—they do not depend on the cash flows from mortgages in the pool.

If a mortgage defaults or is prepaid, the bank has to replenish the cover pool with other mortgages on its balance sheet. If the bank becomes insolvent, the loans in the pool are separated from other assets and are used solely to repay the bank's obligation to covered bondholders. In other words, a covered bond is a secured debt obligation of the bank, for which the mortgages serve as collateral.

---

9. Banks operate with high degrees of leverage. To oversimplify, capital in this context is equity. The bank and its shareholders would like to operate with as little capital as possible—and as much leverage as possible—but capital provides a buffer against insolvency. Because the U.S. government insures bank deposits, it has some interest in making sure banks maintain adequate capital.

20

HEDGE FUNDS AND PRIVATE EQUITY FUNDS

Hedge funds and private equity funds are unlike the other topics in this part of the text, in that they are types of investors rather than financial instruments.

Nonetheless, these funds are important users of many of the instruments previously discussed. For example, if a financial institution facilitates a company's desire to hedge its interest rate exposure by selling the company a swap, the financial institution might hedge its own exposure by selling a countervailing swap to a hedge fund.

As a review exercise, it bears considering what remaining risk the financial institution retains after selling two such mirror image swaps.

Hedge funds account for a large part of the trading volume in New York and London, and in some areas, like convertible debt, hedge fund trading dominates the market. North American-based hedge funds managed over $2.3 trillion as of the end of 2015, which represented over two-thirds of the global assets under management. The world's biggest hedge fund, Connecticut's Bridgewater Associates, had $146 billion of assets under management as of early 2016, down by $23 billion since the first quarter of 2015.

At a high level of abstraction, hedge funds are just like mutual funds. They pool money from investors and then invest that money. As a legal matter, a hedge fund or a mutual fund is just a legal entity—often a trust, in the case of mutual funds, or a limited partnership, in the case of hedge funds—whose business is investing.

As we shall see, hedge funds are expressly structured to avoid much of the regulation that mutual funds gladly accepted after the stock market crash in 1929.[1] Before then, however, it would have been possible for a mutual fund to do most everything a hedge fund at the time could do—if there were any hedge funds.

---

1. Steven M. Davidoff, *Black Market Capital*, 2008 Colum. Bus. L. Rev. 172, 201–216.

The first widely known hedge fund—there might have been earlier funds, especially before the crash—was established by Alfred W. Jones in 1949.[2] Jones combined normal stock picking with short sales to "hedge" against the risks of his portfolio, while also using some degree of leverage.[3] The growth of ever more complex financial products beginning in the 1970s—in parallel with the growth of computing—allowed future hedge fund managers to modify Jones's original idea in myriad ways.

Private equity funds are more recent, and the term *private equity fund* is more recent still. Before the term was widely used, firms like KKR and Forstmann Little essentially were private equity funds.[4] Structured similarly to hedge funds, the key distinction between hedge funds and private equity funds turns on their investment strategies.

Whereas hedge funds are somewhat like mutual funds, private equity funds are somewhat like merchant banks—financial institutions that take long-term stakes in a portfolio of companies.[5] The key innovation with private equity funds is that they typically leverage their investment, so that investors can gain exposure to potential large returns in exchange for comparatively modest principal investments.

Attorneys advise funds regarding compliance with laws governing securities offerings, regulation of investment companies, and regulation of investment managers. Fund attorneys also advise on permitted fund investments and other operations and changes to the management teams of funds.

When considering hedge funds, we actually have to consider two players simultaneously: the fund itself and the fund's manager. While the two are undoubtedly related, they can raise distinct legal issues. Throughout our analysis of hedge funds, we look at Och-Ziff Capital Management Group LLC, "one of the largest institutional alternative asset managers in the world, with approximately $42.0 billion in assets under management as of May 1, 2016."[6] This company is the manager of several hedge funds.

1.   STRUCTURAL ISSUES: HEDGE FUNDS AND FUND MANAGERS

As a legal matter, a *hedge fund* is any professionally managed pool of investments exempt from the definition of "investment company" (*i.e.,* mutual

---

2. Sharon Reier, From Jones to LTCM: A Short (-Selling) History, *International Herald Tribune* (December 2, 2000).

3. http://goo.gl/P7067.

4. Ronald J. Gilson & Charles K. Whitehead, *Deconstructing Equity: Public Ownership, Agency Costs, and Complete Capital Markets*, 108 Colum. L. Rev. 231 (2008); Brian Cheffins & John Armour, *The Eclipse of Private Equity*, 33 Del. J. Corp. L. 1, 18 (2008).

5. *See* Arthur E. Wilmarth Jr., *The Dodd-Frank Act: A Flawed and Inadequate Response to the Too-Big-To-Fail Problem*, 89 Or. L. Rev. 951, 1045 (2011).

6. http://www.ozcap.com/our_firm/index.

fund) under the 1940 Investment Company Act and therefore not required to register with the Securities and Exchange Commission.

As a matter of corporate finance, the term hedge fund generally refers to an investment pool that is relatively liquid. On the other hand, *private equity funds* are investment pools that take longer term positions in companies and have more restrictions on investor withdrawal. Both types of funds can use leverage, but it is private equity funds that are most often associated with leveraged buyouts of companies.

More generally, as a legal matter both private equity and hedge funds present an interesting package of tax, regulatory, and business associations law that make up their structure.[7] Beginning with the last issue first, we can note that typically these funds are structured as a group of related limited partnerships and limited liability companies.

Och-Ziff Capital Management Group's 10-K explains:

> Our funds are typically organized using a "master-feeder" structure. This structure is commonly used in the hedge fund industry and calls for the establishment of one or more U.S. or non-U.S. "feeder" funds, which are managed by us but are separate legal entities and have different structures and operations designed for distinct groups of investors. Fund investors, including our executive managing directors, employees and other related parties, invest directly into our feeder funds. These feeder funds hold direct or indirect interests in a "master" fund that, together with its subsidiaries, is the primary investment vehicle for its feeder funds.

And again, later in the same document:

> The Company's funds are typically organized using a "master-feeder" structure. Fund investors, including the Company's executive managing directors, employees, and other related parties to the extent they invest in a given fund, invest directly into the feeder funds. These feeder funds are typically limited partnerships or limited companies that hold direct or indirect interests in a master fund. The master fund, together with its subsidiaries, is the primary investment vehicle for its feeder funds. The Company generally collects its management fees and incentive income from the feeder funds or wholly owned subsidiaries of the feeder funds ("intermediate funds"), and does not collect any management fees or incentive income directly from the master funds.

Och-Ziff's primary hedge fund is OZ Master Fund, Ltd., a Cayman Islands exempted limited company.

As indicated in the excerpts above, hedge fund investors do not directly invest in the master fund. Instead, investments are typically made through one of two avenues: a domestic entity that is treated as a partnership for U.S. federal income

---

7. See Henry Ordower, *Demystifying Hedge Funds: A Design Primer*, 7 U.C. Davis Business L.J. 323 (2007).

tax purposes or a foreign entity treated as a corporation for U.S. federal income tax purposes. The master fund pools the investments coming from both sources.

The foreign feeder fund is organized in a tax-friendly jurisdiction, most often the Cayman Islands. Non-U.S. investors and certain U.S. tax-exempt investors invest in the non-U.S. feeder fund. U.S. taxable investors invest in the U.S. feeder fund, which is inevitably a Delaware limited partnership. More on the reasons for this split in the section below on taxes.

In the case of the OZ Master Fund, foreign investors and tax-exempt investors buy interests in OZ Overseas Fund II, Ltd., another Cayman Islands exempted limited company. Domestic investors buy limited partner interests in OZ Domestic Partners II, L.P., a Delaware limited partnership, whose general partners are OZ Advisors LP and Och-Ziff Holding Corporation, both formed in Delaware. Both feeder funds pass on cash received from investors to the OZ Master Fund.[8] As of 2016, OZ Domestic Partners II had approximately 450 beneficial owners, while the master fund itself had more than 1,900.

The Delaware limited partnership has issued more than $8.4 billion in securities—limited partnership interests, sold in increments of $100,000. The OZ Overseas Fund II, the Cayman entity that also feeds into the master fund, has issued securities worth more than $15.6 billion.

The OZ Master Fund is managed by OZ Management L.P., again a Delaware limited partnership. Och-Ziff Capital Management Group, the publicly traded entity, is the sole shareholder of Och-Ziff Holding Corporation, a Delaware corporation that is the general partner of OZ Management and also of OZ Advisors LP, mentioned above.

PROBLEM SET 20.1

1. Diagram the Och-Ziff relationships described in the foregoing section (ignore the footnote to make it manageable). Drawing on your knowledge of basic corporate law, what are some of the possible purposes for this structure?
2. Och-Ziff reportedly receives more than a third of its total investments from pension funds. About 12 percent of its investments come from "fund-of-funds." A fund-of-funds is a hedge fund that invests in other hedge funds. Often these funds have lower initial investment requirements, making them the primary way many individuals obtain entry into the more "exclusive" funds. Drawing on earlier discussions,

---

8. Actually, the text simplifies things more than a bit by focusing on a specific pair of feeder funds. The OZ Master Fund is actually fed by the following funds, which include those discussed in the text: OZ Domestic Partners II, L.P.; OZ Domestic Partners, L.P.; OZ Overseas Fund II, Ltd.; OZ Overseas Fund, Ltd.; OZ Overseas Institutional Fund, Ltd.; OZ Overseas Intermediate Fund II, L.P.; and OZ Overseas Intermediate Fund, L.P. The feeder funds with "Intermediate" in their names also are master funds, with several funds feeding into them before they, in turn, feed into the OZ Master Fund.

including the discussion of portfolio theory, what might be the costs and benefits of investing in such a fund?

3.   Despite the increasing popularity of LLCs in other contexts, the most popular choice to structure the fund itself remains the limited partnership. Why might that be?

2.   INVESTMENT TERMS

Setting up a hedge fund involves drafting hundreds of documents. One of the most important is the *offering memorandum* or *private placement memorandum (PPM)*, which is central to the success of the fund. It spells out the fund's strategy, the risks of the strategy, the fund's management and their histories, and the fund's governance.

The key players in a hedge fund or private equity fund are the sponsor, the investment advisor, and, of course, the investors. The fund's general partner controls the fund, but usually is a pure holding company that has no employees. Quite often the entity or people who put together the fund in the first instance, the sponsors, own the general partner.

The sponsors are often also related to the investment advisor or management company, which provides the real people who make investment decisions and the physical office space that a layperson would associate with the fund.

Quite often the manager and the general partner are subsidiaries of an overarching holding company. Although they could be a single entity, fund managers based in New York City tend to bifurcate the general partner and the manager entities, for reasons of local tax law.[9]

The fund, the sponsor, and the manager are all bound together by a compensation scheme known as "2 and 20." The manager is paid an annual fee equal to 2 percent of assets under management, for which the manager not only provides management but also absorbs the "overhead" of the fund. The fund's general partner also receives a performance fee equal to 20 percent of the gains in the fund, referred to as the *carried interest*. Two and 20 are the standard terms, and of course variations might be negotiated by investors and the sponsor.[10]

Often the fund documents prohibit the manager from collecting the 20 percent upside fee again until the investor's account value exceeds the level at which the fund previously accrued an incentive fee.[11] Imagine an investor with $1 million in a fund on January 1, whose account declines in value to $500,000 at the end of the year. If in the next year the value of the account appreciates to $1.5 million,

---

9. In particular, it is preferable to have a separate entity receive the 20 percent "upside" payment discussed below to ensure it remains taxable as a capital gain, rather than as regular income or as subject to the New York City unincorporated business tax.

10. Large sovereign wealth funds and other important and very large investors often obtain preferential terms, including discounted management fees and carried interest.

11. This is known as a "high water mark."

the hedge fund manager's performance fee would only be payable for the second year with respect to the $500,000 gain.

Managers themselves buy some of the limited partnership interests in the fund, a feature often referred to as *co-investment*. The 20 percent share of upside the manager gets can thus be seen as disproportionate allocation of profits, which gives the controlling party more than their pro rata share of the profits.[12]

The OZ Master Fund, or more precisely its feeder funds, charge a *management fee* that varies depending on how long the investor agreed to keep its money in the fund, referred to as the "lock-up" period:

- 2.5 percent for a one-year lock-up
- 2 percent for a two-year lock-up, and
- 1.5 percent for a three-year lock-up

In addition, all investors agree to the standard 20 percent *performance fee*. Only three-year lock-up investments come with a *hurdle rate*—equal to the three-month Treasury bill rate—that limits the performance fee to performance that exceeds the mark set by the hurdle. All investors also benefit from a perpetual high water mark.

Hedge funds often accept capital only at the beginning of calendar months and, if they determine that assets under management exceed their ability to effectively deploy such capital, they may temporarily close themselves to new investor contributions. On the other hand, hedge funds typically limit the ability of investors to withdraw capital or redeem from a fund, so that investors might only be able to exit at certain set points in time, upon tendering advance notice to the fund. In addition, many fund general partners (or boards, in the case of the offshore feeder fund) retain the option of limiting withdrawals in times of market stress by imposing "*gates*" or suspension provisions that cap total withdrawals from the fund.

This differs distinctly from mutual funds, which offer daily liquidity to their investors. Liquidity, of course, simply means the ability to withdraw your investment at its present value—which might be much less than the amount you originally deposited with the fund.

Conversely, although the liquidity offered by mutual funds obviates the need for complex contractual provisions regarding exit from the fund, the lack of liquidity in a hedge fund makes such provisions all the more important.

The minimum initial investment in the OZ Master Fund is $10 million, and subsequent investments have to exceed $1 million. Investments are accepted on the last business day of each month.

The fund allows redemptions after the expiration of the applicable lock-up period. One-year lock-up investors can redeem quarterly, while the other investors are only permitted annual redemptions. In all cases, investors must provide advanced notice, ranging from 30 to 90 days depending on the applicable

12. Lee Sheppard, *News Analysis: Hedge Fund Managers' Tax Benefits Compared*, 119 Tax Notes 243 (2008).

lock-up type. Fund interests can be sold only with the consent of feeder funds' general partners (or boards, again in the case of the offshore feeder fund).

PROBLEM SET 20.2

1. What problems might arise from the fee structure explained above? In particular, what incentives might the fee structure give fund managers?
2. What are the drawbacks of the "high water mark?"

3.   TAXES

Taxes drive many structural considerations, from both the investor and the manager perspective. At the most basic level, note that the entities used throughout much of the fund structure are "pass through" entities. This means the outside investors of the fund—the limited partners—will only pay tax, if at all, as if they had invested in the underlying securities in the fund, avoiding an entity level tax and permitting tax gains and losses to pass through to investors.[13] This allows the investors to realize investment tax subsidies built into the law: for example, long-term capital gains on securities held for more than one year and certain qualifying dividend income are taxed at a maximum rate of about half that of ordinary income.

If the fund generates income that is connected with the conduct of a U.S. trade or business (Effectively Connected Income or (ECI)), the fund will be required to withhold U.S. income tax on the income that is attributable to the fund's non-U.S. investors, regardless of whether it is distributed.[14] In addition, all or a portion of the gain on the disposition by a non-U.S. investor of its interest in the fund can be taxed as ECI to the extent such gain is attributable to assets of the fund that generate ECI.

Moreover, a tax-exempt investor is subject to tax on some income earned from an entity treated as a partnership for tax purposes.[15] This type of tax is especially acute in private equity funds, given special rules for debt-funded investment income.[16]

Both of these issues lead to the widespread use of the master-feeder structure we saw at the outset of the chapter, because neither foreign nor U.S non-profit investors, like university endowments, will want to invest through a domestic entity, like a Delaware limited partnership.

In mid-2013, the large role played by the Cayman Islands in the hedge fund industry became something of a mini controversy. Jeffrey Sachs, an economist at Columbia, wrote several letters to the *Financial Times* in which he noted that

---

13. This status would be lost if the fund were publically traded. 27 U.S.C. §7704(b).

14. http://goo.gl/QqFI3.

15. Emily Cauble, *Harvard, Hedge Funds, and Tax Havens: Reforming the Tax Treatment of Investment Income Earned by Tax-Exempt Entities*, 29 Va. Tax Rev. 695 (2010).

16. Internal Revenue Code §514.

some residents of the Cayman Islands sit on hundreds of fund boards, while the Cayman financial system has $1.4 trillion in liabilities and assets. He termed the entire structure a "house of cards," a characterization that (unsurprisingly) representatives of the Cayman Islands financial industry dismissed.

4.   SEEKING ALPHA: HEDGE FUND GOALS

We have already seen that an investment's return relative to the market can be measured by beta. But what of the return that is not measured by CAPM? We might add an error term to the CAPM equation and call that "alpha," or if you prefer to be Mediterranean, "α."

In a nutshell, alpha is the difference between a fund's expected returns based on its beta and its actual returns. Alpha is sometimes interpreted as the value that a portfolio manager adds.

Hedge funds and private equity funds focus extensively on alpha. After all, why would you pay "2 and 20" to a manger who achieved the same return you could get from buying an index fund that charges 0.03 percent.[17]

Beta investing, as we have already discussed, involves taking on a degree of systematic risk for which the investor is compensated. For example, equity investments provide higher return than cash or safe government debt because they involve higher expected risks.

The other way to make money through investing is by targeting alpha. Alpha investing involves an assumption that the investor is smarter or somehow better informed than other investors and that this superior knowledge can be used to make excess returns. As such, alpha investing involves a zero-sum game, where the investor (in this case the hedge fund manager) looks for assets that the current holder undervalues or does not fully understand. This alpha could be return in addition to the stock market return or return that is uncorrelated with the stock market.

In short, hedge funds seek return that is not explained by CAPM and the ECMH. Of course, the return not explained by CAPM might come from the manager's skill, but it might also come from other sources, too. Such as ... (bet you'll be asked in class).

The OZ Master Fund's performance is shown on the following table, which is taken from data in the Och-Ziff Capital Management Group's 10-K. The OZ Master Fund Composite referred to on the table represents the composite performance of all feeder funds that comprise the OZ Master Fund, net of fees and expenses, and assumes reinvestment of all dividends and other income.

---

17. https://www.schwabetfs.com/summary.asp.

	1 Year	3 Years	5 Years	Since Fund Inception (January 1, 1998)
Net Annualized Return through December 31, 2015				
OZ Master Fund Composite	-0.4%	6.2%	5.9%	9.1%
S&P 500 Index	1.4%	15.1%	12.6%	6.2%
MSCI World Index	2.7%	13.7%	10.2%	5.4%
Volatility: Standard Deviation (Annualized)				
OZ Master Fund Composite	6.1%	5.0%	4.4%	5.0%
S&P 500 Index	13.7%	10.6%	11.7%	15.5%
MSCI World Index	13.9%	10.3%	11.3%	14.6%
Sharpe Ratio				
OZ Master Fund Composite	-0.10	1.21	1.28	1.31
S&P 500 Index	0.09	1.41	1.06	0.24
MSCI World Index	0.18	1.31	0.89	0.20

The *Sharpe ratio* is a measure for calculating risk-adjusted return. It was developed by William Sharpe, whom we learned about in connection with CAPM. The Sharpe ratio is the average return earned in excess of the risk-free rate per unit of volatility or total risk. The top part of the ratio looks at what a fund returned over a set period and subtracts what an investor could have earned in a risk-free investment, typically defined as three-month Treasury bills, over that same period. With short-term Treasury yields near zero at present (0.22 percent, to be precise), the amount subtracted hardly has an effect. The denominator is the fund's standard deviation, which measures how much a fund strays from its average performance—in other words, its volatility.

The higher a fund's Sharpe ratio, the better a fund's returns have been relative to the risk it has taken on. Imagine Monty's Fund gained an average of 12 percent a year over the past three years, and had a standard deviation of 30 percent, giving it a Sharpe ratio of 0.4. Pat's Fund, on the other hand, returned an average of 10 percent over that same period and had a standard deviation of 20 percent, giving it a Sharpe ratio of 0.5. The Sharpe ratio suggests that Pat's Fund is actually the better investment, despite the lower nominal return, because Monty's Fund is taking on a lot more risk to get only a slightly better nominal return.

What does the table tell us about the OZ Master Fund?

Hedge funds delivered their worst performance in years in 2015—with prominent managers David Einhorn and Bill Ackman posting some of their biggest losses ever, each down 20 percent. From 2010 through 2014, annual hedge fund returns averaged 4.5 percent, compared to 15.5 percent for the S&P 500. Perhaps as a result, in 2014 CalPERS, the largest U.S. public pension fund, said it would stop investing in hedge funds entirely. It should be noted, however, that hedge funds beat the S&P from 2000 to 2009.

5.   HEDGE FUND STRATEGIES

Hedge funds employ a variety of investment strategies, many far removed from the original Jones fund that gave "hedge funds" their name. For example, one common hedge fund strategy involves corporate governance activism—the fund takes a small but significant stake in a company and pushes for improvements in the business. This really involves very little in the way of hedging.[18]

BRIAN R. CHEFFINS & JOHN ARMOUR, *THE PAST, PRESENT, AND FUTURE OF SHAREHOLDER ACTIVISM BY HEDGE FUNDS*

37 J. Corp. L. 51, 56–61 (2011)

Shareholder activism has been described as "the exercise and enforcement of rights by minority shareholders with the objective of enhancing shareholder value over the long term." While defining shareholder activism by reference to the use of shareholder rights to enhance shareholder value delineates the basic parameters of this corporate governance tactic, the formulation is too general in nature to distinguish hedge fund interventions from those carried out by mainstream institutional investors such as mutual funds and public pension funds. Law professors Marcel Kahan and Ed Rock have described the different approaches adopted as follows:

> Mutual fund and public-pension fund activism, if it occurs, tends to be incidental and ex post: when fund management notes that portfolio companies are underperforming, or that their governance regime is deficient, they will sometimes be active (footnote omitted). In contrast, hedge fund activism is strategic and ex ante: hedge fund managers first determine whether a company would benefit from activism, then take a position and become active.

Employing the adjectives "defensive" and "offensive" provides a convenient way to distinguish the sort of activism in which mainstream institutional

---

18. Frank A. Partnoy, *Shapeshifting Corporations*, 76 U. Chi. L. Rev. 261, 266 (2009) ("Activist hedge funds purchase (or sell short) concentrated ownership positions in public companies. In the simplest case, one or more hedge funds acquire substantial (typically a 'sweet spot' of 5 to 10 percent) equity stakes and then press for strategic change. Their involvement leads to immediate and dramatic changes in the shareholder base of a company, and typically also results in positive returns for shareholders.").

shareholders engage from the sort for which hedge funds—private investment vehicles that do not necessarily hedge their positions but have historically taken advantage of exclusions and regulatory "safe harbors" to operate largely outside statutory rules on investment companies and investment advisers—have achieved notoriety. Defensive shareholder activism occurs when an investor with a pre-existing stake in a company becomes dissatisfied with corporate performance or corporate governance and reacts by lobbying for changes, whether "behind the scenes" or with a public challenge to management (e.g., proposing the election of directors the dissident supports). A shareholder acting in this sort of ex post fashion will not own enough shares to guarantee victory in a contest for boardroom control or to dictate corporate policy but potentially can use their stake as a departure point in garnering support for the changes they advocate. To the extent pension funds and mutual funds engage in shareholder activism, it will most often be of this reactive ex post sort, as they work "defensively" to protect the value of existing investments.

The key feature that makes activism "defensive" is that the shareholder or shareholders taking the initiative will have held a sizeable stake before stepping forward. This "initial endowment" is not a feature of offensive shareholder activism. What happens instead is that an investor lacking a meaningful stake in a company builds up one "offensively" on the presumption that the company is not currently maximizing shareholder returns and with the intention of agitating for change to unlock shareholder value should this be necessary. The investor crucially will plan ex ante to press for a fresh approach if management does not take the initiative. As the quote from Kahan and Rock indicates, this is precisely the sort of activism for which hedge funds have gained notoriety.

The adjective "offensive" potentially connotes an aggressive posture towards incumbent management. This form of activism does not necessarily imply, however, shareholder/executive antagonism. While hedge fund activists have gained notoriety for their confrontational approach, they often aim for a collegial, if firm, "hands on" approach with incumbent management. As Warren Lichtenstein, the founder of Steel Partners II, a prominent activist hedge fund, said in 2004, "The best situation is where we find a cheap stock with great management and a great business, and we can sit back and make money." Correspondingly, Lichtenstein found when Steel Partners II bought shares, "Many times managements are happy there's a long-term, supportive investor."

Lichtenstein's reference to the desirable properties of a "cheap stock" reveals an overlap in investment philosophies between activist hedge funds and the prototypical "value investor" who seeks through diligent analysis of corporate fundamentals to purchase shares trading at a bargain price, the proverbial dollar for 50 cents. Hedge funds that engage in offensive shareholder activism typically rely on the "value approach" when identifying targets, forming as such a subset of hedge funds that invests in equities in a manner akin to classic, value-oriented investors.

Managers of activist hedge funds correspondingly tend not to be experts in quantitative theories of finance—a typical attribute of a hedge fund manager—

but are often former investment bankers or research analysts used to working hard to understand balance sheets and income statements. Activist hedge funds in turn often justify their investment strategy on the basis the companies they buy stakes in are undervalued, and the targets themselves, despite usually having sound operating cash flows and returns on assets, typically have a low share price relative to book value and low dividend payout ratios.

If an activist hedge fund identifies and invests in an "undervalued" company and the share price subsequently increases due to a belated reaction by the market rather than due to any prompting by the hedge fund, this will be relatively "easy money" for the hedge fund. The situation will be the same if management, on its own initiative, makes changes that serve to increase shareholder returns. Under such circumstances activist hedge funds who buy sizeable stakes in target companies merely need to wait to sell when the time is right and thus will be doing little more than engaging in conventional "stock picking."

The readiness to take a hands-on role to shake things up is the crucial additional dimension to hedge fund activism. Activist hedge funds, rather than merely adopting the passive approach that characterizes value investing and waiting for the market to self-correct—which may well never happen if a company's shares do not get noticed and instead drift lower—are prepared to take the initiative and accelerate matters by lobbying for changes calculated to boost shareholder returns. As a private equity fund manager said in 2007 of various prominent hedge fund activists, "I'd like to thank my friends Carl Icahn, Nelson Peltz, Jana Partners ... for teeing up deals because . . . many times [activist targets] are being driven into some form of auction." Hence, despite Warren Lichtenstein characterizing Steel Partners II as a potentially "supportive investor," activist hedge funds do not give management a full-scale "vote of confidence" when they invest in companies.

. . .

The investment approach activist hedge funds employ is markedly different from the approach private equity adopts. Private equity firms believe that taking a "hands on" role with the management of companies they take private is necessary to set the stage for a profitable exit and thus are comfortable deploying sufficient capital to obtain outright voting control. Activist hedge funds rarely have any interest in going this far with the companies they target. Instead, they prefer not to tie up capital in the form of majority or sole ownership of companies and instead anticipate profiting as minority shareholders when shareholder returns improve due to changes management makes, in response to investor pressure if necessary. This is borne out by a 2009 article by economists Robin Greenwood and Michael Schor, who compiled a dataset of 784 instances between 1993 and 2006 where a hedge fund disclosed pursuant to federal securities law that it owned 5% or more of the shares of a publicly traded company and declared an intention to influence the management of the company. The hedge funds in question held, on average, 9.8% of the shares of the companies they targeted, far short of majority or sole ownership. Hedge fund activists do in some instances propose acquiring outright control of companies they focus upon. Only rarely, though, do they end up with a majority stake, with their bids either fading away as an engagement takes its course or being beaten out by a higher offer.

. . .

Hedge fund activists, when they opt to be proactive, will typically begin by sounding out management with a telephone call, letter, or e-mail pressing the incumbent board to make changes designed to increase shareholder value. Hedge funds often lobby for finance-oriented changes, such as having a target company squeeze value from the balance sheet by spinning off underperforming non-core assets and by using share buy-backs or a sizeable one-off dividend to distribute "excess" cash to shareholders. More radically, a hedge fund activist may advocate an outright sale of the target, either as a going concern or through divestiture of key operations. Hedge funds also sometimes lobby in favor of increased operational efficiency and reputedly began putting more emphasis on strategic changes when the tighter credit markets associated with the 2008 financial crisis made it more difficult for target companies to engage in financial engineering.

If a quiet approach fails to yield the desired results, an activist hedge fund can step up the pressure, perhaps by criticizing management in public or by threatening a lawsuit against the company's directors. A particularly forceful strategy is to threaten what Gilson and Schwartz term a "transfer by vote," this being the securing of managerial control by winning a proxy contest intended to determine who serves on the board. Activist investors say that because of the high costs involved they avoid proxy battles if possible. Moreover, the preference of hedge fund managers to avoid hands-on involvement in the running of target companies implies that securing board control will typically not be a high priority. Nevertheless, Alon Brav, Wei Jiang, Frank Partnoy, and Randall Thomas report in a widely cited study that in 13% of hedge fund activism incidents they uncovered through searches of filings under federal securities law the hedge fund was involved in a proxy contest to replace incumbent directors. A likely explanation for many of the proxy battles that do occur is that hedge funds use contests for board seats to signal to potential future targets that they are prepared to invest heavily in pursuing an activist campaign should this be required.

Some big hedge funds invest across a wide variety of strategies. In these cases, the only unifying theme is that the investments in question tend to be ones that individual investors are unable to implement themselves, due to either regulatory prohibitions or transaction costs.

OCH-ZIFF CAPITAL MANAGEMENT GROUP LLC

Form 10-K, For the Fiscal Year Ended December 31, 2015

As of December 31, 2015, we managed approximately $29.5 billion of assets under management in our multi-strategy funds, or 65% of our total assets under management. The portfolio composition of our multi-strategy funds is determined by evaluating what we believe are the best market opportunities for each fund, consistent with each fund's goal of generating consistent, positive, risk-adjusted returns while protecting fund investor capital. The primary investment strategies we employ in our multi-strategy funds include the following:

- Long/short equity special situations, which consists of fundamental long/short and event-driven investing. Fundamental long/short investing involves analyzing companies and assets to profit where we believe mispricing or undervaluation exists. Event-driven investing attempts to realize gain from corporate events such as spin-offs, recapitalizations and other corporate restructurings, whether company specific or due to industry or economic conditions.
- Structured credit, which involves investments in residential and commercial mortgage-backed securities and other asset-backed securities. This strategy also includes investments in collateralized loan obligations and collateralized debt obligations.
- Corporate credit, which includes a variety of credit-based strategies, such as high-yield debt investments in distressed businesses and investments in bank loans and senior secured debt. Corporate credit also includes providing mezzanine financing and structuring creative capital solutions.
- Convertible and derivative arbitrage, which takes advantage of price discrepancies between convertible and derivative securities and the underlying equity or other security. These investments may be made at multiple levels of an entity's capital structure to profit from valuation or other pricing discrepancies. This strategy also includes volatility trades in equities, interest rates, currencies and commodities.
- Merger arbitrage, which is an event-driven strategy involving multiple investments in entities contemplating a merger or similar business combination. This strategy seeks to realize a profit from pricing discrepancies among the securities of the entities involved in the event.
- Private investments, which encompasses investments in a variety of special situations that seek to realize value through strategic sales or initial public offerings.

The OZ Master Fund, our global multi-strategy fund, opportunistically allocates capital between our investment strategies in North America, Europe and Asia based on market conditions and attractive investment opportunities. The OZ Master Fund generally employs every strategy and geography in which our funds invest and constituted approximately 53% of our assets under management as of December 31, 2015. Our other funds implement geographical—or strategy—

focused investment programs. The investment performance for our other funds may vary from those of the OZ Master Fund, and that variance may be material.

The chart below presents the composition, by strategy (excluding residual assets attributable to redeeming investors), of the OZ Master Fund as of January 1, 2016:

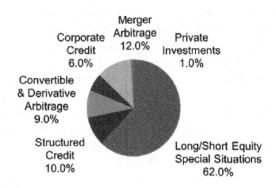

For the third quarter of 2016, the OZ Master Fund generated a gross return of 2.7 percent and a net return of 1.1 percent year-to-date through September 30, 2016. According to the manager's 10-Q, "performance-related depreciation in long/short equity special situations was more than offset by strong positive performance in merger arbitrage, convertible and derivative arbitrage and credit-related strategies." The firm further reported that "we experienced redemptions of approximately $6.7 billion from our funds, and an additional $6.7 billion during the first nine months of 2016. We may continue to experience elevated redemption levels if economic and market conditions remain uncertain or worsen or pressures on the hedge fund industry continue." You can find up-to-date information on Och-Ziff Capital Management Group LLC on www.sec.gov.

6.   REGULATION

As noted, a key consideration in constructing a hedge fund or a private equity fund involves securities regulation. In particular, these funds typically try to avoid the relevant securities law to the greatest extent possible, especially the laws that restrict the investment activities of mutual funds and the compensation of their managers.

PHILLIP GOLDSTEIN v. SECURITIES AND EXCHANGE COMMISSION

451 F.3d 873
United States Court of Appeals, District of Columbia Circuit.
June 23, 2006.

RANDOLPH, Circuit Judge.

This is a petition for review of the Securities and Exchange Commission's regulation of "hedge funds" under the Investment Advisers Act of 1940, 15 U.S.C. §80b-1 et seq. See Registration Under the Advisers Act of Certain Hedge Fund Advisers, 69 Fed.Reg. 72,054 (Dec. 10, 2004) (codified at 17 C.F.R. pts. 275, 279) ("Hedge Fund Rule"). Previously exempt because they had "fewer than fifteen clients," 15 U.S.C. §80b-3(b)(3), most advisers to hedge funds must now register with the Commission if the funds they advise have fifteen or more "shareholders, limited partners, members, or beneficiaries." 17 C.F.R. §275.203(b)(3)-2(a). Petitioners Philip Goldstein, an investment advisory firm Goldstein co-owns (Kimball & Winthrop), and Opportunity Partners L.P., a hedge fund in which Kimball & Winthrop is the general partner and investment adviser (collectively "Goldstein") challenge the regulation's equation of "client" with "investor."

I.

"Hedge funds" are notoriously difficult to define. The term appears nowhere in the federal securities laws, and even industry participants do not agree upon a single definition. . . . The term is commonly used as a catch-all for "any pooled investment vehicle that is privately organized, administered by professional investment managers, and not widely available to the public." President's Working Group on Financial Markets, Hedge Funds, Leverage, and the Lessons of Long-Term Capital Management 1 (1999).

Exemption from regulation under the Investment Company Act allows hedge funds to engage in very different investing behavior than their mutual fund counterparts. While mutual funds, for example, must register with the Commission and disclose their investment positions and financial condition, id. §§80a-8, 80a-29, hedge funds typically remain secretive about their positions and strategies, even to their own investors. The Investment Company Act places significant restrictions on the types of transactions registered investment companies may undertake. Such companies are, for example, foreclosed from trading on margin or engaging in short sales, 15 U.S.C. §80a-12(a)(1), (3), and must secure shareholder approval to take on significant debt or invest in certain types of assets, such as real estate or commodities, id. §80a-13(a)(2). These transactions are all core elements of most hedge funds' trading strategies.

Another distinctive feature of hedge funds is their management structure. Unlike mutual funds, which must comply with detailed requirements for independent boards of directors, and whose shareholders must explicitly approve of certain actions, domestic hedge funds are usually structured as limited partnerships to achieve maximum separation of ownership and management. In the typical arrangement, the general partner manages the fund (or several funds) for a fixed fee and a percentage of the gross profits from the fund. The limited partners are passive investors and generally take no part in management activities.

Hedge fund advisers also had been exempt from regulation under the Investment Advisers Act of 1940, 15 U.S.C. §80b-1 et seq. ("Advisers Act"), a companion statute to the Investment Company Act, and the statute which primarily concerns us in this case. Enacted by Congress to "substitute a philosophy of full disclosure for the philosophy of caveat emptor" in the investment advisory profession, SEC v. Capital Gains Research Bureau, Inc., 375 U.S. 180, 186 (1963), the Advisers Act is mainly a registration and anti-fraud statute. Non-exempt "investment advisers" must register with the Commission, 15 U.S.C. §80b-3, and all advisers are prohibited from engaging in fraudulent or deceptive practices. By keeping a census of advisers, the Commission can better respond to, initiate, and take remedial action on complaints against fraudulent advisers.

Hedge fund general partners meet the definition of "investment adviser" in the Advisers Act. See 15 U.S.C. §80b-2(11). But they usually satisfy the "private adviser exemption" from registration in §203(b)(3) of the Act, 15 U.S.C. §80b-3(b)(3). That section exempts "any investment adviser who during the course of the preceding twelve months has had fewer than fifteen clients and who neither holds himself out generally to the public as an investment adviser nor acts as an investment adviser to any investment company registered under [the Investment Company Act]." Id. As applied to limited partnerships and other entities, the Commission had interpreted this provision to refer to the partnership or entity itself as the adviser's "client." See 17 C.F.R. §275.203(b)(3)-1. Even the largest hedge fund managers usually ran fewer than fifteen hedge funds and were therefore exempt.

Although the Commission has a history of interest in hedge funds . . . the current push for regulation had its origins in the failure of Long-Term Capital Management, a Greenwich, Connecticut-based fund that had more than $125 billion in assets under management at its peak. In late 1998, the fund nearly collapsed. Almost all of the country's major financial institutions were put at risk due to their credit exposure to Long-Term, and the president of the Federal Reserve Bank of New York personally intervened to engineer a bailout of the fund in order to avoid a national financial crisis.

The Hedge Fund Rule first defines a "private fund" as an investment company that (a) is exempt from registration under the Investment Company Act by virtue of having fewer than one hundred investors or only qualified investors, see 15 U.S.C. §80a-3(c)(1), (7); (b) permits its investors to redeem their interests within two years of investing; and (c) markets itself on the basis of the "skills, ability or expertise of the investment adviser." 17 C.F.R. §275.203(b)(3)-1(d)(1). For these private funds, the rule then specifies that "[f]or purposes of section 203(b)(3) of the [Advisers] Act (15 U.S.C. §80b-3(b)(3)), you must count as clients the shareholders, limited partners, members, or beneficiaries...of [the] fund." Id. §275.203(b)(3)-2(a). The rule had the effect of requiring most hedge fund advisers to register by February 1, 2006.

II.

The Commission[] . . . argues that the Hedge Fund Rule amends only the method for counting clients under §203(b)(3), and that it does not "alter the duties or obligations owed by an investment adviser to its clients." 69 Fed.Reg. at 72,070. We ordinarily presume that the same words used in different parts of a statute have the same meaning. The Commission cannot explain why "client" should mean one thing when determining to whom fiduciary duties are owed, 15 U.S.C. §80b-6(1)-(3), and something else entirely when determining whether an investment adviser must register under the Act, id. §80b-3(b)(3).

The Commission also argues that the organizational form of most hedge funds is merely "legal artifice," to shield advisers who want to advise more than fifteen clients and remain exempt from registration. See Hedge Fund Rule, 69 Fed.Reg. at 72,068. But as the discussion above shows, form matters in this area of the law because it dictates to whom fiduciary duties are owed.

The Hedge Fund Rule might be more understandable if, over the years, the advisory relationship between hedge fund advisers and investors had changed. The Commission cited, as justification for its rule, a rise in the amount of hedge fund assets, indications that more pension funds and other institutions were investing in hedge funds, and an increase in fraud actions involving hedge funds. All of this may be true, although the dissenting Commissioners doubted it. But without any evidence that the role of fund advisers with respect to investors had undergone a transformation, there is a disconnect between the factors the Commission cited and the rule it promulgated. That the Commission wanted a hook on which to hang more comprehensive regulation of hedge funds may be understandable. But the Commission may not accomplish its objective by a manipulation of meaning.

The Commission has, in short, not adequately explained how the relationship between hedge fund investors and advisers justifies treating the former as clients of the latter. . . . The Commission points to its finding that a hedge fund adviser sometimes "may not treat all of its hedge fund investors the same." Hedge Fund Rule, 69 Fed.Reg. at 72,069–70 (citing different lock-up periods, greater access to information, lower fees, and "side pocket" arrangements). From this the Commission concludes that each account of a hedge fund investor "may bear many of the characteristics of separate investment accounts, which, of course, must be counted as separate clients." Id. at 72,070. But the Commission's conclusion does not follow from its premise. It may be that different classes of investors have different rights or privileges with respect to their investments. This reveals little, however, about the relationship between the investor and the adviser. Even if it did, the Commission has not justified treating all investors in hedge funds as clients for the purpose of the rule. If there are certain characteristics present in some investor-adviser relationships that mark a "client" relationship, then the Commission should have identified those characteristics and tailored its rule accordingly.

By painting with such a broad brush, the Commission has failed adequately to justify departing from its own prior interpretation of §203(b)(3). As we have discussed, in 1985 the Commission adopted a "safe harbor" for general partners of limited partnerships, enabling them to count the partnership as a single "client" for the purposes of §203 so long as they provided advice to a "collective investment vehicle" based on the investment objectives of the limited partners as a group. This "safe harbor" remains part of the Commission's rules and has since been expanded to include corporations, limited liability companies, and business trusts. The Hedge Fund Rule therefore appears to carve out an exception from this safe harbor solely for investment entities that have fewer than one hundred-one but more than fourteen investors. As discussed above, the Commission does not justify this exception by reference to any change in the nature of investment adviser-client relationships since the safe harbor was adopted. Absent such a justification, its choice appears completely arbitrary.

The petition for review is granted, and the Hedge Fund Rule is vacated and remanded.

So ordered.

Hedge and private equity funds avoid registering their shares under the 1933 Act because they structure their transactions to qualify for the private offering exemption from registration under Section 4(a)(2) of the Securities Act and Regulation D adopted thereunder.[19]

They avoid reporting requirements under the 1934 Act by not listing on stock exchanges and by having fewer than 2,000 total investors in any particular fund.[20] This may explain why the OZ Master Fund has so many feeder funds, as was noted at the outset of the chapter.

---

19. Regulation D requires that each investor in the fund be an accredited investor, which means individuals with a net worth of more than $1 million or income above $200,000 in the last two years and a reasonable expectation of reaching the same income level in the current year, and entities with more than $5 million in assets. Under the Dodd-Frank Act, the accredited investor standard's net-worth test has been revised to exclude the value of the investor's primary residence from the calculation of the investor's total assets and the amount of any mortgage or other indebtedness secured by an investor's primary residence from the calculation of the investor's total liabilities, except to the extent the fair market value of the residence is less than the amount of such mortgage or other indebtedness. *See* 17 CFR 230.501-.508.

20. *See* Securities Exchange Act of 1934 §12(g); Rule 12g-1. Until recently, under Exchange Act Section 12(g)(1), issuers had been required to register a class of equity securities if, at the end of the most recent fiscal year, the issuer had more than $10 million in total assets and a class of equity securities "held of record" by 500 or more persons. In 2012, the JOBS Act raised the holders' threshold of Section 12(g)(1) to either 2,000 holders of record or 500 holders of record that are not "accredited investors." To rely on the higher JOBS Act higher threshold, an issuer must be able to determine which of its holders are accredited investors and must make such determination

The Investment Company Act of 1940 generally requires "investment companies" to register as such with the SEC. Registered investment companies—commonly called mutual funds by humans (non-lawyers)—are subject to a complicated array of tax rules, investment restrictions, liquidity requirements and other constraints. Many of these rules are incompatible with typical hedge fund practices, as noted in *Goldstein*.

Hedge funds and private equity are exempt from the investment company definition under the 1940 Investment Company Act Section 3(c)(1), which exempts privately offered investment funds with up to 100 beneficial owners, and Section 3(c)(7), which exempts "qualified purchaser" funds.[21] Under a section 3(c)(1) structure, however, if the fund is to pay performance fees to its manager, all of the investors in the 3(c)(1) fund also must be "qualified clients."[22]

And both exclusions—3(c)(1) and 3(c)(7)—require that all investors are "accredited investors" within the meaning of Rule 506 of Regulation D under the 1933 Act.

In short, depending on the particular fund structure used, the fund will have to make sure its investors are some combination of qualified purchasers, accredited investors, and qualified clients. Each investor in the fund will typically be required to represent that it is a qualified purchaser as defined in section 2(a)(51) of the 1940 Investment Company Act. In the event that not all of a fund's investors are qualified purchasers, then the fund might still qualify for an exemption by limiting the number of investors to not more than 100, all of which must still be accredited investors. And in that case the fund will likely also want to make sure its investors are qualified clients.

If all of this has given you a headache, take some aspirin and then consider Table 20-1.

TABLE 20-1

	3(c)(1)	*3(c)(7)*
Accredited investor status ($1 million/$200,000)	Applies	Applies
Limitation on number of investors	Not more than 100 persons	No limitation
Qualified client status ($1 million/$2 million)	Applies	Applies
Qualified purchaser status ($5 million portfolio)	Not applicable	Applies

as of the last day of the issuer's most recent fiscal year, as opposed to at the time of sale of the securities.

21. Qualified purchasers are investors who, in the case of individual investors, have at least $5 million net of debt in investments exclusive of the hedge fund in question.

22. The Dodd-Frank Act amended Section 205(e) of the Advisers Act to provide that, by July 21, 2011, and every five years thereafter, the SEC must adjust the dollar amount thresholds included in rules issued under Section 205(e) to account for inflation. Under the first such adjustment, qualified clients are now defined as individuals who had at least $1 million under management immediately after entering into the advisory contract or individuals who the adviser reasonably believed had a net worth of more than $2 million at the time the contract was entered into. Rule 205-3.

PROBLEM SET 20.3

1. It has been predicted that the section 3(c)(1) will become increasingly rare. Why might that be?
2. The OZ Master Fund relies on section 3(c)(7). OZ Domestic Partners II, L.P., the domestic feeder fund for the fund, also relies on section 3(c)(7).
3. Alex Hamilton is the president of a large Gotham City bank, a job that pays him $1 million per year. He has $500,000 ready to invest in a hedge fund, which represents his life savings. Will he find a hedge fund to invest in?

That leaves the Investment Advisers Act of 1940, the subject of much of the *Goldstein* opinion reproduced above. This act generally requires investment advisors to register with the SEC. In 2004, the SEC estimated that just less than half of eligible investment advisers to hedge funds were registered under the Advisers Act.[23] Registration requires fund advisers to expand their disclosures, adopt compliance policies and procedures, appoint a Chief Compliance Officer, and open their doors to the SEC for periodic inspections and examinations.[24]

Until recently, unregistered advisers generally relied on the private adviser exemption of Section 203(b)(3) in the 1940 Advisers Act. That section provided that an investment adviser would not have to register with the SEC if it (1) had fewer than 15 clients in the preceding 12 months, (2) did not hold itself out generally to the public as an investment adviser, and (3) did not act as an investment adviser to a registered investment company or business development company. An unregistered adviser also relied on Rule 203(b)(3)-1 that allowed it to count as clients the funds it advised and not the number of actual investors in the fund. *Goldstein* halted the SEC's attempt to change that method of counting investors.

The Dodd-Frank Act repealed Section 203(b)(3), meaning that the SEC ultimately won the war, if not the battle.[25] With limited exceptions, most funds management companies will be registered with the SEC going forward.[26]

Form ADV is the investment adviser registration form used by the SEC. An asset manager registered as an investment adviser with the SEC must update Part

---

23. Inv. Adv. Act Release No. 2266 (July 20, 2004), 2004 WL 1636422, at *24; Inv. Adv. Act Release No. 2333 (Dec. 10, 2004), 2004 WL 2785492, at *6 n.62.

24. About 75 New York-based examiners are responsible for 2,000 advisers with $11 trillion under management, an SEC representative told a conference in November 2011.

25. William K. Sjostrom Jr., *A Brief History of Hedge Fund Adviser Registration and Its Consequences for Private Equity and Venture Capital Advisers*, Harvard Business L. Rev. (Feb. 1, 2011).

26. Rule 204(b)-1, recently adopted by the SEC, will require registered investment advisers with $150 million or more in private fund assets to file Form PF periodically with the SEC. Under Dodd-Frank, investment advisers who manage between $25 million and $100 million in assets under management, known as "mid-sized" investment advisers, will now be required to register with the state as opposed to the SEC.

1 and Part 2 (comprised of a "Brochure" and a "Brochure Supplement") of its Form ADV on an annual basis.

In the case of Och-Ziff and the OZ Master Fund, the registered investment advisor is OZ Management LP.

Similarly, in early 2012 the Commodities Futures Trading Commission adopted rule changes that rescind the exemption from commodity pool operator registration contained in its Rule 4.13(a)(4), which many hedge funds had used. As a result, unless an exemption is otherwise available, hedge funds will be required to register with the National Futures Association if the fund conducts more than a small amount of speculative trading in futures, commodity options, and other commodity interests. Note that it is the adviser or manager that registers, not the fund itself.

Finally, under the Dodd-Frank Act, many hedge funds also may be subject to additional regulation by the SEC and the CFTC as "major swaps participants."

7.   KEY HEDGE FUND RELATIONSHIPS: PRIME BROKERAGE AGREEMENTS

Hedge Funds enter into myriad contracts that form the basis of their business. While lawyers are rarely involved in the day to day trading operations at a hedge fund, they frequently advise funds with regard to these agreements, which include (i) ISDA agreements, (ii) futures agreements, (iii) repurchase agreements, (iv) stock loan agreements, (v) master netting agreements, (vi) debt prime brokerage agreements, (vii) derivatives intermediation agreements, and, most importantly, (viii) prime brokerage agreements.

1994 WL 808441 (S.E.C. NO-ACTION LETTER)

Publicly Available January 25, 1994

January 25, 1994
Mr. Jeffrey C. Bernstein
Prime Broker Committee
c/o Bear, Stearns & Co., Inc.
One Metrotech Center North
Brooklyn, NY 11201

Re: Prime Broker Committee Request

Dear Mr. Bernstein:

This is in response to your letter dated September 13, 1989 on behalf of the Prime Broker Committee in which you requested the views of the Division of Market Regulation of the Securities and Exchange Commission ("Division") and the Division of Banking Supervision and Regulation of the Board of Governors of the Federal Reserve System ("FRS Division") regarding the applicability of Sections 7, 10, 11(d), 15(c)(3) and 17 of the Securities Exchange Act of 1934 ("Exchange Act") and Regulation T thereunder, and Rules 10a-1, 10b-10, 11d1-1, 15c3-1 and 15c3-3 under the Exchange Act to prime broker arrangements.

I.   BACKGROUND

On the basis of your letter, and subsequent conversations, we understand the facts to be the following.

Prime brokerage is a system developed by full-service firms to facilitate the clearance and settlement of securities trades for substantial retail and institutional investors who are active market participants. Prime brokerage involves three distinct parties: the prime broker, the executing broker, and the customer. The prime broker is a registered broker-dealer that clears and finances the customer trades executed by one or more other registered broker-dealers ("executing broker") at the behest of the customer. Each of the executing brokers receives a letter from the prime broker agreeing to clear and carry each trade placed by the customer with the executing broker where the customer directs delivery of money or securities to be made to or by the prime broker.

The customer maintains its funds and securities in an account with the prime broker. Orders placed with the executing broker are effected through an account with the executing broker in the name of the prime broker for the benefit of the customer. When a customer places a trade order ("trade date"), the executing broker buys or sells securities in accordance with the customer's instructions. On trade date, the customer notifies the prime broker of the trade performed by the executing broker. The transaction is recorded in the customer's cash or margin account with the prime broker. At the same time, the prime broker records the transaction in a "fail-to-receive/deliver" account with the executing broker.

The prime broker issues a confirmation or notification to the customer and computes all applicable credit and Regulation T amounts. The executing broker confirms the transaction with the prime broker through the Depository Trust Company's Institutional Delivery System. The prime broker then will affirm the trade if its information matches successfully with the information received from the executing broker. The trade may then be submitted to the National Securities Clearing Corporation for clearance and settlement following normal settlement procedures. The prime broker then settles with the customer in the normal way.

The prime broker issues a statement of account to its customer at least on a monthly basis. The statement includes all security transactions during that period and the resultant customer security positions and money balances.

The Prime Broker Committee believes that this arrangement is advantageous to prime brokerage customers because the prime broker acts as a clearing facility and accountant for all of the customer's security transactions wherever executed as well as a central custodian for the customer's securities and funds.

In addition to facilitating trading with multiple brokers, all from a single account, the prime broker typically acts as a custodian for the fund, holding all of the fund's securities.

The prime broker also facilitates the fund's use of leverage in its trading strategies. First, the broker can provide the fund with typical margin credit. Moreover, because most prime brokers are part of larger financial institutions— Morgan Stanley and Goldman Sachs are said to dominate the business, with the two together now having about 37 percent of the market—the prime broker can arrange for an unregulated affiliate to provide additional financing to the fund.[27] The prime brokerage business itself is often low margin; it can be a crucial source of stock trading revenue.

As a registered broker-dealer, a prime broker is subject to regulatory oversight by various entities, including by the U.S. Securities and Exchange Commission, the Financial Industry Regulatory Authority ("FINRA"), state securities regulators, and, to the extent that the prime broker is a bank, the Federal Reserve Board. In addition, the prime broker also must comply with the rules and regulations of various securities and commodities exchanges. A number of rules and regulations are intended to protect the rights of prime brokerage customers, including regulations promulgated under the Securities Exchange Act of 1934.

Before Lehman's collapse, the relationship between hedge funds and prime brokers was one-sided, with prime brokers holding most of the bargaining power. When Lehman Brothers went bankrupt many U.S. hedge funds found themselves with significant exposure to Lehman's London subsidiary, where many of the Lehman's prime brokerage customer accounts were held. When Lehman Brothers filed for bankruptcy, many funds were taken by surprise that the vast majority of their assets had been rehypothecated and that they were therefore in the position of unsecured creditors in the U.K. insolvency proceedings concerning the value of those assets. Under English law at the time, broker-dealers were permitted to rehypothecate (or repledge) the assets that clients post as margin or collateral for trades entered into under prime brokerage arrangements. In practice, this meant that the prime broker could use the client's assets, for example, to lend to other hedge funds or to post as collateral itself for another purpose.

As a result of the experience with Lehman, most hedge funds of any size now engage with multiple prime brokers, whereas in the past business was often concentrated with one or two prime brokers. Along these lines, the OZ Master Fund and its affiliated feeder funds report using eleven prime brokers.

---

27. Traditional margin lending by a regulated broker-dealer is subject to section 7 of the 1934 Exchange Act and Regulations T and U, promulgated by the Federal Reserve Board. 12 C.F.R. §§220, 221.

PROBLEM SET 20.4

1. What risks does a hedge fund face with regard to its prime brokerage relationship? How might those risks be mitigated? What risks does the prime broker face?
2. When negotiating a prime brokerage agreement on behalf of a hedge fund client, what terms should be of special import?

Why might the fund want to execute trades with multiple brokers? That is, why not execute all trades with the brokerages that act as prime broker?

8.   PRIVATE EQUITY FUNDS

Private equity funds are essentially hedge funds that focus on illiquid securities or investment strategies with longer-term investment horizons. That is, a private equity fund can be seen as a hedge fund with a specialized investment strategy.

But unlike hedge funds, private equity funds have been doing pretty well lately. That might change with rising interest rates, and more expensive debt finance, but as the book went to print, the *Financial Times* reported that

> CVC, Europe's biggest private equity group, will cut the hurdle rate for its fees and scrap the early-bird discounts typically offered to new investors after identifying between €25bn and €30bn of demand for its latest buyout fund, according to two people familiar with the investor talks.[28]

Within the industry, private equity funds and hedge funds consider themselves quite distinct. The following excerpt provides some important background.

SUN CAPITAL PARTNERS III, LP v.
NEW ENGLAND TEAMSTERS & TRUCKING INDUSTRY PENSION FUND

724 F.3d 129
United States Court of Appeals, First Circuit.
July 24, 2013.

LYNCH, Chief Judge.
This case presents important issues of first impression as to withdrawal liability for the pro rata share of unfunded vested benefits to a multiemployer pension fund of a bankrupt company, here, Scott Brass, Inc. (SBI). *See* Employee Retirement Income Security Act of 1974 (ERISA), 29 U.S.C. §1001 *et seq., as*

---

28. Javier Espinoza, *CVC tightens fundraising terms after strong demand for new fund,* Financial Times (Dec. 20, 2016).

amended by the Multiemployer Pension Plan Amendment Act of 1980 (MPPAA), 29 U.S.C. §1381 *et seq.* This litigation considers the imposition of liability as to three groups: two private equity funds, which assert that they are mere passive investors that had indirectly controlled and tried to turn around SBI, a struggling portfolio company; the New England Teamsters and Trucking Industry Pension Fund (TPF), to which the bankrupt company had withdrawal pension obligations and which seeks to impose those obligations on the equity funds; and, ultimately, if the TPF becomes insolvent, the federal Pension Benefit Guaranty Corporation (PBGC), which insures multiemployer pension plans such as the one involved here. If the TPF becomes insolvent, then the benefits to the SBI workers are reduced to a PBGC guaranteed level. According to the PBGC's brief, at present, that level is about $12,870 for employees with 30 years of service.

The plaintiffs are the two private equity funds, which sought a declaratory judgment against the TPF. The TPF . . . has counterclaimed and sought payment of the withdrawal liability at issue. The TPF is supported on appeal by the PBGC, as amicus.

We conclude that at least one of the private equity funds which operated SBI, through layers of fund-related entities, was not merely a "passive" investor, but sufficiently operated, managed, and was advantaged by its relationship with its portfolio company, the now bankrupt SBI. We also conclude that further factual development is necessary as to the other equity fund. We decide that the district court erred in ending the potential claims against the equity funds by entering summary judgment for them under the "trades or businesses" aspect of the two-part "control group" test under 29 U.S.C. §1301(b)(1).

As a result, we remand for further factual development and for further proceedings under the second part of the "control group" test, that of "common control," in 29 U.S.C. §1301(b)(1). The district court was, however, correct to enter summary judgment in favor of the private equity funds on the TPF's claim of liability on the ground that the funds had engaged in a transaction to evade or avoid withdrawal liability.

I.

The material facts are undisputed.

A.   THE SUN FUNDS

Sun Capital Advisors, Inc. ("SCAI") is a private equity firm founded by its co-CEOs and sole shareholders, Marc Leder and Rodger Krouse. It is not a plaintiff or party in this case. SCAI and its affiliated entities find investors and create limited partnerships in which investor money is pooled, as in the private equity funds here. Moreover, SCAI finds and recommends investment opportunities for the equity funds, and negotiates, structures, and finalizes investment deals. SCAI also provides management services to portfolio companies, and employs about 123 professionals to provide these services.

The plaintiffs here are two of SCAI's private equity funds (collectively the "Sun Funds"), Sun Capital Partners III, LP ("Sun Fund III")[29] and Sun Capital Partners IV, LP ("Sun Fund IV"). They are organized as Delaware limited partnerships. SBI is one of their portfolio companies, and the two Sun Funds have other portfolio companies. The Sun Funds do not have any offices or employees; nor do they make or sell goods, or report income other than investment income on their tax returns. The stated purpose of the Sun Funds is to invest in underperforming but market-leading companies at below intrinsic value, with the aim of turning them around and selling them for a profit. As a result, the Sun Funds' controlling stakes in portfolio companies are used to implement restructuring and operational plans, build management teams, become intimately involved in company operations, and otherwise cause growth in the portfolio companies in which the Sun Funds invest. The intention of the Sun Funds is to then sell the hopefully successful portfolio company within two to five years. In fact, the Sun Funds have earned significant profits from sales of various portfolio companies.[30]

These private equity funds engaged in a particular type of investment approach, to be distinguished from mere stock holding or mutual fund investments. *See, e.g.,* S. Rosenthal, *Taxing Private Equity Funds as Corporate 'Developers,'* Tax Notes, Jan.21, 2013, at 361, 364 & n. 31 (explaining that private equity funds differ from mutual funds and hedge funds because they "assist and manage the business of the companies they invest in"). As one commentator puts it, "[i]t is one thing to manage one's investments in businesses. It is another to manage the businesses in which one invests." C. Sanchirico, *The Tax Advantage to Paying Private Equity Fund Managers with Profit Shares: What Is It? Why Is It Bad?,* 75 U. Chi. L. Rev. 1071, 1102 (2008).

The Sun Funds are overseen by general partners, Sun Capital Advisors III, LP and Sun Capital Advisors IV, LP. Leder and Krouse are each limited partners in the Sun Funds' general partners and, together with their spouses, are entitled to 64.74% of the aggregate profits of Sun Capital Advisors III, LP and 61.04% of such profits from Sun Capital Advisors IV, LP. The Sun Funds' limited partnership agreements vest their respective general partners with exclusive authority to manage the partnership. Part of this authority is the power to carry out all the objectives and purposes of the partnerships, which include investing in securities, managing and supervising any investments, and any other incidental activities the general partner deems necessary or advisable.

---

29. Sun Fund III is technically two different funds, Sun Capital Partners III, LP and Sun Capital Partners III QP, LP. Like the district court, we consider them one fund for purposes of this opinion because they are "parallel funds" run by a single general partner and generally make the same investments in the same proportions.

30. For instance, Sun Fund IV, the larger of the Funds, reported total investment income of $17,353,533 in 2007, $57,072,025 in 2008, and $70,010,235 in 2009.

For these services, each general partner receives an annual fee of two percent of the total commitments (meaning the aggregate cash committed as capital to the partnership)[31] to the Sun Funds, paid by the limited partnership, and a percentage of the Sun Funds' profits from investments. The general partners also have a limited partnership agreement, which provides that for each general partner a limited partner committee makes all material partnership decisions. Leder and Krouse are the sole members of the limited partner committees. Included in the powers of the limited partner committees is the authority to make decisions and determinations relating to "hiring, terminating and establishing the compensation of employees and agents of the [Sun] Fund or Portfolio Companies." The general partners also each have a subsidiary management company, Sun Capital Partners Management III, LLC and Sun Capital Partners Management IV, LLC, respectively. These management companies contract with the holding company that owns the acquired company to provide management services for a fee, and contract with SCAI to provide the employees and consultants. When portfolio companies pay fees to the management companies, the Sun Funds receive an offset to the fees owed to the general partner.

B.   THE ACQUISITION OF SCOTT BRASS, INC.

In 2006, the Sun Funds began to take steps to invest in SBI, the acquisition of which was completed in early 2007. Leder and Krouse made the decision to invest in SBI in their capacity as members of the limited partner committees.

SBI, a Rhode Island corporation, was an ongoing trade or business, and was closely held; its stock was not publicly traded. SBI was a leading producer of high quality brass, copper, and other metals "used in a variety of end markets, including electronics, automotive, hardware, fasteners, jewelry, and consumer products." In 2006, it shipped 40.2 million pounds of metal. SBI made contributions to the TPF on behalf of its employees pursuant to a collective bargaining agreement.

On November 28, 2006, a Sun Capital affiliated entity sent a letter of intent to SBI's outside financial advisor to purchase 100% of SBI. In December 2006, the Sun Funds formed Sun Scott Brass, LLC (SSB–LLC) as a vehicle to invest in SBI. Sun Fund III made a 30% investment ($900,000) and Sun Fund IV a 70% investment ($2.1 million) for a total equity investment of $3 million. This purchase price reflected a 25% discount because of SBI's known unfunded pension liability.[32] SSB–LLC, on December 15, 2006, formed a wholly-owned subsidiary, Scott Brass Holding Corp. (SBHC). SSB–LLC transferred the $3 million the Sun Funds invested in it to SBHC as $1 million in equity and $2 million in debt. *Id.* at 111. SBHC then purchased all of SBI's stock with the $3

---

31. The aggregate capital commitment of Sun Fund IV was $1.5 billion, which the TPF asserts means the management fee at the 2% rate was $30 million.

32. The Sun Funds contend that they reduced the purchase price based on the expectation that a future buyer would pay less for a company with unfunded pension obligations, not because of a concern that they were incurring potential withdrawal liability.

million of cash on hand and $4.8 million in additional borrowed money. The stock purchase agreement to acquire SBI's stock was entered into on February 8, 2007.

On February 9, 2007, SBHC signed an agreement with the subsidiary of the general partner of Sun Fund IV to provide management services to SBHC and its subsidiaries, *i.e.,* SBI. Since 2001, that general partner's subsidiary had contracted with SCAI to provide it with advisory services. In essence, as the district court described, the management company acted as a middle-man, providing SBI with employees and consultants from SCAI.

Numerous individuals with affiliations to various Sun Capital entities, including Krouse and Leder, exerted substantial operational and managerial control over SBI, which at the time of the acquisition had 208 employees and continued as a trade or business manufacturing metal products. For instance, minutes of a March 5, 2007 meeting show that seven individuals from "SCP" attended a "Jumpstart Meeting" at which the hiring of three SBI salesmen was approved, as was the hiring of a consultant to analyze a computer system upgrade project at a cost of $25,000. Other items discussed included possible acquisitions, capital expenditures, and the management of SBI's working capital. Further, Leder, Krouse, and Steven Liff, an SCAI employee, were involved in email chains discussing liquidity, possible mergers, dividend payouts, and concerns about how to drive revenue growth at SBI. Leder, Krouse, and other employees of SCAI received weekly flash reports from SBI that contained detailed information about SBI's revenue, key financial data, market activity, sales opportunities, meeting notes, and action items. According to the Sun Funds, SBI continued to meet its pension obligations to the TPF for more than a year and a half after the acquisition.

C. SBI'S BANKRUPTCY AND THIS LITIGATION

In the fall of 2008, declining copper prices reduced the value of SBI's inventory, resulting in a breach of its loan covenants. Unable to get its lender to waive the violation of the covenants, SBI lost its ability to access credit and was unable to pay its bills.

In October 2008, SBI stopped making contributions to the TPF, and, in so doing, became liable for its proportionate share of the TPF's unfunded vested benefits. In November 2008, an involuntary Chapter 11 bankruptcy proceeding was brought against SBI. The Sun Funds assert that they lost the entire value of their investment in SBI as a result of the bankruptcy.

On December 19, 2008, the TPF sent a demand for payment of estimated withdrawal liability to SBI. The TPF also sent a notice and demand to the Sun Funds demanding payment from them of SBI's withdrawal liability, ultimately calculated as $4,516,539. The TPF asserted that the Sun Funds had entered into a partnership or joint venture in common control with SBI and were therefore jointly and severally liable for SBI's withdrawal liability under 29 U.S.C. §1301(b)(1).

On June 4, 2010, the Sun Funds filed a declaratory judgment action in federal district court in Massachusetts. The Sun Funds sought a declaration that they were not subject to withdrawal liability under §1301(b)(1) because: (1) the Sun Funds were not part of a joint venture or partnership and therefore did not meet the common control requirement; and (2) neither of the Funds was a "trade or business."

The TPF counterclaimed that the Sun Funds were jointly and severally liable for SBI's withdrawal liability in the amount of $4,516,539, and also that the Sun Funds had engaged in a transaction to evade or avoid liability under 29 U.S.C. §1392(c). The parties both filed cross-motions for summary judgment in September 2011.

The district court issued a Memorandum and Order on October 18, 2012, granting summary judgment to the Sun Funds. The district court did not reach the issue of common control, instead basing its decision on the "trade or business" portion of the two-part statutory test. It also decided the "evade or avoid" liability issue.

On the "trade or business" issue, the district court addressed the level of deference owed to a September 2007 PBGC appeals letter that found a private equity fund to be a "trade or business" in the single employer pension plan context. The appeals letter found the equity fund to be a "trade or business" because its controlling stake in the bankrupt company put it in a position to exercise control over that company through its general partner, which was compensated for its efforts.

The district court held that the appeals letter was owed deference only to the extent it could persuade. The district court found the letter unpersuasive for two reasons: (1) the appeals board purportedly incorrectly attributed activity of the general partner to the investment fund; and (2) the appeals board letter supposedly conflicted with governing Supreme Court tax precedent. Engaging in its own analysis, the court found that the Sun Funds were not "trades or businesses," relying on the fact that the Sun Funds did not have any offices or employees, and did not make or sell goods or report income other than investment income on their tax returns. Moreover, the Sun Funds were not engaged in the general partner's management activities.

As to its "evade or avoid" liability analysis, the district court stated that §1392(c) was not meant to apply to an outside investor structuring a transaction to avoid assuming a potential liability. The language of the statute suggested that "it is aimed at sellers, not investors," and imposing liability on investors for trying to avoid assumption of such liability would disincentivize investing in companies subject to multiemployer pension plan obligations, thereby undermining the aim of the MPPAA.

The TPF has timely appealed. It argues that the district court erred in finding that the Sun Funds were not "trades or businesses" and that the Sun Funds should be subject to "evade or avoid" liability under §1392(c). The PBGC has filed an amicus brief on appeal in support of reversal of the district court's "trades or businesses" decision, but has taken no position on the §1392(c) claim.

II.

B.   WITHDRAWAL LIABILITY UNDER THE MPPAA

The MPPAA was enacted by Congress to protect the viability of defined pension benefit plans, to create a disincentive for employers to withdraw from multiemployer plans, and also to provide a means of recouping a fund's unfunded liabilities. As such, the MPPAA requires employers withdrawing from a multiemployer plan to pay their proportionate share of the pension fund's vested but unfunded benefits. An employer withdraws when it permanently ceases its obligation to contribute or permanently ceases covered operations under the plan.

The MPPAA provides: "For purposes of this subchapter, under regulations prescribed by the [PBGC], all employees of trades or businesses (whether or not incorporated) which are under common control shall be treated as employed by a single employer and all such trades and businesses as a single employer." So, "[t]o impose withdrawal liability on an organization other than the one obligated to the [pension] Fund, two conditions must be satisfied: 1) the organization must be under 'common control' with the obligated organization, and 2) the organization must be a trade or business." The Act's broad definition of "employer" extends beyond the business entity withdrawing from the pension fund, thus imposing liability on related entities within the definition, which, in effect, pierces the corporate veil and disregards formal business structures.

While Congress in §1301(b)(1) authorizes the PBGC to prescribe regulations, those regulations "shall be consistent and coextensive with regulations prescribed for similar purposes by the Secretary of the Treasury under [26 U.S.C. §414(c)]" of the Internal Revenue Code. The PBGC has adopted regulations pertaining to the meaning of "common control," but has not adopted regulations defining or explaining the meaning of "trades or businesses."

The phrase "trades or businesses" as used in §1301(b)(1) is not defined in Treasury regulations and has not been given a definitive, uniform definition by the Supreme Court.

C.   FAILING TO HAVE PROMULGATED REGULATIONS, THE PBGC NONETHELESS OFFERS GUIDANCE ON THE MEANING OF "TRADES OR BUSINESSES"

The only guidance we have from the PBGC is a 2007 appeals letter, defended in its amicus brief.

In a September 2007 response to an appeal, the PBGC, in a letter, applied a two-prong test it purported to derive from *Commissioner of Internal Revenue v. Groetzinger,* 480 U.S. 23, 107 S.Ct. 980, to determine if the private equity fund was a "trade or business" for purposes of the first part of the §1301(b)(1) requirement. The PBGC asked (1) whether the private equity fund was engaged in an activity with the primary purpose of income or profit and (2) whether it conducted that activity with continuity and regularity. *See id.* at 35, 107 S.Ct. 980 ("We accept . . . that to be engaged in a trade or business, the taxpayer must be involved in the activity with continuity and regularity and that the taxpayer's primary purpose for engaging in the activity must be for income or profit.").

The PBGC found that the private equity fund involved in that matter met the profit motive requirement. It also determined that the size of the fund, the size of its profits, and the management fees paid to the general partner established continuity and regularity. The PBGC also observed that the fund's agent provided management and advisory services, and received fees for those services. Indeed, the Appeals Board noted that the equity fund's agent, "N," received 20% of all net profits received in exchange for its services and that its acts were attributable to the fund as the fund's agent. In addition, the fund's controlling stake in the portfolio company put it in a position to exercise control through its general partner, consistent with its stated purpose. The approach taken by the PBGC has been dubbed an "investment plus" standard.

D.   SUN FUND IV IS A "TRADE OR BUSINESS" UNDER §1301(B)(1), THE PBGC'S "INVESTMENT PLUS" APPROACH IS PERSUASIVE, AND THE SAME APPROACH WOULD BE EMPLOYED EVEN WITHOUT DEFERENCE

The Sun Funds argue that the "investment plus" test is incompatible with Supreme Court tax precedent. Regardless, they argue, the Sun Funds cannot be held responsible for the activities of other entities in the management and operation of SBI. And even if the Sun Funds had engaged in those activities, they argue, that would not be enough.

Where the MPPAA issue is one of whether there is mere passive investment to defeat pension withdrawal liability, we are persuaded that some form of an "investment plus" approach is appropriate when evaluating the "trade or business" prong of §1301(b)(1), depending on what the "plus" is. Further, even if we were to ignore the PBGC's interpretation, we, like the Seventh Circuit, would reach the same result through independent analysis. In *Central States, Southeast & Southwest Areas Pension Fund v. Messina Products, LLC,* 706 F.3d 874, the Seventh Circuit employed an "investment plus"-like analysis without reference to any PBGC interpretation. We agree with that approach. We see no need to set forth general guidelines for what the "plus" is, nor has the PBGC provided guidance on this. We go no further than to say that on the undisputed facts of this case, Sun Fund IV is a "trade or business" for purposes of §1301(b)(1).

In a very fact-specific approach, we take account of a number of factors, cautioning that none is dispositive in and of itself. The Sun Funds make investments in portfolio companies with the principal purpose of making a profit. Profits are made from the sale of stock at higher prices than the purchase price and through dividends. But a mere investment made to make a profit, without more, does not itself make an investor a trade or business.

Here, however, the Sun Funds have also undertaken activities as to the SBI property. The Sun Funds' limited partnership agreements and private placement memos explain that the Funds are actively involved in the management and operation of the companies in which they invest. Each Sun Fund agreement states, for instance, that a "principal purpose" of the partnership is the "manag[ement] and supervisi[on]" of its investments. The agreements also give the general partner of each Sun Fund exclusive and wide-ranging management authority.

In addition, the general partners are empowered through their own partnership agreements to make decisions about hiring, terminating, and compensating agents and employees of the Sun Funds and their portfolio companies. The general partners receive a percentage of total commitments to the Sun Funds and a percentage of profits as compensation—just like the general partner of the equity fund in the PBGC appeals letter.

It is the purpose of the Sun Funds to seek out potential portfolio companies that are in need of extensive intervention with respect to their management and operations, to provide such intervention, and then to sell the companies. The private placement memos explain that "[t]he Principals typically work to reduce costs, improve margins, accelerate sales growth through new products and market opportunities, implement or modify management information systems and improve reporting and control functions." More specifically, those memos represent that restructuring and operating plans are developed for a target portfolio company even before it is acquired and a management team is built specifically for the purchased company, with "[s]ignificant changes . . . typically made to portfolio companies in the first three to six months." The strategic plan developed initially is "consistently monitored and modified as necessary." Involvement can encompass even small details, including signing of all checks for its new portfolio companies and the holding of frequent meetings with senior staff to discuss operations, competition, new products and personnel.

Such actions are taken with the ultimate goal of selling the portfolio company for a profit. On this point, the placement memos explain that after implementing "significant operating improvements . . . during the first two years[,] . . . the Principals expect to exit investments in two to five years (or sooner under appropriate circumstances)."

Further, the Sun Funds' controlling stake in SBI placed them and their affiliated entities in a position where they were intimately involved in the management and operation of the company. Through a series of appointments, the Sun Funds were able to place SCAI employees in two of the three director positions at SBI, resulting in SCAI employees controlling the SBI board.

Through a series of service agreements described earlier, SCAI provided personnel to SBI for management and consulting services. Thereafter, individuals from those entities were immersed in details involving the management and operation of SBI, as discussed.

Moreover, the Sun Funds' active involvement in management under the agreements provided a direct economic benefit to at least Sun Fund IV that an ordinary, passive investor would not derive: an offset against the management fees it otherwise would have paid its general partner for managing the investment in SBI. Here, SBI made payments of more than $186,368.44 to Sun Fund IV's general partner, which were offset against the fees Sun Fund IV had to pay to its general partner. This offset was not from an ordinary investment activity, which in the Sun Funds' words "results solely in investment returns."

In our view, the sum of all of these factors satisfy the "plus" in the "investment plus" test.

The Sun Funds [argue] that because none of the relevant activities by agents and different business entities can be attributed to the Sun Funds themselves, withdrawal liability cannot be imposed upon them. We reject this argument as well. Without resolving the issue of the extent to which Congress intended in this area to honor corporate formalities, as have the parties we look to the Restatement of Agency. And, because the Sun Funds are Delaware limited partnerships, we also look to Delaware law.

Under Delaware law, a partner "is an agent of the partnership for the purpose of its business, purposes or activities," and an act of a partner "for apparently carrying on in the ordinary course the partnership's business, purposes or activities or business, purposes or activities of the kind carried on by the partnership binds the partnership." To determine what is "carrying on in the ordinary course" of the partnership's business, we may consider the partnership's stated purpose.

Here, the limited partnership agreements gave the Sun Funds' general partners the exclusive authority to act on behalf of the limited partnerships to effectuate their purposes. These purposes included managing and supervising investments in portfolio companies, as well as "other such activity incidental or ancillary thereto" as deemed advisable by the general partner. So, under Delaware law, it is clear that the general partner of Sun Fund IV, in providing management services to SBI, was acting as an agent of the Fund.

Moreover, even absent Delaware partnership law, the partnership agreements themselves grant actual authority for the general partner to provide management services to portfolio companies like SBI. And the general partners' own partnership agreements giving power to the limited partner committees to make determinations about hiring, terminating, and compensating agents and employees of the Sun Funds and their portfolio companies show the existence of such authority. Hence, the general partner was acting within the scope of its authority.

Even so, the Sun Funds argue that the general partner entered the management service contract with SBI on its own accord, not as an agent of the Sun Funds. The Sun Funds' own characterization is not dispositive.

The argument is unpersuasive for at least two reasons. First, it was within the general partner's scope of authority to provide management services to SBI. Second, providing management services was done on behalf of and for the benefit of the Sun Funds. The investment strategy of the Sun Funds could only be achieved by active management through an agent, since the Sun Funds themselves had no employees. Indeed, the management services agreement was entered into just one day after the execution of the stock purchase agreement. In addition, Sun Fund IV received an offset in the fees it owed to its general partner because of payments made from SBI to that general partner. That provided a benefit by reducing its expenses. The services paid for by SBI were the *same services* that the Sun Funds would otherwise have paid for themselves to implement and oversee an operating strategy at SBI.

The Sun Funds also make a policy argument that Congress never intended such a result in its §1301(b)(1) control group provision. They argue that the purpose of the provision is to prevent an employer "from circumventing ERISA obligations by divvying up its business operations into separate entities." It is *not,* they say, intended to reach owners of a business so as to require them to "dig into their own pockets" to pay withdrawal liability for a company they own.

These are fine lines. The various arrangements and entities meant precisely to shield the Sun Funds from liability may be viewed as an attempt to divvy up operations to avoid ERISA obligations. We recognize that Congress may wish to encourage investment in distressed companies by curtailing the risk to investors in such employers of acquiring ERISA withdrawal liability. If so, Congress has not been explicit, and it may prefer instead to rely on the usual pricing mechanism in the private market for assumption of risk.

We express our dismay that the PBGC has not given more and earlier guidance on this "trade or business" "investment plus" theory to the many parties affected. The PBGC has not engaged in notice and comment rulemaking or even issued guidance of any kind which was subject to prior public notice and comment. Moreover, its appeals letter that provides for the "investment plus" test leaves open many questions about exactly where the line should be drawn between a mere passive investor and one engaged in a "trade or business."

Because to be an "employer" under §1301(b)(1) the entity must both be a "trade or business" and be under common control, we reverse entry of summary judgment on the §1301(b)(1) claim in favor of Sun Fund IV and vacate the judgment in favor of Sun Fund III. We remand the §1301(b)(1) claim of liability to the district court to resolve whether Sun Fund III received any benefit from an offset from fees paid by SBI and for the district court to decide the issue of common control. We determine only that the "trade or business" requirement has been satisfied as to Sun Fund IV.

III.

We deny, for different reasons than the district court, the TPF's appeal from entry of summary judgment against its claim under 29 U.S.C. §1392(c). That provision of the MPPAA states "[i]f a principal purpose of any transaction is to evade or avoid liability under this part, this part shall be applied (and liability shall be determined and collected) *without regard to such transaction.*" 29 U.S.C. §1392(c) (emphasis added).

The TPF argues that §1392(c) applies because the Sun Funds, during the acquisition, purposefully divided ownership of SSB–LLC into 70%/30% shares in order to avoid the 80% parent-subsidiary common control requirement of §1301(b)(1). Under Treasury regulations, to be in a parent-subsidiary group under common control, the parent must have an 80% interest in the subsidiary.

26 C.F.R. §1.414(c)–2(b)(2)(i). The TPF asserts that, because a Sun Fund representative testified that a principal purpose of the 70%/30% division was to avoid unfunded pension liability and because an email states that a reason ownership was divided was "due to [the] unfunded pension liability," liability can be imposed on the Sun Funds under §1392(c).

We hold that §1392(c) cannot serve as a basis to impose liability on the Sun Funds because, by applying the remedy specified by the statute, the TPF would still not be entitled to any payments from the Sun Funds for withdrawal liability.

The instruction requires courts to put the parties in the same situation as if the offending transaction never occurred; that is, to erase that transaction. It does not, by contrast, instruct or permit a court to take the affirmative step of writing in new terms to a transaction or to create a transaction that never existed. In order for the TPF to succeed, we would have to (improperly) do the latter because simply doing the former would not give the TPF any relief, but would only sever any ties between the Sun Funds and SBI.

Disregarding the agreement to divide SSB–LLC 70%/30% would not result in Sun Fund IV being the 100% owner of SBI. At the moment SSB–LLC was divided 70%/30%, the transaction to purchase SBI had not been completed. There is no way of knowing that the acquisition would have happened anyway if Sun Fund IV were to be a 100% owner, but it is doubtful.

The TPF argues that because Sun Fund IV had already signed a letter of intent to purchase 100% of SBI before the decision was made to divide ownership between the Sun Funds, we can rely on the letter of intent. The TPF claims that the decision to split ownership to avoid the automatic assumption of withdrawal liability at 80% ownership was made after a binding transaction was entered into through the letter of intent. That is not true. The letter of intent was so named because it was not a binding contract or any sort of purchase agreement. Rather, the letter explicitly contained a clause stating that:

> The first five captioned paragraphs of this letter ('Purchase Price', 'Purchase Agreement Terms,' 'Financing,' 'Timing & Process,' and 'Due Diligence') represent only the intent of the parties, do not constitute a contract or agreement, are not binding, and shall not be enforceable against the Sellers, the Company, or Sun Capital. . . . [N]either party shall have any legally binding obligation to the other unless and until a definitive purchase agreement is executed.

This is simply not a case about an entity with a controlling stake of 80% or more under the MPPAA seeking to shed its controlling status to avoid withdrawal liability. As such, disregarding the agreement to divide ownership of SSB–LLC would *not* leave us with Sun Fund IV holding a controlling 80% stake in SBI.

The Sun Funds are not subject to liability pursuant to §1392(c) and the district court's conclusion that they are not is affirmed.

———————————

The First Circuit remanded the case to the district court to determine whether a related private equity fund was also a trade or business under ERISA and whether the second prong of the test for imposing joint and several liability under ERISA—*i.e.,* "common control"—had been met with respect to the group of related portfolio companies. On remand, the district court concluded in *Sun Capital Partners III, LP v. New England Teamsters & Trucking Indus. Pension Fund*, 2016 BL 95418 (D. Mass. Mar. 28, 2016), that the answer to both of these questions is "yes." That ruling has been appealed to the First Circuit (docket no. 16-1376).

PROBLEM SET 20.5

1. As always, diagram the transaction and be ready to discuss.
2. Recall the discussion of taxation and ECI earlier in this chapter. Does this case present a problem for the common master-feeder structure?
3. Does the Court hold that the fund itself is engaged in a trade or business?

9. DIFFERENCES WITH HEDGE FUNDS

This section briefly details some key differences between hedge funds and private equity funds.

First, private equity funds typically have specified lives, whereas hedge funds typically last as long as the manager wants them to last. The term of a private equity fund begins following the first fund closing and typically runs for ten to twelve years.

Because a private equity fund obtains capital from its investors during the early years of the fund by making a series of capital calls based on each investor's capital commitment (as opposed to a hedge fund, which receives full payment when it issues shares or interests), there is the potential for an investor to refuse or otherwise fail to meet a capital call. In these cases, the private equity fund documents usually provide a number of potential remedies against the defaulting investor. For example, some funds require a defaulting investor to forfeit its entire interest in the fund and thereafter offer the other investors the ability to purchase the forfeited interest. Alternatively, the manager may bring legal action against the defaulting investor.

The operating agreements of private equity funds typically contain an offset mechanism (a management fee offset) requiring an adjustment to the fund management fee against a percentage of management services, transaction, and other fees received by the sponsor and its affiliates from the fund's portfolio companies. The percentage of the fee offset may vary depending on the type of fee.

Similarly, private equity funds often provide a "clawback" provision relating to the sponsor's carried interest. A clawback is triggered if, on calculating the fund's total returns, including events occurring after interim distributions made to the sponsor, the sponsor has received more than its "share" of the fund's distributions (for example, if the return to the investors is less than the hurdle rate or less than 80 percent of the total fund profits).

10. STRATEGIES

Private equity funds, like hedge funds, have expanded into a variety of strategies. Common types include buyout funds, merchant banking funds, venture capital funds, mezzanine funds, "special situations" funds, real estate and other asset-backed funds, distressed debt funds, and infrastructure funds. A hedge fund heavily invested in illiquid assets or a private equity fund engaged in active trading become almost indistinguishable.

As noted, one key area for private equity fund activity involves takeovers of publicly traded firms, often by means of a leveraged buyout that turns the target company into a privately held firm. Approximately 25 percent of all global M&A volume during the first half of 2007 was attributable to such deals. Things changed dramatically with the failure of Lehman and the lack of lending activity that followed.

Whether or not these funds provide real value to investors is the subject of some degree of debate, and whether any value they do provide is not simply the result of a wealth transfer from employees and creditors became the subject of much debate during the 2012 presidential election. Mitt Romney, you will recall, was the founder of a private equity firm, and his holdings in the Cayman Islands did little to help the industry's image as "rapacious asset-strippers who hide their ill-gotten gains in secret bank accounts."[33]

PROBLEM SET 20.6

1. Consider the following swap: Counterparty pays the investor a floating payment equal to the total return on a notional investment in a hedge fund. Investor makes an initial payment to the counterparty, periodic payments equal to a floating interest rate plus a spread on the notional amount less the initial payment, and any depreciation on the notional hedge fund investment. At the end of the term, counterparty returns the initial payment to investor. What type of swap is this? What is the economic equivalent of this investment? What are its risks?

2. What benefits does a private equity fund investor get that could not be obtained by buying a portfolio company's equity while it was still publicly traded?

---

33. *http://goo.gl/yJNzn*

11. UNDERSTANDING THE TERMS

Take a look at the sample term sheet available online. Be prepared to discuss the terms of an investment in the (purely hypothetical) Funk to Funky Capital XIV LP private equity fund.

21

VENTURE CAPITAL FUNDS AND INVESTMENTS

Venture capital funds can be seen as a kind of specialized private equity fund, designed to invest in the early stages of businesses, while traditional private equity funds invest in more mature businesses. Venture capital funds buy stakes in portfolio companies, with the end goal of realizing profit through the sale of a private company or an initial public offering. The fund purchases preferred stock or debt securities convertible into equity, and it usually takes an active role in the direction of the business by becoming a member of a board of directors, as well as by advising the entrepreneurs who started the business.[1]

As part of the Dodd-Frank legislation, the SEC adopted Rule 203(1)-1, which defines a venture capital fund as any private fund that

(i) represents to investors and prospective investors that it pursues a venture capital strategy,

(ii) immediately after the acquisition of any asset (other than qualifying investments or cash, cash equivalents, U.S. Treasury securities with a remaining maturity of 60 days or less and shares of an open-end management investment company registered under Section 8 of the Investment Company Act and regulated as a money market fund ("short-term holdings")), holds no more than 20% of the fund's aggregate capital contributions and uncalled capital commitments in assets (excluding short-term holdings) that are not qualifying investments, valued at cost or fair value, consistently applied by the fund,

(iii) does not borrow, issue debt obligations, guarantee or otherwise incur leverage in excess of 15% of the private fund's aggregate capital contributions and uncalled committed capital, and any such permitted indebtedness or guarantee has a non-renewable term of no longer than 120 calendar days, except that any guarantee by the fund of a qualifying portfolio company's obligations up to the amount of the value of the fund's investment in the portfolio company is not subject to the 120 calendar day limit,

(iv) does not offer its investors withdrawal, redemption, repurchase or other similar liquidity rights, except in extraordinary circumstances, and

---

1. Elizabeth Pollman, *Team Production Theory and Private Company Boards*, 38 Seattle U. L. Rev. 619, 627 (2015).

(v) is not registered under Section 8 of the Investment Company Act and has not elected to be treated as a business development company under Section 54 of the Investment Company Act.

This definition should immediately suggest at least one key difference between private equity and venture capital funds.

1. STRUCTURE OF THE FUND

If you understand the structure of hedge funds and private equity funds, the basic structure of venture capital funds should be easily understood, too. The following case involves an individual's tax dispute, which is, of course, not the subject of this class. But the opinion includes a rare, detailed description of the structure of actual venture capital funds so we read it on that basis.

TODD A. AND CAROLYN D. DAGRES
v. COMMISSIONER OF INTERNAL REVENUE

136 T.C. 263
United States Tax Court
No. 15523-08 | March 28, 2011

GUSTAFSON, Judge:

On March 21, 2008, the Internal Revenue Service (IRS) issued to petitioners Todd and Carolyn Dagres a notice of deficiency pursuant to section 6212, determining a deficiency of $981,980 in income tax for 2003 and an accompanying accuracy-related penalty of $196,369 under section 6662(a). After Mr. Dagres's concession that the $30,000 of interest he received in 2003 constitutes taxable income, the issues for decision are whether: (1) Mr. Dagres is entitled to a $3,635,218 business bad debt deduction for 2003 pursuant to section 166(a); and (2) Mr. Dagres is liable for the accuracy-related penalty under section 6662(a).

On the facts proved at trial, we find that Mr. Dagres was in the trade or business of managing venture capital funds; and we hold that he suffered a bad debt loss in connection with that business in 2003, and that it was a business bad debt loss. As a result, he is entitled to deduct the loss under section 166(a). Because the bad debt deduction offsets all of Mr. Dagres's taxable income, he is not liable for the accuracy-related penalty.

In 1994 Mr. Dagres worked as an analyst for Montgomery Securities, an investment bank based in San Francisco, and he focused on the computer networking industry.

JOINING BATTERY VENTURES

In 1996 . . . Mr. Dagres left Montgomery Securities to engage in venture capital activities in Boston with a group of associated entities generally referred to as Battery Ventures. When Mr. Dagres joined Battery Ventures, four funds had already been established. Mr. Dagres stayed with Battery Ventures for 9 years (and at the time of trial in 2009 he worked at Spark Capital, another venture capital firm).

BATTERY VENTURES' ORGANIZATION

During the relevant years, Battery Ventures was a group of entities that consisted of the following three types:

(1) *Specific venture capital funds.* Each of Battery Ventures' venture capital funds was organized as a limited partnership, and each was governed by a limited partnership agreement. Important in the relevant period were funds named Battery Ventures IV, L.P. (organized in January 1997), Battery Ventures V, L.P. (organized in March 1999), and Battery Ventures VI, L.P. (apparently organized in 2000), which we refer to individually as Fund IV, Fund V, and Fund VI and collectively as the Venture Fund L.P.s. Funds IV, V, and VI were formed during Mr. Dagres's tenure at Battery Ventures. Each Venture Fund L.P. had limited partners (who were its principal investors) and a single general partner.

(2) *Limited liability companies* (L.L.C.s). Battery Ventures' L.L.C.s served as the general partners of the Venture Fund L.P.s, responsible for management and investment. Important in the relevant period were Battery Partners IV, L.L.C. (the general partner of Fund IV), Battery Partners V, L.L.C. (the general partner of Fund V), and Battery Partners VI, L.L.C. (the general partner of Fund VI), which we refer to individually as Partners IV, Partners V, and Partners VI and collectively as the General Partner L.L.C.s. The General Partner L.L.C.s were governed by limited liability company agreements that provided for several types of members ("Member Managers," "Special Members," and "Limited Members") and that set out the members' entitlement to share in the profits of the L.L.C. The members of the General Partner L.L.C.s were Battery Ventures personnel. Mr. Dagres was a Member Manager of Partners IV, V, and VI and was entitled to a 12–to 14– percent share of their profits.

(3) *Management companies.* The Battery Ventures management companies provided services to assist the operation of the Venture Fund L.P.s and their General Partner L.L.C.s. Relevant in this suit is Battery Management Co. (BMC), an S corporation that served as a management company in relevant years. Battery Ventures personnel, including Mr. Dagres, were salaried employees of BMC. BMC's shares were owned by

the Member Managers of the General Partner L.L.C.s, including Mr. Dagres. At the end of each year, the management company paid unspent service fees to its shareholders, in proportion to their ownership interest in the management company (though the record does not show the fact or amount of actual payments in any particular year).

Mr. Dagres contends that, in addition to these specific entities, "'Battery Ventures'*** likely constituted an oral partnership or partnership by estoppel under state law," and that this partnership was engaged in a venture capital business that should be attributed to him as a partner. It is true that Mr. Dagres held himself out as a "General Partner" of "Battery Ventures," and literature evidently published by Battery Ventures entities did the same. However, in view of our finding that the General Partner L.L.C.s were engaged in the business of managing venture capital funds, and our holding that this activity is attributed to Mr. Dagres as a Member Manager of those L.L.C.s, we need not and do not resolve the factual and legal issues prompted by this contention of partnership by estoppel.

SERVICES AND FEES

Under the limited partnership agreement of each Venture Fund L.P., its General Partner L.L.C. was responsible for managing the fund and making its investments, in return for a fee. The General Partner L.L.C. in turn entered into a service agreement with BMC, pursuant to which—in return for the General Partner L.L.C.'s promise of an equivalent fee to BMC—Mr. Dagres and other Battery Ventures personnel actually performed the necessary work of managing and investing for the Venture Fund L.P.

Under the service agreement, BMC assumed all the normal operating expenses of the General Partner L.L.C.s, including all routine expenses incident to serving the venture capital activities of the General Partner L.L.C.s. These included the expenses for investigating investment opportunities, compensating the officers and employees of BMC, paying the salaries of the Member Managers of the General Partner L.L.C.s, and paying the fees and expenses for administrative, accounting, bookkeeping, and legal services, office space, utilities, travel, liability insurance, and other related expenses. BMC provided the facilities and staff needed to perform the venture capital business of Battery Ventures, including staff who helped with identifying and researching potential investment targets, staff who helped perform due diligence on those prospects, staff who helped to manage the investments (by providing management assistance to the target companies themselves), and other support staff, such as receptionists, secretaries, accounting personnel, etc.

Each Venture Fund L.P. paid service fees annually of 2 to 2.5 percent of the partners' total committed capital in the fund. The limited partnership agreements obligated each Venture Fund L.P. to pay these service fees to its respective General Partner L.L.C., but each General Partner L.L.C. in turn agreed to reimburse BMC for organizational expenses incurred in setting up the General Partner L.L.C. and the Venture Fund L.P., and agreed to pay a service fee to BMC equal to the service fee described in the limited partnership agreement. Consequently, each Venture Fund L.P. remitted the service fees directly to BMC, by-passing the General Partner L.L.C. that was immediately obligated to perform the management services and entitled to receive the fees. Those service fees were the revenue source from which BMC paid salaries to its employees.

INVESTMENT AND RETURN

Each Venture Fund L.P. solicited investors to invest (as limited partners) in "developmental and emerging companies primarily in the software, communications and information systems industries primarily in the United States." The total maximum subscription or aggregate investment amount for Fund IV was $200 million, and the maximum for Fund V was $400 million. The aggregate investment amount is also called the amount of pledged funds or the "committed capital" of the fund. Each Venture Fund L.P. had a 10-year life, and each limited partnership agreement provided that the General Partner L.L.C. could not make additional calls for capital contributions by the limited partners after the fifth anniversary of the date of the agreement.[2]

The limited partner investors included insurance companies, pension funds, foundations, and high-net-worth individuals. Each limited partnership agreement required its General Partner L.L.C. to use its best efforts to conduct the partnership's affairs: (1) in a manner to avoid any classification for Federal income tax purposes that the partnership was engaged in the conduct of a trade or business, and (2) in a manner to avoid generating any unrelated business taxable income for any tax-exempt limited partner. The parties therefore agree that the activity of the Venture Fund L.P.s themselves was investment, and not the conduct of a trade or business.

The limited partners contributed 99 percent of each fund's capital. The remaining 1 percent of the funds in the Venture Fund L.P. came from the General Partner L.L.C. The members of that General Partner L.L.C. personally contributed the money to fund that 1 percent, presumably in proportion to their ownership interests in the General Partner L.L.C. (though the record does not show the proportions).

The General Partner L.L.C. was entitled to additional compensation for the management and investment services that it was obliged to provide (with support from the management company): Each Venture Fund L.P. granted a 20-percent profits interest to its General Partner L.L.C. This profits interest is called "carried interest" or "carry." As is explained above, this "carry" is an important feature of

---

2. The limited partnership agreements provided that Fund IV began on January 22, 1997, and would end December 31, 2007, and that Fund V began March 31, 1999, and would end December 31, 2009. At the end of that time, each Venture Fund L.P. was to be liquidated and its cash and securities distributed. Thus a capital call could occur for Fund IV as late as January 22, 2002, and for Fund V as late as March 31, 2004.

the venture capital arrangement. Though the venture capital firm makes only a relatively modest 1-percent contribution to the capital of the fund, it obtains an additional 20-percent interest in the profits. It therefore has a very substantial opportunity for gain—and, from the point of view of the other investors, it has a very substantial incentive to maximize the fund's success.[3]

PROBLEM SET 21.1

1. Diagram the structure of the funds. What precisely do the general partner entities do?
2. What roles did Mr. Dagres play in the funds? In what ways did he receive cash flows from his various roles?
3. In a general sense, what was the cost of an investment in one of these funds? What was the potential return?

2.   STRUCTURE OF THE INVESTMENT

Venture capital funds typically invest in "early-stage" firms.[4] "Early-stage" could mean almost anything from an entity with nothing more than an idea to a business that has operated for some time, but has yet to experience real growth.

The first stage of financing that a startup completes is commonly referred to as a seed round or, if the investors have close connections of the founders, this initial financing round may also be referred to as a friends and family round. Venture capital funds are generally considered to be the second of a three-stage finance process that begins with "angel" investors, who are the first outside investors in the firm, then venture capital investors, and then the public markets.

A venture capital fund typically provides cash to its portfolio companies in exchange for preferred shares in the company. When additional capital is needed, additional preferred stock is purchased by the fund, with each new round of investment receiving specific rights.

---

3. Strictly speaking, it appears that the General Partner L.L.C. obtains slightly less than 21 percent (20 percent plus 1 percent) of the profits. After the investors' capital has been returned to them, 20 percent of the profits is paid to the General Partner L.L.C. in its capacity as manager of the Venture Fund L.P., and then the remaining 80 percent of the profits is distributed to the investors in proportion to their investment. Since the General Partner L.L.C. invested 1 percent of the capital, it receives 1 percent of the investors' share—i.e., 1—percent of 80 percent of the profits. Thus, the General Partner L.L.C. as a 1 percent investor receives 0.8 percent of the profits. For the sake of simplicity, we refer in this Opinion to the 20-percent and 1-percent interests without making this correction.

4. Jennifer S. Fan, *Regulating Unicorns: Disclosure and the New Private Economy*, 57 B.C. L. Rev. 583, 590-98 (2016).

RONALD J. GILSON, *ENGINEERING A VENTURE CAPITAL MARKET:*
LESSONS FROM THE AMERICAN EXPERIENCE

55 Stan. L. Rev. 1067, 1072 (2003)

The venture capital fund's equity investments in portfolio companies typically take the form of convertible preferred stock.[5] While not required by the formal legal documents, the fund is also expected to make important noncash contributions to the portfolio company. These contributions consist of management assistance, corresponding to that provided by management consultants; intensive monitoring of the portfolio company's performance which provides an objective view to the entrepreneur; and the use of the fund's reputation to give the portfolio company credibility with potential customers, suppliers, and employees. While each investment will have a "lead" investor who plays the primary role in monitoring and advising the portfolio company, commonly the overall investment is syndicated with other venture capital funds that invest in the portfolio company at the same time and on the same terms.

The initial venture capital investment usually will be insufficient to fund the portfolio company's entire business plan. Accordingly, investment will be "staged." A particular investment round will provide only the capital the business plan projects as necessary to achieve specified milestones set out in the business plan. While first round investors expect to participate in subsequent investment rounds,[6] often they are not contractually obligated to do so even if the business plan's milestones are met; the terms of later rounds of investment are negotiated at the time the milestones are met and the prior investment exhausted. Like the provision of noncapital contributions, an implicit, not explicit, contract typically governs the venture capital fund's right and obligation to provide additional rounds of financing if the portfolio company performs as expected. The venture capital fund's implicit right to participate in subsequent rounds—by contrast to its implicit obligation to participate—is protected by an explicit right of first refusal.[7]

---

5. Paul Gompers, Ownership and Control in Entrepreneurial Firms: An Examination of Convertible Securities in Venture Capital Investments 2, 314–15 (Harvard Business School, Working Paper, 1997) (on file with author); Sahlman, *supra* note 7, at 504. Steven Kaplan and Per Strömberg report that convertible preferred stock was used in 95% of a sample of 200 financing rounds in 118 portfolio companies made by 14 venture capital firms between 1996 and 1999. Steven N. Kaplan & Per Strömberg, Financial Contracting Theory Meets the Real World: An Empirical Analysis of Venture Capital Contracts 13 (Nat'l Bureau of Econ. Research, Working Paper 7660, 2000), available at http://www.nber.org/papers/w7660. Ronald Gilson and David Schizer argue that this consistency is driven by the tax efficiency of this capital structure in delivering high-powered incentives to management. Ronald J. Gilson & David M. Schizer, *Understanding Venture Capital Structure: A Tax Explanation for Convertible Preferred Stock*, 116 Harv. L. Rev. 874 (2003).

6. Sahlman reports that venture capital funds invest one third of their capital in new investments and two thirds in later round financing of companies already in their portfolios.

7. Kaplan and Strömberg report that some 15% of the financing rounds in their sample conditioned disbursement of a portion of the round on explicit contingencies. Many of these,

The use of staged financing, with multiple rounds, has the potential to lead to the dilution of earlier investors. To protect against this, venture capital investors, as noted at the end of the excerpted article, retain a right to provide the next round of financing and thus maintain their relative ownership interest.

But venture capital investors also want to protect the conversion option in the preferred shares. This is particularly important to the investor if a subsequent round of financing results in a lower valuation of the startup company. This is commonly referred to as a "down round" financing.

The *"full-ratchet"* is the strongest form of protection against a down round. Under a "full ratchet," previous convertible preferred shares have their conversion ratio reset to the lowest subsequent conversion ratio.

For example, if the venture capital investor purchased 1 million shares of convertible preferred stock at $1 per share, and new capital is raised at 50 cents per share, then the venture capital investor's conversion price will be reduced to 50 cents, and the venture capital investor thus will be entitled to convert its preferred stock into 2 million shares instead of 1 million shares.

An alternative approach is referred to as the "weighted average" approach. Preexisting convertible preferred shares are adjusted based on a formula. There are a variety of ways to state the formula, but here is one of the simpler versions:

$$NCP = \frac{(X + Y)}{(Z)}$$

- NCP refers to the new conversion price.
- X equals the original issue price multiplied by the number of shares issued at that price.
- Y equals the new issue price multiplied by the number of shares issued at that price.
- Z equals the number of total number of shares outstanding after the new sale.

---

however, are not inconsistent with the unconstrained option to abandon analysis in the text. First, in some number of these instances, subsequent financing was contingent on "no material deviation" from the business plan. Kaplan & Strömberg, *supra* note 14, at 59 tb1.6. While such a formulation does operate to make exercise of the option to abandon reviewable by a court, it hardly represents state contingent contracting and still leaves the venture capitalist with a great deal of discretion. Since material changes in a business plan are predictable given the nature of an early stage business, in most cases the material deviation contingency will collapse into a pure option to abandon. Second, contingencies are keyed to readily observable and verifiable events like the issuance of a patent, or the hiring of a chief executive officer, again instances when a specific uncertainty can be specified and its resolution observed. Finally, Kaplan and Strömberg do not suggest that the venture capitalists are committed to provide future financing rounds even in the minority of rounds where explicit contingencies are found. Taken as a whole, their data leave intact the general proposition that venture financing is staged, without binding future commitments by existing venture investors.

To give this some concreteness, use the numbers from before and assume a venture capital investor purchased 1 million shares of convertible preferred stock at $1 per share, and $1 million of new capital is raised at 50 cents per share. In all cases the preferred shares convert to common shares on a one for one basis.

X equals 1 million, Y equals 1 million. Two million divided by 3 million gets us the new conversion price of 66 cents per share, 16 cents more than under a full ratchet.

As a result, the original fund will be able to convert their preferred shares into just over 1.5 million common shares: more than their original 1 million, but again less than the 2 million shares they would have received under a full ratchet.

Typically the formula only adjusts the old conversion price if the new financing is a down round. Otherwise the holders of the old preferred shares are perfectly happy to have a discount conversion option.

Venture capital investors must also be concerned about the same things that preferred shareholders of all types worry about.

BENCHMARK CAPITAL PARTNERS IV, L.P. v. RICHARD VAGUE

2002 Del. Ch. LEXIS 90, *aff'd*, 822 A.2d 396 (Del. 2003)
Court of Chancery of Delaware
July 15, 2002

NOBLE, Vice Chancellor.

I.   INTRODUCTION

This is another one of those cases in which sophisticated investors have negotiated protective provisions in a corporate charter to define the balance of power or certain economic rights as between the holders of junior preferred stock and senior preferred stock. These provisions tend to come in to play when additional financing becomes necessary. One side cannot or will not put up more money; the other side is willing to put up more money, but will not do so without obtaining additional control or other diminution of the rights of the other side. In short, these cases focus on the tension between minority rights established through the corporate charter and the corporation's need for additional capital.

In this case, Plaintiff Benchmark Capital Partners IV, L.P. ("Benchmark") invested in the first two series of the Defendant Juniper Financial Corp.'s ("Juniper") preferred stock. When additional capital was required, Defendant Canadian Imperial Bank of Commerce ("CIBC") was an able and somewhat willing investor.[8] As a result of that investment, Benchmark's holdings were relegated to the status of junior preferred stock and CIBC acquired a controlling interest in Juniper by virtue of ownership of senior preferred stock. The lot of a holder of junior preferred stock is not always a happy one. Juniper's Fifth

---

8. CIBC invested in Juniper through a subsidiary, Defendant CIBC Delaware Holdings, Inc. For purposes of this memorandum opinion, I do not distinguish between CIBC and its subsidiary.

Amendment and Restated Certificate of Incorporation (the "Certificate") contains several provisions to protect the holders of junior preferred stock from abuse by the holder of senior preferred stock. Two of those provisions are of particular importance here. The Certificate grants the junior preferred stockholders a series vote on corporate actions that would "[m]aterially adversely change the rights, preferences and privileges of the [series of junior preferred stock]." In addition, the junior preferred stockholders are entitled to a class vote before Juniper may "[a]uthorize or issue, or obligate itself to issue, any other equity security . . . senior to or on a parity with the [junior preferred stock]."

The Certificate provides that those provisions protecting the rights of the junior preferred stockholders may be waived by CIBC. CIBC may not, however, exercise this power "if such amendment, waiver or modification would . . . diminish or alter the liquidation preference or other financial or economic rights" of the junior preferred stockholders or would shelter breaches of fiduciary duties.

Juniper now must seek more capital in order to satisfy regulators and business requirements, and CIBC, and apparently only CIBC, is willing to provide the necessary funds. Juniper initially considered amending its charter to allow for the issuance of another series of senior preferred stock. When it recognized that the protective provisions of the Certificate could be invoked to thwart that strategy, it elected to structure a more complicated transaction that now consists principally of a merger and a sale of Series D Preferred Stock to CIBC. The merger is scheduled to occur on July 16, 2002 with a subsidiary merging with and into Juniper that will leave Juniper as the surviving corporation, but with a restated certificate of incorporation that will authorize the issuance of a new series of senior preferred stock and new junior preferred stock with a reduced liquidation preference and will cause a number of other adverse consequences or limitations to be suffered by the holders of the junior preferred. As part of this overall financing transaction, Juniper, after the merger, intends to issue a new series of preferred, the Series D Preferred Stock, to CIBC in exchange for a $50 million capital contribution. As the result of this sequence of events, the equity holdings of the junior preferred stockholders will be reduced from approximately 29% to 7%. Juniper will not obtain approval for these actions from the holders of the junior preferred stock. It contends that the protective provisions do not give the junior preferred stockholders a vote on these plans and, furthermore, in any event, that CIBC has the right to waive the protective provisions through the Series C Trump.[9]

Benchmark, on the other hand, asserts that the protective provisions preclude Juniper's and CIBC's heavy-handed conduct and brings this action to prevent the violation of the junior preferred stockholder's fundamental right to vote on these corporate actions as provided in the Certificate and to obtain interim protection from the planned evisceration of its equity interest in Juniper. Because of the imminence of the merger and the issuance of the new senior preferred stock,

---

9. Juniper concedes that CIBC does not have the power to waive any junior preferred stockholder's right to vote with respect to a diminished liquidation preference.

Benchmark has moved for a preliminary injunction to stop the proposed transaction. This is the Court's decision on that motion.

II. THE PARTIES

Benchmark, a Delaware limited partnership based in Menlo Park, California, is a venture capital firm specializing in preferred stock investments. It manages more than $2 billion and has made approximately 50 preferred stock investments in the preceding 5 years.

Juniper is a Delaware corporation with its principal place of business in Wilmington, Delaware, where it has more than 300 employees. It is a financial services enterprise with the issuance of credit cards as its core business. Juniper Bank is Juniper's wholly-owned state-chartered banking subsidiary.

CIBC is a Canadian bank based in Toronto and controls Juniper through a subsidiary as the result of a $145 million investment in 2001.

The individual defendants are directors of Juniper. Defendants Richard Vague and James Stewart are founders and officers of Juniper. Defendant John Tolleson is a member of the special committee appointed by the board of Juniper to review the Series D Preferred financing.

III. FACTUAL BACKGROUND

A. BENCHMARK AND CIBC INVEST IN JUNIPER

Benchmark became the initial investor in Juniper when in June 2000, it invested $20 million and, in exchange, was issued Series A Preferred Shares. Juniper raised an additional $95.5 million in August 2000 by issuing its Series B Preferred Shares. Benchmark contributed $5 million in this effort. It soon became necessary for Juniper to obtain even more capital. Efforts to raise additional funds from existing investors and efforts to find new potential investors were unavailing until June 2001 when CIBC and Juniper agreed that CIBC would invest $27 million in Juniper through a mandatory convertible note while CIBC evaluated Juniper to assess whether it was interested in acquiring the company. CIBC also agreed to provide additional capital through a Series C financing in the event that it chose not to acquire Juniper and if Juniper's efforts to find other sources for the needed funding were unsuccessful.

In July 2001, CIBC advised Juniper that it would not seek to acquire Juniper. After reviewing its options for other financing, Juniper called upon CIBC to invest the additional capital. The terms of the Series C financing were negotiated during the latter half of the summer of 2001. A representative of Benchmark, J. William Gurley, and its attorney were active participants in these negotiations. Through the Series C Transaction, which closed on September 18, 2001, CIBC invested $145 million (including the $27 million already delivered to Juniper). With its resulting Series C Preferred holdings, CIBC obtained a majority of the voting power in Juniper on an as-converted basis and a majority of the voting power of Juniper's preferred stock. CIBC also acquired the right to select six of the eleven members of Juniper's board. As required by Juniper's then existing certificate of incorporation, the approval of the holders of Series A Preferred and Series B Preferred Stock, including Benchmark, was obtained in order to close the Series C Transaction.

B.   THE CERTIFICATE'S PROTECTIVE PROVISIONS

In the course of obtaining that consent, CIBC had extensive negotiations regarding the provisions of Juniper's charter designed to protect the rights and interests of the holders of Series A Preferred and Series B Preferred Stock. For example, CIBC had sought the power to waive, modify or amend certain protective provisions held by the Series A Preferred and Series B Preferred stockholders. As the result of those discussions, the Certificate was adopted. CIBC obtained the right to waive certain protective voting provisions, but the right was not unlimited. A review of the Certificate's protective provisions directly involved in the pending dispute follows.

Juniper's Certificate protects the holders of Series A Preferred and Series B Preferred from risks associated with the issuance of any additional equity security that would be senior to those shares by requiring their prior approval through a separate class vote as prescribed in Section C.6.a(i):

> So long as any shares of Series A Preferred Stock or Series B Preferred Stock remain outstanding, the Corporation shall not, without the vote or written consent by the holders of at least a majority of the then outstanding shares of the Series A Preferred Stock and Series B Preferred Stock, voting together as a single class; *provided, however*, that the foregoing may be amended, waived or modified pursuant to Section C.4.c: (i) Authorize or issue, or obligate itself to issue, any other equity security (including any security convertible into or exercisable for any equity security) senior to or on a parity with the Series A Preferred Stock or Series B Preferred Stock as to dividend rights or redemption rights, voting rights or liquidation preferences (other than the Series C Preferred Stock and Series C Prime Preferred Stock sold pursuant to, or issued upon the conversion of the shares sold pursuant to, the Series C Preferred Stock Purchase Agreement. . . .)

Under Section C.6.a(ii), Juniper also must provide the holders of the junior preferred stock with a class vote before it may proceed to dispose of all or substantially all of its assets or to "consolidate or merge into any other Corporation (other than a wholly-owned subsidiary Corporation)." Furthermore, this right to a class vote also applies to efforts to increase the number of Juniper's directors.

Because CIBC was investing a substantial sum in Juniper, it insisted upon greater control than it would have obtained if these voting provisions (and other comparable provisions) could be exercised without limitation by the holders of Series A Preferred and Series B Preferred shares as a class. Thus, it sought and obtained a concession from the Series A Preferred and Series B Preferred holders that it could amend, waive, or modify, *inter alia*, the protective provisions of Section C.6.a. The right of CIBC to waive the voting rights of the Series A Preferred and Series B Preferred holders was limited by excluding from the scope of the waiver authority any action that "would (a) diminish or alter the liquidation preference or other financial or economic rights, modify the registration rights, or increase the obligations, indemnities or liabilities, of the holders of Series A Preferred Stock, Series A Prime Preferred Stock or Series B Preferred Stock or (b) authorize, approve or waive any action so as to violate any fiduciary duties owed by such holders under Delaware law."

Another protection afforded the holders of both the Series A Preferred and Series B Preferred Stock was set forth in Sections C.6.c(ii) & C.6.d(ii) of the Certificate. Those provisions require a vote of the holders of each series, provided that the requirement for a series vote was not amended or waived by CIBC in accordance with Section C.4.c, if that corporate action would "[m]aterially adversely change the rights, preferences and privileges of the Series A Preferred [and Series B] Preferred Stock."

C. ADDITIONAL FINANCING BECOMES NECESSARY

By early 2002, Juniper was advising its investors that even more capital would be necessary to sustain the venture. Because Juniper is in the banking business, the consequences of a capital shortage are not merely those of the typical business. Capital shortfall for a banking entity may carry the potential for significant and adverse regulatory action. Regulated not only by the Federal Reserve Board and the Federal Deposit Insurance Corporation but also by the Delaware Banking Commissioner, Juniper is required to maintain a "well-capitalized" status. Failure to maintain that standard (or to effect a prompt cure) may result in, among other things, regulatory action, conversion of the preferred stock into a "senior common stock" which could then be subjected to the imposition of additional security through the regulatory authorities, and the loss of the right to issue Visa cards and to have its customers serviced through the Visa card processing system.

Juniper, with the assistance of an investment banking firm, sought additional investors. The holders of the Series A Preferred and Series B Preferred Stock, including Benchmark, were also solicited. Those efforts failed, thus leaving CIBC as the only identified and viable participant available for the next round of financing, now known as the Series D Transaction.

D. THE SERIES D PREFERRED TRANSACTION

Thus, Juniper turned to consideration of CIBC's proposal, first submitted through a term sheet on March 15, 2002, to finance $50 million through the issuance of Series D Preferred Stock that would grant CIBC an additional 23% of Juniper on a fully-diluted basis and reduce the equity interests of the Series A Preferred and Series B Preferred holders from approximately 29% to 7%.

The board, in early April 2002, appointed a special committee to consider the CIBC proposal. As the result of the negotiations among Juniper, the special committee, and CIBC, the special committee was able to recommend the Series D Transaction with CIBC. The terms of the Series D Transaction are set forth in the "Juniper Financial Corp. Series D Preferred Stock Purchase Agreement" and the "Agreement and Plan of Merger and Reorganization by and Between Juniper Financial Corp. and Juniper Merger Corp."

In general terms, the Series D Transaction consists of the following three steps:

1. Juniper will carry out a 100–1 reverse stock split of its common stock.
2. Juniper Merger Corp., a subsidiary of Juniper established for these purposes, will be merged with and into Juniper which will be the surviving corporation. The certificate of incorporation will be revised as part of the merger.
3. Series D Preferred Stock will be issued to CIBC (and, at least in theory, those other holders of Series A, B and C Preferred who may exercise preemptive rights) for $50 million.

Each share of existing Series A Preferred and each share of existing Series B Preferred will be converted into one share of new Series A Preferred or Series B Preferred, respectively, and the holders of the existing junior preferred will also receive, for each share, a warrant to purchase a small fraction of a share of common stock in Juniper and a smaller fraction of a share of common stock in Juniper. A small amount of cash will also be paid. Juniper will receive no capital infusion as a direct result of the merger. Although the existing Series A Preferred and Series B Preferred shares will cease to exist and the differences between the new and distinct Series A Preferred and Series B Preferred shares will be significant, the resulting modification of Juniper's certificate of incorporation will not alter the class and series votes required by Section C.6. The changes to Juniper's charter as the result of the merger include, *inter alia*, authorization of the issuance of Series D Preferred Shares, which will be senior to the newly created Series A Preferred and Series B Preferred Stock with respect to, for example, liquidation preferences, dividends, and as applicable, redemption rights. Also the Series D Stock will be convertible into common stock at a higher ratio than the existing or newly created Series A Preferred and Series B Preferred Stock, thereby providing for a currently greater voting power. In general terms, the equity of the existing Series A Preferred and Series B Preferred holders will be reduced from approximately 29% before the merger to approximately 7% after the Series D financing, and CIBC will hold more than 90% of Juniper's voting power.

Juniper intends to proceed with the merger on July 16, 2002 and to promptly thereafter consummate the Series D financing. It projects that, without the $50 million infusion from CIBC, it will not be able to satisfy the "well-capitalized" standard as of July 31, 2002. That will trigger, or so Juniper posits, the regulatory problems previously identified and business problems, such as the risk of losing key personnel and important business relationships. Indeed, Juniper predicts that liquidation would ensue and, in that event (and Benchmark does not seriously contest this), that the holders of Series A Preferred and Series B Preferred Stock would receive nothing (or essentially nothing) from such liquidation.

IV. CONTENTIONS OF THE PARTIES

Benchmark begins its effort to earn a preliminary injunction by arguing that the junior preferred stockholders are entitled to a vote on the merger on a series basis under Sections C.6.c(ii) & C.6.d(ii) because the merger adversely affects, *inter alia*, their liquidation preference and dividend rights and on a class basis under Section C.6.a(i) because the merger, through changes to Juniper's capital structure as set forth in its revised certificate of incorporation, will authorize the issuance of a senior preferred security.[10] Benchmark also invokes its right to a class vote to challenge the Series D Purchase Agreement under Section C.6.a(i) because that agreement obligates Juniper to issue a senior preferred security. Similarly, Benchmark challenges the issuance of the new Series D Preferred Stock after the merger because it will be issued without a class vote by the holders of either the old or the new Series A Preferred Stock and the new Series B Preferred Stock.

In response, Juniper and CIBC argue that the junior preferred stockholders are not entitled to a class or series vote on any aspect of the Series D financing, particularly the merger. The adverse effects of the transaction arise from the merger and not from any separate amendment of the certificate of incorporation, which would have required the exercise of the junior preferred stockholders' voting rights.[11] Juniper and CIBC emphasize that none of the junior preferred stock protective provisions expressly applies to mergers. Finally, Juniper and CIBC assert that the Series C Trump allows for the waiver of all of the voting rights at issue (except for the diminishment of the liquidation preference

---

10. While the Verified Complaint asserts general fiduciary duty and disclosure claims relating to the alleged scheme to dilute wrongfully the interests of the junior preferred stockholders, Benchmark has not relied upon these claims in pursuing its application for a preliminary injunction.

11. Juniper focuses on the separate statutory regimes for amendments of certificates of incorporation and for mergers. A corporation may amend its certificate of incorporation to reclassify its authorized stock, 8 *Del. C.*§242(a)(3), or to create a new class of stock with rights and preferences superior to other classes of stock, 8 *Del. C.*§242(a)(5). By 8 *Del. C.*§242(b)(2), "[t]he holders of the outstanding shares of a class shall be entitled to vote as a class upon a proposed amendment, whether or not entitled to vote thereon by the certificate of incorporation, if the amendment would increase or decrease the aggregate number of authorized shares of such class, increase or decrease the par value of the shares of such class, or alter or change the powers, preferences, or special rights of the shares of such class so as to affect them adversely." Mergers, by contrast, are accomplished in accordance with 8 *Del. C.*§251. A merger agreement, in accordance with 8 *Del. C.*§251(b)(3), and a certificate of merger, in accordance with 8 *Del. C.*§253(c)(4), shall state: "[I]n the case of a merger, such amendments or changes in the certificate of incorporation of the surviving corporation as are desired to be effected by the merger. . . ."

accomplished by the merger). Benchmark, as one might expect, maintains that the exercise of the Series C Trump is precluded because the "economic or financial rights" of the holders of the junior preferred will be adversely affected and, therefore, the limitation on CIBC's right to exercise the Series C Trump is controlling.

Juniper and CIBC also vigorously contest the issuance of a preliminary injunction by arguing that a balancing of the equities (or balancing of the relative harms from granting or not granting the preliminary injunction) heavily counsels against its issuance. They point out that, in the absence of the proposed financing, Juniper would encounter severe regulatory and business problems, that liquidation would be likely, and that, with liquidation, Benchmark and the other junior preferred shareholders would receive little or nothing from their interests in Juniper.

V.   ANALYSIS

A.   PRELIMINARY INJUNCTION STANDARD

The familiar standard for a preliminary injunction places the burden on the movant to demonstrate "(1) a reasonable probability of success on the merits, (2) irreparable harm if the injunction is not granted, and (3) a balance of equities in favor of granting the relief." Because a preliminary injunction is an extraordinary remedy, such relief will not be granted "where the remedy sought is excessive in relation to, or unnecessary to prevent, the injury threatened."

. . .

Thus, there is no question as to Juniper's pressing need for capital. CIBC has come forward and is willing to invest an additional $50 million in the company. In light of Benchmark's failure to challenge effectively the evidence of Juniper's current critical need for additional capital, the lack of any alternate source for such funding, and the onerous consequences that failure to secure such capital will cause Juniper and its constituents, Benchmark's argument that Juniper's position is a mere gloom and doom one is unpersuasive. As such, this case may be distinguished from the one before this Court in *Sorrento* where "the record before the Court indicate[d] that [the company's need for additional cash was] not imminent and that [the defendant company] ha[d] the means to sustain itself well beyond any final determination of th[e challenged] action."

While loss of a shareholder's right to vote would certainly be a factor that must be given serious weight in this analysis, when viewed in light of the factual setting of this case, I am of the opinion that Benchmark's risks are minor when compared to those which would likely result from depriving Juniper of financing through the Series D Transaction. Considering that Benchmark would recover nothing (or almost nothing) if Juniper were forced into liquidation, my conclusion that the equities tip in favor of Juniper is bolstered even more. Accordingly, I find that the potential for harm caused by denying Juniper the much needed financing resulting from the Series D Transaction outweighs any potential harm attributable to any deprivation of Benchmark's class voting rights or dilution of its equity interest.

VI. CONCLUSION

Because Benchmark has failed to meet any of the three criteria which should be satisfied by an applicant for a preliminary injunction, denial of its motion should easily follow. I pause to note, however, that Benchmark has ably advocated several arguments that are not easily dismissed. In addition, Benchmark seeks to preserve its voting rights and the voting rights of other Series A Preferred and Series B Preferred shareholders. Its claims to a right to vote as part of a class implicate significant issues of corporate governance. Nonetheless, as I balance the various well-known factors as I must, I conclude that Benchmark has failed to justify issuance of a preliminary injunction.

Therefore, for the foregoing reasons, Benchmark's motion for a preliminary injunction is denied. An order will be entered in accordance with this memorandum opinion.

PROBLEM SET 21.2

1. Assume that the founder of a company holds all the common shares, and a first round venture capital fund holds convertible preferred shares. Would the founder prefer a full ratchet or weighted average term in the convertible shares? What concerns would the founder have with either?

2. And of course be ready to discuss the Juniper transaction, including the goals of each side as the deal was negotiated and how they might have better positioned themselves through changes in the documents.

3. A certificate of designation for a new class of convertible preferred shares has the following term in the initial draft:

    > The holders shall be entitled to receive dividends in preference to any dividend on the Common Stock at the rate of _____ % of the Original Purchase Price per annum/\$ _____ per share, *when, as and if* declared by the Board of Directors except that if the preferred shares have not converted to common shares by [date], dividends shall begin to accumulate from that date and shall be due and payable quarterly in arrears.

    What would you argue for if you were representing the founders? The venture capital funds?

4. In a 2016 study, Bloomberg found that venture capital portfolio companies exhibited an extreme gender skew:

    > The vast majority of venture capital goes to companies founded by men. Just 7% of the 2,005 founders on our list are women. Companies founded by women also get less money—an average of \$77 million compared

with $100 million for male-led startups. That shortfall parallels the overall U.S. pay gap, where women are paid an average of 79 cents for every dollar earned by men. Among cities with at least 20 founders, South San Francisco startups have the highest ratio of women founders at 16.1% while Santa Monica is second at 15%.

What do you make of this?

3.   GOVERNANCE AND EXIT

The goal of the venture capital fund is to sell all of its portfolio company investments by the end of the fund's life, typically ten years. Obviously, the entire portfolio cannot be sold precisely at year ten, so the second half of the fund's life span is often spent in the gradual process of selling off investments and returning capital to investors. This second step facilitates the sale of newly formed funds to existing investors.

For the duration of the investment, the fund will want to make sure its interests are represented in the governance of the portfolio company. That is, while the fund's investors are passive, the fund itself is far from a passive investor.

Convertible preferred stock issued in venture capital transactions typically has the same voting rights as existing common stock, even before conversion. In addition, the holders of convertible preferred stock, voting separately as a class, usually have the right to veto certain corporate transactions affecting the convertible preferred stock directly. Other voting rights may include a class vote for election of directors and rights to elect a majority of the board of directors upon a breach of the terms of the convertible preferred stock.

ROBERT P. BARTLETT, III, *VENTURE CAPITAL, AGENCY COSTS, AND THE FALSE DICHOTOMY OF THE CORPORATION*

54 UCLA L. Rev. 37, 71 (2006)

VC investors ordinarily seek to exit company investments through one of two principal methods: the sale of shares into the public equity markets after a company's IPO or the acquisition of a company for cash or publicly traded securities. In either case, differences in VC investors' stock ownership may create differences as to what constitutes an acceptable exit event for a company. As one prominent attorney in the industry notes, "[T]he actual exit strategy employed . . . may require cooperation from shareholders who will not (or may not) be in agreement with the timing, price or other terms as proposed by [a particular] VC."

The source of these differences arises from the potentially different investment returns each VC investor in a start-up company will receive on a proposed exit. In FormFactor [a venture-backed company that completed an

IPO], for instance, investors who acquired shares of the company's Series G Preferred Stock at $15.00 per share would view less favorably a proposed IPO in January 2003 at $10.00 per share than would MDV [Mohr Davidow Ventures, an "early stage venture capital firm"], whose average price paid per share was $1.34. MDV would stand to realize at this price a total return on investment of almost 650 percent, or an annual internal rate of return (IRR) of approximately 37 percent. In contrast, a stockholder who only participated in the Series G financing would realize a total return on investment of −33 percent, or an annual IRR of approximately −27 percent.

The extent to which VC investors purchase their pro rata share in each stage of financing does little to mitigate the potential for divergent investment returns among VC investors. . . .

The structure of the VC market encourages VC investors to focus on achieving positive returns for several reasons. As a general matter, venture capitalists must offer LPs the prospect of significant investment returns in order to compensate them for the limited liquidity and significant risks associated with start-up investments. Among early-stage venture capitalists, for instance, it is generally assumed that an investment portfolio should yield an IRR of approximately 30 to 50 percent. Moreover, because many of these investments will ultimately be written off, VC investors commonly make individual company investments with the expectation that each will produce a 40 to 50 percent projected IRR after accounting for the venture capitalist's fees and compensation.

VC fund structure further accentuates this concern with investment returns owing to the capital-time investment constraint and the investment return incentives. First, the intense pressure to raise successive VC funds can encourage a venture capitalist to time exit events so as to accelerate positive returns and to delay negative returns. By exiting an investment with a significant return, a VC investor locks in a gain that helps lift the IRR of a portfolio likely to contain several losing investments. For a VC investor in the process of raising another fund, these early "home runs" may be critical to attracting LPs. Moreover, under the prevailing industry valuation standards, VC investors generally carry a company investment at cost until an exit event or a subsequent financing. IRR calculations will therefore be higher the sooner a fund liquidates a successful investment. For similar reasons, a VC investor faced with a losing investment may present a healthier picture of its overall portfolio to its current and prospective LPs by delaying an exit given that an investment valued at cost looks better to LPs than an investment loss.

In addition to these marketing pressures, the carried interest also encourages venture capitalists to focus on accelerating positive returns and delaying negative returns. As noted above, the carried interest entitles a venture capitalist to receive a specified percentage (usually 20 percent) of the profits realized on a fund's start-up company investments. A corollary of the carry is the so-called "claw-back" provision, which ensures that the venture capitalist receives no more than her specified percentage of fund profits upon the termination of a fund. This result can occur where a VC fund initially liquidates profitable investments and later liquidates losing investments—a common pattern among VC funds. In such situations, the claw-back provision requires a venture capitalist to recontribute capital to the fund in order to avoid receiving excess compensation. Consequently, the ability of a venture capitalist to realize a profit rather than a loss on an investment may potentially mean the difference between receiving an incentive payment from the VC fund and having to recontribute capital to its LPs.

Thus, because of staged investment and investment syndication, a venture capitalist who invests in a start-up company faces a discernable risk that it may disagree at some point with the company's other VC investors concerning what constitutes a proper exit event. In the highly volatile start-up markets, investors holding higher-priced securities may simply be more willing than holders of lower-priced securities to postpone an exit event until the next "up" market. Moreover, the challenge of achieving investor consensus on this issue is made more complicated by the limited life of VC funds. Because of the ten-year term of most funds, an early investor who has held an investment for several years may face a structural incentive to exit at a time when a company's later investors are not subject to these pressures. A company's earlier investors may therefore be less willing to forego a low-value exit yielding a return on investment, even if the investors believe the company could obtain a higher valuation in the long term.

THE CONTRACTUAL RESPONSE

Given the risk that a company's VC investors may disagree over an acceptable exit event, an important aspect of VC contracting centers on mechanisms that contain this risk. The risk is especially acute for VC investors who have lost their original control rights in a company following multiple rounds of staged financing. Even where a new VC investor obtains significant control rights in a company, there can be no guarantee that an exit event will arise during the period in which the investor controls the company. For instance, the company may have to undergo additional rounds of financing before an exit event appears likely, by which time the investor's control may be significantly diminished through dilution. As a result, a VC investor will ordinarily seek specific contract rights that protect its preferences concerning the proper timing and amount of an exit regardless of the level of control it possesses as a result of its equity holdings. In the words of one leading VC lawyer, "[C]ontracts signed at the time of VC's initial investment will generally give VC certain future rights to control its exit strategy. This is especially important where VC will not (or may not) control [the] portfolio company at the back end when the exit strategy is executed."

In the context of an IPO, a VC investor will ordinarily obtain these special control rights by demanding a veto right over the completion of an IPO at an unacceptably low price per share. VC investors accomplish this by relying on the virtually universal practice among investment bankers that, prior to completing an IPO, all shares of a company's preferred stock must convert into common stock. Because of this industry practice, the preferred stock purchased by VC investors will generally have a provision requiring the automatic conversion of preferred stock upon either an IPO at a pre-specified price per share or the requisite vote of preferred stockholders. For many investors, a condition to making a company investment will be setting the automatic conversion price of its preferred stock to a price that equals or exceeds its purchase price. Likewise, with regard to an automatic conversion by means of a stockholder vote, VC investors commonly seek a special veto right with respect to the conversion of its shares of preferred stock. As a result of these two provisions, a VC investor can block the conversion of its preferred stock on an IPO—and thereby block the IPO entirely—if the offering price is less than the investor's purchase price.

An example of each of these techniques appears in FormFactor's charter. Under FormFactor's charter, shares of Series A, Series B, Series C, and Series D Preferred Stock would automatically convert into common stock at an IPO having a price per share of at least $6.90—a price well in excess of the per-share purchase price of each series. For the higher-priced Series E, Series F, and Series G Preferred Stock, the minimum IPO price for automatic conversion of each series was set at exactly its per-share purchase price ($7.50, $11.00, and $15.00, respectively). To convert any series of FormFactor's preferred stock by means of a stockholder vote, it was necessary to obtain the approval of two-thirds of the outstanding shares of each series.

A VC investor will also seek to protect its particular economic preferences concerning the price and timing of a company acquisition. These protections may take the form of either special veto rights or special liquidation preferences. With regard to veto rights, a VC investor may seek specific class veto rights that guarantee it a blocking right over a company's acquisition. Alternatively, where existing investors already hold an approval right over an acquisition, a later-stage investor may seek to increase the voting threshold required for approving an acquisition to ensure that its vote is required.

In addition to veto rights, a new VC investor may seek to protect its preferences concerning an exit event through a senior liquidation preference. As noted above, a liquidation preference entitles a stockholder to a specified preferential return (ordinarily, an investor's purchase price) on its preferred shares prior to any common stock payments in the event of a company's acquisition. A senior liquidation preference entitles one VC investor to receive its liquidation preference in advance of other VC investors. According to one attorney in the industry:

> [L]ater investors typically want to be first in line to get their original investment (and hopefully their return on investment) out. By subordinating the liquidation preferences of earlier investors, later round investors ensure their priority directly behind creditors and ahead of other equity investors including those who invested in earlier rounds, as well as angel investors, founders and employees.

Unfortunately, the manner in which VC investors seek to protect their particular preferences regarding a company's exit strategy is not always easy to discern. The ability to identify how VC investors resolve potential conflicts over a company exit event requires an analysis of VC investor stock ownership, as well as an understanding of how voting rights and liquidation preferences can work in tandem to create a system of reciprocal veto rights. For instance, a straightforward analysis of FormFactor's charter might suggest its VC investors are generally aligned in their preference concerning the company's acquisition. Under its charter, the protective provisions provide merely that an acquisition of the company must be approved by the holders of a majority of the shares of Series B through Series G Preferred Stock. However, analysis of the VC investors' stock ownership reveals a more complicated story: This voting threshold ensured that no acquisition could occur without the collective approval of MDV, IVP, and MSVP [three venture funds].

The voting threshold clearly provided less protection to the Series E through Series G investors, as MDV, IVP, and MSVP could approve an acquisition without their consent. How did these investors protect against the risk that MDV, IVP, and MSVP would approve a low-value acquisition? The answer is in the liquidation preferences negotiated by these investors: The company's charter granted to the holders of Series D through Series G Preferred Stock a senior liquidation preference. This liquidation preference guaranteed that if MDV, IVP, and MSVP approved a low-value acquisition, no proceeds could be paid on their shares of Series B and Series C Preferred Stock until each share of Series D through Series G Preferred Stock had been distributed an amount equal to the share's original cost ($3.45, $7.50, $11.00, and $15.00, respectively). In other words, no VC investor was at risk that an acquisition would be approved against its will where the investor did not receive back at least its original investment cost.

As analysis of FormFactor's charter reveals, the common use among VC investors of series veto rights and liquidation preferences seeks to address a fundamental challenge of VC investment. It is a challenge unrelated to concerns about whether managers will act as good agents. Rather, it is a challenge arising from the potentially conflicting interests among VC investors concerning what constitutes a proper exit event for a start-up company.

PROBLEM SET 21.3

1. Some investment agreements provide that if the venture capital fund is unable to exit through the normal changes—sales, IPO, and so on—the portfolio company may be required to repurchase the fund's shares at a specified price. Such puts are often also triggered by certain events, such as a default on a bank loan. What are the limitations to this sort of a contractual term? *SV Inv. Partners, LLC v. ThoughtWorks, Inc.,* 37 A.3d 205 (Del. 2011).

2. The venture capital investor's block of stock will usually come with the power to appoint at least one member to the board. Often this right of representation means that that fund has a disproportionate influence relative to the size of its stake (especially in early rounds). Based on your knowledge of corporate governance law from prior classes, what risks does this present for the fund? *In re Trados Inc. S'holder Litig.*, 73 A.3d 17 (Del. Ch. 2013).

III

MERGERS AND ACQUISITIONS

22

TENDER OFFERS

This chapter commences our review of *mergers and acquisitions* or M&A. M&A in the United States is governed by a dual federal and state regulatory regime, consisting of state corporation laws (e.g., the Delaware General Corporation Law (DGCL)) and federal securities laws (primarily, the Securities Act of 1933 and the Securities Exchange Act of 1934). Unlike most other jurisdictions, the U.S. patchwork of federal and state regulation of acquisitions is not focused on the substantive issue of regulating changes of control in target companies. The coming chapters focus on the various tools used to effectuate an M&A transaction from the finance side.

Additional regulatory regimes, beyond the scope this class, are also relevant when doing deals. For example, under the Hart-Scott-Rodino Antitrust Improvements Act of 1976 (the HSR Act), an acquirer is normally required to make a filing with federal antitrust authorities before completing an acquisition. Generally, the HSR Act requires filing if, as a result of the transaction, the acquiring person will hold voting securities, assets, or interests valued above $80.8 million (adjusted annually for inflation) after the deal closes. There are also additional industry-specific statutes that may require advance notification to regulators when considering an acquisition. Examples of such regulated industries include airlines, financial institutions, broadcasters, and utilities.

We begin M&A by looking at tender offers. A *tender offer* is an offer to buy shares from the market,[1] typically at a premium over the price at which the shares traded before the announcement of the offer.[2]

Friendly deals are quite often deals done as two-step transactions in which a buyer purchases a majority position through a tender offer and then proceeds to effectuate a merger with the target company, now a subsidiary of the buyer. The merger changes the majority-owned subsidiary into a wholly-owned subsidiary.

---

1. We cover tender offers for debt, commonly called exchange offers, in Chapter 26.

2. In Wellman v. Dickinson, 475 F. Supp. 783, 823-824 (S.D.N.Y. 1979), *aff'd on other grounds*, 682 F.2d 355 (2d Cir. 1982), *cert. denied*, 460 U.S. 1069 (1983). *See* Rand v. Anaconda-Ericsson, Inc., 794 F.2d 843, 848-849 (2d Cir. 1986), *cert. denied*, 479 U.S. 987 (1986).

Hostile deals are the other context in which tender offers are used. If the buyer cannot convince the target board to accept its offer, a tender offer making the buyer the majority shareholder is a key way around that deadlock. Given the power that most boards have, particularly with regard to *poison pills,* as discussed later in this chapter, a fully hostile takeover often needs to be combined with some sort of proxy contest to change the composition of the board or a litigation strategy arguing that the board is breaching its duties by not considering the proffered deal.

By and large, tender offers were unregulated until the late 1960s. State statutory corporate law has little to say about secondary market share purchases, and the federal securities laws originally did not address tender offers except in the general sense of prohibiting fraud in connection with the securities markets. That changed in 1968 when the Williams Act amended the '34 Act. We discuss the Williams Act later, which you perhaps have also covered to some extent in your Business Associations class.

Initially, state fiduciary duty law did not address tender offers either. This provided a strong incentive for deals to be done by tender offer, and if the tender offer obtained more than 90 percent of the outstanding shares, the second step merger could happen by way of a short-form merger, thus avoiding the entire body of law that the Delaware courts had developed to address takeovers by controlling shareholders.[3]

That has begun to change in recent years, although this case law comes from Delaware chancery (trial) courts, so it is hard to say if this development is permanent.

IN RE CNX GAS CORPORATION SHAREHOLDERS LITIGATION

4 A.3d 397
Court of Chancery of Delaware.
May 25, 2010.

LASTER, Vice Chancellor.
Representatives of a putative class of minority stockholders have challenged a controlling stockholder freeze-out structured as a first-step tender offer to be

---

3. In a nutshell, this law requires controlling shareholders who desire to "cash out" the minority shareholders or otherwise engage in a deal in which the controller "stands on both sides" to show the deal's "entire fairness," unless an independent board committee approves the deal or a "majority of the minority" of shareholders approves the deal, in which case the standard stays at entire fairness but the burden of proof shifts to the plaintiffs. If the controller irrevocably commits to using both approval devices at the start of the deal, the deal will be evaluated under the deferential "business judgment" standard.

After a tender offer, the second step of a deal will still involve a controlling shareholder. But the Delaware courts have held this law does not apply in short form mergers. Glassman v. Unocal Exploration Corp., 777 A.2d 242 (Del. 2001) (holding that absent fraud or illegality an appraisal is the exclusive remedy available to stockholders in a §253 short form merger, entire fairness doctrine does not apply, and no need for the target to use a special committee because there is no opportunity to "deal" with majority holder).

followed by second-step short-form merger. The plaintiffs have sued the controlling stockholder, its controlled subsidiary, and the four members of the subsidiary board. Three of the subsidiary directors are also directors of the controller. The fourth is an independent outsider and the sole member of the special committee formed to respond to the controller's tender offer. The plaintiffs have moved for a preliminary injunction against the transaction.

I apply the unified standard for reviewing controlling stockholder freeze-outs described in In re Cox Communications, Inc. Shareholders Litigation, 879 A.2d 604 (Del.Ch.2005). Under that standard, the business judgment rule applies when a freeze-out is conditioned on *both* the affirmative recommendation of a special committee *and* the approval of a majority of the unaffiliated stockholders. Because the special committee did not recommend in favor of the tender offer, the transaction at issue in this case will be reviewed for entire fairness. Although the lack of an affirmative recommendation is sufficient to trigger fairness review under *Cox Communications*, the plaintiffs also have shown that the special committee was not provided with the authority to bargain with the controller on an arms' length basis. The plaintiffs similarly have established a reasonable basis to question the effectiveness of the majority-of-the-minority tender condition.

Because a fairness standard applies to the challenged transaction, any harm to the putative class can be remedied through a post-closing damages action. There are no viable disclosure claims, and the tender offer is not coercive. I therefore decline to issue a preliminary injunction.

Did the plaintiffs win or lose here?

Note that the case law touched on above involves a controlling shareholder. Essentially, the Delaware courts are adopting a heightened standard of review whenever an existing controlling shareholder attempts to squeeze out the minority, regardless of deal structure. State law continues to have little to say about tender offers more generally, save when the *Unocal* standard of review might apply to responses to tender offers, as discussed below. But Delaware courts generally have held that tender offerors who are not controlling shareholders have no duty to offer a "fair" price since the target corporation's shareholders may either accept or reject the offer as they see fit.

1.   STRUCTURAL ISSUES

Why pick a tender offer or a two-step structure instead of just a merger? There are several reasons, beginning with the speed of tender offers. A straight merger requires a shareholder vote, and that usually requires SEC approval of a proxy statement and also a registration statement if stock is to be issued in the transaction.[4]

On the other hand, all-cash tender offers may be consummated quickly, subject only to a minimum offer period of 20 business days from commencement.[5] This reduces the degree of market risk the buyer is exposed to in the period between contract and closing.

The tender offer will typically lead, if it is successful, to a back-end merger, perhaps without the need for a vote of the target's stockholders at the end of the process. But a two-step structure has another timing-related advantage even where the tender offer attracts a majority, but less than the amount necessary to do a short or medium form merger under state law. The advantage is that the buyer will have cut off "interloper risk" once the tender offer is completed, and that alone can be a very important benefit. That is, the parties reduce the risk that their friendly deal will be upset by an uninvited hostile bidder.

A tender offer also does not suffer from the so-called dead vote problem that arises in merger transactions when a substantial number of shareholders sell their shares after the record date and then do not vote, or do not change an outdated vote, after they have sold their economic interest. The only vote in a tender offer is the implicit one involved in taking the consideration offered.

However, a two-step structure involving a tender offer is not necessarily always preferable to a one-step merger. For example, in a deal that involves a regulatory approval process, the tender offer would have to remain open until the regulatory approval was obtained, because the buyer must condition the offer on authorization to buy the target. During that period the parties might have been able to obtain shareholders' votes on a straight merger.

Also tender offers can sometimes be difficult to finance if the buyer is reliant on outside funding. The most obvious source of collateral for the buyer is the target shares that it will be acquiring, but the Federal Reserve Board's margin rules restrict loans secured by public company stock to half of the shares' market value. In a merger, the buyer can have direct access to the target's assets and use those for collateral for the loan. The identity of the buyer—and whether the buyer is a private equity fund, a so-called "financial" buyer, as opposed to a strategic buyer—can matter quite a lot here.

Two-step transactions can also be difficult if the target's shares are widely held by index funds. These mutual funds, or exchange traded funds, will not tender into the first step of a transaction because they must hold the index. In such cases, it is often better to simply do a single step deal that starts and ends with a merger.

Finally, as noted, tender offers are most often used when deals are all cash. If the deal consideration is buyer company shares, those new shares must be

---

4. *See* 15 U.S.C. §78n; 17 C.F.R §§240.14a-1 to-20 (rules for proxy solicitation); *id.* at §240.14a-101 (information required in proxy statement); *id.* at §239.25 (information "for the registration of securities issued in business combination transactions").

5. *See* 17 C.F.R. § 240.14e-1.

registered under the '33 Act. Waiting for the registration process to be complete takes away the speed advantage of doing a tender offer.

2. STANDSTILL PROVISIONS AND NEGOTIATIONS

A standstill agreement or provision is often demanded by the target company. At its core, such a provision prohibits the putative buyer from "going hostile." Standstill provisions are motivated by the inherent problem that the buyer, particularly if it is a strategic buyer, is both a competitor and a potential future ally. During the negotiations that might lead to a deal, the target must provide the buyer with large amounts of confidential information, all of which might help the buyer either compete with the target or launch a low-ball bid for the target's assts.

While in theory the "standstill" could be a separate agreement, it is more often folded into a broader confidentiality agreement. We come back to these agreements in the next chapter, but in short, confidentiality agreements contain a grab bag of provisions that set the ground rules for negotiating a deal.

The standstill provision works hand-in-hand with the general confidentiality provisions that provide: (1) the buyer must not *disclose* confidential information; and (2) the buyer must not *use* confidential information except for the specific purpose of pursuing a transaction with the target company.

The following Canadian case is the key decision exploring the interaction of standstill provisions and general confidentiality provisions.[6]

CERTICOM CORP. v. RESEARCH IN MOTION LIMITED

94 O.R. (3d) 511
Ontario Superior Court.
January 19, 2009.

HOY J.—

[1] This application turns on the interpretation of two non-disclosure agreements and raises the issue of the appropriate remedy for the breach of such an agreement in the context of a hostile takeover bid.

[2] Research In Motion Limited ("RIM"), through its wholly owned subsidiary, Research In Motion Acquisition Corporation Inc. ("RIMAC"), launched a hostile (or "unsolicited") takeover bid for Certicom Corp. on December 10, 2008. Before launching its hostile bid, RIM obtained confidential information about Certicom under the terms of two non-disclosure agreements it had entered into with Certicom. RIM considered that information in assessing the desirability of launching a bid for Certicom. Certicom asserts that the use of the

---

6. *E.g.*, Martin Marietta Materials, Inc. v. Vulcan Materials Co., 56 A.3d 1072, 1114 (Del. Ch.), *aff'd*, 45 A.3d 148 (Del. 2012).

confidential information for this purpose breached the two non-disclosure agreements and, to remedy this breach, RIM and RIMAC should be permanently enjoined from taking any steps to advance their bid.

[3] Certicom is clear that it does not seek to enjoin RIM from making any hostile bid. RIM was not precluded from launching a hostile bid at this time, Certicom argues. It could have properly done so had it set up a "firewall" so that no use was made of the confidential information. Alternatively, Certicom says, RIM could make a "friendly bid."

[4] RIM argues that the use of the confidential information to make a hostile bid was permitted by the two non-disclosure agreements and, in the alternative, in the circumstances the injunction sought by Certicom is not an appropriate remedy for a breach of those agreements.

[6] While I expressed doubts to counsel before they began their submissions that this matter could be resolved without a trial, after hearing their submissions and reviewing all of the evidence, I accept that the determination of this time-sensitive matter can properly be made on the extensive application record before me, and that there is no necessity for viva voce evidence. I note that in arguing the merits of its case, Certicom relied on the evidence of RIM's own deponents.

CONCLUSION

[7] The use of the confidential information provided pursuant to the two non-disclosure agreements at issue—referred to in these reasons as the "2007 NDA" and the "2008 NDA"—to assess the desirability of a hostile takeover bid breached those agreements. RIM and RIMAC shall be enjoined from taking any steps to advance the hostile takeover bid launched by them on December 10, 2008.

BACKGROUND

[8] RIM is a well known and highly successful company with a current market capitalization of over $20 billion. It is a leading designer, manufacturer and marketer of innovative wireless solutions for the worldwide mobile communications market. The BlackBerry is one of its products.

[9] Certicom, a much smaller company, is a leading authority for the cryptography required by software vendors and device manufacturers to embed security in their products.

[10] RIM has been a customer of Certicom since 2000. RIM and Certicom exchanged commercial information in the ordinary course of their relationship pursuant to standard form non-disclosure agreements signed in 2002 and 2005. These agreements are not at issue in this application.

THE 2007 NDA

[11] In February of 2007, Certicom and RIM first discussed the possible acquisition of Certicom by RIM. At the time, the price of Certicom's shares was between $5 and $6. In order to facilitate due diligence of Certicom, Certicom and RIM entered into the "2007 NDA"—the first of the two non-disclosure agreements at issue—on July 11, 2007. At the time that Certicom and RIM entered into the 2007 NDA, the non-disclosure agreement executed by the parties in 2005 (the "2005 NDA") was in effect. The 2005 NDA was RIM's standard form, reciprocal non-disclosure agreement for commercial use.

[12] The 2007 NDA limited the use of "Confidential Information" disclosed pursuant to the 2007 NDA to certain permitted purposes during a five-year term and provided that the disclosing party would have the right to seek injunctive relief for any use of the Confidential Information that was contrary to the terms of the 2007 NDA.

[13] Section 4 of the 2007 NDA provides that "Recipient shall use and reproduce the Confidential Information only to the extent reasonably required to fulfill the Purpose." Section 3 of the 2007 NDA defines "Purpose" to mean "(i) assessing the desirability or viability of establishing or furthering a business or contractual relationship between the Parties which may include, without limitation, some form of business combination between the Parties; and (ii) to the extent this Agreement is incorporated by reference into any other agreement between the Parties, achieving the objectives of that agreement." At issue on this application is whether a hostile takeover bid is some form of a business combination between the parties and therefore whether the Confidential Information could be used for the purpose of assessing the desirability of a hostile bid.

[14] By its terms, the 2007 NDA only applies to information provided within six months of its execution.

[15] At Certicom's request, the 2007 NDA also contained a "standstill" provision pursuant to which RIM specifically agreed, among other things, not to make a hostile take-over bid for Certicom for a 12-month period. The precise wording of this clause, reproduced in Schedule A [set forth below],[7] was

_____

7. Standstill Until the earliest of: (i) the expiration of twelve (12) months from the date hereof, (ii) such date, if any, that the Participant or any of its affiliates or Representatives enters into a legally binding agreement with any third party or a third party makes a public announcement regarding a bona fide unsolicited offer with respect to the potential purchase of the Participant or its outstanding equity securities, assets or operations, including without limitation the granting of an exclusive license to all or substantially all of the Participant's intellectual property, or any other potential transaction that would reasonably be expected to result in a change of control of the Participant, including without limitation any transaction described in paragraph (a) below (each, an "Acquisition Proposal"), (iii) such time as RIM shall not be permitted by the Participant to participate in any process being conducted by the Participant to consider its strategic alternatives or any subsequent "auction" or similar process on terms (including with respect to standstill obligations) at least as favourable as other participants, and (iv) such time as you receive the written consent of the Participant (collectively, the "Standstill Period"), neither RIM nor any of its

negotiated by the parties. The standstill provision expired before RIM launched its bid and is not at issue, except to the extent it affects the interpretation of the definition of the Purpose for which RIM is permitted to use the Confidential Information.

THE FIRST TRANCHE OF DISCLOSURE

[18] In September of 2007, Certicom provided RIM with a large package of disclosure pursuant to the 2007 NDA. This package was the first of three tranches of confidential information provided. It included: Certicom's financial year 2008 strategic growth plan and business plan; a detailed list of Certicom patents pending and issued; patent licence agreements, including confidential

---

affiliates nor any of its Representatives for their account or jointly and in concert with RIM shall directly or indirectly;

(a) effect or seek, offer, agree or propose (whether publicly or otherwise) to effect, or cause to participate in or in any way advise, encourage or assist (including without limitation financial assistance) any other person to effect or seek, offer agree or propose (whether publicly or otherwise) to effect or participate in (i) any acquisition of any securities or rights to acquire any securities (or any other beneficial ownership thereof), assets or properties of the Participant or any of its subsidiaries, whether such agreement or proposal is with the Participant or any of its subsidiaries or shareholders or with a third party, (ii) any merger or other business combination or tender, takeover bid or exchange offer involving the Participant or any of its subsidiaries or shareholders, (iii) any recapitalization, restructuring, liquidation, dissolution or other extraordinary transaction with respect to the Participant or any of its subsidiaries; or (iv) any "solicitation" of "proxies" (as such terms are used in the proxy provisions of the Securities Act (Ontario)) or consent to vote or otherwise with respect to any voting securities of the Participant or any of its subsidiaries;

(b) form, join or in any way participate in a group or act jointly or in concert with any person with respect to voting securities of the Participant or attempt to acquire control of the Participant or acquire any assets thereof;

(c) otherwise act, alone or in concert with others, to seek to control or influence the management, Board of Directors or policies of the Participant (other than negotiations or proposals in accordance with this Agreement);

(d) take any action which might reasonably be expected to cause or require the Participant to make a public announcement regarding any of the types of matters set forth in (a)-(c) above;

(e) disclose any intention, plan or arrangement in contravention of the foregoing; or (f) enter into any discussion or arrangements with any third party with respect to any of the foregoing.

Nothing contained herein shall prohibit RIM from making a private proposal to the Board of Directors of the Participant relating to a proposal for an offer for the assets, securities of the Participant or other business combination. During the Standstill Period, Participant shall promptly notify RIM of any legally binding agreements entered into with third parties in respect of the matters described in this Section 12, including without limitation any such legally binding agreements with third parties for Acquisition Proposals, or other events that would result in the termination of the Standstill Period.
(Emphasis added.)

agreements with Certicom's key customers; a breakdown of Certicom's patent licence revenue; Certicom's patent infringement information; and Certicom's litigation information. The information provided was specifically deemed Confidential Information pursuant to the 2007 NDA.

[19] Mr. Wormwald, RIM's vice-president of Strategic Alliances, conceded on his cross-examination that RIM did not have information of the nature provided before this disclosure, the information was protected by the 2007 NDA and the information was important for its assessment of a potential acquisition of Certicom. The licensing agreements were reviewed by competent people at RIM, including patent counsel. Mr. Wormwald acknowledged that the customer agreements continue to constitute "Confidential Information"; they are still not available to the public.

[20] In November of 2007, Certicom's interim chief executive officer put the possible acquisition "on hold" because Certicom anticipated that a permanent CEO would be named by year-end, and the matter should be left to the new CEO.

[21] A new CEO of Certicom, Karna Gupta, was appointed in January of 2008.

THE SECOND TRANCHE OF DISCLOSURE

[22] Certicom's founder, Scott Vanstone, was not aware that Certicom's interim CEO had shut down RIM's due diligence and acquisition discussions. In February of 2008, he met with Chris Wormwald of RIM and asked why RIM appeared disinterested in making an acquisition of Certicom. He provided Mr. Wormwald with an e-mail with a summary of certain licences, and later, a memory stick containing some, but not all, licensing agreements. The parties agreed to treat this information as though it was provided pursuant to the 2007 NDA, even though the 2007 NDA only applied to information provided within six months after the agreement was executed.

[23] Following Mr. Gupta's appointment, Certicom began to pursue a new strategic direction. In March of 2008, RIM's CEO, Jim Balsillie, spoke to Mr. Gupta about the potential acquisition. Mr. Gupta advised him, by e-mail, that he was focusing on fixing the business fundamentals and would only turn his attention to the potential acquisition in a few quarters.

THE 2008 NDA

[24] Certicom and RIM executed the second non-disclosure agreement at issue—what I refer to as the "2008 NDA"—on June 17, 2008. This agreement was signed in the ordinary course of the parties' commercial relationship and not in contemplation of an acquisition. Like the 2005 NDA, it is RIM's standard form, reciprocal non-disclosure agreement for commercial use. It does not contain a standstill provision. It limits the use of Confidential Information disclosed within three years following execution to certain permitted purposes during a five-year term and provides that an aggrieved party is entitled to seek

injunctive relief. It provides that Confidential Information disclosed may be used only for the Purpose of "(i) assessing the desirability or viability of establishing or furthering a business or contractual relationship between the Parties; and (ii) to the extent this agreement is incorporated by reference into any other agreement between the Parties, achieving the objectives or that agreement." "Purpose" in the 2008 NDA does not include the language "some form of a business combination between the Parties" which was added to the 2007 NDA.

DISCUSSIONS RESUME

[25] Certicom approached RIM again about a potential acquisition in September 2008, after Certicom had commenced discussions with an unidentified multinational company. That company signed a non-disclosure agreement with Certicom that contained a 12-month standstill provision.

[26] RIM expressed interest but indicated that it wanted to undertake further due diligence. It wanted information about Certicom's patent portfolio and its new business plan. At this point, neither Mr. Gupta, on the one hand, nor Mr. Wormwald and Jamie Belcher of RIM, on the other, were aware that the 2008 NDA had been signed. Mr. Gupta indicated that while a non-disclosure agreement was not mandatory for an IP discussion at the "first level," it was mandatory if RIM wished to review the business plan. The multinational company, referred to above, had signed a standstill agreement. It would be unfair to treat potential bidders differently. RIM, which was unhappy that it had agreed to a standstill provision in the 2007 NDA only to have the due diligence and acquisition process shut down by Certicom a few months later, indicated that it was unwilling to sign a non-disclosure agreement with a standstill provision.

[27] Certicom sent RIM a non-disclosure agreement, without a standstill provision.

[28] In response, Jamie Belcher of RIM advised Mr. Gupta on September 29, 2008 that RIM's legal department had advised him of the existence of the 2008 NDA and that RIM was of the view that it was "sufficient for the purposes presently being contemplated and we do not feel another NDA is required." Mr. Gupta responded, "Great. This works." Based on the 2008 NDA, he was willing to proceed with technical and IP disclosure.

[29] Mr. Wormwald's evidence is that because Mr. Gupta had agreed that additional information could be provided without RIM executing a standstill provision, Mr. Wormwald "understood the information disclosed could be used for the potential acquisition of Certicom and RIM was in no way precluded from making an offer directly to Certicom's shareholders." Mr. Wormwald's further evidence was that his preference was to proceed by way of a negotiated acquisition, but that he did not want to preclude RIM from launching a hostile bid.

[30] Mr. Gupta's evidence was that each time he spoke to Mr. Balsillie, which he did on March 19, 2008, October 28, 2008, November 7, 2008 and November 9, 2008, Mr. Balsillie confirmed that RIM would proceed in a "friendly" fashion,

and that Certicom would not have provided RIM with confidential information had it known that RIM would use that information to make an offer directly to Certicom's shareholders. Mr. Gupta's further evidence is that no one at RIM suggested that RIM reserved the right to go directly to Certicom's shareholders until Mr. Balsillie wrote to Certicom to that effect on November 28, 2008. Mr. Gupta's evidence was not challenged on cross-examination, and Mr. Balsillie did not provide any evidence to the contrary.

THE THIRD TRANCHE OF DISCLOSURE

[31] Relying on the provisions of the 2008 NDA, Certicom provided RIM with the third, and final, tranche of "Confidential Information" in October of 2008. The third tranche included slides presented at a meeting held on October 6, 2008 regarding Certicom's patents and Certicom's IP licensing and related oral disclosure; materials sent by Certicom on October 17, 2008 and October 20, 2008 co-relating claims in several patents against particular industry standards (the "Mapping Analysis") and the relevant portions of the applicable standards; disclosures made at a meeting on October 21, 2008 (which primarily entailed explanation of the Mapping Analysis); and further patent mapping information sent in an October 22, 2008 e-mail. The Mapping Analysis was specifically prepared by Certicom for provision to RIM. While RIM could have obtained the relevant industry standards and created the Mapping Analysis from materials publicly available, by providing the information in this manner, Certicom saved RIM a few days to about a week of work. The definition of "Confidential Information" in the 2008 NDA (and the 2007 NDA) includes "proprietary or confidential information." The information provided was at a minimum proprietary and it is not disputed that at the time provided, constituted Confidential Information under the 2008 NDA.

[32] Mr. Wormwald acknowledged on cross-examination that the disclosure went "slightly" beyond that which might occur between businesses engaged in a licensing or supplier relationship, and that the information was being assessed from a mergers and acquisitions point of view.

EVENTS LEADING UP TO THE BID AND THE BID

[33] By November, Certicom's share price had plummeted. On November 7, 2008, Mr. Balsillie told Mr. Gupta that RIM wanted to acquire 100 per cent of Certicom, wanted to proceed in a friendly fashion and wanted exclusivity to complete its due diligence. Certicom indicated that it could not provide exclusivity because another party had executed a non-disclosure agreement. Certicom proposed "refreshing" the 2007 NDA, which as noted above, contains a standstill provision.

[34] On November 28, 2008, Mr. Balsillie sent a non-binding expression of interest to the Certicom board, proposing a price of $1.50 per common share, and

indicating that RIM reserved its right to take its offer directly to Certicom's shareholders.

[35] Mr. Wormwald acknowledged that RIM had the information provided under the 2007 NDA and the October 2008 disclosures when it decided to launch its hostile bid. Mr. Wormwald's evidence is also that RIM made no attempt to use a different group of internal people to prepare its hostile offer from those who had been involved with Certicom in 2007 to the end of October 2008, and that essentially the same group of people was involved.

[36] RIM announced its intention to make an offer on December 3, 2008, and circulated its offer and circular to RIM shareholders on December 10, 2008. Its offer was extended and currently expires January 27, 2009. RIM's offer is conditional, among other things, on not less than 66 and 2/3 per cent of Certicom's shares being deposited under the bid and on the waiver or cease trade of Certicom's shareholder rights plan, or "poison pill." Counsel for RIM advised that RIM has not yet made an application to the Ontario Securities Commission (the "OSC") to cease trade the poison pill, but intends to do so.[8] It is acknowledged that the poison pill would result in an unacceptable level of dilution, and that as a practical matter RIM will not complete its acquisition with the poison pill in place. This raises the possibility that RIM will further extend its offer.

[37] The board of directors of Certicom has determined that the RIM offer is inadequate and recommended that shareholders reject RIM's offer. In response to RIM's bid, Certicom has commenced an auction process in an attempt to secure a superior bid. Confidential information is being made available to interested parties who have signed non-disclosure and standstill agreements.

[38] A commercial contract is to be interpreted:

> (1) as a whole, in a manner that gives meaning to all of its terms and avoids an interpretation that would render one or more of its terms ineffective;
> (2) by determining the intention of the parties in accordance with the language they have used in the written document and based upon the "cardinal presumption" that they have intended what they have said;
> (3) with regard to objective evidence of the factual matrix underlying the negotiation of the contract (what Kentucky Fried Chicken Canada, a Division of Pepsi-Cola Canada Ltd. v. Scott's Food Services Inc., [1998] O.J. No. 4368, 114 O.A.C. 357 (C.A.), at para. 25, refers to as "the general context that gave birth to the document"), but without reference to the subjective intention of the parties; and
> (4) to the extent there is any ambiguity in the contract, in a fashion that accords with good business sense, and that avoids a commercial absurdity.

---

8. Under Canadian law, securities regulators have the power to order a company to deactivate its poison pill. Unlike in the United States, pills are only effective for a maximum of 105 days in any event, so that an offer made after the pill has expired will not be effected by the pill. — AUTHOR.

Ventas, Inc. v. Sunrise Senior Living Real Estate Investment Trust (2007), 85 O.R. (3d) 254, [2007] O.J. No. 1083 (C.A.), at para. 24.

[39] To the extent there is ambiguity after applying principles 1 through 3 above, the court is also entitled to consider the subsequent conduct of the parties as evidence of their intention at the time that the contract was executed: Canadian National Railways v. Canadian Pacific Ltd., [1978] B.C.J. No. 1298, [1979] 1 W.W.R. 358 (C.A.), at para. 48, affd [1979] 2 S.C.R. 668, [1979] S.C.J. No. 62, 105 D.L.R. (3d) 170.

[40] Section 4 of the 2007 NDA provides, in part, that

Recipient shall use and reproduce the Confidential Information only to the extent reasonably required to fulfill the Purpose.

[41] Section 3 defines "Purpose" to mean

(i) assessing the desirability or viability of establishing or furthering a business or contractual relationship between the Parties which may include, without limitation, some form of business combination between the Parties; and (ii) to the extent this Agreement is incorporated by reference into any other agreement between the Parties, achieving the objectives of that agreement.

[43] The evidence established, and it is conceded, that the first two tranches of information provided to RIM constitute Confidential Information under the 2007 NDA.

[44] Certicom argues that an offer by RIM to Certicom's shareholders to purchase their shares in Certicom, which is not endorsed by Certicom, is not a "business or contractual relationship between the Parties which may include, without limitation, some form of business combination between the Parties." An offer from RIM to Certicom's shareholders is not "between" Certicom and RIM.

[45] Certicom argues that its interpretation is supported by wording in the standstill provision, in s. 12 of the 2007 NDA. In that section, RIM agrees, among other things, that neither it nor any of its affiliates will effect or propose to effect, "any merger or other business combination or tender, takeover bid or exchange offer involving [Certicom] or any of its subsidiaries or shareholders." This disjunctive language, Certicom argues, makes clear that a takeover bid is not a business combination. Certicom submits that if the parties had intended to permit RIM to make a takeover bid directly to Certicom shareholders, they would have used the language "take-over bid . . . involving . . . shareholders" used in s. 12.

[46] RIM points to the following sentence in the standstill provision in s. 12 of the 2007 NDA as indicating that a business combination includes an offer by RIM to Certicom's shareholders: "Nothing contained herein shall prohibit RIM from making a private proposal to the Board of Directors of [Certicom] relating to a proposal for an offer for the assets, securities of [Certicom] or other business

combination (emphasis added)." Based on this wording, RIM argues that an offer for the securities of Certicom is a form of business combination, and an offer by RIM to Certicom's shareholders to purchase their shares in Certicom is accordingly a business combination between RIM and Certicom within the meaning of s. 3 of the 2007 NDA.

[47] RIM also argues that where, as in this case, the parties specifically negotiated a standstill provision, the confidentiality obligation should be interpreted in a manner that does not, effectively, extend the duration of the negotiated standstill.

ANALYSIS

[48] I accept RIM's argument that a takeover bid can constitute a business combination for the purposes of the 2007 NDA, based on the language RIM refers to in s. 12 and the factual matrix.

[49] When the 2007 NDA was negotiated, the acquisition by RIM of Certicom through a "friendly" transaction was contemplated. The information was provided to facilitate the assessment of the desirability of an acquisition. Such an acquisition could have taken the form of an offer to the shareholders of Certicom, consented to in writing by the board of directors of Certicom. If a takeover bid does not constitute "some form of business combination," the 2007 NDA would not have permitted RIM to use the information for the very purpose intended.

[50] That being said, a takeover bid is not necessarily a business combination between the parties.

[51] The Shorter Oxford English Dictionary (Oxford University Press, 1973) defines "between" as "Expressing reciprocal action or relation between two agents; Used of relation to two (or more) things or parties acting conjointly or participating in action" and "Of time, quantity or degree: Intermediate to two others."

[52] The word "between" is, on my count, used three other times in the 2007 NDA. In each case, it is used in manner consistent with its conventional meaning and dictionary definition and in two cases it imports the concept of a contractual relationship between Certicom and RIM. The recitals indicated that the 2007 NDA is "entered into by and between" RIM and Certicom. Section 5 indicates that the 2007 applies to Confidential Information that is disclosed "between" the effective date and six months thereafter. Section 14 refers to "any pre-existing non-disclosure agreements between the Parties."

[53] Based on the ordinary and usual meaning and dictionary definition of the word "between" and the manner in which the word is used in the 2007 NDA, a takeover bid would in my view only amount to a business combination between the parties if Certicom consented to, or endorsed, the transaction and in that manner participated with RIM in RIM's bid.

[54] This conclusion is buttressed by the factual matrix. As noted, when the 2007 NDA was negotiated, the parties contemplated a friendly bid for Certicom. This is the context in which the word must be interpreted.

[55] In Aurizon Mines Ltd. v. Northgate Minerals Corp., [2006] B.C.J. No. 2070, 2006 BCSC 1022, affd [2006] B.C.J. No. 1584, 2006 BCCA 340, Northgate signed a combined confidentiality and standstill agreement, but no confidential information was provided to it. It took the position that the standstill provision, which was negotiated in anticipation of disclosure of confidential information, was as a result ineffective and made an unsolicited bid for Aurizon. Northgate was held to be subject to the standstill provision, and enjoined from making a bid for Aurizon. As drafted, the standstill provision was not tied to whether or not confidential information was disclosed and the court concluded that such a term could not be implied. The non-disclosure and standstill provisions were held to be separate obligations that were not inter-linked, each with business efficacy. At paras. 52 and 55, Allan J. endorsed the view of Aurizon's financial advisor, Mr. Sauntry of BMO Nesbitt Burns Inc., who deposed that

> The purpose of confidentiality agreements differs from the purpose of standstill agreements. A confidentiality agreement on its own facilitates, in particular, the exchange of information. Standstill agreements are entered into because companies entering into strategic dialogues do not want to find themselves then exposed to a hostile takeover bid or other unsolicited offer from the party with whom it has had such discussions. Further, where confidential information may be exchanged, standstill agreements typically also remove the need to prove whether information that has been exchanged is confidential at all, or that confidential information has been misused in connection with a bid or other conduct as such conduct itself is simply prohibited.

[56] Thus, a confidentiality provision can independently prohibit the use of the information disclosed for the purpose of assessing the desirability of a hostile bid and thereby hamper the ability of the "disclosee" to make an unsolicited bid. A standstill provision is better protection, removing the need for proof and costly litigation.

[57] In this case, I have concluded that the standstill and the non-disclosure provisions are properly interpreted as separate clauses, providing different protections for different terms. The term of the absolute protection of the negotiated standstill is shorter than that provided by the non-disclosure provision. It applied whether or not RIM obtained disclosure. Indeed, s. 9 of the 2007 NDA specifically provides that Certicom is not obligated to disclose any confidential information to RIM. After the standstill provision falls away, Certicom is left with longer-term protection that, among other things, entails the need for proof of disclosure and proof of use of confidential information. Certicom's patents and patent licences are the heart of its business. The evidence was that Certicom's patent licence agreements are generally for the life of the patent. Longer-term protection is commercially reasonable in this context. After the standstill provision had expired, it was open to RIM to mount a hostile bid, provided that it had not received, and used, any Confidential Information in assessing the bid.

[58] Interpreted in this manner, the provisions are complementary and do not amount to conflicting standstill provisions.

[95] Certicom is a technology company. Its assets consist of patents and patent licence agreements. The information disclosed to RIM included patent licence agreements. RIM is a strategic purchaser, motivated by Certicom's technology. Some of the agreements are sufficiently sensitive that participants in the auction process are given access to the agreements only through their counsel. Which of these commercially sensitive agreements contains change of control provisions and which permit assignment or sub-licensing would be of value to a strategic purchaser. Having regard to the nature of Certicom's business, and Mr. Wormwald's evidence that the information was important for its assessment of a potential acquisition of Certicom, I am able to come to the above conclusion that such disclosure was of value, without the necessity for viva voce evidence.

[96] Nor do I accept that Certicom does not have "clean hands." It broke off discussions with RIM for legitimate reasons. Certicom was not subject to an exclusivity obligation when it commenced discussions with the unidentified multinational, and it re-opened discussions with RIM.

[97] In the result, a permanent injunction shall issue, enjoining RIM and RIMAC from taking any steps to advance the hostile takeover bid launched on December 10, 2008. As Certicom indicated, RIM is free to make a friendly bid, and, should it manage to craft a manner of launching a subsequent hostile bid without breaching the non-disclosure agreements, as Certicom submits it is possible to do, another hostile bid.

PROBLEM SET 22.1

1. A possible problem that may be in evidence in the foregoing is the tendency to think of confidentiality provisions and standstill provisions as distinct clauses. As noted, the confidentiality provisions come in two forms: disclosure restrictions and use restrictions. The second could be written in various ways, some of which will implicate the standstill provision. Consider the following:
    a. "You shall not use the information except in connection with a potential acquisition involving the target," and
    b. "You shall not use the confidential information except in connection with your assessment of a negotiated transaction between the buyer and the target."
2. Imagine you represent a potential buyer in negotiations. Counsel for the target presents you with the provision set forth below. How would you attempt to revise it?

> STANDSTILL PROVISION. The Prospective Acquirer agrees that, during the ten-year period commencing on the date of this Agreement (the "Standstill Period"), neither the Prospective Acquirer nor any of the

Prospective Acquirer's Representatives will, in any manner, directly or indirectly:

(a) make, effect, initiate, cause or participate in (i) any acquisition of beneficial ownership of any securities of Target or any securities of any subsidiary or other affiliate of Target, (ii) any acquisition of any assets of Target or any assets of any subsidiary or other affiliate of Target, (iii) any tender offer, exchange offer, merger, business combination, recapitalization, reorganization, restructuring, liquidation, dissolution or extraordinary transaction involving Target or any subsidiary or other affiliate of Target, or involving any securities or assets of Target or any securities or assets of any subsidiary or other affiliate of Target, or (iv) any "solicitation" of "proxies" (as those terms are used in the proxy rules of the Securities and Exchange Commission) or consents with respect to any securities of Target;

(b) form, join or participate in a "group" (as defined in the Securities Exchange Act of 1934 and the rules promulgated thereunder) with respect to the beneficial ownership of any securities of Target;

(c) act, alone or in concert with others, to seek to control or influence the management, board of directors or policies of Target;

(d) take any action that could reasonably be expected to require Target to make a public announcement regarding any of the types of matters set forth in clause "(a)" of this sentence;

(e) agree or offer to take, or encourage, facilitate or propose (publicly or otherwise) the taking of, any action referred to in clause "(a)," "(b)," "(c)," or "(d)" of this sentence;

(f) induce or encourage any other Person to take any action of the type referred to in clause "(a)," "(b)," "(c)," "(d)," or "(e)" of this sentence;

(g) enter into any discussions, negotiations, arrangement or agreement with any other Person relating to any of the foregoing; or

(h) request or propose that Target or any of Target's Representatives amend, waive or consider the amendment or waiver of any provision set forth in this Section 8.

The expiration of the Standstill Period will not terminate or otherwise affect any of the other provisions of this Agreement.

For purposes of this Agreement, a party's "Representatives" will be deemed to include each Person that is or becomes (i) a subsidiary or other affiliate of such party, or (ii) an officer, director, employee, partner, attorney, advisor, accountant, agent or representative of such party or of any of such party's subsidiaries or other affiliates.

3.   TOP-UP OPTIONS

IN RE COMVERGE, INC. SHAREHOLDERS LITIGATION

2014 WL 6686570
Court of Chancery of Delaware.
November 25, 2014.

PARSONS, Vice Chancellor.

. . . Comverge and HIG executed the Merger Agreement and several related documents. The deal was structured as a two-step acquisition in which HIG would acquire shares in a public tender offer and then execute a back-end merger to complete the takeover. Toward this end, the Merger Agreement granted HIG a "top-up option" that might enable the second step to be completed in a short-form merger. At the $1.75 per share offer price, the acquisition had an equity value of approximately $48 million. In addition, HIG and Comverge entered into a $12 million bridge loan agreement, which HIG funded immediately. The notes issued under the bridge loan agreement bore an interest rate of 15 percent per annum and were convertible at the election of HIG into 8,571,428 shares of Comverge common stock at a conversion price of $1.40 per share (the "Convertible Notes").

The Merger Agreement provided for a 30–day "go-shop" period, which could be extended by 10 days if Comverge received and was negotiating a potentially superior proposal. During the go-shop period, a termination fee of $1.206 million was in effect, and Comverge also agreed to reimburse HIG for up to $1.5 million in expenses. After the go-shop period expired, the termination fee increased to $1.93 million. In addition, Comverge and Grace Bay entered into a forbearance agreement (the "Forbearance Agreement") pursuant to which Grace Bay agreed for a limited time not to exercise its rights under the PFG Note, including the blocking rights by which it otherwise might impede an alternative transaction.

On March 28, two days after the Merger was announced, Raging Capital filed a Schedule 13D with the SEC, in which it addressed the Comverge Board and scathingly criticized the proposed Merger. The Raging Capital letter stated in part:

> To put it simply, we are extremely disappointed with the price, terms and structure of this proposed acquisition and the actions taken by the Board of Directors (the "Board") in furtherance thereof. The proposed acquisition values Comverge at less than $50 million which, in our view, is a grossly inadequate equity valuation for a company with a $500 million multi-year backlog, more than 500 utility and commercial clients, and a leading edge technology platform. By our calculations, the offer price also represents a significant discount to the valuation of the Company's primary publicly traded peer [EnerNOC, Inc.].
>
> Even more troubling, H.I.G. could potentially reap payments worth up to 14% or more of the deal value in the event the deal is terminated, including up to $1.9 million in break-up fees, up to $1.5 million in expense reimbursements, and up to

$3 million or more of profits upon conversion of its new convertible note to common shares (we view this bridge loan as essentially a second break-up fee designed to have a chilling effect on the ability of a third-party to submit a competing bid). Further, Comverge has only a short period of time, just 40 days, to "go shop" for a superior deal, even as H.I.G. retains a right of first refusal to match any superior offer. In short, we believe this deal is a lemon and we seriously question whether the Board has met its fiduciary obligations to shareholders. . . .

We believe it is more than likely that [either Raging Capital or other stockholders would have] stepped up to refinance the Company rather than see it sold for a song to an opportunistic offeror. One must wonder what "package" Comverge's management will receive from H.I.G. to remain with the Company.

While we have not yet decided on next steps, we believe Comverge remains an undervalued asset. We believe the Board, in the exercise of its fiduciary duties, should immediately withdraw its recommendation for H.I.G.'s proposal. We remain open to participating in an alternative transaction if we do not see a materially higher price for our shares.

During the go-shop period, from March 26 through April 25, 2012, JP Morgan contacted multiple potential buyers, several of whom executed confidentiality agreements and conducted due diligence. This process yielded indications of interest from two bidders, one identifying a range of $2.50 to $2.90 per share, the other indicating $3.25 per share. No firm proposal was made, however. Plaintiffs attribute that to concern among potential suitors about completing due diligence during the specified timeframe and repaying the Convertible Note. The first-step tender offer period from April 11 and to May 9 partially overlapped with the go-shop period, and by May 9 approximately 52.2 percent of Comverge's outstanding shares of common stock were tendered. After HIG made another tender offer from May 10 to May 14, the total percentage of tendered shares reached 65.1 percent. HIG then exercised its top-up option, and the Merger became effective on May 15, 2012 . . .

Plaintiffs' . . . *Revlon*-related argument is that, in connection with the Merger Agreement, the Board accepted several deal protection devices that effectively precluded a topping bid from emerging during the go-shop period. Specifically, they challenge: (1) the length of the go-shop period; (2) the top-up option; and (3) the termination fee.

Plaintiffs' challenge to the top-up option is without merit. A top-up option is a device commonly used by transactional planners and not one that conceivably could be called unreasonable in itself when conditioned on the attainment of a majority of the shares in a public tender offer. . . .

PROBLEM SET 22.2

1. A further refinement of the top-up option, the so-called Burger King structure, has been used in several deals, often involving private equity buyers. Under this approach, the minimum condition to the front-end tender offer is set at the percentage that, when added to the maximum

available top-up option, will ensure that the buyer will cross the 90-percent short-form threshold; if the tender fails to meet that higher minimum condition (often much higher than 50 percent), the parties abandon the tender offer and proceed with a one-step merger using a proxy statement that is prepared and filed while the tender offer is pending. What are the drawbacks of this approach?

2. Note that use of a top-up option is checked in cases where there are insufficient authorized but unissued shares to allow the exercise of the option to carry the buyer offer over the 90-percent level. This is something to consider when drafting the certificate of incorporation in the first instance.

4.   "MEDIUM FORM" MERGERS: THE (PROBABLE?) DEATH OF TOP-UP OPTIONS

As you may have learned in your earlier Corporations class, Delaware section 253 has long provided for a *short form merger*, when "at least 90% of the outstanding shares of each class of stock of a corporation . . . is owned by another corporation." A short-form merger does not require any vote of the target's stockholders to complete and accordingly does not require the filing of any proxy statement or information statement. Therefore, if a short-form merger can be effected, it can be concluded immediately upon completion of the front-end tender offer.

Without a "top-up" option, if the buyer holds less than 90 percent of the target company's shares after the first-step tender offer, the target company must hold a stockholders' meeting and incur the expense associated with preparing and filing proxy materials to approve the second-step merger, even though stockholder approval is a certainty (because the buyer acquired a majority of the voting shares through the tender offer).

In 2013, the Delaware state legislature amended the DGCL to add new subsection 251(h). That new subsection allows a buyer who, following consummation of a tender offer, owns a percentage of the shares of a target sufficient to approve the merger agreement under Delaware law (and sufficient under the target's certificate of incorporation, if that requires a higher percentage) to effect a second-step merger without a vote of the target's stockholders. Since its adoption, 251(h) has become a preferred method of accomplishing a tender offer in public M&A transactions, thus reducing the need for top-up options.

To be eligible to use section 251(h), the target corporation's shares must be listed on a national securities exchange or held of record by more than 2,000 stockholders immediately before the execution of the merger agreement. The tender or exchange offer also must be made on the terms provided for in the merger agreement. In addition, the consideration paid to holders of outstanding shares in the second-step merger must be the same amount and kind as that paid in the front-end tender or exchange offer.

Take a look at section 251(h) in your statutory supplement. In what cases, if any, would you still want to include a top-up option in a deal? Would this new section apply to a hostile takeover?

A handful of other states, including Maryland, have recently adopted provisions based on section 251(h).

5. THE WILLIAMS ACT

The Williams Act was passed in 1968 to protect shareholders in the course of takeovers and tender offers by granting the SEC and the courts the power to manage problems that arise. The Act added several provisions to the Securities Exchange Act of 1934.

Section 14(d)(1) of the '34 Act requires compliance with certain disclosure and filing requirements in connection with any tender offer for more than 5 percent of a class of equity security registered under Section 12 of the '34 Act, as well as certain securities of insurance and investment companies. The principal filing, dissemination, and disclosure requirements with respect to third-party tender offers are set forth in Regulation 14D.

All written communications from and including the first public announcement of the tender offer are filed on a Schedule TO no later than the date of the communication.

Under Rule 14e-1(a) a tender offer is required to remain open at least until midnight on the 20th business day from the date of commencement. For an offer to be "open," the bidder must be willing to accept shares for deposit each day during the 20 business-day period. In a hostile tender offer, the 20 business-day period begins on the date when the bidder files its Schedule TO and makes a request to the target under Rule 14d-5 to obtain a shareholder list and, in the case of an offer to exchange existing shares for new shares, files a registration statement with the SEC.

Rule 14e-1(b) requires a tender offer remain open at least 10 business days from the date there is an increase or decrease in the consideration offered, the percentage of securities sought in the tender offer (other than increases of 2 percent or less, a kind of de minimus exception), or the dealer's soliciting fee.

Under the "all holders rule," Rule 14d-10, a tender offer must be open to all shareholders of the class of securities subject to the tender offer. This represents a partial "overruling" of the Delaware Supreme Court's opinion in the famous *Unocal* decision, where the court held that a selective tender offer (that cut out a hostile bidder) did not violate state corporate law. By virtue of the Supremacy Clause, such deals are now impermissible, at least with regard to publicly traded companies.

The tender offer rules also include a "best-price rule" in Rule 14d-10. This requires that the consideration paid to any security holder in a tender offer be the highest consideration paid to any other security holder in the offer. Amounts paid under an employment compensation, severance, or other employee benefits arrangement are exempted from the best-price rule if the amounts payable under the arrangement relate solely to past or future services or future services to be refrained from and are not based on the number of shares the employee owns or tenders.

Rule 14d-7 gives each tendering shareholder the right to withdraw the tendered securities "at any time that the offer remains open," including during any extension. Look back at the *Comverge* case. Do you now understand why the buyer started a new tender offer, rather than keeping the first tender offer open for a bit longer? *See* Rule 14d-11.

6. POISON PILLS

In some cases, the target does not want to do a deal, or it only wants to do a deal at a much higher price. The most effective way to hold off an unwanted acquirer is through a *shareholders' rights plan*. These are more commonly known as *poison pills*.

The key features of a rights plan are the "flip-in" and "flip-over" provisions, the effect of which is to impose unacceptable levels of share dilution on an acquirer. The rights are triggered when the stock ownership of a shareholder, or a group of shareholders acting in concert, exceeds some threshold—often 20 percent. The plan then gives all other shareholders the right to purchase either the target's stock (flip-in) or the acquirer's stock (flip-over) at a substantial discount, effectively diluting the acquirer's stock ownership.

Rights plans also generally provide that, once the triggering threshold is crossed, the target's board may exchange, in whole or in part, the rights of all holders other than the acquirer for shares of the company's common stock. This provision avoids the expense of requiring rights holders to exercise their flip-in rights and eliminates any uncertainty as to whether individual holders will in fact exercise the rights.

But before getting bogged down in the mechanics of the plan, understand that a rights plan is somewhat like a thermonuclear bomb: It's not really intended to be used; instead it is supposed to act as a deterrent. Hopefully the hostile bidder is rational and will never trigger the plan.

Instead, the plan forces the bidder to negotiate with the board, because the board retains the right to deactivate the pill.

With the basic legality of pills established by case law in the 1980s and early 1990s, almost all litigation now focuses on whether or not a board should be required to redeem the rights in response to a particular bid.[9]

---

9. William B. Chandler III, *The Delaware Court of Chancery: An Insider's View of Change and Continuity*, 2012 Colum. Bus. L. Rev. 411, 413 (2012).

IN RE AIRGAS INC. SHAREHOLDER LITIGATION

16 A.3d 48
Court of Chancery of Delaware.
Feb. 15, 2011.

CHANDLER, Chancellor

This case poses the following fundamental question: Can a board of directors, acting in good faith and with a reasonable factual basis for its decision, when faced with a structurally non-coercive, all-cash, fully financed tender offer directed to the stockholders of the corporation, keep a poison pill in place so as to prevent the stockholders from making their own decision about whether they want to tender their shares—even after the incumbent board has lost one election contest, a full year has gone by since the offer was first made public, and the stockholders are fully informed as to the target board's views on the inadequacy of the offer? If so, does that effectively mean that a board can "just say never" to a hostile tender offer?

The answer to the latter question is "no." A board cannot "*just* say no" to a tender offer. Under Delaware law, it must first pass through two prongs of exacting judicial scrutiny by a judge who will evaluate the actions taken by, and the motives of, the board. Only a board of directors found to be acting in good faith, after reasonable investigation and reliance on the advice of outside advisors, which articulates and convinces the Court that a hostile tender offer poses a legitimate threat to the corporate enterprise, may address that perceived threat by blocking the tender offer and forcing the bidder to elect a board majority that supports its bid.

In essence, this case brings to the fore one of the most basic questions animating all of corporate law, which relates to the allocation of power between directors and stockholders. That is, "when, if ever, will a board's duty to 'the corporation and its shareholders' require [the board] to abandon concerns for 'long term' values (and other constituencies) and enter a current share value maximizing mode?" More to the point, in the context of a hostile tender offer, who gets to decide when and if the corporation is for sale?

Since the Shareholder Rights Plan (more commonly known as the "poison pill") was first conceived and throughout the development of Delaware corporate takeover jurisprudence during the twenty-five-plus years that followed, the debate over who ultimately decides whether a tender offer is adequate and should be accepted—the shareholders of the corporation or its board of directors—has raged on. Starting with Moran v. Household International, Inc.[10] in 1985, when the Delaware Supreme Court first upheld the adoption of the poison pill as a valid takeover defense, through the hostile takeover years of the 1980s, and in several recent decisions of the Court of Chancery and the Delaware Supreme Court, this fundamental question has engaged practitioners, academics, and members of the judiciary, but it has yet to be confronted head on.

---

10. 490 A.2d 1059 (Del.Ch.1985).

For the reasons much more fully described in the remainder of this Opinion, I conclude that, as Delaware law currently stands, the answer must be that the power to defeat an inadequate hostile tender offer ultimately lies with the board of directors. As such, I find that the Airgas board has met its burden under *Unocal* to articulate a legally cognizable threat (the allegedly inadequate price of Air Products' offer, coupled with the fact that a majority of Airgas's stockholders would likely tender into that inadequate offer) and has taken defensive measures that fall within a range of reasonable responses proportionate to that threat. I thus rule in favor of defendants. Air Products' and the Shareholder Plaintiffs' requests for relief are denied, and all claims asserted against defendants are dismissed with prejudice.

INTRODUCTION

This is the Court's decision after trial, extensive post-trial briefing, and a supplemental evidentiary hearing in this long-running takeover battle between Air Products & Chemicals, Inc. ("Air Products") and Airgas, Inc. ("Airgas"). The now very public saga began quietly in mid-October 2009 when John McGlade, President and CEO of Air Products, privately approached Peter McCausland, founder and CEO of Airgas, about a potential acquisition or combination. After McGlade's private advances were rebuffed, Air Products went hostile in February 2010, launching a public tender offer for all outstanding Airgas shares.

Now, over a year since Air Products first announced its all-shares, all-cash tender offer, the terms of that offer (other than price) remain essentially unchanged. After several price bumps and extensions, the offer currently stands at $70 per share and is set to expire today, February 15, 2011—Air Products' stated "best and final" offer. The Airgas board unanimously rejected that offer as being "clearly inadequate." The Airgas board has repeatedly expressed the view that Airgas is worth at least $78 per share in a sale transaction—and at any rate, far more than the $70 per share Air Products is offering.

So, we are at a crossroads. Air Products has made its "best and final" offer—apparently its offer to acquire Airgas has reached an end stage. Meanwhile, the Airgas board believes the offer is clearly inadequate and its value in a sale transaction is at least $78 per share. At this stage, it appears, neither side will budge. Airgas continues to maintain its defenses, blocking the bid and effectively denying shareholders the choice whether to tender their shares. Air Products and Shareholder Plaintiffs now ask this Court to order Airgas to redeem its poison pill and other defenses that are stopping Air Products from moving forward with its hostile offer, and to allow Airgas's stockholders to decide for themselves whether they want to tender into Air Products' (inadequate or not) $70 "best and final" offer.

A week-long trial in this case was held from October 4, 2010 through October 8, 2010. Hundreds of pages of post-trial memoranda were submitted by the parties. After trial, several legal, factual, and evidentiary questions remained to be answered. In ruling on certain outstanding evidentiary issues, I sent counsel a

Letter Order on December 2, 2010 asking for answers to a number of questions to be addressed in supplemental post-trial briefing. On the eve of the parties' submissions to the Court in response to that Letter Order, Air Products raised its offer to the $70 "best and final" number. . .

Now, having thoroughly read, reviewed, and reflected upon all of the evidence presented to me, and having carefully considered the arguments made by counsel, I conclude that the Airgas board, in proceeding as it has since October 2009, has not breached its fiduciary duties owed to the Airgas stockholders. I find that the board has acted in good faith and in the honest belief that the Air Products offer, at $70 per share, is inadequate.

Although I have a hard time believing that inadequate price alone (according to the target's board) in the context of a non-discriminatory, all-cash, all-shares, fully financed offer poses any "threat"—particularly given the wealth of information available to Airgas's stockholders at this point in time—under existing Delaware law, it apparently does. Inadequate price has become a form of "substantive coercion" as that concept has been developed by the Delaware Supreme Court in its takeover jurisprudence. That is, the idea that Airgas's stockholders will disbelieve the board's views on value (or in the case of merger arbitrageurs who may have short-term profit goals in mind, they may simply ignore the board's recommendations), and so they may mistakenly tender into an inadequately priced offer. Substantive coercion has been clearly recognized by our Supreme Court as a valid threat.

Trial judges are not free to ignore or rewrite appellate court decisions. Thus, for reasons explained in detail below, I am constrained by Delaware Supreme Court precedent to conclude that defendants have met their burden under *Unocal* to articulate a sufficient threat that justifies the continued maintenance of Airgas's poison pill. That is, assuming defendants have met their burden to articulate a legally cognizable threat (prong 1), Airgas's defenses have been recognized by Delaware law as reasonable responses to the threat posed by an inadequate offer—even an all-shares, all-cash offer (prong 2).

In my personal view, Airgas's poison pill has served its legitimate purpose. Although the "best and final" $70 offer has been on the table for just over two months (since December 9, 2010), Air Products' advances have been ongoing for over sixteen months, and Airgas's use of its poison pill—particularly in combination with its staggered board—has given the Airgas board over a full year to inform its stockholders about its view of Airgas's intrinsic value and Airgas's value in a sale transaction. It has also given the Airgas board a full year to express its views to its stockholders on the purported opportunistic timing of Air Products' repeated advances and to educate its stockholders on the inadequacy of Air Products' offer. It has given Airgas *more time than any litigated poison pill in Delaware history*—enough time to show stockholders four quarters of improving financial results, demonstrating that Airgas is on track to meet its projected goals. And it has helped the Airgas board push Air Products to raise its bid by $10 per share from when it was first publicly announced to what Air Products has now represented is its highest offer. The record at both the

October trial and the January supplemental evidentiary hearing confirm that
Airgas's stockholder base is sophisticated and well-informed, and that essentially
all the information they would need to make an informed decision is available to
them. In short, there seems to be no threat here—the stockholders know what
they need to know (about both the offer and the Airgas board's opinion of the
offer) to make an informed decision.

That being said, however, as I understand binding Delaware precedent, I may
not substitute my business judgment for that of the Airgas board.[11] The Delaware
Supreme Court has recognized inadequate price as a valid threat to corporate
policy and effectiveness.[12] The Delaware Supreme Court has also made clear that
the "selection of a time frame for achievement of corporate goals ... may not be
delegated to the stockholders." Furthermore, in powerful dictum, the Supreme
Court has stated that "[d]irectors are not obliged to abandon a deliberately
conceived corporate plan for a short-term shareholder profit unless there is
clearly no basis to sustain the corporate strategy." Although I do not read that
dictum as eliminating the applicability of heightened *Unocal* scrutiny to a
board's decision to block a non-coercive bid as underpriced, I do read it, along
with the actual holding in *Unitrin*, as indicating that a board that has a good faith,
reasonable basis to believe a bid is inadequate may block that bid using a poison
pill, irrespective of stockholders' desire to accept it.

Here, even using heightened scrutiny, the Airgas board has demonstrated that
it has a reasonable basis for sustaining its long term corporate strategy—the
Airgas board is independent, and has relied on the advice of three different
outside independent financial advisors in concluding that Air Products' offer is
inadequate. Air Products' *own three nominees* who were elected to the Airgas
board in September 2010 have joined wholeheartedly in the Airgas board's
determination, and when the Airgas board met to consider the $70 "best and
final" offer in December 2010, it was one of those Air Products Nominees who
said, "We have to protect the pill." Indeed, one of Air Products' *own directors*
conceded at trial that the Airgas board members had acted within their fiduciary
duties in their desire to "hold out for the proper price," and that "if an offer was
made for Air Products that [he] considered to be unfair to the stockholders of Air
Products . . . [he would likewise] use every legal mechanism available" to hold
out for the proper price as well. Under Delaware law, the Airgas directors have
complied with their fiduciary duties. Thus, as noted above, and for the reasons
more fully described in the remainder of this Opinion, I am constrained to deny
Air Products' and the Shareholder Plaintiffs' requests for relief.

---

11. Paramount Commc'ns, Inc. v. Time, Inc., 571 A.2d 1140, 1154 (Del.1990); *see* City Capital
Assocs. Ltd. P'ship v. Interco, Inc., 551 A.2d 787 (Del.Ch.1988); Grand Metro. Pub. Ltd. Co. v.
Pillsbury Co., 558 A.2d 1049 (Del.Ch.1988).

12. *See* Unitrin, Inc. v. Am. Gen. Corp., 651 A.2d 1361, 1384 (Del.1995) ("This Court has held
that the 'inadequate value' of an all cash for all shares offer is a 'legally cognizable threat.'")
(quoting Paramount Commc'ns, Inc. v. Time, Inc., 571 A.2d 1140, 1153 (Del.1990)).

A Brief Poison Pill Primer—*Moran* and its Progeny

This case unavoidably highlights what former-Chancellor Allen has called "an anomaly" in our corporation law. The anomaly is that "[p]ublic tender offers are, or rather can be, change in control transactions that are functionally similar to merger transactions with respect to the critical question of control over the corporate enterprise." Both tender offers and mergers are "extraordinary" transactions that "threaten [] equivalent impacts upon the corporation and all of its constituencies including existing shareholders." But our corporation law statutorily views the two differently—under DGCL §251, board approval and recommendation is required before stockholders have the opportunity to vote on or even consider a merger proposal, while traditionally the board has been given no statutory role in responding to a public tender offer. The poison pill was born "as an attempt to address the flaw (as some would see it) in the corporation law" giving boards a critical role to play in the merger context but no role to play in tender offers.

These "functionally similar forms of change in control transactions," however, have received disparate legal treatment—on the one hand, a decision not to pursue a merger proposal (or even a decision not to engage in negotiations at all) is reviewed under the deferential business judgment standard, while on the other hand, a decision not to redeem a poison pill in the face of a hostile tender offer is reviewed under "intermediate scrutiny" and must be "reasonable in relation to the threat posed" by such offer....

In Moran v. Household International, Inc., written shortly after the *Unocal* decision in 1985, the Delaware Supreme Court first upheld the legality of the poison pill as a valid takeover defense. Specifically, in *Moran*, the Household board of directors "react[ed] to what it perceived to be the threat in the market place of coercive two-tier tender offers" by adopting a stockholder rights plan that would allow the corporation to protect stockholders by issuing securities as a way to ward off a hostile bidder presenting a structurally coercive offer. The *Moran* Court held that the *adoption* of such a rights plan was within the board's statutory authority and thus was not *per se* illegal under Delaware law. But the Supreme Court cabined the use of the rights plan as follows:

> [T]he Rights Plan is not absolute. When the Household Board of Directors is faced with a tender offer and a request to redeem rights, they will not be able to arbitrarily reject the offer. They will be held to the same fiduciary standards any other board of directors would be held to in deciding to adopt a defensive mechanism, the same standard they were held to in originally approving the Rights Plan.

The Court went on to say that "[t]he Board does not now have unfettered discretion in refusing to redeem the Rights. The Board has no more discretion in refusing to redeem the Rights than it does in enacting any defensive mechanism." Accordingly, while the Household board's adoption of the rights plan was deemed to be made in good faith, and the plan was found to be reasonable in relation to the threat posed by the "coercive acquisition techniques" that were prevalent at the time, the pill at that point was adopted merely as a preventive mechanism to ward off future advances. The "ultimate response to an actual takeover," though, would have to be judged by the directors' actions taken at that time, and the board's "use of the Plan [would] be evaluated when and if the issue [arose]."

In Paramount Communications, Inc. v. Time, Inc., however, the Delaware Supreme Court explicitly rejected an approach to *Unocal* analysis that "would involve the court in substituting its judgment as to what is a 'better' deal for that of a corporation's board of directors." Although not a "pill case," the Supreme Court in *Paramount* addressed the concept of substantive coercion head on in determining whether an all-cash, all-shares tender offer posed a legally cognizable threat to the target's stockholders.

As the Supreme Court put it, the case presented them with the following question: "Did Time's board, having developed a [long-term] strategic plan ... come under a fiduciary duty to jettison its plan and put the corporation's future in the hands of its stockholders?" Key to the Supreme Court's ruling was the underlying pivotal question in their mind regarding the Time board's specific long-term plan—its proposed merger with Warner—and whether by entering into the proposed merger, Time had essentially "put itself up for sale." This was important because, so long as the company is *not* "for sale," then *Revlon* duties do not kick in and the board "is not under any *per se* duty to maximize shareholder value in the short term, even in the context of a takeover." The Supreme Court held that the Time board had not abandoned its long-term strategic plans; thus *Revlon* duties were not triggered and *Unocal* alone applied to the board's actions.

In evaluating the Time board's actions under *Unocal*, the Supreme Court embraced the concept of substantive coercion, agreeing with the Time board that its stockholders might have tendered into Paramount's offer "in ignorance or a mistaken belief of the strategic benefit which a business combination with Warner might produce." Stating in no uncertain terms that "in our view, precepts underlying the business judgment rule militate against a court's engaging in the process of attempting to appraise and evaluate the relative merits of a long-term versus a short-term investment goal for shareholders" (as to do so would be "a distortion of the *Unocal* process"), the Supreme Court held that Time's response was proportionate to the threat of Paramount's offer. Time's defensive actions were not aimed at "cramming down" a management-sponsored alternative to Paramount's offer, but instead, were simply aimed at furthering a pre-existing long-term corporate strategy. This, held the Supreme Court, comported with the board's valid exercise of its fiduciary duties under *Unocal*.

Five years later, the Supreme Court further applied the "substantive coercion" concept in Unitrin, Inc. v. American General Corp. There, a hostile acquirer (American General) wanted Unitrin (the target corporation) to be enjoined from implementing a stock repurchase and poison pill adopted in response to

American General's "inadequate" all-cash offer. Recognizing that previous cases had held that "inadequate value" of an all-cash offer could be a valid threat (i.e. *Interco*), the Court also reiterated its conclusion in *Paramount* that inadequate value is not the only threat posed by a non-coercive, all-cash offer. The *Unitrin* Court recited that "the Time board of directors had reasonably determined that inadequate value was not the only threat that Paramount's all cash for all shares offer presented, but was *also* reasonably concerned that the Time stockholders might tender to Paramount in ignorance or based upon a mistaken belief, i.e., yield to substantive coercion."

Relying on that line of reasoning, the *Unitrin* Court determined that the Unitrin board "reasonably perceived risk of substantive coercion, i.e., that Unitrin's shareholders might accept American General's inadequate Offer because of 'ignorance or mistaken belief' regarding the Board's assessment of the long-term value of Unitrin's stock." Thus, perceiving a valid threat under *Unocal*, the Supreme Court then addressed whether the board of Unitrin's response was proportional to the threat.

Having determined that the Unitrin board reasonably perceived the American General offer to be inadequate, and Unitrin's poison pill adoption to be a proportionate response, the Court of Chancery had found that the Unitrin board's decision to authorize its stock repurchase program was disproportionate because it was "unnecessary" to protect the Unitrin stockholders from an inadequate bid since the board already had a pill in place. The Court of Chancery here was sensitive to how the stock buy back would make it extremely unlikely that American General could win a proxy contest. The Supreme Court, however, held that the Court of Chancery had "erred by substituting its judgment, that the Repurchase Program was unnecessary, for that of the board," and that such action, if not coercive or preclusive, could be valid if it fell within a range of reasonableness.

Under the first prong of *Unocal*, defendants bear the burden of showing that the Airgas board, "after a reasonable investigation...determined in good faith, that the [Air Products offer] presented a threat...that warranted a defensive response."

Although the Airgas board meets the threshold of showing good faith and reasonable investigation, the first part of *Unocal* review requires more than that; it requires the board to show that its good faith and reasonable investigation ultimately gave the board "grounds for concluding that a threat to the corporate enterprise existed." In the supplemental evidentiary hearing, Airgas (and its lawyers) attempted to identify numerous threats posed by Air Products' $70 offer: It is coercive. It is opportunistically timed. It presents the stockholders with a "prisoner's dilemma." It undervalues Airgas—it is a "clearly inadequate" price. The merger arbitrageurs who have bought into Airgas need to be "protected from themselves." The arbs are a "threat" to the minority. The list goes on.

The reality is that the Airgas board discussed essentially none of these alleged "threats" in its board meetings, or in its deliberations on whether to accept or reject Air Products' $70 offer, or in its consideration of whether to keep the pill in place. The board did not discuss "coercion" or the idea that Airgas's stockholders would be "coerced" into tendering. The board did not discuss the concept of a "prisoner's dilemma." The board did not discuss Air Products' offer in terms of any "danger" that it posed to the corporate enterprise. In the October trial, Airgas had likewise failed to identify threats other than that Air Products' offer undervalues Airgas. In fact, there has been no specific board discussion since the October trial over whether to keep the poison pill in place (other than Clancey's "protect the pill" line).

Airgas's board members testified that the concepts of coercion, threat, and the decision whether or not to redeem the pill were nonetheless "implicit" in the board's discussions due to their knowledge that a large percentage of Airgas's stock is held by merger arbitrageurs who have short-term interests and would be willing to tender into an inadequate offer. But the only threat that the board discussed—the threat that has been the central issue since the beginning of this case—is the inadequate price of Air Products' offer. Thus, inadequate price, coupled with the fact that a majority of Airgas's stock is held by merger arbitrageurs who might be willing to tender into such an inadequate offer, is the only real "threat" alleged. In fact, Airgas directors have admitted as much. Airgas's CEO van Roden testified:

> Q. [O]ther than the price being inadequate, is there anything else that you deem to be a threat?
>
> A. No.

In the end, it really is "All About Value." Airgas's directors and Airgas's financial advisors concede that the Airgas stockholder base is sophisticated and well-informed, and that they have all the information necessary to decide whether to tender into Air Products' offer.

PILLS, POLICY AND PROFESSORS (AND HYPOTHETICALS)

When the Supreme Court first upheld the use of a rights plan in *Moran*, it emphasized that "[t]he Board does not now have unfettered discretion in refusing to redeem the Rights." And in the most recent "pill case" decided just this past year, the Supreme Court reiterated its view that, "[a]s we held in *Moran*, the adoption of a Rights Plan is not absolute."[13] The poison pill's limits, however, still remain to be seen.

---

13. Versata Enters., Inc. v. Selectica, Inc., 5 A.3d 586, 607 (Del.2010) (citing *Moran*, 500 A.2d at 1354). Marty Lipton himself has written that "the pill was neither designed nor intended to be an absolute bar. It was always contemplated that the possibility of a proxy fight to replace the board would result in the board's taking shareholder desires into account, but that the delay and uncertainty as to the outcome of a proxy fight would give the board the negotiating position it needed to achieve the best possible deal for all the shareholders, which in appropriate cases could be the target's continuing as an independent company. . . . A board cannot say 'never,' but it can

The merits of poison pills, the application of the standards of review that should apply to their adoption and continued maintenance, the limitations (if any) that should be imposed on their use, and the "anti-takeover effect" of the combination of classified boards plus poison pills have all been exhaustively written about in legal academia.[14] Two of the largest contributors to the literature are Lucian Bebchuk (who famously takes the "shareholder choice" position that pills should be limited and that classified boards reduce firm value) on one side of the ring, and Marty Lipton (the founder of the poison pill, who continues to zealously defend its use) on the other.[15]

The contours of the debate have morphed slightly over the years, but the fundamental questions have remained. Can a board "just say no"? If so, when? How should the enhanced judicial standard of review be applied? What are the pill's limits? And the ultimate question: Can a board "just say never"? In a 2002 article entitled *Pills, Polls, and Professors Redux*, Lipton wrote the following:

> As the pill approaches its twentieth birthday, it is under attack from [various] groups of professors, each advocating a different form of shareholder poll, but each intended to eviscerate the protections afforded by the pill. . . . Upon reflection, I think it fair to conclude that the [] schools of academic opponents of the pill are not really opposed to the idea that the staggered board of the target of a hostile takeover bid may use the pill to "just say no." Rather, their *fundamental disagreement is with the theoretical possibility that the pill may enable a staggered board to "just say never."* However, as . . . almost every [situation] in

---

say 'no' in order to obtain the best deal for its shareholders." Martin Lipton, *Pills, Polls, and Professors Redux*, 69 U. Chi. L.Rev. 1037, 1054 (2002) (citing Marcel Kahan & Edward Rock, *How I Learned to Stop Worrying and Love the Pill: Adaptive Responses to Takeover Law*, 69 U. Chi. L.Rev. 871, 910 (2002) ("[T]he ultimate effect of the pill is akin to 'just say wait.'")). As it turns out, for companies with a "pill plus staggered board" combination, it might actually be that a target board can "just say wait . . . a very long time," because the Delaware Supreme Court has held that having to wait two years is not preclusive.

14. I will not cite them all here, but a sampling of just the early generation of articles includes: Martin Lipton, *Takeover Bids in the Target's Boardroom*, 35 Bus. Law. 101 (1979); Frank Easterbrook & Daniel Fischel, *Takeover Bids, Defensive Tactics, and Shareholders' Welfare*, 36 Bus. Law. 1733 (1981); Martin Lipton, *Takeover Bids in the Target's Boardroom: An Update After One Year*, 36 Bus. Law. 1017 (1981); Frank Easterbrook & Daniel Fischel, *The Proper Role of a Target's Management in Responding to a Tender Offer*, 94 Harv. L.Rev. 161 (1981); Martin Lipton, *Takeover Bids in the Target's Boardroom: A Response to Professors Easterbrook and Fischel*, 55 N.Y.U. L.Rev. 1231 (1980); Ronald J. Gilson, *A Structural Approach to Corporations: The Case Against Defensive Tactics in Tender Offers*, 33 Stan. L.Rev. 819 (1981); Lucian Arye Bebchuk, *The Case for Facilitating Competing Tender Offers*, 95 Harv. L.Rev. 1028 (1982).

15. In addition, Lipton often continues to argue that the deferential business judgment rule should be the standard of review that applies, despite the fact that that suggestion was squarely rejected in *Moran* and virtually every pill case since, which have consistently applied the *Unocal* analysis to defensive measures taken in response to hostile bids. Accordingly, although it is not the law in Delaware, Lipton's "continued defense of an undiluted application of the business judgment rule to defensive conduct" has been aptly termed "tenacious." Ronald Gilson & Reinier Kraakman, *Delaware's Intermediate Standard for Defensive Tactics: Is There Substance to Proportionality Review?*, 44 Bus. Law. 247, 247 n. 1 (1989).

which a takeover bid was combined with a proxy fight show, the incidence of a target's actually saying "never" is so rare as not to be a real-world problem. While [the various] professors' attempts to undermine the protections of the pill is argued with force and considerable logic, none of their arguments comes close to overcoming the cardinal rule of public policy—particularly applicable to corporate law and corporate finance—"If it ain't broke, don't fix it."

Well, in this case, the Airgas board has continued to say "no" even after one proxy fight. So what Lipton has called the "largely theoretical possibility of continued resistance after loss of a proxy fight" is now a real-world situation.

Conclusion

Vice Chancellor Strine recently suggested that:

> The passage of time has dulled many to the incredibly powerful and novel device that a so-called poison pill is. That device has no other purpose than to give the board issuing the rights the leverage to prevent transactions it does not favor by diluting the buying proponent's interests.[16]

There is no question that poison pills act as potent anti-takeover drugs with the potential to be abused. Counsel for plaintiffs (both Air Products and Shareholder Plaintiffs) make compelling policy arguments in favor of redeeming the pill in this case—to do otherwise, they say, would essentially make all companies with staggered boards and poison pills "takeover proof." The argument is an excellent sound bite, but it is ultimately not the holding of this fact-specific case, although it does bring us one step closer to that result.

As this case demonstrates, in order to have any effectiveness, pills do not— and can not—have a set expiration date. To be clear, though, this case does not endorse "just say never." What it does endorse is Delaware's long-understood respect for reasonably exercised managerial discretion, so long as boards are found to be acting in good faith and in accordance with their fiduciary duties (after rigorous judicial fact-finding and enhanced scrutiny of their defensive actions). The Airgas board serves as a quintessential example.

Directors of a corporation still owe fiduciary duties to *all stockholders*—this undoubtedly includes short-term as well as long-term holders. At the same time, a board cannot be forced into *Revlon* mode any time a hostile bidder makes a tender offer that is at a premium to market value. The mechanisms in place to get around the poison pill—even a poison pill in combination with a staggered board, which no doubt makes the process prohibitively more difficult—have been in place since 1985, when the Delaware Supreme Court first decided to uphold the pill as a legal defense to an unwanted bid. That is the current state of Delaware law until the Supreme Court changes it.

---

16. Hollinger Int'l, Inc. v. Black, 844 A.2d 1022, 1083 (Del.Ch.2004).

For the foregoing reasons, Air Products' and the Shareholder Plaintiffs' requests for relief are denied, and all claims asserted against defendants are dismissed with prejudice. The parties shall bear their own costs.

In 2015, Air Liquide SA, a French company, agreed to pay $10.3 billion ($143 a share in cash) for Airgas Inc. Does that change your opinion of the foregoing decision?

Rights plans may also be used to protect a corporation's tax "assets." As we will discuss later in the course, a company with net operating losses (NOLs) can offset those losses against future income. But if the company experiences a change of control, generally a greater than 50 percent increase in ownership by 5-percent shareholders in any three-year period under Section 382 of the Internal Revenue Code, it could lose the right to use those NOLs. Some companies have adopted rights plans to prevent such a change of control, which is a somewhat different thing than preventing a hostile takeover generally.

Please read pages 38 to 39 of the 2010 10-K regarding the Dynegy shareholders' rights plan, and the Dynegy pill available online, and be prepared to discuss in class. Also review DGCL §109 in the Statutory Supplement at the same time.

7. DYNEGY'S TENDER OFFER

As you may recall, Dynegy was involved in a series of transactions in 2010 and 2011. We focus on one proposed deal, in which certain entities affiliated with Carl Icahn offered to take over Dynegy in a two-step transaction.

The Schedule TO for the tender offer describes the background to the tender offer thusly:

On August 13, 2010, the Company announced that it had entered into the Prior Merger Agreement pursuant to which it would be acquired by an affiliate of The Blackstone Group L.P. (the *"Blackstone Merger"*). On October 12, 2010, Icahn Partners, Icahn Master, Icahn Master II, Icahn Master III and High River (collectively, the *"Icahn Parties"*) filed a Schedule 13D with the SEC (the *"13D"*) disclosing an aggregate beneficial ownership of 12,000,000 Shares. The Icahn Parties stated in the 13D that they acquired the Shares believing them to be undervalued. In the 13D, the Icahn Parties also disclosed their belief that the $4.50 per share consideration agreed to in the Prior Merger Agreement was inadequate and disclosed that they may seek to have conversations with the Company to discuss the Blackstone Merger. On October 19, 2010, senior management of the Company and representatives from Greenhill & Co., LLC (*"Greenhill"*), the Company's financial advisor, met with Carl Icahn and other representatives of the Icahn Parties at the offices of the Icahn Parties. At this meeting, senior management of the Company expressed its support for the Blackstone Merger, explained why the Company's Board of Directors recommended it and indicated that the Icahn Parties should also consider supporting the Blackstone Merger.

On November 12, 2010, the Icahn Parties amended the 13D to disclose that they intended to vote against approval of the proposal to adopt the Prior Merger Agreement and would demand appraisal rights. In addition, and in response to concerns raised by the Company that if the Prior Merger Agreement was not approved, the Company would face potential liquidity issues, on November 12, 2010, Carl Icahn and other representatives of the Icahn Parties contacted Bruce Williamson, the Chairman, President and Chief Executive Officer of the Company, and informed Mr. Williamson that the Icahn Parties would consider offering a replacement credit facility if that would mitigate such liquidity concerns. Mr. Williamson and other members of the Company's management responded that the Company required a long-term solution rather than the solution provided by the replacement facility offered by the Icahn Parties.

On November 23, 2010, the Company announced that the Prior Merger Agreement failed to receive the necessary votes to be adopted, and as a result, the Prior Merger Agreement had been terminated. In addition, on November 23, 2010, the Company announced that it had adopted the Rights Agreement.

On November 30, 2010, Carl Icahn and other representatives of the Icahn Parties met with Mr. Williamson, the Company's Chairman and Chief Executive Officer, and other representatives of the Company, at the offices of the Icahn Parties. At that meeting, the parties discussed the Company's strategic options in light of the termination of the Prior Merger Agreement. The parties discussed entering into a confidentiality agreement that would permit the Icahn Parties to receive certain material non-public information concerning the Company. In the following days, representatives from the Icahn Parties and the Company and their respective advisors exchanged drafts of, but did not execute, a confidentiality agreement that also included a standstill agreement that, among other things, restricted the Icahn Parties' ability to buy or sell the Company's securities.

On December 7, 2010, the Icahn Parties and the Company discussed the possibility of entering into a negotiated merger agreement pursuant to which the Icahn Parties would agree to launch a tender offer, followed by a merger. In the following days, the Icahn Parties, the Company and their representatives negotiated such an agreement as well as the Stockholder Support Agreement and the Guarantee.

On December 15, 2010, the Offeror, Merger Sub and the Company entered into the Merger Agreement, pursuant to which Offeror agreed to launch the Offer, and, after the completion of the Offer and the satisfaction or waiver of all of the conditions applicable to the Merger, Merger Sub would be merged with and into the Company, and the Company would survive the Merger as a wholly-owned subsidiary of Offeror and an indirect wholly-owned subsidiary of IEH. In certain circumstances, the parties have agreed to consummate the Merger, without the prior completion of the Offer, after receipt of the vote of the holders of a majority of the issued and outstanding shares of Common Stock on a record date yet to be selected in favor of the adoption of the Merger Agreement. In that case, the consummation of the Merger would be subject to conditions similar to the conditions to the Offer, other than the addition of a condition that the holders of a majority of the issued and outstanding shares of Common Stock have adopted the Merger Agreement and the inapplicability of the Minimum Condition. Also on December 15 and simultaneously with the execution of the Merger Agreement, the Support Parties and the Company entered into a Stockholder Support Agreement, and IEH entered into the Guarantee in favor of the Company. Pursuant to the Stockholder Support Agreement, the Support Parties agreed, subject to the terms and conditions of such agreement, to, among other things, vote shares of Common Stock (and shares of Common Stock underlying call options to the extent exercised), constituting up to approximately 14.92% of the issued and outstanding shares of Common Stock entitled to vote thereon, in favor of the adoption of the Merger Agreement, if necessary. Pursuant to the Guarantee, IEH is guaranteeing the payment and other obligations of the Offeror and Merger Sub under the Merger Agreement and in connection with the Offer (other than certain obligations related to indemnification of directors and officers of the Company).

On December 16, 2010, Dynegy and Icahn Enterprises L.P. issued the following press release:

FOR IMMEDIATE RELEASE
DYNEGY ENTERS INTO AGREEMENT TO BE ACQUIRED BY
ICAHN ENTERPRISES LP FOR $5.50 PER SHARE IN CASH
OPEN STRATEGIC ALTERNATIVES PROCESS TO CONTINUE IN ORDER
TO SOLICIT SUPERIOR ALTERNATIVE PROPOSALS

HOUSTON, DECEMBER 15, 2010—Dynegy Inc. (NYSE: DYN) today announced that its Board of Directors has unanimously approved a definitive agreement to be acquired by Icahn Enterprises LP (NYSE: IEP) in a tender offer followed by a merger for $5.50 per share in cash, or approximately $665 million in the aggregate. Dynegy has approximately $3.95 billion of outstanding debt, net of cash.

Under the terms of the agreement, Dynegy stockholders will receive $5.50 in cash for each outstanding share of Dynegy common stock they own, which is $0.50 per share or 10% higher than the previous offer and represents a 10% premium to Dynegy's average closing stock price over the last 30 trading days. In connection with today's announcement, it is expected that a wholly-owned subsidiary of IEP will commence a tender offer for all of the outstanding shares of Dynegy that they do not already own no later than December 22, 2010. IEP and its affiliates own approximately 9.9% of Dynegy's outstanding shares and have previously acquired options to purchase approximately 5% of Dynegy's outstanding shares. IEP has also agreed that, in certain circumstances, if a "superior" all cash offer is made and supported by Dynegy, and IEP does not wish to top the "superior" offer, it will support it.

The tender offer ultimately failed. The following information, from the 2010 10-K, regarding Dynegy's shares may provide some insight into the failure of the tender offer:

COMMON SHARE DATA*

	2010	2009	2008
Earnings (loss) per diluted common share attributable to Dynegy Inc	$ (1.95)	$ (7.60)	$ 1.04
Annual cash dividend per common share**	–	–	–
Market price at year end	5.62	9.05	10.00
Average common shares outstanding (in millions)			
Diluted	121	165	168
Basic	120	164	168

Of course, by Fall 2012 the Dynegy shares were trading at 2.5 cents per share. Does this suggest anything about the common assumption that shareholders behave rationally? Dynegy's largest shareholder after the Icahn entities was Seneca Capital, which argued that the Icahn offer undervalued Dynegy.[17]

Review Article I of the Dynegy Merger Agreement, available online, and be prepared to discuss it in class. What role does the tender offer play in this transaction? Why does the Article limit the buyer's ability to waive the conditions attached to the tender offer? What are the conditions to the offer?

---

17. http://goo.gl/BsQQS.

23

MERGERS

You might have covered the essentials of mergers in your Corporations or Business Associations class. The basic idea is that two corporations combine, and the target shareholders either become shareholders in the new, combined corporation or they are "cashed-out," which amounts to a forced sale of their shares. Consideration paid to the target shareholders can also consist of a mixture of cash, stock, and even debt.

The seminal duty of care case in the merger context is *Smith v. Van Gorkom*, 488 A.2d 858 (Del. 1985). In *Van Gorkom*, the Delaware Supreme Court held that directors can be personally liable for the difference between the consideration actually paid and a judicially determined "fair price" when the company agrees to a transaction without appropriate board consideration of whether it was in the best interests of shareholders.

The facts of *Van Gorkom* are rather extreme: The court found that the directors approved a deal after thinking about it for two hours, without prior notice, and with only a sketch of the proposed transaction available. And since the case, Delaware has enacted section 102(b)(7), which greatly limits duty of care claims.

Under the *Revlon* doctrine, the board of a company selling itself is obligated to seek the best value reasonably available for shareholders. But in 2009 the Delaware Supreme Court explained that "[n]o court can tell directors exactly how to accomplish that goal [of getting the best price in a sale], because they will be facing a unique combination of circumstances, many of which will be outside their control."[1]

Although management cannot entrench itself in a job for life, the Delaware court has also made it clear that it does not adhere to a strong form of the ECMH, explaining that "it is not a breach of faith for directors to determine that the present stock market price of shares is not representative of true value."[2]

---

1. Lyondell Chemical Corp. v. Ryan, 970 A.2d 235, 242 (Del. 2009). *See* William W. Bratton, *Lyondell: A Note of Approbation*, 55 N.Y.L. Sch. L. Rev. 561, 572 (2011).

2. Paramount Communications, Inc. v. Time Inc., 571 A.2d 1140, 1150 n.12 (Del. 1989).

The board is entitled to select the transaction that they believe provides shareholders the best long-term prospects with the least amount of downside risk; the directors thus have substantial discretion. In its *Time* decision, the Delaware Supreme Court held that the directors' statutory mandate "includes a conferred authority to set a corporate course of action, including time frame, designed to enhance corporate profitability."[3]

Whereas your prior class mostly focused on the duties of the board, in this chapter we focus on the negotiation of the deal itself. Of course, part of that negotiation must involve the board exercising its duties.

1.   MERGER AGREEMENTS

Business combinations are typically achieved by use of either a merger or stock purchase agreement. Stock purchase agreements are used when the target company's shares are concentrated among a few holders, which most often happens with smaller firms. Otherwise deals will typically be done by a merger agreement, which must be approved by the shareholders after the board consents to the deal.[4]

To paraphrase *Casablanca*,[5] a merger agreement is just like any other contract, only more so.[6]

One key thing to understand is that any corporate transaction is like buying a house. The contract is signed, but the actual exchange of assets for consideration does not happen until some later point called the "closing." Thus, the contract must not only set forth the terms of the underlying deal, but also account for the possible changes that might occur during the interregnum.

Moreover, during the interim period the parties will have a chance to investigate each other—much like you might have a house inspected before the closing—and regulators might have an ability to review the deal, depending on the size of the deal and particular industries involved.

The contract has to provide a mechanism for dealing with information learned during this process. For example, if the buyer learns that the target has some previously unknown problem, the buyer will want the right to renegotiate the price or even terminate the deal. If a regulator refuses to approve, or imposes conditions, what happens?

Moreover, the parties must agree on how the parties' confidential information will be treated before it is shared. Typically this is done by a separate contract ingeniously called a "confidentiality agreement."

In addition to the obligation to maintain information in confidence, the confidentiality agreement will limit the uses of the information. This provides

---

3. 571 A.2d at 1150.

4. Del. Gen. Corp. Law §251(c).

5. http://goo.gl/kODiO.

6. Claire A. Hill, *Bargaining in the Shadow of the Lawsuit: A Social Norms Theory of Incomplete Contracts*, 34 Del. J. Corp. L. 191, 203 (2009).

protection against the recipient using confidential information to facilitate a hostile bid in the event discussions fall apart.

In addition to confidentiality provisions, confidentiality agreements sometimes contain provisions limiting the right of the buyer to try to hire away employees of the target that buyer representatives meet or become aware of during the diligence process. Also, confidentiality agreements sometimes contain standstill provisions, which limit the potential buyer's ability to acquire or control the target or any substantial portion of the target for some period of time, outside of the confines of a friendly transaction.

It is in the confidentiality agreement that you will often find the standstill provisions we discussed in the prior chapter.

A. Market Risk

The delay between signing and closing, combined with the frequent use of stock as consideration in mergers, means that a deal is subject to pricing risks over the period between announcement and closing.

For example, a drop in the price of an acquirer's stock between execution of the acquisition agreement and the closing of the transaction results in the seller's shareholders receiving less for their shares. This market risk can be dealt with by a pricing structure that uses a valuation formula instead of a fixed exchange ratio.

But that itself can have risks. For example, several years ago a company called Cendant signed a deal to acquire a target in which each target share would be converted into Cendant common stock. But then Cendant's share price declined tremendously. At the new price, Cendant would have had to issue about four times as many shares as it had anticipated, massively diluting its existing shareholders. Rather than proceed under these circumstances, Cendant paid $400 million to get out of the deal.[7]

This kind of risk is somewhat addressed with a collar, which provides for adjustment of the stock consideration within a specified range. A collar protects the acquirer by placing an upper limit on the amount of stock it will be required to issue in the event of a decline in the price of its stock between signing and closing, and it protects the target shareholders by providing a floor on their compensation under the deal. Once the share price is outside the collar range, no further adjustments are made, and the exchange ratio becomes fixed at its upper or lower limit.

Some transactions also include so-called "walk-away" provisions permitting unilateral termination by the seller-target in the event the acquirer's share price falls below a certain level, set either on an absolute basis or by reference to some index.

---

7. http://goo.gl/u27xl.

Cash consideration, of course, faces no such risk, at least if the buyer and seller are within the same jurisdiction. Buyers operating in different currencies face exchange rate risk.[8]

B.   Covenants, Reps, and Warranties

Representations and warranties appear in many types of agreements, including acquisition, loan, and venture investment agreements and loan agreements and bond indentures, which we have already discussed.

A representation is simply a statement of fact. For example, "The target is properly incorporated in Delaware."

A warranty is a promise of indemnity if a statement of fact is false. The distinction between this and a representation is discussed in the following case.

CBS INC. v. ZIFF-DAVIS PUBLISHING CO.

75 N.Y.2d 496, 553 N.E.2d 997, 554 N.Y.S.2d 449
Court of Appeals of New York.
April 3, 1990.

HANCOCK, Jr., J.

A corporate buyer made a bid to purchase certain businesses based on financial information as to their profitability supplied by the seller. The bid was accepted and the parties entered into a binding bilateral contract for the sale which included, specifically, the seller's express warranties as to the truthfulness of the previously supplied financial information. Thereafter, pursuant to the purchase agreement, the buyer conducted its own investigation which led it to believe that the warranted information was untrue. The seller dismissed as meritless the buyer's expressions of disbelief in the validity of the financial information and insisted that the sale go through as agreed. The closing took place with the mutual understanding that it would not in any way affect the previously asserted position of either party. Did the buyer's manifested lack of belief in and reliance on the truth of the warranted information prior to the closing relieve the seller of its obligations under the warranties? This is the central question presented in the breach of express warranty claim brought by CBS Inc. (CBS) against Ziff-Davis Publishing Co. (Ziff-Davis). The courts below concluded that CBS's lack of reliance on the warranted information was fatal to its breach of warranty claim and, accordingly, dismissed that cause of action on motion under CPLR 3211 (a) (7). We granted leave to appeal and, for reasons stated hereinafter, disagree with this conclusion and hold that the warranty claim should be reinstated.

---

8. The currency swaps you covered in Chapter 18 might have a role to play here.

I

The essential facts pleaded—assumed to be true for the purpose of the dismissal motion—are these. In September 1984, Goldman Sachs & Co., acting as Ziff-Davis's investment banker and agent, solicited bids for the sale of the assets and businesses of 12 consumer magazines and 12 business publications. The offering circular, prepared by Goldman Sachs and Ziff-Davis, described Ziff-Davis's financial condition and included operating income statements for the fiscal year ending July 31, 1984 prepared by Ziff-Davis's accountant, Touche Ross & Co. Based on Ziff-Davis's representations in the offering circular, CBS, on November 9, 1984 submitted a bid limited to the purchase of the 12 consumer magazines in the amount of $362,500,000. This was the highest bid.

On November 19, 1984 CBS and Ziff-Davis entered into a binding bilateral purchase agreement for the sale of the consumer magazine businesses for the price of $362,500,000. Under section 3.5 of the purchase agreement, Ziff-Davis warranted that the audited income and expense report of the businesses for the 1984 fiscal year, which had been previously provided to CBS in the offering circular, had "been prepared in accordance with generally accepted accounting principles" (GAAP) and that the report "present[ed] fairly the items set forth." Ziff-Davis agreed to furnish an interim income and expense report (Stub Report) of the businesses covering the period after the end of the 1984 fiscal year, and it warranted under section 3.6 that from July 31, 1984 until the closing, there had "not been any material adverse change in Seller's business of publishing and distributing the Publications, taken as a whole." Section 6.1(a) provided that "all representations and warranties of Seller to Buyer shall be true and correct as of the time of the closing," and in section 8.1, the parties agreed that all "representations and warranties ... shall survive the closing, notwithstanding any investigation made by or on behalf of the other party." In section 5.1 Ziff-Davis gave CBS permission to "make such investigation" of the magazine businesses being sold "as [it might] desire" and agreed to give CBS and its accountants reasonable access to the books and records pertaining thereto and to furnish such documents and information as might reasonably be requested.

Thereafter, on January 30, 1985 Ziff-Davis delivered the required Stub Report. In the interim, CBS, acting under section 5.1 of the purchase agreement, had performed its own "due diligence" examination of Ziff-Davis's financial condition. Based on this examination and on reports by its accountant, Coopers & Lybrand, CBS discovered information causing it to believe that Ziff-Davis's certified financial statements and other financial reports were not prepared according to GAAP and did not fairly depict Ziff-Davis's financial condition.

In a January 31, 1985 letter, CBS wrote Ziff-Davis that, "[b]ased on the information and analysis provided [to it, CBS was] of the view that there [were] material misrepresentations in the financial statements provided [to CBS] by Touche Ross & Co., Goldman, Sachs & Co. and Ziff-Davis." In response to this letter, Ziff-Davis advised CBS by letter dated February 4, 1985 that it "believe[d] that all conditions to the closing . . . were fulfilled," that "there [was] no merit to the position taken by CBS in its [Jan. 31, 1985] letter" and that the financial statements were properly prepared and fairly presented Ziff-Davis's financial condition. It also warned CBS that, since all conditions to closing were satisfied, closing was required to be held that day, February 4, 1985, and that, if it "should fail to consummate the transactions as provided . . . Ziff-Davis intend[ed] *to pursue all of its rights and remedies as provided by law.*" (Emphasis added.)

CBS responded to Ziff-Davis's February 4, 1985 letter with its own February 4 letter, which Ziff-Davis accepted and agreed to. In its February 4 letter, CBS acknowledged that "a clear dispute" existed between the parties. It stated that it had decided to proceed with the deal because it had "spent considerable time, effort and money in complying with [its] obligations . . . and recogniz[ed] that [Ziff-Davis had] considerably more information available." Accordingly, the parties agreed "to close [that day] on a mutual understanding that the decision to close, and the closing, [would] not *constitute a waiver of any rights or defenses either of us may have"* (emphasis added) under the purchase agreement. The deal was consummated on February 4.

CBS then brought this action claiming . . . that Ziff-Davis had breached the warranties made as to the magazines' profitability. Based on that breach, CBS alleged that "the price bid and the price paid by CBS were in excess of that which would have been bid and paid by CBS had Ziff-Davis not breached its representation and warranties." Supreme Court granted Ziff-Davis's motion to dismiss the breach of warranty cause of action because CBS alleged "it did not believe that the representations set forth in Paragraphs 3.5 and 3.6 of the contract of sale were true" and thus CBS did not satisfy "the law in New York [which] clearly requires that this reliance be alleged in a breach of warranty action." Supreme Court also dismissed CBS's fourth cause of action relating to an alleged breach of condition. The Appellate Division, First Department, unanimously affirmed for reasons stated by Supreme Court. There should be a modification so as to deny the dismissal motion with respect to the . . . cause of action for breach of warranties.

II

In addressing the central question whether the failure to plead reliance is fatal to CBS's claim for breach of express warranties, it is necessary to examine the exact nature of the missing element of reliance which Ziff-Davis contends is essential. This critical lack of reliance, according to Ziff-Davis, relates to CBS's disbelief in the truth of the warranted financial information which resulted from its investigation *after* the signing of the agreement and *prior to* the date of closing. The reliance in question, it must be emphasized, does not relate to whether CBS relied on the submitted financial information in making its bid or relied on Ziff-Davis's express warranties as to the validity of this information when CBS committed itself to buy the businesses by signing the purchase agreement containing the warranties.

Under Ziff-Davis's theory, the reliance which is a necessary element for a claim of breach of express warranty is essentially that required for a tort action based on fraud or misrepresentation—i.e., a belief in the truth of the representations made in the express warranty and a change of position in reliance on that belief. Thus, because, prior to the closing of the contract on February 4, 1985, CBS demonstrated its lack of belief in the truth of the warranted financial information, it cannot have closed in reliance on it and its breach of warranty claim must fail. This is so, Ziff-Davis maintains, despite its unequivocal rejection of CBS's expressions of its concern that the submitted financial reports contained errors, despite its insistence that the information it had submitted complied with the warranties and that there was "no merit" to CBS's position, and despite its warnings of legal action if CBS did not go ahead with the closing. Ziff-Davis's primary source for the proposition it urges—that a change of position in reliance on the truth of the warranted information is essential for a cause of action for breach of express warranty—is language found in older New York cases such as Crocker-Wheeler Elec. Co. v. Johns-Pratt Co. (29 App Div 300, *affd* 164 NY 593).

CBS, on the other hand, maintains that the decisive question is whether it purchased the express warranties as bargained-for contractual terms that were part of the purchase agreement. It alleges that it did so and that, under these circumstances, the warranty provisions amounted to assurances of the existence of facts upon which CBS relied in committing itself to buy the consumer magazines. Ziff-Davis's assurances of these facts, CBS contends, were the equivalent of promises by Ziff-Davis to indemnify CBS if the assurances proved unfounded. Thus, as continuing promises to indemnify, the express contractual warranties did not lose their operative force when, prior to the closing, CBS formed a belief that the warranted financial information was in error. Indeed, CBS claims that it is precisely because of these warranties that it proceeded with the closing, despite its misgivings.

As authority for its position, CBS cites, *inter alia*, Ainger v. Michigan Gen. Corp. and Judge Learned Hand's definition of warranty as "an assurance by one party to a contract of the existence of a fact upon which the other party may rely. It is intended precisely to relieve the promisee of any duty to ascertain the fact for himself; *it amounts to a promise to indemnify the promisee for any loss if the fact warranted proves untrue, for obviously the promisor cannot control what is already in the past*" (Metropolitan Coal Co. v. Howard, 155 F2d 780, 784 [2d Cir 1946]). (Emphasis added.)

We believe that the analysis of the reliance requirement in actions for breach of express warranties adopted in Ainger v. Michigan Gen. Corp. and urged by CBS here is correct. The critical question is not whether the buyer believed in the truth of the warranted information, as Ziff-Davis would have it, but "whether [it] believed [it] was purchasing the [seller's] promise [as to its truth]." This view of "reliance"—i.e., as requiring no more than reliance on the express warranty as being a part of the bargain between the parties—reflects the prevailing perception of an action for breach of express warranty as one that is no longer grounded in tort, but essentially in contract. The express warranty is as much a part of the contract as any other term. Once the express warranty is shown to have been relied on as part of the contract, the right to be indemnified in damages for its breach does not depend on proof that the buyer thereafter believed that the assurances of fact made in the warranty would be fulfilled. The right to indemnification depends only on establishing that the warranty was breached.

If, as is allegedly the case here, the buyer has purchased the seller's promise as to the existence of the warranted facts, the seller should not be relieved of responsibility because the buyer, after agreeing to make the purchase, forms doubts as to the existence of those facts. Stated otherwise, the fact that the buyer has questioned the seller's ability to perform as promised should not relieve the seller of his obligations under the express warranties when he thereafter undertakes to render the promised performance.

The cases which Ziff-Davis cites as authority for the application of its tort-action type of reliance requirement do not support the proposition it urges. None are similar to the case at bar where the warranties sued on are bargained-for terms in a binding bilateral purchase contract. In most, the basis for the decision was a factor other than the buyer's lack of reliance such as, for example, insufficient proof of the existence of the alleged express warranty or that the warranty sued upon was expressly excluded by terms of the contract or that there was insufficient proof that the express warranty had been breached; and some involve implied rather than express warranties....

Viewed as a contract action involving the claimed breach of certain bargained-for express warranties contained in the purchase agreement, the case may be summarized this way. CBS contracted to buy the consumer magazine businesses in consideration, among other things, of the reciprocal promises made by Ziff-Davis concerning the magazines' profitability. These reciprocal promises included the express warranties that the audited reports for the year ending July 31, 1984 made by Touche Ross had been prepared according to GAAP and that the items contained therein were fairly presented, that there had been no adverse material change in the business after July 31, 1984, and that all representations and warranties would "be true and correct as of the time of the closing" and would "survive the closing, notwithstanding any investigation" by CBS.

Unquestionably, the financial information pertaining to the income and expenses of the consumer magazines was relied on by CBS in forming its opinion as to the value of the businesses and in arriving at the amount of its bid; the warranties pertaining to the validity of this financial information were express terms of the bargain and part of what CBS contracted to purchase. CBS was not merely buying identified consumer magazine businesses. It was buying businesses which it believed to be of a certain value based on information furnished by the seller which the seller warranted to be true. The determinative question is this: should Ziff-Davis be relieved from any contractual obligation under these warranties, as it contends that it should, because, prior to the closing, CBS and its accountants questioned the accuracy of the financial information and because CBS, when it closed, did so without *believing in* or *relying on* the truth of the information?

We see no reason why Ziff-Davis should be absolved from its warranty obligations under these circumstances. A holding that it should because CBS questioned the truth of the facts warranted would have the effect of depriving the express warranties of their only value to CBS—i.e., as continuing promises by Ziff-Davis to indemnify CBS if the facts warranted proved to be untrue (*see,* Metropolitan Coal Co. v. Howard, *supra,* at 784).

Ironically, if Ziff-Davis's position were adopted, it would have succeeded in pressing CBS to close despite CBS's misgivings and, at the same time, would have succeeded in *defeating* CBS's breach of warranties action because CBS harbored these *identical misgivings.*

Judges Simons, Alexander and Titone concur with Judge Hancock, Jr.; Judge Bellacosa dissents in part and votes to affirm in a separate opinion; Chief Judge Wachtler and Judge Kaye taking no part.

One way to shift risk in the representations or warranties is with materiality exceptions or qualifications. Depending on the degree of the qualification, a certain number of breaches will be nonactionable. That effectively means the other party bears the risk and costs with respect to any nonmaterial items. And then there are the covenants.

Some covenants apply from the signing of the agreement until the closing date and provide assurance that the proper actions are taken to facilitate the closing of the transaction and preserve the business pending the closing. For example, some of the covenants require the parties to obtain the necessary approvals from various governmental agencies and other third parties that are required for the consummation of the deal. The space between agreement and closing provides the parties with time to perform these covenants.

Other covenants survive the closing for a certain length of time, such as covenants requiring cooperation of the parties with respect to the post-closing operation of the business or sharing of facilities.

C. Conditions

A merger agreement becomes binding and the closing must happen only if any conditions to closing have been satisfied.[9] As noted earlier, a standard agreement will contain representations, warranties, and covenants (often qualified by materiality standards, as also described earlier).

The agreement will also provide that closing is conditional on the truth of the other party's representations and warranties, as well as either specific closing

---

9. Albert Choi & George Triantis, *Strategic Vagueness in Contract Design: The Case of Corporate Acquisitions,* 119 Yale L.J. 848, 863–864 (2010).

conditions. For example, if the other party made no effort to get a needed regulatory approval, that will breach a covenant and closing will be excused.

There will also be conditions in the form of bright line tests that must be met or a general closing condition tied to the nonoccurrence of a "material adverse change," or "material adverse event," which itself might be subject to various materiality exceptions.

That is a long way of saying that any breach of a covenant, representation, or warranty gives the other side an option to terminate the deal or, more likely, to renegotiate the price. But when such an option is triggered is not always clear, and the parties will typically negotiate a settlement in light of the relevant case law.

IN RE IBP, INC. SHAREHOLDERS LITIGATION

789 A.2d 14
Court of Chancery of Delaware, New Castle County
June 15, 2001.

STRINE, Vice Chancellor.

This post-trial opinion addresses a demand for specific performance of a "Merger Agreement" by IBP, Inc., the nation's number one beef and number two pork distributor. By this action, IBP seeks to compel the "Merger" between itself and Tyson Foods, Inc., the nation's leading chicken distributor, in a transaction in which IBP stockholders will receive their choice of $30 a share in cash or Tyson stock, or a combination of the two.

The IBP-Tyson Merger Agreement resulted from a vigorous auction process that pitted Tyson against the nation's number one pork producer, Smithfield Foods. To say that Tyson was eager to win the auction is to slight its ardent desire to possess IBP. During the bidding process, Tyson was anxious to ensure that it would acquire IBP, and to make sure Smithfield did not. By succeeding, Tyson hoped to create the world's preeminent meat products company—a company that would dominate the meat cases of supermarkets in the United States and eventually throughout the globe.

During the auction process, Tyson was given a great deal of information that suggested that IBP was heading into a trough in the beef business. Even more, Tyson was alerted to serious problems at an IBP subsidiary, DFG, which had been victimized by accounting fraud to the tune of over $30 million in charges to earnings and which was the active subject of an asset impairment study. Not only that, Tyson knew that IBP was projected to fall seriously short of the fiscal year 2000 earnings predicted in projections prepared by IBP's Chief Financial Officer in August, 2000.

By the end of the auction process, Tyson had come to have great doubts about IBP's ability to project its future earnings, the credibility of IBP's management, and thought that the important business unit in which DFG was located—Foodbrands—was broken.

Yet, Tyson's ardor for IBP was such that Tyson raised its bid by a total of $4.00 a share after learning of these problems. Tyson also signed the Merger Agreement, which permitted IBP to recognize unlimited additional liabilities on account of the accounting improprieties at DFG. It did so without demanding any representation that IBP meet its projections for future earnings, or any escrow tied to those projections.

After the Merger Agreement was signed on January 1, 2001, Tyson trumpeted the value of the merger to its stockholders and the financial community, and indicated that it was fully aware of the risks that attended the cyclical nature of IBP's business. In early January, Tyson's stockholders ratified the merger agreement and authorized its management to take whatever action was needed to effectuate it.

During the winter and spring of 2001, Tyson's own business performance was dismal. Meanwhile, IBP was struggling through a poor first quarter. Both companies' problems were due in large measure to a severe winter, which adversely affected livestock supplies and vitality. As these struggles deepened, Tyson's desire to buy IBP weakened.

This cooling of affections first resulted in a slow-down by Tyson in the process of consummating a transaction, a slow-down that was attributed to IBP's on-going efforts to resolve issues that had been raised about its financial statements by the Securities and Exchange Commission ("SEC"). The most important of these issues was how to report the problems at DFG, which Tyson had been aware of at the time it signed the Merger Agreement. Indeed, all the key issues that the SEC raised with IBP were known by Tyson at the time it signed the Merger Agreement. The SEC first raised these issues in a faxed letter on December 29, 2000 to IBP's outside counsel. Neither IBP management nor Tyson learned of the letter until the second week of January, 2001. After learning of the letter, Tyson management put the Merger Agreement to a successful board and stockholder vote.

But the most important reason that Tyson slowed down the Merger process was different: it was having buyer's regret. Tyson wished it had paid less especially in view of its own compromised 2001 performance and IBP's slow 2001 results.

By March, Tyson's founder and controlling stockholder, Don Tyson, no longer wanted to go through with the Merger Agreement. He made the decision to abandon the Merger. His son, John Tyson, Tyson's Chief Executive Officer, and the other Tyson managers followed his instructions. Don Tyson abandoned the Merger because of IBP's and Tyson's poor results in 2001, and not because of DFG or the SEC issues IBP was dealing with. Indeed, Don Tyson told IBP management that he would blow DFG up if he were them.

After the business decision was made to terminate, Tyson's legal team swung into action. They fired off a letter terminating the Agreement at the same time as they filed suit accusing IBP of fraudulently inducing the Merger that Tyson had once so desperately desired.

This expedited litigation ensued, which involved massive amounts of discovery and two weeks of trial.

In this opinion, I address IBP's claim that Tyson had no legal basis to avoid its obligation to consummate the Merger Agreement, as well as Tyson's contrary arguments. The parties' extensive claims are too numerous to summarize adequately, as are the court's rulings.

THE BASIC CONTENTIONS OF THE PARTIES

The parties have each made numerous arguments that bear on the central question of whether Tyson properly terminated the Merger Agreement, which is understandable in view of the high stakes. The plethora of theories and nuanced arguments is somewhat daunting and difficult to summarize. But the fundamental contentions are as follows.

IBP argues that Tyson had no valid reason to terminate the contract on March 29, 2001 and that the Merger Agreement should be specifically enforced. In support of that position, IBP argues that it has not breached any of the contractual representations and warranties. In addition, IBP contends that Tyson improperly terminated the Cash Offer on February 28, 2001 because all closing conditions were met as of that date. In this regard, IBP says that Tyson did not need IBP to formally file its Restated Financials in order for Tyson to proceed with the Cash Offer. As a result, IBP says that §2.01(e) and (h) of the Agreement do not provide Tyson with a contractual safe harbor.

Tyson argues that its decision to terminate was proper for several reasons. First, Tyson contends that IBP breached its contractual representations regarding the Warranted Financials, as evidenced by the Restatements. Second, Tyson contends that the DFG Impairment Charge as well as IBP's disappointing first quarter 2001 performance are evidence of a Material Adverse Effect, which gave Tyson the right to terminate.

Finally, Tyson argues that the Merger Agreement should be rescinded because that Agreement (and related contracts) were fraudulently induced. In this respect, Tyson contends that IBP's failure to disclose the Comment Letter and certain DFG-related documents before January 1, 2001 constitutes ground for rescission. Tyson says that the Agreement should also be rescinded because IBP management made oral statements regarding the Rawhide Projections that they knew to be false, on which Tyson reasonably relied to its detriment. For identical reasons, Tyson says that a letter agreement it signed in connection with the Merger Agreement should also be rescinded, thus entitling Tyson to a refund of a $66 million termination fee it paid to the Rawhide group on behalf of IBP.

The parties have chosen to accompany their basic contentions with a variety of subsidiary theories, all of which derive from the same factual issues.

WAS TYSON'S TERMINATION JUSTIFIED BECAUSE IBP HAS SUFFERED A MATERIAL ADVERSE EFFECT?

Tyson argues that it was . . . permitted to terminate because IBP had breached §5.10 of the Agreement, which is a representation and warranty that IBP had not suffered a material adverse effect since the "Balance Sheet Date" of December 25, 1999, except as set forth in the Warranted Financials or Schedule 5.10 of the Agreement.

Under the contract, a material adverse effect (or "MAE") is defined as "any event, occurrence or development of a state of circumstances or facts which has had or reasonably could be expected to have a Material Adverse Effect" . . . "on the condition (financial or otherwise), business, assets, liabilities or results of operations of [IBP] and [its] Subsidiaries taken as whole. . . ."

Tyson asserts that the decline in IBP's performance in the last quarter of 2000 and the first quarter of 2001 evidences the existence of a Material Adverse Effect. It also contends that the DFG Impairment Charge constitutes a Material Adverse Effect. And taken together, Tyson claims that it is virtually indisputable that the combination of these factors amounts to a Material Adverse Effect.

In addressing these arguments, it is useful to be mindful that Tyson's publicly expressed reasons for terminating the Merger did not include an assertion that IBP had suffered a Material Adverse Effect. The post-hoc nature of Tyson's arguments bear on what it felt the contract meant when contracting, and suggests that a short-term drop in IBP's performance would not be sufficient to cause a MAE. To the extent the facts matter, it is also relevant that Tyson gave no weight to DFG in contracting.

The resolution of Tyson's Material Adverse Effect argument requires the court to engage in an exercise that is quite imprecise. The simplicity of §5.10's words is deceptive, because the application of those words is dauntingly complex. On its face, §5.10 is a capacious clause that puts IBP at risk for a variety of uncontrollable factors that might materially affect its overall business or results of operation as a whole. Although many merger contracts contain specific exclusions from MAE clauses that cover declines in the overall economy or the relevant industry sector, or adverse weather or market conditions, §5.10 is unqualified by such express exclusions.

IBP argues, however, that statements in the Warranted Financials that emphasize the risks IBP faces from swings in livestock supply act as an implicit carve-out, because a Material Adverse Effect under that section cannot include an Effect that is set forth in the Warranted Financials. I agree with Tyson, however, that these disclaimers were far too general to preclude industry-wide or general factors from constituting a Material Adverse Effect. Had IBP wished such an exclusion from the broad language of §5.10, IBP should have bargained for it. At the same time, the notion that §5.10 gave Tyson a right to walk away simply

because of a downturn in cattle supply is equally untenable. Instead, Tyson
would have to show that the event had the required materiality of effect.[10]

The difficulty of addressing that question is considerable, however, because
§5.10 is fraught with temporal ambiguity. By its own terms, it refers to any
Material Adverse Effect that has occurred to IBP since December 25, 1999
unless that Effect is covered by the Warranted Financials or Schedule 5.10.
Moreover, Tyson's right to refuse to close because a Material Adverse Effect has
occurred is also qualified by the other express disclosures in the Schedule, by
virtue of (i) the language of the Annexes that permits Tyson to refuse to close for
breach of a warranty unless that breach results from "actions specifically
permitted" by the Agreement; and (ii) the language of the Agreement that makes
all disclosure schedules apply to Schedule 5.10 where that is the reasonably
apparent intent of the drafters. Taken together, these provisions can be read to
require the court to examine whether a MAE has occurred against the December
25, 1999 condition of IBP as adjusted by the specific disclosures of the
Warranted Financials and the Agreement itself. This approach makes commercial
sense because it establishes a baseline that roughly reflects the status of IBP as
Tyson indisputably knew it at the time of signing the Merger Agreement.

But describing this basic contractual approach is somewhat easier than
applying it. For example, the original IBP 10-K for FY 1999 revealed the
following five-year earnings from operations and earnings per share before
extraordinary items:

	1999	1998	1997	1996	1995
Earnings from Operations	$ 528,473	373,735	226,716	322,908	480,096
(in thousands)					
Net Earnings Per Share	$ 3.39	2.21	1.26	2.10	2.96

The picture that is revealed from this data is of a company that is consistently
profitable, but subject to strong swings in annual EBIT and net earnings. The
averages that emerge from this data are of EBIT of approximately $386 million
per year and net earnings of $2.38 per share. If this average is seen as weighting
the past too much, a three-year average generates EBIT of $376 million and net
earnings of $2.29 per share.

The original Warranted Financials in FY 2000 also emphasize that swings in
IBP's performance were a part of its business reality. For example, the trailing
last twelve month's earnings from operations as of the end of third quarter of FY
2000 were $462 million, as compared to $528 million for full year 1999, as
originally reported. In addition, the third quarter 10-Q showed that IBP's

---

10. *But see* Pittsburgh Coke & Chem. Co. v. Bollo, 421 F.Supp. 908, 930 (E.D.N.Y.1976)
(where Material Adverse Condition ("MAC") clause applied to a company's "financial condition,"
"business," or "operations," court read that clause narrowly to exclude "technological and
economic changes in the aviation industry which undoubtedly affected the business of all who had
dealings with that industry").

earnings from operations for the first 39 weeks of 2000 were lagging earnings from operations for the comparable period in 1999 by $40 million, after adjusting for the CFBA Charges.

The financial statements also indicate that Foodbrands was hardly a stable source of earnings, and was still much smaller in importance than IBP's fresh meat operations. Not only that, FY 2000 Foodbrands performance was lagging 1999, even accounting for the unusual, disclosed items.

The Rawhide Projections add another dimension to the meaning of §5.10. These Projections indicated that IBP would not reach the same level of profitability as originally reported *until FY 2004.* In FY 2001, IBP was expected to have earnings from operations of $446 and net profits of $1.93 a share, down from what was expected in FY 2000. This diminishment in expectations resulted from concern over an anticipated trough in the cattle cycle that would occur during years 2001 to 2003. Moreover, the performance projected for FY 2001 was a drop even from the reduced FY 2000 earnings that Tyson expected as of the time it signed the Merger Agreement.

These negotiating realities bear on the interpretation of §5.10 and suggest that the contractual language must be read in the larger context in which the parties were transacting. To a short-term speculator, the failure of a company to meet analysts' projected earnings for a quarter could be highly material. Such a failure is less important to an acquiror who seeks to purchase the company as part of a long-term strategy. To such an acquiror, the important thing is whether the company has suffered a Material Adverse Effect in its business or results of operations that is consequential to the company's earnings power over a commercially reasonable period, which one would think would be measured in years rather than months. It is odd to think that a strategic buyer would view a short-term blip in earnings as material, so long as the target's earnings-generating potential is not materially affected by that blip or the blip's cause.

In large measure, the resolution of the parties' arguments turns on a difficult policy question. In what direction does the burden of this sort of uncertainty fall: on an acquiror or on the seller? What little New York authority exists is not particularly helpful, and cuts in both directions. One New York case held a buyer to its bargain even when the seller suffered a very severe shock from an extraordinary event, reasoning that the seller realized that it was buying the stock of a sound company that was, however, susceptible to market swings.[11] Another case held that a Material Adverse Effect was evidenced by a short-term drop in sales, but in a commercial context where such a drop was arguably quite

---

11. Bear Stearns Co. v. Jardine Strategic Holdings, No. 31371187, slip. op. (N.Y.Supr. June 17, 1988), *aff'd mem.*, 143 A.D.2d 1073, 533 N.Y.S.2d 167 (1988) (Tender offeror who was to purchase 20% of Bear Stearns could not rely on the MAC clause to avoid contract despite $100 million loss suffered by Bear Stearns on Black Monday, October 19, 19[8]7, and the fact that Bear Stearns suffered a $48 million quarterly loss, its first in history. The buyer knew that Bear Stearns was in a volatile cyclical business.).

critical.[12] The non-New York authorities cited by the parties provide no firmer guidance.

Practical reasons lead me to conclude that a New York court would incline toward the view that a buyer ought to have to make a strong showing to invoke a Material Adverse Effect exception to its obligation to close. Merger contracts are heavily negotiated and cover a large number of specific risks explicitly. As a result, even where a Material Adverse Effect condition is as broadly written as the one in the Merger Agreement, that provision is best read as a backstop protecting the acquiror from the occurrence of unknown events that substantially threaten the overall earnings potential of the target in a durationally-significant manner.[13] A short-term hiccup in earnings should not suffice; rather the Material Adverse Effect should be material when viewed from the longer-term perspective of a reasonable acquiror. In this regard, it is worth noting that IBP never provided Tyson with *quarterly* projections.

When examined from this seller-friendly perspective, the question of whether IBP has suffered a Material Adverse Effect remains a close one. IBP had a very sub-par first quarter. The earnings per share of $.19 it reported exaggerate IBP's success, because part of those earnings were generated from a windfall generated by accounting for its stock option plan, a type of gain that is not likely to recur. On a normalized basis, IBP's first quarter of 2001 earnings from operations ran 64% behind the comparable period in 2000. If IBP had continued to perform on a straight-line basis using its first quarter 2001 performance, it would generate earnings from operations of around $200 million. This sort of annual performance would be consequential to a reasonable acquiror and would deviate materially from the range in which IBP had performed during the recent past.

Tyson says that this impact must also be coupled with the DFG Impairment Charge of $60.4 million. That Charge represents an indication that DFG is likely to generate far less cash flow than IBP had previously anticipated. At the very least, the Charge is worth between $.50 and $.60 cents per IBP share, which is not trivial. It is worth even more, says Tyson, if one realizes that the Rawhide Projections portrayed Foodbrands as the driver of increased profitability in an era of flat fresh meats profits. This deficiency must be considered in view of the overall poor performance of Foodbrands so far in FY 2001. The Rawhide Projections had targeted Foodbrands to earn $137 million in 2001. In a January 30, 2001 presentation to Tyson, Bond had presented an operating plan that hoped to achieve $145 million from Foodbrands. As of the end of the first quarter,

---

12. In Pan Am Corp. v. Delta Air Lines, 175 B.R. 438, 492-493 (S.D.N.Y.1994), Pan Am airlines suffered a sharp decline in bookings over a three-month period that was shocking to its management. The court held that a MAC had occurred. It did so, however, in a context where the party relying on the MAC clause was providing funding in a work-out situation, making any further deterioration of Pan Am's already compromised condition quite important.

13. A contrary rule will encourage the negotiation of extremely detailed "MAC" clauses with numerous carve-outs or qualifiers. An approach that reads broad clauses as addressing fundamental events that would materially affect the value of a target to a reasonable acquiror eliminates the need for drafting of that sort.

Foodbrands had earned only $2 million, and thus needed another $135 million in the succeeding three quarters to reach its Rawhide Projection. IBP's overall trailing last twelve month's earnings had declined from $488 million as of the end of the third quarter of 2000 to $330 million.

As a result of these problems, analysts following IBP issued sharply reduced earnings estimates for FY 2001. Originally, analysts were predicting that IBP would exceed the Rawhide Projections in 2001 by a wide margin. After IBP's poor first quarter, some analysts had reduced their estimate from $2.38 per share to $1.44 a share. *Even accounting for Tyson's attempts to manipulate the analyst community's perception of IBP*, this was a sharp drop.

Tyson contends that the logical inference to be drawn from the record evidence that is available is that IBP will likely have its worst year since 1997, a year which will be well below the company's average performance for all relevant periods. As important, the company's principal driver of growth is performing at markedly diminished levels, thus compromising the company's future results as it enters what is expected to be a tough few years in the fresh meats business.

IBP has several responses to Tyson's evidence. IBP initially notes that Tyson's arguments are unaccompanied by expert evidence that identifies the diminution in IBP's value or earnings potential as a result of its first quarter performance. The absence of such proof is significant. Even after Hankins generated extremely pessimistic projections for IBP in order to justify a lower deal price, Merrill Lynch still concluded that a purchase of IBP at $30 per share was still within the range of fairness and a great long-term value for Tyson. The Merrill Lynch analysis casts great doubt on Tyson's assertion that IBP has suffered a Material Adverse Effect.

IBP also emphasizes the cyclical nature of its businesses. It attributes its poor first quarter to an unexpectedly severe winter. This led ranchers to hold livestock back from market, causing a sharp increase in prices that hurt both the fresh meats business and Foodbrands. Once April was concluded, IBP began to perform more in line with its recent year results, because supplies were increasing and Foodbrands was able to begin to make up its winter margins. Bond testified at trial that he expects IBP to meet or exceed the Rawhide Projection of $1.93 a share in 2001, and the company has publicly indicated that it expects earnings of $1.80 to $2.20 a share. Peterson expressed the same view.

IBP also notes that any cyclical fall is subject to cure by the Agreement's termination date, which was May 15, 2001. By May 15, IBP had two weeks of strong earnings that signaled a strong quarter ahead. Moreover, by that time, cattle that had been held back from market were being sold, leading to plentiful supplies that were expected to last for most of the year.

Not only that, IBP notes that not all analyst reporting services had been as pessimistic as Tyson portrays. In March, Morningstar was reporting a mean analyst prediction of $1.70 per share for IBP in 2001. By May, this had grown to a mean of $1.74 a share. Throughout the same period, Morningstar's consensus prediction was an FY 2002 performance of $2.33 range in March, and $2.38 in

May. Therefore, according to Morningstar, the analyst community was predicting that IBP would return to historically healthy earnings next year, and that earnings for this year would fall short of the Rawhide Projections by less than $.20 per share.

IBP also argues that the Impairment Charge does not approach materiality as a big picture item. That Charge is a one-time, non-cash charge, and IBP has taken large charges of that kind as recently as 1999. While IBP does not deny that its decision to buy DFG turned out disastrously, it reminds me that DFG is but a tiny fraction of IBP's overall business and that a total shut-down of DFG would likely have little effect on the future results of a combined Tyson/IBP. And as a narrow asset issue, the charge is insignificant to IBP as a whole.

I am confessedly torn about the correct outcome. As Tyson points out, IBP has only pointed to two weeks of truly healthy results in 2001 before the contract termination date of May 15. Even these results are suspect, Tyson contends, due to the fact that IBP expected markedly better results for the second week just days before the actual results come out. In view of IBP's demonstrated incapacity to accurately predict near-term results, Tyson says with some justification that I should be hesitant to give much weight to IBP's assurances that it will perform well for the rest of the year.

In the end, however, Tyson has not persuaded me that IBP has suffered a Material Adverse Effect. By its own arguments, Tyson has evinced more confidence in stock market analysts than I personally harbor. But its embrace of the analysts is illustrative of why I conclude that Tyson has not met its burden.

As of May 2001, analysts were predicting that IBP would earn between $1.50 to around $1.74 per share in 2001. The analysts were also predicting that IBP would earn between $2.33 and $2.42 per share in 2002. These members are based on reported "mean" or "consensus" analyst numbers. Even at the low end of this *consensus* range, IBP's earnings for the next two years would not be out of line with its historical performance during troughs in the beef cycle. As recently as years 1996–1998, IBP went through a period with a three year average earnings of $1.85 per share. At the high end of the analysts' consensus range, IBP's results would exceed this figure by $.21 per year.

This predicted range of performance from the source that Tyson vouches for suggests that no Material Adverse Effect has occurred. Rather, the analyst views support the conclusion that IBP remains what the baseline evidence suggests it was—a consistently but erratically profitable company struggling to implement a strategy that will reduce the cyclicality of its earnings. Although IBP may not be performing as well as it and Tyson had hoped, IBP's business appears to be in sound enough shape to deliver results of operations in line with the company's recent historical performance. Tyson's own investment banker still believes IBP is fairly priced at $30 per share. The fact that Foodbrands is not yet delivering on the promise of even better performance for IBP during beef troughs is unavailing to Tyson, since §5.10 focuses on IBP as a whole and IBP's performance as an entire company is in keeping with its baseline condition.

Therefore, I conclude that Tyson has not demonstrated a breach of §5.10. I admit to reaching this conclusion with less than the optimal amount of confidence. The record evidence is not of the type that permits certainty.

IBP IS ENTITLED TO AN AWARD OF SPECIFIC PERFORMANCE

Having determined that the Merger Agreement is a valid and enforceable contract that Tyson had no right to terminate, I now turn to the question of whether the Merger Agreement should be enforced by an order of specific performance. Although Tyson's voluminous post-trial briefs argue the merits fully, its briefs fail to argue that a remedy of specific performance is unwarranted in the event that its position on the merits is rejected.

This gap in the briefing is troubling. A compulsory order will require a merger of two public companies with thousands of employees working at facilities that are important to the communities in which they operate. The impact of a forced merger on constituencies beyond the stockholders and top managers of IBP and Tyson weighs heavily on my mind. The prosperity of IBP and Tyson means a great deal to these constituencies. I therefore approach this remedial issue quite cautiously and mindful of the interests of those who will be affected by my decision.

I start with a fundamental question: is this is a truly unique opportunity that cannot be adequately monetized? If the tables were turned and Tyson was seeking to enforce the contract, a great deal of precedent would indicate that the contract should be specifically enforced. In the more typical situation, an acquiror argues that it cannot be made whole unless it can specifically enforce the acquisition agreement, because the target company is unique and will yield value of an unquantifiable nature, once combined with the acquiring company. In this case, the sell-side of the transaction is able to make the same argument, because the Merger Agreement provides the IBP stockholders with a choice of cash or Tyson stock, or a combination of both. Through this choice, the IBP stockholders were offered a chance to share in the upside of what was touted by Tyson as a unique, synergistic combination. This court has not found, and Tyson has not advanced, any compelling reason why sellers in mergers and acquisitions transactions should have less of a right to demand specific performance than buyers, and none has independently come to my mind.

In addition, the determination of a cash damages award will be very difficult in this case. And the amount of any award could be staggeringly large. No doubt the parties would haggle over huge valuation questions, which (Tyson no doubt would argue) must take into account the possibility of a further auction for IBP or other business developments. A damages award can, of course, be shaped; it simply will lack any pretense to precision. An award of specific performance will, I anticipate, entirely eliminate the need for a speculative determination of damages.

Finally, there is no doubt that a remedy of specific performance is practicable. Tyson itself admits that the combination still makes strategic sense. At trial, John

Tyson was asked by his own counsel to testify about whether it was fair that Tyson should enter any later auction for IBP hampered by its payment of the Rawhide Termination Fee. This testimony indicates that Tyson Foods is still interested in purchasing IBP, but wants to get its original purchase price back and then buy IBP off the day-old goods table. I consider John Tyson's testimony an admission of the feasibility of specific performance.[14]

Probably the concern that weighs heaviest on my mind is whether specific performance is the right remedy in view of the harsh words that have been said in the course of this litigation. Can these management teams work together? The answer is that I do not know. Peterson and Bond say they can. I am not convinced, although Tyson's top executives continue to respect the managerial acumen of Peterson and Bond, if not that of their financial subordinates.

What persuades me that specific performance is a workable remedy is that Tyson will have the power to decide all the key management questions itself. It can therefore hand-pick its own management team. While this may be unpleasant for the top level IBP managers who might be replaced, it was a possible risk of the Merger from the get-go and a reality of today's M & A market.

The impact on other constituencies of this ruling also seems tolerable. Tyson's own investment banker thinks the transaction makes sense for Tyson, and is still fairly priced at $30 per share. One would think the Tyson constituencies would be better served on the whole by a specific performance remedy, rather than a large damages award that did nothing but cost Tyson a large amount of money.

In view of these factors, I am persuaded that an award of specific performance is appropriate, regardless of what level of showing was required by IBP. That is, there is clear and convincing evidence to support this award. Such an award is decisively preferable to a vague and imprecise damages remedy that cannot adequately remedy the injury to IBP's stockholders.

CONCLUSION

For all the foregoing reasons, IBP's claim for specific performance is granted. Tyson's claims for relief are dismissed. The parties shall collaborate and present a conforming partial final order no later than June 27. In addition, the parties shall schedule an office conference with the court to occur later that same week.

Suffice to say, this case looms large in the minds of any potential acquirer who is thinking of invoking the MAC clause.

---

14. It may also be Tyson's preference, if it has to suffer an adverse judgment. Any damages award will be huge and will result in no value to Tyson.

PROBLEM SET 23.1

1. What factors might go into the choice of pricing mechanisms in a merger agreement?
2. Consider the MAC clause from both sides of the deal. What considerations go into the negotiation? Should Tyson have bargained for an easier to implement clause?
3. Later cases have expanded on the holding in *Ziff-Davis*. For example, in Galli v. Metz, 973 F.2d 145 (2d Cir. 1992), the Second Circuit determined that "where a buyer closes on a contract in the full knowledge and acceptance of facts disclosed by the seller which would constitute a breach of warranty under the terms of the contract, the buyer should be foreclosed from later asserting the breach. In that situation, unless that buyer expressly preserves his rights under the warranties (as CBS did in *Ziff-Davis*), we think the buyer has waived the breach." Does this new gloss on *Ziff-Davis* represent a workable rule?

2. DEAL STRUCTURES

Companies that want to merge have a variety of choices. They could pursue the following options:

- A merger of the parent holding companies. This is sometimes called a "classic" merger, perhaps because they are rarely done anymore.
- A forward triangular merger where the target company is merged into a newly formed subsidiary of the acquirer and the merger subsidiary survives.
- A reverse triangular merger of a newly formed subsidiary of the acquirer into the target company where the target company survives as a subsidiary of the acquirer. The formation of a new holding company into which both companies are merged, either directly into the holding company or into separate subsidiaries of the new holding company.

Tax, contract, and liability considerations tend to drive the choice of structure. The tax issues are summarized in the next section.

We discuss liability issues in more detail in connection with financial distress later in the course, but in general, concerns about unknown target liability issues in the deal will push in the direction of using a triangular structure.

The basic rule is that a merger results in the pooling of assets and liabilities.[15] Thus, if one company acquires another, and the target has potential tort liabilities (imagine a products liability case), a merger of the two will make the acquiring company's assets available to pay the target's tort creditors. Putting the target

---

15. Del. Gen. Corp. Law §259(a).

into a newly created subsidiary contains the liability, at least so long as there are no grounds for piercing the corporate veil.

If there are significant liability issues, such as a Superfund site or a massively unfunded pension, the deal might be restructured as an asset sale, where the buyer only takes the "good" assets of the target.[16] The normal rule, subject to some important exceptions discussed in later chapters, is that an asset buyer does not take any liabilities not expressly purchased.

If the lingering liabilities are extreme, a sale in bankruptcy becomes an option.[17] We cover that in yet another forthcoming chapter.[18]

In other instances, the form of the transaction will be driven by one party having certain attributes that the parties wish to maintain, regardless of which party is the nominal "acquirer." For example, a change of control provision in a contract or indenture might tilt the balance in favor of having one entity be the "survivor" of the transaction, even if that entity is immediately renamed to reflect the "true" acquiring company.

MESO SCALE DIAGNOSTICS, LLC v. ROCHE DIAGNOSTICS GMBH

62 A.3d 62
Court of Chancery of Delaware.
Feb. 22, 2013.

PARSONS, Vice Chancellor.

This action is before me on a motion for summary judgment relating to, among other things, license rights to sophisticated diagnostic and assay technology. In 2003, a foreign pharmaceutical and diagnostic holding company lost or was in danger of losing its exclusive license to that technology. The holding company sought to acquire a new license from the then-patent holder. In 2003, the holding company entered into a series of contemporaneously executed agreements that granted it a new non-exclusive license from the patent holder. The plaintiffs, two Delaware limited liability companies with disputed springing rights to the same patented technology, consented to the second nonexclusive license. As part of that transaction, the holding company acquired the patent holder, but not before the intellectual property assets were transferred to a separate company. In 2007, the holding company acquired that separate company through a reverse triangular merger.

In 2010, the plaintiffs filed the complaint in this action asserting that the foreign holding company and a number of their affiliates breached two agreements related to the 2003 transaction. In the first count, the plaintiffs claim that the 2007 reverse triangular merger was an assignment by operation of law that required their consent.

The defendants have moved for summary judgment on multiple grounds.

---

16. Del. Gen. Corp. Law §271. Asset sales are the subject of Chapter 24.
17. 11 U.S.C. §363(f).
18. Chapter 29.

I.   BACKGROUND

A.   THE PARTIES

Plaintiffs Meso Scale Diagnostics, LLC ("MSD") and Meso Scale Technologies, LLC ("MST" and, collectively, "Plaintiffs" or "Meso") are Delaware limited liability companies. MST was founded by Jacob Wohlstadter to commercialize his invention of a new application of electrochemiluminescent ("ECL") technology. In 1995, MST and IGEN International, Inc. ("IGEN") formed MSD as a joint venture. The joint venture was created to research and develop the use of various technologies in diagnostic procedures, including procedures utilizing ECL technology. Jacob Wohlstadter is the President and Chief Executive Officer ("CEO") of MSD and MST.

The defendants in this case are all affiliates or subsidiaries of the F. Hoffmann–La Roche, Ltd. family of pharmaceutical and diagnostics companies. Roche Holding Ltd. ("Roche Holding") is a publicly traded joint stock company organized under the laws of Switzerland. IGEN is a Delaware corporation that was acquired by Roche Holding in 2003 and remains a wholly owned subsidiary of Roche Holding.[6] IGEN LS, LLC ("IGEN LS") is a Delaware limited liability company and wholly owned subsidiary of IGEN.[7] BioVeris Corp. ("BioVeris") is a Delaware corporation and wholly owned subsidiary of Roche Holding.[8] BioVeris owns and licenses a portfolio of patents based on and related to ECL technology.[9] Lili Acquisition Corp. ("Lili Acquisition") was a subsidiary of Roche Holding that was merged into BioVeris on June 26, 2007 and no longer exists.

B.   FACTS

1.   THE 1992 LICENSE

In 1992, IGEN granted Boehring Mannheim GmbH ("BMG"), a company acquired by Roche in 1998, a license (the "1992 License") to use its patented ECL technology. The 1992 License was narrow in scope and only allowed BMG to use the licensed technology in hospitals, blood banks, and clinical reference laboratories. The license explicitly excluded use of the technology in the proximity of a patient, such as home, patient bedside, ambulance, and physician office uses.

2.   THE MSD LICENSE

MSD was formed in 1995 as a joint venture between IGEN and MST, and was intended to be the exclusive vehicle for developing and commercializing the use of various technologies in diagnostic procedures, including procedures utilizing ECL technology. IGEN also "granted to MSD an exclusive, worldwide, royalty-free license [*i.e.,* the "MSD License"] to practice the IGEN Technology to make, use and sell products or processes (A) developed in the course of the

Research Program, or (B) utilizing or related to the Research Technologies." Those technologies included "selection and screening methods," "electrodes," and "multi-array diagnostic[s]." The MSD License has a perpetual term and provides that it will survive a termination of the MSD joint venture for any reason. The MSD License also contains a now-disputed springing right under which, if an exclusive license previously granted to a third party, such as the exclusive rights granted to Roche under the 1992 License, was terminated or IGEN was no longer restricted by such a license from licensing to MSD, the technology automatically would be licensed to MSD. Finally, IGEN agreed, as part of the MSD joint venture agreement (the "Joint Venture Agreement") and for the term of that agreement, that it would not use or allow its technology to be used to compete with MSD with respect to the Research Program.

3.   THE FOURTH CIRCUIT LITIGATION

In 1997, IGEN brought suit against Roche for breach of contract for, among other things, failing to pay royalties, failing to share ECL improvements with IGEN, and selling ECL-based products outside the contractually limited field. While the suit was ongoing, Roche allegedly sought to settle with IGEN by acquiring ownership or access to the ECL rights. In 2001, Roche made a public tender offer to acquire IGEN for $1.5 billion. After conducting due diligence, however, Roche became concerned that acquiring IGEN "would *not* achieve the stated objectives of unencumbered ownership, avoidance of future litigation and discontinuation of business relationships with business entities controlled by the Wohlstadter family." Roche ultimately informed IGEN that it could not pursue an acquisition at that time. During later settlement negotiations in 2002, Roche sought to have MSD and MST "consent to and join in the license granted to Roche as necessary to [e]nsure Roche's non-exclusive use of the ECL Technology in Roche's Field."

While negotiations were still ongoing, the jury returned a special verdict in IGEN's favor finding that Roche had materially breached the 1992 Agreement and awarding compensatory and punitive damages against it. As a result, the United States District Court for the District of Maryland then allowed IGEN to terminate the 1992 License; the United States Court of Appeals for the Fourth Circuit affirmed that decision on July 9, 2003. That same day, IGEN sent Roche a notice purporting to terminate the 1992 License. As a result of the termination of the 1992 License and MSD's springing rights in the MSD License, those rights, according to MSD, were automatically and exclusively licensed to MSD. In other words, Plaintiffs appear to contend that the ECL rights IGEN previously had licensed to Roche were now exclusively licensed to MSD.

4.   THE 2003 TRANSACTION

Roche had expressed concern over the possible termination of the 1992 License in its 10–K for the fiscal year ended March 31, 2003, stating that in the event the 1992 License was terminated, its business would be materially adversely affected. Not surprisingly, therefore, just two weeks after the appellate ruling, Roche sought to reacquire ECL licensing rights so as to preserve its immunoassay business, which relied on ECL technology. Ultimately, Roche agreed to purchase IGEN for $1.25 billion and, along with IGEN, MSD, and MST, entered into a transaction (the "2003 Transaction"), which was memorialized in a number of contemporaneous agreements (the "Transaction Agreements").

IGEN's operating business and intellectual property rights (including IGEN's ECL intellectual property) were spun off to IGEN Integrated Healthcare, LLC, *i.e.* "Newco," which eventually became BioVeris. IGEN LS retained its rights as a licensee under the Roche License.

66 Acquisition Corporation II ("Sub"), a wholly owned subsidiary of Roche Holding, then was merged with and into IGEN.

BioVeris Corporation and became a publicly held and publicly traded company. As a result of the 2003 Transaction, which was signed on July 24, 2003, BioVeris obtained IGEN's intellectual property rights and Roche obtained a limited-field license indirectly through IGEN LS.

[Another] document contained an important provision preventing the assignment of rights of Newco (ultimately, BioVeris) without the prior written consent of the other parties. Specifically, Section 5.08 [of that document] stated:

> Neither this Agreement nor any of the rights, interests or obligations under this Agreement shall be assigned, in whole or in part, *by operation of law or otherwise by any of the parties without the prior written consent of the other parties;* provided, however, that the parties acknowledge and agree that the conversion of Newco in accordance with Section 2.01 of the Restructuring Agreement and the continuation of Newco as a result thereof shall be deemed not to be an assignment and shall not require any consent of any party. Any purported assignment without such consent shall be void. Subject to the preceding sentences, this Agreement will be binding upon, inure to the benefit of, and be enforceable by, the parties and their respective successors and assigns.

5.   ROCHE'S ACQUISITION OF BIOVERIS

After the 2003 Transaction was completed, BioVeris alleged that Roche was selling ECL-based products outside of the Field. Roche asserted that the out-of-field sales were minimal and estimated that it owed a $1.5 million fee to BioVeris under the 65% royalty provided for in Section 2.5(b) of the Roche License. BioVeris, however, estimated that the fee due from Roche for out-of-field sales could exceed $30 million annually. The parties therefore engaged Ernst & Young LLP ("Ernst & Young") as a neutral "field monitor" to calculate out-of-field sales.

According to Roche, Samuel Wohlstadter, the CEO of BioVeris, "repeatedly" proposed to Roche that it buy BioVeris to resolve the dispute over out-of-field sales. Consistent with that suggestion, on July 20, 2006, Samuel Wohlstadter waived the four-year restriction in the Post–Closing Covenants Agreement and permitted Roche to discuss a consensual transaction with BioVeris.

As an independent business, BioVeris was not very profitable. For example, in 2006, BioVeris had only $20.6 million in revenues and incurred a net loss of $27.9 million. Nevertheless, in March 2007, Roche offered to pay approximately $600 million in cash for BioVeris, a 58% premium over its pre-announcement market capitalization of approximately $370 million.

The record shows that Roche's sole objective was to acquire BioVeris's intellectual property rights. Roche internally had valued those intellectual property rights at 1.695 billion Swiss francs, or approximately $1.4 billion. Roche also touted the fact that "[b]y acquiring BioVeris, Roche [would] own the complete patent estate of the [ECL] technology deployed in [Roche's] Elecsys product line which gives Roche Diagnostics the opportunity to fully exploit the entire immunochemistry market."

The acquisition of BioVeris (the "BioVeris Merger") was structured as a reverse triangular merger. Lili Acquisition was formed as an "acquisition subsidiary" of Roche and merged into BioVeris on June 26, 2007, with BioVeris as the surviving corporation. As a result of the merger, "all the properties, right, privileges, powers and franchises of [BioVeris] and [Lili Acquisition] [vested] in [BioVeris], and all claims, obligations, debts, liabilities and duties of [BioVeris] and [Lili Acquisition] [became] the claims, obligations, debts, liabilities and duties of [BioVeris]."

In September 2007, BioVeris notified its customers that it was discontinuing certain product lines and that they would need to develop a plan to transition to another supplier or alternate technology. In September and October 2007, Roche closed down BioVeris's research and development plant and delivered exit dates to each employee of BioVeris. At all times after the BioVeris Merger, however, BioVeris continued to hold the intellectual property relevant to this dispute.

C.   PROCEDURAL HISTORY

On June 22, 2010, Meso commenced this action by filing a complaint (the "Complaint") against Roche charging it with breach of contract as to [two agreements].

On September 2, 2012, Roche moved for summary judgment in this Court on both counts of the Complaint. After extensive briefing, I heard argument on November 5, 2012. A trial on the merits of both counts is scheduled to begin on February 25, 2013. This Opinion constitutes my ruling on Roche's motion for summary judgment.

D.   PARTIES' CONTENTIONS

Roche seeks summary judgment on several independent grounds . . . Roche . . . seeks summary judgment on Count I on the bases that ... as a matter of law, a reverse triangular merger cannot be an assignment by operation of law.

Meso disputes all of Roche's contentions and urges denial of Defendants' motion for summary judgment in its entirety.

II.   ANALYSIS

Roche argues that even if this Court concludes that Section 5.08 applies to the assignment of rights, interests, or obligations relating to BioVeris's intellectual property, Roche still is entitled to summary judgment on Count I because no assignment by operation of law or otherwise occurred when Roche acquired BioVeris through a reverse triangular merger. Specifically, Roche asserts that BioVeris remained intact as the surviving entity of the merger, and, therefore, BioVeris did not assign anything. Meso, on the other hand, contends that mergers generally, including reverse triangular mergers, can result in assignments by operation of law.

At the motion to dismiss stage, I noted that Section 5.08 does not require Meso's consent for changes in ownership, but prohibits, absent consent from MSD and MST, an assignment of BioVeris's rights and interests *by operation of law or otherwise.* I concluded that no Delaware case squarely had addressed whether a reverse triangular merger could ever be viewed as an assignment by operation of law. I further stated that "Plaintiffs plausibly argue that 'by operation of law' was intended to cover mergers that effectively operated like an assignment, even if it might not apply to mergers merely involving changes of control."

To interpret an anti-assignment provision, a court "look[s] to the language of the agreement, read as a whole, in an effort to discern the parties' collective intent." Roche contends that the language "by operation of law or otherwise" makes clear that the parties did not intend Section 5.08 to cover reverse triangular mergers. I find Roche's interpretation of Section 5.08 to be reasonable. Generally, mergers do not result in an assignment by operation of law of assets that began as property of the surviving entity and continued to be such after the merger.

When any merger or consolidation shall have become effective under this chapter, for all purposes of the laws of this State the separate existence of all the constituent corporations, or of all such constituent corporations *except the one into which the other or others of such constituent corporations have been merged,* as the case may be, shall cease and the constituent corporations shall become a new corporation, or be merged into one of such corporations ... the rights, privileges, powers and franchises of each of said corporations, and all property, real, personal and mixed, and all debts due to any of said constituent corporations on whatever account ... *shall be vested in the corporation surviving or resulting from such merger or consolidation;* and all property, rights, privileges, powers and franchises, and all and every other interest shall be thereafter as effectually the property of the surviving or resulting corporation as they were of the several and respective constituent corporations.

In *Koppers Coal & Transport Co. v. United States,* the United States Court of Appeals for the Third Circuit concluded that "the underlying property of the constituent corporations is transferred to the resultant corporation upon the carrying out of the consolidation or merger as provided by Section 59." Other courts in Delaware have held that Section 259(a) results in the transfer of the *non-surviving corporation's* rights and obligations to the surviving corporation by operation of law. For example, in *DeAscanis v. Brosius–Eliason Co.,* the Delaware Supreme Court associated Section 259 with assignments by operation of law. The language in Section 259, "except the one into which the other or others of such constituent corporations have been merged," however, suggests that the surviving corporation would not have effected any assignment. In sum, Section 259(a) supports Roche's position that a reverse triangular merger generally is not an assignment by operation of law or otherwise, and that, therefore, Section 5.08 was not intended to cover reverse triangular mergers.

I also note that Roche's interpretation is consistent with the reasonable expectations of the parties. Pursuant to the widely accepted "objective theory" of contract interpretation—a framework adopted and followed in Delaware—this Court must interpret a contract in a manner that satisfies the "reasonable expectations of the parties at the time they entered into the contract." The vast majority of commentary discussing reverse triangular mergers indicates that a reverse triangular merger does not constitute an assignment by operation of law as to the surviving entity. For example, this Court has recognized that "it is possible that the only practical effect of the [reverse triangular] merger is the conversion of the property interest of the shareholders of the target corporation." Similarly, in *Lewis v. Ward,* then-Vice Chancellor Strine observed:

> In a triangular merger, the acquiror's stockholders generally do not have the right to vote on the merger, nor are they entitled to appraisal. If a reverse triangular structure is used, the rights and obligations of the target are not transferred, assumed or affected. Because of these and other advantages to using a triangular structure, it is the preferred method of acquisition for a wide range of transactions.

Leading commentators also have noted that a reverse triangular merger does not constitute an assignment by operation of law. Based on the commentary on this subject, I consider it unlikely that the parties would have expected a clause covering assignments by operation of law to have applied to reverse triangular mergers.

Meso disagrees and has advanced three theories in support of its interpretation of Section 5.08, *i.e.,* that the anti-assignment clause was intended to cover reverse triangular mergers. Those theories are: (1) the acquisition of BioVeris was nothing more than the assignment of BioVeris's intellectual property rights to Roche; (2) Delaware case law regarding forward triangular mergers compels the conclusion that a provision covering assignment "by operation of law" extends to all mergers; and (3) this Court should embrace a California federal court's holding that a reverse triangular merger results in an assignment by operation of law.

First, Meso contends that "the acquisition of BioVeris was nothing more than the assignment of BioVeris's intellectual property rights to Roche" because, as a result of the acquisition, Roche Diagnostics effectively owned the ECL patents. Meso's argument, however, is unavailing because it ignores Delaware's longstanding doctrine of independent legal significance.

Here, Lili Acquisition was merged into BioVeris, with BioVeris as the surviving entity. Under Section 259, the surviving entity continued to "possess[ ] all the rights, privileges, powers and franchises" it had before the merger plus those of each of the corporations merged into it. Thus, no assignment by operation of law or otherwise occurred as to BioVeris with respect to what it possessed before the merger.

Meso also avers that this Court should look to Delaware's forward triangular merger cases for the propositions (1) that a provision covering assignment "by operation of law" extends to *all* mergers and (2) that this Court should assess whether Meso was adversely harmed in construing the parties' intent. Meso relies primarily on two cases for that proposition: *Star Cellular Telephone Co. v. Baton Rouge CGSA, Inc.* and *Tenneco Automotive Inc. v. El Paso Corp.*

Although both *Star Cellular* and *Tenneco* involved a transfer assignment by operation of law, each of those decisions involved a finding that the non-consenting party had not been adversely harmed and that the parties had not intended to require consent to the challenged transaction. It is important to note, however, that the broad statement in *Tenneco* that an assignment by operation of law commonly would be understood to include a merger, appears to rely on *DeAscanis v. Brosius–Eliason Co.* The *DeAscanis* case focused on Section 259 and mergers in connection with which assignments were made by non-surviving constituent entities. Indeed, *Tenneco* acknowledged that, under Section 259, the corporation that was merged into the second corporation "cease[d] to exist." Thus, both *Tenneco* and *Star Cellular* are distinguishable because they involved forward triangular mergers where the target company was not the surviving entity, whereas in this case BioVeris was the surviving entity in a reverse triangular merger.

In both cases, after reading the agreement as a whole, the Court found the anti-assignment language at issue to be ambiguous. The anti-assignment provisions on their own indicated that consent might be required because there had been assignments as a matter of law. In light of other inconsistencies, however, the Court ultimately determined the agreements to be ambiguous. In this case, on the other hand, there was no assignment by operation of law or otherwise. Furthermore, upon examination of Section 5.08, the Global Consent, and the related Transaction Agreements, there are no comparable inconsistencies that might support an inference that the parties intended to depart from the principle that a reverse triangular merger is not an assignment by operation of law. To the contrary, there was a recognition that Roche might acquire BioVeris.

Meso also contends that the proviso at the end of Section 5.08 made clear "that even mere changes of corporate form would result in prohibited assignments (but for the express exception)," and that, therefore, any merger also would result in a prohibited assignment. The conversion of an LLC to a corporation, however, is distinguishable from a reverse triangular merger in that a conversion results in a change in the corporate form. A reverse triangular merger does not. Even if Meso were correct that the proviso reflected the parties' intent that a change in corporate form would constitute an assignment, that conclusion has no bearing on reverse triangular mergers, which do not result in a change in corporate form. Moreover, the proviso arguably operated as a cautious, "belt and suspenders" reaction to a concern that Meso might attempt to extract hold-up value from the contemplated conversion of Newco into a corporation. For these reasons, I conclude that the proviso to Section 5.08 does not create an ambiguity as to whether the "assignment by operation of law or otherwise" language was intended to cover the reverse triangular merger in this case. Thus, Meso has not shown that its proposed interpretation of Section 5.08, like Roche's, is a reasonable one in the circumstances of this case.

As a final argument, Meso suggests that this Court should embrace the United States District Court for the Northern District of California's holding in SQL Solutions, Inc. v. Oracle Corp. that a reverse triangular merger results in an assignment by operation of law. There the court stated, "an assignment or transfer of rights does occur through a change in the legal form of ownership of a business." The court in *SQL Solutions* applied California law and cited a line of California cases for the proposition that whether "an assignment results merely from a change in the legal form of ownership of a business ... depends upon whether it affects the interests of the parties protected by the nonassignability of the contract."

I decline to adopt the approach outlined in *SQL Solutions,* however, because doing so would conflict with Delaware's jurisprudence surrounding stock acquisitions, among other things. Under Delaware law, stock purchase transactions, by themselves, do not result in an assignment by operation of law. For example, in the *Baxter Pharmaceutical Products* case, this Court stated, "Delaware corporations may lawfully acquire the securities of other corporations, and a purchase or change of ownership of such securities (again, without more) is not regarded as assigning or delegating the contractual rights or duties of the corporation whose securities are purchased." Similarly, in *Branmar Theatre Co. v. Branmar, Inc.,* the Court held that "in the absence of fraud . . . transfer of stock of a corporate lessee is ordinarily not a violation of a clause prohibiting assignment. . . ."

Delaware courts have refused to hold that a mere change in the legal ownership of a business results in an assignment by operation of law. *SQL Solutions,* on the other hand, noted, "California courts have consistently recognized that an assignment or transfer of rights does occur through a change in the legal form of ownership of a business." The *SQL Solutions* case, however, provides no further explanation for its apparent holding that any change in ownership, including a reverse triangular merger, is an assignment by operation of law. Both stock acquisitions and reverse triangular mergers involve changes in legal ownership, and the law should reflect parallel results. In order to avoid upsetting Delaware's well-settled law regarding stock acquisitions, I refuse to adopt the approach espoused in *SQL Solutions.*

In sum, Meso could have negotiated for a "change of control provision." They did not. Instead, they negotiated for a term that prohibits "assignments by operation of law or otherwise." Roche has provided a reasonable interpretation of Section 5.08 that is consistent with the general understanding that a reverse triangular merger is not an assignment by operation of law. On the other hand, I find Meso's arguments as to why language that prohibits "assignments by operation of law or otherwise" should be construed to encompass reverse triangular mergers unpersuasive and its related construction of Section 5.08 to be unreasonable.

For the foregoing reasons, I conclude that Section 5.08 was not intended to cover the BioVeris Merger and that Roche is entitled to summary judgment in its favor as to Count I.

As we noted in Chapter 22, quite often you will see deals done as "two-step" transactions. This involves a tender offer followed by a merger. The tender offer involves the purchase of the target's shares, and if sufficiently successful, can allow the second step to be done by a "short form" merger, which requires no minority shareholder voting,[19] or by a "medium form" merger under the relatively new provisions of section 251(h).

3. TAXES AND MERGERS

The type of consideration paid in the deal can influence the taxation, and thus the form, of the merger.

Two tax issues are at play here: those of the corporations involved in the deal, and those of the shareholders, particularly shareholders of the target. The shareholders often desire a "tax-free" merger. In such a merger, the target shareholders will not have to pay taxes on the consideration they receive in the deal. It is important to note that for a target shareholder, a tax-free merger (or "reorganization" to use the Tax Code term) usually only defers taxation. Upon any subsequent sale of the stock received in the deal, tax will be due.

Whether a "tax-free" merger is good from the corporate perspective often depends on whether we are looking at things from the buyer's or the target's perspective. If the reorganization is tax free, the buyer will inherit the target's basis in its assets. As such, the buyer might pay higher taxes in the future. If the

---

19. Del. Gen. Corp. Law §253.

merger is instead taxable for the target and its shareholders, the acquiring corporation is treated as acquiring all of the target corporation's assets for cash, and the acquisition price will be allocated across the various assets in ascribing a tax basis to each asset acquired.

The buyer and the seller boards might also have interests that override tax considerations. For example, as noted below, it is more difficult to conduct a reverse triangular merger on a tax-free basis. But because a reverse triangular merger avoids the problems that can arise from the termination of the target company's existence—breach of loan agreements, lease agreements, and so forth—deals are often done as reverse triangular mergers nonetheless. More generally, if the buyer company does not want to dilute its existing shareholders, a cash-out merger might be attractive regardless of the tax consequences.

If the parties are seeking tax-free treatment, particularly for target shareholders, a key consideration is the "continuity of interest" requirement. The continuity of interest requirement basically mandates that, to qualify as a tax-free merger, a substantial portion of the consideration received by the target shareholders in exchange for their stock must consist of equity interests in the acquiring company. Thus a stock for stock merger will be tax free, while a pure cash-out merger will not.

If the consideration is at least partially in shares, there may be ways in which the parties can avoid incurring taxes at the time of the deal.

In a forward triangular merger, for example, the transferring shareholders often receive the common stock of the parent corporation from the acquisition subsidiary. An all cash forward triangular merger involves the target corporation being merged into a subsidiary of the acquiring corporation, with the target shareholders receiving cash payment for their shares. Obviously, this merger will not qualify as a tax-free merger, as it is essentially the same as the direct cash-out merger discussed above. But what if they receive a mix of cash and stock?

The fundamental question is at what point does the amount of cash or other non-stock consideration tip the transaction over so that it no longer satisfies the "continuity of interest" rules applicable to all corporate reorganizations. Tax attorneys report that a forward triangular merger where each target shareholder is paid 40 percent in acquirer stock and 60 percent in cash in the merger should qualify as a tax-free merger. Forty percent likely represents the absolute minimum amount of stock that can be used, and others will tell you that at least half of the consideration must be stock.

In a reverse triangular merger, the existence of the target corporation is maintained, and the new subsidiary created by the buying corporation for the transaction is merged into the target corporation. However, to qualify for "gain-recognition postponement," the requirements of Tax Code § 368(a)(2)(E) must be met, which means at least 80 percent of the consideration received by the target shareholders must consist of the buyer parent's *voting* stock (in forward triangular mergers, some nonvoting stock is permissible when meeting the applicable targets). In short, it is more difficult to achieve a reverse triangular merger that is tax free for target shareholders.

All of which is to say that you really should take the Corporate Tax class if you want to practice in this area.

4.   BREAKUP FEES

Once the parties sign a deal, they often want to make sure that the deal happens.[20] This is especially true in friendly deals.

But the board has duties in most states—such as the *Revlon* duties in Delaware—that require the board to consider other offers, particularly when those offers value the company at a higher level than the preferred deal.

Moreover, a deal may fail not because of a competing offer, but because one of the closing contingencies was not met. For example, a regulator may not approve the deal. Or the buyer found out that some representation was breached and then exercised its right to cancel the closing. But in either case, the original buyer by that point has expended some degree of effort in making its offer. Management has considered the deal from the business side, while the buyer's lawyers have spent some time drafting an agreement and probably the many letters that preceded the agreement. In addition to these out-of-pocket expenses, the buyer may have incurred less quantifiable costs resulting from the firm's expending time on the deal that could have been put toward other projects (i.e., opportunity costs).

The target can incur costs, too, and sometimes its choice of offers might be influenced by the risk that a deal will not close and the target will have incurred costs for nothing.[21]

The most common way to address these issues is through breakup fees, with fees paid to the target sometimes termed "reverse" breakup fees.[22]

5.   DYNEGY MERGER AGREEMENT

We return to the Dynegy Merger Agreement. The merger agreement is available on the course webpage, and relates to a merger between Dynegy and entities controlled by Carl Icahn, a well-known investor.[23] The Merger Agreement is attached to an 8-K that explains the deal. That's a good place to start reading.

In addition, take a look at the Dynegy 2010 annual report we looked at in connection with Chapter 1. Pages 2 and 3, F-24, F-72, and F-73 to F-74 are relevant here. Be prepared to discuss the merger agreement in light of the above reading.

---

20. Marcel Kahan & Edward Rock, *How to Prevent Hard Cases from Making Bad Law: Bear Stearns, Delaware, and the Strategic Use of Comity*, 58 Emory L.J. 713, 726 (2009).

21. Steven M. Davidoff, *The Failure of Private Equity*, 82 S. Cal. L. Rev. 481, 518 (2009).

22. Afra Afsharipour, *Transforming the Allocation of Deal Risk Through Reverse Termination Fees*, 63 Vand. L. Rev. 1161, 1224 (2010).

23. http://www.forbes.com/profile/carl-icahn/.

24

ASSET SALES

Another way to sell or acquire a business is through an asset sale. This involves a sale of the target's assets to a buyer, or, more often, a newly formed buyer subsidiary, that pays cash or shares to the target. Typically, the target then dissolves under state corporate law, using the sale consideration to pay off its obligations in a manner consistent with the absolute priority rule. A recent example of such a transaction is shown below. Note that one of the assets being sold is the equity the parent company owns in its subsidiary.

PRESS RELEASE
SWISHER HYGIENE INC. ANNOUNCES AGREEMENT TO SELL ITS
U.S. OPERATIONS TO ECOLAB
TRANSACTION EXPECTED TO CLOSE DURING THE
FOURTH QUARTER
PENDING APPROVAL OF THE COMPANY'S STOCKHOLDERS

CHARLOTTE, N.C., Aug. 13, 2015—Swisher Hygiene Inc. ("Swisher") (NASDAQ:SWSH), a leading service provider of essential hygiene and sanitizing solutions, today announced that the Company agreed to sell the stock of its wholly owned U.S. subsidiary Swisher International, Inc. and other assets relating to Swisher's U.S. operations, which comprise all of Swisher's remaining operating interests, to Ecolab Inc. for $40.0 million in cash, of which $2.0 million is subject to a holdback for working capital adjustments. In the transaction, Swisher will retain certain debt and liabilities as set forth in the Purchase Agreement governing the sale. Completion of the transaction is subject to stockholder approval and other customary conditions.

"We believe the transaction is in the best interest of our stockholders and creates a very positive opportunity for our customers and employees. This transaction provides a broader customer base of business, additional service support, and the resources to expand our business and better service our customers. We believe Swisher International's business model complements Ecolab's existing institutional U.S. operations and will benefit our customers and employees," said William M. Pierce, President and Chief Executive Officer of Swisher.

CONFERENCE CALL

Swisher will host a conference call and live webcast to discuss this announcement as well as its second quarter 2015 results today at 8:30 a.m. Eastern Time.

---

1.   THE ASSET PURCHASE AGREEMENT

Having seen a merger agreement, an asset purchase agreement (APA) will be familiar stuff. But there are important differences. For example, and perhaps most obviously, an APA will also contain transfer provisions that differ from those found in a merger agreement or a stock purchase agreement.

The APA will usually provide for the "Acquired Assets"—capitalized to indicate it's a defined term—to be transferred at the closing. But because the law of asset transfers in the United States is largely dependent on the nature of the underlying assets, the parties need different documents to transfer different sorts of assets. Thus, there will be the following:

- A bill of sale covering all the tangible personal property.
- Deeds conveying each piece of real property.
- Assignments of lease rights.
- Assignments of other contractual rights.
- Assignments of intellectual property rights.

The APA will also likely provide for the "Assumed Liabilities" to be transferred at the closing.

Recall that only liabilities that are among the Assumed Liabilities transfer over to the buyer, unless one of the exceptions described in Section 3 below applies. In all other cases, the creditor's rights remain against the seller corporation and the consideration the seller has just received.

As a result, the indemnification section of an APA will differ from that of a merger agreement or SPA. In addition to indemnifying buyer for breaches of representations and covenants, the target shareholders will typically indemnify the buyer for all excluded liabilities. What considerations go into negotiating the scope of this provision?

Review the following section from an APA and be ready to discuss the details of this deal in class.

PURCHASE AGREEMENT

This Purchase Agreement, dated as of August 12, 2015 (this "Agreement"), is by and between ECOLAB INC., a Delaware corporation ("Buyer"), and SWISHER HYGIENE INC., a Delaware corporation ("Seller"). Buyer and Seller are sometimes individually referred to in this Agreement as a "Party" and collectively as the "[Parties]." Capitalized terms not otherwise defined herein have the meanings set forth in Section 1.1.

WHEREAS, Seller and certain of its Affiliates are engaged in the Business;

WHEREAS, in connection with the Business, Seller and certain of its Affiliates own the Purchased Assets, which includes one hundred percent (100%) of the issued and outstanding equity interests (the "Purchased Company Equity Interests") of Swisher International, Inc., a Nevada corporation (the "Purchased Company");

WHEREAS, on the terms and subject to the conditions set forth herein, Seller shall (and shall cause any of its applicable Affiliates to) sell, assign, transfer and convey to Buyer or Affiliates of Buyer, and Buyer shall (and shall cause any of its applicable Affiliates to) purchase and acquire from Seller (or its applicable Affiliates), all of their right, title and interest in and to the Purchased Assets (the "Transaction"); and

WHEREAS, as an inducement and condition to Buyer entering into this Agreement, each Person set forth on Exhibit A-1 attached hereto is entering into a support agreement, in the form set forth in Exhibit A-2 attached hereto, pursuant to which, among other things, such Persons shall agree to approve and vote in favor of the Transaction and this Agreement (the "Support Agreement").

NOW, THEREFORE, in consideration of the representations, warranties, covenants and agreements contained in this Agreement, and for other good and valuable consideration, the receipt and sufficiency of which are hereby acknowledged, on the terms and subject to the conditions of this Agreement, the Parties hereby agree as follows:

ARTICLE I

DEFINITIONS

Section 1.1 Definitions.   As used herein, the following terms have the meanings set forth below:

"Assumed Liabilities" has the meaning set forth in Section 2.6.

"Base Purchase Price" means an aggregate of Forty Million Dollars ($40,000,000) in cash.

"Business" means the chemical service, wholesale and hygiene businesses as conducted by Seller and certain of its Affiliates, in each case outside of Canada, as of the Closing Date, which includes the sale, licensing, manufacturing and marketing of cleaning and sanitizing chemicals, hygiene programs and related products and services, including customer and supplier relationships.

"Excluded Assets" has the meaning set forth in Section 2.5.

"Material Adverse Effect" means (A) any fact, circumstance, event, violation, development, change or effect that, individually or in the aggregate with all such other facts, circumstances, events, developments, changes or effects is, or would be reasonably expected to be, materially adverse to the business, condition, results of operations, assets or Liabilities (excluding, Retained Liabilities) of the Purchased Assets or the Business (taken as a whole); provided, however, that no such fact, circumstance, event, violation, development, change or effect resulting or arising from or in connection with any of the following matters shall be deemed by itself or by themselves, either alone or in combination, to constitute or contribute to a Material Adverse Effect: (a) the general conditions in the industries in which the Business operates; (b) general financial or capital or credit market conditions or trends (including interest rates); (c) changes in global or national political conditions or trends; (d) any act of civil unrest, war or terrorism (including by cyberattack or otherwise), including an outbreak or escalation of hostilities involving the United States or any other country or the declaration by the United States or any other country of a national emergency or war; (e) changes or proposed changes in GAAP; (f) the announcement of this Agreement or the transactions contemplated thereby; (g) actions or omissions of the Seller taken with the consent of Buyer in furtherance of the Transaction or actions of the Seller in accordance with this Agreement, including borrowing money or incurrence of Liens in accordance with the terms hereof; (h) the failure by the Seller to take any action that is prohibited by this Agreement, or (i) without limiting clause (B) below, any failure of the Business to meet any projections, forecasts, guidance, estimates, milestones, budgets or financial or operating predictions of revenue, earnings, cash flow or cash position; provided that any adverse facts, circumstances, events, violations, developments, effects or changes resulting from the matters described in clauses (a), (b), (c), (d) and (e) may be taken into account in determining whether there has been a Material Adverse Effect to the extent that they have a disproportionate effect on the Purchased Assets or the Business in the aggregate relative to similarly situated businesses in the industries in which the Business operates or (B) if aggregate revenue of the Business during the three (3) month period ending on the last day of the month preceding the last full month prior to the Closing Date is less than fifty percent (50%) of aggregate revenue of the Business during the three (3) month period ending on December 31, 2014; provided, however, that aggregate revenue shall be calculated in a manner consistent with the accounting principles used in the preparation of the Seller Financial Statements, and shall include any revenue received by Buyer or its Affiliates after the public announcement of the Transaction and prior to Closing from customers of Seller or its Subsidiaries who became customers of the Buyer or its Affiliates after the public announcement of the Transaction and prior to Closing. For example, with respect to clause (B) above, if revenue of the operations solely with respect to the Business (excluding revenues of the Seller from segments other than the Business) were $14,000,000 for the three (3) month period ending on December 31, 2014; and the Closing Date is scheduled to occur on November 2, 2015; if revenue of the Business for the three (3) months ending on September 30, 2015 were to equal or exceed $7,000,000, no Material Adverse Effect shall have occurred.

"Purchase Price" has the meaning set forth in Section 2.2.

"Purchased Assets" has the meaning set forth in Section 2.4.

"Purchased Company" has the meaning set forth in the Recitals.

"Retained Liabilities" has the meaning set forth in Section 2.7.

"Retained Personnel" has the meaning set forth in Section 5.14(a).

"Target Minimum Working Capital" means $9,500,000.

ARTICLE II

PURCHASE AND SALE; CLOSING

Section 2.1 Purchase and Sale. Subject to the terms and conditions of this Agreement, at the Closing, (a) Seller shall, and shall cause each of its Subsidiaries to, sell, assign, transfer and deliver to Buyer, and Buyer shall purchase and acquire from Seller or such Subsidiaries of Seller, all of Seller's or such Subsidiaries' right, title and interest in and to the Purchased Assets, as further described in Section 2.4, and (b) Buyer will assume the Assumed Liabilities, as further described in Section 2.6.

Section 2.2 Purchase Price. In consideration for the Purchased Assets and the other obligations of Seller pursuant to this Agreement, at the Closing, Buyer shall, on behalf of itself and/or its Affiliates, (a) pay to Seller the Closing Purchase Price and make the other payments payable in accordance with Section 2.8, and (b) assume the Assumed Liabilities. The Closing Purchase Price may be further adjusted in accordance with Section 2.9 (as so adjusted, the "Purchase Price").

Section 2.3 Closing Date. The closing of the Transaction (the "Closing") shall take place at 10:00 a.m. St. Paul time, at the offices of Skadden, Arps, Slate, Meagher & Flom LLP, 155 North Wacker Drive, Chicago, Illinois 60606, on the first Business Day of the month following the date on which the last of the conditions set forth in Article VII (other than those conditions that are to be satisfied by action taken at the Closing, but subject to the satisfaction or waiver of such conditions at the Closing) have been satisfied (or, to the extent permitted, waived by the parties entitled to the benefits thereof) or at such other place, time and date as may be agreed between Seller and Buyer. The date on which the Closing occurs is referred to in this Agreement as the "Closing Date." Unless the parties otherwise agree in writing, the Closing shall be deemed at 12:01 a.m. local time in each applicable jurisdiction on the Closing Date.

Section 2.4 Purchased Assets. Subject to the terms and conditions of this Agreement, on the Closing Date and at the Closing, Seller shall, and shall cause each of its Subsidiaries to, sell, assign, transfer and convey to Buyer or Affiliates of Buyer, and Buyer shall, and shall cause any of its applicable Affiliates to, purchase, acquire and accept from the Seller or such Subsidiaries of Seller, all of Seller's or such Subsidiaries' right, title and interest as of the Closing in and to (a) the Purchased Company Equity Interests, free and clear of all Liens, other than Liens which will be released simultaneously with the Closing, (b) any and all of the assets, rights and properties of every kind and description, whether tangible or intangible or real, personal or mixed primarily used in or held for use in the operation of the Business (other than the Excluded Assets), free and clear of all Liens other than Permitted Liens, and (c) any of the assets set forth on Section 2.4 of the Seller Disclosure Schedule, free and clear of all Liens other than Permitted Liens (collectively the assets specified in clauses (a), (b) and (c), the "Purchased Assets").

Section 2.5 Excluded Assets. Notwithstanding anything to the contrary contained herein, Buyer expressly understands and agrees that the following assets and properties of Seller (the "Excluded Assets") shall be retained by Seller and its Affiliates (other than the Purchased Company and its Subsidiaries), and shall be excluded from the Purchased Assets, notwithstanding any other provision of this Agreement:

(a) Any and all loans and advances, if any, by Seller to any of their Affiliates or otherwise to the Business;

(b) Any and all Contracts set forth on Section 2.5(b) of the Disclosure Schedule;

(c) Any and all assets and rights primarily used or held for use in Seller's or its Affiliates' operation of the Canada Business prior to its sale (excluding any and all intellectual property licensed pursuant to that certain Formula License Agreement, dated as of August 4, 2015, by and between Seller and 7324375 Canada, Inc., and all rights under such license);

(d) Tax Returns and other books and records related to Taxes paid or payable by Seller or any of its Affiliates (other than any such returns and other books and records of the Purchased Company and its Subsidiaries and other than any such returns related to the Purchased Assets);

(e) Any refunds or credits of or against any Seller Taxes;

(f) Any and all Cash Amounts (other than any Cash Amounts of the Purchased Company and its Subsidiaries as of immediately prior to the Closing);

(g) The insurance policies set forth on Section 2.5(g) of the Seller Disclosure Schedules;

(h) All rights exclusively related to matters which are Retained Liabilities;

(i) Any equity interest in any Subsidiary of Seller other than the Purchased Company and the Subsidiaries of the Purchased Company;

(j) Any and all Privileged Communications;

(k) Any marketable or non-marketable securities to the extent any such securities are not otherwise included in Cash Amounts; and

(l) Any receivables of any kind or nature from any Affiliate or Related Person.

Section 2.6 <u>Assumed Liabilities</u>. Subject to the terms of this Agreement (including but not limited to Section 9.2(iv)), the Buyer hereby agrees to assume (or cause its applicable designated Affiliates, which shall include the Purchased Company or its Subsidiaries following the Closing, to assume or perform) and agrees to discharge and perform when due (or cause its applicable designated Affiliates to discharge and perform) (a) any and all Liabilities of Seller or any Subsidiary of Seller, which are related to the Business, properly reflected as Current Liabilities in the Closing Working Capital on the Post-Closing Statement as determined pursuant to Section 2.9 and not otherwise Liabilities Transferring by Operation of Law (defined below) and (b) those Liabilities identified on Section 2.6 of the Seller Disclosure Schedules (collectively, the "<u>Assumed Liabilities</u>"), and no others. For the avoidance of doubt, Buyer acknowledges and agrees that, subject to Section 9.2(iv), any Liability of the Purchased Company or a Subsidiary of the Purchased Company prior to the Closing shall continue to be a Liability of the Purchased Company or such Subsidiary of the Purchased Company following the Closing (collectively, the "<u>Liabilities Transferring by Operation of Law</u>").

Section 2.7 <u>Retained Liabilities</u>. Notwithstanding anything in this Agreement to the contrary, Seller acknowledges and agrees that any Liability of Seller or any Affiliate of Seller prior to the Closing shall continue to be a Liability of Seller or such Affiliate of Seller following the Closing except for (i) the Assumed Liabilities and (ii) the Liabilities Transferring by Operation of Law (collectively, the "<u>Retained Liabilities</u>"). Without limiting the generality of the foregoing, the Retained Liabilities shall include any of the following Liabilities, whether or not relating to the Business:

(a) Any and all Liabilities for which Seller expressly has responsibility pursuant to this Agreement, including the Seller portion of Shared Contract Liabilities pursuant to Section 2.10(b);

(b) Any and all Liabilities that relate to, or arise out of, directly or indirectly Seller's or any of its Affiliates' operation or sale of the Canada Business, and any Taxes associated therewith, including but not limited to any Liabilities of any former Subsidiary of Seller which (i) was domiciled in Canada, (ii) owned another Subsidiary domiciled in Canada or (iii) was engaged in the Canada Business;

(c) Any and all Liabilities to the extent arising out of or related to the Excluded Assets;

(d) Any and all Liabilities for Taxes that are Seller Taxes;

(e) Any and all Liabilities of any Subsidiary of Seller other than the Purchased Company or any Subsidiary of the Purchased Company;

(f) Any and all fees and expenses (including the Seller Transaction Expenses) of brokers, finders, counsel, financial advisors, accountants, consultants and other professional advisors incurred by Seller or any Affiliate of Seller in connection with any auction or other sale process to sell the Business, the Canada Business or any other line of business of Seller or any Affiliate of the Seller, including the negotiation and execution of this Agreement;

(g) Any and all Liabilities related to the matters set forth on Section 2.7(g) of the Seller Disclosure Schedules;

(h) Any and all Liabilities in respect of the Retained Personnel, including with respect to such Retained Personnel's termination of employment or engagement with the Purchased Company or a Subsidiary of the Purchased Company, as applicable, and any Liabilities related thereto;

(i) Any and all Liabilities in respect of the stockholders of Seller, associated with the issuance, sale, redemption or other disposition of any shares of stock or other Securities of Seller, including any options, warrants, calls, purchase rights, subscription rights, exchange rights or other rights, convertible Securities, agreements or commitments of any kind associated with, related to or derived from Securities of Seller, or related to the breach of, or non-compliance with, (i) any rule of any Governmental Entity (including the SEC or NASDAQ) which relates to reporting, disclosure or other securities-related obligations of Seller or (ii) any applicable fiduciary duties owed to the stockholders of the Seller or otherwise arising under the Delaware General Corporation Law; and

(j) except to the extent provided on Section 2.6 of the Seller Disclosure Schedules, any and all Liabilities relating to or arising under any Seller Benefit Plan.

For the avoidance of doubt, neither Buyer nor, following the Closing, the Purchased Company or any Subsidiary of the Purchased Company shall assume or be liable for (and Buyer shall not cause any of its Affiliates to assume or be liable for) any of the Retained Liabilities.

Section 2.8 <u>Closing Deliveries</u>

(a) At the Closing, Buyer shall make or cause to be made the following payments by wire transfer of immediately available funds:

(i) First, the amounts specified in the payoff letters delivered by Seller to Buyer pursuant to Section 2.8(c)(v) to the payees set forth therein; and

(ii) Second, an amount equal to the Closing Purchase Price, <u>less</u> the Holdback Amount, and <u>less</u> the amount of any withholding required under Section 2.11, to one or more bank accounts designated in writing by Seller (such designation to be made by Seller at least two (2) Business Days prior to the Closing Date).

(b) At the Closing, Buyer shall deliver, or cause to be delivered, to Seller the following:

(i) the certificate to be delivered pursuant to Section 7.3(c);

(ii) a counterpart of a transition services agreement, in a form agreed between Buyer and Seller following the execution of this Agreement and prior to the Closing (the "<u>Transition Services Agreement</u>"), duly executed by Buyer (or one or more Affiliates of Buyer designated by Buyer);

(iii) to the extent any Purchased Asset or Assumed Liability is not held by the Purchased Company or a Subsidiary of the Purchased Company, a counterpart of the Assignment and Assumption Agreement and Bill of Sale for such Purchased Assets and Assumed Liabilities, by and between Seller and Buyer (or one or more Affiliates of Buyer designated by Buyer), substantially in the form attached as <u>Exhibit B</u> hereto (the "<u>Assignment Agreement and Bill of Sale</u>"), duly executed by Buyer (or one or more Affiliates of Buyer designated by Buyer).

(c) At the Closing, Seller shall deliver, or cause to be delivered, to Buyer the following:

(i) the certificate to be delivered pursuant to Section 7.2(c);

(ii) a counterpart of the Transition Services Agreement duly executed by Seller;

(iii) certificates evidencing the Purchased Company Equity Interests, duly endorsed in blank or with stock powers duly executed in proper form for transfer;

(iv) a counterpart of the Assignment Agreement and Bill of Sale duly executed by Seller;

(v) a payoff letter or similar instrument in a form reasonably satisfactory to Buyer with respect to any and all Indebtedness (including any prepayment premiums, penalties, breakage costs or similar costs or fees associated with such Indebtedness) set forth on Section 2.8(c)(v) of the Seller Disclosure Schedule, each of which shall include an appropriate release and discharge or commitment to release and discharge upon receipt of funds specified therein which releases and terminates any and all Liens related to such Indebtedness;

(vi) all appropriate releases and discharges releasing and terminating the Liens described on Section 3.11 of the Seller Disclosure Schedule; and

(vii) a duly executed certificate of non-foreign status from Seller substantially in the form of the sample certification set forth in Treasury Regulation Section 1.1445-2(b)(2)(iv)(B).

Section 2.9 <u>Adjustment to Base Purchase Price.</u>

(a) Section 2.9 of the Seller Disclosure Schedules sets forth a calculation of the Working Capital, the calculated Adjustment Amount, the Cash Amounts and the Indebtedness of the Purchased Company and its Subsidiaries, in each case, as of June 30, 2015 (the "<u>Sample Closing Statement</u>"), including the asset and liability line items and general ledger accounts. The Sample Closing Statement has been prepared in accordance with the Transaction Accounting Principles.

(b) At least five (5) Business Days prior to the Closing Date, Seller shall cause to be prepared and delivered to Buyer a closing statement (the "<u>Closing Statement</u>") setting forth its good-faith estimate of (i) the Closing Working Capital, (ii) the Adjustment Amount, (iii) the Closing Cash Amounts and (iv) the Closing Debt and, subject to the proviso in this sentence, such estimates shall be deemed the "<u>Estimated Closing Working Capital</u>," "<u>Estimated Adjustment Amount</u>," "<u>Estimated Closing Cash Amounts</u>" and "<u>Estimated Closing Debt</u>," respectively, for purposes of this Agreement; <u>provided</u>, <u>however</u>, that Buyer shall be given the opportunity to consult with Seller respecting the foregoing estimates and Seller shall use reasonable efforts to consider and incorporate Buyer's reasonable comments in preparing the Closing Statement and any item set forth therein unless Seller reasonably determines in good faith that the Independent Accounting Firm would not agree that such comments are appropriate in the circumstances. The Closing Statement shall set forth the calculations of such amounts in a manner consistent with the Sample Closing Statement, shall be prepared in accordance with the Transaction Accounting Principles and shall be supported by the books and records of the Business. The Estimated Closing Working Capital, the Estimated Adjustment Amount, the Estimated Closing Cash Amounts and the Estimated Closing Debt, shall be used to calculate the Closing Purchase Price to be paid by Buyer to Seller at the Closing.

(c) As promptly as reasonably possible and in any event within sixty (60) days after the Closing Date, Buyer shall prepare or cause to be prepared, and will provide to Seller, a written statement (the "<u>Post-Closing Statement</u>"), setting forth Buyer's calculation of the Closing Working Capital, the Adjustment Amount, the Closing Cash Amounts and the Closing Debt as of 12:01 a.m. Eastern Time on the Closing Date. The Post-

Closing Statement shall set forth in reasonable detail the Buyer's calculations of such amounts in a manner consistent with the Sample Closing Statement and shall be prepared in accordance with the Transaction Accounting Principles.

(d) Within thirty (30) days following receipt by Seller of the Post-Closing Statement, Seller shall deliver written notice to Buyer of any dispute Seller has with respect to the calculation, preparation or content of the Post-Closing Statement (the "Dispute Notice"); provided, however, that if Seller does not deliver any Dispute Notice to Buyer within such fifteen (15) day period, the Post-Closing Statement will be final, conclusive and binding on the Parties. The Dispute Notice shall set forth in reasonable detail (i) any item on the Post-Closing Statement that Seller disputes and (ii) the correct amount of such item; provided, however, that Seller may not dispute the accounting principles, practices, methodologies and policies used in preparing the Post-Closing Statement unless they are not in accordance with the Transaction Accounting Principles. Upon receipt by Buyer of a Dispute Notice, Buyer and Seller shall negotiate in good faith to resolve any dispute set forth therein. If Buyer and Seller fail to resolve any such dispute within thirty (30) days after delivery of the Dispute Notice (the "Dispute Resolution Period"), then Buyer and Seller jointly shall engage, within five (5) Business Days following the expiration of the Dispute Resolution Period, Ernst & Young, or, if Ernst & Young is unavailable or conflicted, another nationally recognized independent accounting firm selected jointly by Seller and Buyer (the "Independent Accounting Firm") to resolve any such dispute; provided that, if Seller and Buyer are unable to agree on the Independent Accounting Firm, then each of Seller and Buyer shall select a nationally recognized independent accounting firm, and the two (2) firms will mutually select a third nationally recognized independent accounting firm to serve as the Independent Accounting Firm. As promptly as practicable, and in any event not more than fifteen (15) days following the engagement of the Independent Accounting Firm, Buyer and Seller shall each prepare and submit a presentation detailing each Party's complete statement of proposed resolution of each issue still in dispute to the Independent Accounting Firm. Buyer and Seller shall instruct the Independent Accounting Firm to, as soon as practicable after the submission of the presentations described in the immediately preceding sentence and in any event not more than twenty (20) days following such presentations, make a final determination along with a written report, binding on the Parties, of the appropriate amount of each of the line items that remains in dispute as indicated in the Dispute Notice. With respect to each disputed line item, such determination, if not in accordance with the position of either Seller or Buyer, shall not be in excess of the higher, nor less than the lower, of the amounts advocated by Seller or Buyer, as applicable, in their respective presentations to the Independent Accounting Firm described above. Notwithstanding the foregoing, the scope of the disputes to be resolved by the Independent Accounting Firm shall be limited to whether any disputed determinations of the Closing Working Capital, the Adjustment Amount, the Closing Cash Amounts and the Closing Debt were properly calculated in accordance with the Transaction Accounting Principles. All fees and expenses relating to the work, if any, to be performed by the Independent Accounting Firm shall be borne equally by Seller and Buyer. All determinations made by the Independent Accounting Firm, and the Post-Closing Statement, as modified by the Independent Accounting Firm, will be final, conclusive and binding on the Parties (absent manifest error). The Parties agree that any adjustment as determined pursuant to this Section 2.9(d) shall be treated as an adjustment to the Purchase Price, except as otherwise required by Law.

(e) For purposes of complying with the terms set forth in this Section 2.9, each of Seller and Buyer shall reasonably cooperate with and make available to each other and their respective Representatives all information, records, data and working papers, in each case to the extent related to the Purchased Assets, Excluded Assets, Assumed Liabilities, Retained Liabilities and Business, and shall permit access to its facilities and personnel, as may be reasonably required in connection with the preparation and analysis of the Post-Closing Statement and the resolution of any disputes thereunder.

Section 2.10 <u>Non-Assignment; Consents</u>.

(a) Seller and Buyer shall use commercially reasonable efforts to obtain, or cause to be obtained, any approval, authorization, or consent of, filing with, notification to, or granting or issuance of any license, order, waiver or permit by, any Person (collectively, "<u>Approvals</u>") (other than Regulatory Approvals, which shall be governed by Section 5.1) required in connection with the sale, assignment or transfer of any Purchased Asset. If such Approval is not obtained prior to Closing, until the earliest of (i) such time as such Approval or Approvals are obtained or (ii) the date Seller is dissolved in accordance with the General Corporation Law of the State of Delaware or (iii) six (6) months following the Closing Date, then Seller will cooperate with Buyer in any arrangement reasonably acceptable to Buyer and Seller intended to both (x) provide Buyer and/or its applicable Affiliates, to the fullest extent practicable, the claims, rights and benefits of any such Purchased Assets (including by means of any subcontracting, sublicensing or subleasing arrangement) and (y) cause Buyer and/or its applicable Affiliates to bear all costs and Liabilities thereunder from and after the Closing in accordance with this Agreement to the extent that Buyer and/or its applicable Affiliates receive the rights and benefits of such Purchased Assets from and after the Closing in accordance with this Agreement. In furtherance of the foregoing, Buyer will, or will cause its Affiliates to, promptly pay, perform or discharge when due any related

Liability (other than any Liability for income, franchise or similar Taxes) arising thereunder after the Closing Date to the extent that Buyer and/or its applicable Affiliates receive the rights and benefits of such Purchased Assets from and after the Closing in accordance with this Agreement.

(b) Any Contract to be assigned, transferred and conveyed in accordance with Section 2.4 that does not primarily relate to the Business (each, a "Shared Contract") shall be assigned, transferred and conveyed only with respect to (and preserving the meaning of) those parts that relate to the Business, to either Buyer or an Affiliate of Buyer designated by Buyer, if so assignable, transferrable or conveyable, or appropriately amended prior to, on or after the Closing, so that Buyer and its Affiliates shall be entitled to the rights and benefit of those parts of the Shared Contract that relate to the Business and shall assume the related portion of any Liabilities contemplated by this Agreement (the "Buyer Portion of the Shared Contract Liabilities"); provided, however, that (i) in no event shall any Person be required to assign (or amend), either in its entirety or in part, any Shared Contract that is not assignable (or cannot be amended) by its terms without obtaining one or more Approvals and (ii) if any Shared Contract cannot be so partially assigned by its terms or otherwise, or cannot be amended, without such Approval or Approvals, until the earliest of (A) such time as such Approval or Approvals are obtained, (B) the date Seller is dissolved in accordance with the General Corporation Law of the State of Delaware or (C) six (6) months following the Closing Date, then Seller will cooperate with Buyer to establish an agency type or other similar arrangement reasonably satisfactory to Seller and Buyer intended to both (x) provide Buyer and/or its applicable Affiliates, to the fullest extent practicable under such Shared Contract, the claims, rights and benefits of those parts that relate to the Business (including by means of any subcontracting, sublicensing or subleasing arrangement) and (y) cause Buyer and/or its applicable Affiliates to bear the costs and Liabilities thereunder from and after the Closing in accordance with this Agreement to the extent that Buyer and/or its applicable Affiliates receive the rights and benefits of the parts of the Shared Contracts that relate to the Business. In furtherance of the foregoing, Buyer will promptly pay, perform or discharge when due any Liability (other than any Liability for income, franchise or similar Taxes) arising thereunder after the Closing Date to the extent that Buyer and/or its applicable Affiliates receive the rights and benefits of the parts of such Shared Contracts that relate to the Business.

Section 2.11 Withholding. Notwithstanding any other provision in this Agreement to the contrary, Buyer and each of its Affiliates shall be entitled to deduct and withhold from amounts otherwise payable to any Person pursuant to this Agreement such amounts as it is required to deduct and withhold with respect to the making of such payment under any provision of any federal, state, local or foreign Tax Law. To the extent that amounts are so withheld by Buyer or any of its Affiliates, Buyer shall remit such amounts to the appropriate Taxing Authority, and such withheld and remitted amounts shall be treated for all purposes of this Agreement as having been paid to the relevant Person in respect of which such deduction and withholding was made.

PRESS RELEASE
SWISHER HYGIENE INC.'S BOARD OF DIRECTORS APPROVES MAY 27, 2016 FILING OF CERTIFICATE OF DISSOLUTION
COMPANY SHARES TO CEASE TRADING ON OTCQB AND CLOSE STOCK TRANSFER BOOK UPON FILING

FORT LAUDERDALE, FL—April 14, 2016—Swisher Hygiene Inc. (the "Company") (OTCQB: SWSH) announced today that its Board of Directors unanimously approved the filing of a Certificate of Dissolution (the "Certificate") on Friday, May 27, 2016 (the "Final Record Date"). The Certificate will be filed with the Secretary of State of the State of Delaware on the Final Record Date. The filing of the Certificate will be made pursuant to a Plan of Dissolution approved by stockholders at the Company's annual meeting held on October 15, 2015.

The Company has notified OTCQB that the Certificate will be filed on the Final Record Date and that as of 6:00 pm Eastern Time on the Final Record Date, the Company's shares will cease to be traded on OTCQB. Also after the Final Record Date, the Company's stock transfer books will be closed and transfers of the shares of the Company's common stock will no longer be recorded. The Company also intends to seek relief from the Securities and Exchange Commission (the "SEC") to suspend certain of its reporting obligations under the Securities Exchange Act of 1934, as amended. If the SEC grants such relief, the Company intends to report any further material events relating to the liquidation and dissolution on Form 8-K.

Pursuant to the Plan of Dissolution, and under Delaware law, the dissolution of the Company shall be effective as of 6:00 pm Eastern Time on the Final Record Date. Under Delaware law, the dissolved corporation is continued for three (3) years (unless extended by direction of the Court of Chancery) to enable the company's directors to wind up the affairs of the corporation, including the discharge of the Company's liabilities and to distribute to the stockholders remaining assets, if any. No assurances can be made as to if or when any such distribution will be made, or the amount of any such distribution, if one is made. Any distribution, however, would be made to the Company's stockholders of record as of the Final Record Date.

2. EARN-OUTS

AIRBORNE HEALTH, INC. v. SQUID SOAP, LP

984 A.2d 126
Court of Chancery of Delaware.
Nov. 23, 2009.

LASTER, Vice Chancellor.
Plaintiffs . . . have moved for judgment on the pleadings against defendant Squid Soap, LP ("Squid Soap"). Except for two minor issues, I grant the motion.

I. FACTUAL BACKGROUND

I assume the following facts to be true for purposes of the motion for judgment on the pleadings. The facts are drawn solely from the pleadings, which consist of Airborne and Weil's complaint, Squid Soap's first amended answer and counterclaims, and Airborne and Weil's replies to the counterclaims. I also have considered the Asset Purchase Agreement (the "Agreement" or the "APA"), which is incorporated by reference in all of the pleadings. Because this is a motion for judgment on the pleadings, I have assumed that all disputed factual allegations would be resolved in favor of Squid Soap, the non-movant. I likewise have given Squid Soap the benefit of all reasonable factual inferences.

A. THE PARTIES.

Defendant Squid Soap is a Texas limited partnership with its principal place of business in Austin, Texas.

Plaintiff Airborne is a Delaware corporation with its principal place of business in Minneapolis, Minnesota. Effective as of June 15, 2007, Airborne and Squid Soap entered into an Asset Purchase Agreement by which Airborne acquired all of Squid Soap's assets, including certain intellectual property.

Plaintiff Weil is a New York limited liability partnership with its headquarters in New York, New York. Weil served as legal counsel to Airborne for purposes of drafting and negotiating the APA.

B. SQUID SOAP'S POTENTIAL.

In the early 1990s, John Lynn saw a business opportunity in society's growing awareness that thorough hand washing limits the spread of germs. Mr. Lynn believed that germ-focused parents, educators, and health professionals would embrace his invention. According to the counterclaims, he was right. Squid Soap received national attention. It was featured in magazines such as Redbook, Woman's Day, InStyle, and Parenting, and it appeared on television shows such as Good Morning America and the Fox Morning Show. Newspapers and websites praised it.

Buoyed by its unique attributes and the same favorable market trends that propelled sales of hand sanitizer and anti-bacterial wipes, Squid Soap became a hit. Retailers like Wal-Mart, Target, CVS, and Walgreen's stocked Squid Soap products. A consumer product paradise beckoned with high recurrent sales and patent-protected margins. All Squid Soap needed was a nationwide marketing platform and brand-name recognition.

C.   SQUID SOAP TALKS WITH POTENTIAL STRATEGIC PARTNERS.

In early 2007, Mr. Lynn was approached by companies and investment groups seeking to capitalize on Squid Soap's potential. Each group expressed great interest in Squid Soap. The suitors included the consumer products powerhouse Procter & Gamble, a multibillion dollar hedge fund HBK Investments, and a publicly traded business development company Capital Southwest Corporation.

D.   AIRBORNE'S STORY.

Like Squid Soap, Airborne started out as a small, single-product company focused on stopping the spread of germs. Airborne's initial product was a cocktail of various vitamins, herbs and other ingredients that Airborne marketed as preventing and even curing the common cold. Indeed, Airborne required vendors to place its product displays on their cough and cold remedy aisles.

Victoria Knight-McDowell founded Airborne in 1997. In 2005, Summit Partners acquired majority ownership of Airborne. Ms. Donahue became CEO, replacing Mrs. Knight-McDowell, who continued her role as a brand spokesperson and board member.

By 2006, propelled by celebrity endorsements and aggressive advertising, Airborne ranked at the top of a list of the fastest-growing privately held companies. It experienced furious growth and at one time projected $300 million in annual sales. Airborne was at the pinnacle of brand recognition. Its name was its product.

E.   SQUID SOAP SELLS TO AIRBORNE.

Airborne's story charmed Mr. Lynn. The counterclaims allege that "[b]ased on Airborne's representations about, among other things, its brand name, sterling reputation, marketing prowess, and in particular its promises to leverage the Airborne name and marketing platform to fully maximize Squid Soap's potential, Squid Soap, relying on and induced by Airborne's representations and promises, re-focused its acquisition talks to Airborne, to the exclusion of its other suitors."

Squid Soap and Airborne eventually agreed on a transaction through which Airborne would purchase Squid Soap's assets (the "Asset Purchase"). The terms of the Asset Purchase are memorialized in the APA. The APA was an integrated contract, and in Section 10.3, the parties agreed that it reflected their complete agreement on the terms for the transaction.

Several aspects of the APA stand out. Most notably, Squid Soap agreed to sell its assets for $1 million in cash at closing, plus the potential for earn-out payments of up to $26.5 million if certain targets were achieved. Squid Soap asserts in the counterclaims that "[t]he high price tag was a reflection of Squid Soap's enormous market value." What an earn-out (and particularly a large one) typically reflects is disagreement over the value of the business that is bridged when the seller trades the certainty of less cash at closing for the prospect of more cash over time. In theory, the earn-out solves the disagreement over value by requiring the buyer to pay more only if the business proves that it is worth more. But since value is frequently debatable and the causes of underperformance equally so, an earn-out often converts today's disagreement over price into tomorrow's litigation over the outcome. Based on an earn-out of this magnitude (viewed in terms of the portion of total potential consideration), the plain inference is that Squid Soap believed that its business had tremendous value and was willing to bet heavily on that proposition.

Reinforcing this inference is a second notable feature of the APA. Airborne purchased Squid Soap's brand name, goodwill, and intellectual property, including the Patents, but the APA required that Airborne return the assets to Squid Soap if certain business targets were not met. Section 3.2 of the APA states:

> Notwithstanding anything herein to the contrary, in the event that (i) Purchaser does not incur at least $1,000,000 of marketing, account retail programs and/or advertising spending (including brand spending but excluding co-op fees, slotting fees and product discounts) specifically focused upon the [Squid Soap] Products within the first twelve months after Closing . . . , and (ii) Net Sales of the [Squid Soap] Products have not reached $5,000,000 within the first twelve months after Closing, then Purchaser shall transfer the Purchased Assets existing as of such date (other than inventory) back to Seller for the consideration of $10.00 and other valuable consideration of which the Purchaser and Seller both agree is valuable and adequate consideration. Upon such transfer, each person's obligations under this Agreement shall terminate except for obligations due and payable up through the date of termination.

Similarly, Section 3.2(g) provides:

> Notwithstanding anything herein to the contrary, in the event Purchaser ceases to market, advertise and sell [Squid Soap] Product(s) at any time prior to reaching aggregate Net Sales of $7,500,000 then Purchaser agrees to transfer the Purchased Assets existing as of such date (other than inventory) back to Seller for $10.00 and other valuable consideration of which the Purchaser and Seller both agree is valuable and adequate consideration. Upon such transfer, each person's obligations under this Agreement shall terminate except for obligations due and payable up through the date of termination.

I will refer to these provisions as the "Asset Return Provisions."

The Asset Return Provisions establish a framework in which Airborne gets to take its shot at making Squid Soap a success, but if things do not work out, then Airborne has to return the assets. Section 3.2 is particularly instructive in this regard. It gives Airborne twelve months. After that point, if Airborne has not spent $1 million on marketing and achieved $5 million in Net Sales, then Airborne must return the assets to Squid Soap. Like the earn-out, this structure indicates that Squid Soap believed its product was a winner, that it was in demand, and that if Airborne could not make a go of it, then Squid Soap would get the assets back and could pursue a relationship with someone else.

A third noteworthy aspect of the APA is the absence of any specific commitments by Airborne regarding the level of efforts or resources that it would devote. Squid Soap alleges that "the APA required Airborne to spend a minimum of $1,000,000.00 on marketing specifically for Squid Soap's products within the first 12 months after the APA was signed." This is not what the APA provides. The $1 million figure appears in Section 3.2, one of the Asset Return Provisions, and establishes a requirement that Airborne must hit if it wants to retain the assets.

A mandatory commitment by Airborne to expend funds easily could have been drafted. All it needed to say was "Purchaser shall incur at least $1,000,000 of marketing, account retail programs and/or advertising spending (including brand spending but excluding co-op fees, slotting fees and product discounts) specifically focused upon the Squid Soap Products within the first twelve months after Closing." Squid Soap did not obtain a commitment of this nature.

A fourth noteworthy feature of the APA is the absence of detailed representations by Airborne regarding the issues that Squid Soap now claims were critically important. Squid Soap alleges:

> In entering the APA, Squid Soap relied on and was induced by Airborne's promises and representations regarding its positive brand name and image, its marketing power, as well as Airborne's intent and, importantly, its ability to market Squid Soap and to leverage Airborne's positive brand image. These representations by Airborne were at the core of Squid Soap's decision to sell to Airborne. Given their importance, Squid Soap relied upon Airborne's repeated assurances about its reputation and brand image and their effect on Airborne's ability to market and leverage that positive brand name.

Yet there are no contractual representations in the APA by Airborne regarding these matters.

The APA called for a simultaneous signing and closing, which took place on June 15, 2007.

F.   AIRBORNE SUFFERS SIGNIFICANT REVERSES.

According to the counterclaims, at the time Squid Soap entered into the APA, Squid Soap did not know that Airborne's product had been severely criticized by a special investigation conducted by ABC News and aired on Good Morning America. The special report found that the clinical study on which Airborne based its germ-fighting claims had been produced by a "two-man operation started up just to do the Airborne study." The news report led to intense scrutiny of Airborne's products, marketing, and claims.

Squid Soap also says it did not know then that there was a class action pending against Airborne in California state court, filed in May 2006, which asserted various claims for false or misleading advertising, consumer fraud, deceptive or unfair business practices, concealment, omission, and unfair competition (the "California Action"). The Center for Science in the Public Interest, a non-profit organization with significant expertise in litigation over product mislabeling, joined the California Action on the plaintiffs' side. The Center's litigation director called the case a "great opportunity for CSPI to participate in a major lawsuit against one of the biggest supplement frauds in the country."

Airborne's post-APA problems immediately became Squid Soap's problems because Airborne owned Squid Soap and because Squid Soap had been repackaged as "Squid Soap by Airborne." Squid Soap alleges that Airborne's difficulties "killed Squid Soap in its infancy."

G. AIRBORNE RETURNS THE SQUID SOAP ASSETS.

Since its legal stumbles, Airborne has engaged in damage control. Mrs. Knight-McDowell reacquired Airborne and launched a highly publicized campaign to restore consumer confidence and rebuild the company. According to the counterclaims, Airborne has focused on its historic products and has done nothing to market or rehabilitate Squid Soap.

Under the Asset Return Provisions, Airborne was required to return Squid Soap's assets, including the Patents, to Airborne if the financial thresholds in those provisions were not met. It is undisputed that the thresholds were not met.

Squid Soap contends that because the thresholds were not met, the assets automatically reverted to Squid Soap on June 15, 2008, one year after the closing of the Asset Purchase. This is not what the Asset Return Provisions say. They obligate Airborne to return the assets, but title does not revert automatically.

Airborne attempted to return the assets to Squid Soap. In an email dated September 9, 2008, Mr. Rainone, President of Airborne's Squid Soap Division, advised Squid Soap that Airborne would be returning the assets. As quoted in the counterclaims, the email stated:

> We [Airborne] understand your need to transition [the Patents and other purchased assets back to Squid Soap] and will do whatever is necessary to make it a smooth one. . . . Our goal is to transition this to you in a way which will make it seamless for our customers. . . . [L]et's discuss a plan for a smooth transition.

It appears that at the same time, Airborne was in the process of securing financing from BNP Paribas, secured by Airborne assets that included the Patents. On September 29, 2008, just three weeks after Mr. Rainone's email, Airborne entered into an agreement assigning an interest in the Patents to BNP Paribas. The interest was recorded the following day with the United States Patent and Trademark Office.

Squid Soap sees further perfidy in Airborne's actions, which it claims "prevent[ed] Squid Soap from marketing or selling Squid Soap to any would-be buyers after the reversion date [allegedly June 15, 2008] but before the onset of the current economic crisis that has solidly dead-stopped private investment into companies like Squid Soap." I take judicial notice of the indisputably troubled state of the financial markets prior to June 2008, including the shotgun acquisition of Bear Stearns by JPMorgan in March of that year. Squid Soap has not identified any potential buyer, interested party, or prospect that it could have pursued.

It is undisputed that Airborne continued to attempt to return the assets to Squid Soap. It is equally undisputed that Squid Soap has refused to accept them.

H.   SQUID SOAP SUES IN TEXAS, BUT THAT ACTION IS DISMISSED.

The APA contains a forum selection clause requiring all disputes arising out of or relating to the Agreement to be heard in this Court or any federal court in the State of Delaware. Section 10.4(b) states:

> All actions and proceedings arising out of or relating to this Agreement shall be heard and determined in the Chancery Court of the State of Delaware or any federal court sitting in the State of Delaware, and the parties hereto hereby irrevocably submit to the exclusive jurisdiction of such courts (and, in the case of appeals, appropriate appellate courts therefrom) in any such action or proceeding and irrevocably waive the defense of an inconvenient forum to the maintenance of any such action or proceeding.

Despite this provision, on December 3, 2008, Squid Soap filed suit in the United States District Court for the District of Texas against Airborne and BNP Paribas asserting various causes of action arising out of and relating to the APA, including conversion, fraud, negligent misrepresentation, breach of fiduciary duty, unjust enrichment, and conspiracy. On February 6, 2009, Squid Soap amended its complaint in the Texas action to drop BNP Paribas and add Weil. On May 14, 2009, the Texas court dismissed the Texas action without prejudice.

Meanwhile, on March 6, 2009, Airborne and Weil sought a declaratory judgment from this Court establishing that they were not liable under the APA. On June 30, Squid Soap amended its answer to assert counterclaims against Airborne and Weil. After Airborne and Weil replied to the counterclaims, they moved for judgment on the pleadings.

THE IMPLIED COVENANT OF GOOD FAITH AND FAIR DEALING

Squid Soap ultimately falls back to the implied covenant of fair dealing. This count recasts both of Squid Soap's basic complaints—Airborne's failure to disclose litigation risks and Airborne's failure to spend on marketing or achieve sales—as breaches of the implied covenant.

The implied covenant of good faith and fair dealing inheres in every contract governed by Delaware law and "requires a party in a contractual relationship to refrain from arbitrary or unreasonable conduct which has the effect of preventing the other party to the contract from receiving the fruits of the bargain." The implied covenant does not apply when "the subject at issue is expressly covered by the contract." At the same time, the covenant exists to fulfill the reasonable expectations of the parties, and thus the implied obligation must be consistent with the terms of the agreement as a whole. The doctrine thus operates only in that narrow band of cases where the contract as a whole speaks sufficiently to suggest an obligation and point to a result, but does not speak directly enough to provide an explicit answer. In the Venn diagram of contract cases, the area of overlap is quite small.

The test for the implied covenant depends on whether it is "clear from what was expressly agreed upon that the parties who negotiated the express terms of the contract would have agreed to proscribe the act later complained of as a breach of the implied covenant of good faith—had they thought to negotiate with respect to that matter." Katz v. Oak Indus., Inc., 508 A.2d 873, 880 (Del.Ch.1986) (Allen, C.). "[I]mplying obligations based on the covenant of good faith and fair dealing is a cautious enterprise." "[C]ourts should be most chary about implying a contractual protection when the contract easily could have been drafted to expressly provide for it."

Squid Soap's implied covenant claim based on litigation disclosure is easily addressed. The parties to the APA agreed upon a specific representation by Airborne relating to litigation in Section 6.3. Squid Soap could have insisted on a broader representation. With the benefit of hindsight, it should have. But the implied covenant is not a means to re-write agreements.

Squid Soap's arguments regarding Airborne's obligation to spend funds on marketing and to achieve sales have a tinge more color. Squid Soap understandably questions what it obtained under the APA if Airborne had no obligation actually to expend resources. The APA does not contain any language that specifically addresses the issue, either by requiring Airborne to expend resources or by saying explicitly that Airborne has no obligation to expend resources. The APA does, however, contain explicit financial targets on which the parties agreed. This allows Squid Soap to contend plausibly that this case falls within the narrow band of the implied covenant. The provision Squid Soap seeks to imply is that Airborne could not arbitrarily refuse to expend resources and thereby deprive Squid Soap of the prospects for the earn-out. In Squid Soap's view, Airborne at least had to make an honest go of it.

There is support in our law for this argument. When a contract confers discretion on one party, the implied covenant requires that the discretion be used reasonably and in good faith. Airborne thus could not have refused arbitrarily or in bad faith to pursue the Squid Soap business. But Squid Soap does not contend that Airborne failed to expend funds to make the business a success arbitrarily, in bad faith, or for no reason. Squid Soap's counterclaims quite clearly allege that Airborne suffered a corporate crisis in its core business and, at least in part as a result of that crisis, did not expend resources on Squid Soap. Squid Soap specifically recognizes that Airborne was "[u]ndoubtedly restrained by the legal and financial burdens of the settlement and systemic market damage." This as-pled scenario does not support a claim that Squid Soap exercised its contractual discretion in bad faith.

Squid Soap's position is also undercut by the ease with which Squid Soap could have insisted on specific contractual commitments from Airborne regarding the expenditure of resources, or some form of "efforts" obligation for Airborne. These provisions are familiar to any transactional lawyer, and Squid Soap was a sophisticated party represented by able counsel. Moreover, Section 7.6, entitled "Obligations of Seller," provides that "[e]ach Selling Partner agrees to take all reasonable actions necessary to cause Seller to perform its obligations hereunder and to otherwise comply with the terms of this Agreement." Squid Soap could have insisted on a provision binding Airborne. Rather than holding out for these types of contractual protections, Squid Soap accepted earn-out provisions that are expressly phrased in conditional terms.

Importantly for purposes of the implied covenant, I do not think it irrational, or even unreasonable, that Squid Soap would have chosen this deal structure. The APA provides contractual downside protection, but in the different form of a requirement that Airborne return the assets so that Squid Soap could go elsewhere. Squid Soap alleges that it had a hot property, and thus the prospect of getting the assets back and linking up with a better partner could well have made sense. At the same time, Airborne had powerful incentives to want Squid Soap to succeed, and thus Squid Soap and Airborne's interests were largely aligned. Squid Soap made an understandable business decision, albeit one it now regrets.

This is not a case in which Squid Soap has been deprived of the fruit of its bargain arbitrarily or in a manner where the implied covenant of good faith and fair dealing should come into play. The price of the greater consideration that Squid Soap hoped to achieve through the earn-out was the risk that Airborne would fail. Unfortunately for Squid Soap, Airborne did not succeed, but that does not allow Squid Soap to rewrite the deal it cut in more optimistic days. I therefore enter judgment on the pleadings against Squid Soap and in favor of Airborne on Squid Soap's implied covenant claim.

3.   VOTING RIGHTS

Under the corporate law of many states, the buyer shareholders do not get to vote on an asset sale. And the target-seller shareholders only get to vote when the sale involves "all or substantially all" of the seller's assets.[1] Others may have contractual rights that are triggered in similar circumstances. But what does "all or substantially all" mean?

HOLLINGER INC. v. HOLLINGER INTERNATIONAL, INC.

858 A.2d 342
Court of Chancery of Delaware, New Castle County.
July 29, 2004.

STRINE, Vice Chancellor.

If the questions resolved in this lengthy opinion could be distilled to three, they would be as follows:

1. Has the judiciary transmogrified the words "substantially all" in §271 of the Delaware General Corporation Law into the words "approximately half"?

[The other questions are omitted.]

This opinion answers each question in the same way: no.

Hollinger Inc. (or "Inc.") seeks a preliminary injunction preventing Hollinger International, Inc. (or "International") from selling the *Telegraph* Group Ltd. (England) to Press Holdings International, an entity controlled by Frederick and David Barclay (hereinafter, the "Barclays"). The *Telegraph* Group is an indirect, wholly owned subsidiary of International and publishes the *Telegraph* newspaper and the *Spectator* magazine. The *Telegraph* newspaper is a leading one in the United Kingdom, both in terms of its circulation and its journalistic reputation.

The key question addressed in this decision is whether Inc. and the other International stockholders must be provided with the opportunity to vote on the sale of the *Telegraph* Group because that sale involves "substantially all" the assets of International within the meaning of 8 *Del.* C. §271. The sale of the *Telegraph* followed a lengthy auction process whereby International and all of Hollinger's operating assets were widely shopped to potential bidders.

As a practical matter, Inc.'s vote would be the only one that matters because although it now owns only 18% of International's total equity, it, through high-vote Class B shares, controls 68% of the voting power.

Inc. argues that a preliminary injunction should issue because it is clear that the sale of the *Telegraph* satisfies the quantitative and qualitative test used to determine whether an asset sale involves substantially all of a corporation's assets. The *Telegraph* Group is one of the most profitable parts of International and is its most prestigious asset. After its sale, International will be transformed from a respected international publishing company controlling one of the world's major newspapers to a primarily American publishing company whose most

---

1. Del. Gen. Corp. Law §271.

valuable remaining asset, the *Chicago Sun-Times*, is the second leading newspaper in the Second City.

In response to these arguments, International makes several points. Initially, it contends that the sale of the *Telegraph* Group does not trigger §271. However prestigious the *Telegraph* Group, International says its sale does not involve, either quantitatively or qualitatively, the sale of substantially all International's assets. Whether or not the *Chicago Sun-Times* is as prestigious as the *Daily Telegraph*, it remains a profitable newspaper in a major city. Along with a group of profitable Chicago-area community newspapers, the *Chicago Sun-Times* has made the "Chicago Group" International's most profitable operating segment in the last two years and its contribution to International's profits has been comparable to that of the *Telegraph* Group for many years. Moreover, International retains a number of smaller newspapers in Canada and the prestigious *Jerusalem Post.* After the sale of the *Telegraph* Group, International therefore will quantitatively retain a sizable percentage of its existing assets and will qualitatively remain in the same business line. Although the *Telegraph* sale is admittedly a major transaction, International stresses that §271 does not apply to every major transaction; it only applies to transactions that strike at the heart of a corporation's existence, which this transaction does not. Only by ignoring the statute's language, International argues, can this court determine that International will have sold substantially all its assets by divesting itself of the *Telegraph* Group.

As an alternative argument, International contends that §271 is inapplicable for another reason. International argues that none of *its* assets are being sold at all, because the *Telegraph* Group is held through a chain of wholly owned subsidiaries and it is only the last link in that chain which is actually being sold to the Barclays.

In this opinion, I conclude that Inc.'s motion for a preliminary injunction motion should be denied as neither its §271 nor its equitable claims have a reasonable probability of success.

I choose not to decide whether International's technical statutory defense has merit. It is common for public companies to hold all of their operating assets through indirect, wholly owned subsidiaries. International wants me to hold that a parent company board may unilaterally direct and control a process by which its indirect, wholly owned subsidiary sells assets that would, if held directly by the parent, possibly comprise substantially all of the parent's assets and by which the sale proceeds under a contract that the parent corporation itself negotiates, signs, and fully guarantees. In that circumstance, International says that §271 would have no application unless the selling subsidiary has no corporate dignity under the strict test for veil piercing. A ruling of that kind would, as a practical matter, render §271 an illusory check on unilateral board power at most public companies. And while that ruling would involve a rational reading of §271, it would not represent the only possible interpretation of that statute. Because this motion can be resolved on substantive economic grounds and because the policy implications of ruling on International's technical defense are important, prudence counsels in favor of deferring a necessarily hasty decision on the interesting question presented.

Instead, I address the economic merits of Inc.'s §271 claim and treat the *Telegraph* Group as if it were directly owned by International. An application of the governing test, which was originally articulated in Gimbel v. Signal Cos.,[2] to the facts demonstrates that the *Telegraph* Group does not come close to comprising "substantially all" of International's assets. Although the *Telegraph* Group is a very important asset of International's and is likely its most valuable asset, International possesses several other important assets. Prominent among these is its so-called Chicago Group, a valuable collection of publications that, by any objective standard approaches the *Telegraph* Group in economic importance to International. In fact, earlier this year, Inc. based its decision to try to sell itself to the Barclays on advice that the Chicago Group was worth more than the *Telegraph* Group. And the record is replete with evidence indicating that the Chicago Group's recent performance in outperforming the profitability of the *Telegraph* Group was not anomalous and that many reasoned observers— including Inc.'s controlling stockholder, Conrad Black—believe that the Chicago Group will continue to generate EBITDA at levels akin to those of the *Telegraph* Group.

Put simply, after the *Telegraph* Group is sold, International will retain considerable assets that are capable of generating substantial free cash flow. Section 271 does not require a vote when a major asset or trophy is sold; it requires a vote only when the assets to be sold, when considered quantitatively and qualitatively, amount to "substantially all" of the corporation's assets.

Inc.'s inability to meet this economically focused test has led it to place great weight on the greater journalistic reputation of the *Telegraph* newspaper when compared to the *Sun-Times* and the social importance of that newspaper in British life. The problem with this argument is that §271 is designed as a protection for rational owners of capital and its proper interpretation requires this court to focus on the economic importance of assets and not their aesthetic worth. The economic value of the *Telegraph's* prestige was reflected in the sales process for the *Telegraph* Group and in the cash flows projected for that Group. The Barclays' bid includes the economic value that bidders place on the *Telegraph's* social cachet and does not approach a price that puts the *Telegraph* Group close to being substantially all of International's assets. Nor does the sale of the *Telegraph* Group break any solemn promise to International stockholders. During its history, International has continually bought and sold publishing assets, and no rational investor would view the *Telegraph* Group as immune from the company's ongoing M & A activity.

---

2. 316 A.2d 599 (Del.Ch.), *aff'd*, 316 A.2d 619 (Del.1974).

A sale of all or substantially all of a company's assets might also trigger *Revlon* duties, although the case law on this point is sparse. Also remember that many credit agreements and indentures contain covenants that restrict asset sales. The most significant case on this issue is *Sharon Steel Corp. v. The Chase Manhattan Bank, N.A.,* which hopefully is vaguely familiar.

Appraisal rights also vary based on the nature of the transaction structure. For example, Delaware law provides that shareholders who do not approve of a merger may exercise appraisal rights if they are dissatisfied with the consideration they receive in the merger. On the other hand, appraisal rights are not available in a stock purchase, either by tender or SPA. Some jurisdictions, but not Delaware, provide for appraisal rights in connection with certain asset sales.[3]

PROBLEM SET 24.1

1. California grants broader voting rights than Delaware in some assets sales, but not others. *See* Cal. Corp. Code. §§181, 1000, 1200, 1201. Why might they draw the distinction that they do? Is this approach preferable to the Delaware approach?

4.   THE LIMITS OF ASSET SALES

DARREL FRANKLIN v. USX CORPORATION

87 Cal.App.4th 615
Court of Appeal, First District, Division 3, California.
March 2, 2001.

WALKER, J.

Jeannette Franklin, now deceased, and her husband, Darrel Franklin (respondents), filed an action for personal injury, premises liability and loss of consortium against several defendants, including appellant USX Corporation (USX). Respondents contended that Jeannette had contracted mesothelioma, an asbestos-caused cancer, as a result of childhood exposure to second hand asbestos carried home by her parents, who worked at the Western Pipe & Steel Shipyard (WPS) in South San Francisco during World War II. Respondents sought to hold USX liable for their injuries on the theory that it was the successor in interest to WPS. By stipulation, the successor in interest issue was tried by the court on a statement of facts that were either agreed to or disputed, along with an agreed-upon documentary record; no testimony was presented in this phase of the trial. The trial court concluded that USX was the successor in interest to WPS, and was therefore liable for any damages caused by WPS. In a bifurcated proceeding, a jury decided the issues of liability and damages, and returned a verdict against USX in excess of $5 million.

---

3. N.Y. Bus. Corp. §910(a)(B).

USX appeals the trial court's conclusion that it was the successor in interest to WPS. It also appeals the jury verdict on several grounds. We hold that the trial court erred in finding USX liable as the successor in interest to WPS. Accordingly, we do not address the issues pertaining to the jury verdict.

GENERAL BACKGROUND

Prior to the beginning of World War II, WPS owned a steel fabrication plant in South San Francisco, which had been used to build ships during World War I. When World War II broke out, WPS entered into a contract with the United States Maritime Commission to again build ships for use in the war. The contract required the use of ship building materials containing asbestos.

Jeannette Franklin was a child during World War II. Both of her parents worked at WPS from 1942 to 1945. Neither of her parents worked directly with asbestos-containing materials, but they both worked in areas where asbestos was present. At times, they were exposed to airborne dust during the mixing of mud, during insulation work, and when workers swept up debris. Franklin alleged that she was exposed to this asbestos-containing dust because her parents brought it home on their clothing and in their car. In 1996, Franklin was diagnosed with peritoneal mesothelioma, which she maintained was caused by her childhood second hand exposure to asbestos.

CORPORATE HISTORY

In December 1945, the assets of WPS were purchased by Consolidated Steel Corporation of California (Con Cal) for over $6.2 million in cash. In connection with the sale, Con Cal agreed to assume all of the liabilities, obligations and commitments of WPS.

On December 14, 1946, Con Cal and some of its affiliates entered into an agreement (the purchase agreement) to sell certain assets (the transfer assets) to Columbia Steel Company (Columbia), a division of U.S. Steel. Although the closing date was set for March 31, 1947, the filing of a Sherman Act antitrust action delayed the closing until the summer of 1948. In August 1948, Columbia assigned its rights under the purchase agreement to a newly formed corporation and subsidiary of U.S. Steel, Consolidated Western Steel Corporation of Delaware (Con Del). On August 31, 1948, Con Cal sold the transfer assets to Con Del for almost $8.3 million in cash, plus additional consideration that brought the total purchase price to over $17 million. Con Del was later merged into U.S. Steel, which thereafter changed its name to USX, the appellant here.[4] After August 31, 1948, Con Cal changed its name to Consolidated Liquidating Corporation, which dissolved on February 29, 1952. Alden G. Roach was Con Cal's president and chairman of the board at the time of the sale; after the sale he

---

4. To avoid confusion, we will hereafter refer to the purchasing party as USX.

continued as president of Con Del and Columbia, and was appointed chairman of Columbia's board.

DISCUSSION

It has been generally stated that "where one corporation sells or transfers all of its assets to another corporation, the latter is not liable for the debts and liabilities of the former unless (1) the purchaser expressly or impliedly agrees to such assumption, (2) the transaction amounts to a consolidation or merger of the two corporations, (3) the purchasing corporation is merely a continuation of the selling corporation, or (4) the transaction is entered into fraudulently to escape liability for debts." In addition, under certain limited circumstances an exception has been judicially created to provide a remedy against the successor when a person has been injured by the predecessor's product. This exception, first enunciated in Ray v. Alad, *supra*, 19 Cal.3d 22, 136 Cal.Rptr. 574, 560 P.2d 3, has become known as the "product line successor" rule. The trial court found USX liable for respondents' injuries under the first three general exceptions to non-liability, as well as under the product line successor exception. We consider each ground, and hold that USX cannot be found to be the successor in interest to Con Cal/WPS under any of the theories asserted.

USX DID NOT EXPRESSLY OR IMPLIEDLY ASSUME THE TORT LIABILITIES OF CON CAL/WPS

Based upon its interpretation of the 1946 purchase agreement and other extrinsic evidence, the trial court found that USX had expressly or impliedly assumed the tort liabilities of Con Cal/WPS. Because no issue of credibility was involved in the trial court's determination, we review the agreement and the extrinsic evidence de novo with an eye toward giving effect to the mutual intentions of the contracting parties. We first consider the language of the purchase agreement itself, which we conclude unambiguously shows that USX did not assume the tort liabilities of Con Cal/WPS. We further hold that, because the unambiguous contract was expressly integrated, it was improper to consider extrinsic evidence to vary or alter its terms. Finally, even if the extrinsic evidence is taken into account, it does not show the parties' intention that USX assume the liabilities at issue in this action.

Pursuant to the 1946 purchase agreement, the bulk of Con Cal's business assets were purchased by USX, with Con Cal retaining certain specified assets and certain existing contracts. With regard to USX's assumption of liabilities, the agreement provided: "The Buyer shall not, except as herein otherwise specifically provided, directly or indirectly, by virtue of any of the provisions of this agreement, become liable for any of the debts, obligations, liabilities, undertakings, agreements or commitments of the Sellers of any nature whatsoever. . . . It further provided that, while USX would assume responsibility for performing "all the obligations of the Sellers with respect to the uncompleted portion of [assumed] contracts, orders and subcontracts ... *in no event* shall the Buyer assume any obligations of the Sellers, or any of them, arising out of deliveries of goods, wares or merchandise made by the Sellers prior to the closing, including, but not limited to, any claims on account of any allegedly defective goods, wares or merchandise delivered by the Sellers pursuant to any such contract or order, or otherwise." (Italics added.)

The quoted language is clear and unambiguous; USX assumed only the liabilities specified in the purchase agreement, which did not include the assumption of contingent tort liabilities. It is equally clear that the purchase agreement was an integrated document. It provided that "[t]here are no agreements, contracts, promises, representations or statements between the parties hereto except as contained in this agreement, and this agreement shall constitute the entire and whole contract between the parties hereto."

Notwithstanding the quoted language of the integrated agreement, the trial court found the "contract documents" to be ambiguous, and considered documents extrinsic to the contract in order to resolve the perceived ambiguity. Based upon the purchase agreement provision rendering USX responsible for all unfilled sales orders and on an indemnity clause contained in a document entitled "Bill of Sale" entered into on August 31, 1948, the court found that the agreement between the parties regarding the assumption of liabilities was ambiguous. The indemnity clause in the bill of sale provided that the seller would use its best efforts to obtain written consent from "third parties to all assignments and transfers of leases, contracts, agreements, licenses, options and other property, assets and business assigned and transferred to the respective Buyers ... in order to make effective as against said third parties any such assignment and transfer, it being understood that, if the respective Buyer shall assume all liabilities thereunder of the Seller to the third party or parties remaining unperformed at the time of such assignment, the Seller will save, defend and keep harmless the respective Buyer of, from and against such part of such unperformed liabilities as shall relate to the period to and including August 31, 1948."

This indemnity provision was itself clear, and did not render ambiguous the parties' intentions with regard to the assumption of tort liabilities, as it had nothing to do with those liabilities. The subject matter of this indemnity clause pertained only to unfinished contracts assumed by USX in the purchase, and to Con Cal's promise to indemnify USX for those parts of the contracts remaining unperformed before the closing date. While USX agreed to assume responsibility to complete those contracts after the closing date, it specifically disavowed responsibility and liability under the contracts to the extent these arose prior to the closing.

In addition, we note that the bill of sale contained specific and clear provisions relating to the buyer's general non-assumption of liability. It stated that "[t]he transfer of the Seller's business and certain of its property and assets to the Buyers is made without the assumption by the Buyers of any of the liabilities of the Seller except those specifically enumerated below, and the Seller hereby covenants and agrees at all times to save, defend and keep harmless the Buyers . . . from and against any and all claims . . . expenses and liabilities whatsoever, based upon, arising out of or in any way connected with the Seller's liabilities except those specifically enumerated. . . ." Those specifically enumerated exceptions were for liabilities on contracts, purchase orders, unfilled sales orders, performance bonds and indemnity contracts arising *after* August 31, 1948. This provision, as well as the indemnity provision relied upon by the trial court, comport completely with the clear and unambiguous terms of the purchase agreement, by which USX assumed no liabilities for the damages at issue in this lawsuit. We thus conclude that, because the contract language was unambiguous, and the parol evidence created no ambiguity and was consistent with the contract, the trial court erred in considering the extrinsic evidence to vary or modify the terms of the contract. (Pacific Gas & Electric v. G.W. Thomas Drayage Co. (1968) 69 Cal.2d 33, 37, 69 Cal.Rptr. 561, 442 P.2d 641.)

Nonetheless, by referring to extrinsic evidence, the court concluded that USX had, expressly or by implication, assumed liability for the personal injury claims asserted by the Franklins. In reaching its conclusion, the trial court looked to two other categories of extrinsic evidence.

First, it considered letters written by USX to third parties after the execution of the purchase agreement. In these letters, Con Cal's customers, vendors and subcontractors were informed of the sale of Con Cal's "business and operating properties" to Con Del, and were told that "[t]he change of ownership will not in any way affect the fulfillment of the contractual obligations of the selling company. All undelivered orders and uncompleted contracts of that company will be assumed by the acquiring company and will be performed by it in strict accordance with their terms." In similar letters, various governmental entities were informed of the sale, and advised that Con Del "will continue to operate the transferred facilities and business without material change in present personnel, management or business policies."

The trial court concluded that the "business policies" referred to in these letters "included, among others, Consolidated California's policy to assume WPS' debts and liabilities of any nature." The fundamental problem with this finding is that it finds absolutely no support in the record. These letters speak for themselves: they were written to inform the recipients of the change in ownership, and assure them that the change would have no effect on the fulfillment of the seller's contractual obligations. Based upon the evidence in the record, the letters were not susceptible to the trial court's interpretation.

The court also looked to a Navy contract that USX assumed as part of the purchase agreement. This contract was the one under which WPS had agreed to build ships during the war, resulting in the employment of Jeannette Franklin's parents. The trial court found that the Navy contract imposed on WPS the obligation to maintain and repair the premises at its South San Francisco shipyard, that "all of USX's potential liability in this premises liability case arises out of WPS' operation of the shipyard under this contract, and therefore arises directly out of the fulfillment of this contract that USX specifically assumed," and that "had WPS fulfilled all of its obligations under this contract, Jeannette Franklin's parents likely would not have endured the asbestos exposures at WPS' shipyard that are the subject of this lawsuit against USX." From this analysis, the trial court concluded that USX expressly assumed the tort liabilities of Con Cal/WPS. Again, our review of the document and of the evidence in the record does not support the trial court's conclusion.

The Navy contract in question imposed upon WPS the responsibility to maintain and repair the facilities prior to their transfer to the government. It made no mention of any obligations that could be interpreted as inuring to the benefit of shipyard employees and their safety. Thus, even if considered for the purpose of shedding light on the intent of the parties with respect to assumption of the seller's tort liabilities, the Navy contract contributed nothing. In addition, there was no evidence in the record to support the trial court's finding that WPS had not fulfilled its obligations under the Navy contract, or that had it done so Jeannette Franklin's parents "likely would not have endured the asbestos exposures."

THERE WAS NO DE FACTO MERGER OR MERE CONTINUATION

The trial court also found that USX could be deemed to have assumed the liabilities of Con Cal/WPS under the de facto merger theory and under the theory that USX was a "mere continuation" of Con Cal. Although these two theories have been traditionally considered as separate bases for imposing liability on a successor corporation, we perceive the second to be merely a subset of the first.[5] The crucial factor in determining whether a corporate acquisition constitutes either a de facto merger or a mere continuation is the same: whether adequate cash consideration was paid for the predecessor corporation's assets.

No California case we have found has imposed successor liability for personal injuries on a corporation that paid adequate cash consideration for the predecessor's assets. The trial court recognized this limitation to its holding, but found "no logical reason why the fact that the consideration for a purchase of corporate assets is cash (with an agreement to liquidate) rather than stock should in itself bar victims from recovering from the purchaser for the seller's tortious conduct." We, however, perceive a very sound reason for the rule of non-liability in adequate cash sales: predictability. "Predictability is vital in the corporate field. Unforeseeable alterations in successor liability principles complicate transfers and necessarily increase transaction costs. [Citations.] Major economic decisions, critical to society, are best made in a climate of relative certainty and reasonable predictability. The imposition of successor liability on a purchasing company long after the transfer of assets defeats the legitimate expectations the

---

5. In fact, it appears to us that the mere continuation theory swallows up the de facto merger theory, because once the two mere continuation elements are satisfied there is no need to further consider the additional elements of the de facto merger theory in establishing successor liability.

parties held during negotiation and sale. Another consequence that must be faced is that few opportunities would exist for the financially troubled company that wishes to cease business but has had its assets devalued by the extension of successor liability. In addition, of course, a sale for adequate cash consideration ensures that at the time of sale there are adequate means to satisfy any claims made against the predecessor corporation. (See Ray v. Alad, *supra*, 19 Cal.3d at p. 29, 136 Cal.Rptr. 574, 560 P.2d 3.)

In reaching its conclusion that the sale of Con Cal's assets to USX constituted a de facto merger, the trial court relied on Marks v. Minnesota Mining & Manufacturing Co. (1986) 187 Cal.App.3d 1429, 232 Cal.Rptr. 594 (*Marks*). In *Marks*, the court . . . noted: "The critical fact is that while there was more than one merger or reorganization, an analysis of each transaction discloses to us that its intrinsic structure and nature, *unlike a sale of assets for cash*, was of a type in which the corporate entity was continued and all liability was transferred."

Marks is not alone in recognizing the overriding significance of the type and adequacy of consideration paid in a corporate asset sale.

In discussing the mere continuation exception to the general rule of successor nonliability, the court in Ray v. Alad stated that liability has been imposed on a successor corporation "only upon a showing of *one or both* of the following factual elements: (1) no adequate consideration was given for the predecessor corporation's assets and made available for meeting the claims of its unsecured creditors; (2) one or more persons were officers, directors, or stockholders of both corporations. [Citations.]" (Ray v. Alad, 19 Cal.3d at p. 29, 136 Cal.Rptr. 574, 560 P.2d 3, italics added.) Respondents make much of the second prong enunciated by Ray v. Alad, asserting that the trial court properly found USX to be a mere continuation of Con Cal because Alden Roach was president and a board member of both the predecessor and the successor corporations. However, a review of the cases cited by the Ray v. Alad court to support its statement reveals that all of the cases involved the payment of inadequate cash consideration, and some also involved near complete identity of ownership, management or directorship after the transfer. None of these cases involved a situation such as the one before us, where the consideration paid was undisputedly adequate, and only a single person with minimal ownership interest in either entity remained as an officer and director.

Thus, although other factors are relevant to both the de facto merger and mere continuation exceptions, the common denominator, which must be present in order to avoid the general rule of successor non-liability, is the payment of inadequate consideration. The evidence presented showed that in 1948 Con Cal was paid in excess of $17 million for its business assets. As was the case in Ray v. Alad, no claim has been made that this consideration was inadequate, or that there were insufficient assets available *at the time of the predecessor's dissolution* to meet the claims of its creditors. Lacking the essential factor of inadequate consideration, there was no de facto merger, nor could USX be deemed a mere continuation of Con Cal.

THE PRODUCT LINE SUCCESSOR THEORY DOES NOT APPLY TO TORT CLAIMS

Finally, contrary to established California precedent, the trial court found that pursuant to Ray v. Alad, USX was liable as a product line successor in interest to Con Cal/WPS, even though respondents had asserted no claim for strict product liability.

In Ray v. Alad, *supra*, 19 Cal.3d 22, 136 Cal.Rptr. 574, 560 P.2d 3, the California Supreme Court imposed liability on Alad Corporation for the plaintiff's injury sustained in a fall from a defective ladder manufactured by Alad Corporation's predecessor. The injury occurred more than six months after Alad Corporation had acquired the assets of the dissolved ladder manufacturer. Although none of the traditional bases for imposing liability on Alad Corporation were present in the plaintiff's action against it for strict product liability, the court held that given the specific circumstances, the plaintiff should recover under a special exception to the general rule. The court explained that "'the paramount policy to be promoted by the [strict product liability] rule is the protection of otherwise defenseless victims of manufacturing defects and the spreading throughout society of the cost of compensating them.'" It held that imposition of strict liability against the successor to the manufacturer was justified where, as in the case before it, the plaintiff had no viable remedy against the then nonexistent manufacturer of the defective product, the successor to the manufacturer continued to manufacture the same product line as its predecessor, retained the same personnel, used the same designs and customer lists, gave no outward indication of the change in ownership and had opportunities to evaluate production risks and pass on the cost of meeting those risks almost identical to its predecessor's. The Ray v. Alad court presented a three-part rationale for imposing strict liability on the successor corporation: "(1) the virtual destruction of the plaintiff's remedies against the original manufacturer caused by the successor's acquisition of the business, (2) the successor's ability to assume the original manufacturer's risk-spreading role, and (3) the fairness of requiring the successor to assume a responsibility for defective products that was a burden necessarily attached to the original manufacturer's good will being enjoyed by the successor in the continued operation of the business."

The trial court here found that the Ray v. Alad product line successor exception should not be limited to product liability claims, but should extend to ordinary negligence actions. Respondents urge us to reach the same conclusion. In Monarch Bay II v. Professional Service Industries, Inc. (1999) 75 Cal.App.4th 1213, 89 Cal.Rptr.2d 778 (*Monarch Bay II*) and *Maloney, supra*, 207 Cal.App.3d 282, 255 Cal.Rptr. 1, this precise argument was presented and rejected. As did those two courts before us, we decline to expand the product line exception beyond the arena of product liability.

We concur with the court's comments in *Monarch Bay II:* "[Appellant] argues there is no significant difference between a plaintiff injured by a defective product and one harmed by corporate negligence and urges us to broaden the *Ray* exception. We agree that in many respects, the distinction is without a difference.

But we see no policy reasons to extend *Ray's* holding beyond strict tort liability. The criticisms levied at the product line exception, which, of course, we are bound to follow under the principles of stare decisis, militate against eroding the traditional rule even further. . . . The trend in other jurisdictions appears to be away from expansion of successor liability. Although the product line exception was adopted by a number of courts following the *Ray* opinion, 'recent cases from a variety of states have rejected the product line exception in favor of retaining the traditional rule on non-liability.' The *Ray* court clearly intended the product line exception to be limited to the circumstances presented in that case, and we decline to extend the rationale to other circumstances." (*Monarch Bay II, supra*, 75 Cal.App.4th at pp. 1218–1219, 89 Cal.Rptr.2d 778.)

The court in *Monarch Bay II* also concluded, as we have in the context of de facto mergers, that an imposition of product line successor liability in non-product-liability cases would upset the predictability so vital to key economic decisions made in the corporate milieu. (*Monarch Bay II, supra*, 75 Cal.App.4th at p. 1218, 89 Cal.Rptr.2d 778.) We, too, view this predictability as crucial. There is no legal basis to support a conclusion that USX was a product line successor liable to respondents for their tort claims.

CONCLUSION AND DISPOSITION

The trial court found USX liable for the Franklins' injuries allegedly caused by WPS. We conclude that no such successor in interest liability attaches. The fully integrated purchase agreement between the predecessor of USX and Con Cal expressly and unambiguously provided that the buyer was not assuming the seller's liabilities except as specifically provided. The specific assumptions pertained only to business related obligations, and not to the liabilities at issue in this action. Because the purchase agreement was unambiguous and fully integrated, the trial court erred in considering extrinsic evidence to vary or alter the terms of the agreement. Even considering that evidence, however, the agreement was not reasonably susceptible to the court's interpretation. Since respondents have not asserted that the consideration for the sale of Con Cal's assets was inadequate or that there were insufficient assets to satisfy creditors' claims at the time of dissolution, USX was not liable as a successor in interest under the theories of de facto merger or mere continuation. Finally, we conclude that the product line successor rule applies only to product liability actions, and is therefore inapplicable to the present case. Based upon these holdings, we reverse the trial court's determination of the successor in interest issue, and do not address the remaining issues raised. The judgment entered against USX is reversed. Appellant shall recover its costs on appeal.

CORRIGAN, Acting P.J., and PARRILLI, J., concur.

Contractual solutions sometimes provide an answer to the question of how a deal can still proceed in the face of the risk of successor liability. But only if they are drafted very carefully, as the next case shows.

FINA, INC. v. ARCO, BP OIL COMPANY

200 F.3d 266
United States Court of Appeals, Fifth Circuit.
Jan. 4, 2000.

WIENER, Circuit Judge:
In this case arising under the Comprehensive Environmental Response, Compensation, and Liability Act ("CERCLA"), 42 U.S.C. §§9601 *et seq.*, Plaintiff-Appellant Fina, Inc. ("Fina") appeals the district court's grant of summary judgment in favor of Defendants-Appellees BP Oil Company ("BP") and Atlantic Richfield Company ("ARCO"). Fina contends that the district court improperly applied Delaware law in holding that cross-indemnities running between the parties bar Fina's CERCLA claims against BP and ARCO. We hold that the indemnities are unenforceable with respect to the CERCLA liability in question, and accordingly reverse and remand for proceedings consistent with this opinion.

I.

FACTS AND PROCEEDINGS

BP acquired a refinery located in Port Arthur, Texas from ARCO in 1969. BP subsequently sold the refinery to Fina in 1973. The ARCO/BP and BP/Fina agreements of sale contain cross-indemnities that apportion responsibility between the contracting parties for liabilities arising from the operation of the refinery. The ARCO/BP agreement provides in relevant part that:

> BP shall indemnify, defend, and hold harmless ARCO . . . against all claims, actions, demands, losses or liabilities arising from the ownership or the operation of the Assets . . . and accruing from and after Closing . . . except to the extent that any such claim, action, demand, loss or liability shall arise from the gross negligence of ARCO.

The BP/Fina agreement provides in relevant part that:

> Fina shall indemnify, defend and hold harmless BP . . . against all claims, actions, demands, losses or liabilities arising from the use or the operation of the Assets . . . . and accruing from and after closing.

In 1989, Fina conducted an environmental investigation covering all areas of the refinery. It found seven areas of the refinery contaminated with solid and hazardous wastes. Investigating the origins of the contamination, Fina unearthed evidence that the pollution was at least in part attributable to the activities of BP and ARCO.

Fina reported its discovery to the State of Texas. The Texas Natural Resource Conservation Commission ordered Fina to conduct several further investigations. Those investigations are still ongoing. Fina has already incurred over $14 million in investigatory and remedial response costs.

In 1996, Fina sued BP and ARCO seeking contribution and cost recovery under the Comprehensive Environmental Response, Compensation, and Liability Act ("CERCLA"), 42 U.S.C. §§9607 and 9613(f). BP filed a declaratory judgment counterclaim against Fina, arguing that Fina's claims are covered by the indemnity provision in the BP/Fina agreement of sale. ARCO filed a similar declaratory judgment cross-claim against BP.

All parties moved for summary judgment. The district court granted the motions of BP and ARCO, ruling that (1) Fina's claims against BP are covered by the BP/Fina indemnity provision, (2) Fina's claims against ARCO are covered by the ARCO/BP indemnity provision, and (3) because ARCO is indemnified by BP which in turn is indemnified by Fina, a "circuitous indemnity obligation" is owed by Fina to ARCO, which obligation covers Fina's claims against ARCO.

ISSUES

We are called on to interpret and determine the enforceability of two related yet distinctly different indemnity provisions. The BP/Fina and ARCO/BP indemnity provisions both allocate responsibility between the contracting parties for liabilities arising from the ownership or operation of the refinery. The two provisions differ, however, in two significant respects. First, whereas the BP/Fina agreement of sale includes a choice of law provision designating Delaware law as the governing law, the ARCO/BP agreement of sale does not contain a choice of law provision. Second, the ARCO/BP indemnity provision, unlike its BP/Fina counterpart, states that it covers all claims "except to the extent that any such claim . . . shall arise from the gross negligence of ARCO." We must therefore analyze the two indemnity provisions separately.

1.   The BP/Fina Indemnity Provision

Fina contends that the BP/Fina indemnity provision does not indemnify BP for retroactive CERCLA liability. Under the indemnity provision, Fina's obligations to BP extend only to those liabilities that accrue after the closing date of the BP/Fina agreement of sale. Fina contends that, although CERCLA was not enacted until 1980, the CERCLA liability "accrued" at the time that BP and ARCO polluted the refinery grounds-well before the closing date of the BP/Fina agreement of sale. Fina argues in the alternative that, even if the BP/Fina indemnity provision does purport within its broad terms to cover the CERCLA liability in question, the provision is unenforceable with respect to that liability because governing Delaware law requires that, to indemnify a party for prospective strict liability claims, an indemnity provision must "clearly and unequivocally" state that it covers such claims. As we conclude that the indemnity provision is unenforceable under Delaware law with respect to the CERCLA liability at issue here, we need not reach the question whether the liability "accrued" prior to closing, within the meaning of the agreement.

Under Delaware law, contracts to indemnify a party against the consequences of its own negligence are strictly construed against the indemnitee. The purpose of this rule is to ensure that the indemnitor is fully cognizant of the extraordinary risk that it is assuming.

Delaware law thus requires that, to be enforceable, "the intent to indemnify must be clear and unequivocal" on the face of an indemnity provision. "To be enforceable, the provision must specifically focus attention on the fact that by the agreement the indemnitor was assuming liability for [the] indemnitee's own negligence." The Delaware courts have often stated that there are no particular words that must be used to render an indemnity provision enforceable. But "[n]o Delaware case has allowed indemnification of a party for its own negligence without making specific reference to negligence of the indemnified party."

The BP/Fina indemnity provision gives no indication that the parties considered the issue of indemnifying BP for the consequences of its own negligence: There is no reference in the indemnity to BP's own negligence, and its use of the phrase "all claims, actions, demands, losses or liabilities" is insufficient as a matter of Delaware law to satisfy the clear and unequivocal test. Thus, the BP/Fina indemnity provision is unenforceable as applied to the prospective CERCLA liability at issue in this case.

We hold, therefore, that (1) the BP/Fina indemnity provision is subject to the clear and unequivocal test under Delaware law as applied to Fina's CERCLA claims against BP; (2) the BP/Fina indemnity provision fails to satisfy the clear and unequivocal test; and (3) the indemnity provision consequently does not bar Fina's claims against BP.

The ARCO/BP agreement of sale does not contain a choice-of-law provision. ARCO and BP agree, however, that the contract is governed by Texas law. Since 1987, Texas has applied the "express negligence" test in lieu of the "clear and unequivocal" test. The "express negligence" test holds that "parties seeking to indemnify the indemnitee from the consequences of its own negligence must express that intent in specific terms." This rule is applicable to claims based on strict liability. And, because the rationale behind the Texas rule is the same as the rationale behind the Delaware rule, we are satisfied that Texas would apply the "express negligence" test to all claims that were merely prospective at the time the indemnity provision was signed.

The ARCO/BP provision indemnifies ARCO for "all claims ... arising from the ownership or the operation of the Assets ... and accruing from and after Closing ... except to the extent that any such claim ... shall arise from the gross negligence of ARCO." It makes no mention of claims based on BP's own negligence or on strict liability. The Texas Supreme Court has held that an indemnification provision is not enforceable as applied to claims based on strict liability unless that provision expressly states the indemnitor's intent to cover such claims. Even if the exclusion of gross negligence from the indemnity's coverage is interpreted as indicating that BP intended to indemnify ARCO for ordinary negligence, claims based on strict liability are of quite a different nature. Texas law requires that each type of claim be separately referenced by an indemnity provision: "Indemnification against strict liability is an exception to usual business practices in the same manner as indemnifying against someone else's negligence. . . . [F]airness dictates against imposing liability on an indemnitor unless the agreement clearly and specifically expresses the intent to encompass strict liability claims." Thus, the ARCO/BP indemnity provision is not enforceable under Texas law as applied to claims based on strict liability. Consequently, ARCO may not seek indemnification from BP for any amounts recovered against it by Fina based on strict liability.

For the reasons discussed above, the district court's grant of summary judgment is reversed and the case is remanded for further proceedings consistent with this opinion.

What are the other limits of these sorts of contractual solutions?

5.   TAX MATTERS

As a general matter, the sale of all of the target's assets will result in a taxable event for the target to the extent it receives more for its assets than the current tax basis of those assets, and its shareholders will recognize gain on the distribution of any proceeds from the sale.

Thus, an asset sale results in two levels of tax on the seller side if proceeds are distributed, an unfavorable result for the seller and its shareholders if significant appreciation in target asset value exists. The parties must weigh this against the other factors that might suggest the need to proceed by APA.

And note that the corporate level tax will not be an issue if the target has sufficient NOLs to offset against any gains realized upon sale. The tax basis of the target's assets is increased at closing to the purchase price paid, which may be of some benefit to the buyer.

25

LEVERAGED BUYOUTS AND
DISTRESSED ACQUISITIONS

Justice Breyer recently explained that in *a leveraged buyout* (LBO)

> the buyer (B) typically borrows from a third party (T) a large share of the funds
> needed to purchase a company (C). B then pays the money to C's shareholders.
> Having bought the stock, B owns C. B then pledges C's assets to T so that T will
> have security for its loan. Thus, if the selling price for C is $50 million, B might
> use $10 million of its own money, borrow $40 million from T, pay $50 million to
> C's shareholders, and then pledge C assets worth $40 million (or more) to T as
> security for T's $40 million loan. If B manages C well, it might make enough
> money to pay T back the $40 million and earn a handsome profit on its own $10
> million investment. But, if the deal sours and C descends into bankruptcy, beware
> of what might happen: Instead of C's $40 million in assets being distributed to its
> existing creditors, the money will go to T to pay back T's loan—the loan that
> allowed B to buy C. (T will receive what remains of C's assets because T is now a
> secured creditor, putting it at the top of the priority list).[1]

LBOs are strongly associated with private equity firms, who often use an
LBO to move a publicly traded firm into the private equity firm's portfolio of
companies. Distressed acquisitions, on the other hand, involve acquisition of a
company that is already highly indebted, and perhaps experiencing or on the
verge of financial distress.

Both types of transactions involve the M&A techniques discussed in earlier
classes, but also invoke a special set of considerations examined in this chapter.
As a general rule, leveraged buyouts tend to peak during good economic times,
when banks are quite willing to lend to potential buyers.

Thus, following Lehman Brothers' chapter 11 filing in September 2008, JC
Flowers & Co. LLC backed out of a $26 billion buyout of SLM Corp.; Goldman
Sachs Capital Partners cancelled an $8 billion deal for Harman International
Industries, Inc.; Bain Capital LLC, Carlyle Group, and Clayton, Dubilier & Rice,
Inc.'s $10.3 billion buyout of Home Depot, Inc.'s H&D Supply, Inc. was reduced

---

1. Czyzewski v. Jevic Holding Corp., 580 U. S. ____ (2017) (slip opinion at p. 5).

to $8.5 billion; and Thomas H. Lee Partners LP and Bain Capital's buyout of Clear Channel Communications, Inc., originally announced for $25 billion, was restructured to involve much less consideration. This represented a rather abrupt end to more than five years of frenzied LBO activity.

Distressed acquisitions, our other yet related topic in this Chapter, can occur during any economic phase, although they obviously increase in volume when more potential sellers are distressed.

For the distressed seller, the choice of transaction structure will be driven by whether the assets sold constitute substantially all the assets of the company, whether the sale proceeds can be maximized by separate assets sales to multiple buyers, and what is the best way to consummate a transaction given the seller's obligations to its creditors.[2] The reasons behind these considerations should be apparent from earlier classes.

In an LBO, the goal is typically to "cash out" the existing shareholders and replace them with the new owners, and quite often new management, too. LBOs come in a few different flavors. For example, a "bust up" LBO is based on the notion that that the whole is worth less than the sum of the parts.

More often recent LBO transactions have been based on an operational turnaround or a cyclical swing. Turnaround deals almost invariably involve the introduction of new management. Cyclical deals are based on a bet that the buyer is right about timing an industry cycle.

1.   FINANCING LBOs

The typical LBO is financed with a combination of devices already seen earlier in this course. The next case examines the typical structure, and the conflicts of interest that can arise.

PARACOR FINANCE, INC. v. GENERAL ELECTRIC CAPITAL CORPORATION

96 F.3d 1151
United States Court of Appeals, Ninth Circuit.
March 13, 1996.

O'SCANNLAIN, Circuit Judge:

In reviewing this saga of a debenture offering turned sour, we must decide whether any of the supporting cast on the offeror's side have violated the securities laws. In particular, we must determine whether the lender in a financial transaction should be considered a "controlling person" of its borrower.

---

2. It is generally accepted that the creditors of an insolvent company can enforce the fiduciary duties that you learned about in your basic Corporations or Business Associations class. *N. Am. Catholic Educ. Programming Fund v. Gheewalla*, 930 A.2d 92 (Del. 2007).

I

We begin with the facts that led up to the debenture offering at issue here as an appeal from a "Final Partial Judgment" under Federal Rule of Civil Procedure 54(b) which recapped a series of prior orders of the district court granting summary judgments. Jordan Schnitzer, a Portland businessman, hired Bear, Stearns & Co. to locate a profitable corporation which he could purchase and merge with an unprofitable corporation he owned in order to utilize his corporation's net operating loss carryforwards and obtain certain tax benefits. He was directed to Casablanca Industries, Inc., a California manufacturer of ceiling fans.

In December 1988, Schnitzer approached General Electric Capital Corp. ("GE Capital") for financing for a leveraged buyout of Casablanca. After undertaking its own due diligence, GE Capital agreed to provide a bridge loan for the acquisition. One condition of the bridge loan was that the acquired Casablanca would immediately sell $27 million in high-yield subordinated debentures (aka "junk bonds"), which would be used partially to pay down the loan. The bridge financing would then be replaced with permanent financing by GE Capital. A bridge loan of $53 million to Casablanca Acquisition Corp., a company formed by Schnitzer to make the acquisition, was eventually made in April 1989.

In March 1989, Shearson Lehman Brothers Inc. ("Shearson") was retained to place the subordinated debentures with investors. Shearson prepared a Private Placement Memorandum ("Placement Memorandum") for this purpose. The Placement Memorandum contained various representations about Casablanca including sales projections of $83.3 million and earnings of $8.5 million for fiscal year 1989. Shearson distributed the Placement Memorandum to various institutional investors active in the subordinated debt market.

Elders Finance, Inc. (now known as Paracor Finance, Inc.), Cargill Financial Services Corp., Lutheran Brotherhood, and Farm Bureau Life Insurance Co. (collectively "the Investors") received the Placement Memorandum. During the following weeks, analysts for the Investors performed their own due diligence on the offering. The analysts inspected Casablanca's books, met with its management, visited Casablanca's offices, and had occasional contacts with GE Capital (the substance of which forms part of this dispute). By early May, the Investors had decided to purchase the debentures. The closing of the deal was delayed until late June, however, by continuing negotiations over its terms.

By June, Schnitzer had successfully completed his tender offer and merged his corporation with Casablanca. In the interim, Casablanca's fortunes had been declining. Casablanca's April sales were only $7.88 million, compared with projections of $10.195 million. May and June sales were also below projections. During this time, Burton Burton was the CEO of Casablanca (though the extent of his involvement in its affairs is disputed), and Jerry Holland was the President.

A Debenture Purchase Agreement ("Purchase Agreement") was eventually negotiated between the Investors and Casablanca. In the Purchase Agreement, Casablanca represented that "[s]ince March 31, 1989, Casablanca has not suffered any Material Adverse Effect." The Investors represented that they "had access to the information [they] requested from [Casablanca]" and that they "made [their] own investment decision with respect to the purchase of the Debentures . . . without relying on any other Person." On June 17, 1989, the parties signed the deal documents. On June 23, the Investors wired $27 million to GE Capital as the escrow agent for the various parties to the transaction.

After its first payment of interest on the debentures in August, Casablanca defaulted. Casablanca filed for bankruptcy a little over a year later in November 1990. The Investors, needless to say, were upset.

In March 1991, the Investors filed suit against everyone involved in the transaction, including Casablanca, GE Capital and Schnitzer, Burton, and Holland (collectively "the defendants"). The Investors claimed (1) primary and secondary violations of section 10(b) and Rule 10b-5 of the Securities Exchange Act of 1934, (2) violations of Oregon Revised Statute §59.115 (the "Oregon Securities Law"), and (3) common-law torts of fraud and negligent misrepresentation. The Investors also brought a claim of unjust enrichment against GE Capital alone. The Investors' claims against Casablanca were subject to the bankruptcy stay.

II

The Investors contend that GE Capital and Burton are primarily liable for violations of section 10(b) and Rule 10b-5 for making affirmative misrepresentations and for failing to disclose material facts about Casablanca's sales. The heart of the Investors' claim is that they were not provided with the negative sales data for the three months immediately prior to the closing.

Rule 10b-5(b), enacted under section 10(b) of the Securities Exchange Act of 1934, 15 U.S.C. §78j(b), makes it unlawful "[t]o make any untrue statement of a material fact or to omit to state a material fact necessary in order to make the statements made, in the light of the circumstances under which they were made, not misleading." 17 C.F.R. §240.10b-5(b). The elements of a Rule 10b-5 claim are: (1) a misrepresentation or omission of a material fact, (2) reliance, (3) scienter, and (4) resulting damages. If one of these elements is missing, the Investors' claim fails.

A

Regarding GE Capital, both of the first two elements pose significant obstacles to the Investors' claims. As this is an appeal from summary judgment, we will look at the facts underlying these elements in the light most favorable to the Investors.

1

The heart of the Investors' Rule 10b-5 claim is that GE Capital knew of Casablanca's poor April-June quarter sales results and failed to disclose them. It takes more than mere knowledge, however, to amount to an actionable omission. "Rule 10b-5 is violated by nondisclosure only when there is a duty to disclose." "[T]he parties to an impersonal market transaction owe no duty of disclosure to one another absent a fiduciary or agency relationship, prior dealings, or circumstances such that one party has placed trust and confidence in the other." A number of factors are used to determine whether a party has a duty to disclose: (1) the relationship of the parties, (2) their relative access to information, (3) the benefit that the defendant derives from the relationship, (4) the defendant's awareness that the plaintiff was relying upon the relationship in making his investment decision, and (5) the defendant's activity in initiating the transaction.

Canvassing these factors, the relationship between GE Capital and the Investors did not rise to the level at which GE Capital assumed a duty to disclose. First, GE Capital had no relationship with the Investors prior to the debenture transaction. During the transaction, it had no contact whatsoever with two of the Investors (Lutheran Brotherhood and Farm Bureau Life Insurance), and its contact with the other two amounted to a couple of brief face-to-face meetings and a handful of telephone calls. Second, the Investors' access to information was comparable to GE Capital's. After GE Capital funded the bridge loan in April, Casablanca was required to provide daily "Open Sales Order" reports and weekly "Tuesday" reports. Although the Investors did not receive these reports, they had their own channels for information. The Investors, sophisticated institutions with competent analysts, conducted their own due diligence. They also signed representations that they were provided with all information that they requested, and conceded that such representations were accurate.

Third, GE Capital certainly benefitted from the Investors' purchase of the debentures by having their exposure on the $53 million unsecured bridge loan effectively reduced. Fourth, GE Capital informed Cargill Financial Services and Elders Finance on more than one occasion and in writing that they could not rely on GE Capital. When GE Capital did provide Elders Finance with a copy of its business survey of Casablanca, it insisted that Elders Finance state in writing that it was not relying on GE Capital. Finally, GE Capital effectively initiated the debenture transaction, because its bridge loan to Schnitzer was conditioned on the debenture offering being made.

Taken together, these factors show that GE Capital initiated a financial transaction from which it stood to benefit. They do not show, however, that GE Capital assumed a relationship of trust and confidence with the Investors.

According to the Investors, GE Capital's employees made several oral misrepresentations to employees of Elders Finance and Cargill Financial Services about Casablanca's performance. For example, at a late April meeting, GE Capital's Steve Read stated that Casablanca was "a good property, a good investment."

It is somewhat troubling that while GE Capital was smiling and nodding to the Investors it may have been grimacing in private. At the same time GE Capital's Bengtson was telling Elders Finance's Gerstel that Casablanca was performing in accordance with expectations, Bengtson had also sent a memo to her superior at GE Capital, Scott Lavie, informing him about Casablanca's declining sales. However, the Investors have not introduced evidence that GE Capital lacked at least a reasonable basis for their various representations, even though in hindsight they may now appear a little too rosy. GE Capital's Lavie stated that, as of the closing date, GE Capital was "aware that [Casablanca's fan division] itself [would] not attain its full projections, but we also realized on the twelve months year-to-date, the results were not significantly off what was projected."

The Investors were not novices in the financial markets; these statements, although hedged with reassurances, were sufficient to put them on notice that Casablanca's fan sales were not breezing along as usual. In light of all of the information available to them, and the generality of GE Capital's statements, the Investors have failed to demonstrate an issue of material fact as to whether GE Capital made actionable misrepresentations.

2

Even if the Investors had succeeded in meeting the first element of a Rule 10b-5 claim, they would also have to demonstrate that they had relied on GE Capital. Justifiable reliance "is a limitation on a rule 10b-5 action which insures that there is a causal connection between the misrepresentation and the plaintiff's harm." Atari Corp. v. Ernst & Whinney, 981 F.2d 1025, 1030 (9th Cir.1992) (internal quotation marks omitted).

The Investors have failed to introduce an issue of material fact that they justifiably relied on GE Capital. Significantly, in Section 4.4 of the Purchase Agreement the Investors recited that they were given "access to the information [they have] requested from the Company" and that they "made [their] own investment decision with respect to the purchase of the Debentures ... without relying on any other Person." Elders Finance's Thomas Goossens conceded that the representations in Section 4.4 were true as of the signing of the Purchase Agreement. These representations do much to defeat the Investors' claims of reliance on GE Capital.

Since the Investors fail to establish either of the first two elements of their Rule 10-b5 claim against GE Capital, we do not reach the remaining two.

III

The Investors claim that GE Capital and Burton are secondarily liable for Casablanca's alleged Rule 10b-5 violations because they were "controlling persons" of Casablanca under section 20(a) of the Securities Exchange Act of 1934, 15 U.S.C. §78t(a).

Section 20(a) provides:

> Every person who, directly or indirectly, controls any person liable under any provision of this chapter or of any rule or regulation thereunder shall also be liable jointly and severally with and to the same extent as such controlled person to any person to whom such controlled person is liable, unless the controlling person acted in good faith and did not directly or indirectly induce the act or acts constituting the violation or cause of action.

To establish "controlling person" liability, the plaintiff must show that a primary violation was committed and that the defendant "directly or indirectly" controlled the violator. The plaintiff need not show the controlling person's scienter or that they "culpably participated" in the alleged wrongdoing. If the plaintiff establishes that the defendant is a "controlling person," then the defendant bears the burden of proving he "acted in good faith and did not directly or indirectly induce the act or acts constituting the violation or cause of action." 15 U.S.C. §78t(a).

Here, a material issue of fact exists as to whether a primary violation was committed by Casablanca, through its President, Holland. The district court denied Holland's motion for summary judgment on the section 10(b) claims, stating: "He signed the no material adverse change certificate. It seems to me having done that, the remaining issues of liability are one of fact that can't be resolved on summary judgment motion." Whether Holland (and Casablanca) violated Rule 10b-5 is a pending issue in the district court. The question thus becomes whether there are issues of material fact as to GE Capital's or Burton's control over Casablanca.

A

Regarding GE Capital, the Investors have introduced evidence that it had a strong hand in Casablanca's debenture offering. GE Capital's bridge loan to Schnitzer was conditioned on the debenture offering taking place. GE Capital, along with Schnitzer, retained Shearson to market the debentures. GE Capital may have indirectly contributed to the Placement Memorandum by working with Casablanca's management to come up with "assumptions" for their long-term projections. GE Capital had the right to select the lead investor and exercised its right to select Elders Finance. Finally, GE Capital participated in the drafting and negotiating of the Purchase Agreement.

However, the Investors have not shown any of the traditional indicia of control of Casablanca in a broader sense. GE Capital had no prior lending relationship with Casablanca. GE Capital did not own stock in Casablanca prior to the closing and did not have a seat on its Board. GE Capital's bridge loan was unsecured by any of Casablanca's assets. In short, there is no evidence that GE Capital exercised any influence whatsoever over Casablanca on a day-to-day basis.

Other courts addressing this situation have been very reluctant to treat lenders as controlling persons of their borrowers....

GE Capital did not exercise control over the "management and policies" of Casablanca, nor did it direct its day-to-day affairs in any sense. As we hold that at least some indicia of such control is a necessary element of "controlling person" liability, the Investors cannot sustain a secondary liability claim against GE Capital.

PROBLEM SET 25.1

1.   As illustrated in the case, leveraged buyouts are typically financed by a loan that is then replaced, in whole or in part, by bond financing. What are the risks of this structure? Why not simply use bonds from inception?
2.   What were the loan's proceeds used for in this transaction? Should the law discourage the intentional creation of a company that is insolvent?
3.   As noted in the opinion, the buyer purchased the target in this LBO to better utilize certain tax losses that the buyer had, but could not use. The issue of "NOLs" will be further considered in the subsequent class on exchange offers.
4.   As we have previously noted, one advantage of financing a company with debt is that interest payments, unlike dividend payments, are typically tax deductible by the corporation. In the late 1980s, following concerns about the growth of leveraged buyouts, Congress enacted rules that limit interest deductions on "applicable high-yield discount obligations" (AHYDO, as the tax lawyers like to call it). Generally, the rules provide that, if a debt obligation has a term of more than five years, has a yield at least equal to the risk-free rate plus 5 percent and has significant OID,[3] then the yield that exceeds the risk-free rate plus 6 percent is not deductible and the rest of the yield is only deductible when actual cash payments are made. What is the likely effect of this rule? Does it represent a sensible policy decision?

2.   FRAUDULENT TRANSFER LAWS

As discussed earlier in the text, corporate law (and, with some qualifications, corporate bankruptcy law) provides for the creditors of a company to be paid before the owners of the company: debt before equity. This is the absolute priority rule.[4]

Fraudulent transfer laws are intended to give the creditors of a company a tool to ensure that the indebtedness of the company is paid before the holders of the equity in the enterprise receive payments in respect of their equity interests.

---

3. Original issue discount; recall the discussion of this in the bond unit.
4. *See* Chapter 3.

Fraudulent transfer laws date back to at least Elizabethan England—most notably the Statute of 13 Elizabeth from 1571[5]—and thus came to the United States as part of the preindependence common law.[6] In present days, fraudulent transfers are addressed by state and federal law, and the occasional state still addresses fraudulent transfer via common law.

State law is more typically based on one of two uniform laws: the Uniform Fraudulent Conveyance Act ("UFCA") or the Uniform Fraudulent Transfer Act ("UFTA"). The UFCA was promulgated in 1918 by the National Conference of Commissioners on Uniform State Laws in an attempt to codify and clarify the common law of fraudulent conveyance. The UFCA remains in effect in three jurisdictions: Maryland, the U.S. Virgin Islands, and, most important, New York.[7]

The UFTA was promulgated by the Commissioners in 1984 to work with the overall design and structure of the then recently enacted 1978 Federal Bankruptcy Code. Forty-four jurisdictions have adopted the UFTA, but some have made changes that reduce the statute's "uniformity."[8]

Under the Bankruptcy Code, the trustee or the debtor will typically have the choice of bringing a fraudulent transfer action under either the applicable state law or the fraudulent transfer provision in the Code. Section 544 of the Bankruptcy Code gives the trustee the right to avoid a transaction that might be avoided under applicable state law. Section 548 of the Bankruptcy Code sets forth the basic right of the "trustee" in bankruptcy (which for this purpose includes a debtor in chapter 11 reorganization case) to avoid any "obligation incurred" by a debtor or any "transfer" of property (including any payments or the grant of a lien) that constitutes a "fraudulent transfer" by the debtor.

A key distinction among all three statutes is the relevant statute of limitations: UFCA, six years; UFTA, four years; and the Bankruptcy Code §548, two years.[9]

The statutes attack two types of fraudulent conveyances: the *intentional fraudulent conveyance* and the *constructive fraudulent conveyance*.

In the case of an *intentional* fraudulent conveyance or transfer, the debtor "conveys" or "transfers" property, or incurs an obligation, with the "actual intent to hinder, delay or defraud creditors." Giving your car, house, dog, and wallet to a friend right after entry of a big tort judgment would be an obvious example.

---

5. 13 Eliz 1, c 5 (1571).

6. Fraudulent transfer was initially a common law concept in colonial America but a statutory concept in England.

7. In New York, a bill to enact the UFTA was before the Senate Judiciary Committee in 2007. However, the bill was not addressed during either the 2007 or the 2008 legislative sessions.

8. In 2014, the National Conference of Commissioners on Uniform State Laws approved the Uniform Voidable Transactions Act (UVTA) as a replacement for the UFTA. To date, the UVTA has been enacted in eight jurisdictions (California, Georgia, Idaho, Kentucky, Minnesota, New Mexico, North Carolina, and North Dakota).

9. UFCA generally uses the time period applicable to fraud claims, which is six years in New York. One exception on the federal side is § 548(e), which looks back ten years from the date of the commencement of the bankruptcy case. *See* 11 U.S.C. § 548(e).

More often fraudulent intent is determined by reference to certain "badges of fraud"—a concept that also dates back to England. Indeed, the most famous badges of fraud case is *Twyne's Case*, a 1601 opinion from the Star Chamber.[10] Don't you just love a good, pre-*Mayflower*, Star Chamber opinion?

UFTA section 7, unlike the Bankruptcy Code or the UFCA, provides a list of "badges of fraud" that a court may consider in determining whether actual intent exists. The UFTA list includes (i) the transfer or obligation was to an insider; (ii) the debtor retained possession or control of the property transferred after the transfer; (iii) the transfer or obligation was concealed; (iv) before the transfer was made or obligation was incurred, the debtor had been sued or threatened with suit; (v) the transfer was of substantially all of the debtor's assets; (vi) the debtor absconded; (vii) the debtor removed or concealed assets; (viii) the debtor was insolvent or became insolvent shortly after the transfer was made or the obligation was incurred; (ix) the transfer occurred shortly before or shortly after a substantial debt was incurred; (x) the debtor transferred the essential assets of the business to a lienor who transferred the assets to an insider of the debtor.

The concept of a constructive fraudulent transfer arises in situations where fraud is presumed because the benefit of the transaction to the debtor is small and the harm to creditors is large. That is, transfers for less than "reasonably equivalent value" can be undone as constructively fraudulent transfers.

In an LBO situation, lenders have to worry that their loan might itself be a fraudulent transfer if the debtor grants a lien in exchange for the proceeds used to buy out the old shareholders. After all, what precisely does the corporation get in such a transaction? In the case of a distressed acquisition, the potential that the asset sale will be challenged after the fact looms large.

IN RE JEVIC HOLDING CORPORATION

2011 WL 4345204

United States Bankruptcy Court, D. Delaware.

Sept. 15, 2011.

Brendan Linehan SHANNON, Bankruptcy Judge.

Before the Court is a motion to dismiss (the "Motion") filed by the CIT Group/Business Credit, Inc. ("CIT"). By the Motion, CIT seeks the dismissal of all claims in the complaint and objection to claims, as amended (the "Complaint") filed by the Official Committee of Unsecured Creditors (the "Committee") of Jevic Holding Corporation ("Jevic") that initiated this adversary proceeding.

I.   BACKGROUND

On May 20, 2008 (the "Petition Date"), Jevic and various of its affiliates (collectively, the "Debtors") each filed voluntary petitions for relief under

---

10. 3 Coke 806 (Star Chamber 1601).

chapter 11 of title 11 of the United States Code (the "Bankruptcy Code") in the U.S. Bankruptcy Court for the District of Delaware. Founded in 1981, Jevic was a trucking company that provided regional and interregional transportation services across the United States and portions of Canada. In 2004, after years of profitability, Jevic began experiencing a prolonged financial downturn from which it never rebounded and which eventually led Jevic into bankruptcy.

Until 2006, Jevic was wholly owned by SCS Transportation, Inc. ("SCS"). Earlier that year, Jevic hired an investment banking firm to explore its financial and strategic alternatives. On June 30, 2006, Sun Capital Partners IV, LP ("Sun") purchased Jevic from SCS for $77.4 million (the "Acquisition").[11] To finance the Acquisition, Sun obtained a $90 million loan (the "Acquisition Facility") from Bank of Montreal to cover the purchase price and transaction costs. The Acquisition Facility was evidenced by a demand note, secured by all assets of Jevic and JHC, and guaranteed by Sun.

Within a month of the Acquisition, Jevic entered into a credit agreement administered by CIT to refinance the Acquisition Facility (the "Refinancing Facility"). Under the Refinancing Facility, Jevic obtained a revolving line of credit in the amount of $85 million (the "Revolver") and a $16.2 million term loan (the "Term Loan"), for a total credit facility in the amount of $101.2 million. The Refinancing Facility was secured by a first lien on all of Jevic's assets including its accounts receivable and stock, but the Term Loan was separately secured by two specific real estate properties owned by Jevic (the "Properties"). The proceeds of the Refinancing Facility were used to pay off the Acquisition Facility and to finance the transaction costs and fees.

Jevic was almost immediately in default of various provisions of the Refinancing Facility. In exchange for relaxing certain covenants, CIT obtained from Jevic various concessions and required Jevic to market the Properties and, upon their sale, to apply the sale proceeds of the Properties toward the outstanding principal of the Term Loan. Accordingly, within several months of the Acquisition, Jevic sold the Properties for approximately $20 million and delivered the proceeds to CIT. Jevic simultaneously entered into 20-year leases with the new owners of the Properties in order to continue to use the Properties for its ongoing business operations. The Committee refers to the sale of the Properties, the turnover of sale proceeds to CIT, and the execution of the leases in the aggregate as the "Sale–Leaseback." After the Sale–Leaseback, Jevic's obligations on the Refinancing Facility diminished: the Term Loan was paid in full and the Revolver was reduced to $55 million.

Notwithstanding these various transactions, Jevic's financial condition continued to deteriorate. Unable to meet its obligations under the Refinancing Facility, Jevic entered into a forbearance agreement with CIT, which was amended several times to extend the expiration date. The forbearance agreement

---

11. For the sake of accuracy, the Court notes that Jevic was formally purchased by Jevic Holding Corporation ("JHC"), Sun's wholly owned investment vehicle, but for the purpose of ruling upon the Motion, the Court generally refers to Sun as the acquiring entity.

finally expired without further extension on May 12, 2008. Eight days later, Jevic declared bankruptcy. Since the Petition Date, the Debtors have shut down their business operations and have liquidated their assets through a sale under 11 U.S.C. §363.[12]

As of the Petition Date, the Debtors' total liability on the Refinancing Facility was $50,417,204, and CIT has filed proofs of claim against the Debtors in this amount.

On December 31, 2008, the Committee timely objected to CIT's claims under the Refinancing Facility by filing a joint objection and complaint to initiate this adversary proceeding.

As it relates to CIT, the Complaint contains ... claims for relief grounded in the following causes of action: constructively fraudulent transfers under 11 U.S.C. §§544 and 548,... aiding and abetting breach of fiduciary duty, and equitable subordination under §510. The Court addresses the sufficiency of the Committee's allegations with respect to each of these causes of action in turn.

A.   FRAUDULENT TRANSFER CLAIMS (CLAIMS I THROUGH IV)

In Claims I and II, the Committee alleges that the Debtors' obligations on the Refinancing Facility, the liens on Jevic's assets which secure the Refinancing Facility, and the payments made on account of the Refinancing Facility, including the turnover of the proceeds from the sale of the Properties, are all constructively fraudulent transfers under 11 U.S.C. §544(b) and the Uniform Fraudulent Transfer Act ("UFTA"). In Claims III and IV, the Committee alleges that these same transfers and obligations are also voidable as fraudulent transfers under 11 U.S.C. §548(a). In support of its fraudulent transfer claims, the Committee argues that the Acquisition, the Acquisition Facility, the Refinancing Facility, and the Sale–Leaseback should all be viewed as component transactions that must be collapsed in a single integrated transaction, which in the aggregate comprise the leveraged buyout ("LBO") of Jevic by Sun. The Court first addresses the Committee's argument for collapsing these transactions and then considers whether the Committee has adequately alleged fraudulent transfer claims against CIT under §§548 or 544, or both.

1.   Collapsing the Transactions

The Third Circuit has recognized the propriety of collapsing multiple transactions and treating them as one integrated transaction for the purpose of assessing a defendant's fraudulent transfer liability. United States v. Tabor Court Realty Corp., 803 F.2d 1288, 1301-03 (3d Cir.1986), *cert. denied*, 483 U.S. 1005 (1987). In *Tabor*, the Third Circuit explained that where a series of transactions were all "part of one integrated transaction," a court could look "beyond the exchange of funds" in one transaction and consider the "*aggregate* transaction."

---

12. Chapter 29 addresses 363 sales. —AUTHOR

An LBO is the classic context in which courts have collapsed multiple transactions for the purpose of assessing and finding fraudulent transfer liability. *See id.* at 1302; HBE Leasing Corp. v. Frank, 48 F.3d 623, 635 (2d Cir.1995) ("This [collapsing] approach finds its most frequent application to lenders who have financed leveraged buyouts of companies that subsequently become insolvent.").

To determine whether a series of transactions should be "collapsed" and viewed as a single integrated transaction, courts focus on the substance rather than on the form of the transactions and consider the overall intent and impact of the transactions. While the transactions that are sought to be collapsed may be structurally independent and distinct from one another, courts focus their analysis "not on the structure of the transaction but the knowledge and intent of the parties involved in the transaction."

The courts in this District have considered the following factors when assessing whether the parties to the transactions sought to be collapsed had the requisite knowledge and intent to warrant consideration of the asserted transactions in the aggregate: whether all parties involved in the individual transactions had knowledge of the other transactions; whether each transaction sought to be collapsed would have occurred on its own; and whether each transaction was dependent or conditioned on the other transactions.

Whether the relevant parties to the various transactions had notice of the overall scheme has been a central issue for courts that have applied the collapsing theory.

Whether the parties had the requisite intent can be ascertained by demonstrating that the transactions sought to be collapsed are interdependent because "[e]ach step of the [collapsed] [t]ransaction would not have occurred on its own, as each relied on additional steps to fulfill the parties' intent." The passage of some time between the various transactions sought to be collapsed is not fatal if they are sufficiently related. Boyer v. Crown Stock Distribution, Inc. *(In re Boyer)*, 587 F.3d 787, 795-96 (7th Cir. 2009). For example, in *Boyer*, the Seventh Circuit collapsed transactions that were about three years apart, finding that they were all "an integral part of the LBO."

Ultimately, in the LBO context, courts will frequently collapse a series of transactions upon a showing that these transactions are part of "an overall scheme to defraud the estate and its creditors by depleting all the assets through the use of a leveraged buyout." Neither time nor transactional formalities can shield a party involved in such a series of transactions. With respect to lender liability specifically, the Third Circuit explained in *Tabor* that where a lender has been "intimately involved" with the overall transaction at issue, "[t]ry as they might to distance themselves from the transaction now, they cannot rewrite history."

Here, the Committee seeks to collapse the Acquisition, the Acquisition Facility, the Refinancing Facility, the liens on Jevic's assets to secure the Refinancing Facility, and the Sale-Leaseback into one integrated transaction which, in the aggregate, should be viewed as Sun's leveraged buyout of Jevic (the "Jevic LBO"). In support of its argument, the Committee alleges that the overall intent of the transacting parties, *viz.*, Sun, Bank of Montreal, CIT, and Jevic—was to enable, facilitate, and effectuate the Jevic LBO. The Committee further asserts that CIT was aware of Sun's intentions to acquire Jevic from the start, even though the Acquisition Facility was initially provided by another bank. According to the Committee, Sun "turned to CIT to provide a 'comprehensive financing solution'" to facilitate its acquisition of Jevic. The Complaint alleges that Sun and CIT negotiated for a June closing date months before the Acquisition occurred, but CIT was unable to close at that time. To avoid delaying the closing, the Committee alleges that Sun obtained the Acquisition Facility from Bank of Montreal to serve as a "bridge facility" for the purpose of effectuating the Acquisition "until CIT was prepared to move forward with what would then be permanent financing." By the end of July, CIT had refinanced the Acquisition Facility through the Refinancing Facility. The Committee contends that "Sun would not have caused [its subsidiary] to borrow $90 million under [the Acquisition Facility], and Sun would not have guaranteed . . . repayment of the [Acquisition Facility], if Sun was not all but certain that CIT would successfully complete the re-financing in a short period of time."

CIT argues that the Committee has failed to allege bad faith or an intent to defraud Jevic's creditors. However, the Court notes that the Complaint includes allegations of collusion between Sun and CIT to maximize the Refinancing Facility. The Committee argues that the Refinancing Facility, which exceeded the Acquisition Facility by more than $10 million, was the result of a collaborative and calculated effort by Sun and CIT to render unrealistically high asset valuations and revenue projections for Jevic with an eye towards obtaining the highest possible loan package. The Committee maintains that CIT would not have funded the Refinancing Facility—the Revolver and the Term Loan— without these allegedly excessive valuations and projections.

The Court is satisfied that the Committee has sufficiently pleaded that there is cause to collapse the series of transactions which are allegedly comprised in the Jevic LBO. Based on the Committee's allegations, the Court could conclude that CIT, Sun, Bank of Montreal, and Jevic were all apprised of the overall goal— Sun's acquisition of Jevic through a highly leveraged buyout—of each of these separate transactions in which the various parties were involved. Assuming the veracity of the Committee's assertions and making all reasonable inferences in its favor, the Committee could establish that CIT had sufficient knowledge and notice of the Jevic LBO. The Court also finds that the Committee has adequately alleged that the various transactions constituting the Jevic LBO would not have occurred independently of each other. Given the short time span within which these transactions occurred and their asserted relatedness, the Court concludes that the Committee has provided enough facts from which the Court could reasonably infer the common aim of these transactions.

CIT attempts to shield itself from liability with respect to the Jevic LBO by maintaining that "[it] did not play any role in the leveraged buyout whatsoever." While the Court acknowledges that the intervening role Bank of Montreal complicates the Committee's case and may ultimately prove fatal to the claims in the Complaint, the purpose of the integration doctrine is to enable a plaintiff to overcome precisely the type of argument against liability which CIT is now asserting. Despite CIT's detachment from the Acquisition Facility pursuant to which Sun initially acquired Jevic, the Court concludes that the Committee has sufficiently alleged that CIT was nonetheless "fully engaged," "actively pursuing the transaction," and intimately involved in the Jevic LBO. Accordingly, the Committee is entitled to develop and present evidence to corroborate its claims with respect to the propriety of collapsing the asserted transactions into Jevic LBO for the purpose of establishing CIT's fraudulent transfer liability.

2. *Constructively Fraudulent Transfer Claims under §548 (Claims III and IV)*

Section §548(a)(1) of the Bankruptcy Code grants a trustee the power to avoid any transfer made or obligation incurred by a debtor of an interest in property, made no more than two years before the debtor files for bankruptcy relief, if the transfer or obligation is deemed to be actually or constructively fraudulent. Here, the Committee has alleged that the Refinancing Facility, and its attendant liens and loan payments by Jevic, are voidable as constructively fraudulent transfers. A transfer or an obligation is deemed constructively fraudulent and thus voidable if the debtor received less than reasonably equivalent value in exchange for such transfer or obligation, and (i) the debtor was insolvent when such transfer was made or obligation was incurred, or became insolvent as a result thereof, (ii) the debtor retained unreasonably small capital to operate its business when the transfer was made or obligation was incurred, or (iii) the debtor made the transfer or incurred the obligation when it was already unable to service its debts. Thus, to survive this Motion with respect to §548(a)(1), the Complaint must include facts sufficient to show that Jevic did not receive reasonably equivalent value in exchange for the obligations it incurred and the attendant transfers it made. The Complaint must also include enough facts to show that Jevic was or became insolvent when these transactions occurred, or that it retained unreasonably small capital as a result thereof, or that it was unable to pay its debts when the transactions occurred.

a. *Reasonably Equivalent Value*

A transfer or obligation is avoidable under §548(a)(1)(B) only if the debtor "received less than a reasonably equivalent value in exchange for such transfer or obligation." The term "reasonably equivalent value" is not defined in the Bankruptcy Code and "courts have rejected the application of any fixed mathematical formula to determine reasonable equivalence." The Third Circuit has held that assessing whether a debtor received reasonably equivalent value in exchange for a transfer or obligation requires a two-step approach. First, "a court must consider whether, 'based on the circumstances that existed at the time' of the transfer, it was 'legitimate and reasonable' to expect some value accruing to the debtor."

Second, if the court finds that the debtor received any value, the court must engage in a fact-driven comparison between such value and the transfer or obligation sought to be avoided to determine "whether the debtor got roughly the value it gave." To assess the reasonable equivalence of the transfer or obligation and the value received by the debtor, a court should "look to the 'totality of the circumstances,' including (1) the 'fair market value' of the benefit received as a result of the transfer, (2) 'the existence of an arm's-length relationship between the debtor and the transferee,' and (3) the transferee's good faith." Courts have previously upheld the reasonable equivalence of indirect value as well.

In the LBO context, courts assess the value transferred to and from the debtor in the aggregate when the plaintiff in an avoidance action—typically the debtor or the trustee—has established that the various transactions which compose the LBO should be collapsed and assessed collectively. The debtor may be deemed to have received reasonably equivalent value in exchange for a transfer or obligation when one of a series of transactions is viewed in isolation and apart from the others. However, when the collapsed transactions are analyzed in the aggregate, courts have often found that the total value accruing to the debtor is not reasonably equivalent to the total value of the transfers made or obligations incurred by the debtor. *See, e.g., Tabor*, 803 F.2d at 1302. For instance, the *Tabor* court found that certain funds which were alleged to have provided the debtor with reasonably equivalent value in fact merely passed through the debtor when the relevant transactions were integrated and viewed in the aggregate, prompting the court to find that the debtor did not receive reasonably equivalent value after all. *Id.*

Here, the Committee alleges that Jevic did not receive reasonably equivalent value in exchange for its obligation with respect to the Refinancing Facility, the liens that secure it, and the various payments made on account thereof. CIT argues that in exchange for Jevic's obligation on the Refinancing Facility and the liens on Jevic's assets, CIT provided value to Jevic in the form of the loan proceeds. CIT also asserts that in exchange for certain payments on account of the Refinancing Facility—specifically, to pay off the Term Loan using the proceeds from the sale of the Properties—CIT gave value via forbearance. However, CIT's argument does not take into account the Committee's argument that when the transactions relating to the Jevic LBO are collapsed, the aggregate value of the obligation incurred and the transfers made by Jevic exceeds and is therefore not reasonably equivalent to the aggregate value that CIT provided to Jevic in return. The Committee alleges that the loan proceeds relating to the Refinancing Facility were used to pay off the Acquisition Facility, on which Sun's wholly owned affiliate was the obligor and Sun the guarantor. Considering all allegations and reasonable inferences in favor of the Committee, the Court concludes that the Complaint contains sufficient allegations that, if true, could support a finding that the loan proceeds received by Jevic merely passed through Jevic and thus failed to provide reasonably equivalent value to Jevic in exchange for the accumulated value Jevic transferred to CIT. While the Committee will still need to marshal evidence to refute CIT's charge that Jevic received reasonably equivalent value, the Court finds that the Committee has adequately alleged the absence of such value at this stage and is entitled to further pursue its claims.

b. Insolvency

The Bankruptcy Code defines insolvency as the "financial condition such that the sum of [an] entity's debts is greater than all of such entity's property." 11 U.S.C. §101(32)(A). When determining liability under §548, a court measures a debtor's solvency "at the time the debtor transferred value, not at some later or earlier time." Here, the Committee alleges that Jevic was "insolvent or would be rendered insolvent by the transactions undertaken in connection with the [Jevic] LBO, the [Refinancing Facility], and Sale-Lease Back." The Court concludes that these allegations are sufficient to survive this motion.

c. Unreasonably Small Capital

Like insolvency, the Bankruptcy Code does not define what constitutes unreasonably small capital. In the context of an LBO, the Third Circuit has held that "the test for unreasonably small capital is reasonable foreseeability. "The problem universal to all LBOs—transactions characterized by their high debt relative to equity interest—is that they are less able to weather temporary financial storms because debt demands are less flexible than equity interest." When determining whether the LBO-related transactions sought to be collapsed and unwound left the target—now the debtor entity—with unreasonably small capital, the court should determine whether the projections for the LBO target, which forecast that the debtor would retain sufficient cash or credit to operate and sustain its business, were reasonable. In other words, "[the court's] task in determining whether a company had sufficient working capital as evidenced by cash flow projections was not to examine what happened to the company but whether the projections employed prior to the LBO were prudent."

The Court finds it significant that the Third Circuit has stated that "leveraged buyouts present great potential for abuse." In a typical LBO, the target company alone—not the buyer—becomes obligated on the LBO debt that is secured by the target company's assets. The target company's capital structure is radically altered as a result of the LBO because its equity is substituted for highly leveraged debt for the benefit of the parties who are driving the LBO deal and to the detriment of the target company and its creditors. The risk of the LBO is thereby externalized to unsecured creditors and away from the parties to the LBO deal. For this reason, "[a]n LBO may be attractive to the buyer, seller, and lender because the structure of the transaction could allow all parties to the buyout to shift most of the risk of loss to other creditors of the corporation if the provisions of section 548(a)(2) were not applied."

Here, the Committee alleges that the transactions related to the Jevic LBO left Jevic with unreasonably small capital. In support of this allegation, the

Committee asserts that following the Jevic LBO, Jevic's equity was reduced from $46 million to $1 million while its debt rose from $55 million to $101.2 million. The Committee further alleges that the projections underlying which the Refinancing Facility, allegedly prepared by Sun and approved by CIT, were unrealistic and highly unreasonable, but were made for the purpose of maximizing the Refinancing Facility. Assuming the truth of the Committee's allegations, the Court concludes that the Committee could establish that Jevic was left with unreasonably small capital within the meaning of §548.

3.   *Fraudulent Transfer Claims under §544 (Claims I and II)*

Under §544(b), a debtor may avoid any transfer of an interest in the debtor's property that is voidable under applicable state law by a creditor holding an allowable unsecured claim. Here, the Committee invokes the Uniform Fraudulent Transfer Act ("UFTA") but has failed to allege the state-specific UFTA law upon which such claim is grounded. As a general matter, UFTA allows a debtor's creditors to recover property that was transferred by a debtor who did not receive reasonably equivalent value for it and who was insolvent when the transfer occurred or became insolvent as a result thereof. Because UFTA generally tracks 11 U.S.C. §548, the Committee's success on a §544(b) action will likely mirror its success on a §548 action that is based upon the same facts. Here, however, the Committee's failure to identify the state-specific UFTA upon which its claims are based leads the Court to conclude that the Committee has failed to put CIT on sufficient notice of the grounds upon which the cause of action against it are based. In light of *Twombly* and *Iqbal* especially, case law provides that such inadequate notice necessitates dismissal of the Committee's §544 claim for failure to state a claim upon which relief can be granted.

D.   AIDING AND ABETTING BREACH OF FIDUCIARY DUTY (CLAIM VI)

In Claim VI, the Committee alleges that CIT aided and abetted Jevic's officers and directors in the breach of their fiduciary duties. The Committee asserts that the officers and directors of Jevic breached their fiduciary duties by supporting and approving the Acquisition, the Refinancing Facility, the transfer of liens on Jevic's assets to CIT, the Sale–Leaseback, the transfer of the proceeds from the sale of the Properties to CIT, and the payments made by Jevic on account of the Refinancing Facility. The Committee also contends that CIT knew the officers and directors and knew that they breached their fiduciary duties by supporting and approving these transactions. The Committee maintains that notwithstanding this knowledge, "CIT directed, encouraged, assisted, facilitated and/or participated" in the conduct that has given rise to the directors' and officers' alleged breach of their fiduciary duties. According to the Committee, by aiding and abetting such conduct, CIT directly and proximately harmed Jevic by diminishing its estate, reducing its ability to operate its business, and increasing the likelihood that its creditors would not be paid in the event that Jevic declared bankruptcy.

Under the internal affairs doctrine, only one state has the authority to regulate a corporation's internal affairs, which include matters peculiar to relationships among or between the corporation and its current officers, directors, and shareholders. Edgar v. MITE Corp., 457 U.S. 624, 645 (1982). The Supreme Court has held that the state under which the corporation is chartered has this authority. *Id.* Courts have long recognized that few, if any, claims are more central to a corporation's internal affairs than those relating to an alleged breach of a fiduciary duty by a corporation's directors and officers.

Here, because Jevic is a Delaware corporation, Delaware law governs the Committee's claim for aiding and abetting the breach of a fiduciary duty. As with a claim for the breach of a fiduciary duty, the internal affairs doctrine compels the Court to also apply Delaware law to a claim for aiding and abetting the breach of a fiduciary duty asserted against CIT.

Delaware courts have articulated four elements that must be proven to establish a claim for aiding and abetting the breach of a fiduciary duty: (1) the existence of a fiduciary relationship; (2) the breach of a duty by the fiduciary; (3) the knowing participation in the breach by the defendant, who is not a fiduciary; and (4) damages to the plaintiff resulting from the concerted action of the fiduciary and the nonfiduciary. Proof of scienter is the crux of a successful claim. "In order to be found liable for aiding and abetting a breach of a fiduciary duty, one must demonstrate that the party knew that the other's conduct constituted a breach of a fiduciary duty and gave substantial assistance or encouragement to the other in committing that breach." A plaintiff must demonstrate the defendant's "knowing participation" with specific facts.

Here, the Committees fails to plead specific facts in support of its allegation that CIT knowingly participated in the breach of a fiduciary duty. The Complaint merely states in general terms that CIT knew the directors and officers of Jevic who breached their fiduciary duties, knew that their conduct amounted to such breach, and directed, encouraged, and assisted such conduct.

E.   EQUITABLE SUBORDINATION UNDER §510(C) (CLAIM VII)

Finally, in Claim VII, the Committee alleges that there is a sufficient factual predicate in support of its request for the equitable subordination under 11 U.S.C. §510(c) of CIT's claims against the estate in the amount of approximately $50.4 million. The Committee asserts that CIT's conduct resulted in injury to the Debtors, conferred an unfair advantage to CIT, or both.

The Bankruptcy Code provides that a court may "under principles of equitable subordination, subordinate for purposes of distribution all or part of an allowed claim to all or part of another allowed claim." Proof of three elements is required to establish equitable subordination: (1) the defendant engaged in some type of inequitable conduct; (2) the misconduct caused injury to the creditors or conferred an unfair advantage on the defendant; and (3) equitable subordination of the claim is consistent with bankruptcy law. Benjamin v. Diamond (In re Mobile Steel Co.), 563 F.2d 692, 699-705 (5th Cir.1977). *See also* United States v. Noland, 517 U.S. 535, 538-39 (1996) (adopting the *Mobile Steel* test for equitable subordination). Courts differentiate between insiders and outsiders when analyzing whether conduct was inequitable. "The most important factor in determining if a claimant has engaged in inequitable conduct for the purposes of equitable subordination is whether the claimant was an insider or outsider in relation to the debtor at the time of the act." In re Mid–Am. Waste Sys., Inc., 284 B.R. 53, 69 (Bankr.D.Del.2002). If a defendant is not an insider, then evidence of more egregious conduct such as fraud, spoliation or overreaching is necessary.

Here, the Committee has alleged only that CIT's conduct, as it is described in the Committee's preceding claims, warrants the equitable subordination of CIT's claims against the Debtors. Based on such sparse allegations, however, the Court cannot conclude that the Committee has sufficiently alleged a claim for equitable subordination against CIT and will therefore dismiss this claim.

As you will see in Chapter 27, our old friend Dynegy also had some fraudulent transfer problems after the Icahn deal fell through. But they did not involve an LBO, so we leave them for the bankruptcy chapters.

PROBLEM SET 25.2

1. Why not leave fraudulent transfer issues to contract and the terms of bond indentures and loan agreements? What are the risks fraudulent transfer laws?
2. And of course, diagram the transaction in the case and be prepared to discuss its motivations in class. In particular, who benefits? Who was hurt?

As you read the next case, think about what it teaches us about structuring LBO deals.

IN RE TRIBUNE COMPANY FRAUDULENT CONVEYANCE LITIGATION

818 F.3d 98
United States Court of Appeals, Second Circuit.
March 29, 2016.

WINTER, Circuit Judge:
Representatives of certain unsecured creditors of the Chapter 11 debtor Tribune Company appeal from Judge Sullivan's grant of a motion to dismiss their state law, constructive fraudulent conveyance claims brought against Tribune's former

shareholders. Appellants seek to recover an amount sufficient to satisfy Tribune's debts to them by avoiding (recovering) payments by Tribune to shareholders that purchased all of its stock. The payments occurred in a transaction commonly called a leveraged buyout ("LBO"), soon after which Tribune went into Chapter 11 bankruptcy.

BACKGROUND

A) THE LBO

Tribune Media Company (formerly known as "Tribune Company") is a multimedia corporation that, in 2007, faced deteriorating financial prospects. Appellee Samuel Zell, a billionaire investor, proposed to acquire Tribune through an LBO. In consummating the LBO, Tribune borrowed over $11 billion secured by its assets. The $11 billion plus, combined with Zell's $315 million equity contribution, was used to refinance some of Tribune's pre-existing bank debt and to cash out Tribune's shareholders for over $8 billion at a premium price—above its trading range—per share. It is undisputed that Tribune transferred the over $8 billion to a "securities clearing agency" or other "financial institution," as those terms are used in Section 546(e), acting as intermediaries in the LBO transaction. Those intermediaries in turn paid the funds to the shareholders in exchange for their shares that were then returned to Tribune. Appellants seek to satisfy Tribune's debts to them by avoiding Tribune's payments to the shareholders. Appellants do not seek money from the intermediaries.

B) BANKRUPTCY PROCEEDINGS

On December 8, 2008, with debt and contingent liabilities exceeding its assets by more than $3 billion, Tribune and nearly all of its subsidiaries filed for bankruptcy under Chapter 11 in the District of Delaware. A trustee was not appointed, and Tribune and its affiliates continued to operate the businesses as debtors in possession. *See* 11 U.S.C. § 1107(a) ("Subject to any limitations on a trustee ... a debtor in possession shall have all the rights ..., and powers, and shall perform all the functions and duties ... of a trustee...."). In discussing the powers of a bankruptcy trustee that can be exercised by a trustee or parties designated by a bankruptcy court, we shall refer to the trustee or such parties as the "trustee *et al.*"

The bankruptcy court appointed an Official Committee of Unsecured Creditors (the "Committee") to represent the interests of unsecured creditors. In November 2010, alleging that the LBO-related payments constituted intentional fraudulent conveyances, the Committee commenced an action under Code Section 548(a)(1)(A) against the cashed out Tribune shareholders, various officers, directors, financial advisors, Zell, and others alleged to have benefitted from the LBO. An intentional fraudulent conveyance is defined as one in which there was "actual intent to hinder, delay, or defraud" a creditor.

In June 2011, two subsets of unsecured creditors filed state law, constructive fraudulent conveyance claims in various federal and state courts. The plaintiffs, the appellants before us, were: (i) the Retiree Appellants, former Tribune employees who hold claims for unpaid retirement benefits and (ii) the Noteholder Appellants, the successor indenture trustees for Tribune's pre-LBO senior notes and subordinated debentures. A constructive fraudulent conveyance is, generally speaking, a transfer for less than reasonably equivalent value made when the debtor was insolvent or was rendered so by the transfer.

Before bringing these actions, appellants moved the bankruptcy court for an order stating that: (i) after the expiration of the two-year statute of limitations period during which the Committee was authorized to bring avoidance actions under 11 U.S.C. § 546(a), eligible creditors had regained the right to prosecute their creditor state law claims; and (ii) the automatic stay imposed by Code Section 362(a) was lifted solely to permit the immediate filing of their complaint. In support of that motion, the Committee argued that, under Section 546(a), the "state law constructive fraudulent conveyance transfer claims ha[d] reverted to individual creditors" and that the "creditors should consider taking appropriate actions to preserve those claims."

In April 2011, the bankruptcy court lifted the Code's automatic stay with regard to appellants' actions. The court reasoned that because the Committee had elected not to bring the constructive fraudulent conveyance actions within the two-year limitations period following the bankruptcy petition imposed by Section 544, fully discussed *infra,* the unsecured creditors "regained the right, if any, to prosecute [such claims]." Therefore, the court lifted the Section 362(a) automatic stay "to permit the filing of any complaint by or on behalf of creditors on account of such Creditor [state law fraudulent conveyance] Claims." The court clarified, however, that it was not resolving the issues of whether the individual creditors had statutory standing to bring such claims or whether such claims were preempted by Section 546(e).

On March 15, 2012, the bankruptcy court set an expiration date of June 1, 2012 for the remaining limited stay on the state law, fraudulent conveyance claims. In July 2012, the bankruptcy court ordered confirmation of the proposed Tribune reorganization plan. The plan terminated the Committee and transferred responsibility for prosecuting the intentional fraudulent conveyance action to an entity called the Litigation Trust. The confirmed plan also provided that the Retiree and Noteholder Appellants could pursue "any and all LBO–Related Causes of Action arising under state fraudulent conveyance law," except for the federal intentional fraudulent conveyance and other LBO-related claims pursued by the Litigation Trust. Under the plan, the Retiree and Noteholder Appellants recovered approximately 33 cents on each dollar of debt. The plan was scheduled to take effect on December 31, 2012, the date on which Tribune emerged from bankruptcy.

C) DISTRICT COURT PROCEEDINGS

Appellants' various state law, fraudulent conveyance complaints alleged that the LBO payments, made through financial intermediaries as noted above, were for more than the reasonable value of the shares and made when Tribune was in distressed financial condition. Therefore, the complaints concluded, the payments were avoidable by creditors under the laws of various states. These actions were later consolidated with the Litigation Trust's ongoing federal intentional fraud claims in a multi-district litigation proceeding that was transferred to the Southern District of New York.

After consolidation, the Tribune shareholders moved to dismiss appellants' claims..

The district court held that Section 546(e) did not bar appellants' actions because: (i) Section 546(e)'s prohibition on avoiding the designated transfers applied only to a bankruptcy trustee *et al.*; and (ii) Congress had declined to extend Section 546(e) to state law, fraudulent conveyance claims brought by creditors.

DISCUSSION

Under the Supremacy Clause, Article VI, Clause 2 of the Constitution, federal law prevails when it conflicts with state law.

Section 546(e)'s reference to limiting avoidance by a trustee provides appellants with a plain language argument that only a trustee *et al.*, and not creditors acting on their own behalf, are barred from bringing state law, constructive fraudulent avoidance claims. However, as discussed *infra,* we believe that the language of Section 546(e) does not necessarily have the meaning appellants ascribe to it. Even if that meaning is one of multiple reasonable constructions of the statutory scheme, it would not necessarily preclude preemption because a preemptive effect may be inferred where it is not expressly provided.

Under the implied preemption doctrine, state laws are "preempted to the extent of any conflict with a federal statute. Such a conflict occurs . . . when [ ] state law stands as an obstacle to the accomplishment and execution of the full purposes and objectives of Congress." *Hillman v. Maretta,* —— U.S. ——, 133 S.Ct. 1943, 1949–50, 186 L.Ed.2d 43 (2013) (citations and internal quotation marks omitted).

Appellants argue that a recognized presumption against preemption limits the implied preemption doctrine. They argue that Section 546(e) preempts creditors' state law, fraudulent conveyance claims only if the claims would do "'major damage' to 'clear and substantial' federal interests." The presumption against inferring preemption is premised on federalism grounds and, therefore, weighs most heavily where the particular regulatory area is "traditionally the domain of state law." *Hillman,* 133 S.Ct. at 1950. According to appellants, the presumption against preemption fully applies in the present context because fraudulent conveyance claims are "among 'the oldest [purposes] within the ambit of the police power.'"

Preemption is always a matter of congressional intent, even where that intent must be inferred. As in the present matter, the presumption against preemption usually goes to the weight to be given to the lack of an express statement overriding state law.

The presumption is strongest when Congress is legislating in an area recognized as traditionally one of state law alone. However, the present context is not such an area. To understate the proposition, the regulation of creditors' rights has "a history of significant federal presence."

Congress's power to enact bankruptcy laws was made explicit in the Constitution as originally enacted, Art. 1, § 8, cl. 4, and detailed, preemptive federal regulation of creditors' rights has, therefore, existed for over two centuries. Charles Jordan Tabb, *The History of the Bankruptcy Laws in the United States,* 3 Am. Bankr.Inst. L.Rev. 5, 7 (1995). Once a party enters bankruptcy, the Bankruptcy Code constitutes a wholesale preemption of state laws regarding creditors' rights.

Consider, for example, the present proceeding. While the issue before us is often described as whether Section 546(e) preempts state fraudulent conveyance laws, that is a mischaracterization. Appellants' state law claims were preempted when the Chapter 11 proceedings commenced and were not dismissed. Appellants' own arguments posit that those claims were, at the very least, stayed by Code Section 362. Whether, as appellants argue, they were restored in full after two years, *see* 11 U.S.C. § 546(a)(1)(A), or by order of the bankruptcy court, *see* 11 U.S.C. § 349(b)(3), is hotly disputed. But if they were restored, it was by force of federal law.

Once Tribune entered bankruptcy, the creditors' avoidance claims were vested in the federally appointed trustee *et al.* 11 U.S.C. § 544(b)(1). A constructive fraudulent conveyance action brought by a trustee *et al.* under Section 544 is a claim arising under federal law. Although such a claim borrows applicable state law standards regarding avoiding the transfer in question, the claim has its own statute of limitations, 11 U.S.C. § 546(a)(1)(A), measure of damages, *see* 11 U.S.C. § 550, and standards for distribution, 11 U.S.C. § 726. A disposition of this federal law claim extinguishes the right of creditors to bring state law, fraudulent conveyance claims. And, if creditors are allowed by a bankruptcy court, trustee, or, as appellants argue, by the Bankruptcy Code, to bring state law actions in their own name, that permission is a matter of grace granted under federal authority. The standards for granting that permission, moreover, have everything to do with the Bankruptcy Code's balancing of debtors' and creditors' rights, *In re Coltex Loop Cent. Three Partners, L.P.,* 138 F.3d 39, 44 (2d Cir.1998), or rights among creditors, *United States v. Ron Pair Enters., Inc.,* 489 U.S. 235, 248, 109 S.Ct. 1026, 103 L.Ed.2d 290 (1989), and nothing to do with the vindication of state police powers.

We also note here, and discuss further *infra,* that the policies reflected in Section 546(e) relate to securities markets, which are subject to extensive federal regulation. The regulation of these markets has existed and grown for over eighty years and reflects very important federal concerns.

In the present matter, therefore, there is no measurable concern about federal intrusion into traditional state domains. Our bottom line is that the issue before us is one of inferring congressional intent from the Code, without significant countervailing pressures of state law concerns.

2. THE LANGUAGE OF SECTION 546(E)

Section 544(b) empowers a trustee *et al.* to avoid a "transfer . . . [by] the debtor . . . voidable under applicable law by a[n] [unsecured] creditor." Section 548(a) also provides the trustee *et al.* with independent federal intentional, 11 U.S.C. § 548(a)(1)(A), and constructive fraudulent conveyance claims, 11 U.S.C. § 548(a)(1)(B).

Section 546(e) provides in pertinent part:

> Notwithstanding sections 544, . . . 548(a)(1)(B) . . . of this title, the trustee may not avoid a transfer that is a . . . settlement payment . . . made by or to (or for the benefit of) a . . . stockbroker, financial institution, financial participant, or securities clearing agency, or that is a transfer made by or to (or for the benefit of) a . . . stockbroker, financial institution, financial participant, or securities clearing agency, in connection with a securities contract . . . except under section 548(a)(1)(A). . . .

Section 546(e) thus expressly prohibits trustees *et al.* from using their Section 544(b) avoidance powers and (generally) Section 548 against the transfers specified in Section 546(e). However, Section 546(e) creates an exception to that prohibition for claims brought by trustee *et al.* under Section 548(a)(1)(A) that, as noted, establishes a federal avoidance claim to be brought by a trustee *et al.* based on an intentional fraud theory. As discussed *supra,* the Litigation Trust has brought a Section 548(a)(1)(A) claim against the same transfers challenged by appellants' actions before us on this appeal. That claim is still pending.

The language of Section 546(e) covers all transfers by or to financial intermediaries that are "settlement payment[s]" or "in connection with a securities contract." Transfers in which either the transferor or transferee is not such an intermediary are clearly included in the language. The Section does not distinguish between kinds of transfers, e.g., settlements of ordinary day-to-day trading, LBOs, or mergers in which shareholders of one company are involuntarily cashed out. So long as the transfer sought to be avoided is within the language quoted above, the Section includes avoidance proceedings in which the intermediary would escape a damages judgment. *But see In re Lyondell Chem. Co.,* 503 B.R. 348, 372–73 (Bankr.S.D.N.Y.2014), that Section 546(e) does not include "LBO payments to stockholders at the very end of the asset transfer chain, where the stockholders are the ultimate beneficiaries of the constructively fraudulent transfers, and can give the money back to injured creditors with no damage to anyone but themselves."

Section 546(e) was intended to protect from avoidance proceedings payments by and to financial intermediaries in the settlement of securities transactions or the execution of securities contracts. The method of settlement through intermediaries is essential to securities markets. Payments by and to such intermediaries provide certainty as to each transaction's consummation, speed to allow parties to adjust the transaction to market conditions, finality with regard to investors' stakes in firms, and thus stability to financial markets. Unwinding settled securities transactions by claims such as appellants' would seriously undermine—a substantial understatement—markets in which certainty, speed, finality, and stability are necessary to attract capital. To allow appellants' claims to proceed, we would have to construe Section 546(e) as achieving the opposite of what it was intended to achieve.

Allowing creditors to bring claims barred by Section 546(e) to the trustee *et al.* only after the trustee *et al.* fails to exercise powers it does not have would increase the disruptive effect of an unwinding by lengthening the period of uncertainty for intermediaries and investors. Indeed, the idea of preventing a trustee from unwinding specified transactions while allowing creditors to do so, but only later, is a policy in a fruitless search of a logical rationale.

The narrowest purpose of Section 546(e) was to protect other intermediaries from avoidance claims seeking to unwind a bankrupt intermediary's transactions that consummated transfers between customers. It must be emphasized that appellants' legal theory would clearly allow such claims to be brought (later) by creditors of the bankrupt intermediary. Even the narrowest purpose of Section 546(e) is thus at risk.

Some judicial and other discussions of these issues avoid addressing the full effects of adopting appellants' arguments. *See In re Lyondell Chem. Co.,* 503 B.R. 348, 359–78 (Bankr.S.D.N.Y.2014). Such analysis always begins by reliance on the "trustee" language, *id.* at 358, but then narrows the scope of the transfers covered by Section 546(e)'s language. For example, appellants argue that the concerns of the *amicus curiae* Securities and Exchange Commission regarding the effect of the district court's decision on the securities markets are misplaced, because appellants are not seeking money from the intermediaries. In doing so, they rely upon the *Lyondell* opinion, which, after relying on the "trustee" language, held that Section 546(e) is not preemptive of state law, fraudulent conveyance actions involving LBOs because such actions do not implicate the purposes of Section 546(e). 503 B.R. at 372–73.

There is no little irony in putting lynchpin reliance on the word "trustee" while ignoring the language that follows. In any event, Section 546(e)'s language clearly covers payments, such as those at issue here, by commercial firms to financial intermediaries to purchase shares from the firm's shareholders. 11 U.S.C. § 546(e) (limitations on avoidance of transfers made to a financial intermediary "in connection with a securities contract"). A search for legislative purpose is heavily informed by language, and analyzing all the language of a provision and its relationship to the Code as a whole is preferable to using literalness here and perceived legislative purpose (without regard to language) there as needed to reach particular results.

We do not dwell on this because we perceive no conflict between Section 546(e)'s language and its purpose. Section 546(e) is simply a case of Congress perceiving a need to address a particular problem within an important process or market and using statutory language broader than necessary to resolve the immediate problem. Such broad language is intended to protect the process or market from the entire genre of harms of which the particular problem was only one symptom. The legislative history of Section 546(e) clearly reveals such a purpose. That history (confirmed by the broad language adopted) reflects a concern over the use of avoidance powers not only after the bankruptcy of an intermediary, but also after a "customer" or "other participant" in the securities markets enters bankruptcy. *See* H.R.Rep. No. 97–420 (1982). To be sure, the examples used by the Section's proponents focused on the immediate concern of creditors of bankrupt brokers seeking to unwind payments by the bankrupt firm to other intermediaries. *Id.* Such actions were perceived as creating a danger of "a ripple effect," *id.,* a chain of bankruptcies among intermediaries disrupting the securities market generally. From these examples, appellants, and others, have argued that when monetary damages are sought only from shareholders, or an LBO is involved, the purposes of Section 546(e) are not implicated. Even apart from using the oil and water mixture of applying a narrow literalness to the word "trustee" and disregarding the rest of the Section's language, we disagree.

As courts have recognized, Congress's intent to "minimiz[e] the displacement caused in the commodities and securities markets in the event of a major bankruptcy affecting those industries," *In re Quebecor World (USA) Inc.,* 719 F.3d 94, 100 (2d Cir.2013) (*quoting Enron Creditors Recovery Corp. v. Alfa, S.A.B. de C.V.,* 651 F.3d 329, 333 (2d Cir.2011)), reflected a larger purpose memorialized in the legislative history's mention of bankrupt "customers" or "other participant[s]" and in the broad statutory language defining the transactions covered. That larger purpose was to "promot[e] finality ... and certainty" for investors, by limiting the circumstances, e.g., to cases of intentional fraud, under which securities transactions could be unwound.

The broad language used in Section 546(e) protects transactions rather than firms, reflecting a purpose of enhancing the efficiency of securities markets in order to reduce the cost of capital to the American economy. As noted, central to a highly efficient securities market are methods of trading securities through intermediaries. Section 546(e)'s protection of the transactions consummated through these intermediaries was not intended as protection of politically favored special interests. Rather, it was sought by the SEC—and corresponding provisions by the CFTC—in order to protect investors from the disruptive effect of after-the-fact unwinding of securities transactions.

A lack of protection against the unwinding of securities transactions would create substantial deterrents, limited only by the copious imaginations of able lawyers, to investing in the securities market. The effect of appellants' legal theory would be akin to the effect of eliminating the limited liability of investors for the debts of a corporation: a reduction of capital available to American securities markets.

For example, all investors in public companies would face new and substantial risks, if appellants' theory is adopted. At the very least, each would have to confront a higher degree of uncertainty even as to the consummation of securities transfers. The risks are not confined to the consummation of securities transactions. Pension plans, mutual funds, and similar institutional investors would find securities markets far more risky if exposed to substantial liabilities derived from investments in securities sold long ago. If appellants were to prevail, a pension plan whose position in a firm was cashed out in a merger would have to set aside reserves in case the surviving firm went bankrupt and triggered avoidance actions based on a claim that the cash out price exceeded the value of the shares. Every economic downturn would expose such institutional investors not only to a decline in the value of their current portfolios but also to claims for substantial monies received from mergers during good times.

Given the occasional volatility of economic events, any transaction buying out shareholders would risk being attacked as a fraudulent conveyance avoidable by creditors if the firm faltered. Appellants' legal theory would even reach investors who, after voting against a merger approved by other shareholders, were involuntarily cashed out. Tender offers, which almost always involve a premium above trading price, Lynn A. Stout, *Are Takeover Premiums Really Premiums? Market Price, Fair Value, and Corporate Law,* 99 Yale L.J. 1235, 1235 (1990), would imperil cashed out shareholders if the surviving entity encountered financial difficulties.

If appellants' theory was adopted, individual investors following a conservative buy-and-hold strategy with a diversified portfolio designed to reduce risk might well decide that such a strategy would actually increase the risk of crushing liabilities. Such a strategy is adopted because it involves low costs of monitoring the prospects of individual companies and emphasizes the offsetting of unsystematic risks by investing in multiple firms. Appellants' legal theory might well require costly and constant monitoring by investors to rid their portfolios of investments in firms that might, under then-current circumstances, be subject to mergers, stock buy-backs, or tender offers (and would otherwise be good investments). Investing in multiple companies, the essence of diversification, would increase the danger of avoidance liability.

The threat to investors is not simply losing a lawsuit. Given the costliness of defending such legal actions and the long delay in learning their outcome, exposing investors to even very weak lawsuits involving millions of dollars would be a substantial deterrent to investing in securities. The need to set aside reserves to meet the costs of litigation—not to mention costs of losing—would suck money from capital markets.

As noted, concern has been expressed that LBOs are different from other transactions in ways pertinent to the Bankruptcy Code. *In re Lyondell Chem. Co.,* 503 B.R. 348, 354, 358–59 (Bankr.S.D.N.Y.2014). However, the language of

Section 546(e) does not exempt from its protection payments by firms to intermediaries to fund ensuing payments to shareholders for stock.

Moreover, securities markets are heavily regulated by state and federal governments. The statutory supplements used in law school securities regulation courses are thick enough to rival Kevlar in stopping bullets. Mergers and tender offers are among the most regulated transactions. *See, e.g.,* Williams Act, 15 U.S.C.A. §§ 78m(d)–(e), 78n(d). Much of the content of state and federal regulation is designed to protect investors in such transactions. Much of that content is also designed to maximize the payout to shareholders cashed out in a merger, *see, e.g., Revlon, Inc. v. MacAndrews & Forbes Holdings, Inc.,* 506 A.2d 173, 182 (Del.1986); *Unocal Corp. v. Mesa Petroleum Co.,* 493 A.2d 946, 955–56 (Del.1985), or accepting a tender offer, *see* Williams Act, 15 U.S.C.A. §§ 78m(d)–(e), 78n(d). Appellants' legal theory would allow creditors to seek to portray that maximization as evidence supporting a crushing liability. A legal rule substantially undermining those goals of state and federal regulation—again, one akin to eliminating limited liability—is a systemic risk.

It is also argued that the Bankruptcy Code has many different purposes and that Section 546(e) does not clearly "trump[ ] all [the] other[s]." The pertinent—and "trumping"—"other" purpose of the Code is said to be the maximization of assets available to creditors. Courts customarily accommodate statutory provisions in tension with one another where the principal purpose of each is attainable by limiting each in achieving secondary goals. However, Section 546(e) is in full conflict with the goal of maximizing the assets available to creditors. Its purpose is to protect a national, heavily regulated market by limiting creditors' rights. Conflicting goals are not accommodated by giving value with the right hand and taking it away with the left. Section 546(e) cannot be trumped by the Code's goal of maximizing the return to creditors without thwarting the Section's purposes.

We therefore conclude that Congress intended to protect from constructive fraudulent conveyance avoidance proceedings transfers by a debtor in bankruptcy that fall within Section 546(e)'s terms.

Contrast the foregoing with the Delaware Bankruptcy Court's recent opinion in *In re Physiotherapy Holdings, Inc.,* 62 Bankr. Ct. Dec. 213 (Bankr.D.Del.2016):

Although *Tribune* . . . settled the split in the Second Circuit, it is nevertheless not binding on the Court. The Court finds the reasoning in *Lyondell* more persuasive and therefore adopts its holding. Because "the purpose of Congress is the ultimate touchstone in every pre-emption case," the Court must look to the purpose and legislative history behind the safe harbors and section 546(e) before it determines whether or not the claims are preempted. Wyeth v. Levine, 555 U.S. 555, 565 (2009) (quoting Medtronic, Inc. v. Lohr, 518 U.S. 470, 485, 116 S. Ct. 2240, 135 L. Ed. 2d 700 (1996)). The Court believes that the *Lyondell* opinion more accurately addresses the history and function of the safe harbors. The second touchstone of preemption analysis, as articulated by the *Wyeth* court, is that "[i]n all pre-emption cases, and particularly in those in which Congress has legislated . . . in a field which the States have traditionally occupied . . . we start with the assumption that the historic police powers of the States were not to be superseded by the Federal Act unless that was the clear and manifest purpose of Congress." *Id.* Once again, the Court believes that the *Lyondell* decision correctly recognized that the States have traditionally occupied the field of fraudulent transfer law, and applying the presumption against preemption is therefore appropriate.

3.   BULK SALES (UCC ARTICLE 6)

If an acquisition is structured as the sale of the assets of the target company, the sale may be subject to the bulk transfer laws contained in Article 6 of the Uniform Commercial Code, if Article 6 is in effect in the jurisdictions that might be applicable to the transaction. Under the bulk sales laws, "bulk transfers" of assets are ineffective against creditors of the seller unless there is compliance with the special procedures of Article 6 that provide notice to the target's creditors. What justifications might exist for such a statute?

Article 6 is a fading statute, still in force in only a small handful of states.[13] New York repealed its version of the statute in 2001. Nonetheless, it remains a concern when dealing with a multistate business. *See, e.g.,* Cal. Com. Code, §§ 6101 to 6111.

4.   A NOTE ON ALTERNATIVE ACQUISITION STRUCTURES

Most commonly distressed acquisitions take the form of asset sales that are structured (as best as possible) to show the payment of "reasonably equivalent value." The buyer hopes to avoid both fraudulent transfer and successor liability as a result.

But a distressed company's assets might also be acquired through the state law foreclosure system. In general, liens on personal property are governed by the Uniform Commercial Code, which authorizes both private and public foreclosure sales. Liens on interests in real estate, or mortgages, are governed by more complex state real property law and the foreclosure procedures will vary from state to state.

A potential purchaser could wait until the secured party exercises its remedies under state law and then buy the assets at the foreclosure sale. Or the buyer could acquire the secured party's debt, which will allow the purchaser to control the foreclosure process and acquire the assets at the foreclosure sale through a credit bid.[14]

---

13. http://www.lawrev.state.nj.us/rpts/ucc6.pdf.

14. Credit bids are discussed in the bankruptcy materials, but essentially involve the lender "bidding" part of its debt at the auction—in place of cash.

As opposed to an asset sale under state corporate law, the foreclosure process has the advantage that the sale may not be challenged as a fraudulent transfer in a subsequent bankruptcy case.[15]

Another state law procedure that can be useful in acquiring assets is known as the assignment for the benefit of creditors. This statutory procedure allows a distressed company to assign all of its assets to a representative who then liquidates the assets and distributes the proceeds to the creditors. In some sense this can be seen as a state law bankruptcy process—although the states are limited by the Contract Clause in the Constitution in their ability to provide full bankruptcy relief.[16]

5. WORKER ADJUSTMENT AND RETRAINING NOTIFICATION ACT ("WARN")

IN THE MATTER OF FLEXIBLE FLYER LIQUIDATING TRUST

511 Fed.Appx. 369, 2013 WL 586823
United States Court of Appeals, Fifth Circuit.
Feb. 11, 2013.

PER CURIAM:

This appeal addresses an employer's duty to notify employees of a plant closing and mass layoff under the Worker Adjustment and Retraining Notification Act ("WARN Act"), where lenders suddenly and without advance notice completely terminated the company's financing. The question presented is whether such circumstance satisfies the WARN Act exception for "unforeseeable business circumstances." The case largely turns on the factual findings of the bankruptcy court. Because the findings are not clearly erroneous, we AFFIRM.

I.

Cerberus Capital Management Corp. ("Cerberus"), a private equity hedge fund, formed the now bankrupt Flexible Flyer in 1997 to purchase the assets of a bankrupt company. Flexible Flyer manufactured swing sets, hobby horses, go-carts, utility vehicles, and fitness equipment. These products were sold to a variety of retailers, including Wal-Mart, Toys-R-Us, K-Mart, and Sam's Club.

Flexible Flyer never made a profit—indeed it constantly lost money—but hope and a few good signs kept it going. Until late 2000, Flexible Flyer was funded entirely by its parent company, Cerberus. During this time, Cerberus infused Flexible Flyer with $85 million in capital. In late 2000, Flexible Flyer obtained an additional source of operating capital when it entered into a factoring arrangement with CIT Group Commercial Systems, LLC ("CIT"). Under this

---

15. BFP v. Resolution Trust Corp., 511 U.S. 531, 545 (1994).

16. *See* Stephen J. Lubben, *A New Understanding of the Bankruptcy Clause,* 64 Case W. Res. L. Rev. 319 (2013).

arrangement, Flexible Flyer assigned its eligible accounts receivables to CIT, and CIT advanced Flexible Flyer 80% of the receivables that it acquired. The factoring arrangement with CIT and occasional capital infusions from Cerberus were Flexible Flyer's primary sources of operating funds during its struggling existence.

CIT and Cerberus closely monitored Flexible Flyer's financial performance, because, as we have indicated, Flexible Flyer consistently operated at a deficit. Each year, Cerberus told Flexible Flyer that it would shut Flexible Flyer down if it did not become profitable within a year. But, despite the failure to make a profit and despite issuing these warnings year after year, Cerberus never took the steps to close Flexible Flyer. Cerberus continued to provide capital and did not refuse Flexible Flyer's requests for additional funding when Flexible Flyer indicated that more funding was essential for its continued operation.

In 2005, Flexible Flyer's situation became even more tenuous. It experienced a number of financial problems, and the company notified its employees in April of possible layoffs in the go-cart section. Two months later, Flexible Flyer was forced to recall 10,000 go-carts because of defective parts. Around this same time, Wal-Mart, K-Mart, and Toys-R-Us notified Flexible Flyer that they would be deferring the purchase of approximately $5 million in swing sets until the next year. Another customer, Tractor Supply Company, withheld $300,000 in payments for merchandise that had already been shipped.

Michael Earrey, Flexible Flyer's Chief Financial Officer, took a number of actions attempting to address these problems. In August 2005, he convinced Wal-Mart to pay its invoices sooner, and several vendors agreed to defer payments due from Flexible Flyer. Earrey was less successful, however, in convincing some customers, most notably Wal-Mart, to provide written commitments regarding projected delivery dates or future orders. Despite the lack of written commitments, Earrey testified that he remained optimistic Flexible Flyer could weather the storm. During this time, Flexible Flyer's primary domestic competitor had filed for bankruptcy protection, leaving Flexible Flyer as the only U.S. manufacturer of swing sets. Fewer competitors gave Earrey a reason to be encouraged about Flexible Flyer's future.

Recognizing that it needed additional funds to operate, Flexible Flyer consulted with an attorney in August 2005 to explore all of its options. Among those options were exiting the go-cart business completely, selling the fitness equipment business, or possibly filing for Chapter 11 bankruptcy protection. Before Flexible Flyer decided on which course of action to take, however, CIT reduced its credit line. Instead of continuing to advance Flexible Flyer 80% of its receivables, CIT cut the amount to 50%. Earrey believed that Flexible Flyer could continue to operate at the 50% rate, but two weeks after the initial cut, CIT informed Flexible Flyer that it would no longer be advancing credit at all. Earrey attempted to get funding from Cerberus, but this time, Cerberus refused. With no cash to operate, Flexible Flyer was forced to file for bankruptcy on September 9, 2005, two days after CIT terminated all funding. That same day, Flexible Flyer notified its employees that it would be terminating business operations, resulting in company-wide layoffs.

A group of over 100 former Flexible Flyer employees filed an adversary action in Flexible Flyer's bankruptcy proceeding, alleging that Flexible Flyer was liable under the WARN Act for failing to give them the required sixty-day layoff notice. Both parties agreed that there were more than 100 employees involved, that Flexible Flyer had failed to give the sixty-day notice, and that consequently the WARN Act applied. After a bench trial, the bankruptcy court determined, however, that Flexible Flyer was excused from providing advance notice because it had established that the shutdown was the result of an unforeseeable business circumstance. The court credited Earrey's testimony, finding that the abrupt unavailability of operating funds caused the layoffs and that the sudden lack of funds was completely unanticipated. The court concluded that "[t]he shutdown of Flexible Flyer and the mass layoffs were not planned, proposed, or foreseeable" and found that Flexible Flyer had provided WARN Act notice at "the earliest practical date that such a notice could be provided."

The employees appealed to the district court, which held that "the factual determinations made by the [bankruptcy] court were not clearly erroneous, and the legal conclusions were thorough and correct." This timely appeal from the district court's judgment followed.

III.

The WARN Act, 29 U.S.C. §§2101–2109, requires covered employers who are planning a plant closing or mass layoff to give affected employees sixty days notice of such action. 20 C.F.R. §639.2. Advance notice is meant to provide "workers and their families some transition time to adjust to the prospective loss of employment, to seek and obtain alternative jobs and, if necessary, to enter skill training or retraining." There are exceptions, however, that excuse employers who fail to provide the required notice. If a WARN Act exception applies, employers are required to give only "as much notice as is practicable."

The unforeseeable business circumstance exception applies when the closing or layoff was "caused by business circumstances that were not reasonably foreseeable as of the time that notice would have been required." Closings and layoffs are not foreseeable when "caused by some sudden, dramatic, and unexpected action or condition outside the employer's control." In assessing the foreseeability of business circumstances, our focus is "on an employer's business judgment. An employer is required only to "exercise such commercially reasonable business judgment as would a similarly situated employer in predicting the demands of its particular market."

We previously have stated that where it only is possible that the business circumstance at issue may occur, such circumstances are not reasonably foreseeable. Rather, "it is the probability of occurrence that makes a business circumstance 'reasonably foreseeable' and thereby forecloses use of the [unforeseeable business circumstances] exception."

Here, the bankruptcy court was the finder of fact. It determined that the September 9, 2005 closing of Flexible Flyer's business was not reasonably foreseeable. The record showed that sixty days before the shutdown, Flexible Flyer was undisputedly experiencing financial difficulties. But, even so, there was no indication that a company shutdown was imminent. Indeed, the bankruptcy court credited Earrey's testimony that, until almost the last moment, he had been working tirelessly to turn the company around and was considering a number of cost-saving measures designed to keep the company operating for as long as possible. Moreover, Flexible Flyer's position in the market had improved as a result of its competitor's demise, and Earrey had presented Wal-Mart with projections for Flexible Flyer's 2006 operations, demonstrating his belief that the company would continue operations into the new year. Earrey also testified that he was considering options for "an orderly downsizing of the business over time, not an immediate shutdown." All of the evidence proffered thus shows that the focus of Flexible Flyer's management was on saving the company, not planning for an upcoming shutdown. Based on Earrey's testimony, the bankruptcy court found that, "Earrey's exercise of his business judgment, in keeping Flexible Flyer going and in anticipating that Flexible Flyer would continue operations into 2006, was completely reasonable." We cannot say that the bankruptcy court clearly erred in crediting Earrey's testimony or in concluding that his exercise of business judgment was reasonable under the circumstances.

The holdings of the bankruptcy and district courts are further supported by the showing that during the time period immediately preceding the closure, Flexible Flyer still had financing in place from CIT, as well as back-up funding from Cerberus, who had never refused Flexible Flyer's previous requests for additional capital. It was only when CIT and Cerberus both decided to cut off funding completely, and did so almost simultaneously without warning, that the shutdown became inevitable. Earrey testified that he had "no clue" that CIT was going to cut funding, and Cerberus's refusal to provide capital was a sudden departure from its prior actions in response to Flexible Flyer's funding requests. Again crediting Earrey's testimony, the bankruptcy court concluded that the "abrupt unavailability of operating funds" caused the layoffs, and that CIT and Cerberus's actions were "completely unanticipated." Nothing in the record suggests that these findings and conclusions were clearly erroneous.

The arguments of the former employees suggest that the sixty days notice should have been issued sometime following the June 2005 go-cart recall. Contrary to the contention of the former employees, Flexible Flyer's financial difficulties in July and in the ensuing weeks do not establish the foreseeability of a complete withdrawal of funding; nor consequently, the company's sudden closure on September 9, 2005. As noted above, the bankruptcy court credited Earrey's testimony that CIT and Cerberus's decision to cut all funding was an unanticipated event taking place two days before the shutdown. Under [case law] and the WARN Act regulations, the focus of the analysis of this appeal must be on the probability that the plant closure and subsequent layoffs would occur, and the employer's exercise of business judgment. It is true that Flexible Flyer's financial condition was perilous for much of its eight-year existence. But it is also true that encouraging events continued to renew probabilities that better days may be ahead. The WARN Act allows good faith, well-grounded hope, and reasonable expectations. Its regulations protect the employer's exercise of business judgment and are intended to encourage employers to take all reasonable actions to preserve the company and the jobs. Holding Flexible Flyer liable for a WARN Act violation on the facts found by the bankruptcy court would serve only to encourage employers to abandon companies even when there is some probability of some success.

Thus, we hold that the bankruptcy court did not err in finding Earrey's testimony credible; based on his testimony, he pursued numerous options to save Flexible Flyer up until the sudden termination of all funding by CIT and Cerberus. Termination of outside funding may have always been possible, but it cannot be said on the record before us that Flexible Flyer probably knew during or before July 2005 that it would be stripped of funding, causing an immediate shutdown. This case presents a convincing example of an event that meets the unforeseeable business circumstance exception. The bankruptcy court correctly concluded that the exception applied in this case. The district court's judgment therefore is AFFIRMED.

The responsibility to notify employees whose employment will be terminated as a result of a sale remains with the seller up to and including the effective date of the transaction, and thereafter is assumed by the buyer.[17]

What transitional considerations does the WARN Act raise in the context of a leveraged buyout or distressed acquisitions?

Many states, including New York, New Jersey, and California (among others), have enacted state mini-WARN Acts, whose provisions differ in various respects from WARN and often are more demanding. For example, under the New York State WARN Act, NY Labor Law §§860 et seq., employers with 50 or more full-time employees in New York State must provide at least 90 days advance written notice for a plant closing.

6.   BANKRUPTCY RISKS OF DISTRESSED ACQUISITIONS

Bankruptcy will be discussed in subsequent chapters, but it bears noting at this point that if a financially distressed company does file for bankruptcy protection after the signing but before the closing of the transaction, the buyer is subject to risk that the now-bankrupt target will exercise its rights under section 365 of the Bankruptcy Code to reject the sale agreement. Alternatively, the target might use its powers under the Bankruptcy Code to attempt to renegotiate the terms of the sale by threatening rejection. Moreover, the representations, warranties, and

---

17. 29 U.S.C. §2101 (b)(1).

indemnities contained in the asset purchase agreement might not be worth very much after the target's bankruptcy filing. In short, because of the risk of future bankruptcy cases, the acquirer has strong incentives to close the transaction quickly.

IV

FINANCIAL DISTRESS

26

EXCHANGE OFFERS AND WORKOUTS

This chapter begins the fourth and final section of the course. The fourth unit deals with corporate finance in the context of financial distress. Just as these chapters are the beginning of the end of your course, these topics are often the beginning of the end of the firm. But not always.

The most obvious way to deal with financial distress is through bankruptcy. But this chapter examines the ways in which a firm can try to solve its problems outside of bankruptcy.

It is generally thought that these sorts of out-of-court processes involve less cost, as bankruptcy is a court-driven process that requires lots of pleadings to be drafted, even when there is general consensus among the firm and its claimants.

1. WORKOUTS

At a basic level a workout is simply an agreement between the debtor firm and its creditors. That presupposes the firm knows who its creditors are—the advent of distressed debt investors and derivatives might make this more complicated than it would appear.

STEPHEN J. LUBBEN & RAJESH P. NARAYANAN, *CDS AND THE RESOLUTION OF FINANCIAL DISTRESS*

24 J. Applied Corp. Fin. 129 (2012)

The ownership of debt conveys to the creditor a bundled set of rights—cash flow rights to principal and interest payments, and control rights to protect and recover these promised payments through the ability to vote on covenant waivers, reorganization plans and liquidation decisions. Hedging in the CDS markets immunizes the creditor to the debtor's financial condition and thus functionally unbundles the cash flow rights from the control rights embodied in the debt contract.

The potential for this unbundling to cause problems in restructurings was first identified by Lubben (2007), and then given the moniker the "empty creditor problem" by Hu and Black (2008a, 2008b). In short, the issue relates to how the altered incentives of hedged creditors result in unexpected behavior after the onset of financial distress.

While it is normally assumed that creditors are interested in keeping a solvent but financially distressed firm out of bankruptcy and hence willing to renegotiate out-of-court, a hedged creditor will lack the incentive to participate in an out of court workout—such as an exchange offer. In extreme cases, the creditor might have incentives to thwart workouts and file involuntary bankruptcy cases, all with an eye toward triggering their CDS contract. This problem could be especially extreme in North America, where, for historical reasons, "restructuring" is often not included as a credit event in standard CDS contracts.

It is also possible that the holder of a large, speculative CDS position could acquire a position in a distressed firm's traded debt to block a potential workout. After the onset of financial distress, it could be that the cost of such a blocking position on the distressed debt markets would be justified given a sufficiently large CDS position. Indeed, if the CDS market is made up of mostly speculators, the prior scenario, or something like it, might be the most plausible. After all, it is unclear how many CDS buyers actually use such swaps to hedge ordinary bonds.

Similarly, it should be noted that such a blocking strategy would not necessarily involve buying debt at the same level in the capital structure as referenced by the investor's CDS contracts. Indeed, it would typically be more effective to purchase senior secured debt, which would result in a higher return upon bankruptcy and facilitate greater blocking power. For example, many syndicated loan agreements require super majority votes to waive defaults. And in chapter 11, secured creditors are separately classified, resulting in greater voting power.

CDS may also place artificial time limits on restructuring negotiations, given that most contracts run for five years, and will presumably have been purchased before financial distress made the cost prohibitive. Credit default swaps expire without value to the protection buyer if no credit event occurs before maturity. Thus, as maturity dates approach on outstanding credit default swaps, protected creditors will have an increasing disincentive to work with the debtor on the terms of a restructuring arrangement that might not be announced or consummated until after the creditors' swaps have terminated. More generally, the protection buyer faces the risk that any workout could extend the underlying debt obligation beyond the duration of the swap.

Even the more extreme cases, such as creditors filing involuntary bankruptcy petitions to manufacture a credit event, are not apt to be easily detected, so long as the creditor has other, more traditional grounds for filing the petition. At present, there is no legal obligation for a petitioning creditor to disclose whether it has hedged its position.

Identifying these problems in actual cases of financial distress is quite difficult. Most workouts require the creditor to balance what they are offered in the workout with what they would receive in a hypothetical chapter 11 or chapter 7 case of the same debtor. CDSs do not change this analysis, but rather places a thumb on the bankruptcy side of the scale. That is, CDSs result in a marginal change of incentives, rather than an absolute change. Detecting such a shift, separate from the underlying attractiveness of the competing offers in the workout, requires subtle analysis.

Press reports on the difficulties facing debtors attempting to reorganize in the presence of hedged creditors first began to appear in connection with British telecom company Marconi's renegotiations with its lenders in 2001–2002. Since then, press coverage on problems with hedged creditors has accompanied the bankruptcies of Mirant, Lyondell-Basell, General Growth Properties, Six Flags, Abitibi-Bowater, featuring most prominently in the 2009 bankruptcies of General Motors and Chrysler.

In 2009, ISDA examined whether the ability to hedge using CDSs made out-of-court restructurings less likely than bankruptcy filings. Positing that "*the correlation between number of defaults and restructurings as percent of defaults should be lower when credit default swaps are available that when they are not*," it reported "*the correlation between number of defaults in a given year and restructurings relative to defaults in the same year is about 9 percent over the entire sample period. But restricting attention to the period of liquid credit default swap markets, which arguably began in 2003 with the publication of the 2003 ISDA Credit Derivative Definitions and the subsequent initiation of trading in the CDX and iTraxx credit indexes, the correlation jumps to 90 percent. While correlations within small data sets should be interpreted carefully, the correlation statistics presented here would not appear to support the empty creditor hypothesis, according to which the availability of credit default swaps would make restructurings less likely.*

Further evidence comes from the list of restructurings that occurred during 2008 and the first half of 2009. During that time, twenty-one firms underwent out-of-court restructurings; credit default swap protection was available on eleven of them (52 percent). And of the restructurings that occurred during that period, four subsequently filed for Chapter 11 bankruptcy; of those four, two had liquid CDS available and two did not. Again, the evidence thus far does not appear to support the empty creditor hypothesis." (Mengle, pp. 8–9)

More generally, exchange offers often fail because of holdout problems associated with disparate creditors. Bedendo, Cathcart, El-Jahel (2010) account for this possibility and attempt to discern whether the failure of exchange offers is due to hedged creditors. They find that ". . . the outcome of the debt renegotiation process seems to be driven by essentially the same variables in both reference and non-reference entities" (p. 3) and is not linked to hedged creditors.

To get at the issue more directly, Danis (2012) examines whether creditor participation rates in exchange offers vary with the ability to hedge in the CDS markets. He finds that average participation rates are lower in exchange offers conducted by reference entities compared to non-reference entities which suggests that hedged creditors may make it more difficult for firms to restructure debt out-of-court.

Debtors may respond by structuring their exchange offers to circumvent hedged creditors. Typically, the reference obligation underlying the CDS is senior unsecured debt. Narayanan and Uzmanoglu (2012) posit that debtors target junior debt in the exchange offer as a way to alleviate distress. They provide evidence that, relative to non-reference entities, reference entities disproportionately restructure junior debt by offering creditors greater concession to tender in the exchange.

Debtors may find it useful to use a coercive exchange offer, to force the "true" stakeholders of a firm to reveal themselves. Of course, this move might also further encourage involuntary bankruptcy petitions, with the attendant risk of an unplanned filing in an unfavorable jurisdiction.

There is some indirect evidence associated with hedged creditors increasing the cost of distress resolution. Subrahmanyam, Tang and Wang (2011) find that both the probability of future credit downgrade and the probability of filing for bankruptcy increase after the introduction of CDS trading on a firm, leading them to state that the "the reluctance of (CDS protected lenders) to restructure is the most likely cause of the increase in credit risk." (p. 1)

More broadly, growth of credit derivatives could well impede the negotiation of workouts, as well as prenegotiated or prepackaged bankruptcy plans, inasmuch as the party with the real risk of loss will often be unknown. Creditors may no longer behave in predictable ways; previously unknown creditors may appear on the scene, demanding a voice in the proceedings, and the debtor's true stakeholders may be subject to dispute.

In short, negotiations on the eve of bankruptcy can be expected to become increasingly complex and opaque (Skeel and Partnoy 2007). In large part this is the result of the design of the credit protection markets, which expressly seek to allow banks and other lenders the ability to offload credit risk without alerting their customers of this fact and incurring the resulting reputation costs. However, this lack of transparency creates obvious and severe information asymmetries that may hinder pre-bankruptcy negotiation and planning, a serious problem after the 2005 amendments to the Bankruptcy Code make it increasingly difficult for a debtor to enter chapter 11 without such planning.

Assuming one can figure out who the creditors are, one of the key creditor groups in any workout situation is typically the syndicated loan holders. Because syndicated loans often have more covenants than other debts, they are often the first to default. Moreover, if the borrower is facing liquidity problems, the first sign may be substantial increases in loan advances.

During the workout negotiations, the agent lender must negotiate both with the borrower and with the other members of the lending group. A "joint defense and confidentiality agreement" among the lenders and their administrative agent often binds the lending group together and will be the first document to be negotiated in a workout. The agreement must also take into account the likelihood that some lenders will sell their positions to distressed debt investors during the workout process.

The end result is often a "forbearance agreement," in which the lenders agree to certain amendments to the loan agreement. Of course, the borrower pays a price for these changes, often in the form of increased interest rates and even more demanding covenants.

2.   EXCHANGE OFFERS

One of the most common methods for effectuating a workout with bondholders, and even sometimes with widely dispersed loan holders, is through an exchange offer. The firm negotiates a deal for the refinancing of its debt with a group of large creditors, and then it commences a tender offer for its outstanding debt.

The tender offer it institutes is an "exchange offer" in that it typically offers new, longer-dated (and perhaps lower-couponed) debt in exchange for the existing debt.

NICHOLAS P. SAGGESE, ET AL., *A PRACTITIONER'S GUIDE TO EXCHANGE OFFERS AND CONSENT SOLICITATIONS*

24 Loy. L.A. L. Rev. 527 (1991)

The general purpose of restructuring transactions is to preserve the going concern value of a financially troubled corporation by modifying its capital structure to reduce interest or dividend expense, or to eliminate or modify covenants in the corporation's existing securities that restrict or prohibit a restructuring, or that the corporation can no longer satisfy.

A corporation can effect a restructuring in a number of ways. One often-used technique involves the consensual exchange (Exchange Offer) of new securities of the corporation (New Securities) for certain of its then outstanding securities (Target Securities).

In addition, a corporation contemplating an out-of-court restructuring may choose to solicit security holders' consents to modify Target Securities (Consent Solicitation), reclassify equity securities pursuant to an amendment to the corporation's charter (Reclassification) or repurchase Target Securities for cash. A financially troubled corporation may also utilize a "pre-packaged" plan of bankruptcy (Prepackaged Bankruptcy) to avoid protracted chapter 11 proceedings. This Article, however, focuses on issues related to out-of-court restructurings generally as well as certain issues unique to Exchange Offers that involve an exchange or a series of exchanges of New Securities for Target Securities pursuant to section 3(a)(9) of the Securities Act of 1933, as amended (the Securities Act).

The issuance of New Securities in exchange for Target Securities requires registration of the offering of the New Securities with the Securities and Exchange Commission (the SEC), unless an exemption is available. Section 3(a)(9) of the Securities Act (Section 3(a)(9)) provides such an exemption and is often relied upon in the context of out-of-court restructurings. This exemption, often called the "exchange exemption," applies when New Securities are exchanged, except in a case under title 11 of the United States Code, "by the issuer with its existing security holders exclusively where no commission or other remuneration is paid or given directly or indirectly for soliciting such exchange."

A restructuring conducted as an exchange of securities pursuant to Section 3(a)(9) (Section 3(a)(9) Exchange) offers a distinct advantage over alternative forms of restructurings—by avoiding the delay associated with the registration of securities with the SEC, a Section 3(a)(9) Exchange can be commenced relatively quickly and relatively inexpensively. A Section 3(a)(9) Exchange, however, also has one significant disadvantage to the corporation—the corporation cannot retain paid agents to solicit the participation of the holders of Target Securities in the proposed exchange. If a corporation believes that professional solicitation efforts are essential to the success of its restructuring, the corporation must either conduct the exchange within the parameters of another Securities Act exemption, or it must register the sale of New Securities offered in the exchange by filing a registration statement with the SEC (Registered Exchange).

From a legal standpoint, Exchange Offers may involve a plethora of regulations and issues, including the following:

- the elements of Section 3(a)(9), if applicable;
- if there is a concurrent Consent Solicitation, the proxy rules ... promulgated under the Securities Exchange Act of 1934, as amended (the Exchange Act);
- the tender offer and "going private" rules promulgated under the Williams Act, as amended;

- if the New Security is a qualifying debt security, the requirements of the Trust Indenture Act of 1939, as amended (the TIA) and the rules promulgated thereunder;
- the continuing concern about the proper timing of public disclosure about the restructuring and related issues from the conception to consummation of the restructuring;
- the laws governing fiduciary duties and contractual obligations owed to various classes of security holders;
- state blue sky and securities laws;
- the rules of securities exchanges;
- the rules of the National Association of Securities Dealers, Inc. (the NASD) [In 2007, the NASD merged with the New York Stock Exchange's regulation committee to form the Financial Industry Regulatory Authority, or FINRA.]; and
- tax and debtor/creditor considerations.

The oil and gas industry has been rife with exchange offers of late, and set forth below is an example of an exchange offer that relies on the section 4(a)(2) under the 1933 Act. How does it differ from the 3(a)(9) approach outline above? What are the *Chesapeake* noteholders getting by tendering into this offer? How does the offer incentivize tenders?

CHESAPEAKE ENERGY CORPORATION ANNOUNCES PRIVATE EXCHANGE OFFERS FOR SENIOR NOTES

OKLAHOMA CITY, December 2, 2015—Chesapeake Energy Corporation (NYSE:CHK) today announced the commencement of private offers of up to $1.5 billion aggregate principal amount (the "Maximum Exchange Amount") of its new 8.00% Senior Secured Second Lien Notes due 2022 (the "Second Lien Notes") in exchange for certain outstanding senior unsecured notes of the Company, upon the terms and subject to the conditions set forth in the Company's confidential offering memorandum and related letter of transmittal, each dated December 2, 2015.

The following table sets forth each series of outstanding senior unsecured notes subject to the exchange offers (the "Existing Notes") and indicates the acceptance priority level for such series and the applicable consideration offered for such series in the exchange offers for the Existing Notes (the "Exchange Offers").

Title of Series	Aggregate Principal Amount Outstanding (in millions)	Acceptance Priority Level[2]	Principal Amount of Second Lien Notes[1]	
			Early Tender Exchange Consideration	Late Tender Exchange Consideration
6.25% euro senior notes due 2017	$363.6[3]	1	$1,000.00	$950.00
6.5% senior notes due 2017	$660.4	2	$970.00	$920.00
7.25% senior notes due 2018	$668.6	3	$825.00	$775.00
Floating rate senior notes due 2019	$1,500.0	4	$600.00	$550.00
6.625% senior notes due 2020	$1,300.0	5	$610.00	$560.00
6.875% senior notes due 2020	$500.0	5	$608.75	$558.75
6.125% senior notes due 2021	$1,000.0	6	$577.50	$527.50
5.375% senior notes due 2021	$700.0	6	$570.00	$520.00
4.875% senior notes due 2022	$1,500.0	6	$565.00	$515.00
5.75% senior notes due 2023	$1,100.0	6	$567.50	$517.50

(1) For each $1,000 principal amount of Existing Notes.

(2) All Existing Notes that are tendered for exchange in an Exchange Offer on or before the Early Tender Date (as defined below) will have priority over Existing Notes that are tendered for exchange after the Early Tender Date, even if such Existing Notes tendered after the Early Tender Date have a higher Acceptance Priority Level than Existing Notes tendered on or before the Early Tender Date and even if we do not elect to have an Early Settlement Date.

(3) The principal amount shown is based on the exchange ratio of $1.0565 to €1.00 as of 5:00 p.m., New York City time, on November 30, 2015, as set forth by the Bloomberg EURUSD Spot Exchange Rate.

The Exchange Offers are being made only to Eligible Holders (as defined below). Eligible Holders must validly tender (and not withdraw) their Existing Notes at or prior to 5:00 p.m., New York City time, on December 15, 2015 (the "Early Tender Date"), in order to be eligible to receive the applicable "Early Tender Exchange Consideration" shown in the table above. Existing Notes tendered after the Early Tender Date but prior to the Expiration Date (as defined below) will be eligible to receive only the applicable "Late Tender Exchange Consideration" set out in such table.

The Exchange Offers will expire at 11:59 p.m., New York City time, on December 30, 2015 (the "Expiration Date"). The settlement date will occur promptly after the Expiration Date and is expected to occur on December 31, 2015 (the "Final Settlement Date"), subject to all conditions to the Exchange Offers having been satisfied or waived by the Company. The Company may elect, in its sole discretion, to settle the Exchange Offers for any or all series of Existing Notes validly tendered prior to the Early Tender Date (and not validly withdrawn) at any time after the Early Tender Date and prior to the Expiration Date (the "Early Settlement Date"), subject to all conditions to the Exchange Offers having been satisfied or waived by the Company.

Eligible Holders of Existing Notes accepted for exchange in the Exchange Offers will also receive a cash payment equal to the accrued and unpaid interest on such Existing Notes from the applicable latest interest payment date to, but not including, the applicable settlement date. Interest on the Second Lien Notes will accrue from the date of first issuance of Second Lien Notes.

Tenders may be validly withdrawn at any time on or prior to 5:00 p.m., New York City time, on December 15, 2015, but not thereafter unless required by law. The Company may, but is not obligated to, increase the Maximum Exchange Amount without extending the Early Tender Date or reinstating withdrawal rights.

In the event that the Exchange Offers are oversubscribed, the principal amounts of each series of Existing Notes that are accepted will be determined in accordance with the "Acceptance Priority Levels" set forth on the table above, with 1 being the highest Acceptance Priority Level and 6 being the lowest Acceptance Priority Level. Accordingly, all Existing Notes with an Acceptance Priority Level 1 will be accepted before any Existing Notes with an Acceptance Priority Level 2, and so on, until the Maximum Exchange Amount is allocated. Once all Existing Notes tendered in a certain Acceptance Priority Level have been accepted, Existing Notes from the next Acceptance Priority Level may be accepted. If the remaining portion of the Maximum Exchange Amount is adequate to exchange some but not all of the aggregate principal amount of Existing Notes tendered within the next Acceptance Priority Level, Existing Notes tendered for exchange in that Acceptance Priority Level will be accepted on a pro rata basis, based on the aggregate principal amount of Existing Notes tendered with respect to that Acceptance Priority Level (with multiple series at a particular Acceptance Priority Level being treated collectively), and no Existing Notes with a lower Acceptance Priority Level will be accepted for exchange.

Notwithstanding the foregoing, all Existing Notes that are tendered for exchange in an Exchange Offer on or before the Early Tender Date will have priority over Existing Notes that are tendered for exchange after the Early Tender Date, even if such Existing Notes tendered after the Early Tender Date have a higher Acceptance Priority Level than Existing Notes tendered on or before the Early Tender Date and even if the Company does not elect to have an Early Settlement Date. If the principal amount of Existing Notes validly tendered on or before the Early Tender Date constitutes a principal amount of Existing Notes that, if accepted by the Company, would result in the issuance of Second Lien Notes having an aggregate principal amount equal to or in excess of the Maximum Exchange Amount, the Company will not accept any Existing Notes tendered for exchange after the Early Tender Date, regardless of the Acceptance Priority Level of such Existing Notes, unless the Company increases the Maximum Exchange Amount.

The Second Lien Notes will be unconditionally guaranteed, jointly and severally, on a senior basis, by certain subsidiaries of the Company. The Second Lien Notes will be secured by second-priority liens on all of the Company's and the guarantors' assets that secure indebtedness, including under the Company's existing credit facility (the "Credit Facility"), on a first-priority basis, subject to certain exceptions. Any Existing Notes that remain outstanding after the Exchange Offers will be effectively subordinated to the Second Lien Notes to the extent of the value of the collateral for the Second Lien Notes.

The Second Lien Notes will be denominated in U.S. dollars. An equivalent U.S. dollar principal amount of the euro-denominated Existing Notes, based on the Bloomberg EURUSD Spot Exchange Rate as of 5:00 p.m., New York City time, on December 11, 2015, will be used when determining the consideration to be received per $1,000 principal amount of such Existing Notes tendered.

The Exchange Offers are conditioned on the satisfaction or waiver of certain customary conditions, as described in the offering memorandum. The Exchange Offers are not conditioned upon any minimum amount of Existing Notes being tendered. The Company may terminate, withdraw, amend or extend any of the Exchange Offers.

The Exchange Offers will only be made, and the offering memorandum and other documents relating to the Exchange Offers will only be distributed to, holders who complete and return an eligibility form confirming that they are (i) "qualified institutional buyers" as defined in Rule 144A under the Securities Act of 1933, as amended ("Securities Act"), or (ii) outside the United States and persons other than "U.S. persons" as defined in Rule 902 under the Securities Act (such persons, "Eligible Holders"). Holders who desire to obtain and complete an eligibility form should either visit the website for this purpose at http://www.gbsc-usa.com/eligibility/Chesapeake or call Global Bondholder Services Corporation, the Information Agent and Depositary for the Exchange Offers at (866) 470-4300 (toll-free) or (212) 430-3774 (collect for banks and brokers).

The Company is making the Exchange Offers only to Eligible Holders through, and pursuant to, the terms of the confidential offering memorandum and related letter of transmittal. The Company and its affiliates do not make any recommendation as to whether Eligible Holders should tender or refrain from tendering their Existing Notes. Eligible Holders must make their own decision as to whether to tender Existing Notes and, if so, the principal amount of the Existing Notes to tender. The Exchange Offers are not being made to holders of Existing Notes in any jurisdiction in which the making or acceptance thereof would not be in compliance with the securities, blue sky or other laws of such jurisdiction.

The securities to be offered have not been registered under the Securities Act or any state securities laws; and unless so registered, the securities may not be offered or sold in the United States or to U.S. persons except pursuant to an exemption from, or in a transaction not subject to, the registration requirements of the Securities Act and applicable state securities laws. This press release shall not constitute an offer to sell or a solicitation of an offer to buy, nor shall there be any sale of these securities, in any jurisdiction in which such an offer, solicitation or sale would be unlawful prior to registration or qualification under the securities laws of any such jurisdiction.

About Chesapeake Energy Corporation

Chesapeake Energy Corporation (NYSE:CHK) is the second-largest producer of natural gas and the 12th largest producer of oil and natural gas liquids in the U.S. Headquartered in Oklahoma City, the company's operations are focused on discovering and developing its large and geographically diverse resource base of unconventional natural gas and oil assets onshore in the U.S. The company also owns substantial marketing and compression businesses.

PROBLEM SET 26.1

1. Review section 3(a)(9) and section 4(a)(2) in your statutory supplement and be prepared to discuss in class. What are the practical limitations of using these sections to reduce a firm's fixed costs?
2. How might you address the issue discussed in the Lubben-Narayanan article? Have the authors identified a real problem?

3.   EXIT CONSENTS

As you will recall from Chapter 14, section 316(b) of the Trust Indenture Act prohibits changes to certain fundamental provisions of an indenture without unanimous bondholder consent.[1] Although bonds issued under an exemption from registration under the Securities Act need not be issued under a qualified indenture subject to the TIA, many nonqualified indentures nevertheless incorporate the TIA by reference, or explicitly import certain provisions of the TIA into the provisions of the indenture, which leads to the same outcome as if the TIA had been incorporated by operation of law.

But in most cases a majority of the bondholders—unless the indenture provides otherwise—can consent to changes in other terms of the indenture. This grant of "exit consents"—given right before the holder exits into a new security

---

1. George W. Shuster, Jr., *The Trust Indenture Act and International Debt Restructurings*, 14 Am. Bankr. Inst. L. Rev. 431, 437 (2006).

under an exchange offer—is both controversial and useful, at least from the issuing firm's perspective.

MOISE KATZ v. OAK INDUSTRIES INC.

508 A.2d 873
Court of Chancery of Delaware, New Castle County.
March 10, 1986.

ALLEN, Chancellor.

A commonly used word—seemingly specific and concrete when used in everyday speech—may mask troubling ambiguities that upon close examination are seen to derive not simply from casual use but from more fundamental epistemological problems. Few words more perfectly illustrate the deceptive dependability of language than the term "coercion" which is at the heart of the theory advanced by plaintiff as entitling him to a preliminary injunction in this case.

Plaintiff is the owner of long-term debt securities issued by Oak Industries, Inc. ("Oak"), a Delaware corporation; in this class action he seeks to enjoin the consummation of an exchange offer and consent solicitation made by Oak to holders of various classes of its long-term debt. As detailed below that offer is an integral part of a series of transactions that together would effect a major reorganization and recapitalization of Oak. The claim asserted is in essence, that the exchange offer is a coercive device and, in the circumstances, constitutes a breach of contract. This is the Court's opinion on plaintiff's pending application for a preliminary injunction.

I.

The background facts are involved even when set forth in the abbreviated form the decision within the time period currently available requires.

Through its domestic and foreign subsidiaries and affiliated entities, Oak manufactures and markets component equipments used in consumer, industrial and military products (the "Components Segment"); produces communications equipment for use in cable television systems and satellite television systems (the "Communications Segment") and manufactures and markets laminates and other materials used in printed circuit board applications (the "Materials Segment"). During 1985, the Company has terminated certain other unrelated businesses. As detailed below, it has now entered into an agreement with Allied-Signal, Inc. for the sale of the Materials Segment of its business and is currently seeking a buyer for its Communications Segment.

Even a casual review of Oak's financial results over the last several years shows it unmistakably to be a company in deep trouble. During the period from January 1, 1982 through September 30, 1985, the Company has experienced unremitting losses from operations; on net sales of approximately $1.26 billion during that period it has lost over $335 million. As a result its total stockholders' equity has first shriveled (from $260 million on 12/31/81 to $85 million on 12/31/83) and then disappeared completely (as of 9/30/85 there was a $62 million deficit in its stockholders' equity accounts). Financial markets, of course, reflected this gloomy history.[2]

Unless Oak can be made profitable within some reasonably short time it will not continue as an operating company. Oak's board of directors, comprised almost entirely of outside directors, has authorized steps to buy the company time. In February, 1985, in order to reduce a burdensome annual cash interest obligation on its $230 million of then outstanding debentures, the Company offered to exchange such debentures for a combination of notes, common stock and warrants. As a result, approximately $180 million principal amount of the then outstanding debentures were exchanged. Since interest on certain of the notes issued in that exchange offer is payable in common stock, the effect of the 1985 exchange offer was to reduce to some extent the cash drain on the Company caused by its significant debt.

About the same time that the 1985 exchange offer was made, the Company announced its intention to discontinue certain of its operations and sell certain of its properties. Taking these steps, while effective to stave off a default and to reduce to some extent the immediate cash drain, did not address Oak's longer-range problems. Therefore, also during 1985 representatives of the Company held informal discussions with several interested parties exploring the possibility of an investment from, combination with or acquisition by another company. As a result of these discussions, the Company and Allied-Signal, Inc. entered into two agreements. The first, the Acquisition Agreement, contemplates the sale to Allied-Signal of the Materials Segment for $160 million in cash. The second agreement, the Stock Purchase Agreement, provides for the purchase by Allied-Signal for $15 million cash of 10 million shares of the Company's common stock together with warrants to purchase additional common stock.

The Stock Purchase Agreement provides as a condition to Allied-Signal's obligation that at least 85% of the aggregate principal amount of all of the Company's debt securities shall have tendered and accepted the exchange offers that are the subject of this lawsuit. Oak has six classes of such long-term debt.[3] If less than 85% of the aggregate principal amount of such debt accepts the offer, Allied-Signal has an option, but no obligation, to purchase the common stock and warrants contemplated by the Stock Purchase Agreement. An additional condition for the closing of the Stock Purchase Agreement is that the sale of the

---

2. The price of the company's common stock has fallen from over $30 per share on December 31, 1981 to approximately $2 per share recently (p. 38). The debt securities that are the subject of the exchange offer here involved ... have traded at substantial discounts.

3. The three classes of debentures are: 13.65% debentures due April 1, 2001, 101/2% convertible subordinated debentures due February 1, 2002, and 117/8% subordinated debentures due May 15, 1998. In addition, as a result of the 1985 exchange offer the company has three classes of notes which were issued in exchange for debentures that were tendered in that offer. Those are: 13.5% senior notes due May 15, 1990, 95/8% convertible notes due September 15, 1991 and 115/8% notes due September 15, 1990.

Company's Materials Segment contemplated by the Acquisition Agreement shall have been concluded.

Thus, as part of the restructuring and recapitalization contemplated by the Acquisition Agreement and the Stock Purchase Agreement, the Company has extended an exchange offer to each of the holders of the six classes of its long-term debt securities. These pending exchange offers include a Common Stock Exchange Offer (available only to holders of the 95/8% convertible notes) and the Payment Certificate Exchange Offers (available to holders of all six classes of Oak's long-term debt securities). The Common Stock Exchange Offer currently provides for the payment to each tendering noteholder of 407 shares of the Company's common stock in exchange for each $1,000 95/8% note accepted. The offer is limited to $38.6 million principal amount of notes (out of approximately $83.9 million outstanding).

The Payment Certificate Exchange Offer is an any and all offer. Under its terms, a payment certificate, payable in cash five days after the closing of the sale of the Materials Segment to Allied-Signal, is offered in exchange for debt securities. The cash value of the Payment Certificate will vary depending upon the particular security tendered. In each instance, however, that payment will be less than the face amount of the obligation. The cash payments range in amount, per $1,000 of principal, from $918 to $655. These cash values however appear to represent a premium over the market prices for the Company's debentures as of the time the terms of the transaction were set.

The Payment Certificate Exchange Offer is subject to certain important conditions before Oak has an obligation to accept tenders under it. First, it is necessary that a minimum amount ($38.6 million principal amount out of $83.9 total outstanding principal amount) of the 95/8% notes be tendered pursuant to the Common Stock Exchange Offer. Secondly, it is necessary that certain minimum amounts of each class of debt securities be tendered, together with consents to amendments to the underlying indentures.[4] Indeed, under the offer one may not tender securities unless at the same time one consents to the proposed amendments to the relevant indentures.

The condition of the offer that tendering security holders must consent to amendments in the indentures governing the securities gives rise to plaintiff's claim of breach of contract in this case. Those amendments would, if implemented, have the effect of removing significant negotiated protections to holders of the Company's long-term debt including the deletion of all financial covenants. Such modification may have adverse consequences to debt holders who elect not to tender pursuant to either exchange offer.

Allied-Signal apparently was unwilling to commit to the $15 million cash infusion contemplated by the Stock Purchase Agreement, unless Oak's long-term

---

4. The holders of more than 50% of the principal amount of each of the 13.5% notes, the 95/8% notes and the 115/8% notes and at least 662/3% of the principal amount of the 13.65% debentures, 101/2% debentures, and 117/8% debentures, must validly tender such securities and consent to certain proposed amendments to the indentures governing those securities.

debt is reduced by 85% (at least that is a condition of their obligation to close on that contract). Mathematically, such a reduction may not occur without the Company reducing the principal amount of outstanding debentures (that is the three classes outstanding notes constitute less than 85% of all long-term debt). But existing indenture covenants (See Offering Circular, pp. 38–39) prohibit the Company, so long as any of its long-term notes are outstanding, from issuing any obligation (including the Payment Certificates) in exchange for any of the debentures. Thus, in this respect, amendment to the indentures is required in order to close the Stock Purchase Agreement as presently structured.

Restrictive covenants in the indentures would appear to interfere with effectuation of the recapitalization in another way. Section 4.07 of the 13.50% Indenture provides that the Company may not "acquire" for value any of the 95/8% Notes or 115/8% Notes unless it concurrently "redeems" a proportionate amount of the 13.50% Notes. This covenant, if unamended, would prohibit the disproportionate acquisition of the 95/8% Notes that may well occur as a result of the Exchange Offers; in addition, it would appear to require the payment of the "redemption" price for the 13.50% Notes rather than the lower, market price offered in the exchange offer.

In sum, the failure to obtain the requisite consents to the proposed amendments would permit Allied-Signal to decline to consummate both the Acquisition Agreement and the Stock Purchase Agreement.

As to timing of the proposed transactions, the Exchange Offer requires the Company (subject to the conditions stated therein) to accept any and all tenders received by 5:00 p.m. March 11, 1986. A meeting of stockholders of the Company has been called for March 14, 1986 at which time the Company's stockholders will be asked to approve the Acquisition Agreement and the Stock Purchase Agreement as well as certain deferred compensation arrangements for key employees. Closing of the Acquisition Agreement may occur on March 14, 1986, or as late as June 20, 1986 under the terms of that Agreement. Closing of the Stock Purchase Agreement must await the closing of the Acquisition Agreement and the successful completion of the Exchange Offers.

The Exchange Offers are dated February 14, 1986. This suit seeking to enjoin consummation of those offers was filed on February 27. Argument on the current application was held on March 7.

II.

Plaintiff's claim that the Exchange Offers and Consent Solicitation constitutes a threatened wrong to him and other holders of Oak's debt securities[5] appear to be summarized in paragraph 16 of his Complaint:

---

5. It is worthy of note that a very high percentage of the principal value of Oak's debt securities are owned in substantial amounts by a handful of large financial institutions. Almost 85% of the value of the 13.50% Notes is owned by four such institutions (one investment banker owns 55% of that issue); 69.1% of the 9 5/8% Notes are owned by four financial institutions (the same investment banker owning 25% of that issue) and 85% of the 11 5/8% Notes are owned by five

The purpose and effect of the Exchange Offers is [1] to benefit Oak's common stockholders at the expense of the Holders of its debt securities, [2] to force the exchange of its debt instruments at unfair price and at less than face value of the debt instruments [3] pursuant to a rigged vote in which debt Holders who exchange, and who therefore have no interest in the vote, *must* consent to the elimination of protective covenants for debt Holders who do not wish to exchange.

As amplified in briefing on the pending motion, plaintiff's claim is that no free choice is provided to bondholders by the exchange offer and consent solicitation. Under its terms, a rational bondholder is "forced" to tender and consent. Failure to do so would face a bondholder with the risk of owning a security stripped of all financial covenant protections and for which it is likely that there would be no ready market. A reasonable bondholder, it is suggested, cannot possibly accept those risks and thus such a bondholder is coerced to tender and thus to consent to the proposed indenture amendments.

It is urged this linking of the offer and the consent solicitation constitutes a breach of a contractual obligation that Oak owes to its bondholders to act in good faith. Specifically, plaintiff points to three contractual provisions from which it can be seen that the structuring of the current offer constitutes a breach of good faith. Those provisions (1) establish a requirement that no modification in the term of the various indentures may be effectuated without the consent of a stated percentage of bondholders; (2) restrict Oak from exercising the power to grant such consent with respect to any securities it may hold in its treasury; and (3) establish the price at which and manner in which Oak may force bondholders to submit their securities for redemption.

III.

In order to demonstrate an entitlement to the provisional remedy of a preliminary injunction it is essential that a plaintiff show that it is probable that his claim will be upheld after final hearing; that he faces a risk of irreparable injury before final judgment will be reached in the regular course; and that in balancing the equities and competing hardships that preliminary judicial action may cause or prevent, the balance favors plaintiff.

I turn first to an evaluation of the probability of plaintiff's ultimate success on the merits of his claim. I begin that analysis with two preliminary points. The first concerns what is not involved in this case. To focus briefly on this clears away much of the corporation law case law of this jurisdiction upon which plaintiff in part relies. This case does not involve the measurement of corporate or directorial conduct against that high standard of fidelity required of fiduciaries when they act with respect to the interests of the beneficiaries of their trust. Under our law—and the law generally—the relationship between a corporation and the holders of its debt securities, even convertible debt securities, is

---

such institutions. Of the debentures, 89% of the 13.65% debentures are owned by four large banks; and approximately 45% of the two remaining issues is owned by two banks.

contractual in nature. Arrangements among a corporation, the underwriters of its debt, trustees under its indentures and sometimes ultimate investors are typically thoroughly negotiated and massively documented. The rights and obligations of the various parties are or should be spelled out in that documentation. The terms of the contractual relationship agreed to and not broad concepts such as fairness define the corporation's obligation to its bondholders.

Thus, the first aspect of the pending Exchange Offers about which plaintiff complains—that "the purpose and effect of the Exchange Offers is to benefit Oak's common stockholders at the expense of the Holders of its debt"—does not itself appear to allege a cognizable legal wrong. It is the obligation of directors to attempt, within the law, to maximize the long-run interests of the corporation's stockholders; that they may sometimes do so "at the expense" of others (even assuming that a transaction which one may refuse to enter into can meaningfully be said to be at his expense) does not for that reason constitute a breach of duty. It seems likely that corporate restructurings designed to maximize shareholder values may in some instances have the effect of requiring bondholders to bear greater risk of loss and thus in effect transfer economic value from bondholders to stockholders. But if courts are to provide protection against such enhanced risk, they will require either legislative direction to do so or the negotiation of indenture provisions designed to afford such protection.

The second preliminary point concerns the limited analytical utility, at least in this context, of the word "coercive" which is central to plaintiff's own articulation of his theory of recovery. If, *pro arguendo*, we are to extend the meaning of the word coercion beyond its core meaning—dealing with the utilization of physical force to overcome the will of another—to reach instances in which the claimed coercion arises from an act designed to affect the will of another party by offering inducements to the act sought to be encouraged or by arranging unpleasant consequences for an alternative sought to be discouraged, then—in order to make the term legally meaningful at all—we must acknowledge that some further refinement is essential. Clearly some "coercion" of this kind is legally unproblematic. Parents may "coerce" a child to study with the threat of withholding an allowance; employers may "coerce" regular attendance at work by either docking wages for time absent or by rewarding with a bonus such regular attendance. Other "coercion" so defined clearly would be legally relevant (to encourage regular attendance by corporal punishment, for example). Thus, for purposes of legal analysis, the term "coercion" itself— covering a multitude of situations—is not very meaningful. For the word to have much meaning for purposes of legal analysis, it is necessary in each case that a normative judgment be attached to the concept ("inappropriately coercive" or "wrongfully coercive," etc.). But, it is then readily seen that what is legally relevant is not the conclusory term "coercion" itself but rather the norm that leads to the adverb modifying it.

In this instance, assuming that the Exchange Offers and Consent Solicitation can meaningfully be regarded as "coercive" (in the sense that Oak has structured it in a way designed—and I assume effectively so—to "force" rational bondholders to tender), the relevant legal norm that will support the judgment whether such "coercion" is wrongful or not will, for the reasons mentioned above, be derived from the law of contracts. I turn then to that subject to determine the appropriate legal test or rule.

Modern contract law has generally recognized an implied covenant to the effect that each party to a contract will act with good faith towards the other with respect to the subject matter of the contract. The contractual theory for this implied obligation is well stated in a leading treatise:

> If the purpose of contract law is to enforce the reasonable expectations of parties induced by promises, then at some point it becomes necessary for courts to look to the substance rather than to the form of the agreement, and to hold that substance controls over form. What courts are doing here, whether calling the process "implication" of promises, or interpreting the requirements of "good faith," as the current fashion may be, is but a recognition that the parties occasionally have understandings or expectations that were so fundamental that they did not need to negotiate about those expectations. When the court "implies a promise" or holds that "good faith" requires a party not to violate those expectations, it is recognizing that sometimes silence says more than words, and it is understanding its duty to the spirit of the bargain is higher than its duty to the technicalities of the language. *Corbin on Contracts* (Kaufman Supp.1984), §570.

It is this obligation to act in good faith and to deal fairly that plaintiff claims is breached by the structure of Oak's coercive exchange offer. Because it is an implied *contractual* obligation that is asserted as the basis for the relief sought, the appropriate legal test is not difficult to deduce. It is this: is it clear from what was expressly agreed upon that the parties who negotiated the express terms of the contract would have agreed to proscribe the act later complained of as a breach of the implied covenant of good faith—had they thought to negotiate with respect to that matter. If the answer to this question is yes, then, in my opinion, a court is justified in concluding that such act constitutes a breach of the implied covenant of good faith.

With this test in mind, I turn now to a review of the specific provisions of the various indentures from which one may be best able to infer whether it is apparent that the contracting parties—had they negotiated with the exchange offer and consent solicitation in mind—would have expressly agreed to prohibit contractually the linking of the giving of consent with the purchase and sale of the security.

IV.

Applying the foregoing standard to the exchange offer and consent solicitation, I find first that there is nothing in the indenture provisions granting bondholders power to veto proposed modifications in the relevant indenture that implies that Oak may not offer an inducement to bondholders to consent to such amendments. Such an implication, at least where, as here, the inducement is offered on the same terms to each holder of an affected security, would be wholly inconsistent with the strictly commercial nature of the relationship.

Nor does the second pertinent contractual provision supply a ground to conclude that defendant's conduct violates the reasonable expectations of those who negotiated the indentures on behalf of the bondholders. Under that provision Oak may not vote debt securities held in its treasury. Plaintiff urges that Oak's conditioning of its offer to purchase debt on the giving of consents has the effect of subverting the purpose of that provision; it permits Oak to "dictate" the vote on securities which it could not itself vote.

The evident purpose of the restriction on the voting of treasury securities is to afford protection against the issuer voting as a bondholder in favor of modifications that would benefit it as issuer, even though such changes would be detrimental to bondholders. But the linking of the exchange offer and the consent solicitation does not involve the risk that bondholder interests will be affected by a vote involving anyone with a financial interest in the subject of the vote other than a bondholder's interest. That the consent is to be given concurrently with the transfer of the bond to the issuer does not in any sense create the kind of conflict of interest that the indenture's prohibition on voting treasury securities contemplates. Not only will the proposed consents be granted or withheld only by those with a financial interest to maximize the return on their investment in Oak's bonds, but the incentive to consent is equally available to all members of each class of bondholders. Thus the "vote" implied by the consent solicitation is not affected in any sense by those with a financial conflict of interest.

In these circumstances, while it is clear that Oak has fashioned the exchange offer and consent solicitation in a way designed to encourage consents, I cannot conclude that the offer violates the intendment of any of the express contractual provisions considered or, applying the test set out above, that its structure and timing breaches an implied obligation of good faith and fair dealing.

One further set of contractual provisions should be touched upon: Those granting to Oak a power to redeem the securities here treated at a price set by the relevant indentures. Plaintiff asserts that the attempt to force all bondholders to tender their securities at less than the redemption price constitutes, if not a breach of the redemption provision itself, at least a breach of an implied covenant of good faith and fair dealing associated with it. The flaw, or at least one fatal flaw, in this argument is that the present offer is not the functional equivalent of a redemption which is, of course, an act that the issuer may take unilaterally. In this instance it may happen that Oak will get tenders of a large percentage of its outstanding long-term debt securities. If it does, that fact will, in my judgment, be in major part a function of the merits of the offer (i.e., the price offered in light of the Company's financial position and the market value of its debt). To answer plaintiff's contention that the *structure* of the offer "forces" debt holders to tender, one only has to imagine what response this offer would receive if the price offered did not reflect a premium over market but rather was, for example, ten percent of market value. The exchange offer's success ultimately depends upon the ability and willingness of the issuer to extend an offer that will be a financially attractive alternative to holders. This process is hardly the functional equivalent of the unilateral election of redemption and thus cannot be said in any sense to constitute a subversion by Oak of the negotiated provisions dealing with redemption of its debt.

Accordingly, I conclude that plaintiff has failed to demonstrate a probability of ultimate success on the theory of liability asserted.

V.

An independent ground for the decision to deny the pending motion is supplied by the requirement that a court of equity will not issue the extraordinary remedy of preliminary injunction where to do so threatens the party sought to be enjoined with irreparable injury that, in the circumstances, seems greater than the injury that plaintiff seeks to avoid. Eastern Shore Natural Gas Co. v. Stauffer Chemical Co., Del.Supr., 298 A.2d 322 (1972). That principal has application here.

Oak is in a weak state financially. Its board, comprised of persons of experience and, in some instances, distinction, have approved the complex and interrelated transactions outlined above. It is not unreasonable to accord weight to the claims of Oak that the reorganization and recapitalization of which the exchange offer is a part may present the last good chance to regain vitality for this enterprise. I have not discussed plaintiff's claim of irreparable injury, although I have considered it. I am satisfied simply to note my conclusion that it is far outweighed by the harm that an improvidently granted injunction would threaten to Oak.

For the foregoing reasons plaintiff's application for a preliminary injunction shall be denied.

As you will recall, most indentures contain either a New York or English choice of law clause. In contrast to New York law-governed debt, where debt is exchanged in a tender offer, English law-governed bonds and notes typically would be amended by a vote of holders at a meeting of the holders.

ASSÉNAGON ASSET MANAGEMENT S.A. v. IRISH BANK RESOLUTION CORPORATION LIMITED

[2012] EWHC 2090 (Ch)
High Court of Justice, Chancery Division
Royal Courts of Justice, Strand, London.
July 27, 2012.

Mr Justice BRIGGS:

INTRODUCTION

1. This [action] test[s], for the first time, the legality under English law of a technique used by the issuers of corporate bonds which has acquired the label "exit consent." The technique may be summarised thus. The issuer wishes to persuade all the holders of a particular bond issue to accept an exchange of their bonds for replacement bonds on different terms. The holders are all invited to offer their bonds for exchange, but on terms that they are required to commit themselves irrevocably to vote at a bondholders' meeting for a resolution amending the terms of the existing bonds so as seriously to damage or, as in the present case substantially destroy, the value of the rights arising from those existing bonds. The resolution is what has become labelled the exit consent.

2. The exit consent has no adverse effect in itself upon a holder who both offers his bonds for exchange and votes for the resolution. That is either because the issuer nonetheless fails to attract the majority needed to pass the resolution (in which case both the resolution and the proposed exchange do not happen) or simply because, if the requisite majority is obtained, his bonds are exchanged for new bonds and cancelled by the issuer. By contrast, a holder who fails to offer his bonds for exchange and either votes against the resolution or abstains takes the risk, if the resolution is passed, that his bonds will be either devalued by the resolution or, as in this case, destroyed by being redeemed for a nominal consideration. This is in part because the efficacy of the technique depends upon the deadline for exchange being set before the bondholders' meeting so that, if the resolution is then passed, the dissenting holder gets no *locus poenitentiae* during which to exchange his bonds on the terms offered, and accepted in time, by the majority.

3. It is readily apparent, and not seriously in dispute, that the purpose of the attachment of the exit consent to the exchange proposal is to impose a dissuasive constraint upon bondholders from opposing the exchange, even if they take the view that the proffered new bonds are (ignoring the exit consent) less attractive than the existing bonds. The constraint arises from the risk facing any individual bondholder that a sufficient majority of his fellow holders will participate in the exchange and therefore (as required to do) vote for the resolution. The constraint is variously described in

textbooks on both sides of the Atlantic as encouraging, inducing, coercing or even forcing the bondholders to accept the exchange.

4. The technique depends for its persuasive effect upon the difficulties faced by bondholders in organising themselves within the time allowed by the issuer in such a way as to find out before the deadline for accepting the exchange whether there is a sufficient number (usually more than 25% by value) determined to prevent the exchange going ahead by voting against the resolution. They were described in argument as facing a variant of the well-known prisoner's dilemma.

5. Exit consents of this type (but falling short of expropriation) have survived judicial scrutiny in the USA, in the face of challenge by minority bondholders. In *Katz v Oak Industries Inc.* (1986) 508 A.2d 873 the attachment of an exit consent designed to devalue the existing bonds in the hands of dissenting holders who declined an associated exchange offer was challenged in the Delaware Chancery Court as amounting to a breach of the contractual obligation of good faith by the issuer, as against the bondholders. It was not suggested that the participation in the process by the majority bondholders (by committing themselves to vote for the proposed amendment devaluing the existing bonds) constituted an abuse by them of their rights under the terms of the bond issue to bind the minority to a variation of those terms. Chancellor Allen concluded that the particular exit consent in that case (which included the removal of significant negotiated protections to the bondholders, and the deletion of all financial covenants), did not despite its coercive effect amount to a breach of the contractual obligation of good faith between issuer and bondholders in what he evidently regarded as an ordinary commercial arms-length contract.

6. By contrast, the challenge made in the present case to the exit consent technique is mainly based upon an alleged abuse by the majority bondholders of their power to bind the minority, albeit at the invitation of the issuer. The challenge is based upon the well recognised constraint upon the exercise of that power by a majority, namely that it must be exercised *bona fide* in the best interests of the class of bondholders as a whole, and not in a manner which is oppressive or otherwise unfair to the minority sought to be bound. Such limited published professional comment as there is upon the use of this technique within an English law context appears to assume that, provided the exchange offer and associated exit consent proposal is made and fairly disclosed to all relevant bondholders, no question of oppression or unfairness can arise. I was told (although it is impossible for the court to know for sure) that this technique has been put into significant, if not yet widespread, use within the context of bonds structured under English law, in particular in connection with the affairs of banks and other lending institutions requiring to be re-structured as a result of the 2008 credit crunch, so that a decision on this point of principle may be of much wider consequence

than merely the amount at issue between the parties to this claim, which relates to subordinated notes in the company then known as Anglo Irish Bank Corporation Limited ("the Bank") acquired by the claimant Assenagon Asset Management S.A. in tranches between September 2009 and April 2010, for an aggregate of just over €17m.

THE FACTS

7. There is no dispute about the primary facts, which consist of the terms of the relevant bonds, the circumstances in which the exchange proposal was launched, succeeded and concluded, so far as affects the claimant, by redemption of its €17m Notes for a payment by the Bank of a mere €170.

8. There is by contrast not a complete unanimity as to background facts. The parties' differences related more to the relevance of parts of the background, and no request was made by either side for cross-examination.

9. The bond issue to which this dispute relates consists of the Bank's subordinated floating rate notes due 2017 ("the 2017 Notes") issued by the Bank on 15 June 2007 pursuant to the terms of a trust deed dated 15 August 2001 between the Bank and Deutsche Bank Trustee Co. Limited ("the Trustee") as subsequently amended and supplemented by six supplemental trust deeds. I shall refer to the re-stated form of the trust deed applicable to the 2017 Notes as "the Trust Deed." Terms particular to the 2017 Notes are also contained in written Final Terms dated 15 June 2007 ("the Final Terms"). The commercial terms of the 2017 Notes may be summarised as follows:

> i) They were to mature in 2017, for redemption at par, unless redeemed earlier at the Bank's election (also at par) on any interest payment date after 19 June 2012.
> ii) In the meantime they carried a floating rate of interest at 0.25% above three months Euribor until 2012 and 0.75% above three months Euribor thereafter.
> iii) The Notes were subordinated, so as to be prioritised for payment in an insolvency after all secured and unsecured creditors (including the Bank's depositors) and ahead only of equity shareholders. They were wholly unsecured.

10. The 2017 Notes were issued as part of the Bank's Euro Medium Term Note Programme. The Bank issued, in addition, subordinated notes due 2014 and 2016 ("the 2014 and 2016 Notes"). The nominal amount of the 2017 Notes was €750m. I am invited to assume that, for the most part, holders of the 2017 Notes were, at the time of the exchange offer, sophisticated professional investors.

11. It is necessary to focus in some detail upon the provisions in the Trust Deed providing what counsel called "note-holder democracy," namely the calling of note-holders' meetings, the extent of the powers of the majority to bind the minority, the requisite quorum and voting majorities, together with a particular voting disability prayed in aid by the claimant.

12. The 2017 Notes were issued in the form of a single global note to a depository, such that investors recorded as holding proportions of the aggregate nominal amount in the books of the depository were to be treated for all purposes under the Trust Deed as note-holders.

13. Clause 38 of the Trust Deed provided for it to be governed by English law, subject to certain irrelevant exceptions, and clause 39 contained a sufficient submission to the jurisdiction of the English courts for the purposes of these proceedings.

14. Paragraph 14 (i) of the First Schedule to the Trust Deed contained provisions as to the quorum for Noteholders' meetings. Paragraph 2 of Schedule 3 permits the Issuer (the Bank) or the Trustee at any time to call a Noteholders' meeting, and required the Issuer to do so upon a requisition signed by the holders of not less than one-tenth in nominal amount of the Notes.

15. Paragraph 5 of Schedule 3 set out three successively stringent quorum requirements. In relation to an ordinary resolution it was one-twentieth of the nominal amount of the Notes. For an Extraordinary Resolution (defined below) it was a clear majority in nominal amount of the Notes. Finally, for seven specified types of Extraordinary Resolution the quorum was two-thirds of the nominal amount of the Notes. Paragraph 5(b) identified "reduction or cancellation of the principal payable on the Notes or the exchange or conversion thereof or the minimum rate of interest payable thereon" as one of the seven types of Extraordinary Resolution calling for a two-thirds quorum.

16. Paragraph 13 of Schedule 3 contained provision as to who might attend or speak at Noteholders' meetings, but continued:

> "Neither the Issuer nor any Subsidiary shall be entitled to vote at any meeting in respect of Notes beneficially held by it or for its account."

17. Paragraph 18 of Schedule 3 set out in detail the powers capable of being exercised by a majority of Noteholders by Extraordinary Resolution. They included:

> "(a) Power to sanction any compromise or arrangement proposed to be made between the Issuer and the Noteholders. . . .
> (b) Power to sanction any abrogation, modification, compromise or arrangement in respect of the rights of the Noteholders . . . against the Issuer or against any of its property whether such rights shall arise under these presents or otherwise.

(c) Power to assent to any modification of the provisions contained in these presents which shall be proposed by the Issuer or the Trustee."

18. Paragraph 20 provided that an Extraordinary Resolution required a three-fourths majority of persons voting. Paragraph 19 provided that a resolution duly passed at a Noteholders' meeting would be binding upon all Noteholders whether present or absent, voting or abstaining.

19. By September 2008 the Bank had become the third largest bank in the Irish domestic market with €101 billion of gross assets on its balance-sheet, representing about 50% of Irish GDP. It had a particular focus on commercial property lending, and as a result of the 2008 financial crisis, with a linked rapid decline in commercial property values, the Bank faced a liquidity crisis which, unless it was rescued by the Irish Government, would have forced it into insolvent liquidation. Nonetheless, being regarded as of systemic importance to the maintenance of the stability of the Irish financial system, it was indeed rescued by the Irish government by a series of steps, which I shall briefly summarise. The first consisted of a guarantee by the Irish government of certain liabilities of Irish financial institutions, including the 2017 Notes, for the period from 30 September 2008 to 29 September 2010 pursuant to the Credit Institutions (Financial Support) Scheme 2008. The Scheme prohibited any call on that guarantee after 29 September 2010.

20. Secondly, in December 2009 the Irish government guaranteed certain eligible liabilities of participating institutions, including the Bank, pursuant to the Credit Institutions (Eligible Liabilities Guarantee) Scheme 2009. Those liabilities did not include the 2017 Notes, because they were subordinated.

21. On 21 January 2009 the Bank was nationalised, because of its systemic importance to the maintenance of the stability of the Irish financial system, pursuant to the Anglo Irish Bank Corporation Act 2009.

22. On 7 April 2009 the Minister for Finance announced the creation of the National Asset Management Agency ("NAMA") formed to purchase certain distressed loans from banks carrying on in business in Ireland. This had no direct effect upon the 2017 Notes.

23. On 29 May 2009, in view of the continued deterioration in the Bank's financial position following nationalisation, the Irish government announced its intention to make urgent provision of up to €4 billion of capital to the Bank through the purchase of new ordinary shares. This support (but not the earlier nationalisation) required approval from the European Commission which was granted on 26 June 2009. The Commission required to be satisfied that financial support by a member state to a domestic bank was provided on terms that minimised the amount of state aid to that necessary to protect the wider financial system in Ireland and, to that end, the Bank proposed to increase its Core Tier 1 capital by engaging in a "Liability Management Exercise" under which it

intended to buy back subordinated loans, at a premium above the prevailing market rates no higher than "necessary only to ensure a participation rate sufficient to make the Liability Management Exercise worthwhile."

24. By December 2009 the Bank had incurred an aggregate loss of some €12.7 billion. In March, May and August 2010 the Irish government increased its support to the Bank by amounts of €8.3 billion, €2 billion and €8.58 billion respectively.

25. On 8 September 2010, just before the expiry of the October 2008 guarantee, the Minister of Finance made an announcement about the proposed re-structuring of the Bank, which contemplated its being split into a depositors' bank and an asset management entity. In the event this did not proceed. By 30 September, the day after expiry of the October 2008 guarantee, the Irish government had provided a total of €22.88 billion of capital to the Bank by way of share subscription and promissory notes, and NAMA had purchased €6.5 billion worth of distressed loans.

26. It was during the staged rescue of the Bank which I have summarised, and the currency of the October 2008 guarantee of (inter alia) the 2017 Notes, that the claimant acquired its holding of 2017 Notes in the market, at prices ranging between 0.418 and 0.420 per nominal Euro, between 23 September 2009 and 1 April 2010. The substantial discount at which the Notes were trading in the market no doubt reflected a perception that the 2008 guarantee was unlikely to be extended indefinitely, and that holders of subordinated debt could not expect to be treated with the same sympathy as the Bank's retail customers. The claimant acquired its holding as manager of two Luxembourg funds. It may safely be inferred that it did so on behalf of sophisticated investors.

27. On 30 September 2010 (immediately after the expiry of the 2008 guarantee) the Minister of Finance made a statement on the banking system in Ireland which, while stating an intention to respect all senior debt obligations in the Bank, continued:

> "The principle of appropriate burden sharing by holders of subordinated debt, however, is one with which I agree. As can be seen from the figures outlined above, the losses in the bank are substantial and it is right that the holders of Anglo's subordinated debt should share the costs which have arisen.
>
> In keeping with this approach, my Department in conjunction with the Attorney General is working on resolution and re-organisation legislation, which will enable the implementation re-organisation measures specific to Anglo Irish Bank and Irish Nationwide Building Society which will address the issue of burden-sharing by subordinated bondholders. The legislation will be consistent with the requirements for the measures to be recognised as a re-organisation under the relevant EU Directive in other EU Member States.

I expect the subordinated debt holders to make a significant contribution towards meeting the costs of Anglo."

28. This announcement contemplated a two-stage approach. The first was to pursue a voluntary re-structuring of subordinated debt, if possible, by agreement with Noteholders (or a qualifying majority of them). The second was to complete the process, if necessary, by legislation, capable of being enforced in relation to an English law regulated note issue in the English courts, pursuant to the EU Directive referred to in the announcement. The exchange proposal to the 2017 Notes was part of the first of those two stages.

THE 2010 EXCHANGE OFFER

29. On 21 October 2010 the Bank announced exchange offers in respect of certain series of its Notes, including the 2017 Notes (as well as the 2014 and 2016 Notes). The Bank issued three documents, the first two of which substantially overlap in terms of content:

    i) The Announcement
    ii) The Exchange Offer Memorandum
    iii) A Notice of a Noteholders' meeting in respect of the 2017 Notes

30. The Announcement and the Memorandum both began (more or less identically) by proposing to Noteholders an exchange of (inter alia) the 2017 Notes for new Notes ("the New Notes") in the exchange ratio 0.20 i.e. an offer of a holding of 20 cents New Notes for every one Euro of 2017 Notes. The New Notes were not to be subordinated. They were to carry a coupon of three month Euribor plus 3.75 per cent, to be guaranteed by the Irish government and to mature in December 2011. The Announcement continued as follows:

> "In connection with the Exchange Offers, the Bank is also convening (at the times specified in the . . . Memorandum) separate meetings inviting the Holders of each Series of Existing Notes (*a definition which included the 2017 Notes*) to approve, by separate Extraordinary Resolution in respect of each Series, proposed amendments to the terms and conditions of each Series including giving the Bank the right to redeem all, but not some only, of the Existing Notes of each Series at an amount equal to €0.01 per €1000 in principal amount of Existing Notes at any time after the relevant Settlement Date. . . .
> The Bank will announce its decision whether to accept valid offers of Existing Notes for exchange pursuant to each Exchange Offer together with the final aggregate principal amount of the Existing Notes of each Series accepted for exchange and the aggregate principal amount of the New Notes to be issued as soon as reasonably practical after the

Expiration Deadline applicable to the relevant Series. Each Exchange Offer begins on 21 October 2010 and will expire at (i) 4.00 p.m. London time on 19 November 2010 in respect of the 2017 Notes … unless extended, re-opened or terminated as provided in the … Memorandum. The expected Settlement Date for the Exchange Offers is (i) 24 November 2010 in respect of the 2017 Notes Exchange Offer.…"

Under the heading Accrued Interest the Bank undertook to pay interest due on the Existing Notes up and until the Settlement Date.

31. At pages 4-6 of the Announcement the Bank provided an intended timetable for the Exchange Offer Process in relation to each Series. The timetable for 2017 Notes was as follows:

"Commencement of Exchange Offers, Notice of Meeting	21 October 2010
2017 Notes Expiration Deadline	4 pm 19 November 2010
2017 Notes Results Announcement (namely whether the Bank intended to accept the offers, and the amount of 2017 Notes accepted for Exchange)	22 November 2010
2017 Notes Meeting	10am 23 November 2010
Announcement Results of 2017 Notes Meeting	23 November 2010
2017 Notes Settlement Date	24 November 2010"

That timetable was followed by a warning that it was subject to the right of the Bank to extend, re-open, amend and/or terminate each Exchange Offer.

32. The Memorandum had annexed to it the notice of Meeting for the 2017 Notes, describing the terms of the Extraordinary Resolution. It is unnecessary to describe it in detail. It provided for the insertion into the Final Terms of a right for the Bank to redeem the 2017 Notes on any date after the Settlement Date (i.e. 24 November 2010, unless amended) upon payment at a rate of €0.01 per €1000. By contrast with the exchange ratio of 0.20 in the Exchange Offer this amounted to a payment ratio of 0.00001.

33. In addition to replicating most of the provisions of the Announcement, the Memorandum contained the following additional provisions, the first paragraph of which (quoted below) is set out in capital letters and heavy type.

"By offering to exchange its Existing Notes, a holder will be deemed to have given instructions for the appointment of the exchange and tabulation agent (or its agent) as its proxy to vote in favour of the relevant Extraordinary Resolution in respect of all Existing Notes of the relevant series offered for exchange by such holder and which are accepted by the Bank at the . . . 2017 Notes Meeting. . . .

It will not be possible for Holders of a Series of Existing Notes to validly offer to exchange Existing Notes pursuant to the Exchange Offer without at the same time appointing the Exchange Tabulation Agent (or its agent) as their proxy to vote in favour of the Extraordinary Resolution in respect of the relevant Series as described above. If a Holder does not offer to exchange its Existing Notes, or if its offer to exchange Existing Notes is not accepted by the Bank, such Holder may (subject to meeting certain deadlines for making such arrangements—see *'Risk Factors and other Considerations—Deadlines for making arrangements to vote at Meetings if Exchange Instruction is rejected'*) separately arrange to be represented, and vote such Holder's Existing Notes, at the relevant Meetings."

34. Under the heading Risk Factors and Other Considerations, the Memorandum provided (inter alia) as follows:

"If an Extraordinary Resolution is passed in respect of any Series of Existing Notes and the approved amendments are implemented by the Bank by way of publication (expected to be part of the announcement confirming the results of the relevant Meeting) of amendments to the Final Terms of the relevant Series, the amendments shall be binding on all Holders of Existing Notes of such Series, whether or not those Holders attended or were otherwise represented at the relevant Meeting and/or voted in favour of the relevant Proposal.

(*heavy type*) If the Bank chooses to exercise such call right (which the Bank currently intends to do shortly after the relevant Settlement Date, although the Bank is under no obligation to do so), the redemption amounts payable to a Holder of Existing Notes (being €0.01 per €1000 in principle amount of Existing Notes) will be significantly less than the principal amount of the New Notes such Holder would have received had such Existing Notes been exchanged pursuant to the relevant Exchange Offer.

The Risk Factors statement continued with a reference to the burden sharing legislation then proposed by the Irish government, including the passage from the ministerial statement of 30 September 2010, which I have quoted above.

35. Under the sub-heading "Deadlines for making arrangements to vote at Meetings if Exchange Instruction is rejected" the Memorandum continued:

"If a Holder's offer to exchange Existing Notes is not accepted by the Bank at the relevant Expiration Deadline and such Holder nevertheless wishes to vote at the ... 2017 Notes Meeting ..., such Holder must either validly request a voting certificate, or otherwise appoint the Exchange Tabulation and Agent (or its agent) as its proxy to vote in favour of or against the relevant Extraordinary Resolution at the relevant Meeting ..., such request to be submitted to the Exchange and Tabulation Agent through the Clearing Systems. Holders must request a voting certificate or appoint the Exchange and Tabulation Agent (or its agent) as proxy not later than 48 hours before the relevant Meeting. (*heavy type*) The indicative timetable for the Exchange Offers is such that, if a Holder's offer to exchange Existing Notes is rejected at or after the relevant Expiration Deadline, such Holder may not have the opportunity—or may have a very limited period of time in which—to make separate voting arrangements in respect of the relevant Meeting, and accordingly may not be able to vote at the relevant Meeting."

When it is borne in mind that the timetable set out both in the Announcement and the Memorandum contemplated that the Bank would announce its decision whether, and how far, to accept Exchange Offers only one day before the 2017 Notes Meeting, that last warning was, if anything, an understatement.

36. The exchange ratio of 0.20 in the Exchange Offer broadly reflected the price at which the 2017 Notes were then trading in the market, although there is some dispute, which I need not resolve, about the then liquidity of that market. No premium over the then market price for the 2017 Notes was added as an incentive, but the combined effect of the exchange offer and the disincentive to rejecting it constituted by the linked resolution to permit the Bank to redeem the 2017 Notes (if not exchanged) for 0.00001 of their face value was sufficient to ensure that 92.03 per cent of the 2017 Noteholders by value offered their notes for exchange and conditionally bound themselves to vote in favour of the Resolution by the stated deadline of 4 pm on 19 November 2010.

37. The Bank notified acceptance of all notes offered for exchange on 22 November and the Resolution was therefore duly passed by at least the same majority at the 2017 Noteholders' meeting held on the following day. Settlement of the exchange of Existing Notes for New Notes duly then occurred in accordance with the advertised timetable and, on 30 November 2010, the Bank exercised its newly acquired right to redeem the remaining 2017 Notes at the nominal price of €0.01 per €1000 face value pursuant to which the claimant received €170 for its €17 million face value of 2017 Notes.

38. The claimant did not attend, or vote by proxy at, the 2017 Noteholders' meeting. It first complained about what had occurred on 30 November. This claim was issued on 15 April 2011.

THE CLAIMANT'S CASE

39. In their skeleton argument and in oral submissions, Mr Richard Snowden QC and Mr Ben Griffiths put the claimant's case for a declaration that the resolution purportedly passed at the 2017 Noteholders' meeting on 24 November 2010 was invalid on three independent but related grounds:

(1) The Resolution constituted, in substance, the conferral of a power on the Bank to expropriate the 2017 Notes for no more than a nominal consideration. It was therefore ultra vires the power of the majority under paragraph 18 of Schedule 3 to the Trust Deed.

(2) At the time of the Noteholders' meeting on 23 November, all those noteholders whose votes were counted in support of the Resolution held their Notes beneficially, or for the account of, the Bank. Accordingly, all those votes are to be disregarded pursuant to paragraph 13 of Schedule 3 to the Trust Deed.

(3) Even if ultra vires, the Resolution constituted an abuse of the power of the voting majority because:

> (i) It conferred no conceivable benefit or advantage upon the 2017 Noteholders as a class; and,
>
> (ii) It affected, and could by then only have affected, the Notes of that minority which had not coupled an offer of their Notes for exchange with a commitment to vote in favour of the resolution. Accordingly it was both oppressive and unfair as against that minority.

48. [E]ven in provisions conferring wide powers, the parties may include bespoke restrictions designed to avoid its exercise otherwise than for the benefit of the relevant class. It is common ground in the present case that the disenfranchisement of Notes beneficially held by or for the account of the Issuer or any Subsidiary was designed with that objective in mind, because of the likelihood that any such Notes would be voted so as to serve the interests of the Bank rather than the Noteholders.

49. [And] a statute may also intervene. There is in England and Wales the statutory remedy for unfairly prejudicial conduct now to be found in Part 30 of the Companies Act 2006. In the USA, the US Trust Indenture Act of 1939 provides at s.316 (b) a general prohibition against the modification of payment terms without the unanimous consent of all the holders of securities issued and registered with the SEC under the US Securities Act of 1933. There are however no statutory safeguards against abuse of power by a majority of the 2017 Noteholders in the present context.

ABUSE OF POWER

82. This form of coercion is in my judgment entirely at variance with the purposes for which majorities in a class are given power to bind minorities, and it is no answer for them to say that it is the issuer which has required or invited them to do so. True it is that, at the moment when any individual member of the class is required (by the imposition of the pre-meeting deadline) to make up his mind, there is at that point in time no defined minority against which the exit consent is aimed. But it is inevitable that there will be a defined (if any) minority by the time when the exit consent is implemented by being voted upon, and its only purpose is to prey upon the apprehension of each member of the class (aggravated

by his relative inability to find out the views of his fellow class members in advance) that he will, if he decides to vote against, be part of that expropriated minority if the scheme goes ahead.

83. Putting it as succinctly as I can, oppression of a minority is of the essence of exit consents of this kind, and it is precisely that at which the principles restraining the abusive exercise of powers to bind minorities are aimed.

———————

The decision was appealed to the U.K. Court of Appeal, but the appeal was withdrawn, so the High Court decision remains the last word in this particular case.

PROBLEM SET 26.2

1. Be prepared to discuss the merits of the U.S. and English approaches in class. Would the exchange offer in this last case have been permissible under U.S. law?
2. How might a bondholder protect against the use of exit consents?
3. Should exit consents be permitted under section 316(b) of the Trust Indenture Act? Recall that section provides in relevant part:

> Notwithstanding any other provision of the indenture to be qualified, the right of any holder of any indenture security to receive payment of the principal of and interest on such indenture security, on or after the respective due dates expressed in such indenture security, or to institute suit for the enforcement of any such payment on or after such respective dates, shall not be impaired or affected without the consent of such holder.
> . . .

4.   WORKOUTS, NOLs, AND COD

No, this section does not involve the Gloucester fisherman. It involves taxes. Again.

To greatly oversimplify the matter—again, you really must take Corporate Tax—the company undergoing the workout faces two key tax issues. First, these sorts of firms often have net operating losses (NOLs). Often lots and lots of NOLs.

Section 382 of the Tax Code limits the firm's ability to use its NOLs if the firm experiences a change of control.[6] For most firms, NOLs can be offset against future income and income earned in the prior three years. But for a firm that experiences a change of control, section 382 severely limits the ability to use the NOLs.

———————

6. 26 U.S.C. §§382(b) & 382(e)(1), I.R.C. §§382(b) & 382(e)(1).

If the firm does not continue in the same line of business, NOLs disappear altogether. This prevents trafficking in old corporate shells. Even if the old line of business is continued, the amount of losses that can be used each year becomes a function of value of the firm's shares immediately before the ownership change.

A change of control can occur upon a more than 50 percentage increase in the ownership of the firm's shares by one or more shareholders owning at least 5 percent of the loss corporation's stock, looking back over the preceding three years. A change of control does not require that the shares be acquired by a single entity or group of related entities, nor does it require the stock be acquired in a single transaction. Accordingly, a change of control may be triggered by a single entity purchasing 51 percent of a corporation's stock in a single transaction or by 10 unrelated investors each purchasing 5.1 percent of the corporation's stock through a series of transactions over a period of three years.

In the workout context, if a creditor owns no shares of a corporation but then receives 10 percent of the firm's shares in exchange for its bonds, a potential change of control has occurred (the 5 percent shareholder stake has increased from zero to 10 percent with regard to this creditor).

A partial exemption from the change in control limitation is available in a formal bankruptcy case, so long as the historic shareholders and "qualified creditors" of the debtor corporation own at least 50 percent of the value and voting power of the firm's shares after the restructuring. Thus, tax issues may influence the choice of structure in financial distress, just as they did in the merger context.

In addition, when old debt is exchanged for new debt it may give rise to cancellation of debt ("COD") income on the old debt.[7] The general rule is straightforward: If a creditor cancels a debt, then the debtor recognizes taxable income. Similarly, the acquisition of debt by a party that is related to the debtor triggers COD income to the debtor. Likewise, if a firm buys back its own debt from a creditor for an amount that is less than the amount of the debt, then COD income is triggered. Similarly, section 108(e)(10) provides that when stock is issued in exchange for outstanding debt, COD income is recognized to the extent that the principal of the debt exceeds the value of the stock.

In short, when a borrower borrows, the borrower is not taxed on those funds because the borrower has an obligation to repay them. If that obligation goes away, then the borrower has taxable income in an amount equal to the forgiven amount of the loan.[8]

If the firm has sufficient NOLs, it can offset those against the COD income, subject to certain limits. Otherwise an exchange offer could result in a substantial tax bill for the distressed company—something most distressed firms are not in a position to deal with. Giving the creditors ample shares in the firm is a way around the COD problem, but it is apt to trigger a change of control.

---

7. *See* 26 U.S.C. §61(a)(12), §61(a)(12); §1273(a), §1273(a).

8. 26 C.F.R. §1.61-12, Treas. Reg. §1.61-12.

COD income is not includible as income on the firm's tax return if the release of indebtedness occurs in a bankruptcy case. Instead, the debtor firm simply reduces its "tax attributes," essentially the firm's basis, by the amount of COD income avoided. This defers the tax on the COD income until such point as the firm is sold.

This bankruptcy treatment, again, can influence the choice between an out-of-court workout and a formal bankruptcy filing.

27

PREPACKAGED CHAPTER 11 CASES

It is commonly believed, at least among bankruptcy attorneys, that exchange offers often fail because the only way to ensure sufficient "buy in" to the offer is to offer terms that a financially distressed firm cannot afford to offer.

As we noted in the prior chapter, only those bondholders that consent to the exchange offer will have their securities exchanged. Those that "hold out" will continue to hold old securities and will be entitled to full payments in accordance with the terms of their existing debt instruments. If exit consents are used, those securities might be less valuable than before the exchange offer, but they still might return more than the new securities given in exchange.

Because of this, most exchange offers provide that the company will only consummate the exchange if a certain percentage of holders agree to the exchange (generally at least 75 percent). This is another reason exchange offers often fail.

The common solution to the holdout problem is a prepackaged bankruptcy case. This is a chapter 11 case where the firm has solicited votes on the reorganization plan before filing for bankruptcy. Often this solicitation will be combined with the solicitation for an exchange offer: If the exchange offer gets sufficient "buy in," that is implemented, but if not, then the debtor firm proceeds with the bankruptcy case. An example of such a two-prong offer is shown in Figure 27-1 on the next page.

At one time, it was common to make this structure somewhat coercive. For example, bondholders would be offered new securities in the exchange offer that provided somewhat better treatment than they would receive under the proposed bankruptcy plan. This difference was spelled out in the solicitation documents.

More recently, the prepackaged bankruptcy case is simply a way to implement the proffered exchange offer. As you will see, bankruptcy allows a majority to bind the minority to a plan under certain conditions. This solves the holdout problem.

Moreover, discharging debt in a formal bankruptcy proceeding receives favorable tax treatment as compared to out-of-court workouts.

Stacked against these considerations are the reputational and out-of-pocket costs associated with filing for bankruptcy. Of course, it could be that the reputational issues are diminishing: Do you avoid flying on United, Delta, or American Airlines simply because they are or were in chapter 11?

FIGURE 27-1
Example of a Combined Exchange Offer/Prepack Solicitation

AMENDED AND RESTATED OFFERING MEMORANDUM, CONSENT SOLICITATION STATEMENT AND DISCLOSURE STATEMENT SOLICITING ACCEPTANCES OF A PREPACKAGED PLAN OF REORGANIZATION

CENTRAL EUROPEAN DISTRIBUTION CORPORATION
CEDC FINANCE CORPORATION INTERNATIONAL, INC.

Offer to exchange (the "*CEDC Exchange Offer*") all of the outstanding 3.00% Convertible Senior Notes due 2013 (collectively, the "*Existing 2013 Notes*") issued by Central European Distribution Corporation for new shares of common stock of Central European Distribution Corporation ("*New Common Stock*")

and

Offer to exchange (the "*CEDC FinCo Exchange Offer*" and, together with the CEDC Exchange Offer, the "*Exchange Offers*") all of the outstanding 9.125% Senior Secured Notes due 2016 (the "*9.125% Existing 2016 Notes*") and the 8.875% Senior Secured Notes due 2016 (the "*8.875% Existing 2016 Notes*" and, together with the 9.125% Existing 2016 Notes, the "*Existing 2016 Notes*" and, together with the Existing 2013 Notes, the "*Existing Notes*") issued by CEDC Finance Corporation International, Inc. for (i) cash consideration and/or (ii) new Senior Secured Notes due 2018 (the "*New Secured Notes*") and new Convertible Secured PIK Toggle Notes due 2018 (the "*New Convertible Secured Notes*" and, together with the New Secured Notes, the "*New Notes*")

and

Solicitation of consents to amendments to the indenture governing the Existing 2016 Notes

and

Solicitation of acceptances of a prepackaged plan of reorganization

The New Secured Notes offered in the CEDC FinCo Exchange Offer will bear interest, payable semi-annually, at an initial rate per annum of 8.0% with a 1.0% step-up per annum to a maximum rate per annum of 10.0% and will mature on April 30, 2018. The New Convertible Secured Notes offered in the CEDC FinCo Exchange Offer will bear interest, payable in cash or in kind, at a fixed rate per annum, payable semi-annually, equal to 10.0% and will mature on April 30, 2018. The New Convertible Secured Notes will be convertible into New Common Stock initially equal to 20% of CEDC's outstanding common stock, and increasing up to 35% depending on the conversion time. Interest on the New Notes will be payable on April 30 and October 31 of each year, commencing October 31, 2013.

THE EXCHANGE OFFERS WILL EXPIRE AT 11:59 P.M., NEW YORK CITY TIME, ON MARCH 22, 2013 UNLESS EXTENDED OR EARLIER TERMINATED BY US (SUCH DATE AND TIME, AS THE SAME MAY BE EXTENDED OR EARLIER TERMINATED, THE "*EXPIRATION TIME*"). IN ORDER TO RECEIVE THE CONSIDERATION (AS HEREINAFTER DEFINED) APPLICABLE TO THE EXISTING NOTES, NOTEHOLDERS (AS HEREINAFTER DEFINED) MUST VALIDLY TENDER AND NOT WITHDRAW THEIR EXISTING NOTES, AT OR PRIOR TO THE EXPIRATION TIME. HOLDERS OF EXISTING NOTES MAY TENDER THEIR NOTES IN THE EXCHANGE OFFERS WITHOUT DELIVERING ACCEPTANCES TO THE PLAN OF REORGANIZATION OR DELIVERING THEIR CONSENTS (AS HEREINAFTER DEFINED), AS APPLICABLE. HOLDERS OF EXISTING 2016 NOTES MAY DELIVER THEIR CONSENTS WITHOUT TENDERING THEIR EXISTING 2016 NOTES IN THE EXCHANGES OFFERS OR DELIVERING THEIR ACCEPTANCES TO THE PLAN OF REORGANIZATION. HOLDERS OF EXISTING NOTES MAY DELIVER ACCEPTANCES TO THE PREPACKAGED PLAN OF REORGANIZATION WITHOUT TENDERING THEIR NOTES IN THE EXCHANGE OFFERS BUT MUST DELIVER THEIR CONSENTS, AS APPLICABLE.

TENDERS OF EXISTING 2013 NOTES AND ACCEPTANCES OF THE PLAN OF REORGANIZATION MAY BE WITHDRAWN AT ANY TIME PRIOR TO THE EXPIRATION TIME. TENDERS OF EXISTING 2016 NOTES AND CONSENTS TO AMENDMENTS TO THE EXISTING 2016 NOTES INDENTURE MAY BE WITHDRAWN AT ANY TIME PRIOR TO THE EARLIER OF (A) THE DATE AND TIME THAT CEDC FINCO NOTIFIES THE TRUSTEE UNDER THE EXISTING 2016 NOTES INDENTURE THAT CEDC FINCO HAS RECEIVED THE REQUISITE CONSENTS (AS DEFINED BELOW), AND (B) 5:00 PM NEW YORK CITY TIME ON MARCH 14, 2013 (THE "*CONSENT TIME*"). HOLDERS OF EXISTING 2016 NOTES WHO VOTE TO ACCEPT THE PLAN OF REORGANIZATION PRIOR TO THE CONSENT FEE DEADLINE (AS DEFINED) BELOW MAY MODIFY THEIR VOTES AT ANY TIME PRIOR TO THE CONSENT TIME. HOLDERS OF EXISTING 2016 NOTES WHO VOTE TO ACCEPT THE PLAN OF REORGANIZATION AFTER THE CONSENT FEE DEADLINE OR WHO VOTE TO REJECT THE PLAN OF REORGANIZATION MAY MODIFY THEIR VOTES AT ANY TIME PRIOR TO THE VOTING DEADLINE (AS DEFINED BELOW).

NOTEHOLDERS SHOULD REFER TO THE SECTIONS HEREIN ENTITLED "THE EXCHANGE OFFERS AND CONSENT SOLICITATION" AND "PROCEDURES FOR VOTING ON THE PLAN OF REORGANIZATION" FOR INSTRUCTIONS ON HOW TO TENDER NOTES, CONSENT TO THE AMENDMENTS TO THE INDENTURE GOVERNING THE EXISTING 2016 NOTES AND VOTE ON THE PLAN OF REORGANIZATION.

Upon the terms and subject to the conditions set forth in this offering memorandum and consent solicitation statement (as it may be amended from time to time, the "*Offering Memorandum*"), disclosure statement soliciting acceptances of the Plan of Reorganization (as hereinafter defined) (as it may be amended from time to time, the "*Disclosure Statement*" and, together with the Offering Memorandum, this "*Offering Memorandum and Disclosure Statement*") and the ballot ("*Ballot*") for accepting or rejecting the Plan of Reorganization,

- Central European Distribution Corporation, a Delaware corporation ("*CEDC*"), is (i) offering to exchange any and all of its outstanding Existing 2013 Notes for the consideration set forth below, and (ii) soliciting acceptances from all holders of Existing 2013 Notes of the prepackaged plan of reorganization attached hereto as Appendix A (the "*Plan of Reorganization*"); and

- CEDC Finance Corporation International Inc., a Delaware corporation ("*CEDC FinCo*") is (i) offering to exchange any and all of its outstanding Existing 2016 Notes for the consideration set forth below; (ii) soliciting consents (the "*Consent Solicitation*") to amendments to the indenture governing the Existing 2016 Notes (the "*Existing 2016 Notes Indenture*" and, together with the indenture governing the Existing 2013 Notes, the "*Indentures*"); and (iii) soliciting acceptances from all holders of Existing 2016 Notes of the Plan of Reorganization.

Each holder of Existing 2016 Notes who delivers Consents with respect to its Existing 2016 Notes by 5:00 PM. New York City time on March 14, 2013 (the "*Consent Fee Deadline*"), and does not validly withdraw such Consents, will receive a cash payment equal to 0.50% of the principal amount of the Existing 2016 Notes for which Consents were delivered and not withdrawn (the "*Consent Fee*") promptly after the Consent Fee Deadline (the "*Consent Fee Payment Date*"), assuming all of the conditions to the payment of the Consent Fee are met. Holders of Existing 2016 Notes that deliver Consents after the Consent Fee Deadline will not be entitled to a Consent Fee. The Consent Fee will be payable in U.S. dollars. Payments of the Consent Fee in respect of Consents from holders of 8.875% Existing 2016 Notes will be paid based upon the prevailing euro/US dollar exchange rate in effect at the time of payment. The Consent Fee will only be payable if the Collateral and Guarantee Amendments are approved by or before the Consent Fee Deadline.

This Offering Memorandum and Disclosure Statement includes a solicitation of acceptances of the Plan of Reorganization from holders of the Existing Notes ("*Noteholders*", and each a "*Noteholder*"). You should rely only on the information contained herein and in the related Ballot, as applicable, in making your decision to participate in the Exchange Offers, to participate in the Consent Solicitation, and/or to vote to accept the Plan of Reorganization. Holders of Existing 2016 Notes may tender their Existing 2016 Notes in the Exchange Offers without delivering acceptances to the Plan of Reorganization or delivering their Consents, as applicable. Holders of Existing 2016 Notes may deliver their Consents without tendering their Existing 2016 Notes in the Exchange Offers or delivering acceptances to the Plan of Reorganization. Holders of Existing 2016 Notes may deliver their acceptances to the Plan of Reorganization without tendering their Existing 2016 Notes in the Exchange Offers but must deliver their Consents.

NEITHER THE SECURITIES AND EXCHANGE COMMISSION (THE "*SEC*") NOR ANY STATE SECURITIES COMMISSION HAS APPROVED OR DISAPPROVED OF THIS TRANSACTION OR THESE SECURITIES, PASSED UPON THE MERITS OR FAIRNESS OF THE TRANSACTION OR DETERMINED IF THIS OFFERING MEMORANDUM IS TRUTHFUL OR COMPLETE. ANY REPRESENTATION TO THE CONTRARY IS A CRIMINAL OFFENSE.

The Exchange Offers are intended to be exempt from the federal registration requirements of the U.S. Securities Act of 1933 (the "*Securities Act*") pursuant to the exemption from such registration contained in Section 3(a)(9) thereof, and, therefore, considered a federal "covered security" by Section 18(b)(4)(D) (formerly, Section 18(b)(4)(C)), of the Securities Act. The Exchange Offers are exempt from state securities registration by virtue of the preemption as a covered security under Section 18(b)(4)(D) and/or the preemption for "listed securities" under Section 18(b)(1) of the Securities Act.

The date of this Offering Memorandum and Disclosure Statement is March 8, 2013.

The statutory requirements for the contents of a prepackaged plan are no different than for a traditional ("free-fall") plan. These requirements are set forth in sections 1122 (classification of claims and equity interests), 1123 (plan contents), and 1124 (impairment of claims and equity interests) of the Bankruptcy Code. Likewise, the requirements for confirmation of the plan are the same, set forth in section 1129.

1. DEAL STRUCTURE

In a traditional chapter 11 case, vote solicitation cannot occur until after the court has approved a disclosure statement as containing "adequate information" on which creditors can base their votes. In a prepack case, solicitation occurs before the court becomes involved. Below is an example of the disclosure document that accompanies that solicitation, from a reasonably well-known firm. Be prepared to discuss it in detail in class.

IN RE: METRO-GOLDWYN-MAYER STUDIOS INC., ET AL.

United States Bankruptcy Court, S.D. New York.
October 7, 2010.

Metro-Goldwyn-Mayer Studios Inc. and certain of its affiliates (collectively, the *"Debtors"*) are sending you this disclosure statement (the *"Disclosure Statement"*) because you may be a creditor entitled to vote on the Joint Prepackaged Plan of Reorganization of Metro-Goldwyn-Mayer Studios Inc. and certain of its Affiliates (the *"Plan"*). This solicitation (the *"Solicitation"*) of votes is being conducted to obtain sufficient acceptances of the Plan *prior* to the filing of voluntary cases under chapter 11 of title 11 of the United States Code (the *"Bankruptcy Code"*). If sufficient votes to obtain confirmation of the Plan are received and certain other conditions are met, the Debtors intend to file voluntary cases under chapter 11 of the Bankruptcy Code to implement the Plan. Because no chapter 11 cases have yet been commenced, this Disclosure Statement has not been approved by any Bankruptcy Court as containing "adequate information" within the meaning of section 1125(a) of the Bankruptcy Code. Following the commencement of their chapter 11 cases, the Debtors expect to seek promptly an order of the Bankruptcy Court (1) approving (a) this Disclosure Statement as having contained "adequate information" and (b) the Solicitation as having been in compliance with Section 1125(b) of the Bankruptcy Code, and (2) confirming the Plan described herein.

DISCLOSURE STATEMENT DATED OCTOBER 7, 2010 PREPETITION
SOLICITATION OF VOTES WITH RESPECT TO JOINT PREPACKAGED
PLAN OF REORGANIZATION OF METRO-GOLDWYN-MAYER STUDIOS
INC. AND CERTAIN OF ITS AFFILIATES SPECIAL NOTICE REGARDING
FEDERAL AND STATE SECURITIES LAWS

Neither this Disclosure Statement nor the Plan has been filed with or reviewed by the Bankruptcy Court, and the securities to be issued on or after the Effective Date (as defined below) are not the subject of a registration statement filed with the United States Securities and Exchange Commission (the *"SEC"*) under the United States Securities Act of 1933, as amended (the *"Securities Act"*), or any securities regulatory authority of any state under any state securities law (*"Blue Sky Law"*). The Debtors are relying on section 4(2) of the Securities Act and similar provisions of state securities law, as well as, to the extent applicable, the exemption from the Securities Act and equivalent state law registration requirements provided by section 1145(a)(1) of the Bankruptcy Code, to exempt from registration under the Securities Act and Blue Sky Law the offer and sale of new securities in connection with the Solicitation and the Plan.

Each holder of a Credit Agreement Claim (as defined in the Plan) or authorized signatory for the beneficial owner of a Credit Agreement Claim will be required to certify on its Ballot whether such holder or beneficial owner is an Accredited Investor, as that term is defined by Rule 501 of Regulation D of the Securities Act.

The Plan has not been approved or disapproved by the SEC or any state securities commission and neither the SEC nor any state securities commission has passed upon the accuracy or adequacy of the information contained herein. Any representation to the contrary is a criminal offense. Neither the Solicitation nor this Disclosure Statement constitutes an offer to sell, or the solicitation of an offer to buy securities in any state or jurisdiction in which such offer or solicitation is not authorized.

This Disclosure Statement and the information set forth herein are confidential. This Disclosure Statement contains material non-public information concerning the Debtors, their subsidiaries, and their respective securities. Each recipient hereby acknowledges that it (a) is aware that the federal securities laws of the United States prohibit any person who has material non-public information about a company, which is obtained from the company or its representatives, from purchasing or selling securities of such company or from communicating the information to any other person under circumstances in which it is reasonably foreseeable that such person is likely to purchase or sell such securities and (b) is familiar with the United States Securities Exchange Act of 1934, as amended (the *"Securities Exchange Act"*), and the rules and regulations promulgated thereunder, and agrees that it will not use or communicate to any person, under circumstances where it is reasonably likely that such person is likely to use or cause any person to use, any confidential information in contravention of the Securities Exchange Act or any of its rules and regulations, including Rule 10b-5.

THE VOTING DEADLINE TO ACCEPT OR REJECT THE JOINT
PREPACKAGED PLAN OF REORGANIZATION OF METRO-GOLDWYN-
MAYER STUDIOS INC. AND CERTAIN OF ITS AFFILIATES IS 5:00 P.M.
PREVAILING EASTERN TIME ON OCTOBER 22, 2010, UNLESS
EXTENDED BY THE DEBTORS (THE *"VOTING DEADLINE"*). THE
RECORD DATE FOR DETERMINING WHETHER A HOLDER OF AN
IMPAIRED CLAIM IS ENTITLED TO VOTE ON THE PLAN IS OCTOBER
4, 2010 (THE *"VOTING RECORD DATE"*).

THE DEBTORS ARE FURNISHING THIS DISCLOSURE STATEMENT
TO EACH MEMBER OF AN IMPAIRED CLASS UNDER THE JOINT
PREPACKAGED PLAN OF REORGANIZATION OF METRO-GOLDWYN-
MAYER STUDIOS INC. AND CERTAIN OF ITS AFFILIATES. THIS
DISCLOSURE STATEMENT IS TO BE USED BY EACH RECIPIENT
SOLELY IN CONNECTION WITH HIS, HER, OR ITS EVALUATION OF
THE PLAN, AND USE OF THIS DISCLOSURE STATEMENT FOR ANY
OTHER PURPOSE IS NOT AUTHORIZED. WITHOUT THE PRIOR
WRITTEN CONSENT OF THE DEBTORS, THIS DISCLOSURE
STATEMENT MAY NOT BE REPRODUCED OR PROVIDED TO OTHERS
(OTHER THAN THOSE ADVISORS OF ANY RECIPIENT OF THIS
DISCLOSURE STATEMENT WHO MAY REVIEW THE INFORMATION
CONTAINED HEREIN TO ASSIST SUCH RECIPIENT IN HIS, HER, OR ITS
EVALUATION OF THE PLAN).

INTRODUCTION AND DISCLAIMER

Metro-Goldwyn-Mayer Studios Inc. (*"MGM Studios"*) and its affiliated
Debtors (collectively, together with their non-Debtor affiliates the *"Company"* or
"MGM") submit this Disclosure Statement to certain holders of claims against
the Debtors in connection with the Solicitation of acceptances of the proposed
Joint Prepackaged Plan of Reorganization of Metro-Goldwyn-Mayer Studios Inc.
and Certain of Its Affiliates, dated as of October 7, 2010 (a copy of which is
annexed hereto as *Appendix A*). The Debtors are soliciting such acceptances from
holders of secured obligations under the Credit Agreement.

I.   OVERVIEW OF THE COMPANY

This Disclosure Statement contains, among other things, descriptions and
summaries of provisions of the Plan. Unless otherwise defined herein, all
capitalized terms contained herein have the meanings ascribed to them in the
Plan.

A.   CORPORATE STRUCTURE OF THE COMPANY

MGM Holdings Inc. (*"Holdings"*) is the ultimate parent of the MGM family of companies. Holdings owns MGM Holdings II Inc. which, in turn, owns Metro-Goldwyn-Mayer Inc. Metro-Goldwyn-Mayer Inc. owns, directly or indirectly, a number of subsidiaries, including various non-Debtor entities. Metro-Goldwyn-Mayer Inc.'s principal direct and indirect subsidiaries are MGM Studios, United Artists Corporation, United Artists Films Inc. and Orion Pictures Corporation.

A list of the Debtors is attached as *Exhibit B* to the Plan. Generally, the Debtors include all the wholly owned domestic subsidiaries of Holdings other than certain special purpose subsidiaries whose organizational documents contain bankruptcy remote provisions.

The Company's executive offices are located at 10250 Constellation Boulevard, Los Angeles, California 90067–6241. The Company's telephone number is (310) 449–3000. The Company's internet address is *www.mgm.com*. Attached hereto as *Appendices D* and *E*, respectively, is the Company's audited financial statement for the fiscal year ending March, 2009, and unaudited financial statement for the fiscal year ending March, 2010 (collectively, the *"Financial Statements"*).

B.   OVERVIEW OF BUSINESS OPERATIONS

MGM is a film entertainment company, with one of the world's largest film and television libraries and a group of important content franchises. The Company is engaged primarily in the development, production and worldwide distribution of feature films, television programming, interactive media, music, and licensed merchandise. The Company's film and television library (the *"MGM Library"*) contains approximately 4,100 theatrically released feature film titles and approximately 10,800 television episodes, and is one of the largest collections of post-1948 feature films in the world. Films in the MGM Library have won over 200 Academy Awards, including fifteen Best Picture Awards. The MGM Library also contains rights to many iconic film and television franchises. More specifically, assets comprising the MGM Library include: (i) MGM (post-1985)/United Artists film library which consists of more than 2,100 MGM, United Artists and Cannon Group titles, including the *James Bond, Pink Panther*, and *Rocky* franchises as well as *Legally Blonde, Hannibal, Rain Man*, and *A Fish Called Wanda;* (ii) the Orion Pictures film library which consists of more than 1,300 titles, including *Silence of the Lambs* and *Dances With Wolves;* (iii) the Polygram film library which consists of more than 700 titles, including *When Harry Met Sally* and *Four Weddings and a Funeral;* and (iv) the television programs library which includes approximately 10,800 episodes of programming, including *Stargate SG-1*, the longest running science fiction series in U.S. television history. The Company also co-owns the rights to produce two films based on *The Hobbit*, a book which has sold more than 100 million copies worldwide.

C. CORPORATE HISTORY

The Metro-Goldwyn-Mayer brand was established in 1924 when Metro Pictures Corporation (founded in 1916), the Goldwyn Picture Corporation (founded in 1917), and Louis B. Mayer Pictures Corporation (founded in 1918) were joined together by Marcus Loew, the owner of a large theatre chain, Loew's Theatres. During the 1930s and 1940s, Metro-Goldwyn-Mayer was the most dominant motion picture studio in Hollywood and since that time has remained one of the most recognizable worldwide film studios. Following a series of corporate transactions, MGM currently owns one of the largest modern (post-1948) collections of feature films in the world, comprised of the post-1985 MGM library, and the historic United Artists, Orion Pictures, and Polygram film libraries. The following timeline notes key events since 1996.

In July 10, 1996, Metro-Goldwyn-Mayer Inc., a Delaware corporation, was formed specifically to acquire from an indirect wholly-owned subsidiary of Consortium de Realisation all of the outstanding capital stock of MGM Studios and its subsidiaries. Metro-Goldwyn-Mayer Inc. was majority owned by an investor group including Kirk Kerkorian, Tracinda Corporation, a corporation that is principally owned by Mr. Kerkorian, and certain current and former executive officers of MGM Studios. On October 10, 1996, Metro-Goldwyn-Mayer Inc. purchased MGM Studios for an aggregate consideration of $1.3 billion.

In July 1997, Metro-Goldwyn-Mayer Inc. acquired all of the outstanding capital stock of Orion Pictures Corporation and its subsidiaries, including the entity formerly known as The Samuel Goldwyn Company and now known as Orion Film Classics Company, from Metromedia International Group, Inc. In connection with the Orion Pictures Corporation acquisition, Metro-Goldwyn-Mayer Inc. obtained the film and television libraries of Orion Pictures Corporation companies consisting of approximately 1,900 film titles and 3,000 television episodes. In January 7, 1999, Metro-Goldwyn-Mayer Inc. acquired certain film libraries, including 1,300 feature films, and film-related rights that were previously owned by PolyGram N.V. and its subsidiaries.

In November 1997, Metro-Goldwyn-Mayer Inc. completed an initial public offering, whereby it issued and sold 9,000,000 new shares of common stock at a price per share of $20.00 for net proceeds of $165 million. Concurrently with the consummation of the initial public offering, Tracinda Corporation purchased 3,978,780 shares of the common stock for an aggregate purchase price of $75 million. From 1998 to 2003, Metro-Goldwyn-Mayer Inc. made subsequent securities offerings, including public offerings and private placements.

On April 8, 2005, Metro-Goldwyn-Mayer Inc. was acquired by Holdings, a Delaware corporation owned by a consortium comprised of Sony Corporation of America, Providence Equity Partners, Texas Pacific Group, Comcast Corporation and DLJ Merchant Banking Partners (the *"Acquisition"*). The consortium acquired Metro-Goldwyn-Mayer Inc. for a total price of $4.9 billion, consisting of $3.0 billion in cash and $1.9 billion in assumed debt. Subsequent to the

Acquisition, Metro-Goldwyn-Mayer Inc.'s shares were de-listed from the New York Stock Exchange and Metro-Goldwyn-Mayer Inc. became privately held. In 2007, Quadrangle Capital Partners purchased a small stake in Holdings from Providence Equity Partners.

D.   CAPITAL STRUCTURE

1.   MGM Credit Facility

In connection with the Acquisition, the Debtors entered into a credit agreement, dated as of April 8, 2005, by and among MGM Holdings II Inc. (*"Holdings II"*), Metro-Goldwyn-Mayer Inc., as Borrower, Bank of America, N.A., Citicorp USA, Inc. and The Royal Bank of Scotland PLC, as Documentation Agents, Credit Suisse, as Syndication Agent, JPMorgan Chase Bank, N.A., as Administrative Agent, and the lenders from time to time party thereto (as amended, the *"Credit Agreement"*). The Credit Agreement provided the Company with a credit facility (the *"MGM Credit Facility"*) consisting of a five-year $250 million revolving credit facility (*"Revolving Facility"*), a six-year $1.05 billion term loan (*"Term Loan A"*) and a seven-year $2.7 billion term loan (*"Term Loan B"*). The proceeds of Term Loan A and Term Loan B were used to finance a portion of the Acquisition and to pay related fees and expenses. The proceeds of the Revolving Facility were used to finance the working capital needs and general corporate purposes of MGM and its subsidiaries.

Holdings II and several of its direct and indirect subsidiaries guarantee the MGM Credit Facility (collectively, the *"Guarantors"*). The MGM Credit Facility is secured by substantially all of the assets of Metro-Goldwyn-Mayer Inc. and the Guarantors, including perfected first-priority security interests in the capital stock and, subject to certain exceptions, substantially all other tangible and intangible assets of MGM and the Guarantors.

On March 9, 2007, Holdings II and Metro-Goldwyn-Mayer Inc. entered into the second amendment to the Credit Agreement which replaced Term Loan A with a five-year $1.1 billion term loan (*"Term Loan B-1"*) that incorporated the same loan amortization payment requirements of Term Loan B. Both Term Loan B and Term Loan B-1 mature on April 8, 2012, while the Revolving Facility maturity date remained April 8, 2010. On September 30, 2009, the parties entered into a Third Amendment to the Credit Agreement, Amendment To Swap Agreements and Forbearance Agreement (the *"Initial Forbearance Agreement"*) extending until December 15, 2009 the time for payment of interest, letter of credit participation fees and swap termination payments that otherwise would be due and payable from and including September 30, 2009 through December 15, 2009. On November 13, 2009, the parties entered into a Fourth Amendment to Credit Agreement, Amendment To Swap Agreements and Second Forbearance Agreement extending the forbearance period to January 31, 2010. On January 31, 2010, the parties entered into a Fifth Amendment to Credit Agreement, Amendment to Swap Agreements and Third Forbearance Agreement extending the forbearance period to March 31, 2010. On March 31, 2010, the parties entered into a Sixth Amendment to Credit Agreement, Amendment to Swap Agreements and Fourth Forbearance Agreement extending the forbearance period to May 14, 2010. On May 14, 2010, the parties entered into a Seventh Amendment to Credit Agreement, Amendment To Swap Agreements and Fifth Forbearance Agreement extending the forbearance period to July 14, 2010. On July 14, 2010, the parties entered into an Eighth Amendment to Credit Agreement, Amendment to Swap Agreements and Sixth Forbearance Agreement extending the forbearance period to September 15, 2010. On September 15, 2010, the parties entered into a Ninth Amendment to Credit Agreement, Amendment to Swap Agreements and Seventh Forbearance Agreement extending the forbearance period to October 28, 2010.

As of the date hereof, the aggregate amount of the outstanding obligations under the Credit Agreement is approximately $4.737 billion plus an additional $152 million outstanding obligations on account of certain interest rate protection arrangements entered into in connection with the Credit Agreement.

2. *Print and Advertising Facility*

On September 19, 2006, MGM Studios and certain of its distribution subsidiaries entered into an Amended and Restated Revenue Participation Agreement with Domestic Distribution Inc. (*"DDI"*) (as amended, the *"P&A Facility"*). Under the P&A Facility, MGM Studios committed to offer to sell to DDI revenue participations in certain qualifying pictures in exchange for a purchase price that is tied to MGM Studio's domestic print and advertising costs for such picture. DDI, in turn, committed to pay the purchase price for such revenue participations, however such commitment was limited to DDI's availability under the DDI Credit Agreement (as defined below).

DDI's revenue participation is secured by a first priority security interest in (i) an interest in a cash collateral account of up to $20 million funded by MGM Studios from receipts generated from exploitation of certain television and home video rights with respect to qualifying pictures, (ii) certain domestic distribution agreements pursuant to which MGM Studios distributes qualifying pictures, (iii) any collateral granted to MGM Studios with respect to such qualifying pictures, and (iv) subject to certain limitations, any interest in the underlying copyright in, and physical materials relating to, such qualifying picture solely to the extent necessary to exercise certain distribution rights for such qualifying picture.

DDI is a non-Debtor special purpose entity that was formed for the sole purpose of providing financing to the Company under the P&A Facility. DDI funded its obligations under the P&A Facility by borrowings under a credit agreement among DDI, as borrower, JP Morgan Chase Bank, N.A., as administrative agent, and the lenders from time to time party thereto (as amended, the *"DDI Credit Agreement"*). The DDI Credit Agreement provided DDI with a $175 million revolving credit facility, the proceeds of which were to be used by DDI to purchase revenue participations under the P&A Facility. The

DDI Credit Agreement is secured by all of the assets of DDI, including all of DDI's rights in and to the P&A Facility as well as a collateral assignment of the security interest in the qualified pictures granted by the Company to DDI in the P&A Facility. The failure to pay principal under the Credit Agreement at the April 8, 2010 maturity date triggered a cross-default under the P&A Facility.

As of the date hereof, the aggregate principal amount of the Debtors' obligations under the P&A Facility is approximately $52 million.

3.   United Artists Entertainment Credit Facility

As set forth above, MGM Studios is a majority owner of United Artists Entertainment. New United Artists was formed to develop and create new theatrically released films under the New United Artists banner.

On August 16, 2007, United Artists Entertainment, through its wholly-owned subsidiary, UAPF, entered into (i) a Credit and Security Agreement (the "*UAPF Credit Agreement*") with certain lenders and others, and (ii) a Note Purchase and Security Agreement (the "*UAPF Note Purchase Agreement*") with certain lenders and others.

The UAPF Credit Agreement provided United Artists Entertainment with a $250 million senior credit facility (the "*UAPF Facility*"). In addition, under the UAPF Note Purchase Agreement, United Artists Entertainment sold mezzanine promissory notes totaling $75 million (the "*Mezzanine Notes*"). The proceeds of this financing were designed to support the production or acquisition by New United Artists of up to 18 films to be produced under the New United Artists banner and distributed by MGM under the Master Distribution Agreement. Obligations under the UAPF Facility and UAPF Note Purchase Agreement are guaranteed by UAPF's domestic subsidiaries and are secured by substantially all of UAPF's and its domestic subsidiaries' assets, including the certain intellectual property rights related to the films produced and developed by New United Artists. To secure MGM Studios' performance of certain obligations under the Master Distribution Agreement, including its obligations to make payments to UAPF, MGM Studios and certain of its subsidiaries granted UAPF a security interest in their rights, title, and interest in and to certain collateral relating to licensed pictures. A "Stop Funding Event" has occurred under the UAPF Facility. Therefore the lenders under the UAPF Facility are not required to make additional loans to UAPF for new films.

Neither United Artists Entertainment nor UAPF are expected to be debtors in the Debtors' Chapter 11 cases.

E.   EVENTS LEADING TO CHAPTER 11 CASES

The Revolving Facility under the Credit Agreement matured in April 2010 and material amortization of Term Loan B and Term Loan B-1 is scheduled to begin in June 2011. Through a combination of industry-wide pressures and Company-specific issues, it became evident to the Debtors' board in the Spring of 2009 that the value of the Company might not support a re-financing or re-payment of the Revolving Facility at maturity. Subsequently, the Company's board determined that a balance sheet restructuring was the only viable alternative for the Company to continue to operate as a going concern post-maturation of the Revolving Facility. The industry-wide factors include a precipitous decline in home video sales and the worldwide economic downturn which has reduced consumer spending on discretionary items, such as entertainment, and has chilled the capital markets for new financial accommodations. The Company has also suffered because it has not had sufficient resources to support new production and thereby maximize the value of the MGM Library by maintaining an optimal level of new production.

1. Industry-Wide Factors

The greatest macroeconomic factor affecting the Company is the dramatic decline in consumer spending which directly affected the home entertainment business. Due to the economic downturn, consumer spending on discretionary items such as home video has decreased significantly, and remains dormant. Similarly, many consumers are delaying new Blu-ray disc purchases until Blu-ray players become more affordable, and those that do purchase Blu-ray discs are generally selecting new titles. The economic downturn has also caused many retailers to stop selling new DVDs as loss-leaders to drive store traffic. Competitors' aggressive pricing strategy on new releases has also affected the sale of older MGM Library titles.

In addition to the foregoing, the home video market has experienced an overall decline due to consumer shifts to cable-based and Internet-based on demand service providers which allow consumers to view movies and other programming without the need for DVDs or similar physical media. Likewise, consumer shifts toward subscription-based rental services, such as Netflix, have led to a decrease in home video sales.

The economic downtown has also resulted in lower advertising spending, which has negatively affected television broadcasting revenues. This decline directly impacts advertising sales on MGM-owned channels as well as third-party owned channels that license MGM Library content.

2. Lack of New Production

After the Acquisition in April, 2005, the Company sought to implement a business plan that attempted to exploit the MGM Library with limited new production. Limiting new production failed to maximize the value of the MGM Library and allowed the MGM Library to become stale. Therefore, the Company determined that a more robust new production slate was necessary to refresh and replenish the MGM Library, drive sales of MGM Library product, and otherwise preserve the inherent value of the MGM Library. To that end, as set forth above, in August, 2007, the Company established New United Artists with its joint venture partners. Thereafter, in March, 2008, Ms. Mary Parent, an executive with extensive entertainment industry and financial management experience, was appointed Chairperson of the Company's Worldwide Motion Picture Group.

The current credit crisis has also restricted the Company's ability to procure third-party production financing. Because a substantial portion of cash flow generated from the MGM Library has been dedicated to debt service requirements, the Company has had insufficient liquidity to fund new production at levels that the Company believes is necessary to maximize the value of the MGM Library.

3.   Evaluation of Restructuring Alternatives

Due to the approaching April 2010 maturity of the Revolving Facility and the issues identified above, in April 2009 the Company retained Moelis & Company (*"Moelis"*), as financial advisor, to assist it in exploring strategic alternatives. Shortly thereafter, a steering committee (the *"Steering Committee"*) of certain lenders under the Credit Agreement was formed in connection with a potential restructuring of the Debtors' obligations under the Credit Agreement, and the Company and the Steering Committee commenced discussions regarding potential alternatives. On August 18, 2009, the Company hired restructuring expert Mr. Stephen Cooper (co-founder and former chairman of the restructuring firm Zolfo Cooper), who was appointed to the newly created office of the Chief Executive Officer together with Mary Parent (Chairperson for Worldwide Motion Picture Group), and Bedi A. Singh (President, Finance and Administration & Chief Financial Officer).

In September 2009 the Company requested, among other things, an extension under the Credit Agreement of the time for payment of interest, letter of credit participation fees and swap termination payments that otherwise would be due and payable from and including September 30, 2009 to December 15, 2009. On September 30, 2009, the parties to the Credit Agreement entered into the Initial Forbearance Agreement, granting such extensions. As set forth in Section I.D.1. hereof, the Company requested and continued to receive additional extensions of the forbearance period from time to time.

Starting in September 2009, the Debtors, by and through a Capital Structure Committee of Holdings' Board of Directors (*"CSC"*), collaborated with Moelis to draft a confidential information memorandum (*"CIM"*) regarding a potential sale of the Company. In this regard, the Debtors, along with Moelis (in consultation with the Steering Committee's advisors), prepared a potential buyers list and Moelis reached out to numerous potential parties to gauge interest. Beginning in December 2009, Moelis began delivering CIMs to eighteen potential buyers and their respective advisors following execution of confidentiality agreements. These potential buyers and their advisors were also granted access to a virtual data room.

In January 2010, the Debtors received non-binding indications of interest from eight parties. Following such indications of interest, the Debtors, working with Moelis and the Steering Committee's advisors, invited six of these parties to participate in a second round of bidding. The parties' indications of interests were evaluated primarily on long term value to the Company's stakeholders, proposed structure, the perceived ability of each party to consummate a transaction on a timely basis, and the ability to obtain the requisite Secured Lender support for the transaction.

During the second round, bidders were granted access to both physical and virtual data rooms. The Debtors also invited the bidders to management presentations to discuss the Company's business. Bidders were later invited to follow-up diligence sessions with the Company's management to address questions following the management presentation as well as questions resulting from the review of documents in the data rooms.

Following the second round, three parties submitted non-binding bid letters by the end of March, 2010, subject to, among other things, continued due diligence and the negotiation of definitive documents. The Steering Committee determined that such bids were inadequate, and informed the Debtors that its members would not support a plan of reorganization embodying a transaction based upon these bids, and as a result, the Debtors did not accept any of the bids. The Steering Committee then requested that the Debtors present their business plan that assumed a stand-alone plan of reorganization. In April 2010, the Steering Committee, with the Company's consent, elected to meet with certain industry experts to inform their perspectives of such standalone plan and formed an informal committee of certain members of the Steering Committee (the *"Subcommittee"*) to do so and to consider additional alternatives. During April and May, 2010, the Subcommittee met with numerous industry experts and potential partners to discuss their perspectives on MGM and potential alternatives for a reorganization of the Company. During the months of June and July, 2010, the discussions narrowed to Spyglass and a handful of other parties.

Ultimately, the Subcommittee, in consultation with the Steering Committee and, separately, the Debtors, negotiated a non-binding letter of intent with Spyglass and the C/G Stockholders, which was presented to the Debtors for their consideration. The Steering Committee advised the Debtors that it supported moving forward with a proposal with Spyglass and the C/G Stockholders. After analyzing the proposed transaction, and considering the viability of any other alternatives, the Debtors, after consultation with their advisors, determined that under the circumstances the Spyglass transaction was the best alternative available to the Debtors at which point the Company, Spyglass and the C/G Stockholders negotiated and signed a non-binding letter of intent.

F.   THE PROPOSED PLAN

After several months of considering their strategic alternatives, the Debtors and the Steering Committee negotiated the terms of the Plan, the Investment Agreement, and related documents with Spyglass and the C/G Stockholders. The Plan is a prepackaged plan of reorganization. The overall purpose of the Plan is to provide for a restructuring of the Debtors' liabilities in a manner designed to maximize value to all stakeholders and to enhance the financial viability of the reorganized Debtors. Generally, the Plan provides for a balance sheet restructuring whereby (i) existing equity in Holdings will be cancelled, (ii) approximately $4.75 billion of claims under the Credit Agreement will be converted into approximately 95.3% of the equity in Reorganized Holdings, (iii) Spyglass will contribute certain assets to the Reorganized Company in exchange for 0.52% of the equity in Reorganized Holdings, and (iv) Cypress and Garoge will merge with and into a special purpose direct limited liability company subsidiary of Reorganized Holdings, with the Debtor affiliate as the surviving entity and the C/G Stockholders receiving approximately 4.17% of the equity in Reorganized Holdings. All other classes of claims are unimpaired under the Plan. Furthermore, all equity interests in Subsidiary Debtors will be reinstated.

In furtherance of the implementation of the Plan, the Debtors have entered into (or will be entering into) the Transaction Documents, which include the Investment Agreement, the Stockholders Agreement, and the Registration Rights Agreement as well as related documents, including the Stock Incentive Plan. Set forth below in Section I.H. are summaries of the terms of such Investment Agreement, Stockholders Agreement, Registration Rights Agreement, and Stock Incentive Plan. The Plan also contemplates that the Reorganized Debtors will enter into a New Credit Facility on the Effective Date. The New Credit Facility is contemplated to be a $500 million credit facility to be entered into between the Reorganized Debtors and the lenders party thereto, which shall have terms substantially as set forth in the commitment letter or term sheet attached to the Plan as *Exhibit A*, which will be filed with the Bankruptcy Court at least five business days prior to the deadline that the Bankruptcy Court sets for parties in interest to file objections to confirmation of the Plan.

The Debtors believe that their businesses and assets have significant value that would not be maximized in a liquidation. Further in connection with the Debtors' decision to pursue the Plan, the Debtors' financial advisors have prepared and delivered a going concern valuation of the business. The Steering Committee has advised the Debtors that its financial advisors have also prepared a going concern valuation. Moreover, the Debtors believe that any alternative to confirmation of the Plan, such as an out-of-court restructuring or attempts by another party in interest to file a plan of reorganization, would result in significant delays, litigation, and additional costs, and ultimately would lower the recoveries for Holders of Allowed Claims. Additionally, based upon feedback during the course of this restructuring from both the Subcommittee and the Steering Committee, the Company concluded that as a practical matter no other plan of reorganization could be proposed that would garner the support of the Secured Lenders, whose support is essential to the success of any plan. *Accordingly, the Debtors strongly recommend that you vote to accept the Plan, if you are entitled to vote.*

The Debtors have been advised that the Subcommittee and the Administrative Agent also support the Plan and will recommend that Holders of Credit Agreement Claims vote in favor of the Plan.

G. SPYGLASS, CYPRESS AND GAROGE

Spyglass is a film and television production company, co-founded by Gary Barber and Roger Birnbaum. Cypress and Garoge (together, *"Cypress/Garoge"*) are affiliates of Messrs. Barber and Birnbaum that own and exploit a library of films. Collectively, these films have grossed over $5 billion in worldwide box office. They enjoyed instant success with the blockbuster *The Sixth Sense* and have produced a slate of successful films including, among others, *Bruce Almighty, Seabiscuit, Memoirs of a Geisha, 27 Dresses*, and *Invictus*. Spyglass and Cypress/Garoge films have amassed over 34 Oscar nominations, including three wins. Spyglass also co-financed the 2009 blockbusters *Star Trek* and *GI Joe: The Rise of Cobra.*

Under the Plan, Messrs. Barber and Birnbaum will be appointed as co-chairmen and co-chief executive officers of Reorganized Holdings. Reorganized Holdings will enter into identical employment agreements with each of Messrs. Barber and Birnbaum, which will be effective as of the Effective Date and have a 5 year term, subject to the terms and conditions of such agreements. Messrs. Barber and Birnbaum will also be issued options for stock in Reorganized Holdings at a strike price equal to or greater than the value of the stock of Reorganized Holdings at the Effective Date, which options will be subject to vesting.

Messrs. Barber and Birnbaum will be subject to noncompetition and nonsolicitation restrictions while employed by Reorganized Holdings for certain periods following a termination of their respective employment. Messrs. Barber and Birnbaum will also continue to act as directors of Spyglass, and under the terms of the Investment Agreement and their employment agreements, they will be subject to restrictions on the scope of activities they may perform in that capacity. Spyglass will remain a separate entity, subject to restrictions on its activities pursuant to the Investment Agreement, and will receive 0.52% of the New Common Stock in Reorganized Holdings in consideration of the contribution of certain assets under the Investment Agreement. The C/G Stockholders (which include the trusts of Messrs. Barber and Birnbaum) will receive 4.17% of the New Common Stock issued under the Plan in connection with the mergers.

II. SUMMARY OF TREATMENT OF CLAIMS AND INTERESTS UNDER THE PLAN

The table set forth below summarizes the classification and treatment of the prepetition Claims and Interests under the Plan.

The Debtors intend to pursue consummation of the Plan and to cause the Effective Date to occur immediately after all conditions to the Effective Date are satisfied or waived. There can be no assurance, however, as to when or whether the Effective Date will occur. *See* Section VI—"Risk Factors To Be Considered" for a further discussion of certain factors that could delay or prevent the occurrence of the Effective Date.

The Debtors believe that the distributions contemplated by the Plan reflect an appropriate resolution of the Claims, taking into account the differing nature and priority of such Claims.

Description And Amount Of Claims Or Interests Summary Of Treatment

Administrative Claims	On, or as soon as reasonably practicable after, the later of (a) the Effective Date, (b) the date on which an Administrative Claim becomes an Allowed Administrative Claim, or (c) the date on which an Allowed Administrative Claim becomes payable under any agreement relating thereto, each Holder of such Allowed Administrative Claim shall receive, in full and final satisfaction, settlement, release, and discharge of, and in exchange for, such Allowed Administrative Claim, Cash equal to the unpaid portion of such Allowed Administrative Claim. Notwithstanding the foregoing, (y) any Allowed Administrative Claim based on a liability incurred by a Debtor in the ordinary course of business during the Chapter 11 Cases may be paid in the ordinary course of business in accordance with the terms and conditions of any agreement relating thereto and (z) any Allowed Administrative Claim may be paid on such other terms as may be agreed to between the Holder of such Claim and the Debtors or the Reorganized Debtors.
Priority Tax Claims	On, or as soon as reasonably practicable after, the later of (a) the Effective Date or (b) the date on which a Priority Tax Claim becomes an Allowed Priority Tax Claim each Holder of an Allowed Priority Tax Claim shall receive, in full and final satisfaction, settlement, release, and discharge of, and in exchange for, such Allowed Priority Tax Claim, in the sole discretion of the Debtors, (i) Cash equal to the unpaid portion of such Holder's Allowed Priority Tax Claim, (ii) treatment in any other manner such that such Holder's Allowed Priority Tax Claim shall not be impaired pursuant to section 1124 of the Bankruptcy Code, including payment in accordance with the

provisions of section 1129(a)(9)(C) of the Bankruptcy Code over a period of not later than five years from the Petition Date, or (iii) such other treatment as to which the Debtors or the Reorganized Debtors and such Holder shall have agreed upon in writing.

Class 1—Non-Tax Priority Claims

Except to the extent that the Holder of an Allowed Non-Tax Priority Claim has agreed to a less favorable treatment of such Claim, on, or as soon as reasonably practicable after the latest of (a) the Effective Date, (b) the date on which such Non-Tax Priority Claim becomes an Allowed Non-Tax Priority Claim, (c) the date on which such Allowed Non-Tax Priority Claim is otherwise due and payable and (d) such other date as mutually may be agreed to by and between the Debtors and the Holder of such Non-Tax Priority Claim, each Holder of an Allowed Non-Tax Priority Claim shall receive, in full and final satisfaction, release, and discharge of, and in exchange for, such Allowed Non-Tax Priority Claim, Cash equal to the unpaid portion of such Allowed Non-Tax Priority Claim.

Class 1 is an Unimpaired Class, and the Holders of Allowed Class 1 Non-Tax Priority Claims are conclusively deemed to have accepted the Plan pursuant to section 1 126(f) of the Bankruptcy Code. Therefore, the Holders of Class 1 Non-Tax Priority Claims are not entitled to vote to accept or reject the Plan.

Class 2—Other Secured Claims

On the Effective Date, or as soon thereafter as is reasonably practicable, each Holder of an Allowed Class 2 Other Secured Claim shall, in the sole discretion of the applicable Debtor, be entitled to the treatment set forth below in option A, B, C, or D. The Debtors and the Reorganized Debtors specifically reserve the right to challenge the validity, nature and perfection of, and to avoid pursuant to the provisions of the Bankruptcy Code and other applicable law, any purported Liens relating to the Other Secured Claims.

Option A: Allowed Other Secured Claims with respect to which the applicable Debtor elects option A shall be Reinstated. The failure of the Debtors to file an objection, prior to the Effective Date, with respect to any Other Secured Claim that is Reinstated hereunder shall be without prejudice to the rights of the Reorganized Debtors to contest or otherwise defend against such Claim in an appropriate forum (including the Bankruptcy Court in accordance with Article X of the Plan) when and if such Claim is sought to be enforced. Any cure amount that the Debtors may be required to pay pursuant to section 1124(2) of the Bankruptcy Code on account of any such Reinstated Other Secured Claim shall be paid on, or as soon as practicable after, the latest of (a) the Effective Date, (b) the date on which such Other Secured Claim becomes Allowed, or (c) such other date as mutually may be agreed to by and between such Holder and the Debtors or Reorganized Debtors.

Option B: Allowed Other Secured Claims with respect to which the applicable Debtor elects option B shall be paid in Cash, in full, including any amounts owed under section 506 of the Bankruptcy Code, on, or as soon as reasonably practicable after, the latest of (a) the Effective Date, (b) the date on which such Other Secured Claim becomes an Allowed Other Secured Claim, (c) the date on which such Other Secured Claim is otherwise due and payable and (d) such other date as mutually may be agreed to by and between such Holder and the Debtors or Reorganized Debtors.

Option C: Allowed Other Secured Claims with respect to which the applicable Debtor elects option C shall be satisfied by the surrender to the Holder of the Claim of the collateral securing the applicable Other Secured Claim.

Option D: Allowed Other Secured Claims with respect to which the applicable Debtor elects option D shall be satisfied in accordance with such other terms and conditions as may be agreed upon by the applicable Debtor or Reorganized Debtors and the Holder of such Allowed Other Secured Claim.

The applicable Debtor shall be deemed to have elected option A with respect to all Allowed Other Secured Claims except those with respect to which the applicable Debtor elects another option in writing prior to the Confirmation Hearing.

Class 2 is an Unimpaired Class, and the Holders of Allowed Class 2 Other Secured Claims are conclusively deemed to have accepted the Plan pursuant to section 1 126(f) of the Bankruptcy Code. Therefore, the Holders of Class 2 Other Secured Claims are not entitled to vote to accept or reject the Plan.

Class 3—Credit Agreement Claims

Each Holder of an Allowed Credit Agreement Claim shall receive, in full and final satisfaction, release, and discharge of, and in exchange for, such Allowed Credit Agreement Claim, its pro rata share of 95.3% of the New Common Stock to be issued and outstanding on the Effective Date, subject to dilution by the Equity Incentive Plan, plus the consideration described in the paragraph immediately below. Distributions on account of Credit Agreement Claims shall be made on the Effective Date to each Holder of an Allowed Credit Agreement Claim in accordance with Section 6.2 of the Plan. As set forth in Section 5.4 of the Plan, the New Common Stock will be subject to the Stockholders Agreement. For the purpose of the Plan all Class 3 Claims shall be deemed Allowed in an amount not less than $4,888,053,018.00 in accordance with the terms of the Credit Agreement and the Loan Documents and shall not be subject to defense, offset, counterclaim or reduction.

With respect to each of the Letters of Credit outstanding on the Effective Date (if any), the Debtors will, at their discretion and in consultation with the Administrative Agent, (i) return such Letter of Credit to the issuing bank undrawn and marked "cancelled," (ii) "roll" such Letters of Credit into the New Credit Facility in a manner and pursuant to documentation reasonably satisfactory to the applicable issuing lenders of such Letters of Credit, or (iii) cash collateralize Claims in respect of their obligations under such Letters of Credit in an amount acceptable to the Administrative Agent that is intended to insure as much as is practicable a recovery on such Claims that is ratable with other Class 3 Claim recoveries. As of the date hereof, there are approximately $78,000 principal amount of letters of credit issued and outstanding under the Credit Agreement.

All fees, costs and expenses of the Administrative Agent as well as reasonable professional fees and expenses for the Administrative Agent and also for the Steering Committee payable shall be paid in full and in cash on the Effective Date or as soon thereafter as is practicable.

Class 3 is Impaired. Pursuant to section 1126 of the Bankruptcy Code, each Holder of an Allowed Class 3 Credit Agreement Claim is entitled to vote to accept or reject the Plan.

Class 4—P&A Facility Claims	Holders of Class 4 P&A Facility Claims shall have such Claims Reinstated on the Effective Date.

Class 4 is an Unimpaired Class, and the Holders of Allowed Class 4 P&A Facility Claims are conclusively deemed to have accepted the Plan pursuant to section 1126(f) of the Bankruptcy Code. Therefore, the Holders of Class 4 P&A Facility Claims are not entitled to vote to accept or reject the Plan.

Class 5—General Unsecured Claims	On the latest of (a) the Effective Date, (b) the date on which such General Unsecured Claim becomes Allowed, and (c) such other date as mutually may be agreed to by and between the Debtors or Reorganized Debtors and the Holder of such General Unsecured Claim, or, in each case, as soon thereafter as practicable, each Holder of an Allowed General Unsecured Claim in Class 5 shall be paid in Cash the amount of such Allowed General Unsecured Claim, in full and final satisfaction of such Holder's Allowed General Unsecured Claim; *provided, however*, a General Unsecured Claim that is not due and payable on or before the Effective Date shall be paid thereafter (i) in the ordinary course of business in accordance with the terms of any agreement governing, or other documents relating to, such General Unsecured Claim or (ii) in accordance with the course of practice between the Debtors and such Holder with respect to such General Unsecured Claim.

Class 5 is an Unimpaired Class, and the Holders of Allowed Class 5 General Unsecured Claims are conclusively deemed to have accepted the Plan pursuant to section 1126(f) of the Bankruptcy Code. Therefore, the Holders of Class 5 General Unsecured Claims are not entitled to vote to accept or reject the Plan.

Class 6—Interests in Subsidiary Debtors	Holders of Allowed Class 6 Interests in Subsidiary Debtors shall have such Interests Reinstated on the Effective Date.
	Class 6 is an Unimpaired Class, and the Holders of Allowed Class 6 Interests are conclusively deemed to have accepted the Plan pursuant to section 1126(f) of the Bankruptcy Code. Therefore, the Holders of Class 6 Interests are not entitled to vote to accept or reject the Plan.
Class 7—Interests in Holdings	All Interests in Holdings shall be cancelled, and each Holder of Allowed Interests in Holdings shall not receive or retain any property on account thereof.
	Holders of Allowed Interests in Holdings are conclusively deemed to have rejected the Plan pursuant to section 1126(g) of the Bankruptcy Code. Therefore, the Holders of Class 7 Interests in Holdings are not entitled to vote to accept or reject the Plan.

THE PLAN IS A SINGLE PLAN OF REORGANIZATION FOR THE JOINTLY ADMINISTERED CHAPTER 11 CASES, BUT DOES NOT CONSTITUTE A SUBSTANTIVE CONSOLIDATION OF THE DEBTORS' ESTATES.

III. PLAN VOTING INSTRUCTIONS AND PROCEDURES

A. NOTICE TO HOLDERS OF CLAIMS

This Disclosure Statement will be transmitted to Holders of Claims that are entitled under the Bankruptcy Code to vote on the Plan. Holders of Claims in Class 3 are the only Holders of Claims that are entitled to vote on the Plan. The purpose of this Disclosure Statement is to provide adequate information to enable such Holders to make a reasonably informed decision with respect to the Plan prior to exercising their right to vote to accept or reject the Plan. With the exception of Class 7 Equity Interests in Holdings, all other Classes are Unimpaired under the Plan and the Holders of Claims and Interests in such classes are deemed to have accepted the Plan.

ALL HOLDERS OF CLAIMS IN CLASS 3 ARE ENCOURAGED TO READ THIS DISCLOSURE STATEMENT AND ITS APPENDICES CAREFULLY AND IN THEIR ENTIRETY BEFORE DECIDING TO VOTE TO ACCEPT OR REJECT THE PLAN. This Disclosure Statement contains important information about the Plan and important considerations pertinent to acceptance or rejection of the Plan.

THIS DISCLOSURE STATEMENT, THE PLAN, AND BALLOTS ARE THE ONLY DOCUMENTS TO BE USED IN CONNECTION WITH THE SOLICITATION OF VOTES ON THE PLAN. No person has been authorized to distribute any information concerning the Company relating to the Solicitation other than the information contained herein.

B.   SOLICITATION PACKAGE

In soliciting votes for the Plan pursuant to this Disclosure Statement from the Holders of Claims in Class 3, the Debtors also will send copies of the Plan (attached hereto as *Appendix A*) and one or more Ballots to be used by Holders of Claims in such Class to vote to accept or reject the Plan.

C.   VOTING PROCEDURES AND BALLOTS AND VOTING DEADLINE

After carefully reviewing the Plan, this Disclosure Statement, and the detailed instructions accompanying your Ballot, please indicate your acceptance or rejection of the Plan by voting in favor of or against the Plan on the enclosed Ballot. Please complete and sign your Ballot and return your Ballot to Donlin, Recano & Company, Inc. (the *"Voting Agent"*) either by first class mail, or by hand delivery, or overnight courier to the address set forth below, so that it is received by the Voting Deadline.

THE VOTING DEADLINE IS 5:00 P.M. PREVAILING EASTERN TIME ON OCTOBER 22, 2010, UNLESS EXTENDED BY THE DEBTORS.

The Voting Record Date for determining whether a Holder of an Impaired Claim is entitled to vote on the Plan is October 4, 2010.

FOR YOUR VOTE TO BE COUNTED, YOUR BALLOT MUST BE PROPERLY COMPLETED AS SET FORTH ABOVE AND IN ACCORDANCE WITH THE VOTING INSTRUCTIONS ON THE BALLOT AND RECEIVED NO LATER THAN THE VOTING DEADLINE BY THE VOTING AGENT BY FIRST CLASS MAIL, HAND DELIVERY, OR OVERNIGHT COURIER AT THE ADDRESS SET FORTH BELOW.

PROBLEM SET 27.1

1. What was the structure of the original acquisition of MGM? What did the lenders who facilitated that transaction receive in exchange for their loans?
2. What is the structure of the reorganization of MGM? What times of transactions that you have seen before do you recognize in the reorganization?

2.   SOLICITATION ISSUES

STEPHEN J. LUBBEN, *THE DIRECT COSTS OF CORPORATE
REORGANIZATION: AN EMPIRICAL EXAMINATION OF PROFESSIONAL
FEES IN LARGE CHAPTER 11 CASES*

74 Am. Bankr. L.J. 509, 516 (2000)

A true prepack involves a prepetition solicitation of votes on a plan. A partial prepack involves both a prepetition solicitation (e.g., of bondholders) and a postpetition solicitation (e.g., of equity). Partial prepacks are usually done to avoid having to conduct a "registered prepack," which is subject to review and comment by the SEC, and takes substantially longer than a nonregistered prepack. A prearranged or prenegotiated case involves no prepetition solicitation, and thus is little different from a traditional Chapter 11 case, save for the fact that a proposed plan and disclosure statement are fully drafted on the first day of the case.

Which type of prepack is the MGM plan? Why would an equity solicitation require registration with the SEC? The next case provides some further indication of why registered prepacks are often avoided.

IN RE ZENITH ELECTRONICS CORPORATION

241 B.R. 92
United States Bankruptcy Court, D. Delaware.
Nov. 2, 1999.

Mary F. WALRATH, Bankruptcy Judge.
This case is before the Court on the request of Zenith Electronics Corporation ("Zenith") for approval of its Disclosure Statement and confirmation of its Pre-Packaged Plan of Reorganization filed August 24, 1999 ("the Plan"). The Plan is supported by Zenith's largest shareholder and creditor, LG Electronics, Inc. ("LGE"), and the holders of a majority of the debentures issued by Zenith pre-petition ("the Bondholders").[1] The Plan is opposed by the Official Committee of Equity Security Holders ("the Equity Committee") and numerous shareholders, including Nordhoff Investments, Inc. ("Nordhoff") (collectively, "the Objectors"). For the reasons set forth below, we overrule the objections, approve the Disclosure Statement and will confirm the Plan, if modified in accordance with this Opinion.

---

1. An ad hoc committee of the Bondholders was formed pre-petition which included Loomis Sayles & Company, L.P., Mariner Investment Group, Inc., and Caspian Capital Partners, L.L.P. ("the Bondholders' Committee").

I.   FACTUAL BACKGROUND

Zenith has been in business for over 80 years. It was a leader in the design, manufacturing, and marketing of consumer electronics for many years. In recent years it has experienced substantial financial difficulties. It incurred losses in 12 of the last 13 years.

In 1995 Zenith persuaded one of its shareholders, LGE which held approximately 5% of its stock, to invest over $366 million in acquiring a total 57.7% stake in the company. Notwithstanding that investment, and loans and credit support in excess of $340 million provided subsequently by LGE, Zenith's financial condition continued to deteriorate. Zenith suffered net losses in 1996 of $178 million, in 1997 of $299 million and in 1998 of $275 million.

In late 1997, the Asian financial crisis and the continuing losses at Zenith, caused LGE (and Zenith) to question LGE's ability to continue to support Zenith and Zenith's need to reorganize. LGE retained McKinsey & Co. ("McKinsey") to evaluate its investment in Zenith and to suggest improvements Zenith could make in its operations and focus. Zenith hired an investment banking firm, Peter J. Solomon Company ("PJSC") in December, 1997, and a new CEO, Jeff Gannon, in January 1998. Under Mr. Gannon, Zenith made substantial operational changes, including a conversion from manufacturer to a marketing and distribution company which outsourced all manufacturing. Zenith's manufacturing facilities were sold or closed in 1998 and 1999. While those operational changes did have some effect on stemming the losses, they were insufficient to eliminate them. Contemporaneously, PJSC evaluated Zenith's assets on a liquidation and going concern basis.

In early 1998, Zenith also attempted to attract a strategic investor or purchaser of part or all of its business or assets. Because of its financial condition, Zenith was advised that it could not raise money through the issuance of more stock or debt instruments. Zenith's strategy was to identify companies which might have an interest and then to have Zenith's CEO approach the target's CEO to discuss the possibilities. Several meetings were conducted with such entities. No offers were received for a sale of substantial assets or business divisions; nor were any offers of equity investments received.

In April 1998, LGE proposed a possible restructuring of its debt and equity in Zenith, contingent on substantial reduction of the bond debt and elimination of the shareholder interests. Zenith appointed a Special Committee of its Board of Directors to evaluate the restructuring proposal and to conduct negotiations on behalf of Zenith. After agreement was reached with the Special Committee, negotiations proceeded with the Bondholders' Committee. Ultimately the restructuring proposal was reduced to a pre-packaged plan of reorganization.

A Disclosure Statement and Proxy Statement-Prospectus for the solicitation of votes on the Plan was prepared and reviewed by the SEC. Discussions with the SEC over the requirements of the Disclosure Statement started in August 1998. On July 15, 1999, after numerous revisions, the SEC declared the Disclosure Statement effective.

On July 20, 1999, Zenith mailed the Plan and Disclosure Statement to the Bondholders and others entitled to vote on the Plan. After voting was completed on August 20, 1999, the Bondholders had voted in favor of the Plan by 98.6% in amount and 97.01% in number of those voting. LGE and Citibank, a secured creditor, had also voted to accept the Plan. Zenith immediately filed its chapter 11 petition on August 24, 1999. At the same time, Zenith filed its Plan and Disclosure Statement and sought prompt approval of both. A combined Disclosure Statement and confirmation hearing was scheduled for September 27 and 28, 1999.

An ad hoc committee of minority shareholders sought a postponement of the confirmation hearing, which was denied. We did, however, grant its motion for appointment of an official committee of equity holders, over the objection of Zenith, LGE and the Bondholders' Committee. We did so to give the equity holders an opportunity to conduct discovery and present their arguments against confirmation of the Plan.

The combined Disclosure Statement and confirmation hearing was held on September 27 and 28, 1999. Post trial briefs were filed by the parties on October 4, 1999.

II. DISCUSSION

As an initial matter, the Equity Committee objects to the adequacy of the Disclosure Statement, asserting that it failed to advise those voting on the Plan of numerous "essential facts" including (1) that LGE had hired PJSC, thus tainting the valuation of Zenith done by PJSC, (2) that different entities had done different analyses of the value of Zenith, including McKinsey, and (3) that alternatives to the Plan had been analyzed but the results not revealed. Zenith, LGE and the Bondholders' Committee all dispute the Equity Committee's contentions.

A. APPROVAL OF THE DISCLOSURE STATEMENT

Typically, under chapter 11 of the Bankruptcy Code, the court approves the debtor's disclosure statement before it, and the plan of reorganization, are sent to creditors and others entitled to vote on the plan. Section 1125(b) provides:

> (b) An acceptance or rejection of a plan may not be solicited after the commencement of the case under this title from a holder of a claim or interest with respect to such claim or interest, unless, at the time of or before such solicitation, there is transmitted to such holder the plan or a summary of the plan, and a written disclosure statement approved, after notice and a hearing, by the court as containing adequate information.

11 U.S.C. §1125(b). *See also,* Fed. R. Bankr.P. 3017 & 3018.

However, Congress recognized the validity of votes solicited pre-bankruptcy (a practice which had developed under chapter X of the Bankruptcy Act). Section 1126(b) provides:

> (b) For the purposes of subsections (c) and (d) of this section, a holder of a claim or interest that has accepted or rejected the plan before the commencement of the case under this title is deemed to have accepted or rejected such plan, as the case may be, if—
>> (1) the solicitation of such acceptance or rejection was in compliance with any applicable nonbankruptcy law, rule, or regulation governing the adequacy of disclosure in connection with such solicitation; or
>> (2) if there is not any such law, rule, or regulation, such acceptance or rejection was solicited after disclosure to such holder of adequate information, as defined in section 1125(a) of this title.

11 U.S.C. §1126(b).

Zenith asserts that the Disclosure Statement meets both criteria. We agree.

1.   Standing

Zenith asserts as a threshold issue that the Equity Committee does not have standing to object to the Disclosure Statement. Under the Plan, equity holders are receiving nothing. Therefore, the equity holders are conclusively presumed to have rejected the Plan and do not have the right to vote. 11 U.S.C. §1126(g).

Since the Disclosure Statement need only contain adequate information for those entitled to vote, some courts have concluded that non-voting classes have no standing to be heard on the issue.

However, the Equity Committee, as an official committee in this case, does have standing to appear and be heard on any issue in the case. 11 U.S.C. §1109(b). Thus, we conclude that it has standing to object to the Disclosure Statement.

2.   Approval by the SEC

Zenith asserts that the adequacy of its Disclosure Statement is governed by section 1126(b), not section 1125. *See, e.g.,* In re The Southland Corp., 124 B.R. 211, 223 (Bankr.N.D.Tex.1991) (where votes are solicited pre-petition, section 1126(b) applies unless there is no applicable nonbankruptcy law dealing with the adequacy of disclosure issue).

In this case, the SEC was required to approve the Disclosure Statement because the Plan provides for the issuance of new securities to the Bondholders. The SEC did approve the Disclosure Statement on July 15, 1999, as containing adequate information (after 11 months of discussions and numerous amendments).

We conclude that the Disclosure Statement, having been approved by the SEC as containing adequate information, complies with the provisions of section 1126(b)(1).

3. *Adequacy of Information*

Even if it did not fit the provisions of section 1126(b)(1), the Disclosure Statement does contain sufficient information to comply with section 1126(b)(2) and 1125(a). The Disclosure Statement is almost 400 pages. It contains numerous financial statements and historical information about Zenith. It has lengthy descriptions of Zenith's efforts to restructure its operations and finances and alternatives to the proposed Plan. It describes LGE's relationship to Zenith. It provides valuation information and a liquidation analysis.

Further, Zenith is a public company. Consequently, substantial information about its finances and operations is publicly available. It files periodic statements with the SEC, and media attention to its plight has been intense.

In considering the adequacy of a disclosure statement, it is important to keep in mind the audience. Here, those entitled to vote on the Plan are sophisticated, institutional investors. They have competent professionals assisting them in analyzing and testing the information provided by Zenith. They have also been involved in negotiations with Zenith and LGE for over a year before voting on the Plan. Significant documents and information (in addition to the Disclosure Statement) were made available to the Bondholders' Committee and its professionals during that time.

Finally, there is no suggestion that the Disclosure Statement contains false information—only that certain additional information was not included. What the Equity Committee asserts is missing, however, is not uncontested, concrete facts, but rather the Equity Committee's interpretation of those facts or duplicative information. We do not believe that such "information" must be included in the Disclosure Statement.

Given the sophistication of the parties, the wealth of information contained in the Disclosure Statement and publicly available elsewhere, the approval by the SEC and the lack of objection by any party entitled to vote on the Plan, we readily conclude that the Disclosure Statement contains adequate information and the votes solicited by it are valid. The Disclosure Statement will be approved, pursuant to section 1126(b) and/or 1125(a).

. . .

III. CONCLUSION

For all the foregoing reasons, we conclude that the objections of the Equity Committee and Nordhoff to approval of the Disclosure Statement should be overruled. We further conclude that the Plan satisfies the requirements of sections 1123 and 1129 of the Bankruptcy Code and may be confirmed if modified in accordance with the comments . . . above. An appropriate Order is attached.

When soliciting votes on a prepacked plan, who you solicit matters. Sometimes you need to find them. For example, during the PennCentral bankruptcy in the 1970s, the bankruptcy attorneys had to find a large group of European bondholders. But the bonds were bearer bonds, so there was no record of who the current owners were. Newspaper advertisements were used to try to reach as many of the bondholders as possible.

In the United States, the complex ownership structure we discussed in Chapter 12 rears its head again in this context.

IN RE PIONEER FINANCE CORP.

246 B.R. 626
United States Bankruptcy Court, D. Nevada
Jan. 21, 2000

Linda B. RIEGLE, Bankruptcy Judge.

A Chapter 11 debtor seeks confirmation of a proposed plan of reorganization pursuant to a prepetition offering made to record bondholders. In conjunction with its motion, the debtor seeks a determination that its offering qualifies as a valid prepetition solicitation under 11 U.S.C. §1126(b), and a finding that the consents of the record bondholders to the offering are binding obligations to support and vote for its proposed plan. The prepetition offering was in the form of a combined exchange offer and consent solicitation. The offering proposed to exchange new bonds for old bonds or, in the alternative, sought consent of the bondholders to (among other things) vote in favor of a plan of reorganization that complied with the terms of the offering. The offering was sent only to the record holders of the bonds. It was not sent to the beneficial holders.

The Court holds that under the wording of the offering, the bondholders consented only to agree to vote on a plan in the *future*, they did not vote on a present plan. The consents obtained are thus not sufficient to constitute acceptances of the plan which is now proposed. The Court further holds that for the purposes of confirmation of a plan under the Bankruptcy Code, there is insufficient notice and authority to constitute valid acceptances where, as here, a prepetition solicitation was sent only to record bondholders, but not to the beneficial bondholders, and no showing has been made that the record holders had the authority to vote on behalf of the beneficial holders.

Factual Summary

Pioneer Finance Corp. is a debtor-in-possession in the jointly administered Chapter 11 cases of Pioneer Finance Corp. ("PFC") and Pioneer Hotel Inc. ("PHI") (collectively the "Debtors").

PFC is a single purpose entity created to finance Santa Fe Gaming Corp.'s acquisition of the Pioneer Hotel, which is located in Laughlin, Nevada. PFC's sole asset is a Note and Deed of Trust on the assets of PHI. On December 1, 1988, PFC issued $120 million in "13.5% First Mortgage Bonds due December 1, 1998" (the "1988 Bonds"). PFC is the obligor on the 1988 Bonds. Santa Fe Gaming Corp. ("SFGC"), the parent of PHI and PFC, is the guarantor of PFC's obligations on the 1988 Bonds.

The 1988 Bonds were issued in accordance with an Indenture by and between PFC as issuer, Sahara Casino Partners, L.P. (predecessor-in-interest to SFGC) as guarantor, and Security Pacific National Bank, predecessor to IBJ Whitehall Bank & Trust Company ("IBJ") as indenture trustee (the "Indenture Trustee").

The 1988 Bonds and the PHI Note and Deed of Trust matured and came due on December 1, 1998. On that date, PHI did not make the principal and interest payments due at maturity of the PHI Note and Deed of Trust. In addition, PFC defaulted on its obligations on the 1988 Bonds and SFGC defaulted on its obligations on the guaranty.

The Offering

Prior to the defaults which occurred on December 1, 1998, SFGC, PHI and PFC began negotiating with Foothill Capital Corp. ("Foothill") to restructure the bond obligation. Foothill then held approximately 26.50% of the face amounts of the outstanding 1988 Bonds.

After the negotiations, PFC issued an "Offer to Exchange All Outstanding 13% First Mortgage Bonds Due December 1, 1998 ($60,000,000 Principal Amount Outstanding) For 13% First Mortgage Notes Due 2006 and Consent Solicitation Statement" ("Exchange Offer and Consent Solicitation").

The Exchange Offer and Consent Solicitation was dated October 23, 1998. It was supplemented by an "Amended Offer to Exchange" which was dated November 14, 1998. (Both are collectively referred to as the "Offering").

The Offering proposed two alternatives. On the one hand it proposed to exchange the 1988 Bonds for new bonds with a later maturity date secured by a pledge of certain assets by the guarantor if 100% of the bondholders agreed and tendered their 1988 Bonds to PFC (the "Exchange Offer").

Alternatively, if less than 100% of bondholders agreed, PFC simultaneously sought the consent ("Consents") of holders of no less than $42,000,000 principal amount of the 1988 Bonds to, among other things: (1) forbear until December 15, 2000 against exercising any rights against PFC or SFGC in the event of PFC's default on the 1988 Bonds; (2) forbear until December 15, 2000 against exercising any rights in the event of PHI's default on the PHI Note; (3) "consent to and support a plan of reorganization" under Chapter 11 of the Bankruptcy

Code which substantially complied with the Offering ("Consent Solicitation"). If the requisite consents were received, the Debtors agreed to repurchase from the Consenting Bondholders up to $6.5 million principal amount of the 1988 Bonds together with accrued interest. Upon receipt of the Consents, SFGC would pledge the common stock of certain of its affiliates for its guaranty.

The Offering was mailed to the registered holders of the 1988 Bonds ("Record Holders") utilizing the lists maintained by IBJ, who served as the exchange and solicitation agent for the Offering. IBJ maintained a list of Record Holders in its capacity as the Indenture Trustee. An information agent, D.F. King & Co., was hired to facilitate the dissemination of the Offering. The Debtors acknowledge that the Offering was transmitted "to the only parties known to them, the record owners of the 1998 Bonds." Each Record Holder was also mailed, among other documents, a form upon which to register its consent to the Offering ("Consent Form").

The Offering expired on November 24, 1998. Less than 100% of the bondholders agreed to the Exchange Offer alternative. Holders of $45,816,750 in principal amount of 1988 Bonds (approximately 76.4% of the outstanding bonds), however, did agree to the Consent Solicitation ("Consenting Bondholders"). Upon this acceptance, Consenting Bondholders received payments on account of the repurchase and SFGC caused the pledge of the assets.

PFC filed its Chapter 11 petition on February 23, 1999. PHI filed a Chapter 11 petition on April 12, 1999. PFC and PHI filed their first joint disclosure statement and their first plan on April 12, 1999. They filed a revised disclosure statement on June 4, 1999, which was approved on August 30, 1999. The Debtors filed their proposed "Second Amended Plan of Reorganization" in conjunction with the instant "Motion to Approve Prepetition Solicitation" ("Motion to Approve") on August 13, 1999.

In support of their revised disclosure statement, the Debtors at first argued that the Consent Solicitation was a pre-negotiated plan, not a pre-packaged plan. They argued that the Consent Solicitation did not have to comply with the notice provisions of the Bankruptcy Code because it was not a prepetition plan solicitation.

Now, in support of their Motion to Approve, the Debtors argue that the Consent Solicitation *does* qualify as a prepetition solicitation under §1126(b) and Bankruptcy Rule 3018(b), and that the Consents are votes in favor of the Second Amended Plan. They further contend that the disclosure requirements of §1125(a) do not apply because, under §1126(b)(1), they have complied with applicable nonbankruptcy law governing the adequacy of disclosure.

LEGAL ANALYSIS

PREPACKAGED REORGANIZATIONS

In a conventional Chapter 11 case, the debtor files a bankruptcy petition, then negotiates a reorganization plan and solicits votes after a disclosure statement has been approved.

With a "prepackaged" plan, however, which is authorized under 11 U.S.C. §1126(b), a plan proponent has negotiated a plan and solicited votes prior to the filing of a Chapter 11 petition and before there is a hearing to determine the adequacy of the disclosure. With prepackaged plans, the adequacy of the disclosure is evaluated under "applicable nonbankruptcy law, rule or regulation" or, if there is none, under the "adequate information" standard set forth in §1125(a)(1). In a "prenegotiated" plan, the details of a plan are negotiated prior to the filing of the petition. Solicitation, however, does not occur until after the filing.

Regardless of whether a plan is prepackaged or "prenegotiated," it must comply with the provisions of the Bankruptcy Code.

11 U.S.C. §1126 governs the acceptance and rejection of Chapter 11 reorganization plans, whether acceptance occurs before or after the commencement of the case. The adequacy of the Debtors' prepetition solicitation process is thus measured by this section, particularly §1126(b), which concerns acceptance of a plan before the commencement of case, and §1126(c), which defines "acceptance" of a plan.

ADEQUACY OF THE DEBTORS' SOLICITATION PROCESS

A.   The Consents Do Not Constitute Acceptance of the Second Amended Plan

Pursuant to 11 U.S.C. §1126(a) the "holder of a claim or interest" is entitled to accept or reject a plan. 11 U.S.C. §1126(c) states that "acceptance" occurs when "such plan has been accepted by creditors ... that hold at least two-thirds in amount and more than one-half in number of the allowed claims...." Under §1126(b), the holder of a claim or interest that has accepted or rejected "the plan" prepetition is deemed to have done so if the solicitation was in compliance with any applicable nonbankruptcy law or, if there is no such law, there was disclosure of "adequate information" under §1125(a).

In the instant case there has been no acceptance of "the plan" under §1126(b). Instead, under the language of the relevant documents, there has merely been an agreement to consent to some plan *in the future*. The Consenting Bondholders merely *agreed* to *agree* on a plan.

THE CONSENT FORM

Under the language of the Consent Form, a Consenting Bondholder merely *agreed* to *agree* on a future plan. The Consent Form stated the following, in pertinent part:

Part II—Consents
(To be completed by Holders who wish to consent to the Proposed Consents)

The undersigned is a Holder . . . of the [1988 Bonds]. As a Holder of such [1988 Bonds], *the undersigned hereby:*
Consents Does Not Consent
to the following in the event the Exchange Offer is not consummated (the "Proposed Consents"):

—— —— ——

3. *To consent to and support a plan of reorganization under Chapter 11 of the United States Bankruptcy Code* which provides for treatment of the [1988 Bonds] in a bankruptcy case under Chapter 11 of the Bankruptcy Code that is substantially similar to the treatment of the [1988 Bonds] offered in the Exchange (the "Plan"). Such support shall include, without limitation, (i) voting to accept the Plan and making reasonable efforts to obtain confirmation of the Plan, even if the Plan involves a "cramdown" under Section 1129(b) of the Bankruptcy Code of classes of claims or equity interests other than the class that includes the [1988 Bonds], (ii) not agreeing to, consenting to or voting for any plan that contains terms inconsistent with the Plan and (iii) not objecting to or otherwise commencing any proceeding to oppose or alter the Plan or making any action that is inconsistent with, or that would delay solicitation, confirmation, effectiveness or substantial consummation of the Plan.

(Emphasis added.)

THE EXCHANGE OFFER AND CONSENT SOLICITATION

The language of the Exchange Offer and Consent Solicitation also shows that the Consenting Bondholders merely *agreed* to *agree* on a future plan. That document states the following, at page 25:

> Concurrently with the Exchange Offer, [PFC] is seeking the Consents so that if the Minimum Condition or any other condition to the Exchange Offer is not satisfied and the Exchange Offer is not consummated, [PFC] will have the Consents of certain holders of [1988 Bonds] pursuant to which, among other things, the consenting Holders *agree to ... vote to accept a plan of reorganization which provides for treatment of the [1988 Bonds] in a bankruptcy case under Chapter 11 of the Bankruptcy Code that is substantially similar to the treatment of the [1988 Bonds] offered in the Exchange (the "Plan").*

(Emphasis added.)

THE AMENDED OFFER TO EXCHANGE

Similarly, the wording of the Amended Offer to Exchange is such that a Consenting Bondholder merely *agreed* to *agree* on a plan, and agreed to vote to accept *some plan in the future.* The Amended Offer to Exchange states the following, at page 11:

[PFC] is soliciting the consents (the "Consents") of the Holders to the following (the "Proposed Consents"), which will be effective only if the Exchange Offer is not consummated and valid consents are properly furnished by the Solicitation Expiration Date with respect to at least $42 million principal amount of [1988 Bonds]:

———————

To consent to and support a plan of reorganization under Chapter 11 of the Bankruptcy Code which provides for treatment of the [1988 Bonds] in a bankruptcy case under Chapter 11 of the Bankruptcy Code that is substantially similar to the treatment of the [1988 Bonds] offered in the Exchange; provided that (1) the additional Event of Default described under "Modifications to the Exchange Offer and Terms of the New Notes to be Issued in the Exchange Offer" will occur if the events contemplated by paragraphs (a) or (b) thereof have not occurred by the later of December 31, 1999 or six months after the date of a plan of reorganization is confirmed in a Chapter 11 case and (2) the Excess Cash Redemption obligation will commence on the first June 30 or December 31 following the date on which a plan of reorganization is confirmed (the "Plan"). Such support shall include, without limitation, (i) voting to accept the Plan and making reasonable efforts to obtain confirmation of the Plan, even if the Plan involves a "cramdown" under Section 1129(b) of the Bankruptcy Code of classes of claims, including the class that includes the [1988 Bonds] or equity interests, (ii) not agreeing to, consenting to, recommending or voting for any plan that contains terms inconsistent with the Plan, and (iii) not objecting to or otherwise commencing any proceeding to oppose or alter the Plan or taking any action that is inconsistent with, or that would delay solicitation, confirmation, effectiveness or substantial consummation of the Plan....

(Emphasis added.)

While it may be argued that the terms of the proposed Second Amended Plan substantially conform to the Offering, the Offering sought only the consent of Record Holders to a *future plan*. The Consents do not constitute acceptance of "the plan" under §1126(b). Indeed, the Debtors themselves have acknowledged that they did not present a plan or disclosure statement to the 1988 bondholders prepetition, and that "1988 Bondholders were not asked to vote on a specific plan, only to agree to support and vote for a plan embodying the Consent Solicitation."

Even if the Consents were to a present plan, however, the Offering is inadequate because it was sent only to the Record Holders.

B.   *Disclosure to Record Holders v. Beneficial Holders*

The Bankruptcy Code requires that a creditor receive adequate notice before its claim is impacted. In this regard, a prepetition solicitation process must be scrutinized to ensure that substantially all creditors who are affected by the plan receive notice. In this case, the Offering was sent only to the Record Holders.

The Record Holders, however, may or may not be the "holder of the claim" which is based upon the 1988 Bonds.

Pursuant to §1126(a), it is only the "holder of a claim or interest" who is entitled to vote on a plan. Under the Code, a holder of a "claim" is one who has a "right to payment." 11 U.S.C. §101(5)(A). Plainly, it is the beneficial holder, not a holder of record, who has the "claim" and the "right to payment."

Although Fed.R.Bankr.P. 3018 makes reference to the acceptance of a plan by a "holder of record," such language is at odds with §1126, which provides that it is the "holder of a claim or interest" who may accept or reject a plan. Nowhere does §1126(b) refer to "record holders." Where a bankruptcy rule affects a substantive change in the Code, the Code must prevail. *See also*, In re Southland Corp., 124 B.R. 211 (Bankr.N.D.Tex.1991) (Bankruptcy Rule 3018 references to "holder of record" as entity who may accept or reject plan is attempted substantive change in Bankruptcy Code, and does not prevail over identification of "holder of claim" as entity who may accept plan under §1126(b)).

Rule 3018(c) ("Form of Acceptance or Rejection") provides that an acceptance or rejection of a Chapter 11 plan may be made by an "authorized agent." Such authority, however, must be established. Here, there has been no showing that the Beneficial Holders authorized the Record Holders to accept the Consent Solicitation.

In In re Southland Corp., 124 B.R. 211 (Bankr.N.D.Tex.1991) the debtor, relying on Fed.R.Bankr.P. 3018, solicited only the record holders of claims by mailing the solicitation materials to broker dealers, who held the securities in street name. The court required that the votes be re-solicited using procedures designed to identify and obtain the vote of the beneficial holders, because there was no evidence of the authority of the record holders to vote on the plan. The court held that if votes were cast by broker-dealers or other representatives, there had to be certification of the representative's authority to vote. *Id.* at 227. As the *Southland* court stated:

> If the record holder of a debt is not the owner of a claim, or a true creditor, he may not vote validly to accept or reject, unless he is an authorized agent of the creditor, and this authority is established under appropriate bankruptcy law and rules.

Southland, 124 B.R. 211, 227 (Bankr.N.D.Tex.1991).

It is true that Section 308 of the Indenture states that the person in whose name the 1988 Bond is registered is treated as the "owner" for all purposes, and that §101 of the Indenture defines "bondholder" and "holder" as "a person in whose name a bond is registered on the bond register." The Indenture, however, does not control who has the authority to vote for a plan of reorganization under the Bankruptcy Code. While record holders may vote on behalf of beneficial holders outside of bankruptcy under the federal securities laws, under §1126 of the Bankruptcy Code it is the "holder of a claim or interest" who is entitled to receive a plan solicitation package and to vote. Having made the decision to file bankruptcy in order to restructure a debt which could not otherwise be contractually restructured outside bankruptcy, the Debtors must comply with the provisions of the Bankruptcy Code. There is simply no indication in the Bankruptcy Code or Rules that the notice required during a Chapter 11 solicitation process is superceded by federal securities law practices.

Although record holders may vote shares pursuant to the instructions of the beneficial owners under the securities laws, that process is designed to facilitate the rapid trading and marketability of securities. The Bankruptcy Code, however, concerns itself with providing full disclosure to creditors so that those creditors can cast their ballots intelligently. The Bankruptcy Code and the federal securities laws are simply different sets of laws with different purposes. There is no suggestion in Rule 3017(e) or the Committee Notes that practices developed under the federal securities laws have binding application to the chapter 11 voting process.

Moreover, Fed.R.Bankr.P. 3017(e) requires that the beneficial holders of bonds, not merely the record holders, must receive the disclosure statement, plan and ballot.

Thus, a pre-petition solicitation process is invalid where there is no evidence that the solicitation has been sent to beneficial bondholders, and no showing has been made that record holders have been authorized by beneficial holders to vote on their behalf.

The Debtors argue that outside bankruptcy, brokers cannot disclose the names of their customers to third parties, citing SEC Rule 14b-1(c) and 17 CFR §240.14(b)-1(c). The Court appreciates that there might be obligations outside bankruptcy to keep the identities of beneficial holders confidential. In a bankruptcy proceeding, however, Fed. R. Bankr.3017(e) provides a bankruptcy court wide latitude to fashion procedures to protect the confidentiality of the beneficial bondholders. Rule 3017(e) empowers a bankruptcy court to "determine the adequacy of the procedures" for transmitting disclosure to beneficial holders and to "enter any orders the court deems appropriate." While such procedures will most likely vary according to the specific facts of a case, they might include requiring affidavits from record holders who attest that a solicitation was transmitted to the beneficial holders. Alternatively, a consent form could contain a place where a beneficial bondholder could indicate that he or she has seen the solicitation and either does or does not authorize the record holder to vote in its behalf.

Given the Court's holding that there has not been an acceptance of a plan as provided for under §1126(b), the Court need not reach the Debtors' argument that §1125(a) does not have to be satisfied because the debtors have complied with "applicable nonbankruptcy law" governing disclosure.

For the reasons set forth above, the motion is hereby denied.

It is often difficult to identify the beneficial holders of publicly held debt. As such, firms soliciting votes from beneficial holders must do so through the cooperation of the record holders, which will then pass the solicitation information down the chain to the beneficial holders and seek instructions on how to vote. The information must then be passed back up the chain to the debtor firm. The entire process must be documented and presented to the bankruptcy court to enable a finding that votes were properly solicited from the beneficial holders.

3.   TAX ISSUES

Knowing you are already expert in the issue of tax and debt, here is the relevant tax discussion from the MGM disclosure statement:

A. Certain U.S. Federal Income Tax Consequences to the Debtors

1. Cancellation of Indebtedness Income

In general, the discharge of a debt obligation in exchange for cash and other property having a fair market value (or, in the case of a new debt instrument, an "issue price") less than the "adjusted issue price" of the debt gives rise to cancellation of indebtedness (*"COD"*) income to the debtor. However, COD income is not taxable to the debtor if the debt discharge occurs in a Title 11 bankruptcy case. Rather, under the Tax Code, such COD income instead will reduce certain of the Debtors' tax attributes, generally in the following order: (a) net operating losses (*"NOLs"*) and NOL carryforwards; (b) general business credit carryforwards; (c) minimum tax credit carryforwards; (d) capital loss carryforwards; (e) the tax basis of the Debtors' depreciable and nondepreciable assets (but not below the amount of its liabilities immediately after the discharge); and (f) foreign tax credit carryforwards. A debtor may elect to alter the preceding order of attribute reduction and, instead, first reduce the tax basis of its depreciable assets (and, possibly, the depreciable assets of its subsidiaries). Where the debtor joins in the filing of a consolidated U.S. federal income tax return, applicable Treasury Regulations require, in certain circumstances, that certain tax attributes of the consolidated subsidiaries of the debtor and other members of the group be reduced. The reduction in tax attributes occurs only after the tax for the year of the debt discharge has been determined (i.e., such attributes may be available to offset taxable income that accrues between the date of discharge and the end of the Debtors' tax year). Any excess COD income over the amount of available tax attributes is not subject to United States federal income tax and has no other United States federal income tax impact.

The Debtors expect to realize a substantial amount of COD income as a result of the discharge of obligations pursuant to the Plan, which, under the attribute reduction rules described above, is expected to result in the substantial reduction of the Debtors' NOLs, and of certain other U.S. federal income tax attributes of the Debtors, including basis in the assets (the *"Attribute Reduction"*).

2. *Net Operating Losses—Section 382*

In 2005, the Debtors experienced an "ownership change" (within the meaning of Section 382 of the Tax Code) (the *"Ownership Change"*) as a result of which the Debtors' ability to use any pre-Ownership Change NOLs and certain other tax attributes is subject to an annual limitation. The Debtors anticipate that they will experience a second "ownership change" on the Effective Date as a result of the issuance of the New Common Stock to the Holders of Claims, Spyglass, and the C/G Stockholders pursuant to the Plan. As a result, the Debtors' ability to use any pre-Effective Date NOLs or other tax attributes to offset their income in any post-Effective Date taxable year (and in the portion of the taxable year of the ownership change following the Effective Date) to which such a carryforward is made generally (subject to various exceptions and adjustments, some of which are described below) will be subject to a second annual limitation. Subject to the discussion below, the annual limitation under Section 382 of the Tax Code is generally equal to the product of (i) the "long-term tax exempt" (for example, 3.98% for ownership changes occurring during the month of October 2010) and (ii) the fair market value of the stock of the corporation immediately before the ownership change occurs. Under section 382 of the Tax Code, NOLs attributable to a period preceding an earlier ownership change are treated as pre-change losses with respect to later ownership changes with the result that such NOLs always will be subject to the smaller of the earlier annual limitation and any later annual limitations. Thus, the second ownership change may cause pre-Ownership Change NOLs which survive the Attribute Reduction, if any, to be more significantly limited than they currently are and will subject the use of NOLs generated following the earlier ownership change which survive Attribute Reduction, if any, to an annual limit. Section 382 of the Tax Code may also limit the Debtors' ability to use "net unrealized built-in losses" to offset future taxable income. Moreover, the Debtors' loss carryforwards will be subject to further limitations if the Debtors experience additional future ownership changes and could potentially be reduced to zero if they do not continue their business enterprise for at least two years following the Effective Date.

If the Debtors are qualified to use the special rules for corporations in bankruptcy provided in section 382(1)(5) of the Tax Code, and do not elect out of that provision, then, to the extent that the Debtors have post-Ownership Change NOLs that survive the Attribute Reduction, the application of section 382 of the Tax Code will be materially different from that just described. In that case, the Debtors' ability to utilize post-Ownership Change NOLs generated prior to the Effective Date would not be limited as described in the preceding paragraph. However, several other limitations would apply to the Debtors under section 382(1)(5) of the Tax Code, including (a) the Debtors' NOLs would be calculated without taking into account deductions for interest paid or accrued in the portion of the current tax year ending on the Effective Date and all other tax years ending during the three-year period prior to the current tax year with respect to the Claims that are exchanged for New Common Stock pursuant to the Plan, and (b) if the Debtors undergo another ownership change within two years after the Effective Date, the Debtors' section 382 limitation with respect to that ownership change will be zero. Even if section 382(1)(5) of the Tax Code is available, the Debtors could elect not to apply the special rules of section 382(1)(5).

If the Debtors do not qualify for, or elect not to apply, the special rule under section 382(1)(5) of the Tax Code for corporations in bankruptcy described above, then, to the extent that the Debtors have post-Ownership Change NOLs that survive the Attribute Reduction, a different rule under section 382(1)(6) of the Tax Code applicable to corporations under the jurisdiction of a bankruptcy court may apply in calculating the annual section 382 limitation applicable to post-Ownership Change NOLs generated prior to the Effective Date. Under this rule, the limitation will be calculated by reference to the lesser of the value of the company's new stock (with certain adjustments) immediately after the ownership change or the value of such company's assets (determined without regard to liabilities) immediately before the ownership change. Although such calculation may substantially increase the annual section 382 limitation, the Debtors' use of NOLs or other tax attributes remaining after implementation of the Plan, if any, may still be substantially limited after an ownership change.

Because Holders of Class 3 Claims will hold a significant equity position in Reorganized Holdings following the consummation of the Plan, disposition by such persons or entities of all or a significant amount of this position after the Effective Date, could cause the Reorganized Debtors to undergo a subsequent ownership change. This would generally further limit (or possibly eliminate) the Reorganized Debtors' ability to use NOLs and other tax attributes.

In the prior chapter it was indicated that reorganization under the Bankruptcy Code was generally preferable to an exchange offer from a tax standpoint. Why then does MGM's discussion appear so gloomy?

4.   VENUE ISSUES

Very large chapter 11 cases tend to file either in the Southern District of New York or in Delaware. Under current law, debtors can file in one of three places: (a) their state of incorporation, (b) their principal place of business, or (c) a district where a related bankruptcy case is already pending.

The first one helps Delaware attract cases, the second helps the SDNY, since many businesses can argue that they have a key corporate office in New York City, and the third helps corporate groups file in either New York or Delaware, as one company in the group is apt to qualify under either the first or second test. While in practice, your author more than once filed the bankruptcy petition for an obscure subsidiary, only to then hand over the "related" petition of a Fortune 500 parent company.

Because Delaware and New York are obvious locales for so many large chapter 11 cases, the judges have lots of corporate restructuring experience. This in turn brings yet more large chapter 11 cases, from bankruptcy attorneys who appreciate having a judge who "gets it."

Prepackaged chapter 11 cases are especially likely to file in one of these two jurisdictions, because having a judge who "gets it" is important to realizing the benefits of a prepackaged case. But it is generally indisputable that prepackaged cases have a much higher refiling rate than other, more traditional types of chapter 11 cases. That is, a debtor reorganized under a prepackaged case is apt to need to go through a traditional chapter 11 case nonetheless.

Not everyone thinks this forum shopping is ideal. Most notably, UCLA law professor Lynn LoPucki, often with various coauthors, has argued in a controversial book and several articles that this represents "corruption" of the bankruptcy system.[2] And he argues that cases that file in New York or Delaware more often "fail"—his word for refiling—because of these jurisdictions' desire to appease large New York law firms that bring interesting cases to their courts. That is, the courts go easy on debtors, leading to a higher refiling rate.

But not everyone agrees with professor LoPucki's characterization of the issue.[3] Nonetheless, there are some indications that the United States Trustee's Office, part of the Justice Department that monitors bankruptcy cases, is sensitive to suggestions that prepackaged cases, in particular, engage in forum shopping.

IN RE HOUGHTON MIFFLIN HARCOURT PUBLISHING COMPANY

474 B.R. 122
United States Bankruptcy Court, S.D. New York.
June 22, 2012.

Robert E. GERBER, Bankruptcy Judge.
In this contested matter in the jointly administered chapter 11 cases of debtor Houghton Mifflin Harcourt Publishing Company ("**Publishing**") and 24 affiliates, who filed these cases with a prepackaged plan of reorganization that secured the unanimous support of their creditors, the United States Trustee Program ("**UST** ") moves, pursuant to 28 U.S.C. §1406 and Fed.R.Bankr.P. 1014(a)(2), to transfer the venue of these cases elsewhere.

The UST, over the objection of the Debtors and all of the creditors who have weighed in on the matter, contends that venue in this district never was proper, for failure to satisfy the requirements of the relevant statute, 28 U.S.C. §1408. Under these circumstances, the UST contends, dismissal or transfer is mandatory under §1406. The UST further contends that the fact that a transfer would be much more expensive and much less convenient for the Debtors' creditors— especially since we here have a prepack, where the case otherwise would be over in 30 days—does not matter.

For the latter reason, the UST's prosecution of this motion has been perplexing to the Court—not because it is in any way improper, but as a matter of

---

2. *E.g.,* Lynn M. LoPucki, *Courting Failure: How Competition for Big Cases Is Corrupting the Bankruptcy Courts* (2005); Lynn M. LoPucki & Joseph W. Doherty, *Delaware Bankruptcy: Failure in the Ascendancy,* 73 U. Chi. L. Rev. 1387, 1418-1419 (2006); Lynn M. LoPucki & Sarah D. Kalin, *The Failure of Public Company Bankruptcies in Delaware and New York: Empirical Evidence of a "Race to the Bottom,"* 54 Vand. L. Rev. 231, 271 (2001).

3. Melissa B. Jacoby, *Fast, Cheap, and Creditor-Controlled: Is Corporate Reorganization Failing?,* 54 Buff. L. Rev. 401 (2006); Stephen J. Lubben, *Delaware's Irrelevance,* 16 Am. Bankr. Inst. L. Rev. 267 (2008); Todd J. Zywicki, *Is Forum Shopping Corrupting America's Bankruptcy Courts?,* 94 Geo. L.J. 1141 (2006).

prosecutorial discretion, since venue concerns can be waived, by creditors and the UST alike, and here any venue deficiencies were not a matter of concern to the Debtors' creditors. Venue objections of course should be raised, by the UST and creditors alike, when a debtor's venue choice is prejudicial to the creditor community. But here the venue choice was exactly what the creditors wanted; the case, if not slowed down by the UST's motion, would be over in 30 days; and the UST's motion was opposed by every party in the case with money on the line.

But with that said, the Court acts in accordance with the requirements of law. Once a §1406 motion has been filed, §1406 and its related caselaw leave the Court with no discretion. Here the Court must find, as a mixed question of fact and law, that the statutory requirements for venue in this district were not satisfied. The UST's motion having been filed, it thus must be granted, subject only to determining when and where to effect the transfer.

But while the Court has no discretion to retain the case, it still has the ability to reduce the prejudice to the creditors that an immediate transfer would entail. Venue, even if improper, is not jurisdictional. While §1406 mandates transfer or dismissal when statutory venue requirements have not been met, it does not dictate *when* the transfer must take place, nor does it foreclose steps in the interim to protect the creditors who might be harmed thereby.

Thus the Court will effect the transfer at a time that decreases the resulting prejudice to creditors, the Debtors, and the Debtors' employees. The case will be transferred on the first to occur of the Effective Date or three weeks from the date of entry of the confirmation order, if for some reason the Plan has not gone effective by then.

The Court's Findings of Fact, Conclusions of Law, and bases for the exercise of its discretion follow.

FACTS

1.   BACKGROUND

The Debtors are in the publishing business, most significantly in textbooks used in elementary and secondary schools. Their enterprise is large. At the time of filing, the Debtors' combined assets (at book value) were reported to be $2.68 billion, and their total liabilities were said to be $3.54 billion. They had combined revenues of approximately $1.3 billion, and adjusted EBITDA of $238 million, in calendar year 2011. As described in their first day papers (and as unchallenged by the UST), the Debtors' financial difficulties were occasioned by excessive debt and a sharp decrease in demand for their product, particularly as a consequence of financial stress on their customers—state and municipal governments who were victims of the financial crisis of 2007-2008 and decreases in financial assistance from the federal government.

To address their difficulties, the Debtors engaged in prepetition discussions with their creditors to restructure their debt, leading to prepetition agreement on a consensual reorganization plan. Acceptances of a prepackaged plan of reorganization were sought and obtained before the filing of the Debtors' chapter 11 cases.

The prepackaged plan emerged from an agreement between the Debtors and an informal creditor group ("**Informal Creditor Group**") of holders of secured debt, which is one of the several parties that, along with the Debtors, oppose the UST's motion. The ultimately successful negotiations led to a plan support agreement (the "**Plan Support Agreement**") embodying the deal points that found their way into the ultimately accepted prepackaged plan. Though it is not relevant to matters that are purely questions of law (and is relevant only to matters of discretion, if that), the Plan Support Agreement *required* that the chapter 11 cases be filed in the Southern District of New York.[4]

In its simplest terms, the prepackaged plan provided for the conversion of billions of dollars of secured debt into equity. Significantly, the plan left general unsecured claims—most significantly, trade claims from the vendor community and tort claims—unimpaired. The idea, to be implemented by a confirmation hearing based on the plan acceptances that had been obtained prepetition, was to make the Debtors' chapter 11 cases as quick and painless for their creditors (especially their trade creditors) as possible. The plan was unanimously accepted by the Debtors' creditors. A confirmation hearing on the already-accepted plan was scheduled for a date only slightly after the earliest date permissible under the Federal Rules of Bankruptcy Procedure. Unless delayed as a consequence of the UST's motion, the case could be over in about 30 days.

While the UST was free to solicit membership in an official committee of unsecured creditors, no creditors' committee was formed, as there was insufficient interest in forming one. The unsecured creditors who, in another case, would form the natural constituency for such a creditors' committee here would be unimpaired.

2. THE DEBTORS' CHAPTER 11 FILINGS

On May 21, 2012, the 25 Debtors commenced these chapter 11 cases, one after another in quick succession. The first of the cases to be filed on the Court's docket (assuming that it matters) was Publishing, the Debtors' primary operating company. Publishing is a Delaware corporation, with its principal place of business in Boston, Massachusetts. The fourth of the Debtors to file was

---

4. Apart from choice of law issues that were articulated by Debtors' counsel in oral argument, the desire for a filing in New York is partly explained by a point made by the Informal Creditor Group. The latter notes that the agent for the DIP Credit Facility and proposed exit facility, Citibank, N.A. ("Citibank") (which likewise opposes the UST's motion), and substantially all of the senior creditors who are parties to the Plan Support Agreement are located in New York—as are the attorneys for each of the Debtors, the Informal Creditor Group, the first lien secured debt agents and the DIP lenders. The Informal Creditor Group points out that "transferring venue to a different district would appreciably increase professional fees and expenses in these cases." (Informal Creditor Group Br. at 4.) That point is not disputed by the UST, but is argued to be irrelevant.

Houghton Mifflin Holding Company ("**HoldCo**"), also a Delaware corporation, the location of whose principal assets is a matter of dispute between the parties, but whose principal place of business is indisputably in Boston, Massachusetts. The Debtors assert that venue in New York was proper for each of Publishing and HoldCo, and thus that venue in New York for their debtor affiliates was proper as well.

To the extent that the principal places of business of the other Debtors are relevant (though the Court does not believe that they are), they are likewise in Massachusetts, or at least in places other than New York. None of the Debtors is organized under the laws of New York. Most of the Debtors (15 of the 25) are Delaware corporations.

To the extent that the "nerve center" of the entire corporate enterprise—as contrasted to that of any individual Debtor—is relevant (though again, given the underlying basis for the motion here, the Court does not believe that it is), the "nerve center" of the entire corporate enterprise is in Boston, Massachusetts— where "Houghton Mifflin Harcourt Publishing" (without being more specific as to what individual corporations were encompassed under that appellation) was identified by the Boston Redevelopment Authority as one of Boston's largest employers.

3.   FACTS AS TO PUBLISHING AND HOLDCO

The first of the two key debtors, Publishing, has an office at 215 Park Avenue South in Manhattan, where Publishing leases the 12th floor and a portion of the 11th floor. At that office, Publishing employs 60 full-time employees; it also has 15 sales representatives associated with its New York office who work from their homes. That is enough for the Court to find that Publishing does business in the state of New York. But the Court does not understand the Debtors to argue, and in any event does not find, that such is sufficient for the Court to find that Publishing's principal place of business is in New York.

The second of the two key debtors, HoldCo, identified its basis for venue as the presence of its corporate affiliates when it first filed its petition on May 21. Eleven days later, HoldCo filed an amended petition, changing its stated basis for venue to its "domicile, residence, principal place of business or principal assets." HoldCo also changed the location of its principal assets from "N/A" to an address in Manhattan. Later, in their brief in opposition to the motion, the Debtors made clear that HoldCo was relying on the "principal assets" basis, premised on leased and subleased space in New York City.

HoldCo premised its venue assertions on space it leased and then subleased— described on the lease as "Room 815, 1350 Avenue of the Americas" (the "**Sixth Avenue Space**")—in Manhattan. The Sixth Avenue Space formerly served as the domestic office of a previous parent company, Education Media and Publishing Group International. However, HoldCo does not currently conduct operations in the Sixth Avenue Space or otherwise occupy it. Instead, it "is currently subleased *entirely* to an outside, nonaffiliated entity."

HoldCo pays its lessor approximately $415,000 per year for the Sixth Avenue Space, while receiving only $220,000 per year from its sublessee. The prime lease is a net cash drain, which might nevertheless have value if benefits were being obtained from it, but there is no showing of benefits here. Based on the record before the Court, the Sixth Avenue Space is money losing on a cash flow basis. Nor does the Court have evidence from which it could find, if that were so, that the Sixth Avenue Space is at a below-market rate—and thus would have intrinsic economic value to HoldCo as a valuable asset to be retained or that could be put up for sale to a prospective purchaser. The Court can and does find that the lease and sublease are assets of the HoldCo estate, but it cannot find, on the record before it, that they have any material value.

Additionally, however, the Court is compelled to find that the Debtor's presentation of HoldCo's asset mix was, until corrected at oral argument, materially inaccurate. In the Debtors' objection, the Court was told that "[HoldCo] has no other assets besides its rights under the lease and sublease described herein." But the Court cannot find that to be true. Rather, the Court finds that HoldCo was called a "Holding Company" for a reason. It had 15 direct and indirect subsidiaries. When HoldCo filed, it owned the stock of a subsidiary, Houghton Mifflin, LLC ("**LLC Sub**"), a Delaware corporation that also is a debtor in this case. LLC Sub had two subsidiaries of its own, debtor Houghton Mifflin Finance, Inc. ("**Finance**"), a Delaware corporation, and debtor Houghton Mifflin Holdings, Inc. ("**Holdings**"), also a Delaware corporation. And while Finance had no lower level subsidiaries, Holdings did: HM Publishing Corp. ("**HM Publishing**"), which also is a debtor in this case.

Then, HM Publishing had two subsidiaries, debtor Publishing (the first company to file, as discussed above), and HM Receivables Co. II, LLC ("**Receivables**"), apparently a nondebtor.

Finally, but importantly, one of the two subsidiaries of HM Publishing—debtor Houghton Mifflin Harcourt Publishing Company (the same company that was defined above as "Publishing")—which was the first of the 25 debtors to file, and which was designated by the Debtors as the "lead" case (though such designation is of no significance on this motion), had *nine* subsidiaries (the "**Nine Subsidiaries**"), seven of which are debtors here. Unlike the other debtors, Publishing showed very substantial assets on its petition. Publishing checked the "More than $1 billion" box for "Estimated Assets." More significantly, assets of $2.407 billion were reported for Publishing in the Debtors' Rule 1007-2 Declaration (though these were at book value, which for most businesses is not necessarily the same as market value), and Publishing was the source of the overwhelming bulk of the Debtors' $238 million in 2011 EBITDA, an important metric by which companies are valued.

All 12 of the direct and indirect subsidiaries of HoldCo that are debtors showed a street address in Boston. There was no argument here that the locale of any of the Debtors' stock should be found to be anywhere other than in Boston.

No evidence was introduced as to the value of the LLC Sub stock, or (as such might affect the value of LLC Sub stock) the value of the stock of LLC Sub's direct and indirect subsidiaries Finance, Holdings, HM Publishing, Receivables, Publishing, or the Nine Subsidiaries. Nor was evidence submitted as to the extent to which HoldCo had other contractual rights or intangible assets, like tax attributes, such as net operating losses ("**NOLs**"), though it appears that at least some of these subsidiaries, or their predecessors, at least once had business operations, and lost money, requiring a restructuring of their operations—facts that tend to telegraph the presence of NOLs, though of course any NOLs might belong to another entity. HoldCo reported "Estimated Assets" of "$100,001 to $500,000" on its amended petition (a change from "$0 to $50,000" on its original petition), but was otherwise silent as to their nature or value. However, since competent debtor counsel do not put entities into chapter 11 for no reason, the Court must infer, and finds, that one or more of LLC Sub, Finance, Holdings, HM Publishing, the Nine Subsidiaries, and, of course, Publishing had significant assets to protect. They generated nearly a quarter of a billion dollars in EBITDA.

In any event, the Court is not in a position to find, and cannot find, that HoldCo's money-losing contractual rights for the Sixth Avenue Space were worth more than its direct and indirect ownership of no less than 15 separate subsidiaries, one of which represented its assets as worth more than a billion dollars, and was the source of nearly all of the Debtors' $238 million in EBITDA.

4.   PROCEDURAL MATTERS

During the first day hearings on May 22, the UST articulated venue as a concern. The UST's rights were reserved; findings in the proposed orders that venue was proper were removed; and the Debtors' first day motions were otherwise granted.

One of those motions was to set a date for the confirmation hearing with respect to the previously solicited, and unanimously accepted, plan. Another was a routine motion for joint administration of the Debtors' 25 separate chapter 11 cases. As the Debtors put it, "[Publishing] initially was selected by the Debtors as the lead-filing entity and the lead-captioned entity in the Debtors' motion for joint administration." As the UST put it, the joint administration motion was granted, "under the caption, 'In re Houghton Mifflin Publishing Company, *et al.*;' thus identifying the first-filed debtor, [Publishing], as the 'lead debtor' of these mega cases." Each statement is true, but irrelevant.

On May 30, with confirmation scheduled for June 21, the UST moved to transfer these cases. The UST sought to file its motion on shortened notice. By endorsed order, the Court denied the request for a shortening of time, stating, among other things, that "[t]his matter is too important to be heard without giving the stakeholders in this case, whose money is on the line, the normal opportunity to respond."

DISCUSSION

I. STATUTORY & RULE PROVISIONS

Venue for cases—as contrasted to proceedings[5]—under the Bankruptcy Code is addressed under 28 U.S.C. §1408, one of the several provisions of chapter 87 of the Judicial Code (which starts with §1390 and goes on to §1413) that address venue for matters in the federal district courts.
Section 1408 provides:

> Except as provided in section 1410 of this title,[6] a case under title 11 may be commenced in the district court for the district—
>
> (1) in which the domicile, residence, principal place of business in the United States, or principal assets in the United States, of the person or entity that is the subject of such case have been located for the one hundred and eighty days immediately preceding such commencement, or for a longer portion of such one-hundred-and-eighty-day period than the domicile, residence, or principal place of business, in the United States, or principal assets in the United States, of such person were located in any other district; or
>
> (2) in which there is pending a case under title 11 concerning such person's affiliate, general partner, or partnership.

Thus a non-chapter 15 case under the Bankruptcy Code may properly be brought in a district passing muster under one of the four enumerated bases for venue set forth in §1408(1) (*i.e.*, domicile, residence, principal place of business or principal assets), or under the fifth basis, set forth in §1408(2), a district "in which there is pending" a case "concerning such person's affiliate, general partner, or partnership."

From time to time, a case under the Bankruptcy Code may be filed in a district that passes muster under one of the five bases just noted, but is less convenient for parties or otherwise less than optimum in the interests of justice. Also, from

---

5. As the Court has previously explained, *see, e.g.*, Buena Vista Television v. Adelphia Communications Corp. *(In re Adelphia Communications Corp.)*, 307 B.R. 404, 413 n. 22 (Bankr.S.D.N.Y.2004), "case" as used in bankruptcy parlance is a word of art—referring to that which is commenced by the filing for a petition for relief under the Bankruptcy Code, and refers to the umbrella case under which many individual proceedings—applications, motions, contested matters and adversary proceedings—are heard. "Case" is the modern way of referring to what was commonly referred to as a "proceeding" under the former Bankruptcy Act. Though many unfamiliar with bankruptcy practice still refer to a bankruptcy "proceeding" when they should be referring to a bankruptcy "case," it should be understood that a "proceeding" as used in the Judicial Code, 28 U.S.C., is a matter that comes up in a "case," or is a separate proceeding (like an adversary proceeding) brought in connection with a "case." The appropriate venue for "proceedings" under the Bankruptcy Code is governed by a different provision of the Judicial Code, 28 U.S.C. §1409.

6. The exception addressed in §1410 is for cases, in aid of foreign insolvency proceedings, that are brought under chapter 15 of the Bankruptcy Code.

time to time, a case under the Bankruptcy Code may be filed in a district where none of the five enumerated bases has been satisfied. Two of the Judicial Code's venue provisions deal with changes in the venue for bankruptcy cases under such circumstances—one plainly, and one under the bulk of the applicable authority.

Without doubt, 28 U.S.C. §1412 applies to transfers of cases (and also, though not relevant here, proceedings) under the Bankruptcy Code. It provides:

> A district court[7] may transfer a case or proceeding under title 11 to a district court for another district, in the interest of justice or for the convenience of the parties.

Notably, §1412 is permissive; it says that a district court "*may* transfer a case" "in the interest of justice or for the convenience of the parties." It does not say that the court *must* do so.

Nevertheless, the Court concludes, reluctantly, that it should follow the majority on this issue. The Court comes to that view not by counting noses, but by an amalgam of textual analysis; comparison of former §1477 with §1406 and §1412;36 Bankruptcy Rule 1014(a)'s 1987 Advisory Committee comment; and respect for precedent in the Southern District of New York.

Thus the Court concludes that §1406 applies, at least in the first instance, if the Court cannot find one of §1408's five bases for venue to have been satisfied.

II.   COMPLIANCE WITH §1408

Turning then to consideration of those prospective bases for venue, the Court is compelled to find that none here has been satisfied.

The Debtors base venue for the 25 cases in their corporate enterprise on an amalgam of §1408(2) (providing venue for corporate affiliates if venue is proper for any of them), and §1408(1) compliance by either Publishing or HoldCo. But the Court cannot find satisfaction of any of the four bases under §1408(1) for either of those two key Debtors.

III.   CONVENIENCE OF PARTIES AND INTERESTS OF JUSTICE

The Debtors and their creditors speak at length as to how transfer would be destructive to creditor interests, to the great expense and inconvenience of the parties (especially creditors), and the exact opposite of the interests of justice. Their showing in that regard is overwhelming. They would win in a heartbeat if this were a motion under §1412.

---

7. It will be remembered that bankruptcy courts are arms of the district court, with bankruptcy judges presiding over cases under the Bankruptcy Code under orders of reference from their respective district courts. Thus, as a practical matter, while district judges occasionally preside over bankruptcy cases and may be called upon to make like decisions when sitting as bankruptcy courts of original jurisdiction, most decisions under 28 U.S.C. §1412 are made by bankruptcy judges.

But the problem is that this motion is under §1406. On a §1406 motion, the Court's hands are tied by statutory and case law when venue is unsupportable under §1408. That is the exact point of the majority in the split between the majority and minority courts construing §1406. The parties, and the Court, are ultimately subject to the good sense of parties who have standing to make §1406 motions, including the UST, which has the power to make a motion like this under section 307 of the Bankruptcy Code, and the ability, like any other party, to waive any deficiencies that might otherwise lie. The answer, to the extent there is an answer, is for the UST to exercise prosecutorial discretion in deciding when to make motions like this one, keeping in mind the interests of the creditors who would be affected by the motion's outcome.

IV. TIMING OF TRANSFER

As is apparent from the foregoing, the Court acts in accordance with the requirements of law. With the UST having made this motion, and the Court having found insufficient compliance with §1408, the Court will order the requested transfer. But §1406 requires only that the Court dismiss or transfer. It does not say when, and does not tie the hands of a court in mitigating the resulting damage to the creditor community.

The UST has cited no case, nor is the Court aware of one, that has determined that the Court must effect any required dismissal or transfer under any particular timetable dictated by law. Undoubtedly, any required action cannot be pocket vetoed or delayed for an indefinite period, but everything in the venue jurisprudence emphasizes the goal, and ability, of judges to protect the creditors and other stakeholders in the cases on those judges' watch. The Court will implement the decision it is required to make under a timetable that minimizes (though it may not wholly eliminate) the harm to the creditors and other stakeholders that this motion engendered.

As it announced that it would at the conclusion of oral argument on the UST's motion, the Court went forward with the confirmation hearing that was scheduled for this week, denying a UST request (in its objection to confirmation) that the confirmation hearing not be held. Similarly, the Court believes that it should not stay the Plan's Effective Date by reason of the UST's venue concerns. Venue objections, even if valid, are not jurisdictional. *Collier* notes that "[a]s is true with respect to venue generally, venue of a case can be waived by express agreement or by conduct." And the venue statute upon which the UST moves, §1406, effectively says the same thing.

It was shown, without dispute by the UST, that delaying the confirmation hearing, or the Effective Date if the Plan were confirmed, would materially prejudice the creditors in this case (who, it will be recalled, unanimously approved the prepackaged plan) and the Debtors and their employees—whose understandable goal was, as Citibank notes, to achieve their reorganization quickly and without the resulting damage of a lengthy chapter 11 case.[8] Delaying that confirmation hearing would have been materially prejudicial to the interests of the creditors whose money here is on the line.

The case will be transferred on the first to occur of the Effective Date or three weeks from the date of entry of the confirmation order, if for some reason the Plan has not gone effective by then. The Court understands and will respect the desires of the stakeholders here to conclude this case quickly, but will have doubts as to their commitment to that goal if the Plan has not gone effective by that time.

V.   FUTURE PROCEEDINGS

Though the Court has determined that it must transfer this case, another question remains: to where? The leading contender might well be Massachusetts. But any other district in which the cases could properly have been filed (as the Court now knows the facts, the Districts of Colorado, Delaware, New Hampshire or Wyoming, or one of the districts in California, Illinois or Texas) would also appear to be permissible.

The Debtors, the Informal Creditor Group, Citibank and the UST (if it cares) are to consult with each other to reach agreement, if possible, on the particular district to which these cases will be transferred. In the event of an inability to agree, they are to submit simultaneous letters to the Court, explaining the bases for their preferences, after which the Court will decide.

CONCLUSION

For the foregoing reasons, the Court determines that the requirements for venue in the Southern District of New York, as set forth in 28 U.S.C. §1408, were not satisfied. Though a transfer would here be prejudicial to the interests of creditors, the Court has sworn to comply with the law. The Court thus will transfer these cases to a district where venue would be proper under §1408.

The Court will, however, effect the transfer at a time that minimizes the resulting prejudice to creditors, the Debtors, and the Debtors' employees. The case will be transferred on the first to occur of (x) the Effective Date or (y) three weeks from the date of entry of the confirmation order, if for some reason the Plan has not gone effective by then.

---

8. In its decision in *General Motors*, the Court noted, repeatedly, how debtors and their stakeholders can be grievously injured, and value can be destroyed, when chapter 11 cases are not concluded quickly. *See* In re General Motors Corp., 407 B.R. 463, 479, 480, 484, 485, 491, 493 (Bankr.S.D.N.Y.2009), *stay pending appeal denied*, 2009 WL 2033079 (S.D.N.Y.2009) (Kaplan, J.), *appeal dismissed and aff'd*, 428 B.R. 43 (S.D.N.Y.2010) (Buchwald, J.) and 430 B.R. 65 (S.D.N.Y.2010) (Sweet, J.), *appeal dismissed*, No. 10-4882-bk (2d Cir. Jul. 28, 2011). Those concerns are even more applicable with respect to prepacks, which are agreed to by creditors on the assumption that they will proceed through bankruptcy with the unusual speed for prepackaged plans for which the Bankruptcy Code provides.

Provisions consistent with the foregoing may appear in the confirmation order, if the Debtors desire, or in a separate order if they prefer. In either case, decretal language implementing this ruling must be submitted promptly. If the plan supporters and the UST cannot agree upon the form of the order or any implementing decretal provisions, either side may settle an order.

28

INTRODUCTION TO CHAPTER 11

Even if you have not taken Bankruptcy, the coming chapters should be easy because you've now completed a lot of corporate law classes. Chapter 11 is simply another type of corporate negotiation, although bankruptcy attorneys have a certain kind of mystique (a nerdy mystique, granted) because they understand "the Code." In this respect they are kind of like tax lawyers.

To become a truly good corporate lawyer you will want some understanding of bankruptcy because it will help you be a better transactional lawyer: You will be able to anticipate future problems and address them up front in the deal documents. Moreover, from a self-interested perspective, knowing something about chapter 11 makes you more valuable in economic downturns.

We begin at the beginning, with the consideration of what kinds of firms can file chapter 11 bankruptcy petitions.

IN RE INTERVENTION ENERGY HOLDINGS, LLC

553 B.R. 258
United States Bankruptcy Court, D. Delaware.
June 3, 2016.

KEVIN J. CAREY, U.S. BANKRUPTCY JUDGE

BACKGROUND

Before the Court is the EIG Energy Fund XV–A, L.P. Motion to Dismiss the Chapter 11 Cases of Intervention Energy Holdings, LLC and Intervention Energy, LLC (the "EIG MTD").

PROCEDURAL BACKGROUND

On May 20, 2016, Intervention Energy Holdings, LLC ("IE Holdings") and Intervention Energy, LLC ("IE") (together, in these jointly administered proceedings, the "Debtors") filed a voluntary chapter 11 bankruptcy petition in the United States Bankruptcy Court for the District of Delaware (the "Voluntary Petition"). On May 24, 2016, EIG Energy Fund XV–A, L.P. (hereinafter referred to as "EIG")[1] filed the EIG MTD asserting, among other things, that IE Holdings was not authorized to file the Voluntary Petition. EIG argues that, absent its consent to commence a chapter 11 case, IE Holdings lacked authority to file the Voluntary Petition under the Intervention Energy Holdings, LLC Second Amended and Restated Limited Liability Company Agreement (the "Operating Agreement"), which requires "approval of *all* Common Members ... [to] commence a voluntary case under any bankruptcy." For purposes of disposition of this part of the EIG MTD, the material facts are not in dispute.

At the May 26, 2016, hearing on first day motions, the Court scheduled briefing and argument, limited to the issue of whether IE Holdings lacked authority to file its chapter 11 petition.

FACTUAL BACKGROUND

IE Holdings and IE are limited liability companies formed in 2007, and governed under the laws of the State of Delaware. They are private, non-operated oil and natural gas exploration and production companies, almost entirely located in North Dakota. IE Holdings is owned as follows: 84.73%— Intervention Energy Investment Holdings, LLC ("IEIH"); 15.27%–various business and individual investors. IE Holdings issued 22,000,001 Common Units: IEIH holds 22,000,0000 Common Units and EIG holds but one Common Unit. IE is a wholly-owned subsidiary of IE Holdings. EIG is an institutional investor specializing in private investments in global energy, resource, and related infrastructure projects and companies.

On January 6, 2012, the Debtors and EIG entered into a Note Purchase Agreement (the "Note Purchase Agreement"), whereby EIG provided up to $200 million in senior secured notes (the "Secured Notes"). As of the date of the Voluntary Petition, the principal amount outstanding under the Secured Notes was approximately $140 million. The Secured Notes are secured by liens on certain of the Debtors' assets, including, among other things, all inventory, accounts, equipment, fixtures, deposit accounts, and cash collateral. Specifically, with respect to cash collateral, the Debtors granted EIG a lien on all amounts held in any deposit account of the Debtors, as well as a lien on the Debtors' rights to payment under any contract.

On September 15, 2014, the Debtors and EIG entered into Amendment No. 3 to the Note Purchase Agreement (the "Third Amendment") to expand EIG's funding commitment from $110 million to $150 million. In connection with the Third Amendment, the parties amended certain elements of the positive debt covenant calculations (the "Maintenance Covenants"). In October 2015, EIG

---

1. EIG Energy Fund XV, L.P., movant EIG Energy Fund XV–A, L.P., EIG Energy Fund XV–B, L.P., and EIG Energy Fund XV (Cayman), L.P. are funds managed and advised by EIG Management Company LLC. For ease of reference, the movant, EIG Energy Fund XV–A, L.P., is hereinafter referred to as "EIG."

declared an event of default based on the Debtors' failure to comply with the Maintenance Covenants.

On December 28, 2015, the Debtors and EIG negotiated and entered into Amendment No. 5, Forbearance Agreement and Contingent Waiver (the "Forbearance Agreement"). The Forbearance Agreement provided that EIG would waive all defaults if the Debtors raised $30 million of equity capital to pay down a portion of the existing Secured Notes by June 1, 2016. As a condition to the effectiveness of the Forbearance Agreement, the Debtors were required to fulfill the following conditions precedent:

> The Administrative Agent shall have received a fully executed amendment to the limited liability company agreement of the Parent in form and substance satisfactory to the Administrative Agent (i) admitting EIG or its Affiliate as a member of the Parent with one common unit and (ii) amending such limited liability company agreement to require approval of each holder of common units of the Parent prior to any voluntary filing for bankruptcy protection for the Parent of the Company.

Also on December 28, 2015, IE Holdings enacted Amendment No. 1 to the Intervention Energy Holdings, LLC Second Amended and Restated Limited Liability Company Agreement (the "Amendment") to include the unanimous consent requirement to file bankruptcy (the "Consent Provision"). To give effect to the Consent Provision, IE Holdings then issued a single common unit to EIG for a common capital contribution of $1.00, making EIG a common member.

It is not disputed that, but for the Amendment, IE Holdings would have been authorized to seek federal bankruptcy relief.

DISCUSSION

The parties have made several interesting arguments with respect to state law and contractual treatment of fiduciary obligations. EIG argues that an LLC that has abrogated its fiduciary responsibilities to the extent permitted by Delaware law may contract away its right to file bankruptcy at will. In contrast, the Debtors, relying upon the recent case of *In re Lake Michigan Beach Pottawatamie Resort LLC,* draw a parallel between the "golden share"[2] given to EIG and a blocking director installed on the board of a special purpose entity (SPE), arguing that abrogating fiduciary duties is exactly what is fatal to EIG's argument—that the blocking member (or, in this case, holder of the "golden

---

2. This term has been used mainly to refer to a government retaining control over privatized companies. Investopedia—Golden Share, INVESTOPEDIA, http://www.investopedia.com/terms/g /goldenshare.asp (last visited June 2, 2016). "A type of share that gives its shareholder veto power over changes to the company's charter. A golden share holds special voting rights, giving its holder the ability to block another shareholder from taking more than a ratio of ordinary shares. Ordinary shares are equal to other ordinary shares in profits and voting rights. These shares also have the ability to block a takeover or acquisition by another company." Id. Golden shares are now outlawed in the European Union. Id.

share") must retain a duty to vote in the best interest of the potential debtor to comport with federal bankruptcy policy.

In light of my disposition of the federal public policy issue which follows, and reluctant to accept the parties' invitation to decide what may well be a question of first impression of state law (i.e., determining the scope of LLC members' freedom to contract under applicable state law provisions) when an alternate ground for decision is present, I find it unnecessary to address these arguments.

The Debtors note in their Response that it is axiomatic that a debtor may not contract away the right to a discharge in bankruptcy. It has been said many times and many ways. "[P]repetition agreements purporting to interfere with a debtor's rights under the Bankruptcy Code are not enforceable." "If any terms in the Consent Agreement ... exist that restrict the right of the debtor parties to file bankruptcy, such terms are not enforceable." "[A]ny attempt by a creditor in a private pre-bankruptcy agreement to opt out of the collective consequences of a debtor's future bankruptcy filing is generally unenforceable. The Bankruptcy Code pre-empts the private right to contract around its essential provisions." "[I]t would defeat the purpose of the Code to allow parties to provide by contract that the provisions of the Code should not apply." "It is a well settled principal that an advance agreement to waive the benefits conferred by the bankruptcy laws is wholly void as against public policy."

The rule is not new:

> The agreement to waive the benefit of bankruptcy is unenforceable. To sustain a contractual obligation of this character would frustrate the object of the Bankruptcy Act, particularly of section 17 (11 U.S.C. § 35). This was held by the Supreme Judicial Court of Massachusetts, Federal Nat. Bank v. Koppel, 148 N.E. 379, 380 (Mass.1925), where it was said: "It would be repugnant to the purpose of the Bankruptcy Act to permit the circumvention of its object by the simple device of a clause in the agreement, out of which the provable debt springs, stipulating that a discharge in bankruptcy will not be pleaded by the debtor. The Bankruptcy Act would in the natural course of business be nullified in the vast majority of debts arising out of contracts, if this were permissible. It would be vain to enact a bankruptcy law with all its elaborate machinery for settlement of the estates of bankrupt debtors, which could so easily be rendered of no effect. The bar of the discharge under the terms of the Bankruptcy Act is not restricted to those instances where the debtor has not waived his right to plead it. It is universal and unqualified in terms. It affects all debts within the scope of its words. It would be contrary to the letter of section 17 of the Bankruptcy Act as we interpret it to uphold the waiver embodied in this note. So to do would be incompatible with the spirit of that section. Its aim would largely be defeated."

> There are other grounds for sustaining the action of the referee, but the one mentioned is enough.[3]

---

3. In re *Weitzen*, 3 F.Supp. 698, 698–99 (S.D.N.Y.1933) (individual debtor).

Even so long ago as 1912, the United States Supreme Court was forced to address parties attempting to circumvent the bankruptcy laws by "circuity of arrangement."[4] Today's resourceful attorneys have continued that tradition.

Yet, to contract away the right to seek bankruptcy relief is precisely what both parties here have attempted to accomplish. EIG "specifically negotiated Intervention's ability to file a voluntary bankruptcy proceeding." Throughout the EIG MTD, EIG emphasizes and insists upon its "***contracted-for protections, including the Consent Provision***" indisputably meant to block any voluntary bankruptcy filing. In its Reply, EIG again emphasizes that "EIG [ ] ***bought and paid*** for its Common Unit (including all rights related thereto). . . ." Because § 7(b) of the Forbearance Agreement requires, as a condition to the effectiveness of the agreement, that IE both amend its LLC Agreement to institute the unanimous Consent Provision and grant the blocking share, the intent of the parties is unmistakable.

Both parties argue that, were I to decide this issue for the other side, systemic disruption will follow. EIG warns that if I were to declare the Consent Provision here void as contrary to federal public policy, not only would I vitiate the will of state legislatures that LLC members be free to contract, but also that confusion will reign about the breadth of an LLC's right to contract.[5]

The Debtors, on the other hand, argue that if I permit the enforcement of the Consent Provision, the landscape in debtor-creditor relations will be dramatically altered—that lenders will henceforth demand such a provision in every loan/forbearance agreement. True, lenders usually are not reticent to demand provisions that borrowers may often consider oppressive, but, as EIG's counsel replied at argument, as unwelcome as the consequence of doing so may be, a borrower can always say, "No." A borrower can also choose to seek bankruptcy relief sooner than it would prefer, rather than agree to any provision in a forbearance agreement that a borrower finds unacceptable.

The federal public policy to be guarded here is to assure access to the right of a person, including a business entity, to seek federal bankruptcy relief as authorized by the Constitution and enacted by Congress. It is beyond cavil that a state cannot deny to an individual such a right. I agree with those courts that hold the same applies to a "corporate" or business entity, in this case an LLC.

A provision in a limited liability company governance document obtained by contract, the sole purpose and effect of which is to place into the hands of a single, minority equity holder the ultimate authority to eviscerate the right of that entity to seek federal bankruptcy relief, and the nature and substance of whose primary relationship with the debtor is that of creditor—not equity holder—and

---

4. *Nat'l Bank of Newport v. Nat'l Herkimer Cnty. Bank*, 225 U.S. 178, 184 (1912) ("To constitute a preference, it is not necessary that the transfer be made directly to the creditor. It may be made to another, for his benefit. If the bankrupt has made a transfer of his property, the effect of which is to enable one of his creditors to obtain a greater percentage of his debt than another creditor of the same class, circuity of arrangement will not avail to save it.").

5. EIG urges consideration of *CML V, LLC v. Bax*, 28 A.3d. 1037 (Del.2011), to emphasize the breadth of discretion afforded to Delaware LLCs. *Bax* nowhere addresses federal bankruptcy law.

which owes no duty to anyone but itself in connection with an LLC's decision to seek federal bankruptcy relief, is tantamount to an absolute waiver of that right, and, even if arguably permitted by state law, is void as contrary to federal public policy.[25] Under the undisputed facts before me, to characterize the Consent Provision here as anything but an absolute waiver by the LLC of its right to seek federal bankruptcy relief would directly contradict the unequivocal intention of EIG to reserve for itself the decision of whether the LLC should seek federal bankruptcy relief. Federal courts have consistently refused to enforce waivers of federal bankruptcy rights. I now join them, and conclude that the Debtors possessed the necessary authority to commence their chapter 11 proceedings.

To what extent should federal bankruptcy courts simply accept the capital structure, and legal structure, of firms that arrive at their doorstep? As a matter of state agency law, who had the authority to sign this debtor's bankruptcy petition?

1.   A BRIEF INTRODUCTION TO BANKRUPTCY

JOHN D. AYER ET AL., *WELCOME TO THE JUNGLE*

Am. Bankr. Inst. J. 24 (July/August 2003)

The overwhelming majority of bankruptcy cases involve debtors who have no assets to distribute to creditors and who are filing just to get the discharge. There were about a million and a half such cases in the past year. These are important cases for the people involved, and they provide work for a lot of lawyers. But they aren't our department, and we won't spend a lot of time on them. Instead, we will spend most of our time on the cases where the debtor does have assets, and where the goal is to "reorganize" (whatever that may mean—of which more will be discussed later).

Bankruptcy law is federal. It is federal because the Constitution says that Congress shall have the power to make bankruptcy law. Congress exercised the power through the Bankruptcy Reform Act of 1978 (BRA), including the Bankruptcy Code, which is codified in Title 11 of the U.S. Code.

The BRA creates bankruptcy courts that operate as "a unit of" the U.S. district courts. Formally, the big distinction is in the power of the judge: The district judge exercises his judicial power under Article III of the Constitution and is a lifetime appointee, while the bankruptcy judge is a term appointee (14 years), deriving his or her power from the bankruptcy clause in Article I of the Constitution. Because the bankruptcy judges are "Article I" judges, case law holds that there must be limitations on the power of a bankruptcy judge in order for the bankruptcy system to be constitutional. As a result, Title 28 of the U.S. Code was amended to put the bankruptcy judge under the "supervision" of the district judge: Certain decisions by a bankruptcy judge must be reviewed by a district judge, and the district judge can withdraw matters that are pending before the bankruptcy judge and instead decide them herself. But practically speaking, the overwhelming majority of what happens in bankruptcy cases takes place in the bankruptcy court, under the supervision of the bankruptcy judge.

Who are the players in the bankruptcy game?

We have already mentioned the bankruptcy judge; he or she presides over the bankruptcy court. There are about 325 bankruptcy judges around the country, give or take. Some came to the bankruptcy bench with a lot of bankruptcy experience, some did not. But it may not make much difference: Lots of those without bankruptcy experience are fast learners, and some of them brought valuable experience from elsewhere—*e.g.*, good trial skills....

In the mass of ordinary bankruptcies (the "chapter 7 cases" discussed below), the case is administered by a trustee....

Chapter 11 is different. There is no trustee unless the judge orders the appointment of one. In lieu of a trustee, the debtor remains in control of its business and assets as debtor-in-possession (DIP). The DIP has most of the powers and responsibilities of a trustee. In the typical case, it is the debtor who initiates the bankruptcy case through its (pre-bankruptcy) lawyer. Once it has filed, the debtor—now DIP—seeks court approval to retain its former lawyer as counsel for the DIP. The DIP's counsel becomes a kind of "point person" in the chapter 11 case.

Another important player in the bankruptcy system is the Office of the U.S. Trustee, a division of the Department of Justice that is charged with oversight of the bankruptcy system. The U.S. Trustee appoints and supervises panel trustees, appoints official committees (see below), reviews and comments on applications to employ and compensate professionals, investigates bankruptcy fraud and abuse, and can be heard on any other issue in a bankruptcy case. The U.S. Trustee is often active in the very early stages of a chapter 11 case, although once the case is up and running, and particularly if there is active creditor participation, the U.S. Trustee often backs off a bit.

Another player well worth noting in a chapter 11 case (they are permitted in chapter 7 too, but it rarely happens) is the creditors' committee. The committee typically consists of the five or seven largest unsecured creditors that are willing to serve. It hires counsel (and sometimes financial advisors or other professionals) who are paid for by the debtor's estate. The committee has standing to be heard on any issue in a chapter 11 case, and its views tend to be taken seriously by the bankruptcy judges. An active and well-represented committee can play a major role in the outcome of the case. In some cases, other committees will also be appointed, such as equity-holder committees, retiree committees, bondholder committees, etc. Other important players include secured parties, especially banks that may have liens on substantially all of a debtor's assets, and counter-parties to executory contracts.

Now, a word about the structure of the Code. As we said above, the Bankruptcy Code is in Title 11 of the U.S. Code and is divided into chapters. Chapters 1, 3 and 5 are "general" chapters designed to govern all cases.

Chapter 11 contains definitions, delineates who can be a debtor, describes the courts' powers and contains some other general rules. Chapter 3 governs "administration of the case," including matters such as the filing of new cases, employment of professionals, the automatic stay, the use, sale and lease of estate assets, post-petition financing, executory contracts, the dismissal and closing of cases, and some other matters. Chapter 5 covers a wide variety of matters relating to the rights of debtors and creditors, including claims and priorities, matters relating to exemptions and discharge of debts, and the "avoidance" provisions, which permit a trustee or DIP to claw back certain transfers made prior to the petition date....

Chapter 11, entitled "reorganization," is the chapter that governs the small number of "big" cases that entail a lot of lawyer time and effort, and generate a lot of professional fees. If you ask a chapter 11 lawyer what it means to reorganize, he will likely say something like this: The reorganization case allows the debtor to preserve the business as a going concern, and thereby to maximize value for creditors, shareholders, employees and other stakeholders.

This is a beguiling picture and not entirely false. But there are all kinds of difficulties. The most obvious is that not all businesses are worth more as a going concern than they are in liquidation. A notorious example is the case of the Penn Central Railroad, one of the largest bankruptcies in American history. Penn Central went into bankruptcy as an unprofitable network of railroads, then emerged as a valuable real estate company.

A second difficulty is that chapter 11 specifically provides that a reorganization plan may provide for the liquidation of some or all of the debtor's assets—so chapter 11 is not only about reorganization, and the Code implicitly recognizes that in some cases value is maximized through liquidation. Third, the debtor does not need to choose chapter 11 if he wants the business to continue; the trustee may, with court approval, continue to operate the business in chapter 7 (although it is not often done). Finally, the distinction between "liquidation" and "going concern" may be less clear in practice than it is in theory. One can perfectly well "liquidate" a business by selling it as a going concern, in which case the distinction does not mean anything at all. Indeed, "going concern" sales—and the use of asset sales to circumvent the chapter 11 plan process—seem to be a popular trend these days.

Why this muddle? The point is that bankruptcy law conflates two concepts that are overlapping but fundamentally quite different. One is the notion of maximizing the value of the assets. The other is the notion of saving the residual stake of the pre-bankruptcy owners. This confusion is apparent in the classic chapter 11 case. The old residual owners (equity-holders), still in control of the enterprise, will file the petition. They will remain in control (as DIP) and will propose "a plan" to "save the going concern." If all goes well, the effect will be to maximize the payout to creditors and to leave something on the table for the owners (while preserving jobs, generating future tax revenues and serving other social goods that are often touted as benefits of reorganization).

Such a scenario appears to be a self-evident win-win situation. The interests of creditors and equity appear to be allied. But it is rarely that simple. "Saving the going concern" means continuing the business, which means continuing to bear risk. Where the business is insolvent, equity always gains from taking risks: Liquidate today, and they get nothing; keep the business going, and they may have a chance. Creditors are correspondingly risk-averse: Liquidate today, and they get paid. Take a gamble, and the rewards go to equity, while the creditors bear the risk of loss. The point is not that creditors always favor liquidation— clearly, they don't—but the risk-reward calculation is different for creditors than it is for equity-holders.

There can be no doubt that chapter 11 obscures, rather than resolves, this tension—almost as if deliberately to allow the court to choose, from case to case and even from time to time within a case, whether "assets" or "equity" will dominate.

In the biggest chapter 11 cases, is it clear that the managers and board who file the petition represent the "owners" of the corporation?[6] What if management has been revamped in connection with the various forbearance agreements and other workouts that might have occurred in the "pre-petition" days?

A chapter 11 case may be commenced on a voluntary or involuntary basis. Most are voluntary, especially with regard to big firms.[7]

As we noted with regard to prepacks, many of the largest cases are filed in either the Southern District of New York or the District of Delaware. Figure 28-1 provides an answer to how GM managed to file in New York, despite being a Delaware corporation headquartered in Detroit. Remember that each corporate entity within a "firm" files its own bankruptcy case, unless you want to concede grounds for piercing the corporate veil or its bankruptcy counterpart, substantive consolidation. When the firm has international subsidiaries, the choices become more complex.

Filing a bankruptcy petition creates something called the "bankruptcy estate."[8] In individual chapter 7 cases, the estate is easy to understand: It is comprised of all the debtor's nonexempt assets; that is, all assets the creditors can get at state law. The trustee takes charge of the estate and liquidates the assets therein for the benefit of creditors. Essentially the debtor trades his or her assets for relief from creditors.

In chapter 11 the estate is a bit more abstract because the DIP remains "in possession" of its estate. Thus the estate is created, but it looks remarkably just like the prebankruptcy debtor.

---

6. Adolf Berle & Gardiner Means, *The Modern Corporation and Private Property* (1932).

7. 11 U.S.C. §301. These Code provisions are in your statutory supplement, of course.

8. 11 U.S.C. §541.

FIGURE 28-1
Pages from General Motors Bankruptcy Petition

(Official Form 1) 09-50026-reg Doc 1 Filed 06/01/09 Entered 06/01/09 07:57:51 Main Document Pg 1 of 24

United States Bankruptcy Court
Southern District of New York

Voluntary Petition

Name of Debtor (if individual, enter Last, First, Middle): **GENERAL MOTORS CORPORATION**	Name of Joint Debtor (Spouse) (Last, First, Middle): **N/A**
All Other Names used by the Debtor in the last 8 years (include married, maiden, and trade names): **See Schedule 1 Attached**	All Other Names used by the Joint Debtor in the last 8 years (include married, maiden, and trade names): **N/A**
Last four digits of Soc. Sec. or Individual-Taxpayer I.D. (ITIN) No./Complete EIN (if more than one, state all): **38-0572515**	Last four digits of Soc. Sec. or Individual-Taxpayer I.D. (ITIN) No./Complete EIN (if more than one, state all): **N/A**
Street Address of Debtor (No. and Street, City, and State): **300 Renaissance Center** **Detroit, Michigan** ZIP CODE **48265-3000**	Street Address of Joint Debtor (No. and Street, City, and State): **N/A** ZIP CODE
County of Residence or of the Principal Place of Business: **Wayne County**	County of Residence or of the Principal Place of Business: **N/A**
Mailing Address of Debtor (if different from street address): ZIP CODE	Mailing Address of Joint Debtor (if different from street address): **N/A** ZIP CODE

Location of Principal Assets of Business Debtor (if different from street address above):
767 Fifth Avenue, New York, New York ZIP CODE **10153**

Type of Debtor (Form of Organization) (Check one box.)
- ☐ Individual (includes Joint Debtors) *See Exhibit D on page 2 of this form.*
- ☒ Corporation (includes LLC and LLP)
- ☐ Partnership
- ☐ Other (If debtor is not one of the above entities, check this box and state type of entity below.)

Nature of Business (Check one box.)
- ☐ Health Care Business
- ☐ Single Asset Real Estate as defined in 11 U.S.C. § 101 (51B)
- ☐ Railroad
- ☐ Stockbroker
- ☐ Commodity Broker
- ☐ Clearing Bank
- ☒ Other

Automotive Manufacturing

Tax-Exempt Entity (Check box, if applicable.)
- ☐ Debtor is a tax-exempt organization under Title 26 of the United States Code (the Internal Revenue Code).

Chapter of Bankruptcy Code Under Which the Petition is Filed (Check one box)
- ☐ Chapter 7
- ☐ Chapter 9
- ☒ Chapter 11
- ☐ Chapter 12
- ☐ Chapter 13
- ☐ Chapter 15 Petition for Recognition of a Foreign Main Proceeding
- ☐ Chapter 15 Petition for Recognition of a Foreign Nonmain Proceeding

Nature of Debts (Check one box)
- ☐ Debts are primarily consumer debts, defined in 11 U.S.C. § 101(8) as "incurred by an individual primarily for a personal, family, or household purpose."
- ☒ Debts are primarily business debts.

Filing Fee (Check one box)
- ☒ Full Filing Fee attached
- ☐ Filing Fee to be paid in installments (applicable to individuals only) Must attach signed application for the court's consideration certifying that the debtor is unable to pay fee except in installments. Rule 1006(b). See Official Form 3A.
- ☐ Filing Fee waiver requested (applicable to chapter 7 individuals only). Must attach signed application for the court's consideration. See Official Form 3B.

Chapter 11 Debtors

Check one box:
- ☐ Debtor is a small business debtor as defined in 11 U.S.C. § 101(51D).
- ☒ Debtor is not a small business debtor as defined in 11 U.S.C. § 101(51D).

Check if:
- ☐ Debtor's aggregate noncontingent liquidated debts (excluding debts owed to insiders or affiliates) are less than $2,190,000.

Check all applicable boxes:
- ☐ A plan is being filed with this petition.
- ☐ Acceptances of the plan were solicited prepetition from one or more classes of creditors, in accordance with 11 U.S.C. § 1126(B).

Statistical/Administrative Information
- ☒ Debtor estimates that funds will be available for distribution to unsecured creditors.
- ☐ Debtor estimates that, after any exempt property is excluded and administrative expenses paid, there will be no funds available for distribution to unsecured creditors.

THIS SPACE IS FOR COURT USE ONLY

Estimated Number of Creditors (on a Consolidated Basis)

☐	☐	☐	☐	☐	☐	☐	☐	☐	☒
1-49	50-99	100-199	200-999	1,000-5,000	5,001-10,000	10,001-25,000	25,001-50,000	50,001-100,000	Over 100,000

Estimated Assets (on a Consolidated Basis)

☐	☐	☐	☐	☐	☐	☐	☐	☐	☒
$0 to $50,000	$50,001 to $100,000	$100,001 to $500,000	$500,001 to $1 million	$1,000,001 to $10 million	$10,000,001 to $50 million	$50,000,001 to $100 million	$100,000,001 to $500 million	$500,000,001 to $1 billion	More than $1 billion

Estimated Liabilities (on a Consolidated Basis)

☐	☐	☐	☐	☐	☐	☐	☐	☐	☒
$0 to $50,000	$50,001 to $100,000	$100,001 to $500,000	$500,001 to $1 million	$1,000,001 to $10 million	$10,000,001 to $50 million	$50,000,001 to $100 million	$100,000,001 to $500 million	$500,000,001 to $1 billion	More than $1 billion

NY2:\1991951\13\16_ZZ11!.DOC\72240.0635

To keep creditors from pulling the estate apart, and to allow time for a reorganization plan to come together, the Code provides for an "automatic stay."[9] Think of it as a statutory, no-notice injunction that prevents creditors from using the remedies available under state and federal debtor-creditor law, like getting the marshal to sell the debtor's stuff to pay off the debts.

9. 11 U.S.C. §362.

In chapter 11, the stay protects the debtor's estate, but not anyone else, such as officers or shareholders. Sometimes the debtor will ask the bankruptcy court to enter a regular injunction to protect these parties—and sometimes the court will do so, but not as often as most debtors would probably like (keep in mind who it is that gets the debtor-firm to make the request in the first place).

The Code also expressly carves out a number of exceptions to the scope of the automatic stay, which are listed in section 362(b) of the Code. And a creditor may seek relief from the automatic stay, as provided in section 362(d).

The stability of the case in the early days is also protected by giving the debtor and only the debtor the first crack at coming up with a plan. But that is the subject of a future chapter.

09-50026-reg   Doc 1   Filed 06/01/09   Entered 06/01/09 07:57:51   Main Document
Pg 2 of 24

(Official Form 1) (1/08)		FORM B1, Page 2
Voluntary Petition *(This page must be completed and filed in every case.)*	Name of Debtor(s): **GENERAL MOTORS CORPORATION**	

All Prior Bankruptcy Case Filed Within Last 8 Years (If more than two, attach additional sheet.)		
Location Where Filed: **N/A**	Case Number: **N/A**	Date Filed: **N/A**
Location Where Filed: **N/A**	Case Number: **N/A**	Date Filed: **N/A**

Pending Bankruptcy Case Filed by any Spouse, Partner or Affiliate of this Debtor (If more than one, attach additional sheet.)		
Name of Debtor: **Chevrolet-Saturn of Harlem, Inc.**	Case Number: **As filed**	Date Filed: **June 1, 2009**
District: **Southern District of New York**	Relationship: **Wholly-Owned Direct Subsidiary of General Motors Corporation**	Judge: **Undetermined**

Exhibit A	Exhibit B
(To be completed if debtor is required to file periodic reports (e.g., forms 10K and 10Q) with the Securities and Exchange Commission pursuant to Section 13 or 15(d) of the Securities Exchange Act of 1934 and is requesting relief under chapter 11.)	(To be completed if debtor is an individual whose debts are primarily consumer debts.) I, the attorney for the petitioner named in the foregoing petition, declare that I have informed the petitioner that [he or she] may proceed under chapter 7, 11, 12, or 13 of title 11, United States Code, and have explained the relief available under each such chapter. I further certify that I have delivered to the debtor the notice required by § 342(b).
☒ Exhibit A is attached and made a part of this petition.	X_____ Signature of Attorney for Debtor(s) Date

Exhibit C
Does the debtor own or have possession of any property that poses or is alleged to pose a threat of imminent and identifiable harm to public health or safety?
☐ Yes, and Exhibit C is attached and made a part of this petition.
☒ No.

Exhibit D
(To be completed by every individual debtor. If a joint petition is filed, each spouse must complete and attach a separate Exhibit D.)
☐ Exhibit D completed and signed by the debtor is attached and made a part of this petition.
If this is a joint petition:
☐ Exhibit D also completed and signed by the joint debtor is attached and made a part of this petition.

Information Regarding the Debtor - Venue (Check any applicable box.)
☐ Debtor has been domiciled or has had a residence, principal place of business, or principal assets in this District for 180 days immediately preceding the date of this petition or for a longer part of such 180 days than in any other District.]
☒ There is a bankruptcy case concerning debtor's affiliate, general partner, or partnership pending in this District.
☐ Debtor is a debtor in a foreign proceeding and has its principal place of business or principal assets in the United States in this District, or has no principal place of business or assets in the United States but is a defendant in an action or proceeding [in a federal or state court] in this District, or the interests of the parties will be served in regard to the relief sought in this District.

Certification by a Debtor Who Resides as a Tenant of Residential Property (Check all applicable boxes)
☐ Landlord has a judgment against the debtor for possession of debtor's residence. (If box checked, complete the following.)
_____ (Name of landlord that obtained judgment)
_____ (Address of landlord)
☐ Debtor claims that under applicable nonbankruptcy law, there are circumstances under which the debtor would be permitted to cure the entire monetary default that gave rise to the judgment for possession, after the judgment for possession was entered, and
☐ Debtor has included with this petition the deposit with the court of any rent that would become due during the 30-day period after the filing of the petition.
☐ Debtor certifies that he/she has served the Landlord with this certification. (11 U.S.C. § 362(l)).

NY2\1991951\14.DOC\ZZ11!.DOC\72240.0635

2.   MORE ON THE DIP

If you read sections 1101 and 1107 of the Code, you will begin to understand the concept of the DIP. The basic idea is that management of the debtor stays in place, without a trustee, but acts with the duties and powers of a bankruptcy trustee.

MICHELLE M. HARNER, *THE SEARCH FOR AN UNBIASED FIDUCIARY IN CORPORATE REORGANIZATIONS*

86 Notre Dame L. Rev. 469 (2011)

The primary goals of Chapter 11 are to rehabilitate corporate debtors and maximize recoveries to creditors. The Bankruptcy Code also generally seeks to level the playing field among a debtor's stakeholders, thereby providing a more equitable distribution. Achieving one or more of the Bankruptcy Code's objectives is difficult in any individual or business bankruptcy case. That task is even more onerous in a Chapter 11 case because the corporate debtor and its various stakeholders often have their own, competing agendas.

Creditors are not benevolent by nature. Rather, they endeavor to maximize their individual returns. If other creditors also benefit, that result typically is inadvertent and of secondary concern.

Early U.S. bankruptcy law did not address corporate reorganization. The laws primarily focused on merchants and "straight" bankruptcy (i.e., liquidation). Troubled corporations thus were left to their own devices, negotiating workouts with their major creditors in a largely unsupervised forum. The Great Depression of the 1930s produced the first federal bankruptcy laws covering corporate reorganizations, and aspects of those laws continue under the U.S. Bankruptcy Code. An understanding of the law's development is helpful in analyzing control contests and conflicts in bankruptcy and the role that DIPs and statutory committees do or should play.

In the late nineteenth century, creative lawyers and federal judges crafted a procedure to fill a void in U.S. bankruptcy laws and address the financial distress of the country's railroads. The procedure, commonly referred to as an equity receivership, allowed a troubled railroad—with the assistance of its major creditors—to invoke the jurisdiction of the federal courts to achieve a restructuring of its debt. Technically, the railroad's creditors would petition the court to appoint a receiver and the receiver would take title to the railroad's assets. The receiver's primary task was to find a buyer for the assets and to continue the railroad's operations until the time of the sale.

Although the basic description of an equity receivership leaves the impression that the railroad, its management and its creditors turned over control of the restructuring to a receiver, that result did not occur in most cases. Rather, management typically encouraged friendly creditors to petition for the appointment of a receiver, and then management and those creditors would negotiate a restructuring plan. Those creditors were sometimes referred to as a protective committee or a reorganization committee. Those creditors also were frequently the only (and therefore successful) bidders at the sale of the railroad's assets. Consequently, in most cases, the receiver played an insignificant role.

Other troubled corporations soon adopted equity receivership procedures similar to those invoked by the railroads. The process not only provided a structured forum in which corporations could reorganize, but it also facilitated a quick restructuring with little interference from outsiders, such as the court, the receiver, and the Securities and Exchange Commission (SEC). Corporate management thus frequently favored the process.

The insular nature of equity receiverships, however, lent the process to abuse and generated substantial criticism. The most notable critic was William O. Douglas. As discussed below, Justice Douglas launched his campaign against equity receiverships after the process was codified by Congress in 1934. He asserted that management and those creditors aligned with management controlled most aspects of the equity receivership process, providing no representation for, and frequently small returns to, other creditors. In fact, creditors not participating in the reorganization committee's plan could be cashed out for a fraction of their debt holdings.

Equity receivership was the preferred means of corporate reorganization well into the 1930s. Congress even adopted key features of equity receiverships in the first U.S. corporate reorganization laws, enacted in 1934 as section 77B of the 1898 Bankruptcy Act. Congress enacted section 77B in response to the Great Depression.

The codification of equity receiverships generated substantial criticism from the SEC and others. The result was a substantial overhaul of corporate reorganization laws, culminating in the Chandler Act of 1938. What equity receiverships and section 77B gave management and key creditors' groups, the Chandler Act essentially took away, at least with respect to public corporations.

The Chandler Act of 1938 established two business reorganization options—Chapter X for public companies and Chapter XI for small businesses. Chapter X stood in stark contrast to equity receiverships and section 77B. For example, it mandated the appointment of an independent bankruptcy trustee, SEC involvement in the plan process and significantly increased court involvement in the solicitation of votes on, and approval of, the plan of reorganization.

Not surprisingly, public corporations resisted filings under Chapter X. Managers and large creditors disliked the loss of control and corresponding uncertainty. Consequently, many corporations first tried to qualify for Chapter XI or negotiate a restructuring outside of the formal process. They viewed Chapter X as a last resort.

A sharp rise in consumer bankruptcy in the 1960s energized bankruptcy reform efforts that produced the Bankruptcy Code of 1978. Corporate reorganization received substantial attention in the reform process as well. The Bankruptcy Code consolidated the business reorganization chapters into one chapter (i.e., Chapter 11) and eliminated what corporations found most offensive about Chapter X: the mandatory trustee and SEC participation.

Notably, the two key proposals set forth during the bankruptcy reform process did not directly recommend the elimination of trustees and the SEC's involvement in the plan process. For example, the proposal by the National Bankruptcy Review Commission contemplated a presumption in favor of a trustee in large cases and the appointment of a bankruptcy administrator to perform the tasks assigned to the SEC under Chapter X. Similarly, the proposal by the National Conference of Bankruptcy Judges maintained the role of the trustee and SEC in public corporation cases. The bankruptcy bar was, however, a strong proponent of a presumption that a trustee would not be appointed, leaving a corporation's restructuring in management's hands.

Chapter 11 of the Bankruptcy Code adopted much of the flexibility built into Chapter XI. Debtors (as DIPs) remain in possession of their assets and can operate their businesses and pursue their restructurings with oversight primarily from a creditors' committee. The Bankruptcy Code also created the U.S. trustee program, which serves some of the administrative functions assigned to the SEC under Chapter X. The U.S. trustee oversees both individual and business bankruptcies and rarely plays a substantive oversight role in any particular case. In addition, Chapter 11 permits the appointment of a trustee or examiner under certain circumstances.

Overall, the Bankruptcy Code was largely viewed as prodebtor legislation at the time of its enactment. In early Chapter 11 cases, courts granted the debtor's management lengthy periods of exclusivity in which only the debtor could propose a plan of reorganization; allowed the debtor to defer decisions on the treatment of most all contracts and leases until plan confirmation; and enjoined most all actions against the debtor and sometimes its directors, officers and nondebtor affiliates. The debtor's control of the process has weakened, however, as creditors have become more sophisticated, lobbied for favorable legislative amendments and created control opportunities.

As discussed above, Chapter 11 allows a DIP and its management to lead the debtor's restructuring efforts and contemplates the appointment of a statutory committee to oversee those efforts. Sections 1101 and 1107 of the Bankruptcy Code facilitate the DIP's role by recognizing the existence of a DIP and granting it "all the rights ... and powers, and [authority to perform] all the functions and duties ... of a trustee serving in a case under" Chapter 11. Section 1102 in turn provides that, in all but a few excluded cases, "the United States trustee shall appoint a committee of creditors or ... of equity security holders as the United States trustee deems appropriate." The committee's duties are listed in §1103 and include consulting with the DIP; investigating the DIP's prepetition and postpetition conduct and affairs; and participating in the plan process.

The Bankruptcy Code itself does not use the term "fiduciary" or expressly designate either the DIP or the committee as a fiduciary. Nevertheless, case law recognizes the fiduciary nature of both statutory representatives. Specifically, courts treat the DIP as a fiduciary for the bankruptcy estate, and the committee as a fiduciary for those it represents. Courts also have suggested in certain circumstances that the committee's efforts must generally benefit the bankruptcy estate.

A fiduciary relationship traditionally exists where "one party to a fiduciary relation (the entrustor) is dependent on the other (the fiduciary)." The role envisioned for the DIP and the committee under the Bankruptcy Code certainly satisfies this basic definition. The debtor's stakeholders—i.e., parties with economic interests in the bankruptcy estate—rely on the DIP to propose and confirm a plan that maximizes the estate's value. Likewise, creditors or equity holders represented by a committee expect the committee to act in their best interests.

The United States is the only country that allows management such freedom upon insolvency. In England management is replaced by administrators, employees of a large accounting firm. In Canada, reorganization involves the appointment of a monitor, a kind of neutral party that opines on the debtor's proposed actions during the reorganization. Most continental countries simply replace management with a trustee, which is only routinely done in chapter 7 liquidations in the United States.

If the debtor's management is not to be trusted, a trustee can be appointed. Appointment of a trustee, however, is often associated with conversion to chapter 7.[10] A less draconian solution is to appoint an examiner under section 1104 (also the provision for appointment of a trustee).

An examiner investigates the debtor or some related party, and reports back. But they do not take over control of the debtor. We saw an example of an examiner's report in Chapter 1 regarding Lehman's use of certain, odd repo transactions. Here's another examiner's report; this one involves an old friend.

IN RE: DYNEGY HOLDINGS, LLC, ET AL., DEBTORS

United States Bankruptcy Court, S.D. New York.
March 9, 2012,
Jointly Administered

Report of Susheel Kirpalani, Examiner

I.   **EXECUTIVE SUMMARY OF THE EXAMINER'S CONCLUSIONS**

A.   **EXAMINER APPOINTMENT AND MANDATE**

On January 11, 2012, Tracy Hope Davis, the United States Trustee for Region 2, appointed Susheel Kirpalani as Chapter 11 Examiner in the bankruptcy cases

---

10. Oscar Couwenberg & Stephen J. Lubben, *The Costs of Chapter 11 in Context: American and Dutch Business Bankruptcy*, 85 Am. Bankr. L.J. 63 (2011).

of Dynegy Holdings, LLC and its debtor affiliates. On January 12, 2012, the Honorable Cecelia G. Morris of the United States Bankruptcy Court for the Southern District of New York approved the appointment. The Examiner was asked to complete an independent, unfettered investigation of certain issues relating to the Debtors' conduct in the months leading up to the bankruptcy filing, and to file a report containing his findings within 60 days. The Examiner was also charged to serve as a court-appointed mediator to attempt to forge a consensual Chapter 11 plan among the Debtors' various constituents.

B.   SUMMARY OF FINDINGS AND CONCLUSIONS

Dynegy Inc. is a publicly traded holding company whose stock is listed on the New York Stock Exchange. Before September 1, 2011, Dynegy Inc.'s only asset was ownership of 100% of the equity in Dynegy Holdings, which in turn owned, through a variety of subsidiaries, all of Dynegy's operations. Dynegy's debt was issued by Dynegy Holdings or its subsidiaries.

Dynegy Holdings and certain of its indirect subsidiaries filed for bankruptcy protection on November 7, 2011. In the three months prior to filing, Dynegy Holdings had transferred or authorized the transfer of billions of dollars of its assets (stock or other direct or indirect ownership interests of subsidiaries) as part of a multi-step plan to reorganize Dynegy's business segments and restructure Dynegy's debts. The first phase of the restructuring facilitated a refinancing of Dynegy Holdings's secured bank debt, which, in the absence of a refinancing, was in danger of a covenant breach. Once the crisis of the potential bank default was averted, Dynegy implemented the next phase of its restructuring plan. The goal of this second phase was to reduce the amount of Dynegy's unsecured debt, while simultaneously increasing value for stockholders. To those familiar with the basic tenets of corporate finance, this may seem paradoxical, as it is a bedrock principle that a company's creditors must be paid in full before its stockholders can receive or retain any value—unless, of course, creditors agree otherwise. Over the spring and summer of 2011, Dynegy devised and implemented a plan to move assets away from the reach of Dynegy Holdings's unsecured creditors in order to encourage, for lack of a better word, such creditors to accept less than full payment and at the same time permit a recovery for stockholders. This report examines whether the techniques that Dynegy employed were legally permissible.

The Bankruptcy Court directed the Examiner to investigate Dynegy's pre-bankruptcy transactions and to report on the conduct of the Debtors, the existence of any fraudulent transfers, and whether Dynegy Holdings is capable of confirming a Chapter 11 plan. In carrying out its restructuring strategy, Dynegy was principally concerned with whether it was violating any of the contractual prohibitions contained in Dynegy Holdings's debt agreements. If it did not violate the letter of the contracts, then Dynegy believed it was free to implement the strategy of moving assets and, potentially, control away from Dynegy Holdings in the hope of convincing creditors to accept less than full payment for their debt. Dynegy expected that creditors would challenge this strategy and, to maximize its defenses, Dynegy tried to structure its transfers of assets away from Dynegy Holdings in a manner that it could claim were transfers in exchange for fair value. Put simply, Dynegy believed that, even if Dynegy Holdings was insolvent, as long as it transferred assets in exchange for what the law considers "reasonably equivalent value," then creditors would have no legitimate cause to complain.

Dynegy's strategy was permissible with respect to the transfers relating to the first phase of the restructuring, *i.e.*, transfers incident to the creation of two distinct silos of assets, CoalCo and GasCo,[11] because those transfers did not injure creditors and were not, in and of themselves, intended to do so. Indeed, following these so-called "ring-fencing" transactions, both silos of assets continued ultimately to be owned (as they had been) by Dynegy Holdings. While it is true that as a result of the ring-fencing and attendant refinancing of pre-existing secured bank debt, unsecured creditors of Dynegy Holdings could look only to the residual equity value of CoalCo and GasCo, this was, as a practical matter, always the case for unsecured creditors of Dynegy Holdings, regardless of whether the silos were created.[12]

Dynegy's strategy was ill-conceived, however, with respect to the second phase of the restructuring, *i.e.*, the transfer or purported "sale" of CoalCo by Dynegy Holdings to Dynegy Inc. in exchange for a piece of paper that Dynegy actively avoided valuing. This transfer of CoalCo, which the board of Dynegy Inc. then valued at $1.25 billion, was made in exchange for an illiquid, unsecured, highly unusual financial instrument called an "undertaking." In addition, the undertaking had no covenants to protect the holder's value against other actions that might be taken by Dynegy Inc. The Examiner believes that this undertaking had a midpoint value at the time (even prior to its amendment in a manner adverse to Dynegy Holdings) of approximately $860 million. Immediately after Dynegy Inc. provided the undertaking, Dynegy Inc. and Dynegy Holdings agreed to amend it so Dynegy Inc. could reduce its payment

---

11. The terms "CoalCo" and "GasCo" are sometimes used for convenience in this report to refer to the holding companies that were newly formed as part of a "ring-fencing" strategy to hold coal and gas assets previously held by subsidiaries of Dynegy Holdings.

12. To be clear, the amount of refinancing indebtedness did exceed the aggregate amount of Dynegy's funded, secured bank debt and the Sithe Debentures, all of which were repaid with the proceeds of the refinancing. Excess net proceeds of more than $250 million were set aside for general corporate purposes within the CoalCo and GasCo chains. In addition, $400 million of excess net proceeds essentially replaced the same amount of cash previously residing at Dynegy Holdings, which had been used to repay funded, secured bank debt, and was also set aside for general corporate purposes. Those purposes did ultimately include aspects of the second phase of the restructuring, but the Examiner has not found that the lenders under the refinancing loans had clear knowledge that this second phase would definitely occur ... or, if it did, what the precise terms would be or how it might impact Dynegy Holdings, which was not obligated under the new facilities. As such, this type of financing is distinguishable from those where "collapsing" a loan with the use of the proceeds of such loan (*e.g.*, leveraged buyouts) may well be appropriate to determine the economic substance of a transaction on the borrower.

obligations by $1.678 over the course of the payment stream (an amount apparently designed to mimic a dollar-for-dollar present value reduction) for each dollar face amount of Dynegy Holdings bonds that was acquired or otherwise retired by Dynegy Inc., even if such debt was acquired or retired at a discount to the face amount. Dynegy took the position that Dynegy Inc.'s future satisfaction of Dynegy Holdings's debt would constitute value, as a matter of law, measured by the face amount of such debt—no matter what Dynegy Inc. paid for such debt, and regardless of whether Dynegy Inc. paid for such debt by pledging the stock of its newly acquired direct subsidiary, CoalCo. In this way, Dynegy Holdings transferred to Dynegy Inc. not only CoalCo, but also the corporate opportunity to use CoalCo as a vehicle for exchanging its outstanding bonds for structurally senior bonds at a discount, or otherwise to control its own restructuring of indebtedness with its own assets. Moreover, the addition of the payment reduction mechanism into the amended undertaking rendered the undertaking unsalable to third-parties, and thereby further eroded the value of the undertaking to Dynegy Holdings.

In other words, if creditors of Dynegy Holdings had been willing to compromise their indebtedness at less than face value in exchange for new debt backed by a pledge of CoalCo stock (which was a Dynegy Holdings asset), absent Dynegy Holdings's transfer of CoalCo to Dynegy Inc., that reduction of indebtedness would have appropriately inured to the benefit of Dynegy Holdings, and not to Dynegy Inc. Reduced to its essence, the transaction transferred hundreds of millions of dollars away from Dynegy's creditors in favor of its stockholders.

The decision to "sell" CoalCo to Dynegy Inc. in exchange for an undertaking and amended undertaking was made and implemented by directors and officers of Dynegy Inc. The three senior-most Dynegy Inc. officers also served as board members of Dynegy Holdings and its newly formed shell subsidiary, Dynegy Gas Investments, LLC. The boards of Dynegy Holdings and DGI did not appreciate that what may be good for Dynegy's ultimate parent, Dynegy Inc., may not be good for Dynegy Inc.'s insolvent[13] subsidiary, Dynegy Holdings. The Examiner believes that these officers did not understand the distinction, from a corporate and fiduciary perspective, between Dynegy Holdings and Dynegy Inc.—a lapse perhaps caused by having the same professionals advise all entities within the consolidated Dynegy family of companies. Indeed, when authorizing the transfer of CoalCo away from Dynegy Holdings, they believed they were attempting to obtain creditor concessions for the benefit of the "company" or "enterprise" as a whole.

The same cannot be said, however, for the board members of Dynegy Inc. Certain members of the Dynegy Inc. board did not even understand the transfer

---

13. For the reasons given in the Examiner's Work Plan, filed with the Bankruptcy Court on January 24, 2012, the Examiner has assumed that Dynegy Holdings was insolvent throughout the relevant period. While a solvency analysis is outside the scope of this report, the Examiner believes that such an assumption is reasonable and has ample support in the record.

that was being made, or why the CoalCo transfer was prudent or appropriate; others did not even know whether there was a separate Dynegy Holdings board. But other members knew exactly what was happening, and why the CoalCo transfer was being made. In reviewing the CoalCo transfer, the board of Dynegy Inc. relied on the recommendations of the Dynegy Inc. board's Finance and Restructuring Committee.[14] The Chair of the FRC is an experienced investor who is employed by Dynegy Inc.'s largest stockholder. Certain members of the FRC understood that the goal was to capture any value attainable by acquiring Dynegy Holdings's bonds at a discount for the benefit of Dynegy Inc. They did not believe this was inappropriate so long as it did not violate the contractual restrictions in Dynegy Holdings's debt agreements. Indeed, given certain other actions that the FRC Chair believed Dynegy Inc. could have lawfully accomplished in the first phase of the restructuring—such as taking on extensive additional debt in what others called an "extend and pretend" strategy—Dynegy Inc. was, in his view, "entitled" to compensation from Dynegy Holdings's creditors for forgoing such options.

The Examiner concludes that the conveyance of CoalCo to Dynegy Inc. was an actual fraudulent transfer and, assuming that Dynegy Holdings was insolvent on the date of the transfer (approximately two months before the bankruptcy filing), a constructive fraudulent transfer, and a breach of fiduciary duty by the board of directors of Dynegy Holdings. Dynegy Inc., through its board of directors, used its power to control the affairs of Dynegy Holdings—an insolvent subsidiary whose property should have been maximized, or at least safeguarded, for the benefit of Dynegy Holding's creditors—to disadvantage Dynegy Holdings for the benefit of Dynegy Inc. Dynegy Inc.'s conduct provides a basis for disregarding the corporate separateness among Dynegy Inc., Dynegy Holdings, and Dynegy Holdings's newly formed shell subsidiary, DGI. As such, DGI should be considered the alter ego of Dynegy Holdings, and DGI's transfer of CoalCo should be deemed a transfer to Dynegy Inc. of an interest in property of Dynegy Holdings. In that event, Dynegy Holdings would have a claim against Dynegy Inc. for the fraudulent transfer of CoalCo. Alternatively, to remedy the injustice occasioned upon Dynegy Holdings and, derivatively, its creditors, CoalCo should be deemed property of Dynegy Holdings's bankruptcy estate. Finally, the breach of fiduciary duty by the board of directors of Dynegy Holdings should be equally attributed to the board of directors of Dynegy Inc.

Throughout the planning and execution of the Prepetition Restructuring, the Dynegy Inc. board favored paths that benefited Dynegy Inc. and its stockholders to the detriment of Dynegy Holdings and its creditors. Indeed, a key purpose of the Prepetition Restructuring, which was identified as early as spring 2011 and ultimately implemented on September 1, 2011, was to transfer value from Dynegy Holdings to and for the benefit of Dynegy Inc., cloaking the central

---

14. The members of the FRC installed themselves as the majority of the members of the board of Dynegy Holdings shortly before the commencement of these Chapter 11 Cases. As such, as of the date of this report, the Debtors are controlled by the FRC.

transaction with the semblance of fair value. The Examiner concludes that the Bankruptcy Court could confirm a chapter 11 plan for Dynegy Holdings, but, in light of the conduct of all but one of the members of the board of Dynegy Inc. as of September 1, 2011, four of whom now constitute the majority of the board of Dynegy Holdings, any plan that provides for these individuals to continue as directors would not be consistent with the interests of creditors and with public policy. That being said, the Examiner does not believe the continued service by senior management of Dynegy Inc., even in director or officer capacities, would be contrary to creditor interests or public policy.

In the Dynegy case, the United States Trustee read the examiner's report and on March 11 moved for the appointment of a trustee. Ultimately the issue was settled, as you will see in a coming chapter.

3.   THE ROLE OF COMMITTEES

Section 1102 of the Bankruptcy Code provides for the appointment by the United States Trustee of a committee of unsecured creditors willing to serve. As noted in the Ayer excerpt above, the firm filing a chapter 11 case is required to attach to its petition a list of its 20 largest unsecured creditors; however, in large chapter 11 cases, a list of the 30 or 40 largest unsecured creditors is often filed for the consolidated group.

Section 1103 of the Code sets forth the powers and duties of creditors' committees. Among other things, the committee consults with the debtor concerning the administration of the chapter 11 case; investigates the acts, conduct, assets and liabilities, and financial condition of the debtor and the operation of the debtor's business; and, of special importance, participates with the debtor in the formulation of a plan of reorganization. Section 1103 of the Bankruptcy Code also authorizes the creditors' committee to employ professionals to assist the committee in the performance of its duties. The fees of these professionals are treated as administrative expenses of the chapter 11 case. That is, the debtor-firm pays for the committee's expenses, and committee members are not responsible for payment.

The court may authorize the committee to pursue fraudulent or preferential transfers if for some reason the debtor refuses to pursue those claims. (Can you imagine why a reorganizing firm might not want to bring a fraudulent transfer action, even if it has a good case?) Often, the committee will bring actions to generate funds for the bankruptcy estate or will use the ability to pursue these actions as a negotiating tactic in formulating a plan of reorganization.

While creditors' committees are common—at least in big cases—equity committees have become less common in recent years.

IN RE ADELPHIA COMMUNICATIONS CORPORATION

544 F.3d 420
United States Court of Appeals, Second Circuit.
Sept. 24, 2008.

SOTOMAYOR, Circuit Judge:

The Official Committee of Equity Security Holders (the "Equity Committee") appeals from a May 17, 2007 order of the United States District Court for the Southern District of New York (Shira A. Scheindlin, J.), dismissing the Equity Committee's appeal of the confirmation order of the United States Bankruptcy Court for the Southern District of New York (Robert E. Gerber, J.) approving a Chapter 11 plan of reorganization (the "Plan") for Adelphia Communications Corporation ("Adelphia") and certain affiliated debtors. Pursuant to the Plan, the Equity Committee's derivative claims were transferred to a litigation trust. The Equity Committee argues, *inter alia,* that the bankruptcy court lacked the authority to transfer the derivative claims, without its consent, and therefore the district court erred in dismissing its appeal. We disagree and affirm the judgment of the district court.

FACTUAL AND PROCEDURAL BACKGROUND

The facts of this case are set forth in the bankruptcy court's opinion. We recite only those facts relevant to the issue of the bankruptcy court's authority to transfer the Equity Committee's derivative claims to a litigation trust, without the Equity Committee's consent.

In the bankruptcy proceedings of Adelphia and its subsidiaries (collectively, the "Debtors"), the United States Trustee for the Southern District of New York appointed the Equity Committee to protect equity holder interests because, at that time, the ultimate value of the Debtors' assets was uncertain and there existed a possibility of residual value for the equity holders. After the Debtors rejected a demand to bring certain claims against the Debtors' bank lenders and investment banks, the Equity Committee moved for standing to assert those claims on behalf of Adelphia. The Debtors neither supported nor opposed this motion, and, on August 30, 2005, the bankruptcy court allowed the Equity Committee to pursue the claims derivatively. Although acknowledging that it was not "particularly optimistic" about the "ultimate prognosis ... for all but a few of the Equity Committee's claims," the bankruptcy court nonetheless concluded that the prosecution of the claims was in the best interests of the estate because the claims were sufficiently "colorable."

On January 5, 2007, the bankruptcy court entered an order confirming the Plan for the Debtors. The Plan provided for the transfer of various estates' claims, including those of Adelphia asserted by the Equity Committee, to a litigation trust managed by five trustees who were appointed by the Official Committee of Unsecured Creditors (the "Creditors' Committee"). Recoveries by the litigation trust would first be paid to all Debtors' unsecured creditors that had not yet realized the full value of their claims, without regard to which of the Debtors' claims had generated the recoveries. Remaining funds would be distributed to shareholders.

Although the Equity Committee objected to the transfer of the derivative claims to a litigation trust, the bankruptcy court rejected its arguments. The court calculated that for "value to pour down all the way to equity, the [litigation trust] would have to recover at least $6.5 billion—an ambitious goal, which seemingly is so ambitious that it could fairly be said that equity is hopelessly out of the money." *In re Adelphia Commc'ns Corp.,* 368 B.R. at 272. It further explained that it had

> leaned over backward in this case to give the Equity Committee a fair shot at maximizing value in these cases, and to ensure that value wasn't unfairly taken away from it by senior classes, but the time for that has come and gone. The Equity Committee served responsibly and well. But now its job is done.

Id. at 276.

The district court subsequently dismissed the Equity Committee's appeal.

The Equity Committee argues that, as a result of its derivative standing, it acquired ownership and control over the claims asserted against pre-petition lenders and investment banks on behalf of Adelphia. Accordingly, the Equity Committee asserts that its claims could not be transferred to a litigation trust without the Committee's consent. We hold that, to the contrary, a court may withdraw a committee's derivative standing and transfer the management of its claims, even in the absence of that committee's consent, if the court concludes that such a transfer is in the best interests of the bankruptcy estate.

The Bankruptcy Code does not expressly authorize committees or individual creditors—in contrast to trustees and debtors-in-possession—to sue on behalf of an estate. Nevertheless, this Circuit has recognized an "implied, but qualified" right under 11 U.S.C. §§ 1103(c)(5) and 1109(b) for an unsecured creditors' committee to assert claims where the trustee or debtor-in-possession unjustifiably failed to bring suit or abused its discretion in not suing on colorable claims likely to benefit the reorganization estate. *Unsecured Creditors Comm. of Debtor STN Enters., Inc. v. Noyes (In re STN Enters.),* 779 F.2d 901, 904–05 (2d Cir.1985). This Court subsequently expanded *STN Enterprises* to confer derivative standing upon a committee with the consent of either the debtor-in-possession or trustee, *Commodore Int'l Ltd. v. Gould (In re Commodore Int'l Ltd.),* 262 F.3d 96, 100 (2d Cir.2001), or when the committee acts as co-plaintiff with the debtor-in-possession or trustee, *Glinka v. Murad (In re Housecraft Indus. USA, Inc.),* 310 F.3d 64, 70–72 (2d Cir.2002).

Although *STN Enterprises, Commodore* and *Housecraft* expanded the scope of derivative standing, our precedent did not undermine either the debtor's central role in handling the estate's legal affairs or the court's responsibility to monitor for abuses by the parties. It remains "the debtor's duty to wisely manage the estate's legal claims," and this duty "is implicit in the debtor's role as the estate's only fiduciary."[15] The debtor-in-possession may not always fulfill its responsibilities, and we have recognized that a debtor-in-possession may unjustifiably fail to bring valid claims or abuse its discretion by not suing. Yet it is the court's role—and not that of a derivative plaintiff—both to oversee the litigation and "to check any potential for abuse by the parties."

Despite this precedent, the Equity Committee argues that this Circuit concluded in *Smart World* that derivative standing equates to ownership of claims. In that case, creditors argued that the right to "appear and be heard on any issue" provided by 11 U.S.C. § 1109(b) included the right to move for settlement of an adversary proceeding despite the debtor-in-possession's objections. In rejecting the creditors' argument, our Court contrasted the limited bundle of rights provided by intervention under § 1109(b) with "ownership of the causes of action," which the Court suggested required derivative standing under *STN.* The Equity Committee seizes upon this dicta regarding "ownership"—used by the Court only for the sake of comparison—to argue that the Equity Committee's derivative standing under *STN* vested it with ownership over its derivative claims. But that is not so. Although an *STN* plaintiff's rights may exceed those of intervenors under § 1109(b), it does not follow—and our Court in *Smart World* did not hold—that an *STN* plaintiff's control over the estate's claims rivals that of the debtor-in-possession. Instead, *Smart World* emphasized the debtor's central role as the "estate's legal representative," and our Court concluded that the bankruptcy court had erred in granting derivative standing to creditors to settle a cause of action over the objection of a Chapter 11 debtor-in-possession.

It would be contrary to the reasoning of this Circuit's precedent to hold that the bankruptcy court's grant of derivative standing vested the Equity Committee with a veto over both the court and the debtor-in-possession. The bankruptcy court not only had the authority to confer derivative standing upon the Equity Committee, it also had the authority to—and did—effectively withdraw that standing when it concluded that the Equity Committee's role was no longer in the best interests of the estate, and to transfer the derivative claims to a litigation trust. Although the bankruptcy court originally conferred *STN* standing upon the Equity Committee because the Debtors had "unjustifiably failed" to bring the Equity Committee's claims, the bankruptcy court emphasized that it had not found any improper motive on the part of the Debtors in failing to pursue the claims. In fact, the bankruptcy court stated that the Equity Committee's proceeding to obtain derivative standing resembled one in which the debtor-in-possession consented.

Having concluded that the bankruptcy court possessed the authority to confirm a plan that transferred the Equity Committee's claims to a litigation trust, we next decide whether the bankruptcy court abused its discretion in determining that the transfer was in the best interests of the estate.

---

15. In contrast, a committee owes a fiduciary duty to the class it represents, but not to the debtor, other classes, or the estate. *Smart World,* 423 F.3d at 175 n. 12.

The Equity Committee argues that the litigation trust will pursue the derivative claims less effectively than it would because the trustees, appointed by the Creditors' Committee, possess conflicts of interest. According to this line of reasoning, the trustees will quickly resolve litigation in order to satisfy creditors' senior claims without pursuing larger resolutions whose benefits might trickle down to shareholders. But the Plan requires the trustees to "maximize the value of the transferred Causes of Action, whether by litigation, settlement or otherwise," and the trustees are liable for deliberately intending to injure, or recklessly disregarding the best interests of, interest holders in the litigation trust (including equity holders). In light of these guarantees and the Equity Committee's failure to put forth any evidence suggesting that the trustees have violated their fiduciary duties, we conclude that there is no reason to second-guess the bankruptcy court's judgment.

Moreover, the bankruptcy court conducted a reasonable analysis of the costs and benefits of the Equity Committee's continued management of the claims. Approximately seventeen months after granting *STN* standing to the Equity Committee, the bankruptcy court concluded that Adelphia's equity holders were unlikely to realize any recovery because of the significant sums due to more senior classes.[16] In fact, because equity holders were entitled to nothing, the Plan—which gave interests in the litigation trust to equity holders—gave them "*more* than their legal entitlement." The bankruptcy court also concluded that while the benefits of the Equity Committee's continued litigation were questionable, the costs risked being considerable. When the bankruptcy court granted *STN* standing to the Equity Committee, the Committee provided an assurance that it would cooperate with the Creditors' Committee. The bankruptcy court concluded that "the joint nature of the process would render [the Equity Committee's] claims only incrementally more costly to prosecute" because of the two committees' overlapping claims. But the bankruptcy court interpreted the Equity Committee's subsequent assertion of exclusive standing over the claims to be inconsistent with its earlier, cooperative stance. This raised the specter of an expensive, "independent full-blown litigation." Given the court's cost-benefit analysis, it was not an abuse of discretion for the court to conclude that the litigation trust was in the estate's best interest.

CONCLUSION

For the foregoing reasons, the order of the district court dismissing the Equity Committee's appeal is AFFIRMED.

---

16. Although the Equity Committee contests the bankruptcy court's conclusion that Adelphia's equity holders were $6.5 billion "out of the money," it does not provide even a cursory analysis that would suggest that the equity holders could ever realistically be "in the money."

Should equity committees be required in all cases? What risks might arise if shareholders are unrepresented by a committee in a chapter 11 case? *See* Diane Lourdes Dick, *Grassroots Shareholder Activism in Large Commercial Bankruptcies*, 40 J. Corp. L. 1 (2014).

4.   STABILIZING THE BUSINESS

In the days and weeks before a chapter 11 filing, bankruptcy attorneys begin to understand the debtor's business and documents are prepared to ease the company into chapter 11 with minimal disruption to its business. Ideally.

In Lehman, the bankruptcy attorneys reportedly had a few hours to prepare to file the biggest bankruptcy case ever.

This prebankruptcy preparation has to be done carefully and confidentially. Otherwise the debtor risks having an involuntary case filed against it, vendors may stop supplying the debtor, forcing an earlier filing than planned, and there is always the risk of insider trading. Remember the discussion of short selling from earlier chapters.

Beyond the petition, the debtor will usually file motions to retain their bankruptcy counsel, motions to approve new financing arrangements (the subject of the next section of this chapter), and a series of "first day" motions. For example, the Code generally prohibits a debtor from paying any prepetition debts, so a debtor might file a motion seeking permission to pay prepetition employee wages or prepetition claims of critical trade vendors—imagine the railroad that delivers coal to the debtor's power plant.

The idea is that despite what the Code might require, the debtor will lose value by not paying employees and critical trade vendors who have no legal obligation to continue to work with the debtor after bankruptcy. In the days when these motions were done in paper form, they typically comprised a large black, four-inch-thick binder that had a partner binder with all of the petitions for the case.

Not everyone thinks that first day motions are a good idea.

IN THE MATTER OF: KMART CORPORATION

---

359 F.3d 866
United States Court of Appeals, Seventh Circuit
May 6, 2004

EASTERBROOK, Circuit Judge.

On the first day of its bankruptcy, Kmart sought permission to pay immediately, and in full, the pre-petition claims of all "critical vendors." (Technically there are 38 debtors: Kmart Corporation plus 37 of its affiliates and subsidiaries. We call them all Kmart.) The theory behind the request is that some suppliers may be unwilling to do business with a customer that is behind in payment, and, if it cannot obtain the merchandise that its own customers have come to expect, a firm such as Kmart may be unable to carry on, injuring all of its creditors. Full payment to critical vendors thus could in principle make even the disfavored creditors better off: they may not be paid in full, but they will receive a greater portion of their claims than they would if the critical vendors cut off supplies and the business shut down. Putting the proposition in this way implies, however, that the debtor must *prove*, and not just allege, two things: that, but for immediate full payment, vendors *would* cease dealing; and that the business will gain enough from continued transactions with the favored vendors to provide some residual benefit to the remaining, disfavored creditors, or at least leave them no worse off.

Bankruptcy Judge Sonderby entered a critical-vendors order just as Kmart proposed it, without notifying any disfavored creditors, without receiving any pertinent evidence (the record contains only some sketchy representations by counsel plus unhelpful testimony by Kmart's CEO, who could not speak for the vendors), and without making any finding of fact that the disfavored creditors would gain or come out even. The bankruptcy court's order declared that the relief Kmart requested—open-ended permission to pay any debt to any vendor it deemed "critical" in the exercise of unilateral discretion, provided that the vendor agreed to furnish goods on "customary trade terms" for the next two years—was "in the best interests of the Debtors, their estates and their creditors." The order did not explain why, nor did it contain any legal analysis, though it did cite 11 U.S.C. §105(a). (The bankruptcy court issued two companion orders covering international vendors and liquor vendors. Analysis of all three orders is the same, so we do not mention these two further.)

Kmart used its authority to pay in full the pre-petition debts to 2,330 suppliers, which collectively received about $300 million. This came from the $2 billion in new credit (debtor-in-possession or DIP financing) that the bankruptcy judge authorized, granting the lenders super-priority in post-petition assets and revenues. Another 2,000 or so vendors were not deemed "critical" and were not paid. They and 43,000 additional unsecured creditors eventually received about 10¢ on the dollar, mostly in stock of the reorganized Kmart. Capital Factors, Inc., appealed the critical-vendors order immediately after its entry on January 25, 2002. A little more than 14 months later, after all of the critical vendors had been paid and as Kmart's plan of reorganization was on the verge of approval, District Judge Grady reversed the order authorizing payment. 291 B.R. 818 (N.D.Ill.2003). He concluded that neither §105(a) nor a "doctrine of necessity" supports the orders.

Appellants insist that, by the time Judge Grady acted, it was too late. Money had changed hands and, we are told, cannot be refunded. But why not?

Thus we arrive at the merits. Section 105(a) allows a bankruptcy court to "issue any order, process, or judgment that is necessary or appropriate to carry out the provisions of" the Code. This does not create discretion to set aside the Code's rules about priority and distribution; the power conferred by §105(a) is one to implement rather than override. We agree with this view of §105. "The fact that a [bankruptcy] proceeding is equitable does not give the judge a free-floating discretion to redistribute rights in accordance with his personal views of justice and fairness, however enlightened those views may be." In re Chicago, Milwaukee, St. Paul & Pacific R.R., 791 F.2d 524, 528 (7th Cir.1986).

A "doctrine of necessity" is just a fancy name for a power to depart from the Code. Although courts in the days before bankruptcy law was codified wielded power to reorder priorities and pay particular creditors in the name of "necessity"—see Miltenberger v. Logansport Ry., 106 U.S. 286, 1 S.Ct. 140, 27 L.Ed. 117 (1882); Fosdick v. Schall, 99 U.S. 235, 25 L.Ed. 339 (1878)—today it is the Code rather than the norms of nineteenth century railroad reorganizations that must prevail. *Miltenberger* and *Fosdick* predate the first general effort at codification, the Bankruptcy Act of 1898. Today the Bankruptcy Code of 1978 supplies the rules. Congress did not in terms scuttle old common-law doctrines, because it did not need to; the Act curtailed, and then the Code replaced, the entire apparatus. Answers to contemporary issues must be found within the Code (or legislative halls). Older doctrines may survive as glosses on ambiguous language enacted in 1978 or later, but not as freestanding entitlements to trump the text.

So does the Code contain any grant of authority for debtors to prefer some vendors over others? Many sections require equal treatment or specify the details of priority when assets are insufficient to satisfy all claims. E.g., 11 U.S.C. §§507, 1122(a), 1123(a)(4). Appellants rely on 11 U.S.C. §§363(b), 364(b), and 503 as sources of authority for unequal treatment. Section 364(b) reads: "The court, after notice and a hearing, may authorize the trustee to obtain unsecured credit or to incur unsecured debt other than under subsection (a) of this section, allowable under section 503(b)(1) of this title as an administrative expense." This authorizes the debtor to obtain credit (as Kmart did) but has nothing to say about how the money will be disbursed or about priorities among creditors. To the extent that In re Payless Cashways, Inc., 268 B.R. 543 (Bankr.W.D.MO.2001), and similar decisions, hold otherwise, they are unpersuasive. Section 503, which deals with administrative expenses, likewise is irrelevant. Pre-filing debts are not administrative expenses; they are the antithesis of administrative expenses. Filing a petition for bankruptcy effectively creates two firms: the debts of the pre-filing entity may be written down so that the post-filing entity may reorganize and continue in business if it has a positive cash flow. Treating pre-filing debts as "administrative" claims against the post-filing entity would impair the ability of bankruptcy law to prevent old debts from sinking a viable firm.

That leaves §363(b)(1): "The trustee [or debtor in possession], after notice and a hearing, may use, sell, or lease, other than in the ordinary course of business, property of the estate." This is more promising, for satisfaction of a pre-petition debt in order to keep "critical" supplies flowing is a use of property other than in the ordinary course of administering an estate in bankruptcy. Capital Factors insists that §363(b)(1) should be limited to the commencement of capital projects, such as building a new plant, rather than payment of old debts—as paying vendors would be "in the ordinary course" but for the intervening bankruptcy petition. To read §363(b)(1) broadly, Capital Factors observes, would be to allow a judge to rearrange priorities among creditors (which is what a critical-vendors order effectively does), even though the Supreme Court has cautioned against such a step. Yet what these decisions principally say is that priorities do not change unless a statute supports that step; and if §363(b)(1) is such a statute, then there is no insuperable problem. If the language is too open-ended, that is a problem for the legislature. Nonetheless, it is prudent to read, and use, §363(b)(1) to do the least damage possible to priorities established by contract and by other parts of the Bankruptcy Code. We need not decide whether §363(b)(1) could support payment of some pre-petition debts, because *this* order was unsound no matter how one reads §363(b)(1).

The foundation of a critical-vendors order is the belief that vendors not paid for prior deliveries will refuse to make new ones. Without merchandise to sell, a retailer such as Kmart will fold. If paying the critical vendors would enable a successful reorganization and make even the disfavored creditors better off, then all creditors favor payment whether or not they are designated as "critical." This suggests a use of §363(b)(1) similar to the theory underlying a plan crammed down the throats of an impaired class of creditors: if the impaired class does at least as well as it would have under a Chapter 7 liquidation, then it has no legitimate objection and cannot block the reorganization. For the premise to hold true, however, it is necessary to show not only that the disfavored creditors *will* be as well off with reorganization as with liquidation—a demonstration never attempted in this proceeding—but also that the supposedly critical vendors would have ceased deliveries if old debts were left unpaid while the litigation continued. If vendors will deliver against a promise of current payment, then a reorganization can be achieved, and all unsecured creditors will obtain its benefit, without preferring any of the unsecured creditors.

Some supposedly critical vendors will continue to do business with the debtor because they must. They may, for example, have long term contracts, and the automatic stay prevents these vendors from walking away as long as the debtor pays for new deliveries. See 11 U.S.C. §362. Fleming Companies, which received the largest critical-vendors payment because it sold Kmart between $70 million and $100 million of groceries and related goods weekly, was one of these. No matter how much Fleming would have liked to dump Kmart, it had no right to do so. It was unnecessary to compensate Fleming for continuing to make deliveries that it was legally required to make. Nor was Fleming likely to walk away even if it had a legal right to do so. Each new delivery produced a profit; as long as Kmart continued to pay for new product, why would any vendor drop the account? That would be a self-inflicted wound. To abjure new profits because of old debts would be to commit the sunk-cost fallacy; well-managed businesses are unlikely to do this. Firms that disdain current profits because of old losses are unlikely to stay in business. They might as well burn money or drop it into the ocean. Again Fleming illustrates the point. When Kmart stopped buying its products after the contract expired, Fleming collapsed (Kmart had accounted for more than 50% of its business) and filed its own bankruptcy petition. Fleming was hardly likely to have quit selling of its own volition, only to expire the sooner.

Doubtless many suppliers fear the prospect of throwing good money after bad. It therefore may be vital to assure them that a debtor will pay for new deliveries on a current basis. Providing that assurance need not, however, entail payment for pre-petition transactions. Kmart could have paid cash or its equivalent. (Kmart's CEO told the bankruptcy judge that COD arrangements were not part of Kmart's business plan, as if a litigant's druthers could override the rights of third parties.) Cash on the barrelhead was not the most convenient way, however. Kmart secured a $2 billion line of credit when it entered bankruptcy. Some of that credit could have been used to assure vendors that payment would be forthcoming for all post-petition transactions. The easiest way to do that would have been to put some of the $2 billion behind a standby letter of credit on which the bankruptcy judge could authorize unpaid vendors to draw. That would not have changed the terms on which Kmart and any of its vendors did business; it just would have demonstrated the certainty of payment. If lenders are unwilling to issue such a letter of credit (or if they insist on a letter's short duration), that would be a compelling market signal that reorganization is a poor prospect and that the debtor should be liquidated post haste.

Yet the bankruptcy court did not explore the possibility of using a letter of credit to assure vendors of payment. The court did not find that any firm would have ceased doing business with Kmart if not paid for pre-petition deliveries, and the scant record would not have supported such a finding had one been made. The court did not find that discrimination among unsecured creditors was the only way to facilitate a reorganization. It did not find that the disfavored creditors were at least as well off as they would have been had the critical-vendors order not been entered. For all the millions at stake, this proceeding looks much like the Chapter 13 reorganization that produced *In re Crawford*, 324 F.3d 539 (7th Cir.2003). Crawford had wanted to classify his creditors in a way that would enable him to pay off those debts that would not be discharged, while stiffing the creditors whose debts were dischargeable. We replied that even though classification (and thus unequal treatment) is possible for Chapter 13 proceedings, see 11 U.S.C. §1322(b), the step would be proper only when the record shows that the classification would produce some benefit for the disfavored creditors. Just so here. Even if §362(b)(1) allows critical-vendors orders in principle, preferential payments to a class of creditors are proper only if the record shows the prospect of benefit to the other creditors. This record does not, so the critical-vendors order cannot stand.

For a while there were three common venues for filing big chapter 11 cases: New York, Wilmington, and Chicago. Now there are two. Chicago is trying to get back in the game, however, and the Southern District of Texas has been capturing many of the recent oil and gas bankruptcy cases.

PROBLEM SET 28.1

1. Think about how the Kmart attorneys could have avoided this problem in the first instance. In the interest of full disclosure, you might want to know that your author worked on the Kmart case—but not this issue.
2. The necessity of payment doctrine that undergirds most first day motions has its roots in the old railroad reorganization cases. As a matter of public policy, railroads were not allowed to liquidate, which gave the "critical" vendors extreme bargaining power. Should that influence the analysis today?

5.   FINANCING THE BUSINESS

Many bankruptcy filings are caused by liquidity problems. And if the debtor did not have a liquidity problem before, after chapter 11 they likely will, as vendors demand cash upon delivery.

The Bankruptcy Code provides ways for the debtor to obtain new, post-bankruptcy financing. Section 364 is the place to look with regard to post-bankruptcy financing. But you might first look at section 363 with regard to cash collateral. The normal rule in bankruptcy is that the debtor can continue to use its property, even property that secured a pre-bankruptcy loan, in the ordinary course of business.

There is one important exception for cash collateral, which is cash that a lender has a lien on or has a right to set off against. For example, if Chase makes a loan to Bogartco, and Bogartco has its bank account at Chase, the bank can set the two off if Bogartco defaults on the loan.

How might Bogartco avoid this threat to its continued operations?

To use cash collateral, a debtor must either get the consent of the secured party or court authorization. If the creditor does not consent to the use of its cash collateral, then the debtor must provide "adequate protection" to the lender—essentially, the debtor must compensate the creditor for any loss the creditor might experience from not being able to take the collateral back right now.

If the debtor has no cash whatsoever, then they will require a loan. Section 364 of the Bankruptcy Code permits a debtor to borrow funds and offers protections and priorities to induce lenders to make these loans, which are called "DIP loans."

Take a look at section 364 before reading the next case.

IN RE LOS ANGELES DODGERS LLC

457 B.R. 308
United States Bankruptcy Court, D. Delaware.
July 22, 2011.

Kevin GROSS, Bankruptcy Judge.

On June 27, 2011, Los Angeles Dodgers LLC,[17] and affiliates, debtors and debtors in possession in the above-captioned cases (the "Debtors"), filed the Emergency Motion for Interim and Final Orders (I) Authorizing Debtors to Obtain Postpetition Financing pursuant to 11 U.S.C. §§105, 362, and 364, and (II) Scheduling a Final Hearing Pursuant to Bankruptcy Rule 4001(b) and (c) [D.I. 13] (the "Motion"). Debtors sought the Court's approval of proposed financing further described below.

The Debtors and objecting parties reached agreement on revised terms. The Court entered an order on June 28, 2011 [D.I. 52] (the "Interim DIP Order") that, among other things, approved the Motion on an interim basis on the terms set forth in the Interim DIP Order and scheduled and held an evidentiary hearing on July 20, 2011.

Debtors seek authority to obtain final approval of postpetition financing consisting of a superpriority delayed draw term loan facility in an aggregate principal amount of up to $150,000,000 (the "DIP Facility"). Debtors received an initial draw of $60 million upon entry of the Interim Order and the remaining $90 million would be available from time to time following entry of a final order.

The proposed lenders are a group in the Highbridge Senior Loan Fund II family of funds ("Highbridge"), with whom Debtors have entered into a Credit and Security Agreement on terms more fully described below (the "Highbridge Loan"). The Office of the Commissioner of Baseball (the "Commissioner"), doing business as Major League Baseball ("Baseball") has objected to the Motion and the terms of the Highbridge Loan and has proposed its own loan (the "Baseball Loan") which it characterizes as an unsecured loan. Debtors dispute the nature of the loan.

Baseball fairly counters that, to date, Debtors have flatly refused to negotiate its proposal. Baseball is prepared immediately to engage in good faith negotiations toward an unsecured loan on the terms placed on the record.

---

17. This entity owns the Los Angeles Dodgers Major League Baseball team (the "Dodgers") whose rich and successful history is of mythical proportions. Its great former players, managers and executives could justify their own hall of fame. Formerly the Brooklyn Dodgers, the team name is derived from fans who used to "dodge" that city's trolleys.

The essential terms of the Highbridge Loan are as follows:

Amount:	$150,000,000 multiple draw term loans (of which $60,000,000 has been funded)
Rate:	LIBOR plus 6.00% for LIBOR Loans with a LIBOR floor of 3.00%
Timing of Interest Payments:	Paid at the end of an Interest Period/monthly during term of the facility
Number of Borrowings:	Borrower may only specify up to two Borrowing Dates during any 30-day period
Fees:	Closing date fees paid per Fee Letter:

- Closing commitment payment: 3.5% of the DIP Loan Commitment ($5,250,000), which has already been paid

Agent fee: $50,000 (paid annually)

Additional Credit Agreement Fees:

- Delayed draw fee: 0.50% of undrawn commitment
- Deferred commitment fee: $4,500,000 upon earlier of repayment in full and maturity
- Audit and collateral monitoring fees

Maturity:	June 27, 2012 (before expiration of Fox Sports' right of first negotiation)
Security:	All Assets of the Loan Parties
Debt Priority:	Super-priority administrative expense claims under section 364(c), senior to all other administrative expense claims

The Court will decide the Motion on the narrowest grounds possible, i.e., applying the applicable section of the Bankruptcy Code to the dispute and leaving to a later, more appropriate day, the issues surrounding the underlying feud between the Commissioner and Debtors' principal, Frank McCourt ("Mr. McCourt").[18] It is clear that Baseball needs and wants the Dodgers to succeed and the Debtors are best served by maintaining Baseball's good will and

---

18. Mr. McCourt blames the Commissioner for Debtors' woes while the Commissioner alleges Mr. McCourt's mismanagement and self-dealing are the cause. It appears that their dispute will shortly be before the Court. Their acrimonious relationship and Mr. McCourt's belief that the Commissioner is hostile toward him is an unhelpful distraction which obfuscates the uncontroverted testimony from Debtors' representative, Mr. Jeffrey Ingram, that Baseball is not hostile to the Debtors.

contributing to the important and profitable franchise group under the Commissioner's leadership.

A comparison of the Highbridge Loan and the proposed Baseball Loan clearly shows the substantial economic superiority of the Baseball Loan, as follows:

	Highbridge DIP Facility	*MLB DIP Facility*
Fees:	0.50% Delayed Draw Fee	None
	$4.5 MM Deferred Comm Fee	
	$5.25 MM Closing Comm Fee	
	$50,000 Annual Agent Fee	
Interest Rate:	LIBOR + 6%	LIBOR + 5.5%
	(3% Floor)	(1.5% Floor)
	Base Rate + 6.0%	Base Rate + 4.5%
Security:	All Estate Assets	Unsecured
Priority:	Super–Priority Administrative	Administrative
Events of Default:	Case Dismissal	No Onerous Events of Default
	Trustee or Examiner Appointed	
	Termination of Debtors' Rights under Baseball Agreement	
Maturity Date:	June 27, 2012	November 30, 2012
	(Before Fox Sports' Right of First Negotiation)	(After Fox Sports' Right of First Negotiation)

The Court will deny the Motion, premised upon of Section 364(b) of the Bankruptcy Code, 11 U.S.C. §364(b), which explicitly precludes the Highbridge Loan where, as here, Debtors are unable to prove that they are "unable to obtain unsecured credit allowable under section 503(b)(1) . . . as an administrative expense." The opposite holds true, *viz.*, Baseball is ready, anxious and able to provide unsecured financing and has committed to do whatever it takes to do just that. The Court will insure that Baseball honors its commitment.

In seeking approval of the Highbridge Loan, the Debtors have the burden of proving that:

(1) They are unable to obtain unsecured credit per 11 U.S.C. §364(b), i.e., by allowing a lender only an administrative claim per 11 U.S.C. §503(b)(1)(A);

(2) The credit transaction is necessary to preserve the assets of the estate; and

(3) The terms of the transaction are fair, reasonable, and adequate, given the circumstances of the debtor-borrower and the proposed lender.

The Court "may not approve any credit transaction under subsection (c) [of Section 364] unless the debtor demonstrates that it has attempted, but failed, to obtain unsecured credit under section 364(a) or (b)." In re Ames Dep't Stores, Inc., 115 B.R. 34, 37 (Bankr.S.D.N.Y.1990).

Debtors not only failed to attempt to obtain unsecured financing, they refused to engage Baseball in negotiations because, they explained, Baseball has been hostile to Debtors.

Debtors correctly posit that courts will almost always defer to the business judgment of a debtor in the selection of the lender. The business judgment rule is a standard of judicial review designed to protect the wide latitude conferred on a board of directors in handling the affairs of the corporate enterprise. The rule refers to the judicial policy of deferring to the business judgment of corporate directors in the exercise of their broad discretion in making corporate decisions. Under the rule, courts will not second-guess a business decision, so long as corporate management exercised a minimum level of care in arriving at the decision. The business judgment rule under Delaware law and the law of numerous other jurisdictions establishes a presumption that in making a business decision, the directors of a corporation acted on an informed basis, in good faith, and in the honest belief that the action taken was in the best interests of the company.

Under this formulation, the business judgment rule governs unless the opposing party can show one of four elements: (1) the directors did not in fact make a decision; (2) the directors' decision was uninformed; (3) the directors were not disinterested or independent; or (4) the directors were grossly negligent. Baseball relies on the third exception to argue that the business judgment rule does not apply. Baseball says Mr. McCourt did not make a disinterested or independent decision.

The evidence shows that if Debtors, controlled by Mr. McCourt, did not seek court approval for the Highbridge Loan, Mr. McCourt would personally owe $5.25 million to Highbridge. Such potential personal liability clearly compromised Debtors'/McCourt's independent judgment. Therefore, Debtors' decision is not entitled to review using the business judgment standard. Instead, the Court must review Debtors' decision to accept the Highbridge Loan applying the entire fairness standard. This requires proof of fair dealing and fair price and terms. Moran v. Household Int'l, Inc., 500 A.2d 1346 (Del.Supr.1985). The Debtors did not establish that the terms of the Highbridge Loan are entirely fair, particularly given Baseball's competing terms.

Additionally, Debtors refused to negotiate terms with Baseball to obtain a better and unsecured loan because of Mr. McCourt's poor relationship with the Commissioner. In this case, the Debtors decision to select the Highbridge Loan and refuse to negotiate with Baseball arises from recent dealings which Debtors claim show clearly an unworkable relationship with Baseball which will be harmful to reorganization efforts.[19] Further, Debtors contend that Highbridge is motivated to lend for commercial purposes unlike Baseball which Debtors fear has a nefarious strategy, namely, to seize control of the Dodgers away from Mr. McCourt. The Court finds that the Baseball Loan is not a vehicle for Baseball to control Debtors. Had Debtors negotiated with Baseball, a more economically viable loan may have developed—but at a high cost to the Debtors' decision-maker, Mr. McCourt. The Court therefore concludes that Debtors' decision is not entitled to deference as a matter of business judgment. Consequently, Debtors had to prove the entire fairness of the Highbridge Loan—fair dealing and fair price. Baseball's willingness to extend unsecured credit on better terms and Debtors' refusal to negotiate with Baseball precludes a finding of entire fairness.

The Court is confident that Baseball will propose to Debtors a short form credit agreement that is genuinely unsecured in nature and contains minimal—if any—representations, covenants and warranties, no releases for prepetition actions and no default triggers for violations of Baseball's rules and regulations. The Baseball Loan must be independent of and uncoupled from Baseball's oversight and governance of the Dodgers under the Major League Baseball Constitution. The Court, if necessary and as always, will provide ready access to Debtors in the hopefully unlikely event that Baseball strays from its obligations to act in good faith as Debtors' lender.

At the same time, Debtors are directed to negotiate with Baseball cooperatively and in good faith. Debtors and Baseball are entitled to the other's full cooperation in finalizing and administering an unsecured loan facility.

Therefore, based foremost on Debtors' failure to satisfy the statutory predicate for the Highbridge Loan and, secondarily, for failure to prove the entire fairness of the Highbridge Loan, the Court hereby denies the Motion.

6. DYNEGY IN BANKRUPTCY

Available online is a bundle of Dynegy materials related to the commencement of its chapter 11 case. Review them and be prepared to discuss them in class. Consider the purpose of the various pleadings and how you might respond to them if you were representing a large bondholder in the Dynegy case. Pay special attention to the DIP loan motion. What exactly is going on there?

---

19. It is unclear to the Court how Debtors think they can successfully operate a team within the framework of Baseball if they are unwilling to sit with Baseball to consider and negotiate even more favorable loan terms while under the Court's protection.

29

SELL AND LIQUIDATE
REORGANIZATIONS

Chapter 11 as drafted in the late 1970s was designed to facilitate the negotiation and implementation of a reorganization plan. But after a few notable missteps in the 1980s—including the ultimate liquidation of PanAm and Eastern, two major airlines, following lengthy chapter 11 cases—senior creditors began to look to new ways to use the bankruptcy process in ways that would increase their power. After all, these creditors were held at bay while these unsuccessful reorganization attempts took place.

The power of senior secured lenders, particularly lenders who have granted debtor-firms a lifeline in bankruptcy under section 364, became the obvious tool.

STEPHANIE BEN-ISHAI & STEPHEN J. LUBBEN, *INVOLUNTARY CREDITORS AND CORPORATE BANKRUPTCY*

45 U. British Columbia L. Rev. 253 (2012)

Traditional corporate reorganization involves the acceptance of a plan by creditors, with a concomitant reduction of the debtors fixed claims and realignment of its operations. In the U.S., this process is facilitated by an automatic stay of actions against the debtor, and a similar stay is typically entered in Canadian *CCAA [Companies' Creditors Arrangements Act]* proceedings. In chapter 11, unsecured creditors are typically represented by a committee, while in *CCAA* this role is taken up by the monitor. The debtor formulates a plan, and the creditors then vote on the same. After the creditors approve the plan, the court will consider the plan and, if it meets the provisions of the statute, sanction it and it becomes binding on all claimants.

This traditional form of corporate bankruptcy is increasingly rare in larger corporate insolvency cases.[1] Instead, debtors utilize their power to sell their

---

1. Stephanie Ben-Ishai & Stephen J Lubben, "Sales or Plans: A Comparative Account of the 'New' Corporate Reorganization" (2011) 56:3 McGill LJ 591. See also *Re Chrysler LLC*, 576 F (3d) 108 at 115 (2d Cir 2009), rev'd on other grounds (2009), 130 S Ct 1015 (Mem 2009), citing

assets first, and then proceed to formulate a plan that distributes the sale proceeds to creditors.

Take, for example, the well-known case of Lehman Brothers. The Lehman holding company filed under chapter 11 in New York on 15 September 2008 and then sold office buildings and the North American investment-banking business to Barclays one week later. It recently confirmed a plan that will distribute the proceeds of this and other asset sales to creditors over time.

This change in approach has been attributed to the growing power of secured lenders. This is particularly true in the U.S., where it is argued that secured lenders have learned the lessons of the Eastern Airlines case—a major airline case from the 1980s that is said to typify debtor control, and which ultimately resulted in the eventual liquidation of Eastern—and now understand how they can use their prebankruptcy power over the debtor's liquidity to control the chapter 11 process.

But this is more a story of how, than why. Aside from the implicit benefits of avoiding a lengthy reorganization process, the reasons for why this turn to quick sales has happened, and whether it benefits anyone besides the senior lenders, is still open to debate. And some argue that the trend is affirmatively harmful to the goal of maximizing the value of the debtor.

The nearest thing to a normative justification for quick sales has been Baird and Rasmussen's argument that current American chapter 11 debtors generally lack substantial debtor-specific value, and thus the sale of these assets is apt to realize as much as any reorganization of the same.[2] This "no harm, no foul" argument was very likely a product of the specific time when Baird and Rasmussen wrote their papers: during the early part of this century the American bankruptcy system was still dealing with the remnants of the "tech bubble" of the late 1990s, meaning that many debtors of that era had fewer fixed assets than before, and, as we now know all too well, there was also a simultaneous credit bubble that allowed for purchasers to easily finance the acquisition of distressed assets, which no doubt reduced the risk that quick sales would result in reduced prices.

In this paper we present a new justification for quick sales that turns on the presence of involuntary creditors, especially environmental claims. Particularly in the U.S. . . . the existing case law on environmental claims in reorganization proceedings strongly encourages the breakup of the firm: untainted assets are transferred to a new owner, while the old debtor liquidates the contaminated property along with a distribution of the sale proceeds.

In Canada a similar set of issues are at stake, although the law is less developed on this point—especially since the asset sale provision of the *CCAA* is relatively new, its current form only coming into being with the 2009 reforms to

---

Douglas G Baird & Robert K Rasmussen, "The End of Bankruptcy" (2002) 55:3 Stan L Rev 751 at 751–52.

2. Douglas G. Baird & Robert K. Rasmussen, "Chapter 11 at Twilight" (2003) 56:3 Stan L Rev 673.

the *CCAA*. In the past, without any express provisions dealing with asset sales in the *CCAA*, Canadian courts relied on their powers to impose terms and conditions under a stay order.

The tendency to move towards sales as opposed to reorganization plans is driven by two related factors: the focus on environmental obligations status as "claims," and the development in both chapter 11 and the *CCAA* of a strong ability to sell assets free and clear of charges on those assets.

The question of whether an environmental obligation is a claim has been particularly significant in the U.S., but the apparent victory of environmental regulators on this point is apt to be hollow, as it depends on the debtor's continued operations postinsolvency. And the growing strength of sale orders, transferring assets free and clear of obligations, means that the debtor and its controlling creditors are increasingly unconcerned about the ability to obtain a discharge at the end of the reorganization process. As the discharge loses its significance, the power of involuntary creditors is apt to dwindle. . . .

If a debtor stays largely intact during its reorganization, the scope of its discharge at the end of the *CCAA* or chapter 11 process is key. But if the debtor sells most of its assets, discharge wanes in importance. And if the debtor can create a new entity to buy its assets, then the distinction between "normal" reorganization and sale vanishes from an operational perspective, and the only question is which process better rids the assets of past errors, thus maximizing the value of the same.

Outside of reorganization, the general rule is that an asset sale does not result in a transfer of liabilities, unlike a merger. But several other doctrines limit the general rule. For example, in many jurisdictions in the U.S., courts have developed successor liability doctrines that lead to continued liability for a purchaser for product defects. Moreover, a buyer outside of reorganization takes subject to the risk that the transaction will be challenged *ex post* as a fraudulent transfer, if the debtor is deemed to have sold its assets "too cheap."

Thus, in the chapter 11 or *CCAA* sale context, the vital feature of reorganization law is the ability to sell assets free and clear of claims to the buyer. For example, section 363(f) of the *Bankruptcy Code* authorizes the trustee or a debtor in possession to sell property of a debtor "free and clear of any interest in such property." An interest in property includes claims that arise from the assets being sold.

Essentially, section 363(f) authorizes the bankruptcy court to grant relief similar to the discharge enjoyed by debtors under the Bankruptcy Code, exonerating a buyer from successor liability, including liability for the debtor's environmental claims that are unrelated to the purchased assets.

The excerpt foreshadows the discussion of successor liability and bankruptcy sales late in the chapter, but also suggests a reason to prefer a sale over a traditional plan.

Many large chapter 11 cases involve Canadian subsidiaries, or even Canadian parent companies; so learning a bit about the CCAA doesn't hurt either.

Asset purchase agreements used in chapter 11 mirror those used in normal corporate circumstances. The key difference is that the buyer knows they will inevitably have to subject their bid to an auction process, which essentially means that all asset sales in bankruptcy invoke something like the *Revlon* duties in the board. And the agreement will typically include detailed procedures for conducting the sale of the debtor.

1.   THE AUCTION PROCESS

Before the sale can happen, the debtor needs to set up an auction process to prove that it is obtaining the highest possible value for its creditors. The Bankruptcy Code provides no guidance on how such an auction should be conducted, but over the years courts, particularly in New York and Delaware, have developed a series of routine procedures that are typically put in place before the auction.

IN RE INNKEEPERS USA TRUST

448 B.R. 131
United States Bankruptcy Court, S.D. New York.
April 1, 2011.

Shelley C. CHAPMAN, Bankruptcy Judge.

Before the Court is the Motion of Innkeepers USA Trust and certain of its debtor affiliates (collectively, the "Debtors") for entry of an order (i) authorizing the Debtors to enter into a commitment letter (the "Commitment Letter") with Five Mile Capital II Pooling REIT LLC ("Five Mile"), Lehman ALI Inc. ("Lehman"), and Midland Loan Services, a division of PNC Bank, National Association, in its capacity as special servicer for the Debtors' fixed rate mortgage loan ("Midland"),[3] (ii) approving the New Party/Midland Commitment between the Debtors and Midland, (iii) approving bidding procedures (the "Bidding Procedures"), (iv) approving bid protections, (v) authorizing an expense reimbursement to "Bidder D," and (vi) modifying cash collateral order to increase expense reserve (the "Motion").

I.   BACKGROUND: EVENTS LEADING TO THE SELECTION OF THE STALKING HORSE BIDDER

In late September 2010, the Debtors began working with their advisors to discuss and develop restructuring alternatives which would maximize value. In

---

3. Midland is the special servicer for that certain secured loan in the amount of not less than $825,402,542 plus interest, costs, and fees (the "Fixed Rate Loan"), owed by certain of the Debtors (the "Fixed Rate Debtors").

October 2010, Moelis & Company LLC ("Moelis"), the Debtors' investment banker, proposed and the Board of Trustees of Innkeepers USA Trust (the "Board") approved a timeline for selecting a stalking horse bidder. During that period, the Debtors identified five stalking horse candidates, including Five Mile. On or before the November 23, 2010 deadline established by the Debtors, four of the five stalking horse candidates responded with proposals. After further discussions with the candidates, the Debtors were left with two proposals, one from Five Mile and Lehman (together, "Five Mile/Lehman") and one from the bidder known as "Bidder D."[4]

At a board meeting on December 3, 2010, the Board selected Bidder D as the stalking horse bidder, subject to certain continuing discussions between the parties regarding modifications to Bidder D's bid. On December 11, 2010, Five Mile/Lehman informed the Debtors that it had substantially improved its proposal and that commitment letters had been signed between (i) Five Mile and Lehman and (ii) Five Mile and Midland. After approximately ten days of negotiation between the Debtors and Five Mile/Lehman, including a weekend of "near around-the-clock" negotiations regarding modifications to certain terms of the proposed Commitment Letter, the Independent Committee of the Board and the Board selected Five Mile/Lehman as the stalking horse bidder. As set forth in the Declaration of Mr. William Q. Derrough of Moelis which was filed in support of the Motion, while the Debtors would have preferred the exclusion of certain provisions from the bid, the Debtors determined that the Five Mile/Lehman bid represented the most favorable economic proposal received by the Debtors and provided an opportunity to forge consensus among the Debtors' constituents.

A.   THE MOTION

As originally filed with the Court on January 14, 2011, the Motion sought (among other things) authorization for the Debtors to enter into the Commitment Letter with Five Mile and Lehman, which contemplated an enterprise-level transaction involving the Debtors' entire portfolio of 71 hotels. In connection with this stalking horse proposal (the "Original Five Mile/Lehman Bid"), Midland agreed to provide "stapled financing" to fund the Original Five Mile/Lehman Bid or any other qualified bid at the auction which (i) contained a debt-to-capitalization ratio for the reorganized enterprise of not greater than 70% and (ii) provided for payment to Lehman of not less than $200.3 million in cash. Although the Original Five Mile/Lehman Bid was supported by Lehman (as holder of the Floating Loan[5]) and Midland (as special servicer for the Fixed Rate

---

4. Due to the highly confidential nature of the bid process, the parties early on adopted the convention of referring to bidders by letter designation.

5. The "Floating Rate Loan" is comprised of (a) that certain senior secured loan in the face amount of $250,000,000, plus interest, costs and fees and (b) that certain junior mezzanine loan in the face amount of $118 million, plus interest, costs, and fees, owed by certain of the Debtors (the "Floating Rate Debtors").

Loan), together comprising over $1 billion in principal amount of secured debt, the chorus of objections to the Motion remained loud and clear.

After the filing of the Motion, the Debtors and their advisors actively continued the marketing process. Moelis compiled a list of potential buyers and made contact with over 200 of these parties, sending teasers to nearly 120 of them. The Debtors also executed more than thirty non-disclosure agreements and responded to detailed diligence requests from approximately thirty potential investors. Moelis also contacted nine potential financing sources, four of which executed non-disclosure agreements.

On January 24, 2011, the Debtors circulated a more detailed and updated process letter to potential bidders (the "Revised Process Letter"). The Revised Process Letter, which was also filed with the Court, further reminded potential bidders that the Debtors were open to all types of proposals for the Debtors' assets; it stated that the Debtors were willing to consider, in addition to superior enterprise-based transactions, *all* value-maximizing restructuring proposals, including those for pools of assets or individual assets. That same day, the Debtors also issued a widely-publicized press release announcing the Original Five Mile/Lehman Bid and the related Motion and indicating the Debtors' willingness to consider any and all other bids.

To date, as a result of these efforts, the Debtors have received multiple competing bid proposals, which were described in the sealed pleadings filed with the Court. Indeed, it appears that, as late as March 10, 2011, the date on which the hearing on the Motion commenced, interested parties continued to contact the Debtors to express interest in the Debtors' assets. The number of bids and their varying structures (each of which was for less than the entire enterprise) are evidence that there was no confusion in the market as to the Debtors' desire to receive bids in varying forms.

On February 25, 2011, formal objections to the Motion were filed by (i) the Ad Hoc Committee of Preferred Shareholders (the "Ad Hoc Committee"), (ii) LNR Securities Holdings, LLC and the ML-CFC 2006-4 and CSFB 2007-C1 Trusts (collectively, "LNR"), (iii) TriMont Real Estate Advisors, Inc. ("TriMont"), (iv) Appaloosa Investment L.P. I, Palomino Fund Ltd., Thoroughbred Fund L.P., and Thoroughbred Master Ltd. (collectively, "Appaloosa"), (v) CWCapital Asset Management LLC and CIII Asset Management LLC (together, "CW"), and (vi) the Official Committee of Unsecured Creditors.

A statement in response to the objections was filed by Apollo Investment Corporation ("Apollo"). Midland, in its capacity as special servicer, filed (i) a Statement in Support of the Motion, (ii) an Omnibus Reply to the Objections to the Motion, and (iii) a Supplemental Statement in Support of the Motion. Five Mile also filed a Reply to Objections and Statement in Support of the Motion.

B.   THE REVISED FIVE MILE/LEHMAN BID AND THE FINAL FIVE MILE/LEHMAN BID

What happened next exemplifies a chapter 11 process at its best. The Original Five Mile/Lehman Bid was modified—not once, but twice. First, it was revised to remove the seven hotel properties that are secured by individual mortgages (commonly referred to by the parties as the "Seven Sisters"), leaving only the hotels covered by the Fixed Rate Loan and Floating Rate Loan in the revised proposed transaction (the "Revised Five Mile/Lehman Bid"). The Revised Five Mile/Lehman Bid was described for the first time in the Debtors' Omnibus Reply in Support of the Motion, which was filed on March 6, 2011. Drafts of the revised Commitment Letter and Bidding Procedures were served on the Court and the Debtors' key constituents on March 8, 2011, and the final forms of such documents were filed with the Court on March 10, 2011, the date on which the hearing on the Motion commenced. Prior to the continuation of the hearing on March 11, 2011, the Revised Five Mile/Lehman Bid was altered again, and the Debtors submitted further revised, final documents to the Court (the "Final Five Mile/Lehman Bid") which eliminated the payment of any break-up fee to Five Mile/Lehman. Simply put, the creditors and preferred shareholders spoke and the Debtors listened.

It is the Final Five Mile/Lehman Bid and related Bidding Procedures that are before the Court today. The Final Five Mile/Lehman Bid proposes the following significant terms:

- The Final Five Mile/Lehman Bid contemplates an enterprise transaction involving the Debtors identified in Exhibit A to the Commitment Letter (the "Fixed/Floating Debtors") and is valued at $970.7 million. The Final Five Mile/Lehman Bid is comprised of a capital structure that includes approximately $622.5 million of debt financing and approximately $348.2 million of equity.
- The bid covers only the properties securing the Fixed Rate Loan and the Floating Rate Loan, and the Debtors will continue to market the Seven Sisters independent of the Fixed/Floating Debtors.
- Midland will provide "stapled financing" for the Final Five Mile/Lehman Bid as more fully set forth in the Commitment Letter and its related exhibits.
- General unsecured creditors with claims against the Fixed/Floating Debtors will share in a distribution of up to $3.75 million, but not to exceed a recovery of 65% of the face amount of allowed general unsecured claims against such Debtors.
- Apollo will contribute $375,000, all of which will be included in the amounts distributed to general unsecured creditors of the Fixed/Floating Debtors. Apollo will retain whatever rights it may have with respect to Debtors and property that are not covered by the Final Five Mile/Lehman Bid.
- Nothing in the Final Five Mile/Lehman Bid will impact the rights of any person or entity with respect to the $7.4 million in cash that is currently held in a bank account of Debtor Innkeepers USA Limited Partnership, which is

not subject to the Final Five Mile/Lehman Bid. No amount of the cash will be distributed in connection with the bid.

- Confirmation of the plan encompassing the Final Five Mile/Lehman Bid will not be tied to the confirmation of any plan related to the Seven Sisters' Debtors.
- Five Mile/Lehman will receive an expense reimbursement of up to $3.0 million.

C.   OBJECTIONS TO THE FINAL FIVE MILE/LEHMAN BID

On March 9 and 10, 2011, each of the objecting parties filed a statement indicating to the Court whether or not it intended to pursue its objection to the Motion in light of the revisions to the Original Five Mile/Lehman Bid. Based on each of the statements and the representations made at the hearing held on March 10 and 11, 2011, only Appaloosa continues to object to the Motion. The bases for its objection can be summarized as follows. Appaloosa believes that the revised Bidding Procedures are an impediment to competitive bidding; it specifically asserts that the revised Bidding Procedures do not permit a non-enterprise bid to be "Qualified" for the purpose of an auction and that, along with the "Overbid Allocation," the Bidding Procedures restrict bidders' ability to separately value and bid on "pool assets." Appaloosa further contends that the Lehman "cash-out" provision is a further deterrent to competitive bidding and that the "fiduciary out" contained in the Bidding Procedures does not cure any of these shortcomings. Appaloosa further objects on the basis that the revised Bidding Procedures improperly mandate terms of a plan of reorganization.

II.   APPALOOSA'S STANDING TO BE HEARD

As a preliminary matter, the Court must address whether Appaloosa, as an owner of certificated interests in the Fixed Rate Loan serviced by Midland as special servicer, has standing to be heard and to object to the Motion—specifically, standing to object to the approval of the Final Five Mile/Lehman Bid which now covers only the Fixed/Floating Debtors.

Section 1109(b) of the Bankruptcy Code provides that "[a] party in interest, including the debtor, the trustee, a creditors' committee, an equity security holders' committee, a creditor, an equity security holder, or any indenture trustee, may raise and may appear and be heard on any issue in a case under this chapter." 11 U.S.C. §1109(b). Appaloosa asserts that it has standing in the Debtors' cases under section 1109(b) as a "party in interest." This court has held that a party in interest is one that has a sufficient interest in the outcome of the case that would require representation, or a pecuniary interest that will be directly affected by the case. Courts in this District, while generally interpreting section 1109(b) broadly, have limited "party in interest" standing where a party's interest in the proceeding is not a direct one.

While it appears to be the case that no court has specifically addressed CMBS/REMIC certificateholder standing in a chapter 11 case, several courts have come close. . . . Appaloosa holds beneficial interests in the REMICS, the C-6 Trust and the C-7 Trust, that own the Fixed Rate Loan, making it merely an investor in a creditor.

This Court is unpersuaded by Appaloosa's argument that "shutting [it] out of the Bankruptcy Case inevitably will result in litigation in other venues, which ultimately will impede the implementation of a confirmable plan." In light of the consensus the Debtors have achieved in the week prior to the hearing on the Motion with respect to the Final Five Mile/Lehman Bid, it appears that the Debtors can and will propose a confirmable plan for the Fixed/Floating Debtors—and for the Excluded Debtors—in the very near term.

III.   DECISION ON THE MOTION

I will now turn to the ruling on the Motion before the Court. The standards applicable to a motion of this character appear in numerous decisions issued by courts in this Circuit, most significantly (i) the Second Circuit's decision in In re Lionel Corp., 722 F.2d 1063, 1071 (2d Cir.1983); (ii) the District Court's opinion in In re Integrated Resources, 147 B.R. 650 (S.D.N.Y.1992), and (iii) the Bankruptcy Court's decision in In re Global Crossing, 295 B.R. 726 (Bankr.S.D.N.Y.2003), in which Judge Gerber discussed the decisions in *Lionel* and *Integrated Resources*. In each of these decisions, the courts have applied a business judgment test to evaluate whether a sound business purpose justifies the use, sale, or lease of property under section 363 of the Bankruptcy Code.

In *Lionel*, the Court of Appeals for the Second Circuit held that a proposed sale under section 363(b) of the Bankruptcy Code outside of a plan of reorganization should only be approved if the proponents of the sale present "some articulated business justification, other than appeasement of major creditors." In *Integrated Resources*, Judge Mukasey concluded that business judgment rule's presumption shields corporate decision makers and their decisions from judicial second-guessing only when the following elements are present: (i) a business decision, (ii) disinterestedness, (iii) due care, (iv) good faith, and (v) according to some courts and commentators, no abuse of discretion or waste of corporate assets.

I note that today I evaluate only the Debtors' business decision in seeking approval of the stalking horse bid set forth in the final commitment letter, the Bidding Procedures, and the other relief requested in the Motion; plan confirmation issues are not before the Court and all parties' rights are reserved in that regard.

The Court finds that the Debtors have appropriately exercised their business judgment in determining to enter into the Final Five Mile/Lehman Bid and to propose the revised Bidding Procedures. The Debtors have successfully modified the initial stalking horse bid to achieve consensus among their stakeholders, and the Court has found that the only remaining objector, Appaloosa, does not have standing as a certificateholder to be heard on its objections to the Motion and the Final Five Mile/Lehman Bid. After reviewing the uncontroverted declarations of Mr. Ruisi, Mr. Derrough, and Mr. Beilinson, the Court finds that the Debtors have a sound business justification for entering into the Final Five Mile/Lehman Bid. Since Five Mile submitted its initial proposal to the Debtors in August 2010, the Debtors have successfully negotiated four subsequent proposals from Five Mile or Five Mile/Lehman, generating approximately $100 million in additional enterprise value. After months of hard-fought negotiations among the parties, which continued through the hearing on the Motion, the Debtors have demonstrated that the Final Five Mile/Lehman Bid constitutes the best bid received to date for the assets of the Fixed/Floating Debtors. For the reasons set forth herein, the Court grants the Motion and authorizes the Debtors to enter into the commitment letter supporting the Final Five Mile/Lehman Bid.

Even if the Court had granted standing to Appaloosa to be heard as a certificateholder with respect to its objections to the Motion, or if the Court considers Appaloosa's objections to be properly asserted in its capacity as a preferred shareholder or a DIP lender, the Court finds each of those objections to be without merit, for the following reasons.

First, Appaloosa argues that the revised Bidding Procedures are improper. Specifically, Appaloosa criticizes (i) the "enterprise only" limitation on bids, which mandates that all bids be structured on terms comparable to the Final Five Mile/Lehman Bid and include a debt to capitalization ratio of not greater than 70%, (ii) the "Overbid Allocation" requiring competing bids to be allocated in the same manner as the Final Five Mile/Lehman Bid, and (iii) the Leman "cash-out" provision, which requires payment in cash to Lehman of at least $200.3 million. Appaloosa asserts that each of these provisions will improperly restrict bidders and "chill" bidding.

The Court disagrees. I note that while, ideally, there would be total flexibility on each of these points in the Debtors' Bidding Procedures, the evidence in the record reveals that the Debtors by all accounts tried but failed to remove the Lehman cash-out provision. Notwithstanding the Debtors' inability to remove this provision, the Debtors have demonstrated to the Court that the other benefits of the Final Five Mile/Lehman Bid, including the fact that it is supported by the two largest secured creditors of the affected Debtors, outweighed this concern. Even LNR's financial advisor, Mr. Ronen Bojmel of Miller Buckfire, testified at his deposition (which, I note, was taken during the period in which LNR strenuously objected to the Motion) that a serious bidder would not have an issue obtaining the leverage in the market to fund a cash portion of its bid as required by the Bidding Procedures.

Similarly, Mr. Greenspan's Declaration indicates that the "not greater than 70%" leverage ratio required for Qualified Bids under the final Bidding Procedures is, if anything, higher than what a buyer may receive in the market. According to Mr. Greenspan, typical financing for hospitality assets in the current marketplace is often limited to 60% or 65% of market value and is very unlikely to exceed the 70% being offered to overbidders by Midland. Based on the entirety of the record—including the fact that interested bidders continued to engage in discussions with the Debtors through the night before the hearing on the Motion—the Court declines to second-guess the business judgment of the Debtors in agreeing to these terms. Far from being "chilled," the bidding process appears to be quite heated.

Appaloosa also criticizes the marketing process through which the Final Five Mile/Lehman Bid was obtained as "flawed" due to the Debtors' "adherence" to an enterprise-level restructuring. While the Court does not believe the Debtors' marketing process was perfect—no such process is—it was not flawed. Without question, the process has continued over an extended period of time and substantial concerns of stakeholders have been addressed as the process evolved. The allegations that the Debtors sent "mixed messages" which confused potential bidders as to whether parties could submit non-enterprise bids are unsubstantiated. To the contrary, as Mr. Derrough states in his Second Supplemental Declaration, contrary to these assertions, he has seen no evidence to support a conclusion that the marketplace is confused. Mr. Derrough declares that

> [P]otential buyers have communicated that they understand the flexibility of the Debtors' marketing process and many potential investors are taking advantage of that flexibility by working to formulate proposals either on an enterprise or non-enterprise basis. Further, the fact that the Debtors have received multiple bids for less than the entire enterprise indicates that potential investors were quite clear that the Debtors were, and continue to be, willing to accept bids in all forms.

The Court also notes that the Debtors' assets have been "in play" since September 1, 2010, the date on which the Court declined to approve the Debtors' Plan Support Agreement. Accordingly, for the past six months, the market has been keenly aware of the availability of these assets—as an enterprise, as pools, or individually. There is no evidence that a potential bidder has sat on the sidelines because of the limitations on what constitutes a "Qualified Bid," because it has not had enough time, because the Lehman cash-out provision is a "show-stopper," or because it is "confused" by the Bidding Procedures and Revised Process Letter.

Sophisticated investors and bankers who identify an asset that they believe is undervalued by the marketplace will not be shy about joining the fray here. Strategic and financial buyers who want these valuable hotel properties will step forward if they have not done so already. In that regard, should other bidders wish to come to the table and bid on all or a portion of the Debtors' assets, the Debtors still have a marketing period of forty-five days after the approval of the Motion. For now, the time has come to give the market and the Debtors the certainty and the "rules" that they need to complete the auction process and move on to plan confirmation.

Moreover, as in *Innkeepers I*, the Debtors urge that, in any event, there is a "fiduciary out" and that the Debtors may and will consider any and all bids whether they are "Qualified Bids" under the revised Bidding Procedures or not. Unlike in *Innkeepers I*, however, the "fiduciary out" contained in the current transaction trumps every other provision in the controlling documents. Contained in Section 11 of the revised Bidding Procedures, it provides that "[u]pon the determination by the Debtors' directors, trustees, or members, as applicable, and upon advice of counsel, no term or provision of the Term Sheet or the Commitment Letter shall prevent, amend, alter, or reduce the Debtors' ability to exercise their fiduciary duties under applicable law." In other words, if a competing bidder submits a bid that reflects a higher return to either the Debtor obligors under the Fixed Rate Loan, the Floating Rate Loan, or both, albeit comprised of a different mix of cash, debt, and equity than that in the Final Five Mile/Lehman Bid, the Debtors can and should exercise their fiduciary duty to give it their full consideration.

Finally, it is worth noting that the Debtors need not have pursued an auction process at all; they could simply have proceeded directly to a plan. They ought not to be faulted for attempting to create a framework for additional value to be realized for creditors. *See, e.g.,* In re Neff Corp., Case No. 10-12610(SCC) (Bankr.S.D.N.Y.2010) (debtors' use of "payout event procedures" in plan process resulted in increased return for stakeholders from original proposal).

In that regard, the Court notes that certain of the remaining objections asserted by Appaloosa (and previously asserted by LNR, the Ad Hoc Committee, TriMont, and CW) are best categorized as confirmation objections. For example, Appaloosa contends that (i) the Final Five Mile/Lehman Bid and the revised Bidding Procedures dictate plan terms that go beyond the scope of the investment terms encompassed by the bid, (ii) the Term Sheet requires that the negotiated terms apply to any successful overbid, and (iii) the release provisions are overly broad and should not be approved absent the consent of each releasing party.

The Court finds that these concerns need not be addressed at this time. The Debtors are asking the Court to approve Bidding Procedures and a stalking horse bid so that they may conduct an auction. The winner of the auction will gain the right to sponsor a plan of reorganization. The proposed plan will still be required to meet all confirmation requirements set forth in the Bankruptcy Code, and parties in interest will be afforded the right to make relevant objections in the event that they believe the proposed plan falls short of such requirements. Ultimately, the transaction contemplated in the Final Five Mile/Lehman Bid, or any other bid ultimately selected by the Debtors, will not be consummated absent confirmation of a plan. The rights of all parties in interest to object to confirmation at the appropriate time are reserved and preserved.

With respect to the issue of releases, while releases may be important to the ultimate success of a plan, it is impossible to properly analyze the releases that have been proposed in the Term Sheet. Deciding whether a release is appropriate before a plan has been formulated or filed has the potential to short-circuit negotiations among the Debtors and their creditors. It remains to be seen if the proposed releases, including the Special Servicer Release, the Apollo Release, and the Global Release (as each is defined in the relevant documents comprising the Final Five Mile/Lehman Bid) are appropriate. These issues will be considered if they are raised once a plan of reorganization is proposed.

Accordingly, for all of the foregoing reasons, the Motion is granted.

Do you see any similarities between the standing issue here and the complaints that arose in *Chrysler?* Refer back to Chapter 16.

2.   CREDIT BIDDING

What stops the debtor from selling its assets to insiders at some lowball price? Extreme cases are apt to be checked by the court, but what if the price is low, but not so low as to be ridiculous? The Code, in section 363(k), provides an answer.

IN RE: SUBMICRON SYSTEMS CORPORATION

432 F.3d 448
United States Court of Appeals, Third Circuit.
Jan. 6, 2006.

AMBRO, Circuit Judge.

Appellant Howard S. Cohen ("Cohen"), as Plan Administrator for the bankruptcy estates of SubMicron Systems Corporation, SubMicron Systems, Inc., SubMicron Wet Process Stations, Inc. and SubMicron Systems Holdings I, Inc. (jointly and severally, "SubMicron"), challenges the sale to an entity created by Sunrise Capital Partners, LP ("Sunrise") of SubMicron's assets under 11 U.S.C. §363(b), which authorizes court-approved sales of assets "other than in the ordinary course of business." Sunrise negotiated directly with several—but not all—of SubMicron's creditors before presenting its bid to the District Court. These creditors—The KB Mezzanine Fund II, LP ("KB"), Equinox Investment Partners, LLC ("Equinox"),[6] and Celerity Silicon, LLC ("Celerity") (collectively, the "Lenders")—agreed to contribute toward the purchase of SubMicron's assets new capital along with all of their claims in bankruptcy against SubMicron in exchange for equity in the entity formed by Sunrise to acquire the assets—Akrion LLC ("Akrion"). Akrion in turn "credit bid" the full value of the Lenders' secured claims contributed to it as part of its bid for SubMicron's assets pursuant to 11 U.S.C. §363(k). The District Court approved the sale.[7]

Cohen, seeking as Plan Administrator of the SubMicron estates to aid unsecured creditors "cut out of the deal" by the Lenders and Sunrise, attacks the sale on several fronts. First, he argues that the purportedly secured debt

---

6. Equinox was formed in 1996 to manage KB after it was acquired by Dresdner Bank. For the sake of simplicity, we shall refer to both entities simply as "KB/Equinox."

7. This bankruptcy case is before the District Court because it withdrew, pursuant to 28 U.S.C. §157(d), the reference of the case to the Bankruptcy Court for the District of Delaware.

investments made by the Lenders and contributed to Akrion should have been recharacterized by the District Court as equity investments. In the alternative, if the District Court did not err in declining to recharacterize the investments as equity, Cohen contends that it erred by failing to conclude that the debt was unsecured. Even if the District Court properly considered the debt secured, Cohen challenges the propriety of the District Court's allowance of the credit bid portion of Akrion's offer. As a last option, Cohen asserts that the District Court erred by declining to equitably subordinate the Lenders' secured claims to those of creditors with inferior claims. For the reasons discussed below, we reject these arguments and affirm the judgment of the District Court.

I.   FACTS AND PROCEDURAL POSTURE

A.   SUBMICRON'S FINANCING

Before its sale in bankruptcy, SubMicron designed, manufactured and marketed "wet benches"[8] for use in the semiconductor industry. By 1997, it was experiencing significant financial and operational difficulties. To sustain its operations in the late 1990s, SubMicron secured financing from several financial and/or investment institutions. On November 25, 1997, it entered into a $15 million working capital facility with Greyrock Business Credit ("Greyrock"), granting Greyrock first priority liens on all of its inventory, equipment, receivables and general intangibles. The next day, SubMicron raised another $20 million through the issuance of senior subordinated 12% notes (the "1997 Notes") to KB/Equinox (for $16 million) and Celerity (for $4 million) secured by liens behind Greyrock on substantially all of SubMicron's assets. Submicron subsequently issued a third set of notes in 1997 (the "Junior 1997 Notes") for $13.7 million, comprising $8.7 million of 8% notes and a $5 million note to The BOC Group, Inc. The Junior 1997 Notes were secured but junior to the security for the 1997 Notes. Despite this capital influx, SubMicron incurred a net loss of $47.6 million for the 1997 fiscal year.

A steep downturn in the semiconductor industry made 1998 a similarly difficult year for SubMicron. By August of that year, it was paying substantially all of the interest due on the 1997 Notes as paid-in-kind senior subordinated notes. On December 2, 1998, SubMicron and Greyrock agreed to renew the Greyrock line of credit, reducing the maximum funds available from $15 to $10 million and including a $2 million overadvance conditioned on SubMicron's securing an additional $4 million in financing. To satisfy this condition, on December 3, SubMicron issued Series B 12% notes (the "1998 Notes") to KB/Equinox (for $3.2 million) and Celerity (for $800,000). The 1998 Notes ranked *pari passu* with the 1997 Notes and the interest was deferred until

---

8. Wet benches are automatic process tools used for cleaning and etching operations in semiconductor processing. *See* http:// www.semiconductorglossary.com/default.asp?searchterm =wet+bench (last visited Dec. 27, 2005).

October 1, 1999. SubMicron incurred a net loss of $21.9 million for the 1998 fiscal year, and at year's end its liabilities exceeded its assets by $4.2 million.

SubMicron's financial health did not improve in 1999. By March of that year, its management determined that additional financing would be required to meet the company's immediate critical working capital needs. To this end, between March 10, 1999 and June 6, 1999, SubMicron issued a total of eighteen Series 1999 12% notes (the "1999 Tranche One Notes") for a total of $7,035,154 (comprising nine notes to KB/Equinox totaling $5,888,123 and nine notes to Celerity totaling $1,147,031). The 1999 Tranche One Notes proved insufficient to keep SubMicron afloat. As a result, between July 8, 1999 and August 31, 1999, KB/Equinox and Celerity made periodic payments to SubMicron (the "1999 Tranche Two Funding") totaling $3,982,031 and $147,969, respectively. No notes were issued in exchange for the 1999 Tranche Two Funding. Between the 1999 Tranche One Notes and the 1999 Tranche Two Funding (collectively, the "1999 Fundings"), KB/Equinox and Celerity advanced SubMicron a total of $9,870,154 and $1,295,000, respectively. (The 1999 Fundings were recorded as secured debt on SubMicron's 10-Q filing with the Securities and Exchange Commission.) Despite the cash infusions, during the first half of 1999 SubMicron incurred a net loss of $9.9 million. On June 30, 1999, SubMicron's liabilities exceeded its assets by $3.1 million.

By January 1999, KB/Equinox had appointed three members to SubMicron's Board of Directors. All appointees were either principals or employees of KB/Equinox. By June 1999, following resignations of various SubMicron Board members, KB/Equinox employees Bonaparte Liu and Robert Wickey, and Celerity employee Mark Benham, represented three-quarters of the Board, with SubMicron CEO David Ferran the lone Board member not employed by KB/Equinox or Celerity.

B. THE ACQUISITION

SubMicron began acquisition discussions with Sunrise in July of 1999. By all accounts, it was generally understood that if SubMicron failed to reach a deal with Sunrise, it would be forced to liquidate, leaving secured creditors—with the exception of Greyrock—with pennies on the dollar and unsecured creditors and shareholders with nothing. KB/Equinox, not SubMicron's management, conducted negotiations with Sunrise, developing and agreeing on the terms and financial structure of an acquisition to occur in the context of a prepackaged bankruptcy.

On August 31, 1999, SubMicron entered into an asset purchase agreement with Akrion, the entity created by Sunrise to function as the acquisition vehicle. The following day, SubMicron filed a Chapter 11 bankruptcy petition and an associated motion seeking approval of the sale of its assets to Sunrise outside the ordinary course of business pursuant to §363(b) of the Bankruptcy Code.

The asset purchase agreement reiterated, *inter alia*, that KB/Equinox and Celerity would contribute their secured claims (*i.e.*, the 1997 Notes, the 1998

Notes and the 1999 Fundings) in order for Akrion to credit bid these claims under §363 of the Bankruptcy Code—but only contingent on the closing of the sale. The agreement also required SubMicron, at the closing of the sale, to pay $5,500,000 immediately to the holders of the 1999 Fundings. In return, KB/Equinox and Celerity would receive a 31.475% interest in Akrion (KB/Equinox received a 30% interest and Celerity received a 1.475% interest). The Court and Official Committee of Unsecured Creditors (the "Creditors' Committee") were apprised of the terms of this agreement prior to the sale.

At the sale hearing Akrion submitted a bid of $55,507,587 for SubMicron. The cash component of the bid totaled $10,202,000 and included $5,500,000 in cash from Akrion, $3,382,000 to pay pre- and post-petition Greyrock secured debt, and $850,000 to cover administrative claims. The credit portion of the bid consisted of the $38,721,637 outstanding for the 1997 Notes, the 1998 Notes, and the 1999 Fundings (all of which KB/Equinox and Celerity had contributed to Akrion), plus $1,324,138 in individual secured claims, for a total of $40,045,775. Finally, the bid included SubMicron's liabilities that would be assumed by Akrion—$681,346 in lease obligations and $4,578,466 in other assumed liabilities for a total of $5,259,812. No other bid for SubMicron's assets was made, SubMicron's Board and the Court both approved Akrion's bid over the objection of the Creditors' Committee, and on October 15, 1999, the asset sale closed.

On April 18, 2000, the Creditors' Committee brought against the Lenders, among others, an adversary proceeding in which it made the claims before us on appeal. (Cohen was subsequently substituted for the Creditors' Committee.) After a bench trial before Judge Sue Robinson in late July/early August 2001, she ruled against Cohen, setting out her reasoning in a comprehensive opinion. Cohen appeals.

V.   PROPRIETY OF §363 CREDIT BID

Having determined that the 1999 Fundings represented an extension of secured debt, we turn to Cohen's argument that the §363(k) credit bid was improper because the Lenders did not (and could not) demonstrate that some portion of their claims remained secured by collateral as defined in Bankruptcy Code §506(a). The District Court determined that "there was no collateral available to actually secure the 1999 fundings." As a result, Cohen argues that, because the secured debt had no actual (or economic) value, it could not be credit bid under §363(k). Because that section empowers creditors to bid the total *face* value of their claims—it does not limit bids to claims' economic value—we disagree and hold that the District Court did not err in allowing the Lenders to credit bid their claims.

It is well settled among district and bankruptcy courts that creditors can bid the full face value of their secured claims under §363(k).

In fact, logic demands that §363(k) be interpreted in this way; interpreting it to cap credit bids at the economic value of the underlying collateral is theoretically nonsensical.

A hypothetical is illustrative.

> Assume that Debtor has a single asset: a truck, T. Lender is a secured creditor that has loaned Debtor $15, taking a security interest in T. Debtor is in Chapter 11 bankruptcy and has filed a §363 motion to sell T to Bidder for $10. Debtor argues that Lender can only credit bid $10 for T and must bid any excess in cash if it wishes to outbid B.

This hypothetical reveals the logical problem with an actual value bid cap. If Lender bids $12 for T, by definition $12 *becomes* the value of Lender's security interest in T. In this way, until Lender is paid in full, Lender can always overbid Bidder. (Naturally, Lender will not outbid Bidder unless Lender believes it could generate a greater return on T than the return for Lender represented by Bidder's offer.) As Lender holds a security interest in T, any amount bid for it up to the value of Lender's full claim becomes the secured portion of Lender's claim by definition. Given the weight of reason's demand that "it must be so," we see no reason to catalog the myriad other arguments that have been advanced to support this "interpretation."

Cohen is not out of plausible arguments, however, as he claims that because the Lenders were not *partially* undersecured but *completely* undersecured— that is, because the collateral was found to have no economic value—this case is different. Yet nothing about the logic of allowing credit bids up to the full face value of the collateral changes if the collateral has no actual value. Because the Lenders had a valid security interest in essentially all the assets sold, by definition they were entitled to the satisfaction of their claims from available proceeds of any sale of those underlying assets. Their credit bid did nothing more than preserve their right to the proceeds, as credit bids do under §363(k).

Unable squarely to rest this argument on a theoretically sound construction of the Bankruptcy Code's credit bidding provisions, Cohen enlists the aid of 11 U.S.C. §506(a), which provides for the splitting of partially secured claims into their secured claim and unsecured claim components. Yet §506(a) is inapplicable. As one member of the Supreme Court has explained, "[w]hen ... the Bankruptcy Code means to refer to a secured party's entire allowed claim, *i.e.*, to both the 'secured' and 'unsecured' portions under §506(a), it uses the term *'allowed claim'—as in 11 U.S.C. §363(k)*...." Dewsnup v. Timm, 502 U.S. 410, 422 (1992) (Scalia, J., dissenting) (first emphasis in original). That is, §363(k) speaks to the full face value of a secured creditor's claim, not to the portion of that claim that is actually collateralized as described in §506.

Moreover, as a practical matter, no §506 valuation is required before a §363 sale of the underlying collateral can be approved. Section 363 attempts to *avoid* the complexities and inefficiencies of valuing collateral altogether by substituting the theoretically preferable mechanism of a free market sale to set the price. The provision is premised on the notion that the market's reaction to a sale best reflects the economic realities of assets' worth. Naturally, then, courts are not required first to determine the assets' worth before approving such a market sale. This would contravene the basis for the provision's very existence.

For these reasons, we conclude that the District Court properly allowed the Lenders to contribute their credit bids under the §363 sale.

PROBLEM SET 29.1

1. Some argue that credit bidding distorts an auction, because the lender does not have to bid actual cash. What do you make of this?
2. The ultimate effect of section 363(k) is that if the debtor's assets will not sell for more than the secured debt, the secured lender takes the assets if it wants them. That amounts to a foreclosure, but in this case the foreclosure is done in federal court. Should the bankruptcy courts be used for this purpose?
3. In the prior section we noted the tendency to adopt bidding procedures that include restrictions on who can become an actual participant in the 363 sale. Why?

3.   SUCCESSOR LIABILITY AND 363 SALES

In Chapter 24 we noted that the normal rule was that an asset sale does not transfer any liabilities, unless certain exceptions applied. These exceptions are lumped under the general category of successor liability.

Now read section 363(f) of the Code:

(f) The trustee [or DIP] may sell property under subsection (b) or (c) of this section free and clear of any interest in such property of an entity other than the estate, only if—

(1) applicable nonbankruptcy law permits sale of such property free and clear of such interest;
(2) such entity consents;
(3) such interest is a lien and the price at which such property is to be sold is greater than the aggregate value of all liens on such property;
(4) such interest is in bona fide dispute; or
(5) such entity could be compelled, in a legal or equitable proceeding, to accept a money satisfaction of such interest.

Does this provision allow assets sales that happen under the Bankruptcy Code to rid assets of successor liability claims? Is a successor liability claim an "interest," and if so, can it be detached from the debtor's assets via bankruptcy?

JUSTIN LEFEVER v. K.P. HOVNANIAN ENTERPRISES, INC.

160 N.J. 307
Supreme Court of New Jersey.
July 29, 1999.

O'HERN, J.

This appeal concerns the meaning of the product-line exception in Ramirez v. Amsted Industries Inc., 86 N.J. 332, 431 A.2d 811 (1981), when a successor corporation acquires the predecessor's product line through a bankruptcy sale.

The general rule of corporate-successor liability is that when a company sells its assets to another company, the acquiring company is not liable for the debts and liabilities of the selling company simply because it has succeeded to the ownership of the assets of the seller. Traditionally, there have been only four exceptions: (1) the successor expressly or impliedly assumes the predecessor's liabilities; (2) there is an actual or *de facto* consolidation or merger of the seller and the purchaser; (3) the purchasing company is a mere continuation of the seller; or (4) the transaction is entered into fraudulently to escape liability. 15 William & Fletcher, *Cyclopedia of the Law of Corporations* §7122, nn. 9-15 (1990).

New Jersey, along with several other jurisdictions, has adopted a product-line exception to the general rule. Under that doctrine, by purchasing a substantial part of the manufacturer's assets and continuing to market goods in the same product line, a corporation may be exposed to strict liability in tort for defects in the predecessor's products. The question in this appeal is whether the product-line exception is applicable when the successor has purchased the predecessor's assets at a bankruptcy sale. Our task is made easier in this case because the bankrupt was not the manufacturer of the defective product, but rather an intermediary owner of the product line against whom no claim had been made by the injured party.

I

The facts of this case are more fully set forth in the reported opinion of the Appellate Division, 311 *N.J.Super.* 1, 709 *A.*2d 253 (1998). For convenience, we shall eliminate reference to certain intermediate business entities used by the parties. Conceptually, there were three distributors of the product line. Plaintiff, Justin Lefever, was injured in 1989 when a forklift he was operating tipped over and caused him to suffer crushing injuries. The Lull Engineering Corporation, Inc., whom we shall refer to as "Lull I," had manufactured and distributed the forklift. Through a series of transfers, Lull I's assets were acquired in 1986 by Lull Corporation ("Lull II"). In 1992, Lull II went into bankruptcy. In November 1993, the trustee in the bankruptcy proceedings conveyed to Lull Industries Inc. ("Lull III"), interests in substantially all of Lull II's assets.

On September 24, 1990, plaintiff sued "Lull Engineering Co., Inc." in the Superior Court, Law Division, Middlesex County.[9] Plaintiff never sued Lull II. During the course of discovery, plaintiff learned that Lull II had acquired the assets of Lull I, and that Lull II had transferred its assets to Lull III through a bankruptcy sale. Plaintiff joined Lull III as a party defendant. Lull III moved to dismiss plaintiff's claim on the basis that the bankruptcy sale was free and clear of any interests in the property, including any successor-liability claims. The trial court granted Lull III's motion.

On appeal, the Appellate Division reversed.

II

After analyzing the differences between the continuity exception formulated by the Michigan Supreme Court in *Turner* and the product-line exception [adopted by the California Supreme Court] in *Ray*, the *Ramirez* Court adopted the rule of *Ray* with its focus on the product causing the injury. Concerning its own justifications for the "product line" exception, the Court in *Ramirez* emphasized the two latter justifications of spreading the risk and enjoyment of the predecessor manufacturer's good will.

III

Does the supremacy of federal bankruptcy law prevent the application of state common law to claims against a successor business enterprise that has acquired its assets through a bankruptcy sale?

The short answer to this question is "yes," but only if the federal bankruptcy court has "dealt with" the claim. The long answer requires us to examine the function of a bankruptcy sale and to determine what effect a bankruptcy sale may have on other principles of law affecting the liability of a successor business enterprise. For purposes of this analysis, we will draw essentially on a summary of the law of bankruptcy sales set forth by Michael H. Reed in *Successor Liability and Bankruptcy Sales*, 51 Bus.Law. 653 (1996). This recital is not intended to be a digest of bankruptcy law but only a brief outline of what we understand to be the governing principles that apply in federal courts.

There are essentially two ways [in which] a bankruptcy trustee or debtor-in-possession can sell assets: (i) a sale pursuant to section 363 of the Code; or (ii) a sale pursuant to a confirmed Chapter 11 plan of reorganization.

---

9. Although plaintiff in fact named as defendant a company that purchased Lull I's assets and later sold them to Lull II, it appears that plaintiff intended to sue Lull I, whose name is virtually identical to the name of its immediate successor. The named defendant has been a dormant corporation with no assets since 1986.

A. DOES A SECTION 363 SALE CUT OFF PRODUCT LIABILITY CLAIMS?

Section 363(f) of the Bankruptcy Code (the Code), 11 U.S.C.A. §363(f) (1978), authorizes the trustee or debtor-in-possession to sell property of the estate "free and clear of the 'interest' of another entity in such property. . . ." The primary purpose of that provision is "to permit the sale of property free and clear of the liens of secured creditors."

Some courts have held that notwithstanding the use of the term "interest" in section 363(f), the bankruptcy court has

> "the power to convey assets free and clear of not only property interests, such as liens and encumbrances, but also preconveyance claims, or in personam liabilities of the transferor
>
> "Other courts, however, have held that, because the plain language of section 363(f) speaks only of 'interests' and makes no mention of 'claims,' it does not provide authority for a sale free and clear of preconveyance claims because claims, as distinguished from 'liens' and 'encumbrances,' are not property interests."

Again, the author explains:

> [I]t is difficult to quarrel with these [latter] decisions. The term "interest," while undefined, clearly connotes some form of property interest as it is utilized throughout the Code. It includes the property interest of an equity security holder . . . as well as the property interest of a lienholder. . . . Creditor-held interests clearly include not only "liens" but also "charges."

There is nothing in the Code, however, to suggest that the term "interest" was intended to embrace rights to payment, which are the substantive nuclei of bankruptcy "claims." *See*...§101(5) [of the Code]; *see also* Fairchild Aircraft, Inc. v. Campbell (In re Fairchild Aircraft Corp.) [discussed *infra* at 318, 734 A.2d at 296], wherein Judge Clark explained: "Section 363(f) does not authorize sales free and clear of any interest, but rather of any interest in such property. . . . The sorts of interests impacted by a sale free and clear are *in rem* interests which have attached to the property." *Id.* at 917–18.

That a Chapter 11 sale will resolve the question of successor liability is thus by no means clear. Courts analyzing the scope of the power of bankruptcy courts to sell property free and clear of claims reason that the breadth of such power is coextensive with the courts' power to discharge claims under the Code.

Thus, a claimant asserting successor liability would argue that even if, as a general proposition, the bankruptcy court has the power to convey assets free and clear of "claims," it does not have the power to cut off obligations or rights, such as environmental agency injunctions or future products liability claims, which are not cognizable as claims for dischargeability purposes. Such claims could not be divested, regardless of whether the sale is made within or outside of a plan of reorganization.

Although the asset purchase agreement between the trustee and the buyer at the bankruptcy sale expressly recites that the purchaser "will not assume, undertake, accept or be bound by or responsible for ... any liabilities or obligations of Lull or Erickson or their affiliates that arise or have arisen prior to the Closing Date," such disclaimers are ineffective in insulating the buyer from successor liability when other principles of law require the imposition of liability.

Congress appears to have recognized the foregoing limitation on the scope of a bankruptcy discharge by expressly providing that in the case of debtors liable for personal injury due to asbestos-containing products, bankruptcy courts shall have the authority to insulate a successor from liability "with respect to any claim or demand made against such entity by reason of its becoming such a transferee or successor." In *Fairchild Aircraft, supra*, 184 *B.R.* at 931–33, which involved personal injury claims arising out of an airplane crash that occurred after a bankruptcy sale, the court refused to cut off those claims because of (1) insufficient or impossible notice to the putative successor liability claimants, (2) insufficient representation of the interests of such claimants, and (3) absence of any provision for such claimants under the plan of reorganization. Thus, even if a bankruptcy court were to seek to "deal with" preconfirmation conduct, at a minimum there probably should be notice to the class of claimants who would be subject to the claims, and some provision for such claimants should be made under the plan of reorganization. For example, in the silicone breast-implant cases, one of the manufacturers, Dow Corning, entered Chapter 11 and then sought to reach a settlement with its comprehensive general liability insurers. Although the court approving the settlement held that third parties injured as the alleged result of the defendant's silicone breast implants did not have an interest in the insurance policies, the court noted that "competing claims to the insufficient assets [would] be settled through the reorganization process...."

Justin Lefever's claim was simply not dealt with in the bankruptcy proceedings. Plaintiff was not a creditor of the bankrupt. He filed no claim in the bankruptcy proceedings. In addition, the sale here was under Section 363 and Lefever had no "interest" in the sense of a lien or encumbrance on the property. In fact, the bankruptcy trustee specifically authorized plaintiff to proceed with his suit against Lull III because the suit was not against the bankrupt. *But see* In re All Am. of Ashburn, Inc., 56 B.R. 186 Bankr.N.D.Ga.1986) (enjoining claim against successor because bankruptcy sale of assets was free and clear of all claims). The most that can be said is that the debtor, Lull II, listed plaintiff's claim in its schedule of affairs, but there was no attempt to "deal with it."

IV

If federal law permits it, should the principles of Ramirez call for successor liability after bankruptcy sales?

This is by far the harder of the two main issues in the case. Respected commentators find the "policies behind the 'product line' exception inapplicable to the purchase of assets at a bankruptcy sale. Not only does this extension of strict liability violate basic principles of tort law, but it also contradicts the fundamental goals of the Bankruptcy Code. . . ." David R. Kott & Walter A. Effross, *Forgive Us Our Predecessors: Bankruptcy Sales and the Product Line Exception*, 4 Prod.Liab.L.J. 123, 123 (May 1993). They argue that imposing successor liability amounts to creating a lien on the assets in favor of future products liability claimants and thereby decreases the sale price and effectively minimizes the assets available for the debtors. Future products liability claimants will have "jumped the line" to come out ahead of the debtor's current creditors who may be deprived of compensation for the claims. Although the argument is appealing, it has equal application to that wide variety of other contexts in which liability may be imposed on a successor. *See Chicago Truck Drivers, supra*, 59 F.3d at 51. For example, a purchaser of contaminated assets will be responsible for environmental cleanup costs even though the property has been acquired at a bankruptcy sale free and clear of liens. James B. Holden & Debora D. Jones, *Representing Purchasers of Assets from Bankruptcy Estates*, 20 Colo.Law. 2259, 2261 (1991). Liability also may be imposed on transferees in other contexts. *See, e.g.*, Upholsterers' Int'l Union Pension Fund v. Artistic Furniture of Pontiac, 920 F.2d 1323 (7th Cir.1990) (delinquent pension fund contributions); Klegerman v. F.G. Apparel, Inc., No. 85C7887, 1986 WL 2531 (N.D.Ill. Feb. 11, 1986) (considering successor's liability for age-discrimination claims despite acquisition of assets at bankruptcy sale).

We acknowledge that California, the jurisdiction that initiated the product-line exception, has declined to apply the exception to the acquisition of a product line through a bankruptcy sale. In Stewart v. Telex Communications, Inc., 1 Cal.App.4th 190, 1 Cal.Rptr.2d 669, 675 (1991), the California Court of Appeals adopted the reasoning of the Washington Supreme Court in Hall v. Armstrong Cork, Inc., 103 Wash.2d 258, 692 P.2d 787, 792 (1984), that "'[t]he traditional corporate rule of nonliability is . . . counterbalanced by the policies of strict liability [only] when acquisition by the successor, and not some [other] event or act, virtually destroys the ability of the plaintiff to seek redress from the manufacturer of the defective product.'" We believe, however, that the California court has focused on the first justification for the product-line exception, specifically, that strict liability is appropriate when the successor's acquisition of the business has virtually destroyed the plaintiff's remedies, to the exclusion of the more dominant themes.

We must first remember that in *Ramirez* the defendant did not cause the destruction of the plaintiff's remedies against the original manufacturer. On the same day that the Court decided *Ramirez*, the Court decided *Nieves, supra*, 86 N.J. 361, 431 A.2d 826. In that case, an intermediate producer of the product line argued that an essential justification for the imposition of liability was missing, namely, the nonavailability of a functioning manufacturer of the product line. The intermediate manufacturer argued that the first prong of the *Ray* doctrine is concerned solely with finding one viable extant corporate defendant that had succeeded to the manufacturing operation and that it was not such a defendant. The Court disagreed. In its view, "the imposition on [the intermediary] of potential liability for injuries . . . is justified as a fair and equitable burden necessarily attached to the substantial benefit that [the intermediary] enjoyed in the 'deliberate, albeit legitimate, exploitation of [the manufacturer's] established reputation as a going concern producing a specific product line.'" *Nieves, supra,* 86 N.J. at 369, 431 A.2d 826 (quoting *Ray, supra,* 136 Cal.Rptr. 574, 560 P.2d at 11). Both the intermediary and the final successor had the ability to assume the original manufacturer's risk-spreading and cost-avoidance roles.

One may fairly assume that a prudent purchaser of assets makes the cost-benefit analysis that renders the acquisition profitable. The *Ramirez* doctrine rests on principles of justice and fairness. "[T]he legal limitation on the scope of [products] liability is associated with policy—with our more or less inadequately expressed ideas of what justice demands, or of what is administratively possible and convenient."

Ultimately, the question is whether the imposition of a duty on the successor to respond to the complaints of its predecessor's customers is fair, when the successor trades on the loyalty of those customers.

In these circumstances, we do not consider it unfair to impose liability on the successor manufacturers of the Lull forklift.

The judgment of the Appellate Division is affirmed.

POLLOCK, J., dissenting.

With limited exceptions, successor corporations are not liable for harm caused by defective products made or distributed by a predecessor. *Restatement (Third) of Torts* sec. 12 (1997). Contrary to the rule in most jurisdictions, this Court recognizes the "product-line" exception. . . .

The product-line exception represents our perception of the appropriate balance in the ordinary case between compensating injured parties and the uninhibited transfer of assets.

This appeal questions the weight to be placed in striking that balance when the selling corporation at the time of sale is in bankruptcy. The majority holds that the bankruptcy is of no weight. I believe, however, that when an injury occurs before bankruptcy and the injured party had the opportunity to file a claim in the bankruptcy proceeding, a court should weigh the bankruptcy when striking the balance of interests in the "product line" exception.

To place the matter in perspective, some facts in addition to those set forth in the majority opinion may help. Plaintiff, Justin Lefever, was injured in 1989 in an employment-related accident arising out of the operation of a forklift that had been manufactured by the corporation identified by the majority as "Lull I." Previously, in 1973, Lull I had sold its manufacturing assets to "Lull II," which assumed responsibility for product liability claims such as plaintiff's. Initially, plaintiff sued "Lull Engineering Co., Inc.," for manufacturing and design defects in producing the forklift. Plaintiff also joined as defendants Giles & Ransome, the distributor of the forklift, and K.P. Hovananian Enterprises, the owner of the work site where the accident occurred. Thereafter, plaintiff settled his claims against Giles and Ransome and K.P. Hovananian.

On March 3, 1992, nearly twenty years after acquiring Lull I's assets, Lull II filed a petition for a Chapter 11 bankruptcy. The trustee in bankruptcy promptly notified plaintiff of the bankruptcy, but plaintiff decided not to file a claim. In 1993, Badger R. Bazen (Badger) bought Lull II's assets "free and clear of all interests pursuant to Sections 363(b), 363(f) of the Bankruptcy Code" and with an express disclaimer of any of Lull II's liability for products manufactured or sold before the closing date. The bankruptcy court approved the sale. Also in 1993, Badger sold the assets to the corporation identified by the majority as Lull III.

The bankruptcy court stayed all actions against the debtor. In January 1995, however, the trustee sent plaintiff's counsel a letter stating that the stay did not apply because the present action is not against the debtor, Lull II. On November 14, 1996, plaintiff joined Lull III as a defendant.

One justification for the product line exception when the original manufacturer no longer exists at the time of the injury is that an injured party may be left without a remedy. *Mettinger, supra,* 153 N.J. at 383, 709 A.2d 779. When, however, the injured party has recourse against the original manufacturer, that consideration should yield to the unfairness of imposing liability on an innocent successor. The scale could tilt back toward the imposition of liability, if the successor agreed to assume liability in the asset-purchase agreement or if it knowingly participated in a fraudulent asset transfer. Here, the purchaser of Lull II's assets expressly disclaimed liability. Plaintiff, moreover, does not allege that Lull III participated in a fraudulent asset transfer or engaged in a sham transaction.

Significantly, plaintiff had recourse against Lull II, which had assumed contractually the liability of the manufacturer, Lull I. Admittedly, Lull II's bankruptcy could affect the amount paid on plaintiff's claim, but no more so than it would affect the claims of other creditors.

As the Third Circuit Court of Appeals stated, "If a remedy against the original manufacturer was available ... the consumer has not been obliged to bear the risk and the justification for imposing successor liability evaporates." Conway v. White Trucks, 885 F.2d 90, 95 (1989). To the same effect, the Seventh Circuit Court of Appeals has written:

> Had the [plaintiffs] been parties to the bankruptcy proceeding, they would have had no possible basis for a suit against [the successor] . . . because the successorship doctrine on which they rely is inapplicable if the plaintiff had a chance to obtain a legal remedy against the predecessor, even so limited a remedy as that afforded by the filing of a claim in bankruptcy. [Zerand-Bernal, Inc. v. Cox, 23 F.3d 159, 163 (7th Cir.1994) (Posner, J.).]

The majority suggests that plaintiff should be permitted to proceed with his suit against Lull III because his claim was not "dealt with" in the bankruptcy proceedings. Continuing, the majority remarks that "even if a bankruptcy court were to seek to 'deal' with preconfirmation conduct, at a minimum there probably should be notice to the class of claimants . . . and some provision for such claimants should be made under the plan of reorganization." *See ante* at 320-21, 734 A.2d at 298. Plaintiff's claim was not "dealt with," however, only because he failed to file a claim in the bankruptcy proceedings, not because he had no notice of the bankruptcy.

The majority opinion limits the power of the bankruptcy court by denying it the power to permit the sale of the debtor's assets free of liability for tort claims. Section 363(f) of the Bankruptcy Code provides, however, that the bankruptcy court shall have the power to sell assets "free and clear of any interest in ... property." 11 U.S.C. 363(f). Indeed, the sale of Lull II's assets, as approved by the bankruptcy court, so provided. A question remains whether such a sale is free and clear of tort claims that arise after the sale. No case, however, has ever held a successor corporation liable for a tort claim that arose before court approval of the sale.

When a tort occurs before bankruptcy, courts have treated a tort claimant like all other claimants. In that context, a sale of assets "free and clear" does not result in the imposition of liability on the successor corporation. To impose successor liability would frustrate "the orderly scheme of the bankruptcy law by allowing some unsecured creditors to recover without regard to the priority order of the bankruptcy proceedings." A bankruptcy court's authority to sell assets free and clear of existing tort claims is "implicit in the court's general equitable powers and its duty to distribute debtor's assets." The effect of subjecting the successor to the risk of liability is to diminish the value of the assets to the extent of the cost of that risk.

That diminution in value will redound to the detriment of all other creditors who seek to participate in the distribution of the bankruptcy estate. Permitting a tort claimant to pursue a successor after a bankruptcy sale would grant that claimant a priority over other claimants who were paid in accordance with the Bankruptcy Code and would produce a negative impact on the trustee's ability to sell assets of the estate at a fair price. Those considerations should tip the scale back toward the general rule of not imposing liability on a successor when a claimant has been injured before the bankruptcy proceedings and provided with notice and the opportunity to participate in the proceedings. In sum, the imposition of liability on the purchaser of assets from a bankrupt estate "free and clear of any interests in property" skews the balance of interests in the product line exception.

I respectfully dissent. Justices GARIBALDI and COLEMAN join in this opinion.

––––––––––––––

Does it seem odd to you that a state court doctrine could trump the federal Bankruptcy Code? How might the buyer have better addressed this issue?

IN RE GENERAL MOTORS CORP.

407 B.R. 463
United States Bankruptcy Court, S.D. New York.
July 5, 2009.

Robert E. GERBER, Bankruptcy Judge.

In this contested matter in the jointly administered chapter 11 cases of Debtors General Motors Corporation and certain of its subsidiaries (together, "**GM**"), the Debtors move for an order, pursuant to section 363 of the Bankruptcy Code, approving GM's sale of the bulk of its assets (the "**363 Transaction**"), pursuant to a "Master Sale and Purchase Agreement" and related documents (the "**MPA**"), to Vehicle Acquisitions Holdings LLC (the "**Purchaser**")[10]—a purchaser sponsored by the U.S. Department of the Treasury (the "**U.S. Treasury**")—free and clear of liens, claims, encumbrances, and other interests. The Debtors also seek approval of the assumption and assignment of the executory contracts that would be needed by the Purchaser, and of a settlement with the United Auto Workers ("**UAW**") pursuant to an agreement (the "**UAW Settlement Agreement**") under which GM would satisfy obligations to an estimated 500,000 retirees.

GM's motion is supported by the Creditors' Committee; the U.S. Government (which has advanced approximately $50 billion to GM, and is GM's largest pre- and post-petition creditor); the Governments of Canada and Ontario (which ultimately will have advanced about $9.1 billion); the UAW (an affiliate of which is GM's single largest unsecured creditor); the indenture trustees for GM's approximately $27 billion in unsecured bonds; and an ad hoc committee representing holders of a majority of those bonds.

But the motion has engendered many objections and limited objections, by a variety of others. The objectors include, among others, a minority of the holders of GM's unsecured bonds (most significantly, an ad hoc committee of three of them (the "**F & D Bondholders Committee**"), holding approximately .01% of GM's bonds),[11] who contend, among other things, that GM's assets can be sold only under a chapter 11 plan, and that the proposed section 363 sale amounts to an impermissible "*sub rosa*" plan.

Objectors and limited objectors also include tort litigants who object to provisions in the approval order limiting successor liability claims against the Purchaser; asbestos litigants with similar concerns, along with concerns as to

---

10. When discussing the mechanics of the 363 Transaction, the existing GM will be referred to as "**Old GM**," and the Purchaser will be referred to as "**New GM**."

11. When it filed its objection, the F & D Bondholders Committee, identifying itself as the "Family & Dissident" Bondholders Committee, said it was "representing the interests of" 1,500 bondholders, with bond holdings "believed to exceed $400 million." But even after it filed the second of its Fed.R.Bankr.P.2019 statements, it identified no other bondholders for whom it was speaking, or provide the holdings, purchases and sales information for any others that Rule 2019 requires. Under these circumstances, the Court must consider that the committee speaks for just those three bondholders.

asbestos ailments that have not yet been discovered; and non-UAW unions ("**Splinter Unions**") speaking for their retirees, concerned that the Purchaser does not plan to treat their retirees as well as the UAW's retirees.

On the most basic issue, whether a 363 sale is proper, GM contends that this is exactly the kind of case where a section 363 sale is appropriate and indeed essential—and where under the several rulings of the Second Circuit and the Supreme Court in this area, GM's business can be sold, and its value preserved, before the company dies. The Court agrees. GM cannot survive with its continuing losses and associated loss of liquidity, and without the governmental funding that will expire in a matter of days. And there are no options to this sale—especially any premised on the notion that the company could survive the process of negotiations and litigation that characterizes the plan confirmation process.

As nobody can seriously dispute, the only alternative to an immediate sale is liquidation—a disastrous result for GM's creditors, its employees, the suppliers who depend on GM for their own existence, and the communities in which GM operates. In the event of a liquidation, creditors now trying to increase their incremental recoveries would get nothing.

Neither the Code, nor the caselaw—especially the caselaw in the Second Circuit—requires waiting for the plan confirmation process to take its course when the inevitable consequence would be liquidation. Bankruptcy courts have the power to authorize sales of assets at a time when there still is value to preserve—to prevent the death of the patient on the operating table.

Nor can the Court accept various objectors' contention that there here is a *sub rosa* plan. GM's assets simply are being sold, with the consideration to GM to be hereafter distributed to stakeholders, consistent with their statutory priorities, under a subsequent plan. Arrangements that will be made by the Purchaser do not affect the distribution of the *Debtor's* property, and will address wholly different needs and concerns—arrangements that the Purchaser needs to create a new GM that will be lean and healthy enough to survive.

Issues as to how any approval order should address *successor liability* are the only truly debatable issues in this case. And while textual analysis is ultimately inconclusive and caselaw on a nationwide basis is not uniform, the Court believes in *stare decisis;* it follows the caselaw in this Circuit and District in holding that to the extent the Purchaser has not voluntarily agreed to accept successor liability, GM's property—like that of Chrysler, just a few weeks ago—may be sold free and clear of claims.

Those and other issues are addressed below. GM's motion is granted.

10.   SPECIFICS OF THE TRANSACTION

The sale transaction, as embodied in the MPA and related documents, is complex. Its "deal points" can be summarized as follows:

(A)   ACQUIRED AND EXCLUDED ASSETS

Under the Sale, New GM will acquire all of Old GM's assets, with the exception of certain assets expressly excluded under the MPA (respectively, the **"Purchased Assets"** and the **"Excluded Assets"**). The Excluded Assets chiefly consist of:

(i) $1.175 billion in cash or cash equivalents;

(ii)   equity interests in certain Saturn and other entities;

(iii)   certain real and personal property;

(iv)   bankruptcy avoidance actions;

(v)   certain employee benefit plans; and

(vi)   certain restricted cash and receivables.

(B)   ASSUMED AND EXCLUDED LIABILITIES

Old GM will retain all liabilities except those defined in the MPA as **"Assumed Liabilities."** The Assumed Liabilities include:

(i)   product liability claims arising out of products delivered at or after the Sale transaction closes (the "*Closing*");

(ii)   the warranty and recall obligations of both Old GM and New GM;

(iii)   all employment-related obligations and liabilities under any assumed employee benefit plan relating to employees that are or were covered by the UAW collective bargaining agreement; and—by reason of an important change that was made in the MPA after the filing of the motion—

(iv)   broadening the first category substantially, *all* product liability claims arising from accidents or other discrete incidents arising from operation of GM vehicles occurring subsequent to the closing of the 363 Transaction, *regardless of when the product was purchased.*

The liabilities being retained by Old GM include:

(i)   product liability claims arising out of products delivered prior to the Closing (to the extent they weren't assumed by reason of the change in the MPA after the filing of objections);

(ii)   liabilities for claims arising out of exposure to asbestos;

(iii)   liabilities to third parties for claims based upon "[c]ontract, tort or any other basis";

(iv)   liabilities related to any implied warranty or other implied obligation arising under statutory or common law; and

(v)   employment-related obligations not otherwise assumed, including, among other obligations, those arising out of the employment, potential employment, or termination of any individual (other than an employee covered by the UAW collective bargaining agreement) prior to or at the Closing.

(C) CONSIDERATION

Old GM is to receive consideration estimated to be worth approximately $45 billion, plus the value of equity interests that it will receive in New GM. It will come in the following forms:

(i)   a credit bid by the U.S. Treasury and [Export Development Canada ("EDC")], who will credit bid the majority of the indebtedness outstanding under their DIP facility and the Treasury Prepetition Loan;

(ii)   the assumption by New GM of approximately $6.7 billion of indebtedness under the DIP facilities, plus an additional $1.175 billion to be advanced by the U.S. Treasury under a new DIP facility (the "**Wind Down Facility**") whose proceeds will be used by Old GM to wind down its affairs;

(iii)   the surrender of the warrant that had been issued by Old GM to Treasury in connection with the Treasury Prepetition Loan;

(iv)   10% of the post-closing outstanding shares of New GM, plus an additional 2% if the estimated amount of allowed prepetition general unsecured claims against Old GM exceeds $35 billion;

(v)   two warrants, each to purchase 7.5% of the post-closing outstanding shares of New GM, with an exercise price based on a $15 billion equity valuation and a $30 billion equity valuation, respectively; and

(vi)   the assumption of liabilities, including those noted above.

(D) OWNERSHIP OF NEW GM

Under the terms of the Sale, New GM will be owned by four entities.

(i)   Treasury will own 60.8% of New GM's common stock on an undiluted basis. It also will own $2.1 billion of New GM Series A Preferred Stock;

(ii)   EDC will own 11.7% of New GM's common stock on an undiluted basis. It also will own $400 million of New GM Series A Preferred Stock;

(iii)   A New Employees' Beneficiary Association Trust ("**New VEBA**") will own 17.5% of New GM's common stock on an undiluted basis. It also will own $6.5 billion of New GM's Series A Preferred Stock, and a 6-year warrant to acquire 2.5% of New GM's common stock, with an exercise price based on $75 billion total equity value; and

(iv)   Finally, if a chapter 11 plan is implemented as contemplated under the structure of the Sale transaction, Old GM will own 10% of New GM's common stock on an undiluted basis. In addition, if the allowed prepetition general unsecured claims against Old GM exceed $35 billion, Old GM will be issued an additional 10 million shares, amounting to approximately 2% of New GM's common stock. Old GM will also own the two warrants mentioned above.

(E)   OTHER ASPECTS OF TRANSACTION

New GM will make an offer of employment to all of the Sellers' non-unionized employees and unionized employees represented by the UAW. Substantially all of old GM's executory contracts with direct suppliers are likely to be assumed and assigned to New GM.

After the Closing, New GM will assume all liabilities arising under express written emission and limited warranties delivered in connection with the sale of new vehicles or parts manufactured or sold by Old GM.

One of the requirements of the U.S. Treasury, imposed when the Treasury Prepetition Loan was put in place, was the need to negotiate a new collective bargaining agreement which would allow GM to be fully competitive, and "equitize"—*i.e.*, convert to equity—at least one half of the obligation GM had to the UAW VEBA. Ultimately GM did so. New GM will make future contributions to the New VEBA that will provide retiree health and welfare benefits to former UAW employees and their spouses. Also, as part of the 363 Transaction, New GM will be the assignee of revised collective bargaining agreements with the UAW, the terms of which were recently ratified—though contingent upon the approval of the entirety of these motions.

(F)   THE PROPOSED SALE ORDER

Though GM's request has been narrowed, as noted above, to provide that New GM will assume liability for product liability claims arising from operation of GM vehicles occurring after the closing of the 363 Transaction (regardless of when the product was purchased), GM asks this Court, as in the *Chrysler* case, to authorize the Sale free and clear of all other "liens, claims, encumbrances and other interests," including, specifically, "all successor liability claims."

To effectuate this result, GM has submitted a proposed order to the Court (the **"Proposed Sale Order"**) that contains provisions directed at cutting off successor liability except in the respects where successor liability was contractually assumed.

First, the Proposed Sale Order contains a finding—and a decretal provision to similar effect—that the Debtors may sell the Purchased Assets free and clear of all liens, claims, encumbrances, and other interests, including rights or claims based on any successor or transferee liability.

Second, the Proposed Sale Order would enjoin all persons (including "litigation claimants") holding liens, claims, encumbrances, and other interests, including rights or claims based on any successor or transferee liability, from asserting them against New GM or the Purchased Assets.

2.   SUCCESSOR LIABILITY ISSUES

Many objectors—including the Ad Hoc Committee of Consumer Victims (the "**Consumer Victims Committee**"), individual accident litigants ("the **Individual Accident Litigants**"), and attorneys for asbestos victim litigants (collectively, "the **Asbestos Litigants**") object to provisions in the proposed sale order that would limit any "successor liability" that New GM might have. Successor liability claims normally are for money damages—as, for example, the claims by the Individual Accident Litigants are. If permitted, such claims would be asserted against the successor in ownership of property that was transferred from the entity whose alleged wrongful acts gave rise to the claim.

"As a general rule, a purchaser of assets does not assume the liabilities of the seller unless the purchaser expressly agrees to do so or an exception to the rule exists." Successor liability is an equitable exception to that general rule. Successor liability depends on state law, and the doctrines vary from state to state, but generally successor liability will not attach unless particular requirements imposed by that state have been satisfied.

If a buyer cannot obtain protection against successor liability, "it may pay less for the assets because of the risk."[12] When the transfer of property takes place in a 363 sale, and the buyer has sought and obtained agreement from the debtor that the sale will be free and clear, the bankruptcy court is invariably asked to provide, in its approval order, that the transferee does not assume liability for the debtor's pre-sale conduct.

Such a request was likewise made here. Under the proposed order, in its latest form, New GM would voluntarily assume liability for warranty claims, and for product liability claims asserted by those injured after the 363 Transaction—even if the vehicle was manufactured before the 363 Transaction. But New GM would not assume any Old GM liabilities for injuries or illnesses that arose before the 363 Transaction. And the proposed order has a number of provisions making explicit findings that New GM is not subject to successor liability for such matters, and that claims against New GM of that character are enjoined.[13]

---

12. Whether the U.S. and Canadian Governments would have lent and ultimately bid a lesser amount here is doubtful, but this consideration provides the context for deciding legal issues that presumably will extend beyond this case.

13. The principal provisions in the proposed order provide, in relevant part:

Except for the Assumed Liabilities, pursuant to sections 105(a) and 363(f) of the Bankruptcy Code, the Purchased Assets shall be transferred to the Purchaser in accordance with the MPA, and, upon the Closing, shall be free and clear of all liens, claims, encumbrances, and other interests of any kind or nature whatsoever ... including rights or claims based on any successor or transferee liability....

The issues as to the successor liability provisions in the approval order are the most debatable of the issues now before the Court. Textual analysis is ultimately inconclusive as to the extent to which a 363 order can bar successor liability claims premised upon the transfer of property, and cases on a nationwide basis are split. But principles of *stare decisis* dictate that under the caselaw in this Circuit and District, the Court should, and indeed must, rule that property can be sold free and clear of successor liability claims.

(A) TEXTUAL ANALYSIS

As before, the Court starts with textual analysis.

Application of section 363(f)'s authority to issue a "free and clear" order with respect to a successor liability claim turns, at least in the first instance, on whether such a claim is an "interest in property." But while "claim" is defined in the Code, neither "interest" nor "interest in property" is likewise defined.

So in the absence of statutory definitions of either "interest" or "interest in property," what can we discern from the text of the Code as to what those words mean?

First, we know that "interest" includes more than just a lien. Subsection (f)(3) makes clear that "interest" is broader, as there otherwise would be no reason for (f)(3) to deal with the subset of interests where "such interest is a lien."

Second, we know that an "interest" is something that may accompany the transfer of the underlying property, and where bankruptcy policy, as implemented by the drafters of the Code, requires specific provisions to ensure that it *will not* follow the transfer.

The Individual Accident Litigants contend that here the Court should presume that "equivalent words have equivalent meaning when repeated in the same statute." But while that is often a useful aid to construction, we cannot do so here. That is because "interest" has wholly different meanings as used in various places in the Code,[14] and assumptions that they mean the same thing here are unfounded.

...[A]ll persons and entities ... holding liens, claims, encumbrances, and other interests of any kind or nature whatsoever, including rights or claims based on any successor or transferee liability, against or in a Seller or the Purchased Assets (whether legal or equitable, secured or unsecured, matured or unmatured, contingent or noncontingent, senior or subordinated), arising under or out of, in connection with, or in any way relating to, the Sellers, the Purchased Assets, the operation of the Purchased Assets prior to the Closing, or the 363 Transaction, are forever barred, estopped, and permanently enjoined from asserting against the Purchaser, its successors or assigns, its property, or the Purchased Assets, such persons' or entities' liens, claims, encumbrances, and other interests, including rights or claims based on any successor or transferee liability.

14. *See* Postings of Stephen Lubben, Professor at Seton Hall Law School, to Credit Slips, http://www.creditslips.org/creditslips/2009/06/claim-or-interest.html (June 13, 2009, 8:25 PM EST); and http://www.creditslips.org/creditslips/2009/06/claim-or-interest-part-2.html (June 14, 2009, 6:42 PM EST). Blogs are a fairly recent phenomenon in the law, providing a useful forum for

Thus, those in the bankruptcy community know, upon considering the usage of "interest" in any particular place in the Code, that "interest" means wholly different things in different contexts:

(i)   a nondebtor's *collateral*—as used, for example, in consideration of adequate protection of an interest under sections 361 and 362(d)(1), use of cash collateral under section 363(c)(2), or in many 363(f) situations, such as where a creditor has a lien;

(ii)   *a legal or equitable ownership of property*—as used, for example, in section 541 of the Code, or in other section 363(f) situations, where a nondebtor asserts competing ownership, a right to specific performance, or the like—or, quite differently,

(iii)   *stock* or other equity in the debtor, *as contrasted to debt*—as used, for example, in section 1111 ("[a] proof of claim or interest is deemed filed under section 501"), or where a reorganization plan is to establish classes of claims and interests, under sections 1122 and 1123.

The Individual Accident Litigants place particular emphasis on section 1141(c) of the Code, asking this Court to compare and contrast it. They argue that

> In contrast, §1141(c) of the Bankruptcy Code provides that "property dealt with by the plan is free and clear of all *claims and interests* ... *in* the debtor." (Emphasis added). Section 363 and 1141(c) are two mechanisms for transfer of estate property (one through a sale, the other through a plan). The difference between the words chosen by Congress in these two closely related sections shows that Congress did not intend a sale under §363(f) to be free and clear of "*claims*," but only of "*interests in* such property" because "'it is generally presumed that Congress actions intentionally and purposely' when it 'includes particular language in one section of a statute but omits it in another.'"

But this is not an apt comparison, since when "interests" is used in section 1141(c), it is used with the wholly different definition of (iii) above—*i.e.*, as stock or another type of equity—in contrast to the very different definitions in (i) and (ii) above, which are ways by which "interests in property" may be used in section 363(f).

Thus, as Lubben suggests, and the Court agrees, in section 1141 "interest" matches up with "equity," and "claim" matches up with debt.[15]

---

interchanges of ideas. While comments in blogs lack the editing and peer review characteristics of law journals, and probably should be considered judiciously, they may nevertheless be quite useful, especially as food for thought, and may be regarded as simply another kind of secondary authority, whose value simply turns on the rigor of the analysis in the underlying ideas they express.

15. *See* Posting of Stephen Lubben, Professor at Seton Hall Law School, to Credit Slips, http://www.creditslips.org/creditslips/2009/06/claim-or-interest.html (June 13, 2009, 8:25 PM EST).

Section 1141 is of no assistance in determining whether litigation rights transmitted through transfers of property fall within the meaning of "interests in property." Section 1141 does not provide a yardstick by which section 363(f)'s meaning can be judged.

So where does textual analysis leave us? It tells us that "interest" means more than a lien, but it does not tell us how much more. Textual analysis does not support or foreclose the possibility that an "interest in property" covers a right that exists against a new party solely by reason of a transfer of property to that party. Nor does textual analysis support or foreclose the idea that an "interest" is a right that travels with the property—or that it would do so unless the Code cut it off. Ultimately textual analysis is inconclusive. Neither the Code nor interpretive aids tells us how broadly or narrowly—in the particular context of section 363(f)—"interest in property" should be deemed to be defined.[16]

(B) CASELAW

Therefore, once again—as in the Court's earlier consideration of *Lionel* and its progeny and the cases establishing the judge-made law of *sub rosa* plans—the Court must go beyond the words of the Code to the applicable caselaw.

Viewed nationally, the caselaw is split in this area, both at the Circuit Court level and in the bankruptcy Courts. Some courts have held that section 363(f)

---

16. The Individual Accident Litigants also place heavy reliance on Butner v. United States, 440 U.S. 48, 99 S.Ct. 914, 59 L.Ed.2d 136 (1979), *see* Indiv. Accident Litigants Br. 8, suggesting that *Butner* requires deference to state law that might impose successor liability and that this would require excluding successor liability damages claims from any definition of "interest." But the Court cannot agree. First, when quoted in full, *Butner* (whose bottom line was that the issue of whether a security interest extended to rents derived from the property was governed by state law) stated:

> The Bankruptcy Act does include provisions invalidating certain security interests as fraudulent, or as improper preferences over general creditors. Apart from these provisions, however, Congress has generally left the determination of property rights in the assets of a bankrupt's estate to state law.

440 U.S. at 54, 99 S.Ct. 914. *Butner* further stated (in language the Individual Accident Litigants did not quote):

> Unless some federal interest requires a different result, there is no reason why such interests should be analyzed differently simply because an interested party is involved in a bankruptcy proceeding.

Id. at 55, 99 S.Ct. 914. But the *Butner* court laid out principles by which we determine what is property of the estate; it did not address the different issue of whether a state may impose liability on a transferee of estate property by reason of something the debtor did before the transfer. Moreover, *Butner* noted that provisions of the Code can and do sometimes trump state law. And section 363(f), for as much or as little as it covers, is exactly such a provision. In fact, 363(f) is a classic example of an instance where a "federal interest requires a different result." *Butner* neither supports nor defeats either party's position here.

provides a basis for selling free and clear of successor liability claims,[17] and others have held that it does not.[18]

But the caselaw is *not* split in this Circuit and District. In *Chrysler*, Judge Gonzalez expressly considered and rejected the efforts to impose successor liability. And more importantly, the Second Circuit, after hearing extensive argument on this issue along with others, affirmed Judge Gonzalez's *Chrysler* order for substantially the reasons Judge Gonzalez set forth in his *Chrysler* decision.

This Court has previously noted how *Chrysler* is so closely on point, and this issue is no exception. Judge Gonzalez expressly considered it. In material reliance on the Third Circuit's decision in *TWA*, "the leading case on this issue," Judge Gonzalez held that *TWA:*

> makes clear that such tort claims are interests in property such that they are extinguished by a free and clear sale under section 363(f)(5) and are therefore extinguished by the Sale Transaction. The Court follows *TWA* and overrules the objections premised on this argument....[I]n personam claims, including any potential state successor or transferee liability claims against New Chrysler, as well as in rem interests, are encompassed by section 363(f) and are therefore extinguished by the Sale Transaction.

This Court has already noted its view of the importance of *stare decisis* in this district, and feels no differently with respect to this issue. This Court follows the decisions of its fellow bankruptcy judges in this district, in the absence of plain error, because the interests of predictability in commercial bankruptcy cases are of such great importance. Apart from the underlying reasons that have caused *stare decisis* to be embedded in American decisional law, *stare decisis* is particularly important in commercial bankruptcy cases because of the expense and trauma of any commercial bankruptcy, and the need to deal with foreseeable events, by pre-bankruptcy planning, to the extent they can be addressed. Likewise, litigation, while a fact of life in commercial bankruptcy cases, takes money directly out of the pockets of creditors, and predictability fosters settlements, since with predictability, parties will have an informed sense as to how any disputed legal issues will be decided.

---

17. *See, e.g., Chrysler*, 405 B.R. at 111; In re Trans World Airlines, Inc., 322 F.3d 283, 288-90 (3d Cir.2003) ("*TWA*"); *United Mine Workers of Am.1992 Benefit Plan v. Leckie Smokeless Coal Co. (In re Leckie Smokeless Coal Co.)*, 99 F.3d 573, 581-82 (4th Cir.1996).

18. *See, e.g.*, Michigan Empl. Sec. Comm. v. Wolverine Radio Co., Inc. (In re Wolverine Radio Co.), 930 F.2d 1132, 1147-48 (6th Cir.1991); Precision Indus., Inc. v. Qualitech Steel SBQ, LLC (In re Qualitech Steel Corp.), 327 F.3d 537, 545-46 (7th Cir.2003); Fairchild Aircraft Corp. v. Cambell (In re Fairchild Aircraft Corp.), 184 B.R. 910, 918 (Bankr.W.D.Tex.1995), *vacated as moot on equitable grounds*, 220 B.R. 909 (Bkrtcy.W.D.Tex.1998). *See also* Volvo White Truck Corp. v. Chambersburg Beverage, Inc. (In re White Motor Credit Corp.), 75 B.R. 944, 948 (Bankr.N.D.Ohio 1987) (concluding that 363(f) could not be utilized, but that section 105(a) could be used to effect 363 sale free and clear of claims).

Though for all of these reasons, this Court would have followed *Chrysler* even if that case had no subsequent history, we here have a hugely important additional fact. The Circuit affirmed *Chrysler, and* for "substantially for the reasons stated in the opinion below."

This Court fully understands the circumstances of tort victims, and the fact that if they prevail in litigation and cannot look to New GM as an additional source of recovery, they may recover only modest amounts on any allowed claims—if, as is possible, they do not have other defendants who can also pay. But the law in this Circuit and District is clear; the Court will permit GM's assets to pass to the purchaser free and clear of successor liability claims, and in that connection, will issue the requested findings and associated injunction.

PROBLEM SET 29.2

1. What steps did the buyer take in *GM* that the buyer in *Lefever* did not? Will these steps matter? *See* In re Emoral, Inc., 740 F.3d 875, 876 (3d Cir. 2014).

2. The appellants in the *Chrysler* case sought review in the Supreme Court following the Second Circuit's decision. The Supreme Court dismissed the appeal as moot—the Chrysler sale had already closed by that point—but also instructed the Circuit to dismiss its opinion on the same basis. Thus, Judge Gerber's opinion stands simply on the basis of his deference to the prior decision of his colleague in *Chrysler*, which is largely based on the Third Circuit's opinion in *TWA*. In re Trans World Airlines, Inc., 322 F.3d 283, 288-90, 293 (3d Cir. 2003). *See also* Nelson v. Tiffany Indus., Inc., 778 F.2d 533 (9th Cir. 1985).

3. Should section 363(f) overcome state law successor liability claims? Is a successor liability claim an "interest" in the debtor's property at the time of the sale?

4. How does a 363 sale facilitate "reorganization"?

5. Not long after the GM bankruptcy, it became known that some GM cars had long suffered from an ignition switch defect, which can cause cars to lose power abruptly and prevent airbags from deploying. This defect caused 84 deaths and led to subsequent recalls that ultimately involved 27 million GM vehicles. In 2015, Judge Gerber ruled that "New GM" was shielded from a substantial portion of the lawsuits based on ignition switch defects in cars manufactured prior to New GM's acquisition of the assets of Old GM in 2009. Judge Gerber determined that the lawsuits were barred by the provisions of the sale order, discussed in the opinion above. The judge concluded that, while these claimants were denied their due process notice rights in connection with the sale, no due process violation ultimately occurred, because showing such a violation requires that the claimant demonstrate that it was prejudiced as a result of the notice deficiency. The finding of lack of prejudice stemmed from the fact that, while the plaintiffs did not get notice of the sale, other similarly

situated creditors did get notice of the sale, filed objections, raised the very same successor liability arguments that these claimants asserted, and the court overruled all of these objections and permitted the sale of Old GM's assets to New GM free and clear of successor liability claims. The court did hold, however, that a subset of claimants were prejudiced by the lack of notice: they missed an opportunity to advance one argument in opposition to the proposed sale order that had not been raised by other claimants at the sale hearing in 2009. These claimants argued, and the court agreed, that the sale order should not have barred causes of action against New GM arising out of New GM's own, independent, post-sale acts so long as the claims are not based on acts committed by Old GM. In re Motors Liquidation Co., 529 B.R. 510 (Bankr.S.D.N.Y.2015). On July 13, 2016, the Second Circuit ruled that the sale order did indeed apply to successor liability claims, but that the plaintiffs were prejudiced by the lack of notice, and thus remanded the case for further proceedings. The company had a pending petition for *certiorari* as this book went to press (Case No. 16-764).

30

CHAPTER 11 PLANS

The traditional end of chapter 11 is confirmation of a plan. That plan often will be a reorganization plan, but sometimes it will be a liquidation plan. The latter is especially true if the debtor previously sold most of its assets under section 363. A chapter 11 plan can be seen as a contract. But unlike most contracts, this one can be imposed on dissenting parties. Namely, if the plan meets certain requirements that we talk about in this chapter, it becomes binding on all of the debtor's creditors and shareholders, regardless of whether they voted for the plan or participated in the chapter 11 case.

Moreover, the bankruptcy court has nationwide jurisdiction, so the binding effects of the plan are enforceable on any creditor that has minimum contacts with the United States. This means that large financial institutions, even if based in a foreign country, will typically be bound by a plan, since the financial institution will often have a presence in New York City.

1. EXCLUSIVITY, PLAN SOLICITATION, DISCLOSURE STATEMENTS, AND VOTING

The debtor-in-possession enjoys the exclusive right to file a plan for the first 120 days of a chapter 11 bankruptcy case.[1] The debtor's exclusive period ends

- upon the appointment of a Chapter 11 trustee,
- if the debtor has not filed a plan before the expiration of the 120-day period, or
- if the debtor has not filed a plan that has been accepted by each impaired class of claims or interests within the first 180 days of the bankruptcy case.[2]

Before 2005, courts could and routinely did extend the exclusive period for "cause." Competing plans were rare, especially in big cases.

---

1. 11 U.S.C. §1121(b).
2. 11 U.S.C. §1121(c).

Since 2005, bankruptcy courts are not permitted to extend the date for filing a plan beyond 18 months and the date for acceptance beyond 20 months. Both are measured from the date of filing.

After exclusivity lapses, any party in interest may propose a plan. In such cases, the court, and perhaps voting creditors, may have multiple plans to choose from. In all cases, creditors considering a plan must be provided with a disclosure statement that explains the plan. You saw examples of prepetition disclosure statements in Chapter 27.

IN RE OXFORD HOMES, INC., DEBTOR

204 B.R. 264
United States Bankruptcy Court, D. Maine.
Jan. 6, 1997.

James B. HAINES, Jr., Bankruptcy Judge.
Invoking §503(b)(3)(D) and §503(b)(4), Peter N. Connell, a former shareholder and prepetition creditor of Oxford Homes, Inc., seeks administrative expense treatment for $85,085.00 in counsel fees and $1,830.17 in counsel's expenses that he incurred in connection with Oxford's successful reorganization. For the reasons set forth below, I conclude that Connell's request will not be granted. To do so would subvert the disclosure statement and plan confirmation process and would be fundamentally unfair to Oxford's creditors, who voted to accept Oxford's reorganization plan with no inkling that Connell would request administrative treatment for any portion of his counsel's fees.

PROCEDURAL HISTORY

Oxford filed its voluntary Chapter 11 petition on February 22, 1994. After a rocky beginning, during which the case nearly converted to Chapter 7, the reorganization proceeded under the supervision of a Chapter 11 trustee. Along the way, the trustee's efforts were assisted mightily by Connell. Connell and the trustee jointly devised and proposed Oxford's reorganization plan. After a series of amendments and modifications, the joint plan was confirmed on December 23, 1994.

FACTS

1.   WHAT CONNELL AND HIS COUNSEL DID.

No party in interest disputes that Connell's active alliance with the Chapter 11 trustee fostered, indeed fathered, Oxford's reorganization. From a point soon after the trustee's appointment, Connell drew upon the assistance of Steven E. Cope, Esq., of Cope & Cope, a Portland, Maine, law firm specializing in bankruptcy matters. Cope provided comprehensive legal services to Connell, working to negotiate and structure Oxford's reorganization. Cope authored and reportedly revised the plan and disclosure statement that Connell and the trustee proposed.

Cope asserts that his activities on Connell's behalf substantially contributed to Oxford's reorganization; reasonably required 486.2 hours of his time, billed at $175.00 per hour; and entailed reasonable expenses and disbursements amounting to $1,830.17. Cope performed additional services for Connell, generating approximately 50 hours of billable legal work, for which Connell does not seek administrative allowance.

The original disclosure statement, and each ensuing version, described in detail the administrative claims category and the Connell claims class. Nowhere did they advert to the possibility that Connell might seek to have his attorney's fees paid "off the top" through the plan as an administrative expense.

Notwithstanding the plan trustee's concession that as much as half of the $85,085.00 fee application is properly allowable as an administrative expense, and notwithstanding the absence of objection from any other quarter, I must review Connell's request by my own lights. "The bankruptcy judge has an independent duty to examine the propriety and reasonableness of fees, even if no party in interest objects to the application."

Although I am convinced of the necessity, reasonableness, and value of Cope's work, I am unconvinced of the *propriety* of *any* administrative fee award in this instance.

3.   WHY THE APPLICATION MUST BE DISALLOWED.

A plan of reorganization may not be submitted to a debtor's creditors unless and until a disclosure statement has been approved by the court as containing "adequate information." 11 U.S.C. §1125(b). Adequate information is defined in the Code as:

> information of a kind, and in sufficient detail, as far as is reasonably practicable in light of the nature and history of the debtor and the condition of the debtor's books and records, that would enable a hypothetical reasonable investor typical of holders of claims or interests of the relevant class to make an informed judgment about the plan . . . ;

11 U.S.C. §1125(a)(1). As the Third Circuit recently observed:

> [D]isclosure requirements are crucial to the effective functioning of the federal bankruptcy system. Because creditors and the bankruptcy court rely heavily on the debtor's disclosure statement in determining whether to approve a proposed reorganization plan, the importance of full and honest disclosure cannot be overstated.

Ryan Operations G.P. v. Santiam–Midwest Lumber Co., 81 F.3d 355, 362 (3rd Cir.1996). The precise contours of "adequate information" were vaguely drawn by Congress so that bankruptcy courts might exercise their discretion to limn them in view of each case's peculiar circumstances.[3]

Although what constitutes "adequate information" will vary from case to case, a good faith estimate of administrative expenses, incurred and upcoming, is a virtual constant. Creditors deserve to be fairly informed of the transaction costs entailed in the reorganization plan they are being asked to back.

As a plan proponent whose counsel was intimately involved in drafting Oxford's disclosure statement[s] and plan[s], it was incumbent on Connell to reveal any intention he entertained to seek administrative payment of his legal expenses. This he failed to do.

At each stage of their evolution, the plan and disclosure statement not only neglected to reveal the possibility that Connell would seek administrative payment of 90% of his attorney's fees, their comprehensive explanation of the scope of administrative claims and the extent of Connell's claims seemingly ruled out such a possibility. Connell, who asked creditors to support the plan on that record, may not now ask them to pay his fees before realizing their plan distributions.

The result I reach is based on the need to honor the trust creditors are entitled to repose in the disclosure, solicitation, and confirmation processes that are at the heart of Chapter 11. Because Connell, through Cope, authored the disclosure

---

3. Categories of information that ought to be considered for inclusion in a disclosure statement include:

1.　　The circumstances that gave rise to the filing of the bankruptcy petition;
2.　　A complete description of the available assets and their value;
3.　　The anticipated future of the debtor, with accompanying financial projections;
4.　　The source of the information provided in the disclosure statement;
5.　　The condition and performance of the debtor while in chapter 11;
6.　　Information regarding claims against the estate, including those allowed, disputed, and estimated;
7.　　A liquidation analysis setting forth the estimated return that creditors would receive under chapter 7;
8.　　The accounting and valuation methods used to produce the financial information in the disclosure statement;
9.　　Information regarding the future management of the debtor, including the amount of compensation to be paid to any insiders, directors, and/or officers of the debtor;
10.　　A summary of the plan of reorganization;
11.　　An estimate of all administrative expenses, including attorneys' fees and accountants' fees;
12.　　The collectibility of any accounts receivable;
13.　　Any financial information, valuations or *pro forma* projections that would be relevant to creditors' determinations of whether to accept or reject the plan;
14.　　Information relevant to the risks being taken by the creditors and interest holders;
15.　　The actual or projected value that can be obtained from avoidable transfers;
16.　　The existence, likelihood and possible success of nonbankruptcy litigation;
17.　　The tax consequences of the plan;
18.　　The relationship of the debtor with affiliates.

statement and plan, it is only fair that he be bound by them. To the extent that the principle upon which I base my decision need be further defined, it represents a form of judicial estoppel.

Administrative allowance of Connell's attorney's fees was not an immaterial point when the disclosure statement was approved or at confirmation. It is not today.

Moreover, the fees being sought today were more than just "foreseeable." As of the date the disclosure statement was finally approved, the lion's share of them had already accrued.

A class entitled to vote on a plan is deemed to accept a plan if creditors holding at least two-thirds in amount and more than one-half in number of the allowed claims in the class accept the plan.[4]

But certain classes have votes presumed for them. Unimpaired classes are conclusively presumed to have accepted the plan, making solicitation from the holders of claims or interests in such classes unnecessary.[5]

Conversely, a class is deemed to have rejected a plan if the plan provides that the holders of the claims or interests in such class will not receive or retain any property under the plan on account of such claims or interests.[6]

PROBLEM SET 30.1

1. Monkey Industries has recently filed a chapter 11 petition and begun to work on a plan. Hugo Capital Investors has its doubts about the management of the debtor and has begun sending a memorandum with the outlines of an alternative plan to other large creditors to gauge their support. Does this present any problems under the Bankruptcy Code? *See, e.g.,* In re The Heritage Org., LLC, 376 Bankr. 783, 791 (Bankr.N.D.Tex.2007).

2. Disclosure statements tend to be almost as long as the form 10-Ks filed with the SEC. And then it is typical to attach a 10-K to the disclosure statement as well. Is this what is meant by "adequate information" in §1125(b) of the Bankruptcy Code? Why not write a shorter disclosure statement and incorporate the 10-K by reference?

2. CHAPTER 11 PLANS

Section 1123 provides what a plan must do, and also provides some examples of what it could do. But the permissive parts of 1123 are quite open ended, which

---

4. 11 U.S.C. §1126(c).
5. 11 U.S.C. §1126(f).
6. 11 U.S.C. §1126(g).

leaves the parties open to negotiation of almost any creative solution they might imagine, so long as it does not violate some affirmative provision of the Code.

In the prior section we discussed the voting requirements for particular classes to approve a plan. But how are the classes constructed?

The Code is maddeningly vague on this point. Section 1123 requires classification "subject to section 1122." Section 1122(a) provides that "a plan may place a claim or an interest in a particular class only if such claim or interest is substantially similar to the other claims or interests of such class." That, of course, begs the question of what "substantially similar" means.

IN RE TRIBUNE COMPANY, ET AL.[7]

476 B.R. 843
United States Bankruptcy Court, D. Delaware.
July 13, 2012.

Kevin J. CAREY, Bankruptcy Judge.

Before the Court for consideration is the Fourth Amended Joint Plan of Reorganization for Tribune Company and Its Subsidiaries Proposed by the Debtors, the Official Committee of Unsecured Creditors, Oaktree Capital Management, L.P., Angelo Gordon & Co., L.P., and JPMorgan Chase Bank, as revised (the "Fourth Amended Plan"). The DCL Plan Proponents seek confirmation of the Fourth Amended Plan, but objections to confirmation filed by the following parties remained unresolved: (i) Aurelius Capital Management, L.P. ("Aurelius") (docket nos. 11664 and 11753), (ii) Law Debenture Trust Company of New York ("Law Debenture") (docket no. 11668), (iii) Deutsche Bank Trust Company of Americas ("Deutsche Bank") (docket no. 11667), (iv) Wilmington Trust Company ("WTC") (docket no. 11666), (v) Citadel Equity Fund Ltd. and Camden Asset Management LP (together, "Citadel Camden") (docket no. 11659), (vi) EGI-TRB LLC ("EGI") (docket no. 11658), (vii) certain former directors and officers of the Debtors (the "D & Os") (docket no. 11657), and (viii) F. Ashley Allen, Catherine M. Hertz, Michael D. Slason, and Louis J. Stancampiano ("Certain Former Employees") (docket no. 11661).

The DCL Plan Proponents responded to the objections to confirmation of the Fourth Amended Plan by filing the Memorandum of Law in Support of Confirmation and Omnibus Reply to Objections to Confirmation (docket no. 11746). Other parties weighed in by filing replies to some of the objections, including (i) the Statement of Robert R. McCormick Tribune Foundation (the

---

7. The chapter 11 case filed by Tribune Media Services, Inc. (Bky. Case No. 08-13236) is jointly administered with the Tribune Company bankruptcy case and 109 additional affiliated debtors pursuant to the Order dated December 10, 2008 (docket no. 43). An additional debtor, Tribune CNLBC, LLC (formerly known as Chicago National League Baseball Club, LLC) filed a voluntary petition for relief under chapter 11 of the Bankruptcy Code on October 12, 2009 (Bky. Case No. 09-13496), and is also jointly administered with the Tribune Company bankruptcy case pursuant to this Court's Order dated October 14, 2009 (docket no. 2333). The debtors in the jointly administered cases are referred to herein as the "Debtors."

"McCormick Foundation") and Cantigny Foundation in Response to Objection of Aurelius Capital Management, LP (docket no. 11725), (ii) the D & Os' Reply to the Objection of Aurelius Capital Management, LP (docket no. 11739), (iii) the D & Os' Joinder to the Statement of the Robert R. McCormick Tribune and Cantigny Foundations (docket no. 11740), and (iv) the Bridge Agent's Reply, and Joinder to the DCL Plan Proponents' Reply, to the Objection of Aurelius Capital Management, LP (docket no. 11748).

A hearing to consider confirmation of the Fourth Amended Plan was held on June 7 and 8, 2012, and continued via conference call on June 11, 2012 (together, the "Fourth Amended Plan Confirmation Hearing").

On June 18, 2012, the DCL Plan Proponents filed the revised Fourth Amended Plan (docket no. 11836) to incorporate modifications that resolved a number of objections to confirmation. On the same date, the DCL Plan Proponents also filed revised exhibits and other documents related to the Fourth Amended Plan, including (i) Plan Exhibit 13.1—the Litigation Trust Agreement, the Litigation Trust Loan Agreement, the proposed Agreement Respecting Transfer of Documents, Information, and Privileges from Debtors and Reorganized Debtors (the "Debtors' LT Agreement"), the proposed Agreement Respecting Transfer of Documents, Information, and Privileges from the Official Committee of Unsecured Creditors (the "Committee's LT Agreement").

On June 20, 2012, Aurelius filed a letter objection with the Court (docket no. 11856) arguing that changes made to the proposed Committee's LT Agreement regarding the Litigation Trustee's discovery rights with respect to the Creditors' Committee did not address its concerns. The Creditors' Committee filed a letter in response (docket no. 11867) and a telephonic hearing was held on June 21, 2012 to discuss the issue.

On July 11, 2012, a further hearing was held to address the Certain Former Employees' objection and Aurelius' objection to the Committee's LT Agreement. After colloquy with counsel at the July 11, 2012 hearing, the objection by the Certain Former Employees was withdrawn. At the July 11, 2012 hearing, the Court also suggested language to address Aurelius' objection to provisions in the proposed Committee's LT Agreement concerning certain discovery rights of the Litigation Trustee vis-a-vis the Creditors' Committee (including its retained professionals). The parties discussed the Court's proposed language and agreed to make further revisions to the affected paragraphs. However, Aurelius requested one additional change to which the Creditors' Committee did not agree. The revised language as otherwise agreed to by the parties at the July 11, 2012 hearing (without Aurelius' final change), was submitted under Certification on July 12, 2012 (docket no. 12001). The proposed Committee's LT Agreement, as revised, fairly addresses Aurelius' concerns. Accordingly, Aurelius' last remaining request is denied.

For the reasons set forth herein, the remaining objections by Aurelius, Law Debenture, Deutsche Bank, WTC, EGI, Citadel Camden, the McCormick Foundation, and the D & Os will be overruled. Subject to submission of final revisions to the Fourth Amended Plan consistent with various resolutions that

have been made, by agreement and consistent with this Memorandum, the Fourth
Amended Plan will be confirmed.

BACKGROUND

The arduous journey for confirmation of a plan is chronicled in three previous
decisions.... A detailed description of the Debtors (including an overview of the
Debtors' business, their pre-petition debt structure, the 2007 leveraged buy-out
(the "LBO")), and the chapter 11 proceedings (including the appointment of and
investigation by the Examiner, plan mediation efforts, and the filing of four
competing plans of reorganization) can be found in the Confirmation Opinion.
Tribune I, 464 B.R. at 136-46, [the relevant parts of which are reproduced
below:]

[A.   OVERVIEW OF THE DEBTORS' BUSINESS

Tribune Company is a Delaware corporation with its principal place of
business in Chicago, Illinois. Tribune Company directly or indirectly owns all (or
substantially all) of the equity in 128 subsidiaries (the "Tribune Entities"), of
which 110 are Debtors. The Tribune Entities are a leading media and
entertainment conglomerate reaching more than eighty percent (80%) of
households in the United States through their newspapers, other publications and
websites, their television and radio stations, and their other news and
entertainment offerings.

The Tribune Entities' operations are divided into two primary industry
segments: the "Publishing Segment" and the "Broadcasting Segment." The
Publishing Segment accounted for seventy percent (70%) of the Tribune Entities'
consolidated revenues in 2009. The Publishing Segment includes operation of
eight major-market daily newspapers: *The Los Angeles Times, Chicago Tribune,
South Florida Sun–Sentinel, Orlando Sentinel, The Sun, Hartford Courant, The
Morning Call*, and *The Daily Press. (Id.)*.

The Broadcasting Segment accounted for thirty percent (30%) of the Tribune
Entities' consolidated operating revenues in 2009 and includes 23 television
stations in 19 markets. Various Tribune entities also have investments (typically
minority equity interests) in a number of private corporations, limited liability
companies, and partnerships, including CareerBuilder, Classified Ventures, TV
Food Network, Homefinder, Topix, quadrantONE and Metromix.

In September 2006, the Tribune board of directors (the "Board") created a
Special Committee to oversee a formal process of exploring strategic alternatives
for Tribune, including a sale of all Tribune Entities, a leveraged recapitalization
of Tribune, the sale of the Broadcasting Segment, a spin-off of the Broadcasting
Segment, and a split-off of the Publishing Segment. As a result of that process,
on April 1, 2007, based on the recommendation of the Special Committee, the
Board approved a series of transactions with a newly formed Tribune Employee
Stock Ownership Plan (the "ESOP"), EGI-TRB, LLC, a Delaware limited

liability company wholly owned by Sam Investment Trust, a trust established for the benefit of Samuel Zell and his family ("EGI" or the "Zell Entity") and Samuel Zell ("Zell"). This Leveraged ESOP Transaction (also referred to as the "2007 Leveraged Buy-out" or the "LBO") was consummated in two principal steps, commonly referred to as "Step One" and "Step Two."

In Step One, the newly formed ESOP purchased 8,928,571 shares of Tribune common stock at $28 per share. The Zell Entity also made an initial investment of $250 million in Tribune in exchange for 1,470,588 shares of Tribune's common stock at a price of $34 per share and an unsecured subordinated exchangeable promissory note of Tribune in the principal amount of $200 million.

Thereafter, Tribune commenced a cash tender offer (at a price of $34 per share) to repurchase approximately 52% of its outstanding common stock. Tribune retired the repurchased shares on June 4, 2007. To finance the tender offer, Tribune entered into the $8.028 billion senior secured credit agreement (the "Senior Loan Agreement"). A number of Tribune's domestic subsidiaries (the "Guarantor Subsidiaries") provided unsecured guarantees of indebtedness under the Senior Loan Agreement. The proceeds from the Senior Loan Agreement were also used to refinance Tribune's 2006 Credit Facility and 2006 Bridge Credit Facility.

In Step Two, consummated in December 2007, Tribune merged with a Delaware corporation wholly owned by the ESOP, with Tribune surviving the merger. Upon completion of the merger, all issued and outstanding shares of Tribune's common stock (other than shares held by Tribune or the ESOP) were cancelled and Tribune became wholly owned by the ESOP. The merger was financed through additional borrowings of $2.1 billion under the Senior Loan Agreement (known as the "Incremental Facility") and $1.6 billion under the Bridge Loan Agreement. Incremental Facility and the Bridge Loan Facility are unsecured but guaranteed by the Guarantor Subsidiaries. The proceeds of the additional borrowings were used for, among other things, the consummation of the merger, the repurchase of outstanding Tribune shares not held by the ESOP at $34 per share, and the Step Two financing fees, costs and expenses.

As of the Petition Date, Tribune's pre-LBO indebtedness and LBO indebtedness, totaled approximately $12.706 billion in principal amount.]

The Confirmation Opinion addressed two proposed competing plans of reorganization for the Debtors: (i) the Second Amended Joint Plan of Reorganization for Tribune Company and Its Subsidiaries (the "Debtor/Committee/Lender Plan" or the "DCL Plan") proposed by the Debtors, the Creditors' Committee, Oaktree, Angelo Gordon, and JPM, and (ii) the Joint Plan of Reorganization for Tribune Company and Its Subsidiaries (the "Noteholder Plan") proposed by Aurelius, Deutsche Bank, Law Debenture and WTC. After a confirmation hearing spanning more than two weeks, followed by post-hearing briefing and closing arguments, I determined that both plans failed to meet the requirements of Bankruptcy Code §1129, for the reasons detailed in the Confirmation Opinion, and I denied confirmation of both plans.

However, the Confirmation Opinion contained detailed analyses and determined a number of disputed issues related to confirmation, including, among other things, the Debtors' valuation, and the reasonableness of the Settlements proposed in the DCL Plan. The Confirmation Opinion also analyzed the competing plans under §1129(c) and decided that, assuming the proponents of the competing plans could correct the flaws that prevented confirmation under §1129, and then refiled the corrected plans with substantially similar terms and similar voting results, then the DCL Plan would have the edge for confirmation.

On November 18, 2011, the DCL Plan Proponents filed the Third Amended Joint Plan of Reorganization for Tribune Company and Its Subsidiaries (docket no. 10273) (the "Third Amended Plan"). The Third Amended Plan included an "Allocation Dispute Protocol" which proposed to establish reserves for distributions to holders of allowed claims in certain classes that would be impacted by unresolved disputes regarding inter-creditor priorities, particularly with respect to the PHONES Notes and the EGI-TRB LLC Notes (the "EGI Notes"). Upon the request of certain parties, I agreed to resolve the "Allocation Disputes," as defined in the Order dated January 24, 2012 (docket no. 10692) before parties were required to vote on or object to confirmation of the Third Amended Plan. On April 9, 2012, I issued the Allocation Decision which, among other things, determined the applicability of subordination provisions and the order of priority of distributions under the DCL Plan Proponents' amended plan, contingent upon and subject to confirmation of a plan substantially in the form of the Third Amended Plan.

On April 17, 2012, the DCL Plan Proponents filed the Fourth Amended Plan, which incorporated the previously-approved DCL Plan Settlement, as well as Third Amended Plan modifications that addressed the issues raised in the Confirmation Opinion. Further, in light of the Allocation Decision, the Fourth Amended Plan eliminated the Allocation Dispute Protocol and provided for the allocation of distributions that had been proposed under the DCL Plan and Third Amended Plan (which, the DCL Plan Proponents assert, was upheld by the Allocation Decision).

On April 17, 2012, the DCL Plan Proponents also filed the Supplemental Disclosure Document relating to the Fourth Amended Plan. Following a hearing on the adequacy of the Supplemental Disclosure Document, the Court entered the DCL Plan Solicitation Order which, among other things, (i) approved the Supplemental Disclosure Document pursuant to section 1125 of the Bankruptcy Code, (ii) established procedures for the solicitation and tabulation of votes to accept or reject the Fourth Amended Plan, and (iii) scheduling the Confirmation Hearing and related deadlines.

The DCL Plan Proponents solicited votes to accept or reject the Fourth Amended Plan from the Revoting Classes in accordance with the DCL Plan Solicitation Order. As summarized in the Epiq Voting Declaration, the Fourth Amended Plan was accepted by most Holders of Claims in the Revoting Classes, as follows:

Classes	Number of Voting Creditors	% Number Accepting	Amount Voted	% Amount Accepting	Result
Class 1C: Senior Loan Claims against Tribune Company	352	99.72%	$8,275,396,770.39	99.97%	Accept
Class 1D: Bridge Loan Claims against Tribune Company	30	100%	$1,600,000,000.00	100%	Accept
Class 1E: Senior Noteholder Claims against Tribune Company	196	85.20%	$1,143,639,844.07	9.95%	Reject
Class 1F: Other Parent Claims against Tribune Company	278	98.92%	$ 286,027,485.95	91.57%	Accept
Class 1I: EGI-TRB LLC Notes Claims against Tribune Company	1	0%	$ 167,047,531.55	0%	Reject
Class 1J: PHONES Notes Claims against Tribune Company	23	4.35%	$ 734,994,736.40	0.45%	Reject
Classes 2E, 4E–7E, 10E, 12E–15E, 18E–20E, 22E–29E, 31E38E, 40E, 42E, 43E and 46E–49E: General Unsecured Claims against Filed Subsidiary Debtors	1	100%	$ 1.00	100%	Accept
Classes 50C–111C: Senior Guaranty Claims	358	99.72%	$8,426,345,592.39	99.97%	Accept

Prior to the Confirmation Hearing for the Fourth Amended Plan, the DCL Plan Proponents negotiated with objecting parties and resolved a number of the objections. The remaining unresolved objections are discussed in detail below.

OBJECTIONS TO CONFIRMATION OF THE FOURTH AMENDED PLAN

C.   OBJECTION TO THE FOURTH AMENDED PLAN'S CLASSIFICATION OF THE SENIOR NOTES INDENTURE TRUSTEE ATTORNEY FEES CLAIM

Deutsche Bank, in its capacity as successor indenture trustee under the DBTCA Indentures, and Law Debenture, in its capacity as successor indenture trustee under the 1996 Indenture, each objected to the Fourth Amended Plan's classification of their claims based upon their asserted contractual rights to recover fees, costs and other amounts due in connection with their roles as indenture trustees under the DBTCA Indentures and the 1996 Indenture, respectively (collectively, the "Indenture Trustee Expense Claims").

The Fourth Amended Plan classifies the Indenture Trustee Expense Claims as Senior Noteholder Claims in Class 1E. "Senior Noteholder Claims" are defined as "all Claims arising under or evidenced by the Senior Notes Indentures and related documents and any Claim of the Senior Noteholders arising under the Pledge Agreement."

Deutsche Bank and Law Debenture argue that the Indenture Trustee Expense Claims are contractual obligations under the Senior Notes Indentures and are separate from the claims for payment of principal and interest owed to the Senior Noteholders. They argue that Bankruptcy Code §1122(a) requires claims within a class to be "substantially similar" and, therefore, contend that the Indenture Trustee Expense Claims should be classified as "Other Parent Claims" in Class 1F, which includes "General Unsecured Claims against Tribune and the Swap Claim (and for the avoidance of doubt includes all Claims against Tribune under Non-Qualified Former Employee Benefit Plans, but does not include Convenience Claims)." The definition of General Unsecured Claims also includes any allowed claim by WTC for fees and expenses arising under the PHONES Notes Indenture.

The DCL Plan Proponents respond that the Indenture Trustee Expense Claims are properly classified because (i) the claims arise under the Senior Notes Indentures, (ii) the claims are asserted against the same entity (Tribune Company), (iii) the claims have the same priority against Tribune, and (iv) the claims are asserted in the same proofs of claim that were filed for the other Senior Noteholder Claims for principal and interest due on the Senior Notes.

Section 1122(a) of the Bankruptcy Code provides that "a plan may place a claim or an interest in a particular class only if such claim or interest is substantially similar to the other claims or interests of such class." 11 U.S.C. §1122(a). Section 1122(a) is mandatory in one respect: only substantially similar claims may be classified together. Yet, Section 1122(a) is permissive is this respect: it does *not* provide that *all* similar claims must be placed in the same class.

Although plan proponents have discretion to classify claims, the Third Circuit has recognized that the Code does not allow a plan proponent complete freedom to place substantially similar claims in separate classes. Instead, a classification scheme must be reasonable. The *John Hancock* Court wrote:

> [When] the sole purpose and effect of creating multiple classes is to mold the outcome of plan voting, it follows that the classification scheme must provide a reasonable method for counting votes. In a "cram down" case, this means that each class must represent a voting interest that is sufficiently distinct and weighty to merit a separate voice in the decision whether the proposed reorganization should proceed. Otherwise, the classification scheme would simply constitute a method for circumventing the requirement set out in 11 U.S.C. §1129(a)(10).

The threshold issue is whether the claims are "substantially similar" and presents two questions: first, are the claims within Class 1E (*i.e.*, the Indenture Trustee Expense Claims and the Senior Notes Claims) substantially similar, and, second, are the Indenture Trustee Expense Claims and the Other Parent Claims in Class 1F substantially similar?

Courts in this Circuit have interpreted "substantially similar" as a reflection of the "legal attributes of the claims, not who holds them." This analysis focuses on how the "legal character of [a] claim relates to the assets of the debtor" and whether the claims "exhibit a similar effect on the debtor's bankruptcy estate." For example, in *AOV*, the Court determined that a plan may classify all unsecured creditors in a single class, rejecting the argument that an unsecured claim with a third-party guaranty should be classified separately, writing:

> The existence of a third-party guarantor does not change the nature of a claim vis-a-vis the bankruptcy estate and, therefore, is irrelevant to a determination of whether claims are "substantially similar" for classification purposes.

Deutsche Bank and Law Debenture argue that the claims in Class 1E are of different character and effect because the Indenture Trustee Expense Claims are contractual obligations to reimburse fees and expenses, while the Senior Notes Claims seek to recover principal and interest under the Notes. However, both types of claims are contractual claims arising from the Senior Notes Indentures. More importantly, as the DCL Plan Proponents point out, the Indenture Trustee Expense Claims and the Senior Notes Claims have the same priority as unsecured claims and are asserted against Tribune. Therefore, the Indenture Trustee Expense Claims and the Senior Notes Claims are substantially similar as to their rights against the Debtors' assets and may be placed within the same class.

Employing the reasoning above, I also conclude that the Indenture Trustee Expense Claims are substantially similar to the Other Parent Claims in Class 1F because all are unsecured claims asserted against Tribune. Is the Fourth Amended Plan's classification of the Indenture Trustee Expense Claims with the Senior Notes Claims, and separate from the Other Parent Claims, reasonable?

The parties have not alleged—and there is no evidence to indicate—that the Fourth Amended Plan's classification scheme was intended to gerrymander votes. Nor is there any indication that the Indenture Trustee Expense Claims were included in Class 1E with the Senior Notes Claims arbitrarily or for a fraudulent purpose.

In *Coram*, the Court noted that separate classification was reasonable when it determined that a group of unsecured noteholders represented a voting interest that was sufficiently distinct from the trade creditors to merit a separate voice in the reorganization. The Senior Noteholders merit a separate voice in this bankruptcy case and, therefore, the Fourth Amended Plan reasonably classifies the Senior Noteholder Claims separately from the Other Parent Claims. Moreover, throughout this bankruptcy case, the Indenture Trustees have represented the interests of their respective noteholders. Accordingly, the interests of the Indenture Trustees align with Senior Noteholders and the Plan reasonably includes the Indenture Trustees Expense Claims within Class 1E. The classification objections by Deutsche Bank and Law Debenture will be overruled.

3.   CONFIRMATION

The bankruptcy court will confirm a plan if the requirements of section 1129(a) are met. Review the provisions of 1129(a) before reading the next case.

IN RE ADELPHIA COMMUNICATIONS CORP.

United States Bankruptcy Court, S.D. New York.
Jan. 3, 2007.

ROBERT E. GERBER, BANKRUPTCY JUDGE.
In this contested matter in the jointly administered chapter 11 cases of Adelphia Communications Corporation and its subsidiaries (the "Debtors"), I have before me, for confirmation, the First Modified Fifth Amended Joint Chapter 11 Plan (the "Plan")—a much-revised plan of reorganization for all of the 230-odd Debtors in these cases—now jointly proposed by the Debtors and the Official Committee of Unsecured Creditors (the "Creditors Committee"), and bank lender agents Wachovia, the Bank of Montreal, and the Bank of America (collectively, the "Plan Proponents"). The Plan would distribute the approximately $15 billion in value remaining after the Debtors' $17.6 billion sale of the Company this summer to Time Warner and Comcast, and after the distribution of the first $2.6 billion in value under an earlier confirmed plan for joint venture debtors in the Adelphia chapter 11 cases.

After 4-1/2 years in chapter 11 in a case that has been among the most challenging—and contentious—in bankruptcy history (and after seven predecessor plans that made one creditor constituency or another—and in some cases nearly everybody—extremely unhappy), the Plan now has overwhelming support. It has satisfied the Bankruptcy Code's assent thresholds for all 30 of the 30 impaired classes that were entitled to, and did, vote on the Plan, holding approximately $10.7 billion of the Debtors' $12.7 billion total in debt. But the Plan nevertheless has been faced with objections to confirmation—including not just the usual, relatively minor, confirmation objections that normally accompany any chapter 11 plan (and are easily resolved, either by negotiation or judicial determination), but also extremely bitter objections by creditors who were outvoted in the balloting on the plan.

Significantly—as this underlies much of the Plan's support, and the vociferous objection to it—the Plan has as its cornerstone a settlement, described more fully below (the "Settlement"), of intercreditor disputes that have plagued the Adelphia cases for years (and that, if not settled, would continue to do so), and that came very close to torpedoing the Time Warner/Comcast sale.

Principally by reason of the settlement of the interdebtor disputes, the Plan has been vigorously opposed by a group of holders of Senior Notes of ACC (the "ACC Bondholder Group") who vociferously oppose the Settlement. They argue that notwithstanding the overwhelming support for the Plan (including within their own class and the six other classes of ACC creditors and equity holders), the Plan is unconfirmable.

Some minor aspects of the ACC Bondholder Group's objections have merit (or did until they were cured), but the great bulk of them do not. And those that lack merit include, most significantly, the objections to the Settlement, which I have reviewed with considerable care to ensure that it passes muster for reasonableness. Significantly, as relevant to the remaining objections that do have merit (which are minor, in the scheme of things, and which will not require resolicitation of the Plan), the Plan provides for automatic corrections, as the impermissible provisions apply only to the extent permissible under law, or are trumped by an order of the Court directing otherwise. As I am now telling the parties how I will address those matters (as discussed below), the Plan will be confirmed.

The following are my Findings of Fact and Conclusions of Law in connection with this determination.

FINDINGS OF FACT

A. BACKGROUND

Adelphia, until the sale of nearly all of its operations to Time Warner and Comcast, was the fifth largest operator of cable systems in the United States. It provided residential customers with analog and digital video services, high-speed Internet access, and other advanced services over its broadband networks. It was founded by John J. Rigas, who later brought his sons and other members of his family into the business. Over the years, Adelphia grew substantially, principally as a result of acquisitions, many of which were financed by borrowings. With the acquisitions, Adelphia became much larger, and its operations became much more complex. The Rigases themselves owned a number of cable companies and other, non-cable assets, through a variety of corporations, partnerships, and LLCs (the "Rigas Family Entities"). The day-to-day affairs of the Rigas Family Entities that were cable companies (the "Managed Entities") were managed by Adelphia.[8] By 2002, John Rigas and members of his family occupied the top officer positions at Adelphia, and many (but not all) of the seats on the board of directors of ACC (the "Board").

In March 2002, the Debtors disclosed that they were jointly and severally liable for more than $2 billion of borrowings attributed to certain of the Managed Entities under credit facilities (the "Co–Borrowing Facilities") that were not reflected as debt on the Debtors' consolidated financial statements. It also appeared that a portion of the borrowings for which Adelphia entities were jointly and severally liable had been advanced to various Rigas Family Entities to finance purchases of Adelphia securities. In the aftermath of this disclosure, the stock of ACC was delisted from the NASDAQ National Market; Deloitte & Touche LLP, the Debtors' independent auditor at that time, suspended its auditing work on Adelphia's consolidated financial statements for the year that ended December 31, 2001, and withdrew its opinion for prior consolidated financial statements; and, ultimately, the Debtors defaulted under all six credit facilities and all of the indentures to which they were a party.

In the Spring of 2002, a special committee of the Board, comprised of three members of the Board who were not members of the Rigas Family, commenced a formal investigation into related party transactions between Adelphia entities and members and the Rigas Family Entities. This investigation led to the public disclosure of previously undisclosed information about the Rigas Family's co-borrowing activities, related party transactions, and involvement in accounting irregularities. In May 2002, the Rigases resigned their positions as officers and directors of Adelphia. After the Rigases' resignation, only four directors, unaffiliated with the Rigases (the "Carry–Over Directors") remained on the ACC Board, who managed Adelphia, to the extent anyone could, until new directors and officers came on board.

With no access to traditional sources of liquidity in the capital markets, pending governmental agency investigations, mounting litigation, default notifications under various credit instruments, and the resulting risk of collection and foreclosure actions by creditors, substantially all of the Debtors filed for chapter 11 protection in June 2002.

In July 2002, the United States Trustee for the Southern District of New York (the "UST") appointed the Creditors Committee, as a fiduciary to represent the interests of the unsecured creditors of the Debtors. The membership of the Creditors Committee changed over the course of time, as creditors sold their claims, and others acquired claims as an investment. The current members of the Creditors Committee are: W.R. Huff Asset Management Co., LLC; Appaloosa Management; Law Debenture Trust Debtors of New York, as Indenture Trustee; Sierra Liquidity Fund, LLC; U.S. Bank National Association, as Indenture

---

8. As used here, "Adelphia" refers to enterprise as a whole and "ACC" refers to Adelphia Communications Corporation, the parent company.

Trustee; Tudor Investment Corporation; Wilmington Trust, as Indenture Trustee; Highfields Capital Management; and Dune Capital Management LP.

When it looked like there might also be sufficient value in the estate to provide recoveries to equity holders, the UST also appointed an Equity Committee, as a fiduciary to protect equity holder interests.

On November 21, 2005, after several previous iterations of a plan of reorganization had been filed with the Bankruptcy Court, the Debtors filed the Fourth Amended Plan (referred to here, for simplicity, as the "November 2005 Plan"). Among other things, it provided for implementing the sale of the Company to Time Warner and Comcast. Shortly thereafter, I approved a disclosure statement for soliciting acceptances of the November 2005 Plan (the "November 2005 Disclosure Statement"). Solicitation of votes with respect to the November 2005 Plan commenced on or about December 5, 2005, and the hearing to consider confirmation of the November 2005 Plan was originally scheduled to begin on February 5, 2006.

Though everyone in the case who spoke to the matter expressed approval of the sale of the Company to Time Warner and Comcast, the November 2005 Plan was in all other material respects exceedingly unpopular with creditors. Over 50 objections to the confirmation of the November 2005 Plan were filed, including objections by all of the formal and ad hoc committees in these cases. And a multitude of stakeholders stated their intention to oppose vigorously any attempt by the Debtors to seek to confirm the November 2005 Plan over their rejecting vote. Further complicating matters, a number of the objections asserted diametrically opposed positions, demonstrating a lack of common ground among the Debtors' stakeholders.

As a result, in many cases, the Debtors could not amend the November 2005 Plan to assuage the concerns of one creditor faction without further alienating another. Moreover, once the Debtors submitted the November 2005 Plan to their creditors for a vote, it became clear that the November 2005 Plan was at risk of being rejected by multiple classes of creditors. This effectively froze progress on the confirmation of a reorganization plan, with the deadlock increasingly threatening the Time Warner/Comcast sale, whose deadline for closing, after confirmation of a reorganization plan, was just a few months down the road, at the end of the upcoming July. ...

By the end of May 2006, with twice weekly (or more) negotiations ... ongoing for nearly four months, with no agreement that could lead to a plan having been reached, the Debtors determined that they had to do something to save the Time Warner/Comcast deal. With the agreement of Time Warner and Comcast, and the support of many of the Debtors' creditor constituencies, the Debtors sought to get the deal closed with a section 363 sale, instead of a global plan which would be dependent on resolution of the intercreditor disputes.

In furtherance of this approach, on May 26, 2006, the Debtors filed a motion (the "363 Motion") seeking authority to, among other things ... consummate the Sale Transaction for all of the Debtors under a section 363 sale. ...

On August 17, 2006, the ACC Bondholder Group moved to terminate exclusivity, asking me to allow the ACC Bondholder Group to propose its own plan for all of the Debtors. In the Exclusivity Motion, the ACC Bondholder Group argued that the filing of a plan incorporating the Plan Agreement was "extremely inappropriate," and a "blatant abuse of the privilege of exclusivity"—contending that the plan violated neutrality requirements and my earlier orders governing prior plans. At the hearing on the Exclusivity Motion, counsel to the ACC Bondholder Group continued this argument, stating that "[t]here is no settlement," because it was not "negotiated and agreed to by the parties authorized to control it."

On September 19, 2006, I issued a bench decision in which I denied the relief sought by the Exclusivity Motion. I ruled, among other things, that: (a) the Plan containing the Settlement should be put up for a vote; (b) the Plan "was the result of weeks of effort to bring seemingly intractable disagreements to a consensual conclusion;" and (c) that I "disagreed with the contentions that the process that led up to the term sheet that underlies it was in any way unlawful or illegitimate."

… Thereafter, and after further negotiations and amendments to improve the settlement from an ACC creditor perspective, three additional major holders of ACC Senior Notes—OZ Management, L.L.C. ("Oz"), C.P. Management, LLC ("C.P.") and Satellite Asset Management, L.P. ("Satellite") (the "Additional ACC Settling Parties") agreed to support the settlement. After additional rounds of discussions, on October 11, 2006, an agreement (the "Plan Support Agreement") was reached on the terms of the Settlement that is now embodied in the Plan. The Plan Support Agreement was executed by the Plan Proponents, Committee II, Huff, the Arahova Noteholders Committee, Appaloosa Management LP, Deutsche Bank Securities, Inc., the Initial ACC Settling Parties and the Additional ACC Settling Parties. Among other terms, the Plan Support Agreement generally provides that at least approximately $1.08 billion in value will be transferred from certain unsecured creditors of various Subsidiary Debtors to certain unsecured senior, trade and other unsecured creditors of ACC and certain other holding company debtors, subject, in some cases, to repayment from contingent sources of value, including the proceeds of the CVV. As the ACC Senior Notes Claims Class has voted to accept the Plan, the $1.08 billion in value has been increased by $50 million in accordance with the Plan to $1.13 billion.

On August 18, 2006, the Debtors and the Creditors Committee filed the Fifth Amended Plan—a first version of the current iteration of the Plan—which reflected the understanding reached in the Amended Term Sheet, and a related disclosure statement supplement (the "Second Disclosure Statement Supplement"). Thereafter, subsequent iterations of these documents, reflecting the additional agreements reached and the added disclosure requirements from the disclosure approval process, were filed. On October 17, 2006, I approved the Second Disclosure Statement Supplement, relating to the Fifth Amended Plan.

DISCUSSION

It's unnecessary for me here to make this decision even longer by discussing all of the extensive law relating to confirmation of a reorganization plan, but I think I should take a moment to discuss the more important aspects of the key provisions of chapter 11 that bear on this controversy. Section 1123 of the Code addresses what a reorganization plan must, and may, contain; section 1123(a) discusses what a plan *must* contain, and section 1123(b) discusses what it *may* contain. Section 1126 discusses, among other things, the requisite acceptances that must be obtained to confirm a plan. And section 1129 of the Code sets forth the substantive requirements for confirmation of a reorganization plan—cross-referencing in several instances, either explicitly or under the caselaw, other sections of the Code, principally other sections in chapter 11.

Listed among the things that a plan must contain, under section 1123(a), are classes for various kinds of claims, which, if impaired, will then be entitled to vote, individually, for or against acceptance of the plan. Section 1126 then discusses what levels of support are required for classes of claims and interests to accept, setting forth the familiar requirement for approval by a class of creditors, that it be supported by creditors (other than those disqualified from voting) holding a majority in number, and at least 2/3 in amount, of the allowed claims of such class held by creditors that have either accepted or rejected the plan. The combination of those two requirements, and especially the supermajority requirement embodied in the "2/3 in amount," has the result that a class of claims will not have voted in favor of a plan in the absence of a great deal of consensus.

But classes of claims, like individual holders, can have different perspectives, and in the typical large chapter 11 case, there will be many classes of impaired claims and interests. It is sometimes the case, but not common, that every single class accepts, and the Bankruptcy Code deals with both acceptance scenarios by a combination of two sections of the Code, 1129(a) and 1129(b).

[S]ection 1129(a) provides, in substance, that a court may confirm a reorganization plan only if all of its requirements are met. Those requirements include, as relevant to the Adelphia cases, 13 subsections of section 1129(a). Satisfaction of some of those 1129(a) requirements is disputed here, and I'll discuss those in due course.

As noted above, getting the affirmative vote of every single impaired class of claims and interests isn't common in large chapter 11 cases, if indeed it's common in any. But it has happened here. The Plan was approved by 30 of the 30 impaired classes that voted on the Plan.

As noted above, section 1123(b)(3), which describes what a plan may contain, expressly includes settlements, and the Settlement that this Plan contains is one of its most important, and controversial features. All parties agree, as do I, that while a Plan may contain a settlement, any such settlement (like the Fed. R. Bankr.P. 9019 settlements that are more common in chapter 11 cases) must pass muster for fairness, under standards articulated by the Supreme Court, the Second Circuit and lower courts. . . .

In my view, the Settlement, looking initially solely at its economic terms, is plainly reasonable (and even more plainly, well within the range of reasonableness), fair and equitable, and in the best interests of the ACC estate, and I so find, as a mixed question of fact and law. When one adds to the equation the additional *TMT* and *Texaco* factors—most significantly, the complexity of the underlying litigation, and the huge expense and delay that would be occasioned by prosecuting it—this decision as to the Settlement's reasonableness becomes quite an easy one. The Settlement is eminently reasonable, fair and equitable, and in the best interests of the ACC estate (and, to the extent relevant, the other Debtor estates), and I so find.

V. BEST INTERESTS OF CREDITORS

The "Best Interests" test embodied in section 1129(a)(7) of the Bankruptcy Code requires that, with respect to an impaired class of claims or interests, each holder that rejects a plan receive or retain under such plan property of a value, as of the effective date, that is no less than such holder would receive in a hypothetical chapter 7 liquidation of the debtor on such date.

The ACC Bondholder Group contends that the Plan does not meet the best interests test under section 1129(a)(7)—principally because, it argues, an independent chapter 7 trustee exercising its fiduciary duties on behalf of ACC would not conclude that the Settlement is in ACC's best interest, and because a chapter 7 trustee would be able to achieve greater recoveries for the ACC Bondholder Group than those provided in the Plan. The ACC Bondholder Group also argues that the Plan Proponents have overstated the liquidation costs that would have to be satisfied in a chapter 7 case, and the interest that would have to be paid to other creditors. I disagree with the ACC Bondholder Group's contentions in this regard, to the extent they need to be addressed, and find that the Plan easily meets the requirements of the Best Interests test.

The plan proponent has the burden of proof to establish by a preponderance of the evidence that its plan meets the Best Interests test. In determining whether the best interests standard is met, the court must measure what is to be received by rejecting creditors in the impaired classes under the plan against what would be received by them in the event of liquidation under chapter 7. In doing so, the court must take into consideration the applicable rules of distribution of the estate under chapter 7, as well as the probable costs incident to such liquidation.

Under chapter 7, a debtor's estate is liquidated by a trustee appointed by the bankruptcy court. Here, substantially all of the Debtors' businesses have been sold to Time Warner and Comcast, and the estates consist primarily of cash, TWC stock (which is not now freely marketable), and the value to be realized from the Contingent Value Vehicle. Accordingly, the determination of whether the Plan satisfies the Best Interests test here necessarily focuses on the incremental costs that may accrue in a chapter 7 that the estates need not absorb under the Plan, and, to the extent applicable, any incremental cost savings they might enjoy.

Comparing the estimated recovery for each impaired creditor under the Plan with its estimated recovery in a hypothetical chapter 7 case requires examining, among others, five significant factors: (i) the costs and discounts associated with an initial public offering of the TWC stock; (ii) the additional administrative expense costs of having one or more chapter 7 trustees appointed to liquidate the estates; (iii) the loss of value associated with losing the expertise of the Debtors' employees and professionals; (iv) increased claims against the Debtors and resulting delays in distribution; and (v) the Settlement embodied in the Plan. Also, in the event the Plan is not confirmed, the Debtors will be required to continue to pay postpetition interest to holders of Bank Claims, which approximates $42 million a month (offset by approximately $22 million earned in interest on the bank debt).

The first two alone are determinative, but I will discuss them all. I conclude, after doing the liquidation analysis, that nonaccepting creditors of impaired classes (including, in particular, those of ACC) would receive more in chapter 11 than in a hypothetical chapter 7 liquidation on the effective date.

IPO Costs

First, a huge cost of a chapter 7 liquidation of the Estates would be the cost of liquidating $6.5 billion in TWC stock. In chapter 11, the Debtors could distribute that stock without going through an underwriting and registering it with the SEC, by reason of the Code's exemption, under section 1145, for securities distributed under a plan. But section 1145 is inapplicable to liquidations under chapter 7, and one or more chapter 7 trustees would have the expensive task of distributing that huge block of stock in an underwriting, by means of an initial public offering of the TWC stock.

Costs associated with an IPO would include, among others, an IPO discount, which I have found above, as a fact, reasonably should be estimated to be 7%. Such costs would also include underwriting fees, which I have found, as a fact, reasonably should be estimated to be 4%. Together, the costs associated with the IPO of all of the TWC stock (or, in the case of a partial IPO, additional costs associated with subsequent public sales) would amount to about 11% of its value. As I've valued the TWC stock at $6.5 billion, the IPO costs can reasonably be estimated to be $715 million.

The ACC Bondholder Group disagrees with the Plan Proponents' estimate of the IPO costs. It argues that because cable is a well-performing sector, and in light of the high quality of TWC's assets and investor familiarity with Time Warner, the TWC stock would not need to be priced at a discount to attract investors. Furthermore, the ACC Bondholder Group asserts that the Debtors control the amount of TWC stock that would be offered to the public above a threshold of 33-1/3% of the Debtors' holdings. It contends that if only the minimum required amount is offered to the public, a 4% underwriters fee would result in IPO costs of approximately $85 million.

I can't accept the ACC Bondholder Group's argument. First, even assuming that cable stocks are in demand, there has been no testimony or evidence that today's cable market will vitiate the need to price shares at a discount; the argument is only speculation. Furthermore, there has been no testimony that the scarcity of TWC shares on the market will drive up the price per share with the effect of obliterating the need for or the desired effect of the IPO discount.

Second, I agree with the Plan Proponents that in the event of a liquidation, *all* of the TWC stock would need to be sold to the public in order for a chapter 7 trustee to liquidate the estate. In one way or another, the stock will have to be liquidated, and it will have to be liquidated in accordance with law. It is therefore reasonable to use the numbers which represent the cost of the IPO for all of the TWC shares held by Adelphia for the purposes of Best Interests test, because secondary offerings would incur comparable costs and expenses to the IPO. Thus, it is reasonable to assume that all of the TWC stock held by the Debtors would be sold during the IPO.

Administrative costs of chapter 7 trustee and professionals

Second, the estimated aggregate amount of cash available for distributions would be lower in a hypothetical chapter 7 because of increased administrative costs. Under section 326(a) of the Code, a chapter 7 trustee is entitled to a statutory fee of up to 3% on all distributions made by the trustee in excess of $1 million. In addition, the chapter 7 trustee's advisors would be entitled to reasonable compensation for services rendered and related expenses incurred, which would be entitled to treatment as administrative expense claims. Given the amount of time such professionals would be required to devote to become familiar with the Debtors and the issues related to these cases, such fees and costs would reduce overall recoveries. Furthermore, if the MIA weren't settled, one would have to factor in the very substantial cost of litigating it. If multiple trustees were appointed, for each of the affected Debtor groups, each would have to have its own counsel, with the associated costs. Alternatively, if a single trustee were to be put in place, once again deputizing creditor groups to do the litigation (as they did before), it is reasonable to exact that each would look to the estate for compensation for that counsel, under "substantial contribution" requests.

While section 326(c) of the Code doesn't permit the aggregate compensation of all trustees in the case to exceed the maximum compensation prescribed for a single trustee by section 326(a), the professionals of each chapter 7 trustee would be entitled to professional fees and costs. Under such circumstances, a hypothetical chapter 7 liquidation would add at least several million dollars of costs, further reducing creditor recoveries. While I assume that in an estate of this size, a chapter 7 trustee would not get the maximum fee authorized under law, or close to it, even if a single chapter 7 trustee were appointed and received a 0.5% fee on all distributions, assuming approximately $15 billion in distributions, the trustee's fee would exceed $70 million.

Furthermore, if a plan is not confirmed, additional fees and expenses of professionals (already approaching $1 billion) will continue to accrue, and, in the event the MIA process is resumed, will be significant.

Familiarity with business

Third, a chapter 7 liquidation would likely involve the appointment of chapter 7 trustees unfamiliar with the Debtors' business, assets and/or liabilities. In contrast, the Plan contemplates the appointment of a Plan Administrator, Quest, that has been serving as an advisor to the Creditors Committee since August 2006 and has been working with the Debtors, the Creditors Committee and their professionals to familiarize itself with the Debtors' cases and steps needed to implement the Plan. Quest is in the best position to determine which of the Debtors' employees should be retained to consummate and administer the Plan. These employees have significant experience and background knowledge relating to (a) the Causes of Action included in the CVV, (b) the Sale Transaction, for purposes of negotiating the release of reserves or protecting the Estates against indemnity claims under the Purchase Agreements, (c) assumed or rejected executory contracts and related cure and rejection damage Claims, (d) general Claims reconciliation, and (e) tax strategies. The need to replace an organization like Quest could result in reduced recovery in certain litigation for the Estates and the diminished ability of the Estates to defend against Claims and requested closing adjustments in connection with the Time Warner/Comcast sale.

Delay in Receiving Distributions

Fourth, in a hypothetical chapter 7, the Debtors' creditors would likely be forced to wait a significant period of time before receiving distributions, either due to the IPO (and any resulting lock up period) or the delayed and perhaps disrupted prosecution of the CVV litigation, for example. There is a risk that distribution of the proceeds of a hypothetical chapter 7 liquidation might not occur for one or more years after the completion of such liquidation in order to resolve Claims and prepare for distribution, and the "time value" of distributions must be factored into the "best interests" analysis. Delayed distributions would be less valuable than the near-term distributions.

Adoption of Settlement

The Plan proposes distributions to creditors based on a settlement of disputed issues, including the MIA and a settlement with Bank Lenders. The Plan Proponents believe it is reasonable to assume that a chapter 7 trustee would adopt settlements similar to the Settlement and the settlement with the Bank Lenders embodied within the Plan in order to avoid the risks, length, cost and uncertainties of litigation. I agree with the Plan Proponents. I think that there's no realistic basis to conclude that a chapter 7 trustee for ACC would come to a different view as to the desirability of the Settlement than Tudor, Highfields, Oz, C.P., Satellite, and all of the accepting ACC classes of claims and interests did.

Even if there were individual trustees for individual estates, and an ACC trustee took positions, as an advocate, allied with the interests of ACC creditors, there is no reasonable basis for a conclusion that he or she could argue anything other than the same merits that have been discussed at length above, or that the trustees for other estates would agree as to the merits of a chapter 7 trustee's positions. It is much more likely that taking into account the complexity and expense of litigating the MIA and the risk of protracted litigation, the chapter 7 trustee for the ACC estate will adopt the Settlement, concluding, as I do, that it is in the best interests of the ACC estate and its creditors.

XIII. STAY UNDER FRBP 3020 AND 8005

For the foregoing reasons, I'll be confirming the Plan, and will be entering a confirmation order. We then have to turn to the issue of the extent, if any, to which I should stay its effectiveness pending appeal.

I've considered that matter at length, in the context of the two Bankruptcy Rules that govern stays. FRBP 3020(e) provides that "[a]n order confirming a plan is stayed until the expiration of 10 days after the entry of the order, unless the court orders otherwise." It was added in 1999 to provide sufficient time for a party to seek a stay pending appeal before the plan is implemented and appeal becomes moot. Fed. R. Bankr.P. 8005, which governs stays (of any kind of order or judgment) pending appeal, provides that motions for stays pending appeal must ordinarily be presented to the bankruptcy judge in the first instance.

I conclude, in the exercise of my discretion, that fairness to the ACC Bondholder Group—and to the district court, which will have a lengthy decision to plow through, and which may not deal with bankruptcy issues on a daily basis—requires that I not take an affirmative step that would foreclose all opportunities for judicial review, and that I should not "order[ ] otherwise" to take away the normal period for asking for a further stay. But I further conclude, based on a very extensive knowledge of this case, and the merits of the objections, that I would grant no further stay, and that if a further stay is to come, it must come only from the district court or a higher court.

Here I do not believe that an appeal would have a likelihood of success. Sometimes I decide matters of first impression or where the issue is close, but this is not one of them. The ACC Bondholder Group's principal complaint is its objection to the settlement, but an issue of that character is reviewed on an abuse of discretion basis, and the appellant must show that the settlement falls below the lowest range of reasonableness. As hopefully is apparent, I've canvassed the Settlement at great length and with great care, and I think it's not remotely close to the level where any appellate court would find that it falls below the lowest level of reasonableness. In fact, 72% of the members of the ACC Senior Notes Class voted in favor of the Plan, with its Settlement (with other classes of ACC creditors supporting the Plan, in comparable or even higher numbers)—and the ACC Bondholder Group, even with its extensive solicitation materials, was unsuccessful in convincing more than 2.5% of the other ACC Bondholders that the Settlement was a bad idea. Those creditors were free to disapprove the Settlement based on a standard *much less demanding* than that the appellate courts would have to apply—*e.g.,* if any simply wanted to hold out for a little more—but the support for the Plan and its Settlement was overwhelming.

Ultimately the dissatisfaction with the Plan and the Settlement is the desire on the part of ACC Bondholder Group members to obtain relatively modest incremental recoveries for the ACC Senior Notes, and/or to advance other investment strategies unrelated to the recoveries for creditors of ACC. Either may be an understandable reason for voting against a plan, or for trying to convince other creditors to do so, but these do not constitute legally cognizable bases for declaring a settlement to be below the range of reasonableness.

I have likewise found other arguments by the ACC Bondholder Group to be unpersuasive, and see no material likelihood that an appellate court would regard them as any more persuasive than I did.

In this case, 30 of 30 classes that voted on the plan supported it, holding debt in excess of $10 billion of the more than $12 billion outstanding. It would be grossly unconscionable, in my view, to thwart the will of such an overwhelming majority to accommodate the desires of such a small minority, who are simply dissatisfied with the Settlement under the Plan. Aside from the interests of the estate as a whole, I must think of the 72% of the ACC Senior Notes that accepted the Plan (and even higher percentages of ACC Sub Debt, Trade Claims, Other Unsecured Claims, Preferred Stock and Common Stock holders) whose will would be frustrated, and whose recoveries will suffer more than any as a consequence of delay. The public interest requires bankruptcy courts to consider the good of the case as a whole, and not individual creditors' investment concerns. Particularly where, as here, the incremental recoveries to ACC Senior Noteholders, if their contentions were accepted, would be modest, and the desire to block consummation of this Plan seemingly must be driven by other factors, the public interest cannot tolerate any scenario under which private agendas can thwart the maximization of value for all.

Thus, under the facts of this case, where every single class has accepted the Plan, where the holders of more than $10 billion in claims would be prejudiced by the objection to confirmation of a vocal few, and where there will huge costs to the estate resulting from delay in the Plan's going effective, I will not grant a longer stay. The requirements of Fed. R. Bankr.P. 8005 for action in this Court shall be deemed satisfied, and further application to me is waived. Any further application for a stay shall be made to the district court.

CONCLUSION

The Plan has secured the assent of over $10 billion in claims, representing approximately 84% of the claims in this case, and, as more relevant to section 1126 and 1129 requirements, the assent, in both number and amount, of 30 of the 30 classes who voted on the Plan. But I fully recognize that confirmation of a plan is not just a popularity contest, but also requires consideration of whether the substantive requirements of the Bankruptcy Code have been satisfied.

After having reviewed, with care, all of the requirements of section 1129 of the Code (and, additionally, the reasonableness of the Settlement), I've determined that the Plan fully conforms to the requirements of the Code. I will enter an order confirming the Plan. Matters that I require by this decision that do not require Plan revisions, but which nevertheless require implementation, can be effected through either the Confirmation Order or one or more supplemental orders. With a proposed confirmation order having been circulated in advance, the Plan proponents are to settle such an order on one day's notice by fax, e-mail or hand.

If all classes voted for the plan, why does the "best interests of the creditors" test apply? Should it apply? What is the significance of a stay pending appeal following confirmation of a chapter 11 plan?

4.   CRAMDOWN

A plan need not satisfy the absolute priority rule so long as any class affected by the deviation from absolute priority has accepted the plan. That is, deviations from absolute priority must be consensual—although consent is measured at the class level.

A plan also can be confirmed even if not every class has accepted it. This is the so-called cramdown power. Colorful term, no? You will find it in section 1129(b).

Indeed, this is quite common because, as we have already discussed, classes that receive no recovery under a plan are automatically deemed to reject the plan. Thus, if the old shares are cancelled and new shares issued to creditors, the shareholders will be deemed to have rejected the plan.

In such a case, at least one impaired class must have accepted the plan (not counting the votes of any insider) and the plan must be fair and equitable, which includes satisfying the absolute priority rule as to the nonaccepting class. It also must not unfairly discriminate against the dissenting class.

You know what the absolute priority rule requires. The next case looks at unfair discrimination too.

IN RE GENCO SHIPPING & TRADING LIMITED

513 B.R. 233
United States Bankruptcy Court, S.D. New York.
JULY 2, 2014.

SEAN H. LANE, UNITED STATES BANKRUPTCY JUDGE

Before the Court is a dispute over the Debtors' proposed plan of reorganization, with the parties primarily disagreeing about the value of the Debtors, a dry bulk shipping company. Using four different valuation methods and their many component parts, the Debtors and the Official Committee for the Equity Holders (the "Equity Committee") arrive at significantly different values for the Debtors' estate. Based on their differing approaches, the Equity Committee appointed in this case argues that there is enough value in this company that the proposed plan of reorganization should not be confirmed because it does not give a sufficient recovery to equity holders, whose recovery comes only after all creditors have been paid. As a related matter, the Equity Committee contends that the plan is not proposed in good faith given the problematic valuation methods used by the Debtors' management. The Debtors and supporting creditors counter that the proper valuation here demonstrates that equity is entirely out of the money and is fortunate to receive the recovery contemplated by the plan, which is based on the restructuring support agreement negotiated by the majority of creditors prior to the filing of these cases.

For the reasons set forth below and based on the evidence at trial, the Court agrees for the most part with the Debtors' views on valuation and concludes that the equity holders are not entitled to any recovery.

BACKGROUND

Genco Shipping and Trading Limited together with its affiliated Debtors (collectively, "Genco" or "the Company") is one of the world's largest dry bulk shippers, operating with a fleet of 53 shipping vessels. Genco has a highly leveraged capital structure, with over $1.3 billion of senior secured debt and $125 million of unsecured convertible notes. The senior secured debt is held in three separate credit facilities. The first is referred to as the "2007 Credit Facility," with Wilmington Trust, National Association serving as agent, under which the Debtors owe approximately $1.069 billion (exclusive of interest). The 2007 Credit Facility holds a first and second lien on substantially all of the Debtors' assets. The second facility is referred to as the "$100 Million Credit Facility," with Credit Agricole serving as agent, under which approximately $74 million is owed (exclusive of interest). The $100 Million Credit Facility holds a first lien on the five vessels purchased with the proceeds of its loan. Finally, there is the "$253 Million Credit Facility," with Deutsche Bank serving as agent, under which approximately $176 million is owed (exclusive of interest). The $253 Million Credit Facility is secured by liens on thirteen vessels purchased with the proceeds of the loan. In addition to these three levels of secured debt, Genco also has convertible unsecured notes, in the amount of $125 million, that reach maturity in August 2015. Genco also owes various ordinary course creditors, including charterers, vendors and suppliers, all of whom are unsecured.

On April 21, 2014, the Debtors filed voluntary petitions in this Court seeking relief under Chapter 11 of the Bankruptcy Code. The filing is a prepackaged Chapter 11 case, pursuant to which Genco seeks to implement a consensual debt conversion restructuring that is supported by the majority of the Debtors' lenders.

Prior to the petition date, Genco negotiated a restructuring support agreement (the "RSA"), which established the framework for a prepackaged plan of reorganization that would deleverage Genco's balance sheet and provide new liquidity through a fully backstopped $100 million rights offering. The RSA was executed on April 3, 2014, by the Debtors and approximately 98% of the lenders under the 2007 Credit Facility, 100% of the lenders under the $100 Million Credit Facility and the $253 Million Credit Facility, and approximately 82% of the holders of the convertible notes (the "Noteholders").

The parties to the RSA were required to support approval of the Prepack Plan. Through the RSA, the Debtors also obtained agreement for consensual use of cash collateral. At a hearing held on April 23, 2014, the Debtors established that, absent the use of cash collateral, they would have insufficient funds to pay employees, maintain business relationships with vendors and suppliers, and otherwise could not finance their operations.

The RSA includes a fiduciary out for Genco. It provides: "in order to fulfill the Company Parties' fiduciary obligations, the Company may receive (but not solicit) proposals or offers for Alternative Transactions from other parties and negotiate, provide due diligence, discuss, and/or analyze such Alternative Transactions received without breaching or terminating this agreement...." If Genco announces its intention to pursue an alternative transaction, however, the RSA may be terminated by two-thirds of the supporting creditors on five days' notice. If the RSA is terminated to allow Genco to pursue an alternative transaction, and that alternative transaction is consummated, the RSA requires that Genco pay to the supporting 2007 Credit Facility lenders and supporting Noteholders a termination fee of $26.5 million plus expense reimbursements. The termination fee will be treated as an administrative expense and will serve as the sole and exclusive remedy of the supporting 2007 Credit Facility lenders and the Noteholders under the RSA. *Id.*

In accordance with the terms of the RSA, the Debtors and the Supporting Creditors finalized the terms of the Prepack Plan and disclosure statement. The Prepack Plan, as contemplated by the RSA, converts approximately $1.2 billion of debt to equity in the reorganized Genco, provides the Debtors with $100 million of additional new money through a fully backstopped rights offering, and extends the maturity dates of the $253 and $100 Million Credit Facilities. In exchange for the conversion of debt to equity, the 2007 Credit Facility will receive 81.1 % of the reorganized Genco equity and the right to participate in 80% of the rights offering. The Noteholders will receive 8.4% of the equity and the right to participate in up to 20% of the rights offering. Under the RSA, the

Debtors will reinstate allowed general unsecured claims and pay them in the ordinary course of business. The Plan also provides for existing equity holders to receive warrants in exchange for the surrender or cancellation of their equity interests. The warrants cover 6% of the new equity.

The Debtors began solicitation of votes on the Prepack Plan on April 16, 2014. At the time of filing on April 21, 2014, 100% of the Credit Facility claims had voted to accept the Plan, but the Debtors were still accepting votes from the Noteholders. The Court authorized the assumption of the RSA in May. In approving the RSA, the Court concluded that the Debtors were overleveraged, that they needed to restructure their debt, and that a Chapter 11 proceeding was an appropriate vehicle for doing so. The Court found that the RSA could accomplish those goals through a comprehensive restructuring of the Debtors on a consensual basis, while avoiding a long, drawn out Chapter 11 process and the attendant costs. For those reasons, among others, the Court approved assumption of the RSA because it met the business judgment standard under Section 365 of the Bankruptcy Code.

On May 9, 2014, the United States Trustee appointed the Equity Committee, consisting of three equity holders: (i) Aurelius Capital Partners LP, (ii) Mohawk Capital LLC, and (iii) OZ Domestic Partners, LP.[9]

The Court held a confirmation hearing and trial on June 12, 13, 23, and 24, 2014, during which the parties presented a variety of evidence, most of it concerning valuation. The Debtors called Harry Perrin, a Genco board member; John James O'Connell, of Blackstone Advisory Partners LP ("Blackstone"); and John Wobensmith, CEO of Genco, as fact witnesses. The Debtors relied on three expert witnesses to further support their case: (1) Dr. Adam Kent, of Maritime Strategies International Limited ("MSI"), who conducted a valuation of each vessel in the Debtors' fleet; (2) Dr. Arlie Sterling, of Marsoft, Inc. ("Marsoft"), who testified regarding projected dry bulk shipping rates; and (3) Timothy Coleman, of Blackstone, who testified regarding the valuation methods used by the Debtors. The Equity Committee called two experts: Neil Augustine, of Rothschild Inc. ("Rothschild"), to testify regarding his opinion on the valuation of Genco; and Morton Arntzen, of CMG Advisory Services LLC ("CMG"),[5] who testified regarding the shipping industry and market predictions.[10]

---

9. OZ Domestic Partners, LP also has been colloquially referred to in this case as "Och Ziff."

10. In addition to these seven witnesses, the parties also designated the deposition testimony of another five witnesses: Peter Georgiopoulos, chairman of the board of Genco; Richard Morgner, managing director and global joint head of restructuring and recapitalizations at Jefferies, LLC; Jason Scheir, of Apollo Management Holdings LP; Bao Truong, of Centerbridge Partners LP; and Scott Vogel, of Midtown Acquisitions, LP.

DISCUSSION

A. THE APPLICABLE LAW

1. *Section 1129(a)(8)—Cramdown*

The Debtors, as the proponents of the Plan, bear the burden of establishing by a preponderance of the evidence that the Plan meets the requirements of Section 1129 of the Bankruptcy Code.

Section 1129(a)(8) of the Bankruptcy Code requires that each class of claims or interests under a plan have either accepted the plan or be unimpaired by the plan. Thus, the affirmative consent of all impaired classes is required for the consensual confirmation of a plan. However, if a plan meets all of the other confirmation criteria in Section 1129(a), it may still be confirmed over the rejection of a class of claims or interests, so long as the plan "does not discriminate unfairly, and is fair and equitable, with respect to each class of claims or interests that is impaired under, and has not accepted, the plan." § 1129(b)(1).

The Debtors' Plan classifies Equity Interests in Class 11. Class 11 is impaired under the Plan and holders of Equity Interests are deemed to reject the Plan pursuant to Section 1126(g) of the Bankruptcy Code. Because the requirements of Section 1129(a)(8) have not been met with respect to Class 11, the Debtors must establish that the Plan is fair and equitable and does not unfairly discriminate against the holders of Equity Interests.

Neither the Bankruptcy Code nor legislative history provides clear guidance for determining what constitutes "unfair discrimination." "Generally speaking, this standard ensures that a dissenting class will receive relative value equal to the value given to all other similarly situated classes...." Thus, a plan will be found to unfairly discriminate "where similarly situated classes are treated differently without a reasonable basis for the disparate treatment "To determine whether a plan discriminates unfairly, courts consider whether (1) there is a reasonable basis for discriminating, (2) the debtor cannot consummate the plan without the discrimination, (3) the discrimination is proposed in good faith, and (4) the degree of discrimination is in direct proportion to its rationale."

A plan is considered to be fair and equitable to a class of equity holders if it provides that each equity holder in the class "receive or retain on account of such interest property of a value, as of the effective date of the plan, equal to the ... value of such interest; or the holder of any interest that is junior to the interests of such class will not receive or retain under the plan on account of such junior interest any property." 11 U.S.C. § 1129(b)(2)(C). "It's undisputed that the 'fair and equitable' requirement encompasses a rule that a senior class cannot receive more than full compensation for its claims." Courts will therefore deny confirmation "if a plan undervalues a debtor and therefore would have resulted in paying senior creditors more than full compensation for their allowed claims." Therefore, "[a] determination of the Debtor's value directly impacts the issues of whether the proposed plan is 'fair and equitable,' as required by 11 U.S.C. § 1129(b)."

2. Valuation Methodologies

Valuation is not an exact science. *In re Spansion, Inc.,* 426 B.R. 114, 130 (Bankr.D.Del.2010) ("It has been aptly observed that entity valuation is much like a guess compounded by an estimate.") (Internal quotations omitted.)

"Fair valuation for a company that can continue day-to-day operations is based on a 'going concern' or 'market price' valuation." There are three main methodologies commonly used to determine reorganization value: (1) discounted cash flow analysis ("DCF"); (2) market multiple approach; and (3) comparable transaction approach. But courts have "broad discretion to determine the extent and method of inquiry necessary for a valuation ... depend[ing] on the facts of each case." "The goal of all methods is the same: to determine the 'present worth of future anticipated earnings' of the debtor corporation."

The first method, DCF, estimates the net present value of a company by:

(i) projecting unlevered free cash flows over a given fixed forecast period, then discounting those cash flows back to the present using an estimated discount rate based upon the company's weighted average cost of capital ("WACC"); and

(ii) deriving the value of all unlevered free cash flows beyond the explicit forecast period—the "terminal value"—and then discounting that terminal value back to the present by applying the estimated discount rate. The enterprise value is determined by adding the numbers derived from (i) and (ii).

DCF analysis may be problematic where management's projections are inaccurate or unreliable. [S]ee also In re DBSD N. Am., Inc., 419 B.R. 179, 197 (S.D.N.Y.2009) (noting serious problems with DCF analysis based on negative cash flows).

The second method, the market multiple or comparable company analysis, estimates the value of a company by using the value of comparable companies as an indicator of the subject company. "Values are standardized using one or more common variables such as revenue, earnings, or cash flow, with the expert then applying a multiple of the financial metric or metrics that yields the market's valuation of these comparable companies." The key to this analysis is the choice of appropriate comparable companies relative to the company in question.

The third method, precedent transactions, looks at the purchase prices of comparable companies in recent transactions and uses the subject company's earnings, cash flow, or earnings before interest, taxes, depreciation, and amortization ("EBITDA") to determine a range of total enterprise value, or TEV. "This method requires qualitative judgments in light of the unique circumstances of each precedent transaction and inherent differences between the precedent acquired companies and the subject company."

The Debtors maintain that a fourth methodology, net asset value ("NAV"), is the appropriate methodology to value a dry bulk shipping company. NAV is "based on independent appraisals that incorporate an impartial assessment of the broadest, most concrete consensus regarding future earnings." NAV is a method that adds together the appraisal values and any other assets, such as ownership stakes in other companies, service contracts, and cash on hand.

B. THE VALUE OF GENCO

The question before the Court is whether Genco's value, as calculated using these various methodologies, exceeds $1.48 billion, the amount that would entitle equity holders to any recovery.[11] In addressing this question, the Debtors urge the Court to adopt a NAV analysis, which the Debtors contend is between $1.36 billion to $1.44 billion. The Equity Committee, however, advocates using all four valuation methods and then assigning a weight to each; the Committee weighs DCF and comparable companies most heavily at 37.5%, NAV is weighed at 15%, and precedent transactions is given only a 10% value. Using the Equity Committee's analysis, Genco's value ranges from $1.54 billion to $1.91 billion, with a midpoint of $1.725 billion.

As explained below, the Court concludes that NAV should not be the exclusive basis for valuation in this case, but nonetheless should be given substantial weight given the nature of the dry bulk shipping industry. The Court finds that a comparable companies analysis is equally useful in determining Debtors' value and that the precedent transaction analysis is of some limited utility. But the Court concludes that the DCF analysis is not an appropriate method of valuation, largely due to the highly speculative nature of rate projections for the dry bulk shipping industry. The Court also concludes that there are other significant flaws with Rothschild's DCF analysis. Turning to the three remaining methodologies other than DCF, none produces a valuation figure above the $1.48 billion mark that would entitle the equity holders to a recovery. In other words, using NAV and the comparable companies analysis—and to a

---

11. This $1.48 billion figure is comprised of the following claims that must be paid in full before equity holders could recover anything under the rule of absolute priority: $1.069 billion due under the 2007 Credit Facility; $176 million due under the $253 Million Credit Facility; $74 million due under the $100 Million Credit Facility; $125 million of Convertible Notes; $4 million of accrued interest; $6 million in swap liability; $1 million owed under lease agreements; and $26 million of other administrative claims. Rothschild claimed that this number should be $1.443 billion, because they subtracted $37 million cash on hand from the $1.48 billion claims total. Given the Court's conclusion that Mr. Coleman provided credible testimony and that he provided a convincing detailed breakdown of the required cash on hand for each vessel, the Court adopts Mr. Coleman's $1.48 billion figure.

The Debtors also point out that, when taking into account the value of the warrants being gifted to the equity holders, that $1.48 billion figure rises even higher. Although the Equity Committee disputes the value of the warrants, as discussed in further detail below, the Debtors value the warrants at $32.9 million, which would mean that the value of Genco would have to exceed $1.51 billion for equity holders to recover more than they will receive under the Plan.

lesser extent the precedent transactions methodology—the Court concludes that the Debtors have established by a preponderance of the evidence that the Debtors' value does not exceed the $1.48 billion figure. ...

4. Discounted Cash Flow

The last of the valuation methodologies here is the DCF method, which takes the sum of two future cash flow streams to determine the net present value of a company. The DCF method can be summed up as follows:

A discounted cash flow analysis entails estimating the periodic cash flow that a company will generate over a discrete time period, determining the "terminal value" of the company at the end of the period, and discounting each of the cash flows and terminal value to determine the total value as of the relevant date.

In applying the DCF method, Rothschild relied on adjusted rate projections provided by the Equity Committee's expert CMG to calculate Genco's terminal value using both the EBITDA exit multiple approach and the perpetuity growth rate approach.[12] The DCF results generated by Rothschild's inputs are significantly higher than those from the other three methodologies that Rothschild applied.

But the Court concludes that there are many good reasons that the DCF method should not be applied here. Although DCF is a traditional methodology used in valuation exercises, courts have recognized its limitations, particularly when the assumptions are unreliable or difficult to ascertain. As Judge Gerber of this Court has observed, "DCF works best (and, arguably, only) when a company has accurate projections of future cash flows...." When "the factual underpinnings of the DCF computation become unreliable ... the propriety of any use of DCF (and the weight DCF conclusions should be given) becomes debatable at best." Other courts have reached similar conclusions. In *In re JCC Holding Co., Inc. Shareholders Litigation,* for example, the court rejected the argument that a particular corporation was obliged to perform a DCF analysis in determining the fairness of a proposed merger transaction to satisfy its requirement of "fair disclosures." *In re JCC Holding Co., Inc. S'holders Litig.,* 843 A.2d 713, 721 (Del.Ch.2003). The court noted that there were no "reliable recent long-term projections from which [the financial advisor] could perform a DCF valuation analysis."

In another case, the Delaware Chancery court noted:

The utility of a DCF analysis, however, depends on the validity and reasonableness of the data relied upon. ... The problem in this case is that the most

---

12. The cash flows were discounted applying a weighted average cost of capital ("WACC") range, which considers the cost of capital of the peer group in the comparable companies analysis and certain company specific factors. The Court notes that at the trial, there was little discussion of the WACC ranges applied in both the Rothschild and Blackstone analyses, although it appears the respective WACC rates actually applied by both experts varied. (Rothschild's WACC was 8.5% to 10.5%, while Blackstone used 10.1% "sensitized to 9.1% and 11.1%.").

fundamental input used by the experts—the projections of future revenues, expenses, and cash flows—were not shown to be reasonably reliable.

The court's primary reason for rejecting DCF was that there was an absence of "reasonably reliable contemporaneous projections." More specifically, the court explained that the "degree of speculation and uncertainty characterizing the future prospects of [the company] and the industry in which it operates make a DCF analysis of marginal utility. . . ." "[T]he industry was so new and volatile that reliable projections were impossible . . . it was difficult to forecast the next quarter, let alone five years out."

No accurate projections exist in this case. Despite the numerous disputed issues at trial, all parties agree that dry bulk shipping rates are extremely volatile and difficult to predict. Rothschild conceded, for example, that "shipping rates are volatile and the industry can be characterized as cyclical. . . ." The Equity Committee's shipping expert, Mr. Arntzen, similarly testified that "[i]t is difficult to accurately forecast freight rates in drybulk shipping . . . [and that] the drybulk market is dynamic and volatile. . . ." Blackstone agreed, concluding that:

> In the global drybulk shipping industry, charter rates are inherently volatile and can change drastically on a daily basis. This makes charter rates difficult to predict and cash flow projections inherently unreliable. . . . As a result, DCF analyses are fundamentally unreliable for valuing companies in the drybulk shipping industry. . . .

This unpredictability in rates is consistent with the credible evidence at trial that the dry bulk market is highly fragmented, with low barriers to entry, and affords market participants little, if any, opportunity to differentiate themselves. Little if any of that evidence was disputed. Thus, the dry bulk shipping market parallels what classical economists would call "perfect competition," where "rates are determined on a daily basis by supply and demand in the market ... [and] [c]onsequently, a company's ability to predict long term revenues is severely constrained."

While the volatility of the industry is a sufficient basis by itself to reject a DCF analysis, there are other problems with Rothschild's analysis. Notably, Rothschild's heavy reliance on DCF is inconsistent with other aspects of its own analysis. For example, Rothschild relied on a survey of thirteen equity analysts for its views of the future of the dry bulk shipping industry. But only five of these analysts rely on the DCF method in making their assessments. Indeed, Rothschild conceded that the DCF method is less frequently used in the dry bulk shipping industry. Rothschild did not present any facts or analysis that credibly resolved these inconsistencies in its approach.

Similarly, Rothschild's reliance on DCF is undercut by the views it expressed on Genco prior to the bankruptcy filing. In March 2014, Rothschild discussed Genco with equity holder Och Ziff. As part of these discussions, Rothschild provided written presentations to Och Ziff. In comments on two recent shipping cases, Rothschild's written presentation to Och Ziff noted that (1) "neither OSG nor General Maritime used traditional [valuation] methodologies"; (2) "more emphasis was placed on fleet valuation and a market indication of value based on financing and M & A transaction proposals from interested parties"; and (3) "some market commentators also dismiss traditional valuation methodologies given the highly cyclical nature of the shipping industry." All of these comments are consistent with the position Debtors have taken regarding valuation.

In its efforts to persuade the Court that DCF should be used, the Equity Committee spent considerable time on "fairness opinions"—in both its cross examination of Mr. Coleman, and its re-direct examination of Mr. Augustine. The Equity Committee introduced evidence from two transactions in the shipping industry, where documents filed with the SEC include a fairness opinion. In both of these referenced at trial, the Equity Committee suggested that DCF was relied upon in determining the fairness of such transactions.

But for each of the transactions where Equity Committee pointed to the use of DCF in the fairness opinion, there is other evidence to suggest that those transactions focused more on the NAV methodology for purposes of valuation.

Additionally, there is conflicting testimony on the usefulness of fairness opinions in this context. While the Equity Committee and Mr. Augustine emphasized the importance of fairness opinions, Mr. Coleman had an entirely different perspective. Mr. Coleman testified that Blackstone had not relied on fairness opinions in its valuation analysis and that he had never seen them used in the context of a court hearing on valuation. Moreover, Mr. Coleman noted that a fairness opinion will traditionally use all methodologies due to the legal ramifications of such opinions and the desire to avoid liability, but they are not valuations *per se*. The Court credits Mr. Coleman's testimony on this issue.

Last but not least, the data used by Rothschild to compute DCF is flawed. One key input of cash flow projections in the dry bulk shipping industry are the relevant shipping rates. The parties used different experts to compute these rates and arrived at different conclusions. The Debtors employed Dr. Arlie Sterling of Marsoft, while the Equity Committee hired Morten Arntzen, of CMG. The Court finds Marsoft to be far more persuasive than CMG for a variety of reasons.

Marsoft was founded almost 30 years ago and employs 25 individuals who service over one hundred clients in the maritime industry, providing ongoing evaluation and forecasting of market conditions including a quarterly report on the dry bulk market . . .

On the other hand, CMG was formed just a few weeks prior to the hearing. Mr. Arntzen has never previously been paid for his rate forecasts, and any that he did perform were not subject to review by others (i.e., analysts or other market participants). It is not clear from Mr. Arntzen's testimony exactly the nature of CMG's services. Rather, the qualifications described in his declaration focus solely on Mr. Arntzen's 35 years of experience in the shipping industry, which includes his tenure as CEO of a shipping company and various positions held in maritime lending. While Mr. Arntzen clearly has a wealth of experience in and knowledge of the shipping industry (and managing shipping companies), his credentials and experience in the specific area of forecasting rates were less impressive.

Turning to the substance of Mr. Arntzen's opinion, the Court is not convinced that his conclusions are the result of applying rigorous scientific or other specialized methods . . .

5. Other Factors Relevant to Genco's Value

The Court finds it telling that no equity holder, including large hedge funds on the Equity Committee, has expressed any interest in investing its own money in a transaction involving the Debtors. As Mr. Coleman noted, there has been no inquiry or expression of interest by any other party about buying Genco, including from any of the equity holders. He explained, "if you had a valuation such as Rothschild's that suggest almost a half billion dollars of potential difference[ ] [from] our valuation ... I would think we would have a line out the door like a Starbucks where people would be clamoring to take advantage of this situation. In particular, I would have thought Och–Ziff and Aurelius would be standing there with their checkbooks buying this company and we don't have that."

Even Mr. Augustine seemed aware of this tension. In its early conversations with Och Ziff, Rothschild recognized that it would be "difficult to establish credibility in [a] valuation fight if [the equity holders are] unwilling to 'buy into' [the] capital structure at a higher valuation post-emergence." Thus, although equity holders are not required to put up any money, the Debtors' views on value are supported by the lack of interest in the Debtors' assets by equity holders and the market.

Finally, the Equity Committee complains that the warrants they will receive under the Plan are inadequate. They seek anti-dilution protections to guard against future decreases in value of those warrants and a compensatory feature for "loss of time value" if a sale of the Reorganized Debtors occurs prior to the end of the seven-year tenor. But the warrants offered under the Plan contain terms that are customary for public company warrants and there is evidence that the anti-dilution protections are indeed not appropriate for public companies. In any event, the Equity Committee's argument fails given the Court's conclusion that Genco is insolvent and, therefore, the equity holders are not entitled to any recovery.

In the end, it all comes back to valuation.

5.   DISCHARGE AND EXIT

Typically, a chapter 11 plan will not become "effective" upon confirmation. Instead, the plan usually specifies an effective date, which is often contingent on a variety of events happening first. In this way the plan is like other important corporate transactions that "close" some point after the deal is actually signed.

Upon confirmation, section 1141(d) provides that the provisions of a confirmed plan bind the debtor, any entity issuing securities or acquiring property under the plan, creditors, and the equity security holders. Except as provided in the plan or in the confirmation order, property of the estate vests in the debtor and the property dealt with by the plan vests free and clear of all claims and interests of creditors and equity security holders.

All claims that were or could have been filed against the debtor are discharged, and the creditors are prohibited by operation of federal law from attempting to collect such claims.

Before we close, a brief note on Dynegy. The examiner's report led to mediation—with the examiner as the mediator—that resulted in Dynegy's revised reorganization plan, which was confirmed in September 2012. Dynegy Inc. decided to put itself into bankruptcy and merged itself with Dynegy Holdings LLC. Dynegy Inc. was the "surviving entity."

The plan gave the company's unsecured creditors a 99 percent stake in Dynegy. Dynegy Inc. shareholders received 1 percent, plus warrants to potentially boost their stake to 13.5 percent over five years. As your author noted in his column on the *New York Times* webpage, the shareholders "probably could have gotten that deal in 2011."

In May 2013, Bloomberg reported that Dynegy had sold new debt, but it had been compelled to pay an "abuse premium" of 42 basis points.

TABLE OF CASES

Italics indicate principal cases.

INDEX